KT-221-414

THE LAWS
OF SCOTLAND

_____●_____

STAIR MEMORIAL
ENCYCLOPAEDIA

Volume 11

THE LAWS
OF SCOTLAND

———•———

STAIR MEMORIAL
ENCYCLOPAEDIA

Volume 11

The Law Society of Scotland
Butterworths

Edinburgh   1990

The Law Society of Scotland
The Law Society's Hall, 26 Drumsheugh Gardens, EDINBURGH EH3 7YR

Butterworths	
United Kingdom	Butterworth & Co (Publishers) Ltd, 88 Kingsway, LONDON WC2B 6AB and 4 Hill Street, EDINBURGH EH2 3JZ
Australia	Butterworths Pty Ltd, SYDNEY, MELBOURNE, BRISBANE, ADELAIDE, PERTH, CANBERRA and HOBART
Canada	Butterworth & Co (Canada) Ltd, TORONTO and VANCOUVER
Ireland	Butterworth (Ireland) Ltd, DUBLIN
Malaysia	Malayan Law Journal Sdn Bhd, KUALA LUMPUR
New Zealand	Butterworths of New Zealand Ltd, WELLINGTON and AUCKLAND
Singapore	Butterworth & Co (Asia) Pte Ltd, SINGAPORE
USA	Butterworth Legal Publishers, ST PAUL, Minnesota, SEATTLE, Washington, BOSTON, Massachusetts, AUSTIN, Texas and D & S Publishers, CLEARWATER, Florida

All rights reserved. No part of this publication may be reproduced in any material form (including photocopying or storing it in any medium by electronic means and whether or not transiently or incidentally to some other use of this publication) without the written permission of the copyright owner except in accordance with the provisions of the Copyright, Designs and Patents Act 1988 or under the terms of a licence issued by the Copyright Licensing Agency Ltd, 33–34 Alfred Place, London, England WC1E 7DP. Applications for the copyright owner's written permission to reproduce any part of this publication should be addressed to the publisher.

Warning: The doing of an unauthorised act in relation to a copyright work may result in both a civil claim for damages and criminal prosecution.

First published 1990

© The Law Society of Scotland 1990

British Library Cataloguing in Publication Data

The Laws of Scotland: Stair memorial encyclopaedia.
Vol 11
1. Law — Scotland — Dictionaries
I. Law Society of Scotland
344.1108'6   KDC150

ISBN (complete set) 0 406 237 00 X
(this volume) 0 406 237 11 5

Typeset and printed in Scotland by Thomson Litho Ltd, East Kilbride, on Bannockburn Fine Wove made by Guardbridge Papers Co Ltd of Fife and supplied by James McNaughton Paper Group. Bound by Hunter & Foulis Ltd of Edinburgh using cloth supplied by Watson Grange of Linwood, Paisley.

GENERAL EDITORS

1981–88
THE LATE SIR THOMAS SMITH QC, DCL, LLD, FRSE, FBA
Honorary Bencher of Gray's Inn
Professor Emeritus of Scots Law in the University of Edinburgh

1988–
ROBERT BLACK QC, LLB, LLM
Professor of Scots Law in the University of Edinburgh
Formerly Deputy and Joint General Editor

DEPUTY GENERAL EDITORS

HAMISH McN HENDERSON MA, LLB
Advocate in Aberdeen
University Fellow and formerly Senior Lecturer in
Scots Law in the University of Edinburgh

JOSEPH M THOMSON LLB
Professor of Law in the University of Strathclyde

ASSISTANT GENERAL EDITOR

KENNETH MILLER LLB, LLM, PHD
Senior Lecturer in Law in the University of Strathclyde

CO-ORDINATOR TO THE GENERAL EDITORS

JOAN ROSE BA

OFFICE BEARERS OF THE LAW SOCIETY OF SCOTLAND

President 1990–91
A T F Gibb LLB, SSC

Vice-President 1990–91
James H Campbell BL

Secretary
Kenneth W Pritchard BL, WS

Convener, Encyclopaedia Committee
Professor J Ross Harper CBE, MA, LLB

Members of the Encyclopaedia Committee
Sheriff John S Boyle BL
C W R Gemmill BA, LLB

BUTTERWORTHS' EDITORIAL STAFF

Text Editor
R Peter Moore, LLB
of Lincoln's Inn, Barrister

Editorial Manager
Margaret Cherry LLB

Sub-editor
Margaret Hannan

INDEXER
Ann Barrett
Member, the Society of Indexers

Contributors to this volume

FISHERIES

SALMON AND FRESHWATER FISHERIES

G W S Barry BA(Oxon), WS

SEA FISHERIES

Professor Patricia Birnie BA(Oxon), PHD, Barrister of Gray's Inn,
Director, International Maritime Organization,
International Maritime Law Institute, Malta

FOOD, DAIRIES AND SLAUGHTERHOUSES

The late John Angus Beaton CB, BL

FORESTRY

R W G Weir BL, WS
Solicitor to the Forestry Commissioners in Scotland

TAXATION

Colin J Tyre LLB, DESU(Aix-Marseille), Advocate

FRAUD

Joseph M Thomson LLB
Professor of Law in the University of Strathclyde

GAME

Stanley Scott Robinson MBE, TD, SSC
Sheriff of Grampian, Highland and Islands (retired)

G W S Barry BA(Oxon), WS

GENERAL LEGAL CONCEPTS

D Neil MacCormick MA, LLD, JUR DR HC, FRSE, FBA,
Barrister of the Inner Temple,
Regius Professor of Public Law and the Law of Nature and Nations
in the University of Edinburgh

GUARDIANSHIP

John D Campbell, Advocate

J W G Blackie BA(Cantab), LLB, Advocate
Senior Lecturer in Scots Law in the University of Edinburgh

HARBOURS

The Hon Lord Weir
Senator of the College of Justice

HEALTH SERVICES

Alistair F Neilson CBE, SSC
Former legal adviser to the Scottish Health Service

HERALDRY

Sir Crispin Agnew of Lochnaw, Bt, Advocate
Rothesay Herald of Arms

HOTELS AND TOURISM

John J Downes LLB, M INST TT
Senior Lecturer in Law in Dundee Institute of Technology
Director and Chairman of the European section of the
International Forum of Travel and Tourism Advocates
Consultant to the World Tourism Organisation

HOUSING

C M G Himsworth BA, LLB
Senior Lecturer in Law in the University of Edinburgh

HOMELESSNESS

Peter Robson LLB, PHD, Solicitor
Reader in Law in the University of Strathclyde

Paul Q Watchman LLB, Solicitor

**The law stated in this volume is in general that in force on 31 December
1989 but later developments have been noted wherever possible.**

Contents

GAME

GENERAL LEGAL CONCEPTS

GUARDIANSHIP

HARBOURS

Abbreviations

AC	Law Reports, Appeal Cases (House of Lords and Privy Council) 1890–
AD	Appellate Division (S Africa) 1910–46
AD	Annual Digest and Reports of Public International Law Cases 1919–1949
A-G	Attorney-General
AJIL	American Journal of International Law
ALR	Argus Law Reports (Australia) 1895–1973, and Australian Law Reports 1973–
AMS	Ancient Manuscripts of Scotland
APS	Acts of the Parliament of Scotland
AS	Act of Sederunt
AYIL	Australian Yearbook of International Law
Act of Adj	Act of Adjournal
Ad & El	Adolphus and Ellis's Reports (King's Bench and Queen's Bench) (England) 1834–42
Adam	Adam's Justiciary Reports 1894–1919
All ER	All England Law Reports 1936–
All ER Rev	All England Law Reports Annual Review 1982–
App Cas	Law Reports, Appeal Cases (House of Lords) 1875–90
App D	Appellate Division (S Africa) 1910–46
App Div	Appellate Division (New York Supreme Court) 1896–1955; 2d, 1955–
Arkley	Arkley's Justiciary Reports 1846–48
Arnot	Arnot's Criminal Trials 1536–1784
Asp MLC	Aspinall's Maritime Law Cases 1870–1943
ATC	Annotated Tax Cases 1922–
Aust	Australia
B & Ad	Barnewall and Adolphus's Reports (King's Bench) (England) 1830–34
B & Ald	Barnewall and Alderson's Reports (King's Bench) (England) 1817–22
B & C	Barnewall and Cresswell's Reports (King's Bench) (England) 1822–30
B & CR	Bankruptcy and Companies Winding up Reports 1918–41
B & S	Best and Smith's Reports (Queen's Bench) (England) 1861–70
BCLC	Butterworths Company Law Cases 1983–
BCR	British Columbia Reports 1867–1947
BILC	British International Law Cases
BTLC	Butterworths Trading Law Cases 1986–
BTR	British Tax Review 1956–
BYIL	British Yearbook of International Law 1920–
Beav	Beavan's Reports (Rolls Court) (England) 1838–66
Bell App	S S Bell's Scotch Appeals (House of Lords) 1842–50
Bell Fol Cas	P Bell's Folio Cases (Court of Session) 1794–95
Bell Oct Cas	P Bell's Octavo Cases (Court of Session) 1790–92
Bing	Bingham's Reports (Common Pleas) (England) 1822–34
Bing NC	Bingham's New Cases (Common Pleas) (England) 1834–40
Biss & Sm	Bisset and Smith's Digest (S Africa)
Bligh	Bligh's Reports (House of Lords) 1819–21
Bligh NS	Bligh's Reports, New Series (House of Lords) 1827–37
Broun	Broun's Justiciary Reports 1842–45

Brown's Supp	Brown's Supplement to Morison's Dictionary of Decisions (Court of Session) 1622–1794
Brown's Syn	Brown's Synopsis of Decisions (Court of Session) 1532–1827
Bruce	Bruce's Decisions (Court of Session) 1714–15
Buchan	Buchanan's Reports (Court of Session) 1800–13
C	Command Papers 1833–99
CA	Court of Appeal
CAR	Commonwealth Arbitration Reports 1905–65
C & P	Carrington and Payne's Reports (Nisi Prius) (England) 1823–41
CB	Common Bench (England) 1845–56
CBNS	Common Bench, New Series (England) 1856–65
CCR	County Court Rules (England)
CDE	Cahiers de Droit Européen
CL	Current Law 1947–
CLJ	Cambridge Law Journal
CLR	Commonwealth Law Reports (Australia) 1903–
CLY	Current Law Year Book 1947–
CMLR	Common Market Law Reports 1962–
CPD	Law Reports, Common Pleas Division (England) 1875–80
CYIL	Canadian Yearbook of International Law
Camb LJ	Cambridge Law Journal 1921–
Camp	Campbell's Reports (Nisi Prius) (England) 1807–16
Cas tep Talb	Cases in Equity temp Talbot
Cd	Command Papers 1900–18
Ch	Law Reports, Chancery Division (England) 1890–
Ch App	Law Reports, Chancery Appeals (England) 1865–75
Ch D	Law Reports, Chancery Division (England) 1875–90
Ch Rob	Christopher Robinson's Reports (Admiralty) (England) 1798–1808
Cl & Fin	Clark and Finnelly's Reports (House of Lords) 1831–46
Cm	Command Papers 1986–
C-MAC	Courts-Martial Appeal Court
Cmd	Command Papers 1919–56
Cmnd	Command Papers 1956–86
Com Cas	Commercial Cases 1895–1941
Com Dig	Comyn's Digest 1792 (England)
Com LR	Commercial Law Reports 1981–
Cornell ILJ	Cornell International Law Journal
Coup	Couper's Justiciary Reports 1868–85
Cox CC	Cox's Criminal Cases (England) 1843–1941
Cr App Rep	Criminal Appeal Reports (England) 1908–
Crim LR	Criminal Law Review (England) 1954–
D	Dunlop's Session Cases 1838–62
DC	Divisional Court
D (HL)	House of Lords cases in Dunlop's Session Cases 1838–62
DLR	Dominion Law Reports (Canada) 1912–55; 2d, 1956–67; 3d, 1968–83; 4th 1984–
DNB	Dictionary of National Biography
Dalr	Dalrymple's Decisions (Court of Session) 1698–1718
Deas & And	Deas and Anderson's Decisions (Court of Session) 1829–32
De G & J	De Gex and Jones's Reports (Chancery) (England) 1857–59
De G & Sm	De Gex and Smale's Reports (Chancery) (England) 1846–52
De G F & J	De Gex, Fisher and Jones's Reports (Chancery) (England) 1859–62
De G J & Sm	De Gex, Jones and Smith's Reports (Chancery) (England) 1862–65

De G M & G	De Gex, Macnaghten and Gordon's Reports (Chancery) (England) 1851–57
Dirl	Dirleton's Decisions (Court of Session) 1665–77
Dods	Dodson's Reports (Admiralty) (England) 1811–22
Dow	Dow's Reports (House of Lords) 1812–18
Dow & Cl	Dow and Clark's Reports (House of Lords) 1827–32
Durie	Durie's Decisions (Court of Session) 1621–42
EAT	Employment Appeal Tribunal
E & B	Ellis and Blackburn's Reports (Queen's Bench) (England) 1852–58
E & E	Ellis and Ellis's Reports (Queen's Bench) (England) 1858–61
E B & E	Ellis, Blackburn and Ellis's Reports (Queen's Bench) (England) 1858–60
EC	European Communities
ECHR	European Court of Human Rights
ECJ	European Court of Justice (Court of Justice of the European Communities)
ECR	European Court of Justice Reports 1954–
ECSC	European Coal and Steel Community
EEC	European Economic Community
EG	Estates Gazette 1858–
EGD	Estates Gazette Digest 1902–
EHD	English Historical Documents
EHR	Economic History Review
EHRR	European Human Rights Reports 1979–
ER	English Reports 1220–1865
Edgar	Edgar's Decisions (Court of Session) 1724–26
Elchies	Elchies' Decisions (Court of Session) 1733–54
Eng Judg	Decisions of English Judges during the Usurpation 1655–61
Eq Rep	Equity Reports (England) 1853–55
Euratom	European Atomic Energy Community
Ex D	Law Reports, Exchequer Division (England) 1875–80
Exch	Exchequer Reports (England) 1847–56
F	Fraser's Session Cases 1898–1906 (preceded by year and volume number); Federal Reporter (USA) 1880–1924; 2d, 1924– (preceded by volume number and followed by year)
FC	Faculty Collection (Court of Session) 1752–1825
F (HL)	House of Lords cases in Fraser's Session Cases 1898–1906
F (J)	Justiciary cases in Fraser's Session Cases 1898–1906
FLR	Family Law Reports (1980–)
FSR	Fleet Street Reports 1963–
F Supp	Federal Supplement (USA) 1932–
Falc	Falconer's Decisions (Court of Session) 1744–51
Fam	Law Reports, Family Division (England) 1972–
Ferg	Ferguson's Consistorial Decisions 1811–17
Forbes	Forbes' Journal of the Sessions 1705–13
Fount	Fountainhall's Decisions (Court of Session) 1678–1712
GA Resoln	General Assembly Resolution
GWD	Green's Weekly Digest 1986–
GYIL	German Yearbook of International Law
Gaz LR	Gazette Law Reports (New Zealand) 1898–1953
Gil & Fal	Gilmour's and Falconer's Decisions (Court of Session) 1661–66, 1681–86
H & C	Hurlstone and Coltman's Reports (Exchequer) (England) 1862–66

H & N	Hurlstone and Norman's Reports (Exchequer) (England) 1856–62
HC	High Court
HL	House of Lords
HL Cas	House of Lords Cases 1847–66
HLR	Housing Law Reports 1981–
Hague Recueil	Hague Academy of International Law Recueil de Cours
Hailes	Hailes' Decisions (Court of Session) 1766–91
Hale PC	Hale's Pleas of the Crown 1678
Harc	Harcarse's Decisions (Court of Session) 1681–91
Hawk PC	Hawkin's Pleas of the Crown
Home	Clerk Home's Decisions (Court of Session) 1735–44
Hume	Hume's Decisions (Court of Session) 1781–1822
ICJ	International Court of Justice
ICJR	International Court of Justice Reports
ICLQR	International and Comparative Law Quarterly Review 1952–
ICR	Industrial Cases Reports (England) 1972–
IH	Inner House
IL	The International Lawyer
ILJ	Industrial Law Journal
ILM	International Legal Materials
ILR	Irish Law Reports 1838–50
ILT	Irish Law Times 1867–
ILT Jo	Irish Law Times Journal 1867–
IR	Irish Reports 1893–
IRLR	Industrial Relations Law Reports 1972–
ITR	Industrial Tribunal Reports 1966–78
Imm AR	Immigration Appeal Reports 1972–
Int LR	International Law Reports
Irv	Irvine's Justiciary Reports 1851–68
J	Justice
JC	Justiciary Cases 1917–
J Juris	Journal of Jurisprudence 1857–91
JLSS	Journal of the Law Society of Scotland 1956–
JP	Justice of the Peace Reports (England) 1837–
JP Jo	Justice of the Peace and Local Government Review (England) 1837–
JPL	Journal of Planning Law 1948–53; Journal of Planning and Property Law 1954–72; and Journal of Planning and Environment Law 1973–
J Shaw	J Shaw's Justiciary Reports 1848–51
JR	Juridical Review 1889–
JSPTL	Journal of the Society of Public Teachers of Law
Jur Soc P	Juridical Society Papers 1858–74
KB	Law Reports, King's Bench Division (England) 1900–52
KIR	Knight's Industrial Reports (England) 1966–75
K & W Dic	Kames' and Woodhouselee's Dictionary of Decisions (Court of Session) 1540–1796
Kames Rem Dec	Kames' Remarkable Decisions (Court of Session) 1716–28
Kames Sel Dec	Kames' Select Decisions (Court of Session) 1752–68
Kilk	Kilkerran's Decisions (Court of Session) 1738–52
LA	Lord Advocate
LC	Lord Chancellor

LCJ	Lord Chief Justice
LGR	Knight's Local Government Reports 1902–
LJ	Law Journal newspaper (England) 1866–1965; Lord Justice
L J-C	Lord Justice-Clerk
LJ Ch	Law Journal, Chancery (England) 1831–1946
LJ Ex	Law Journal, Exchequer (England) 1831–75
L J-G	Lord Justice-General
LJKB	Law Journal, King's Bench (England) 1900–52
LJP	Law Journal, Probate, Divorce and Admiralty (England) 1875–1946
LJPC	Law Journal, Privy Council 1865–1946
LJQB	Law Journal, Queen's Bench Division (England) 1831–1900
LJR	Law Journal Reports (England) 1947–49
LQR	Law Quarterly Review 1885–
LR A & E	Law Reports, Admiralty and Ecclesiastical (England) 1865–75
LRCCR	Law Reports, Crown Cases Reserved (England) 1865–75
LRCP	Law Reports, Common Pleas (England) 1865–75
LR Eq	Law Reports, Equity (England) 1865–75
LR Exch	Law Reports, Exchequer (England) 1865–75
LRHL	Law Reports, House of Lords (England and Ireland) 1866–75
LR Ir	Law Reports, Ireland 1877–93
LR P & D	Law Reports, Probate and Divorce (England) 1865–75
LRPC	Law Reports, Privy Council 1865–75
LRQB	Law Reports, Queen's Bench (England) 1865–75
LRRP	Law Reports, Restrictive Practices 1957–
LR Sc & Div	Law Reports, House of Lords (Scotch and Divorce) 1866–75
LS Gaz	Law Society's Gazette (England) 1903–
LT	Law Times Reports (England) 1859–1947
LT Jo	Law Times newspaper (England) 1843–1947
LTOS	Law Times Reports, Old Series (England) 1843–59
LVAC	Lands Valuation Appeal Court
Land Ct	Scottish Land Court
Law Com	Law Commission (England)
Ll L Rep	Lloyd's List Law Reports 1919–50
Lloyd's Rep	Lloyd's List Law Reports 1951–67; Lloyd's Law Reports 1968–
LoNJ	League of Nations Journal
LoNTS	League of Nations Treaty Series
Lyon Ct	Court of the Lord Lyon
M	Macpherson's Session Cases 1862–73
M (HL)	House of Lords cases in Macpherson's Session Cases 1862–73
MLR	Modern Law Review 1937–
MR	Master of the Rolls
Mac & G	Macnaghten and Gordon's Reports (Chancery) (England) 1849–52
MacF	MacFarlane's Jury Trials (Court of Session) 1838–39
Macl & R	Maclean and Robinson's Scotch Appeals (House of Lords) 1839
Maclaurin	Maclaurin's Arguments and Decisions 1670–1770
Macq	Macqueen's House of Lords Reports 1851–65
Misc	New York Miscellaneous Reports 1892–1955; 2d, 1955–
Moore Int Arb	Moore's History and Digest of International Arbitrations
Mor	Morison's Dictionary of Decisions (Court of Session) 1540–1808
Mun LR	Municipal Law Reports 1903–13
Murr	Murray's Jury Court Cases 1815–30
NI	Northern Ireland Law Reports 1925–
NLJ	New Law Journal (England) 1965–

NMS	National Manuscripts of Scotland
NY	New York Court of Appeals Reports 1847–1955; 2d, 1956–
NYS	New York Supplement 1888–1937; 2d, 1938–
NZ	New Zealand
NZLR	New Zealand Law Reports 1883–
NZULR	New Zealand University Law Review 1963–
OCR	Ordinary Cause Rules
OH	Outer House
OJ	Official Journal of the European Communities; C, Information; L, Legislation
OLR	Ontario Law Reports 1901–30
OR	Ontario Reports 1931–73; 2d, 1974–
P	Law Reports, Probate, Divorce and Admiralty Division (England) 1890–1971
P & CR	Planning and Compensation Reports 1949–67; Property and Compensation Reports 1968– (England)
PC	Judicial Committee of the Privy Council
PCIJ	Permanent Court of International Justice Reports
PD	Law Reports, Probate, Divorce and Admiralty Division (England) 1875–90
PL	Public Law
Pat	Paton's House of Lords Appeal Cases 1726–1821
Paters	Paterson's House of Lords Appeals 1851–73
Pitc	Pitcairn's Criminal Trials 1488–1624
Pol Q	Political Quarterly
QB	Queen's Bench Reports (England) 1841–52 (volume number precedes)
QB	Law Reports, Queen's Bench Division (England) 1891–1901, 1952– (year precedes)
QBD	Law Reports, Queen's Bench Division (England) 1875–90
QC	Queen's Counsel
R	Rettie's Session Cases 1873–98
RA	Rating Appeals 1965–
RC	Rules of the Court of Session
RGS	Register of the Great Seal of Scotland
R (HL)	House of Lords cases in Rettie's Session Cases 1873–98
RICS	Royal Institution of Chartered Surveyors, Scottish Lands Valuation Appeal Reports
R (J)	Justiciary cases in Rettie's Session Cases 1873–98
RPC	Reports of Patents, Designs and Trade Marks Cases 1884–; Restrictive Practices Court
RRC	Ryde's Rating Cases (England) 1956–
RSC	Rules of the Supreme Court (England)
RTR	Road Traffic Reports 1970–
RVR	Rating and Valuation Reports (England) 1960–
Robert	Robertson's Scotch Appeals (House of Lords) 1707–27
Robin	Robinson's Scotch Appeals (House of Lords) 1840–41
Ross LC	G Ross's Leading Cases in the Law of Scotland (Land Rights) 1638–1849
S	P Shaw's Session Cases 1821–38
SA	South African Law Reports 1947–
SALJ	South African Law Journal
SAL Rev	South African Law Review

SAR	South African Supreme Court Reports 1881–92
S & D Just	Shaw and Dunlop's Justiciary Cases 1819–31
SC	Session Cases 1907–; Supreme Court
SCCR	Scottish Criminal Case Reports 1981–
SCCR Supp	Scottish Criminal Case Reports Supplement 1950–80
SC (HL)	House of Lords cases in Session Cases 1907–
SC (J)	Justiciary Cases in Session Cases 1907–16
SCLR	Scottish Civil Law Reports 1987–
SCOLAG	The journal of the Scottish Legal Action Group
SCR	Summary Cause Rules
SC Resoln	Security Council Resolution
Sel Cas Ch	Select Cases in Chancery (England) 1724–33
SI	Statutory Instruments
SJ	Scottish Jurist 1829–73
SLCR	Scottish Land Court Reports in Scottish Law Review (1913–63) (preceded by year and volume number), and Scottish Land Court Reports 1982– (preceded by year)
SLCR App	Appendix to the annual reports of the Scottish Land Court 1963–
SLG	Scottish Law Gazette 1933–
SLJ	Scottish Law Journal and Sheriff Court Record 1858–61
SLM	Scottish Law Magazine and Sheriff Court Reporter 1862–67
SLR	Scottish Law Reporter 1865–1925
SL Rev	Scottish Law Review and Sheriff Court Reporter 1885–1963
SLT	Scots Law Times 1893–1908 (preceded by year and volume number), and 1909– (preceded by year)
SLT (ECCN)	Scots Law Times European Court Case Notes (1984–)
SLT (Land Ct)	Scottish Land Court Reports in Scots Law Times 1964–
SLT (Lands Trib)	Lands Tribunal for Scotland Reports in Scots Law Times 1971–
SLT (Lyon Ct)	Lyon Court Reports in Scots Law Times 1950–
SLT (Notes)	Notes of Recent Decisions in Scots Law Times 1946–1981
SLT (Sh Ct)	Sheriff Court Reports in Scots Law Times 1893–
SN	Session Notes 1925–48
SO	Standing Orders
SPD	State Papers Domestic
SPLP	Scottish Planning Law and Practice 1980–
SR & O	Statutory Rules and Orders
SRR	Scots Revised Reports 1707–1873, 1898–1908
STC	Simon's Tax Cases 1973–
Scot Law Com	Scottish Law Commission
Scot Hist Rev	Scottish Historical Review
Sh & Macl	P Shaw and Maclean's House of Lords Appeal Cases 1835–38
Sh App	P Shaw's Scotch Appeals (House of Lords) 1821–26
Sh Ct Rep	Sheriff Court Reports in Scottish Law Review 1885–1963
Shaw Just	P Shaw's Justiciary Reports 1819–31
Shaw Teind	P Shaw's Teind Court Decisions 1821–31
Sim	Simon's Reports (Chancery) (England) 1826–52
Sim & St	Simon & Stuart's Reports (Chancery) (England) 1822–26
Sim NS	Simon's Reports, New Series (Chancery) (England) 1850–52
Smith LC	Smith's Leading Cases (England)
Sol Jo	Solicitors' Journal (England) 1856–
Stair Rep	Stair's Reports (Court of Session) 1661–81
Stair Soc	Stair Society
State Tr	State Trials 1163–1820
State Tr NS	State Trials, New Series 1820–58
Stuart	Stuart, Milne and Peddie's Reports (Court of Session) 1851–53
Swin	Swinton's Justiciary Reports 1835–41
Syme	Syme's Justiciary Reports 1826–29

TC	Tax Cases 1875–
TLR	Times Law Reports (England) 1884–1952
TR	Taxation Reports 1939–
TS	United Kingdom Treaty Series
Taunt	Taunton's Reports (Common Pleas) (England) 1807–19
Term Rep	Term Reports (England) 1785–1800
UNRIAA	United Nations Reports of International Arbitral Awards
UNTS	United Nations Treaty Series
US	United States Supreme Court Reports 1754–
VATTR	Value Added Tax Tribunal Reports 1973–
V-C	Vice-Chancellor
VLR	Victorian Law Reports 1875–1956
VR	Victorian Reports 1870–72, and 1957–
Ves	Vesey Junior's Reports (Chancery) (England) 1789–1817
Ves Sen	Vesey Senior's Reports (Chancery) (England) 1747–56
WALR	West Australian Law Reports 1898–1959
WAR	Western Australian Reports 1960–
W & S	Wilson and Shaw's House of Lords Cases 1825–34
WLR	Weekly Law Reports (England) 1953–
WN	Law Reports, Weekly Notes (England) 1866–1952
WR	Weekly Reporter (England) 1852–1906
WS	Writer to the Signet
WWR	Western Weekly Reports (Canada) 1911–1950, and 1955–
West	West's House of Lords Reports 1839–41
White	White's Justiciary Reports 1885–93
YB	Year Books
YBILC	Yearbook of the International Law Commission
YBWA	Yearbook of World Affairs
YEL	Yearbook of European Law

Table of Statutes

Table of Orders, Rules and Regulations

Table of Other Enactments

Table of Cases

A

References are to paragraphs

References are to paragraphs

C

References are to paragraphs

References are to paragraphs

References are to paragraphs

References are to paragraphs

References are to paragraphs

References are to paragraphs

References are to paragraphs

References are to paragraphs

References are to paragraphs

References are to paragraphs

References are to paragraphs

Q

R

References are to paragraphs

References are to paragraphs

References are to paragraphs

References are to paragraphs

References are to paragraphs

References are to paragraphs

X

References are to paragraphs

Y

Z

References are to paragraphs

FISHERIES

The General Editors and author acknowledge with appreciation valuable comments and suggestions made by Mr Robert B Williamson, Inspector of Salmon and Freshwater Fisheries for Scotland.

1. SALMON AND FRESHWATER FISHERIES

(1) SALMON FISHING RIGHTS

1. Meaning of 'salmon'. For the purposes of the Salmon and Freshwater Fisheries (Protection) (Scotland) Act 1951, 'salmon' includes all migratory fish of the species *Salmo salar* and *Salmo trutta* and commonly known as salmon and sea trout respectively or any part of such fish[1].

> 1 Salmon and Freshwater Fisheries (Protection) (Scotland) Act 1951 (c 26), s 24(1). A similar definition appears in the Salmon Act 1986 (c 62), s 40(1), save that the word 'means' is used instead of 'includes', so that the 1986 definition is more restrictive. That 1986 definition is applied by the Salmon Fisheries (Scotland) Act 1868 (c 123), s 1A (added by the Salmon Act 1986, s 41(1), Sch 4, para 1). Under repealed nineteenth-century legislation 'salmon' meant and included salmon, grilse, sea trout, bull trout, smolts, parr and other migratory fish of the salmon kind: Salmon Fisheries (Scotland) Act 1862 (c 97), s 2 (repealed), which was originally applied to the Salmon Fisheries (Scotland) Act 1868 by s 2 (repealed).

2. History of regulation of salmon fishing. The value attributed to salmon fishing in Scotland since time immemorial is evidenced by the fact that statutory protection is said to have been first given by David I (1124–1153) and William the Lion (1165–1214), when the principle of a weekly close time was introduced[1]. It was also enacted that in mid-stream there should be a gap wide enough to allow a three-year-old swine, well fed, to stand in it '*ita quod neque grunnus porci appropinquet sepi nec cauda*' — 'sua that nothes the gronzie (snout) na the tayl may wyn (reach) till ony side'[2]. An Act of 1424 prohibited inter alia the construction of cruives in tidal waters[3], and was clearly directed to maintaining stocks of fish. A further Act of 1696, entitled 'An Act against Killers of Black Fish and Destroyers of the Fry and Smolts of Salmon'[4], has only recently been repealed[5].

The basis for modern statutory protection of salmon fishing was provided by a succession of Acts[6] which, after a gap of some 120 years, culminated in the Salmon Act 1986 (c 62).

> 1 Assise Regis Willemi c 10 (APS i, 374), which enacts that there should be no fishing from Saturday evening until Monday sunrise. 'Among the problems presented to the historian of the reign of King William is the measure of credit to be given to the "assizes" or laws of his reign': A A M Duncan *Scotland: the Making of the Kingdom* (1975) p 185. However, Duncan accepts Assise Regis Willemi c 10 as 'probably genuine': p 200, note 30. Nevertheless, Lord Cooper of Culross suspected 'that these provisions were invented by some medieval A P Herbert': 'Early Scottish Statutes Revisited' in Lord Cooper *Selected Papers 1922–1954* (1957) pp 242, 243. Robert Bruce's legislation of 1318 (c 11) requires that cruives in salmon rivers have measurements of such a size as not to impede young salmon smolt or fry of other kinds of fish.
> 2 Assise Regis Willemi c 10.
> 3 Salmon Act 1424 (c 12) (repealed). A cruive is a dyke or low dam built across a river with one or more traps built into it. Examples of cruives can now be found only in two or three places in Scotland. See *Second Report of the Committee on Scottish Salmon and Trout Fisheries* (the 'Hunter Report') (Cmnd 2691) (1965) para 191. See further para 11 below.
> 4 Salmon Act 1696 (c 35). A black fish is a female salmon that has recently spawned. A male that has recently spawned is a red fish.
> 5 Salmon Act 1986 (c 62), s 41(2), Sch 5.
> 6 Ie the Salmon Fisheries (Scotland) Act 1828 (c 39) (repealed), the Salmon Fisheries (Scotland) Act 1844 (c 95) (repealed), the Salmon Fisheries (Scotland) Act 1862 (c 97) (repealed), the Salmon Fisheries (Scotland) Act 1868 (c 123), and the Salmon Fisheries (Scotland) Act 1951 (c 26).

3. Nature of the right of salmon fishing. As the right of salmon fishing will be dealt with in greater detail elsewhere in this work[1], it is necessary here only to give a brief outline of the nature of the right, the acquisition of title to it and its extent and limitations.

While salmon in their natural state are *res nullius* and, as such, are wild and belong to no one until caught, the right of catching them is vested in the Crown[2]. This would appear to refer to the fishings rather than to the fish themselves, as any person convicted of certain offences under the Salmon and Freshwater Fisheries (Protection) (Scotland) Act 1951 is liable under the Act to the forfeiture of any fish illegally taken by him or in his possession at the time of the offence[3], and if the salmon had been regarded as Crown property this provision would have been unnecessary[4].

The exclusive right of salmon fishing in Scotland and within Scottish territorial waters[5], except in Orkney and Shetland[6], and without regard to whether the waters are tidal or non-tidal[7], vested originally in the Crown. Thus all proprietors of salmon fishing in Scotland today (except on these islands) derive their right directly or indirectly from a Crown grant.

It was at one time contended that the Crown's exclusive right to salmon fishings extended only to net and coble[8], and did not include the right of angling by rod and line, but it is now settled law that such a right is an exclusive right to take salmon by all lawful means, including rod and line[9].

1 See PROPERTY (treatment of salmon fishing by K Reid).
2 Stair *Institutions* II, 3, 69; Erskine *Institute* II, 1, 10; J Rankine *The Law of Land-ownership in Scotland* (4th edn, 1909) p 304.
3 Salmon and Freshwater Fisheries (Protection) (Scotland) Act 1951 (c 26), s 19(1), which is expressed to apply to offences against Pt I (ss 1–9) and s 13, being offences in respect of which no provision for forfeiture is expressly made.
4 Erskine states that 'though the fishing of salmon be a royal right . . . yet the salmon themselves which are so caught are not *inter regalia*, and therefore belong to the catcher': *Institute* II, 1, 10.
5 As to territorial waters, see paras 71 ff below.
6 *Lord Advocate v Balfour* 1907 SC 1360, 15 SLT 7, OH.
7 *Comrs of Woods and Forests v Gammell* (1851) 13 D 854, affd 3 Macq 419, HL; *Joseph Johnston & Son v Morrison* 1962 SLT 322, OH.
8 As to net and coble, see para 11 below. A coble was traditionally a short flat-bottomed rowing boat, used especially in salmon fishing or lake- or river-fishing: *Concise Scots Dictionary* (1985).
9 *Anderson v Anderson* (1867) 6 M 117.

4. The acquisition of the right. The right of salmon fishing comprises a separate feudal estate, and is not an incident of land ownership[1]. It was classified as a right *inter regalia minora*, and consequently as a legally separate tenement which could be acquired by express grant from the Crown or by prescription on a habile title. The ways in which such rights may be acquired are listed by Craigie as follows:

'(1) by express grant thereof from the Crown, either alone or by a clause *cum piscationibus salmonum* in the dispositive clause or a Crown charter of lands;
(2) by prescriptive possession of salmon fishing on a barony title with or without a general clause of fishings;
(3) by prescriptive possession of salmon fishing on a Crown charter of lands not a barony, with a general clause of fishings; *ie, cum piscationibus* or *cum privilegio piscendi, cum piscariis,* or probably *cum piscibus*;
(4) by prescriptive possession of salmon fishing on an express grant thereof in a conveyance granted by a subject-superior; and
(5) by prescriptive possession of salmon fishing on a title to land with a general clause of fishings'[2].

The period of possession which must be established by a person relying on prescription is ten years, except in a question with the Crown, when it is twenty years[3].

1 Contrast trout fishing: see para 48 below.
2 J Craigie *The Scottish Law of Conveyancing — Heritable Rights* (3rd edn, 1899) p 121, who cites cases in support.
3 Prescription and Limitation (Scotland) Act 1973 (c 52), s 1(1), (4).

5. The extent of the right. The only lawful method of fishing for or taking salmon in any inland water[1] is by rod and line[2] or by net and coble[3], although any right of fishing for salmon in existence on 10 May 1951 may continue to be exercised[4]. In many cases the size of the river will dictate the appropriate method. In practice it will be more often exercised by rod and line than by net and coble[4].

Is a right to fish for salmon in a river unrestricted? If the right includes fishing from both banks, then clearly there can be no impediment to the exclusive right to fish anywhere within the bounds of the right. Difficulties may arise where the right extends to one bank only, with the right to fish from the other bank vested in another proprietor, which is frequently the case. The boundaries of the right will be fixed either by the respective titles of the parties or by prescriptive possession, but in the absence of either the generally accepted rule to be applied was that the limit of the right was the *medium filum* or centre line of the river[5]. This rule was examined, and the authorities reviewed, by the House of Lords in 1984 in *Fothringham v Passmore*[6], as a result of which there emerged a new rule which was to the effect that each proprietor is entitled to stand on his own bank, or to wade out or row his boat for the purposes of harling to the limit of his property up to the *medium filum*, and to fish as far across the river as he could reach by normal casting or spinning: he was not restricted to casting or spinning, or to allowing his fly or lure to be carried by the current when harling, only up to the *medium filum*.

In practice, whatever the size of the river, arrangements are usually made whereby each proprietor fishes the whole width of the river at certain times. A rule whereby a proprietor was limited to casting, or rowing his boat when harling, to the *medium filum* only, would be almost impossible to enforce. Reference was made in the House of Lords to the power of the court to regulate the respective rights of opposite proprietors 'if their enjoyment of their respective rights is seriously prejudiced in consequence'[7].

The right of salmon fishing includes the right to fish for brown trout and other freshwater fish in the same waters. As is discussed below[8], the right to fish for brown trout is not a separate heritable right like salmon fishing, but pertains to the ownership of the lands which border, and are *adverso*, the water. The result may therefore be that one proprietor owns the salmon fishings and a separate proprietor of the lands adjoining the water will have the right to fish for freshwater fish[9] such as trout and eels in the same water. The 'greater' right of salmon fishing includes the 'lesser' right to fish for freshwater fish, whereas the converse is not so. Strictly speaking, therefore, a person who has the right to fish for trout in a salmon river and who accidentally catches a salmon in the course of pursuing his right to catch trout is required to return the salmon to the river.

1   'Inland waters' includes all rivers above estuary limits and their tributary streams, and all waters, watercourses and lochs whether natural or artificial draining into the sea; and 'estuary limits' means limits which divide each river including its mouth or estuary from the sea as fixed by any enactment, byelaw or the decision of a court: Salmon and Freshwater Fisheries (Protection) (Scotland) Act 1951 (c 26), s 24(1).
2   Ibid, s 2(1). 'Rod and line' means single rod and line with such bait or lure as was lawful on 10 May 1951 and, in the case of fishing for salmon in an area to which and at a time during which regulations made under the Salmon Act 1986 (c 62), s 8, apply, is not specified in such regulations in respect of that area and time: Salmon and Freshwater Fisheries (Protection) (Scotland) Act 1951, s 24(1) (amended by the Salmon Act 1986, s 8(6)). Under s 8(1)–(5), Sch 1, paras 3–9, the Secretary of State may make regulations specifying baits and lures for the purposes of this definition: see para 23 below.
3   Salmon and Freshwater Fisheries (Protection) (Scotland) Act 1951, s 2(1). For a detailed description of net and coble, see para 11 below. Section 2 does not apply to activities within a fish farm

(defined in para 57 below) in the course of the operations of a fish farm: Freshwater and Salmon Fisheries (Scotland) Act 1976 (c 22), s 7(1), Sch 3, para 8(a).

4 Salmon and Freshwater Fisheries (Protection) (Scotland) Act 1951, s 2(1) proviso. An example is by harling, ie trolling or drawing a line baited with a fly or minnow, especially from a boat, discussed by Lord Fraser of Tullybelton in *Fothringham v Passmore* 1984 SC (HL) 96 at 130, 1984 SLT 401 at 408, HL.

5 *Gay v Malloch* 1959 SC 110 at 121, 1959 SLT 132 at 138, per Lord President Clyde, referring to *Earl of Zetland v Tennent's Trustees* (1873) 11 M 469 at 474, per Lord Cowan. The Lord President went on to discuss arrangements which might be made if it were impossible to fish without crossing the *medium filum*. The First Division held that fishing by net and coble beyond the *medium filum* was not permitted without the consent of the opposite proprietor, but interdict was withheld to give the parties an opportunity to come to an arrangement, in the absence of which the court could supply one.

6 *Fothringham v Passmore* 1984 SC (HL) 96, 1984 SLT 401.

7 1984 SC (HL) 96 at 130, 1984 SLT 401 at 408. See also *Gay v Malloch* 1959 SC 110 at 121, 1959 SLT 132 at 138, per Lord President Clyde.

8 See para 48 below.

9 'Freshwater fish' means any fish living in fresh water, including trout, and eels and the fry of eels, but exclusive of salmon and of any kind of fish which migrate between the open sea and tidal waters; and 'trout' means non-migratory trout of the species *Salmo trutta* living in fresh waters or estuaries: Salmon and Freshwater Fisheries (Protection) (Scotland) Act 1951, s 24(1).

6. Restrictions on the exercise of the right. The proprietor of salmon fishings is subject to certain restrictions in the exercise of his right, in addition to those limitations referred to above as to the actual methods of fishing. A proprietor has certain obligations to other holders of salmon fishing rights in the same waters[1]. For example, he must not interfere with the *alveus* of the river in a way which might affect the natural flow of the river and which, as a consequence, damages the rights of others[2]; nor may a proprietor erect barriers to prevent the free passage of salmon. A proprietor may, however, restore the *alveus* on his own side to its original condition by carrying out engineering works when it has been disturbed by a flood, but any such works must be carried out within a reasonable time, for example in the same year as the flooding took place[3]. Other proprietors also have rights as to the quantity of water abstracted from the river, if such abstraction interferes with the free passage of salmon up the river[4]. Proprietors of salmon fishings also have rights against those who discharge pollutants into a river[5].

1 For further discussion, see PROPERTY.

2 *Robertson v Foote & Co* (1879) 6 R 1290, where the Second Division held that a salmon proprietor was not entitled to improve his fishings by removing massive boulders from the river bed on his own side of the *medium filum*, as the effect on other proprietors was impossible to predict.

3 *Town of Nairn v Brodie, Lord Lyon* (1738) Mor 12779; *Aberdeen Magistrates v Menzies* (1748) Mor 12787; *Mather v Machraire* (1873) 11 M 522.

4 *Duke of Roxburghe v Waldie's Trustees* (1879) 6 R 663; *Alex Pirie & Sons Ltd v Earl of Kintore* (1906) 8 F (HL) 16, 14 SLT 215.

5 *Countess of Seafield v Kemp* (1899) 1 F 402, 6 SLT 289. Such discharges could also comprise an offence under the Control of Pollution Act 1974 (c 40), ss 31, 32 (both substituted by the Water Act 1989 (c 15), s 169, Sch 23, para 4), and the Water (Scotland) Act 1980 (c 45), s 75.

7. Salmon rights and rights of navigation. Salmon proprietors may not exercise their rights of fishing in such a way as to interfere with the public right of navigation[1]. The law on navigable rivers required to be restated and applied to modern conditions mainly because of the advent of the fibreglass canoe and its ability successfully to be navigated down swift-flowing Scottish rivers. The passage of canoes down such rivers has posed problems for salmon proprietors and these questions had therefore to be answered: whether a right of salmon fishing in non-tidal waters took precedence over a right of passage of a canoe down a salmon river and, if so, whether the owners of the salmon rights could prevent such passage. As the answer is given so succinctly, it is worth quoting the heading to *The Times* law report of 3 March 1976, when reporting the decision in the *Wills' Trustees* case[2] — '1782 decision allows canoes to disturb the fish'. This refers to an early case[3] in which it was held finally, after prolonged litigation, that the floating of timber down the River Spey constituted a public right of passage which was, as Lord Wilberforce said, based not on a private right or servitude, and later decisions and writers of authority had accepted that the case was a decision 'in favour of a public right'[4]. The House of Lords therefore held in 1976 that the River Spey was a public navigable river so that the owners of the salmon fishings along the non-tidal stretch of that river could not prevent the public use of the waters for canoeing. The effect of the 1976 decision is that where a river is held to be 'navigable', canoeists will have an equal right with the owners of the rights of salmon fishing to the use of that river, but such right of passage is not unlimited. To establish any right of passage successfully, navigation must be shown to have taken place during at least part of the year for a period of forty years or more.

As regards the extent of the exercise of the right of passage, this would appear to be confined to a genuine 'passage' down a river by conventional propulsion of the canoe. Lord Fraser of Tullybelton, in the *Wills' Trustees* case, did not consider such right of passage to be unlimited, but said that it should be exercised in a manner which had regard to the interests of other persons such as anglers legitimately exercising their rights in the river, and would not include 'operations which would be more like acrobatic feats than navigation'[5]. This would seem to mean that a right of passage is not to be equated with performing 'eskimo rolls' in a salmon pool, in which case it would be unlikely that the canoeist would obtain the protection of the law. In practice, proprietors reach agreements with canoe clubs as to their use of a particular stretch of river, with the result that both uses of the water can co-exist in harmony. The right of passage does not imply a right of access to the river, other than at a public place, with the result that canoeists require specific permission from the owner of the land adjoining the river in order to obtain access to, or to leave, the river.

1 See further PROPERTY, and also *Wills' Trustees v Cairngorm Canoeing and Sailing School Ltd* 1976 SC (HL) 30, 1976 SLT 162, and *Burton's Trustees v Scottish Sports Council* 1983 SLT 418, Vacation Ct.
2 *Wills' Trustees v Cairngorm Canoeing and Sailing School Ltd* 1976 SC (HL) 30, 1976 SLT 162.
3 *Grant v Duke of Gordon* (1782) 2 Pat 582, HL.
4 *Wills' Trustees v Cairngorm Canoeing and Sailing School Ltd* 1976 SC (HL) 30 at 120, 1976 SLT 162 at 189.
5 1976 SC (HL) 30 at 169, 1976 SLT 162 at 216.

8. Rights ancillary to salmon fishing rights. A right to salmon fishing implies a right to such accessories as are necessary for the beneficial enjoyment of the principal right. The most important of these ancillary rights is clearly that of access to the water, as otherwise it would be impossible to exercise the right. This will become particularly important where the salmon fishing rights and the land adjoining the water are in different ownerships. The general principle is that the proprietor of salmon fishings may make all uses of the adjacent banks, or the foreshore where fishing in the sea is concerned, which are reasonably required for the proper exercise of his right. This includes the use of the foreshore, beach and waste land adjoining for drawing and drying salmon nets[1]. He may therefore have access across land to reach the waters[2]. The authorities concerning access to salmon fishings were reviewed by Lord Davidson in the *Middletweed* case, where he concluded:

'. . . these passages tend to reinforce the view that the necessary right of access which attaches to property in salmon fishings is restricted not merely to access which is least prejudicial to the riparian owner, but also to access which is necessary for the beneficial enjoyment of the fishings'[3].

On arrival at the fishing the salmon proprietor is entitled to use the bank for casting and other such necessary purposes but, as specified by Lord Davidson, the use must be such as is least prejudicial to the riparian owner. Doubt has been expressed as to the legal basis of such accessory rights[4]. Certain judicial statements would appear to support the view that such rights are rights in property and not servitudes[5].

1 *Miller v Blair* (1825) 4 S 214 (NE 217); *Lord Advocate v Sharp* (1878) 6 R 108. See also PROPERTY.
2 *Miller v Blair* (1825) 4 S 214 (NE 217).
3 *Middletweed Ltd v Murray* (1989) SLT 11 at 14, OH. See also J Rankine *The Law of Land-ownership in Scotland* (4th edn, 1909) p 315.
4 See PROPERTY.
5 *Miller v Blair* (1825) 4 S 214 at 217, per Lord Craigie; *Berry v Wilson* (1841) 4 D 139 at 147, per Lord Justice-Clerk Hope.

9. Leases of salmon fishings. Salmon fishings are often the subject of lease, either of rod and line or of netting. Net and rod fishings in the same water may be let to different lessees. A proprietor may reserve to himself the right of fishing, say by rod and line, and thereafter lease it to another[1]. A lease of salmon fishings, being a separate heritable estate, is protected against claims by singular successors by the Leases Act 1449[2]. It is probable that such a lease will exclude sub-tenants and assignees, unless specially stipulated[3], since such a lease, like 'a lease of shootings implies *delectus personae* in a sense more emphatic than almost any other kind of lease'[4].

1 *Gemmill v Riddell* (1847) 9 D 727.
2 *Leith v Leith* (1862) 24 D 1059. The Leases Act 1449 (c 6) was applied by the Freshwater and Salmon Fisheries (Scotland) Act 1976 (c 22), s 4.
3 *Earl of Fife v Wilson* (1864) 3 M 323, approved in *Mackintosh v May* (1895) 22 R 345, 2 SLT 471.
4 *Earl of Fife v Wilson* (1864) 3 M 323, per Lord Kinloch, cited by Lord Stormonth-Darling in *Mackintosh v May* (1895) 22 R 345 at 348n.

(2) REGULATION OF SALMON AND FRESHWATER FISHING

10. Modern statutory basis. The basis for the modern administration of salmon fisheries in Scotland was created by the Salmon Fisheries (Scotland) Acts of 1862, 1863 and 1868, which together set up the machinery for the management and enforcement of salmon fishery legislation today. These three Acts, which were to be read and construed as one[1], provided for the setting up of salmon fishery district boards to manage and administer salmon fisheries throughout Scotland, as well as creating offences and establishing the ground rules for the regulation of salmon fisheries. Reference to these Acts will continue to be made hereafter, although they were largely repealed by the Salmon Act 1986[2].

The Freshwater Fish (Scotland) Act 1902 (c 29) established a close season for trout, and was amended by the Trout (Scotland) Act 1933 (c 35). There was then no fundamental change in the law until 1951, when the Salmon and Freshwater Fisheries (Protection) (Scotland) Act 1951 came into force following the Maconochie Report[3] on methods of combating poaching and illegal fishing for salmon, which had increased after the 1939–45 war. This Act, which remains in force, being primarily an anti-poaching measure, created new offences and substantially increased the penalties for others[4], but concessions were made to fish farmers and those acting on their behalf[5]. It should be noted that while the legislation referred to applies generally to all waters in Scotland, certain waters, namely the River Tweed and the Solway Firth, also have their own private legislation[6]. The Sea Fish Industry Act 1962 (c 31) enabled orders to be made prohibiting the use of drift nets to catch salmon or sea trout in Scottish waters. Following this, there was no further change in the law relating to salmon fisheries until the Salmon Act 1986 was passed, of which the greater part applies to Scotland only[7]. Pressure for amending legislation had been exerted following the publication in 1965 of the Hunter Report[8], which contained a number of recommendations for the radical reform of the administration and management of Scottish salmon fisheries. These recommendations were never implemented, and although eventually the 1986 Act was passed it was not in general based on the Hunter Committee proposals.

To advise the electricity industry and the Secretary of State a Fisheries Committee was appointed under the Electricity (Scotland) Act 1979[9] and is continued in existence by the Electricity Act 1989 and charged with the duty of giving advice and assistance on questions relating to the effect in Scotland on fisheries or fish stocks in any waters of generating stations wholly or mainly driven by water[10].

1 Salmon Fisheries (Scotland) Act 1868 (c 123), s 2 (repealed).
2 The Salmon Act 1986 (c 62), s 41(2), Sch 5, repealed the whole of the Salmon Fisheries (Scotland) Acts 1862 (c 97) and 1863 (c 50), and part of the Salmon Fisheries (Scotland) Act 1868.
3 *Report on Poaching and Illegal Fishing of Salmon and Trout in Scotland* (the Maconochie Report) (Cmd 7917) (1949).
4 Salmon and Freshwater Fisheries (Protection) (Scotland) Act 1951 (c 27), ss 1–4 (amended by the Salmon Act 1986 (c 62), s 21): see paras 11, 21, 54, below.
5 Freshwater and Salmon Fisheries (Scotland) Act 1976 (c 22), s 7, Sch 3, para 8: see para 63 below.
6 See the Tweed Fisheries Act 1857 (c cxlviii), the Tweed Fisheries Amendment Act 1859 (c lxx) and the Tweed Fisheries Act 1969 (c xxiv); and the Solway Act 1804 (c xlv) and the Solway Salmon Fisheries Commissioners (Scotland) Act 1877 (c ccxl).
7 Salmon Act 1986, s 43(5).
8 *Second Report of the Committee on Scottish Salmon and Trout Fisheries* (The Hunter Report) (Cmnd 2691) (1965).
9 See the Electricity (Scotland) Act 1979 (c 11), s 5, Sch 4, and ENERGY, vol 9, paras 616, 635. The Act is prospectively repealed by the Electricity Act 1989 (c 29), s 112(4), Sch 18 from a day to be appointed by order under s 113(2). The committee was originally established under the Hydro-Electric Development (Scotland) Act 1943 (c 32), s 9(2) (repealed).
10 See the Electricity Act 1989, s 38, Sch 9, para 5, which comes into force on a day to be appointed by order under s 113(2), and para 39 below.

11. Permitted methods of fishing. The lawful methods by which fishing may take place will depend on where the right is exercised. Within inland waters[1] the only permitted methods of fishing for salmon[2] are by rod and line[3] or by net and coble[4]. Within these waters the only lawful method of fishing for freshwater fish, including trout[5], is by rod and line[6], but for freshwater fish other than trout proprietors and occupiers may use a net or trap[7]. Nothing in these provisions is to be construed as prohibiting the use of a gaff, tailer or landing-net as auxiliary to the taking of any fish by rod and line[8]. Fishing for any freshwater fish by net is permitted on any pond or loch where all the proprietors so agree[9]. Nothing in the Salmon and Freshwater Fisheries (Protection) (Scotland) Act 1951 renders legal any method of fishing which was, or would have been, illegal at the date of its commencement[10] on 10 May 1951. Various lures and methods of using a rod and line were expressly prohibited by statutes in force when the 1951 Act was passed[11]. However, any right of fishing for salmon in existence at that date may continue to be exercised as if the 1951 Act had not been passed[12]. This covers fishing by cruive[13], a form of trap used very rarely and then only by the holders of cruive charter rights, and fishing by privileged fixed engines, a method of fishing in the Solway Firth[14].

Persons using any of the permitted methods must first have either the legal right to fish or written permission from a person with a legal right to fish. Any person who fishes for salmon without such right or permission commits the offence of poaching, for which the maximum penalty on summary conviction is a fine not exceeding level 3 on the standard scale, and the forfeiture of any fish illegally taken by him or in his possession at the time of the offence[15]. Contravention of the other provisions set out above is an offence against the 1951 Act and is punishable on summary conviction by a fine not exceeding level 4 on the standard scale[16].

While 'rod and line' is suitably defined by statute[17], the term 'net and coble' is nowhere so defined, and it is therefore necessary to rely on judicial pronouncements for a definition[18]. The judges in the *Bermoney Boat* case[19] set out the principles of what constitutes 'fair net and coble', and these have been followed ever since. It is worth quoting in full a general description of net and coble fishing based on a study of authoritative texts and relevant court decisions:

> 'Net and coble is a lawful form of fishing for salmon within estuary limits whereby the fish are surrounded by a net and drawn to the shore; the net and any warps being both shot and hauled as quickly as practicable and kept in unchecked motion by the fisherman and under his effectual command and control for the purpose of enclosing the fish within the sweep of the net and bringing them to the shore. It is not permitted for the net to be held or left to lie stationary relative to either the land or the water or to use it to enmesh the fish or to obstruct, turn or drive them; there may be some obstruction as the net is shot but this must be momentary only and merely incidental to the rapid encirclement of the fish. It is unlawful to use obstructing devices such as other nets, stakes, dykes, heaps of stones etc, in conjunction with the net even if the net is shot and hauled as described above. The throwing of stones or other things, splashing or other activities designed to drive fish into the area of the sweep, or to keep them there, is not fair net and coble and therefore unlawful'[20].

If fishing for salmon takes place in a salmon fishery district[21] outside estuary limits[22], the permitted methods (on the coming into force of the relevant provisions of the Salmon Act 1986) include not only rod and line and net and coble but also bag net, fly net or other stake net[23].

1　For the meaning of 'inland waters', see para 5, note 1, above.
2　For the meaning of 'salmon', see para 1 above.
3　For the meaning of 'rod and line', see para 5, note 2, above.
4　Salmon and Freshwater Fisheries (Protection) (Scotland) Act 1951 (c 26), s 2(1). As to the meaning of 'net and coble', see below.
5　For the meaning of 'freshwater fish' and 'trout', see para 5, note 9, above.
6　Salmon and Freshwater Fisheries (Protection) (Scotland) Act 1951, s 2(2).
7　Ibid, s 2(2) proviso (b).
8　Ibid, s 2(3).
9　Ibid, s 2(2) proviso (a).
10　Ibid, s 24(2).
11　Eg the use of any fish roe as a lure (Salmon Fisheries (Scotland) Act 1868 (c 123), s 18 (amended by the Freshwater and Salmon Fisheries (Scotland) Act 1976 (c 22), s 6(1), Sch 2, and by the Salmon Act 1986 (c 62), s 41(1), Sch 4, para 3(1)); and striking salmon with a hook (sniggering or dragging) (Salmon Fisheries (Scotland) Act 1868, s 17 (repealed)).
12　Salmon and Freshwater Fisheries (Protection) (Scotland) Act 1951, s 2(1) proviso.
13　See para 2, note 3, above. General regulations as to the construction and use of cruives were set out in a byelaw reproduced in the Salmon Fisheries (Scotland) Act 1868, Sch (F) (repealed).
14　See the Solway Salmon Fisheries Commissioners (Scotland) Act 1877 (c ccxl), s 5. These engines were defined as including only those in use for taking salmon in the open season of one or more of the years 1861 to 1864 in accordance with any grant, charter or immemorial usage. The Special

Commissioners for Solway Fisheries granted certificates of privileged engines after inquiry, and a list of all fixed engines approved by them was then published.

15 Salmon and Freshwater Fisheries (Protection) (Scotland) Act 1951, s 1 (amended by the Freshwater and Salmon Fisheries (Scotland) Act 1976 (c 22), Sch 2, and the Salmon Act 1986 (c 62), Sch 4, para 7); Criminal Procedure (Scotland) Act 1975 (c 21), ss 289E–289G (added by the Criminal Justice Act 1982 (c 48), s 54). Level 3 is £400: Increase of Criminal Penalties etc (Scotland) Order 1984, SI 1984/526, art 4. Under the forfeiture provision fish obtained lawfully but in the poacher's possession at the time of the offence would be liable to forfeiture.

16 Salmon and Freshwater Fisheries (Protection) (Scotland) Act 1951, s 2(4); Freshwater and Salmon Fisheries (Scotland) Act 1976, Sch 2; Criminal Procedure (Scotland) Act 1975, ss 289E–289G (as so added). Level 4 is £1,000: Increase of Criminal Penalties etc (Scotland) Order 1984, art 4.

17 See para 5, note 2, above.

18 *Hay v Perth Magistrates* (1863) 4 Macq 535, 1 M (HL) 41 (the 'Bermoney Boat Case'). However, from a day to be appointed by order under the Salmon Act 1986, s 43(2), the Secretary of State, after consulting such persons as he considers appropriate, may by regulations made by statutory instrument subject to annulment in pursuance of a resolution of either House of Parliament define fishing for salmon by net and coble: see the Salmon and Freshwater Fisheries (Protection) (Scotland) Act 1951, s 2(2A)–(2C) (prospectively added by the Salmon Act 1986, s 21(b)).

19 See note 18 above.

20 R B Williamson, Inspector of Salmon Fisheries, Scotland, *Powers of Bailiffs* (Dept of Agriculture and Fisheries for Scotland, revised 1988).

21 As to salmon fishery districts, see the Salmon Act 1986, s 1, and para 33 below.

22 Ie waters in the district other than inland waters. For the meaning of 'inland waters' and 'estuary limits', see para 5, note 1, above.

23 Salmon and Freshwater Fisheries (Protection) (Scotland) Act 1951, s 2(1A) (prospectively added by the Salmon Act 1986, s 21(a)). The Secretary of State will have power under the provisions cited in note 18 above to make regulations defining 'bag net, fly net or other stake net'. There are, however, generally accepted definitions brought about through usage and recognised by fishermen.

12. Unlawful methods of fishing. The Salmon and Freshwater Fisheries (Protection) (Scotland) Act 1951 prescribes that only certain methods of fishing are to be legal in inland waters, whereas provisions in earlier statutes had been directed against certain specified methods of fishing. This makes the law easier to enforce and more certain. It is therefore possible to state as a generality that anyone who fishes for salmon by any other means other than rod and line or net and coble in inland waters, or for freshwater fish in inland waters except by rod and line (or, in certain cases, net or trap[1]), will be using an unlawful method, and therefore commits an offence against the 1951 Act[2]. The unlawful methods in common use today, which are prohibited in any waters, may be listed shortly as follows:

(1) use of explosives with intent to take or destroy fish in any waters, including the sea up to 12 nautical miles from the baselines from which the breadth of the territorial sea is measured[3];

(2) use of any poison or other noxious substance with intent to take or destroy fish in any such waters[4];

(3) use of an electrical device to stun or destroy salmon or freshwater fish in any such waters[5];

(4) use of gaffs, spears or illegal baits and lures, that is by dragging hooks and thereby ripping, even when using rod and line[6];

(5) use of nets with meshes smaller than laid down by statute[7];

(6) use of nets in rivers and estuaries otherwise than by the permitted method of net and coble[8];

(7) fishing from any fishing boat[9] for salmon or migratory trout in the sea by drift net[10] or other gill net[11], trawl net, seine net (other than beach seining or fishing from shore by net and coble), troll or long-line, within the fishery limits off the Scottish coast[12];

(8) fishing for salmon or migratory trout with any gill net[13] within a specified sea area[14];

(9) setting or using a net or any other engine to catch salmon when leaping etc at falls[15];

(10) taking salmon at a fish pass[16].

1 See para 11, text to notes 7, 9 above.

2 See the Salmon and Freshwater Fisheries (Protection) (Scotland) Act 1951 (c 26), ss 2(4), 3, 4.

3 Ibid, s 4(a) (amended by the Fishery Limits Act 1976 (c 86), s 9(1), Sch 2, para 12). Note that whereas heads (1) and (2) refer to 'fish' generally, head (3) refers specifically to salmon (defined in para 1 above) and to freshwater fish (defined in para 5, note 9, above). A person committing an offence under any of heads (1)–(3) is liable on summary conviction to a fine not exceeding the prescribed sum or imprisonment for a term not exceeding three months, or both, and on conviction on indictment to a fine or imprisonment for a term not exceeding two years, or both: Salmon and Freshwater Fisheries (Protection) (Scotland) Act 1951, s 4; Freshwater and Salmon Fisheries (Scotland) Act 1976 (c 22), s 6, Sch 2; Criminal Procedure (Scotland) Act 1975 (c 21), s 289B (added by the Criminal Law Act 1977 (c 45), s 63(1), Sch 11, para 5, and substituted by the Criminal Justice Act 1982 (c 48), s 55(2)). The prescribed sum is £2,000: Increase of Criminal Penalties etc (Scotland) Order 1984, SI 1984/526, art 3. As to forfeiture, see para 22 below.

4 Salmon and Freshwater Fisheries (Protection) (Scotland) Act 1951, s 4(b). Heads (2) and (3) do not apply to any act carried out within a fish farm (defined in para 57 below) in the course of the operations of the farm: Freshwater and Salmon Fisheries (Scotland) Act 1976 (c 22), s 7(1), Sch 3, para 8(b). For the penalties, see note 3 above.

5 Salmon and Freshwater Fisheries (Protection) (Scotland) Act 1951, s 4(c). See also note 4 above. For the penalties, see note 3 above.

6 *Heatlie v Kellett* 1955 SLT (Sh Ct) 29, where the accused was charged under the Salmon and Freshwater Fisheries (Protection) (Scotland) Act 1951, s 2(1) (see para 11 above), of 'dragging and ripping' the water with rod and line using artificial minnow and hooks and tackle known as a 'spoon bait'. It was held that, though these methods were not expressly forbidden in the 1951 Act (as they had been in the Salmon Fisheries (Scotland) Act 1868 (c 123), s 17 (repealed)), the definition of 'rod and line' (see para 5, note 2, above) as being with 'such bait or lure as is lawful at the passing of this Act' rendered them illegal. For the exception permitting the auxiliary use of a gaff, tailer or landing-net, see para 11 above.

7 Ibid, s 15(4), prohibits fishing for salmon with a net having a mesh contrary to any byelaw. Schedule (E) (repealed) regulated the size of meshes. This head, and heads (9) and (10), do not apply to the River Tweed (for which see paras 40 ff below): s 41. The penalty on summary conviction is a fine not exceeding level 3 on the standard scale (for which see para 11, note 15, above): s 15 (amended by the Salmon Act 1986 (c 62), s 5(1)); Freshwater and Salmon Fisheries (Scotland) Act 1976, Sch 2; Criminal Procedure (Scotland) Act 1975, ss 289E–289G (added by the Criminal Justice Act 1982 (c 48), s 54). The provisions of the Salmon and Freshwater Fisheries (Protection) (Scotland) Act 1951, s 19, as to forfeiture (see para 22 below) apply to persons convicted of offences under the Salmon Fisheries (Scotland) Act 1868, s 15: s 15 (amended by the Salmon Act 1986, s 5(1)).

8 See the Salmon and Freshwater Fisheries (Protection) (Scotland) Act 1951, s 2(1), and para 11 above.

9 'Fishing boat' means a vessel of whatever size, and in whatever way propelled, for the time being employed in sea fishing: Sea Fish (Conservation) Act 1967 (c 84), s 22(1).

10 'Drift-net' means any length of net allowed to float or drift, being either attached to or released from a fishing boat and not being a length of net attached to or held on the shore: Salmon and Migratory Trout (Prohibition of Fishing) (No 2) Order 1972, SI 1973/207, art 3(2).

11 'Gill net' here means any length of net designed for the purpose of catching fish by enmeshing them: ibid, art 3(2) (amended by SI 1975/844).

12 Ibid, art 3(1), (2) (extended by SI 1983/60), made under the Sea Fish (Conservation) Act 1967, s 5. As to the fishery limits, see para 130 below. The penalty on summary conviction is a fine not exceeding £50,000 or, on conviction on indictment, a fine, and in addition, in either case, a fine equal to the value of the fish: s 11(1), (3), (5) (amended by the Fisheries Act 1981 (c 29), s 24(1)).

13 'Gill net' here means any net designed or set to catch fish by enmeshing them, whether the net is set on its own or attached to, or part of, other fishing equipment: Inshore Fishing (Salmon and Migratory Trout) (Prohibition of Gill Nets) (Scotland) Order 1986, SI 1986/59, art 2. See also note 14 below.

14 Ibid, art 3. This provision is of particular importance as it closed a legal loophole whereby under head (7) a boat was an essential element to create the offence, either being used to fish from or to assist in setting the gill net. The provision under head (8) was introduced so that the setting of a

gill net from the shore without the use of a boat was created an offence. Similarly, under head (7) there was some doubt as to whether salmon taken in the 'leader' of an otherwise legal bag net could be said to have been taken illegally. The new definition of 'gill net' (see note 13 above) made it clear that any salmon taken in such a 'leader' would be illegally caught as being enmeshed in a net 'attached to, or part of, other fishing equipment'. The specified sea area referred to in head (8) is the sea area adjacent to certain parts of the coast of Scotland extending from the mean high-water mark of ordinary spring tides for half a mile seawards from the mean low-water mark of ordinary spring tides: see art 2. The order was made under the Inshore Fishing (Scotland) Act 1984 (c 26), s 1. The penalty on summary conviction is a fine not exceeding £5,000 or, on conviction on indictment, a fine: s 4(1), (2). Another order, made under s 2 (the Inshore Fishing (Prohibition of Carriage of Monofilament Gill Nets) (Scotland) Order 1986, SI 1986/60), was held to be illegal under Community and United Kingdom law since the necessary consultation required under the Act had not taken place: *Stranraer Procurator Fiscal v Marshall* [1988] 1 CMLR 657, Sch Ct (in which an appeal is, in April 1990, awaiting a reference to the European Court of Justice).

15 Salmon Fisheries (Scotland) Act 1868, s 15(5). See also note 7 above. The penalty on summary conviction under head (9) or head (10) is a fine not exceeding level 4 on the standard scale (for which see para 11, note 16, above): s 15 (amended by the Salmon Act 1986, s 5(1); Freshwater and Salmon Fisheries (Scotland) Act 1976, Sch 2; Criminal Procedure (Scotland) Act 1975, ss 289E–289G (as added: see note 7 above). As to forfeiture, see note 7 above.

16 Salmon Fisheries (Scotland) Act 1868, s 15(6). See also note 7 above. For the penalties, see note 15 above.

13. Exemptions from prosecution.

A person is not, in respect of any act or omission relating to salmon, salmon roe or salmon eggs, guilty of a contravention of an enactment prohibiting or regulating that act or omission, if the purpose is scientific, or for the protection, improvement or development of stocks of fish, or for conservation, and written permission has first been obtained from the Secretary of State or the appropriate district salmon fishery board[1].

Nor, in respect of any act or omission relating to fishing for or taking salmon, is a person guilty of a contravention of an enactment prohibiting the act or omission if the act or omission has been exempted by the Secretary of State[2]. He may grant an exemption only if satisfied that the proprietor of every salmon fishery in the relevant district entered in the valuation roll likely to be affected by the exemption, and the relevant district salmon fishery board, have previously consented[3]. The exemption, which must be in writing, may relate only to a specified person, must specify the waters concerned, the duration of the exemption and the enactment to which it relates, and may be subject to conditions specified in it[4].

There are also a series of exemptions in respect of the operation of a fish farm[5].

1 Salmon Act 1986 (c 62), s 28(1). As to district salmon fishery boards, see para 35 below. The board's consent is appropriate if the act or omission takes place in the board's district and is a contravention of the Salmon Fisheries (Scotland) Act 1868 (c 123), s 18, s 19 or s 20 (sale and possession of salmon roe; taking, destruction, sale or possession of young salmon or disturbing spawning beds; taking, selling or possession of unclean or unseasonable salmon); of the Salmon and Freshwater Fisheries (Protection) (Scotland) Act 1951 (c 26), s 2 or s 4(c) (methods of fishing; using electrical device); or of the Tweed Fisheries Act 1857 (c cxlviii), s 45 (using nets in annual close time); or of the Tweed Fisheries Amendment Act 1859 (c lxx), s 6 (fishing in annual close times): Salmon Act 1986, s 28(2).
2 Ibid, s 27(1).
3 Ibid, s 27(2), (3).
4 Ibid, s 27(4).
5 See para 63 below.

14. Permitted times.

It has been recognised from time immemorial that there should be 'close times' when salmon could freely run the rivers without the danger of being caught. For this reason also there were prohibitions against the erection of barriers in rivers, in order to enable salmon to have free access to the upper stretches of rivers to spawn, and to ensure that they should be able to return to the sea. To this end, particularly during the spawning season (which usually occurs during November to January) there have been statutory provisions prohibiting the catching and taking of salmon during this period, which is termed 'the close season'. There are two such close times to be considered: the annual close time[1] and the weekly close time[2].

1 See paras 15, 16, below.
2 See para 17 below.

15. Annual close time. The annual close times for net fishing and rod fishing were formerly laid down in the Salmon Fisheries (Scotland) Act 1868[1]. They varied from river to river, with specific extensions during which rod fishing might be carried on, and could be, and were, varied by the Secretary of State on the petition of a district salmon fishery board[2]. In general the commencement of the close time varied between 21 August and 14 September, and between 4 and 28 February for the close, and the rod extensions varied from 30 September to 15 November, the earliest date for commencing rod fishing being 11 January.

Today the annual close time for a salmon fishery district is a continuous period of not less than 168 days[3]. It applies to every mode of fishing for and taking salmon except to the extent that provision is made within that time during which salmon may be fished for and taken by rod and line[3]. The dates of the annual close time and the periods for rod fishing are, in the case of any particular district:

(1) the dates and periods specified in the designation order made in respect of that salmon fishery district, or

(2) where no such order has been made, the dates and periods determined under the Salmon Fisheries (Scotland) Act 1862[4], subject to any variation under the Salmon Fisheries (Scotland) Act 1868[5], which, immediately before 7 January 1987, were in force as respects the district which had the same coastal limits as that salmon fishery district[6].

Notwithstanding the foregoing, the Secretary of State may, subject to the above provision as to the overall length of the annual close time, by order (called an 'annual close time order') prescribe for any salmon fishery district the dates of the annual close time and the periods within it for rod fishing, and may make different provision for different parts of a district[7]. However, an annual close time order may only be made on the application of the district salmon fishery board for the district or, where there is no such board, of two proprietors of salmon fisheries in the district[8].

1 Salmon Fisheries (Scotland) Act 1868 (c 123), s 10, Sch (C) (repealed).
2 Ibid, s 9(1) (repealed).
3 Salmon Act 1986 (c 62), s 6(1). References in other enactments to regulations or byelaws made under the earlier Acts relating to the annual close time, or to the Salmon Fisheries (Scotland) Act 1868, Sch (C), are to be construed as including references to an annual close time order or to such part of a designation order as provides for the annual close time: Salmon Act 1986, s 6(7).
4 Ie under the Salmon Fisheries (Scotland) Act 1862 (c 97), s 6(5) (repealed), which gave Commissioners the power to fix the annual close time and the periods within it for rod fishing. As to the Commissioners, see para 32 below.
5 Ie under the Salmon Fisheries (Scotland) Act 1868, s 9 (repealed), which enabled the board to petition the Secretary of State to vary the annual close time.
6 Salmon Act 1986, s 6(2)(a), (b). As to designation orders, see para 23 below.
7 Ibid, s 6(3). For the procedure for making an annual close time order, see Sch 1, paras 3–9, as modified and applied by s 6(6).
8 Ibid, s 6(4). The application must state the proposed dates of the annual close time and the period within it proposed for rod fishing, and the general effect of the proposals, which may include different dates and periods for different parts of the district: s 6(5).

16. Offences relating to the annual close time. The following are statutory offences in respect of the annual close time:

(1) fishing for salmon during the annual close time other than by rod and line[1];

(2) fishing for salmon during the annual close time by rod and line, except as allowed for by annual close time order or designation order[2];

(3) failure to remove boats, nets and tackle from a salmon fishery, and all obstructions in a cruive to the free passage of fish through the cruive, within thirty-six hours before the start of the annual close time[3];

(4) buying, selling, exposing for sale or having in possession any salmon taken between the commencement of the latest and the termination of the earliest annual close time in force at the time for any salmon fishery district[4];

(5) shipping or exporting salmon between the commencement of the latest and the termination of the earliest annual close time for any salmon fishery district in Scotland without proof of legal capture[5];

(6) shipping or exporting salmon caught by rod and line during the close time for net fishing[5].

These offences do not apply in the Tweed district[6].

1 Salmon Fisheries (Scotland) Act 1868 (c 123), s 15(1). The penalty on summary conviction is a fine not exceeding level 4 on the standard scale (for which see para 11, note 16, above): s 15 (amended by the Salmon Act 1986 (c 62), s 5(1)); Freshwater and Salmon Fisheries (Scotland) Act 1976 (c 22), s 6, Sch 2; Criminal Procedure (Scotland) Act 1975 (c 21), ss 289E–289G (added by the Criminal Justice Act 1982 (c 48), s 54). As to forfeiture, see para 12, note 7, above.

2 Salmon Fisheries (Scotland) Act 1868, s 15(3). The penalty on summary conviction is a fine not exceeding level 3 on the standard scale (for which see para 11, note 15, above): s 15 (as so amended); Freshwater and Salmon Fisheries (Scotland) Act 1976, Sch 2; Criminal Procedure (Scotland) Act 1975, ss 289E–289G (as so added). As to forfeiture, see para 12, note 7, above. In *Haydon v Cormack* (1885) 5 Coup 608, it was held that when a salmon was caught during the close time in a stake net set for catching white fish this did not constitute 'taking' the salmon under the Salmon Fisheries (Scotland) Act 1868.

3 Ibid, s 23. The penalty on summary conviction is a fine not exceeding level 4 on the standard scale: Freshwater and Salmon Fisheries (Scotland) Act 1976, Sch 2; Criminal Procedure (Scotland) Act 1975, ss 289E–289G (as so added). As to forfeiture, see para 12, note 7, above. In *Joseph Johnston & Sons Ltd v Ingram* 1976 SLT (Notes) 30, the accused were charged with failure to remove equipment used for taking salmon. The nets themselves had been removed, but not the pins used to attach the nets to poles driven into the sand. On appeal the court questioned the conviction as fair notice might have enabled the applicants to show the impracticability of removing the pins.

4 Salmon Fisheries (Scotland) Act 1868, s 21. Thus a prosecution cannot be taken under this section when any river in Scotland is open (ie, currently any time except from 15 September to 10 February). It also seems to be settled that the period of extension for fishing by rod and line is held to be part of the close time and so a prosecution may be brought even though rod fishing was permitted in some districts because of such extensions: *Porteous v M'Naughton* 1971 JC 12, 1971 SLT 94, where charges were laid under this provision against the accused for being in possession of salmon taken from the River Tay on 25 September. The close time for nets on the Tay was then 27 August to 10 February, while rod fishing was permitted from 27 August to 15 October. He was found not guilty but, on appeal by the complainer, it was held that the close time included the period when rod fishing only was permitted, and that possession of salmon during that period raised a prima facie presumption against the accused, so that the onus lay on him to show that the salmon had been taken legally by rod and line. It is a good defence to a charge under this provision to prove that the salmon was taken by rod and line at a permitted time and place by a legal method of fishing: *Fairley v Wardens of the City of London Fishmongers* 1951 JC 14, 1951 SLT 54, following *Fishmongers of the City of London v Stiven* 1912 SC(J) 28, 1912 1 SLT 313. The penalty on summary conviction is a fine not exceeding level 3 on the standard scale: Freshwater and Salmon Fisheries (Scotland) Act 1976, Sch 2; Criminal Procedure (Scotland) Act 1975, ss 289E–289G (as added: see note 1 above). As to forfeiture, see the Salmon Fisheries (Scotland) Act 1868, s 31.

5 Ibid, s 22. The salmon are liable to forfeiture, and the offender is liable to a penalty not exceeding £25 for each salmon: s 22; Criminal Procedure (Scotland) Act 1975, s 289C (added by the Criminal Law Act 1977 (c 45), s 63(1), Sch 11, para 5, and amended by the Criminal Justice Act 1982 (c 48), s 55(3)).

6 Salmon Fisheries (Scotland) Act 1868, s 41. As to the Tweed, see para 40 ff below.

17. Weekly close time. In general no fishing for salmon is permitted, even in the open season, during the weekly close time[1], which extends from 6 pm on Friday evening to 6 am on the following Monday morning[2]. However, salmon fishing by rod and line is permitted during Friday, Saturday and Monday[3], but fishing for salmon is absolutely prohibited on Sunday[4]. The following are offences in respect of the weekly close time:
(1) fishing for or taking salmon on a Sunday[5];
(2) fishing for or taking salmon during the weekly close time other than by rod and line[6];
(3) failing to comply with weekly close time byelaws relating to fixed salmon nets[7].
There is an exception in respect of heads (1) and (2) for fish farms[8], and head (3) does not apply to the Tweed[9].

1 Salmon and Freshwater Fisheries (Protection) (Scotland) Act 1951 (c 26), s 13(2) (substituted by the Salmon (Weekly Close Time) (Scotland) Regulations 1988, SI 1988/390, reg 2).
2 Salmon and Freshwater Fisheries (Protection) (Scotland) Act 1951, s 13(3) (as so substituted).
3 Ibid, s 13(2) (as so substituted).
4 Ibid, s 13(1).
5 Ibid, s 13(1), (4). A person guilty of an offence under s 13 is liable on summary conviction to a fine not exceeding level 4 on the standard scale (for which see para 11, note 16, above): Freshwater and Salmon Fisheries (Scotland) Act 1976 (c 22), s 6, Sch 2; Criminal Procedure (Scotland) Act 1975 (c 21), ss 289E–289G (added by the Criminal Justice Act 1982 (c 48), s 54). As to forfeiture, see the Salmon and Freshwater Fisheries (Protection) (Scotland) Act 1951, s 19, and para 22 below.
6 Ibid, s 13(2), (4) (as substituted: see note 1 above). For the penalties, see note 5 above.
7 Salmon Fisheries (Scotland) Act 1868 (c 123), s 24. Byelaws in Sch (D) (repealed) governed the means of preventing nets from fishing during the weekly close times. The byelaws provided for such matters as the removal of the leaders of bag nets. The obligation was laid exclusively on the proprietor or, where the fishing was let, the occupier of a fishing station, and did not apply to a servant or agent locally in charge: *Fishmongers' Co v Bruce* 1980 SLT (Notes) 35, citing *Don v Johnston* (1897) 25 R (J) 34 at 37, per Lord Moncreiff. A person guilty of an offence under the Salmon Fisheries (Scotland) Act 1868, s 24, is liable on summary conviction to forfeiture of the nets and a fine not exceeding level 4 on the standard scale: s 24; Freshwater and Salmon Fisheries (Scotland) Act 1976, Sch 2; Criminal Procedure (Scotland) Act 1975, ss 289E–289G (as added: see note 5 above).
8 See the Freshwater and Salmon Fisheries (Scotland) Act 1976, s 7(1), Sch 3, para 8(c), and para 63 below.
9 Salmon Fisheries (Scotland) Act 1868, s 41. As to the Tweed, see paras 40 ff below.

18. Unclean salmon. Any person who takes or fishes for unclean or unseasonable salmon, or who helps with or attempts these activities, or who buys, sells, exposes for sale or possesses such salmon, commits an offence[1]. An unclean salmon has been held to be one which has spawned (that is, a kelt), and not one which is very near to spawning[2]. The offence is independent of the close time offences[3]. A person who commits the offence is liable on summary conviction to a fine not exceeding level 3 on the standard scale for each fish, and each fish is liable to forfeiture[4]. It is a defence to show that the salmon was taken accidentally and immediately returned to the water with the least possible injury[5], or that it was taken for scientific or other appropriate purposes with the necessary written permission, or under an exemption granted by the Secretary of State, or in the course of fish farming[6].

1 Salmon Fisheries (Scotland) Act 1868 (c 123), s 20 (amended by the Salmon Act 1986 (c 62), s 41(1), Sch 4, para 2(3)).
2 *Nixon v White* 1958 SLT (Sh Ct) 38, where the sheriff accepted as authoritative the definition of 'foul fish' in C Stewart *Rights of Fishing in Scotland* (2nd edn, 1892 by J C Shairp) p 207. The

Salmon and Freshwater Fisheries Act 1923 (c 16), s 92(1) (repealed) (see now the Salmon and Freshwater Fisheries Act 1975 (c 51), s 41(1)), which defines an unclean fish as one that is about to spawn or has recently spawned or has not recovered from spawning, does not apply to Scotland.

3 As to these offences, see paras 16, 17, above.

4 Salmon Fisheries (Scotland) Act 1868, s 20 (amended by the Freshwater and Salmon Fisheries (Scotland) Act 1976 (c 22), s 6(1), Sch 2); Criminal Procedure (Scotland) Act 1975 (c 21), ss 289E–289G (added by the Criminal Justice (Scotland) Act 1982 (c 48), s 54). For level 3, see para 11, note 15, above.

5 Salmon Fisheries (Scotland) Act 1868, s 20.

6 See para 63 below.

19. Obstruction etc of salmon. A number of statutory provisions have as their main objectives the free passage of salmon upriver and, thereafter, freedom to spawn. The related offences are:

(1) preventing the passage of a salmon through a fish pass[1];

(2) failure to comply with byelaws relating to fish passes, screens, sluices, etc at dams and mill lades[2], although there is a specific exemption for some hydro-electric installations[3];

(3) failure to comply with byelaws relating to cruives[4];

(4) obstructing the passage of salmon to the spawning beds during the annual close time, or using any device for purposes of obstructing the passage of juvenile salmon[5].

1 Salmon Fisheries (Scotland) Act 1868 (c 123), s 15(6). This does not apply to the Tweed (as to which see paras 40 ff below): s 41. A person guilty of an offence under s 15(6) or s 15(8) is liable on summary conviction to a fine not exceeding level 4 on the standard scale (for which see para 11, note 16, above): s 15 (amended by the Salmon Act 1986 (c 62), s 5(1)); Freshwater and Salmon Fisheries (Scotland) Act 1976 (c 22), s 6, Sch 2; Criminal Procedure (Scotland) Act 1975 (c 21), ss 289E–289G (added by the Criminal Justice Act 1982 (c 48), s 54). As to forefeiture, see para 12, note 7, above.

2 Salmon Fisheries (Scotland) Act 1868, s 15(8). For the byelaws, see Sch (G) (amended by the Salmon and Freshwater Fisheries (Protection) (Scotland) Act 1951 (c 26), s 25(1), Sch 1); *Hardie v Walker* 1948 SC 674, 1949 SLT 13. For the penalty, see note 1 above. This provision does not apply to the Tweed: Salmon Fisheries (Scotland) Act 1868, s 41 (amended by the Salmon and Freshwater Fisheries (Protection) (Scotland) Act 1951, Sch 1, and the Salmon Act 1986 (c 62), s 41(1), Sch 4, para 5).

3 Salmon Fisheries (Scotland) Act 1868, Sch (G), para 8 (added by the Electricity (Scotland) Act 1979 (c 11), s 46(1), Sch 11).

4 Salmon Fisheries (Scotland) Act 1868, s 15(8). For the byelaws, see Sch (F). This does not apply to the Tweed: s 41. For the penalty, see note 1 above.

5 Ibid, s 19, which also provides an exception for acts done for the purpose of artificial propagation of salmon or other scientific purpose, or in the course of cleaning or repairing any dam of mill-lade, or in the course of the exercise of rights of property in the bed of any river or stream (s 19 proviso). This provision applies to the Tweed: s 41 (amended by the Salmon and Freshwater Fisheries (Protection) (Scotland) Act 1951, Sch 1). An offender is liable on summary conviction to a fine not exceeding level 3 on the standard scale (for which see para 11, note 15, above) and forfeiture of fishing equipment and any smolt or salmon fry found in his possession: Salmon Fisheries (Scotland) Act 1868, s 19; Freshwater and Salmon Fisheries (Scotland) Act 1976, Sch 2; Criminal Procedure (Scotland) Act 1975, ss 289E–289G (as added: see note 1 above).

20. Further provisions relating to the protection of salmon stocks. Other offences under enactments designed to protect salmon stocks are:

(1) taking, destroying, buying, selling or possessing or knowingly injuring juvenile salmon[1];

(2) disturbing salmon spawning beds[1];

(3) buying, selling or possessing salmon roe[2];

(4) introducing salmon or salmon eggs into inland waters[3] except with the written consent of the district salmon fishery board or where the waters constitute or are included in a fish farm[4];

(5) importing, keeping or releasing any live non-native fish (or its eggs) designated under the Import of Live Fish (Scotland) Act 1978 as likely to harm
native fish, except in accordance with the provisions of that Act[5];

(6) importing live salmon or live salmon eggs except under a licence[6].

1 Salmon Fisheries (Scotland) Act 1868 (c 123), s 19. For the extent and penalties, see para 19, note
   5, above.
2 Ibid, s 18. See *Crook v Duncan* (1899) 1 F (J) 50, 6 SLT 292. A person committing the offence is
   liable on summary conviction to a fine not exceeding level 3 on the standard scale (for which see
   para 11, note 15, above) and to forfeiture of any salmon roe in his possession: Salmon Fisheries
   (Scotland) Act 1868, s 18; Freshwater and Salmon Fisheries (Scotland) Act 1976 (c 22), s 6, Sch 2;
   Criminal Procedure (Scotland) Act 1975 (c 21), ss 289E–289G (added by the Criminal Justice Act
   1982 (c 48), s 54). It is a defence to a charge of possessing salmon roe to give to the court of trial a
   satisfactory reason for the possession: Salmon Fisheries (Scotland) Act 1868, s 18 (amended by
   the Salmon Act 1986 (c 62), s 41(1), Sch 4, para 3(1)). There are exemptions in the case of acts for
   scientific purposes etc: see para 13 above.
3 Ibid, s 24(1). An offender is liable on summary conviction to a fine not exceeding level 2 on the
   standard scale: s 24(1). Level 2 is £100: Increase of Criminal Penalties etc (Scotland) Order 1984,
   SI 1984/526, art 4. For the meaning of 'inland waters', see para 5, note 1, above. That definition is
   applied by the Salmon Act 1986, s 40(1).
4 Ibid, s 24(2). As to district salmon fishery boards, see para 35 below. For the meaning of 'fish
   farm', see para 57 below. That definition is applied by s 24(2).
5 Import of Live Fish (Scotland) Act 1978 (c 35), s 1. An offender is liable to forfeiture of the fish or
   eggs and to a fine not exceeding level 4 on the standard scale (for which see para 11, note 16,
   above): s 3(1); Criminal Procedure (Scotland) Act 1975, s 289G (added by the Criminal Justice
   Act 1982 (c 48), s 54). For a designation order, see the Import of Live Fish (Coho Salmon)
   (Prohibition) (Scotland) Order 1980, SI 1980/376.
6 Diseases of Fish Act 1937 (c 33), s 1(1), (2) (amended by the Diseases of Fish Act 1983 (c 30), s 1).
   Live fish of the salmon family may not be imported into Great Britain, even under licence, unless
   the fish are of a description specified in an order made by the Secretary of State: Diseases of Fish
   Act 1937, s 1(6) (added by the Diseases of Fish Act 1983, s 1). For an order relating to live salmon
   from Northern Ireland, see the Importation of Live Fish of the Salmon Family Order 1986, SI
   1986/283. A person who contravenes the prohibition is liable on summary conviction to a fine
   not exceeding level 4 on the standard scale, and the fish or eggs are subject to forfeiture: Diseases
   of Fish Act 1937, ss 1(4), 8(1) (amended by the Diseases of Fish Act 1983, s 5, Schedule, para 6).

21. Miscellaneous offences. A number of important additional provisions
have been introduced in an attempt to combat the illegal trade in salmon. The
most significant of the offences created by these provisions are:

(1) illegal fishing[1] by two or more persons acting together[2];

(2) unlawfully taking or removing dead salmon or trout from any waters,
including any part of the sea within 1 mile of low water mark[3];

(3) possession of salmon or trout or any instrument, explosive, poison or other
noxious substance which could be used to take salmon or trout, in circumstances affording reasonable ground for suspecting that possession of it has
been obtained as a result of or for the purpose of committing certain
offences[4] relating to illegal fishing[5];

(4) possession of salmon by a person who believes, or by a person in circumstances in which it would be reasonable for him to suspect that a relevant
offence[6] has at any time been committed in relation to the salmon[7];

(5) attempting or doing any act preparatory to the commission of any of the
foregoing offences or any offence of illegal fishing[8];

(6) consigning or sending salmon, sea trout or trout in a package not conspicuously marked 'salmon', 'sea trout' or 'trout', as the case may be, and with
the sender's name and address[9];

(7) fishing by means of trawls or other moving gear within half a mile of any
fixed salmon net[10];

(8) the carriage of monofilament gill nets in British fishing boats within a
specified sea area in Scottish inshore waters[11].

1 Ie doing an act which constitutes an offence against the Salmon and Freshwater Fisheries (Protection) (Scotland) Act 1951 (c 26), s 1 or s 2, for which see para 11 above.

2 Ibid, s 3. The courts treat this as a serious offence, hence the severe penalties. Offenders are liable on summary conviction to a fine not exceeding the prescribed sum (for which see para 12, note 3, above) or imprisonment for a term not exceeding three months, or both, and on conviction on indictment to a fine or imprisonment for a term not exceeding two years, or both: s 5; Freshwater and Salmon Fisheries (Scotland) Act 1976 (c 22), s 6, Sch 2; Criminal Procedure (Scotland) Act 1975 (c 21), s 289B (added by the Criminal Law Act 1977 (c 45), s 63(1), Sch 11, para 5, and substituted by the Criminal Justice Act 1982 (c 48), s 55(2)).

3 Salmon and Freshwater Fisheries (Protection) (Scotland) Act 1951, s 6, which provides an exemption for water bailiffs or constables in the exercise of their respective duties, persons authorised by the Secretary of State or a district salmon fishery board, and persons with a right to fish in the waters, and the agents of any such persons. Where waters are suspected of being infected, a district salmon fishery board may remove dead or dying fish: see the Diseases of Fish Act 1937 (c 33), s 3. An offender is liable to a fine not exceeding level 4 on the standard scale (for which see para 11, note 16, above): Freshwater and Salmon Fisheries (Scotland) Act 1976, Sch 2; Criminal Procedure (Scotland) Act 1975, ss 289E–289G (added by the Criminal Justice Act 1982 (c 48), s 54).

4 Ie offences under the Salmon and Freshwater Fisheries (Protection) (Scotland) Act 1951, ss 1–4 (see paras 11, 12, above and the text above).

5 Ibid, s 7(1). A conviction may be obtained on the evidence of one witness: s 7(3). The penalty is as for the appropriate illegal fishing offence: s 7(2). It is clear from the decisions that suspicious possession enables proceedings to be taken under these provisions of the 1951 Act and so avoids the necessity of specifying a *locus* for unlawful taking, but there can be no conviction without proof of the substantive offence or proposed offence, albeit by inference or the evidence of one witness: *Aitchison v Bartlett* 1963 JC 27, 1963 SLT 65; *Corbett v MacNaughton* 1984 SCCR 401, 1985 SLT 312.

6 An offence is a 'relevant offence' in relation to a salmon if (1) it is committed by taking, killing or landing that salmon, either in Scotland or in England and Wales, or (2) that salmon is taken, killed or landed there in the course of the commission of the offence; and 'offence' here means an offence under the law of the place where the salmon is taken, killed or landed: Salmon and Freshwater Fisheries (Protection) (Scotland) Act 1951, s 7A(4), (5) (added by the Salmon Act 1986, s 22(1)).

7 Salmon and Freshwater Fisheries (Protection) (Scotland) Act 1951, s 7A(1) (as so added). It is a defence to show that no relevant offence had in fact been committed: s 7A(2) (as so added). A person is not guilty of this offence in respect of conduct constituting a relevant offence in relation to any salmon or in respect of anything done in good faith for purposes connected with the prevention or detection of crime or the investigation or treatment of disease: s 7A(6) (as so added). A person may be convicted on the evidence of one witness: s 7A(3) (as so added). Under head (3) the offence of illegal possession requires the possessor himself being suspected of having committed the original illegal fishing offence. The new provision widens the scope of the offence. The penalties are the same as those stated in note 2 above: see s 7A(1) (as so added).

8 Ibid, s 8 (amended by the Criminal Procedure (Scotland) Act 1975, s 460(1)). The offences referred to are offences under the Salmon and Freshwater Fisheries (Protection) (Scotland) Act 1951, Pt I (ss 1–9) (see paras 11, 12, above, and this paragraph). The offence is punishable in like manner as the attempted or proposed offence: s 8.

9 Ibid, s 16(1). The penalty on summary conviction is a fine not exceeding level 3 on the standard scale (for which see para 11, note 15, above): s 16(3); Freshwater and Salmon Fisheries (Scotland) Act 1976, Sch 2; Criminal Procedure (Scotland) Act 1975, ss 289E–289G (as added: see note 3 above). For powers of persons authorised by the Secretary of State, of officers of district salmon fishery boards and of constables to open packages suspected of containing salmon, sea trout or trout, and to detain the contents, see the Salmon and Freshwater Fisheries (Protection) (Scotland) Act 1951, s 16(2).

10 Inshore Fishing (Scotland) Act 1984 (c 26), s 3. The penalty on summary conviction is a fine not exceeding £5,000 or, on conviction on indictment, a fine: s 4(1), (2). Where a fishing boat is involved, the master, owner and charterer are each guilty of the offence: s 4(1).

11 Inshore Fishing (Scotland) Act 1984, s 2; Inshore Fishing (Prohibition of Carriage of Monofilament Gill Nets) (Scotland) Order 1986, SI 1986/60. As to a challenge to the legality of this order, see para 12, note 14, above.

22. Forfeiture.

The Acts relating to salmon fisheries give power to the courts to order the forfeiture of illegally taken fish[1] and tackle or gear used in committing offences[2], as well as vehicles or boats used to assist in the commission of offences[3]. Any fish seized as liable to forfeiture may be sold by the person who seized it, and the net proceeds of the sale are similarly liable to forfeiture[4], although no person is to be subject to any liability if he neglects or fails to exercise these powers[5].

1 See the Salmon Fisheries (Scotland) Act 1868 (c 123), s 15 (amended by the Salmon Act 1986 (c 62), s 5(1)) (in respect of offences under the Salmon Fisheries (Scotland) Act 1868, s 15), and ss 18, 20, 21; and the Salmon and Freshwater Fisheries (Protection) (Scotland) Act 1951 (c 26), s 1 and s 19(1) (in respect of offences under ss 2–4, 6–8, 13).

2 See the Salmon Fisheries (Scotland) Act 1868, s 15 (as so amended) (in respect of offences under s 15), ss 19, 24, and ss 31, 33 (in respect of offences under that Act); and the Salmon and Freshwater Fisheries (Protection) (Scotland) Act 1951, s 19(1) (in respect of offences under ss 2–4, 6–8, 13).

3 See the Salmon Fisheries (Scotland) Act 1868, s 15 (as so amended) (vehicles and boats) (in respect of offences under s 15) and ss 31, 33 (boats) (in respect of offences under the Act); and the Salmon and Freshwater Fisheries (Protection) (Scotland) Act 1951, s 19(2), (3) (amended by the Salmon Act 1986, s 41(1), Sch 4, para 10) (vehicles and boats) (in respect of offences under the Salmon and Freshwater Fisheries (Protection) (Scotland) Act 1951, ss 1–4, 6–8, 13). Any vehicle or boat forfeited under s 19 is to be disposed of as the court may direct: s 19(3). 'Cart' in the forfeiture provisions of the Tweed Fisheries Amendment Act 1859 (c lxx) s 10, has been held to include any conveyance: *Leadbetter v Hutchison* 1934 JC 70, 1934 SLT 319.

4 Salmon and Freshwater Fisheries (Protection) (Scotland) Act 1951, s 20 (which applies to forfeiture under that Act).

5 Ibid, s 20 proviso.

23. Powers of the Secretary of State to make orders and regulations. Although limited powers had been available to the Secretary of State since 1868[1], he had until recently only limited powers to make orders and regulations under the Acts relating to salmon fisheries. He now has power under the Salmon Act 1986 to regulate salmon fisheries in the fields mentioned below.

First, he may by designation order designate any area as a salmon fishery district[2]. The purpose may be to abolish old districts created under earlier Acts and create new ones, or to amalgamate two or more existing districts[3]. The order will define the boundaries of the district, will apply to the district regulations made under other powers[4], and will specify the annual close time to apply within the district and when it is permitted to fish for salmon by rod and line, making different provision, if desired, for different parts of the district[5].

Secondly, the Secretary of State has extensive powers to make regulations, after consultation with such persons as he considers appropriate, with respect to:
(1) the observance of the weekly close time;
(2) the construction and use of cruives;
(3) the construction and alteration of dams (including mill dams, lades or water wheels) so as to allow a reasonable means for the passage of salmon;
(4) the meshes, materials and dimensions of nets used in salmon fishing;
(5) obstructions in rivers or estuaries to the passage of salmon; and
(6) the construction, alteration and use, for the control of the passage of salmon, of screens in off-takes from inland waters, and structures associated with those screens[6].
The Secretary of State has by regulations increased the weekly close time for salmon from forty-two hours to sixty hours during a weekend, from 6 pm on Friday to 6 am on Monday[7].

Thirdly, he has power to revoke any regulations made under previous legislation and, in particular, those made under the Salmon Fisheries (Scotland) Acts 1862 to 1868[8]. These older regulations otherwise continue to apply to the districts to which they applied under the former legislation until revoked expressly or by implication by new regulations[9].

Fourthly, he may make annual close time orders. These have already been discussed[10].

Fifthly, he has power to make an estuary limits order, on the application of a district salmon fishery board or, where there is no such board, of two proprietors in the district, prescribing the limits which divide each river, including its mouth or estuary, from the sea[11]. Otherwise the estuary limits are fixed by judicial decision or are fixed and defined under the Salmon Fisheries (Scotland) Act 1862[12].

Sixthly, the Secretary of State, on the application of a district salmon fishery board or the joint application of more than one such board, may make regulations specifying baits and lures or classes of baits and lures for the purposes of the statutory definition of 'rod and line', and the times when and areas to which the regulations apply[13].

Seventhly the Secretary of State may by order introduce a system for licensing dealers in salmon within the existing machinery[14] for licensing[15].

1 Under the Salmon Fisheries (Scotland) Act 1868 (c 123), s 9 (repealed), district boards could petition the Secretary of State to vary the annual and weekly close times: see para 15 above.

2 Salmon Act 1986 (c 62), s 1(2). As to salmon fishery districts, see para 33 below. The order may be made only on written application (1) by a district salmon fishery board for a district affected by the proposed order; (2) if there is no such body, by two proprietors so affected; or (3) by any number or combination of such boards or proprietors so affected: s 2(5), Sch 1, para 1. The Secretary of State may proceed even if the applicants do not represent the whole of the area affected: Sch 1, para 1. The application must be accompanied by written proposals as to the area to be designated, the identity of the existing salmon fishery district or districts wholly or partly within that area, the reasons for the proposal, the proposed annual close time and dates within it permitting rod and line fishing, and the general effect of the proposals: Sch 1, para 2. The Secretary of State must consult such persons as he considers appropriate, may request further information, may dismiss the application or may proceed with the application: Sch 1, para 3. He must direct newspaper advertisement of the proposals at the applicants' expense, inviting representations and objections: Sch 1, para 4. He may at any time alter the proposals and if necessary have further consultation and require further advertisement: Sch 1, para 5. If no representations or objections are made, or if any made are withdrawn, he may make the order; otherwise, after considering them, he may make the order, dismiss the application or cause a local inquiry to be held: Sch 1, paras 6, 7. After considering the report of any inquiry and any representations or objections duly made he may make the order: Sch 1, para 8. The power to make the order is exercisable by statutory instrument: Sch 1, para 9.

3 Ibid, ss 1(2), 2(1). The power does not extend to the River Tweed: s 2(4).

4 Ibid, s 2(2). These are regulations made under s 3 (see below), and regulations made under earlier Acts as respects the matters specified in the Salmon Fisheries (Scotland) Act 1862 (c 97), s 6(6) (which are the same as those listed in the Salmon Act 1986, s 3(2)(a)–(e)): s 2(2).

5 Ibid, s 2(3). See eg the East Lewis Salmon Fishery District Designation Order 1989, SI 1989/1869, which defines and designates the area of the district, abolishes earlier superseded districts, applies general regulations, fixes the annual close time as 27 August to 10 February, inclusive, and specifies 27 August to 31 October, inclusive, as the period within which rod and line fishing is permitted.

6 Salmon Act 1986, s 3(2)(a)–(f). For an exemption for fish farms in respect of regulations under s 3(2)(a), (b), see para 63 below.

7 See the Salmon (Weekly Close Time) (Scotland) Regulations 1988, SI 1988/390, substituting the Salmon and Freshwater Fisheries (Protection) (Scotland) Act 1951 (c 26), s 13(2), and para 17 above.

8 Salmon Act 1986, s 3(4).

9 Ibid, s 3(1).

10 See ibid, s 6, and para 15 above.

11 Ibid, s 7(2), (3), (6). This does not apply to the River Tweed: s 7(6). For the procedure for making the order, see Sch 1, paras 3–9, as modified and applied by s 7(5).

12 Salmon Act 1986, s 7(1). See the Salmon Fisheries (Scotland) Act 1862, s 6(1). For estuary limits in Scotland, see the Salmon Fisheries (Scotland) Act 1868, Sch (B).

13 Salmon Act 1986, s 8(1)–(3). For the definition referred to, see the Salmon and Freshwater Fisheries (Protection) (Scotland) Act 1951, s 24(1), and para 5, note 2, above. The application must be accompanied by details of the applicant's proposals and the reasons for them: Salmon Act 1986, s 8(4). For the procedure for making the order, see Sch 1, paras 3–9, as modified and applied by s 8(5).

14 Ie the machinery under the Civic Government (Scotland) Act 1982 (c 45), Pts I, II (ss 1–8, 9–44): see LOCAL GOVERNMENT, vol 14, paras 529 ff.
15 See the Salmon Act 1986, s 20. After consideration of proposals in 1988 and 1989 it was announced that this power will not be implemented.

24. Authority to enforce legislation. There are three main categories of persons with the requisite statutory powers to enforce salmon and freshwater fisheries legislation (apart from the police[1] and British sea-fishery officers[2]), namely water bailiffs[3], persons authorised by the Secretary of State[4] and wardens appointed by the Secretary of State[5].

A water bailiff has various statutory powers of entry, search, seizure and arrest[6]. These powers may be exercised in the district of the board by which he was appointed or in any adjoining district[7].

1 Any constable may exercise in relation to any water any of the powers specified in the Salmon and Freshwater Fisheries (Protection) (Scotland) Act 1951 (c 26), s 10(1) (for which see paras 25 ff below): s 10(4).
2 As to British sea-fishery officers, see para 171 below.
3 Water bailiffs are appointed by district salmon fishery boards on such terms and conditions as the boards think fit: Salmon Act 1986 (c 62), s 16(3)(b). In the Salmon and Freshwater Fisheries (Protection) (Scotland) Act 1951 'water bailiff' means any water bailiff or other duly appointed officer of a district salmon fishery board: s 24(1). The production by a water bailiff of the instrument of his appointment purporting to be signed on behalf of the board, or of any badge or other device indicating his appointment is sufficient warrant for the exercise of his powers: s 10(3). See further R B Williamson *Powers of Water Bailiffs and Wardens to enforce the Salmon and Freshwater Fisheries Acts* (Dept of Agriculture and Fisheries for Scotland, revised 1988).
4 Any person appointed by the Secretary of State in that behalf may exercise in relation to any water any of the powers specified in the Salmon and Freshwater Fisheries (Protection) (Scotland) Act 1951, s 10(1): s 10(5). See further para 30 below.
5 See the Freshwater and Salmon Fisheries (Scotland) Act 1976 (c 22), s 2(1), and para 56 below. See also the publication cited in note 3 above.
6 See paras 25 ff below.
7 Salmon and Freshwater Fisheries (Protection) (Scotland) Act 1951, s 10(1), (2). As to salmon fishery districts, see para 33 below.

25. Powers of entry. A water bailiff, constable, watcher, officer of a district salmon fishery board or any police officer may, at any hour of the day or night, enter and remain upon any land in the vicinity of a river or of the sea coast, for the purpose of preventing a breach of the Salmon Fisheries (Scotland) Act 1868 or the Salmon and Freshwater Fisheries (Protection) (Scotland) Act 1951, or for detecting persons guilty of a breach of those Acts[1]. The owner or occupier of the land is entitled to ask him to leave the land and, if he refuses to leave, may treat him as a trespasser, and the onus will then be on him to prove to the sheriff principal or justices that he had reason to believe that an offence had been or was about to be committed[2].

A water bailiff or other authorised person[3] may enter land[4] for the purpose of examining a dam, fixed engine, obstruction or lade[5]. He may also enter, on the authority of a warrant issued by a sheriff or justice of the peace, and by force if necessary, any premises or vehicle on or in which there is reasonable ground to suspect that there is evidence of any of certain offences[6].

1 Salmon Fisheries (Scotland) Act 1868 (c 123), s 27 (amended by the Salmon and Freshwater Fisheries (Protection) (Scotland) Act 1951 (c 26), s 25(1), Sch 1).
2 Salmon Fisheries (Scotland) Act 1868, s 27 proviso (amended by the Sheriff Courts (Scotland) Act 1971 (c 58), s 4).
3 Ie a constable or a person authorised by the Secretary of State: see para 24, notes 1, 4, above.
4 'Land' here includes land covered by water, but not a dwellinghouse or any yard, garden, outhouses and pertinents belonging thereto or usually enjoyed therewith: Salmon and Freshwater Fisheries (Protection) (Scotland) Act 1951, s 10(7)(b).

5 Ibid, s 10(1)(a). 'Dam' means any weir, dam, dyke, cauld, mill dam or other structure con-structed in the bed of any stream, river or loch for the purpose of controlling, impounding or diverting water therefrom; 'fixed engine' means any engine, net or trap used for taking salmon, other than a sweep net which when in use is hauled through the water continuously and not allowed to be stationary or to drift with the current; and 'lade' includes any artificial channel through which water is diverted from any inland water (defined in para 5, note 1, above) in which salmon or trout are present: s 24(1).

6 Ibid, s 11(1) (amended by the Salmon Act 1986 (c 62), s 22(2)(a)). The offences referred to are offences under the Salmon and Freshwater Fisheries (Protection) (Scotland) Act 1951, ss 1–4, 7, 7A. This provision is applied to offences against the Sea Fish (Conservation) Act 1967 (c 84), s 4, and orders under ss 5, 6, by s 18(2), and to orders under the Inshore Fishing (Scotland) Act 1984 (c 26), s 1, by s 7(2). 'Vehicle' includes any conveyance other than a vehicle used for the purposes of a passenger transport service: Salmon and Freshwater Fisheries (Protection) (Scotland) Act 1951, s 24(1).

26. Powers of search. A water bailiff or other authorised person[1] may stop and search any boat which is used in fishing or which there is reasonable cause to suspect contains salmon or trout[2]. He may also search and examine nets or other instruments used in fishing or any basket, pocket or other receptacle capable of carrying fish, which there is reasonable cause to suspect contains salmon or trout illegally taken[3]. Where he has reasonable ground for suspecting that evidence of any of certain offences[4] is to be found in any vehicle on private land adjoining any water within his district or an adjoining district, or in any stationary vehicle on a road[5] adjoining any such water or such land, he may search that vehicle[6].

An important extension of the powers of search enables a constable (but not a water bailiff) to search premises (other than a dwellinghouse or any yard, garden, outhouses or pertinents belonging thereto and usually enjoyed there-with), without warrant where by reason of urgency it is impracticable to apply for one, where there are reasonable grounds for suspecting that the offence of possessing salmon which have been illegally taken[7] has been committed and that evidence of the commission of the offence may be found in the premises[8]. A constable may similarly, without warrant where necessary, stop and search any vehicle where he has reasonable grounds for suspecting that any of certain offences[9] has been committed and that evidence of the commission of the offence may be found in the vehicle[10]. This power extends to the search of any person found in the vehicle or whom the constable has reasonable grounds to believe to have recently left or to be about to enter it[10].

The powers of entry already described[11] are for the purposes of search. A warrant granted by a sheriff principal or justice of the peace will provide the necessary authority to search for the purpose of detecting offences against the Salmon Fisheries (Scotland) Act 1868 or the Salmon and Freshwater Fisheries (Protection) (Scotland) Act 1951 or concealed salmon or other articles[12]. A bailiff, constable or person authorised by the Secretary of State holding such a warrant to search premises or a vehicle may also search every person found thereon or therein or whom he has reasonable grounds to believe has recently left or is about to enter the premises or vehicle[13].

In any search, a female may be searched only by another female[14].

1 Ie a constable or a person appointed by the Secretary of State: see para 24, notes 1, 4, above.

2 Salmon and Freshwater Fisheries (Protection) (Scotland) Act 1951 (c 26), s 10(1)(b). 'Boat' includes any craft or vessel used in fishing: s 24(1).

3 Ibid, s 10(1)(c). It seems that the reference to 'pocket' does not imply authority to conduct pre-arrest searches of persons.

4 For these offences, see para 25, note 6, above.

5 Ie a road within the meaning of the Roads (Scotland) Act 1984 (c 54), s 151(1), or a highway within the meaning of the Highways Act 1980 (c 66), s 328.

6 Salmon and Freshwater Fisheries (Protection) (Scotland) Act 1951, s 11(4) (amended by the Salmon Act 1986 (c 62), s 22(2)(c)).

7 Ie an offence against the Salmon and Freshwater Fisheries (Protection) (Scotland) Act 1951, s 7A: see para 21 above.
8 Ibid, s 11(3A) (added by the Salmon Act 1986, s 22(2)(b)).
9 Ie an offence against the Salmon and Freshwater Fisheries (Protection) (Scotland) Act 1951, ss 1, 4, 7, 7A.
10 Ibid, s 11(3) (amended by the Salmon Act 1986, s 22(2)(a)).
11 See para 25 above.
12 Salmon Fisheries (Scotland) Act 1868 (c 123), s 26 (amended by the Salmon and Freshwater Fisheries (Protection) (Scotland) Act 1951, s 25(1), Sch 1); Salmon and Freshwater Fisheries (Protection) (Scotland) Act 1951, s 11(1) (amended by the Salmon Act 1986, s 22(2)(a)).
13 Salmon and Freshwater Fisheries (Protection) (Scotland) Act 1951, s 11(2).
14 Ibid, s 11(6).

27. Powers of seizure. A water bailiff or other authorised person[1] may seize any fish, instrument or article, boat or vehicle that is liable to be forfeited in pursuance of the Salmon and Freshwater Fisheries (Protection) (Scotland) Act 1951[2]. This power has been extended to include fish, instruments or articles (but not boats or vehicles) liable to forfeiture in connection with salmon offences under the Sea Fish (Conservation) Act 1967 and the Inshore Fishing (Scotland) Act 1984[3].

Water bailiffs, constables, watchers, other officers of district salmon fishery boards and police officers may seize any salmon illegally taken, illegal nets, engines and other instruments that they may find during a search under warrant[4]. A water bailiff, constable or person appointed for the purpose by the Secretary of State has power to prevent the transmission of illegally caught fish whereby, if he suspects that salmon, sea trout or trout which he has found in a package consigned by common or other carrier has been dealt with contrary to law, or if the package is not properly marked[5], he may detain the contents pending proceedings for an offence and, if the fish become unfit for human consumption, may destroy them[6]. Additional powers of seizure are given to 'authorised persons', namely water bailiffs, under the Diseases of Fish Act 1937[7].

1 Ie a constable or a person authorised by the Secretary of State: see para 24, notes 1, 4, above.
2 Salmon and Freshwater Fisheries (Protection) (Scotland) Act 1951 (c 26), s 10(1)(d). The forfeiture powers (see s 19, and para 22 above) extend to the Salmon Fisheries (Scotland) Act 1868 (c 123), s 15. For the meaning of 'boat' and 'vehicle' see respectively para 26, note 2, and para 25, note 6, above.
3 See the Sea Fish (Conservation) Act 1967 (c 84), s 18(2), and the Inshore Fishing (Scotland) Act 1984 (c 26), s 7(2), and para 25, note 6, above.
4 Salmon Fisheries (Scotland) Act 1868, s 26: see para 26 above.
5 See the Salmon and Freshwater Fisheries (Protection) (Scotland) Act 1951, s 16, and para 21 above.
6 Ibid, s 16(2).
7 See the Diseases of Fish Act 1937 (c 33), s 6(1).

28. Powers of arrest. A water bailiff, constable or person appointed by the Secretary of State may, without warrant, arrest any person found committing any of the principal offences[1] relating to salmon fishing and carry him before any sheriff principal or justice of the peace[2]. They have similar powers on the River Tweed[3].

1 Ie any offence against the Salmon Fisheries (Scotland) Act 1868 (c 123), ss 15(1)–(6), 18–22, the Salmon and Freshwater Fisheries (Protection) (Scotland) Act 1951 (c 26), ss 1–8, the Sea Fish (Conservation) Act 1967 (c 84), s 4, or orders under ss 5, 6, or orders under the Inshore Fishing (Scotland) Act 1984 (c 26), s 1.
2 Salmon Fisheries (Scotland) Act 1868, s 29 (amended by the Salmon and Freshwater Fisheries (Protection) (Scotland) Act 1951, ss 12(2), 25(2), Sch 2, and the Sheriff Courts (Scotland) Act 1971 (c 58), s 4), extended and applied by the Salmon and Freshwater Fisheries (Protection)

(Scotland) Act 1951, s 12(1), which is in turn applied by the Sea Fish (Conservation) Act 1967, s 18(2), and the Inshore Fishing (Scotland) Act 1984 (c 26), s 7(2).

3 Tweed Fisheries Act 1857 (c cxlviii), s 38 (amended by the Salmon and Freshwater Fisheries (Protection) (Scotland) Act 1951, ss 12(3), 25(1), Sch 1, and applied by ss 12(1), 22(2)).

29. Obstruction of enforcing officer. Any person who refuses to allow a water bailiff, constable or any person appointed by the Secretary of State to exercise any of his statutory powers in relation to salmon fisheries or who obstructs him in the exercise of any such power is guilty of an offence[1]. This applies to any river in Scotland, including the Tweed[2].

1 Salmon and Freshwater Fisheries (Protection) (Scotland) Act 1951 (c 26), s 10(6). He is liable on summary conviction to a fine not exceeding level 4 on the standard scale (for which see para 11, note 16, above) or imprisonment for a term not exceeding three months, or both: Freshwater and Salmon Fisheries (Scotland) Act 1976 (c 22), s 6, Sch 2; Criminal Procedure (Scotland) Act 1975 (c 21), ss 289E–289G (added by the Criminal Justice Act 1982 (c 48), s 54).

2 Salmon and Freshwater Fisheries (Protection) (Scotland) Act 1951, s 10(7)(a).

30. Persons appointed by the Secretary of State. The powers in respect of salmon fisheries of persons appointed by the Secretary of State[1] are in almost all respects identical to those that may be exercised by water bailiffs, subject to the following restrictions:

(1) persons so appointed have no authority to exercise their powers beyond those waters in respect of which they are authorised;

(2) they are not explicitly empowered to enter and remain on land, as are water bailiffs[2];

(3) they do not appear to have the wider powers available to water bailiffs under the Salmon Fisheries (Scotland) Act 1868 to search premises under warrant in connection with certain offences[3];

(4) they do not have the power, automatically available to water bailiffs, to open and detain packages suspected of containing salmon or trout, although they can be expressly appointed for this purpose[4].

In all other respects a person so appointed has the same powers of entry, search, seizure and arrest as a water bailiff[5], and it is an offence to refuse to allow him to exercise his functions or to obstruct him in the exercise of those functions[6]. The production of the instrument of his appointment purporting to be signed by or on behalf of the Secretary of State is sufficient warrant for the exercise of his powers[7].

1 See the Salmon and Freshwater Fisheries (Protection) (Scotland) Act 1951 (c 26), s 10(5), and para 24 above.

2 See the Salmon Fisheries (Scotland) Act 1868 (c 123), s 27, and para 25 above.

3 See ibid, s 26, and para 26 above. However, they do have these powers in connection with offences under the Salmon and Freshwater Fisheries (Protection) (Scotland) Act 1951 (see s 11), and in connection with salmon offences under the Inshore Fishing (Scotland) Act 1984 (c 26) (see s 7).

4 Salmon and Freshwater Fisheries (Protection) (Scotland) Act 1951, s 16(2)(a).

5 See paras 25 ff above.

6 See para 29 above.

7 Salmon and Freshwater Fisheries (Protection) (Scotland) Act 1951, s 10(5).

(3) ADMINISTRATION OF SALMON FISHINGS

31. Introduction. Prior to 1828, although the salmon had long been recognised as a valuable source of food, and had accordingly been afforded statutory protection, there was no attempt to provide for local organisation of the management of salmon fisheries. The Salmon Fisheries (Scotland) Act 1828 (c 39) set up machinery for local administration of salmon fisheries which foreshadowed the later district boards. This provision was superseded by the Salmon Fisheries (Scotland) Acts 1862 (c 97), 1863 (c 50), 1864 (c 118) and 1868 (c 123) which, until 1987, formed the code of management and regulation of Scottish salmon fisheries, but the Salmon Act 1986, by which the greater part of the previous legislation has been repealed, does no more than restate in modern form, with certain additions, the 1862 to 1868 Acts which established the framework for the administration of salmon fisheries. The modern legislation has retained a great deal of this framework by specifically providing that such regulations and byelaws as had been made under those earlier Acts, as applicable to salmon fishing districts, are still to have effect[1].

1 Salmon Act 1986 (c 62), s 3(1): see para 23 above.

32. Early administration. Under the Salmon Fisheries (Scotland) Act 1862 each river in Scotland flowing into the sea, and every tributary stream or lake flowing into or connected with such river, and the mouth or estuary of such river and the sea coasts adjoining thereto was to form a district[1]. The Secretary of State, who remained the central authority, was empowered to appoint three Commissioners[2], whose duties inter alia were:

(1) to define the limits dividing each river from the sea and the limits of the Solway Firth[3];

(2) to fix the limits of each district and the portions of the sea coast adjoining the mouth of any river to be included in the district[4];

(3) to fix a point on each river below which the proprietors of salmon fisheries were to be 'lower proprietors' and above which they were to be 'upper proprietors'[5];

(4) to determine the annual close time and the periods within that time when rod fishing was to be permitted[6]; and

(5) to make general regulations as to weekly close times, cruives, obstructions in the river and the meshes of nets[7].

The 1862 Act also provided for the constitution, election, powers and duties of district boards[8]. The Salmon Fisheries (Scotland) Act 1868 was passed largely to improve the operation of the district board system[9] and to give further effect to the exercise of the Commissioners' powers[10].

The appointment of Commissioners continued until 1882, when a Fishery Board for Scotland was established[11] to have the general superintendence of Scottish salmon fisheries and the powers and duties of the Commissioners, but without prejudice to or interference with the powers of district boards[12]. The functions of the Fishery Board were transferred to the Secretary of State in 1939[13]. Provision was also made in 1882 for the appointment of an inspector of salmon fisheries for Scotland to inspect salmon fisheries, inquire into the operation of the relevant legislation and report thereon to the Fishery Board (and subsequently the Secretary of State)[14]. The inspector continues to this day to advise the Secretary of State on matters relating to salmon fisheries in Scotland.

1 Salmon Fisheries (Scotland) Act 1862 (c 97), s 4 (repealed).
2 Ibid, s 5 (repealed).
3 Ibid, s 6(1), (2) (repealed). See now the Salmon Fisheries (Scotland) Act 1868 (c 123), Sch (B).
4 Salmon Fisheries (Scotland) Act 1862, s 6(3) (repealed). See the Salmon Fisheries (Scotland) Act 1868, Sch (A).
5 Salmon Fisheries (Scotland) Act 1862, s 6(4) (repealed). See the Salmon Fisheries (Scotland) Act 1868, Sch (A).
6 Salmon Fisheries (Scotland) Act 1862, s 6(5) (repealed). See the Salmon Fisheries (Scotland) Act 1868, Sch (C).

7 Salmon Fisheries (Scotland) Act 1862, s 6(6) (repealed). See the Salmon Fisheries (Scotland) Act 1868, Schs (D)–(G).

8 Salmon Fisheries (Scotland) Act 1862, ss 18–24 (repealed). The boards were elected by the upper and lower proprietors from among themselves: see s 18.

9 See the Salmon Fisheries (Scotland) Act 1868, ss 2–14 (largely repealed). The boards acted for the protection or improvement of the fisheries within their districts: see s 13.

10 See ibid, s 10, Schs (A)–(G).

11 Fishery Board (Scotland) Act 1882 (c 78), s 4 (repealed).

12 Ibid, s 5(2) (repealed).

13 Reorganisation of Offices (Scotland) Act 1939 (c 20), s 1(1).

14 Fishery Board (Scotland) Act 1882, s 6.

33. Salmon fishery districts. Provision for the administration of salmon fisheries within prescribed districts by district boards, originally made in 1862 and continued in 1868[1], has been continued by the Salmon Act 1986, the long title to which states inter alia that it is 'an Act to make fresh provision for the administration of salmon fisheries in Scotland'.

Salmon fishery districts under the 1986 Act are based on the districts established under the earlier Acts[2]. Thus a salmon fishery district is the area within the coastal limits of such a district and extending seaward for 3 miles from mean low water springs and landward to include the catchment area of each river which flows directly or indirectly into the sea within those limits, but excluding any area designated as a salmon fishery district by a designation order made by the Secretary of State[3]. Districts within the meaning of the earlier Acts are abolished and replaced by the new salmon fishery districts, although a salmon fishery district with the same coastal limits as an old district retains the name of the old district[4]. Except as otherwise provided in the 1986 Act, the River Tweed is not a salmon fishery district[5].

After consulting such persons as he thinks fit the Secretary of State may by order made by statutory instrument include within a salmon fishery district any island or part of an island which is not within a salmon fishery district and the sea within 3 miles from mean low water springs on that island or part, or remove any doubt as to whether a particular place is within a salmon fishery district, or change a reference used in describing a salmon fishery district where the suitability of a reference for that purpose has lessened or ceased; but such an order cannot create a salmon fishery district[6].

1 See para 32 above.

2 See para 32, text and note 4, above.

3 Salmon Act 1986 (c 62), s 1(1). As to designation orders, see s 1(2), 2, and para 23 above.

4 Ibid, s 1(3).

5 Ibid, s 1(5). As to the Tweed, see paras 40 ff below.

6 Ibid, s 1(4).

34. Proprietors. A qualified proprietor is a proprietor of a salmon fishery entered in the valuation roll[1]. Each qualified proprietor continues to be classified as an 'upper proprietor' or a 'lower proprietor' according to whether his salmon fishery is upstream or downstream of a division of a river[2]. This division is either a line from bank to bank prescribed by the Secretary of State at the request of the district salmon fishery board or, failing that, a point of division fixed under earlier legislation, or, failing that, the normal tidal limit[3]. It is possible for an individual qualified proprietor to come within both categories of proprietor if he has one fishery above and another below this division[4], but, subject to this, a proprietor is not eligible to sit on the district salmon fishery board in respect of more than one salmon fishery[5]. The clerk of the salmon fishery board must maintain a roll of proprietors, showing which category they fall into and the values of their fisheries as entered in the valuation roll, and the board may add or remove names to or from the roll[6].

To cover situations where there may be joint proprietors or timeshare schemes of salmon fishings, with several persons owning fishing rights in the same fishery, it was considered necessary to define very carefully the meaning of 'proprietor' in the Salmon Act 1986, to avoid possible difficulties which might have been encountered when electing members to district salmon fishery boards. 'Proprietor' is therefore defined as meaning any person, partnership, company or corporation which is the proprietor of a salmon fishery or which receives or is entitled to receive the rents of such fishery on its own account or as trustee, guardian or factor for any person, company or corporation[7]. However, 'proprietor' includes not more than one person authorised by:

(1) in the case of a fishery in which more than one person has a *pro indiviso* share, such persons, or

(2) in the case of a fishery in which the rights to the fishery are shared by more than one person in any other way, such persons,

but in neither case does 'proprietor' include (except by virtue of this provision) a person whose right to the fishery is so shared[8]. Notwithstanding the provisions about qualified proprietors, it is provided that any proprietor (whether entered on the valuation roll or not) is entitled to vote at a district salmon fishery board election and is eligible for election[9].

1 Salmon Act 1986 (c 62), s 11(1). As to entry in the roll, see s 11(2), (3).
2 Ibid, s 11(4).
3 Ibid, s 11(7), (8).
4 Ibid, s 11(5).
5 Ibid, s 11(6).
6 Ibid, s 11(9). As to applications to the sheriff in respect of the roll, see s 11(10).
7 Ibid, s 40(1).
8 Ibid, s 40(3).
9 Ibid, s 14(3), Sch 2, para 3(4).

35. District salmon fishery boards. The Salmon Act 1986 provided for existing district boards under the earlier legislation[1] to continue as transitional district boards, each being deemed to be a district salmon fishery board and having the powers and duties of such a board, for a transitional period[2], on the expiry of which district salmon fishery boards had to be constituted under the 1986 Act. If the proprietors in a salmon fishery district form an association for the purpose of protecting or improving the fisheries within their district and duly elect a committee to act for them, that committee will be the district salmon fishery board[3] for a limited three-year period[4]. However, on the coming into force of a designation order made by the Secretary of State any transitional district board for or committee in respect of a district superseded by the designated district ceased to be a district salmon fishery board, and the committee duly constituted in anticipation of the order in respect of that district became the district salmon fishery board[5]. There may be a district salmon fishery board for a district whether or not there are any salmon in the waters there[6].

The 1986 Act provides for the formation of district salmon fishery boards by setting out detailed rules as to the qualifications for membership and the methods of election. The procedure can be summarised as follows: Qualified proprietors of salmon fisheries, both 'upper' and 'lower', meet and elect a chairman from among themselves[7]. Not more than three representatives of each category of proprietors are then elected as members by the proprietors constituting each category[8]. If there are fewer than three eligible in either category, then no more than that number may be elected from the other category[9]. Finally, not more than three representatives of salmon anglers and three representatives of tenant netsmen in the district are to be co-opted as members by the members already elected[10]. The maximum number of members, both elected and co-opted, must not exceed thirteen, including the chairman, and may be less[11]. The detailed rules are somewhat complicated, but it is clearly expressed that if the numbers of members do not permit the maximum of three for each of the four categories, then the number elected or co-opted from any category must not exceed the number eligible for election or co-option in the other categories[12].

The co-option of tenant netsmen to membership of district salmon fishery boards is likely to cause some difficulty. On a strict interpretation of the rules applying to their co-option it would seem that only individual tenant netsmen may be eligible, which rules out those who are partnerships or limited companies.

A district salmon fishery board under the 1986 Act takes the form of an association of proprietors of salmon fisheries in the district, who elect a committee which becomes the board, the election of the committee being carried out in accordance with the procedure outlined above. For the election it should be noted that each proprietor may have up to four votes as respects each of his fisheries, depending on the valuation of each fishery as entered in the valuation roll[13].

The members of a district salmon fishery board hold office for three years and, before the expiry of the three-year period, a meeting of qualified proprietors must be held to go through the election procedure outlined above[14]. There is a procedure for filling vacancies on the board during the normal tenure of office[15].

1 See para 32 above.
2 See the Salmon Act 1986 (c62), s 14(8), Sch 3, paras 1, 6. The latest date for phasing out any transitional boards was 6 January 1990: see s 43(1), Sch 3, para 6.
3 Ibid, s 14(1). For the mode of election, see Sch 2.
4 Ibid, s 14(3).
5 Ibid, s 14(4).
6 Ibid, s 14(9).
7 Ibid, Sch 2, paras 3(1), 6(1). As to qualified proprietors, see para 34 above. As to the calling of the meeting, see Sch 2, paras 1, 2. The chairman has both a deliberative and a casting vote: s 17(3)(a).
8 Ibid, Sch 2, paras 3(2), 4(1), 6(1).
9 Ibid, Sch 2, para 4(2). For the position where there is a sole proprietor, see para 36 below.
10 Ibid, s 16(2), Sch 2, paras 5, 6(1)–(3).
11 Ibid, Sch 2, para 6(3).
12 Ibid, Sch 2, paras 4(2), 5(1).
13 Ibid, Sch 2, para 3(3), (4).
14 Ibid, s 18(1), (2), Sch 2, paras 2–6.
15 Ibid, s 18(5).

36. Sole proprietor in a salmon fishery district. For the rare occasion where there is only one proprietor of salmon fisheries in a salmon fishery district there are special provisions. Under the Salmon Fisheries (Scotland) Acts 1862–68, where there was only one proprietor in a district, he was able to exercise all the powers conferred on a district board[1]. Such powers may not now be exercised by a sole proprietor[2] and, similarly, any water bailiff previously appointed by that sole proprietor may no longer exercise the powers of water bailiff[3]. In respect of other provisions of the Salmon Act 1986 a sole proprietor will have the rights conferred elsewhere on two proprietors[4], so that he will have some administrative control over the salmon fisheries in his district.

1 Salmon Fisheries (Scotland) Act 1862 (c97), s 19 (repealed).
2 Salmon Act 1986 (c62), s 12(2).

3 Ibid, s 12(3). A sole proprietor may, however, apply to the Secretary of State for him to appoint a person under the Salmon and Freshwater Fisheries (Protection) (Scotland) Act 1951 (c 26), s 10(5), for which see paras 24, 30, above.
4 Salmon Act 1986, s 12(1).

37. Mandatories. A qualified proprietor of a salmon fishery or an elected member or a chairman of a district salmon fishery board may at any time authorise a person to act for him, known as a 'mandatory'[1]. It is also permitted for a mandatory as such to be elected[2] as a member of a district salmon fishery board to represent qualified proprietors or as chairman, but it is not permitted for a person to authorise another, as mandatory, to act as a co-opted member, nor is it permitted for a mandatory to be co-opted to represent salmon anglers or tenant netsmen[3]. It seems that the element of *delectus personae* was considered to be of overriding importance when it came to co-opting representatives of both salmon anglers and tenant netsmen to district fishery boards[4].

1 Salmon Act 1986 (c 62), s 13(1). As to proprietors, see para 34 above, and as to boards, see para 35 above. A person who is both an upper and a lower proprietor may authorise a mandatory in either or both of his capacities or may do so in each capacity: s 13(3).
2 Ie under the rules contained in ibid, Sch 2: see para 35 above.
3 Ibid, s 13(2).
4 However, contrast the position as regards mandatories of qualified proprietors: see above.

38. Powers and duties of district salmon fishery boards. The purpose of district salmon fishery boards is to protect or improve salmon fisheries within their districts[1]. That was the reason behind their original creation, and the principle has remained unchanged. They have been required to implement their obligation under the various Acts relating to salmon fisheries, but have no title beyond this. District salmon fishery boards alone have a title to enforce byelaws under the Salmon Fisheries (Scotland) Act 1868[2], but prosecutions may be brought only by the procurator fiscal[3]. It is also doubtful whether a district salmon fishery board may proceed at common law for the protection of the fisheries, the right to do so resting with the individual salmon proprietors alone[4].

District salmon fishery boards were intentionally given powers under the Salmon Act 1986 in broad and unspecific terms, on the basis that the less specification the less likelihood there was of subsequent challenge to their exercise. This is in direct contrast to the provisions under previous repealed legislation which specified the powers available to district boards[5], and which provided difficulties of interpretations.

The powers now available to a district salmon fishery board are to do such acts, execute such works and incur such expenses as may appear to it expedient for (1) the protection or improvement of the fisheries within its district, (2) the increase of salmon, or (3) the stocking of the waters of the district with salmon[6]. These provisions have not yet been tested in the courts as to their extent or limitations, but they would appear to give boards wider powers of enforcement than were available to them before. A board may sue and be sued in the name of its clerk[7]. It has power to appoint a clerk to the board, and water bailiffs[8].

A district salmon fishery board has had, since the inception of district boards[9], the power to impose a fishery assessment on all salmon fishery proprietors in its district, according to the valuation of their fisheries as entered in the valuation roll. Additional financial powers and duties have been given by the Salmon Act 1986, which enables a board, whose members are themselves not entitled to any salary or fees from their work as members[10], (a) to continue to levy the fishery assessment on each salmon fishery in its district[11], (b) to recover arrears of assessments, with interest if more than three months overdue, by civil action[12], (c) to borrow money to assist in carrying out its purposes under the Act[13], and, in particular, (d) to authorise expenditure, including expenditure for the purpose of acquiring heritable property, which may be financed not only from the proceeds of the fishery assessment, or by borrowing, but also from 'any other source'[14]. This power to purchase heritable property will enable boards not only to acquire property to house their staff, but also to purchase fisheries, either rod or net. It is significant that at the time of writing a number of netting rights of lower proprietors had already been acquired in order to abandon them, to enable salmon to run the rivers free of netting stations, for the ultimate benefit of salmon rod anglers.

A district salmon fishery board has power to apply to the Secretary of State to seek changes or variations in the existing legislation. This has already been described[15]. The powers so vested in the Secretary of State may only be exercised by him on the application of a district salmon fishery board, where it exists, which failing by two proprietors or a sole proprietor of salmon fisheries in the district[16].

Each year a district salmon fishery board must prepare a report and a statement of accounts (which must be audited) relating to its activities, and the clerk must call an annual meeting of qualfied proprietors, to consider the report and accounts[17].

 1 See the Salmon Act 1986 (c 62), s 14(1).
 2 *Lyall v Carnegy* (1900) 2 F 423 at 429, 7 SLT 341 at 342, per Lord President Balfour, relating to proceedings under the Salmon Fisheries (Scotland) Act 1862 (c 97), s 29 (repealed), and the Salmon Fisheries (Scotland) Act 1868 (c 123), Sch (G).
 3 See the Salmon Act 1986, s 30(1).
 4 *Tay District Fishery Board v Robertson* (1887) 15 R 40.
 5 See the Salmon Fisheries (Scotland) Act 1868, s 13 (repealed).
 6 Salmon Act 1986, s 16(1)(a)–(c).
 7 Ibid, s 16(4).
 8 Ibid, s 16(3).
 9 See the Salmon Fisheries (Scotland) Act 1862, s 23 (repealed). The Salmon Fisheries (Scotland) Act 1828 (c 39), s 10 (repealed), contained provisions for two or more proprietors to initiate the holding of meetings to make assessments on all the proprietors of salmon fisheries in any river for the purposes of enforcing that Act.
10 Salmon Act 1986, s 15(10).
11 Ibid, s 15(2), (3).
12 See ibid, s 15(5)–(7).
13 See ibid, s 15(8), (9).
14 Ibid, s 15(10).
15 See paras 15, 23, above.
16 See the Salmon Act 1986, ss 6(4), 7(3), 8(2), Sch 1, para 1.
17 Ibid, s 15(1).

39. Miscellaneous points on the administration of salmon fisheries. For the most part the Salmon Act 1986 does not apply to the River Tweed[1], where the salmon fisheries are administered by a council on behalf of the Tweed Commissioners[2]. There are also special provisions relating to the River Esk (Dumfriesshire) and the Solway Firth[3].

A district salmon fishery board may be established for a district even though there may not be salmon in the waters of that district[4]. This provision has been specifically included in order to provide for the cleaning up and restocking of rivers, which is now in fact taking place, the River Clyde being a good example of a river where salmon are once again spawning after an absence of many years, as a result of effective anti-pollution measures.

Notwithstanding a vacancy in the membership of a district salmon fishery board, or a defect in the qualification or appointment of any of its members, it is not possible to question or vitiate any act or proceedings of that board[5].

Under previous legislation the clerk of a district board was empowered to prosecute offences under the legislation[6]. This is no longer permitted[7], and such prosecutions may now be brought only by the procurator fiscal. The need for corroboration of evidence is not required in respect of certain offences committed under the Salmon Fisheries (Scotland) Act 1868[8].

Provision has been included in the 1986 Act for a review of certain salmon net fishing. The Minister of Agriculture, Fisheries and Food and the Secretary of State are required as soon as practicable after 7 November 1989 to prepare a report for Parliament reviewing the nature and extent of salmon fishing in the areas of the Yorkshire and Northumbrian water authorities and the salmon fishery districts from the River Tweed to the River Ugie[9]. This will involve monitoring the effects of the salmon net fisheries of the north-east coast of England (drift netting being still a lawful method of fishing in England and Wales, while prohibited in Scottish waters[10]) on the migration of salmon up the east coast of Scotland into the Scottish rivers. The purpose is to ensure that sufficient salmon are returning to spawn in those rivers and that the net fishing in those specified areas is being properly managed[11]. The necessity to have this review timeously and effectively carried out is of vital importance to the future of salmon stocks in the waters of the east coast of Scotland.

Provision is included in the 1986 Act to bind the Crown, but only in respect of the part of the Act dealing with the administration of salmon fisheries in Scotland[12]. Thus the Crown Estate Commissioners will be required to continue their involvement in the administration of salmon fisheries in Scotland.

The Fisheries Committee appointed by the Secretary of State under the Electricity (Scotland) Act 1979[13] has the function of giving, to him and to persons engaged in, or proposing to engage in, the operation of a generating station wholly or mainly driven by water, advice and assistance (whether specifically requested or not) on questions relating to the effect in Scotland on fisheries, or on the stock of fish in any waters, of such generating stations[14]. Persons engaged in or proposing to engage in such a generating station must furnish to the committee such maps, plans, drawings and information as it may require and must give it reasonable inspection facilities[15]. A person seeking the consent of the Secretary of State to the construction of such a generating station must consult the committee[16].

1 See eg the Salmon Act 1986 (c 62), ss 1(5), 2(4), 7(6), 41(3). See, however, eg ss 10, 27(2), 28(4), 29(1).
2 See the Tweed Fisheries Act 1969 (c xxiv), s 6, and para 41 below.
3 See paras 44–46 below.
4 Salmon Act 1986, s 14(9).
5 Ibid, s 17(4).
6 Salmon Fisheries (Scotland) Act 1868 (c 123), ss 30, 38–40 (repealed).
7 Salmon Act 1986, s 30(1).
8 Ibid, s 30(2), referring to the Salmon Fisheries (Scotland) Act 1868, ss 15, 18–24.
9 Salmon Act 1986, s 39(1)–(3) (amended by the Water Act 1989 (c 15), s 141(5), Sch 17, para 9(2), so as to refer, after the transfer date, to the areas which before then were the areas of the Yorkshire and Northumbrian Water Authorities for the purposes of their fisheries functions).
10 See para 12 above.
11 Salmon Act 1986, s 39(1)(a), (b).
12 Ibid, s 42(1), which provides that Pt I (ss 1–19) is to apply to land an interest in which belongs to Her Majesty in right of the Crown and land an interest in which belongs to a government department or is held in trust for Her Majesty for the purposes of a government department, but that otherwise the Act does not bind the Crown. 'Land' includes salmon fisheries: s 42(2).
13 See the Electricity (Scotland) Act 1979 (c 11), s 5(2) (repealed) (replacing the Hydro-Electric Development (Scotland) Act 1943 (c 32), s 9(2)). For the constitution of the committee, see now

the Electricity Act 1989 (c 29), s 38, Sch 9, para 5(2), (3), which comes into force on a day to be appointed by order under s 113(2).
14 Ibid, Sch 9, para 5(1).
15 Ibid, Sch 9, para 5(4).
16 Ibid, s 36, Sch 9, para 5(5). On being consulted the committee may make recommendations: see Sch 9, para 5(6).

(4) THE RIVER TWEED

40. Introduction. The River Tweed lies partly in Scotland and partly in England. From this fact stems the special legislation applying to the Tweed. There has been such legislation since 1771[1]. The principal existing Acts are the Tweed Fisheries Act 1857, the Tweed Fisheries Amendment Act 1859 and the Tweed Fisheries Act 1969. In addition, parts of the Salmon Fisheries (Scotland) Act 1868[2] and all of the Salmon and Freshwater Fisheries (Protection) (Scotland) Act 1951 apply to the whole of the River Tweed[3]. Under these Acts the administration of the salmon fisheries in the River Tweed is carried out by the River Tweed Council on behalf of the River Tweed Commissioners[4]. For the purposes of the Salmon Act 1986, the River Tweed is not a salmon fishery district except as otherwise provided by that Act[5], whereas references in the 1951 Act and in any other enactment as amended by that Act to a district are construed as including references to the River Tweed[6].

In the Tweed Fisheries Acts 'the river' means the River Tweed and every river, brook or stream which flows or runs into it, and also the mouth or entrance of the river[7]. At present the Tweed limits run from Cockburnspath in Berwickshire to Beal Point in Northumbria, and extend for 5 miles seaward. For the purposes of those Acts 'salmon' includes salmon, grilse, sea trout, bull trout and whiting[8].

1 Tweed Fisheries Act 1771 (c 27) (repealed).
2 Ie the Salmon Fisheries (Scotland) Act 1868 (c 123), ss 13, 18–20, 33, Schs (A), (G).
3 Ibid, s 41 (amended by the Salmon and Freshwater Fisheries (Protection) (Scotland) Act 1951 (c 26), s 25(1), Sch 1, and the Salmon Act 1986 (c 62), s 41(1), Sch 4, para 5 — but see also s 10(1)); Salmon and Freshwater Fisheries (Protection) (Scotland) Act 1951, s 22(2).
4 Tweed Fisheries Act 1969 (c xxiv), s 6(1). References in the Tweed Fisheries Act 1857 (c cxlviii) and the Tweed Fisheries Amendment Act 1859 (c lxx) to the commissioners under those Acts are now construed as references to the commissioners appointed under the Tweed Fisheries Act 1969: s 2(3).
5 Salmon Act 1986, s 1(5).
6 Salmon Act 1986, s 1(6).
7 Tweed Fisheries Act 1857, s 2; Tweed Fisheries Amendment Act 1859, s 2, applied by the Tweed Fisheries Act 1969, s 2(1).
8 Tweed Fisheries Act 1857, s 2 (amended by the Tweed Fisheries Act 1969, s 13(1), Sch 2, and applied by s 2(1)); Tweed Fisheries Amendment Act 1859, s 2.

41. Administration of Tweed salmon fisheries. As already described above, responsibility for administering salmon fisheries on the River Tweed lies with the River Tweed Council on behalf of the River Tweed Commissioners[1]. The council consists of thirty-eight elected proprietary commissioners[2] and forty-three representative commissioners[3]. The powers and duties of the commissioners have been vested since 1 February 1970 in the council, which exercises and complies with all the powers and duties of the commissioners under the Tweed Fisheries Act 1857 and the Tweed Fisheries Amendment Act 1859[4].

The proprietary commissioners are required to meet annually on or before the first Monday in March in Kelso to elect thirty-eight of their number as members of the council[5]. At the meeting they must elect one of their number to act as chairman, and he has a second or casting vote[6]. Each proprietor elected to the council holds office for one year unless he previously dies, resigns, becomes disqualified or ceases to be a proprietary commissioner[7]. In the event of a casual vacancy, the clerk to the council must convene a special meeting of the proprietary commissioners to elect a replacement for the remaining period of office of the member replaced[8].

The annual general meeting of the council takes place on the first Monday in March[9]. This and all ordinary meetings, which are held when the council so decides, must be held in Kelso[10]. At each annual general meeting the council members elect a chiarman and vice-chairman from among their number, to hold office until the next annual general meeting[11]. Any casual vacancy is filled at an ordinary meeting held for the purpose[12]. All meetings are presided over by the chairman, whom failing the vice-chairman, and if neither is present the members elect one of their number to preside[13]. At all meetings the chairman or acting chairman has a second or casting vote[14]. Every member may nominate a proxy in writing to represent him and vote on his behalf at any council meeting[15].

The powers and duties of the commissioners, which are set out mainly in the 1857 Act (which was a consolidating Act), are much the same as those performed by district salmon fishery boards in respect of their districts[16]. The commissioners may appoint a clerk, a superintendent and water bailiffs[17]. Their source of finance is by means of an annual assessment levied on owners of salmon fisheries in the River Tweed within the limits of its mouth, as defined[18], in proportion to the rents or yearly value of their fisheries, such valuation being fixed by the council itself[19]. Their duties include the enforcement of the Acts and regulations relating to salmon fisheries[20], as they apply to the River Tweed, and in this connection it should be particularly noted that the Salmon Act 1986 has excepted the River Tweed from the repeal of the provision contained in previous legislation which empowered district boards by agreement to purchase, for the purpose only of removal, dams, weirs, cruives or other fixed engines and remove any natural obstructions and generally to execute such works and incur such expense as may appear to the River Tweed Council expedient for the protection or improvement of its fisheries[21]. Similarly, the powers and duties of the River Tweed Council are not affected by the provisions in the 1986 Act relating to the formation and regulation and the powers and duties of district salmon fishery boards.

 1 See para 40 above.
 2 Proprietary commissioners are all proprietors of specified salmon fishings, namely those of the annual value of not less than £30, or which extend for half a mile on one side of the river or for a quarter of a mile on both sides: Tweed Fisheries Act 1969 (c xxiv), s 2(1) ('proprietary commissioner' and 'specified salmon fishing'), and ss 2(3), 4. No distinction is drawn between upper and lower proprietors (cf para 34 above (district salmon fishery boards)).
 3 Ibid, s 6(1). The representative commissioners are appointed by the district councils of Berwickshire, Roxburgh, Ettrick and Lauderdale, Tweeddale and Berwick on Tweed: s 2(1) ('representative commissioner'), and s 5(1), Sch 1 (amended by the Local Government (Scotland) Act 1973 (c 65), s 213(3), Sch 26, paras 2(a), 5).
 4 Tweed Fisheries Act 1969, s 6(1).
 5 Ibid, s 6(2)(a) (amended by the Local Government (Scotland) Act 1973, Sch 26, para 3).
 6 Tweed Fisheries Act 1969, s 6(2)(b).
 7 Ibid, s 6(3).
 8 Ibid, s 6(4).
 9 Ibid, s 7(1).
10 Ibid, s 7(2), (3) (amended by the Local Government (Scotland) Act 1973, Sch 26, para 4).
11 Tweed Fisheries Act 1969, s 8(1).
12 Ibid, s 8(2).
13 Ibid, s 8(3).
14 Ibid, s 9(1).

15 Ibid, s 9(3).
16 Tweed Fisheries Act 1969, s 6(1).
17 Tweed Fisheries Act 1857 (c cxlviii), ss 24, 36 (amended by the Tweed Fisheries Act 1969, s 13(1), Sch 2).
18 This must now mean the limits as defined by the Salmon Fisheries (Scotland) Act 1868 (c 123), Sch (A).
19 Tweed Fisheries Act 1857, s 79 (as amended: see note 17 above).
20 See ibid, s 82, and the Tweed Fisheries Amendment Act 1859 (c lxx), s 19.
21 Salmon Fisheries (Scotland) Act 1868, s 13, which, as respects the River Tweed, was excepted from repeal by the Salmon Act 1986, s 41(3). Section 16 of the 1986 Act (for which see para 38 above) does not apply to the River Tweed Council: see s 1(5).

42. Regulation of salmon fisheries on the River Tweed. The regulatory measures contained in the Salmon and Freshwater Fisheries (Protection) (Scotland) Act 1951 are all applicable to the River Tweed, together with those already specified contained in the Salmon Fisheries (Scotland) Act 1868[1]. Measures applicable to the River Tweed only are contained in the special legislation already referred to. The most important such measures are those relating to close times and fixed nets and engines.

The annual close time for nets in the River Tweed is 153 days extending from 14 September to 15 February, with an exception for rod and line fishing, with artificial fly only, from 15 September to 30 November and 1 to 14 February[2]. There is also a provision permitting the taking of salmon, with the written permission of the Tweed Commissioners and the owner of the fishery, for the purpose of artificial propagation[3]. The weekly close time is regulated by the 1951 Act as described above[4].

The use of fixed nets or engines in the River Tweed is prohibited[5]. Such nets and fixed engines may be used beyond the river limits as fixed by the Tweed Fisheries Act 1857[6], but such use is subject to regulations in the Tweed Fisheries Amendment Act 1859 regarding the size of the mesh, and construction of stake nets and bag nets and the way in which they are to be put out of fishing order during the weekly close time[7]. Failure to remove boats, nets and other tackle from the fishery on or before 17 September in each year constitutes an offence, and they must be kept securely lodged until 13 February; and boats used for rod fishing must be removed on or before 3 December and stored until 30 January[8].

Water bailiffs appointed by the Tweed Commissioners have all the necessary powers of entry, search, seizure and arrest as are given to water bailiffs by district salmon fishery boards in terms of the 1951 Act[9]. It is an offence to obstruct or restrict a Tweed bailiff in the performance of his duties[10].

1 See para 40 above.
2 Tweed Fisheries Amendment Act 1859 (c lxx), s 6, under which contravention is an offence. For an exception for fish farms, see the Freshwater and Salmon Fisheries (Scotland) Act 1976 (c 22), s 7(1), Sch 3, para 3.
3 Tweed Fisheries Amendment Act 1859, s 6 proviso.
4 See the Salmon and Freshwater Fisheries (Protection) (Scotland) Act 1951 (c 26), s 13 (as amended), and para 17 above.
5 Ibid, s 2(1) (for which see para 11 above), replacing the Tweed Fisheries Act 1857 (c cxlviii), s 55 (repealed).
6 Tweed Fisheries Act 1857 (c cxlviii), s 41.
7 Tweed Fisheries Amendment Act 1859, ss 12, 13. For an exception from s 13 for fish farms, see the Freshwater and Salmon Fisheries (Scotland) Act 1976, Sch 3, para 3.
8 Tweed Fisheries Amendment Act 1859, s 11. For an exception for fish farms, see the Freshwater and Salmon Fisheries (Scotland) Act 1976, Sch 3, para 3.
9 See the Salmon and Freshwater Fisheries (Protection) (Scotland) Act 1951, ss 10–12, and paras 25 ff above. Tweed bailiffs also have similar powers of arrest in respect of offences against the Tweed Acts and against ss 13 and 16 of the 1951 Act: Tweed Fisheries Act 1857, s 38 (amended by the Salmon and Freshwater Fisheries (Protection) (Scotland) Act 1951, s 25(1),

Sch 1). However, they do not have the powers of entry on land given to water bailiffs by the Salmon Fisheries (Scotland) Act 1868 (c 123), s 27: see s 41.

10 See the Salmon and Freshwater Fisheries (Protection) (Scotland) Act 1951, s 10(6), and para 29 above.

43. Miscellaneous points relating to the River Tweed. There are a number of provisions in the Tweed Acts which constitute specific offences[1].

Certain provisions in the Salmon Act 1986 refer to the River Tweed and, as such, require consideration. In terms of that Act the Secretary of State is empowered to make regulations in respect of certain matters on application being made to him. These powers have already been considered[2], and certain of them may be exercised in respect of the River Tweed. On application being made to him, by the River Tweed Council he may make regulations as to the following matters:

(1) the annual close time, being a continuous period of not less than 153 days[3];
(2) the use of baits and lures, specifying the types and classes of baits and lures that may be used as the lawful 'rod and line' method[4].

The exercise of such powers by the Secretary of State in respect of the River Tweed will require the amendment of various provisions in the Tweed Acts, and he is given power to make regulations effecting the necessary amendments[5].

Exemption from certain offences in respect of certain acts and omissions may be granted by the Secretary of State. An act or omission relating to the fishing for or taking of salmon which otherwise would have constituted an offence may be so exempted[6]. In such a case the River Tweed Council is first required to give its consent[7]. A similar exemption is available in cases where the act or omission is for some scientific purpose, or for the purpose of protecting, improving or developing stocks of fish, or of conservation[8]. In such cases the written permission of either the Tweed River Council or the Secretary of State is required if the act is one which would otherwise contravene certain statutory provisions, including the Tweed Acts[9]. There are also certain exemptions for fish farms[10].

1 See eg the Tweed Fisheries Act 1857 (c cxlviii), s 45 (use of nets in annual close time), s 52 (use of ferry boats etc in fishing), s 53 (regulation of private boats), s 54 (use of distinguishing marks on boats), s 60 (beating the water etc), s 62 (wrongful use of wear shot nets), s 70 (taking foul or unseasonable fish), s 72 (putting such fish back in the river), s 73 (restoration to owner of salmon taken when fishing for trout), and s 74 (destruction of spawn or fry); and the Tweed Fisheries Amendment Act 1859 (c lxx), s 10 (contravention of annual close time) and s 16 (use of cleek in landing fish).
2 See para 23 above.
3 Salmon Act 1986 (c 62), s 10(4), (5).
4 Ibid, s 10(6)(d), applying s 8 (for which see para 23 above) with a modification.
5 Ibid, s 10(6)(a)–(c), under which regulations under s 3(2)(a), (d), (e) may respectively amend the Tweed Fisheries Amendment Act 1859, s 12 and ss 12, 13, and the Tweed Fisheries Act 1857, s 57. Further, under the Salmon Act 1986, s 10(6), an annual close time order may amend the Tweed Fisheries Amendment Act 1859, ss 6, 10, 11.
6 See the Salmon Act 1986, s 27, and para 13 above.
7 Ibid, s 27(2).
8 See ibid, s 28, and para 13 above.
9 Ibid, s 28(1)(b), (2), (4)(a).
10 See the Freshwater and Salmon Fisheries (Scotland) Act 1976 (c 22), s 7(1), Sch 3, paras 2, 3, referring to the Tweed Fisheries Act 1857, ss 45, 72, 74, and the Tweed Fisheries Amendment Act 1859, ss 6, 10, 11, 13. See also the Freshwater and Salmon Fisheries (Scotland) Act 1976, s 7(4), referring to the Tweed Fisheries Amendment Act 1859, s 11.

(5) THE SOLWAY FIRTH

44. Introduction. Like the River Tweed, the area of the Solway Firth is difficult to administer as it lies partly in Scotland and partly in England and is divided by the national boundary. The configuration of the bed of the firth is liable to change, and with it the main channel. Special legislation was therefore necessary, hence the Solway Firth Fisheries Act 1804 (c xlv). Although this Act has not been specifically repealed (except in so far as it applied to England and the Annan District[1]), most of its provisions have been superseded by general Scottish salmon fishing legislation and are impliedly repealed. The limits dividing the Solway from the sea were fixed in 1864[2] and confirmed by the Salmon Act 1986[3]. For this purpose the area of the Solway Firth is defined as including all the waters east of a line drawn from the Mull of Galloway to Hodbarrow Point in Cumbria.

1 See the Annan Fisheries Act 1841 (c xviii).
2 Ie by the Commissioners under the Salmon Fisheries (Scotland) Act 1862 (c 97), s 6(2), re-enacted in the Salmon Fisheries (Scotland) Act 1868 (c 123), Sch (B).
3 Salmon Act 1986 (c 62), s 9.

45. Regulation of salmon fisheries in the Solway Firth. Salmon fisheries and their regulation are covered generally by the Salmon Fisheries (Scotland) Act 1868, the Salmon and Freshwater Fisheries (Protection) (Scotland) Act 1951 and the Salmon Act 1986. However, the control of 'fixed engines' has been the subject of special treatment. The Salmon Fisheries (Scotland) Act 1862 (repealed) applied the Salmon Fishery Act 1861 to the Scottish part of the waters of the Solway Firth[1], thus prohibiting the use of fixed engines for salmon fishing, subject to a proviso which preserved certain ancient rights[2]. A special commission was later set up[3] to decide which nets qualified under the proviso. The commissioners issued certificates of privilege in respect of those fixed engines it judged to be lawful[4], and all others were required to be removed. Although the original statutory provisions have been repealed, the effects have been retained in the 1986 Act, which makes it an offence for any person to place or use an uncertificated fixed engine within the limits of the Solway Firth for the purpose of taking or obstructing the free passage of salmon[5]. There is some doubt as to whether a particular type of net (the 'haaf (or paidle) net') used as a traditional method by salmon fishermen to take salmon in the Solway Firth is lawful or unlawful. The haaf net is held stationary by fishermen. In English waters it appears to be lawful[6], but it is certainly the view of some that, traditional though its use may be, the haaf net may well be an unlawful method of taking salmon in Scotland in terms of the Scottish legislation[7]. It is certainly uncertificated, but is it a 'fixed engine'[8]?

1 Salmon Fisheries (Scotland) Act 1862 (c 97), s 33 (amended by the Salmon Fisheries (Scotland) Act 1863 (c 50), s 3).
2 Salmon Fishery Act 1861 (c 109), s 11 (repealed). This was an English Act. In that act 'fixed engine' included stake nets, bag nets, putts, putchers and all fixed engines for catching or facilitating the catching of fish: s 4 (repealed).
3 Ie under the Solway Salmon Fisheries Commissioners (Scotland) Act 1877 (c ccxl).
4 Ibid, s 5.
5 Salmon and Freshwater Fisheries (Protection) (Scotland) Act 1951 (c 26), s 7B(1) (added by the Salmon Act 1986 (c 62), s 25), under which the offence is punishable on summary conviction by a fine not exceeding level 4 on the standard scale (for which see para 11 note 16, above).
6 See the Salmon and Freshwater Fisheries Act 1975 (c 51), s 6. This is an English Act.
7 Ie in terms of the Salmon and Freshwater Fisheries (Protection) (Scotland) Act 1951, s 7B: see above. See J H Tait *Game Laws, Trout and Salmon Fishing* (2nd edn, 1928) p 236.

8 In ibid, s 7B, 'fixed engine' includes any net or other implement for taking fish which is fixed to
the soil or made stationary in any other way: s 7B(2) (as added: see note 5 above).

(6) THE RIVER ESK

46. Regulation of salmon fishing in the River Esk. The River Esk in the
former county of Kirkcudbright gives rise to difficulties, as it is a Border river
partly in Scotland and partly in England. Until recently salmon fishing in the
Esk has been entirely regulated by English statute[1], with the unsatisfactory
result that regulation of the fishings there was difficult and uncertain. The
situation has been improved by the Salmon Act 1986, which applies to the
Scottish parts of the Esk the poaching provisions of the Salmon and Freshwater
Fisheries (Protection) (Scotland) Act 1951[2], so that in future it will be an offence
to fish for salmon in the Esk without legal right or permission. In all other
respects, however, the position remains that the 1951 Act will not apply to that
part of the Esk situated in Scotland[3]. The new poaching provisions may be
enforced by the appropriate English authority[4], and Scottish water bailiffs have
no powers on the Esk.
   On the Esk the annual close time, which must extend for at least 153 days, and
the close time for rod and line fishing, which must extend for at least 92 days, are
fixed by byelaw made by the appropriate authority[5]. In the absence of any such
byelaw, the annual close time for salmon is from 31 August to 1 February and
the close time for rod and line fishing is from 31 October to 1 February[6]. The
weekly close time, which must be at least 42 hours, is also to be fixed by byelaw,
but is otherwise from 6 am on Saturday to 6 am on Monday[7]. Sunday rod
fishing for salmon is not prohibited, but it is understood that it is little exercised
in practice.

1 The Salmon and Freshwater Fisheries Act 1975 (c 51) applies to so much of the River Esk, with its
banks and tributary streams up to their source, as is situated in Scotland: s 39(1)(b). See also
s 39(1A) (added by the Salmon Act 1986 (c 62), s 26(2)). For the Salmon and Freshwater Fisheries
Act 1975 (c 51), 'salmon' means only salmon (sea trout are 'trout'): s 41(1).
2 Ibid, s 1, and ss 3, 18–20 so far as relating to an offence under s 1, are applied by s 21(2) (added by
the Salmon Act 1986, s 26(1)).
3 Salmon and Freshwater Fisheries (Protection) (Scotland) Act 1951, s 21(1) (amended by the
Salmon Act 1986, s 26(1)).
4 Ie the National Rivers Authority established under the Water Act 1989 (c 15), s 1, as successor to
the North West Water Authority: see s 4. As to the functions of the National Rivers Authority in
respect of the Scottish parts of the Esk, see s 141(1), (4).
5 Salmon and Freshwater Fisheries Act 1975, s 19(1), Sch 1, paras 1, 3 (amended by the Water Act
1989, s 141(5), Sch 17, para 7(12)).
6 Salmon and Freshwater Fisheries Act 1975, Sch 1, para 6(a).
7 Ibid, Sch 1, paras 1, 3, 6(c).

(7) TROUT FISHING

47. Nature of trout. The indigenous brown trout (*Salmo fario*) or common
trout is a freshwater fish that does not migrate to the sea, although it may move
between fresh and salt water in certain rivers, and is then known as a 'slob'. The
Salmon and Freshwater Fisheries (Protection) (Scotland) Act 1951 defines
'trout' as non-migratory trout of the species *Salmo trutta* living in fresh waters or
estuaries[1], but the Freshwater Fish (Scotland) Act 1902 refers to the common
trout *Salmo fario*[2]. *Salmo trutta* and *Salmo fario* are not two species of fish: the
different names reflect changing fashion in scientific nomenclature.

Trout in a natural stream or loch are, like all wild animals (*ferae naturae*), the property of no one until they are reduced into possession[3]. Being *res nullius*, therefore, no one can be convicted of theft of trout while in their natural state in a private river, stream or loch. If trout are enclosed in a fishpond, however, they become the property of the person having the right to, and enclosing them in, the pond[4]. A person who takes trout from such a fishpond or 'stank' without the permission of the owner commits theft[5], on the basis that the owner has a property in them. It seems certain, therefore, that small lochs within the ownership of one proprietor which are stocked with trout and which have devices on the outlet burn to prevent fish escaping would constitute 'stanks' in terms of the Theft Act 1607. As regards waters which have been artificially stocked with fish (whether brown trout, rainbow trout or other fish) and which may not comply with the definition of 'stank', the law is not so certain, although there is a view that an angler who took such artificially introduced fish without permission would probably also be committing theft[6].

1 Salmon and Freshwater Fisheries (Protection) (Scotland) Act 1951 (c 26), s 24(1).
2 Freshwater Fish (Scotland) Act 1902 (c 29), s 1.
3 Stair *Institutions* II, 1, 5.
4 *Copland v Maxwell* (1871) 9 M (HL) 1.
5 The Theft Act 1607 (c 6) imposes a penalty on 'quhasoevir . . . steillis . . . fisches in propir stanks and loches'. In *Pollok v M'Cabe* 1910 SC (J) 23, 1910 1 SLT 83, it was held that a reservoir without inlet or outlet was a 'proper stank' and theft of trout by rod and line established.
6 Lord Jauncey *Fishing in Scotland — Law for the Angler* (2nd edn, 1984) p 16.

48. Right to fish for trout. The right of fishing for brown trout in a private river, stream or loch is not a separate feudal estate but pertains to the ownership of the land which borders the water: 'a right to fish is a privilege to the proprietor of the land'[1]. In other words, 'a right of trout-fishing is an incident to the right of property'[2].

Where a river or stream runs between the properties of different proprietors, each has the right of fishing for brown trout *ex adverso* of his own land. The other *alveus* (river bed) belongs to the proprietor of each bank up to the middle line of the river (*medium filum*)[3]. This gives rise to the question as to what rights of fishing the respective proprietors may have: can they cast their flies across the full width of the river or are they restricted to casting up to the *medium filum* only? In the case of a small river the full width of which can be covered from one bank, it has been held that there is no rule limiting the proprietor on one side of the river to his own side of the *medium filum* in fishing for brown trout, and that consequently the proprietors of each bank have a common interest entitling them to take joint action against anyone fishing without permission from either side, but only as regards that stretch of the river which flows between their estates[4]. As regards rights of fishing for brown trout in larger rivers, it seems likely that, as a result of a recent decision relating to salmon fishing[5], the exercise of the right would not necessarily be restricted to the *medium filum*, although opinion was given in decisions earlier that such right would not extend beyond it[6]. It is clear that any such rights must not be exercised *in aemulationem vicini*[7].

Where a loch is surrounded entirely by the land of a single proprietor, then the whole of the loch and the *solum* belongs to that proprietor, so he has the exclusive right to fish for brown trout in the whole loch[8]. But where a private loch is surrounded by land owned by more than one proprietor, the presumption is that each proprietor has a common right of fishing for brown trout in the loch[9]. When there are joint rights, each proprietor has an exclusive right to the *solum* from his own share up to the middle of the loch[10], but he must not exercise his right to fish in such a way as to interfere with the enjoyment by the other owners of their rights, that is, by an excessive use of them to the detriment of others. If he were to abuse his rights in this manner the court, at the instance of the injured party, would be entitled to regulate the enjoyment of the right[11]. All proprietors have the right to sail and fish over the whole loch, but the court may restrict or regulate the number of boats each proprietor may put on it in the particular case concerned to prevent the destruction of, or damage to, the fishing[12]. The authorities are not entirely clear as to the common law rights of owners of land which adjoin or surround an artificial loch or reservoir created under statutory authority[13], although the observations of the First Division would tend to support the claims of adjoining landowners over such waters.

Where salmon fishing rights in a river are owned separately from the adjoining land, the salmon rights carry with them the lesser right of fishing for brown trout. Such right of trout fishing is not exclusive, and it is settled that the holder of the salmon and trout rights is not entitled to prevent the owner of land bounding the water from fishing for brown trout in the salmon water, so far as it is *ex adverso* of his property[14]. The two rights may therefore be exercised in the same water by different persons, but in such a way that the holder of the trout rights does not damage or cause injury to the holder of the salmon rights[15].

1 *Copland v Maxwell* (1871) 9 M (HL) 1 at 4, per Lord Westbury, approving words of Lord Neaves.
2 *Maxwell v Copland* (1868) 7 M 142 at 149, per Lord Neaves.
3 Bell *Principles* s 1101.
4 *Arthur v Aird* 1907 SC 1170, 15 SLT 209.
5 *Fothringham v Passmore* 1983 SLT 444 (revsd 1984 SC (HL) 96, 1984 SLT 401): see para 5 above.
6 *Stuart v M'Barnet* (1867) 5 M 753 at 762, per Lord Deas, and at 765 per Lord Ardmillan.
7 *Campbell v Muir* 1908 SC 387, 15 SLT 737 .
8 *Montgomery v Watson* (1861) 23D 635.
9 *Macdonald v Farquharson* (1836) 15 S 259.
10 *Cochrane v Earl of Minto* (1815) 6 Pat 139, HL.
11 *Menzies v Macdonald* (1854) 16 D 827, affd (1856) 2 Macq 463, HL, per Lord Cranworth.
12 *Menzies v Wentworth* (1901) 3 F 941, 9 SLT 107.
13 *Kilsyth Fish Protection Association v M'Farlane* 1937 SC 757, 1937 SLT 562.
14 *Lord Somerville v Smith* (1859) 22 D 279.
15 *Mackenzie v Rose* (1832) 6 W & S 31, HL, affirming (1830) 8 S 816.

49. Leases. The right of fishing for brown trout, not being a separate heritable right, cannot be owned by persons who do not own land adjoining the water concerned. It is incapable of being disposed of, other than with the land of which it is a pertinent. A right to fish for brown trout is considered to be a personal right and is therefore incapable of being made the subject of a proper lease, good against singular successors under the protection of the Leases Act 1449 (c 6). It is now possible, however, for an owner of land to create a lease of trout fishing pertaining to that land and which will be binding on future owners of that land, the lease to be in writing for a consideration and for a period of not less than one year[1]. The Leases Act 1449 will apply to such a lease, and the right of fishing authorised by it will, 'for the purposes of succession to that right, be deemed to be heritable property'[1].

It is common practice, where land bordering on water is leased, for the tenant to be given permission to fish for brown trout so long as he remains a tenant. In the case of an agricultural tenancy, where there is no express stipulation to that effect in the lease, the right of the tenant to fish for trout will not be implied, even where the water concerned is situated wholly within the boundaries of the leased property[2]. It is settled that a right of angling is not an accessory to an agricultural lease.

1 Freshwater and Salmon Fisheries (Scotland) Act 1976 (c 22), s 4.
2 *Copland v Maxwell* (1871) 9 M (HL) 1.

50. Extent of the right to fish for trout. Contrary to a generally held belief, the right to fish for brown trout in many waters in Scotland is not public. A person wishing to fish for brown trout in private waters must first obtain the permission of the owner of the land, of which the trout fishing is a pertinent. If a person fishes private waters without the required permission, the only remedy available in the normal course to an owner is under the common law of trespass[1], and anyone found trespassing on the waters may be turned off, provided no undue violence is used. In the event of actual damage being caused by the trespassing fisherman, he will be liable in damages to the owner. Similarly if the trespass is likely to be repeated, the remedy of interdict will be available to an owner.

No common right of fishing for brown trout is available to the public at large or to such persons as may have access to the water by virtue of a right of passage along the banks of that water[2]. Nor does a right to navigate a non-tidal water carry with it a right to fish for brown trout[3]. It is also settled that the continuous use and practice of fishing a stream for brown trout for forty years or more will not establish a right in the public or in local inhabitants of a neighbourhood, but must be ascribed to toleration on the part of the proprietors[3], which use can be stopped by the proprietors at any time.

What has been said as to brown trout fishing applies only to private waters. The only place where a right to fish for brown trout is public is in the tidal reaches of a river or sea loch, that is to say that the tide must ebb and flow at the place where the public right to fish is claimed[4]. It is settled that this right to fish extends as far up the river as the ordinary spring tides[5].

1 See, however, para 55 below.
2 *Fergusson v Shirreff* (1844) 6 D 1363.
3 *Grant v Henry* (1894) 21 R 258, 1 SLT 448.
4 *Bowie v Marquis of Ailsa* (1887) 14 R 649; *Grant v Henry* (1894) 21 R 358, 1 SLT 448.
5 *Bowie v Marquis of Ailsa* (1887) 14 R 649 at 661n, per Lord Trayner.

51. Regulation of brown trout fishing. In sharp contrast with salmon fishing, the statutory controls and restrictions on trout fishing lack force, mainly due to the fact that there is no statutory prohibition of poaching brown trout in Scotland, other than where protection orders are in force[1]. It has already been seen that brown trout, being wild and the property of no one until captured, are not capable of being stolen, other than where they are confined in a 'stank'. The only remedy available for fishing without permission is by the application of the law of common trespass. Although certain statutory restrictions have been introduced, and will be considered generally speaking, it is still true to say that there is very little control over fishing for brown trout in Scotland, with the result that the majority of people still believe, wrongly, that trout fishing in private waters in Scotland is freely available to all.

1 As to protection orders, see para 55 below.

52. Statutory controls on trout fishing. General controls on trout fishing were first introduced by the Trout (Scotland) Acts 1845 and 1860, now repealed[1]. The former prohibited fishing for trout by means of nets without permission, and the latter prohibited fishing for trout by means of nets, double rods, cross lines, set lines or others[1]. Further Acts dealing with brown trout were passed in 1902 and 1933[2] and are still in force. The Salmon and Freshwater Fisheries (Protection) (Scotland) Act 1951, the principal recent anti-poaching measure in respect of salmon, also included brown trout in its definition of 'freshwater fish'. Whereas the definition of 'trout' in the 1902 and 1933 Acts was restricted to brown trout[3], the wider definition of 'freshwater fish' in the 1951 Act refers to any fish living in fresh water, including trout[4], which will thus include rainbow trout, a species introduced from North America.

 1 The Trout (Scotland) Acts 1845 (c 26) and 1860 (c 45) were both repealed by the Salmon and Freshwater Fisheries (Protection) (Scotland) Act 1951 (c 26), s 25(2), Sch 2.
 2 Ie the Freshwater Fish (Scotland) Act 1902 (c 29) and the Trout (Scotland) Act 1933 (c 35).
 3 Freshwater Fish (Scotland) Act 1902, s 1(a) (common trout: *Salmo fario*) (see para 47 above); Trout (Scotland) Act 1933, s 3 (which excludes rainbow trout or migratory trout).
 4 Salmon and Freshwater Fisheries (Protection) (Scotland) Act 1951 (c 26), s 24(1): see para 5, note 9, above.

53. Annual close time for trout. The annual close time during which brown trout may not be fished for or taken in any river, water or loch in Scotland by net, rod, line or otherwise, and may not be possessed, is from 7 October to 14 March[1]. Contravention is an offence[2], although there are limited exceptions for stews and artificial hatcheries[3] and fish farms[4]. It is also an offence to purchase, sell, expose or consign for sale, export or consign for export any trout between 1 September and 31 March, both inclusive[5].

 1 Freshwater Fish (Scotland) Act 1902 (c 29), s 1 (amended by the Trout (Scotland) Act 1933 (c 35), ss 1, 5).
 2 Freshwater Fish (Scotland) Act 1902, s 1. An offender is liable on summary conviction to a fine not exceeding level 3 on the standard scale (as to which see para 11, note 15, above): s 1 (amended by the Salmon and Freshwater Fisheries (Protection) (Scotland) Act 1951 (c 26), s 25(1), Sch 1, the Freshwater and Salmon Fisheries (Scotland) Act 1976 (c 22), s 6, Sch 2, and the Criminal Procedure (Scotland) Act 1975 (c 21), ss 289E–289G (added by the Criminal Justice Act 1982 (c 48), s 54)).
 3 See the Freshwater Fish (Scotland) Act 1902, s 1 (amended by the Trout (Scotland) Act 1933, s 5).
 4 See the Freshwater and Salmon Fisheries (Scotland) Act 1976, s 7(1), Sch 3, para 6.
 5 Trout (Scotland) Act 1933, s 2(1)(b), (2). An offender is liable on summary conviction to a fine as mentioned in note 2 above: s 2(2); Freshwater and Salmon Fisheries (Scotland) Act 1976, Sch 2; Criminal Procedure (Scotland) Act 1975 ss 289E–289G (as added: see note 2 above).

54. Illegal methods of fishing for trout. The only legal method of fishing for trout in inland waters is by rod and line[1], although this is subject to netting being permitted in a pond or loch where all the proprietors are so agreed[2]. Any other method of fishing for trout is illegal, including the use of explosives, poison or electrical devices[3]. Examples of illegal methods commonly used in Scotland are otterboards (planks of wood with rows of hooks set in them) and set lines, which are left overnight. It is also not unusual to see people on the shores of lochs with one or two, or more, rods beside them supported on stones or forked sticks. Such a method is illegal as not being fishing 'by rod and line'[4].

 1 Salmon and Freshwater Fisheries (Protection) (Scotland) Act 1951 (c 26), s 2(2). For the meaning of 'trout' in this Act, see para 47 above, and for the meaning of 'inland waters' and 'rod and line', see para 5, notes 1, 2, above. It is permissible to use a gaff, tailer or landing-net as an auxiliary to the taking of trout by rod and line: s 2(3).
 2 Ibid, s 2(2) proviso (a). Contravention of s 2 is an offence: see s 2(4), and para 11 above. If two or more persons acting together do any act which would constitute an offence against s 2, each is liable to the penalties set forth in s 5 (for which see para 21, note 2, above): s 3.
 3 See ibid, s 4(a)–(c), and para 12 above.
 4 *Lockhart v Cowan* 1980 SLT (Sh Ct) 9, where it was held that fishing by set lines was prohibited by the Trout (Scotland) Act 1860 (c 45), s 1, and therefore an illegal method at the passing of the Salmon and Freshwater Fisheries (Protection) (Scotland) Act 1951 (s 24(2)), and was thus a contravention of s 2(2).

55. Protection orders. Where fishing for trout takes place without the permission of the proprietor the only method by which statutory protection may be given is by way of protection order. The Freshwater and Salmon Fisheries (Scotland) Act 1976 was passed principally to encourage the proprietors of land (and thus of trout fishings[1]) to make more freshwater fishing in inland waters[2] available for public use and in return, where this was done, to give proprietors protection for their fishings[3]. The scheme has not been taken up as anticipated, mainly because of the lengthy and complex procedure required before a protection order under the Act can be made. Six protection orders have been made.

Where the Secretary of State has made a protection order in relation to a prescribed catchment area or part thereof of any river prohibiting persons without legal right or written permission from a person having such a right from fishing for or taking freshwater fish[4] (including trout) in the inland waters in the prescribed area[5], it becomes an offence to fish for freshwater fish in that area without such right or permission[6]. The offence of poaching for trout was thus created, but only in those areas of Scotland where protection orders are in force. Such an offence does not exist outside these specific areas and is thus of limited scope.

Before a protection order may be made by the Secretary of State, a written application containing detailed proposals specifying inter alia the limits of the waters to which they relate and the amount of fishing that will be made available to fishermen etc, has to be made by the owner or occupier of the land to which freshwater fishing rights belong, advertised and posted up, and considered by a special committee set up by the Secretary of State to advise him[7]. Representations and objections may be made, and the Secretary of State may hold a local inquiry[8]. Only after an application has passed through all the required stages may he make a protection order[9], which must then be advertised and posted up on the banks of the waters concerned[10].

1 See para 48 above.
2 'Inland waters' includes all rivers (other than their tidal parts) and their tributary streams, and all waters, watercourses and lochs, whether natural or artificial, which drain or drain to some extent into the sea: Freshwater and Salmon Fisheries (Scotland) Act 1976 (c 22), s 9(1).
3 See ibid, s 1(1).
4 For the meaning of 'freshwater fish', see para 5, note 9, above. That definition is applied by ibid, s 9(1).
5 Ibid, s 1(2).
6 Ibid, s 1(8). The penalty on summary conviction is a fine not exceeding level 3 on the standard scale (for which see para 11, note 15, above): s 1(8); Criminal Procedure (Scotland) Act 1975 (c 21), ss 289E–289G (added by the Criminal Justice Act 1982 (c 48), s 54).
7 Freshwater and Salmon Fisheries (Scotland) Act 1976, s 1(3), (4), (10), Sch 1, paras 1–3.
8 Ibid, Sch 1, paras 5, 6.
9 The order must be made by statutory instrument and may be varied or revoked by a subsequent order so made: ibid, s 1(10). As to revocation, see Sch 1, para 9. For the matters which the Secretary of State must consider before making the order, see s 1(3), (5). As to the duration of the order, see s 1(7). See eg the River Tay Catchment Area Protection Order 1986, SI 1986/1590, and the River Tay Catchment Area Protection (Renewal) Order 1990, SI 1990/49, which prohibit freshwater fishing in that area during the periods from 7 October 1986 to 6 October 1989 and from 30 January 1990 to 29 January 1993 without legal right or written permission from a person having such a right. See also the River Earn Catchment Area Protection Order 1990, SI 1990/50.
10 Freshwater and Salmon Fisheries (Scotland) Act 1976, Sch 1, para 7. Each year the Secretary of State must publish a list of the prescribed areas which are the subject of protection orders: Sch 1, para 10.

56. Wardens to enforce protection orders. Once a protection order has been made for a prescribed area the Secretary of State may appoint as wardens to secure compliance with the order such persons as he thinks fit from among persons nominated by the owner of the fishing rights or an occupier of such a right[1]. Such a warden has no power under any Act other than the Freshwater and Salmon Fisheries (Scotland) Act 1976, and is authorised solely to deal with offences under that Act. He may exercise his powers within the area covered by the protection order. Production by a warden of his instrument of appointment is sufficient warrant for the exercise of the powers conferred on him[2].

A warden or a constable may make inquiry as to the legal right or written permission of any person to fish in the area if he has reasonable cause to suspect that the person has no such right or permit, and may require him to produce written evidence of the right or permission within fourteen days[3]. If he has reasonable cause to suspect that a contravention of a prohibition contained in a protection order has taken place or is being attempted or that an act preparatory to a contravention has been done, he may within the prescribed area seize any instrument or article used or calculated to be of use in such contravention[4]. The phrase 'may make inquiry' can be construed as allowing a warden to ask the person concerned for proof of identity to assist in any subsequent identification. The warden may also stipulate to whom the written evidence of right or permission is to be produced, for example to the owner or occupier or to the warden himself. Any equipment seized in exercise of these powers would be taken for the purpose of evidence but could also ultimately be forfeited[5].

A warden has a right to enter any land[6] in the vicinity of any waters in the prescribed area for the purpose of exercising any of the above powers of inquiry and seizure[7]. He may also enter any land to affix or maintain an order or notice required to be affixed or maintained thereon[8], and may enter any land in the vicinity of those waters and remain there during any period to prevent a breach of a protection order or detect a person contravening it[9]. Any person who wilfully obstructs a warden or refuses to allow him to exercise any of these powers is guilty of an offence[10].

1 Freshwater and Salmon Fisheries (Scotland) Act 1976 (c 22), s 2(1).
2 Ibid, s 3(4).
3 Ibid, s 2(2)(a).
4 Ibid, s 2(2)(b), impliedly extended to attempts and preparations by s 1(9).
5 Ie under the Criminal Procedure (Scotland) Act 1975 (c 21), s 436.
6 'Land' does not include any building thereon (Freshwater and Salmon Fisheries (Scotland) Act 1976, s 3(5)), but includes land covered by water (s 9(1)).
7 Ibid, s 3(1)(a).
8 Ibid, s 3(1)(b). Similar power may be exercised by a person authorised in writing by the Secretary of State: see s 3(2).
9 Ibid, s 3(1)(c). No warden so remaining on land for such a purpose is deemed to be a trespasser: s 3(1)(c).
10 Ibid, s 3(3). He is liable on summary conviction to a fine not exceeding level 3 on the standard scale (for which see para 11, note 15, above) or to imprisonment for a term not exceeding three months: s 3(3); Criminal Procedure (Scotland) Act 1975, ss 289E–289G (added by the Criminal Justice Act 1982 (c 48), s 54).

(8) FISH FARMING FOR SALMON AND TROUT

57. Meaning of 'fish farm'. For the purposes of the Diseases of Fish Act 1937, 'fish farm' means any pond, stew, fish hatchery or other place used for keeping, with a view to their sale or their transfer to other waters (including any other fish farm), live fish, live eggs of fish, fish or foodstuff for fish, and includes any buildings used in connection therewith, and the banks and margins of any water therein[1]. For the purposes of the provisions of the Diseases of Fish Act 1983 relating to the collection of information, a fish farm may be an inland fish farm or a marine fish farm. 'Inland fish farm' means any place where inland waters[2] are used for the keeping of live fish with a view to their sale or to their transfer to other waters (whether inland or not)[3]. A marine fish farm comprises any cage, pontoon or other structure anchored or moored in marine waters[4] which is used for the purposes of a business of fish farming[5] carried on by the owner (whether or not for profit)[6].

Another kind of fish farming is shellfish farming, namely the cultivation or propagation of shellfish (whether in marine or inland waters or on land) with a view to their sale or to their transfer to other waters or land[7].

1 Diseases of Fish Act 1937 (c 33), s 10(1) (amended by the Diseases of Fish Act 1983 (c 30), s 4(3)), applied by the Freshwater and Salmon Fisheries (Scotland) Act 1976 (c 22), s 9(1).
2 'Inland waters' means waters within Great Britain which do not form part of the sea or of any creek, bay or estuary or of any river as far as the tide flows: Diseases of Fish Act 1983, s 7(8).
3 Ibid, s 7(8).
4 'Marine waters' means waters (other than inland waters) within the seaward limits of the territorial sea adjacent to Great Britain: ibid, s 7(8).
5 'Fish farming' means the keeping of live fish with a view to their sale or to their transfer to other waters: ibid, s 7(8).
6 Ibid, s 7(8).
7 Ibid, s 7(8). 'Shellfish' includes crustaceans and molluscs of any kind, and includes any brood, ware, half-ware, spat or spawn of shellfish: s 7(8).

58. Introduction. Inland fish farms have been operated in Scotland for many years, mainly for trout, both brown and rainbow, for food and for restocking of lochs and rivers for angling purposes. This has developed and is now on a large scale. Salmon farming is comparatively new, and it was not until the late 1970s that anyone was confident that salmon could be farmed commercially. Since then the growth has been dramatic, with Scottish farms producing some 28,500 tonnes of salmon and 3,500 tonnes of rainbow trout in 1989. The rearing of salmon in captivity is principally for production as food, although restocking of rivers is still an important factor which must be taken into account.

59. Inland fish farms and development. The obvious requirement for the establishment of an inland fish farm[1], whether it be for the rearing and production of trout or salmon, is an area of suitable ground for the siting of the ponds or fish tanks and an adequate supply of fresh water. The provision of such facilities will be the subject of private agreement between the landowner and the fish farm operator, but clearly certain outside bodies may also require to be involved as 'development' of the land will be necessary to provide the ponds, tanks and ancillary buildings. Planning permission is normally a prerequisite of development under the town and country planning legislation, but certain development is 'permitted', whereby planning permission is deemed to have been granted and no specific application is required[2]. This includes development affecting certain operations on agricultural land[3]. 'Agricultural land' formerly extended to certain fish farms[4], but this is no longer the case[5], so planning permission is now required for the development of any fish farm and *a fortiori* any buildings associated with it.

1 For the meaning of 'inland fish farm', see para 57 above.
2 Town and Country Planning (General Development) (Scotland) Order 1981, SI 1981/830, art 3(1) (substituted by SI 1983/1620).
3 See ibid, Sch 1, Pt I, Class V. By virtue of art 2(1), 'agricultural land' has the same meaning as in the Agriculture (Scotland) Act 1948 (c 45). Thus it means land used for agriculture (defined in AGRICULTURE, vol 1, para 712, note 4) which is so used for the purposes of a trade or business or which is designated by the Secretary of State for this purpose: s 86(1).
4 Town and Country Planning (General Development) (Scotland) Order 1981, Sch 1, Pt I, Class V, para (4) (added by SI 1985/2007). See, however, note 5 below.
5 See ibid, art 2(1) (definition of 'agricultural land' and 'agricultural unit'), amended by the Town and Country Planning (General Development) (Scotland) Amendment Order 1990, SI 1990/508, so as to add 'but shall not include land or a unit respectively used for the purposes of fish farming'. The 1990 Order also revoked the provision referred to in note 4 above.

60. Regulation of inland fish farms. There is as yet no general legislation dealing with the development, operation or control of inland fish farms[1]. Two specific aspects of their operation are, however, regulated by statute: the control of fish diseases and the registration of fish farming businesses. The Secretary of State is empowered to make orders to obtain information for the purpose of preventing the spread of disease among fish[2] and to designate areas where infections of fish have occurred[3].

Any person who occupies an inland fish farm for the purposes of a business of fish farming carried on by him (whether or not for profit), or who owns or possesses any cage, pontoon or other structure anchored or moored in marine waters[4] which is used by him for the purposes of such a business so carried on, or who carries on a business of shellfish farming (whether or not for profit), must within two months of the commencement of the business register the business with the Secretary of State by notifying him in writing of prescribed particulars[5]. Not later than 31 December each year the person required to be registered must furnish in writing to the Secretary of State specified information as to the number of fish etc moved on to and from the site during the twelve months ending 30 November[6], and, if so requested by the Secretary of State, must furnish information to him as to the accuracy of the registered particulars[7]. He must also keep prescribed records[8].

Many orders have been made since 1983 designating areas where fish disease has occurred, imposing restrictions on the movement of live fish in and out of the designated area, and requiring fish farm owners to take steps to prevent the spread of disease etc. The intention is to isolate an affected area to halt the spread of the disease and to encourage producers to take action to eradicate disease where it has occurred.

In parallel with the statutory 'disease' provisions, the Department of Agriculture and Fisheries for Scotland, in conjunction with the National Farmers Union of Scotland, issues guidelines on notifiable diseases which set out the likely course of action which would be taken by the department if a notifiable disease were suspected or confirmed at a fish farm. These guidelines follow the statutory framework of the Disease of Fish Acts 1937 and 1983.

It is the duty of any person entitled to take fish from any inland waters, or employed to have the care of such waters, and who has reasonable grounds for suspecting that the waters are infected waters[9] to report the facts in writing to the Secretary of State, and if without reasonable excuse he fails to do so he is guilty of an offence[10].

---

1 For the meaning of 'inland fish farm', see para 57 above.
2 Diseases of Fish Act 1983 (c 30), s 7(1), and s 7(8) ('the Minister'). See the Registration of Fish Farming and Shellfish Farming Businesses Order 1985, SI 1985/1391.
3 Diseases of Fish Act 1937 (c 33), s 2(1) (substituted by the Diseases of Fish Act 1983, s 2).
4 For the meaning of 'marine waters', see para 57, note 4, above.
5 Registration of Fish Farming and Shellfish Farming Businesses Order 1985, art 3(1), (2), Sch 1. Any change in the particulars, or the cessation of the business, must also be notified: art 3(3), (4).
6 Ibid, art 4(1), (3), Sch 2.
7 Ibid, art 4(2).
8 See ibid, art 5, Sch 3.
9 'Infected waters' means waters in which any of certain prescribed diseases exists among fish or in which the causative organisms of any of those diseases are present: Diseases of Fish Act 1937, s 10(1) (amended by the Diseases of Fish Order 1983, SI 1983/2093), read with the definition of 'infected' in the Diseases of Fish Act 1937, s 10(1) (substituted by the Diseases of Fish (Definition of 'Infected') Order 1984, SI 1984/301, and amended by SI 1986/213 and SI 1988/195).
10 Diseases of Fish Act 1937, s 4(6) (substituted by the Diseases of Fish Act 1983, s 3). The penalty on summary conviction is a fine not exceeding level 4 on the standard scale (for which see para 11, note 16, above): Diseases of Fish Act 1937, s 8(1) (amended by the Diseases of Fish Act 1983, s 5, Schedule, para 6(2)).

61. Marine fish farms. In order to establish a fish farming operation in marine waters, different legal requirements have to be considered from those applying to inland fish farms[1]. A proprietary right in the sea bed within the limits of the territorial waters of Scotland is vested in the Crown: this was conceded in the leading *Fairlie Yacht Slip* case[2]. Because the right to the sea bed lying between low water mark and the limit of territorial waters is vested in the Crown, any person wishing to operate a marine fish farm is required to apply to the Crown Estate Commissioners for the grant of a right to anchor or moor a cage or pontoon to the sea bed. In considering whether a lease may be granted for this purpose the Crown Estate Commissioners undertake a non-statutory consultation processs involving public advertisement of the proposal and direct consultation with a number of authorities and bodies. A fee is payable for each application. Any lease subsequently granted by the Crown will be in respect of a defined area of the sea bed, for the purposes of anchoring a specified number and size of cages and other equipment for the rearing and cultivation of salmon or trout. A necessary feature of such a lease is the need to ensure that the salmon cages and other equipment that are anchored to the sea bed do not constitute a hazard to the public right of navigation on the sea[3]. It is usual for such a lease to oblige the tenant of a marine fish farm first to obtain consent for his operation from the Department of Transport under provisions of the Coast Protection Act 1949 which empower the Secretary of State for Transport to withhold consent to such an application, or to grant consent subject to conditions, if he considers that the proposed marine fish farming operation will, or is likely to, result in obstruction, or provide a hazard to, navigation[4]. Buildings associated with the operation of a marine fish farm will usually be constructed above high water mark and will therefore normally require to be the subject of a planning application for their erection. The operator of a marine fish farm will also require the grant of a right to the ground on which any such buildings are to be erected, and for access to the site from the owner of the ground adjoining the sea (unless the operator is himself the landowner). Where the foreshore used for access purposes is not in the ownership of the Crown the consent of the owner (if not the operator or the adjoining landowner) will also be required.

Licences may be necessary for the establishment of marine fish farms within the jurisdiction of port or harbour authorities under the terms of their individual Harbour Acts. Under the Merchant Shipping Act 1988 these licences may supplant the need for a Department of Transport consent under the 1949 Act[5]. In addition, all marine fish farms in the coastal waters off the Shetland Islands require a works licence from the Shetland Islands Council[6].

The provisions of the Diseases of Fish Acts 1937 and 1983 already referred to apply equally to the operators of marine fish farms as to inland fish farms, including the statutory requirements as to registration and the supply of information and the reporting of outbreaks of disease etc[7].

1 For the meaning of 'marine waters' and 'inland fish farm', see para 57 above.
2 *Crown Estate Comrs v Fairlie Yacht Slip Ltd* 1976 SC 161, 1977 SLT 19, OH, affd 1979 SC 156.
3 *Walford v Crown Estate Comrs* 1988 SLT 377 at 379, OH, per Lord Clyde.
4 See the Coast Protection Act 1949 (c 74), s 34.
5 See the Merchant Shipping Act 1988 (c 12), s 37.
6 Zetland County Council Act 1974 (c viii).
7 See para 60 above.

62. Pollution. The legal authority for controlling pollution from fish farms is contained in the Control of Pollution Act 1974 and in the Rivers (Prevention of Pollution) (Scotland) Acts 1951 (c 66) and 1965 (c 13). Under the 1974 Act it is an offence to permit any poisonous, noxious or polluting matter to enter any controlled waters unless the discharge is authorised by statute or licence or made with the consent of the Secretary of State or of the river purification authority[1]. As the discharge from a fish farm is considered to come within the definition of 'trade effluent'[2], the fish farmer is required to apply to the river purification authority for consent to make this new discharge[3]. As premises used for the carrying on of any trade or industry include land used for the same purpose[4], and 'land' includes land covered with water, this control can therefore be extended to caged sites. In such a case the premises are the land on which the cages are anchored and the cages containing the fish.

1 Control of Pollution Act 1974 (c 40), s 31(1)(a), (2), s 106(2) (s 31 being substituted by the Water Act 1989 (c 15), s 169, Sch 23, para 4). A notice imposing conditions with respect to discharges which was given under the Rivers (Prevention of Pollution) (Scotland) Act 1951 (c 66), s 28(4), or the Rivers (Prevention of Pollution) (Scotland) Act 1965 (c 13), s 1(5), is treated for this purpose as having given the authority's consent: see the Control of Pollution Act 1974, s 56(5) (as so substituted).
2 Ibid, s 105(1).
3 Ibid, s 34(1) (as substituted: see note 1 above), and s 106(2).
4 See ibid, s 106(1) ('premises').

63. Exceptions and exemptions for fish farms.

Other than those statutory provisions already described there is a notable absence of law applicable to fish farming operations, both inland and marine. Fish farmers are, in fact, the subject of a great number of exceptions to and exemptions from the law applying to Scottish fisheries in general. It is, for example, normally an offence to introduce salmon eggs into inland waters without the previous written consent of the appropriate district salmon fishery board, but fish farmers are excluded from this provision if the inland waters constitute or are included in a fish farm[1]. A fish farmer does, however, require consent if he wishes to release fish into open water for restocking purposes etc.

There are many statutory exceptions from the Acts relating to fisheries under which fish farmers are held not to be guilty of contravening various enactments[2] in respect of any act or omission if he carries out the act or the omission takes place within a fish farm in the course of the operation of a fish farm[3]. It is thus no defence for a fish farmer to contravene any of the provisions affected outside the fish farm and to aver that the contravention was necessary for the purpose of the operation of the fish farm. However, the act of selling or exporting fish by or on behalf of the person who reared it in a fish farm is deemed to be an act carried out within a fish farm in the course of the operation of the farm[4]. In proceedings for any of certain offences[5] in relation to a boat or other thing mentioned in the enactment creating the offence which is not a fish farm, it is a defence to prove that the act or omission complained of was necessary for the purpose of the operation of a fish farm[6]. These provisions now apply also to those parts of the River Tweed which are outwith Scotland[7].

1 See the Salmon Act 1986 (c 62), s 24(1), (2), and para 20 above.
2 Ie offences under (1) the Solway Act 1804 (c xlv), ss 1, 2, 11, 15; (2) the Tweed Fisheries Act 1857 (c cxlviii), ss 45, 72, 74; (3) the Tweed Fisheries Amendment Act 1859 (c lxx), ss 6, 10, 11, 13; (4) the Salmon Fisheries (Scotland) Act 1868 (c 123), ss 15(1), (2), (4), 20, 21, 23 (salmon fishing in close season other than by rod and line or in weekly close time; salmon fishing by net with illegal mesh; taking etc unclean or unseasonable salmon; removal of boats and nets in close season); (5) the Freshwater Fish (Scotland) Act 1902 (c 29), s 1 (trout fishing in close season); (6) the Trout (Scotland) Act 1933 (c 35), s 2 (purchase etc of undersized trout or of trout out of season); (7) the Salmon and Freshwater Fisheries (Protection) (Scotland) Act 1951 (c 26), ss 2, 4(b), (c), 13 (illegal methods of fishing; fishing by poison or electrical; devices; salmon fishing in weekly close time); and (8) regulations made under the Salmon Act 1986, s 3(2)(a), (b) (weekly close time; cruives): Freshwater and Salmon Fisheries (Scotland) Act 1976 (c 22), Sch 3, Pt I (paras 1–3, 5–8A) (amended by the Salmon Act 1986, s 41(1), Sch 4, para 15).
3 Freshwater and Salmon Fisheries (Scotland) Act 1976, s 7(1), Sch 3. There is no contravention of the Salmon and Freshwater Fisheries (Protection) (Scotland) Act 1951, s 4(b) or (c) (for which see

para 12 above), by virtue of this provision in respect of an act referred to in s 4(b) or (c) only if the act is carried out with the consent of the Secretary of State: Freshwater and Salmon Fisheries (Scotland) Act 1976, s 7(2).

4 Ibid, s 7(3).

5 Ie offences under (1) the Solway Act 1804, s 3; (2) the Tweed Fisheries Amendment Act 1859, s 11; and (3) the Salmon Fisheries (Scotland) Act 1868, s 23 (removal of boats and nets in close season): Freshwater and Salmon Fisheries (Scotland) Act 1976, Sch 3, Pt II (paras 9–11).

6 Ibid, s 7(4).

7 Ibid, s 7(5) (added by the Fisheries Act 1981 (c 29), s 38(2), and amended by the Salmon Act 1986, Sch 4, para 15).

64. Derating of fish farms. Fish farms have been exempted from assessment to rating, and lands and heritages (other than dwellinghouses) used solely for or in connection with fish farming are not to be entered in the valuation roll[1].

1 See the Valuation and Rating (Scotland) Act 1956 (c 60), s 7A (added by the Local Government, Planning and Land Act 1980 (c 65), s 32, and amended by the Abolition of Domestic Rates Etc (Scotland) Act 1987 (c 47), s 34, Sch 6), and VALUATION FOR RATING, vol 24, paras 654–656. 'Fish farm' for this purpose is defined in s 7A(8) of the 1956 Act.

2. SEA FISHERIES

(1) INTRODUCTION

65. The need for an international legal framework. Scotland, as part of an island state with many offshore islands, both when independent and since it became part of the United Kingdom, has always had a major interest in securing the maximum access to the maximum benefit from the fisheries adjacent to its extensive coastlines. But most fish are migratory species and frequently travel considerable distances, traversing the jurisdictions of one or more foreign states or the open seas. Though they may spawn in the sheltered waters off one state, at their harvestable stage they may be found in the waters of another. The extent to which the coastal state can exercise its sovereignty or jurisdiction over fisheries has therefore to be determined by reference to international law. Moreover, the management of fisheries, especially in semi-enclosed seas such as the North Sea or Irish Sea but even in the open areas of the North Atlantic Ocean, requires international co-operation if fisheries are not to become over-exploited and depleted. Fishing for most species has to be maintained, on the basis of scientific advice, at levels which will ensure their conservation and sustainable yield. Conclusion of international agreements is necessary both for allocation of the competence to control access to fisheries and to regulate them for purposes of conservation. States thus need to legislate pursuant to the international law not only to control their offshore waters but also to control their fishing vessels and fishermen when fishing areas within the jurisdiction of other states or on the high seas. Historically, both the geographical and material scope of national fisheries law has given rise to disputes. The new international customary law generated by the Third United Nations Law of the Sea Confer-ence and the conclusion of the European Community's Common Fisheries Policy in 1983 now provide an accepted international framework which has done much to resolve past controversies. Much of the present law affecting Scottish fisheries, however, was developed before these events although it has been adapted to take account of them. An understanding of the historical development of international fisheries law is thus essential to an understanding of the kinds of problems that are likely to arise today, since many of these derive from the fact that some fishermen, both Scottish and foreign, fishing in United Kingdom waters resent the solutions now adopted and occasionally return to practices sanctioned by the former law.

66. Jurisdictional zones. An understanding of the way access to fisheries is regulated requires first a description of the various zones of coastal state jurisdiction, namely internal waters[1], the territorial sea[2], exclusive fisheries or economic zones[3], and the continental shelf[4]. It also requires a description of the high seas regime[5] and identification of the extent to which states had to control their registered vessels fishing on the high seas. The legal status of these zones has not been affected by the European Community's Common Fisheries Policy: that requires merely that common conditions of access are applied to zones subject to 'the maritime jurisdiction' of member states, as well as promulgation of a common conservation policy[6].

1 As to internal waters, see para 79 below.
2 As to the territorial sea, see paras 71 ff below.
3 As to the exclusive fishery zone, see paras 80, 81 below.
4 As to the continental shelf, see paras 82 ff below.
5 As to the high seas, see paras 86 ff below.
6 See further AGRICULTURE, vol 1, paras 893, 943.

67. Conservation. An understanding of the conservatory regime and the regulations which implement it requires a description both of the principles of conservation and the system of international co-operation now organised, so far as Scotland is concerned, indirectly through the European Community but to some extent also through international fishery commissions: the North-East Atlantic Fisheries Commission (NEAFC), the Northwest Atlantic Fisheries Organisation (NAFO, formerly the ICNAF (International Commission for Northwest Atlantic Fisheries)) and the North Atlantic Salmon Conservation Organisation (NASCO)[1].

1 As to these commissions, see paras 92 ff below.

68. Scientific research. Effective conservation requires scientific knowledge and advice. The right to conduct research is, therefore, also an important element in the conservatory regime. It is related both to existing rights in the various jurisdictional zones and to mechanisms for international co-operation. Some states, but not the United Kingdom, now include controls over marine scientific research within their exclusive fisheries or exclusive economic zones, requiring that their consent be obtained for the conduct of such research as is permitted in the 1982 United Nations Convention on the Law of the Sea[1], subject to certain conditions. The United Kingdom to date has not introduced such requirements within its 200-mile[2] fishery limits.

1 See the United Nations Convention on the Law of the Sea (Montego Bay, 10 December 1982; Misc 11 (1983); Cmnd 8941), art 56, and Pt XIII (Marine Scientific Research) (arts 238–265).
2 As to the United Kingdom fishery limits, see para 130 below. All references to miles in this title are to international nautical miles of 1,852 metres: see the Fishery Limits Act 1976 (c 86), s 8.

69. Resolution of conflicts. Conflicts frequently arise concerning not only access to fishing resources but also the implementation of conservatory regulations such as those prescribing the kind of gear fishermen may use[1] to capture the fish and the areas and periods of fishing. Conflicts can also arise between fisheries and other uses of the sea such as oil and gas exploration or exploitation (including the removal of offshore installations[2]), the disposal of wastes, and sand and gravel extraction.

1 Eg the types of nets, gear and vessels.
2 See para 85 below.

70. Development of international law. The international law in all these respects has developed through customary law and the conclusion of ad hoc treaties with other states in the region or states fishing a particular stock, whether in waters subject to coastal state jurisdiction or on the high seas. More recently it has developed through the conclusion of multilateral law of the sea conventions concluded under the auspices of United Nations Conferences on the Law of the Sea (UNCLOS).

The United Nations endeavoured to solve some of the problems by convening at Geneva in 1958 the First United Nations Conference on the Law of the Sea (UNCLOS I) which adopted four conventions, known as the Geneva Conventions on the Law of the Sea: the Convention on the Territorial Sea and Contiguous Zone[1]; the Convention on the High Seas[2]; the Convention on Fishing and Conservation of the Living Resources of the High Seas[3]; and the Convention on the Continental Shelf[4]. All relate directly or indirectly to fisheries, inter alia; all remain in force, and the United Kingdom is party to all four. None of them, however, sets any outer limit for the territorial sea; nor did they endorse the concept of a fisheries zone extending beyond the territorial sea in which the coastal state could exercise preferential or exclusive rights over fisheries.

A Second United Nations Conference on the Law of the Sea (UNCLOS II) convened in 1960 specifically to settle these questions failed to reach the necessary agreement, and no further Law of the Sea conventions were concluded until 1982 when the Third United Nations Conference on the Law of the Sea (UNCLOS III) adopted a comprehensive convention on virtually all aspects of the law of the sea, the United Nations Convention on the Law of the Sea[5], which set, inter alia, the maximum limit of the territorial sea at 12 miles[6] and provided for the institution of 200-mile exclusive economic zones (measured from the baselines of the territorial sea)[7] within which coastal states have sovereign rights over fisheries, inter alia, subject to various international and national terms and conditions. The United Kingdom has not become a party to this convention but accepts that certain provisions of it have already become part of customary international law, based on state practice, and have thus superseded relevant parts of the 1958 Geneva Conventions. These provisions include those concerning the coastal states' sovereignty or sovereign rights over the exploration and exploitation of fisheries resources within a 200-mile zone and the 12-mile limit for the territorial sea, both of which the United Kingdom has now enacted[8]. However, since the United Kingdom became a member of the European Community in 1972, these zones are subject to the Community's Common Fisheries Policy.

These developments will first be considered up to 1976.

1 Convention on the Territorial Sea and the Contiguous Zone (Geneva, 29 April 1958; TS 3 (1965); Cmnd 2511).
2 Convention on the High Seas (Geneva, 29 April 1958; TS 5 (1963); Cmnd 1929).
3 Convention on Fishing and Conservation of the Living Resources of the Sea (Geneva, 29 April 1958; TS 39 (1966); Cmnd 3028).
4 Convention on the Continental Shelf (Geneva, 29 April 1958; TS 39 (1964); Cmnd 2422).
5 United Nations Convention on the Law of the Sea (Montego Bay, 10 December 1982; Misc 11 (1983); Cmnd 8941). See further paras 106ff below.
6 Ibid, art 3.

7 Ibid, art 57.
8 As to the 200-mile zone and the 12-mile limit, see paras 80, 81, 130, below.

(2) THE TERRITORIAL SEA

71. Origin of division between territorial seas and high seas. For nearly 300 years from the seventeenth to the twentieth centuries disputes concerned such issues as whether the exclusive competence of a coastal state over fisheries should be restricted to the narrow belt of territorial sea over which it was accepted that it exercised sovereignty, subject only to a right of innocent passage for foreign vessels, including fishing vessels; what the breadth of that belt should be; and from which basepoints it should be measured. The areas beyond were regarded as high seas, open to unrestricted access to fisheries for all states, under the doctrine of the freedom of the high seas. From time to time, however, certain states asserted the right to close some areas of the sea beyond the territorial sea to foreign fishing[1]. Until recently the doctrine that the territorial sea should be narrow and that the high seas should be subject to freedom of fishing had become widely settled, following the great doctrinal debate between Grotius and Selden and Welwod in the seventeenth century[2].

  1 The history of these claims and counterclaims is documented in T W Fulton *The Sovereignty of the Sea* (1911).
  2 As to this debate, see para 72 below.

72. The debate between Grotius, Welwod and Selden. For the purposes of ensuring freedom of trade for the Netherlands, which depended on freedom of navigation, Hugo Grotius, a Dutch lawyer, advocated a *mare liberum*. He thus maintained that the territorial sea should be confined to a narrow coastal belt and that the high seas beyond, which were not susceptible to occupation, were free for use by all states[1]. He regarded the resources of the high seas as common property resources (*res communis*) which could be reduced to ownership only by capture and possession by individual fishermen. Fisheries science was not then in being and it was thought inconceivable, given the simple technology and small populations that then existed, that fish could ever be over-exploited. Catch levels were low and remained so until the industrial revolution and its intensification in the twentieth century. Despite the development of modern techniques and the present extension of fisheries jurisdiction beyond the territorial sea, fish retain today the status Grotius ascribed to them.

William Welwod or Welwood[2], a lawyer at St Andrews University, and Selden[3], in England, however, argued in favour of a *mare clausum*, insisting that parts of the high seas could be appropriated by coastal states, a policy that had been followed for certain areas by James I and VI and for which Charles I subsequently sought legal support. Welwod, following the Scottish practice, held that coastal fisheries could be exhausted and that the coastal population had a prior right to the fruits of the seas against foreigners. But these claims were abandoned in the eighteenth century and Grotius's view that the maximum area of high seas should be free to all prevailed, though Welwod's and Selden's arguments were revived in the twentieth century and are now generally accepted. Thereafter, the main problem was to settle the limit of the territorial sea and the precise nature of the rights exercisable there, including those over fisheries.

  1 Grotius *Mare Liberum* (1609; 2nd edn 1618).
  2 W Welwod *An Abridgement of all Sea-Lawes* (1613); *De Dominio Maris Juribusque ad Dominium praecipue spectantibus Assertio brevis et methodica* (1615) (cited in T W Fulton *The Sovereignty of the*

Sea (1911) p 354), Grotius prepared a reply to this: see A R G McMillan 'Admiralty and Maritime Law' in *Sources and Literature of Scots Law* (Stair Soc vol 1, 1936) p 325 at p 330.
3 J Selden *Mare Clausum, Seu, de Dominio Maris libriduo* (1635).

73. The limits of the territorial sea. The limits of the territorial sea have never been settled on a uniform international basis. From time to time different states have claimed different limits, generally ranging from 3 to 12 miles, but a few have claimed up to 200 miles and continue to do so although the position is likely to change once the 1982 United Nations Convention on the Law of the Sea, which provides for a maximum of 12 miles, enters into force[1]. In the fifteenth century the Scottish fishermen kept foreign fishermen away from their shores by asserting exclusive rights to a distance determined by a system of 'land-kenning' based on the range of vision from sea to land, determined at about 14 miles[2]. Later, Scotland sometimes claimed a double land-kenning of 28 miles, and for bays and firths measured the limit from closing lines drawn from headland to headland[3]. The majority of states in the nineteenth and early twentieth centuries, however, maintained a limit of 3 nautical miles, and until 1987 the United Kingdom still continued so to do despite the fact that the majority of coastal states claimed the 12 nautical miles limit provided for in the 1982 convention. In 1987, however, Parliament enacted the Territorial Sea Act 1987 extending the territorial sea of the United Kingdom to 12 miles, measured from the baselines[4], and subsequently, by Order in Council, the baselines from which the new limit is to be measured were also adjusted[5].

1 See para 106 below.
2 As to land-kenning, see also UDAL LAW, vol 24, para 315. See also T W Fulton *The Sovereignty of the Sea* (1911) pp 84, 192, 223.
3 *Fulton* pp 77, 545.
4 Territorial Sea Act 1987 (c 49), s 1(1)(a). The Territorial Sea (Limits) Order 1987, SI 1987/1269, delimits, on the basis of a simplified median line, the areas in the Straits of Dover where the territorial seas of France and the United Kingdom overlap.
5 See the Territorial Sea (Limits) Order 1987, which supplements those laid down in the Territorial Waters Order in Council 1964 of 25 September 1964 and the Territorial Waters (Amendment) Order in Council of 23 May 1979.

74. The baselines of the territorial sea. The baselines are the lines from which the outer limits of the territorial sea are measured. For many years, despite the early Scottish practice described above[1], the United Kingdom, as did most states, used the low-water line along the coast as its baseline for this purpose although some states, including Norway, used a system of straight baselines across deep coastal indentations, enclosing fringes of islands that lay close to the coast. In 1950 the United Kingdom belatedly challenged the Norwegian system following the arrest of British fishermen fishing within the 4-mile territorial sea claimed by Norway, which was measured from straight baselines. The United Kingdom contended that only the natural baseline system was acceptable in international law. The dispute was referred to the International Court of Justice, which adjudged that the straight baselines in question did not constitute a violation of international law and were binding on the United Kingdom as they had not been protested by it when they were first asserted by a Norwegian decree in 1869[2].

The court found that the straight baselines might be drawn not only across certain bays but also between islands, islets, rocks and across the seas separating them, though the lines should follow the general direction of the coast. In arriving at this conclusion the court took into account 'geographical realities' and 'economic interests peculiar to a region'. Nonetheless, it emphasised that the delimitation of the sea areas always has an international aspect since the areas newly enclosed by such baselines were formerly part of the high seas. Delimitation, according to the court,

> 'cannot be dependent merely upon the will of the coastal state as expressed in municipal law. The validity of the delimitation with regard to other states depends upon international law'[3].

That is to say, extension of national jurisdiction over further areas of the high seas requires the consent or acquiescence of other states, especially those directly affected. So far as is known to the writer, there has been no protest concerning the extension in 1987 of the territorial sea limits of the United Kingdom to 12 nautical miles or its extension of its baselines.

1 See para 73 above.
2 *Anglo-Norwegian Fisheries Case* (1951) ICJ Rep 116.
3 (1951) ICJ Rep 116 at 132.

75. Conflicts between international and municipal law concerning jurisdictional limits. It is nonetheless possible for a municipal court, following the doctrine of parliamentary sovereignty, to hold that international law is not binding upon it unless that law has been specifically incorporated into municipal law by statute or custom, and thus for it to enforce the municipal law even if it conflicts with the international law if the latter has not been so incorporated[1]. Since under Scottish law domestic statutes are regarded as prevailing over international customary or treaty law in such circumstances, in a case in which the Danish captain of a Norwegian-registered vessel fishing in the Moray Firth beyond the 3-mile limit was convicted for fishing in contravention of a Scottish conservatory byelaw made pursuant to a fisheries statute in force[2], the High Court of Justiciary had held that even if the municipal law were contrary to international law (as it was, since the area, according to international law, was part of the high seas, where freedom of fishing prevailed), the court was bound to apply the statute and could not override the presumed intention of Parliament[3]. The terms of the statute were general, applying to every person committing the offence of trawling within the area of the Moray Firth headlands. In such cases where the decisions of municipal courts conflict with international law, the government has to resort to diplomatic remedies. Following this decision the fishermen concerned were granted a royal pardon and their fines were repaid.

1 See PUBLIC INTERNATIONAL LAW, vol 19, paras 652 ff.
2 Ie Byelaw no. 10 made by the Fishery Board for Scotland in 1892 (amended by Byelaw no 14 made in 1896) under the Herring Fishery (Scotland) Act 1889 (c 23), s 7 (repealed).
3 *Mortensen v Peters* (1906) 8 F (J) 93, 14 SLT 227. See PUBLIC INTERNATIONAL LAW, vol 19, para 655; T W Fulton *The Sovereignty of the Sea* (1911) pp 726, 727; D Johnston 'European Fishery Limits' in *Developments in the Law of the Sea 1958–1964* (British Institute of International and Comparative Law, 1965) pp 326–331.

76. The Geneva Convention on the Territorial Sea. Having lost the 1958 *Anglo-Norwegian Fisheries Case*[1], the United Kingdom supported the inclusion of the straight as well as the natural baseline system in the Convention on the Territorial Sea[2] concluded by the United Nations at its First Conference on the Law of the Sea (UNCLOS I) in 1958[3], and became a party to that convention. Article 3 provides that:

> 'Except when otherwise provided in these articles, the normal baseline for measuring the breadth of the territorial sea is the low-water line along the coast as marked on large-scale charts officially recognized by the coastal state'.

Article 4 provides that:

'In localities when the coastline is deeply indented and cut into, or if there is a fringe of islands along the coast in its immediate vicinity, the method of straight baseline joining approximate points may be employed . . .'.

Various qualifications are added, as well as a requirement that these also be marked on charts, to which publicity must be given. Provision is also made, subject to various conditions, for taking account of low-tide elevations[4], bays other than so-called 'historic bays'[5], harbour works[6] and roadsteads[7], and river mouths[8]. An island, defined as a naturally formed area of land surrounded by water, which is above water at high tide, can have its own territorial sea and baselines[9]. These provisions have not been substantially changed in the 1982 United Nations Convention on the Law of the Sea. In the view of the United Kingdom the provision relating to islands[10] applies equally to uninhabited rocky islets such as Rockall, incorporated into the United Kingdom in the Island of Rockall Act 1972 (c 2), since that provision does not lay down any requirement that the island be inhabited or capable of habitation, though the 1982 convention, to which the United Kingdom is not a party, whilst accepting that such islets can have a territorial sea, denies rights to exclusive economic zones or continental shelves to islands which are uninhabited and incapable of sustaining human habitation or economic life on their own[11]. The Territorial Sea Act 1987 applies to Rockall[12] (though not to any of the Channel Islands or the Isle of Man, the possibility of these further extensions by Order in Council being, however, reserved[13]). The Pentland Firth, it should be noted, now falls within United Kingdom territorial seas, and passage is limited to innocent passage; foreign fishing boats (subject to any exceptions permitted and the Common Fisheries Policy) must, therefore, observe the international requirements for such passage.

1 *Anglo-Norwegian Fisheries Case* (1951) ICJ Rep 116: see para 74 above.
2 Convention on the Territorial Sea and Contiguous Zone (Geneva, 29 April 1958; TS 3 (1965); Cmnd 2511).
3 For a good account of the baseline system for the territorial sea and the fisheries zone laid down in this convention and in the United Nations Convention on the Law of the Sea (Montego Bay, 10 December 1982; Misc 11 (1983); Cmnd 8941), as followed by the United Kingdom, and of claims relating thereto, see R Churchill and A V Lowe *The Law of the Sea* (2nd edn, 1988) ch 2, 4, 5, 13.
4 Convention on the Territorial Sea and Contiguous Zone, arts 3, 11.
5 Ibid, art 7.
6 Ibid, art 8.
7 Ibid, art 9.
8 Ibid, art 13.
9 Ibid, art 10.
10 Convention on the Territorial Sea and Contiguous Zone, art 10.
11 United Nations Convention on the Law of the Sea, art 121.
12 The Territorial Sea Act 1987 (c 49), s 1(1)(a), defines the territorial sea 'adjacent to the United Kingdom', and Rockall is part of the United Kingdom.
13 Ibid, s 4(4).

77. Outer limit of the territorial sea. The Convention on the Territorial Sea and Contiguous Zone did not set any outer limit to the territorial sea. It merely provides that:

'the outer limit of the territorial sea is the line every point of which is at a distance from the nearest point of the baseline equal to the breadth of the territorial sea'[1].

Charts are not required to show any outer limit, and relevant United Kingdom charts do not do so. As this convention also provides for a contiguous zone, beyond the territorial sea, which is not to exceed a limit of 12 nautical miles from the baseline of the territorial sea[2], it was concluded by many states that this provision also impliedly set this figure as a maximum limit for the territorial sea. Though a party to the convention, the United Kingdom did not set its limits at 12 miles until 1987[3]; it does not claim a contiguous zone, which merely provides additional enforcement powers to prevent infringements of certain specified regulations (other than fisheries regulations) and does not confer any additional fisheries jurisdiction, although there has been some argument that it does not restrict such application.

1 Convention on the Territorial Sea and Contiguous Zone (Geneva, 29 April 1958; TS 3 (1965); Cmnd 2511), art 6.
2 Ibid, art 24.
3 Territorial Sea Act 1987 (c 49), s 1(1)(a).

(3) UNITED KINGDOM PRACTICE ON BASELINES AND LIMITS

(a) Straight Baselines; Bays

78. The Scottish coasts. Following the entry into force of the Convention on the Territorial Sea and Contiguous Zone[1], the United Kingdom promulgated by Order in Council a straight baseline system along the north-west coast of Scotland including the Outer Hebrides[2]. The whole of the Minches has thus become part of internal waters. The United Kingdom has not, however, done this for any part of the east coast, nor has the Moray Firth been included within internal waters as a bay. The convention lays down strict tests for qualification as a bay across or within which a 24-mile closing line can be drawn[3]. A line has first to be drawn across the natural entrance points; a semi-circle has to be constructed on it; if the area of water within the bay exceeds the area within this, the indentation can be counted as a bay. Although this test does not apply to so-called 'historic bays' (not defined in the convention but generally regarded in customary international law as bays claimed over a considerable period of time as part of internal waters, subject to international acceptance of or acquiescence in this claim), Scotland has not claimed the Moray Firth as such a bay in recent times[4]. Current fishery limits extend from 'the baselines from which the breadth of the territorial sea adjacent to the United Kingdom, the Channel Islands and the Isle of Man is measured'[5].

1 The Convention on the Territorial Sea and Contiguous Zone (Geneva, 29 April 1958; TS 3 (1965); Cmnd 2511) entered into force on 10 September 1964.
2 Territorial Waters Order in Council 1964 of 25 September 1964, which came into force on 30 September 1964.
3 Convention on the Territorial Sea and Contiguous Zone, art 7.
4 For earlier practice, see T W Fulton *The Sovereignty of the Sea* (1911) pp 233–239, 720–728, and *Mortensen v Peters* (1906) 8 F (J) 93, 14 SLT 227.
5 See the Fishery Limits Act 1976 (c 86), s 1(1), and para 130 below.

(b) Internal Waters

79. The landward side of the baseline. Waters on the landward side of the territorial sea baselines, according to the Convention on the Territorial Sea and the Contiguous Zone, form part of the internal waters of the state[1]. These are part of the territory of the coastal state; other states have no access to fisheries in them without the specific consent of the coastal state, which may be given under international agreement[2]. A right of innocent passage for foreign vessels, including fishing vessels, continues to exist in areas enclosed by straight base-lines which previously had been considered as part of the territorial sea or the high seas. The convention provides that the passage of foreign fishing vessels is not to be considered innocent if they do not observe such laws and regulations as the coastal state may make and publish in order to prevent those vessels from fishing in the territorial sea[3]. Innocent passage must not be hampered.

1 Convention on the Territorial Sea and the Contiguous Zone (Geneva, 29 April 1958; TS 3 (1965); Cmnd 2511), art 5.
2 For the impact of the Common Fisheries Policy of the European Community in this respect, see para 109 below.
3 Convention on the Territorial Sea and the Contiguous Zone, art 14(5).

(c) The Exclusive Fishery Zone

80. Origin of 200-mile claims. Although historically, from time to time, Scotland, as did some other states, briefly closed some areas beyond the terri-torial sea to foreign fishing, the concept was not accepted internationally. The claims to 200-mile exclusive maritime zones by a few Latin American states from 1947 onwards were originally resisted by other states. But the First (1958) and Second (1960) United Nations Conferences on the Law of the Sea did attempt to meet the demand for extended coastal state control of fisheries by endeavouring to negotiate a proposal for a 6-mile territorial sea in which the coastal state would have exclusive or preferential rights, with a 6-mile zone beyond in which the coastal state would determine the rights of access of foreign fishermen. Difficulty arose concerning so-called 'historic rights' claimed by foreign fishermen on the basis of long-standing fishing practices in the area. Such rights are a contentious issue in international law[1] and are not recognised in any of the United Nations Law of the Sea Conventions[2], which make no reference to them. In the 1958 and 1960 conferences no agreement could be reached on a period for phasing out such rights in the outer belt. The proposal therefore failed. Following this, many states began to make unilateral claims to fisheries zones of up to 12 miles or more. The United Kingdom maintained a 12-mile fishing zone from 1964 to 1976[3]. In 1974 the International Court of Justice accepted, in the *Icelandic Fisheries Jurisdiction Case*[4], that the 12-mile fisheries zone had become established as a rule of customary international law; beyond that limit the court held that coastal states had 'preferential rights' but that the interests of states whose fishermen had established long-standing fish-ery practices in that area must also be taken into account in any negotiations with a coastal state concerning fishing quotas in such areas, the limits of which were left unspecified. Iceland at that date was unilaterally asserting a fishery limit of 50 miles (later extended to 200 miles). The United Kingdom did not extend its fishery limits to 200 miles until 1976[5], by which time consensus had been reached on such extension at the Third United Nations Conference on the Law of the Sea[6], which accepted and so provided in the resulting convention that coastal states have 'sovereign-rights for the purpose of exploring and exploit-ing, conserving and managing the natural resources, whether living or non-living, of the waters superjacent to the sea-bed and of the sea-bed and its subsoil'[7]. The United Kingdom accepts that this is now part of customary international law.

1 See R Churchill and A V Lowe *The Law of the Sea* (2nd edn, 1988) ch 3.
2 As to these conventions, see para 70 above.
3 Fishery Limits Act 1964 (c 72), s 1(1) (repealed by the Fishery Limits Act 1976 (c 86), s 9(3), Sch 3, except for waters adjacent to both Northern Ireland and the Republic of Ireland, for which the limit remains 12 miles: see s 10(2)(a)).

4 *Icelandic Fisheries Jurisdiction Case* 1974 ICJ Rep 3.
5 See para 130 below.
6 See para 106 below.
7 United Nations Convention on the Law of the Sea (Montego Bay, 10 December 1982; Misc 11 (1983); Cmnd 8941), art 56.

81. The Fisheries Convention of 1964. In 1964 seventeen states, including the United Kingdom and most member states of the European Community, signed a Fisheries Convention[1], which accorded the coastal state the exclusive right to fish, and exclusive jurisdiction over fisheries, in a 6-mile belt measured from the baselines of the territorial sea. It did not accord foreign fishermen any rights in internal waters, but provided that, in a further 6-mile belt, from 6 to 12 miles from the baselines, the right to fish could be exercised only by the coastal state and by such other contracting parties whose fishing vessels had 'habitually fished' in that belt during a ten-year reference period from 1 January 1953 to 31 December 1962, as long as they confined their efforts to the stocks of fish or fishing grounds that they had habitually exploited. Use of the term 'historic rights' was avoided. In the outer belt the coastal state could only enforce internationally agreed conservation measures. Foreign fishermen who had habitually fished in the inner 6-mile belt could be, and were, gradually phased out, but in the outer 6-mile belt some states (including present member states of the European Community) still exercised fishing rights under agreements concluded with the coastal state (including the United Kingdom). These rights eventually formed a basis of the derogations from the Common Fisheries Policy that were conceded in the 1972 Treaty of Accession[2]. The 1964 convention was of unlimited duration and is still in force. It can, however, be denounced twenty years from the date of its entry into force in 1966. It provides that 'nothing in the present Convention shall prevent the maintenance or establishment of a special regime in matters of fisheries . . . as between members and Associated States of the European Economic Community'[3]. The convention has, however, now largely been superseded by the Common Fisheries Policy and the declaration of 200-mile exclusive fishery or economic zones by many of its parties.

1 Fisheries Convention (London, 9 March 1964; TS 35 (1966); Cmnd 3011). Signatories are Austria, Belgium, Denmark, France, the Federal Republic of Germany, Iceland, Ireland, Italy, Luxembourg, the Netherlands, Norway, Poland, Portugal, Spain, Sweden, Switzerland and the United Kingdom. Of these, Austria, Iceland, Luxembourg, Norway and Switzerland did not ratify the convention. For an analysis of its history and provisions, see D Johnston 'European Fishery Limits' in *Developments in the Law of the Sea 1958–1964* (British Institute of International and Comparative Law, 1965); and E D Brown 'British Fisheries and the Common Market' (1972) 25 *Current Legal Problems* pp 37–51.
2 See AGRICULTURE, vol 1, para 943.
3 Fisheries Convention, art 10.

(d) The Continental Shelf

82. The Convention on the Continental Shelf. Following the proclamation in 1945 by President Truman of the United States exclusive rights over the natural resources (that is, the living as well as non-living resources) of the continental shelf contiguous to United States territory[1], this doctrine rapidly became widely accepted as part of customary international law, and the rules emerging from state practice were to a large extent codified in the Convention on the Continental Shelf[2]. In 1969, in the *North Sea Continental Shelf Cases*[3], the International Court of Justice found that articles 1 to 3 of this convention represented customary international law. The United Kingdom is a party to the convention, and enacted the doctrine in the Continental Shelf Act 1964 (c 29). The convention defines the term continental 'shelf' for the purposes of the convention as referring:

'(a) to the seabed and subsoil of the submarine areas adjacent to the coast, but outside the area of territorial sea, to a depth of 200 metres or, beyond that limit, to where the depth of the superadjacent waters admits of the exploitation of the natural resources of the said areas;

(b) to the seabed and subsoil of similar submarine areas adjacent to the coasts of islands[4]'.

In the North Sea there are no significant areas deeper than 200 metres, though these can be found on the outer Hebridean Shelf. In the *North Sea Continental Shelf Cases* the court concluded that it was the character of the shelf as a natural prolongation of the land territory of the coastal state that gave rise to that state's inherent right to explore and exploit the natural resources of the area. This has given rise to an expansive interpretation of the above definition in state practice to include not only the area covered by the depth criterion and the areas that are, or become, exploitable, but all those that can be regarded as having a geological, geophysical or geomorphological affinity with the land territory of the adjacent state. The term has thus been redefined in the 1982 United Nations Convention on the Law of the Sea to bring together the concepts of the 200-mile fisheries or maritime zone, within the new exclusive economic zone, and of the 'natural' shelf, by including within the definition of 'continental shelf' the whole of the continental margin, where this exists (subject to a precise formula for delimitation of its outer limit[5]), as well as the seabed within 200 miles distance from the coastal baselines, without any need for proof of 'natural prolongation' based on geological or other factors[6]. As the continental shelf for legal purposes begins only beyond the territorial sea according to both the 1958 and 1982 conventions, its outer limit is measured from the baselines of the latter, but its outer limit can extend beyond the 200-mile fisheries zone. Though it is most unlikely, however, that any living resources that are exploitable exist on such outer areas of the continental shelf off Scotland, including its offshore islands, such as Rockall, the United Kingdom can and does assert sovereign rights over these resources.

In 1988 the United Kingdom and the Republic of Ireland concluded an agreement delimiting parts of the continental shelf that lie between them[7].

1 M Whiteman 4 *Digest of International Law* 756.
2 Convention on the Continental Shelf (Geneva, 29 April 1958; TS 39 (1964); Cmnd 2422), which entered into force on 10 June 1964.
3 *North Sea Continental Shelf Cases* (1969) ICJ Rep 3 at 40.
4 Convention on the Continental Shelf, art 1.
5 See ibid, art 76.
6 United Nations Convention on the Law of the Sea (Montego Bay, 10 December 1982; Misc 11 (1983); Cmnd 8941), art 76.
7 Agreement between the United Kingdom and the Republic of Ireland concerning the Delimitation of Areas of the Continental Shelf between the Two Countries (Dublin, 7 November 1988; Cm 535). See the Petroleum Royalties (Relief) and Continental Shelf Act 1989 (c 1), s 3, the Continental Shelf Act 1989 (c 35), s 1(2), and the Continental Shelf (Designation of Areas) Order 1989, SI 1989/2398.

83. Rights to natural resources. The Convention on the Continental Shelf accords to the coastal state 'sovereign rights for the purpose of exploring and exploiting its natural resources'[1]. These rights are stated to be exclusive in the sense that if the coastal state does not explore the continental shelf or exploit its natural resources, no one else may undertake these activities, or make a claim to the continental shelf, without the express consent of the coastal state[2].

1 Convention on the Continental Shelf (Geneva, 29 April 1958; TS 39 (1964); Cmnd 2422), art 2(1). For the meaning of 'natural resources', see para 84 below.
2 Ibid, art 2(2).

84. Meaning of 'natural resources'. 'Natural resources' are defined in the Convention on the Continental Shelf in legal terms as consisting of the mineral and other non-living resources of the seabed and subsoil,

> 'together with the living organisms belonging to the sedentary species, that is to say, organisms which, at the harvestable stage, either are immobile on or under the seabed or are unable to move except in constant physical contact with the seabed or the subsoil'[1].

Further, 'the rights do not depend on occupation, effective or notional, or on any express proclamation'[2], a view supported by the International Court of Justice in the *North Sea Continental Shelf Cases*[3], although it is contrary to views expressed by earlier jurists[4].

The convention does not further identify 'sedentary species'. There is no annex listing them; nor does the Continental Shelf Act 1964 (c 29) list them. The term is not a scientific one and thus, while the legal definition clearly includes all shellfish (molluscs such as oysters, clams and mussels are clearly covered), there has been controversy concerning whether the term includes crustaceans such as crabs and lobsters[5]. The official United Kingdom view is that it includes crabs but not lobsters, which can swim. The importance of the distinction lies in the possible application of different policies and regulations and instruments to enforce them, whether under internal, Community or United Kingdom law, to swimming fish, which are the resources of the fisheries zone, and to sedentary species which fall under the continental shelf regime. Under neither the 1958 Convention on the Continental Shelf nor the 1982 United Nations Convention on the Law of the Sea, which repeats the 1958 convention in all these respects, is the coastal state under any obligation to make any part of the resources of the continental shelf available to foreign states, although, being in an area under the 'maritime jurisdiction' of the coastal state concerned, sedentary species technically come within the scope of the Common Fisheries Policy.

1 Convention on the Continental Shelf (Geneva, 29 April 1958; TS 39 (1964); Cmnd 2422), art 2(2).
2 Ibid, art 2(3).
3 *North Sea Continental Shelf Cases* (1969) ICJ Rep 3.
4 See D Johnston 'European Fishery Limits' in *Developments in the Law of the Sea 1958–1964* (British Institute of International and Comparative Law, 1965) pp 226–240.
5 See *Johnston* pp 7, 8, 226–240.

85. Conflicts with other uses of the sea. The Convention on the Continental Shelf requires that exploration and exploitation of the shelf's natural resources must not result in any 'unjustifiable interference' with navigation, fishing or the conservation of the living resources of the sea, nor any interference with fundamental oceanographic or other scientific research carried out with the intention of open publication[1]. Neither 'unjustifiable' nor 'interference' is defined. They are left to interpretation by the coastal state through its laws and practice in the context of its obligations under the convention and the objects and purposes of the convention. The coastal state must not impede the laying or maintenance of submarine cables or pipelines on the shelf, though it may take 'reasonable measures' in relation to them to further its right to explore and exploit the natural resources[2].

Due notice must be given of the construction of installations on the shelf, permanent means of giving warning of their presence must be maintained, and any installations that are abandoned or disused must be 'entirely removed'[3]. However, this provision is beginning to be overtaken by practice based on the 1982 United Nations Convention on the Law of the Sea, which requires that abandoned or disused installations be removed to ensure safety of navigation, taking into account any generally accepted international standards established in this regard by the competent international organisation, and that removal must have due regard to fishing, the protection of marine environment and the rights and duties of other states[4]. The United Kingdom made provision in the Petroleum Act 1987 for the relevant Secretary of State to order at his discretion only partial removal of some of the larger installations[5]. No reference is made in this Act to the need to take account of international standards, and none existed when it was passed. Fishermen unsuccessfully opposed this legislation. They subsequently pressed the International Maritime Organisation, which accepted that it was the 'appropriate international organisation' to take account of their interests when considering the promulgation of guidelines concerning the means and extent of removal, including partial removal, of installations. Fishermen's organisations have no status at IMO, but their views were made known by non-governmental observers and the United Nations Food and Agriculture Organisation. Fishermen pressed for total removal and, if not, removal to a depth which would not injure their nets. The guidelines now adopted take some account of the points raised by the fishermen, but the 1987 Act does not specifically require the Secretary of State to take account of such guidelines, nor does it provide any formal mechanism for objecting to particular decisions that any installation need not be wholly removed when abandoned. It is expected that most installations in United Kingdom waters will be removed, and that only a few of the largest will be left partially *in situ*.

1 Convention on the Continental Shelf (Geneva, 29 April 1958; TS 39 (1964); Cmnd 2422), art 5(1).
2 Ibid, art 4.
3 Ibid, art 5(4).
4 United Nations Convention on the Law of the Sea (Montego Bay, 10 December 1982; Misc 11 (1983); Cmnd 8941), art 60(3).
5 See the Petroleum Act 1987 (c 12), Pt I (ss 1–16).

(e) The High Seas

86. Meaning of 'high seas'. According to the 1958 Geneva Convention on the High Seas, to which the United Kingdom is party and which entered into force on 30 September 1962, the term 'high seas' means all parts of the sea that are not included in the territorial sea or in the internal waters of a state[1]. The preamble states that the parties to the convention desire to codify the relevant international law. The 1982 United Nations Convention on the Law of the Sea arguably limits this definition by excluding from the application of high seas provisions the 200-mile exclusive economic zone, which concedes exclusive fisheries rights to the coastal state on certain conditions[2]. Following the widespread adoption of 200-mile fisheries or exclusive economic zones, the area open to high seas freedom of fishing, which was regulated by the North-East Atlantic Fisheries Commission and the International Commission for North-West Atlantic Fisheries, has been much reduced, and this led to the renegotiation of their constituent conventions[3].

1 Convention on the High Seas (Geneva, 29 April 1958; TS 5 (1963); Cmnd 1929), art 1.
2 United Nations Convention on the Law of the Sea (Montego Bay, 10 December 1982; Misc 11 (1983); Cmnd 8941), art 86.
3 See paras 93–100 below.

87. Legal status of the high seas. The Convention on the High Seas and the United Nations Convention on the Law of the Sea provide that the high seas cannot be appropriated or subjected to sovereignty by any state under either convention; since the high seas also are open to use by all states, vessels of all states, including land-locked states, can exercise the freedom of fishing and also of navigation, overflight and laying of submarine cables and pipelines, and 'others which are recognised by the general principles of international law'[1]. They are, however, required to exercise each freedom with 'reasonable regard to the interests of other states' in their exercise of these freedoms[1], and to exercise their jurisdiction and control in administrative, technical and social matters for fisheries and other purposes over ships flying their flag[2].

1 Convention on the High Seas (Geneva, 29 April 1958; TS 5 (1963); Cmnd 1929), art 2.
2 Ibid, art 5. This the United Kingdom does through the Acts referred to in para 110 ff below.

88. Jurisdiction of flag state over fishing vessels. Under the Convention on the High Seas, ships have the nationality of the state whose flag they fly, and each state must fix the conditions for granting its nationality, registering ships in its territory and the right to fly its flag, issuing confirmatory documents to each ship[1]. Each ship must be subject to the exclusive jurisdiction of its flag state on the high seas[2], though, of course, if it enters into the fisheries zone or territorial waters of another, it becomes subject to the concurrent jurisdiction of that state for the purposes accepted under international law as appropriate for that zone.

1 Convention on the High Seas (Geneva, 29 April 1958; TS 5 (1963); Cmnd 1929) art 5.
2 Ibid, art 6.

89. Problems of open access to high seas fisheries. The lack of restriction on entry into high seas fisheries encourages more vessels to enter than eventually many fisheries can sustain. This leads both to over-exploitation and collapse of particular fisheries and to economic inefficiency; the history of herring fisheries off Scotland is a case in point. At this stage states in the region or those fishing in that area, or for the species affected, generally become willing to enter into co-operative agreements for the regulation of access or for the allocation of the catches or to ensure conservation, or for all these purposes, through the conclusion of treaties, which frequently establish international regulatory commissions. But the doctrine of freedom of fishing and the resultant over-capacity of fishing effort makes it difficult for such commissions to establish sufficiently strict measures effectively to achieve their ends. Such problems beset the two commissions in which the United Kingdom formerly participated — the North East and North West Atlantic Commissions established by the North-East Atlantic Fisheries Convention of 1959[1] and the International Convention for the North-West Atlantic Fisheries 1949[2] respectively. Both conventions have now been denounced following the widespread adoption of 200-mile exclusive economic or fishery zones from 1976 onwards by their parties. They have been replaced by two new co-operative conventions for the North-East Atlantic Fisheries (1980)[3] and for the Northwest Atlantic Fisheries (1978)[4] respectively. The former itself replaced a Permanent Commission established under the 1946 Convention for the Regulation of Meshes of Fishing Nets and the Size Limits of Fish[5] (the so-called 'Over-fishing Convention'); unlike the 1959 convention the 1946 convention had established no power to set catches or allocate quotas internationally, only to lay down the measures indicated in its title in order to restrict catches of young and immature fish. These proved ineffective in countering over-exploitation of various species; the measures did not even cover herring, the most over-exploited fish. In the seas surrounding Scotland the solution of extended coastal state fisheries jurisdiction, which immediately became subject to the Common Fisheries Policy, has now been adopted, and the role of such commissions has declined though some continue to exist and in 1982 a new one for conservation of North Atlantic salmon was established[6].

1 North-East Atlantic Fisheries Convention (London, 24 January 1959; TS 68 (1963); Cmnd 2190).

2 International Convention for the North-West Atlantic Fisheries (Washington, 8 February 1949; TS 62 (1950); Cmd 8071).

3 Convention on Future Multilateral Co-operation in North-East Atlantic Fisheries (London, 18 November 1980; Misc (1982); Cmnd 8474; OJ L227, 12.8.81, p 22). The convention has thirteen signatories, of whom the following twelve have ratified it: Bulgaria, Denmark (in respect of the Faroe Islands and Greenland), the European Community, the German Democratic Republic, Iceland, Norway, Poland, Portugal, Spain, Sweden, the United Kingdom and the USSR. Cuba signed the convention but has neither ratified it nor denounced the 1959 North-East Atlantic Fisheries Convention. Finland has denounced the 1959 convention but has not signed the 1981 convention. See further paras 93 ff below.

4 Convention on Future Multilateral Co-operation in the Northwest Atlantic Fisheries (Ottawa, 24 October 1978; Misc 9 (1979); Cmnd 7569; OJ L378, 30.12.78, p 16). The convention has thirteen parties: Bulgaria, Denmark (in respect of the Faroe Islands), Canada, Cuba, the European Community, the German Democratic Republic, Iceland, Japan, Poland, Portugal, Norway, Romania and the USSR. See further paras 97 ff below.

5 Convention for the Regulation of the Meshes of Fishing Nets and the Size Limits of Fish (London, 5 April 1946; TS 8 (1956); Cmd 9704) (as amended: see TS 11 (1963); Cmnd 1942).

6 Convention for the Conservation of Salmon in the North Atlantic Ocean (Reykjavik, 2 March 1982; Misc 7 (1982); Cmnd 8830; OJ L378, 31.12.82, p 5): see paras 101 ff below.

90. Conservation. Provision for conservation was made in the Convention on Fishing and Conservation of the Living Resources of the High Seas of 1958[1]. This convention was the fourth of those concluded at the First United Nations Conference on the Law of the Sea. The United Kingdom is a party to it, and it entered into force on 20 March 1966. It has not been denounced by the United Kingdom to date. The convention does not purport to be codifying and has attracted less support than the others; its scope and effectiveness has been much diminished in any event by the widespread adoption of exclusive economic zones or fisheries zones, provided for in the 1982 United Nations Convention on the Law of the Sea[2] and now accepted in state practice. As the 1958 convention has not been denounced it remains in force, though much of its area of application falls now within the 200-mile zones of coastal states. The convention recognises that all states have the right for their nationals to engage in fishing on the high seas but subject to their treaty obligations[3], the interests and rights of coastal states under the convention and its provisions on conservation, and stipulates that all states have the duty to adopt, or to co-operate with other states in adopting, the necessary measures for their nationals to ensure conservation of the high seas living resources[4]. It defines 'conservation' as the aggregate of the measures rendering possible the optimum sustainable yield from those resources so as to secure a maximum supply of food and other marine products[5]. The need to give priority in conservation to securing a supply of food for human consumption is stressed. The convention requires states whose nationals fish the same stocks of fish in any area, on request, to enter into negotiations with a view to prescribing by agreement for their nationals the necessary measures for the conservation of the resources affected[6]. In case agreement cannot be reached, procedures for settling disputes are provided[7], though these have never been used.

1 Convention on Fishing and Conservation of the Living Resources of the Sea (Geneva, 29 April 1958; TS 39 (1966); Cmnd 3028).

2 United Nations Convention on the Law of the Sea (Montego Bay, 10 December 1982; Misc 11 (1983); Cmnd 8941), art 55.
3 So far as the United Kingdom is concerned, these are outlined in paras 92 ff below.
4 Convention on Fishing and Conservation of the Living Resources of the Sea, art 1.
5 Ibid, art 2.
6 Ibid, art 4.
7 See ibid, art 9.

91. Rights of coastal state over the living resources of the high seas. Because the high seas remained open to all states and the concept of fisheries zones was not universally accepted in 1958, the Convention on Fishing and Conservation of the Living Resources of the Sea could not accord the coastal state any exclusive rights, either to take the fish or to enforce measures for their conservation on foreign flag vessels. The convention merely recognised that 'A coastal state has a special interest in the maintenance of the productivity of the living resources in any area of the high seas adjacent to its territorial sea' and that other states, at its request, should enter into negotiations 'with a view to prescribing by agreement' the necessary conservation measures[1]. Subsequently, the International Court of Justice in the *Icelandic Fisheries Jurisdiction Case* concluded that there was a rule of customary international law under which in certain circumstances a coastal state whose economy was particularly dependent on fishing could assert preferential (but not exclusive) rights of access to high seas fishery resources adjacent to its territorial sea but that it should have regard to the interests of those who had fished in these areas for many years and enter into negotiations with them[2]. This decision has been much criticised and the basis of the court's findings have not been followed in state practice. Though the convention does not go so far as to recognise the preferential rights of a coastal state on the high seas, only its 'interest' in conservation, the 1982 United Nations Convention on the Law of the Sea went further in recognising the sovereign rights of a coastal state to living resources in 200-mile exclusive economic zones[3].

1 Convention on Fishing and Conservation of the Living Resources of the Sea (Geneva, 29 April 1958; TS 39 (1966); Cmnd 3028), art 6.
2 *Icelandic Fisheries Jurisdiction Case* (1974) ICJ Rep 3 at 93–97.
3 United Nations Convention on the Law of the Sea (Montego Bay, 10 December 1982; Misc 11 (1983); Cmnd 8941), art 57: see para 107 below.

(4) INTERNATIONAL REGIME NOW APPLYING IN WATERS OFF SCOTLAND

(a) Introduction

92. The situation until 1976: fisheries commissions. Until 1976, when the United Kingdom enacted the Fishery Limits Act 1976 (c 86) and extended these limits to 200 miles, fisheries beyond the then 3-mile limit of the territorial sea were subject to the requirement of the Geneva Conventions of 1958[1], the Fisheries Convention of 1964[2] and the North-East Atlantic Fisheries Convention of 1959[3], enforced by national and international means, under a Joint Enforcement Scheme negotiated in 1967[4], though not in force until 1976. This scheme enabled limited mutual inspection of the fishing vessels of participating states on the high seas, but any vessels found offending against the regulations could only be reported to their flag state and the North East Atlantic Fisheries Commission; they could not be arrested by the foreign vessel concerned. This scheme has now been superseded by the reduction of most of its area of application to the jurisdiction of its members' 200-mile zones within which enforcement is exclusively by national means, supplemented for European Community member states by the Community's own more limited inspection scheme[5]. Fisheries in the North-West Atlantic area were governed under similar arrangements established by the International Convention for the North-West Atlantic Fisheries[6], executed by the Northwest Atlantic Fisheries Commission instituted by it.

1 As to the Geneva Conventions of 1958, see para 70 above.
2 Fisheries Convention (London, 9 March 1964; TS 35 (1966); Cmnd 3011) (referred to in practice as the 'London' or 'European' Convention).
3 North-East Atlantic Fisheries Convention (London, 24 January 1959; TS 68 (1963); Cmnd 2190).
4 Convention on Conduct of Fishing Operations in the North Atlantic (London, 1 June 1967; TS 40 (1977) Cmnd 6799). Though superseded in practice, this convention has not been denounced.
5 See AGRICULTURE, vol 1, para 948. See also para 173, text and note 6, below.
6 International Convention for the North-West Atlantic Fisheries (Washington, 8 February 1949; TS 62 (1950); Cmd 8071).

(b) The North-East Atlantic Fisheries

93. The North-East Atlantic Fisheries Commission before 1982. The North-East Atlantic Fisheries Commission (NEAFC) originated from the Permanent Commission established in 1953 under the 1946 Convention for the Regulation of Meshes of Fishing Nets and the Size Limits of Fish[1]. The powers of that Permanent Commission were limited. A commission with wide powers was therefore established under the North-East Atlantic Fisheries Convention of 1959[2]; but although it had powers to establish closed seasons and fishing areas and to regulate catch and fishing effort it could not fix the tonnage of the total allowable catch (TAC)[3]. It took years for the approval necessary to enable this to be negotiated, and even after this was concluded in 1974 the commission still could not allocate catch quotas to individual member states or restrict the types of species caught by them. Moreover, though NEAFC received scientific advice on the necessary conservation measures through a Liaison Committee established under the long-standing and respected International Council for the Exploration of the Sea (ICES, whose Headquarters are in Denmark), the political and economic concerns of NEAFC members prevented it from acting fully or timeously on the advice of ICES. Even the measures it did adopt were expressed as non-binding regulations and could, under the 1959 convention, be objected to by any member state. Enforcement was often poor, but prior to 1977 the United Kingdom enacted a number of conservatory measures agreed by NEAFC through orders promulgated under its national legislation. However, the weakness of the NEAFC system, coupled with the move to 200-mile fisheries zones, the decision in the *Icelandic Fisheries Jurisdiction Case*[4] and the subsequent failure of the United Kingdom to negotiate further access to Icelandic fishing grounds for Scottish and English fishermen, in particular, led the United Kingdom to propose to the European Community in 1976 that its member states should concert their declarations of 200-mile fisheries jurisdiction, despite the fact that the Common Fisheries Policy, as already adopted by the Community, would immediately be applicable within these limits. The gradual adoption of 200-mile jurisdictions by the United Kingdom and other member states bordering the North Atlantic necessitated that they denounce the existing NEAFC convention to take account of this development and renego-tiate it. Athough not all NEAFC parties were member states of the Com-munity, most had also declared 200-mile zones.

1 Convention for the Regulation of Meshes of Fishing Nets and the Size Limits of Fish (London, 5 April 1946; TS 8 (1956); Cmd 9704) (amended: see TS 11 (1963); Cmnd 1942).
2 North-East Atlantic Fisheries Convention (London, 24 January 1959; TS 68 (1963); Cmnd 2190), art 3.
3 See AGRICULTURE, vol 1, para 947.
4 *Icelandic Fisheries Jurisdiction Case* (1974) ICJ Rep 3.

94. The North-East Atlantic Fisheries Commission after 1981. A new convention relating to the North-East Atlantic Fisheries was negotiated in 1978, and came into force in 1982. The Convention on Future Multilateral Co-operation in North-East Atlantic Fisheries of 1980[1] differs from the North-East Atlantic Fisheries Convention of 1959[2] in providing for the European Com-munity to be a signatory in place of its individual member states. The area covered by the 1980 convention includes the Atlantic and Arctic Oceans, excluding part of the Baltic Sea and the Belts and the Mediterranean Sea[3]. It applies to all fishery resources except sea mammals and sedentary species[4]. All effect on rights, claims and views of parties concerning the limits or extent of jurisdiction over fisheries is disclaimed[5].

The convention established a new North-East Atlantic Fisheries Com-mission[6]. Each party has one vote, and decisions are taken by a simple majority or, as specified in the convention, by a two-thirds majority of parties casting affirmative or negative votes[7]. The commission is required to function in the interests of both conservation and optimum utilisation of the fishery resources of its area, taking account of the best scientific evidence available to it[8] (to be supplied by the International Council for the Exploration of the Sea[9]), and providing a forum for consultation and exchange of information on the state of the fishery resources in the convention area and on management policies, including examination of the overall effect of such policies on those resources[10].

1 Convention on Future Multilateral Co-operation in North-East Atlantic Fisheries (London, 18 November 1980; Misc 2 (1982); Cmnd 8474; OJ L227, 12.8.81, p 22). For the parties, see para 89, note 3, above.
2 North-East Atlantic Fisheries Convention (London, 24 January 1959; TS 68 (1963); Cmnd 2190).
3 Ibid, art 1(1).
4 Ibid, art 1(2).
5 Ibid, art 2.
6 Ibid, art 3(1).
7 Ibid, art 3(9).
8 Ibid, art 4(1).
9 Ibid, art 14.
10 Ibid, art 4(2).

95. Powers of the commission. The North-East Atlantic Fisheries Com-mission, which meets annually[1], makes recommendations concerning fisheries conducted beyond areas under the fisheries jurisdiction of its contracting par-ties, seeking to ensure consistency between recommendations that apply to stocks that occur both within the parties' jurisdictional areas and beyond and those affecting the latter through species inter-relationships, and with measures and decisions taken by a contracting party for the management of such stocks within their own jurisdictional areas[2]. The commission may make recommen-dations to parties concerning fisheries conducted in their jurisdictional areas, but

only at their request and if the particular recommendation receives the affirmative vote of that party[3]. Subject to these limitations, the commission may
consider inter alia measures regulating gear and net mesh sizes, size limits of
fish, closed seasons and closed areas, and for the improvement and increase of
the fishery resources, the setting of a total allowable catch, the allocation of
national quotas and the regulation of and allocation of fishing effort[4]. The
commission may also recommend the collection of statistical data in areas in and
beyond national jurisdiction[5]. A recommendation becomes binding only if not
objected to within a specified period, and even then cannot bind any objecting
party — and if three parties object it is not binding on any party[6]. Parties must be
notified of any recommendations[7]. By 1985 the commission had made only one
recommendation[8].

1 Convention on Future Multilateral Co-operation in North-East Atlantic Fisheries (London,
  18 November 1980; Misc 2 (1982); Cmnd 8474; OJ L227, 12.8.81, p 22), art 3(6).
2 Ibid, art 5.
3 Ibid, art 6.
4 Ibid, art 7.
5 Ibid, art 8.
6 Ibid, art 12.
7 Ibid, art 11(1).
8 This was a recommendation that a minimum mesh size of 16 mm should be used when fishing
  for capelin in its regulatory area (ie in waters beyond the jurisdictional zones of its parties):
  Recommendation 1 — Minimum Mesh Size when Fishing for Capelin, made at the 1984 annual
  meeting of the North-East Atlantic Fisheries Commission and effective from 1 May 1985:
  Handbook of Basic Texts (NEAFC 1985), p 49.

96. Enforcement. Contracting parties are required to take adequate measures
for the punishment of infractions in order effectively to implement the Convention on Future Multilateral Co-operation in North-East Atlantic Fisheries[1].
They must submit to the North-East Atlantic Fisheries Commission an annual
statement of the actions they have taken[2], inform it of relevant legislative
measures and agreements they have concluded[3] and furnish it with scientific,
statistical and other information[4]. The commission publishes reports of its
activities and other information relating to fisheries[5], including details of the
technical conservation measures in force in the zones under the fisheries jurisdiction of its contracting parties as well as in its own regulatory area[6].

1 Convention on Future Multilateral Co-operation in North-East Atlantic Fisheries (London,
  18 November 1980; Misc 2 (1982); Cmnd 8474; OJ L227, 12.8.81, p 22), art 15(1).
2 Ibid, art 15(2).
3 Ibid, art 16(1).
4 Ibid, arts 9, 16(2).
5 Ibid, art 11(2).
6 *North-East Atlantic Fisheries Commission, Technical Conservation Measures* (1986). These are
  categorised under Convention Area; Minimum Fish Sizes; Minimum Net Sizes; By-Catch
  Rules; Attachment to Nets; Measurement of Net Sizes; and Logbooks. Legislation of European
  Community member states is listed as within 'EEC waters'. This manual is stated to be for
  reference only and has no legal status as such.

(c) The Northwest Atlantic Fisheries

97. Introduction. For reasons similar to those requiring the renegotiation of
the North-East Atlantic Fisheries Convention, the International Convention for
the North-West Atlantic Fisheries[1] was also renegotiated in 1978 and replaced
by the Convention on Future Multilateral Co-operation in Northwest Atlantic
Fisheries[2].

1 International Convention for the North-West Atlantic Fisheries (Washington, 8 February 1949;
   TS 62 (1950); Cmd 8071).
2 Convention on Future Multilateral Co-operation in the Northwest Atlantic Fisheries (Ottawa,
   24 October 1978; Misc 9 (1979); Cmnd 7569; OJ L378, 30.12.78, p 16). For the parties, see para
   89, note 4, above.

98. Application of the convention. The Convention on Future Multilateral
Co-operation in Northwest Atlantic Fisheries applies to a 'convention area' of
the Northwest Atlantic Ocean as defined therein, but within this convention
area there is a 'regulatory area' comprising that part of the convention area
which lies beyond the areas in which the coastal states exercise fisheries jurisdiction[1]. The convention applies to all fishery resources of the convention area
except salmon, tuna and marlin (also called 'spear fish'), cetaceans managed by
the International Whaling Commission or its successor and sedentary species[2],
but coastal states are obliged neither to seek nor to accept the advice of the
Northwest Atlantic Fisheries Commission on the remaining species in the
convention area.

Nothing in the convention affects or prejudices the positions or claims of any
contracting party in regard to internal waters, the territorial sea or the limits or
extent of the fisheries jurisdiction of any party, or the views or positions of any
contracting party with respect to the law of the sea[3].

1 Convention on Future Multilateral Co-operation in the Northwest Atlantic Fisheries (Ottawa,
   24 October 1978; Misc 9 (1979); Cmnd 7569; OJ L378, 30.12.78, p 16), art I(1), (2). 'Coastal state'
   means a contracting party exercising fisheries jurisdiction in waters forming part of the convention area: art I(3).
2 Ibid, art I(4).
3 Ibid, art I(5).

99. The organisation and its councils and commission. A new body, the
Northwest Atlantic Fisheries Organisation, is established by the Convention on
Future Multilateral Co-operation in the Northwest Atlantic Fisheries to contribute through consultation and co-operation to the optimum utilisation,
rational management and conservation of the fishery resources of the convention area[1]. The organisation consists of a General Council, a Scientific Council,
a Fisheries Commission and a Secretariat[2]. The General Council is the main
administrative and co-ordinating body, dealing with external relations[3]; all
parties are members and have one vote at its annual meetings[4]. The Scientific
Council provides a forum for consultation and co-operation on scientific aspects
including environmental and ecological factors affecting the fisheries of the
convention area, but provides scientific advice to coastal states only when
requested by them to do so[5]. The Fisheries Commission may refer questions
concerning management and conservation of fishery resources in the regulatory
area, for which it is responsible[6], to the Scientific Council, which provides
advice by consensus[7]. The Fisheries Commission also seeks to ensure consistency of proposals relating to the regulatory and non-regulatory (coastal state)
areas, taking account of those having effect through species inter-relationships
on stocks in the latter areas[8]. In adopting proposals for allocation of catches in
the regulatory area the commission must take account of the interests of its
members whose vessels have 'traditionally fished' within that area[9]. It may also
adopt proposals for international measures of control and enforcement within
that area[10]. Proposals are subject to objection procedures, and members are not
bound if they duly object[11]. If a majority of members object, none is bound[11].
Decisions are taken by a majority of votes of commission members present and
casting affirmative or negative votes[12].

1 Convention on Future Multilateral Co-operation in the Northwest Atlantic Fisheries (Ottawa, 24 October 1978; Misc 9 (1979); Cmnd 7569; OJ L378, 30.12.78, p 16), art II(1).
2 Ibid, art II(2)(a)–(d).
3 See ibid, art III.
4 See ibid, arts IV, V.
5 See ibid, art VI.
6 See ibid, art XI(1).
7 See ibid, arts VIII, X.
8 Ibid, art XI(3).
9 Ibid, art XI(4).
10 Ibid, art XI(5).
11 See ibid, art XII(1).
12 Ibid, art XIV(2).

100. Enforcement. All parties must take the measures necessary to implement the Convention on Future Multilateral Co-operation in the Northwest Atlantic Fisheries, and must impose adequate sanctions for violations[1]. They must submit to the Northwest Atlantic Fisheries Commission annual statements of the actions taken[1]. A joint international enforcement scheme is established for the regulatory area, providing for reciprocal rights of boarding and inspection and for flag state prosecution and sanctions, reports of which must be included in the annual statement[2].

1 Convention on Future Multilateral Co-operation in the Northwest Atlantic Fisheries (Ottawa, 24 October 1978; Misc 9 (1979); Cmnd 7569; OJ L378, 30.12.78, p 16), art XVII.
2 Ibid, art XVIII.

(d) The Conservation of Salmon in the North Atlantic

101. Introduction. The over-fishing of salmon both on the high seas and within the jurisdictional zones of coastal states led to a serious decline in catches and in numbers of salmon returning to their spawning grounds, many of which in the case of the Atlantic salmon are found in the rivers of Scotland. Atlantic salmon, the only native salmon of the North Atlantic originating in Scottish rivers, have been found off Greenland, the return journey to which covers 3,500 miles. The discovery of the grounds on which salmon congregate off Greenland and their over-exploitation by Denmark led to a decline in the number of salmon returning to Scottish rivers. As the capital value of Scottish salmon fisheries has been estimated at £3,500 per fish, international co-operation is essential to ensure the conservation and management of salmon stocks. Early attempts to reach agreement with Denmark were not successful in sufficiently reducing catches.

102. The United Nations Convention on the Law of the Sea and anadromous species. The 1982 United Nations Convention on the Law of the Sea in its provisions concerning the establishment of an exclusive economic zone made special provision[1] for anadromous species, namely species, such as salmon, which, though spending part of their life cycle in sea water, whether on the high seas or in coastal zones, spawn in fresh water areas lying exclusively within national territorial jurisdiction. Measures taken by the states of origin to protect the salmon on, and en route to, their spawning grounds are undermined if the salmon protected there are over-exploited by other states when they reach the high seas where freedom of fishing pertains, or when they enter the exclusive 200-mile fisheries zones of other states, where the coastal state alone otherwise decides the allowable catch and determines which states, if any, are to have access to it, and on what terms.

The convention provides that states in whose rivers anadromous stocks originate (such as the United Kingdom) are to have the primary interest in and responsibility for such stocks. This so-called 'state of origin' must in return ensure the conservation of the stocks by establishing appropriate regulatory measures for fishing in all waters landward of the outer limits of its exclusive economic zone and for minimising economic dislocation in such other states as may be fishing the stock beyond this limit. It may, after consultation with these states and with those states through whose zones anadromous stocks migrate, establish total allowable catches for stocks originating in its rivers. Fisheries for anadromous stocks are, however, to be carried out only in waters on the landward side of the outer limits of the exclusive economic zone, unless so to require would result in economic dislocation for other states; in such cases the states concerned must consult to try to reach agreement on the terms and conditions of fishing beyond the limit of that zone, with regard to the conservation measures of the state of origin and other needs for the stocks. It in turn must co-operate and take into account the normal catch and operating methods of these states and all the areas in which they have previously fished the stocks concerned. Such states, if they participate with the state of origin in agreements undertaking the necessary measures to renew stocks (especially if they contribute to the costs involved), must be given special consideration in harvesting stocks originating in the rivers of the state of origin. Enforcement of resultant regulations on the high seas requires agreement between all states concerned. States through whose zones anadromous species migrate also must co-operate with the state of origin on conservation management measures.

The state of origin and other states fishing the stocks must make the above arrangements, where appropriate (which is likely to be in most cases) through regional organisations. The first to be established exclusively to implement the convention regime was the North Atlantic Salmon Organisation, whose area covers inter alia all Scottish rivers and all waters off Scotland. Although the convention does not directly bind the United Kingdom since it has neither signed nor ratified it, the United Kingdom accepts that these provisions represent the basis of the new customary law and, as a member state of the European Community, which has become a party to the Convention for the Conservation of Salmon in the North Atlantic Ocean[2], must implement any measures it adopts.

1 United Nations Convention on the Law of the Sea (Montego Bay, 10 December 1982; Misc 11 (1983); Cmnd 8941), art 66.
2 Convention for the Conservation of Salmon in the North Atlantic Ocean (Reykjavik, 2 March 1982; Misc 7 (1982); Cmnd 8830; OJ L378, 31.12.82, p 25). The convention has been ratified by Canada, Denmark (in respect of the Faroe Islands and Greenland), the European Community, Finland, Iceland, Norway, Sweden, the United States and the USSR.

103. The North Atlantic salmon convention. The Convention for the Conservation of Salmon in the North Atlantic Ocean recognises that salmon originating in the rivers of different states intermingle in certain parts of the North Atlantic, and takes into account international law, including the provisions concerning anadromous stocks in the then Draft Convention of the Third United Nations Conference on the Law of the Sea[1]. Its expressed aims are to promote the acquisition, analysis and dissemination of scientific information pertaining to salmon stocks in the North Atlantic and the conservation, restoration, enhancement and rational management of those salmon stocks through international co-operation[1].

The convention applies to the salmon stocks which migrate beyond the areas subject to the fisheries jurisdiction of coastal states of the Atlantic Ocean north of 36 degrees latitude and throughout their migratory range[2]. It prohibits the fishing of salmon in areas beyond the limits of this fisheries jurisdiction and also in areas of coastal fisheries jurisdiction beyond 12 nautical miles[3].

1 Convention for the Conservation of Salmon in the North Atlantic Ocean (Reykjavik, 2 March 1982; Misc 7 (1982); Cmnd 8830; OJ L378, 31.12.82, p 25), preamble.
2 Ibid, art 1(1). The 36 degree line is a line of latitude drawn approximately between Gibraltar and Cape Hatteras, North Carolina.
3 See ibid, art 2.

104. The North Atlantic Salmon Conservation Organisation and its regional commissions. An international organisation known as the North Atlantic Salmon Conservation Organisation has been established to contribute through consultation and co-operation to the conservation, restoration, enhancement and rational management of salmon stocks subject to the Convention for the Conservation of Salmon in the North Atlantic Ocean of 1982[1]. The organisation consists of a council, three regional commissions and a secretariat[2].

The North Atlantic is divided into three areas, for each of which a regional commission is established, namely the North American Commission, the West Greenland Commission and the North-East Atlantic Commission[3]. The regional commissions provide the forum for consultation and co-operation between the members, propose regulatory measures and make recommendations to the council on the needs for scientific research[4]. The commissions must obtain the best available scientific information, including the advice of the International Council for the Exploration of the Sea[5].

A commission must, in making proposals and recommendations, take into account (1) measures taken and other factors, both inside and outside the commission's areas, that affect stocks; (2) the efforts of states of origin to implement and enforce measures for the conservation, restoration, enhancement and rational management of salmon stocks in their rivers and areas of fisheries jurisdiction; (3) the extent to which salmon stocks feed in the areas of jurisdiction of the respective parties; (4) the relative effects of harvesting salmon at different stages of their migration route; (5) the contribution of parties other than states of origin to the conservation of salmon which migrate into their areas of jurisdiction by limiting their catches; and (6) the interests of communities which are particularly dependent on salmon fisheries[6].

Although the promulgation of measures by a commission involves complex decisions involving political and economic as well as scientific considerations, the convention provides the forum within which Scottish interests in preventing an excessive proportion of fish originating in Scotland from being intercepted by the Faroese and Greenlanders can be protected.

1 Convention for the Conservation of Salmon in the North Atlantic Ocean (Reykjavik, 2 March 1982; Misc 7 (1982); Cmnd 8830; OJ L378, 31.12.82, p 25), art 3(1), (2). The organisation's headquarters are at 11 Rutland Square, Edinburgh EH1 2AS: see art 3(7).
2 Ibid, art 3(3)(a)–(c). For the functions and constitution of the council, see arts 4–6.
3 Ibid, art 3(3)(b). The area of each commission is defined in art 3(4).
4 Ibid, art 7(1).
5 Ibid, art 9(a).
6 Ibid, art 9(b)–(g).

105. Progress of North Atlantic salmon conservation. The Council of the North Atlantic Salmon Conservation Organisation has identified the basic scientific questions involved in conservation and management of these species and has received advice from the International Council for the Exploration of the Sea. The West Greenland Commission has reduced the total allowable catch off Greenland (established for thirteen years only by bi-lateral agreement) by

27 per cent; rights of both so-called 'grazing' states and states of origin have been discussed; and information is exchanged on relevant laws, regulations and programmes of member states, who are reconsidering their national management plans.

(e) Effect on Fisheries in Waters off Scotland of the United Nations Convention on the Law of the Sea

106. United Kingdom position on the convention; relation with Common Fisheries Policy. The United Nations Convention on the Law of the Sea (UNCLOS) has been signed by 159 states but, as at 31 December 1989, had been ratified by only forty-two states and entities. It requires sixty ratifications and the lapse of one year following the sixtieth ratification for entry into force[1].

Although the United Kingdom has not become a party to the convention, it accepts that as large parts of it, especially those of Part V concerning fisheries jurisdiction[2], were negotiated by consensus, or represent a codification of existing customary and treaty law as outlined in this title of the Encyclopaedia, and have been enacted in state practice, such parts have now become part of international customary law. However, whilst adopting and enacting the extended jurisdictional limits that UNCLOS provides, inter alia, for the territorial sea fisheries and, additionally, for a 200-mile fisheries zone[3], the United Kingdom has not enacted the detailed terms and conditions laid down in Part V of the convention. Nonetheless, in practice the United Kingdom observes these requirements, albeit most are fulfilled through implementation by the United Kingdom of the Common Fisheries Policy of the European Community by means of ad hoc statutes and orders. All member states of the Community except the United Kingdom and the Federal Republic of Germany have signed, though not ratified, the convention. The objection of the United Kingdom and the Federal Republic to UNCLOS relates to its provisions concerning the terms and conditions for exploitation of the deep seabed area beyond national jurisdiction[4] and does not relate in any respect to its provisions concerning living resources.

1 United Nations Convention on the Law of the Sea (Montego Bay, 10 December 1982; Misc 11 (1983); Cmnd 8941), art 308(1).
2 Ibid, Pt V (Exclusive Economic Zone) (arts 55–75).
3 See para 130 below.
4 United Nations Convention on the Law of the Sea, Pt XI (The Area) (arts 133–191). See also Pt VI (Continental Shelf) (arts 76–85).

107. Relevant provisions on fisheries. The United Nations Convention on the Law of the Sea provides for the establishment by coastal states of a 200-mile exclusive economic zone beyond the territorial sea[1], an area subject to the specific legal regime set out in the convention in which the rights and jurisdiction of the coastal state and the rights and freedoms of other states are governed by the convention. In it the coastal state has 'sovereign rights for the purpose of exploring and exploiting, conserving and managing the natural resources, whether living or not living, of the waters superjacent to the sea bed and its subsoil'[2]. It also has jurisdiction, as set out in other parts of the convention, over marine scientific research[3] and the protection and preservation of the marine environment[4]. States retain in the exclusive economic zone the freedoms of navigation and overflight and of laying submarine cables and pipelines, subject to the provisions of the convention, and also other internationally lawful uses of the sea related to these freedoms and compatible with them, such as those associated with operation of ships, aircraft, submarine cables and pipelines[5]. In exercising these rights as well as in performing duties under the convention in the exclusive economic zone, states must have due regard to the rights and duties of the coastal state and must comply with its laws, adopted under and compatible with the convention[6]. The exclusive economic zone seabed rights are subject to the continental shelf regime as set out in the convention[7]; sedentary species living on or in relation to the shelf fall under the shelf regime as they did before under the 1958 Conventions[8]. These rights can, if the shelf is naturally prolonged beyond 200 miles, extend through all that area of natural prolongation up to a maximum of 350 miles from the territorial sea baselines, or to 100 miles from the 2,500 metre isobath (a line connecting the 2,500 metre depth)[9].

1 United Nations Convention on the Law of the Sea (Montego Bay, 10 December 1982; Misc 11 (1983); Cmnd 8941), art 57.
2 Ibid, art 56(1)(a).
3 See ibid, Pt XIII (arts 238–265).
4 See ibid, Pt XII (arts 192–237).
5 Ibid, art 58(1).
6 Ibid, art 58(3).
7 Ibid, art 56(3).
8 As to the 1958 Conventions, see para 70 above.
9 United Nations Convention on the Law of the Sea, art 76.

108. Conservation. Subject to the above limitations, the United Nations Convention on the Law of the Sea requires the coastal state to determine the total allowable catch of living resources in its exclusive economic (or fisheries) zone[1]. It must take into account the best scientific evidence available to it to ensure the taking of measures that will avoid over-exploitation[2]. It must also ensure by taking proper conservation and management measures that harvested species in the zone are maintained at or restored to levels that produce the maximum sustainable yield, but this can be qualified by economic and environmental factors, including the economic needs of coastal fishing communities and of developing states, fishing patterns, interdependence of stocks, and any recommended international minimum standards, whether global, regional or sub-regional[3]. Scientific information, catch and fishing effort statistics and other such conservation related data must be provided and exchanged through competent international organisations[4].

1 United Nations Convention on the Law of the Sea (Montego Bay, 10 December 1982; Misc 11 (1983); Cmnd 8941), art 61(1).
2 Ibid, art 61(2).
3 Ibid, art 61(3).
4 Ibid, art 61(5).

109. Access to fisheries. To ensure that the concession of exclusive coastal states rights to fisheries neither leads to their non- or partial exploitation and that other states are not unnecessarily denied access to foreign fisheries, the United Nations Convention on the Law of the Sea requires that coastal states promote the objective of optimum utilisation of these resources[1] and, that, having determined their own capacity to harvest the total allowable catch, they allow other states access to the surplus catch by means of agreements or other arrangements[2]. The convention indicates some factors to be taken into account in granting such access, such as the significance of the fisheries to the economy of the coastal state, the need to minimise economic dislocation in states whose nationals have habitually fished in the zone involved in research on the stocks, and the requirements of developing states in the region[3]. It should be noted that if the coastal state declares that it can itself harvest all the total allowable catch there is no clear obligation to allow other states access. Moreover, in the case of the so-called sedentary species of the continental shelf, which come under other provisions of the convention, it is neither required that optimum use be promoted, that a total allowable catch be set nor that other states be given access to any surplus if it is[4].

Foreign nationals fishing in the zone must comply with the conservation measures and other laws and regulations of the coastal state[5]. The convention lists eleven topics to which they can, inter alia, relate, including licensing; the usual conservatory measures limiting species caught, areas and periods of fishing, gear etc; placing coastal state observers or trainees on board and training their personnel; and enforcement procedures[5]. In the case of the United Kingdom these requirements and measures are determined mainly by the European Community through the Common Fisheries Policy, though executed by national laws.

The United Kingdom has neither declared nor enacted an exclusive economic zone as laid down in the convention, although some European Community member states have provided for this. The United Kingdom has, however, adopted an exclusive fisheries zone by extending its fishery zone to 200 miles and introducing a system of licensing therein[6]. The new United Kingdom fishery limits are measured from the baselines of the territorial sea, as provided in the 1958 conventions[7] and in the 1982 convention[8].

1 United Nations Convention on the Law of the Sea (Montego Bay, 10 December 1982; Misc 11 (1983); Cmnd 8941), art 62(1).
2 Ibid, art 62(2).
3 Ibid, art 62(3).
4 See ibid, art 77.
5 Ibid, art 62(4).
6 See paras 130, 131, below.
7 As to the 1958 conventions, see para 70 above. As to the baselines, see paras 74, 76, above.
8 See the United Nations Convention on the Law of the Sea, art 3.

(5) FISHERIES IN SCOTTISH WATERS AND FISHING BY SCOTTISH FISHING BOATS

(a) Introduction

110. General purposes and objects of United Kingdom fishery laws. United Kingdom fishery laws are the instruments for achieving the aims of British fisheries policy, namely to maintain the economic viability of the British fishing industry and, more recently, to protect from over-fishing both United Kingdom waters and other waters where United Kingdom fishermen fish. These laws thus reflect various changes in such aims and the methods of achieving them, particularly since the 1939-45 war when the need to maintain a balance between the level of fishing activity and the need for conservation of stocks began to take precedence over encouraging the industrial performance of the fishing fleets by the provision of an appropriate legislative framework and financial support[1]. Until 1974–76 the larger part of the British fishing fleet operated on the high seas, where stock depletion by over-fishing presented fewer problems and national conservation measures were not regarded as essential. The promulgation of 200-mile exclusive economic zones and fishery zones, however, resulted in loss of access for Scottish fishermen, among others, to traditional grounds formerly part of the high seas, and increased the pressure on stocks in coastal waters, which themselves became subject to increasing requirements of conservation emanating from the Common Fisheries Policy of the European Community, during and after its negotiation between 1972 and 1983. United Kingdom law now reflects the new concern for extending coastal state jurisdiction and control and promoting conservation by stricter regulation. It also reflects the fact that changes in limits have resulted in changes in the species caught and landed by British fishermen and in a search for new stocks hitherto unregulated, such as mackerel. Conditions for the British fishing industry worsened considerably from 1974 onwards. But to date many of the necessary changes in the law brought about by these events have been achieved by amending existing statutes rather than introducing new legislation. Only a few of the presently relevant Acts have been introduced since 1976.

1 For a discussion of these aspects, see R Lawson *Fisheries Economics* (1985).

111. Regulatory techniques. Fisheries laws, particularly since the 1960s, have consisted of a series of major enabling Acts providing for subsequent detailed regulation to reflect changes in national and international requirements and practices, implemented by statutory instruments or orders. This allows the flexibility in regulation necessitated by the need to follow changing scientific advice concerning the conservation measures required. However, the provisions in the Sea Fisheries Regulation (Scotland) Act 1895 for the making of byelaws by fishery district committees[1] were never implemented, and were repealed by the Inshore Fishing (Scotland) Act 1984[2]. The corresponding provisions of the Sea Fisheries Regulation Act 1888[3], applicable to England and Wales, were re-enacted as amended in the Sea Fisheries Regulation Act 1966[4]. The result of the use of these techniques, though enabling change, is that the law is contained in a number of ancient and ad hoc statutes, and since the 1960s has developed in a pragmatic, piecemeal fashion, including through a large number of ad hoc licensing and other orders. In the 1960s most United Kingdom orders implemented biological measures of the International Council for the Exploration of the Sea, the International Commission for Northwest Atlantic Fisheries, the Northwest Atlantic Fisheries Organisation and the North-East Atlantic Fisheries Commission, and thus took the form of closed areas and closed seasons, minimum net sizes, minimum landing sizes for fish, and gear controls, which were all to be enforced on vessels flying the United Kingdom flag fishing in areas of the high seas.

1 Sea Fisheries Regulation (Scotland) Act 1895 (c 42), ss 5–8.
2 Inshore Fishing (Scotland) Act 1984 (c 26), s 10(2), Sch 2.
3 Sea Fisheries Regulation Act 1888 (c 54), ss 1, 2.
4 Sea Fisheries Regulation Act 1966 (c 38), ss 1–5: see para 133 below.

112. The Cameron Report. The Report entitled *Regulation of Scottish Inshore Fisheries*[1] was received in 1970 from the Scottish Inshore Fisheries Committee under the chairmanship of Lord Cameron, appointed by HM Government in 1967 to review the law governing the methods of sea fishing in Scottish coastal waters. This was, of course, before the entry of the United Kingdom into the European Community. The terms of reference of the committee thus included the changing patterns of sea fishing at that date, the requirements of fishing communities, conservation of fish stocks, costs and methods of enforcement and the cost effectiveness thereof, inter alia; having reviewed these it recommended changes in the then existing fisheries law, having concluded that the present body of legislation[2] was 'excessively difficult of accurate ascertainment and in certain particulars obsolete in function and irrelevant to modern conditions' as well as being widely evaded, due in part to weaknesses therein and low penalties. The committee noted that there was a need for clarification and restatement of the law and of the powers exercisable by the executive in 'a comprehensive, enabling and declaratory statute and for excision from the law of all obsolete and irrelevant provisions'.

In 1979 the Sheriff Court at Dingwall held that the ban on beam or otter trawling within 3 miles of the low-water mark of any part of the coast of Scotland applied only to bottom trawling, and that mid-water trawling for pelagic species was lawful[3]. Subsequently a committee of officials was set up to review the Cameron Report in the light of this judgment, the likely outcome of the negotiations establishing the Common Fisheries Policy, and developments occurring in the decade following publication of the report. This committee issued its report in 1981 as a departmental consultative paper circulated to the industry and other interested parties. The Inshore Fishing (Scotland) Act 1984 (c 26) is the fruit of these efforts.

Despite several changes since 1976, the fundamental problem has not been tackled and this need remains. Such changes as have been made have been introduced in other ad hoc statutes.

The Cameron Committee, though noting the possibility of Britain's entry into the European Community and the possible adoption of a Common Fisheries Policy based on equal access, disregarded this possibility in making its recommendations. It concluded, however, that conservation was mainly an international problem and that conservation measures applying only to waters within United Kingdom fishery limits were of value only in relation to localised or sedentary stocks, that is, a small number of species.

1 *Regulation of Scottish Inshore Fisheries* (the 'Cameron Report') (Cmnd 4453) (1970).
2 This is listed in ibid, App II, pp 180, 181.
3 *Aitchison v Taylor* 1980 SLT (Sh Ct) 8.

113. Conflict between European Community and national measures.

From 1977, during the Common Fisheries Policy negotiations and after the United Kingdom enacted its 200-mile fishery limit[1], the United Kingdom enacted conservation measures applicable within that limit, some of which implemented European Community requirements and some of which were purely national[2]. Some of these orders have been held by the European Court of Justice to be illegal, for example the extension of the Norwegian pout box east of the Shetland Isles[3], a ban on herring fishing in two areas[3] and a minimum net size for nephrops[4], and remained contentious until the conclusion of the Common Fisheries Policy in 1983.

1 Fishery Limits Act 1976 (c 86), s 1(1).
2 For an exhaustive account of the state of the British fishery industry up to 1977 see *Fifth Report from the Expenditure Committee together with minutes of evidence taken before the Trade and Industry Sub-committee in Sessions 1976–1978* (HC Paper (1977–78) no. 356), especially vol 1 *The Fishing Industry*. Appendix I, Memorandum by P W Birnie, gives a short history of the Common Fisheries Policy and the international legal background. For a fuller account, see R Churchill *EEC Fisheries Law* (1987), and for a succinct account of the current Common Fisheries Policy, see 18 *Halsbury's Statutes of England* (4th edn) pp 57–60.
3 Case 32/79 *EC Commission v United Kingdom* [1980] ECR 2403, [1981] 1 CMLR 219, ECJ.
4 Case 141/78 *France v United Kingdom* [1979] ECR 2923, [1980] 1 CMLR 6, ECJ.

114. Licensing before 1983.

Before the conclusion of the Common Fisheries Policy licences were issued freely; licensing was used not for purposes of restricting entry (except in two cases) but to monitor the amount of effort expended by fishing vessels and to provide an administrative system for allocation and enforcement of quotas. The first exception to the free issue of licences was the Manx herring fishing, for which only a limited number of licences were allocated in the 1977 season (twenty-four to Irish and a hundred to British vessels). The system was abandoned in 1980, when the European Court of Justice held that the scheme was discriminatory in fact and thus illegal[1]. The second exception was the mackerel fishing, licensed from 1977 and initially subject only to catch restrictions on licence holders but from 1980 subject to restriction of entry — only purse seiner and freezer vessels which had previously participated in the fishing were awarded licences. Plans to introduce a fully restrictive licensing system were dropped because of intense opposition from the fishing industry.

1 Case 32/79 *EC Commission v United Kingdom* [1980] ECR 2403, [1981] 1 CMLR 219, ECJ.

115. Licensing after 1983. When the Common Fisheries Policy was concluded, new proposals for restrictive licensing were introduced for species, including mackerel, for which United Kingdom Community quotas were insufficient to allow unrestricted fishing (so-called 'pressure stocks'). From 1984, therefore, no licences have been issued to British boats of over 10 metres which do not have a record of fishing one or more pressure stocks. The transfer of a licence from any vessel which had received a recently-introduced decommissioning grant was also prohibited. Both measures were introduced for a trial three-year period.

The number of species now subjected to restrictions on the total allowable catch has resulted in an increase in licensing orders. Orders in 1982 and 1983 extended the licensing system from catching to trans-shipment of most pelagic (deep water) species from British or foreign boats within British fishery limits[1], and revoked seventeen ad hoc orders adopted since 1973 and extended licensing to all appropriate quota species and areas[2]. The existing orders were consolidated, with amendments, in 1989[3].

1 Receiving of Trans-shipped Sea Fish (Licensing) Order 1982, SI 1982/80 (varied by SI 1983/1139).
2 Sea Fish Licensing Order 1983, SI 1983/1206 (amended by SI 1983/1881, SI 1986/1438, and SI 1987/1565) (revoked).
3 Sea Fish Licensing Order 1989, SI 1989/2015: see para 195, note 4, below.

116. Need for consolidating legislation. Many of the existing fisheries laws are based on several ancient statutes, revised ad hoc, to achieve the objectives enunciated above; the oldest appears to be the Fisheries Act 1705 (c 48). A plethora of orders has been issued under some of these. The United Kingdom government is understood to have considered a consolidation Bill, but the idea appears to have been dropped. The account given below is based on the fisheries legislation currently in force, but all references will, of course, have to be amended in the light of any forthcoming enactment. It should be noted that all references to the British fishery limits in current legislation refer, following the enactment of the Fishery Limits Act 1976, to a 200-mile limit[1], expressed in international nautical miles of 1,852 metres[2].

1 Fishery Limits Act 1976 (c 86), s 1(5).
2 Ibid, s 8 ('miles').

117. Implementation of fisheries Acts by statutory instruments and bye-laws. Many of the Acts discussed below are implemented by subordinate legislation enacted by means of statutory instruments, and some Acts also enable the making of byelaws. The very nature of fisheries regulation and conservation necessitates frequent changes in the regulations, to adapt them both to changing fishing quotas and practices and to scientific advice concerning biological and other measures required to maintain fish stocks exploited by the fishing industry at the maximum or optimum levels required to sustain further exploitation. These measures may include, if necessary, the cessation of catching certain stocks or species from time to time and the closure of particular areas. Changes in regulations and directives implementing the Common Fisheries Policy of the European Community also necessitate changes in relevant United Kingdom secondary legislation, as do changes in measures adopted by the North-East Atlantic Fisheries Commission, the Northwest Atlantic Fisheries Organisation and the North Atlantic Salmon Conservation Organisation.

A large number of United Kingdom orders have been made, especially since the extension of United Kingdom fishery limits and the negotiation and conclusion of the Common Fisheries Policy. Many of these orders have been revoked, varied or substituted, and many are of a transient nature and require periodic renewal or variation. Thus it is neither practicable nor desirable to list them all in this work. However, in ascertaining the current state of the law on most aspects of fisheries and fishing boats it is necessary to check the extent of orders made under the various United Kingdom Acts in the current biennial *Index to Government Orders*[1]. The state of the orders there listed may be ascertained in the annual *Table of Government Orders* as at the date of that Table, but it is necessary to investigate in the monthly *List of Government Orders* any changes made subsequently.

Only a selection of orders and regulations is listed or described in the paragraphs below.

1 In the *Index to Government Orders* relevant orders are listed under 'MERCHANT SHIPPING — 4 Fishing boats and sea fishing service' and '6 Safety', and under 'SEA FISHERIES'.

(b) Early Legislation on Sea Fisheries in Distant and Coastal Waters

118. Obsolete Acts. Many of the early Acts relating to fisheries in waters adjoining Scotland and to Scottish fishing boats, though some are still partly in force, have been superseded. These include the Fisheries (Scotland) Act 1756 (c 23), which gave local inhabitants the power to take, buy from fishermen and cure herring and white fish free of any obstruction or claim for payment in cash or kind by others; the Fishery Board (Scotland) Act 1882 (c 78), which established a Fishery Board for Scotland to replace the Board of British White Herring Fishery established by the Sea Fisheries Acts 1868 (c 45) and 1875 (c 15)[1]; and the Herring Fishery (Scotland) Act 1889 (c 23), which prescribed the cran measure, prohibited daylight and Sunday fishing on the west coast and beam and other trawling in certain areas; the Sea Fisheries Regulation (Scotland) Act 1895 (c 42), which reconstituted the Fishery Board for Scotland, originally established by the 1882 Act, provided for the establishment of sea fishery districts and sea fishery committees with power to make byelaws for regulating sea fisheries in certain circumstances, and for the appointment of sea fishery officers to enforce them, and extended the powers of the Fishery Board to clams and mussels; and the Sea Fisheries (Scotland) Application of Penalties Act 1907 (c 42), which provided for the payment to the Fishery Board of penalties and other money received in respect of illegal sea fishing in Scotland. A number of other older Acts, however, still have some, albeit limited, relevance[2].

1 These Acts are named the Herring Fishery Act 1868 (c 45) and the Sea Fishery Act 1875 (c 15) in the Fishery Board (Scotland) Act 1882 (c 78), s 5(1). The names given in the text appear in the *Chronological Table of the Statutes*.

2 See paras 119 ff below.

119. The Fisheries Act 1705. The Fisheries Act 1705[1] empowers all Scottish subjects to take, buy and cure herring and white fish in 'all and sundry seas, channells, bays, firths, lochs, rivers, &c' throughout the kingdom and islands, wheresoever such fish are taken, and to have free use of all 'ports, harbours, shoares, fore-lands and others, for bringing in, pickeling, drying, unloading, and loading the same' on payment of ordinary harbour dues.

1 The Fisheries Act 1705 (c 48) was repealed in part by the Statute Law Revision (Scotland) Act 1906 (c 38), Schedule.

120. The White Herring Fisheries Act 1771. The White Herring Fisheries Act 1771 was adopted to encourage the white herring fisheries, but has largely been repealed[1]. The surviving sections provide for persons employed in white herring fisheries to have the free use of all ports, harbours, shores and forelands in Great Britain and the islands belonging to the Crown, for a variety of purposes related to the conduct of the white herring industry. Anyone violating the Act by demanding dues or obstructing the fishermen and others employed in connection with the industry is liable to a penalty[2]. Dues are payable for the use of artificial harbours and piers[3]. Penalties can be prosecuted and determined in Scotland in the Court of Session, half the penalty accruing to the Crown and half to the person suing and prosecuting therefor[4].

1 The Sea Fisheries Act 1868 (c 45), s 71, repealed most of the White Herring Fisheries Act 1771 (c 31).

2 Ibid, s 11.

3 Ibid, s 12.

4 Ibid, s 13; Exchequer Court (Scotland) Act 1856 (c 56), s 1.

121. The Oyster Fisheries (Scotland) Act 1840. Provision for the better protection of oyster fisheries in Scotland is made by the Oyster Fisheries (Scotland) Act 1840. Those wilfully and knowingly taking and carrying away oysters or oyster broods that belong to any person or body corporate or politic, marked out or known as such, are guilty of theft and liable to a prison term of up to one year[1]. Anyone undertaking an illegal use of a dredge or other equipment that drags the ground of an oyster fishery, whether or not oysters or broods are taken, is deemed guilty of attempted theft and is liable to a fine or imprisonment for up to three months[2]. Floating fish within the oyster fishing limits may, however, legitimately be taken[3], and the Act has no effect on any existing rights relating to the fishing[4].

1 Oyster Fisheries (Scotland) Act 1840 (c 74), s 1.

2 Ibid, s 2.

3 Ibid, s 3.

4 Ibid, s 4.

122. The Mussel Fisheries (Scotland) Act 1847. Provision for the protection of mussel fisheries in Scotland is made by the Mussel Fisheries (Scotland) Act 1847 in terms similar to those of the Oyster Fisheries (Scotland) Act 1840[1]. Persons unlawfully taking mussels or mussel broods that are the property of others are deemed guilty of theft and similarly penalised[2]. Persons unlawfully dredging or trespassing in any mussel fishery are deemed guilty of an attempted theft punishable by a fine or up to three months' imprisonment[3]. But there is nothing in the Act of 1847 to prevent persons from exercising any legal rights they may have, including the taking of bait[4], or those lawfully so entitled from fishing for floating fish within the mussel fishery limits[5].

1 As to the Oyster Fisheries (Scotland) Act 1847 (c 74), see para 121 above.
2 Mussel Fisheries (Scotland) Act 1847 (c 92), s 1.
3 Ibid, s 2.
4 Ibid, s 4.
5 Ibid, s 3.

123. The Sea Fisheries Act 1868. The Sea Fisheries Act 1868 has been much amended[1], but it was for many years the basis of the law concerning the regulation of sea fisheries. In its amended form, however, it deals only with the requirement that sea-fishing boats carry official papers[2].

1 The Sea Fisheries Act 1868 (c 45) has been amended, principally by the Sea Fisheries Act 1968 (c 77), s 22(2), Sch 2, Pt I, the Fishery Limits Act 1964 (c 72), s 3(4), Sch 2, and the Sea Fisheries (Shellfish) Act 1967 (c 83), s 24(2), Sch 3. The provisions of the 1868 Act concerning the registry of sea-fishing boats were replaced by those of the Merchant Shipping Act 1894 (c 60), Pt V (ss 369–417), by the Merchant Shipping (Scottish Fishing Boats) Act 1920 (c 39). See now the Merchant Shipping Act 1988 (c 12), Pt II (ss 12–25), and paras 188 ff below.
2 See the Sea Fisheries Act 1868, s 26, and para 196 below.

124. The Sea Fisheries Acts 1883 to 1891. The Sea Fisheries Act 1883 gave effect to the Convention for Regulating the Police of the North Sea Fisheries[1]. The Act has been prospectively repealed with certain savings as to Orders in Council extending the application of the Act in accordance with subsequent conventions, treaties and arrangements with foreign states[2]. The Act, with the Sea Fisheries (Scotland) Amendment Act 1885 (c 70) and Part I of the Fisheries Act 1891 are known collectively as the Sea Fisheries Acts 1883 to 1891[3]. Part I of the 1891 Act put into effect the Declaration respecting the North Sea Fisheries[4]. Parts II and III of the 1891 Act, which amend the law relating to sea fisheries[5] and salmon and freshwater fisheries[6], have been repealed[7]. The remaining provision (which is not included in the collective title) concerns the power to take legal proceedings for enforcing certain provisions relating to salmon and freshwater fisheries[8].

1 Convention for Regulating the Police of the North Sea Fisheries (The Hague, 6 May 1882; 73 BFSP 39), set out in the Sea Fisheries Act 1883 (c 22), Sch 1.
2 Sea Fisheries Act 1968 (c 77), s 22(2), (6), Sch 2, Pt II. The repeal takes effect from a day to be appointed by order under s 23(2).
3 Fisheries Act 1891 (c 37), s 6(3). Part I comprises ss 1–6 (though s 5 has been repealed).
4 Declaration respecting the North Sea Fisheries (Brussels, 2 May 1891; TS 1 (1892); C 6587), set out in the Fisheries Act 1891, Schedule.
5 Ibid, Pt II, comprised ss 7–11. It applied to England and Wales only.
6 Ibid, Pt III, comprised s 12.
7 Salmon and Freshwater Fisheries Act 1923 (c 167), s 93, Sch 5; Sea Fisheries Regulation Act 1966 (c 38), s 21, Schedule, Pt I.
8 Fisheries Act 1891, s 13 (amended by the Sea Fisheries Act 1968, s 22(1), (2), Sch 1, para 31, Sch 2, Pt II).

125. Penalties under the Sea Fisheries Act 1883. The Sea Fisheries Act 1883[1] enables Her Majesty by Order in Council to make, alter and revoke regulations to execute the Act, to further its intent and object, to keep order among sea-fishing boats and to impose fines for breach of such regulations[2]. If any person within British fishery limits[3], or any person belonging to a British sea-fishing boat outside those limits, contravenes specific provisions of the appropriate convention[4] or causes injury to fishing boats or persons belonging thereto or fishes for prohibited oysters, he may be fined or imprisoned for up to three months[5]. A similar penalty, coupled with forfeiture of any instrument used, may be applied if any such person uses an instrument to damage or destroy any fishing implement used by another sea-fishing boat or has on board an instrument dedicated to this purpose[6].

1 As to the prospective repeal of the Sea Fisheries Act 1883 (c 22), see para 124, text and note 2, above.
2 Ibid, s 3. 'Sea-fishing boat' includes every vessel, of whatever size and however propelled, used by any person in sea-fishing or in carrying on the business of a sea-fisherman, 'sea-fishing' means the fishing for every description both of fish and of shellfish found in the relevant seas, and 'sea-fisherman' is to be construed accordingly: ibid, s 28; Fishery Limits Act 1964 (c 72), s 3(2). Similar definitions appear in the Sea Fisheries Act 1868 (c 45), s 5.
3 As to these limits, see the Fishery Limits Act 1976 (c 86), s 1, and para 130 below.
4 Ie the Declaration respecting the North Sea Fisheries (Brussels, 2 May 1891; TS 1 (1892); C 6587), arts 13–22. These provisions concern concealing nationality (art 13), anchoring at night, or using nets etc, where drift-net fishing is going on (arts 14, 17), injuring other boats or interfering with other fishing operations (arts 15, 16), making fast a boat to another fisherman's tackle (art 18), injuring drift-net or long-line fishermen (art 19), cutting fouled nets or lines, and cutting, hooking or lifting up tackle, belonging to different fishermen (arts 20–22). The convention is set out in the Fisheries Act 1891 (c 37), Schedule.
5 Sea Fisheries Act 1883, s 4 (amended by the Fishery Limits Act 1964, s 3(3), (4), Schs 1, 2, and the Fishery Limits Act 1976, s 9(1), Sch 2, para 5).
6 Sea Fisheries Act 1883, s 5 (as so amended).

126. Enforcement of the Sea Fisheries Act 1883 by sea-fishery officers.

The provisions of the Sea Fisheries Act 1883 and of orders made under it may be enforced by sea-fishery officers, either British[1] or foreign[2]. For the purpose of enforcing those provisions, British sea-fishery officers may, inter alia, board any sea-fishing boat[3] within British fishery limits[4] or any British sea-fishing boat beyond those limits, require the production of certificates and other relevant documents, muster the crew, require explanations of the master, examine equipment, seize instruments designed or intended to be used to damage or destroy fishing implements, make examinations and inquiries necessary to detect contraventions or to fix the amount of compensation due for damage etc, and take suspected offenders and the boat and crew concerned to the nearest or most convenient port and detain them there until the alleged contravention has been adjudicated upon[5]. British and foreign sea-fishery officers are given these powers also for enforcing the Convention for Regulating the Police of the North Sea Fisheries of 1882 with respect to British sea-fishing boats or foreign ones to which the Act of 1883 applies[6].

Sea-fishery officers are protected by the Act, and anyone obstructing them in various ways is liable to penalties[7]. The Act also provides for compensation for damage arising out of contraventions[8]. For the purpose of giving jurisdiction to courts, a sea-fishing boat is deemed to be a ship within the meaning of any Act relating to offences committed on board a ship, and every court has jurisdiction over foreign sea-fishing boats within British fishery limits, and persons belonging thereto, as it has over British sea-fishing boats[9]. Summonses and other matters in legal proceedings may be served personally on the person to be served or at his last place of abode or by leaving it for him on board any ship to which he belongs with the person in charge[10]. The master of a sea-fishing boat is deemed to be guilty of any offence against the 1883 Act committed by any person belonging to his boat, and liable for any fine imposed, although certain defences are available to him[11].

Fines or compensation adjudged under the Act may be recovered in the ordinary way or, if the court so orders, by poinding and sale of the boat concerned and of tackle, apparel, furniture and any property on board or, in the case of a foreign sea-fishing boat, by detention in a British port for up to three months[12].

1 British sea-fishery officers include every officer of or appointed by the Secretary of State for Trade and Industry, every commissioned officer of Her Majesty's ships on full pay, every officer authorised in that behalf by the Secretary of State for Defence, every British colonial officer, every Customs and Excise collector and principal officer in any place in the British Islands and every customs officer there authorised in that behalf by the Customs and Excise Commissioners, every coastguard divisional officer and every principal officer of a coastguard station: Sea Fisheries Act 1883 (c 22), s 11(2); Defence (Transfer of Functions) Act 1964 (c 15), s 3(2); Secretary of State for Trade and Industry Order 1970, SI 1970/1537, arts 2(1), 7(4); Secretary of State (New Departments) Order 1974, SI 1974/692; Transfer of Functions (Trade and Industry) Order 1983, SI 1983/1127. As to the prospective repeal of the Sea Fisheries Act 1883, see para 124, text and note 2 above. British sea-fishery officers may also be appointed by the Minister of Agriculture, Fisheries and Food or the Secretary of State under the Sea Fish Industry Act 1951 (c 30), s 25 (prospectively repealed by the Sea Fisheries Act 1968 (c 77), s 22(2), Sch 2, Pt II). As to sea-fishery officers under the 1968 Act and their powers, see ss 7, 8, and paras 171, 172, below.
2 Foreign sea-fishery officers include the commander of any vessel belonging to the government of a foreign state bound by the Convention for Regulating the Police of the North Sea Fisheries (The Hague, 6 May 1882; 73 BFSP 39), set out in the Sea Fisheries Act 1883 (c 22), Sch 1, and any officer appointed by a foreign state for the purpose of enforcing it or otherwise recognised by Her Majesty as a sea-fishery officer of a foreign state: s 11(3).
3 For the meaning of 'sea-fishing boat', see para 125, note 2, above.
4 As to these limits, see the Fishery Limits Act 1976 (c 86), s 1, and para 130 below.
5 Sea Fisheries Act 1883, s 12(1)–(8) (amended by the Fishery Limits Act 1976, s 9(1), Sch 2, para 5).
6 Sea Fisheries Act 1883, s 13.
7 See ibid, s 14. Offences are prosecuted and fines recovered in a summary manner: see s 16(1). As to appeals, see s 16(2).
8 See ibid, s 15.
9 Ibid, s 18 (as amended: see note 5 above).
10 Ibid, s 19.
11 Ibid, s 20(1).
12 Ibid, s 20(2).

127. Enforcement of the Sea Fisheries (Scotland) Amendment Act 1885 by sea-fishery officers. For the purpose of carrying out the provisions of the Sea Fisheries (Scotland) Amendment Act 1885, a British sea-fishery officer may exercise all the powers conferred on him by the appropriate provisions of the Sea Fisheries Act 1968[1] for the purpose of enforcing an order regulating sea fishing operations[2] or the statutory provisions[3] restricting access to British fishery limits[4].

1 Ie by the Sea Fisheries Act 1968 (c 77), s 8: see para 172 below.
2 Ie an order under ibid, s 5: see para 170 below.
3 Ie the Fishery Limits Act 1976 (c 86), s 2: see para 131 below.
4 Sea Fisheries (Scotland) Amendment Act 1885 (c 70), s 10 (amended by the Sea Fisheries Act 1968, s 22(1), Sch 1, para 30, and the Fishery Limits Act 1976, s 2(2)). Further, the Sea Fisheries Act 1968, s 10, applies for the purposes of the 1885 Act as if for any reference to s 8 or s 9 of the 1968 Act there were substituted a reference to the Sea Fisheries (Scotland) Amendment Act 1885, s 10: s 10 of the 1885 Act (amended by the Fishery Limits Act 1976, s 4(4)).

128. The Sea Fishing Boats (Scotland) Act 1886. The Sea Fishing Boats (Scotland) Act 1886 dealt with the division into shares of property in a boat, questions of joint ownership, the purchase and sale of boats, loans on the security of a boat and various aspects of the mortgage of a boat, and applied to all sea-fishing boats as defined in the Sea Fisheries Act 1868[1] and Orders in Council relating to the prosecution of the sea fishing industry in Scotland[2]. 'Boat' here included ropes, sails, oars and other appurtenances required for navigation, but not nets, lines or other fishing gear[3]. The property in the boat was divided into sixteen shares; consequently no more than sixteen people could be registered as the owners of one boat[4]. Up to five persons could be registered as joint owners of a boat or of a share or shares in a boat[5]. Subject to various provisions, registered boats could be made the security for loans under a so-called 'mortgage' instrument[6]. The Act was repealed by the Merchant Shipping Act 1988[7], which makes fresh provision for the 'mortgaging' of fishing boats[8].

1 See the Sea Fisheries Act 1868 (c 45), s 5, and cf para 125, note 2, above.
2 Sea Fishing Boats (Scotland) Act 1886 (c 53), s 2 (repealed).
3 Ibid, s 17 (repealed).
4 Ibid, s 3 (repealed).
5 Ibid, s 4 (repealed).
6 See ibid, ss 6–12, 15 (repealed).
7 Merchant Shipping Act 1988 (c 12), s 57(5), Sch 7.
8 See ibid, s 21, and para 194 below.

129. The North Sea Fisheries Act 1893. The Convention respecting the Liquor Traffic in the North Sea of 1887[1] is implemented by the North Sea Fisheries Act 1893[2]. If a person on board or belonging to a British vessel either:
(1) supplies, by exchange or sale, or
(2) exchanges articles not belonging to him or purchases,
within North Sea limits[3] but outside territorial waters, spirituous liquors[4] to any person on board or belonging to a sea-fishing boat, he is liable to penalties[5]. Unlicensed dealing on board in provisions or articles other than spirits is also penalised[6]. These rules also apply if the vessel does not carry required markings or if licence conditions are contravened[6]. Regulations concerning the necessary licences may be made by Order in Council[7].

1 Convention respecting the Liquor Traffic in the North Sea (The Hague, 16 November 1887; TS 13 (1894); C 7354), with Protocol (The Hague, 14 February 1893; TS 13 (1894); C 7354). The convention, which was concluded between the United Kingdom, Germany, Belgium, France and the Netherlands, and which is set out, with the Protocol, in the North Sea Fisheries Act 1893 (c 17), Schedule, was designed to redress abuses arising from traffic in spirits among North Sea fishermen outside territorial waters.
2 Ibid, s 1.
3 'North Sea limits' is defined in ibid, s 9, by reference to the Convention for Regulating the Police of the North Sea Fisheries (The Hague, 6 May 1882; 73 BFSP 39), art 4, set out in the Sea Fisheries Act 1883 (c 22), Sch 1.
4 'Spirituous liquors' includes every liquid obtained by distillation and containing more than 5 per cent of alcohol: North Sea Fisheries Act 1893, s 8.
5 Ibid, s 2 (exchange or sale), and s 3 (exchange or purchase). In the case of fines, offences and legal proceedings, the Sea Fisheries Act 1883, ss 16, 18–22 (see para 126 above), are applied by the North Sea Fisheries Act 1893, s 7.
6 Ibid, s 4.
7 Ibid, s 5.

(c) Fishery Limits

130. The fishery limits. Fishery limits were first extended beyond the territorial sea (then 3 miles) by the Fishery Limits Act 1964[1] in conjunction with the ratification by the United Kingdom of the 1958 Geneva conventions on the law of the sea[2] and the Fisheries Convention 1964[3]. The base points from which the new limits were to be measured were laid down by Order in Council[4]. These placed many baselines on the north-west coast of Scotland a considerable distance from the natural coastline. The limit of the British territorial sea was subsequently extended from 3 to 12 nautical miles[5].

The Fishery Limits Act 1976, which also amended a number of earlier Acts, extended the fishery limits to 200 miles[6], following the agreement of the Council of Ministers of the European Community to concert the extension by member states bordering the Atlantic Ocean of their fishery limits. The British limits are measured from the baseline from which the breadth of the territorial sea adjacent to the United Kingdom, the Channel Islands and the Isle of Man is measured[7]. Her Majesty may by Order in Council adjust these limits in order to implement any international agreement or international arbitral award, or otherwise[8]. The limits extend to the median line[9] where that line is less than 200 miles from the baseline and no other line has been specified by Order in Council[10].

1 The Fishery Limits Act 1964 (c 72), s 1, established 12-mile fishery limits, and 6-mile exclusive fishery limits, beyond the territorial sea. The Act was effectively repealed by various subsequent Acts, the most important of which is the Fishery Limits Act 1976 (c 86). For an exception to the repeal, see para 80, note 3, above.
2 As to these conventions, see para 70 above.
3 Fisheries Convention (London, 9 March 1964; TS 35 (1966); Cmnd 3011): see para 81 above.
4 See para 78 above.
5 Territorial Sea Act 1987 (c 49), s 1.
6 Fishery Limits Act 1976 (c 86), s 1(1). References in other extant enactments to British fishery limits are adjusted by s 1(5), read with s 10(2)(b).
7 Ibid, s 1(1).
8 Ibid, s 1(2).
9 'Median line' means a line every point of which is equidistant from the nearest points of (1) the baselines referred to above and (2) the corresponding baselines of other countries: ibid, s 1(4).
10 Ibid, s 1(3).

131. Access to British fisheries. Access by foreign fishing boats[1] to fisheries within British fishery limits is (subject to the requirements of the European Community Common Fisheries Policy) governed by order made by the ministers[2] by statutory instrument designating not only the country concerned whose registered boats may fish therein but also the areas within those limits in which and the species for which they may fish[3]. These are subject to change, according to the current Common Fisheries Policy and agreements concluded by the Community with third states.

A fishing boat registered in a designated country must not fish, or attempt to fish, for any other species or in any other area than that specified in the order, and must stow its gear when in an area in which it is prohibited from fishing[4]. No other foreign fishing boat may enter British fishery limits except for purposes recognised by international law (which might include distress or *force majeure*) or in treaties in force between the United Kingdom and the flag state of the vessel concerned[5].

Fishing for the purpose of scientific research under arrangements made between the flag state of the vessel concerned and the United Kingdom government is exempted from these restrictions[6].

1 'Fishing boat' means any vessel employed in fishing operations or any operations ancillary thereto; and 'foreign fishing boat' means a fishing boat which is not (1) registered in the United Kingdom, the Channel Islands or the Isle of Man; or (2) excluded from registration by regulations under the Merchant Shipping Act 1988 (c 12), s 13 (see para 188 below); or (3) owned wholly by one or more qualified persons or companies within the meaning of s 14 (see para 189, note 1, below): Fishery Limits Act 1976 (c 86), s 8 (amended by the Merchant Shipping Act 1988, s 57(4), Sch 6).
2 'The ministers' means the Minister of Agriculture, Fisheries and Food and the Secretaries of State concerned with sea fishing in Scotland and Northern Ireland respectively: Fishery Limits Act 1976, s 8.
3 Ibid, s 2(1). See eg the Fishing Boats (European Economic Community) Designation Order 1983, SI 1983/253 (amended by SI 1986/382), which designates the several member states of the

Community and specifies the areas in which their fishing boats may fish and the descriptions of sea fish for which those boats may fish.

4 Fishery Limits Act 1976, s 2(3), (4).
5 Ibid, s 2(2).
6 Ibid, s 2(6).

132. Penalties for unlawful access. The master of a vessel offending against the restrictions on access to British fisheries is liable on summary conviction to a fine not exceeding £350,000 or on conviction on indictment to a fine[1]. The court convicting him may order forfeiture of fish and fishing gear and, where the contravention takes place in Scotland, any such fish or fishing gear may be destroyed or disposed of as the court thinks fit[2]. Proceedings may be taken, and the offence may for all incidental purposes be treated as having been committed, in any place in the United Kingdom[3].

1 Fishery Limits Act 1976 (c 86), s 2(5)(a).
2 Ibid, s 2(5)(b), (c).
3 Sea Fisheries Act 1968 (c 77), s 14 (amended by the Fishery Limits Act 1976, s 2(8)).

(d) Inshore Fisheries

(A) ENGLAND AND WALES

133. Introduction. Inshore fisheries are dealt with differently in Scotland and in England and Wales. In England and Wales local authorities exercise some control through local districts and with local fisheries committees under the Sea Fisheries Regulation Act 1966, which is one of the most important Acts concerning sea fisheries. It does not extend to Scotland[1]. It consolidated with corrections and improvements various earlier enactments relating to England and Wales only. It provided that the Minister of Agriculture, Fisheries and Food can, on application by a county council, create by revokable or variable order sea fisheries districts in England and Wales comprising any part of the sea within the 'national or territorial waters'[2] of the United Kingdom adjacent to England and Wales, with or without any part of the adjoining coast; define the limits of the districts and the areas chargeable with expenses under the Act; and constitute local fisheries committees for the regulation of the sea fisheries carried on within the districts[3], the constitution[4] and powers of which are prescribed. The local committees can, subject to certain restrictions[5] and to any regulations the minister may issue and to confirmation by him, make byelaws restricting or prohibiting fishing for all or specified kinds of sea fish for any specified period, or methods of fishing or use of fishing instruments or for determining the size of mesh or form and dimensions of such instruments[6]. They can also make byelaws to prohibit or regulate the deposit or discharge of solid or liquid substances detrimental to sea fish or fishing and to regulate, protect and develop shell fisheries[6]. Such byelaws may be applicable in all or part of a district[7], subject to certain restrictions preserving any effects on rights of several fisheries to the seashore and preserving byelaws of water authorities and powers of local authorities to discharge sewage[8]. The byelaws can be enforced by fishery officers appointed by the committee, though this does not affect the duties of British sea-fishery officers to enforce the laws affecting vessels engaged in sea fishing[9]. Fishery officers have all the powers of constables, and may stop and search vessels and vehicles, examine fishing gear and containers used in carrying fish and seize sea fish and gear[10]. Obstructing fishery officers and contravening byelaws are offences[11].

1 Sea Fisheries Regulation Act 1966 (c 38), s 22(2).
2 The distinction between national and territorial waters is not explained but the phrase is
   presumably intended to include internal waters landward of the baselines of the territorial sea.
3 Sea Fisheries Regulation Act 1966, s 1.
4 Ibid, s 2 (amended by the Water Act 1989 (c 15), s 141(5), Sch 17, para 5(2)).
5 Sea Fisheries Regulation Act 1966, s 6.
6 Ibid, s 5(1) (amended by the Sea Fisheries (Shellfish) Act 1967 (c 83), s 24(1), Sch 2, and prospectively amended by the Control of Pollution Act 1974 (c 40), s 108(2), Sch 4).
7 Sea Fisheries Regulation Act 1966, s 5(2).
8 Ibid, s 6.
9 Ibid, s 10(1).
10 Ibid, s 10(2), (3).
11 Ibid, s 11.

134. Powers of local fisheries committees. Local fisheries committees in
England and Wales may make byelaws and appoint fishery officers[1], stock or
restock public fisheries for shellfish[2], with ministerial approval destroy preda-
tory fish, marine animals and birds and their eggs[3], contribute to certain
harbour expenses[4], and enforce within their districts any Act relating to sea
fisheries[5]. They are required to collect statistics and make returns to the Minister
of Agriculture, Fisheries and Food[6].

1 See para 133 above.
2 Sea Fisheries Regulation Act 1966 (c 38), s 13(1).
3 Ibid, s 13(2).
4 Ibid, s 13(3), (4).
5 Ibid, s 13(5) (amended by the Sea Fisheries Act 1968 (c 77), s 22(1), (2), Sch 1, para 37, Sch 2,
   Pt II).
6 Sea Fisheries Regulation Act 1966, s 14.

(B) SCOTLAND

135. The Inshore Fishing (Scotland) Act 1984. The Secretary of State for
Scotland is given wide general powers to regulate inshore fishing under the
Inshore Fishing (Scotland) Act 1984, which repealed in whole or in part previous Acts that had regulated Scottish inshore fishing ad hoc since the eighteenth
century, and made fresh provision for the regulation of inshore fishing and for
connected purposes. It was enacted partly to implement the European Community Common Fisheries Policy and partly to deal with conflict between those
fishermen that used static and those that used mobile gear following the decision
in *Aitchison v Taylor* that it was lawful to engage in mid-water pelagic trawling
within 3 miles of the Scottish coast[1]. 'Scottish inshore waters' are defined in the
Act as the sea adjacent to the coast of Scotland and to the landward of a limit of
6 miles from the baseline from which the breadth of the territorial sea is
measured, up to the mean high-water mark of ordinary spring tides[2]. The miles
referred to are nautical miles of 1,852 metres, and 'sea fish' means fish of any
kind found in the sea, including shellfish, salmon and migratory trout[2]. For the
purpose of the Act 'fishing boat' means any vessel which is for the time being
employed in sea fishing, and 'British fishing boat' means a fishing boat registered in the United Kingdom, excluded[3] from registration or wholly owned by
a person who is qualified to own a British ship[4].

1 *Aitchison v Taylor* 1980 SLT (Sh Ct) 8.
2 Inshore Fishing (Scotland) Act 1984 (c 26), s 9(1).
3 Ie by regulations under the Merchant Shipping Act 1988 (c 12), s 13.
4 Inshore Fishing (Scotland) Act 1984, s 9(1) (amended by the Merchant Shipping Act 1988,
   s 57(4), Sch 6).

136. Prohibition of sea fishing in specified areas. After consulting such bodies as he considers appropriate, the Secretary of State may make orders by statutory instrument, subject to annulment in pursuance of a resolution of either House of Parliament[1], regulating fishing for sea fish in any specified area within Scottish inshore waters[2]. Such an order may, within the specified waters, prohibit all or any of the following: (1) all fishing for sea fish, (2) fishing for a specified description of sea fish, (3) fishing by a specified method, and (4) fishing from a specified description of fishing boat; and may specify the periods during which any prohibition is to apply and make exceptions to any prohibition[3]. Contravention of an order is an offence[4]. The first comprehensive order was made under the Inshore Fishing (Scotland) Act 1984 on its entry into force: it designated twenty-three sea areas, generally known as 'static gear reserves', within which it is now prohibited to fish for sea fish with mobile gear during specified periods with an exception for fishing for sea fish for the purpose of scientific research[5].

1 Inshore Fishing (Scotland) Act 1984 (c 26), s 9(2).
2 Ibid, s 1(1). For the meaning of 'sea fish' and 'Scottish inshore waters', see para 135 above.
3 Ibid, s 1(2). For the meaning of 'fishing boat', see para 135 above.
4 Ibid, s 4(1). For penalties etc, see para 140 below.
5 Inshore Fishing (Prohibition of Fishing and Fishing Methods) (Scotland) Order 1989, SI 1989/2307. See also the Inshore Fishing (Salmon and Migratory Trout) (Prohibition of Gill Nets) (Scotland) Order 1986, SI 1986/59.

137. Discarding of illegally caught fish. If an order[1] is in force in an area and, incidental to lawful fishing operations, prohibited species are caught or fish are caught by a method prohibited for that species, such fish must, unless it is provided otherwise in the order, be returned to the sea forthwith[2]. This requirement has provoked controversy and criticism on the grounds that good marketable fish are thus wasted, but the need for effective enforcement was regarded by the government as overriding this disadvantage. Contravention is an offence[3].

1 Ie an order under the Inshore Fishing (Scotland) Act 1984 (c 26), s 1(2)(b) or (c): see para 136, heads (2) and (3), above.
2 Ibid, s 1(3).
3 Ibid, s 4(1). For penalties etc, see para 140 below.

138. Prohibitions concerning nets. After consultation with such bodies as he considers appropriate, the Secretary of State for Scotland may make orders by statutory instrument, subject to annulment in pursuance of a resolution of either House of Parliament[1], prohibiting the carriage, for any purpose, in any British fishing boat in any specified sea area of Scottish inshore waters of any specified type of net[2]. Contravention of such an order is an offence[3].

1 Inshore Fishing (Scotland) Act 1984 (c 26), s 9(2).
2 Ibid, s 2. For the meaning of 'British fishing boat' and 'Scottish inshore waters', see para 135 above. For an order, see the Inshore Fishing (Prohibition of Carriage of Monofilament Gill Nets) (Scotland) Order 1986, SI 1986/60, but as to this order see para 12 above.
3 Inshore Fishing (Scotland) Act 1984, s 4(1). For penalties etc, see para 140 below.

139. Prohibition of fishing near salmon nets. No person may fish by means of a trawl, seine or other gear designed for fishing from a moving vessel within half a mile of any fixed salmon net[1]. Contravention is an offence[2].

1 Inshore Fishing (Scotland) Act 1984 (c 26), s 3.
2 Ibid, s 4(1). For penalties etc, see para 140 below.

140. Offences and penalties. It is an offence for any person to contravene an order prohibiting sea fishing in inshore waters or the carriage of specified types of net there, or to fail to discard fish wrongfully taken there, or to use certain fishing gear near a fixed salmon net[1], and where a fishing boat is used in the commission of such an offence the master, owner and charterer are each guilty of the offence[2]. A person guilty of such an offence is liable on summary conviction to a fine not exceeding £5,000 or, on conviction on indictment, to a fine[3]. Proceedings may be taken in any sheriff court, and the offence may be dealt with by the sheriff in every respect as if the offence had been committed wholly within his jurisdiction[4]. In addition to fining an offender the court may order the forfeiture of fish (or impose an additional fine not exceeding its value) and the forfeiture of any net or other fishing gear used in the commission of the offence, and forfeited fish and gear are to be disposed of as the court may direct[5].

1 See paras 136 ff above.
2 Inshore Fishing (Scotland) Act 1984 (c 26), s 4(1). 'Master' includes the person for the time being in command or charge of the boat, s 9(1).
3 Ibid, s 4(2). As to the recovery of fines, see s 8(2). As to offences by bodies corporate, see s 8(1), and para 143 below.
4 Ibid, s 4(3).
5 Ibid, s 4(4).

141. Powers of sea-fishery officers. Extensive powers are exercisable under the Inshore Fishing (Scotland) Act 1984 by British sea-fishery officers in relation to British fishing boats within British fishery limits[1]. Any such officer may board any such boat, with or without persons assigned to assist him, and may require the boat to stop and do anything to facilitate the boarding of the boat[2]. He may require the attendance of the master and any other persons on board a boat which he has boarded and may make any examination and inquiry which appears necessary[3]. In particular, he may examine fish and equipment on board, require the production of relevant documents, search the boat if necessary and seize and detain documents for production in evidence if he has reason to suspect that an offence has been committed, though no document required by law to be carried on board may be seized and detained except while the boat itself is detained in port[4]. If an offence appears to have been committed, the officer may require the master to take (or himself may take) the boat to port and, under written notice, detain it[5]. He may seize the offending fish, nets and gear[6], at any reasonable time enter premises used for carrying on business related to fishing boats or their activities or ancillary thereto, and require persons on the premises to produce relevant documents, and if the officer suspects that an offence has been committed he may even search the premises for documents, require the assistance of those there in order so to do and seize and detain documents for evidence[7]. Those obstructing or assaulting the officer in various specified ways are guilty of an offence and liable on summary conviction to a fine not exceeding £5,000 or, on conviction on indictment, to a fine[8].

1 Inshore Fishing (Scotland) Act 1984 (c 26), s 5(1). For the meaning of 'British fishing boat', see para 135 above, and as to British fishery limits, see para 130 above. As to sea-fishery officers, see para 171 below.
2 Ibid, s 5(2).
3 Ibid, s 5(3). For the meaning of 'master', see para 140, note 2, above.
4 Ibid, s 5(4).
5 Ibid, s 5(5).
6 Ibid, s 5(6).
7 Ibid, s 5(7).
8 Ibid, s 6.

142. Powers of water bailiffs and others. If an order under the Inland Fishing (Scotland) Act 1984[1] prohibits or restricts fishing for salmon or

migratory trout in waters which form part of the district of a district salmon
fishery board², any water bailiff, constable or other appointed person³ may
exercise appropriate powers⁴ in relation to a contravention of such an order⁵.

1 Ie an order under the Inland Fishing (Scotland) Act 1984 (c 26), s 1: see para 136 above.
2 As to such districts and boards, see paras 33, 35, above.
3 Ie a person appointed by the Secretary of State under the Salmon and Freshwater Fisheries
  (Protection) (Scotland) Act 1951 (c 26), s 10(5): see para 24, note 4, above. As to water bailiffs, see
  para 24, note 3, above.
4 Ie powers of search and seizure under ibid, ss 11, 12 (see paras 26, 28, above), and ss 10(1)(d), 20
  (see paras 22, 27, above) so far as they relate to the seizure of fish and gear liable to forfeiture or
  the disposal of fish.
5 Inshore Fishing (Scotland) Act 1984, s 7(1), (2).

143. Offences by bodies corporate. Where an offence under the Inshore
Fishing (Scotland) Act 1984 is committed by a body corporate with the consent
or approval of any director or other officer of the body corporate, he, as well as
the body corporate, is guilty of the offence¹.

1 Inshore Fishing (Scotland) Act 1984 (c 26), s 8(1).

(e) Conservation of Sea Fish

144. The Sea Fish (Conservation) Act 1967. Although many other Acts
contribute in various ways to conservation, the important Sea Fish Conservation Act 1967 consolidated, with corrections and improvements, various
enactments dating back to 1933¹ providing for the regulation of the commercial
use of, and the fishing for and landing of, sea fish, and for authorising measures
for the increase or improvement of marine resources². 'Sea fish' here means fish,
whether fresh or cured, of any kind found in the sea, including shellfish, and any
parts of such fish, but (except in certain provisions of the Act³) does not include
salmon or migratory trout⁴. The Act prescribes size limits for sea fish and
minimum net sizes⁵, provides for the licensing of fishing boats⁶, regulates the
trans-shipment of fish from vessel to vessel⁷, restricts fishing in certain areas⁸
and the landing of foreign-caught fish⁹, makes provision for the implementation of internationally agreed measures for conserving marine resources¹⁰,
and gives the appropriate minister power to regulate sea fishing for salmon and
migratory trout¹¹.

1 Ie the Sea-Fishing Industry Act 1933 (c 45) (repealed).
2 Sea Fish (Conservation) Act 1967 (c 84), long title.
3 Ie except in ibid, ss 4, 4A, 5–7, 9.
4 Ibid, s 22(1) (amended by the Fisheries Act 1981 (c 29), s 21(2)(c)).
5 See ibid, ss 1–3, and paras 145, 146, below.
6 See ibid, s 4, and para 195 below.
7 See ibid, s 4A (added by the Fisheries Act 1981, s 21(1)), and para 147 below.
8 See the Sea Fish (Conservation) Act 1967, s 5, and para 148 below.
9 See ibid, ss 6–8, and paras 149, 150, below.
10 See ibid, s 10, and para 151 below.
11 See ibid, s 18 (amended by the Salmon and Freshwater Fisheries Act 1975 (c 51), ss 42(2), 43(2),
  the Fishery Limits Act 1976 (c 86), s 9(1), Sch 2, para 16, and the Water Act 1989 (c 15), s 141(5),
  Sch 17, para 6). This power may be used eg to implement measures agreed by the North Atlantic
  Salmon Conservation Organisation.

145. Size limits for fish. No one may, in Great Britain, land, sell, expose or
offer for sale, or possess for that purpose sea fish smaller in size than that

prescribed by ministerial order[1], and contravention is an offence[2]. The size for landing may differ from that prescribed for other purposes[3]. Landing even part of a fish smaller than the size prescribed contravenes the order[4]. Undersized fish must not be carried on a British fishing boat inside or outside British fishery limits[5], and the master, owner and charterer are liable for this offence[6]. Foreign boats are subject to similar prohibitions within British fishery limits[7]. Any order under these provisions may confer exemptions[8].

Though officers authorised so to do by the appropriate minister may grant exemptions in this respect[9], it is an offence for anyone to possess undersized fish for purposes of processing or otherwise putting them to business use[10].

1 Sea Fish (Conservation) Act 1967 (c 84), s 1(1), (2) (substituted by the Fisheries Act 1981 (c 29), s 19(1)). The restriction on landing undersized fish is subject to an exception for fish landed for the purpose of scientific investigation: Sea Fish (Conservation) Act 1967, s 9(1) (amended by the Fisheries Act 1981, s 19(2)). The fish sizes prescribed change from time to time according to the requirements of the Common Fisheries Policy. The orders are thus frequently varied. For an example of an order, see the Undersized Crabs Order 1986, SI 1986/497 (varied by SI 1989/2443), which prescribes the minimum size for the edible crab (*Cancer pagurus*) of each sex which may be landed in various areas of the coast of Great Britain. For Scotland the minimum is 115 mm, measured across the broadest part of the back. The order also lays down a minimum size of 115 mm for the sale of edible crabs and their carriage on a British fishing boat. Similar provision for velvet crabs (*Liocarcinus puber*) is made by the Undersized Velvet Crabs Order 1989, SI 1989/919, under which the minimum size is 65 mm. For the meaning of 'sea fish', see para 144 above.
2 Sea Fish (Conservation) Act 1967, s 1(8) (as so substituted). For penalties, see para 152 below.
3 Ibid, s 1(4) (as so substituted).
4 See ibid, s 1(5) (as so substituted).
5 See ibid, s 1(3) (as so substituted): contravention is deemed to be an offence under s 1(1). 'Fishing boat' means a vessel of whatever size and in whatever way propelled which is for the time being employed in sea fishing or the sea fishing service: s 22(1). 'British fishing boat' means a fishing boat registered in the United Kingdom, excluded from registration by regulations under the Merchant Shipping Act 1988 (c 12), s 13 (see para 188 below), or wholly owned by a person who is qualified to own a British ship: Sea Fish (Conservation) Act 1967, s 1(9) (as so substituted; and amended by the Merchant Shipping Act 1988, s 57(4), Sch 6). For exceptions from the Sea Fish (Conservation) Act 1967, s 1(3), relating to scientific investigation and the transplanting of sea fish from one fishing ground to another, see s 9(2).
6 Ibid, s 1(8) (as so substituted). 'Master' includes the person in command or charge of the vessel: s 22(1).
7 In the case of a foreign fishing boat only the master is liable: ibid, s 1(8) (as so substituted).
8 Ibid, s 1(6) (as so substituted).
9 Ibid, s 2(3).
10 Ibid, s 2(1), (2), (4) (amended by the Fisheries Act 1981, ss 19(2)(a), 46(6)). For penalties, see para 152 below.

146. Regulation of fishing for sea fish. The ministers[1] may make orders requiring that nets and other fishing gear carried in British fishing boats registered in the United Kingdom comply with specific requirements for size, design, material and construction and the mesh size of nets; such orders may be limited to specified descriptions of fish or methods of fishing or specified areas or periods[2]. Orders may extend to foreign boats within the British fishery limits or to unregistered boats[3]. Methods of measuring nets and the manner of using gear may be prescribed as well as measures to avoid evasion of the requirements, but exceptions may be made[4]. Contravention of an order is an offence, for which masters, owners and charterers are liable[5].

1 'The ministers' means the Minister of Agriculture, Fisheries and Food and the Secretaries of State concerned with the sea fishing industry in Scotland, Wales and Northern Ireland, acting in conjunction: Sea Fish (Conservation) Act 1967 (c 84), s 22(2), (3).
2 Ibid, s 3(1). For the meaning of 'British fishing boat', see para 145, note 5, above. For exceptions relating to scientific investigation and the transplanting of sea fish from one fishing ground to another, see s 9(2).

3 Ibid, s 3(2).
4 Ibid, s 3(3), (4).
5 Ibid, s 3(5). For penalties, see para 152 below.

147. Prohibition on trans-shipment of fish. The ministers may by order provide that within British fishery limits or in any specified area within those limits the receiving by any vessel (whether British or foreign) of fish trans-shipped from any other vessel is prohibited unless authorised by a licence granted by one of the ministers[1]. Such an order, which may provide for exceptions, may apply to the receiving of fish generally or the receiving of a specified description of fish, or fish caught by a specified method or in a specified area or caught or trans-shipped during a specified season or caught or trans-shipped by vessels of a specified description or registered in a specified country[2]. The use of a vessel in contravention of such an order is an offence for which the master, owner and charterer are each liable[3].

A licence may be granted to the owner or charterer in respect of a named vessel and may authorise the receiving of fish generally or may confer limited authority by reference to area, period, description and quantities of fish and description of fishing vessel and method of fishing[4], and may authorise the receiving of fish either unconditionally or conditionally[5]. A charge may be made for a licence[6]. The minister granting the licence may require statistical information to be provided to him[7]. The furnishing of false information in response to such a requirement or for the purpose of obtaining a licence is an offence[8]. This licensing power may be exercised so as to limit the number of vessels or of any description of vessel (including vessels registered in a specified country) engaged in receiving fish to such an extent as appears to the ministers necessary or expedient for the regulation of trans-shipment[9].

1 Sea Fish (Conservation) Act 1967 (c 84), s 4A(1) (added by the Fisheries Act 1981 (c 29), s 21(1)). For the meaning of 'the ministers', see para 146, note 1, above, and as to British fishery limits, see para 130 above. For exceptions relating to scientific investigation and the transplanting of sea fish from one fishing ground to another, see the Sea Fish (Conservation) Act 1967, s 9(4), (5).
2 Ibid, s 4A(2) (as so added).
3 Ibid, s 4A(3) (as so added). For penalties, see para 152 below.
4 Ibid, s 4A(5) (as so added). As to the variation, revocation and suspension of licences, see s 4A(10), (11) (as so added). The ministers may delegate their licensing powers: see s 4A(12) (as so added).
5 Ibid, s 4A(6) (as so added). Breach of a condition is an offence for which the master, owner and charterer are each liable: s 4A(6).
6 Ibid, s 4A(4) (as so added).
7 Ibid, s 4A(7) (as so added).
8 Ibid, s 4A(8) (as so added).
9 Ibid, s 4A(9) (as so added).

148. Restriction on fishing for sea fish. The ministers may by order prohibit in any area for a specified or unlimited period all fishing for sea fish[1], or fishing for specified descriptions of sea fish, or fishing by any specified method, by any fishing boat to which the order applies, and if a fishing boat is used in contravention of such an order the master, owner and charterer are each liable for an offence[2]. An order may make different provision in relation to fishing boats of different descriptions[3]. Sea fish taken by a vessel to which an order applies in contravention of the order must be returned to the sea forthwith unless the order otherwise provides[4], though there is an exemption where the fishing operations are conducted for the purpose of scientific investigation or of transplanting fish from one fishing ground to another[5]. Failure to do so is an offence for which the master, owner and charterer are each liable[6].

The prohibitions under such orders relating to areas outside British fishery limits may apply only to British fishing boats registered in the United Kingdom or, in relation to salmon or migratory trout, to British owned and British registered fishing boats, but orders relating to areas within those limits may apply to any fishing boat[7].

1 For the meaning of 'sea fish', which here includes salmon and migratory trout, see para 144 above.
2 Sea Fish (Conservation) Act 1967 (c 84), s 5(1) (substituted by the Fisheries Act 1981 (c 29), s 22(1)). For penalties, see para 152 below. For the meaning of 'fishing boat', see para 145, note 5, above. For examples of orders, which are frequently changed and which often apply for only a limited period, see the Sole (Irish Sea and Sole Bank) (Prohibition of Fishing) Order 1986, SI 1986/1936, the Sole (Specified Sea Areas) (Prohibition of Fishing) Order 1988, SI 1988/1264, the Plaice (Prohibition of Fishing) Order 1988, SI 1988/2197, the Haddock (Specified Sea Areas) (Prohibition of Fishing) Order 1989, SI 1989/2096, the Mackerel (Specified Sea Areas) (Prohibition of Fishing) Order 1989, SI 1989/2447, and the Anglerfish (Specified Sea Areas) (Prohibition of Fishing) Order 1989, SI 1989/2449.
3 Sea Fish (Conservation) Act 1967, s 5(2) (as so substituted).
4 Ibid, s 5(6) (amended by the Fisheries Act 1981, s 22(2)).
5 See the Sea Fish (Conservation) Act 1967, s 9(3)–(5).
6 Ibid, s 5(6), (7).
7 Ibid, s 5(8) (substituted by the Fisheries Act 1981, s 22(3)).

149. Prohibition on landing or trans-shipment of sea fish. After consultation with the Secretary of State for Trade and Industry the ministers may by order prohibit the landing in the United Kingdom of sea fish, or any particular description of sea fish, caught in such waters as are specified in the order[1]. An order may similarly be made prohibiting the trans-shipment of such fish within British fishery limits[2].

Any prohibition, which may be subject to exceptions specified in the order[3], may be for a specified or unlimited period and may be subject to any or all, or be free of any or all, specified limitations whereby the prohibition has effect, in relation to sea fish generally or those of a particular description, as to their condition or the method by which or times at which they are caught[4]. If fish are landed or trans-shipped from or into a vessel in contravention of such an order, the master, owner and charterer are each guilty of an offence[5].

A British sea-fishery officer may require masters, inter alia, on written notice to make written declarations on each occasion when sea fish are about to be landed in the United Kingdom that those fish are not subject to such a prohibition order[6]. The notice expires six months after the date of service[7]. A British sea-fishery officer may also require a similar written declaration from masters where sea fish are brought to land in the United Kingdom in respect of any fish which have been, are being or are about to be landed[8], and similar declarations may be required in respect of trans-shipments[9]. The making of a false declaration is an offence[9].

1 Sea Fish (Conservation) Act 1967 (c 84), s 6(1). For the meaning of 'the ministers', see para 146, note 1, above, and for the meaning of 'sea fish', which here includes salmon and migratory trout (s 6(6)), see para 144 above. For exceptions relating to scientific investigation and the transplanting of sea fish from one fishing ground to another, see s 9(4), (5). For an example of an order, see the Sea Fishing (Specified Western Waters) (Restrictions on Landing) Order 1987, SI 1987/1566, which prohibits, subject to some exceptions, the landing in the United Kingdom from British fishing boats (including boats registered in the Isle of Man or the Channel Islands) of specified sea fish caught in ICES sub-areas VII or VIII.
2 Sea Fish (Conservation) Act 1967, s 6(1A) (added by the Fisheries Act 1981 (c 29), s 23).
3 Sea Fish (Conservation) Act 1967, s 6(3).
4 Ibid, s 6(2).
5 Ibid, s 6(5) and s 6(5A) (as added: see note 2 above). For penalties, see para 152 below.
6 Ibid, s 7(1) (amended by the Fisheries Act 1981, s 23). As to service of the notice, see the Sea Fish (Conservation) Act 1967, s 7(4) (as so amended).
7 Ibid, s 7(1) proviso.

8 Ibid, s 7(2) (as amended: see note 6 above).
9 See ibid, s 7(2A), (2B) (as added: see note 2 above).
10 Ibid, s 7(3) (as amended: see note 6 above). For penalties, see para 152 below.

150. Regulation of landing of foreign-caught sea fish. The Secretary of State for Trade and Industry, after consultation with the ministers[1], may by order regulate the landing in the United Kingdom of sea fish which have neither been taken by British fishing boats registered in the United Kingdom, the Isle of Man or the Channel Islands, nor brought to land in the United Kingdom without having been previously landed outside it, on certain terms and conditions relating to descriptions and quantities of fish[2], taking into account the interest of consumers and the effect the regulation is likely to have on commercial relations between the United Kingdom and other countries[3]. Such orders must not conflict with treaties in force between the United Kingdom and other countries[3].

1 For the meaning of 'the ministers', see para 146, note 1, above.
2 Sea Fish (Conservation) Act 1967 (c 84), s 8(1). For exceptions relating to scientific investigation and the transplanting of sea fish from one fishing ground to another, see s 9(4), (5). For the meaning of 'sea fish', see para 144 above, and for the meaning of 'fishing boat', see para 145, note 5, above.
3 Ibid, s 8(4).

151. Measures for increase or improvement of marine resources. A very general provision of the Sea Fish (Conservation) Act 1967 allows the ministers[1] to take or assist in taking such measures for the increase or improvement of marine resources as may be required for giving effect to any convention for the time being in force between the United Kingdom and any other country[2]. This allows, for example, implementation not only of the EEC Treaty but of measures relating to the North-East Atlantic Fisheries Commission, the Northwest Atlantic Fisheries Organisation and the North Atlantic Salmon Conservation Organisation and measures under any other relevant treaties to which the United Kingdom has become a party and which are in force for it.

1 For the meaning of 'the ministers', see para 146, note 1, above.
2 Sea Fish (Conservation) Act 1967 (c 84), s 10.

152. Penalties. Penalties for offences under the Sea Fish (Conservation) Act 1967, as amended by the Fisheries Act 1981, are more severe than in the past, ranging from fines on summary conviction for some offences of up to £1,000[1] and for others of up to £5,000[2] or up to £50,000[3] or, on conviction on indictment (in any case), to unlimited fines[4]. For certain offences the court may order the forfeiture of fish in respect of which the offence was committed[5] or of the net or other fishing gear involved[6], or of the fish, net and gear[7], or may order that the owner or charterer of the fishing boat used to commit the offence, or of the vessel named in the licence whose condition is broken, be disqualified for a period from holding a licence for that boat[8]. A person guilty of certain offences[9] is liable on summary conviction to a fine not exceeding the value of the fish involved[10] in addition to any other penalty (pecuniary or otherwise), save that the court may not order both the forfeiture of the fish and this supplementary fine[11].

1 This applies to offences under the Sea Fish (Conservation) Act 1967 (c 84), ss 4(3), 4A(3), 5(1), 6(5A)(a): see paras 147–149, above, and para 195 below.
2 This applies to offences under ibid, ss 3, 4(6), (9A), 4A(6), 5(6): see paras 146–148 above, and para 195 below.

3 This applies to offences under ibid, ss 1, 2, 4(7), (7A), 4A(7), (8), 6(5), (5A)(b), 7(3): see paras 145, 147, 149, above, and para 195 below.
4 Ibid, s 11(1) (substituted by the Fisheries Act 1981 (c 29), s 24(1)).
5 This applies to offences under the Sea Fish (Conservation) Act, s 1 (size limits of fish).
6 This applies to offences under ibid, s 3 (breach of order regulating nets and other fishing gear).
7 This applies to offences under ibid, ss 4(3), (6), (9A) (breach of rules concerning licensing of fishing boats), s 5(1), (6) (breach of prohibition on fishing for specified fish in specified areas and failure to return such fish to the sea), and s 6(5), (5A)(b) (landing or trans-shipping fish caught in prohibited areas).
8 Ibid, s 11(2) (as so substituted). This applies to offences under ss 4(3), (6), (9A) (see note 7 above), and s 4A(3), (6) (breaches of rules as to trans-shipment of fish).
9 This applies to offences under ss 1, 3, 4(3), (6), (9A), 4A(3), (6), 5(1), (6), 6.
10 Ibid, s 11(3) (as substituted: see note 4 above).
11 Ibid, s 11(4), (5).

153. Offences by bodies corporate. If any of certain offences under the Sea Fish (Conservation) Act 1967 is committed by a body corporate, any director, manager, secretary or other officer of the body corporate with whose consent or approval the offence was committed is (as well as the body corporate) deemed guilty and may be prosecuted and punished accordingly[1].

1 Sea Fish (Conservation) Act 1967 (c 84), s 12 (amended by the Fisheries Act 1981 (c 29), ss 19(2)(c), 28), which applies to offences under the Sea Fisheries (Conservation) Act 1967, ss 1(1)–(3), 3, 4, 4A, 5 and 6.

154. Enforcement. British sea-fishery officers are given various enforcement powers under the Sea Fish (Conservation) Act 1967. They may seize fish, nets or other fishing gear in respect of which offences or contraventions of orders or prohibitions have been committed[1], may enter business premises and require the production of, search for, copy, and seize and detain, relevant documents[2], and may board vessels used for trans-shipment, require the production of, or search for, and copy, relevant documents, inspect fish and equipment on board and observe any trans-shipment of sea fish into the vessel[3]. Further, they may exercise in relation to fishing boats in any waters adjacent to the United Kingdom and within British fishery limits, and in relation to British fishing boats registered in the United Kingdom and any British-owned fishing boat (not so registered) anywhere outside those limits, such statutory powers[4] of a British sea-fishery officer as may be conferred on them by ministerial order[5].

In addition, powers of entry, boarding, search and seizure to enforce orders relating to size limits for fish[6] are given to officers appointed by the Secretary of State, British sea-fishery officers, police officers and officers of local market authorities within the relevant market limits[7]. Provision is also made for the enforcement of orders regulating nets and other fishing gear[8], and orders in relation to salmon and migratory trout[9].

For the purpose of enforcing the provisions of an order relating to trans-shipment or the conditions of any trans-shipment licence[10], a British sea-fishery officer is empowered under the Fisheries Act 1981 to exercise enforcement powers in relation to any British or foreign vessel within British fishery limits[11]. He may board the vessel, which he may require to stop and do anything necessary to facilitate the boarding, he may require the master and others on board to attend and he may make any necessary examination and inquiry[12]. Where it appears that a contravention has taken place, he may require the master to take, or may himself take, the vessel and crew to the nearest convenient port and may detain or require the master to detain the vessel there, subject to service of a written notice[13].

1 See the Sea Fish (Conservation) Act 1967 (c 84), s 15(1), (2) (amended by the Fishery Limits Act 1976 (c 86), s 9(1), Sch 2, para 16, and the Fisheries Act 1981 (c 29), s 25(1)).

2 See the Sea Fish (Conservation) Act 1967, s 15(2A) (added by the Fisheries Act 1981, s 25(2)).
3 See the Sea Fish (Conservation) Act 1967, s 15(2B) (as so added).
4 Ie powers under the Sea Fisheries Act 1968 (c 77), s 8(2)–(4): see para 172 below.
5 Sea Fish (Conservation) Act 1967, s 15(3) (substituted by the Sea Fisheries Act 1968, s 22(1), Sch 1, para 38, and amended by the Fishery Limits Act 1976, Sch 2, para 16).
6 Ie orders under the Sea Fish (Conservation) Act 1967, ss 1, 2: see para 145 above.
7 Ibid, s 16 (amended by the Fisheries Act 1981, ss 25(3)–(5), 46(6)).
8 See the Sea Fish (Conservation) Act 1967, s 17, relating to orders under s 3.
9 See ibid, s 18 (amended by the Salmon and Freshwater Fisheries Act 1975 (c 51), ss 42(2), 43(2), the Fishery Limits Act 1976, Sch 2, para 16, and the Water Act 1989 (c 15), s 141(5), Sch 17, para 6).
10 Ie an order under the Sea Fish (Conservation) Act 1967, s 4A or s 6(1A), or a licence under s 4A: see paras 147, 149, above.
11 Fisheries Act 1981, s 27(1).
12 Ibid, s 27(2), (3).
13 Ibid, s 27(4).

(f) Shellfish

155. The Sea Fisheries (Shellfish) Act 1967. The Sea Fisheries (Shellfish) Act 1967 consolidated existing legislation dating back to part of the Sea Fisheries Act 1868 (c 45) concerning shellfish fisheries. 'Shellfish' includes crustaceans and molluscs of any kind, and includes any part of a shellfish and any (or any part of) brood, ware, halfware or spat of shellfish, and any spawn of shellfish, and the shell or any part of the shell of a shellfish, and references in the Act of 1967 to shellfish of any particular description are to be construed accordingly[1]. The Act provides inter alia for the establishment, improvement, maintenance and regulation of fisheries for certain shellfish[2]. An especially notable feature is provision for the conferring of several rights, that is an exclusive right of fishing in a given place, either with or without property in the seabed, which may be granted to one or more persons[3].

1 Sea Fisheries (Shellfish) Act 1967 (c 83), s 22(2). See also para 156, text and note 2 below.
2 Ibid, s 1(1) (amended by the Sea Fisheries Act 1968 (c 77), s 15(1), (2)): see para 156 below.
3 Sea Fisheries (Shellfish) Act 1967, s 1(3): see para 157 below.

156. Orders as to fisheries for shellfish. Power to make orders concerning fisheries for shellfish is conferred on the Secretary of State for Scotland who may, on application made in the prescribed form[1], make orders for the maintenance and regulation of a fishing for certain shellfish[2] on any part of the shore, seabed, estuary or tidal river partly or wholly above or below low mark and within waters adjacent to Great Britain to a distance of 6 nautical miles measured from the territorial sea baseline, and for the constitution of boards or bodies corporate for the purposes of the orders[3]. At the end of each year the Secretary of State must lay before each House of Parliament a report respecting applications to him and his proceedings[4] respecting such orders during that year[5].

1 See the Several and Regulated Fisheries (Form of Application) Regulations 1987, SI 1987/217.
2 Ie oysters, mussels, cockles and clams and other molluscs of kinds specified in regulations (namely scallops and queens: Shellfish (Specification of Molluscs) Regulations 1987, SI 1987/218). For the general meaning of 'shellfish', see para 155 above.
3 Sea Fisheries (Shellfish) Act 1967 (c 83), s 1(1), (2) (amended by the Sea Fisheries Act 1968 (c 77), s 15(1), (2)). As to the procedure for making orders, see the Sea Fisheries (Shellfish) Act 1967, Sch 1. Such orders, being local, are not listed in the *Table of Government Orders*.
4 Ie under ibid, ss 1–5.
5 Ibid, s 6.

157. Grant of right of several fishery. An order as to fisheries for shellfish[1] may confer on the person specified in it a right (limited to sixty years) of several fishery with respect to the whole area of the fishery or a specified part of it[2], or a right of regulating the fishery with respect to the whole area or in that portion of the area not included in a right of fishery[3]. Any parts of the seashore belonging to the Crown or the Duchy of Lancaster or the Duchy of Cornwall may be subject to orders only with the consent of the Crown Estate Commissioners or of the appropriate Duchy authorities[4]. The grant of a right of several fishing includes the exclusive right of depositing, propagating, dredging, fishing for and taking shellfish of any description to which the order applies[5]. This covers the making and maintaining of beds for shellfish, the collecting, removing and depositing of the shellfish as the grantees think fit, and the doing of all other things they think proper for obtaining, storing and disposing of the produce of their fishery[6].

1 Ie an order under the Sea Fisheries (Shellfish) Act 1967 (c 83), s 1(1): see para 156 above. For the meaning of 'shellfish', see para 155 above.
2 Ibid, s 1(3)(a), (c).
3 Ibid, s 1(3)(b), (c).
4 Ibid, s 1(4).
5 Ibid, s 2(1).
6 Ibid, s 2(1)(a)–(c).

158. Effect of grant of right of regulating a shellfish fishery. Where an order[1] confers on the grantees a right of regulating a fishery for any specified description of shellfish and imposes restrictions on or makes regulations respecting the dredging, fishing for and taking those shellfish within the limits of the regulated fishery, or part of it, or imposes tolls or royalties on persons dredging, fishing for and taking shellfish there, the grantees have power to carry into effect and enforce the restrictions and regulations, levy the tolls and royalties and provide for depositing and propagating the shellfish within those limits and improving and cultivating the fishery[2]. Contravention of any restriction or regulation or non-payment of tolls or royalties is an offence rendering the offender liable to a fine and forfeiture of the shellfish taken or, if they have been sold, their value[3]. District courts as well as sheriff courts have jurisdiction in this matter[4].

1 Ie an order under the Sea Fisheries (Shellfish) Act 1967 (c 83), s 1, for which see paras 156, 157, above.
2 Ibid, s 3(1), which is expressed to be subject to the order and to s 12 (orders prohibiting deposit of shellfish), for which see para 163 below. For the meaning of 'shellfish', see para 155 above.
3 Ibid, s 3(3). The forfeited shellfish or their value may be directed to be handed to the grantees to be applied for the improvement or cultivation of the fishery: s 3(4).
4 See ibid, s 19(2), (4).

159. Licensing powers in relation to regulated fishery. An order made by the Secretary of State for Scotland[1] may impose restrictions and make regulations prohibiting all persons from dredging, fishing for or taking, within the limits of the fishery or part of it, shellfish of the description to which the order applies except under a licence issued by the grantees of the right of regulation[2]. Subject to the provisions of the order, the grantees have wide discretion as to the number of licences issued, to whom and for what time they are issued and as to the manner and extent of dredging, fishing and taking shellfish under them[3]. The grantees must notify the Secretary of State if they do not propose to issue licences to all applicants, and he must give them directions as to the exercise of their powers[4]. Failure by the grantees to observe these statutory provisions or directions does not of itself invalidate any licence so issued[5]. A licence does not expire before its due date unless the licensee dies, surrenders the licence or the licence is cancelled by the grantees following a second conviction of the licensee of an offence of contravening a restriction or regulation imposed by the order[6].

1 Ie an order under the Sea Fisheries (Shellfish) Act 1967 (c 83), s 1, for which see paras 156, 157, above.
2 Ibid, s 4(1), (2), (8). For the meaning of 'shellfish', see para 155 above.
3 Ibid, s 4(4).
4 Ibid, s 4(5).
5 Ibid, s 4(6).
6 Ibid, s 4(7), (8).

160. Cesser of rights. The right of several fishery, or of regulating a fishery, may be lost in the whole or in any part of the area where it is exercisable if the Secretary of State for Scotland is not satisfied that the grantees are properly cultivating the ground for shellfish as described in the relevant order, or if he is not satisfied that they are properly giving effect to any restrictions and regulations contained in the order, and levying the required tolls or other royalties[1]. He may make a certificate to that effect so that the right is brought to an end in all or part of the area, and so that the provisions of the Sea Fisheries (Shellfish) Act 1967 cease to operate there[1]. In coming to his decision, he may have any inquiries or examinations carried out by an inspector or otherwise, and request from the grantees any information that he thinks necessary and proper, and the grantees must afford all the necessary facilities for these activities[2]. The inspector or other appointee may take evidence, require individuals by signed order to attend and be examined (under oath or otherwise), or take any affidavit or declaration necessary[3]. He may enter land within the limits of the fishery after twenty-four hours' notice to the occupier or grantees, as appropriate, to obtain and take away samples of shellfish found[4]. He must see that the samples are properly labelled or otherwise capable of identification, and may dispose of them as he likes when he has finished with them[5]. The maximum penalty for causing obstruction or failure without reasonable excuse to provide information reasonably required is a fine on summary conviction not exceeding level 3 on the standard scale[6].

1 Sea Fisheries (Shellfish) Act 1967 (c 83), s 5(1). For the meaning of 'shellfish', see para 155 above.
2 Ibid, s 5(2).
3 Ibid, s 5(3), (9).
4 Ibid, s 5(4), (5).
5 Ibid, s 5(4).
6 Ibid, s 5(7); Criminal Procedure (Scotland) Act 1975 (c 21), s 289F (added by the Criminal Justice Act 1982 (c 48), s 54). For level 3, see para 11, note 15, above.

161. Protection of shellfish fisheries. Where a right of several fishery has been granted by order[1] under the Sea Fisheries (Shellfish) Act 1967, or a sufficiently marked out or sufficiently known private oyster-bed is owned independently of the Act, all shellfish in the area or bed become the absolute property of the grantees or owner of the bed[2]. All shellfish removed by any person from the area or bed, unless disposed of with the authority of the grantees or owner, are the absolute property of the grantees or owner[3]. Any person committing any of various actions incompatible with the maintenance of these fisheries is guilty of an offence and liable on summary conviction to fines not exceeding level 3 on the standard scale and also to make full compensation for damage suffered by the grantees or owner, subject to certain exceptions mentioned below[4]. These actions are:

(1) using any implement of fishing except a line and hook or a net adapted solely for catching floating fish without detriment to shellfish of the kind in question, or any bed or fishery of these fish;

(2) dredging for any ballast or other substance except under lawful authority for improving navigation;

(3) depositing any ballast, rubbish or other substance;

(4) placing anything prejudicial to or likely to be prejudicial to, or disturbing or injuring, any shellfish of the kind in question, or bed or fishery of these shellfish, except for lawful purposes of navigation or anchorage[5].

District courts, as well as sheriff courts, have jurisdiction in these matters[6].

The exceptions arise where the limits of the area or parts of the area where a right of several fishery is exercisable or the limits of a private oyster bed are not sufficiently marked out in the prescribed manner (according to any relevant order) or if notice of the limits has not been given to the alleged offender in the prescribed manner; or, in the case of a private oyster bed, if the bed is not sufficiently marked out and known as such[7].

1 Ie by order under the Sea Fisheries (Shellfish) Act 1967 (c 83), s 1, for which see paras 156, 157, above.
2 Ibid, s 7(1), (2). For the meaning of 'shellfish', see para 155 above.
3 Ibid, s 7(3).
4 Ibid, s 7(4); Criminal Procedure (Scotland) Act 1975 (c 21), s 289F (added by the Criminal Justice Act 1982 (c 48), s 54). For level 3, see para 11, note 15, above.
5 Sea Fisheries (Shellfish) Act 1967, s 7(4)(a)–(e).
6 Ibid, s 19(2), (4).
7 Ibid, s 7(5)(a), (b).

162. Grants and loans for restoration of shellfish fisheries. Grants and loans may be made by the Secretary of State, with Treasury approval, for expenses incurred in cleansing, reinstating and restocking shellfish beds[1] which have been affected by disease or pest[2].

1 This applies both to shellfish beds within the limits of a fishery to which an order under the Sea Fisheries (Shellfish) Act 1967 (c 83), s 1 (see paras 156, 157, above), applies and to shellfish beds in respect of which a person has an exclusive right to take oysters, mussels or cockles: s 9(2).
2 Ibid, s 9(1). For the meaning of 'shellfish', see para 155 above.

163. Power to prohibit the deposit or taking of shellfish to inhibit the spread of diseases or pests. The Secretary of State for Scotland may by order prohibit the deposit, in designated waters, of shellfish of any description or of a specified description which have been taken from any shellfish bed outside these waters or elsewhere as specified[1]. Such an order may apply to any tidal waters within the seaward limits of British territorial waters and to any inland waters which the Secretary of State considers to be a source of diseases or pests carried by shellfish[2], and to adjacent land which may be a similar source[3]. A ban on depositing shellfish in these waters will also apply to this land[3]. The order may also prohibit the taking of shellfish of any description or as specified from any designated water or land, to prevent the spread of pests or diseases carried by shellfish[4]. It may make exceptions for shellfish deposited or taken in accordance with conditions under a licence from the Secretary of State[5].

If anyone is convicted of depositing shellfish[6] in contravention of such an order, the Secretary of State may remove these shellfish and any other shellfish which are in his opinion affected by any disease or pest carried by the deposited shellfish[7]. The Secretary of State may dispose of these shellfish by destruction, sale or otherwise, and recover reasonable expense from the convicted person[8].

1 Sea Fisheries (Shellfish) Act 1967 (c 83), s 12(1). Such an order may be varied or revoked by a subsequent order: s 12(8). See the Molluscan Shellfish (Control of Deposit) (Scotland) Order 1978, SI 1978/560, and the Lobsters (Control of Deposit) Order 1981, SI 1981/994. For the meaning of 'shellfish', see para 155 above.
2 Sea Fisheries (Shellfish) Act 1967, s 12(2).
3 Ibid, s 12(3).
4 Ibid, s 12(3A) (added by the Diseases of Fish Act 1983 (c 30), s 6(1)).

5 Sea Fisheries (Shellfish) Act 1967, s 12(4) (amended by the Diseases of Fish Act 1983, s 6(2)).
6 A person who causes shellfish to enter particular waters is taken to deposit them there: Sea Fisheries (Shellfish) Act 1967, s 12(7).
7 Ibid, s 12(5).
8 Ibid, s 12(6).

164. Power to prohibit the importation of shellfish. The Secretary of State for Scotland may by order prohibit the importation[1] of shellfish of any specified description into any designated area that consists of part of the coast or other land adjacent to waters designated by order[2] for the purposes of prohibiting the deposit or taking of shellfish to inhibit the spread of diseases or pests[3]. The order may make exceptions for specified places within the designated area[3]. A person is presumed to have contravened an order if he is in possession of, or is entitled to custody or control of, any prohibited shellfish at the time when they are imported, whether as owner, consignor, consignee, agent or broker[4].

1 'Importation' means importation on board any vessel, hovercraft or aircraft, whether from a place outside Great Britain or not: Sea Fisheries (Shellfish) Act 1967 (c 83), s 12(4) (amended by the Hovercraft (Application of Enactments) Order 1972, SI 1972/971).
2 Ie by order under the Sea Fisheries (Shellfish) Act 1967, s 12: see para 163 above.
3 Ibid, s 13(1). The order may be varied or revoked by a subsequent order: s 13(3). See the Lobsters (Control of Importation) Order 1981, SI 1981/995. For the meaning of 'shellfish', see para 155 above.
4 Sea Fisheries (Shellfish) Act 1967, s 13(2).

165. Further provisions concerning prohibition of the deposit, taking and importation of shellfish. The Secretary of State, having made an order prohibiting the deposit, taking or importation of shellfish[1], must take steps to inform everyone concerned of the effect of the order[2].

The maximum penalty for contravention of an order or of conditions attached to a licence granted under an order is, on summary conviction, a fine not exceeding level 4 on the standard scale, or imprisonment up to three months, or both[3].

Inspectors authorised on behalf of the Secretary of State for Scotland have extensive powers, on at least twenty-four hours' notice, to enter designated land, waters or land covered by water and to obtain, take away and dispose of samples of any shellfish found there, being samples duly marked, labelled or otherwise identifiable[4]. The penalty for obstruction of an inspector is, on summary conviction, a fine not exceeding level 3 on the standard scale[5].

1 Ie an order under the Sea Fisheries (Shellfish) Act 1967 (c 83), s 12 or s 13: see paras 163, 164, above.
2 Ibid, s 14(1).
3 Ibid, s 14(2); Criminal Procedure (Scotland) Act 1975 (c 21), ss 289E, 289F (added by the Criminal Justice Act 1982 (c 48), s 54). For level 4, see para 11, note 16, above.
4 Sea Fisheries (Shellfish) Act 1967, s 14(3), (4).
5 Ibid, s 14(5); Criminal Procedure (Scotland) Act 1975, s 289F (as added: see note 3 above). For level 3, see para 11, note 15, above.

166. Elimination of disease or pest affecting shellfish at public fisheries. The Secretary of State for Scotland may, in waters where the public has a right to fish, take any requisite action to destroy shellfish affected by disease or pest and to eliminate such disease or pest from these waters, and for having waters restocked[1]. However, this power may not be exercised in waters where there is a right of several fishery or of regulating a fishery conferred by a current order under the Sea Fisheries (Shellfish) Act 1967[2], nor in other waters where anyone has an exclusive right to take shellfish of any description[3].

1 Sea Fisheries (Shellfish) Act 1967, s 15(2). For the meaning of 'shellfish', see para 155 above.
2 Ie an order under ibid, s 1, for which see paras 156, 157, above.
3 Ibid, s 15(1).

167. Prohibition on the sale of oysters. There is a prohibition on the sale of any description of oysters between 14 May in any year and the following 4 August[1]. This applies also to exposing them for sale, buying them for sale and consigning them to any person for the purposes of sale[1].

An offender is liable on summary conviction to a fine not exceeding level 1 on the standard scale and to forfeiture of the oysters concerned[2]. However, an offender is not guilty of an offence if he satisfies the court that the oysters concerned were:

(1) originally taken within the waters of a foreign state, or
(2) preserved in tins or otherwise cured, or
(3) intended for the purpose of oyster cultivation within the same district in which the oysters were taken, or
(4) taken from any place for cultivation with the consent of the Secretary of State for Scotland, or
(5) Pacific or Japanese oysters (*Crassostrea gigas*), Portuguese oysters (*Crassostrea angulata*) or other members of the genus *Crassostrea*[3].

Any person with power under any Act, charter or byelaw to search for, seize, remove or condemn any food unfit for human consumption or to order it to be destroyed or otherwise disposed of may exercise the like power with regard to any oysters found in situations contravening these provisions[4].

1 Sea Fisheries (Shellfish) Act 1967 (c 83), s 16(1).
2 Ibid, s 16(1); Criminal Procedure (Scotland) Act 1975 (c 21), ss 289E, 289F (added by the Criminal Justice Act 1982 (c 48), s 54). Level 1 is £50: Increase of Criminal Penalties etc (Scotland) Order 1984, SI 1984/526, art 4. For the purposes of the exercise of jurisdiction by the sheriff court, the offence is deemed to have been committed either in the place where it was actually committed or in any place in which the offender may for the time being be found: Sea Fisheries (Shellfish) Act 1967, s 19(1).
3 Ibid, s 16(2)(a)–(e) (amended by the Sea Fisheries (Shellfish) Act 1973 (c 30), s 1). As to districts under head (3), see the Sea Fisheries (Shellfish) Act 1967, s 16(3), (4). For a defence where the offender reasonably believes that the oysters were produced by fish farming, see the Fisheries Act 1981 (c 29), s 33(5), (6), Sch 4, para 30.
4 Sea Fisheries (Shellfish) Act 1967, s 18. As to the examination and seizure of suspected food by authorised officers of local authorities, see the Food and Drugs (Scotland) Act 1956 (c 30), s 9, and FOOD, para 397 below.

168. Prohibition on the taking and sale of certain crabs and lobsters. It is an offence to sell any edible crab carrying any spawn attached to its tail or other exterior part, or one which has recently cast its shell[1]. The prohibition applies also to taking such crabs, having them in one's possession, exposing them for sale or consigning them to any person for the purpose of sale[1]. However, it is a defence to satisfy the court that the crabs concerned were intended for bait for fishing[2]. The Secretary of State may by order direct that similar provisions are to apply to the landing or sale of lobsters carrying any spawn attached to the tail or some other exterior part, or in a condition showing that when it was taken it was carrying spawn attached in these ways[3]. The penalty on summary conviction for an offence is a fine not exceeding level 3 on the standard scale, with forfeiture of all crabs and lobsters found in the possession of the accused or alleged to have been sold, exposed or offered for sale, or bought or consigned for sale[4]. Any person with power under any Act, charter or byelaw to search for, seize, remove or condemn any food unfit for human consumption or to order it to be destroyed or otherwise disposed of may exercise the like power with regard to any crabs or lobsters found in situations contravening these provisions[5].

1 Sea Fisheries (Shellfish) Act 1967 (c 83), s 17(1).
2 Ibid, s 17(2). For a defence where an offender under s 17(1) or (3) reasonably believes that the edible crabs or lobsters were produced by fish farming, see the Fisheries Act 1981 (c 29), s 33(5), (6), Sch 4, paras 31, 32.
3 Sea Fisheries (Shellfish) Act 1967, s 17(3). No such order was in force at the date at which this volume states the law. Any such order may be varied or revoked by a subsequent order: s 17(5).
4 Ibid, s 17(4); Criminal Procedure (Scotland) Act 1975 (c 21), ss 289E, 289F (added by the Criminal Justice Act 1982 (c 48), s 54). For level 4, see para 11, note 16, above. For the purposes of the exercise of jurisdiction by the sheriff court, the offence is deemed to have been committed either in the place where it was actually committed or in any place in which the offender may for the time being be found: Sea Fisheries (Shellfish) Act 1967, s 19(1).
5 Ibid, s 18. As to the examination and seizure of suspected food by authorised officers of local authorities, see the Food and Drugs (Scotland) Act 1956 (c 30), s 9, and FOOD, para 397 below.

(g) Sea Fisheries

169. The Sea Fisheries Act 1968. The Sea Fisheries Act 1968 was originally designed to provide for subsidies payable to and levies imposed on the white fish and herring industries[1], to amend the Sea Fisheries (Shellfish) Act 1967 (c 83) and the Sea Fish (Conservation) Act 1967 (c 84)[2], to make provision with respect to fishing boats and gear lost or abandoned at sea[3], to remove anomalies in Acts relating to sea fisheries and to the white fish and herring industries and to repeal obsolete and unnecessary enactments[4]. But it no longer relates to the provision of subsidies, and its importance today lies in the provisions regulating sea fishing operations[5].

1 See the Sea Fisheries Act 1968 (c 77), ss 1–4 (repealed).
2 See the Sea Fisheries Act 1968, s 15, and s 16 (repealed).
3 See ibid, s 17, and para 198 below.
4 Ibid, long title. For amendments and repeals, see Schs 1, 2.
5 See ibid, ss 5–14, and paras 170 ff below.

170. Regulation of conduct of fishing operations. The ministers[1] may make orders, whenever it appears to them necessary or expedient, for regulating the conduct of and safeguarding fishing operations and operations ancillary thereto, including provision with respect to the identification and marking of fishing boats and fishing gear[2], applicable (1) to all British fishing boats, and things done by such boats and their crews, wherever they may be, and (2) to all foreign fishing boats, and things done by such boats and their crews, in waters within British fishery limits[3]. In relation to foreign fishing boats, orders may make corresponding provision for boats entering British fishery limits to fish pursuant to an arrangement between the United Kingdom and another country, and may regulate the movement of those boats within those limits[4]. Failure to comply with an order renders the master, owner or charterer, as prescribed by the order, liable to a fine on summary conviction not exceeding the prescribed sum, and on conviction on indictment to a fine[5].

1 'The ministers' means the Minister of Agriculture, Fisheries and Food and the Secretaries of State respectively concerned with the sea fishing industry in Scotland and Northern Ireland: Sea Fisheries Act 1968 (c 77), s 19(1).
2 Ibid, s 5(1) (amended by the Fishery Limits Act 1976 (c 86), s 4(1)). 'Fishing boat' means any vessel for the time being employed in fishing operations or any operations ancillary thereto: Sea Fisheries Act 1968, s 19(1).
3 Ibid, s 5(2)(a), (b) (amended by the Fishery Limits Act 1976, s 4(2), (3)). 'British fishing boat' means a fishing boat registered in the United Kingdom, excluded from registration by regulations under the Merchant Shipping Act 1988 (c 12), s 13 (see para 188 below), or owned wholly by a person who is qualified to own a British ship; and 'foreign fishing boat' means a fishing boat

which is not so registered, excluded or owned: Sea Fisheries Act 1968, s 19(1) (amended by the
Merchant Shipping Act 1988, s 57(4), Sch 6). As to British fishery limits, see para 130 above.
4 Sea Fisheries Act 1968, s 5(3) (amended by the Fishery Limits Act 1976, s 9(1), Sch 2, para 17).
5 Sea Fisheries Act 1968, s 5(4); Criminal Procedure (Scotland) Act 1975 (c 21), s 289B(6) (added by
the Criminal Law Act 1977 (c 45), s 63(1), Sch 11, para 5, and substituted by the Criminal Justice
Act 1982 (c 48), s 55(2)). For the prescribed sum, see para 12, note 3, above. Proceedings may be
taken, and the offence may for all incidental purposes be treated as having been committed, in
any place in the United Kingdom: Sea Fisheries Act 1968, s 14.

171. Sea-fishery officers. Five categories of person are designated as British
sea-fishery officers under the Sea Fisheries Act 1968[1]. They are:
(1) officers of the sea-fishery inspectorates of each of the appropriate ministers
     (namely the Minister of Agriculture, Fisheries and Food, the Secretary of
     State for Scotland and the Department of Agriculture for Northern Ireland),
     but not assistant fishery officers;
(2) commissioned officers of any of Her Majesty's ships;
(3) persons in command or charge of any aircraft or hovercraft of the Royal
     Navy, the Army or the Royal Air Force;
(4) officers of the fishery protection service of the Secretary of State holding the
     rank of commander, first officer or second officer; and
(5) other persons appointed as British sea-fishery officers by one of the appro-
     priate ministers, subject to the limitations specified in their instruments of
     appointment[2].
'Foreign sea-fishery officer', in relation to any convention with respect to the
conduct or safeguarding of fishing or ancillary operations to which the United
Kingdom is a party, means a person of any class specified in an order made by
the ministers, being a person appointed by another country which is a party to
the convention to enforce its provisions or any other person empowered under
the laws of that country to enforce those provisions[3].

1 As to British sea-fishery officers under the Sea Fisheries Act 1883 (c 22), see para 126, note 1,
   above.
2 Sea Fisheries Act 1968 (c 77), s 7(1)(a)–(d), (g), (2), (5); Northern Ireland Constitution Act 1973
   (c 36), s 40, Sch 5, para 8(1). An appointment under head (5) may be limited to particular matters,
   particular areas or particular orders or classes of orders: Sea Fisheries Act 1968, s 7(3). Formerly
   customs officers and certain coastguard officers were also British sea-fishery officers: s 7(1)(e),
   (f) (repealed by the Fisheries Act 1981 (c 29), ss 26(1), 46(2), Sch 5, Pt II).
3 Sea Fisheries Act 1968, s 7(4). For the meaning of 'the ministers', see para 170, note 1, above.

172. General powers of British sea-fishery officers. In relation to any
fishing boat within British fishery limits and in relation to a British fishing boat
anywhere outside those limits[1] a British sea-fishery officer may board the boat,
with or without persons assigned to assist him, and for that purpose may require
the boat to stop and do anything else to facilitate the boarding[2]. He may require
the attendance of the master and other persons on board, may make any
examination and inquiry which appears necessary for the purpose of enforcing
the provisions of any order regulating the conduct of fishing operations[3] or of
the provisions governing access to British fisheries[4] or any order thereunder[5],
and in particular he may examine fish, equipment and fishing gear, require the
production of documents, search the boat for documents and seize and detain
documents save (when at sea) for those required by law to be carried on board[6].
   If it appears to the sea-fishery officer that any of the orders mentioned above
have been contravened, he may take the boat concerned and its crew into port
and detain the boat until notice of detention is withdrawn[7]. If it appears to him
that a British fishing boat or a fishing boat of a country which is party to a
convention with the United Kingdom is being navigated or stationed so close as
to interfere with fishing operations within British fishery limits, he may require

the boat to move away or to move in a specified direction or to a specified position[8]. He also has power to take steps to enforce collision regulations[9] and the Sea Fish (Conservation) Act 1967[10].

  1   For the meaning of 'fishing boat' and 'British fishing boat', see para 170, notes 2, 3, above, and as to British fishing limits, see para 130 above.

  2   Sea Fisheries Act 1968 (c 77), s 8(1), (2) (amended by the Fishery Limits Act 1976 (c 86), s 9(1), Sch 2, para 17).

  3   Ie any order under the Sea Fisheries Act 1968, s 5, for which see para 170 above.

  4   Ie the provisions of the Fishery Limits Act 1976, s 2, for which see para 131 above.

  5   Sea Fisheries Act 1968, s 8(1), (3) (amended by the Fishery Limits Act 1976, s 2(8)).

  6   See the Sea Fisheries Act 1968, s 8(3)(a)–(d) (amended by the Fisheries Act 1981 (c 29), s 26(2)).

  7   Sea Fisheries Act 1968, s 8(4) (substituted by the Fisheries Act 1981, s 26(3)).

  8   Sea Fisheries Act 1968, s 8(5).

  9   Ibid, s 8(6) (as amended: see note 2 above), referring to regulations made under the Merchant Shipping Act 1894 (c 60), s 418, and the enforcement powers under s 723.

10   See the Sea Fish (Conservation) Act 1967 (c 84), s 15, and para 154 above.

173. Powers of sea-fishery officers to enforce conventions. Sea-fishery officers have power to enforce conventions with respect to the conduct or safeguarding of fishing operations to which the United Kingdom is a party[1]. Both British and foreign sea-fishery officers may reciprocally exercise the general powers of British sea-fishery officers[2] anywhere in the convention area outside British fishery limits[3]. However, this does not empower a sea-fishery officer to do anything not authorised by the convention or to exercise in relation to a boat belonging to a party to the convention any power which that country has informed the other parties is not to be exercised in relation to its fishing boats[4].

This power was more significant for enforcement on the high seas, under the 1967 Convention on Conduct of Fishing Operations in the North Atlantic[5], of the old 1959 regulations of the North-East Atlantic Fisheries Commission before the extension of British fishery limits to 200 nautical miles on 1 January 1977 undermined the regulations. This convention has not been denounced, but as its area of application has been so drastically reduced the enforcement provision described above is now effectively relevant only to operation under the limited inspection scheme of the European Community[6].

Both British and foreign sea-fishery officers are protected from civil and criminal proceedings in respect of acts done in good faith on reasonable grounds[7], and it is an offence to obstruct or assault them[8]. Written reports by sea-fishery officers on their legitimate enforcement activities are admissible as evidence in any civil or criminal proceedings[9].

  1   Sea Fisheries Act 1968 (c 77), s 9(1). As to British and foreign sea-fishery officers, see para 171 above.

  2   Ie the powers under ibid, s 8(2), (3): see para 172 above.

  3   Ibid, s 9(1) (amended by the Fishery Limits Act 1976 (c 86), s 9(1), Sch 2, para 17).

  4   Sea Fisheries Act 1968, s 9(2).

  5   Convention on Conduct of Fishing Operations in the North Atlantic (London, 1 June 1967; TS 49 (1977); Cmnd 6799).

  6   See R Churchill *EEC Fisheries Law* (1987) pp 141–143, and EC Council Regulation 2241/87 (OJ L207, 29.7.87, p 1) establishing certain control measures for fishing activities (replacing EC Council Regulation 2057/82 (OJ L229, 29.7.82, p 1) (as amended)).

  7   Sea Fisheries Act 1968, s 10(1) (substituted by the Fisheries Act 1981 (c 29), s 26(4)).

  8   See the Sea Fisheries Act 1968, s 10(2), (2A), (3) (amended by the Fishery Limits Act 1976, Sch 2, para 17, and the Fisheries Act 1981, s 26(5)). The penalty on summary conviction is a fine not exceeding £5,000 or on conviction on indictment is a fine: Sea Fisheries Act 1968, s 10(4) (amended by the Fisheries Act 1981, s 24(3)). Proceedings may be taken, and the offence may for all incidental purposes be treated as having been committed, in any place in the United Kingdom: Sea Fisheries Act 1968, s 14.

  9   Ibid, s 11.

174. Recovery of fines. Where a fine is imposed by a sheriff in Scotland on the master, owner, charterer or a crew member of a fishing boat who is convicted by him of an offence relating to the regulation of the conduct of fishing operations[1], obstruction of or assault on a sea-fishery officer[2] or access to British fisheries[3], the sheriff may issue a warrant for the poinding and sale of the boat and its gear and catch and of any property of the convicted person and, if the boat is a foreign fishing boat, may order it to be detained for a period of up to three months from the date of conviction or until the fine is paid, whichever occurs first[4].

1 Ie an offence under the Sea Fisheries Act 1968 (c 77), s 5: see para 170 above.
2 Ie an offence under ibid, s 10: see para 173 above.
3 Ie an offence under the Fishery Limits Act 1976 (c 86), s 2: see para 131 above.
4 Sea Fisheries Act 1968, s 12(2) (amended by the Fishery Limits Act 1976, s 2(8)).

175. Court for the prosecution of offenders under the Sea Fisheries Acts. Cases under the Sea Fisheries Acts[1] may be prosecuted in any sheriff court declared by the Secretary of State to be the court nearest the spot where the offence was committed or that is otherwise most convenient[2].

1 'Sea Fisheries Act' means any enactments for the time being in force relating to sea fishing, including any enactment relating to fishing for shellfish, salmon or migratory trout: Sea Fisheries Act 1968 (c 77), s 19(1), applied by virtue of the Sea Fisheries (Scotland) Amendment Act 1885 (c 70), s 1 (amended by the Sea Fisheries Act 1968, s 22(1), Sch 1, para 24).
2 Sea Fisheries (Scotland) Amendment Act 1885, s 7.

176. Compensation for damage. If a person is brought for trial before a sheriff in Scotland for an offence relating to the regulation of the conduct of fishing operations[1], obstruction of or assault on a sea-fishery officer[2] or access to British fisheries[3], any person who considers that personal injury to him or damage to his property has been caused by the offence may, before the trial begins, by notice in writing to the accused and to the sheriff clerk, intimate that at the trial the sheriff will be called on to award compensation for the injury or damage[4]. If such notice is given and the accused is convicted, the sheriff must thereupon dispose of the question of compensation, giving decree as in any ordinary action brought before him, but the maximum amount he may award is a sum not exceeding level 5 on the standard scale[5]. Evidence led at the trial is admissible for the disposal of the compensation question, and any report of a British sea-fishery officer is sufficient evidence for the disposal of that question unless the sheriff considers it necessary in the interests of justice that additional evidence should be allowed[6]. The provisions relating to poinding and sale, and of detention of a foreign fishing boat to meet a fine[7], apply also to securing payment of compensation[8]. These provisions do not derogate from the right to receive damages under the general law[9].

1 Ie an offence under the Sea Fisheries Act 1968 (c 77), s 5: see para 170 above.
2 Ie an offence under ibid, s 10: see para 173 above.
3 Ie an offence under the Fishery Limits Act 1976 (c 86), s 2: see para 131 above.
4 Sea Fisheries Act 1968, s 13(2)(a) (amended by the Fishery Limits Act 1976, s 2(8)).
5 Sea Fisheries Act 1968, s 13(2)(b), (d) (amended by the Criminal Justice Act 1982 (c 48), s 56(3), Sch 7, para 2). Level 5 is £2,000: Increase of Criminal Penalties etc (Scotland) Order 1984, SI 1984/526, art 4.
6 Sea Fisheries Act 1968, s 13(2)(c).
7 Ie ibid, s 12: see para 174 above.
8 Ibid, s 13(3) (amended by the Fishery Limits Act 1976, s 5, Sch 1, para 3(4)).
9 Sea Fisheries Act 1968, s 13(4) (as amended: see note 4 above).

177. Sea fisheries statistics. The Secretary of State may require fishermen and other persons belonging to British sea-fishing boats, and fish curers, catching or curing any kind of sea fish in Scotland or any part of the sea adjoining Scotland to make returns, in a prescribed form and at prescribed periods, of all sea fish caught or cured by them[1].

  1 Sea Fisheries (Scotland) Amendment Act 1885 (c 70), s 6 (amended by the Reorganisation of Offices (Scotland) (Adaptation of Enactments) Order 1939, SR & O 1939/782, the Sea Fisheries Act 1968 (c 77), s 22(1), Sch 1, para 26, and the Fishery Limits Act 1976 (c 86), s 2(8)), which provides that failure to make full and correct returns is an offence. The master of the boat concerned is vicariously liable, though some defences are available to him: see the Sea Fisheries (Scotland) Amendment Act 1885, s 6A (added by the Sea Fisheries Act 1968, Sch 1, para 27).

178. Enforcement of Community rules. The Fisheries Act 1981 introduced provisions concerning enforceable European Community restrictions and obligations relating to sea fishing[1] (except where other provision is made under ministerial order[2]). If any fishing boat fishes within British fishery limits in contravention of any such restriction, the master, owner and charterer are each guilty of an offence[3]. The provisions of the Sea Fish (Conservation) Act 1967 concerning penalties, jurisdiction and the powers of seizure of sea-fishery officers[4] apply to these offences just as they apply to offences under that Act[5] relating to ministerial powers to restrict fishing for sea fish[6]. The general enforcement powers of sea-fishery officers under the Sea Fisheries Act 1968[7] are exercisable in relation to such restrictions[8].

  1 Fisheries Act 1981 (c 29), s 30(1). 'Enforceable Community restriction' and 'enforceable Community obligation' mean a restriction or obligation to which the European Communities Act 1972 (c 68), s 2(1), applies: Fisheries Act 1981, s 30(3).
  2 Ibid, s 30(2). See the Sea Fishing (Enforcement of Community Licensing Measures) (North of Scotland Box) Order 1984, SI 1984/1956; the Sea Fishing (Enforcement of Community Control Measures) Order 1985, SI 1985/487 (amended by SI 1986/926 and SI 1987/1536); the Sea Fishing (Enforcement of Community Conservation Measures) Order 1986, SI 1986/2090 (amended by SI 1988/2300); the Sea Fishing (Enforcement of Community Quota Measures) Order 1988, SI 1988/2301; and the Third Country Fishing (Enforcement) Order 1989, SI 1989/217. See paras 179 ff below.
  3 Fisheries Act 1981, s 30(1)(a). 'Fishing boat' means any vessel for the time being employed in fishing operations or any operations ancillary thereto: s 30(3).
  4 Ie the Sea Fish (Conservation) Act 1967 (c 84), ss 11, 12, 14, 15(2): see paras 152–154 above.
  5 Ie under ibid, s 5(1): see para 148 above.
  6 Fisheries Act 1981, s 30(1)(b).
  7 Ie under the Sea Fisheries Act 1968 (c 77), s 8: see para 172 above.
  8 Fisheries Act 1981, s 30(1)(c).

179. Enforcement of Community control measures. The Sea Fishing (Enforcement of Community Control Measures) Order 1985[1] implemented European Community regulations[2] laying down detailed rules for recording information as to the catches of fish of member states. It creates offences, for which fines may be imposed, for contravention of the regulations[3]. These offences relate to the requirements of the regulations concerning co-operation in inspections, keeping log books, making declarations concerning catches landed or trans-shipped after the quota is exhausted, and the stowing of nets[4]. Convicted offenders are also liable to forfeiture of fish, nets and other gear involved[5]. When these penalties are imposed by a sheriff in Scotland on a convicted master, owner, charterer or crew member, the sheriff may issue a warrant for the poinding and sale of the boat and its gear and catch and anything on board belonging to the convicted person and, if the boat is a foreign fishing boat, may order it to be detained for a period of up to three months from the date of conviction, or until the fine is paid, whichever occurs first[6]. The powers of British sea-fishery officers are prescribed[7]. Obstruction of or assault on such an officer is an offence[8]. Any log book kept under the Community regulations and any declaration submitted under them are sufficient evidence in any relevant proceedings of the matters stated therein[9].

1 The Sea Fishing (Enforcement of Community Control Measures) Order 1985, SI 1985/487 (amended by SI 1986/926 and SI 1987/1536), was made under the Fisheries Act 1981 (c 29), s 30(2).
2 See EC Council Regulation 2241/87 (OJ L207, 29.7.87, p 1), establishing control measures for fishing activities, and EC Commission Regulation 2807/83 (OJ L276, 10.10.83, p 21), laying down the rules referred to in the text.
3 Sea Fishing (Enforcement of Community Control Measures) Order 1985, arts 3, 4 (as amended: see note 1 above).
4 Ibid, Schedule (substituted by SI 1986/926 and amended by SI 1987/1536).
5 Ibid, art 4 (amended by SI 1986/926).
6 Ibid, art 5(2).
7 Ibid, arts 6–8 (as amended: see note 1 above).
8 Ibid, art 9.
9 Ibid, art 12 (amended by SI 1987/1536).

180. Enforcement of Community conservation measures. The Sea Fishing (Enforcement of Community Conservation Measures) Order 1986[1] implemented European Community regulations[2] laying down certain technical measures for the conservation of fishery resources. It makes provision similar to that made by the order discussed in the preceding paragraph[3]. The offences with which the order is concerned include contraventions of specified provisions of the regulations relating to specified gear, mesh sizes and the composition of catches; attachments to nets; the disposal of undersized fish; prohibitions on landing lobster tails or claws; the disposal of salmon and sea trout, prohibitions on retaining herring on board and retaining on board mackerel caught in specified waters; notification requirements; limitations on the use of specified vessels or gear; and prohibitions on processing operations on board[4].

1 The Sea Fishing (Enforcement of Community Conservation Measures) Order 1986, SI 1986/2090 (amended by SI 1988/2300), was made under the Fisheries Act 1981 (c 29), s 30(2).
2 See EC Council Regulation 3094/86 (OJ L288, 11.10.86, p 1) (amended by EC Council Regulations 4026/86 (OJ L376, 31.12.86, p 1), 2968/87 (OJ L280, 3.10.87, p 1), 3953/87 (OJ L371, 30.12.87, p 9), 1555/88 (OJ L140, 7.6.88, p 1), 2024/88 (OJ L179, 9.7.88, p 1) and 3287/88 (OJ L292, 26.10.88, p 5)).
3 See para 179 above.
4 Sea Fishing (Enforcement of Community Conservation Measures) Order 1986, Sch 1.

181. Enforcement of Community quota measures. The Sea Fishing (Enforcement of Community Quota Measures) Order 1988[1] implemented a European Community regulation[2] fixing, for certain fish stocks and groups of fish stocks, the total allowable catches for 1989 and certain conditions under which they may be fished. A new regulation and consequently a new order is made each year. The order holds the master, owner and charterer each guilty of an offence if a British fishing boat anywhere or any other fishing boat within British fishery limits contravenes or fails to comply with the Community quota provisions, and renders them liable to fines and the forfeiture of fish, nets and gear[3].

1 The Sea Fishing (Enforcement of Community Quota Measures) Order 1988, SI 1988/2301, was made under the Fisheries Act 1981 (c 29), s 30(2).
2 See EC Council Regulation 4194/88 (OJ L369, 31.12.88, p 3).

3 Sea Fishing (Enforcement of Community Quota Measures) Order 1988, arts 3, 4. Similar provision is made in art 5 as to poinding and sale as those referred to in para 179 above, and sea-fishery officers are given powers by art 6.

182. Enforcement of Community measures as to fishing by third countries.
The Third Country Fishing (Enforcement) Order 1989[1] implements European Community regulations[2] concerning fishing by third countries. The order makes specified contraventions of the regulations within British fishery limits an offence for which the master is liable to fines, enforceable in Scotland by warrant for arrestment and sale[3]. The contraventions concerned relate to the keeping of log books, the transmission of information, the keeping on board of documents certifying the calibration of sea-water tanks, the marking of vessels with registration letters and numbers, the holding on board of the licence or regulations and the observation of their conditions and, in the case of Norwegian vessels, restrictions on fishing methods for certain fish in certain areas[4]. British sea-fishery officers are given enforcement powers[5].

1 The Third Country Fishing (Enforcement) Order 1989, SI 1989/217, was made under the Fisheries Act 1981 (c 29), s 30(2).
2 See EC Council Regulations 4195/88 (OJ L369, 31.12.88, p 38), 4197/88 (OJ L369, 31.12.88, p 47) and 4199/88 (OJ L369, 31.12.88, p 56), laying down for 1989 certain measures for the conservation and management of fishery resources applicable respectively to vessels from Norway, Sweden and the Faroe Islands.
3 Third Country Fishing (Enforcement) Order 1989, arts 2, 3.
4 Ibid, Schedule.
5 Ibid, art 4. As to obstruction of and assault on officers, see art 5.

(h) Fishing Boats

183. Restrictions on fishing etc by unqualified British fishing boats.
The British Fishing Boats Act 1983 prohibits the fishing for and trans-shipment of sea fish[1] in any specified area[2] by or from, and the landing in the United Kingdom of sea fish by, a British fishing boat[3] unless the boat satisfies qualifying conditions prescribed in an order made by the ministers for use in carrying out operations of that description[4]. This provision was enacted to end the practice of nationals of countries other than member states of the European Community registering their vessels in a member state in order to gain access to United Kingdom fishery limits. Where a British fishing boat is not appropriately qualified for carrying out the above operations in a restricted fishing area, and is in such an area, its fishing gear must be stowed in accordance with an order made by the ministers[5]. On any contravention of these restrictions, the master, owner and charterer are each liable on summary conviction to a fine not exceeding £50,000 or on conviction on indictment to a fine, and any fish or fishing gear found in the boat or taken and used by any person from the boat may be ordered to be forfeited, and, in Scotland, may be destroyed or disposed of as the convicting court may direct[6].

1 'Sea fish' includes shellfish, salmon and migratory trout: British Fishing Boats Act 1983 (c 8), s 9.
2 Ie in any area for the time being specified in an order made by the ministers: ibid, s 1(2). The ministers have specified an area consisting of all waters within British fishery limits: British Fishing Boats Order 1983, SI 1983/482, art 3. 'The ministers' means the Minister of Agriculture, Fisheries and Food and the Secretaries of State respectively concerned with the sea fishing industry in Scotland, Wales and Northern Ireland: British Fishing Boats Act 1983, s 9.
3 'Fishing boat' means any vessel for the time being employed in fishing operations or any operations ancillary to fishing operations, and 'British fishing boat' means a fishing boat registered in the United Kingdom, excluded from registration by regulations under the Mer-

chant Shipping Act 1988 (c 12), s 13 (see para 188 below), or owned wholly by a person who is qualified to own a British ship: British Fishing Boats Act 1983, s 9 (amended by the Merchant Shipping Act 1988, s 57(4), Sch 6).
4 British Fishing Boats Act 1983, s 1(1), (2). For the conditions referred to, see para 184 below. See R Churchill *EEC Fishing Law* (1987) pp 125–128.
5 Ibid, s 1(5). For the prescribed manner of stowage, see the British Fishing Boats Order 1983, art 5.
6 British Fishing Boats Act 1983, s 1(6), (7).

184. Conditions for qualification as a British fishing boat. An order[1] prescribing qualifications for British fishing boats for use in carrying out the operations described above may prescribe conditions with respect to the nationality of the crew or of any proportion of them[2]. The conditions must be those appearing to the ministers to be necessary or expedient for the protection of the British sea fishing industry, but must not discriminate between British citizens and nationals of other member states of the European Community[3]. The ministers have by order imposed a condition that in order for a British fishing boat to be qualified at least 75 per cent of the members of the crew must be British citizens or nationals of another member state[4].

1 Ie an order under the British Fishing Boats Act 1983 (c 8), s 1(1): see para 183 above.
2 Ibid, s 1(3).
3 Ibid, s 1(4). For the meaning of 'the ministers', see para 183, note 2, above.
4 British Fishing Boats Order 1983, SI 1983/482, art 4. As to the legality of this provision in EEC law, see Joined Cases C3, C126/87 *The Queen v Ministry of Agriculture, Fisheries and Food, ex parte Agegate Ltd and Jaderow Ltd* (1990) Times, 19 January, ECJ.

185. Powers of British sea-fishery officers at sea and in port. Like previous Acts, the British Fishing Boats Act 1983 enables British sea-fishery officers, in relation to any British fishing boat within a restricted fishing area, to exercise powers to enforce the restrictions on fishing etc by unqualified boats[1]. These powers include boarding the boat and requiring it to stop; requiring the master or other persons on board to attend; making any necessary examination or inquiry; requiring any person on board to produce any document that he has on board that may be relevant for determining his nationality and any other document relating to the boat, its fishing operations or persons on board that is in that person's custody or possession; searching the boat for documents relating to the possible commission of an offence and requiring the help of those on board so to do[2]. If the officer has reason to suspect that an offence has been committed, he may seize and detain any document produced or found on board to use in evidence in the relevant proceedings, but a document required by law to be carried on board may be seized only when a boat is detained in port[3]. If it appears that an offence has been committed, the officer may require the master of the boat to take, or may himself take, the boat and its crew to the nearest convenient port and detain the boat or require the master so to do, subject to service on him of a written notice[4].

Anyone failing to comply with the officer's requirements, or obstructing or assaulting him in the exercise of his duties, is liable on summary conviction to a fine not exceeding £50,000 or, on conviction on indictment, to a fine[5]. The officer himself is protected against civil or criminal proceedings relating to legitimate acts done in the exercise of these powers[6].

1 British Fishing Boats Act 1983 (c 8), s 2(1), referring to the enforcement of s 1, for which see para 183 above. As to British sea-fishery officers, see para 171 above.
2 Ibid, s 2(2)–(4)(a), (b).
3 Ibid, s 2(4)(c).
4 Ibid, s 2(5).

5 Ibid, s 4(1).
6 Ibid, s 4(2).

186. Powers of British sea-fishery officers in relation to premises on land. In Scotland, if a sheriff or a justice of the peace is satisfied by information given on oath that there is reasonable ground for suspecting that an offence of contravening the restrictions on fishing etc by unqualified fishing boats under the British Fishing Boats Act 1983[1] has been committed, he may grant a search warrant to look in specified premises for documents relevant to determining whether such an offence has been committed in relation to the boat concerned[2]. The premises specified must be those used for carrying on a relevant business, but may not be a dwellinghouse[3]. Relevant documents are those concerning the suspected boat, its fishing or related operations, or the nationality of its crew members[4]. The warrant authorises any British sea-fishery officer named in it, with or without constables, to enter the premises specified in the information and to search them for any relevant document[5]. The officer may require anyone on the premises to produce any such document which he has in his possession, and the officer may take copies of it and seize and detain it[6]. He may also require anyone on the premises to do anything the officer considers necessary to facilitate the search[7].

Anyone failing to comply with the officer's requirements, or obstructing or assaulting him in the exercise of his duties, is liable on summary conviction to a fine not exceeding £50,000 or, on conviction on indictment, to a fine[8]. The officer himself is protected against civil or criminal proceedings relating to legitimate acts done in the exercise of these powers[9].

1 Ie an offence under the British Fishing Boats Act 1983 (c 8), s 1, for which see para 183 above.
2 Ibid, s 3(1). The warrant remains in force for one month: s 3(8).
3 Ibid, s 3(2), referring to a business in connection with the operation of fishing boats or activities connected with or ancillary to the operation of such boats.
4 Ibid, s 3(3).
5 Ibid, s 3(4).
6 Ibid, s 3(5), (7).
7 Ibid, s 3(6).
8 Ibid, s 4(1).
9 Ibid, s 4(2).

187. Offences and fines. Proceedings for an offence against the British Fishing Boats Act 1983 may be instituted, and the offence may for all incidental purposes be treated as having been committed, in any place in the United Kingdom[1]. When an offence is committed by a body corporate, any director, manager, secretary or other officer involved in the commission of the offence is guilty of the offence and liable to be proceeded against and punished accordingly[2].

When fines have been imposed by a sheriff in Scotland on masters, owners, charterers or crew members of fishing boats convicted by him of offences under the Act, the sheriff may issue a warrant for the poinding and sale of the boat and its gear and catch and any property of the person convicted, and may order the boat to be detained for up to three months from the date of conviction or until the fine is paid, whichever occurs first[3].

1 British Fishing Boats Act 1983 (c 8), s 7.
2 Ibid, s 6.
3 Ibid, s 5(2).

188. Separate registration of fishing vessels. A fishing vessel[1] will no longer be registered under the general registry provisions of the Merchant Shipping

Act 1894[2] or the provisions of that Act for the registry of British fishing boats[3], or under the Sea Fishing Boats (Scotland) Act 1886[4]. Instead an eligible fishing vessel will be registered in the register of British fishing vessels established and maintained under regulations made by the Secretary of State[5].

Registration is of two kinds: (1) registration of vessels as vessels to which the statutory provisions relating to transfers by bill of sale and the registration of mortgages[6] do not apply (called 'simple registration'); and (2) registration of vessels to which those provisions do apply (called 'full registration')[7].

The Secretary of State may by regulations exclude from registration any specified class or description of vessel[8]. Under this power he has excluded salmon cobles[9].

1 'Fishing vessel' means a vessel for the time being used or intended to be used for or in connection with fishing for sea fish, other than a vessel used or intended to be used for fishing otherwise than for profit; and 'sea fish' includes shellfish, salmon and migratory trout: Merchant Shipping Act 1988 (c 12), s 12(1).
2 Ie the Merchant Shipping Act 1894 (c 60), Pt I (ss 1–91).
3 Ie ibid, s 373 (which is repealed by the Merchant Shipping Act 1894, s 57(5), Sch 7).
4 Merchant Shipping Act 1988, s 13(2). For the Sea Fishing Boats (Scotland) Act 1886 (c 53) (which is repealed by the Merchant Shipping Act 1988, Sch 7), see para 128 above.
5 Merchant Shipping Act 1988, s 13(1); Merchant Shipping (Registration of Fishing Vessels) Regulations 1988, SI 1988/1926, reg 2. For transitional provisions and the position of vessels registered under the law of a country outside the United Kingdom, see the Merchant Shipping Act 1988, s 13(3)–(5).
6 See ibid, ss 19–21, and paras 192–194 below.
7 Merchant Shipping (Registration of Fishing Vessels) Regulations 1988, reg 3.
8 Merchant Shipping Act 1988, s 13(1), (7), Sch 2, para 2(j). The Secretary of State for Transport is the responsible minister in the context of this Act.
9 Merchant Shipping (Registration of Fishing Vessels) Regulations 1988, reg 57.

189. Eligibility for registration. A fishing vessel is eligible for registration only if it is British-owned, it is managed and its operations are directed and controlled from within the United Kingdom, and any charterer, manager or operator of the vessel is a qualified person or company[1]. For the purpose of determining eligibility, the Secretary of State may appoint a person to investigate the eligibility and report back to him[2]. If it appears to the Secretary of State that a registered vessel may no longer be eligible he may serve on the owner or on any charterer, manager or operator a notice calling for specified documents and information[3], and if not then satisfied as to eligibility he must serve notice stating that fact and the vessel's registration will be terminated[4]. Any change affecting eligibility or the percentage of the property in a vessel which is beneficially owned by qualified persons or companies must be notified by the owner to the Secretary of State[5].

1 Merchant Shipping Act 1988 (c 12), s 14(1)(a)–(c). As to when a vessel is British-owned, see s 14(2). 'Qualified person' means a person who is a British citizen resident and domiciled in the United Kingdom or a local authority in the United Kingdom; and 'qualified company' means a company which is incorporated in the United Kingdom, has its principal place of business there, has at least the prescribed percentage of its shares and of each class of its shares legally and beneficially owned by one or more qualified persons or companies and has at least the relevant percentage of its directors as qualified persons: s 14(7). The Secretary of State has limited power under s 14(4) to dispense with the requirement that any individual qualified person be a British citizen.
2 Ibid, s 14(6).
3 Ibid, s 16(1).
4 Ibid, s 16(3), (6). As to the consequences of termination, see s 17.
5 Ibid, s 23(1). Failure to do so is an offence: s 23(2). For the penalties, see s 24(1), and para 191, note 4, below. For the mode of notification, see the Merchant Shipping (Registration of Fishing Vessels) Regulations 1988, SI 1988/1926, reg 33.

190. Application for registration. Application for registration of a fishing vessel must be made to the Secretary of State at the office of the Registrar General of Shipping and Seamen in person or by post or through a local office[1]. The application must be in a form approved by the Secretary of State, must state whether it is for full or simple registration, and must contain specified particulars[2] and be supported by evidence of title and either a declaration of British character or, where the ownership of the vessel has not yet passed to the persons who are to be its owners when it is registered, a declaration of intent with a draft declaration of British character[3].

On receipt of the application the Secretary of State, if satisfied that the vessel is eligible, will allocate to it a register number ('RSS number'), together with the appropriate port letters[4] and a number within that port, and will issue to the owner a 'Carving and Marking Note'[5]. When he receives this note, the owner must cause the vessel to be measured and to be carved with its RSS number and marked with its name, port of registry and port letters and number in the prescribed manner, and must have the work inspected by an inspector of marks[6].

When the Secretary of State is satisfied that all is in order he must register the vessel with full or simple registration, as appropriate, by entering in the register specified particulars of the vessel and its owners, and issue and send to the owner a certificate of registry[7]. However, if the Secretary of State is not satisfied that all is in order he must refuse the application[8], and in particular he may refuse registration if the appropriate safety certificate is not in force in respect of the vessel[9].

Where a fishing vessel acquired outside the United Kingdom which the owner intends should be registered as a British fishing vessel is at the material time at a port outside the United Kingdom, the owner may, instead of applying to the Secretary of State for registration, apply to the appropriate person locally for provisional registration[10]. The application is forwarded to the Secretary of State, and if he notifies the appropriate person that he is satisfied that the vessel is eligible, the appropriate person may register the vessel provisionally for three months and issue a certificate of provisional registry[11]. It is a condition of provisional registry that the vessel does not fish for profit[12].

For the purposes of the registration the property in the fishing vessel is to be divided into sixty-four shares, and the number of registered owners must not exceed sixty-four[13]. A person may not be registered as the owner of a fractional part of a share in the vessel[14].

1 Merchant Shipping (Registration of Fishing Vessels) Regulations 1988, SI 1988/1926, reg 4. As to who may apply, see reg 5.
2 Ibid, reg 6. The particulars are the name of the vessel, the port of registry, year and place of build, construction material, name of builder, length, engine make, model and power, name and address of applicant and, if relevant, specified details of any previous registry: Sch 1, Pts I, II. As to full and simple registration, see para 188 above. As to change from full to simple registration, see reg 7. Any previous certificate of registry must accompany the application: reg 8. Before applying for registration, the applicant must obtain the approval of the Registrar General of Shipping to the proposed name of the vessel: see the Merchant Shipping (Fishing Vessels' Names) Regulations 1988, SI 1988/2003, made under the Merchant Shipping Act 1906 (c 48), s 50.
3 See the Merchant Shipping (Registration of Fishing Vessels) Regulations 1988, regs 9–16, Sch 2.
4 Eg AH for Arbroath or LK for Lerwick: port letters for thirty-eight Scottish ports of registry are set out in ibid, Sch 3, Table B.
5 Ibid, reg 18.
6 Ibid, reg 19. As to measuring, see reg 60, Sch 6, and for the method of marking and carving, see Sch 4.
7 Merchant Shipping Act 1988 (c 12), s 15(1); Merchant Shipping (Registration of Fishing Vessels) Regulations 1988, regs 23, 24. For the specified particulars, see Sch 2, and for the particulars to be recorded on the certificate, see Sch 5. Registry is valid for five years (reg 26), but is renewable

(regs 30, 31). As to termination of registration where the vessel ceases to be eligible, see the Merchant Shipping Act 1988, s 16.

8 Ibid, s 15(3).
9 Ibid, s 15(2), referring to the certificate required by the Fishing Vessels (Safety Provisions) Act 1970 (c 27), s 4, for which see para 201 below.
10 Merchant Shipping (Registration of Fishing Vessels) Regulations 1988, regs 48, 49. The appropriate person is eg a consular officer, High Commissioner or Governor: see reg 1(2).
11 Ibid, regs 50–52.
12 Ibid, reg 53.
13 Merchant Shipping Act 1988, s 18(1)(a), (b). However, any number of persons not exceeding five may be registered as joint owners of the vessel or any share in it, and count as one person: s 18(1)(c). A joint owner may not dispose of his interest separately from the interests of the other joint owners: s 18(1)(d).
14 Ibid, s 18(1)(e).

191. Fishing by unregistered vessel. If a fishing vessel which is eligible for registration[1] or which is wholly owned by one or more persons qualified[2] to be owners of British ships is neither registered nor excluded from registration[3], nor registered under the law of any country outside the United Kingdom, fishes for profit, the skipper, owner and charterer are each guilty of an offence and the vessel is liable to forfeiture[4].

If prescribed marks are displayed on an unregistered fishing vessel, the skipper, owner and charterer are each guilty of an offence[5]; and if the skipper or owner of such a vessel does anything or permits anything to be done for the purpose of causing the vessel to appear to be a registered vessel, the skipper, owner and charterer are each guilty of an offence and the vessel is liable to forfeiture[6].

A fishing vessel which is not a British ship and is not registered under the law of a country outside the United Kingdom, but which is eligible for registration or is wholly owned by persons qualified to be owners of British ships, or which is displaying prescribed marks, is to be dealt with as if it were a British ship for the purposes of the payment of dues, fees or other charges, liability to fines and forfeiture, and the punishment of offences committed on board or by persons belonging to it[7].

1 As to eligibility for registration, see para 189 above. For the meaning of 'fishing vessel', see para 188, note 1 above.
2 Ie for the purposes of the Merchant Shipping Act 1894 (c 60), Pt I (ss 1–91).
3 As to exclusion from registration, see para 188 above.
4 Merchant Shipping Act 1988 (c 12), s 22(1), (2). A person guilty of an offence under s 22 (or s 23) is liable on summary conviction to a fine not exceeding £50,000 or, on conviction on indictment, to imprisonment for a term not exceeding two years or a fine or both: s 24(1). Proceedings for such an offence may be taken, and the offence may for all incidental purposes be treated as having been committed, in any part of the United Kingdom: s 24(3).
5 Ibid, s 22(4). For the penalties, see note 4 above.
6 Ibid, s 22(5). For the penalties, see note 4 above.
7 Ibid, s 22(6), (7).

192. Transfers of registered vessels or shares. Any transfer of a registered fishing vessel or of a share in such a vessel, unless the transfer will result in the vessel ceasing to be British-owned, must be effected by bill of sale in an approved or prescribed form identifying the vessel[1]. Where a vessel or share has been so transferred, the transferee may not be registered as owner of the vessel or share unless he has applied for registration in the prescribed manner, has produced the bill of sale to the Secretary of State and the Secretary of State is satisfied that the vessel is eligible for registration and that all formalities have been complied with[2]. If the application is granted, the Secretary of State must register the bill of sale by causing the applicant's name to be entered in the register as owner of the vessel or share, and indorse that fact on the bill of sale[3]. Bills of sale are registered in the order in which they are produced to the Secretary of State for registration[4]. If on the application the Secretary of State is not satisfied that the vessel is eligible for registration he must serve on the owner a notice stating that fact and stating that the vessel's registration will terminate, and the registration will accordingly terminate[5].

1 Merchant Shipping Act 1988 (c 12), s 19(1), (2); Merchant Shipping (Registration of Fishing Boats) Regulations 1988, SI 1988/1926, reg 11.
2 Merchant Shipping Act 1988, s 19(3), which also applies s 15(2), (3), for which see para 190 above.
3 Ibid, s 19(4).
4 Ibid, s 19(5).
5 Ibid, s 19(6), (7).

193. Transmission of interest in registered vessel or share. Where a registered fishing vessel or a share in such a vessel is transmitted to any person by any lawful means other than by transfer by bill of sale, that person may not be registered as owner of the vessel or share unless he has applied for registration in the prescribed manner, has produced prescribed evidence of the transmission to the Secretary of State and the Secretary of State is satisfied that the vessel is eligible for registration and that all formalities have been complied with[1]. If the application is granted the Secretary of State must cause the applicant's name to be entered in the register as owner of the vessel or share[2]. If on the application the Secretary of State is not satisfied that the vessel is eligible for registration he must serve on the owner a notice stating that fact and stating that the vessel's registration will terminate, and the registration will accordingly terminate[3].

1 Merchant Shipping Act 1988 (c 12), s 20(1) (which also applies s 15(2), (3), for which see para 190 above); Merchant Shipping (Registration of Fishing Boats) Regulations 1988, SI 1988/1926, reg 12.
2 Merchant Shipping Act 1988, s 20(2).
3 Ibid, s 20(4), (5).

194. Mortgage of registered vessel or share. Any registered fishing vessel or share in such a vessel may be made a security for the repayment of a loan or the discharge of any other obligation[1]. The instrument creating such a security, which is called a 'mortgage', must be in a form prescribed or approved by the Secretary of State[2]. Where a duly executed mortgage is presented to the Secretary of State he must register it by causing it to be recorded in the register and indorse on it the fact that it has been recorded[3]. Mortgages are to be registered in the order in which they are produced to the Secretary of State for registration[4]. A registered mortgagee has power, if the mortgage money or part of it is due, to sell the vessel or share, although where there are two or more mortgagees a court order is requisite unless every prior mortgagee concurs[5]. Provision is made for the transfer, transmission and discharge of registered mortgages[6].

1 Merchant Shipping Act 1988 (c 12), s 21(1), Sch 3, para 2(1).
2 Ibid, Sch 3, para 2(2); Merchant Shipping (Registration of Fishing Vessels) Regulations 1988, SI 1988/1926, reg 39.
3 Merchant Shipping Act 1988, Sch 3, para 2(3). As to notices to the Secretary of State of intended mortgages, and the recording in the register of the interests of the intending mortgagees, see Sch 3, para 4, and the Merchant Shipping (Registration of Fishing Vessels) Regulations 1988, reg 47.
4 Merchant Shipping Act 1988, Sch 3, para 2(4). As to the priority of mortgages, see Sch 3, paras 3, 4(3), and the Merchant Shipping (Registration of Fishing Vessels) Regulations 1988, regs 43, 46.
5 Merchant Shipping Act 1988, Sch 3, para 5.
6 See ibid, Sch 3, paras 6–8.

195. Licensing of fishing boats. Under the Sea Fish (Conservation) Act 1967 the ministers[1] may provide by order:

(1) that in any specified area within British fishery limits[2] fishing by fishing boats (whether British or foreign)[3] is prohibited unless authorised by a licence granted by one of the ministers;

(2) that in any specified area outside those limits fishing by British fishing boats is prohibited unless so authorised[4].

Such an order may (subject to any exceptions for which it may provide) apply to fishing generally in the specified area or to fishing (a) for a specified description of sea fish, (b) by a specified method, (c) during a specified season or other period, or (d) in the case of an order under head (1), by fishing boats registered in a particular country[5]. The order may authorise the making of a charge for the licence[6].

The licence must be granted to the owner or charterer in respect of a named vessel, and may authorise fishing generally or may confer limited authority by reference to, in particular, the area, the periods, times or voyages, the descriptions and quantities of fish, and the method of sea fishing[7], and conditions may be attached to the licence, particularly with regard to the landing of fish at particular ports and the use to which the fish taken may be put[8]. A licence may be varied or revoked[9]. The licensing powers may be exercised so as to limit the number of boats operating in any area or fishing for any description of fish there[10]. The minister granting a licence may require the master, owner and charterer of the vessel to provide specified statistical information, and any person failing without reasonable excuse to comply with the requirement, or furnishing false information in purported compliance with the requirement or for the purpose of obtaining a licence, commits an offence[11].

Where any fishing boat is used in contravention of any prohibition imposed by any such order, the master, owner and charterer are guilty of an offence[12]. They are also guilty of an offence if a licence condition is broken[13] or if fish caught in contravention of an order are not returned to the sea forthwith[14]. Penalties for offences are laid down[15].

1 For the meaning of 'the ministers', see para 146, note 1, above.

2 As to British fishery limits, see para 130 above.

3 'Fishing boat' means a vessel of whatever size, and in whatever way propelled, for the time being employed in sea fishing or the sea-fishing service: Sea Fish (Conservation) Act 1967 (c 84), s 22(1). 'British fishing boat' means a fishing boat registered in the United Kingdom or British-owned, and 'foreign fishing boat' means one which is not so registered or owned: s 4(12) (substituted by the Fishery Limits Act 1976 (c 86), s 3).

4 Sea Fish (Conservation) Act 1967, s 4(1)(a), (b) (as so substituted). For exceptions relating to scientific investigation and the transplanting of sea fish from one fishing ground to another, see s 9(4), (5). The Sea Fish Licensing Order 1989, SI 1989/2015 (which consolidates and replaces earlier orders), prohibits fishing by British fishing boats (with certain exceptions for small boats) in specified sea areas (defined by reference to ICES statistical divisions and sub-areas of the International Council for the Exploration of the Sea) for specified descriptions of sea fish unless authorised by a licence, and confers enforcement powers on British sea-fishery officers. See also eg the Herring and White Fish (Specified Manx Waters) Licensing Order 1983, SI 1983/1204 (varied by SI 1983/1879, SI 1986/1439 and SI 1987/1564), which prohibits fishing for herring and certain white fish within a 12-mile belt round the Isle of Man but outside territorial waters unless authorised by a licence, and the Sandeels Licensing Order 1989, SI 1989/1066, which prohibits fishing for sandeels by any British fishing boat within Scottish inshore waters unless authorised by a licence.

5 Sea Fish (Conservation) Act 1967, s 4(2)(a)–(d) (as so substituted). For the meaning of 'sea fish', see para 144 above. It here includes salmon and migratory trout: s 22(1).

6 Ibid, s 4(4) (as so substituted).

7 Ibid, s 4(5) (as so substituted).

8 Ibid, s 4(6) (as so substituted). The conditions may differ as between different vessels or vessels of different descriptions: s 4(6A) (added by the Fisheries Act 1981 (c 29), s 20).

9 See the Sea Fish (Conservation) Act 1967, s 4(9) (as so substituted).

10 Ibid, s 4(8) (as so substituted).
11 Ibid, s 4(7) (as so substituted), and s 4(7A) (as added: see note 8 above).
12 Ibid, s 4(3) (as so substituted).
13 Ibid, s 4(6) (as so substituted).
14 See ibid, s 4(9A), (9B) (as added: see note 8 above).
15 These are, on conviction on indictment, a fine, and, on summary conviction, a fine not exceeding (under ibid, s 4(3)) £50,000 or (under s 4(6) or s 4(9A)) £5,000 or (under s 4(7) or s 4(7A)) £1,000: s 11(1) (substituted by the Fisheries Act 1981, s 24(1)). On conviction under s 4(3), (6) or (9A) the owner or charterer may also be disqualified for a specified period from holding a licence in respect of that vessel, the fish and gear may be forfeited and an additional fine not exceeding the value of the fish may be imposed: Sea Fish (Conservation) Act 1967, s 11(2)(c)(d), (3) (as so substituted) and s 11(5).

196. Sea-fishing boats to have official papers. The master of every registered sea-fishing boat[1], whether his boat is within British waters[2] or not, must have on board his certificate of registration[3], and the master of every foreign sea-fishing boat within British waters must have on board official papers evidencing its nationality[4]. Any person contravening these provisions without reasonable excuse (the proof of which lies on him) is liable on summary conviction to a fine not exceeding level 2 on the standard scale, and in the case of a foreign boat the court may order the boat to be detained for up to three months from the date of conviction or until the fine is paid, whichever period is the shorter[5]. British sea-fishery officers have power to take offending fishing boats to the nearest port and detain them[6].

1 Ie every sea-fishing boat registered under the Merchant Shipping Act 1988 (c 12), Pt II (ss 12–25), for which see paras 188 ff above. For the meaning of 'sea-fishing boat', see the Sea Fisheries Act 1868 (c 45), s 5, and para 125, note 2, above.
2 'British waters' means waters within the seaward limits of the territorial waters adjacent to the United Kingdom, the Channel Islands and the Isle of Man: ibid, s 26(5) (substituted by the Merchant Shipping Act 1988, s 57(4), Sch 6).
3 Sea Fisheries Act 1868, s 26(1) (as so substituted). As to the certificate of registry, see the Merchant Shipping (Registration of Fishing Vessels) Regulations 1988, SI 1988/1926, reg 24, Sch 5.
4 Sea Fisheries Act 1868, s 26(2) (as so substituted). 'Foreign sea-fishing boat' means a sea-fishing boat which is not registered in the United Kingdom, the Channel Islands or the Isle of Man, is not excluded from registration by regulations made under the Merchant Shipping Act 1988, s 13 (see the Merchant Shipping (Registration of Fishing Vessels) Regulations 1988, reg 57 (salmon cobles)), and is not wholly owned by persons qualified to be owners of British ships for the purposes of the Merchant Shipping Act 1894 (c 60), Pt I (ss 1–91): Sea Fisheries Act 1868, s 26(5) (as so substituted).
5 Ibid, s 26(3) (as so substituted). For level 2, see para 20, note 3, above.
6 Ibid, s 26(4) (as so substituted), applying the Sea Fisheries Act 1968 (c 77), s 8(4), for which see para 172 above.

197. Letters and numbers on fishing boats. A fishing boat must bear, in white paint on a black ground on each bow and on the stern, the initial letter or letters of the port to which she belongs and the registry number in the series of numbers for that port, as determined by the competent authority, together with the name of the boat on the stern, and the letter or letters and numbers on any sail, and these must remain legible[1]. In addition to these requirements, every British sea-fishing boat propelled by steam, if fishing in any part of the sea adjoining Scotland, must have these letters and figures painted on its funnel and quarter[2]. These requirements may be enforced by sea-fishery officers[2].

1 Convention for Regulating the Police of the North Sea Fisheries (The Hague, 6 May 1882; 73 BFSP 39), arts 5–10, set out in the Sea Fisheries Act 1883 (c 22), Sch 1.

2 Sea Fisheries (Scotland) Amendment Act 1885 (c 70), s 5 (prospectively repealed by the Sea Fisheries Act 1968 (c 77), s 22(2), Sch 2, Pt II).

198. Fishing boats and gear lost or abandoned at sea. Fishing boats or fishing gear lost or abandoned at sea and found or taken possession of either within United Kingdom territorial waters or beyond those waters and brought within those waters are to be treated as wreck for the purposes of the wreck and salvage provisions[1] of the Merchant Shipping Act 1894[2].

1 Ie the Merchant Shipping Act 1894 (c 60), Pt IX (ss 510–571).
2 Sea Fisheries Act 1968 (c 77), s 17. For the meaning of 'fishing boat', see para 170, note 2, above.

199. Inquiry into complaint of injury to boat or gear. If a person belonging to a British sea-fishing boat in Scotland or any part of the sea adjoining Scotland commits an offence against the Sea Fisheries Acts[1] resulting in injury by one sea-fishing boat to another or to its gear etc, a British sea-fishery officer may inquire into the complaint of any injured party and, subject to various formalities (including giving the respondent an opportunity of being heard), report on it to the Secretary of State[2]. This report generally provides conclusive evidence in the appropriate sheriff court of the damage incurred, though if the damage is found to exceed £12 an appeal is permitted[2].

1 Offences under the Sea Fisheries Act 1968 (c 77), s 5 or s 10, or the Fishery Limits Act 1976 (c 86), s 2 (see paras 131, 170, 173, above) are, however, excluded. For the meaning of 'Sea Fisheries Acts', see para 175, note 1, above.
2 Sea Fisheries (Scotland) Amendment Act 1885 (c 70), s 7 (amended by the Sea Fisheries Act 1968, s 22(1), Sch 1, para 28, and the Fishery Limits Act 1976, s 2(8)).

(j) Safety Measures

200. Safety measures generally. Several Acts concerning merchant shipping generally apply to fishing boats, including the Merchant Shipping Acts 1894 (c 60) and 1906 (c 48), the Merchant Shipping (Scottish Fishing Boats) Act 1920 (c 39), the Merchant Shipping (Safety Conventions) Act 1949 (12 & 13 Geo 6 c 43), the Merchant Shipping Act 1950 (c 9), the Fishery Limits Act 1964 (c 72), the Merchant Shipping Acts 1965 (c 47) and 1970 (c 36), the Customs and Excise Management Act 1979 (c 2), and the Merchant Shipping Acts 1979 (c 39) and 1988 (c 12). Various suggestions have been made for relevant improvement[1].

1 See *Trawler Safety: Final Report of the Committee of Inquiry into Trawler Safety* (the Holland-Martin Report) (Cmnd 4114) (1969); and *Report of the Working Group on Discipline in the Fishing Industry* (the Service Report) (1975).

201. Fishing vessel certificates and safety rules. The Fishing Vessels (Safety Provisions) Act 1970 makes provisions for the safety of all fishing vessels[1] registered in the United Kingdom. It provides for the making of fishing vessel construction rules[2] and of rules for surveying and periodically inspecting fishing vessels[3]. If the Secretary of State for Transport is satisfied, on receipt of a declaration of survey, that the vessel complies with the applicable requirements of the fishing vessel construction rules, the rules for life-saving appliances[4], the radio rules[5], the rules for direction-finders[6] and the rules for radio navigational aids[7], he must, on the application of the owner, issue a fishing vessel certificate[8] without which no fishing vessel required to be surveyed under the fishing vessel survey rules may go to sea[9]. If it goes or attempts to go to sea without such a certificate, the owner or master commits an offence[10]. Notice must be given of any alteration in the vessel or its equipment which affects the certificate[11].

Regulations and rules under the Act are made by statutory instrument, but before rules are made the Secretary of State must consult United Kingdom organisations appearing to him to represent persons likely to be affected[12]. The Act may be extended to specified territories outside the United Kingdom and to fishing vessels registered therein[13].

1 'Fishing vessel' means a fishing vessel as defined in para 188, note 1, above: Fishing Vessels (Safety Provisions) Act 1970 (c 27), s 9(1) (amended by the Merchant Shipping Act 1988 (c 12), s 57(4), Sch 6).
2 Fishing Vessels (Safety Provisions) Act 1970, s 1. See the Fishing Vessels (Safety Provisions) Rules 1975, SI 1975/330 (amended by SI 1975/471, SI 1976/432, SI 1977/252, SI 1977/313, SI 1977/498, SI 1978/1598, SI 1978/1873, and SI 1981/567), and para 202 below.
3 Fishing Vessels (Safety Provisions) Act 1970, s 2. See the rules cited in note 2 above.
4 Ie rules made under the Merchant Shipping Act 1894 (c 60), s 427. See eg the Merchant Shipping (Life-Saving Appliances) Rules 1965, SI 1965/1105 (now in effect replaced by the Merchant Shipping (Life-Saving Appliances) Regulations 1980, SI 1980/538, and the Fishing Vessels (Life-Saving Appliances) Regulations 1988, SI 1988/38 (see para 203 below), made under the Merchant Shipping Act 1979 (c 39), s 22), and the rules cited in note 2 above.
5 Ie rules made under the Merchant Shipping (Safety Conventions) Act 1949 (12 & 13 Geo 6 c 43), s 3 (substituted by the Merchant Shipping Act 1970 (c 36), s 85(1), Sch 1). See the Merchant Shipping (Radio) (Fishing Vessels) Rules 1974, SI 1974/1919 (amended by SI 1982/1292), and para 205 below.
6 Ie rules made under the Merchant Shipping (Safety Convention) Act 1949, s 5. No rules are in force under that power, but see the many instruments made under the Merchant Shipping Act 1979, ss 21, 22.
7 Ie rules made under the Merchant Shipping (Safety Convention) Act 1949, s 6. No rules are in force under that power, but see the many instruments made under the Merchant Shipping Act 1979, ss 21, 22.
8 Fishing Vessels (Safety Provisions) Act 1970, s 3(1); Fishing Vessels (Safety Provisions) Rules 1975, r 126, Sch 1. The certificate remains in force for forty-eight months (r 127) unless extended (r 128) or cancelled (r 129). Periodical inspection of vessels in respect of which a certificate is in force is required by r 130 (amended by SI 1978/1598). The Secretary of State for Transport exercises functions under the 1970 Act which were originally those of the Board of Trade: see the Transfer of Functions (Trade and Industry) Order 1983, SI 1983/1127.
9 Fishing Vessels (Safety Provisions) Act 1970, s 4(1).
10 Ibid, s 4(2).
11 Ibid, s 5.
12 Ibid, s 7.
13 Ibid, s 8.

202. The safety rules. The Fishing Vessels (Safety Provisions) Rules 1975 apply to every mechanically propelled sea-going fishing vessel registered in the United Kingdom[1]. The rules contain fishing vessel construction rules[2], rules for life-saving appliances[3] and provisions as to surveys and certificates[4].

The fishing vessel construction rules cover the structural strength of the hull and superstructure, requiring watertight collision bulkheads[5]; the watertight integrity of the vessel[6]; freeboard and stability[7]; boilers and machinery[8]; bilge pumping arrangements[9]; electrical equipment[10]; miscellaneous plant and equipment, including watertight doors, steering gear, communications on board, refrigerating plants, anchors, winches and lifting gear[11]; structural fire protection and fire detection[12]; the protection of the crew by the provision of bulwarks, guard rails and wires and the safety of deck openings, stairways and ladders[13]; such nautical equipment as compasses, sounding equipment, nautical publications, flags and signalling equipment and pilot ladders[14]; and the documentation to be carried on board[15].

The rules for life-saving appliances contain different requirements for lifeboats, liferafts, lifeboat davits, portable radio equipment and line-throwing appliances for vessels of different lengths[16], as well as general requirements for such equipment[17], and cover equipment and rations for lifeboats and liferafts[18], stowage of lifeboats and other equipment[19]; embarkation into lifeboats etc[20]; and the storage of pyrotechnic distress signals[21]. They also contain different fire appliance requirements for vessels of different lengths[22]; general requirements for fire pumps, pipes, hydrants, hoses, nozzles, extinguishers, alarms and detectors, water spraying systems, foam installations and firemen's outfits, the means of stopping machinery etc, fire control plans and the availability of fire-fighting appliances[23]; and make provision for musters and drills[24].

Where the rules require that the hull or machinery be constructed in a particular manner or that any particular equipment, fitting, material, appliance or apparatus be provided or that particular provision be made, it is sufficient compliance if provision is made which is at least as effective as that required by the rules[25].

Every vessel of 12 metres or over in length must be surveyed and periodically inspected by a surveyor[26], who must provide the Secretary of State with a declaration of survey, a prescribed record of particulars and a report[27]. It is on the basis of this survey that the Secretary of State issues the necessary fishing vessel certificate[28].

1 Fishing Vessels (Safety Provisions) Rules 1975, SI 1975/330, r 1(2).
2 Ibid, Pt II (rr 2–75).
3 Ibid, Pt III (rr 76–121).
4 Ibid, Pt V (rr 123–130).
5 Ibid, r 2.
6 Ibid, rr 3–14 (amended by SI 1976/432).
7 Ibid, rr 15, 16.
8 Ibid, rr 17–35.
9 Ibid, rr 36, 37 (amended by SI 1976/432).
10 Ibid, rr 38–43.
11 Ibid, rr 44–54.
12 Ibid, rr 55–62 (amended by SI 1976/432).
13 Ibid, rr 63–65 (as so amended).
14 Ibid, rr 66–72.
15 Ibid, rr 73–75.
16 Ibid, rr 76–81 (amended by SI 1976/432 and SI 1978/1873).
17 Ibid, rr 82–89.
18 Ibid, rr 90–94.
19 Ibid, rr 95–98.
20 Ibid, r 99.
21 Ibid, r 100.
22 Ibid, rr 101–106.
23 Ibid, rr 107–118.
24 Ibid, rr 119–121.
25 Ibid, r 122.
26 Ibid, rr 123, 124 (amended by SI 1977/313 and the Fisheries Act 1981 (c 29), s 13(2), Sch 3, para 8(3)).
27 Fishing Vessels (Safety Provisions) Rules 1975, r 125, Sch 2.
28 See para 201 above.

203. Equipment requirements. The equipment requirements of the Safety at Sea Act 1986, despite the short title of the Act, apply only to United Kingdom fishing vessels[1]. At the date at which this volume states the law these provisions had not been brought into force[2].

Under the Act (when brought into force) every United Kingdom fishing vessel of 12 metres or more in length[3], and such other United Kingdom fishing vessels as may be prescribed by the Secretary of State by regulations made by statutory instrument[4], must carry a radio beacon which in an emergency will indicate its position by transmitting on a prescribed frequency[5], and the life rafts which it carries must be secured so that they are automatically released and float free if the vessel sinks[6]. Every United Kingdom fishing vessel of less than 12 metres in length must carry a lifejacket of an appropriate size for each person on board, together with extra lifejackets for each different size[7]. The Secretary of State may by regulations made by statutory instrument amplify or extend any of these requirements, in particular by laying down further technical require-ments[8]. Before making any regulations the Secretary of State must carry out consultations with such organisations or persons likely to be affected as appear to him appropriate[9].

No fishing vessel to which the above requirements apply may go to sea unless they are complied with, and if it does the owner and skipper are each liable on summary conviction to a fine not exceeding level 5 on the standard scale[10], although it is a defence for the accused to show that he used all due diligence and took all reasonable precautions to prevent the commission of the offence[11].

The Secretary of State may exempt a fishing vessel or description of fishing vessel from any of these requirements generally, or for a specified time or with respect to a specified voyage or to voyages in a specified area, and may do so subject to any specified conditions[12].

The Secretary of State has a general power to made safety regulations under the Merchant Shipping Act 1979[13]. Under this power he has made regulations laying down requirements for fishing vessels over 12 metres in length to carry emergency position-indicating radio beacons[14], requiring fishing vessels of less than 12 metres in length to carry lifejackets with lifejacket lights[15], and prescrib-ing float-free arrangements for life rafts[16]. A vessel not complying with these requirements is liable to be detained[17], and if it goes to sea the owner and skipper are each guilty of an offence and liable on summary conviction to a fine not exceeding £2,000 or, in the case of non-compliance with the lifejacket require-ments, £500, although it is a defence to prove that the person charged took reasonable steps to avoid the commission of the offence[18].

1 See the Safety at Sea Act 1986 (c 23), ss 1(2), 2(2), 3(2). 'United Kingdom fishing vessel' means a fishing vessel (as defined in para 188, note 1, above) registered in the United Kingdom: s 13(1) (amended by the Merchant Shipping Act 1988 (c 12), s 57(4), Sch 6).
2 As at 1 December 1989 the only commencement order made under the Safety at Sea Act 1986, s 15(3), brought into force the amending provisions of ss 10, 11, 14(2), (3): Safety at Sea Act 1986 (Commencement No 1) Order 1986, SI 1986/1759.
3 'Length' means length as shown in the vessel's certificate of registry: Safety at Sea Act 1986, s 13(1).
4 Ibid, ss 4(1)(a), 9(2).
5 Ibid, s 1(1), (2). Fishing vessel survey rules may be made for the surveying and periodical inspection of United Kingdom fishing vessels or any description of them to ensure compliance with these rules for radio beacons and the automatic release of life rafts: Fishing Vessels (Safety Provisions) Act 1970 (c 27), s 2(1) (as prospectively amended by the Safety at Sea Act 1986, s 5(1)).
6 Ibid, s 2(1), (2). As to survey rules, see note 5 above.
7 Ibid, s 3(1). If the lifejackets are all of the same size, there must be an extra one if there are ten or fewer persons on board, and two if there are eleven or more on board: s 3(1). The lifejackets must comply with the requirements of the Fishing Vessels (Safety Provisions) Rules 1975, SI 1975/330, Sch 11, Pt I (amended by SI 1975/471) or, as the case may be, Sch 11, Pt II: Safety at Sea Act 1986, s 3(2).
8 Ibid, s 4(1)(b), 9(2).
9 Ibid, s 9(3).
10 Ibid, s 6(1), (2). For level 5, see para 176, note 5, above.
11 Ibid, s 6(3).
12 Ibid, s 8(1), (2). No procedure is laid down as to how exemptions are to be applied for or granted.
13 Merchant Shipping Act 1979 (c 39), ss 21, 22.
14 Fishing Vessels (Life-Saving Appliances) Regulations 1988, SI 1988/38, reg 3.
15 Ibid, reg 4, Schs 1, 2.

16 Ibid, reg 5, Sch 3, supplementing the Fishing Vessels (Safety Provisions) Rules 1975, SI
   1975/330, Pt IIIA (rr 76–100) (Life-Saving Applicances and Equipment) (amended by SI 1976/432
   and SI 1978/1873).
17 Fishing Vessels (Life-Saving Appliances) Regulations 1988, reg 7.
18 Ibid, reg 8.

204. Training in safety matters. The Secretary of State may make regulations for securing that the skipper of and every seaman employed or engaged
in a United Kingdom fishing vessel is trained in safety matters[1]. The regulations
may provide that if a person goes to sea on a fishing vessel in contravention of a
requirement of the regulations he and the skipper and owner commit offences[2].
The Secretary of State may grant exemptions from these requirements[3].

The Secretary of State has a general power to make safety regulations under
the Merchant Shipping Act 1979[4]. Under this power he has made regulations
under which no person other than a certificated deck officer or certificated
engineer may be employed or engaged on a fishing vessel registered in the
United Kingdom after specified dates[5] unless he holds a certificate or certificates
issued by the Sea Fish Industry Authority certifying that he has undergone an
approved training course in basic survival at sea, basic fire-fighting and prevention and basic first aid, although holders of skipper or second hand certificates
born before 1 March 1954 do not require first aid certificates[6]. If a person goes to
sea on a fishing vessel registered in the United Kingdom in contravention of
these requirements he is guilty of an offence and liable on summary conviction
to a fine not exceeding level 2 (or, if he is the skipper or owner, level 5) on the
standard scale, and the skipper and owner (except in respect of a contravention
by himself) is liable on summary conviction to a fine not exceeding level 5 on
the standard scale[7]. The Secretary of State may grant exemptions from these
requirements[8].

1 Safety at Sea Act 1986 (c 23), s 7(1). For the meaning of 'United Kingdom fishing vessel', see para
  203, note 1, above. Section 7 has not yet been brought into force: see para 203, note 2, above.
2 See ibid, s 7(2).
3 See ibid, s 8(1), (2), and para 203 above.
4 Merchant Shipping Act 1979 (c 39), ss 21, 22.
5 For new entrants the training must be completed before going to sea, and for serving fishermen
  the specified date is 1 March 1990, 1991, 1992 or 1993, depending on age, the youngest coming
  first: Fishing Vessels (Safety Training) Regulations 1989, SI 1989/126, reg 2(3). Serving fishermen born before 1 March 1954 are exempt from training requirements: reg 2(1).
6 Ibid, reg 2(1).
7 Ibid, reg 3. As to level 2 and level 5, see para 20, note 3, and para 176, note 5, above respectively.
8 Ibid, reg 4.

205. Radios. Detailed provision is made by regulations[1] for the radio equipment required to be installed in fishing vessels of different classes, depending on
the size of the vessel and the voyages on which they are engaged, and for the
aerials with which they must be fitted and the range of transmission they must
have[2]. The vessels must carry suitably qualified radio operators, who have
prescribed duties[3]. Continuous radio watch must be maintained whilst the
vessel is at sea, and a radio log book must be kept and maintained[4]. The vessel
may be boarded and inspected at all reasonable times to ensure that these
provisions are complied with[5].

1 See the Merchant Shipping (Radio) (Fishing Vessels) Rules 1974, SI 1974/1919 (amended by SI
  1982/1292). These regulations were made under the Merchant Shipping (Safety Convention)
  Act 1949 (12 & 13 Geo 6 c 43), s 3 (substituted by the Merchant Shipping Act 1970 (c 36), s 85(1),
  Sch 1).
2 Merchant Shipping (Radio) (Fishing Vessels) Regulations 1974, regs 3, 6, 7 (as so amended).
3 Ibid, regs 9, 10, 12.

4 Ibid, regs 11, 13 (amended by SI 1982/1292).
5 Merchant Shipping Act 1970, s 76(1). For the fees for inspection on the application of the owner, see the Merchant Shipping (Fishing Vessels) (Radios) (Fees) Regulations 1986, SI 1986/680.

206. Medical stores. Every United Kingdom fishing vessel or fishery research vessel proceeding beyond a specified area must carry specified medicines and medical stores[1] of an approved standard[2] packaged, labelled and stored in a prescribed manner[3]. Contravention renders the owner liable on summary conviction to a fine not exceeding £2,000, and contravention of the storage requirements also renders the skipper liable on summary conviction to a fine not exceeding £1,000, although no offence is committed if a deficiency is caused by the proper use of medicines etc which could not reasonably be replaced[4].

1 Merchant Shipping (Medical Stores) (Fishing Vessels) Regulations 1988, SI 1988/1547, reg 3. The requirements differ depending on the length of the voyage and whether or not the vessel is fitted with sleeping accommodation. 'Fishing vessel' means a vessel for the time being employed in sea fishing for profit: reg 1(3). The regulations were made under the Merchant Shipping Act 1979 (c 39), ss 21, 22.
2 Merchant Shipping (Medical Stores) (Fishing Vessels) Regulations 1988, reg 5.
3 Ibid, regs 6, 7.
4 Ibid, reg 9.

207. Reporting of accidents. Every accident on board a United Kingdom fishing vessel of 10 metres or more registered length[1], or during embarking or disembarking, to any person[2] which results in death or personal injury involving incapacity for more than three days following the day of the accident must be notified by the skipper[3].

1 Fishing Vessels (Reporting of Accidents) Regulations 1985, SI 1985/855, reg 2. 'Fishing vessel' means a vessel for the time being employed in sea fishing, but not a vessel used otherwise than for profit: reg 1(2). The regulations were made under the Merchant Shipping Act 1979 (c 39), ss 21, 22.
2 The regulations do not apply to a person employed on board as a docker, shiprepairer or shipbuilder, or a person on board without authority: see the Fishing Vessels (Reporting of Accidents) Regulations 1985, reg 3 proviso.
3 Ibid, reg 3. The skipper notifies the accident by completing and signing a form approved by the Secretary of State and forwarding it to the Department of Transport within seven days of the accident or, if later, the vessel's arrival at the next port of call: reg 4. Failure to comply renders the skipper liable on summary conviction to a fine not exceeding £100 unless he shows that he took all reasonable precautions and exercised all due diligence to avoid the commission of the offence: reg 5.

208. Loading and unloading fishing vessels. A safe place of work must be provided and properly maintained for any person engaged in Great Britain in loading, unloading, moving or handling wet fish on, at or nearby any quay or on any fishing vessel moored there, with safe access to and egress therefrom and adequate lighting[1]. Floors, decks, surfaces, stairs, passages and gangways must be kept free from things likely to cause persons to slip or vehicles to skid[2], and dangerous places must be properly fenced[3]. Adequate and suitable rescue and life-saving equipment, means to effect escape from danger and fire-fighting equipment must be provided[4]. The fish loading process must be so planned and executed as to avoid exposure to danger, and safe plant and equipment must be provided and maintained[5]. It is the duty of every employer, self-employed person, fishing vessel skipper and person otherwise concerned with premises to comply with these requirements so far as they concern matters within his control[6].

1 Loading and Unloading of Fishing Vessels Regulations 1988, SI 1988/1656, regs 2, 3, 5(1), (4). These regulations were made under the Health and Safety at Work etc Act 1974 (c 37), s 15.

2 Loading and Unloading of Fishing Vessels Regulations 1988, reg 5(2).
3 Ibid, reg 5(3).
4 Ibid, reg 5(5).
5 Ibid, reg 6.
6 Ibid, reg 4.

(k) The Sea Fish Industry

209. The white fish industry. The Sea Fish Industry Act 1938 provided for the establishment of the White Fish Commission to review matters relating to the white fish industry and to advise the Secretary of State for Scotland and the then Minister of Agriculture and Fisheries on these matters[1]. 'White fish' included shellfish, but not herring, fish of the salmon species nor migratory trout[2]. The White Fish Commission was replaced by the White Fish Authority constituted under the Sea Fish Industry Act 1951 to reorganise, develop and regulate the white fish industry and to keep matters relating to it under review[3]. The Scottish Committee was constituted to advise the White Fish Authority as to the exercise and performance of its functions in Scotland[4], and further advice as to the exercise and performance of its functions generally was to be given by the White Fish Industry Advisory Council[5]. The legislation was re-enacted in a consolidating Act, the Sea Fish Industry Act 1970[6], most of which was repealed in 1981[7].

1 Sea Fish Industry Act 1938 (c 30), s 1 (repealed).
2 Ibid, s 62(1) (repealed).
3 Sea Fish Industry Act 1951 (c 30), s 1 (repealed).
4 Ibid, s 2 (repealed).
5 Ibid, s 3 (repealed).
6 Sea Fish Industry Act 1970 (c 11), ss 1–3 (repealed).
7 Fisheries Act 1981 (c 29), s 46(2), Sch 5, Pt I.

210. The herring industry. The Herring Industry Act 1935 provided for the establishment of the Herring Industry Board to ascertain the opinion of persons engaged in the herring industry and to prepare a scheme to effect the reorganisation, development and regulation of the industry, and extensive powers to further this aim were given to the board[1]. Provision was also made for the appointment of a consumers' committee and a committee of investigation[2]. The board was reconstituted under the Herring Industry Act 1938[3], and the Herring Industry Advisory Council was constituted to give the board advice and assistance in the discharge of its functions[4]. The legislation was re-enacted in a consolidating Act, the Sea Fish Industry Act 1970, which provided for the continued existence of the board and the advisory council[5] as well as the consumers' committee and the committee of investigation[6], but most of the Act was repealed in 1981[7].

1 Herring Industry Act 1935 (c 9), ss 1–3 (repealed).
2 Ibid, s 4, Sch 2 (repealed).
3 Herring Industry Act 1938 (c 42), s 1 (repealed).
4 Ibid, s 2 (repealed).
5 Sea Fish Industry Act 1970 (c 11), ss 29–32 (repealed).
6 Ibid, s 32 (repealed).
7 Fisheries Act 1981 (c 29), s 46(2), Sch 5, Pt I.

211. Abolition of the White Fish Authority and the Herring Industry Board. Both the White Fish Authority and the Herring Industry Board (which had their headquarters in Edinburgh), and their associated councils and committees, were, following the extension of British fishery limits, and the subjection of these limits to the Common Fisheries Policy of the European Community[1], abolished by the Fisheries Act 1981[2], which established a single Sea Fish Industry Authority with a somewhat different role, to promote the efficiency of the sea fish industry and to serve the interests of that industry as a whole[3].

1 As to the enforcement of Community rules, see para 178 above.
2 Fisheries Act 1981 (c 29), ss 13, 46(2), Sch 5, Pt I.
3 Ibid, s 2(1).

212. The Sea Fish Industry Authority. The Fisheries Act 1981 introduced a number of new policies following the extension of British fishery limits. The main purpose of the Act was to establish a Sea Fish Industry Authority[1] to promote the efficiency of the sea fish industry[2], having regard to consumers' interests[3], and to provide financial assistance for it[4]. The authority has power to carry out research and development on matters relating to the sea fish industry, to give advice on such matters, to provide or provide for training, to promote marketing, consumption and exports and to give financial assistance[5]. For the purpose of financing its activities the authority may impose a levy on persons engaged in the industry[6]. It may borrow, and government grants, and loans and guarantees may be made[7].

1 Fisheries Act 1981 (c 29), s 1(1). For the constitution of the authority, see s 1(2)–(5), Sch 1.
2 Ibid, s 2(1).
3 Ibid, s 2(2).
4 Ibid, Pt II (ss 15–18).
5 Ibid, s 3.
6 Ibid, s 4.
7 Ibid, ss 6–8.

213. Financial assistance for the sea fish industry. The ministers[1] may, in accordance with a scheme made by them with Treasury approval, make grants or loans for the purpose of reorganising, developing or promoting the sea fish industry in the United Kingdom or of contributing to the expenses of those engaged in it[2]. The ministers may require the Sea Fish Industry Authority to administer such a scheme for them[3].

Among the schemes made under this power are schemes for grants to recognised fish producers' organisations or associations of such organisations in respect of their administrative expenses during a specified period to the extent permitted under European Community rules[4]; for grants in respect of the expenditure incurred in acquiring new fishing vessels or in the acquisition, installation, modification, renewal or replacement of any part of a fishing vessel registered in the United Kingdom[5]; and for 'exploratory voyage grants' to engage in fishing operations for commercial purposes in a specified area with a view to assessing the profitability of long-term exploitation of the fishery resources there, and 'joint venture grants' for participation in a contractual association for a limited period with natural or legal persons of third countries with which the European Community maintains fishing relations for the purpose of the joint exploitation and use of the fishery resources of those countries[6].

1 'The ministers' means the Minister of Agriculture, Fisheries and Food and the Secretary of State concerned with the sea fish industry in Scotland, Wales and Northern Ireland or one or more of them, depending on the countries to which the scheme extends: see the Fisheries Act 1981 (c 29), s 18(1).
2 Ibid, s 15(1), read with s 18(2), which also explains who is to be regarded as being engaged in the industry.

3 Ibid, s 16.
4 See the Fish Producers' Organizations (Formation Grants) Scheme 1982, SI 1982/498 (amended
   by SI 1985/987). The rules referred to are contained in EC Council Regulations 106/76 (OJ L20,
   28.1.76, p 42), 3796/81 (OJ L379, 31.12.81, p 1) and 3140/82 (OJ L331, 26.11.82, p 7), and EC
   Commission Regulations 457/72 (OJ L54, 3.3.72, p 31) and 1452/83 (OJ L149, 7.6.83, p 5).
5 See the Fishing Vessels (Acquisition and Improvement) (Grants) Scheme 1987, SI 1987/1135
   (amended by SI 1990/685).
6 See the Fishing Vessels (Financial Assistance) Scheme 1987, SI 1987/1136, which implements EC
   Council Regulation 4028/86 (OJ L376, 31.12.87, p 7) on Community measures to improve and
   adapt structures in the fisheries and aquaculture sector.

214. Financial assistance for fish farming. The ministers[1] may, in accordance with a scheme made by them with Treasury approval, make such grants as
appear to them desirable for the purpose of reorganising, developing or promoting fish farming in Great Britain[2]. Such a scheme has been made, extending
to the whole of Great Britain[3]. Under it the appropriate minister[4] may make to
any person a grant of up to 10 per cent of the expenditure incurred or to be
incurred in connection with a project for fish farming if the grant appears to the
minister to be desirable for the above purpose and requisite to enable that person
to benefit from European Community aid for an appropriate fish farming
project[5]. In certain circumstances grants are revokable and repayable[6]. Application for approval of expenditure for the purpose of a grant is to be made in
such form and manner and at such time, and with such information, as the
appropriate minister determines[7].

1 'The ministers' means, in relation to a scheme extending throughout Great Britain, the Minister
   of Agriculture, Fisheries and Food and the Secretaries of State respectively concerned with
   fisheries in Wales and Scotland and, in relating to a scheme extending only to Scotland, the
   Secretary of State: see the Fisheries Act 1981 (c 29), s 31(5).
2 Ibid, s 31(1). 'Fish farming' means the breeding, rearing or cultivation of fish (including shellfish)
   for the purpose of producing food for human consumption: s 31(2).
3 Fish Farming (Financial Assistance) Scheme 1987, SI 1987/1134.
4 In relation to Scotland 'the appropriate minister' means the Secretary of State for Scotland: ibid,
   para 2.
5 Ibid, paras 3(1), 4(1). The Community aid is given under EC Council Regulation 4028/86 (OJ
   L376, 31.12.86, p 7), title IV, on Community measures to improve and adapt structures in the
   fisheries and aquaculture sector.
6 Fish Farming (Financial Assistance) Scheme 1987, para 5.
7 Ibid, para 3(6). The giving of false information is an offence: Fisheries Act 1981, s 17, applied by
   s 31(8).

(6) MARINE MAMMALS

(a) Introduction

215. General. Although marine mammals such as seals (*Pinnepedia*) and
whales (*Cetacea*) are warm blooded, air breathing creatures and different in
many other ways from fish, they have been traditionally regarded for legal
purposes as fish and to be therefore a *res communis* like fish. Because both species
have these special characteristics they are more vulnerable to capture than fish,
however, and, as both species are highly migratory, they need international
agreements to protect them throughout their migratory range. United Kingdom legislation reflects this. Seals in particular also require protection on land,
where they repair for pupping. Unlike the United States and some other
countries, the United Kingdom has no legislation referring to marine mammals, as such, as a category, but it does have several statutes relating separately
to seals and to whales.

(b) Seals

216. The Seal Fishery Act 1875. The first Act of the United Kingdom to provide a close time for seal fishing was the Seal Fishery Act 1875, which applies to the harp or saddleback seal, the bladder-nosed or hooded seal, the ground or bearded seal, and the floe seal or floe rat[1]. To these may be added any animal of the seal kind specified by Order in Council[1], exercisable by statutory instrument. If and when other states engaged in seal fishing made similar provisions, the Act could be applied, by Order in Council, to certain areas of the seas adjacent to the eastern coasts of Greenland[2].

The Order may provide for a close season, prohibiting the killing, capturing, or attempting to kill or capture of any seal within that area[3]. The penalty for any breach of the Act, by act or default, is a fine not exceeding level 3 on the standard scale[4]. An Order in Council of 28 November 1876 fixes the annual close season as from 1 January to 2 April. If the offence is committed by the fault or with the connivance of the master or owner of the ship, he is liable to the same penalty as any person committing the offence[5]. In addition the court may direct that payment of any fine be secured by arrestment and sale of the ship and her tackle[6].

1 Seal Fishery Act 1875 (c 18), s 6.
2 Ibid, s 1. For the sea areas referred to, see Schedule.
3 Ibid, s 2.
4 Ibid, s 2; Criminal Procedure (Scotland) Act 1975 (c 21), ss 289F, 289G (added by the Criminal Justice Act 1982 (c 48), s 54). For level 3, see para 11, note 15, above.
5 Seal Fishery Act 1875, s 4.
6 Ibid, s 5.

217. The Behring Sea Award Act 1894. The articles of the regulations assented to by a majority of the members of the Tribunal of Arbitration constituted under a treaty concluded in 1892 between the United Kingdom and the United States of America[1] were enacted in the United Kingdom in the Behring Sea Award Act 1894, which is not affected by the Merchant Shipping Act 1894[2]. The regulations remain in force until they have been, in whole or in part, abolished or modified by agreement between the two governments, and must be examined by them every five years with a view to making any modifications seen to be necessary[3]. These modifications are to be given effect by Order in Council[4], but no Order had been made up to 1 December 1989. The regulations provide for

(1) the prohibition by the governments of the United States and of Great Britain (*sic*) of the killing, capture or pursuit by their citizens and subjects respectively of fur-seals within a zone of 60 geographical miles (of 60 to a degree of latitude) around the Pribiloff Islands, including the territorial waters[5];

(2) an annual close season from 1 May to 31 July for sealing on the high sea (including the Behring Sea), north of 35 degrees N, and east of 180 degrees of longitude from Greenwich until it strikes the water boundary described in Article 1 of the Treaty of 1867 between the United States and Russia, following that line up to the Behring Straits[6].

Only sailing boats, or canoes or undecked boats propelled by paddles, oars or sails commonly used as fishing boats, may be used during the open season[7]. Sailing vessels authorised to fish for fur-seals must have a licence issued by their respective governments, and carry a distinguishing flag prescribed by them[8].

Other provisions of the Award require masters of vessels engaged in fur-seal fishing to keep detailed records of their activities, the information recorded being exchanged between the two governments at the end of each open season[9]; ban the use of nets, firearms and explosives for fur-seal fishing in this area[10]; and require the two governments to ensure that men engaged in these operations have the proper skills[11].

There are certain general exemptions to permit American Indians living on the coasts of American and British territory to continue to use traditional vessels for fur-seal fishing for their own purposes, but they do not extend to the waters of the Behring Sea or the waters of the Aleutian Pass[12].

The Behring Sea Award Act 1894 re-enacts certain provisions of the Merchant Shipping Act 1854 which accord powers to specified British officers to seize, detain offending vessels and bring them to trial in the High Court of England or Northern Ireland[13]. It also prescribes legal procedures for imposition of penalties and punishment, in all places in the Queen's dominions except Scotland[14]. Legal procedures in Scotland are provided for separately[15]. The provisions of the Merchant Shipping Act 1894 should now be read to take account of the Sheriff Courts (Scotland) Act 1971 (c 58), the Local Government (Scotland) Act 1973 (c 65), and the Criminal Procedure (Scotland) Act 1975 (c 21).

1 Treaty with the United States of America relating to Behring's Sea (Washington, 29 February 1892; TS 8 (1892); C 6639).
2 Behring Sea Award Act 1894 (c 2), s 1, Sch 1 (where the articles of the award are set out); Merchant Shipping Act 1894 (c 60), s 745(1).
3 Behring Sea Award Act 1894, Sch 1, art 9.
4 Ibid, s 8.
5 Ibid, Sch 1, art 1.
6 Ibid, Sch 1, art 2.
7 Ibid, Sch 1, art 3.
8 Ibid, Sch 1, art 4.
9 Ibid, Sch 1, art 5.
10 Ibid, Sch 1, art 6.
11 Ibid, Sch 1, art 7.
12 Ibid, Sch 1, art 8.
13 Ibid, Sch 2; Merchant Shipping Act 1854 (c 104), s 103.
14 Behring Sea Award Act 1894, Sch 2; Merchant Shipping Act 1854, ss 518–539.
15 Behring Sea Award Act 1894, Sch 2; Merchant Shipping Act 1854, ss 530–543.

218. The Seal Fisheries (North Pacific) Act 1895. The Seal Fisheries (North Pacific) Act 1895 supplemented the Behring Sea Award Act 1894[1] by further providing for the prohibition by Order in Council of fur-seal catching at certain periods in the Behring Sea and other parts of the Pacific adjacent thereto[2], and for the regulation of seal fisheries in those seas by British ships[3]. No Orders in Council have been made under this Act since 1913[4]. The Act may be applied by Order in Council to any marine animal[5], but has never been so extended.

1 For the Behring Sea Award Act 1894 (c 2), see para 217 above.
2 Seal Fisheries (North Pacific) Act 1895 (c 21), ss 1, 7(1).
3 Ibid, s 2.
4 Seal Fisheries (North Pacific) Order in Council 1913, SR & O 1913/485.
5 Seal Fisheries (North Pacific) Act 1895, s 7(1).

219. The Seal Fisheries (North Pacific) Act 1912. Provision was made in the Seal Fisheries (North Pacific) Act 1912 for the prohibition of catching of seals and sea otters in certain parts of the Pacific Ocean and for enforcement of these prohibitions, in order to implement an international agreement concluded between the United Kingdom, the United States and the Emperors of Japan and all the Russias, based on the recommendations of the Behring Sea arbitral tribunal. Since the consequence of the Behring Sea Award was continued over-exploitation of the seals in that area because, as the award applied only to the United States and the United Kingdom (for Canada), the vessels concerned re-registered under the flags of Japan and other states, which were not restricted by the award and continued to exploit the seals without regulation. As the herds of seals declined rapidly under this pressure it was eventually realised by all participants that only a multilateral agreement between the major participants could save the fishing. In 1911, therefore, Russia and Japan agreed to subscribe to the system of regulation followed by the United States and the United Kingdom, and the four states concluded a Treaty for the Preservation and Protection of Fur Seals[1]. The 1912 Act extends the area laid down in the Seal Fisheries (North Pacific) Act 1895 (c 21) within which pelagic sealing may be prohibited[2]; allows for prohibition by Order in Council of killing and hunting sea otters[3]; prohibits the use of United Kingdom ports for the purposes of sealing contrary to an Order[4] and prohibits the importation of seal skins taken in contravention of an Order[5]. The Act was made permanent in 1931[6]. Following the 1939–45 war, the United States, the Soviet Union, Japan and Canada (in its own right) have concluded a series of new conventions replacing the 1911 convention[7].

1 Treaty for the Preservation and Protection of Fur Seals (1911).
2 Seal Fisheries (North Pacific) Act 1912 (c 10), s 1.
3 Ibid, s 2.
4 Ibid, s 3.
5 Ibid, s 4.
6 Expiring Laws Act 1931 (22 & 23 Geo 5 c 2) (repealed).
7 See the Interim Convention on the Conservation of North Pacific Fur Seals (9 February 1957; 314 UNTS 105), which has been repeatedly renewed.

220. The Conservation of Seals Act 1970. The earlier Acts provided for regulation of sealing by British vessels on the high seas. The Conservation of Seals Act 1970, however, repealing the earlier Grey Seals Protection Act 1932[1], provides for the protection and conservation of all seals in England and Wales and Scotland and in the adjacent territorial sea[2] (now extended to 12 nautical miles). The Act proscribes certain methods of killing or taking seals (using any poisons or certain kinds of firearms)[3] and sets an annual close season for grey seals (*Halichoerus grypus*) from 1 September to 31 December and for common seals (*Phoca vitulina*) from 1 June to 31 August[4]. Offences are created for any breach of or attempt to breach these requirements[5]. The Secretary of State may, after consultation with the Natural Environment Research Council, by order prohibit the killing, injuring or taking of seals in any specified area if it appears necessary for the proper conservation of seals, and it then becomes an offence so to do or to attempt so to do[6].

Constables are given certain enforcement powers if they suspect with reasonable cause that someone has committed an offence. A constable may stop a suspected offender if he fails to give his name and address to the constable's satisfaction, search without warrant any vehicle or boat then being used by that person and seize any seal, seal skin, firearm, ammunition or poisonous substance[7].

The penalty on summary conviction of an offence is a fine not exceeding level 4 on the standard scale[8], and the court may order the forfeiture of any seal or seal skin in respect of which the offence was committed, as well as any seal, seal skin, firearm, ammunition or poisonous substance in the offender's possession at the time of the offence[9].

1 The Grey Seals Protection Act 1932 (c 23) was repealed by the Conservation of Seals Act 1970 (c 30), s 16(1).
2 Ibid, long title and s 17(2).
3 Ibid, s 1(1). For exceptions, see para 221 below.
4 Ibid, s 2(1). For exceptions, see para 221 below.

5 Ibid, ss 1(1), 2(2), 8(1).
6 Ibid, ss 3, 8(1). For exceptions, see para 221 below.
7 Ibid, s 4(1)(a)–(c). The repeal of s 4(1)(a) by the Police and Criminal Evidence Act 1984 (c 60),
   ss 26(1), 119(1), Sch 7, Pt I, does not extend to Scotland: s 120(1).
8 Conservation of Seals Act 1970, s 5(2); Criminal Procedure (Scotland) Act 1975 (c 21), ss 289F,
   289G (added by the Criminal Justice Act 1982 (c 48), s 54). For level 4, see para 11, note 16, above.
9 Conservation of Seals Act 1970, s 6.

221. Exceptions. There are certain general exceptions to the provisions for
the protection of seals[1]. A person is not guilty of any offence[2] by reason only of
killing a seal which had been so seriously disabled otherwise than by his act that
there was no reasonable chance of its recovering[3]. Further, a person is not guilty
of an offence under the close season provisions or under an order prohibiting
killing seals[4] by reason only of the taking or attempted taking of a seal which had
been disabled otherwise than by his act and was taken solely for the purpose of
tending it and releasing it when recovered; or the unavoidable killing or injuring
of a seal as an incidental result of a lawful action; or the killing or attempted
killing of a seal to prevent it from damaging a fishing net or fishing tackle or any
fish in the net, provided the seal was then in the vicinity of the net or tackle[5].

1 Ie the provisions discussed in para 220 above.
2 Ie under the Conservation of Seals Act 1970 (c 30), ss 1–3: see para 220 above.
3 Ibid, s 9(2).
4 Ie an offence under ibid, s 2 or s 3.
5 Ibid, s 9(1)(a)–(c).

222. Licences. The Secretary of State, who is required first to consult the
Natural Environment Research Council, may grant licences to anyone authorising that person, subject to specified conditions, in specified areas to take or kill
(by any specified means other than the use of strychnine) a specified number of
seals for scientific or educational purposes, to take by specified means a specified
number of seals for zoos or collections, to take or kill (by any specified means
other than the use of strychnine) a specified number of seals to prevent damage
to fisheries, to reduce a population surplus for management purposes (popularly
referred to as 'culling'), to use a population surplus of seals as a resource or to
protect flora or fauna in certain areas[1]. Failure to comply with any of the
conditions set is an offence[2]. Licences may not, however, be granted (except in
the case of damage to fisheries) to take or kill seals in certain areas[3].

1 Conservation of Seals Act 1970 (c 30), s 10(1)(a)–(c), (3)(a) (amended by the Wildlife and
   Countryside Act 1981 (c 69), ss 12, 73(1), Sch 7, para 7(1), Sch 17, Pt II). The areas referred to
   include nature reserves, areas of special scientific interest and marine nature reserves: see the
   Conservation of Seals Act 1970, s 10(4) (added by the Wildlife and Countryside Act 1970, Sch 7,
   para 7(3)).
2 Conservation of Seals Act 1970, s 10(2).
3 Ibid, s 10(3)(b) (amended by the Nature Conservancy Act 1973 (c 54), s 1(1), (7), Sch 1, para 10,
   and the Wildlife and Countryside Act 1981, Sch 7, para 7(2)). For the areas referred to, see note 1
   above.

223. Entry upon land. For the purposes of obtaining information on seals for
the purpose of any of his functions under the Conservation of Seals Act 1970 or
of the killing or taking of seals to prevent damage to fisheries by seals, the
Secretary of State, after consulting the Natural Environment Research Council,
may authorise in writing any person to enter upon any land[1]. It is an offence
wilfully to obstruct a person so authorised[2].

The authorisation must specify the land to be entered upon, and for how long
(not exceeding eight weeks), the purpose of the entry, and the numbers, species

and age of seals that may be killed or taken where the purpose is to prevent
damage to fisheries by seals[3]. Other conditions may also be attached to the
authorisation[4], and the authorised person, who may take with him on to the
land such other persons as are necessary, must produce his authority on request
to the occupier of the land[5]. Normally the Secretary of State must give forty-
eight hours' notice of his intention to issue an authorisation, but if it is for the
purpose of taking or killing seals, twenty-eight days' notice must be given, and
during that time he must have regard to any representations made by the
occupier[6]. If within that period the occupier satisfies him that he has killed or
taken the number of seals proposed in the authorisation, the Secretary of State
must not issue the authorisation[6]. Seals killed or taken by an authorised person
are the property of the Secretary of State, for disposal as he thinks fit[7].

1 Conservation of Seals Act 1970 (c 30), s 11(1).
2 Ibid, s 11(7).
3 Ibid, s 11(2).
4 Ibid, s 11(3).
5 Ibid, s 11(6).
6 Ibid, s 11(4).
7 Ibid, s 11(5).

224. Scientific advice. The Natural Environment Research Council is
required to provide the Secretary of State with scientific advice on matters
related to the management of seal populations[1].

1 Conservation of Seals Act 1970 (c 30), s 13.

225. Cessation of seal killing. No sealing now takes place in the territorial
sea adjacent to the United Kingdom or by British registered vessels on the high
seas or in the territorial waters or fisheries or economic zones by other states.
Although the culling of seals has occasionally been permitted within the United
Kingdom waters, it has not been carried out for some years following public
protest, though demanded from time to time by fishermen. It could still be
permitted by application of the powers awarded under the Conservation of
Seals Act 1970. The European Community has adopted a directive banning the
importation of seal skins and seal products into the Community[1] which reflects
widespread public opposition to seal killing.

1 EC Council Directive 83/129 (OJ L91, 9.4.83, p 30) (amended by EC Council Directive 85/444
   (OJ L259, 1.10.85, p 70)).

(c) Whales

226. Establishment of the International Whaling Commission. The
United Kingdom was one of the first states to introduce a unilateral licensing
system for whaling[1]. It also participated in the Convention for the Regulation of
Whaling[2] concluded under the auspices of the League of Nations in 1931 and a
subsequent agreement[3] and ad hoc Protocols up to and during the 1939–45 war.
After that war, when whale stocks had recovered somewhat after the wartime
cessation of whaling, the United Kingdom became a party to a new International Convention for the Regulation of Whaling[4] concluded in 1946, which
established the International Whaling Commission[5].

1 For a detailed account of the history of the whaling industry in Scotland, see W Vamplew
   Salvesen of Leith (1975), and as to the regulation of whaling, including most relevant documents,
   see P Birnie *International Regulation of Whaling* (2 vols) (1985).

2 Convention for the Regulation of Whaling (Geneva, 24 September 1931; TS 33 (1934); Cmnd 4751).
3 International Agreement for the Regulation of Whaling (London, 8 June 1937; TS 37 (1938); Cmd 5757). This agreement revised, for one year only, the 1931 convention cited in note 2 above.
4 International Convention for the Regulation of Whaling (Washington, 2 December 1946; TS 5 (1949); Cmd 7604). Copies of the convention are available from the International Whaling Commission, The Red House, Station Road, Histon, Cambridge. The text of the convention (but not of the Schedule of Regulations) also appears in S Lyster *International Wildlife Law* (1985), pp 333 ff.
5 International Convention for the Regulation of Whaling, art 3.

227. Scope. The International Convention for the Regulation of Whaling[1] of 1946 (ICRW) does not yet in practice regulate small cetaceans, only the great whales that were in 1946 or later became the basis of the commercial industry: the blue, humpback, right, bowhead, pygmy right, gray, sei, fin, minke, Bryde's and sperm whales; although it has categorised, under the New Management Procedures that it now applies, the bottlenose whale in the North Atlantic as a 'protection stock' (which thus cannot be exploited[2]). Small cetaceans such as the pilot, beaked, killer (orca) and other bottlenose whales do not at the date at which this volume states the law come within the existing management procedures of the International Whaling Commission, although some of its member states consider that they should. There remains in the commission a contentious issue as to whether the provisions of the ICRW can be interpreted as extending to small as well as large cetaceans. Hence the killing of pilot whales in the Faroe Islands is not regulated under the ICRW, although the issue has been discussed. Elsewhere, for example in Alaska, small takes of otherwise protected whales by aborigines are in practice permitted, subject to quotas established by the commission.

1 International Convention for the Regulation of Whaling (Washington, 2 December 1946; TS 5 (1949); Cmd 7604).
2 Ibid, Schedule, para 10(c).

228. Schedule of Regulations. The International Convention for the Regulation of Whaling[1] of 1946 includes, as an integral part, a Schedule of Regulations amendable at the annual meetings of the International Whaling Commission[2]. United Kingdom law now implements its requirements but it can, and does, also regulate whaling in the territorial sea adjacent to the United Kingdom and the 200-mile British fishery limits and by British vessels anywhere more strictly than the international requirements. No whaling whatsoever, for any purposes, is now licensed by the United Kingdom and has not been so licensed since the United Kingdom gave up industrial whaling in 1963.

1 International Convention for the Regulation of Whaling (Washington, 2 December 1946; TS 5 (1949); Cmd 7604).
2 Ibid, art 5.

229. Cessation of commercial whaling. In 1984 the International Whaling Commission, by amendment of the Schedule of Regulations in the International Convention for the Regulation of Whaling[1], set zero catch limits from 1986 for the coastal and from 1985–86 for the pelagic seasons for all species of whales taken for commercial purposes[2]. These quotas are to be reviewed on the basis of the best scientific advice, and by 1990 at the latest the commission was due to undertake a comprehensive assessment of the effects of this decision on whale stocks and consider modification of this provision and establishment of other catch limits. It is unlikely that the United Kingdom will ever resume whaling even if the zero catch limits are removed, though some states may seek to do so. The convention provides for a right to object to any Schedule amendments[3]. Although a few of the states then still whaling did so, the United Kingdom did not object to the zero quotas.

1 International Convention for the Regulation of Whaling (Washington, 2 December 1946; TS 5 (1949); Cmd 7604).
2 Ibid, Schedule, para 10(e).
3 Ibid, art 5(3).

230. Scientific permits. The International Convention for the Regulation of Whaling of 1946 allows states, at their sole discretion, to grant permits for the taking and killing of whales for scientific purposes from stocks and species otherwise prohibited from such taking[1]. Some states still issue such permits, despite advice of the International Whaling Commission, which reviews recommendations from its Scientific Committee on such permits that it is neither necessary nor desirable to do so for scientific purposes. The United Kingdom does not now issue any such permits.

1 International Convention for the Regulation of Whaling (Washington, 2 December 1946; TS 5 (1949); Cmd 7604), art 8.

231. The current situation. The various Acts enabling the licensing of the taking of whales remain in force, although no licences are now issued under them. The Acts remain important for the purposes of maintaining the moratorium on whaling in United Kingdom waters and zones and by British vessels and are summarised in the paragraphs which follow.

232. The Whale Fisheries (Scotland) Act 1907. Although the Whale Fisheries (Scotland) Act 1907[1] was repealed by the Fisheries Act 1981[2], it is cited here as an illustration of the pioneering role adopted by the regulation of whaling in Scotland when the whaling industry still had a basis in Scotland. The 1907 Act prohibited any person in any part of Scotland from landing any whale or engaging in any way in the manufacture from whales of oil or other primary products without a licence granted and issued subject to conditions laid down in the Act[3]. Licences could be issued by the Fishery Board for Scotland, and subsequently the Secretary of State for Scotland, on various conditions including the payment of a fee of £100 for each whaling steamer[4]. To land whales or engage in manufacture contrary to the Act was an offence for which a penalty of £500 could be imposed on conviction[5]. It was also an offence to contravene various specified requirements concerning the use of vessels and harpoons, or the killing of whales without licence in the existing British fishery limits or in contravention of other specified requirements[6]. The board or the Secretary of State was empowered to appoint inspectors for factories, stations and vessels used by licence holders[7]. The Act did not apply to the smaller whales known as bottle-nose and caa-ing whales or to whaling or related activities in Arctic or Antarctic waters[8].

1 The Whale Fisheries (Scotland) Act 1907 (c 41) was amended by the Fishery Limits Acts 1964 (c 72) and 1976 (c 86) and the Sea Fish Industry Act 1970 (c 11).
2 Fisheries Act 1981 (c 29), s 46(2), Sch 5, Pt II.
3 Whale Fisheries (Scotland) Act 1907, s 1 (repealed).
4 Ibid, s 2 (repealed); Reorganisation of Offices (Scotland) Act 1939 (c 20), s 1(1).
5 Whale Fisheries (Scotland) Act 1907, s 1 (repealed).
6 Ibid, s 3 (repealed). For penalties, see s 6 (repealed).
7 Ibid, s 4 (repealed).
8 Ibid, s 5 (repealed).

233. The Whale Fisheries (Scotland) (Amendment) Act 1922. The Whale Fisheries (Scotland) (Amendment) Act 1922 enabled the Secretary for Scotland, and subsequently the Secretary of State for Scotland, to make inquiries on the application of any interested person, and by order cancel or suspend whaling licences in order to protect herring and other fisheries[1]. The Act was repealed by the Fisheries Act 1981[2].

1 Whale Fisheries (Scotland) (Amendment) Act 1922 (c 34), s 1 (repealed).
2 Fisheries Act 1981 (c 29), s 46(2), Sch 5, Pt II.

234. The Whaling Industry (Regulation) Act 1934. The Whaling Industry (Regulation) Act 1934 was originally enacted to implement the 1931 Convention for the Regulation of Whaling[1] in relation to species of whale covered by it. Later it was used to implement the International Convention for the Regulation of Whaling of 1946[2]. As zero catch limits are now set under this convention on the species of whales commercially exploited[3], no licences are now issued under the 1934 Act, nor are any scientific permits, as the majority of members of the International Whaling Commission no longer consider that it is necessary to kill or take whales to further scientific research[4]. Although the Act is no longer used, it still serves the purposes of providing for a licensing system should whaling ever be resumed and for enforcement powers that can be used against a vessel that engages in whaling contrary to International Whaling Commission regulations or British regulations in British fishery limits.

As amended, however, by the Fisheries Act 1981, the 1934 Act now applies to any cetacean (including dolphins and porpoises) and any products thereof, except when the contrary is specifically stated[5], but so far as application to a ship registered in or licensed under the law of a colony or associated state is concerned certain provisions of the Act[6] apply only to whales known as whalebone whales or baleen whales and to whales known as sperm whales, spermacet whales, cachalots or pot whales, though the number of species can be extended by Order in Council[7].

1 As to the Convention for the Regulation of Whaling (Geneva, 24 September 1931; TS 33 (1934); Cmd 4751), see para 226 above.
2 As to the International Convention for the Regulation of Whaling (Washington, 2 December 1946; TS 5 (1949); Cmd 7604), see para 226 above.
3 Ibid, Schedule, para 10(e).
4 As to licences and scientific permits, see paras 237, 238, below.
5 Whaling Industry (Regulation) Act 1934 (c 49), s 1(1) (substituted by the Fisheries Act 1981 (c 29), s 35(2)).
6 Ie the Whaling Industry (Regulation) Act 1934, ss 3–6.
7 Ibid, s 1(2) (as substituted: see note 5 above).

235. Prohibition of catching or treating whales within United Kingdom waters. It is unlawful for any ship to be used within the coastal waters of the United Kingdom[1] for taking or treating whales, and if any ship is so used, the master is liable on summary conviction to a fine not exceeding £50,000 or on conviction on indictment to a fine[2].

1 'Coastal waters of the United Kingdom' means so much of the waters adjoining the United Kingdom as is within British fishery limits: Whaling Industry (Regulation) Act 1934 (c 49), s 17(1) (amended by the Fishery Limits Act 1964 (c 72), s 3(3), Sch 1, and the Fishery Limits Act 1976 (c 86), s 9(1), Sch 2, para 11).
2 Whaling Industry (Regulation) Act 1934, s 2 (amended by the Fisheries Act 1981 (c 29), s 35(3)).

236. Protection for certain classes of whales. If any person on a British ship within the scope of the Whaling Industry (Regulation) Act 1934 kills or takes or attempts to take or kill, while outside the coastal waters of the United Kingdom, a right whale or a grey whale, an immature whale[1] or a female while accompanied by a calf that person and the master and, as provided in the Act, the owner and any charterer, are liable to a fine on summary conviction up to £50,000 or on conviction on indictment to a fine[2].

1 An immature whale is a whale of any description which is of less than such a length as is prescribed for whales of that description: Whaling Industry (Regulation) Act 1934 (c 49), s 3(2). See the Whaling Industry (Ship) Regulations 1955, SI 1955/1973, reg 2(1).
2 Whaling Industry (Regulation) Act 1934, s 3(1) (amended by the Sea Fish Industry Act 1938 (c 30), s 43, and the Fisheries Act 1981 (c 29), s 35(3)). For the meaning of 'coastal waters of the United Kingdom', see para 235, note 1, above.

237. Licensing of whaling ships and whale oil factories. British ships to which the Whaling Industry (Regulation) Act 1934 applies may not be used outside the coastal waters of the United Kingdom for taking or treating whales, nor may a factory in Great Britain be used for treating whales, unless the owner or charterer of the ship, or occupier of the factory, is the holder of a licence in force under the Act so authorising[1]. Contravention of these requirements makes the owner and charterer of the ship, or the manager and occupier of the factory, liable in respect of each whale taken or treated to a fine of up to £50,000 on summary conviction or a fine on conviction on indictment[2].

Licences may be issued to owners or charterers of British ships or occupiers of factories in Britain on application being made in a prescribed manner and payment of a prescribed fee[3]. A licence remains in force for one year or such shorter period as it may specify[4], and may be refused to a person convicted of an offence under the Act[5]. It is an offence to forge or lend a licence[6].

Various conditions may be attached to a licence. The remuneration of gunners, crew and those engaged in treating whales on board the ship or at the factory, if related to their work, may be related only to size, species, oil-yield and value of whales taken[7]: thus it may not be related to the numbers of whales taken. The taking of any whales of less than the prescribed length or whose taking is prohibited may not be remunerated[8]. Detailed records must be kept and transmitted, as required, to the licensing authority, including accounts showing the remuneration paid[9]. Additional conditions may be added to prevent excessive destruction or waste of whales and whale products, or the taking of whales in particular areas or by other than a particular method[10]. A licence authorising a ship or factory to treat whales must contain conditions as to the keeping of records, the use of approved plant and methods and, in the case of a factory, arrangements for utilising residual products[11]. Contravention of or non-compliance with licence conditions may result in fines on the master, owner and charterer of the ship or the owner and occupier of the factory, on summary conviction, of up to £50,000 and on conviction on indictment to a fine[12]. Persons failing to keep proper records may be fined up to £1,000 on summary conviction or fined on conviction on indictment[13].

1 Whaling Industry (Regulation) Act 1934 (c 49), s 4(1). For the meaning of 'coastal waters of the United Kingdom', see para 235, note 1, above.
2 Ibid, s 4(2) (amended by the Fisheries Act 1981 (c 29), s 35(3)).
3 Whaling Industry (Regulation) Act 1934, s 5(1), (2). See the Whaling Industry (Ship) Regulations 1955, SI 1955/1973, regs 3–5, Sch 1.
4 Whaling Industry (Regulation) Act 1934, s 5(3) (amended by the Sea Fish Industry Act 1938 (c 30), s 44).
5 Whaling Industry (Regulation) Act 1934, s 5(4).
6 Ibid, s 9(1).
7 Ibid, s 6(1), and s 6(1A) (added by the Sea Fish Industry Act 1938, s 45).
8 Whaling Industry (Regulation) Act 1934, s 6(1).

9 Ibid, s 6(3) (amended by the Sea Fish Industry Act 1938, s 45).
10 Whaling Industry (Regulation) Act 1934, s 6(4) (amended by the Sea Fish Industry Act 1938, s 45).
11 Whaling Industry (Regulation) Act 1934, s 6(2).
12 Ibid, s 6(7) (amended by the Fisheries Act 1981, s 35(4)).
13 Whaling Industry (Regulation) Act 1934, s 6(8) (amended by the Fisheries Act 1981, s 35(5)).

238. Permits for scientific purposes. A special permit may be granted to any person authorising him to kill, take and treat whales for purposes of scientific research or for other exceptional purpose, but subject to whatever restrictions as to number and such other conditions as the Secretary of State thinks fit, and acts done in accordance with such a permit are exempt from restrictions imposed under the Whaling Industry (Regulation) Act 1934[1]. No such permits are currently issued.

1 Whaling Industry (Regulation) Act 1934 (c 49), s 7.

239. Powers of whale fishery inspectors. A whale fishery inspector[1] may board or enter any ship or factory reasonably believed to be used for taking or treating whales, inspect the ship or factory and its plant and equipment, require production of licences, records and documents and make inquiries[2]. An inspector specially authorised in writing may board any British ship to which the Whaling Industry (Regulation) Act 1934 applies which is used for treating whales, and remain on board, being provided with sustenance and accommodation (for which he must pay), and be present at all relevant operations[3]. It is an offence to refuse to produce required documents or answers or wilfully to obstruct the inspector or to refuse him facilities, subjecting the offender on summary conviction to a fine of up to £5,000 or on conviction on indictment to a fine[4].

1 'Whale fishery inspector' means a person appointed by the Secretary of State to be such an inspector, or any commissioned Royal Navy officer on full pay: Whaling Industry (Regulation) Act 1934 (c 49), s 8(4).
2 Ibid, s 8(1).
3 Ibid, s 8(2).
4 Ibid, s 8(3) (amended by the Fisheries Act 1981 (c 29), s 35(6)).

240–300. Application to non-British ships. The provisions of the Whaling Industry (Regulation) Act 1934 may be applied by Order in Council, subject to such exceptions, adaptations and modifications as may be specified in the Order, to non-British ships registered in or licensed under the law of colonies or British protectorates[1]. Exemptions may also be made by Order in Council of whaling operations in the coastal waters of some British possessions where local law makes provision substantially corresponding with the provisions of the Act[2].

1 Whaling Industry (Regulation) Act 1934 (c 49), s 11. See the Whaling Industry (Regulation) Act (Newfoundland, Colonies, Protectorates and Mandated Territories) Order 1936, SR & O 1936/716 (amended by SR & O 1941/790).
2 Whaling Industry (Regulation) Act 1934, s 12. See the Order cited in note 1 above.

FOOD, DAIRIES AND SLAUGHTERHOUSES

1. FOOD

(1) STATUTORY SOURCES

(a) General

301. Early food legislation and its later development. Before 1860 there was no legislation which dealt specifically with any aspect of food, although it appears from the introduction to the Adulteration of Food and Drink Act 1860 (c 84) that there had, for some time before it was passed, been a need for statutory control of the quality and purity of food and drink sold to the public. The 1860 Act applied throughout Great Britain and, before it was passed, while England seems to have had some legal provisions for securing the purity and genuineness of specific food stuffs, in Scotland there does not appear to have been more than the general provisions of the Public Health (Scotland) Act 1867[1] to rely on for the purpose.

Enforcement defects of the 1860 Act were partially dealt with by the Adulteration of Food and Drugs Act 1872 (c 74), but these statutes were replaced by the first effective statute dealing with food, namely the Sale of Food and Drugs Act 1875 (c 63). It was followed by a number of statutes dealing with specific foods, such as margarine, milk, butter and other dairy produce[2] and with imported meat. These statutes were mainly concerned with the composition and labelling of the food which they sought to control. But the addition of preservatives to food was also touched on, and they applied throughout Great Britain as did the Food and Drugs (Adulteration) Act 1928 (c 31), which was the first consolidating Act. All these Acts have long since been repealed. The Public Health (Scotland) Act 1897 (c 38) also contained provisions about food.

1 See eg the Public Health (Scotland) Act 1867 (c 101), s 66 (repealed).
2 As to dairy produce, see paras 438 ff below.

302. Legislation about milk. The earliest statute devoted to provisions about food still on the statute book is the Milk and Dairies (Scotland) Act 1914 (c 46), which was primarily concerned to prevent the transmission of bovine infections to human beings by ensuring safe and cleanly production, treatment and sale of milk and other dairy products. The Act has been the subject of many amendments dealing with these processes and other aspects of milk production, sale etc, the most important amending Act being the Milk (Special Designations) Act 1949 (c 34). The provisions of these Acts are dealt with subsequently in this title[1].

The Food and Drugs (Adulteration) Act 1928 (c 31), although applying to Scotland as well as to the remainder of Great Britain, was expressed in terms of English law and contained a minimum of provisions for its application to Scotland. It also made a small number of additions to milk legislation. The Defence (Sale of Food) Regulations 1943[2] made under emergency legislation during the 1939–45 war made many fresh amendments to the then existing legislation, but all of them were revoked by the Food and Drugs (Scotland) Act 1956 except such as were specifically saved[3], and that Act also repealed earlier statutory provisions including the whole of the 1928 Act[4].

The Food Safety Bill, which was passing through Parliament in the Spring of 1990, makes new provision in place of the Milk and Dairies (Scotland) Act 1914, the Milk and Dairies (Amendment) Act 1922 (c 54) and the Milk (Special Designations) Act 1949. The new legislation, when passed, will require to be considered wherever there are references in this title to the 1914, 1922 and 1949 Acts.

1 See paras 438 ff below.
2 SR & O 1943/1553 (revoked).
3 See the Food and Drugs (Scotland) Act 1956 (c 30), s 60(3), (4).
4 Food and Drugs (Scotland) Act 1956, s 60(2), Sch 3.

303. Legislation about slaughterhouses and the slaughter of animals. In 1928 came the enactment also of separate provisions in the Slaughter of Animals (Scotland) Act 1928 (c 29) dealing with slaughterhouses, the slaughter of animals and the maintenance of hygienic conditions of meat in bulk. The Slaughter of Animals (Pigs) Act 1953 (c 27) made special provisions about the slaughter of pigs. These Acts were substantially amended by the Slaughterhouses Act 1954 (c 42) and the Slaughter of Animals (Amendment) Act 1954 (c 59). But all four of them were repealed by the Slaughter of Animals (Scotland) Act 1980 (c 13). A further Act dealing with a similar subject reached the statute book with the enactment of the Slaughter of Poultry Act 1967 (c 24). The provisions of the 1967 and the 1980 Acts and relevant regulations are considered subsequently in this title[1].

1 See paras 496 ff below.

(b) Scottish Legislation relating to Food

304. General. The first measure enacting, in consolidated form, all legislation relating to Scotland only dealing with food (other than milk and dairy products in general) is the Food and Drugs (Scotland) Act 1956 (c 30), which, however, left untouched except marginally all the legislation relating to the slaughter of animals and slaughterhouses now dealt with by the Slaughter of Animals (Scotland) Act 1980 (c 13). The provisions about drugs contained in the 1956 Act disappeared on their repeal by the Medicines Act 1968[1]. In the result the statute law concerning the preparation, safety, hygiene, composition, labelling, advertising and sale of food for human consumption is contained broadly in the 1956 Act. But that Act contained very wide powers enabling the Secretary of State to make, by subordinate legislation, provisions about these and other aspects of food[2]. The powers have been used extensively, and there is much greater coverage of the regulation of food in subordinate legislation than in statute law.

Changes in local government have affected the 1956 Act, and the Control of Food Premises (Scotland) Act 1977 (c 28) enacted provisions for the better enforcement of food hygiene regulations made under the 1956 Act.

The Food Safety Bill, which was passing through Parliament in the Spring of 1990, makes new provision in place of the Food and Drugs (Scotland) Act 1956 and the Control of Food Premises (Scotland) Act 1977. The new legislation, when passed, will require to be considered wherever there are references in this title to the 1956 and 1977 Acts.

1 Medicines Act 1968 (c 67), s 135(2), Sch 6.
2 As to subordinate legislation generally, see paras 321 ff below.

305. The European Communities Act 1972. Further powers were conferred by the European Communities Act 1972 (c 68) to make Orders in Council and other subordinate legislation on the accession of the United Kingdom to the

European Economic Community. In the case of any directly applicable Community provisions relating to food for which, in the opinion of the Secretary of State, it is appropriate to make provision under the 1972 Act, he may by regulations make such provision as he considers necessary or expedient for securing that the Community provisions are administered, executed and enforced under the Food and Drugs (Scotland) Act 1956 (c 30) and has power to apply such of the provisions of the 1956 Act as may be specified in the regulations in relation to the Community provision with such modifications, if any, as may be so specified[1].

On the harmonisation of Scottish food laws with those of the European Community it is important to note the difference between a Community regulation, which is binding in its entirety and directly applicable in all member states, and a Community directive, which is binding as to the result to be achieved upon each member state to whom it is addressed but which leaves to the national authorities the choice of form and methods[2]. The Food and Drugs (Scotland) Act 1956 relates to 'any directly applicable Community provisions', and thus enables any Community regulation to be enforced under that Act. As the implementing directives are left to the individual member states, the provisions of the Act conferring power to make regulations are largely sufficient for the purpose. So far as they are not, the provisions of the 1972 Act give the necessary powers to implement the Community obligations[3].

1 Food and Drugs (Scotland) Act 1956 (c 30), s 56A(1) (added by the European Communities Act 1972 (c 68), s 4(1), Sch 4, para 3(2)(b)). See eg the Tetrachloroethylene in Olive Oil (Scotland) Regulations 1989, SI 1989/837, which implements EC Commission Regulation 1860/88 (OJ L166, 1.7.88, p 16).
2 EEC Treaty, art 189.
3 See the text and note 1 above.

306. Principal regulations. The principal powers to make regulations and orders relate to the composition, labelling and description of food[1], food hygiene[2], and milk and dairies[3]; as well as the power to make regulations for the purpose of securing that a directly applicable Community provision relating to food is administered, executed and enforced under the Food and Drugs (Scotland) Act 1956[4].

1 See paras 352, 359 ff, 383 ff below.
2 See paras 407 ff below.
3 See paras 438 ff below.
4 Food and Drugs (Scotland) Act 1956 (c 30), s 56A(2) (added by the European Communities Act 1972 (c 68), s 4(1), Sch 4, para 3(2)(b)).

307. Application to the Crown. Her Majesty may by Order in Council provide for the application to the Crown of such of the provisions of the Food and Drugs (Scotland) Act 1956 (c 30) and of any regulations or order made under it as may be specified with such exceptions, adaptations and modifications as may be so specified[1]. Further, without prejudice to that generality, an Order may make special provision for the enforcement of any provisions applied by the Order, and, where any provision so applied imposes a liability on a person by reason that he is the occupier or owner of premises or the owner of a business or the principal on whose behalf any transaction is carried out, the Order may make provision for determining, in a case where the premises are occupied or owned, or the business is owned by the Crown or the transaction is carried out on behalf of the Crown, the person who is to be treated as so liable[2]. Any exemption, immunity or privilege subsisting in respect of the provisions of the Act by virtue of the rules of law about the application of enactments to the

Crown has been extended to certain visiting forces and international head-quarters[3].

1 Food and Drugs (Scotland) Act 1956 (c 30), s 52(1). This power has not been exercised. Any such Order is subject to annulment in pursuance of a resolution of either House of Parliament: s 56(1). The making of an Order applying regulations under s 13 (food hygiene) does not have the effect of applying the provisions of the Control of Food Premises (Scotland) Act 1977 (c 28) to the Crown: s 8.
2 Food and Drugs (Scotland) Act 1956, s 52(2). For the meaning of 'premises', see para 334, note 6, and for the meaning of 'business', see para 342, note 2, below.
3 Visiting Forces and International Headquarters (Application of Law) Order 1965, SI 1965/1536, art 12(1), Sch 2.

(c) Alteration of Local Legislation

308. Powers of the Secretary of State to make orders. The provisions of the Food and Drugs (Scotland) Act 1956 or of any order or regulation made under it are to have effect in substitution for the provisions of any local enactment relating to food and of like effect, and any such enactment in so far as inconsistent with the provisions of the Act or of such order or regulation is to cease to have effect[1]. However, the Secretary of State has power, if representations are made by a local authority[2], to restrict or exclude by order the operation of the provisions of any such order or regulation in the area of that authority[3]. Local Acts which contain provisions of the kind mentioned above or which are no longer required or require to be amended having regard to those provisions may by order made by the Secretary of State be repealed or amended[4]. The powers thus conferred on the Secretary of State have not so far been exercised.

1 Food and Drugs (Scotland) Act 1956 (c 30), s 59(1).
2 Subject to contrary specific provisions, 'local authority' in the 1956 Act means an islands or district council: ibid, ss 26(4), 58(1) (amended by the Local Government (Scotland) Act 1973 (c 65), s 214(2), Sch 27, Part II, para 123, and the Local Government and Planning (Scotland) Act 1982 (c 43), s 22(a)).
3 Food and Drugs (Scotland) Act 1956, s 59(1) proviso.
4 Ibid, s 59(2).

309. Procedure for making orders. An order repealing or amending a local Act may be made only if the prescribed procedure is followed[1]. The Secretary of State, after consulting the local authority concerned, must prepare a draft order and publish in the *Edinburgh Gazette* and in one or more newspapers circulating in the area affected by the order a notice stating the general effect of the draft order and the time and manner for making objections[2]. A copy of the notice and of the draft order is thereafter served on every local authority concerned, and a copy of the draft order is, on payment of a fixed charge, provided to any person interested[3]. The order may then be made either in the terms of the draft or in those terms as modified in such manner as the Secretary of State thinks fit, but if the modifications will adversely affect any persons other than those to whom the order relates additional notices must be published[4]. A local inquiry must be held if an objection is made by a local authority or person affected and is not withdrawn[5]. Where such an order is, notwithstanding any objection, thereafter made the Secretary of State must give notice of the making of the order[6]. The order does not have effect until twenty-eight days after the giving of the notice, and if within that period an objection to the order is made and not withdrawn the order becomes subject to special parliamentary procedure[6]. Provision is also made enabling Commissioners under the Private Legislation Procedure (Scotland) Act 1936 to hold any such inquiry, and the Statutory Orders (Special Procedure) Act 1945 is applied[7]. The Secretary of State must publish in the *Edinburgh Gazette*, and in some other manner appropriate for informing persons affected, a notice that an order which has not been confirmed by Parliament has been made and stating where a copy may be obtained[8].

1 Food and Drugs (Scotland) Act 1956 (c 30), s 59(3), Sch 1, Part I (paras 1–7).
2 Ibid, Sch 1, para 1.
3 Ibid, Sch 1, paras 2, 3.
4 Ibid, Sch 1, para 4.
5 Ibid, Sch 1, para 5.
6 Ibid, Sch 1, para 6.
7 Ibid, Sch 1, para 7. As to the Private Legislation Procedure (Scotland) Act 1936 (c 52), see PROVISIONAL ORDERS AND PRIVATE LEGISLATION, vol 19, paras 5 ff, and as to the Statutory Orders (Special Procedure) Act 1945 (9 & 10 Geo 6 c 18), see vol 19, paras 117 ff.
8 Food and Drugs (Scotland) Act 1956, Sch 1, para 8.

310. Challenging validity of orders. Provision is made to enable the validity of an order repealing or amending a local Act to be questioned on certain grounds by application to the Court of Session, which may quash the order in whole or in part if satisfied that the ground on which it is being questioned is good[1].

1 See the Food and Drugs (Scotland) Act 1956 (c 30), s 59(3), Sch 1, para 9.

(2) STATUTORY PROVISIONS RELATING TO FOOD GENERALLY

311. Meaning of 'food' and 'drug'. The provisions of the Food and Drugs (Scotland) Act 1956 are concerned only with food for human consumption. The Act is not now concerned with drugs[1]. For the purposes of the Act 'food' includes drink, chewing gum and other products of a like nature and use, and articles and substances[2] used as ingredients in the preparation of food or drink or of such products[3]. 'Food' does not, however, include water, live animals or birds, fodder or feeding stuffs for animals, birds or fish, or articles or substances used only as drugs[4].

'Drug' includes medicine for internal or external use[4]. In any case of doubt it will be a question of fact for determination by the court whether an article is a drug or not, and the answer will depend upon whether or not it was sold for use as a medicine[5]. An article is not necessarily a drug because it is included in the British Pharmacopoeia and may be used in the preparation of medicine, nor is an article a drug merely because it is sold under a designation which implied that it contains a drug in its composition which in fact it does not[6].

Chambers 20th Century Dictionary defines 'food' as what one feeds on; that which, being digested, nourishes the body; whatever sustains or promotes growth. The definition makes clear that 'food' includes things consumed by humans to maintain life and growth, whether they are consumed alone or whether they are ingredients or additives intended to be mixed with other foods before consumption.

1 See para 304, text and note 1, above.
2 'Article' does not include a live animal or bird, and 'substance' includes any liquid or gas: Food and Drugs (Scotland) Act 1956 (c 30), s 58(1). As to water for human consumption, see WATER SUPPLY, vol 25, especially paras 506, 508, 509.
3 Ibid, s 58(1). 'Preparation' in relation to food includes manufacture and any form of treatment: s 58(1).

4 Ibid, s 58(1). 'Animal' does not include bird or fish: s 58(1).
5 See *Fowle v Fowle* (1896) 75 LT 514; *Armstrong v Clark* [1957] 2 QB 391 at 394, [1957] 1 All ER 433 at 435, DC, per Lord Goddard CJ.
6 *Houghton v Taplin* (1897) 13 TLR 386, per Hawkins J.

312. Fish, wild birds and game. The Food and Drugs (Scotland) Act 1956 contains provisions for the control of the preparation and sale of fish as food[1], and in particular for facilitating the cleansing of shellfish[2]. There are also restrictions on the buying, selling, exposing for sale or having possession for sale, of fish of various kinds[3]. These restrictions concern salmon, sea trout, trout and other freshwater fish, and relate to close and other seasons of the year, to size and to methods or means of catching and taking fish.

Similar restrictions apply to some animals. Hares are dealt with in the Hares Preservation Act 1892 (c 8) and venison in the Deer (Scotland) Act 1959 which, as amended[4], contains detailed provisions for the licensing of dealers in venison and the keeping of records[5].

1 See eg the Meat Products and Spreadable Fish Products (Scotland) Regulations 1984, SI 1984/1714.
2 See the Food and Drugs (Scotland) Act 1956 (c 30), s 20, and para 403 below.
3 See eg the Salmon Fisheries (Scotland) Act 1868 (c 123), the Freshwater Fish (Scotland) Act 1902 (c 29), the Trout (Scotland) Act 1933 (c 35), the Salmon and Freshwater Fisheries (Protection) (Scotland) Act 1951 (c 26), the Freshwater and Salmon Fisheries (Scotland) Act 1976 (c 22), and the Salmon Act 1986 (c 62), and FISHERIES, paras 16, 18, 20, 21, above.
4 See the Deer (Amendment) (Scotland) Act 1982 (c 19), s 11, which adds to the Deer (Scotland) Act 1959 (c 40) a new Part IIIA (ss 25A–25F): see para 433 below, and GAME, paras 944 ff below.
5 See para 433 below.

313. Sale of food by weight, measure or number. The sale of food by weight, measure or number is not dealt with in the food legislation, whether statutory or subordinate. It is the subject of provisions in the Weights and Measures Act 1985 and in subordinate legislation having effect under that Act. Misrepresentation about the quantity of food sold is an offence[1], and specific restrictions are imposed in respect of various foods on their sale by, or marking with, net weight and the quantities and manner in which they may be pre-packed[2].

1 See the Weights and Measures Act 1985 (c 72), s 29, and CONSUMER PROTECTION, vol 6, para 250.
2 See the Weights and Measures Act 1963 (Intoxicating Liquor) Order 1984, SI 1984/1314 (amended by SI 1985/1980); the Weights and Measures Act 1963 (Cheese, Fish, Fresh Fruits and Vegetables, Meat and Poultry) Order 1984, SI 1984/1315 (amended by SI 1985/988 and SI 1985/1980), and the Weights and Measures Act 1963 (Miscellaneous Foods) Order 1984, SI 1984/1316 (amended by SI 1985/988, SI 1985/1980 and SI 1986/1260) (which deals among other foods with biscuits and shortbread, bread, cocoa and chocolate products, coffee and chicory products, liquid edible oil, milk and potatoes).

314. Price control and value added tax. Various statutory provisions relate to the control of the price of food, and the price of milk is dealt with in subordinate legislation[1]. The Prices Act 1974 provides for food subsidies to reduce, prevent or limit the increase of food prices and gives power to regulate prices[2]. It also provides for the making of orders requiring the marking of prices on retail sale[3].

Value added tax is charged on foods in and imported into Great Britain, but food of a kind used for human consumption, except food supplied in the course of catering and otherwise in specified exceptional circumstances, is zero-rated[4].

1 See eg the Milk Prices (Scotland) Amendment Order 1983, SI 1983/491. See also the Welfare Food Order 1980, SI 1980/1648 (amended by SI 1980/1836, SI 1981/1292, SI 1983/379 and SI 1985/1932), and para 432 below.

2 Prices Act 1974 (c 24), s 1.
3 Ibid, s 2.
4 See the Value Added Tax Act 1983 (c 55), ss 1, 16, Sch 5, Group 1.

315. Sale and supply of excisable liquor. Trafficking in any excisable (otherwise alcoholic) liquor in any premises or place without holding a licence issued by the licensing board for the area or licensing division in which the premises or place is located, the bartering or selling of spirits by retail without holding such a licence or the hawking of excisable liquor is prohibited[1]. A person on selling excisable liquor delivered from a vehicle or receptacle must (except in a limited number of cases) keep a record of the quantity, description and price of the liquor; the name and address of the person to whom it is supplied and other particulars connected with the sale[2]. Further provisions on excisable liquor are referred to subsequently[3].

1 Licensing (Scotland) Act 1976 (c 66), s 90. As to evidence of trafficking, see s 122.
2 Ibid, s 91.
3 See para 431 below.

316. Trade descriptions. The Trade Descriptions Act 1968 applies to food and thus offences created by that Act also apply where relevant. One such offence is to apply a false trade description to any goods or to supply or offer to supply any goods to which a false trade description is applied[1]. However, a description applied to goods in accordance with any provision of the Food and Drugs (Scotland) Act 1956 (c 30) is deemed not to be a trade description[2].

1 Trade Descriptions Act 1968 (c 29), s 1(1). As to trade descriptions and false trade descriptions, see ss 2, 3, and as to applying trade descriptions, see s 4 and the Trade Descriptions Act 1972 (c 34), s 3.
2 Trade Descriptions Act 1968, s 2(5).

317. Infestation of food. Any person whose business consists of or includes the manufacture, storage, transport or sale of food must give written notice to the Secretary of State of the occurrence of infestation in any premises or vehicle or any equipment used or likely to be used for any of those purposes or in the food or goods likely to be in contact with the premises or equipment[1]. Regulations may be made relaxing or excluding such requirements in special cases[2]. The Secretary of State has power to give such directions as he thinks expedient to prevent or mitigate damage to food when he is made aware of the infestation[3].

There are statutory provisions about the prevention and eradication of diseases in animals[4], the slaughter of diseased animals[5] and the disposal of carcases[6] and about the importation and landing in Scotland of animals, carcases, fodder and other things[7]. The milk of a diseased cow must not be sold[8]. Other provisions for the prevention of infestation of food are to be found in the Animal Health Act 1981.

1 Prevention of Damage by Pests Act 1949 (c 55), s 13(1).
2 Ibid, s 13(2).
3 Ibid, s 14.
4 Animal Health Act 1981 (c 22), ss 3–6.
5 Ibid, ss 31–34.
6 Ibid, ss 35, 36.
7 Ibid, s 10.
8 Milk and Dairies (Scotland) Act 1914 (c 46), s 13(1): see para 447 below.

318. Emergency orders on contamination of food. The Secretary of State for Scotland and the Minister of Agriculture, Fisheries and Food, or either of them, may make an emergency order if in their or his opinion:

(1) there has been or may have been an escape of substances of such descriptions and in such quantities and in such circumstances as are likely to create a hazard to human health through human consumption of food; and

(2) in consequence food which is or may in the future in an area of land in the United Kingdom, or an area of sea within British fishery limits, or an area both of such land and of such sea, or which is derived from anything in such an area, is, or may be, or may become, unsuitable for human consumption[1].

An emergency order, which is made by statutory instrument, refers to the escape or suspected escape (the 'designated incident'), designates the area (the 'designated area'), and contains appropriate prescribed emergency prohibitions[2]. These may prohibit particular activities in the designated area (for example agricultural activities, gathering wild plants, slaughtering creatures or fishing), may prohibit movements of food into or out of or within that area, and may prohibit particular activities throughout the United Kingdom (for example using things taken from that area, landing fish taken from there, slaughtering animals that were there, and feeding to animals food that was there)[3]. Contravention of an emergency order is an offence[4].

The Secretary of State may consent to the doing in a particular case of anything prohibited by an emergency order[5]. He may give directions appearing necessary or expedient to prevent human consumption of food which he believes is or may be or may become unsuitable for human consumption in consequence of a designated incident, and may do anything which appears to him necessary or expedient for that purpose[6]. Extensive powers of investigation and entry are given to authorised investigating officers and enforcement officers for these purposes[7].

1 Food and Environment Protection Act 1985 (c 48), s 1(1)(a), (b).
2 Ibid, s 1(1), (2), (5). The order must be laid before Parliament, and ceases to have effect after twenty-eight days unless approved by resolution of each House: s 1(8). For an example of such an order, see the Food Protection (Emergency Prohibitions) (No 6) Order 1986, SI 1986/1331 (amended by SI 1986/1360 and 1986/1410), which imposes emergency prohibitions restricting various activities in Dumfries and Galloway, Ross and Cromarty, Strathclyde and the Western Isles arising out of the Chernobyl incident.
3 Food and Environment Protection Act 1985, s 1(2), Sch 1, Pts I–III.
4 Ibid, s 1(6). For defences, see ss 1(7), 2(2).
5 Ibid, s 2(1).
6 Ibid, s 2(3). Failure to comply with such a direction is an offence: s 2(4).
7 Ibid, ss 3, 4, Sch 2.

319. Pesticides. With a view to the continuous development of means to protect the health of human beings, creatures and plants, to safeguard the environment and to secure safe, efficient and humane methods of controlling pests, and with a view to making information about pesticides available to the public, statutory provision has been enacted relating to the control of pesticides[1]. The Minister of Agriculture, Fisheries and Food and the Secretary of State may jointly by regulations prohibit the importation, sale, offer or exposure for sale or possession for the purpose of sale, supply or offer to supply, storage, use or advertisement of any pesticide, make exclusions from any prohibition, provide for approval of specified pesticides and for consent to acts otherwise prohibited, and generally provide for the control of pesticides[2]. In particular, in the context of food, they may specify how much pesticide or pesticide residue may be left in any crop, food or feeding stuff, and direct that if the limit is exceeded they may seize or dispose of the crop, food or feeding stuff or direct the taking of specified remedial action[3]. They may also prepare and issue codes of practice providing practical guidance in respect of these provisions[4]. Detailed enforcement powers, including powers of entry, are given to authorised persons[5].

1 Food and Environment Protection Act 1985 (c 48), s 16(1). 'Pesticide' means any substance, preparation or organism prepared or used for destroying any pest, and 'pest' means any organism harmful to plants or to wood or other plant products, any undesired plant and any harmful creature: s 16(15).
2 Ibid, s 16(2), (3).
3 Ibid, s 16(2)(k), (l). See the Pesticides (Maximum Residue Levels in Food) Regulations 1988, SI 1988/1378, which express maximum residue levels of a wide range of pesticides in terms of milligrams of residue per kilogram of specified cereals, products of animal origin, fruits, vegetables and mushrooms.
4 Food and Environment Protection Act 1985, s 17.
5 Ibid, s 19, Sch 2.

320. Emergency powers. If a state of emergency is declared by Her Majesty to exist, regulations may be made for ensuring and regulating the supply and distribution of food[1].

1 Emergency Powers Act 1920 (c 55), ss 1, 2; Emergency Powers Act 1964 (c 38), s 1.

(3) SUBORDINATE LEGISLATION

321. General. The Food and Drugs (Scotland) Act 1956 confers extensive powers on the Secretary of State for the making of provisions, including transitional and saving provisions, by regulation, order and other means, controlling in detail the general enactments of the Act itself[1]. He also has a general power to make regulations in the interests of public health or otherwise for the protection of the public, or which may be required to comply with any European Community obligation, for any of certain purposes[2].

Powers also appear in the Milk and Dairies (Scotland) Act 1914[3], the Milk and Dairies (Amendment) Act 1922[4], the Milk (Special Designations) Act 1949[5], and in a number of other Acts which, though not specifically concerned with food, are closely connected with the preparation, storage, ingredients, standards and other matters relating to food. An example of the latter is the subordinate legislation relating to slaughterhouses[6]. The provisions of the orders and regulations made are considered in more detail subsequently[7], as is the extent to which provision has been made to cater for the effect of the accession of the United Kingdom to the European Communities[8].

1 See eg the Food and Drugs (Scotland) Act 1956 (c 30), ss 4, 5, 7, 13, 14, 16, 23, 52, 55, 56, 59, 61.
2 Ibid, s 4(1); European Communities Act 1972 (c 68), s 4(1), Sch 4, para 3(1): see para 352 below.
3 Milk and Dairies (Scotland) Act 1914 (c 46), s 12.
4 Milk and Dairies (Amendment) Act 1922 (c 54), s 3 (substituted by the Milk Act 1934 (c 51), s 10).
5 Milk (Special Designations) Act 1949 (c 34), ss 5, 8, 11.
6 Slaughterhouses Hygiene (Scotland) Regulations 1978, SI 1978/1273 (amended by SI 1984/842, SI 1985/1068, SI 1985/1856, SI 1986/1808 and SI 1987/1957).
7 See paras 352 ff below.
8 See para 437 below.

322. Byelaws. The Milk and Dairies (Scotland) Act 1914 imposes on every local authority a duty to make byelaws for its district providing for the inspection of cattle in dairies; for prescribing and regulating the structure and other features of dairies; for the prevention of impurities in milk, for securing the cleanliness and health of cows, the persons and clothing of those engaged in the business and of the milk, cows, dairies, utensils, vehicles and vessels used for the reception, conveyance, storage or sale of milk; and for prescribing precautions to be taken by dairymen against infection or contamination[1]. The procedure to be followed in the making of byelaws is that prescribed by the Local Government (Scotland) Act 1973[2].

1 Milk and Dairies (Scotland) Act 1914 (c 46), s 8(1).
2 Milk and Dairies (Scotland) Act 1914, s 8(2). See the Local Government (Scotland) Act 1973 (c 65), ss 201–204, and LOCAL GOVERNMENT, vol 14, paras 279 ff.

323. Saving for pre-1956 subordinate legislation. Any appointment, agreement or any provision in a regulation or order made under any enactment repealed by the Food and Drugs (Scotland) Act 1956 is not invalidated by the repeal by the Act of the statutory or other provision under which it was made in so far as it could have been made under a corresponding provision of the Act, but is to have effect as if it had been made under that corresponding provision[1]. Similar provision is made for saving notices, directions, consents and other things given under earlier legislation[1], and all these savings apply to certain orders[2] made under defence regulations[3].

1 Food and Drugs (Scotland) Act 1956 (c 30), s 60(3). Among the enactments repealed by the 1956 Act are the Public Health (Regulations as to Food) Act 1907 (c 32), the Food and Drugs (Adulteration) Act 1928 (c 31), the Artificial Cream Act 1929 (c 32), the Public Health (Cleansing of Shell-fish) Act 1932 (c 28) and the Food and Drugs Act 1938 (c 56).
2 Ie orders made under the Defence (Sale of Food) Regulations 1943, SR & O 1943/1553, reg 2 (revoked), relating to the labelling, marking, advertisement and composition of food.
3 Food and Drugs (Scotland) Act 1956, s 60(4).

324. Procedure for making regulations and orders. Any power conferred by the Food and Drugs (Scotland) Act 1956 on the Secretary of State to make orders (except under section 55) or regulations is exercisable by statutory instrument[1], and before making any such orders (except under sections 55, 59 and 61) or regulations the Secretary of State must consult with representative organisations[2]. An order made under section 5, an Order in Council made under section 52 and regulations made under the Act are subject to annulment by resolution of either House of Parliament[3], and an order made under section 14 must be laid in draft before and approved by each House of Parliament[4]. Regulations made under section 13 and orders made under section 14 may apply to the whole or any specified part of Scotland[5]. Any orders and Orders in Council made under the Act, and orders made under the Milk and Dairies (Scotland) Act 1914 (c 46), may be varied or revoked by subsequent orders[6].

All regulations made under Part I of the 1956 Act[7] may (1) modify provisions of the Act relating to samples, (2) apply any provision of any Act with modifications and adaptations, (3) provide for appeals from local authorities to the sheriff or the Secretary of State, (4) authorise the making of charges for certain purposes, (5) impose penalties for offences, (6) require the keeping and production of records and the making of returns, and (7) make necessary consequential, ancillary and incidental provisions[8]. These powers apply also to an order made under section 5, and the powers under heads (2) and (7) apply to an order made under section 14[9].

Orders requiring the furnishing of particulars of the composition and the use of substances sold for use in the preparation of food for human consumption may contain provisions similar to those which may be contained in regulations made under Part I of the 1956 Act[10].

1 Food and Drugs (Scotland) Act 1956 (c 30), s 56(2). For s 55, see para 331 below.
2 Ibid, s 56(6). For s 59, see paras 308–310 above. Orders under s 61 are commencement orders. Consultation must be made in full. Thus sufficient information must be supplied to the organisation to enable it to give advice and sufficient opportunity must be afforded for the advice to be given. Whether consultation has or has not taken place is a question of fact: *Fletcher v*

Minister of Town and Country Planning [1947] 2 All ER 496. The consultation may be made by officials: *Carltona Ltd v Comrs of Works* [1943] 2 All ER 560, CA.

3　Food and Drugs (Scotland) Act 1956, s 56(1), (2). For s 5, see para 351 below, and for s 52, see para 307 above.

4　Ibid, s 56(3). For s 14, see para 420 below.

5　Ibid, s 56(4). For s 13, see para 407 below.

6　Food and Drugs (Scotland) Act 1956, s 56(5).

7　Ibid, Pt I, comprises ss 1–24.

8　Ibid, s 56(8)(a)–(g), (8A) (amended by the Criminal Justice Act 1982 (c 48), s 77, Sch 15, para 8, and the Law Reform (Miscellaneous Provisions) (Scotland) Act 1985 (c 73), s 41(c)).

9　Food and Drugs (Scotland) Act 1956, s 56(9).

10　Ibid, s 56(2), applying s 56(8). Such regulations are made under s 5.

(4) COGNATE LAW

325. Offences. It is accepted by English law that it is an indictable offence at common law knowingly to give any person unwholesome food which is not fit for man to eat or to mix noxious ingredients with food intended for the use of man[1]. There does not appear to be authority for the view that such a rule is part of Scots law.

A director or a member of a body corporate established for the purpose of carrying on any industry or undertaking may be convicted of an offence as well as the body itself if it is proved to have been committed with the consent or connivance of, or to be attributable to any neglect on the part of, the director or any person purporting to act in such capacity[2]. This is also the position in the case of a body corporate established for the purpose of carrying on under national ownership any industry[2].

Sections of the Food and Drugs (Scotland) Act 1956 and provisions in orders and regulations made under it create a wide variety of offences[3].

1　*R v Treeve* (1796) 2 East PC 821, CCR.

2　Food and Drugs (Scotland) Act 1956 (c 30), s 41(6).

3　These are referred to throughout this work. As to prosecutions and penalties, see paras 423 ff below.

326. Implied conditions of sale. As articles of food are goods which may be sold or be the subject of a contract of sale, they are, if sold or subject to such a contract, subject to the same rules of law as other goods sold or contracted for, and the condition of fitness for the purpose for which they are purchased as laid down by statute applies. Where, for instance, a buyer expressly or by implication makes known to the seller a particular purpose for which he is purchasing the goods, and the sale takes place in the ordinary course of business, there is an implied condition that the goods are fit for that purpose except where the circumstances show that the buyer did not rely, or that it is unreasonable for him to rely, on the seller's skill or judgment[1].

A breach of any provision of the Food and Drugs (Scotland) Act 1956 which makes it a penal offence to sell any food to the prejudice of the purchaser as being not of the nature or not of the substance, or not of the quality demanded[2], does not itself give ground for an action for damages for breach of a statutory duty.

1　See the Sale of Goods Act 1979 (c 54), s 14(3).

2　See the Food and Drugs (Scotland) Act 1956 (c 30), s 2, and para 343 below.

(5) ADMINISTRATION

327. Central administration. The central administration of the provisions of the law relating to food generally (there are exceptions for the more detailed administrative executive and enforcement functions[1]) is in the hands of the Secretary of State for Scotland[2]. In a small number of cases, the approval or consent of another authority may be required[3]. In England and Wales central administrative functions are shared between the Minister of Agriculture, Fisheries and Food, the Secretary of State for Social Services and the Secretary of State for Wales[4].

1 See para 329 below.
2 See generally the Food and Drugs (Scotland) Act 1956 (c 30). See eg s 5.
3 See eg ibid, s 21.
4 See the Food Act 1984 (c 30), s 132(1) ('the Ministers').

328. The Scottish Food Hygiene Council. The Scottish Food Hygiene Council, which was appointed by the Secretary of State with advisory but no executive functions[1], has been abolished[2].

1 See the Food and Drugs (Scotland) Act 1956 (c 30), s 25 (repealed).
2 Local Government (Miscellaneous Provisions) (Scotland) Act 1981 (c 23), s 30.

329. Administrative authorities. The enforcement and execution of the provisions of the Food and Drugs (Scotland) Act 1956 is a duty of local authorities within their own areas unless the duty is expressly or by necessary implication placed on some other authority[1].

Regulations made under Part I of the Act (sections 1 to 24) may specify the authorities by whom they are to be enforced and executed and may provide for the giving of assistance and information by any authority enforcing the regulations or the Act, to any other authority[2]. The authorities concerned are islands councils and district councils (each of which is referred to as a 'local authority'), port local authorities (including joint port local authorities) or the Commissioners of Customs and Excise[2].

Where a duty is not imposed in any area on an authority other than the local authority of the area, it is the duty of that authority to enforce and execute the provisions of the Act in its area[3]. This duty may be assigned by order made by the Secretary of State to a port local authority[4]. However, no administrative authority may institute prosecution proceedings for any offence relating to food[5]. The institution, investigation and prosecution of offences are matters for the Lord Advocate and his office, that is the Crown Office and procurators fiscal.

1 Food and Drugs (Scotland) Act 1956 (c 30), s 26(1). An example is a port local authority. 'Local authority' means an islands or district council: see para 308, note 2, above. Regional councils no longer have any powers and duties under the 1956 Act (save under s 27, for which see para 330 below): Local Government and Planning (Scotland) Act 1982 (c 43), s 22.
2 Food and Drugs (Scotland) Act 1956, s 26(3) (amended by the Local Government (Scotland) Act 1973 (c 65), s 214(2), Sch 27, Pt II, para 123, and the Local Government and Planning (Scotland) Act 1982, s 22(a)).
3 Food and Drugs (Scotland) Act 1956, s 26(1).
4 Ibid, s 26(2). 'Port local authority' includes joint port local authority: s 26(5).
5 Ibid, s 26(6).

330. Public analysts. Every regional or islands council is under a duty to appoint as public analysts one or more persons who possess the qualifications approved by, or prescribed by regulations made by, the Secretary of State[1]. A person may not be appointed to such a post if he is engaged directly or indirectly in any trade or business connected with the sale of food[2]. A public analyst is remunerated by the local authority that appoints him, and he may also receive fees from other persons for whom he makes analyses[3]. Fees paid to a public analyst in respect of samples submitted to him by the sampling officer of a district council are generally fixed by the council which appointed the analyst[4]. A deputy analyst may also be appointed on the same terms as the analyst[5]. A public analyst must make a report to the council that appointed him on the last day of March, June, September and December each year on the number of articles he has and has had analysed and the result of each analysis[6].

1 Food and Drugs (Scotland) Act 1956 (c 30), s 27(1), (2), (7); Local Government (Scotland) Act 1973 (c 65), s 214(2), Sch 27, Pt II, para 124. See the Public Analysts (Scotland) Regulations 1956, SI 1956/1162, reg 2. As to evidence of public analysts, see para 424 below.
2 Food and Drugs (Scotland) Act 1956, s 27(2).
3 Ibid, s 27(4).
4 Ibid, s 27A (added by the Local Government and Planning (Scotland) Act 1982 (c 43), s 22(b)).
5 Food and Drugs (Scotland) Act 1956, s 27(5), (6).
6 Ibid, s 35(1). The requirement of s 35(2) that a copy of each report be sent to the Secretary of State was repealed by the Local Government (Miscellaneous Provisions) (Scotland) Act 1981 (c 23), ss 25, 41, Sch 2, para 8, Sch 4.

331. Default of local authority. If the Secretary of State after communication with a local authority[1] is of the opinion that the authority has failed to exercise any of its statutory functions relating to food, he may by order empower an officer of his department to exercise or procure the exercise of that function[2]. If no public analyst is appointed by an authority this provision applies. Expenses incurred by the Secretary of State in carrying out any such default powers if certified by him are recoverable from the authority concerned[3]. Any other power of the Secretary of State with respect to defaults of a local authority is not affected by these default provisions[4].

1 For the meaning of 'local authority', see para 308, note 2, above.
2 Food and Drugs (Scotland) Act 1956 (c 30), s 55(1).
3 Ibid, s 55(2).
4 Ibid, s 55(3).

332. Acquisition of land by local authority. A local authority may be authorised by the Secretary of State to purchase compulsorily any land, whether situated within or outside its area, for the purpose of any of their functions under the Food and Drugs (Scotland) Act 1956[1]. The Acquisition of Land (Authorisation Procedure) (Scotland) Act 1947 (c 42) applies for this purpose[2].

1 Food and Drugs (Scotland) Act 1956 (c 30), s 53(1).
2 Food and Drugs (Scotland) Act 1956, s 53(2). See COMPULSORY ACQUISITION, vol 5.

(6) ANALYSIS OF SAMPLES OF FOOD

333. Duty to analyse food. Where a sampling officer has procured a sample of any food or substance and considers that it should be analysed, he must submit it to be analysed by the public analyst for the area in which the same was procured[1]. A person, other than a sampling officer, who has purchased any food or substance capable of being used in the preparation of food may submit it for analysis in the same way[2]. The public analyst is obliged to analyse, as soon as practicable, any sample submitted to him and give to the person by whom it was submitted a certificate in the prescribed form setting out the result of the analysis[3]. Where the sample is submitted otherwise than by an officer of the local authority who appointed the analyst, the analyst may obtain in advance a fee fixed by the authority[4]. Where the public analyst of the area where the sample was obtained is unable to perform an effective analysis, it may be analysed by the analyst of some other area, and the analyst of that other area must, on payment to him of an agreed sum, analyse it and give a certificate as mentioned above[5]. He must also certify that the sample analysed has undergone no change which would affect the opinion he has expressed.

Where a sample has been analysed by a public analyst, any person to whom part of the sample is given is entitled on payment of a fixed sum to be supplied with a copy of the certificate[6]. Any certificate given by an analyst must be signed by the analyst but the analysis may be made by any person acting under his direction[7].

1 Food and Drugs (Scotland) Act 1956 (c 30), s 29(1). As to sampling officers, see para 334 below, and as to public analysts, see para 330 above. 'Analysis' includes micro-biological assay, but no other form of biological assay, and 'analyse' is to be construed accordingly: s 58(1).
2 Ibid, s 29(2).
3 Ibid, s 29(3). See the Public Analysts (Scotland) Regulations 1956, SI 1956/1162, reg 3, Schedule.
4 Food and Drugs (Scotland) Act 1956, s 29(3) proviso (amended by the Local Government (Scotland) Act 1973 (c 65), s 214(2), Sch 27, Pt II, para 125; and the Local Government and Planning (Scotland) Act 1982 (c 43), s 22(c)), which is expressed not to apply where the fee falls to be fixed under the Food and Drugs (Scotland) Act 1956, s 27A, for which see para 330 above.
5 Ibid, s 29(4).
6 Ibid, s 29(5).
7 Ibid, s 29(6).

334. Procuring of samples. An 'authorised officer' of a local authority may exercise such powers of procuring samples for analysis or bacteriological or other examination as are conferred on him by the Food and Drugs (Scotland) Act 1956, such a person being known as a 'sampling officer'[1]. Such an officer must be authorised in writing either generally or specially and may be a constable so authorised with the approval of the police authority[2]. The designated medical officer and the sanitary inspector of a local authority are deemed to be authorised officers, and for the purposes of food hygiene regulations[3] a veterinary officer employed by a local authority is also so deemed[4].

A sampling officer may purchase samples of food or of any substance used in the preparation of food (including excisable liquor)[5], and he may take a sample of food or of any substance capable of being used in the preparation of food which appears to him to be intended for sale or to have been sold for human consumption or is found by him in or on any premises, stall, vehicle, ship, aircraft or place other than premises he is authorised to enter for the purposes of the execution of the Act[6]. A sampling officer may also, at the request of a person to whom any food or substance is or is to be delivered on sale, take a sample of it[7]. But a sample of any food or substance which appears to the officer to have been sold by retail while in the course of delivery to the purchaser at any time after delivery may not be taken, nor may a sample be taken of any food or substance in a ship not being a home-going ship or in any aircraft, other than food imported or otherwise carried as part of the cargo of that ship or aircraft for unloading at a place in Scotland[8].

Any person, other than a sampling officer, who purchases any food or substance may have a sample of it analysed[9].

1 Food and Drugs (Scotland) Act 1956 (c 30), ss 29(1), 58(1).
2 Ibid, s 58(1).
3 Ie regulations under ibid, s 13: see para 407 below.
4 Ibid, s 58(1) (amended by the National Health Service (Scotland) Act 1972 (c 58), s 64(1), Sch 6, para 97).
5 Food and Drugs (Scotland) Act 1956, s 28(2), (6) (amended by the Medicines Act 1968 (c 67), s 135(2), Sch 6). For the meanings of 'food' and 'substance', see para 311 above.
6 Food and Drugs (Scotland) Act 1956, s 28(3). 'Premises' means a building or any part of it and any forecourts, yards and places of storage used in connection with it: s 58(1). For the meaning of 'preparation', see para 311, note 3, above. 'Preparation for sale' includes packaging and wrapping: s 58(1).
7 Ibid, s 28(4).
8 Ibid, s 28(5).
9 Ibid, s 29(2).

335. Direction to take samples. If it appears to the Secretary of State in relation to any matter appearing to him to affect the general interests of consumers that a sample of any specified food should be analysed, he may direct an officer of his department to procure samples of the food and the officer then has all the powers of a sampling officer, except that any fee is payable by the Secretary of State[1].

1 Food and Drugs (Scotland) Act 1956 (c 30), s 32.

336. Sampling of milk. The provisions of the Food and Drugs (Scotland) Act 1956 relating to the procuring of samples by sampling officers and subsequent procedure have effect in relation to milk subject to the following provisions[1]. A sampling officer has the same powers to obtain samples of milk as he has in relation to any other food, but, in addition, where milk sold or exposed for sale within the area of any local authority is obtained from a dairy in the area of another authority, an authorised officer of the former may, by notice in writing to an officer of the latter, or to an officer of an authority through whose area the milk is transported, require him to procure a sample of the milk and to forward the appropriate parts of the sample to the officer who gave the notice or to such person as that officer may direct[2]. A sample so procured is deemed to have been obtained within the area for which the last-mentioned officer acts[3]. Expenses incurred by the officer to whom the notice is given are payable by the authority whose officer gave the notice[4].

If the authority of an area from which milk is supplied to the area of another authority consents to officers of that other authority taking samples of milk in its area, any samples so procured are deemed to have been procured in the area for which the officer acts[4]. The other authority must not reasonably withhold such consent[4].

A provision in a contract for the sale, whether wholesale or retail, of milk, requiring the person who supplied the milk of which a sample has been taken under the powers conferred by the Act to supply a part of the sample to the person from whom he obtained the milk, or to give notice to the latter that a sample has been procured, is void[5].

A sample of milk taken from a container is presumed, unless the contrary is proved, in any proceedings for any offence in respect of the sample, to have remained unaltered from the time the milk was placed in the container until the sample was taken[6]. The defender in any such proceedings may, as a defence, prove that the container was effectively closed and sealed at the time it left his control but had been opened before the sampling officer had access to it[7].

1 Food and Drugs (Scotland) Act 1956 (c 30), s 31(1).
2 Ibid, s 31(2).

3 Ibid, s 31(2). As to the effect of this on the place of prosecution, see s 41(1) proviso, and para 423 below.
4 Ibid, s 31(2) proviso.
5 Ibid, s 31(4).
6 Ibid, s 31(5).
7 Ibid, s 31(6).

337. Authority of sampling officer. There is no provision requiring that an officer when purchasing a sample of food or substance for analysis must produce his authority[1] for so doing. If the seller asks for a sight of his authority it should be produced. Again it is not expressly required that, in a subsequent prosecution, the officer should prove that he is acting under the authority or direction of the local authority[2].

1 As to this authority, see para 334 above.
2 If the sampling officer is unknown to the seller and does not produce his authority, the prosecution will fail: *Payne v Hack* (1893) 58 JP 165.

338. Division and disposal of samples. A sampling officer who procures a sample[1] of any food or substance for the purpose of analysis or a person (being neither a sampling officer nor a person having the powers of such an officer) who purchases such a sample must forthwith divide it into three parts, each part to be marked and sealed or fastened up in such manner as its nature will permit[2]. Where an act or omission constitutes an offence both under the Food and Drugs (Scotland) Act 1956 and the Trade Descriptions Act 1968, evidence for the prosecution concerning any sample procured for analysis is not admissible in proceedings under the 1968 Act unless the relevant 1956 Act procedure has been complied with[3].

If a sample has been purchased, the sampling officer or other person must give one part of it to the vendor[4]; if the sample is from goods consigned from outside Scotland, and taken before delivery to the consignee, a part must be given to the consignee; if the sample is of milk, a part must be given to the person who caused the milk to be placed in the container from which the sample was taken; if the sample is of a food or substance taken at the request of the purchaser (not being a case to which any of the foregoing apply), a part must be given to the vendor; if the sample is taken in transit (otherwise than as mentioned in any of the above cases), a part must be given to the consignor; and in any other case a part must be given to the person appearing to be the owner of the food or substance[5]. In each case the officer or other person must inform the person to whom the part is given that the sample was procured or taken for analysis by a public analyst[6].

Where the sample is one which was manufactured or put into its wrapper or container by a person (not being someone to whom a part of the sample has been given) having his name and an address in the United Kingdom displayed on the wrapper or container, a notice must be sent to that person, within three days of the procuring of the sample, informing him that the sample has been obtained and specifying where and from whom it was purchased[7].

1 The provisions as to samples do not apply where the whole article is taken for analysis: *Robertson v Gateway Foodmarkets Ltd* 1989 SCLR 305, 1989 SLT 583.
2 Food and Drugs (Scotland) Act 1956 (c 30), s 30(1), (7). The division of the sample must be done forthwith. This has been interpreted stringently in England, but in *Brown v Bonnyrigg and Lasswade Magistrates* 1936 SC 258, 1936 SLT 304, a different view was taken of the meaning of 'forthwith' in the Housing (Scotland) Act 1930 (c 40), s 16(3) (repealed), as regards the making of a demolition order.
3 Trade Descriptions Act 1968 (c 29), s 22(2).
4 If the sample was purchased from an automatic machine, the part of the sample must instead be sent either (1) if the proprietor's name and address (being an address in Scotland) appears on the

machine, to the proprietor; (2) in any other case, to the occupier of the premises on which the machine stands: Food and Drugs (Scotland) Act 1956, s 30(5).
5 Ibid, s 30(2)(a)–(f).
6 Ibid, s 30(2).
7 Ibid, s 30(4). This applies only to samples taken by a sampling officer: s 30(7).

(7) POWERS OF ENTRY

339. Power to enter premises. Except in the case of premises used only as a private dwellinghouse (in respect of which twenty-four hours' notice of intended entry must be given to the occupier), an authorised officer of a local authority has a right to enter any premises at all reasonable hours, upon production, if so required, of some duly authenticated document showing his authority, (1) for the purpose of ascertaining whether there is or has been on, or in connection with, the premises any contravention of the provisions of the Food and Drugs (Scotland) Act 1956 or of any regulation made under it which the local authority is required or empowered to enforce; (2) generally for the purpose of the performance by the authority of its functions under the Act or such regulations[1].

A justice of the peace, sheriff or magistrate may by warrant under his hand authorise a local authority by any authorised officer to enter any premises, if need be by force, if he is satisfied on sworn information in writing that there is reasonable ground for entry for any of the foregoing purposes, and either (a) that admission has been refused or refusal is apprehended and that notice of intention to apply for a warrant has been given to the occupier, or (b) that an application for admission, or the giving of such a notice, would defeat the object of the entry, or that the case is one of urgency, or that the premises are unoccupied or the occupier is temporarily absent[2].

An authorised officer entering any premises by virtue of the foregoing powers or of a warrant so issued may take with him such other persons as may be necessary, and on leaving any unoccupied premises must leave them as effectively secured against trespassers as he found them[3]. If any person who enters a factory or workplace under these powers discloses any information obtained there with regard to any manufacturing process or trade secret, then, unless the disclosure was made in the performance of his duty, he is guilty of an offence[4].

1 Food and Drugs (Scotland) Act 1956 (c 30), s 36(1). For the meaning of 'premises', see para 334, note 6; for the meaning of 'authorised officer', see para 334; and for the meaning of 'local authority', see para 308, note 2, above.
2 Ibid, s 36(2), (8). The warrant remains in force for one month: s 36(4).
3 Ibid, s 36(3).
4 Ibid, s 36(5). As to prosecutions and penalties, see para 423 below.

340. Power to enter ships, aircraft, vehicles etc. An authorised officer of a local authority, on producing, if so required, some duly authenticated document showing his authority, has a right at all reasonable hours to enter any ship or aircraft to ascertain if any food imported as part of the ship's or aircraft's cargo for unloading in Scotland contravenes regulations which the authority is required or empowered to enforce[1]. The right extends to any vehicle, stall or place other than premises, or to any home-going ship, for the same purposes as those which apply in the case of the right to enter premises[2], and the position with regard to the issue of warrants, the power of authorised officers to be accompanied when entering the premises and the duty to leave them secure, is the same as in the case of premises, with necessary modifications[3].

1 Food and Drugs (Scotland) Act 1956 (c 30), s 37(1)(a), referring to regulations made under Pt I (ss 1–24). 'Ship' includes any boat or craft: s 58(1).
2 Ibid, s 37(1)(b). As to the right to enter premises, see s 36, and para 339, above.
3 Ibid, s 37(2).

(8) INJURIOUS FOOD

341. Preparation and sale of injurious food. No substance may be added to food nor used as an ingredient in the preparation of food nor may any constituent of food be abstracted[1] from it nor may food be subjected to any other process or treatment so as (in any such case) to render the food injurious to health[2] with intent that the food be sold for human consumption in that state[3]. Further, no person may sell[4], offer[5], expose[6], or advertise[7] for sale for human consumption, or have in his possession[8] for the purpose of such sale, any food so rendered injurious to health[9]. Contravention of any of these restrictions is an offence against the Food and Drugs (Scotland) Act 1956[10].

In determining whether an article of food is injurious to health, regard must be had not only to the probable effect of that article on the health of the consumer but also to the probable cumulative effect of articles of substantially the same composition on the health of a person consuming such articles in ordinary quantities[11].

In proceedings for prosecution of an offence consisting of the advertisement for sale of any food it is a defence for the person charged to prove that, being a person whose business it is to publish, or arrange for the publication of, advertisements, he received the advertisement for publication in the ordinary course of business[12].

1 See (as analogies) *Knowles v Scott* 1918 JC 32, 1918 1 SLT 28; *Penrice v Brander* 1921 JC 63, 1921 1 SLT 288; *McCallum v Brooks* 1926 JC 39, 1926 SLT 80.
2 The material question is whether the food after it has been added to or subjected to abstraction is injurious.
3 Food and Drugs (Scotland) Act 1956 (c 30), s 1(1). For the meaning of 'food' and 'substance', see para 311 above. 'Human consumption' includes use in the preparation of food for human consumption: s 58(1).
4 There is no sale unless the property in the goods passes from seller to buyer: see *Watson v Coupland* [1945] 1 All ER 217, DC.
5 In order that there may be an offer for sale there must be some evidence that the offer was communicated or put on its way, although it need not be shown that the offer reached the person to whom it was made: *Wiles v Maddison* [1943] 1 All ER 315, DC.
6 An article may be exposed for sale even if it is wrapped and not in the view of the customer: see *Wheat v Brown* [1892] 1 QB 418; *Clark v Strachan* 1940 JC 29, 1940 SLT 125.
7 'Advertisement' includes any notice, circular, label, wrapper, invoice or other document, and any public announcement made orally or by any means of producing or transmitting light or sound, and 'advertise' is to be construed accordingly: Food and Drugs (Scotland) Act 1956, s 58(1).
8 It would appear that 'possession' must be given a wide and not a narrow construction: see *Webb v Baker* [1916] 2 KB 753 at 759.
9 Food and Drugs (Scotland) Act 1956, s 1(3)(a).
10 Ibid, s 1(4). As to prosecutions and penalties, see paras 423 ff below.
11 Ibid, s 1(5).
12 Ibid, s 1(6). See *Robertson v Watson* 1949 JC 73, 1949 SLT 119.

342. Supplying food otherwise than by sale. The supply[1] of food for human consumption, otherwise than by sale at, in or from any place where food is supplied in the course of a business[2], is deemed to be a sale of that food; and where, in connection with any business in the course of which food is supplied, the place where the food is served to the customers is different from the place where the food is consumed, both places are deemed to be places where food is sold[3].

1 'Supply' is not defined in the Food and Drugs (Scotland) Act 1956 (c 30). *Chambers 20th Century Dictionary* defines it as 'to make good, to satisfy, to provide, furnish'.
2 'Business' includes the undertaking of a canteen, club, school, hospital or institution, whether carried on for profit or not, and any undertaking or activity carried on by a public or local authority: Food and Drugs (Scotland) Act 1956, s 58(1).
3 Ibid, s 58(2)(a), (b).

(9) FOOD SUPPLIED NOT OF THE KIND DEMANDED

343. Sale of food not of the proper nature, substance or quality demanded. Subject to certain defences[1], if a person sells for human consumption to the prejudice of the purchaser[2] any food which is not of the nature, or not of the substance, or not of the quality, of the food demanded by the purchaser, he is guilty of an offence against the Food and Drugs (Scotland) Act 1956[3]. Proof of guilty knowledge is not necessary to establish the offence[4]; it is sufficient to prove that the purchaser has not received the article he asked for or which he had a right to expect to receive[5], and, for example, the presence of a small piece of extraneous matter in the article of food demanded may render the selling of it to be in contravention of the provision[6]. It is no defence to allege that the purchaser bought for analysis or examination and therefore was not prejudiced[7]. A person may be prosecuted for this offence even where the facts would support a conviction under other provisions.

1 See para 349 below.
2 If the purchaser is given notice at the time of the sale that the article sold is not of the nature, substance or quality demanded he cannot be prejudiced. See *Preston v Grant* [1925] 1 KB 177, DC, and *Patterson v Findlay* 1925 JC 53, 1925 SLT 277.
3 Food and Drugs (Scotland) Act 1956 (c 30), s 2(1), (3). These are three separate offences: *Bastin v Davies* [1950] 2 KB 579, [1950] 1 All ER 1095, DC. As to prosecutions and penalties, see paras 423 ff below.
4 *Betts v Armstead* (1888) 20 QBD 771.
5 *Goulder v Rook* [1901] 2 KB 290 at 296. See also *Robertson v M'Kay* 1924 JC 31, 1924 SLT 92.
6 *J Miller Ltd v Battersea Borough Council* [1956] 1 QB 43, [1955] 3 All ER 279, DC.
7 Food and Drugs (Scotland) Act 1956, s 2(2).

344. Sale to the prejudice of the purchaser. A customer is prejudiced if he does not get what he asked and paid for[1]. However, it is not an offence to give to a purchaser an article superior to that for which he asks[2]. The prejudice is not, however, confined to pecuniary prejudice, or to prejudice arising from the consumption of unwholesome food, or to prejudice or damage to the actual purchaser in the particular case[3]. A purchaser is not prejudiced if the seller clearly brings to his knowledge the fact that the article is not of the nature, substance or quality demanded[4], but it is not necessary for the seller to disclose precisely what the composition of the article sold is[5]. There is prejudice, however, whenever there is a sale of an article in such a state that an ordinary unskilled person would have been prejudiced if he had received it in response to his demand for an article of that description even though for some reason, peculiar to himself, the actual purchaser is not prejudiced[6]. The price charged for the article is irrelevant to the matter of prejudice[7].

1 *Souter v Lean* (1903) 6 F (J) 20, 11 SLT 526.
2 *Hoyle v Hitchman* (1879) 4 QBD 233 at 240.

3 For instance, an expert in foodstuffs on going into a shop may know at once that an article he sees there, and asks for, is not the article usually sold by that name, and if he insists on having it he cannot be said to be prejudiced in the ordinary sense of the word. Nevertheless an offence may have been committed.
4 *Sandys v Small* (1878) 3 QBD 449.
5 *Williams v Friend* [1912] 2 KB 471.
6 See *Pearks, Gunston and Tee Ltd v Ward* [1902] 2 KB 1, DC.
7 See *A J Mills & Co v Williams* (1964) 62 LGR 354, DC.

345. Notice to purchaser. A notice to a purchaser that the article bought is not of the nature, substance or quality demanded must be clear[1]. Notice may be given by oral communication[2], by a printed notice[3], by a label on a package containing the article or in any other manner which demonstrates that the purchaser did know, from information given by the seller, that the article was different[4]. A notice in a shop that any articles sold there are not of any guaranteed strength is not sufficient to make it clear to the purchaser that articles have been diluted[5], and if the object of the notice is to conceal fraud it will not protect the seller against conviction[6].

1 *Souter v Lean* (1903) 6 F (J) 20, 11 SLT 526; *Wilson and M'Phee v Wilson* (1903) 6 F (J) 10, 11 SLT 578; *Robertson v M'Kay* 1924 JC 31, 1924 SLT 92.
2 *Higgins v Hall* [1886] 51 JP 293.
3 *Preston v Grant* [1925] 1 KB 177, DC.
4 *Morris v Johnson* [1890] 54 JP 612.
5 *Rodbourn v Hudson* [1925] 1 KB 225, DC.
6 *Brander v Kinnear, Kelso v Soutar, Williamson v Soutar* 1923 JC 42, 1923 SLT 354; *Patterson v Findlay* 1925 JC 53, 1925 SLT 277.

346. False representation. If a seller discloses to the purchaser, at the time of sale, the true nature, substance and quality of an article, an earlier misrepresentation made by him about the article is not an offence[1], but the making of a misrepresentation at the time of sale may be an offence even if the purchaser must have known that the representation was incorrect[2]. If an article is asked for and something is handed over as that article, there is an implied representation that the article is of the nature, substance and quality demanded[3].

1 *Kirk v Coates* (1885) 16 QBD 49.
2 *Heywood v Whitehead* (1897) 76 LT 781.
3 *Fitzpatrick v Kelly* (1873) LR 8 QB 337.

347. Question of fact. Whether an article sold is of the nature, substance or quality of the article demanded is a question of fact to be decided by the court[1] unless there is a statutory or recognised standard established in respect of the article[2]. In the absence of any evidence to contradict the certificate of analysis of an analyst who has not been called as a witness, the statement of facts and the opinions expressed in it should be accepted by the court[3].

The evidence should be directed to what the purchaser meant when he demanded a particular article; an expert's opinion that the description of an article purchased by that description is such that it is desirable that it should contain certain ingredients is not sufficient to prove that the purchaser demanded an article containing these ingredients[4].

Where the article has no statutory or recognised standard the court must fix its own standard on the evidence before it[5], bearing in mind that in such cases no offence is committed by selling a genuine article of a low quality[6].

1 *Pashler v Stevenitt* (1876) 35 LT 862.
2 See *Webb v Jackson Wyness Ltd* [1948] 2 All ER 1054.

3 *Bowker v Woodroffe* [1928] 1 KB 217, DC.
4 *Collins Arden Products Ltd v Barking Corpn* [1943] 1 KB 419, [1943] 2 All ER 249.
5 *Wilson and M'Phee v Wilson* (1903) 6 F (J) 10, 11 SLT 578.
6 *Morton v Green* (1881) 8 R (J) 36.

348. Standard of quality. If there is a statutory standard of quality for an article, the article must not be inferior to that standard, and if the article demanded has some recognised standard of composition or quality, the article sold must meet that standard[1]. Standards for a large number of foods have been fixed by statute and subordinate legislation[2].

1 *White v Bywater* (1887) 19 QBD 582. Cf *MacLean v G and W Riddell* 1960 SLT (Sh Ct) 35.
2 See para 353 below.

349. Statutory defences. Where the offence[1] consists in the sale of food to which any substance has been added, or in the preparation of which any substance has been used as an ingredient, or from which any constituent has been abstracted or which has been subjected to any other process or treatment (other than food thereby rendered injurious to health), it is a defence for the person charged to prove[2] that the operation in question was not carried out fraudulently[3], and that the article was sold having attached thereto a notice of adequate size, distinctly and legibly printed[4] and conspicuously visible[5], stating explicitly[6] the nature of the operation, or was sold in a wrapper or container displaying such a notice[7].

Where the offence consists of the sale of food containing extraneous matter it is a defence for the person charged to prove that the presence of that matter was an unavoidable consequence of the process of collection or preparation[8].

Where the offence relates to diluted whisky, brandy, rum or gin, it is a defence for the person charged to prove that the spirit was diluted with water only and that its strength was not lower than 35 degrees under proof[9].

It is a defence for a person charged with a contravention of any provision of the Food and Drugs (Scotland) Act 1956 to prove that the contravention was due to the act or default of some other person[10], and there are defences available also in the case of warranties and certificates of analysis[11].

1 Ie an offence under the Food and Drugs (Scotland) Act 1956 (c 30), s 2: see para 343 above.
2 The onus is on him.
3 This is primarily a question of fact.
4 This is to be treated as a question of fact by the court, which must apply reasonable standards.
5 These words have not yet been construed in this context.
6 See *Star Tea Co Ltd v Neale* (1909) 73 JP 511.
7 Food and Drugs (Scotland) Act 1956, s 3(1). The fact that statute provides defences does not preclude proof that the sale was not to the prejudice of the purchaser: see *Gage v Elsey* (1883) 10 QBD 518.
8 Food and Drugs (Scotland) Act 1956, s 3(3); *Warnock v Johnstone* (1881) 8 R (J) 55. For the meaning of 'preparation', see para 311, note 3, above.
9 Food and Drugs (Scotland) Act 1956, s 3(4), nothing in which affects the Alcoholic Liquor Duties Act 1979 (c 4), s 70, relating to the dilution of spirits after computation of duty: *Brander v Kinnear, Kelso v Soutar, Williamson v Soutar* 1923 JC 42, 1923 SLT 354.
10 See the Food and Drugs (Scotland) Act 1956, s 45, and para 428 below.
11 See ibid, ss 46, 47(2), and paras 426, 427, below.

(10) PROVISIONS RELATING TO THE SALE ETC OF FOOD APPLYING GENERALLY

350. False labelling or advertisement. A person who gives with any food sold by him for human consumption, or displays with any food exposed by him for such sale a label[1], whether attached to or printed on the wrapper or container[2] or not, which falsely describes[3] that food or is calculated to mislead[4] as to its nature, substance or quality, is guilty of an offence against the Food and Drugs (Scotland) Act 1956 unless he proves that he did not know and could not with reasonable diligence[5] have ascertained that the label was of such a character[6]. It is unnecessary for the label to be attached to or printed on the wrapper or container[6].

It is also an offence for a person to publish[7] or to be a party to the publication of any advertisement (other than such a label) which falsely describes any food or is calculated to mislead as to its nature, substance or quality[8]. Where the manufacturer, producer or importer[9] of such food is charged with an offence the onus is on him to prove that he did not publish and was not a party to the publication of the advertisement[10]. It is a defence for the person accused to prove either that he did not know and could not with reasonable diligence have ascertained that the advertisement was of such a character as has been mentioned, or that his business was that of publishing or arranging for the publication of advertisements and that he received it in the ordinary course of that business[11].

In proceedings for any such offence the fact that a label or advertisement in respect of which the offence is alleged to have been committed contained an accurate statement of the composition of the food does not preclude the court from finding that the offence was committed[12].

1 Labels to which orders made under the Agriculture Act 1970 (c 40), s 25, apply are in a special position.
2 'Container' includes a package or receptacle of any kind, whether open or closed: Food and Drugs (Scotland) Act 1956 (c 30), s 58(1).
3 A statement while literally true may be false by reason of what it omits: *R v Lord Kylsant* [1932] 1 KB 442, CCA.
4 Ie likely to mislead: *Concentrated Foods Ltd v Champ* [1944] KB 342 at 350, [1944] 1 All ER 272 at 276, DC.
5 This is a question of fact: *R C Hammett Ltd v Crabb* (1931) 145 LT 638, DC.
6 Food and Drugs (Scotland) Act 1956, s 6(1), (6). A label or advertisement which is calculated to mislead as to the nutritional or dietary value of any food is calculated to mislead as to its quality: s 6(3). As to labelling regulations, see paras 383 ff below.
7 To publish is to make public: *Lambert and Lambert v Roberts Drug Stores Ltd* [1933] 2 WWR 508 (Man. CA).
8 Food and Drugs (Scotland) Act 1956, s 6(2). For the meaning of 'advertisement', see para 341, note 7, above.
9 'Importation' has the same meaning as it has for the purposes of the customs legislation: see ibid, s 58(1).
10 Ibid, s 6(2).
11 Ibid, s 6(4).
12 Ibid, s 6(5).

351. Power of the Secretary of State to obtain particulars of ingredients.

To enable him to exercise his functions of making regulations as regards the composition of food[1], the Secretary of State may by order require every person either then or later carrying on a business[2] which includes the production, importation or use of any class of specified substances to furnish to him, within a specified time, specified particulars of the composition and use of any such substance sold in the course of that business for use in the preparation of food for human consumption, or used for that purpose in the course of that business, including their chemical formulae, the manner of their use in the preparation of food and particulars of any investigations carried out to determine their effect, including their cumulative effect if consumed in ordinary quantities, whether injurious or otherwise, upon a person's health[3].

No particulars or information so obtained may be disclosed, without the previous written consent of the person whose business is involved, except in accordance with directions of the Secretary of State for the purpose of regulations as to the composition of food or for the purposes of any proceedings for an offence against the order, or of any report of those proceedings[4]. Any unauthorised disclosure is an offence against the Food and Drugs (Scotland) Act 1956[4].

1 Ie his functions under the Food and Drugs (Scotland) Act 1956 (c 30), s 4: see para 352 below.
2 For the meaning of 'business', see para 342, note 2, above.
3 Food and Drugs (Scotland) Act 1956, s 5(1), (2).
4 Ibid, s 5(3). As to prosecutions and penalties, see paras 423 ff below.

(11) ORDERS AND REGULATIONS APPLYING TO PARTICULAR ASPECTS OF FOOD

(a) Introduction

352. Regulations as to the composition, treatment etc of food. The Secretary of State may, so far as appears to him necessary or expedient in the interests of public health, or otherwise for the protection of the public, or to be called for by any European Community obligation, make regulations for:

(1) requiring, prohibiting or regulating the addition of any specified substance[1], or any substance of any specified class, to food[2] (or any class of food) intended for sale for human consumption, or the use of any such substance as an ingredient in the preparation[3] of such food, and generally for regulating the composition of such food;

(2) requiring, prohibiting or regulating the use of any process or treatment in the preparation of any food (or any class of food) intended for sale for human consumption;

(3) prohibiting or regulating the sale, possesion for sale, offer or exposure for sale, consignment or delivery of food which does not comply with the regulations, or in relation to which an offence against the regulations has been committed or would have been committed if any relevant act or omission had taken place in Scotland, or the importation of any such food;

(4) prohibiting or regulating the sale, possession for sale, or offer, exposure or advertisement[4] for sale, of any specified substance, or of any substance of a specified class, with a view to its use in the preparation of food for human consumption, and the possession of any such substance for use in the preparation of food intended for sale for human consumption[5].

In the exercise of these functions the Secretary of State must have regard to the desirability of restricting, so far as practicable, the use of substances of no nutritional value as foods or as ingredients of foods[6].

Regulations dealing with the composition of food may apply to cream and separated milk and to any food containing milk, but not to any other milk[7]. Regulations may provide that where a public analyst certified a substance as being food which does not comply with regulations under head (3), it is to be subject to seizure and condemnation as food unfit for human consumption[8].

1 For the meaning of 'substance', see para 311, note 2, above.
2 For the meaning of 'food', see para 311 above.
3 For the meaning of 'preparation', see para 311, note 3, above.
4 For the meaning of 'advertisement', see para 341, note 2, above.
5 Food and Drugs (Scotland) Act 1956 (c 30), s 4(1)(a)–(d) (amended by the European Communities Act 1972 (c 68), s 4(1), Sch 4, para 3(1)).

6 Food and Drugs (Scotland) Act 1956, s 4(2).
7 Ibid, s 4(3). 'Milk' includes cream and separated milk, but not dried or condensed milk; 'separated' includes skimmed; and 'cream' means that part of milk rich in fat which has been separated by skimming or otherwise: s 58(1).
8 Ibid, s 4(4). As to seizure, see s 9, and para 397 below.

353. Food standards. Orders and regulations have been made prescribing standards for ensuring the composition of food generally, and of baking powder and golden raising powder, mustard, self-raising flour, curry powder, tomato ketchup, fish cakes, suet and preserves[1]. Earlier orders were made under the Defence (Sale of Food) Regulations 1943[2] as amended and later revoked. But orders made under the 1943 Regulations were saved by the Food and Drugs (Scotland) Act 1956[3], and many provide that they are to be construed as one with the Food Standards (General Provisions) Order 1944. Since 1953 over fifty other orders have been made dealing with standards and other aspects of the composition of a wide variety of foods.

1 See the Food Standards (General Provisions) Order 1944, SR & O 1944/42; Food Standards (Mustard) (No 2) Order 1944, SR & O 1944/275; Food Standards (Self-Raising Flour) Order 1946, SR & O 1946/157; Food Standards (Curry Powder) Order 1949, SI 1949/1816; Food Standards (Tomato Ketchup) Order 1949, SI 1949/1817; Food Standards (Fish Cakes) Order 1950, SI 1950/589; Food Standards (Suet) Order 1952, SI 1952/2203; Jam and Similar Products (Scotland) Regulations 1981, SI 1981/1320; Bread and Flour (Scotland) Regulations 1984, SI 1984/1518. Several of these orders and regulations have been amended.
2 SR & O 1943/1553.
3 See the Food and Drugs (Scotland) Act 1956 (c 30), s 60(3), and para 323 above.

(b) Special Treatment of Specific Foods

354. Heat treatment of ice cream. Except in certain cases where a complete cold mix is used in its manufacture, the ingredients of ice cream are required to be subject to one of three different methods of pasteurisation or a method of sterilisation[1]. No person may sell or offer for sale ice cream unless one of these methods are employed and prescribed temperature-keeping conditions have been followed[2].

1 Ice Cream (Scotland) Regulations 1948, SI 1948/960, regs 8, 9 (substituted by SI 1960/2108). Otherwise one of the prescribed processes must be complied with.
2 Ibid, reg 10 (as so substituted).

355. Heat treatment of cream. No person may sell cream in Scotland (unless not intended for human consumption or intended for export to a place outwith the United Kingdom) unless prescribed heat treatment requirements are satisfied[1].

1 Cream (Heat Treatment) (Scotland) Regulations 1983, SI 1983/1515, reg 4. As to cream brought into Scotland from England, Wales or Northern Ireland, see reg 5. A person may nevertheless sell untreated cream if he holds a valid certificate issued by the Secretary of State: see reg 4A (added by SI 1985/1222).

356. Pasteurisation of liquid egg. No person may use as an ingredient in the preparation of food intended for sale for human consumption, or import into Scotland for such use, liquid egg unless (1) it satisfies prescribed pasteurisation requirements; or (2) is removed from the shell on the premises where the food is prepared and is either used forthwith or is kept at a temperature not exceeding 50 degrees Fahrenheit (10 degrees Celsius) and used within twenty-four hours[1].

1 Liquid Egg (Pasteurisation) (Scotland) Regulations 1963, SI 1963/1591, reg 4.

357. Irradiation control. No person may, in the preparation of any food, subject it to ionising radiation, except in some cases relating to the quantity of radiation used and if the purchase is certified by a medical practitioner as being a medical one[1]. Nor may any person sell, consign, deliver or import into Scotland food which has been subjected to prohibited ionising radiation[2].

  1 Food (Control of Irradiation) (Scotland) Regulations 1967, SI 1967/388, reg 4 (substituted by SI 1972/307).
  2 Ibid, reg 5.

358. Uncooked meat products. No person may sell, offer or expose for sale, or possess for sale, an uncooked meat product[1] in the preparation of which any specified parts of the carcase[2] has been used as an ingredient unless that part has been used solely as a sausage skin[3].

  1 'Meat product' is defined in the Meat Products and Spreadable Fish Products (Scotland) Regulations 1984, SI 1984/1714, reg 2(1). Exclusions specified in Sch 3 include uncooked chickens, haggis, broth and potted head.
  2 These include brains, feet, intestines, lungs, spleen, stomach and udder: ibid, Sch 2, Pt II.
  3 Ibid, reg 14. Contravention is an offence: reg 15.

(c) Composition, Labelling and Advertisement of Specific Foods

359. Bread and flour. Extensive provisions about the composition, labelling and advertisement of many varieties of bread and of flour appear in regulations. White, brown, wholemeal, wheatgerm or soda bread and bread containing milk solids or added protein which are intended for sale for human consumption may contain only the ingredients specified in the regulations[1]. They must comply with provisions in the regulations about labelling and advertising[2]. Bread containing certain other ingredients is also dealt with. But these provisions do not apply to food intended for export to a place outside the United Kingdom, for consumption by persons in Her Majesty's forces or by a visiting force or not intended for human consumption[3].

A whole loaf of bread of a net weight exceeding 300 g (10 oz), when not pre-packed, may be made for sale only if it is of a net weight of 400 g (14 oz) or a multiple of 400 g, unless the bread is sold in pursuance of a contract for the supply of bread for consumption on the buyer's premises and the contract provides for each delivery to be of not less than 25 kg and for the bread to be weighed on delivery[4].

  1 Bread and Flour (Scotland) Regulations 1984, SI 1984/1518, regs 4–6.
  2 Ibid, regs 5–7.
  3 Ibid, reg 3.
  4 Weights and Measures Act 1963 (Miscellaneous Foods) Order 1984, SI 1984/1316, art 7.

360. Butter. Butter may not be sold, consigned or delivered unless it complies with a prescribed composition[1], and food must not be sold under such a description as to lead an intending purchaser to believe he is purchasing butter if the food does not comply with the prescribed composition[2].

A person may not give with any butter sold by him, or display with any butter offered by him for sale, any label, whether attached to or printed on a container or not, or publish or be a party to the publication of any advertisement for butter, if the label or advertisement includes the word 'butter' unless the food complies with the prescribed composition for butter[3]. If the butter does not contain added salt the label or advertisement must include the words 'unsalted butter', but if the butter contains the permitted amount of salt, the label or advertisement must include the words 'salted butter'[4].

These provisions do not apply to sales for exportation to a place outside the United Kingdom, or for consumption by members of Her Majesty's forces or of visiting forces or for manufacturing purposes[5]. Nor do the provisions as to labelling apply for catering purposes[6].

1 Butter (Scotland) Regulations 1966, SI 1966/1252, reg 5. See also the Colouring Matter in Food (Scotland) Regulations 1973, SI 1973/1310.
2 Butter (Scotland) Regulations 1966, reg 6.
3 Ibid, reg 7(1)(a).
4 Ibid, reg 7(1)(b), (c).
5 Ibid, reg 4.
6 Ibid, reg 4 (amended by the Food Labelling (Scotland) Regulations 1981, SI 1981/137, reg 43, Sch 7, para 3).

361. Cheese and cheese products. Standards for the composition of hard cheese, soft cheese, whey cheese, processed cheese, cheese spread and compound products are prescribed by regulations, and cheese which does not comply with the relevant standards may not be sold, consigned or delivered[1]. Any such food sold, consigned or delivered with or without a container must bear a label or have near it a ticket with a description of the food in accordance with prescribed specifications[2].

Any advertisement for cheese, processed cheese, cheese spread or a cheese product must include the description of the cheese according to the prescribed standards, except that in the case of hard or soft cheese the name of the variety of the cheese may be given instead, but in the case of processed cheese the word 'processed' may be used[3]. The composition of any cheese that is advertised must comply with the relevant requirements[4], and the labelling and advertisement of cream cheese is regulated[5].

Exemptions are made for sales, consignments and deliveries for exportation to a place outside the United Kingdom or to a visiting force or a manufacturer, but advertisement, other than by labels or wrappers is not exempted[6].

The addition of preservatives and colouring matter is also regulated[7].

1 Cheese (Scotland) Regulations 1970, SI 1970/108, regs 4–9, Sch 1.
2 Ibid, regs 12, 14, Sch 2. Generally as to composition and labelling, see reg 10, and as to ingredients, see reg 11 (substituted by SI 1984/847).
3 Ibid, reg 13(1), (3).
4 Ibid, reg 13(2), (3).
5 Ibid, reg 15.
6 Ibid, reg 3.
7 See the Preservatives in Food (Scotland) Regulations 1989, SI 1989/581, and the Colouring Matter in Food (Scotland) Regulations 1973, SI 1973/1310.

362. Cocoa and chocolate products. Cocoa and chocolate products are the subject of detailed regulations which deal with a wide variety of subjects including reserved descriptions of cocoa and chocolate products, the labelling and description of these products, the labelling and advertisement of filled chocolate and declarations of the presence of certain ingredients in chocolate products.

There is a prohibition on the use on any label, display or advertisement of a reserved description, or any derivative thereof or any word or description substantially similar thereto, in relation to any food offered or exposed for sale which is not a cocoa or chocolate product to which the reserved description relates or unless such description, derivative or word makes clear that the substance to which it relates is an ingredient of that food or that the food either is not or does not contain a cocoa or chocolate product[1]. However, there is a reservation for the use of the words 'choc ice' or 'choc bar'[1].

There is also prohibited the sale, consignment or delivery pursuant to a sale of any cocoa or chocolate product unless a true statement is applied to the product specifying a relevant reserved description and other prescribed relevant information[2]. Provision is made as to the placing of the statement on the container in which the product is sold, consigned or delivered, on a document accompanying the product, on a label marked or attached to the container or on a ticket displayed on or in immediate proximity to the product, and special provision is made about information to be given in the case of a sale otherwise than by retail of any prepacked fancy chocolate product and the retail sale of any chocolate product which is not prepacked and has not previously been exposed for sale[3].

The presence of certain ingredients in chocolate products must be declared on labels or containers except declarations which are exempted[4]. Certain special varieties of chocolate product are dealt with separately[5], and natural sources of flavouring substances are also dealt with[6]. Methods of marking and labelling are regulated[7] and other aspects of the sale of both cocoa and chocolate products, including additional ingredients permitted in both, are covered[8]. The addition of preservatives and colouring matter is also regulated[9].

Cocoa and chocolate products sold, consigned or delivered for exportation to any place outside the United Kingdom are exempted from all the provisions of the regulations, as are products supplied for consumption by members of Her Majesty's forces or by visiting forces[10]. The regulations implement EEC directives[11].

1 Cocoa and Chocolate Products (Scotland) Regulations 1976, SI 1976/914, reg 4.
2 Ibid, reg 5(1)–(4) (amended by SI 1982/108).
3 Ibid, reg 5(5)–(7).
4 Ibid, reg 7.
5 Ibid, regs 6, 8, 9.
6 Ibid, reg 10.
7 Ibid, reg 11.
8 Ibid, regs 12–15.
9 See the Preservatives in Food (Scotland) Regulations 1989, SI 1989/581, and the Colouring Matter in Food (Scotland) Regulations 1973, SI 1973/1310.
10 Cocoa and Chocolate Products (Scotland) Regulations 1976, reg 3.
11 Ie EC Council Directive 73/241 (amended by EC Council Directives 74/411, 74/644, 75/155, 76/628, 78/609, 78/842, 80/608).

363. Coffee and coffee products. No person may give with any food sold by him for human consumption any label, whether attached to or borne on the container or not, or display with any food offered or exposed by him for sale any ticket or notice, or apply to any food so sold by him any statement, or publish or be party to the publication of any advertisement for food, which bears, comprises, or includes any reserved description or any derivative thereof unless specified conditions are complied with[1]. The use of the word 'coffee' to describe a beverage prepared from coffee or certain designated products or the use of the words 'dandelion coffee' to describe certain specified products is not prohibited[2].

A designated product[3] must not be sold, consigned or delivered in a container unless it is correctly marked or labelled with prescribed particulars[4].

A raw material which is not sound, wholesome and in marketable condition may not be used in the preparation of any designated product[5], and a designated product which contains any added ingredient may not, with certain exceptions, be sold, consigned or delivered[6]. There are provisions as to products sold from vending machines[7].

The regulations do not apply to designated products for exportation to any place outside the United Kingdom or supplied for consumption by Her Majesty's forces or visiting forces[8].

1 Coffee and Coffee Products (Scotland) Regulations 1979, SI 1979/383, reg 4(1).
2 Ibid, reg 4(2), (3).
3 Ie a coffee or coffee mixture, coffee or chicory extract product, blend of extracts or extract of blends: see ibid, art 2(1), Sch 1 (substituted by SI 1987/2014).
4 Ibid, regs 5, 5A, 6 (as so substituted).
5 Ibid, reg 7.
6 Ibid, reg 8 (amended by SI 1987/2014).
7 Ibid, reg 9.
8 Ibid, reg 3.

364. Ice cream. Various aspects of the substance known as ice cream are controlled by regulations which deal not only with the substance itself and its manufacture and sale but also with the registration of premises and vehicles and with appeals to the sheriff against the refusal or cancellation of registration[1]. There are also provisions about apparatus, equipment and utensils used in the manufacture of ice cream, about its storage and sale and the material construction, type and quantity used in all these cases[2]. There are general public health provisions including provisions for the prevention of contamination of ice cream and the notification to the medical officer of health by a dealer that he believes a person living or working in ice cream premises or a vehicle is suffering from certain diseases[3].

The composition of ice cream and Parev ice is prescribed[4], and there are detailed provisions about the manufacture of ice cream by the reconstitution of a complete cold mix and certain other mixtures[5]. Subject to certain exceptions it is an offence for any person to sell, consign or deliver any ice cream or Parev ice which does not comply with prescribed standards and composition[6], and there are requirements as to the labelling and description of ice cream[7].

A person may not give or display with any ice cream or Parev ice sold or exposed for sale any label, or publish or be party to the publication of any advertisement which bears or includes specified expressions or any word or pictorial device which refers to or is suggestive of butter, cream, milk or anything connected with the dairy interest unless the ice cream contains no fat other than milk fat (save such as may be introduced by egg, flavouring or any emulsifying or stabilising agent)[8]. There are exemptions from all of those provisions, except those relating to advertisements, for ice cream or Parev ice sold, consigned or delivered for exportation to any place outside the United Kingdom, or supplied for consumption by a visiting force, or for manufacturing or catering purposes[9].

1 Ice Cream (Scotland) Regulations 1948, SI 1948/960, regs 4–6.
2 Ibid, reg 7.
3 Ibid, regs 12, 13.
4 Ice-Cream (Scotland) Regulations 1970, SI 1970/1285, reg 4 (amended by the Sweeteners in Food (Scotland) Regulations 1983, SI 1983/1497, reg 12, Sch 2, para 3).
5 Ice Cream (Scotland) Regulations 1948, regs 8, 9 (substituted by SI 1960/2108).
6 Ice-Cream (Scotland) Regulations 1970, reg 5.
7 Ibid, reg 6 (amended by the Food Labelling (Scotland) Regulations 1981, SI 1981/137, reg 43, Sch 7, para 12).

8 Ice-Cream (Scotland) Regulations 1970, reg 7.
9 Ibid, reg 3 (amended by the Food Labelling (Scotland) Regulations 1981, Sch 7, para 6).

365. Margarine. Margarine must contain not less than 80 per cent fat (of which not more than one-tenth by weight may be derived from milk), and not more than 16 per cent water, and a person may not sell, consign or deliver margarine which does not comply with these standards[1]. Nor may a person sell by retail margarine which does not contain, in every ounce, not less than 760 and not more than 940 units of vitamin A, and not less than 80 and not more than 100 international units of vitamin D[2].

There are detailed provisions about the labelling and advertisement of margarine, one of the main objects of which is to ensure that a label, ticket or notice describing magarine does not confuse it with butter or anything connected with the dairy interest[3]. More extensive provisions having a similar object are made in relation to the publications of advertisements[4].

Margarine sold, consigned or delivered for exportation to any place outside the United Kingdom, or to manufacturers or caterers or supplied for consumption by Her Majesty's Forces or by a visiting force is exempt[5].

1 Margarine (Scotland) Regulations 1970, SI 1970/1286, reg 5.
2 Ibid, reg 6.
3 Ibid, reg 8.
4 Ibid, reg 9 (amended by the Food Labelling (Scotland) Regulations 1981, SI 1981/137, reg 43, Sch 7, para 13).
5 Margarine (Scotland) Regulations 1970, reg 3 (amended by the Food Labelling (Scotland) Regulations 1981, Sch 7, para 7).

366. Meat and fish products. Meat products described as burgers, hamburgers, chopped or corned meat, luncheon meat, pies or puddings, pasties, bridies, sausages, pastas, pâtés or spreads must comply with prescribed requirements[1]. Any meat product appearing to be a cut, joint, slice, portion or carcase of raw, cooked or cured meat must be labelled with its ingredients[2]. Provision is made as to the list of ingredients, declaration of meat or fish content, corned meat content, added water content and lean meat content[3], and as to the calculation of content of the different ingredients[4]. The provisions apply to food ready for delivery to the ultimate consumer or to a catering establishment, but not to food which is not intended for human consumption, to food intended for export to a place outside the United Kingdom, to food for consumption by members of Her Majesty's forces or a visiting force or to food marked or labelled as intended exclusively for babies or young children[5]. Contravention of the provisions is an offence[6].

1 Meat Products and Spreadable Fish Products (Scotland) Regulations 1984, SI 1984/1714, reg 4, Sch 4. As to the meaning of 'meat product', see para 358, note 1, above.
2 Ibid, reg 5.
3 Ibid, regs 6–11.
4 Ibid, regs 12–14.
5 Ibid, reg 3.
6 Ibid, reg 15.

367. Salad cream. Standards for the composition of salad cream are prescribed[1]. Labels or advertisements must not contain the words 'salad cream' or 'mayonnaise' unless the product complies with the relevant standard[2]. The use of the description 'salad dressing' is prescribed[3]. The provisions do not apply to salad cream sold for exportation to any place outside the United Kingdom, supplied for consumption by members of Her Majesty's forces or a visiting force or sold to a manufacturer or caterer[4].

1 Salad Cream (Scotland) Regulations 1966, SI 1966/1206, reg 5.
2 Ibid, reg 7.
3 Ibid, reg 8.
4 Ibid, reg 4 (amended by the Food Labelling (Scotland) Regulations 1981, SI 1981/137, art 43, Sch 7, para 2).

368. Soft drinks. The composition of soft drinks is regulated, and the sale of any soft drink which does not comply with the compositional requirements is prohibited[1]. The addition of acids to soft drinks is restricted to those specified in the appropriate regulations and in regulations dealing with preservatives and colouring matters[2]. In addition, any soft drink other than a fruit squash, a fruit crush, or a comminuted citrus drink may contain acetic acid and phosphoric acid[3]. Particular soft drinks may not be sold in a container unless the container bears a label with a specified description of the drink, and a soft drink which does not comply with the prescribed requirements, but is in a container having a label indicating a fruit content, may not be sold[4]. The labelling of semi-sweet, diabetic and low calorie soft drinks is regulated, and the sale of soft drinks from vending machines requires descriptive labelling[5].

Soft drinks intended for exportation to any place outside the United Kingdom or for use as ships stores, or for consumption by Her Majesty's forces or a visiting force, or for sale to a manufacturer or otherwise than in a container are in general exempt from these requirements[6].

1 Soft Drinks (Scotland) Regulations 1964, SI 1964/767, reg 6 (amended by SI 1969/1847 and by the Sweeteners in Food (Scotland) Regulations 1983, SI 1983/1497, reg 12, Sch 2, para 1(2)).
2 Soft Drinks (Scotland) Regulations 1964, reg 7(1)(a), which is deemed to refer to the Colouring Matter in Food (Scotland) Regulations 1973, SI 1973/1310, and the Preservatives in Food (Scotland) Regulations 1989, SI 1989/581.
3 Soft Drinks (Scotland) Regulations 1964, reg 7(1)(b).
4 Ibid, regs 8, 9.
5 Ibid, regs 10–12 and reg 13 (substituted by the Labelling of Food (Scotland) Amendment Regulations 1972, SI 1972/1790, reg 4(4), and amended by the Sweeteners in Food (Scotland) Regulations 1983, Sch 2, para 1(3)).
6 Soft Drinks (Scotland) Regulations 1964, reg 5.

369. Sugar products. The use of certain reserved descriptions in connection with specified sugar products is regulated[1]. Such products must not be sold, consigned or delivered in a container unless there is marked on or securely attached to it a label with a true statement specifying (1) its reserved description; (2) in the case of extra white sugar the reserved description or the description 'sugar' or 'white sugar'; or (3) in the case of dextrose monohydrate or dextrose anhydrous sold by retail, the reserved description or the description 'dextrose'[1]. In the case of certain syrups, solutions and icing preparations, the statement must also include a declaration relating to its composition, and in all cases the name and address of the manufacturer, packer or seller[1].

There are restrictions on the use of the word 'white' in relation to sugar solutions and syrups, and on the sale of glucose syrups with a sulphur dioxide content in excess of a specified amount, as well as on the sale of sugar products with added ingredients[2].

Reserved descriptions, or their derivatives or words substantially similar, must not be used in connection with the sale or advertisement of food unless such food is the specified sugar product to which it relates, or it is clearly indicated that the substance to which it relates is an ingredient of that food, or such description is used in a context clearly indicating that such food is not or does not contain a specified sugar product[3].

The requirements do not apply to specified sugar products sold, consigned or delivered for exportation to any place outside the United Kingdom, or supplied to Her Majesty's forces or a visiting force[4].

1 Specified Sugar Products (Scotland) Regulations 1976, SI 1976/946, regs 5, 7. The regulations implement EC Council Directive 73/437 (OJ L356, 27.12.73, p 71).
2 Specified Sugar Products (Scotland) Regulations 1976, regs 6, 8, 9, Schs 2, 3. Schedule 2 was substituted by SI 1982/410.
3 Ibid, reg 4.
4 Ibid, reg 3.

370. Olive oil. Under European Community legislation olive oil with a tetra-chloroethylene content of more than 0.1 milligram per kilogram may not be offered for sale by retail[1]. Contravention of this provision is an offence[2].

1 EC Commission Regulation 1860/88 (OJ L166, 1.7.88, p 16), art 1.
2 Tetrachloroethylene in Olive Oil (Scotland) Regulations 1989, SI 1989/837, reg 3(1), (2). District and islands councils are responsible for enforcing and executing the regulations: reg 3(3). Regulation 5 applies certain provisions of the Food and Drugs (Scotland) Act 1956 (c 30) for the purposes of the regulations.

(d) Control of Substances used as Ingredients of Food

371. Antioxidants. Regulations are in force which provide that, subject to certain exceptions, no food sold, consigned, delivered in or imported into Scotland may have in it or on it any added antioxidant other than a permitted antioxidant[1]. It follows that the regulations provide that a person may not sell, consign, deliver, import into Scotland or advertise for sale any antioxidant (including any antioxidant with which any other substance has been mixed) for use as an ingredient in the preparation of food except a permitted antioxidant in a container bearing a label on which is printed a true statement about the permitted antioxidants present[2].

Food which has in it or on it certain antioxidants may not be sold along with a label, or be offered or exposed for sale with any ticket or notice, bearing any words, device or description calculated to indicate that the food is intended for babies or young children; and a person may not publish or be party to any advertisement, or use on or in connection with the sale of any food any words, which have a similar indication[3].

Food which does not comply with these provisions may be seized and destroyed as being unfit for human consumption[4]. The regulations do not apply to food for exportation to any place outside the United Kingdom[5].

1 Antioxidants in Food (Scotland) Regulations 1978, SI 1978/492, reg 4, Sch 3. For permitted antioxidants and permitted diluents, see reg 2(1), Schs 1, 2 (amended by SI 1980/1886). The regulations implement EC Council Directive 70/357 (OJ L157, 19.7.70, p 3 (S Edn 1970 (II) p 429)) (as amended).
2 Antioxidants in Food (Scotland) Regulations 1978, reg 5, Sch 4.
3 Ibid, reg 6.
4 Ibid, reg 7.
5 Ibid, reg 3.

372. Colouring matter. Food sold, consigned, delivered or imported into Scotland may not have in it or on it any colouring matter other than a permitted colouring matter, and food may not have in it or on it a mark in any other than a permitted colouring matter[1]. Permitted colouring matters and permitted diluents which may be combined with such colouring matters are prescribed, together with purity criteria[2].

The use of permitted colouring matter in or on certain named foods is limited[3]. Some foods may not have in or on them any colouring matter except for marking purposes, and colouring matter is not permitted to be in tea, coffee, coffee products, condensed milk or dried milk sold, consigned, delivered or imported for human consumption[4].

A person may not sell, consign, deliver, import into Scotland or advertise for sale any colouring matter for use as an ingredient in the preparation of food unless it is a permitted colouring matter, and any such colouring matter must be in a container bearing a prescribed label[5]. Other labelling requirements for permitted colouring matter are prescribed[5].

Colouring matter, diluents combined with such matter, and food containing either, intended for exportation to any place outside the United Kingdom are exempt, as is also such matter intended for scientific testing[6].

1 Colouring Matter in Food (Scotland) Regulations 1973, SI 1973/1310, regs 4(1), (2), 6. These regulations implement EEC Council Directive 62/1 (OJ L115, 12.11.62, p 2645 (S Edn 1959–62 p 279)) (as amended).
2 Colouring Matter in Food (Scotland) Regulations 1973, Schs 1, 2 (amended by SI 1975/1595, SI 1976/2232, SI 1979/107 and SI 1987/1985).
3 Ibid, reg 4(3), Sch 3 (amended by SI 1976/2232).
4 Ibid, reg 5(1), (2) (amended by SI 1987/1985).
5 Ibid, reg 7(1), (2), Sch 4.
6 Ibid, reg 3.

373. Emulsifiers and stabilisers. Any food which contains an added emulsifier or stabiliser, other than a permitted emulsifier or stabiliser, may not be sold or imported into Scotland[1]. Flour intended for sale as such may not contain any emulsifier or stabiliser[2], and bread, soft cheese, whey cheese, processed cheese, cheese spread and cocoa and chocolate products may contain only limited quantities of certain permitted emulsifiers and stabilisers[3]. No food may have in it or on it more than specified proportions of certain permitted emulsifiers and stabilisers[4].

Only a permitted emulsifier or stabiliser may be sold, imported or advertised for use in the preparation of food, and such an emulsifier or stabiliser may be sold only in a container bearing a label which complies with prescribed requirements[5]. No label may be given and no ticket or notice may be displayed with any permitted emulsifier or stabiliser which bears an indication that the emulsifier or stabiliser is a substitute for fat or eggs[6]. This prohibition applies also in the case of advertisements of emulsifiers and stabilisers[6].

Food wrongfully containing emulsifiers or stabilisers may be seized and destroyed as unfit for human consumption[7].

Food having any emulsifier or stabiliser in or on it intended for exportation to any place outside the United Kingdom is exempt[8].

1 Emulsifiers and Stabilisers in Food (Scotland) Regulations 1989, SI 1989/945, reg 4(1). As to permitted emulsifiers and stabilisers, see Sch 1. The regulations implement EC Council Directive 74/329 (OJ L189, 12.7.74, p 1) (as amended); EC Council Directive 78/663 (OJ L223, 14.8.78, p 7) (as amended); EC Council Directive 78/664 (OJ L223, 14.8.78, p 30); and EC Council Directive 86/102 (OJ L88, 3.4.86, p 40).
2 Emulsifiers and Stabilisers in Food (Scotland) Regulations 1989, reg 4(7).
3 Ibid, reg 4(4), Sch 2, Pt II.
4 Ibid, reg 4(2), (3), Sch 2, Pts I, II.
5 Ibid, reg 5, Sch 3.
6 Ibid, reg 6.
7 Ibid, reg 7.
8 Ibid, reg 3.

374. Meat treatment. Raw and unprocessed meat must not contain any added specified substance, and no person may sell, consign or deliver any such meat which contains any such added substance thus masking the condition of the meat[1]. If meat is certified as having been masked it may be treated as condemned meat[2].

1 Meat (Treatment) (Scotland) Regulations 1964, SI 1964/44, reg 4. The specified substances are ascorbic acid, erythorbic acid, nicotinic acid, nicotinamide and any salt or derivative of any of them: reg 2(1), Schedule.
2 Ibid, reg 5.

375. Mineral hydrocarbons. Subject to certain exemptions relating to dried fruit, citrus fruit, sugar confectionary, food of which dried fruit, citrus fruit or sugar confectionary is an ingredient, lubricants, the rind of pressed cheese, eggs and food intended for exportation to any place outside the United Kingdom[1], the use of any mineral hydrocarbon in the composition or preparation of food is prohibited by regulations, which also prohibit the sale and the consignment, delivery or importation of any food containing any mineral hydrocarbon[2].

Specifications are laid down for mineral hydrocarbons the use of which is regulated in relation to the permitted exemptions, together with a test for limits of control of certain polycyclic aromatic hydrocarbons[3].

Provision is made for the condemnation of food containing mineral hydrocarbons in contravention of the regulations[4].

1 Mineral Hydrocarbons in Food (Scotland) Regulations 1966, SI 1966/1263, reg 4.
2 Ibid, reg 5.
3 Ibid, Schedule.
4 Ibid, reg 6.

376. Miscellaneous additives. Food sold or imported must not have in it or on it any added miscellaneous additive other than a permitted miscellaneous additive, and the use in or on any such food of certain permitted additives is restricted[1].

The sale, importation or advertisement for sale for use as an ingredient in the preparation of food of any miscellaneous additive other than a permitted miscellaneous additive is prohibited, and any permitted miscellaneous additive for use as an ingredient must not be sold except in a container bearing a label in accordance with prescribed requirements[2]. Food containing certain additives may not be sold for babies and young children[3]. Food wrongfully containing additives may be seized and destroyed as unfit for human consumption[4].

Food intended for exportation to a place outside the United Kingdom is exempt from these requirements[5].

1 Miscellaneous Additives in Food (Scotland) Regulations 1980, SI 1980/1889, reg 4 (amended by SI 1982/515). As to permitted miscellaneous additives, see Sch 1 (amended by SI 1982/515, SI 1983/1497 and SI 1984/1518). The regulations implement EEC Council Directive of 23 October 1962 (JO 1962, p 1645 (S Edn 1959–62, p 279)); EEC Council Directive 64/54 (JO 1964, p 161 (S Edn 1963–64, p 99)); EEC Council Directive 65/66 (JO 1965, p 373 (S Edn 1965–66, p 25)); EC Council Directive 70/357 (OJ L157, 18.7.70, p 31 (S Edn 1970 (II), p 429)); EC Council Directive 74/329 (OJ L189, 12.7.74, p 1); EC Council Directive 78/612 (OJ L197, 22.7.78, p 22); EC Council Directive 78/663 (OJ L223, 14.8.78, p 7); and EC Council Directive 78/664 (OJ L223, 14.8.78, p 30).
2 Miscellaneous Additives in Food (Scotland) Regulations 1980, reg 5, Sch 3 (amended by SI 1983/1497).

3 Ibid, reg 5A (added by SI 1982/515).
4 Ibid, reg 6.
5 Ibid, reg 3.

377. Preservatives. Save as permitted by regulations, no food sold or imported into Scotland may have in it or on it any added preservative[1]. There are,
however, specified foods any of which may have in it or on it permitted
preservatives of prescribed descriptions in prescribed proportions, and there are
special provisions about specified food in relation to which two or more
permitted preservatives are prescribed[2]. Further, any specified food and any
food intended for use in the preparation of a specified food (with some exceptions) may on importation into Scotland or on a sale other than a retail sale have
in it or on it prescribed permitted preservatives in any proportion if on or before
the sale a prescribed document is provided to the importer or buyer[3]. There are
also special provisions about preservatives in compounded food[4].

Food having not more than 5 milligrams per kilogram of formaldehyde
derived from any wet strength wrapping containing a formaldehyde-based
resin or from plastic food containers or utensils made from resin containing
formaldehyde is exempt from these provisions[5]. The permitted miscellaneous
additive dimethylpolysiloxane may contain formaldehyde in any proportion
not exceeding 1,000 milligrams per kilogram[6]. Cheese, clotted cream or any
canned food may have in it or on it the permitted preservative nisin, and any
food may have in it or on it nisin introduced in the preparation of that food by
the use of any such cheese, clotted cream or canned food[7]. Flour may contain
sulphur dioxide or sodium metabisulphite as prescribed in the appropriate bread
and flour regulations[8], and Community controlled wine may contain certain
permitted preservatives authorised by Community regulations[9]. Food for
babies or young children may not contain added sodium nitrate or sodium
nitrite[10].

The sale, advertisement and labelling of preservatives is regulated[11], as is the
quantitative and qualitative analysis of citrus fruit[12]. Food intended for exportation to any place outside the United Kingdom is exempt[13].

 1 Preservatives in Food (Scotland) Regulations 1989, SI 1989/581, reg 4(1), (12). The regulations
    implement EEC Council Directive 64/54 (JO 1964, p 161 (S Edn 1963–64, p 99)) on the
    approximation of the laws of member states concerning the preservatives authorised for use in
    foodstuffs intended for human consumption, and EEC Council Directive 65/66 (JO 1965, p 373
    (S Edn 1965–66, p 25)) laying down criteria of purity for such preservatives.
 2 Preservatives in Food (Scotland) Regulations 1989, reg 4(2), (3), Sch 2. As to permitted
    preservatives, see Sch 1.
 3 Ibid, reg 4(4), Schs 1–3.
 4 Ibid, reg 5.
 5 Ibid, reg 4(5).
 6 Ibid, reg 4(6). As to formaldehyde introduced in the preparation of food by the use of dimethyl-
    polysiloxane, see reg 4(9).
 7 Ibid, reg 4(7), (8).
 8 Ibid, reg 4(10).
 9 Ibid, reg 4(11).
10 Ibid, reg 7.
11 Ibid, reg 6, Sch 3.
12 Ibid, reg 7, Schs 4–6.
13 Ibid, reg 3.

378. Solvents. Only a permitted solvent[1] may be sold, consigned, delivered
or imported into Scotland, and food which contains a solvent which is not a
permitted solvent must not be sold, consigned, delivered or imported into
Scotland[2]. The publication of an advertisement for any solvent with a view to its
use in the preparation of food is restricted, and so also is the labelling of the

container in which a permitted solvent is sold, consigned or delivered[3]. Food certified as not complying with the regulations may be treated as being unfit for human consumption[4]. These provisions do not apply to food intended for exportation to any place outside the United Kingdom[5].

1　A solvent is a liquid substance, other than a natural food substance and the primary use of which is not flavouring, generally used to facilitate the incorporation of ingredients in food: see the Solvents in Food (Scotland) Regulations 1968, SI 1968/263, reg 2(1). For the permitted solvents, see Sch 1 (amended by SI 1980/1887).
2　Ibid, reg 5.
3　Ibid, regs 6, 7.
4　Ibid, reg 8.
5　Ibid, reg 4.

379. Sweeteners. No person may sell or import any food which has added to it or onto it any sweetener other than a permitted sweetener, or sell or import any such sweetener intended for catering use or for use by the ultimate consumer, or sell or advertise for sale any such sweetener for use in the preparation of food, or sell any food specially prepared for babies or young children (except those with special dietary requirements) if any sweetener has been added[1]. The labelling of permitted sweeteners is regulated[2], and food wrongfully containing sweeteners may be seized and destroyed as being unfit for human consumption[3].

The requirements do not apply to food not intended for human consumption or intended for exportation to any place outside the United Kingdom[4].

1　Sweeteners in Food (Scotland) Regulations 1983, SI 1983/1497, regs 4–6.
2　Ibid, reg 7.
3　Ibid, reg 8.
4　Ibid, reg 3.

(e) Restrictions on the Use of Certain Ingredients of Food

380. Arsenic. The sale, consignment, delivery or importation into Scotland of food which contains arsenic in a proportion exceeding one part per million (by weight) is prohibited, but any specified food may contain specified proportions of arsenic and certain foods are exempt[1]. Food which contravenes these requirements may be treated as unfit for human consumption[2].

1　Arsenic in Food (Scotland) Regulations 1959, SI 1959/928, reg 4, Schedule (amended by SI 1960/2344, SI 1966/1384, SI 1972/1489, SI 1973/1039, SI 1973/1310 and SI 1975/1597).
2　Ibid, reg 5.

381. Erucic acid. No person may sell, consign or deliver any oil or fat, or any mixture thereof, if erucic acid constitutes more than 5 per cent of its fatty acid content; or any food to which oil or fat or a mixture thereof has been added if the erucic acid constitutes more than 5 per cent of the fatty acid content of all the oil and fat in the food[1].

Exempted from these provisions are oil, fat or food intended for exportation to any place outside the United Kingdom; food which contains not more than 5 per cent oil or fat unless it is described directly or by implication as specially prepared for infants or young children; oil, fat or food for use by a manufacturer or caterer; and oil, fat or food manufactured before 21 July 1977[2].

1　Erucic Acid in Food (Scotland) Regulations 1977, SI 1977/1028, reg 4. 'Erucic acid' means the fatty acid cis-docos-13-enoic acid: reg 2(1). As to determining erucic acid content, see reg 5

(added by SI 1982/18). The regulations implement EC Council Directive 76/621 (OJ L202, 28.7.76, p 35).
2 Erucic Acid in Food (Scotland) Regulations 1977, reg 3.

382. Lead. A person may not sell, consign, deliver or import into Scotland any food of a specified description which contains lead in any proportion exceeding that specified in relation to that food[1]. No other food may contain lead in any proportion exceeding 1.0 milligrams per kilogram of such food[2].

These provisions do not apply to any food in respect of which the maximum permitted lead content is prescribed by any other regulations made under the Food and Drugs (Scotland) Act 1956 or by any order having effect as if contained in regulations so made, or which is intended for exportation to any place outside the United Kingdom[3].

Food which does not comply with these requirements may be treated as unfit for human consumption[4].

1 Lead in Food (Scotland) Regulations 1979, SI 1979/1641, reg 4(1), (3), Sch 1 (amended by SI 1985/1438).
2 Ibid, reg 4(2).
3 Lead in Food (Scotland) Regulations 1979, reg 3.
4 Ibid, reg 5.

(f) Labelling of Food

383. General. The marking or labelling of food is regulated by the Food Labelling (Scotland) Regulations 1984, which require all food, subject to certain exemptions, to be marked or labelled with the name of the food, a list of ingredients, an indication of minimum durability, any special storage conditions or conditions of use, and the name and address of the manufacturer or packer or of a seller, and, in certain cases, particulars of the place of origin of the food and instructions for use[1]. The presentation of food must not be such that a purchaser is likely to be misled to a material degree as to the nature, substance or quality of the food[2].

Where special emphasis is placed by a label on the presence or low content of an ingredient in a food, an indication of the minimum or maximum percentage, as the case may be, of that ingredient must be provided[3]. Special provision is made for the labelling of food which is or is not prepacked and for food prepacked in special materials, for fancy confectionary products, for food packed in small packages and for food for immediate consumption[4]. There are additional labelling requirements for food sold from vending machines and for alcoholic drinks[5].

The manner of marking or labelling is prescribed[6]. There are restrictions on the making of claims relating to foods for particular nutritional purposes, and the use of certain words and descriptions in the labelling and advertising of food is restricted[7]. The use of the word 'wine' in composite names for drinks other than wine or table wine is permitted[8].

The regulations do not apply to milk, or, except so far as relating to advertising, to food not intended for sale for human consumption, to food intended for export to any place outside the United Kingdom, and to food for consumption by Her Majesty's forces or a visiting force[9], or (apart from provisions relating to claims and misleading descriptions) to certain products whose labelling is controlled by certain other regulations or EEC Council Regulations[10]. The regulations have only limited application to natural mineral water[11].

1 Food Labelling (Scotland) Regulations 1984, SI 1984/1519, reg 6. See further paras 384 ff below. The regulations were made under the Food and Drugs (Scotland) Act 1956 (c 30), s 7(1), which

empowers the Secretary of State to make regulations imposing requirements as to, and otherwise regulating, the labelling, marking or advertising of food intended for sale for human consumption, and the descriptions which may be applied to such food. The regulations implement EC Council Directives 76/766, 77/94 and 79/112 (OJ L262, 27.9.76, p 149; OJ L26, 31.1.77, p 55; and OJ L33, 8.2.79, p 1). The regulations may not apply to milk, but may apply to cream and separated milk and any food containing milk: Food and Drugs (Scotland) Act 1956, s 7(4).

2 Food Labelling (Scotland) Regulations 1984, reg 4.
3 Ibid, reg 20: see para 385 below.
4 Ibid, regs 24, 25, 27–29: see paras 387–389, below.
5 Ibid, regs 30, 31, 31A (amended by SI 1989/809): see paras 390, 391, below.
6 Ibid, regs 32–35 (as so amended): see para 392 below.
7 Ibid, regs 36–38 (as so amended): see paras 393, 394, below.
8 Ibid, reg 39 (as so amended): see para 395 below.
9 Ibid, reg 3(1), (2).
10 Ibid, reg 5 (amended by SI 1987/26, SI 1987/2014 and SI 1989/809).
11 Ibid, reg 3(3), (4) (added by SI 1989/809).

384. Names for food. Where a particular name is required by law to be used for a food, that name must be used as the name of the food, but where no name is prescribed by law a name which is customary in the area where the food is sold may be used for it[1]. If there is no name prescribed by law for a food and there is no customary name for it, the name used must be sufficiently precise to distinguish the food from products with which it could be confused[2]. The food may have a name or description or both[3]. A trade mark, brand or fancy name may not be substituted for the true name of a food[4]. If the omission of an indication that some feature of the food (for example that it is powdered or freeze-dried) could mislead a purchaser, the name must include such an indication[5].

1 Food Labelling (Scotland) Regulations 1984, SI 1984/1519, regs 7, 8. As to names prescribed by law for fish, melons, potatoes and vitamins, see Sch 1.
2 Ibid, reg 9.
3 Ibid, reg 10.
4 Ibid, reg 11.
5 Ibid, reg 12. As to indications of treatment of frozen food, tenderised meat and processed peas, see Sch 2.

385. Ingredients. The list of ingredients of any food with which the food must be marked or labelled[1] must have a heading which includes the word 'ingredients', and the ingredients must be listed in descending order of weight[2]. There are, however, specific rules about the calculation of the weight of water and volatile products, food in certain forms (for example dehydrated) and food which consists of mixed fruit and other products[3].

Ingredients must be named. If the ingredient could itself be sold as a food the name by which it could be sold will be used for it, with any indication which would be required if it were so sold[4], but a generic name may be used in certain cases[5], and an ingredient added to or used in a food to serve as a specified additive is to have a specified name[6]. Certain additives must be identified by specific names[7]. There are special provisions about the names to be given to a compound ingredient, that is, an ingredient which is itself composed of more than one ingredient[8]. Where water is added as an ingredient, the fact must be declared unless it is used solely for the reconstitution of some other ingredient or is used as part of a medium which is not normally consumed or if it does not exceed 5 per cent of the whole[9].

Certain ingredients, mainly associated with subsidiary additives, need not be named[10], and a considerable number of foods do not require a list of ingredients unless the foods are marked or labelled with a complete list of ingredients as if this were required[11]. There are also provisions about the indications to be given of the minimum or maximum percentages of ingredients which food contains[12].

1 See para 383 above.
2 Food Labelling (Scotland) Regulations 1984, SI 1984/1519, regs 13, 14(1).
3 Ibid, reg 14(2)–(5).
4 Ibid, reg 15(1), (2).
5 See ibid, reg 15(3), Sch 3 (amended by SI 1984/1714 and SI 1986/836).
6 See ibid, reg 15(4), Sch 4.
7 Ibid, reg 15(5), Sch 4.
8 Ibid, reg 16.
9 Ibid, reg 17.
10 Ibid, reg 18.
11 Ibid, reg 19.
12 Ibid, reg 20.

386. Indication of durability and use of food. The minimum durability of a food must be indicated on the label or mark. Subject to some qualifications this is to be effected by the use of the words 'best before', followed by the date up to and including which the food can reasonably be expected to have retained its specific properties if properly stored, and any storage conditions which must be observed[1]. Except in certain cases the date is to be expressed in terms of a day, month and year in that order[2]. Special provisions apply to perishable goods[3]. A large number of foods do not need to bear an indication of minimum durability[4]. Examples of these are fresh fruit and vegetables, cider, beer, bread, vinegar, chewing gum, deep-frozen food, certain cheeses and food with a minimum durability of more than eighteen months[4].

Instructions for the use of the food must be such as to enable appropriate use to be made of the food[5].

1 Food Labelling (Scotland) Regulations 1984, SI 1984/1519, reg 21(1). Such a formula as 'best before date printed on stopper' is permitted by reg 21(3).
2 Ibid, reg 21(2).
3 Ibid, reg 21(4), (5).
4 Ibid, reg 22 (amended by SI 1989/809).
5 Ibid, reg 23(1). For a concentrate, dry mix or similar food (other than custard or blancmange powder) intended to be made into another food by adding another substance, the instructions must specify every other such substance (other than water): reg 23(2). Every advertisement for the sale of such a concentrate etc must list every substance (other than water) which must be added: reg 23(3).

387. Marks or labels from which certain particulars may be omitted. Food which is not prepacked, or is prepacked for direct sale[1], and flour confectionary which is packed in a crimp case or is unmarked or marked only with a price need not be marked or labelled with the required particulars except, generally, for the name of the food[2]. Individually wrapped fancy confectionary products not enclosed in any further packaging and intended for sale as single items need not be marked or labelled except with the name of the food[3].

Any food mentioned above which contains an additive must, notwithstanding the exemptions mentioned above, be marked or labelled with an indication of the categories of additives present in the food except in the case of an edible ice or flour confectionary sold in premises where a notice is displayed that these foods may contain such categories of additives, although these provisions do not apply to food which is not exposed for sale[4].

1 For the meaning of 'prepacked for direct sale', see the Food Labelling (Scotland) Regulations 1984, SI 1984/1519, reg 24(3).

2 Ibid, reg 24(1), (2). For the required particulars, see reg 6, and para 383 above. As to food sold for immediate consumption, see para 388 below.
3 Ibid, reg 25(1). 'Fancy confectionary product' means a confectionary product in the form eg of a figure, animal, cigarette or egg: reg 25(2).
4 Ibid, reg 26.

388. Food sold for immediate consumption. It is not necessary to mark or label with the prescribed particulars (1) food not prepacked which is sold in a catering establishment for immediate consumption there but which is not food mentioned in heads (a) to (e) below; (2) food which is prepacked and is sold at a catering establishment for immediate consumption there as an individual portion and is intended to be an accompaniment to other food; and (3) any prepacked sandwich, filled roll or similar bread product or any prepacked prepared meal which (in either case) is sold in a catering establishment for immediate consumption there; although foods under heads (2) and (3) must be marked or labelled with the name of the food[1].

The following foods need not be marked or labelled with any of the prescribed particulars: (a) sandwiches, filled rolls and similar bread products, (b) food sold hot and ready for consumption, (c) prepared meals, (d) food sold from a vending machine for heating, (e) any food not prepacked or food prepacked for direct sale or food packed in a crimp case or in transparent packaging and which is sold either at a catering establishment or at an establishment concerned mainly with selling food in any of the foregoing categories[2]. However, except in the case of a vending machine, food sold at a catering establishment for immediate consumption is not included in this provision[2]. Food to which this provision applies must be marked or labelled in a specific manner depending on the circumstances in which it is being sold[3].

1 Food Labelling (Scotland) Regulations 1984, SI 1984/1519, reg 28(1)–(3) (amended by SI 1982/2177). As to the prescribed particulars, see reg 6, and para 383, supra. For the meaning of 'prepared meal', see reg 28(4).
2 Ibid, reg 29(1), (2). For the meaning of 'prepacked for direct sale', see reg 24(3).
3 Ibid, reg 29(3), (4).

389. Small packages. With the exception of food prepacked for direct sale, certain flour confectionary, fancy confectionary products and food for immediate consumption[1], any prepacked food the largest surface of whose packaging has an area of less than 10 square centimetres need not be marked or labelled with any of the prescribed particulars[2] except the name of the food and, unless the food is not required to be marked or labelled with such an indication, an indication of minimum durability[3].

1 Ie food to which the Labelling of Food (Scotland) Regulations 1984, SI 1984/1519, regs 24, 25, 28, 29, apply: see paras 387, 388, above.
2 See ibid, reg 6, and para 383 above.
3 Ibid, reg 27.

390. Food sold from vending machines. Unless the name of food sold from a vending machine is easily visible through the outside of the machine, a notice indicating the name of the food must appear on the front of the machine[1].

1 Food Labelling (Scotland) Regulations 1984, SI 1984/1519, reg 30, which is expressed to be without prejudice to any other labelling requirement imposed by the regulations.

391. Alcoholic drinks. Any prepacked alcoholic drink (other than Community controlled wine) having an alcoholic strength by volume of more than

1.2 per cent must be marked or labelled with an indication of its alcoholic strength (determined at 20 degrees Celsius) in the form of a figure, to not more than one decimal place, and the symbol '% vol'[1]. Whisky with an alcoholic strength by volume of less than 40 per cent, and brandy, gin, rum or vodka with an alcoholic strength by volume of less than 37.2 per cent, must, when sold prepacked, bear the words 'under strength' except where, in the case of brandy, its alcoholic strength has fallen to less than 37.2 per cent only through maturing in the cask[2].

In the case of alcoholic drinks sold otherwise than prepacked, including Community controlled wine, having an alcoholic strength by volume of more than 1.2 per cent, the alcoholic strength by volume of a representative sample[3] must be displayed in the form of a figure, to not more than one decimal place, and the symbol '% vol'[4]. This does not apply to cocktails or other mixed drinks, or to drinks customarily served in such a way that the intending purchaser can readily see information in respect of the alcoholic strength by volume[5].

1 Food Labelling (Scotland) Regulations 1984, SI 1984/1519, reg 31(1), (3) (substituted by SI 1989/809). For permitted positive and negative tolerances, see reg 31(2), Sch 5A (as so substituted).
2 Ibid, reg 31(4) (as so substituted).
3 The sample need not exceed thirty, or six in the case of Community controlled wine: ibid, reg 31A(2) (added by SI 1989/809).
4 Ibid, reg 31A(1), (2) (as so added). As to lists of figures, see reg 31A(3) (as so added).
5 Ibid, reg 31A(4) (as so added).

392. Manner of marking or labelling. Where any food (other than food which is not prepacked or prepacked for direct sale, or packed in a special fashion, or fancy confectionary, or food sold for immediate consumption in specified places, or unprepacked alcoholic drinks[1]) is sold, whether to, or otherwise than to, the ultimate consumer, the particulars with which it must be marked or labelled must appear on the packaging or on a label attached to the packaging or on a label which is clearly visible through the packaging; and also, when it is sold otherwise than to the ultimate consumer, in any relevant trade document furnished on or before delivery[2].

In the case of any food excepted above[3], where it is sold, whether to, or otherwise than to, the ultimate consumer, the particulars with which it must be marked or labelled must appear on a label attached to the food or on a ticket or notice displayed in close proximity to it; and also (except in the case of food sold for immediate consumption) when it is sold otherwise than to the ultimate consumer, in any relevant trade document furnished on or before delivery[4].

The particulars with which a food is required to be marked or labelled must be easy to understand, clearly legible and indelible and, when food is sold to the ultimate consumer, must be marked in a conspicuous place in such a way as to be clearly visible[5]. The particulars must not be hidden, obscured or interrupted by any other written or pictorial matter[6]. There is an exception for seasonal selection packs where the contents are individually prepacked and properly marked or labelled[7].

Where a food is required to be marked or labelled with an indication of minimum durability, or, in the case of an alcoholic drink, of alcoholic strength by volume, that indication must appear in the labelling of the food in the same field of vision as the name of the food[8]. Where required by weights and measures legislation, an indication of net quantity, and, where also required, of minimum durability or alcoholic strength by volume must appear in the same field of vision[9].

1 Ie any food other than food to which any of the Food Labelling (Scotland) Regulations 1984, SI 1984/1519, regs 24, 25, 28, 29 or 31A, applies.

2 Ibid, reg 32 (amended by SI 1989/809).
3 Ie any food to which any of ibid, regs 24, 25, 28, 29 or 31A, applies.
4 Ibid, reg 33 (amended by SI 1989/809).
5 Ibid, reg 34(1).
6 Ibid, reg 34(2).
7 Ibid, reg 34(4), (5).
8 Ibid, reg 35(1) (substituted by SI 1989/809).
9 Ibid, reg 35(2) (as so substituted).

393. Prohibited and restricted claims. A claim that a food has tonic properties, or that a food intended for babies is equivalent to or superior to the milk of a healthy mother, may not be made, either expressly or by implication, in the labelling or advertising of a food[1].

A wide variety of prescribed claims may not be made, either expressly or by implication, in the labelling or advertising of a food except in accordance with the appropriate prescribed conditions[2]. The prescribed claims relate to foods for particular nutritional needs; claims relating to babies or young children; diabetic, slimming, medicinal, protein, vitamin, mineral, polyunsaturated fatty acid, cholesterol and energy claims; and claims which depend on another food[3].

However, nothing in these provisions prevents the dissemination of useful information or recommendations intended exclusively for persons having qualifications in dentistry, medicine, nutrition, dietetics or pharmacy[4]. A claim is not constituted merely by:

(1) a reference to a substance other than vitamins, minerals, polyunsaturated fatty acids or cholesterol in the name of a food;
(2) a reference to a substance in a list of ingredients or in a statement of the total nutrient content of a food;
(3) a statement of the energy value of a food[5].

1 Food Labelling (Scotland) Regulations 1984, SI 1984/1519, reg 36(1), Sch 6, Pt I (which provides an exception for the use of the word 'tonic' to denote a soft drink complying with the Soft Drinks (Scotland) Regulations 1964, SI 1964/767, Sch 2, Pt I).
2 Food Labelling (Scotland) Regulations 1984, reg 36(2). Where more than one prescribed claim is made, the conditions prescribed for each must be observed: reg 36(3).
3 Ibid, Sch 6, Pt II.
4 Ibid, reg 37(2).
5 Ibid, reg 37(3)(a)–(c). As to energy value, see also reg 37(4)–(6).

394. Misleading descriptions. The use of certain descriptions in the labelling or advertising of food is prohibited as being misleading except where used in accordance with appropriate prescribed conditions[1].

1 Food Labelling (Scotland) Regulations 1984, SI 1984/1519, reg 38. The descriptions and conditions appear in Sch 7. The descriptions include 'butter', 'cream', 'dietary', 'fresh', 'garden', 'milk', 'starch-reduced', 'vitamin', 'alcohol-free', 'dealcoholised', 'non-alcoholic', 'tonic wine', 'vintage' and 'Scotch whisky'.

395. Use of the word 'wine'. Provision is made for the use of the word 'wine' in circumstances other than those to which it is restricted by EEC regulations[1]. Where the word 'wine' is used in a composite name in the labelling or advertising of food for a drink which is derived from fruit other than grapes or other vegetable, plant or carbohydrate material, the word must be immediately preceded by an indication of that fruit, vegetable, plant or carbohydrate[2]. Where the word is used as a composite name in the labelling or advertising of food for a drink derived from a mixture of such ingredients, it is sufficient to specify in the indication of the ingredients such of them as characterise the drink[3]. The composite name 'non-alcoholic wine' may not be used except for a drink derived from unfermented grape juice which is intended, and clearly labelled or advertised as, exclusively for communion or sacramental use[4].

The use of 'wine' as part of a composite name is prohibited where it is likely to cause confusion with wine or table wine as defined in EEC regulations[5]. Provision is made about the lettering of the composite name of a wine[6].

1 Food Labelling (Scotland) Regulations 1984, SI 1984/1519, reg 39(1) (amended by SI 1989/809). See EC Council Regulation 355/79 (OJ L54, 5.3.79, p 99), art 45(1), which restricts the name 'wine' to wine as defined in what is now EC Council Regulation 822/87 (OJ L84, 27.3.87, p 1), Annex I. The rules here set out apply to wine other than wine as so defined. See also EC Council Regulation 355/79, art 45(2), and EC Commission Regulation 997/81 (OJ L106, 16.4.81, p 1), art 20 (replacing EC Commission Regulation 1608/76), laying down rules for the description and presentation of wines and grape musts.
2 Food Labelling (Scotland) Regulations 1984, reg 39(2).
3 Ibid, reg 39(3).
4 Ibid, reg 39(4).
5 Ibid, reg 39(5) (amended by SI 1989/809), referring to EC Commission Regulation 822/87, Annex I.
6 Food Labelling (Scotland) Regulations 1984, reg 39(6).

396. Labelling offences. It is an offence for a person:
(1) to sell any food the presentation of which is misleading[1];
(2) to sell any food which is not marked or labelled in accordance with the provisions of the appropriate labelling regulations[2];
(3) to sell or advertise for sale any food in respect of which a claim is made or a description is used in contravention of those regulations[3];
(4) to advertise for sale any concentrate, dry mix or similar food without indicating every substance (other than water) which must be added to it[4];
(5) to sell any food from a vending machine in contravention of the regulations[5];
and an offender is liable on summary conviction to a fine not exceeding £2,000 or, on conviction on indictment, to a fine or imprisonment for a term not exceeding one year or both[6]. District and islands councils are responsible for enforcing and executing the regulations within their areas[7].

1 Ie which contravenes the Food Labelling (Scotland) Regulations 1984, SI 1984/1519, reg 4: see para 383, text and note 2, above.
2 Ie in accordance with ibid, Pt III (regs 5–35): see paras 383 ff above.
3 Ie in contravention of ibid, Pt IV (regs 36–39): see paras 393 ff above.
4 Ie in contravention of ibid, reg 23(3): see para 386 above.
5 Ie in contravention of ibid, reg 30: see para 390 above.
6 Ibid, reg 40(a)–(e), (i), (ii) (substituted by SI 1985/1068). For defences, see reg 42.
7 Ibid, reg 41.

(12) FOOD UNFIT FOR HUMAN CONSUMPTION

397. Examination and seizure of food. An authorised officer of a local authority[1] may at all reasonable times[2] examine any food intended for human consumption[3] which has been sold or is offered or exposed for sale[4] or is in the possession of, or has been deposited with or consigned to, any person for the purpose of sale or of preparation for sale[5]. Further, if it appears to the authorised officer to be unfit for human consumption he may seize[6] it and remove it in order to have it dealt with by a justice of the peace[7]. The officer must inform the person in whose possession the food is found of his intention to have it so dealt with[8], but does not have to follow any other procedure. It has, however, been held that such food must be brought before a justice with all reasonable speed[9].

The person in whose possession the food is found and any other person who might be liable to prosecution in respect of the food are entitled to be heard by the justice and to call witnesses[10].

1 For the meaning of 'authorised officer' and 'local authority', see para 334 and para 308, note 2, above.
2 The time during which premises are open for business purposes will ordinarily be deemed reasonable.
3 For the meaning of 'human consumption', see para 341, note 3, above.
4 Sale or intention to sell is essential.
5 For the meaning of 'preparation for sale', see para 334, note 6, above.
6 'Seizure' amounts to something more than a mere taking possession of the food; it must be taken other than on the invitation or with the permission of the owner: see *Vintner v Hind* (1882) 10 QBD 63; *R v Dennis* [1894] 2 QB 458, CCR.
7 Food and Drugs (Scotland) Act 1956 (c 30), s 9(1). 'Justice of the peace' includes a sheriff and a magistrate: s 9(5).
8 Ibid, s 9(2).
9 *Burton v Bradley* (1886) 51 JP 118, DC.
10 Food and Drugs (Scotland) Act 1956, s 9(2).

398. Condemnation of food. If food is brought before a justice of the peace[1], whether it has been seized under the statutory power[2] or is liable to be so seized, and it appears to him on sworn information in writing to be unfit for human consumption, he must condemn it and order it to be destroyed or to be so disposed of as to prevent it from being used for human consumption[3]. There is no right of appeal against his decision because the proceedings are part of the administrative and not the legal process[4].

If he refuses to condemn any food so seized and brought before him the local authority must compensate the owner of the food for any depreciation in its value[5]. The owner cannot refuse to accept any such food back[6]. If there is a dispute about compensation to be paid it is to be settled by arbitration[7].

1 As to justices of the peace, see para 397, note 7, above.
2 See para 397 above.
3 Food and Drugs (Scotland) Act 1956 (c 30), s 9(3). Any such order is sufficient evidence of the unfitness of the food in any proceedings under the Act: s 9(3). As to the information, see *Stakis plc v Boyd* 1989 SCLR 290, 1989 SLT 333, OH.
4 See *R v Cornwall Quarter Sessions Appeal Committee, ex parte Kerley* [1956] 2 All ER 872, [1956] 1 WLR 906, DC.
5 Food and Drugs (Scotland) Act 1956, s 9(4).
6 *Re Bater and Birkenhead Corpn* [1893] 2 QB 77, CA.
7 Food and Drugs (Scotland) Act 1956, s 48.

399. Sale of unsound food. It is an offence against the Food and Drugs (Scotland) Act 1956
(1) to sell or offer or expose for sale, or have in possession[1] for the purpose of sale or of preparation for sale[2], or
(2) to deposit with[3], or consign to, any person for the purpose of sale or of preparation for sale[4],
any food intended[5] but unfit[6] for human consumption[7].

In the case of an offence under head (1), the person who sold the food to the offender is also guilty of an offence[8]. If a person is charged with an offence under head (2), it is a defence for him to prove either that he had no reason to suppose that the person with whom he deposited or to whom he consigned or sold the food intended it for human consumption and that he gave notice to that person that the food was unfit, or that, at the time he delivered or dispatched it to that person, either it was fit for human consumption or he did not know, or could not with reasonable diligence[9] have ascertained, that it was unfit for human consumption[10].

1 It appears from English cases that 'possession' must be read in connection with the purposes of sale or preparation for sale. Possession is then possession in fact and is to be given a wide and not a narrow construction. See eg *Webb v Baker* [1916] 2 KB 753 at 759, per Lord Reading LCJ. As to 'possession for sale', see *Birkett v McGlassons Ltd* [1957] 1 All ER 369, [1957] 1 WLR 269, DC.
2 Food and Drugs (Scotland) Act 1956 (c 30), s 8(1)(a).
3 See *Ollett v Henry* [1919] 2 KB 88, DC.
4 Food and Drugs (Scotland) Act 1956, s 8(1)(b).
5 The burden of proving the contrary is on the accused: see ibid, s 43.
6 Whether the food is unfit is a question of fact: *Wayne v Thompson* (1885) 15 QBD 342. In an English case it was held that the presence of a small piece of extraneous matter in an article of food does not of itself make the article unfit for human consumption for this purpose: see *J Miller Ltd v Battersea Borough Council* [1956] 1 QB 43, [1955] 3 All ER 279, DC.
7 Food and Drugs (Scotland) Act 1956, s 8(1). See *Hooper v Petrou* (1973) 71 LGR 347.
8 Food and Drugs (Scotland) Act 1956, s 8(2). See *Fisher v Barnett and Pomeroy (Bakers) Ltd* [1954] 1 All ER 249, [1954] 1 WLR 351, DC.
9 That this is a question of fact has been held in the English case of *R C Hammett Ltd v Crabb* (1931) 145 LT 638, DC.
10 Food and Drugs (Scotland) Act 1956, s 8(3). As to the burden of proof, see *Cant v Harley & Sons Ltd* [1938] 2 All ER 768.

400. Food offered as prizes or rewards. The provisions governing the sale or examination and seizure of unsound food[1] apply equally to food intended for human consumption which is (1) offered as a prize or reward or given away in connection with any entertainment[2] to which the public is admitted[3], whether on payment of money or not, or (2) offered as a prize or reward or given away for the purposes of advertisement or in furtherance of any trade or business[4], or (3) exposed or deposited in premises[5] for the purpose of being so offered or given away[6].

1 Ie the Food and Drugs (Scotland) Act 1956 (c 30), ss 8, 9: see paras 397–399, above.
2 'Entertainment' includes any social gathering, amusement, exhibition, performance, game, sport, trial of skill or lottery: ibid, s 10(2).
3 Admission in fact is sufficient: *Buchanan v Motor Insurers' Bureau* [1955] 1 All ER 607, [1955] 1 WLR 488.
4 It may be that the trade or business does not yet exist: cf *R v Tearse* [1945] 1 KB 1 at 5, 6, [1944] 2 All ER 403 at 405, CCA.
5 For the meaning of 'premises', see para 334, note 6, above.
6 Food and Drugs (Scotland) Act 1956, s 10(1)(a)–(c).

401. Examination of food in transit. If an authorised officer of a local authority has reason to suspect that any vehicle or container has in it food which is intended for sale for human consumption or is in the course of delivery after such sale, he may examine the contents and, for that purpose, may detain the vehicle or container, and if on examination he finds any food which appears to him to be intended, but is unfit, for human consumption, he may seize and remove it to be dealt with by a justice of the peace as food unfit for human consumption[1]. Where the duties of a customs and excise officer with respect to any goods have not been wholly discharged, the goods may not be examined under these powers without his consent[2].

This provision does not authorise the detention of any vehicle or container belonging to any board established by the Transport Act 1962 or any subsidiary of such a board, or any authorised vehicle used by a carrier of goods holding an operator's licence[3].

1 Food and Drugs (Scotland) Act 1956 (c 30), s 11(1). For the meaning of 'authorised officer', see para 334, supra; for the meaning of 'local authority', see para 308, note 2, supra; and for the meaning of 'container', see para 350, note 2, supra. 'Vehicle' is not defined. The food will be dealt with under s 9(1), and s 9(2)–(4) then applies (see paras 397, 398, supra): *Semple v Dunbar* (1904) 6 F (J) 65, 12 SLT 253.

2 Food and Drugs (Scotland) Act 1956, s 11(3).
3 Food and Drugs (Scotland) Act 1956, s 11(2) (amended by the Transport Act 1962 (c 46), s 32(1), Sch 2, Pt I, and the Transport Act 1968 (c 73), s 156(2), Sch 16, para 7).

402. Suspected food. If a designated medical officer[1] or a sanitary inspector has reasonable ground for suspecting that any food is likely to cause food poisoning[2] he may give notice to the person in charge of the food that, until his investigations are completed, the food or any specified portion of it is not to be used for human consumption and either is not to be removed or is not to be removed except to some place specified in the notice[3]. It is an offence against the Food and Drugs (Scotland) Act 1956 for the person concerned to use or remove the food in any other way[4].

If, as a result of his investigations, the designated medical officer or sanitary inspector is satisfied that the food in question may safely be used for human consumption he must withdraw his notice, but if he is not so satisfied he must have it destroyed[5]. Where a notice is withdrawn by the person who gave it or that person causes the food to which it relates to be destroyed, the Health Board must compensate the owner for any depreciation in the value of the food, although in certain circumstances no compensation is payable[6].

1 See the National Health Service (Scotland) Act 1972 (c 58), s 21.
2 'Food poisoning' includes any disease transmissible by food: Food and Drugs (Scotland) Act 1956 (c 30), s 24(4).
3 Ibid, s 24(1) (amended by the National Health Service (Scotland) Act 1972 (c 58), s 64(1), Sch 6, para 96). The notice should be in writing.
4 Food and Drugs (Scotland) Act 1956, s 24(1). As to prosecutions and penalties, see paras 423 et seq, infra.
5 Ibid, s 24(2) (as amended: see note 3, supra).
6 Ibid, s 24(3) (as amended: see note 3, supra). Disputes as to compensation are to be referred to arbitration: see s 48. As to Health Boards, see the National Health Service (Scotland) Act 1978 (c 29), s 2, and HEALTH SERVICES, para 1410 below.

(13) FOOD HYGIENE

(a) Statutory Provisions

403. Cleansing of shellfish. A local authority[1] has power to provide, in or outside its area, tanks or other apparatus for cleansing shellfish[2] and may make charges in respect of their use, and may contribute towards the expenses incurred by any other authority under this provision by any other person in providing means for cleansing shellfish[3]. Any such tank or other apparatus or the execution of any other work on, over or under land below high water mark of ordinary spring tides may not be established except with the approval of the Secretary of State, who must give his approval before the work is commenced[4].

1 'Local authority' means an islands or district council: Food and Drugs (Scotland) Act 1956 (c 30), s 20(5) (added by the Local Government (Scotland) Act 1973 (c 65), s 214(2), Sch 27, Pt II, para 121).
2 'Cleansing shellfish' includes the subjection of shellfish to any germicidal treatment: Food and Drugs (Scotland) Act 1956, s 20(3).
3 Ibid, s 20(1), (2).
4 Ibid, s 20(4).

404. Slaughter of animals. No animal[1], the meat derived from which is intended for sale for human consumption, may be slaughtered in any place other than a slaughterhouse[2] unless accident, illness or other emergency affecting the animal requires that it be slaughtered elsewhere[3]. No person may sell or offer or expose for sale, or have in his possession for the purpose of sale or of preparation for sale, for human consumption, any part of, or produce derived wholly or partly from, an animal[4] which has been slaughtered in a knacker's yard or of which the carcase has been brought into a knacker's yard[5]. Contravention of any of these provisions is an offence against the Food and Drugs (Scotland) Act 1956[6].

1 'Animal' here means cattle, sheep, goats, swine and horses, and 'horses' includes asses and mules: Food and Drugs (Scotland) Act 1956 (c 30), s 12(4)(a) (substituted by the Slaughter of Animals (Scotland) Act 1980 (c 13), s 23, Sch 1, para 1).
2 'Slaughterhouse' means any premises (defined in para 334, note 6, above) used for slaughtering animals the flesh of which is intended for sale for human consumption, and includes any place other than premises used in connection therewith: Food and Drugs (Scotland) Act 1956, s 12(4)(a) (as so substituted). As to slaughterhouses, see further paras 499 ff below.
3 Ibid, s 12(1), which is expressed to be subject to the other provisions of s 12 and to s 13, for which see para 407 below.
4 'Animal' here includes poultry: ibid, s 12(4)(b).
5 Ibid, s 12(2).
6 Ibid, s 12(3). As to prosecutions and penalties, see paras 423 ff below.

405. Cold stores. A local authority[1] may provide a cold store for the storage and preservation of meat and other articles of food, and may make charges for its use[2]. Any proposal to provide a cold store within the area of another local authority requires the consent of that authority, which must not be unreasonably withheld[3].

1 'Local authority' means an islands or district council: Food and Drugs (Scotland) Act 1956 (c 30), s 21(2) (added by the Local Government (Scotland) Act 1973 (c 65), s 214(1), Sch 27, Pt II, para 122).
2 Food and Drugs (Scotland) Act 1956, s 21(1) (amended by the Local Government (Scotland) Act 1973, ss 209(1), 237(1), Sch 25, para 27, Sch 29).
3 Food and Drugs (Scotland) Act 1956, s 21(1) proviso (as amended: see note 2, supra).

406. Food poisoning. If a registered medical practitioner becomes aware or suspects that a patient whom he is attending within the area of any Health Board is suffering from food poisoning (other than a disease notifiable under some other provision), he must forthwith send to the chief administrative officer of the board a certificate stating the patient's name, age, sex and whereabouts, particulars of the poisoning, and whether the case occurs in the practitioner's general medical practice or in his practice as a medical officer of a public body or institution[1].

1 Food and Drugs (Scotland) Act 1956 (c 30), s 22(1) (amended by the National Health Service (Scotland) Act 1972 (c 58), s 64(1), Sch 6, para 95).

(b) Provisions in Regulations

407. Regulations about hygiene. The Secretary of State may make regulations for securing the observance of sanitary and cleanly conditions and practices in connection with the sale of food for human consumption or the importation, preparation, transport, storage, packaging, wrapping, exposure for sale, service or delivery of food intended for sale or sold for human consumption, or otherwise for the protection of the public health in connection with such matters[1].

Apart from, and without prejudice to these general provisions, the Secretary of State has power to make regulations dealing with many ancillary matters, including (1) the construction, maintenance, cleanliness, water supply to and use of premises[2] where food is sold or offered, exposed, stored or prepared for sale; (2) the provision, maintenance and cleanliness of sanitary and washing facilities in connection with such premises; (3) the prohibition or regulation of the use of specified materials in the manufacturing of apparatus used in the preparation of food; (4) the prohibition of spitting on premises where food is sold; (5) the prescribing of clothing to be worn by persons in such premises; (6) the securing of the inspection of animals (including poultry) intended for slaughter and of carcases to ascertain whether the meat is fit for human consumption; (7) the staining or sterilisation of meat unfit for human consumption or derived from animals slaughtered in knackers' yards or from carcases brought into such yards; (8) the treatment of meat, and of any other food, unfit for human consumption; and (9) the sale of shellfish[3].

The regulations may make different provisions in relation to different classes of business, may apply generally throughout Scotland or to specified areas, may impose responsibility for compliance with them on the occupier and, in the case of structural requirements, on any owner who lets premises for use for a purpose to which the regulations apply or permits their use after notice from the enforcing authority[4]. Further, subject to safeguards and limitations, the regulations may exempt premises from provisions under heads (1) and (2) while there is in force a local authority certificate to the effect that compliance with them cannot reasonably be required[5].

Requirements which may be imposed by regulations in respect of premises may also be applied to home-going ships and to vehicles, stalls and places other than premises[6].

The Secretary of State must take such steps as he thinks expedient for publishing codes of practice in connection with matters which may be made the subject of regulations, for the purpose of giving advice and guidance to persons responsible for compliance with them[7].

1 Food and Drugs (Scotland) Act 1956 (c 30), s 13(1).
2 For the meaning of 'premises', see para 334, note 6, above.
3 Food and Drugs (Scotland) Act 1956, s 13(2)(a)–(i), (3).
4 Ibid, ss 13(4)(a), 56(4).
5 Ibid, ss 13(4)(b), 56(4).
6 Ibid, s 13(5). 'Home-going ship' means a ship plying in inland waters or engaged in coastal passenger services (namely a passenger service or excursion between places in Scotland which does not involve calling at any place outside Scotland): s 58(1).
7 Ibid, s 13(6).

408. Outline of hygiene provisions. The principal regulations requiring hygienic practices in relation to food and the conditions under which it is handled are aimed at the prevention of contamination of the food and ensuring the cleanliness of the premises in which food businesses are carried out[1]. The personal cleanliness of those who handle food and of their clothing are dealt with[2], as are also the steps to be taken if any such person is suffering from certain infections or illnesses transmissible in or caused by food[3]. There are detailed requirements relating to food premises including matters such as the provision of proper drainage and sanitation, cleanliness of forecourts, sanitary conveniences, water supply, washhand basins, and sinks, lighting and ventilation, food rooms, storage of food and accommodation for clothing[4]. Special provision is made about vehicles, stalls and places where food is on sale[5], and about the methods and practices in food businesses, including the cleansing and condition of equipment and utensils and the material of which containers are made[6]. The practices regulated include the treatment of certain food such as gelatine and bakers' confectionery and the reheating of food, the storage of food and the disposal of refuse[7].

Exemption of premises from some of those provisions may be granted by the local authority by certificate, and appeal lies to the sheriff against the refusal of any exemption[8]. There are also provisions about offences and penalties[9].

1 See the Food Hygiene (Scotland) Regulations 1959, SI 1959/413, reg 5 (amended by SI 1978/173). As to food, see reg 2(1); as to handling, see reg 2(3) (amended by SI 1966/967); and as to contamination, see reg 8.
2 See ibid, reg 6 (amended by SI 1978/173).
3 See ibid, reg 7.
4 See ibid, regs 18–28, and para 419 below.
5 See ibid, reg 30 (substituted by SI 1966/967).
6 See ibid, regs 8–12 (amended by SI 1961/622 and SI 1978/173).
7 See ibid, regs 13–17 (amended by SI 1978/173).
8 See ibid, reg 31 (amended by SI 1959/1153).
9 See ibid, regs 32, 33 (amended by SI 1959/1153).

409. Requirements about hygiene applying generally. No food business[1] may be carried on in any premises, vehicle, stall or place, the situation of which would expose the food to the risk of contamination or in which any other business is also carried on which would expose the food to such a risk[2]. Equipment with which food comes, or is liable to come, into contact must be kept clean and must be of such materials and be kept in such a condition as to enable it to be cleaned and to prevent, so far as is reasonably practicable, any matter being absorbed by it and any risk of contamination[3].

Utensils in or on which food sold for immediate consumption is served to a consumer must be cleaned after each occasion on which they are used and, unless they are not to be used again, must be washed and rinsed in water of a certain temperature and dried with a clean cloth or by evaporation[4]. There are also special provisions for the cleansing of drinking vessels[4]. Similar provision is made in respect of equipment used for preparing or storing certain meat, fish or bakery products and, in particular, in respect of tubs used for the brining of meat[5]. Containers, wrappers and packages in which food is placed must be clean and of materials that will not expose the food to risk of contamination[6].

1 'Food business' means any trade or business involving the selling, exposure, service, preparation, transport, storage, packaging, wrapping or delivery of food, but does not include (1) any such business carried on at a boarding house letting not more than three bedrooms, a private house or a registered dairy; (2) so much of any such trade or business carried on otherwise than for the sale of food by retail and which is carried on at such places as docks, warehouses, the premises of a common carrier, a slaughterhouse or meat market or premises used only for the sale of raw vegetables; (3) an agricultural activity: Food Hygiene (Scotland) Regulations 1959, SI 1959/413, reg 3.
2 Ibid, reg 8 (amended by SI 1978/173).
3 Ibid, reg 9.
4 Ibid, reg 10 (substituted by SI 1961/622).
5 Ibid, reg 11.
6 Ibid, reg 12 (amended by SI 1978/173).

410. Prevention of risk of contamination. Food of specified kinds[1] must not be kept on food premises otherwise than in a refrigerator or refrigerating chamber or in a cool ventilated place and must not be at a temperature above 145 degrees Fahrenheit unless the food (1) is being prepared for sale; (2) is exposed for sale or sold to a consumer; (3) after cooking is being cooled under hygienic conditions as quickly as is reasonably practicable; (4) is being made conveniently available for sale on the premises to consumers and it is reasonable to keep it otherwise[2]. Food previously heated must, if reheated, be brought up to a specified temperature for a specified time, and similar provision is made about gelatine and bakers' confectionary filling[3].

Refuse, other than liquid or comminuted refuse in liquid suspension, produced in the course of a food business must be deposited in a suitable receptacle which is to be kept covered and cleaned after emptying[4]. Liquid refuse must be drained into a drainage system or, if produced other than on premises, so disposed of as to obviate risk of contamination of food[5].

1 Ie food consisting of or containing meat, fish, gravy, imitation cream, egg or milk; but not pastry etc which contains egg or milk, chocolate or sugar confectionery, lard etc, uncooked bacon or ham, dried pudding mixes, dried soup mixes etc, unskinned rabbits or unplucked birds, or ice cream: Food Hygiene (Scotland) Regulations 1959, SI 1959/413, reg 13(2).
2 Ibid, reg 13(1).
3 Ibid, regs 14–16.
4 Ibid, reg 17(1), (2).
5 Ibid, reg 17(3) (amended by SI 1978/173).

411. Stalls and vehicles. Every stall[1] or vehicle used in the course or for the purposes of a food business[2] must be kept clean, must be so constructed and so kept as to enable it to be effectively cleaned, and its layout must be such as will enable the food business to be conducted hygienically[3]. Every stall or vehicle must bear conspicuously the name and address of the person carrying on the business[4]. No stall or vehicle may be used as a sleeping place, and every stall and vehicle (other than one in a covered market place) from which food (other than raw vegetables or food in closed containers) is sold or on which it is exposed for sale must be closed and screened so as to prevent risk of contamination of the food[5].

Certain of the general hygiene regulations[6] apply to stalls and vehicles as they apply to food premises or food rooms, although certain stalls and vehicles are exempted from this provision[7].

Any article commonly used, or any substance capable of being used, for human consumption found on any vehicle, stall or place other than premises is, until the contrary is proved, to be presumed to be intended for sale or for manufacturing products for sale for human consumption[8].

1 'Stall' includes a marquee and a tent: Food Hygiene (Scotland) Regulations 1959, SI 1959/413, reg 2(1).
2 For the meaning of 'food business', see para 409, note 1, above.
3 Food Hygiene (Scotland) Regulations 1959, reg 30(1) (substituted by SI 1966/967).
4 Ibid, reg 30(2) (substituted by SI 1966/967).
5 Ibid, reg 30(3), (4) (substituted by SI 1966/967).
6 Ie ibid, regs 13, 22, 24 and 27 and, unless exemption is granted to the owner by the local authority, reg 31. Regulation 23 applies unless utensils are cleaned in accordance with reg 10 elsewhere than on the stall or vehicle: Food Hygiene (Scotland) Amendment Regulations 1966, SI 1966/967, reg 4(2).
7 Ibid, reg 4(1), (3). For exemptions, see reg 4(1) proviso.
8 Food and Drugs (Scotland) Act 1956 (c 30), s 43: see para 429 below.

412. Meat markets. Detailed provisions are made relating to premises used as meat markets, the facilities for the supply etc of water and the management of such markets[1]. Requirements are laid down as to the layout and design arrangements for the hanging of carcases and sides of meat and the construction of the premises and associated forecourts[2]. A piped supply of wholesome water and a supply of piped hot water must be provided[3]. There are provisions about drainage and about facilities to enable persons working in the market to secure their personal cleanliness and to enable equipment and other facilities to be kept clean[4]. Sanitary conveniences are similarly provided for, and the materials and construction of which equipment and fittings, utensils and receptacles are to be made are specified, as also are the cloths, dressings, bandages and first-aid equipment which are to be available[5]. Lastly the management of a meat market is regulated[6]. There are exemptions from the operation of some of these provisions[7].

1 Food (Preparation and Distribution of Meat) (Scotland) Regulations 1963, SI 1963/2001, Pt IV (regs 36–53).
2 Ibid, regs 37–41.
3 Ibid, reg 42.
4 Ibid, regs 43–45 (amended by SI 1967/1507).
5 Ibid, regs 46–50.
6 Ibid, regs 51–53.
7 Ibid, reg 68 (amended by SI 1978/1273).

413. Inspection of animals to be slaughtered and of carcases, preparation of meat for human consumption and hygiene. There are detailed provisions in regulations the purpose of which is to ensure that meat intended for sale or human consumption is fit for that purpose and is produced[1], prepared and transported[2] by hygienic means. Animals the meat of which is intended for sale for human consumption must be inspected by an inspector or veterinary surgeon before slaughter, and after slaughter the carcase of the animal must be inspected. Imported food is also dealt with[3]. Separate regulations make provisions about meat to be exported to other countries in the European Community and with the animals from which such meat is to be derived[4]. Poultry meat is also dealt with separately[5].

No animal the meat from which is intended for sale for human consumption may be slaughtered elsewhere than in a slaughterhouse save in an emergency[6], but meat from a knackers yard must not in any circumstances be sold for human consumption[7].

A fuller statement of these provisions is to be found elsewhere in this title[8].

1 See the Food (Meat Inspection) (Scotland) Regulations 1961, SI 1961/243 (amended by SI 1963/1231, SI 1975/629, SI 1979/1563, SI 1981/996, SI 1983/702 and SI 1985/1068).
2 See the Food (Preparation and Distribution of Meat) (Scotland) Regulations 1963, SI 1963/2001 (amended by SI 1967/1507, SI 1978/1273 and SI 1985/1068).
3 See the Imported Food (Scotland) Regulations 1985, SI 1985/913.
4 See the Fresh Meat Export (Hygiene and Inspection) (Scotland) Regulations 1987, SI 1987/800.
5 See the Poultry Meat (Hygiene) (Scotland) Regulations 1976, SI 1976/1221 (amended by SI 1979/768, SI 1981/1169 and SI 1985/1068).
6 Food and Drugs (Scotland) Act 1956 (c 30), s 12(1).
7 Ibid, s 12(2). See para 404 above.
8 See paras 503 ff below.

414. Protection of public health from imported food. The importation of food into Scotland is controlled by the Imported Food (Scotland) Regulations 1985[1], which contain provisions dealing with all imported food[2]. There are special provisions dealing with imported meat and meat products[3] and regulations that deal with general matters including the keeping of records, penalties, examination outside business hours, compensation disputes, evidence of analysis and third party or warranty defences[4].

The most important provisions are those concerned with the importation of meat[5]. A person may not import into Scotland for sale for human consumption:
(1) any fresh meat[6], meat product[7] or bulk lard[8] unless it bears the appropriate health mark[9], or
(2) any fresh meat or meat product unless any wrapping, packaging and transportation accords with prescribed requirements[10], or

(3) any fresh meat derived from domestic bovine animals, swine, sheep, goats, solipeds or poultry, or (with certain exceptions) meat products in the preparation of which any such fresh meat was used, unless it is accompanied by the appropriate health certificate[11].

Provision is made for lost, damaged or defective health marks and certificates[12]. Where imported meat appears to contravene the regulations, the importer, the master of the ship or aircraft or the driver of the vehicle must be notified, and the meat must not be removed except for exportation from Scotland, but the importer is given the opportunity to show that the importation was not contrary to the regulations[13].

Any food (including meat) commonly used for human consumption, if imported for sale or for use in the preparation of food for sale, is to be presumed until the contrary is proved to have been imported for a relevant purpose[14]. The regulations make provision for the examination of all imported food, the analysis of samples, special examination of food and the functions and powers of customs officers[15]. Local authorities have enforcement responsibilities[16].

1 Imported Food (Scotland) Regulations 1985, SI 1985/913. The regulations give effect to EEC Council Directive 64/433 (OJ 1964 p 2012 (S Edn 1963–64 p 185)) and EC Council Directives 71/118 (OJ L55, 8.3.71, p 23 (S Edn 1971 (I) p 106)), 72/462 (OJ L302, 31.12.72, p 28), 77/99 (OJ L26, 31.1.77, p 85) and 83/643 (OJ L359, 22.12.83, p 8).
2 Imported Food (Scotland) Regulations 1985, Pt II (regs 6–11).
3 Ibid, Pt III (regs 12–18).
4 Ibid, Pt IV (regs 19–25).
5 These provisions do not apply to the following articles of food: vitamin concentrates containing meat, pharmaceutical products containing meat, gelatine, rennet, and meat products of which meat is not a principal ingredient and which do not contain fragments of meat: ibid, reg 12(2), Sch 1.
6 'Fresh meat' means the flesh or other edible parts of a mammal or bird, which has not been subjected to any treatment or process other than chilling, freezing, vacuum packing etc, and includes minced, chopped or mechanically recovered meat and seasoned meat: ibid, reg 2(1).
7 'Meat product' means any product prepared wholly or partly from fresh meat (which has undergone treatment to ensure a certain degree of preservation) but excluding fresh meat and the products specified in note 5 above: ibid, reg 12(1).
8 'Bulk lard' means lard or any other rendered mammal or poultry fat transported unpackaged in the tank of a ship, aircraft, hovercraft or road vehicle: ibid, reg 12(1).
9 Ibid, reg 13(1), (3), (5), Schs 3, 5.
10 Ibid, reg 13(2), Sch 4.
11 Ibid, reg 14, Schs 6–10.
12 Ibid, reg 15.
13 Ibid, reg 16.
14 Ibid, reg 3.
15 Ibid, regs 7–11.
16 Ibid, reg 4.

415. Meat and food handlers. A person engaged in the handling of meat or any other food must take such measures as are reasonably necessary to protect the food from risk of contamination[1], and must keep his person and clothing clean[2]. Such a person must ensure that his hands are clean, must wash his hands after using a sanitary convenience, keep all parts of his clothing liable to come into contact with the food clean, cover any area of skin showing signs of infection on any exposed part of his person, and must not smoke, chew tobacco, take snuff or spit[3].

As soon as any person engaged in the handling of food becomes aware that he is suffering from, or is a carrier of, any of certain infectious diseases he must forthwith give notice to the person having the management and control of the business for the purpose of which he is so engaged, and that manager, upon receiving the notice, must forthwith notify the proper officer of the local authority[4]. If that manager becomes aware that he himself is suffering from any such condition or disease he must notify the proper officer of that also[4].

1 Food Hygiene (Scotland) Regulations 1959, SI 1959/413, reg 5 (amended by SI 1978/173); Food (Preparation and Distribution of Meat) (Scotland) Regulations 1963, SI 1963/2001, reg 5(a).
2 Food Hygiene (Scotland) Regulations 1959, reg 6 (as so amended); Food (Preparation and Distribution of Meat) (Scotland) Regulations 1963, reg 5(b).
3 Food Hygiene (Scotland) Regulations 1959, reg 6 (as so amended); Food (Preparation and Distribution of Meat) (Scotland) Regulations 1963, reg 6 (amended by SI 1978/1273).
4 Food Hygiene (Scotland) Regulations 1959, reg 7; Food (Preparation and Distribution of Meat) (Scotland) Regulations 1963, reg 7; Local Government (Scotland) Act 1973 (c 65), s 214(1), Sch 27, Pt I, para 2(1).

416. Distribution of meat. Detailed provision is made as to the conditions to be complied with in the transportation of meat, the vehicles to be used for the purpose and the handling of imported meat. Different provisions apply to unwrapped meat from those which apply to wrapped meat[1]. The vehicles, containers and equipment in which meat may be transported are specified, as is also their construction and maintenance[2].

There are conditions applying to unwrapped meat of all kinds and of particular kinds and to blood[3]. Conditions applying to wrapped meat and wrapped frozen offal as well as to certain parts of animals not being meat are also prescribed[4]. The handling of imported meat is regulated, as is the procedure to be followed in the transportation of meat by sea[5]. The handling and placing on the dock of imported meat so as to prevent damage to and contamination of it are also regulated[6].

1 Food (Preparation and Distribution of Meat) (Scotland) Regulations 1963, SI 1963/2001, regs 55–59 (amended by SI 1967/1507).
2 Ibid, regs 61–63.
3 Ibid, regs 55–57, 60 (amended by SI 1967/1507).
4 Ibid, regs 58, 59 (amended by SI 1967/1507).
5 Ibid, regs 64–66.
6 Ibid, reg 67.

417. Inspection of fresh meat for exportation. Provisions as to the hygiene and inspection of fresh meat for exportation apply to fresh meat of domestic bovine animals, swine, sheep, goats and solipeds[1]. They prescribe conditions which must be satisfied for the production, cutting up, storage and transport of such meat when it is intended for export or for sale for export to a member state of the European Economic Community for human consumption[2]. Certain categories of meat listed in Community legislation[3] are subject to these provisions, but also remain subject to national provisions of member states prohibiting or restricting importation into other territories[4].

In particular, the regulations as to hygiene and inspection provide that only premises which are approved by the Secretary of State may be used for the production, cutting up, storage and loading of fresh meat for intra-Community trade, and that such premises must comply with prescribed requirements as to structure and hygiene[5]. They also lay down requirements as to slaughter, dressing and cutting practices, ante- and post-mortem inspection, hygiene, health, control of cut meat, health marking and certification, storage, wrapping, packing and transport of such meat[6].

Apart from the approval, suspension and revocation of approval of premises for intra-Community trade, which are functions of the Secretary of State[7], enforcement is the function of the islands and district authorities[8]. They are required to provide the resources necessary for supervision and inspection of approved premises for which they may make provision[9].

The regulations do not affect the application, as appropriate, to export premises of the provisions of certain regulations relating to meat inspection[10].

1 Fresh Meat Export (Hygiene and Inspection) (Scotland) Regulations 1987, SI 1987/800, reg 2(1). These regulations implement EEC Council Directive 64/433 (OJ 121, 29.7.64, p 2012 (S Edn 1963–64 p 185)) on health problems affecting intra-Community trade in fresh meat (amended by EC Council Directive 66/601 (OJ 192, 27.10.66, p 3302 (S Edn 1965–66 p 244)). EC Council Directive 69/349 (OJ L256, 11.10.69, p 5 (S Edn 1969 (II) p 432)), EC Council Directive 83/90 (OJ L59, 5.3.83, p 10), and EC Council Directive 86/587 (OJ L399, 2.12.86, p 26). 'Fresh' meat is meat (including chilled or frozen meat, meat vacuum wrapped or wrapped in a controlled atmosphere) which has not undergone any preserving process: Fresh Meat Export (Hygiene and Inspection) (Scotland) Regulations 1987, reg 2(1).
2 Ibid, regs 4–7. The regulations do not apply to meat exported with the authority of the country of destination and intended exclusively for supplies for international organisations and military forces there serving under another flag: reg 3.
3 See EEC Council Directive 64/433, art 6(1)A.
4 See eg the Slaughter of Animals (Prevention of Cruelty) (Scotland) Regulations 1955, SI 1955/1993; the Food Hygiene (Scotland) Regulations 1959, SI 1959/413; and the Food (Meat Inspection) (Scotland) Regulations 1961, SI 1961/243.
5 Fresh Meat Export (Hygiene and Inspection) (Scotland) Regulations 1987, regs 4–7, Schs 1–4.
6 Ibid, regs 8–11, Schs 5–15.
7 Ibid, regs 4–6.
8 Ibid, regs 2(1), 17.
9 Ibid, reg 12.
10 See ibid, reg 19, which refers to certain provisions of the 1961 regulations cited in note 4 above.

418. Poultry meat. The Poultry Meat (Hygiene) (Scotland) Regulations 1976 apply to poultry meat derived from domestic fowls, turkeys, guinea fowls, ducks and geese[1], and prescribe conditions which must be satisfied for the production, cutting up and storage of such poultry meat intended for sale for human consumption[2]. In particular they (1) require that poultry meat be produced and cut up in slaughterhouses and cutting premises licensed for the purpose and complying with the requirements as to structure and hygiene practice[3], and (2) lay down requirements as to slaughter and evisceration procedures[4], ante- and post-mortem inspections[5], hygiene and control of operations in cutting premises[6], health marking of poultry meat by the official veterinary surgeon in accordance with the regulations[7] and the storage, wrapping, packaging and transport of poultry meat[8]. The requirements relating to cutting up, storage, wrapping and packaging of poultry meat do not apply to these operations when carried out at the retail level[9].

Certain sales of poultry meat by those who keep live poultry are excluded from the operation of the regulations[10], and there is provision for other specific exemptions from particular requirements[11] and for appeals against licensing decisions[12].

The enforcement and execution of the regulations is assigned to islands and district councils[13], which are empowered to make reasonable charges for the grant of exemptions, the issue of licences and for the inspection of poultry meat[14], and are required to maintain records of licences and exemptions issued by them and to furnish information to the Secretary of State for Scotland[15]. The regulations also make provision for powers of entry by authorised officers of the Secretary of State and of local authorities[16]. There are provisions about offences and penalties[17].

1 Poultry Meat (Hygiene) (Scotland) Regulations 1976, SI 1976/1221, reg 2(1). 'Poultry meat' means the flesh or other edible parts of poultry: reg 2(1). The regulations implement EEC Council Directive 71/118 (OJ L55, 8.3.71, p 23 (S Edn 1971(I) p 106) on health problems affecting trade in fresh poultry meat (amended by EC Council Directives 74/387 (OJ L202, 24.7.74, p 1) and 75/431 (OJ L192, 24.7.75, p 6)).
2 Poultry Meat (Hygiene) (Scotland) Regulations 1976, reg 3 (amended by SI 1979/768).

3 Ibid, reg 3(1)(a)(i), (iii) (substituted by SI 1979/768), (b)(i)–(iii). 'Slaughterhouse' and 'cutting premises' are defined in reg 2(1). See also regs 12(a), 24(1) (as so substituted), 27(2), Schs 1, 2. As to licences, see regs 11–21. Application for a licence must be made to the islands or district council of the area, and will be granted if the appropriate officer and local authority are satisfied that the relevant requirements have been satisfied: reg 12, Schs 1–3 (Sch 3 being amended by SI 1979/768).
4 Ibid, regs 3(1)(b)(iii), 4(1)(c) (as so amended), 24(1) (as so substituted), 27(1), Sch 4 (as so substituted).
5 Ibid, regs 3(1)(a)(ii), (iv), 6(2), Schs 5, 6.
6 Ibid, regs 3(1)(b)(v), 24(1) (substituted by SI 1979/768), Sch 7 (amended by SI 1979/768), Sch 8.
7 Ibid, regs 3(1)(a)(v), (b)(vi), (2), 5, 24(1) (as so substituted), Sch 7 (as so amended), Sch 8.
8 Ibid, regs 3(1)(a)(vi)–(viii), (b)(iv), (vii), (viii), 4(3), Schs 10–12.
9 Ibid, reg 3(1)(a)(vi) proviso, (vii) proviso.
10 Ibid, reg 3(1)(a) proviso.
11 Ibid, reg 4 (amended by SI 1979/768).
12 Ibid, reg 15.
13 Ibid, reg 30.
14 Ibid, reg 22, and reg 24 (substituted by SI 1979/768).
15 Ibid, regs 20, 21.
16 Ibid, reg 25 (amended by SI 1979/768).
17 Ibid, regs 27, 28, and reg 29 (substituted by SI 1985/1068).

(14) FOOD PREMISES

419. Requirements applying generally to food premises. All food premises must have such a drainage system as may be necessary for the disposal of soil and waste water from the premises, and such water must be disposed of only through such a system as is provided for those premises[1]. Every forecourt or yard forming part of any food premises and on which food is handled must be capable of being readily cleaned[2]. All sanitary conveniences on food premises must be supplied with water through a suitable flushing apparatus, and must be kept clean and be in efficient working order[3]. Every room or compartment in which there is a convenience must be suitably lighted and ventilated[4], and no such room or compartment must communicate directly with a food room[5]. At or near every convenience used by persons handling food there must be a notice requiring such persons to wash their hands after using a sanitary convenience[6].

A supply of wholesome water must be provided in all food premises[7]. Suitable and sufficient readily accessible washhand basins must be provided in all food premises and adequate supplies of hot and cold water or of warm water at a controlled temperature[8], of soap, nail brushes and of towels or other hygienic drying facilities must be provided there[9]. All washhand basins, soaps, nail brushes and towels are to be used only for securing personal cleanliness, and all such basins and any fitting or connections thereof must be kept clean and in working order[10].

Sinks or other facilities for washing food and equipment must be provided in all food premises, and every sink must have an adequate supply of hot and cold water or of warm water at a controlled temperature[11]. Sinks used only for the washing of fish and other specified foods and for washing drinking vessels in an apparatus manufactured and sold for the cleaning of such vessels require to have supplies of cold water only[12]. Sinks must be kept clean and in working order and have supplies of soap and drying facilities near at hand[13].

Every food room must be sufficiently lighted and ventilated[14], all parts of the structure of every food room must be kept clean and in such a state of repair as to prevent so far as is reasonably practicable the entry of birds or infestation by rats, mice or insects[15]. There must be suitable and sufficient accommodation for the storage of food[16] and provision must be made for storing clothing and footwear[17]. First-aid equipment must be provided[18]. No food room may be used as a sleeping place or communicate directly with any bedroom[19].

1 Food Hygiene (Scotland) Regulations 1959, SI 1959/413, reg 18. 'Food premises' means premises on or from which a food business as defined in reg 3 is carried on: reg 2(1).
2 Ibid, reg 19.
3 Ibid, reg 20(1), which is expressed to be subject to exemption under reg 31: see para 408 above.
4 Ibid, reg 20(2).
5 Ibid, reg 20(3), which is expressed to be subject to exemption under reg 31. 'Food room' means a room where persons handle food or clean equipment for the purposes of a food business, but there are certain exceptions: see reg 2(1).
6 Ibid, reg 20(4).
7 Ibid, reg 21(1). Unless exempted under reg 31, the water supply must be piped: reg 21(2).
8 Ibid, reg 22(1), (2), which are expressed to be subject to exemption under reg 31.
9 Ibid, reg 22(3).
10 Ibid, reg 22(4), (5). Soiled towels must be replaced: reg 22(6) (amended by SI 1978/173).
11 Ibid, reg 23(1), (2).
12 Ibid, reg 23(2) proviso (substituted by SI 1961/622).
13 Ibid, reg 23(3), (4) (amended by SI 1961/622). Soiled drying cloths must be replaced: reg 23(5) (amended by SI 1978/173).
14 Ibid, reg 24.
15 Ibid, reg 25.
16 Ibid, reg 26 (amended by SI 1978/173).
17 Ibid, reg 28.
18 Ibid, reg 27.
19 Ibid, reg 29, which is expressed to be subject to exemption under reg 31.

420. Registration of food premises, manufacturers and traders. Subject to such exceptions as the Secretary of State may by order prescribe, no person may use any premises for the preparation, exposure or offer for sale or sale of food for human consumption, or the storage of food intended for sale for human consumption, in the course of any business of a class prescribed by order made by the Secretary of State unless he is registered in respect of the premises for that purpose by the local authority[1]. Subject to such exceptions as the Secretary of State may by order prescribe, no person may engage otherwise than in, at or from premises, in any business of a class so prescribed and consisting of or including the preparation, exposure or offer for sale or sale of food for human consumption, or the storage of food intended for sale for that purpose, unless he is registered by the local authority[2]. The provisions discussed in this and the following paragraph[3] apply to persons so registered and, where applicable, to vehicles, stalls or places in, at or from which any business of such a class is carried on, but those provisions may be adapted or modified by order in their application to such a business[4].

An application for registration under these provisions must be made, by the person who proposes to use the premises, to the local authority, to which certain information and plans must be supplied[5]. Unless the local authority decides to refuse to grant registration, it must register in respect of the premises the person who made the application and issue to him a certificate[6].

Registers of persons to whom certificates are granted are open to public inspection[7], and a certificate granted must be kept fixed in a conspicuous place in the premises to which it relates[8]. Provision is also made about the use of premises and the right to use them when an application made has yet to be decided, where, on a change of occupation of registered premises, the incoming occupier makes such an application, and where a person registered in respect of premises dies[9]. A person who uses premises for any prescribed class of business without having complied with the provisions about registration or the fixing of a certificate in the premises to which it relates is guilty of an offence against the Food and Drugs (Scotland) Act 1956[10].

1 Food and Drugs (Scotland) Act 1956 (c 30), s 14(1). For the meaning of 'premises', see para 334 above, and for the meaning of 'local authority', see para 308, note 2, above. No order has been made under s 14.
2 Ibid, s 14(2).
3 Ie the provisions of ibid, ss 14, 15.
4 Ibid, s 14(2).
5 Ibid, s 14(3), (4).
6 Ibid, s 14(5). As to refusal of registration, see para 421 below.
7 Ibid, s 14(6).
8 Ibid, s 14(7).
9 See ibid, s 14(8)–(10).
10 Ibid, s 14(11). As to prosecutions and penalties, see paras 423 ff below.

421. Refusal etc of registration of food premises, manufacturers and traders. A local authority to which application for registration of food premises or a manufacturer or trader is made may refuse, cancel or vary it as the case may be, if it appears to the authority (1) that the applicant is not suitable on certain grounds to make use of the premises for the purpose stated in the application having regard to special considerations, (2) that regulations which apply to the business carried on in the registered premises are not being complied with, or (3) that the premises or any part of them are otherwise unsuitable, having regard to certain circumstances, for use for that purpose[1].

The authority, however, must not refuse, cancel or vary any registration unless (a) it has notified the applicant or the person registered in respect of the premises of the decision it proposes to make and of the place and time at which it will consider the matter, and has informed him that he may attend or be represented before the authority (with witnesses) to show cause why it should not so decide, and (b) the applicant or registered person fails to show such cause[2]. Notice of the decision must be given by the authority forthwith[3]. In certain circumstances an application is deemed to have been refused[4]. A person aggrieved by the decision of the authority may appeal to the sheriff, who may make such order as he thinks equitable, and any such order is conclusive[5].

1 Food and Drugs (Scotland) Act 1956 (c 30), s 15(1)(a)–(c). As to appeals, see para 434 below.
2 Ibid, s 15(2)(a), (b).
3 Ibid, s 15(3).
4 See ibid, s 15(4).
5 Ibid, s 15(5), (6).

422. Order closing food premises. The Control of Food Premises (Scotland) Act 1977 prohibits the sale of food in circumstances where there is a risk of danger to health. Where a person is convicted of an offence under any food hygiene regulations[1] and the offence includes the carrying on of a food business either at premises which are insanitary or the condition, situation or construction of which exposes food to risk of contamination, or on, at or from a stall, vehicle or place which is insanitary or so situated, constructed or in such a condition as to expose food to such a risk, the sheriff may, if satisfied on certain matters and after specified procedure[2], make a closure order prohibiting the carrying on of the food business there[3]. If there is imminent risk of danger to health an interim order may be made[4]. There is a right of appeal against the sheriff's decision[5]. Contravention of a closure order or interim order is an offence[6].

A person who wishes to carry on a food business at any premises etc in respect of which a closure order or interim order is in force may apply to the local authority and, if satisfied that the measures specified in the closure order have been carried out, or, in the case of an interim order, that there is no longer any risk of danger to health, the local authority may issue a certificate to that effect[7].

1 Ie regulations under the Food and Drugs (Scotland) Act 1956 (c 30), s 13: see para 407 above.
2 The procurator fiscal must give the accused and, if he is not the accused, the owner of the
   premises etc not less than seven days' notice of his intention to apply for the order, specifying the
   measures which the local authority considers should be taken to remove any danger to health:
   Control of Food Premises (Scotland) Act 1977 (c 28), s 1(2), (3). As to the service of notices, see
   s 5.
3 Ibid, s 1(1).
4 Ibid, s 2(1). As to notice of intention to apply for an interim order, see s 2(2), (3) (which are
   similar to s 1(2), (3)). As to the duration of an interim order, see s 2(1), (5).
5 Ibid, s 3(1), (2). Appeal lies at the instance of the procurator fiscal or any person on whom notice
   of intention to apply was served: s 3(1), (2). Appeal lies to the High Court of Justiciary in the case
   of a closure order, or to the sheriff principal in the case of an interim order: s 3(1), (2).
6 Ibid, s 4.
7 Ibid, ss 1(4), 2(4). A closure order continues in effect until such a certificate is issued: s 1(1).
   Appeal from a refusal or failure to issue a certificate lies to the sheriff: s 3(3). The Food and Drugs
   (Scotland) Act 1956, s 50 (see para 434 below), applies to such an appeal: Control of Food
   Premises (Scotland) Act 1977, s 3(4).

(15) PROSECUTIONS AND PENALTIES

423. Place and nature of prosecution. Where a sample has been procured
under the Food and Drugs (Scotland) Act 1956, any proceedings in respect of the
article or substance sampled must be taken before a court having jurisdiction in
the place where the sample was procured[1]. However, in the case of a sample of
milk procured within one area which is, for the purposes of the Act, deemed to
have been procured in another area[2], proceedings may be taken, at the option of
the prosecution, in a court in either area[3]. Any prosecution for an offence against
any regulations or orders made under the Act may be prosecuted summarily or,
if the regulation or order so provides, on indictment[4].

In any proceedings in respect of an article or substance sampled, the case must
not proceed to trial less than fourteen days from the day on which the complaint
or the indictment was served, and a copy of any certificate of analysis obtained
by the prosecution must be served with the complaint or indictment[5]. No such
proceedings may be begun after two months of the date when the sample was
procured except where earlier proceedings were impracticable[6] or the proceedings are summary and relate to the giving of a false warranty[7]. In the last-
mentioned cases the proceedings may be commenced within twelve months[7].
Where a sample is divided into two parts, the part retained by the person who
obtained the sample must be produced at the trial[8].

There is a provision, which applies generally, about an offence committed by
a body corporate[9].

1 Food and Drugs (Scotland) Act 1956 (c 30), s 41(1).
2 See ibid, s 31(2), and para 336 above.
3 Ibid, s 41(1) proviso.
4 Ibid, s 41(7).
5 Ibid, s 41(2).
6 Ibid, s 41(3).
7 Ibid, s 41(4), which applies notwithstanding the six-month limit normally provided by the
   Criminal Procedure (Scotland) Act 1975 (c 21), s 331(1).
8 Food and Drugs (Scotland) Act 1956, s 41(5).
9 See ibid, s 41(6), and para 325 above.

424. Evidence of certificates of analysis. In any proceedings under the Food
and Drugs (Scotland) Act 1956 the production by one party of a certificate of a
public analyst or of a copy of such a certificate is sufficient evidence of the facts
stated therein unless, in the first-mentioned case, the other party requires that

the analyst be called as a witness, and in that event the evidence of the analyst is sufficient evidence of those facts[1]. Where the proceedings relate to a sample of milk taken by an officer of one authority at the request of an officer of another, a certificate signed by the officer who took the sample is, if a copy has been served on the accused with the complaint or indictment, sufficient evidence of compliance with the provisions of the Act with respect to the manner in which samples are to be dealt with unless the accused requires that the officer be called as a witness, and in that event the evidence of the officer is sufficient evidence of compliance[2]. If an accused person intends to produce a certificate of a public analyst or to require that an analyst or a sampling officer be called as a witness, he must give at least three days' notice to the other party[3].

The Secretary of State has power to make regulations prescribing methods of analysing food[4].

1 Food and Drugs (Scotland) Act 1956 (c 30), s 42(1). As to public analysts, see para 330 above.
2 Ibid, s 42(2).
3 Ibid, s 42(3).
4 See ibid, s 42(4).

425. Analysis by the Government Chemist. The court before which any proceedings are taken under the Food and Drugs (Scotland) Act 1956 may, and must upon the request of either party, require the part of any sample produced before the court[1] to be sent to the Government Chemist for analysis[2]. A certificate of the result of his analysis is sent to the court[2]. The same provision applies in any appeal proceedings[3]. There are provisions about the conduct of the analysis and the sufficiency of the evidence of the person who signs the certificate[4].

1 Ie under the Food and Drugs (Scotland) Act 1956 (c 30), s 41(5): see para 423 above.
2 Ibid, s 44(1).
3 Ibid, s 44(2).
4 See ibid, s 44(3).

426. Warranty as a defence. In any proceedings for an offence against the Food and Drugs (Scotland) Act 1956 or regulations made thereunder consisting of selling or offering, exposing or advertising for sale or having in possession for the purpose of sale any article or substance (other than milk or butter-milk[1]), it is a defence for the accused[2] to prove:
(1) that he purchased it as being an article or substance that could be lawfully so sold or otherwise dealt with, or, as the case may be, could be lawfully so sold or dealt with under the name or description or for the purpose under or for which he sold or dealt with it, and with a written warranty to that effect[3]; and
(2) that he had no reason to believe at the time of the offence that it was otherwise[4]; and
(3) that it was then in the same state as when he purchased it[5].
A warranty is a defence only if the accused has within seven days of the service of the complaint or indictment given notice to the prosecutor that he intends to rely on it and has provided certain other information[6]. Where the warranty is given by a person outside the United Kingdom the accused must prove that he had taken reasonable steps to ascertain and did in fact believe in the accuracy of the statement contained therein[7]. The person by whom the warranty is alleged to have been given is entitled to appear at the diet and give evidence[8].

1 Food and Drugs (Scotland) Act 1956 (c 30), s 46(6).
2 Where the accused is employed by the purchaser, the accused may rely on ibid, s 46, in the same way as his employer could have done had he been the accused: s 46(3).

3 Ibid, s 46(1)(a). For the purposes of ss 46 and 47 a name or description entered in an invoice is deemed to be a warranty that the article etc referred to can lawfully be sold or dealt with under that name or description: s 46(5).
4 Ibid, s 46(1)(b).
5 Ibid, s 46(1)(c).
6 Ibid, s 46(2)(a).
7 Ibid, s 46(2)(b).
8 Ibid, s 46(4).

427. Offences in relation to warranties and certificates of analysis. An accused who, in proceedings under the Food and Drugs (Scotland) Act 1956, wilfully applies to any article or substance a warranty or certificate of analysis not given in relation to it is guilty of an offence under the Act[1].

A person who gives to the purchaser of an article or substance a false warranty in writing is guilty of an offence under the Act unless he proves that when he gave the warranty he had reason to believe it was accurate[2]. Any proceedings in such a case may, at the option of the prosecution, be taken either in the court of the place where the sample to which the proceedings relate was procured or in the court of the place where the warranty was given[3].

1 Food and Drugs (Scotland) Act 1956 (c 30), s 47(1). As to an invoice constituting a warranty, see para 426, note 3, above.
2 Ibid, s 47(2).
3 Ibid, s 47(3).

428. Contravention due to act or default of some other person. Where any person is liable to a penalty for a contravention of the Food and Drugs (Scotland) Act 1956 or any regulation or order made under that Act and the contravention was due to the act or default of another person then, whatever action is taken in regard to the first person, the other person may be charged with any such contravention[1], but if he proves that he used all due diligence to ensure compliance with the provision in question and that some other person was responsible for the contravention he must be acquitted[2].

1 Food and Drugs (Scotland) Act 1956 (c 30), s 45(1).
2 Ibid, s 45(2).

429. Presumptions. The following presumptions apply for the purposes of the Food and Drugs (Scotland) Act 1956 and regulations made under that Act, until the contrary is proved:
(1) any article commonly used for human consumption is, if sold or offered, exposed or kept for sale, presumed to have been sold or, as the case may be, to have been or to be intended for sale, for human consumption[1];
(2) any article commonly so used which is found on premises or on any vehicle, stall or place other than premises used for the preparation, storage or sale of that article, and any article commonly used in the manufacture of products for human consumption which is so found is presumed to be intended for sale, or for manufacturing products for sale, for human consumption[2];
(3) any substance capable of being used in the composition or preparation of any article commonly used for human consumption which is found in premises or on any vehicle, stall or place other than premises on which that article is prepared is presumed to be intended for such use[3].

1 Food and Drugs (Scotland) Act 1956 (c 30), s 43(a). For the meaning of 'article', see para 311, note 2, above, and for the meaning of 'human consumption', see para 341, note 3, above.

2 Ibid, s 43(b). For the meaning of 'premises', see para 334, note 6, above, and for the meaning of 'preparation', see para 311, note 3, above.
3 Ibid, s 43(c). For the meaning of 'substance', see para 311, note 2, above.

430. Penalties. A person found guilty of any offence against the Food and Drugs (Scotland) Act 1956 is liable on summary conviction to a fine not exceeding the prescribed sum[1], or on conviction on indictment to a fine of unlimited amount or imprisonment for a term not exceeding one year or to both[2].

Regulations and certain orders under the general provisions of the Act relating to food[3] may impose on a person convicted of an offence triable only summarily a fine not exceeding level 5 on the standard scale[4], and on a person convicted of an offence triable either summarily or on indictment a fine on summary conviction not exceeding the statutory maximum or, on conviction on indictment, a fine of unlimited amount or imprisonment for a term not exceeding one year or both[5].

1 Food and Drugs (Scotland) Act 1956 (c 30), s 40(1)(a) (amended by the Law Reform (Miscellaneous Provisions) (Scotland) Act 1985 (c 73), s 41(a)); Criminal Procedure (Scotland) Act 1975 (c 21), s 289B(1) (added by the Criminal Law Act 1977 (c 45), s 63(1), Sch 11, para 5, and substituted by the Criminal Justice Act 1982 (c 48), s 55(2)). The prescribed sum is £2,000: Criminal Procedure (Scotland) Act 1975, s 289B(6) (as so added and substituted); Increase of Criminal Penalties etc (Scotland) Order 1984, SI 1984/526, art 3.
2 Food and Drugs (Scotland) Act 1956, s 40(1)(b) (amended by the Law Reform (Miscellaneous Provisions) (Scotland) Act 1985, s 41(b)); Criminal Procedure (Scotland) Act 1975, s 193A (added by the Criminal Law Act 1977, Sch 11, para 1 (amended by the Criminal Justice (Scotland) Act 1980 (c 62), s 83(2), Sch 7, para 37, and the Criminal Justice Act 1982, s 77, Sch 15, para 17).
3 Ie regulations under the Food and Drugs (Scotland) Act 1956, Pt I (ss 1–24), and orders under s 5.
4 Ibid, s 56(8)(e), (8A)(a), (9) (amended by the Criminal Justice Act 1982, Sch 15, para 8, and the Law Reform (Miscellaneous Provisions) (Scotland) Act 1985, s 41(c)). Level 5 is £2,000: Increase of Criminal Penalties etc (Scotland) Order 1984, art 4.
5 Food and Drugs (Scotland) Act 1956, s 56(8)(e), (8A)(b), (9) (as so amended). 'The statutory maximum' means the prescribed sum referred to in note 1 above: Interpretation Act 1978 (c 30), Sch 1 (amended by the Criminal Justice Act 1988 (c 33), s 170(1), Sch 15, para 58(b)).

(16) MISCELLANEOUS

431. Sale of excisable liquor. Since under the Food and Drugs (Scotland) Act 1956 'food' includes drink[1], the general provisions prohibiting the sale of injurious food, food not of the nature, substance or quality demanded[2] and the false labelling or advertisement of food[3] apply to excisable liquor[4]. There is also a provision in the Licensing (Scotland) Act 1976 making it an offence for a licence-holder or his employee or agent to adulterate food or alcoholic liquor fraudulently[5].

1 Food and Drugs (Scotland) Act 1956 (c 30), s 58(1).
2 Ibid, s 2: see para 343 above.
3 Ibid, s 6: see para 350 above.
4 As to excisable liquor, see also para 315 above.
5 Licensing (Scotland) Act 1976 (c 66), s 88. As to licences for premises for the sale of liquor, see ALCOHOLIC LIQUOR, vol 2, paras 8 ff.

432. Miscellaneous foodstuffs. The European Communities have grading standards in respect of fresh fruit and vegetables at all stages of distribution[1]. These apply in Scotland.

No person may sell or offer or expose for sale, or have in his possession for the purpose of sale, any horseflesh for human consumption elsewhere than in premises or in a stall, vehicle or place other than premises over or on which a notice in legible letters not less than 4 inches in height stating that horseflesh is sold there is at all times conspicuously displayed². If horseflesh is exposed for sale otherwise than in such a manner, the onus of proving that it was not intended for human consumption is on the person exposing it for sale³. Horseflesh may not be supplied to a person who has not asked to be supplied with it⁴.

The Meat and Livestock Commission⁵ may compile and operate systems of classifying meat and marking and labelling it in accordance with the classification, and may compile standard codes of practice about the way in which meat is cut and the description of the cuts⁶. The commission may also submit to the Secretary of State for Scotland schemes requiring information to be given as to retail meat prices and for regulating the way in which the information is given⁷. Under the schemes, price lists, prices and weights of particular pieces of meat and the price per pound weight may have to be displayed⁸.

Welfare food and welfare milk may be obtained by certain beneficiaries free of charge on presentation of tokens⁹. Application for the food or milk is made to the Secretary of State for Scotland on a form provided by him and he also issues the tokens¹⁰.

1 See the Agriculture and Horticulture Act 1964 (c 28), Pt III (ss 11–24), and the Grading of Horticultural Produce (Amendment) Regulations 1973, SI 1973/22, and 1983, SI 1983/1053.
2 Food and Drugs (Scotland) Act 1956 (c 30), s 19(1). 'Horseflesh' means the flesh of horses, asses and mules: see s 19(5).
3 Ibid, s 19(4).
4 Ibid, s 19(2).
5 As to the commission, see the Agriculture Act 1967 (c 22), s 1, Sch 1.
6 Ibid, s 7.
7 Ibid, ss 8(1), 25(1).
8 Ibid, s 8(2).
9 Welfare Food Order 1980, SI 1980/1648, art 4(1), (2) (amended by SI 1983/379 and SI 1985/1932) and art 5 (substituted by SI 1983/379). As to tokens, see art 9 (amended by SI 1985/1932). 'Welfare food' means milk, dried milk, children's vitamin drops and vitamin tablets, and 'welfare milk' means milk or dried milk: art 2(1). 'Beneficiary' means expectant or nursing mothers in families in special circumstances as defined in art 3 (as so substituted), all children in such families aged not more than five years and one month or who have not yet started full time school, and handicapped children: arts 2(1), 4(3).
10 Ibid, arts 7, 8.

433. Sale of venison. An islands or district council may grant to any person whom it thinks fit a venison dealer's licence¹. The regulation of applications for licences, the manner in which they are to be dealt with (including the charging of fees), the procedure by which licences may be surrendered, and the handing in of licences on forfeiture or on cessation of dealing are regulated by the Secretary of State². A licence is valid for three years (subject to disqualification), and may be renewed³. A copy of every licence issued must be sent to the Secretary of State, to whom a return of all persons with licences on 1 January in each year must be made⁴.

A licensed venison dealer must keep a book in which a record of all purchases and receipts of venison by him must, along with certain other particulars, be kept⁵. The book may be inspected by a person authorised by the Deer Commission or the Secretary of State or by any constable, and so also may any venison in the dealer's possession, under his control or on his premises or vehicles and all invoices and other documents needed to verify entries in the book⁶. If venison is purchased or received by a licensed dealer from another licensed dealer, different information from that referred to above must be recorded by the former⁷.

It is an offence for any person who is not a licensed venison dealer to sell, offer or expose for sale or have in his possession any venison, or the carcase of a deer believed to have been killed unlawfully, or to transport it or cause it to be transported for the purpose of sale unless, in the case of venison, the sale is to a licensed venison dealer, or to obstruct a person entitled to inspect books or other things, or for a licensed venison dealer to fail to keep proper records[8].

1 Deer (Scotland) Act 1959 (c 40), s 25A(1) (added by the Deer (Amendment) (Scotland) Act 1982 (c 19), s 11).
2 Deer (Scotland) Act 1959, s 25A(2) (as so added). See the Licensing of Venison Dealers (Prescribed Forms etc) (Scotland) Order 1984, SI 1984/899, and the Licensing of Venison Dealers (Application Procedures etc) (Scotland) Order 1984, SI 1984/922.
3 Deer (Scotland) Act 1959, s 25A(3) (as so added).
4 Ibid, s 25A(4), (5) (as so added).
5 Ibid, s 25B(1) (as so added).
6 Ibid, s 25B(2) (as so added).
7 Ibid, s 25C (as so added).
8 See ibid, s 25D (as so added), which also prescribes penalties, including disqualification from holding or obtaining a licence.

434. Appeal against decision of local authority. Where the Food and Drugs (Scotland) Act 1956 or a regulation made under it provides for an appeal against a refusal or other decision of a local authority[1], the appeal must be brought within one month from the date on which notice of the authority's refusal or decision was given to the appellant, or was deemed to have been made[2]. Where such an appeal lies, the document notifying the authority's decision must state the grounds on which the decision is based, the right of appeal and the time within which an appeal may be brought[3].

Where a decision refusing, cancelling or varying a registration makes it unlawful for a person to carry on any business lawfully being carried on when the decision was given, or to use any premises for any purpose for which they were then lawfully being used, that person may carry on the business and use the premises for that purpose until the time for appealing has expired and, if an appeal is lodged, until the appeal is finally disposed of or abandoned or has failed for want of prosecution[4].

1 See eg the Food and Drugs (Scotland) Act 1956 (c 30), s 15, and para 421 above.
2 Ibid, s 50(1). For the meaning of 'local authority', see para 308, note 2, above.
3 Ibid, s 50(2).
4 Ibid, s 51.

435. Apportionment of expenses of altering premises. If the owner or occupier of any premises who incurs expense in order to secure that hygiene regulations[1] are complied with alleges that another person interested in the premises ought to bear the expense, he may apply to the sheriff, who may make such order concerning the expenses or their apportionment as appears to him just and equitable[2]. His order may direct that any contract between the parties is to cease to have effect in so far as it is inconsistent with his order[2].

1 Ie regulations under the Food and Drugs (Scotland) Act 1956 (c 30), s 13: see para 407 above.
2 Ibid, s 49.

436. Borrowing by local authorities. The maximum period for the repayment of sums borrowed by a local authority for the purposes of the Food and Drugs (Scotland) Act 1956 is such period not exceeding sixty years as may be sanctioned by the Secretary of State[1].

1 Food and Drugs (Scotland) Act 1956 (c 30), s 54. For the meaning of 'local authority', see para 308, note 2, above.

437. European Community provisions. The European Communities Act 1972 gives the Secretary of State power, as respects any directly applicable

European Community provisions relating to food, to make such provisions as he considers necessary and expedient to secure that the Community provisions are administered, executed and enforced under the Food and Drugs (Scotland) Act 1956[1]. Special provisions for sampling and analysing, testing or examining samples may also be made for complying with a Community obligation[2]. Reference is made above to Community directives which are implemented by regulations under the 1956 Act[3].

In the harmonisation of Scottish food laws with those of the Community, it is important to remember the difference between a Community regulation, which is binding in its entirety and directly applicable to all member states, and a Community directive, which is binding, as to the result to be achieved, upon each member state but which leaves to the national authority the choice of form and method[4]. The provisions of the 1956 Act relate to 'any directly applicable community provision', which enables any Community regulations to be enforced under the 1956 Act. As the implementing directives are left to the individual member states, the provisions of the 1956 Act conferring powers to make regulations are largely sufficient for the purpose. So far as they are not, the provisions of the 1972 Act give the necessary powers to implement the Community obligations.

1 Food and Drugs (Scotland) Act 1956 (c 30), s 56A(1) (added by the European Communities Act 1972 (c 68), s 4(1), Sch 4, para 3(2)(b)). See eg the Poultry Meat (Hygiene) (Scotland) (Amendment) Regulations 1981, SI 1981/1169; the Fresh Meat Export (Hygiene and Inspection) (Scotland) Regulations 1987, SI 1987/800; and the Materials and Articles in Contact with Food Regulations 1987, SI 1987/1523.
2 Food and Drugs (Scotland) Act 1956, s 56A(2) (as so added).
3 See eg paras 362, 369, 371–373, 377, 381, 383, 395, 414, 417, 418, above.
4 EEC Treaty, art 189.

2. MILK AND DAIRIES

(1) INTRODUCTION

438. Milk. Milk is, of necessity, defined in different ways in different contexts[1], but basically it means, so far as this title is concerned, the white liquid secreted by female mammals for the nourishment of their young[2]. From the time man ceased to live primarily by hunting and, instead of killing animals, kept and tended them for his own livelihood and other purposes, milk surplus to the requirements of the young has been taken from the mother by artificial means and used as food and drink. The animals from which milk is most commonly taken are cows — the females of bovine animals — and over the centuries, with improving methods of farming, feeding, genetic variation by breeding and the increase in other aspects of scientific understanding and usage, the quantity of cow's milk available as food has increased and its quality improved. The milk of female goats and of ewes is also used in small quantities in Scotland for human consumption.

The word 'milk' has come to have many related, onomatopoeic and derivative meanings (some having a slang significance), but these are not looked at here.

Cheese, which is made from the curd of milk, coagulated by rennet, separated from the whey and pressed or otherwise made into a solid mass, is excluded from this part of the title.

1 For the meaning of 'milk', see para 443 below.
2 *Chambers Twentieth Century Dictionary*.

439. Cream. Cream[1] is the only substance that rises on, or is separated by machinery from, milk, and yields butter when churned[2]. Butter is, by other methods, also made from cream and from whole milk. Like 'milk', 'cream' has come to have many related, onomatopoeic and derivative meanings which are not considered here.

  1 For the meaning of 'cream', see para 474 below.
  2 *Chambers Twentieth Century Dictionary*.

440. Dairies. A dairy is, in common usage, a place where milk is kept, cream separated and butter and cheese made, and is also a shop where milk and dairy produce is sold[1]. But the Milk and Dairies (Scotland) Act 1914 expands its meaning to include any creamery, farm, farmhouse, cowshed, byre, milk store, milk shop or other premises from which milk is sold or supplied for sale or in which it is kept for the purpose of sale[2].

  1 *Chambers Twentieth Century Dictionary*.
  2 Milk and Dairies (Scotland) Act 1914 (c 46), s 2: see para 488 below.

441. Historical background. There is little or nothing to be found in non-statutory law about milk, dairies or milk products. The earliest statute in which milk is dealt with by name is the Milk and Dairies (Scotland) Act 1914 (c 46). There had been earlier legislation which by and large was concerned with the prevention of the spread of bovine diseases and diseases of which cows are carriers and all of which are transmissible to human beings, instances being tuberculosis, murrain, rinderpest and foot and mouth disease. The aim of these earlier statutes was, however, to control the animals not the product. One of the earliest was given the long title 'An Act to prohibit the importation of sheep, cattle or other animals for the purpose of preventing the introduction of contagious or infectious disorders'[1]. It conferred power to make Orders in Council for that purpose[2]. Later Acts with similar objectives but with short durations were passed in 1866 and 1867[3] and in 1869 these Acts were consolidated and made 'perpetual'[4]. In 1878 'An Act for the making of better provision respecting contagious and infectious diseases of cattle and other animals'[5] was passed, and in 1886 was amended[6], and the earlier legislation was repealed.

Provision was made in the 1878 Act for the making of orders by the Board of Supervision regulating the trade of persons selling milk[7], and the Dairies, Cowsheds and Milk Shops Order of 1885, with an amending order of 1887, made fairly detailed provisions to this end. The Local Government Board for Scotland took over these functions from the Board of Supervision in 1894[8]; they were passed on to the Scottish Board of Health in 1919[9], and in 1928 the Department of Health for Scotland succeeded to them[10]. The most recent transfer of functions was made by the Reorganisation of Offices (Scotland) Act 1939, when all milk and dairies functions were transferred to the Secretary of State and thence to local authorities[11].

In the meantime the Cattle Sheds in Burghs (Scotland) Act 1866, the Burgh Police (Scotland) Acts of 1892 and 1903 and the Public Health (Scotland) Acts of 1867 and 1897 made provisions more concerned with the sanitation of premises and of articles of use in milk production[12]. Regulations first made in 1901 under food and drugs legislation were concerned with the quality of milk. Since 1 September 1925, when the 1914 Act was brought into operation[13], there have been a number of statutes and much subordinate legislation having as its main objective the treating of milk after production in a variety of ways so as to eliminate from it bacteria and other causes of infectious diseases harmful to human beings if consumed by them. All this legislation earlier than 1878 has either been repealed or has expired.

The 1878 and 1886 Acts were repealed by the 1914 Act along with those sections of the 1897 Act which applied to milk and dairies. The law now in force is thus to be found in the 1914 Act, the 1922 Act, the Milk Act 1934 (all except one provision of which[14] has been repealed), the Milk (Special Designations) Act 1949 and part of the Food and Drugs (Scotland) Act 1956[15], all as amended and not repealed. Orders and regulations made under these Acts also contain extensive provisions about milk and dairies. The 1914, 1922, 1934 and 1949 Acts may be cited together as the Milk and Dairies (Scotland) Acts 1914 to 1949[16].

1 Importation of Sheep Act 1848 (c 105) (repealed).
2 Ibid, ss 2–5 (repealed).
3 Cattle Diseases Prevention Amendment Act 1866 (c 110); Contagious Diseases (Animals) Act 1867 (c 125) (both repealed).
4 Contagious Diseases (Animals) Act 1869 (c 70) (repealed).
5 Contagious Diseases (Animals) Act 1878 (c 74) (repealed).
6 Contagious Diseases (Animals) Act 1886 (c 32) (repealed).
7 Contagious Diseases (Animals) Act 1878, s 34 (repealed).
8 Local Government (Scotland) Act 1894 (c 58), s 2 (repealed).
9 Scottish Board of Health Act 1919 (c 20), s 4, Sch 1 (repealed).
10 Reorganisation of Offices (Scotland) Act 1928 (c 34), s 1 (repealed).
11 Reorganisation of Offices (Scotland) Act 1939 (c 20), s 1.
12 Cattle Sheds in Burghs (Scotland) Act 1866 (c 17); Public Health (Scotland) Act 1867 (c 101), s 16; Burgh Police (Scotland) Act 1892 (c 55); Public Health (Scotland) Act 1897 (c 38), ss 60, 61; Burgh Police (Scotland) Act 1903 (c 33), ss 83–92 (all repealed).
13 Milk and Dairies (Amendment) Act 1922 (c 54), s 1(1) (substituted by s 14(b)); Milk and Dairies (Scotland) Act 1914 Commencement Order 1925, SR & O 1925/533.
14 This provision, the Milk Act 1934 (c 51), s 10, amends the 1922 Act.
15 Ie the Food and Drugs (Scotland) Act 1956 (c 30), ss 16–18.
16 Milk (Special Designations) Act 1949 (c 34), s 16(4).

442. General prohibition on additions to milk. A person is guilty of an offence against the Food and Drugs (Scotland) Act 1956[1] if he:

(1) adds any water or colouring matter, or any dried or condensed milk or liquid reconstituted therefrom, to milk intended for sale for human consumption[2]; or

(2) adds any separated milk, or mixture of cream and separated milk, to unseparated milk intended for such sale[3]; or

(3) sells or offers or exposes for sale or has in his possession for the purpose of sale, for human consumption, any milk to which any addition has been made in contravention of heads (1) and (2)[4]; or

(4) sells or offers or exposes for sale or has in his possession for the purpose of sale as milk any liquid in the making of which separated milk or any dried or condensed milk has been used[5].

1 Food and Drugs (Scotland) Act 1956 (c 30), s 17(3). For penalties, see para 430 above.
2 Ibid, s 17(1)(a). For the meaning of 'milk', see para 443 below.
3 Ibid, s 17(1)(b). For the meaning of 'cream', see para 474 below.
4 Ibid, s 17(1)(c).
5 Ibid, s 17(2).

(2) COW'S MILK

443. Meaning of 'milk'. The term 'milk' is defined in wide terms in the Milk and Dairies (Scotland) Act 1914 as including cream, skimmed milk, separated milk and buttermilk[1]. It is defined in the Milk (Special Designations) Act 1949, for the purposes of that Act, as cow's milk but not as including cream, or separated, skimmed, dried, condensed or evaporated milk or buttermilk[2]. For the purposes of the Food and Drugs (Scotland) Act 1956, however, 'milk' includes cream and separated milk but not dried or condensed milk[3]. Subordinate legislation also defines 'milk' for its purposes[4]. It is thus essential to be clear, when considering any provision about milk in any statute or item of subordinate legislation, which definition applies. For instance, no special designation within the meaning of the 1949 Act can apply to any milk other than cow's milk.

1 Milk and Dairies (Scotland) Act 1914 (c 46), s 2.
2 Milk (Special Designations) Act 1949 (c 34), s 14(1), (3).
3 Food and Drugs (Scotland) Act 1956 (c 30), s 58(1). See also para 352, note 7, above.
4 See eg the Milk (Special Designations) (Scotland) Order 1988, SI 1988/2191, art 2(1), which defines 'milk' in the same terms as in the Milk (Special Designations) Act 1949, s 14(3) (see above).

444. Inspection of cattle in dairies. The veterinary inspector[1] must from time to time and once at least in every year inspect the cattle in every dairy[2] in the district and report to the local authority[3] the result of the inspection[4]. Where milk consigned from one district to another is believed by the proper officer of the receiving district to be impure or likely to cause infectious disease or other illness, the proper officer or veterinary inspector of the receiving district may examine the cattle in the dairy from which the milk has been consigned[5]. Dairy byelaws must provide for the inspection of cattle in dairies[6].

Within its district the local authority and its officers, or an officer of the Secretary of State, may enter, inspect and examine any dairy; the designated medical officer, the proper officer or an officer of the Secretary of State may examine any person at a dairy and require such person to provide him with specimens for bacteriological examination; and the veterinary inspector or an officer of the Secretary of State may examine the cattle in any dairy[7]. Every dairyman and his employees must give all reasonable facilities and assistance to the local authority and its officers in this regard[8].

1 The Milk and Dairies (Scotland) Act 1914 (c 46), s 3(1), which required every local authority to appoint veterinary inspectors, was repealed by the Agriculture Act 1937 (c 70), s 34(4), Sch 3. Under s 19 of that Act (since repealed) the functions of veterinary inspectors under inter alia enactments relating to milk and dairies were to be discharged by veterinary inspectors appointed by the Minister of Agriculture and Fisheries under the Board of Agriculture Act 1889 (c 30), s 5. In England and Wales that provision is now contained in the Food Act 1984 (c 30), s 37, but there appears to be no corresponding provision in Scotland. However, a local authority has a general power under the Local Government (Scotland) Act 1973 (c 65), s 64(1), to appoint such officers as it thinks necessary for the proper discharge of its functions, and this enables local authorities to appoint veterinary inspectors. A local authority also has power to appoint inspectors under the Animal Health Act 1981 (c 22), s 52(1), although in that Act 'veterinary inspector' is confined to inspectors appointed by the minister (s 89(1)).
2 For the meaning of 'dairy', see para 488 below.
3 'Local authority' means an islands or district council: Milk and Dairies (Scotland) Act 1914, s 2 (amended by the Local Government (Scotland) Act 1973, s 214(2), Sch 27, Pt II, para 51). It is the duty of the local authority to enforce the provisions of the Milk and Dairies (Scotland) Act 1914 and byelaws under it: s 9.
4 Milk and Dairies (Scotland) Act 1914, s 4(2).
5 Ibid, s 4(3) (amended by the National Health Service (Scotland) Act 1972 (c 58), s 64(1), (2), Sch 6, para 61, Sch 7, Pt II, and the Local Government (Scotland) Act 1973, s 214(1), Sch 27, Pt I, para 2(1)).
6 Milk and Dairies (Scotland) Act 1914, s 8(1)(a).
7 Ibid, s 20 (amended by the National Health Service (Scotland) Act 1972, Sch 6, para 68, and the Local Government (Scotland) Act 1973, Sch 27, Pt I, para 2(1)). As to the Secretary of State, see para 446, note 1, below. As to the designation of medical officers, see the National Health Service (Scotland) Act 1972, s 21.

8 Milk and Dairies (Scotland) Act 1914, s 20. 'Dairyman' includes any occupier of a dairy and any person carrying on the trade of a cowkeeper or purveyor of milk or maker of butter or cheese or other milk products for sale for human consumption, but not a person who sells milk only in small quantities and for their own consumption to employees or neighbours: s 2.

445. Inspection of cattle elsewhere than in dairies.

The proper officer of a local authority may examine cattle in any premises from which the occupier sells milk in small quantities and for their own consumption to his employees or neighbours[1]. The premises need not necessarily be a dairy. Where an officer of a local authority proposes to inspect the cattle in any dairy in the district of a local authority other than that by which he is employed, he must give notice to the proper officer of the authority in whose district the dairy is situated of his intention to do so, so that an officer or inspector of that authority may be present if circumstances permit[2].

1 Milk and Dairies (Scotland) Act 1914 (c 46), s 5 (amended by the National Health Service (Scotland) Act 1972 (c 58), s 64(2), Sch 7, Pt II, and the Local Government (Scotland) Act 1973 (c 65), s 214(1), Sch 27, Pt I, para 2(1)). For the meaning of 'local authority', see para 444, note 3, above.
2 Milk and Dairies (Scotland) Act 1914, s 6 (amended by the National Health Service (Scotland) Act 1972, s 64(1), (2), Sch 6, para 62, Sch 7, Pt II, and the Local Government (Scotland) Act 1973, Sch 27, Pt I, para 2(1)).

446. Securing compliance by consigning authority with legislation.

If a local authority believes that the provisions of the Milk and Dairies (Scotland) Act 1914 or of byelaws under it are not being complied with by an authority from the district of which milk is consigned to its district, and the latter authority, after complaint from the former to the latter, fails to remove the cause of complaint within a reasonable time, the former may apply to the Secretary of State[1] to take steps to secure compliance with the Act or byelaws[2].

1 The powers of the Local Government Board for Scotland under the Milk and Dairies (Scotland) Act 1914 (c 46) have been transferred to the Secretary of State for Scotland: Scottish Board of Health Act 1919 (c 20), s 4(1), (5), Sch 1 (repealed); Reorganisation of Offices (Scotland) Act 1928 (c 34), s 1 (repealed); Reorganisation of Offices (Scotland) Act 1939 (c 20), s 1.
2 Milk and Dairies (Scotland) Act 1914, s 11.

447. Precautions against spread of disease.

It is an offence to sell, expose or keep for sale for human food, or to use or suffer to be used in the manufacture of products for human consumption, milk taken from a cow suffering from tuberculosis or certain other specified diseases liable to infect or contaminate the milk, but it is a defence for an accused person to prove that he did not know and had no reason to suspect that the milk had been taken from such a cow[1].

A dairyman must give written notice to the local authority that any cow in his dairy is suffering from any such disease[2]. Where infectious disease or symptoms of such a disease occur among persons employed or residing in a dairy, the dairyman must report that fact to the chief administrative officer of the Health Board for the area[3], and where milk is consigned from such a dairy the dairyman may be required to furnish the designated medical officer with a list of the districts to which it is consigned[4].

1 Milk and Dairies (Scotland) Act 1914 (c 46), s 13(1). See also the Milk and Dairies (Amendment) Act 1922 (c 54), s 5(1). A person guilty of a contravention of or failure to comply with the provisions of the 1914 Act or of any order made under it, or who wilfully obstructs any person acting in the execution thereof, may be proceeded against and punished as if he were guilty of an offence under the Food and Drugs (Scotland) Act 1956 (c 30) (see paras 423 ff above): Milk and Dairies (Scotland) Act 1914, s 24(1) (substituted by the Food and Drugs (Scotland) Act 1956,

s 40(2)). On conviction, a person is also liable to lose his registration as a dairyman or purveyor of milk: see paras 494, 495, below.

2 Milk and Dairies (Scotland) Act 1914, s 14. For the meaning of 'local authority' and 'dairyman', see para 444, notes 3, 8, above, and for the meaning of 'dairy', see para 488 below.

3 Ibid, s 15 (amended by the National Health Service (Scotland) Act 1972 (c 58), s 64(1), Sch 6, para 63).

4 Milk and Dairies (Scotland) Act 1914, s 16 (substituted by the National Health Service (Scotland) Act 1972, Sch 6, para 64). As to the designation of medical officers, see s 21 of the 1972 Act.

448. Persons suffering from disease. It is an offence for a person suffering from an infectious disease to milk cows or otherwise to assist in a dairy unless authorised to do so by a certificate from a duly qualified medical practitioner, and for a person recently in contact with such a person to do so unless proper precautions are taken[1]. A dairyman must not permit any person to contravene these provisions[1].

1 Milk and Dairies (Scotland) Act 1914 (c 46), s 17 (amended by the National Health Service (Scotland) Act 1972 (c 58), s 64(1), Sch 6, para 65). For the meaning of 'dairy', see para 488 below, and for the meaning of 'dairyman', see para 444, note 8, above. As to offences, see para 447, note 1 above.

449. Stoppage of milk supplies. If a designated medical officer[1] or the proper officer of a local authority has evidence that a person is suffering from any infectious disease or illness attributable to milk supplied from a dairy in the district, or that milk from such a dairy is likely to cause such disease or illness to any person consuming it, he must visit and examine the dairy and every person there, and if necessary require the veterinary inspector[2] to examine the animals there, and report to the local authority[3]. He may also make an interim order requiring the dairyman not to supply any milk or butter from the dairy[4]. The local authority must consider the report, and any other evidence submitted, at a meeting at which the dairyman may appear, and must either make an order (stating the grounds) that the dairyman is not to supply milk or butter from the dairy until the order is withdrawn, or resolve that no such order is necessary[4]. Such an order must be withdrawn when it is clear that the milk is no longer likely to cause disease[5]. Appeal lies to the sheriff against the making or withdrawal of such an order, the making of such a resolution, or failure to make such an order[6]. Proceedings for contravention of such an order are to be taken before the sheriff[7].

1 As to designated medical officers, see the National Health Service (Scotland) Act 1972 (c 58), s 21.

2 As to veterinary inspectors, see para 44, note 1, above.

3 Milk and Dairies (Scotland) Act 1914 (c 46), s 18(1) (amended by the National Health Service (Scotland) Act 1972, s 64(1), (2), Sch 6, para 66, Sch 7, Pt II, and the Local Government (Scotland) Act 1973 (c 65), s 214(1), Sch 27, Pt I, para 2(1)). For the meaning of 'dairy', see para 488 below, and for the meaning of 'local authority', see para 444, note 3, above.

4 Milk and Dairies (Scotland) Act 1914, s 18(3) (amended by the National Health Service (Scotland) Act 1972, Sch 6, para 66). A dairyman (defined in para 444, note 8, above) is not liable in damages for breach of contract due to such an order: Milk and Dairies (Scotland) Act 1914, s 18(9). In certain circumstances where he is not at fault he may be able to claim compensation from the local authority: see s 18(10).

5 Ibid, s 18(6) (as so amended).

6 Ibid, s 18(7).

7 Ibid, s 18(8). As to offences, see para 447, note 1, above.

450. Lists of customers and suppliers. Where there is an outbreak or spread of infectious disease or another illness within the district of a local authority and it has been certified to it by the designated medical officer or the proper officer that the outbreak or any spread of it is or would, in his opinion, be attributable to milk supplied by one or more dairymen or that milk so supplied is contaminated or impure, the authority may require the dairymen to furnish a confidential list of the names and addresses of all their customers[1] and a confidential list of the names and addresses of the farmers, dairymen or other persons from whom the milk, or any part of it, which they sell or distribute is obtained[2]. Certain other information must also be given if required[2]. It is an offence to fail to comply with these provisions[3].

1 Milk and Dairies (Scotland) Act 1914 (c 46), s 19, para (1) (amended by the National Health Service (Scotland) Act 1972 (c 58), s 64(1), Sch 6, para 67, and the Local Government (Scotland) Act 1973 (c 65), s 214(1), Sch 27, Pt I, para 2(1)). For the meaning 'local authority' and 'dairyman', see para 444, notes 3, 8, above.
2 Milk and Dairies (Scotland) Act 1914, s 19, para (2).
3 Ibid, s 19, paras (1), (2). As to offences, see para 447, note 1, above.

451. Depots for the sale of milk to children. A local authority has power to establish and maintain depots for the sale of milk specially prepared for children under two years of age[1].

1 Milk and Dairies (Scotland) Act 1914 (c 46), s 28 (amended by the Local Government (Scotland) Act 1973 (c 65), ss 209(1), 237(1), Sch 25, para 6, Sch 29). For the meaning of 'local authority', see para 444, note 3, above.

(3) SPECIAL DESIGNATIONS OF MILK

452. Power to prescribe special designations. The Secretary of State[1] has power to prescribe by order in relation to any description of milk such designation ('a special designation') as he considers appropriate[2]. The use of a special designation must be authorised by a 'milk licence' granted by the Secretary of State or the local authority[3], and the periods for which and the conditions subject to which licences either in general or in particular may be used are prescribed[4]. Such matters as are necessary for giving effect to or as are incidental to or consequential on any provisions in the order may also be prescribed[5]. No designation may be used for the purpose of the sale or advertisement of any milk unless a licence exists authorising its use in relation to that milk, and milk may not be described (otherwise than by special designation) in any way calculated falsely to suggest that the milk is free from tubercular or other disease or infection or that the milk is tested, approved or graded by any competent person[6]. If a person is charged with an offence against the last narrated provision he is required to prove the truth of the suggestion[7].

1 There have been transferred to the Secretary of State for Scotland the powers of the Board of Health under the Milk and Dairies (Amendment) Act 1922 (c 54) (Reorganisation of Offices (Scotland) Act 1928 (c 34), s 1 (repealed); Reorganisation of Offices (Scotland) Act 1939 (c 20), s 1), and the powers of the Minister of Food under the Milk (Special Designations) Act 1949 (c 34) (Transfer of Functions (Minister of Food) Order 1955, SI 1955/554).
2 Milk and Dairies (Amendment) Act 1922, s 3(1)(a) (substituted by the Milk Act 1934 (c 51), s 10(1), and amended by the Reorganisation of Offices (Scotland) (Adaptation of Enactments) Order 1939, S R & O 1939/782), read with the Milk and Dairies (Amendment) Act 1922, s 14(a). For the meaning of 'milk' in the Milk (Special Designations) Act 1949 (which, by virtue of s 16(4), is construed as one with the 1922 Act), see para 443 above.
3 See the Milk and Dairies (Amendment) Act 1922, s 3(1)(b) (as so substituted). 'Local authority' means an islands or district council: Milk and Dairies (Scotland) Act 1914 (c 46), s 2 (amended by the Local Government (Scotland) Act 1973 (c 65), s 214(2), Sch 27, Pt II, para 51); Milk (Special Designations) Act 1949, s 16(4). As to licences, see paras 457 ff below. The provisions of the

Milk and Dairies (Amendment) Act 1922, s 3, are to be enforced by islands or district councils: s 10 (substituted by s 14(f) and amended by the Local Government (Scotland) Act 1973, Sch 27, Pt II, para 62).
4 Milk and Dairies (Amendment) Act 1922, s 3(1)(c) (as so substituted).
5 Ibid, s 3(1)(f) (as so substituted).
6 Ibid, s 3(2)(a), (b) (as so substituted).
7 Ibid, s 3(3) (as so substituted). A person guilty of a contravention of or failure to comply with the provisions of the 1922 Act or of any order made under it, or who wilfully obstructs any person acting in the execution thereof, may be proceeded against and punished as if he were guilty of an offence under the Food and Drugs (Scotland) Act 1956 (see paras 423 ff above): Milk and Dairies (Amendment) Act 1922, s 9(1) (substituted by the Food and Drugs (Scotland) Act 1956, s 40(2)). Where it appears to a prosecutor that an offence has been committed in respect of which proceedings might be taken under the 1922 Act against a purveyor of milk, the prosecutor, if reasonably satisfied that the offence was due to an act or default of the purveyor's servant or agent without the purveyor's knowledge, consent or connivance, may proceed against the servant or agent without first proceeding against the purveyor: s 9(2) and s 14(e) (amended by the Food and Drugs (Scotland) Act 1956 (c 30), s 60(1), Sch 2).

453. Use of special designations. Milk sold by retail for human consumption in an area (called a 'specified area') in which this provision is in operation[1] may be sold only under a special designation[2]. This is also the position if, although the place of sale is not a specified area, the milk is delivered from an establishment where milk in relation to the sale of which a special designation must be used is sold[3]. These provisions do not apply to catering sales[4], nor to sale by a milk producer to persons employed by him in or in connection with milk production or otherwise than in agriculture[5]. The Secretary of State has power to consent to the sale of milk in a specified area in special circumstances without the use of a special designation[6]. The designation 'standard' attached to milk does not satisfy an obligation to use a special designation[7].

It is an offence to sell milk for the sale of which a special designation is obligatory without using such a designation[8]. Failure to comply with other provisions of the Milk (Special Designations) Act 1949 is also an offence[9]. It is the duty of islands and district councils to carry into execution and enforce the Act in their areas, but not to institute proceedings for offences[10].

1 See the Milk (Special Designations) Act 1949 (c 34), s 5, and para 455 below.
2 Ibid, s 1(1). For the meaning of 'milk' in the 1949 Act , see para 443 above. As to special designations, see para 452 above. 'Sale' means sale in the course of a business, and includes supply under arrangements for free supply: see s 14(1). For the meaning of 'sale by retail', see s 1(4).
3 Ibid, s 1(2).
4 Ibid, s 1(1), (2). 'Catering sale' means a sale of milk, or of things made from milk or of which milk is an ingredient as, or as part of, a meal or refreshments: s 14(1). For provisions as to catering sales in specified areas, see s 2.
5 Ibid, s 1(3).
6 Ibid, s 3(1). Catering sales in specified areas are not unlawful if made with such consent: s 3(2). As to the Secretary of State, see para 452, note 1, above.
7 See ibid, s 4. As to permitted special designations, see para 459 below.
8 Ibid, s 1(5).
9 See ibid, ss 2(4), 4(2), 8(1). A person guilty of an offence under the 1949 Act is liable to the like penalties as a person guilty of an offence under the Food and Drugs (Scotland) Act 1956 (c 30) (see para 430 above): Milk (Special Designations) Act 1949, s 15(1) (amended by the Food and Drugs (Scotland) Act 1956, s 60(1), Sch 2).
10 Milk (Special Designations) Act 1949, ss 1(6), 2(5), 4(2), 8(5), 15(2), read with s 16(4).

454. Place where milk is sold. If a contract of sale of milk is made in one place and the milk is delivered in another place, the place of sale is the place where it is delivered, save that if it is delivered to a carrier for transport to a third place, the place of sale is that third place[1].

1 Milk (Special Designations) Act 1949 (c 34), s 5(4).

455. Establishment of specified areas. An area becomes a specified area when the Secretary of State, after consultation with representative organisations[1], makes an order creating such an area, and an area may cease to be such an area on the making of an order to that effect[2].

1 Milk (Special Designations) Act 1949 (c 34), s 5(2).
2 Ibid, s 5(1). These orders, though statutory instruments (s 5(3)), are classified as local in character and do not appear in the *Index to Government Orders*. As to the Secretary of State, see para 452, note 1, above. Information about the existence of a specified area would thus have to be obtained from the islands or district council in whose area the specified area is situated, or from the Secretary of State who, presumably, keeps a list of areas which have been specified as, or removed by him from the list of, specified areas.

456. Provision of facilities for treatment of milk. The Secretary of State has power to provide, in certain circumstances, facilities for the treatment of milk which is required to be subjected to any particular process as a condition of a special designation being used in relation to it[1]. Where he provides such facilities, he may either buy the milk to be treated and resell it, otherwise than by retail sale, or apply the treatment to the milk of others[2]. He may make arrangements with local authorities and others for the doing, on his behalf and at his expense, of things he is authorised by these provisions to do[3].

1 Milk (Special Designations) Act 1949 (c 34), s 6(1). As to the Secretary of State, see para 452, note 1, above.
2 Ibid, s 6(2).
3 Ibid, s 6(3).

457. Conditions of licences. A licence authorising the use of a special designation held by a person carrying on a business which includes sales which are sales for the purpose of which the use of a special designation is obligatory and are of milk in relation to which the licence authorises the use of a special designation is subject to certain conditions[1]. If such a condition is breached, the licence holder is guilty of an offence[2], but there are extensive restrictions on the liability of licence holders to punishment for being in breach. Thus a licence holder is not guilty of the offence of being in breach of a condition if he is liable to punishment under another enactment for the act or omission constituting the breach[3], or unless the breach was the later or a later of two or more such breaches within a twelve-month period and was committed after warning or conviction[4], or if he proves certain matters which constitute special defences[5]. There are also restrictions on the circumstances in which a licence may be revoked on a breach of its conditions[6].

1 Milk (Special Designations) Act 1949 (c 34), s 8(2), (3). For the conditions, see Schedule. See also the Milk (Special Designations) (Scotland) Order 1988, SI 1988/2191, art 9, Schs 1–4.
2 Milk (Special Designations) Act 1949, s 8(1). As to penalties, see para 453, note 9, above.
3 Ibid, s 9(1).
4 Ibid, s 9(2).
5 See ibid, s 9(3).
6 See ibid, s 10.

458. Regulations as to revocation etc of licences. The Secretary of State has power to make by regulation or order further provisions for enabling a licensing authority[1] or, on appeal, the Secretary of State to revoke or suspend a licence authorising the use of a special designation on the ground of a breach of a condition having been proved by the finding of a tribunal or to the satisfaction of the licensing authority or the Secretary of State[2]. Such regulations must contain procedural provisions including the conferring on the holder of a licence or an applicant for such a licence of a right to be heard before a decision is made[3] and affording the person affected an opportunity of making representations to a tribunal[4], which must report its findings on any question of fact[5]. There is also provision about the case where a breach of licence to use a designation has been committed but the licence has not been suspended or revoked. In such a case the designation may continue to be used[6].

1 'Licensing authority' means the authority having power to grant or renew a licence authorising the use of a special designation: Milk (Special Designations) Act 1949 (c 34), s 14(1). Islands and district councils have such power: Milk (Special Designations) (Scotland) Order 1988, SI 1988/2191, reg 3, read with reg 2(1) ('local authority').
2 Milk (Special Designations) Act 1949, s 11(1). See also para 461 below. As to the Secretary of State, see para 452, note 1, above.
3 Ibid, s 11(2)(a).
4 See ibid, s 11(2)(b), (d)–(f).
5 Ibid, s 11(2)(c). As to the tribunal, see the Milk (Special Designations) (Scotland) Order 1988, art 15, Sch 7, and para 463 below.
6 Milk (Special Designations) Act 1949, s 12(1).

459. Grant of licence to use special designation. The special designations the use of which may be authorised by a licence are 'Pasteurised', 'Sterilised' and 'Ultra Heat Treated'[1]. Licences to use the former designations 'Premium' and 'Standard' expired in 1983[2]. There are five types of licence:
(1) a pasteuriser's licence, authorising the holder to use the special designation 'Pasteurised' in relation to milk pasteurised by him[3] and sold by him by wholesale at or from the premises where it is pasteurised[4], subject to specified conditions[5];
(2) a steriliser's licence, authorising the holder to use the special designation 'Sterilised' in relation to milk sterilised by him[6] and sold by him by wholesale at or from the premises where it is sterilised[7], subject to specified conditions[8];
(3) a licence to treat milk by the ultra high temperature method, authorising the holder to use the special designation 'Ultra Heat Treated' in relation to milk treated by that method by him[9] and sold by him by wholesale at or from the premises where it is so treated[10], subject to specified conditions[11];
(4) a dealer's licence, authorising a dealer[12] to use a special designation in relation to milk sold by him[13]; and
(5) a dealer's supplementary licence, authorising a dealer to use a special designation in relation to milk sold by him by retail in the area of a local authority[14] other than that in whose area the premises from which the milk is sold are situated[15].
Application for the grant or renewal of a licence must be in writing, and must specify the special designation which the applicant intends to use[16]. Application for the grant or renewal of a licence under any of heads (1) to (3) must also state whether the applicant intends to sell any of the milk by retail[16], and must be made to the local authority of the area in which his premises are situated[17]. Application for the grant or renewal of a dealer's licence must be made to the local authority of the area in which are situated the premises at or from which the milk will be sold[18], and application for the grant or renewal of a dealer's supplementary licence must be made to the local authority of the area in which the milk will be sold[19].

The local authority must grant the licence applied for[20], although it, or the Secretary of State on appeal, may refuse to do so if it or he is not satisfied that the applicant's handling, treatment, storage and distribution arrangements are such as would enable him to comply with the relevant requirements, or if it or he is satisfied that, by reason of his having been convicted of any offence relating to milk and dairies, the applicant is unsuitable to hold a licence[21]. Subject to this, a dealer's supplementary licence must be granted if the local authority has satisfied itself that the applicant has already been granted a dealer's licence by the authority in whose area are situated the premises from which he intends to sell milk, but the supplementary licence may authorise only the use of the special designation authorised by the dealer's licence[22].

A licence may authorise the use of a special designation only in relation to milk sold at or from the premises named in it and, in the case of milk sold by retail, only in relation to milk so sold within the area of the authority granting the licence[23]. The use of a special designation in relation to milk sold by retail may be authorised only by a dealer's licence[24].

1 Milk (Special Designations) (Scotland) Order 1988, SI 1988/2191, art 3(1).
2 Milk (Special Designations) (Scotland) Order 1980, SI 1980/1866, art 7(1)(a), (b) (revoked).
3 The milk must be pasteurised in accordance with the provisions of the Milk (Special Designations) (Scotland) Order 1988, Sch 2.
4 Ibid, art 2(1). For the form of licence, see Sch 8, Form A.
5 See ibid, art 9(1), Schs 1, 2.
6 The milk must be sterilised in accordance with the provisions of ibid, Sch 3.
7 Ibid, art 2(1). For the form of licence, see Sch 8, Form A.
8 See ibid, art 9(2), Schs 1, 3.
9 The milk must be heat treated in accordance with the provisions of ibid, Sch 4.
10 Ibid, art 2(1). For the form of licence, see Sch 8, Form B.
11 See ibid, art 9(3), Schs 1, 4.
12 'Dealer' means a person who carries on a business which consists of or comprises the selling of milk, but not the holder of a pasteuriser's or steriliser's licence, or a licence to treat milk by the ultra high temperature method, who sells the milk pasteurised, sterilised or heat treated by him by wholesale only, and only at or from the premises where the milk is pasteurised, sterilised or heat treated, and who sells no other milk: ibid, art 2(1).
13 Ibid, art 2(1). For the forms of licence, see Sch 8, Forms C, D. A dealer's or dealer's supplementary licence may include a condition that the special designation be used only in relation to milk received by the dealer in retail containers and sold by him in those containers with unbroken caps or fastenings: art 10.
14 'Local authority' means an islands or district council: ibid, art 2(1).
15 Ibid, art 2(1). For the form of licence, see Sch 8, Form E. See also note 13 above.
16 Ibid, art 4(2).
17 Ibid, art 4(1)(a).
18 Ibid, art 4(1)(b).
19 Ibid, art 4(1)(c). The grant, or application for the grant, of such a licence does not authorise the authority to exercise outwith its area any powers conferred on it by any milk and dairies legislation: art 18.
20 Ibid, art 3(2).
21 Ibid, art 6.
22 Ibid, art 5.
23 Ibid, art 3(3).
24 Ibid, art 3(4).

460. Duration of licences. A licence to use a special designation remains in force until the expiry of the period of five years in which it comes or came into force, being one of the periods of five calendar years ending on 31 December 1990 and in any fifth succeeding year[1], save that a dealer's supplementary licence remains in force for such period as the dealer's licence on which it depends remains in force[2]. Where an application for the renewal of a licence is not determined before the date on which the existing licence expires, that licence generally remains in force until the application is determined[3].

1 Milk (Special Designations) (Scotland) Order 1988, SI 1988/2191, art 7(1).
2 Ibid, art 8.
3 Ibid, art 7(2). However, if the renewal application is refused, the existing licence remains in force pending any appeal: see art 7(2) proviso.

461. Suspension, revocation and refusal of renewal of licence. A licence to use a special designation, other than one held by a retailer for a specified area, may be suspended or revoked or the grant of a licence by way of renewal of an existing licence may be refused by the local authority or, on appeal, by the Secretary of State on the ground of a breach of a condition proved to the satisfaction of the one or the other, as the case may be, to have been committed by the holder[1]. A licence may also be suspended or revoked on the ground that the holder has been convicted of an offence under any milk and dairies legislation and is thus unsuitable to hold a licence[2].

A licence held by a retailer for a specified area may be revoked or renewal may be refused by the local authority or, on appeal, the Secretary of State if the holder has been convicted of an offence arising from a breach of certain conditions of the licence[3] or if such a breach has taken place within certain periods[4]. Such a licence may also be suspended on the ground of a breach of a condition of it[5].

Any breach upon which action may be taken as aforesaid must, where the holder of the licence is a retailer for a specified area, have been proved by the finding of a tribunal or, in any other case, to the satisfaction of the local authority or the Secretary of State as the case may be[6]. The holder of a licence who is alleged to be in breach of a condition of it has available to him certain grounds upon which he can show that suspension, revocation or refusal of renewal of the licence should not be decided on[7].

1 Milk (Special Designations) (Scotland) Order 1988, SI 1988/2191, art 11(a).
2 Ibid, art 11(b).
3 Ie conditions to which the Milk (Special Designations) Act 1949 (c 34), s 8, applies: see para 457 above.
4 Milk (Special Designations) (Scotland) Order 1988, art 12(1).
5 See ibid, art 12(2).
6 See ibid, art 12(3). As to the tribunal, see art 15, Sch 7, and para 463 below.
7 See ibid, art 13.

462. Procedure for suspension, revocation or refusal of licence. Where a local authority proposes to suspend, revoke or refuse to grant or renew a licence, the holder or applicant must be informed of the proposal, with the authority's reasons[1], and within twenty-one days of being so informed he may make written representations and may require to be heard by the appropriate committee of the authority[2]. At any hearing, which must be in public, he may be heard himself or by counsel, solicitor or other representative[3]. In other respects the procedure is as the committee may determine[4].

If the authority duly decides to suspend or revoke the licence or to refuse it, it must notify the holder or applicant of its decision and advise him of his right to appeal to the Secretary of State[5]. A decision to suspend or revoke a licence does not have effect until twenty-one days after the holder has received this notification, and, if he appeals, until the determination of the appeal[6].

1 Milk (Special Designations) (Scotland) Order 1988, SI 1988/2191, art 14(1)(a).
2 Ibid, art 14(1)(b).
3 Ibid, art 14(1)(c).
4 Ibid, art 14(1)(d).
5 Ibid, art 14(2).
6 Ibid, art 14(3).

463. Appeal against suspension, revocation or refusal of licence. The holder of a licence which has been suspended or revoked or an applicant to whom a local authority has refused to grant or renew a licence may, within twenty-one days of receiving notification of the authority's decision, appeal to the Secretary of State[1]. The Secretary of State must notify the appellant that he may within twenty-one days make written representations to him and, where the issue is the suspension or revocation of a licence held by a retailer for a specified area or the refusal to renew such a licence, that he may within that period request the Secretary of State to refer the matter to a tribunal[2].

Where such a request is made the Secretary of State must refer the matter to a tribunal[3] of three members, all appointed by him, being a neutral chairman and persons respectively representative of the milk distributive trade and of the consumers' interest[4]. The Secretary of State informs the chairman of the reference and the appellant's name and address, and sends him and the other members copies of the necessary papers[5]. The chairman fixes a public hearing[6] at which the appellant may be heard by himself or by counsel, solicitor or other representative and the local authority may be represented by any person instructed in that behalf[7]. Each side may address the tribunal and call and cross-examine witnesses[8], and the tribunal may visit and inspect any premises[9].

The tribunal's decision, which may be by a majority, is reported in writing to the Secretary of State, with reasons[10]. On receiving the report the Secretary of State sends copies to the appellant and the local authority, and must consider the report before determining the appeal[11]. His decision, which must be given in writing, with reasons, is final[12]. The tribunal is subject to the supervision of the Scottish Committee of the Council on Tribunals[13].

1 See the Milk (Special Designations) (Scotland) Order 1988, SI 1988/2191, art 15(1). The appellant may at any time send notice of withdrawal of the appeal to the Secretary of State: art 15(4).
2 Ibid, art 15(2)(a).
3 Ibid, art 15(2)(b).
4 Ibid, art 15(5), Sch 7, para 1. As to the chairman's tenure of office, see Sch 7, para 2.
5 Ibid, Sch 7, para 3.
6 Ibid, Sch 7, paras 4, 13.
7 Ibid, Sch 7, para 5.
8 Ibid, Sch 7, para 6.
9 Ibid, Sch 7, para 7.
10 Ibid, Sch 7, paras 8, 11, 12.
11 Ibid, art 15(1)(c).
12 Ibid, art 15(3).
13 Tribunals and Inquiries Act 1971 (c 62), ss 1, 4, Sch 1, Pt II, para 40.

464. Sampling. One of the conditions of a licence to use a special designation is that any person duly authorised by the Secretary of State or local authority may take samples of milk free of charge[1]. Further, raw milk may not be accepted for heat treatment unless samples have been taken and have satisfied certain tests[2], and criteria are laid down for the results of tests to which samples are submitted[3]. Provision is made as to the taking, identification and transportation of samples[4], and as to the various tests to be carried out on them[5].

1 See the Milk (Special Designations) (Scotland) Order 1988, SI 1988/2191, art 9(1)–(3), Sch 1, para 7.
2 Ibid, Sch 1, paras 12, 13.
3 Ibid, Sch 2, Pt I, para 7; Sch 3, Pt I, para 7; Sch 4, Pt I, para 6.
4 See ibid, art 16, Sch 5.
5 See ibid, art 16, Sch 6.

465. Designated milk brought from elsewhere in the United Kingdom. The use in relation to milk of a designation whose use is authorised in England and Wales authorises the use in Scotland of a corresponding special designation in relation to that milk if the milk is brought into Scotland from England and Wales[1]. Similar provisions apply to milk brought into Scotland from Northern Ireland[2].

1 Milk (Special Designations) (Scotland) Order 1988, SI 1988/2191, art 17(1).
2 Ibid, art 17(2).

466. Channel Islands and South Devon milk. Milk of the Channel Islands breeds (Jersey and Guernsey) and the South Devon breed is subject to special regulations about composition, description, labelling, offences, penalties and other matters[1].

1 Milk and Dairies (Channel Islands and South Devon Milk) (Scotland) Regulations 1967, SI 1967/81 (amended by SI 1985/1068).

467. Price of milk. The Secretary of State had power to make orders providing for controlled maximum prices to be charged for liquid milk[1]. In exercise of that power he made orders providing maximum prices for raw milk sold for heat treatment and resale for human consumption, and for pasteurised milk for human consumption[2], but the orders have been revoked[3] and the power has expired[4].

1 See the Emergency Laws (Re-enactments and Repeals) Act 1964 (c 60), s 6, which was continued in force by a succession of orders, of which the latest (the Milk (Extension of Period of Control of Maximum Prices) Order 1979, SI 1979/1602) continued the power until the end of 1984.
2 Milk Prices (Scotland) Order 1981, SI 1981/1261 (amended by SI 1981/1852, SI 1982/456 and SI 1983/491).
3 Milk Prices (Scotland) Amendment Order 1983, SI 1983/491, revoking the orders on 31 December 1983.
4 See note 1 above.

(4) LABELLING OF MILK

468. Labelling of milk containers. Every container in which milk[1] is sold[2] to the ultimate consumer[3] or to a catering establishment[4] must be marked or labelled with the name of the milk[5], an indication of minimum durability[6], the net quantity of the milk[7], the name or business name of the packer and the address of the premises where the milk was put into the container (whether in the United Kingdom or elsewhere in the European Community)[8], and particulars of the place of origin or provenance of the milk if failure to give these particulars might mislead a purchaser[9].

1 'Milk' includes whole milk and separated milk produced from cows or other animals and intended for human consumption, but not cream, dried milk, condensed or evaporated milk or buttermilk: Milk Labelling (Scotland) Regulations 1983, SI 1983/938, reg 2(1). These regulations, made under the Food and Drugs (Scotland) Act 1956, s 56A (see para 437 above), implement EC Council Directive 77/94 (OJ L26, 31.1.77, p 55) and EC Council Directive 79/112 (OJ L33, 8.2.79, p 1).
2 'Sold' includes offered or exposed for sale and had in possession for sale: Milk Labelling (Scotland) Regulations 1983, reg 2(1).
3 'Ultimate consumer' means any person who buys otherwise than for the purpose of resale, or of a catering establishment, or of a manufacturing business: ibid, reg 2(1).
4 'Catering establishment' means a restaurant, canteen, club, public house, school, hospital or other establishment (including a vehicle or stall) where, in the course of a business, food is prepared for delivery to the ultimate consumer for immediate consumption: ibid, reg 2(1).
5 Ibid, reg 4(a). For the names which may be given see reg 5.
6 Ibid, reg 4(b), which does not apply to containers of milk prepacked for direct sale and bottles intended for re-use: reg 3(2), (3). 'Milk prepacked for direct sale' means milk put into containers by a milk producer for sale to the ultimate consumer on the premises where the milk is produced or from a vehicle used by him: reg 2(1).
7 Ibid, reg 4(c).

8 Ibid, reg 4(d).
9 Ibid, reg 4(e), which does not apply to containers of milk prepacked for direct sale: reg 3(2).

469. Marks and labels. Provision is made as to the location of marks and labels on milk containers[1] and the manner of marking and labelling[2]. There are special provisions about the marking and labelling of bulk containers in which milk is sold to catering establishments[3] and about the placing of emphasis on particular qualities of milk[4]. The marking, labelling, presentation and advertising of milk about its characteristics and other properties and claims about its nutritional value are also regulated[5].

1 Milk Labelling (Scotland) Regulation 1983, SI 1983/938, reg 7.
2 Ibid, reg 8.
3 Ibid, reg 9. For the meaning of 'catering establishment', see para 468, note 4, above.
4 Ibid, reg 10.
5 Ibid, reg 11, Schedule.

470. Offences and proceedings. A person commits an offence if he sells any milk which is not properly marked or labelled[1], or if he sells any milk whose marking, labelling or presentation for sale contravenes the appropriate regulation[2] or advertises any milk in contravention of that regulation[3]. An offender is liable on summary conviction to a fine not exceeding £2,000, or on indictment to a fine or imprisonment for a term not exceeding one year, or both[4]. It is, however, a defence for him to prove that before offering or advertising the milk he took all reasonable steps to ensure compliance with the requirements[5]. Certain provisions of the Food and Drugs (Scotland) Act 1956[6] apply to proceedings for such an offence[7]. Each district and islands council must enforce and execute within its area the regulations as to milk labelling[8].

1 Ie in accordance with the Milk Labelling (Scotland) Regulations 1983, SI 1983/938, regs 4–10: see paras 468, 469, above.
2 Ie ibid, reg 11: see para 469 above.
3 Ibid, reg 12(1).
4 Ibid, reg 12(2) (substituted by SI 1985/1068).
5 Ibid, reg 14.
6 Ie the Food and Drugs (Scotland) Act 1956 (c 30), ss 41(2), (5), 42(1)–(3), 44 and 47: see paras 423–425, 427, above.
7 Milk Labelling (Scotland) Regulations 1983, reg 15.
8 Ibid, reg 13.

471. Labelling and cap colouring of milk bottles. Bottles closed and fastened by a cap of aluminium foil[1] and containing cow's milk[2] must be labelled with a special designation[3] unless the bottle bears the words 'Undesignated Milk'[4]. Milk contained in a bottle must, if the bottle is labelled with a milk description, be so labelled in embossed lettering or in lettering of a colour specified in relation to that description of milk or partly in embossed lettering and partly in lettering of such a colour, on a cap of a specified colour[5].

1 Milk Bottles (Labelling and Cap Colour) (Scotland) Order 1976, SI 1976/875, art 2(1) ('bottle'). The order was made under the Milk and Dairies (Scotland) Act 1914 (c 46), s 12(2) (amended by the Reorganisation of Offices (Scotland) Act 1939 (c 20), s 5, Schedule), under which the Secretary of State may make orders relating inter alia to the labelling or distinctive marking of receptacles of milk for sale for human consumption.
2 'Milk' means cow's milk for sale for human consumption, but not cream, or skimmed, separated, dried, condensed or evaporated milk or buttermilk: Milk Bottles (Labelling and Cap Colour) (Scotland) Order 1976, art 2(1).
3 As to special designations, see paras 452 ff above.
4 Milk Bottles (Labelling and Cap Colour) (Scotland) Order 1976, art 3.

5 Ibid, art 4. For the colour of lettering and the cap colour for milk of each different description, see Schedule.

(5) DRINKING MILK

472. Sale and composition of drinking milk. Only certain categories of milk[1] may be sold as drinking milk for human consumption in Scotland. No person may deliver, on or in pursuance of any such sale, milk not included in any of these categories[2]. Any alteration in the composition of drinking milk except as specified in relation to the fat content of skimmed and semi-skimmed milk is prohibited[3], and no person may sell or offer or expose for sale any drinking milk the composition of which has been altered in contravention of this requirement[4].

1 These categories are (1) raw milk; (2) non-standardised whole milk produced in the United Kingdom; (3) standardised whole milk imported during any milk year (which runs from 1 April to 31 March) from another member state of the European Community and having a fat content of not less than the guideline figure fixed for that year or any part of that year by the EC Council in accordance with EC Council Regulation 1411/71 (OJ L148, 1.7.71, p 74 (S Edn 1971 (II) p 412)), art 3(7) (added by EC Council Regulation 566/76 (OJ L67, 14.3.76, p 23); (4) semi-skimmed milk; and (5) skimmed milk: Drinking Milk (Scotland) Regulations 1976, SI 1976/1888, reg 4(a)–(e), read with art 2(1). The following definitions (applied by art 2(1)) appear in EC Council Regulation 1411/71, art 3(1) (amended by EC Council Regulation 566/76):
  'milk' means the milk-yield of one or more cows;
  'drinking milk' means the following products for delivery as such to the consumer;
  'raw milk' means milk which has not been heated or subjected to treatment having the same effect;
  'whole milk' means milk which has been subjected to at least one heat treatment or an authorised treatment of equivalent effect by a milk processor, and with respect to fat content meets one of the following requirements: (a) standardised whole milk: milk with a fat content of at least 3.5 per cent; (b) non-standardised whole milk: milk with a fat content that has not been altered since the milking stage either by the addition or separation of milk fats or by mixture with milk, the natural fat content of which has been altered (however, the fat content may not be less than 3 per cent);
  'semi-skimmed milk' means milk which has been subject to at least one heat treatment or an authorised treatment of equivalent effect by a milk processor and whose fat content has been brought to at least 1.5 per cent and at most 1.8 per cent;
  'skimmed milk' means milk which has been so subject and whose fat content has been brought to not more than 0.3 per cent.
2 Drinking Milk (Scotland) Regulations 1976, reg 4.
3 Ibid, reg 5(1).
4 Ibid, reg 5(2).

473. Labelling, records and enforcement. Any container in which standardised whole milk is sold or offered or exposed for sale must be properly labelled[1]. Milk purveyors must keep, retain and produce to an authorised officer or an islands or district council accurate records of his purchases and sales of standardised whole milk[2]. It is an offence to contravene these requirements and those relating to the sale and composition of drinking milk[3], and appropriate provisions of the Food and Drugs (Scotland) Act 1956 are applied to proceedings for such offences[4]. Each district and islands council must enforce and execute within its area the provisions as to drinking milk[5] and must assist other local authorities in this respect[6].

1 Drinking Milk (Scotland) Regulations 1976, SI 1976/1888, reg 6.
2 Ibid, reg 7.
3 Ibid, reg 8(1), (2).

4 Drinking Milk (Scotland) Regulations 1976, reg 9. The provisions are those referred to in para 470, note 6, above.
5 Ibid, reg 8(3).
6 Ibid, reg 8(4).

(6) CREAM

474. Meaning of 'cream'. The Food and Drugs (Scotland) Act 1956 defines 'cream' as that part of milk rich in fat which has been separated by skimming or otherwise[1], but that Act defines 'milk' as including cream[1], though it is silent as to the meaning of 'skimming'. While 'milk' includes cream for the purposes of the 1956 Act, in other contexts it does not do so — for example in the Milk (Special Designations) Act 1949 and regulations made under it[2].

The Cream (Scotland) Regulations 1970 contain no definition of 'milk', and the word must thus have there the same meaning as it has in the 1956 Act under which the regulations are made. The 1970 regulations, however, define such derivative substances as 'clotted cream', 'pasteurised cream', 'sterilised cream', 'ultra heat-treated cream' and 'untreated cream'[3]. In those regulations 'cream' is defined in the same terms as in the 1956 Act save that it must be intended for sale for human consumption[3].

1 Food and Drugs (Scotland) Act 1956 (c 30), s 58(1).
2 Milk (Special Designations) Act 1949 (c 34), s 14(1); Milk (Special Designations) (Scotland) Order 1988, SI 1988/2191, art 2(1).
3 Cream (Scotland) Regulations 1970, SI 1970/1191, reg 2(1).

475. Description and composition of cream. Any cream sold, consigned or delivered to any place within the United Kingdom must bear one of the following descriptions: 'cream', 'clotted cream', 'single cream', 'double cream', 'whipping cream', 'whipped cream', 'half cream' and 'sterilised half cream'[1]. The composition of each of these descriptions of cream is prescribed[2]. If any cream (other than clotted cream) is pasteurised, ultra heat treated or untreated cream, the specified description must be appropriately qualified[3], and if the cream is derived from milk other than cow's milk, the description must name the kind of animal from which the milk came[4]. It is an offence to sell, consign or deliver cream which does not comply with these requirements[5].

1 Cream (Scotland) Regulations 1970, SI 1970/1191, regs 3(a), 4(1).
2 Ibid, reg 4(1).
3 Ibid, reg 4(2).
4 Ibid, reg 4(3).
5 Ibid, reg 4(5).

476. Ingredients and flavouring in cream. Cream sold, consigned or delivered in the United Kingdom must not contain any flavouring or added ingredient, whether or not the ingredient is a constituent of milk[1], although there are numerous exceptions which apply to specific descriptions of cream[2], and others which apply to cream sold, consigned or delivered to a manufacturer or caterer for the purposes of his business as such[3]. No product derived from milk and resembling cream is to be deemed not to be cream simply because it has a flavouring or other added ingredient, or any ingredient in excess of the permitted amount[4]. Cream which is sold under any permitted description must comply with the compositional requirements for that description[5], and when a person sells cream to a purchaser who requests a specified description of cream he is deemed to sell cream of that kind[6].

1 Cream (Scotland) Regulations 1970, SI 1970/1191, regs 3(a), 5(1).
2 Ibid, reg 5(1) proviso.
3 Ibid, reg 5(2).
4 Ibid, reg 5(3).
5 Ibid, reg 7(1).
6 Ibid, reg 7(2).

477. Cream substitutes. No person may sell, offer or expose for sale for human consumption any substance which resembles cream in appearance, but is not cream, or any article of food containing such a substance, under a description or designation which includes the word 'cream' unless the description or designation identifies the substance as reconstituted or imitation cream or as not being for use as, or as a substitute for, cream[2].

1 Food and Drugs (Scotland) Act 1956 (c 30), s 18(1). A person who contravenes this provision is guilty of an offence under the Act: s 18(5). For penalties, see para 430 above.
2 Ibid, s 18(2). 'Reconstituted cream' and 'imitation cream' are defined in s 18(3).

478. Labelling of cream. A person must not sell any food which bears a label, or display any food with a ticket, or publish any advertisement, which includes the word 'cream' or any derivative thereof unless (1) the food is cream which complies with the compositional requirements for that description of cream, or (2) the word is used in such a context as to make it clear that the cream is an ingredient only, and complies with those compositional requirements, or (3) the word is used in such a context as to make it clear that the food is not, or does not contain, cream[1]. The word 'creamed' may, however, be used in relation to food unconnected with or not derived from milk[2]. Cream which contains sugar may not be sold, consigned or delivered to a manufacturer or caterer for the purposes of his business as such unless its presence is made clear, on the label borne on or securely attached to the container of such cream, in the manner prescribed, or is made clear on an associated invoice[3]. There are further detailed provisions about the sale by retail of cream containing certain substances and the sale by retail of cream dispensed from an aerosol container or cream described as 'whipped cream' unless information about the substances it contains appear on an attached ticket[4]. The required description must appear clearly, legibly and conspicuously on any label, ticket or notice borne on the container of or displayed on or near to the cream[5].

1 Cream (Scotland) Regulations 1970, SI 1970/1191, reg 8(a), (b), (i)–(iii).
2 Ibid, reg 8 proviso.
3 Ibid, reg 9(1).
4 Ibid, reg 9(2).
5 Ibid, reg 11 (substituted by the Food Labelling (Scotland) Regulations 1981, SI 1981/137, reg 43, Sch 7, para 11 (revoked)).

479. Heat treatment of cream. Cream intended for human consumption and not intended for export[1] may not be sold unless either it has been heat-treated by pasteurisation, sterilisation or the ultra high temperature method in accordance with prescribed requirements or the seller holds a certificate from the Secretary of State permitting him to sell untreated cream[2]. There are also specific provisions as to the sampling of cream for testing purposes[3], and reciprocal provisions for cream from England and Wales or Northern Ireland[4]. Cream processors must keep and retain accurate records of their milk purchases and cream purchases and sales[5].

1 Cream (Heat Treatment) (Scotland) Regulations 1983, SI 1983/1515, reg 3.

2 Ibid, reg 4(1) (amended by SI 1985/1222). As to the requirements, see Sch 1 (amended by SI 1986/789) and Sch 2, and as to such certificates, see reg 4A (added by SI 1985/1222).
3 Ibid, reg 4(2), Sch 3 (amended by SI 1985/1222 and SI 1986/789).
4 Ibid, reg 5 (amended by SI 1986/789).
5 Ibid, reg 6.

(7) SKIMMED MILK

480. Skimmed milk with non-milk fat. The sale, labelling and advertisement of skimmed milk with non-milk fat, condensed skimmed milk with non-milk fat and dried skimmed milk with non-milk fat are subject to conditions and restrictions imposed by regulations[1]. All three of these substances are referred to in the regulations as 'specified food', and all three are there defined, together with condensed milk, dried milk, skimmed milk and other milk derivatives[2]. These three substances have the appearance of milk, condensed milk or dried milk and contain skimmed milk with non-milk fat. The regulations are designed to regulate the uses to which they are put by ensuring that the labels given with, or displayed on any container which encloses any of them does not mislead as to their composition. In particular they make clear that all, except those specifically excepted[3], are unfit for use for babies[4].

1 See the Skimmed Milk with Non-Milk Fat (Scotland) Regulations 1960, SI 1960/2437, regs 3–5.
2 Ibid, reg 2(1).
3 Ibid, reg 3(1), Sch 2 (substituted by SI 1976/294 and amended by SI 1981/1319. These amendments are designed to keep pace with improvements that have been made in the composition and preparation of substances to which the regulations apply.
4 Ibid, reg 3(1), Sch 1, Pt I.

481. Sale of specified food. No person may sell by retail[1] any 'specified food'[2] except in a container bearing a prescribed label[3]. If the container is wrapped in paper or some other wrapper the label must be visible through the wrapper[4]. These provisions do not apply to sale for immediate consumption of the food at the seller's premises or at a stall or mobile refreshment vehicle[5]. No person may give or display a label with any specified food or with any beverage (of which skimmed milk, condensed skimmed milk or dried skimmed milk is an ingredient) sold by him any label which bears any description of food or beverage or any ingredient or constituent thereof or any brand or descriptive name or pictorial device suggestive of milk or of anything connected with the dairy interest[6], although there are exceptions from this provision[7]. An advertisement for a specified food must use the appropriate description of the food clearly and prominently, although some qualifications of those descriptions are permitted[8], and again there are exceptions[9].

It is an offence to fail to comply with any of these provisions, and penalties are laid down[10]. Certain grounds of defence are available in the case of advertisements[11].

1 'Sale by retail' means any sale to a person buying otherwise than for the purposes of resale, but does not include a sale to a manufacturer for the purposes of his business: Skimmed Milk with Non-Milk Fat (Scotland) Regulations 1960, SI 1960/2437, reg 3(2) (amended by the Food Labelling (Scotland) Regulations 1981, SI 1981/137, reg 43, Sch 7, para 1 (repealed)).
2 For the meaning of 'specified food', see para 480 above.
3 Skimmed Milk with Non-Milk Fat (Scotland) Regulations 1960, reg 3(1)(a), Sch 1, Pt I.
4 Ibid, reg 3(1)(b).
5 Ibid, reg 3(3).
6 Ibid, reg 4.
7 See ibid, reg 6.

8 Ibid, reg 5(1), Sch 1, Pt II.
9 See ibid, reg 6.
10 See ibid, reg 7.
11 See ibid, reg 5(3), (4).

482. Semi-skimmed and skimmed milk. Except where milk is sold to a milk processor[1] for heat treatment, no person may sell any semi-skimmed or skimmed milk unless specific requirements as to heat treatment are satisfied[2]. Such milk brought into Scotland from England or Wales or Northern Ireland does not require to satisfy these requirements if it complies with the requirements of corresponding local regulations[3]. Failure to comply with these provisions is an offence for which penalties are laid down[4].

> 1 'Milk processor' means a person who pasteurises or sterilises milk or treats it by the ultra high temperature method, and 'milk' means cows' milk intended for sale for human consumption, but not such milk intended for manufacture into products for sale for human consumption: Milk and Dairies (Semi-skimmed and Skimmed Milk) (Heat Treatment) (Scotland) Regulations 1988, SI 1988/2190, reg 2(1). These regulations implement EC Council Directive 85/397 (OJ L226, 24.8.85, p 13) on health and animal health problems affecting intra-Community trade in heat-treated milk.
> 2 Milk and Dairies (Semi-skimmed and Skimmed Milk) (Heat Treatment) (Scotland) Regulations 1988, reg 3(1), (4). These requirements are (1) the general requirements of Sch 1 as to heat treatment (which apply even where the sale is to a milk processor: reg 3(4)); (2) the applicable special requirements of Sch 2, Pts I–III, as to pasteurisation, sterilisation or treatment by the ultra-high temperature method respectively; (3) the requirements of Sch 3 as to sampling; and (4) the applicable requirements of Sch 4 as to the testing of samples: reg 3(2).
> 3 Ibid, reg 3(3).
> 4 Ibid, reg 5.

(8) CONDENSED MILK AND DRIED MILK

483. Definitions. 'Condensed milk' means milk, partly skimmed milk or skimmed milk or any combination thereof, whether with or without the addition of cream, dried milk or sucrose, which has been concentrated by the partial removal of water, but does not include dried milk[1]. 'Dried milk' has the same meaning, with the exception that the concentrate takes the form of powder, granule or solid by the total removal of water[2].

'Condensed milk product' and 'dried milk product' mean any food comprising condensed milk or, as the case may be, dried milk, which has been subjected to prescribed treatment or which has a prescribed content, but not any product which contains such a food as an ingredient and which is sold, consigned or delivered as a compound product; and for each such condensed milk product or dried milk product a 'reserved description' is prescribed, such as 'evaporated milk' or 'unsweetened condensed milk'[3].

> 1 Condensed Milk and Dried Milk (Scotland) Regulations 1977, SI 1977/1027, reg 2(1). 'Milk' means cows' milk: reg 2(1). These regulations (as amended) implement EC Council Directive 76/118 (OJ L24, 30.1.76, p 49) on the approximation of laws relating to dehydrated preserved milk for human consumption (amended by EC Council Directive 83/635 (OJ L357, 21.12.83, p 37)), EC Commission Directive 79/1067 (OJ L327, 24.12.79, p 29), and EC Commission Directive 87/524 (OJ L306, 28.10.87, p 24).
> 2 Condensed Milk and Dried Milk (Scotland) Regulations 1977, reg 2(1).
> 3 See ibid, reg 2(1) (amended by SI 1982/1209), Sch 1 (substituted by SI 1982/1209).

484. General restrictions on the use of reserved descriptions. No person may give with any food sold by him any label, or display with food offered or exposed by him for sale any ticket or notice, or publish any advertisement for food, which bears a reserved description[1] unless:

(1) the food is a condensed milk product or dried milk product to which the description relates, or

(2) the description is so used as to indicate that the substance to which it relates is an ingredient in the food, or

(3) the description is so used as to indicate that the food is not a condensed milk product or a dried milk product and does not contain one[2].

1 As to reserved descriptions, see para 483 above.
2 Condensed Milk and Dried Milk (Scotland) Regulations 1977, SI 1977/1027, reg 4.

485. Labelling of condensed milk products and dried milk products. Without prejudice to the general provisions as to the labelling of food[1], no condensed milk product or dried milk product may be sold by retail or consigned or delivered pursuant to a sale by retail in a container unless the container is correctly marked or labelled with a reserved description of the product[2] and certain other particulars depending on the nature of the product, including, where appropriate, a warning that it is not to be used for babies except under medical advice[3].

No such product may be sold otherwise than by retail or consigned or delivered pursuant to a sale otherwise than by retail in a container unless the container is correctly marked or labelled with a reserved description; the name or business name and address of the manufacturer or packer or of a seller established within the European Community; the country of origin if outside the Community; the date of manufacture or a batch marking; and, where appropriate, a declaration that it is for use in vending machines only[4].

These provisions do not apply to condensed milk or dried milk specially prepared for infant feeding and labelled as such[5].

1 For the Food Labelling (Scotland) Regulations 1984, SI 1984/1519, see paras 383 ff above.
2 As to reserved descriptions, see para 483 above. This description is the name prescribed by law for that product for the purposes of ibid, reg 7, for which see para 384 above: Condensed Milk and Dried Milk (Scotland) Regulations 1977, SI 1977/1027, reg 5(1)(a) (substituted by SI 1987/26).
3 Ibid, reg 5(1)(b)–(h) (as so substituted). When the product is packed in units of less than 20 grammes each within an outer package, the particulars may appear on the outer package only: reg 5(2) (as so substituted). As to the manner of marking or labelling, and the indication of minimum durability, see reg 6 (as so substituted).
4 Ibid, reg 5A (added by SI 1987/26). As to the manner of marking or labelling, see reg 6A (as so added).
5 Ibid, reg 3(2).

486. Sale, preparation and ingredients. Dried or condensed milk or liquid reconstituted therefrom may not be added to milk intended for human consumption[1], and any liquid in the making of which dried or condensed milk has been used may not be sold, offered or exposed for sale as milk[2].

No person may sell by retail, or consign or deliver pursuant to a sale by retail, any condensed milk other than a condensed milk product or any dried milk other than a dried milk product[3]; and no person may use as an ingredient in the preparation of any such product any milk, partly skimmed milk, skimmed milk, cream or dried milk, or any combination thereof, which has not been subject to heat treatment at least equivalent to pasteurisation, unless the product is itself subject to such heat treatment during its preparation[4]. Only specified ingredients may be added to such products[5]. These provisions do not apply to condensed milk or dried milk specially prepared for infant feeding and labelled as such[6]. Provision is made for the methods of sampling for the analysis of these products[7]. No condensed milk or dried milk sold, consigned, delivered or imported into Scotland for human consumption may have in it or on it any added colouring matter[8].

1 Food and Drugs (Scotland) Act 1956 (c 30), s 17(1)(a).
2 Ibid, s 17(2). Contravention of s 17 is an offence against the Act: s 17(3). For penalties, see para 430 above.
3 Condensed Milk and Dried Milk (Scotland) Regulations 1977, SI 1977/1027, reg 7.
4 Ibid, reg 8. As to the test for verifying whether reg 8 is satisfied, see reg 8 (amended by SI 1982/1209), and EC Commission Directive 79/1067 (OJ L327, 24.12.79, p 29), Annex II, methods 7, 8.
5 Condensed Milk and Dried Milk (Scotland) Regulations 1977, reg 9.
6 Ibid, reg 3(2).
7 Ibid, reg 9A (added by SI 1989/1975).
8 Colouring Matter in Food (Scotland) Regulations 1973, SI 1973/1310, reg 5(2) (substituted by SI 1987/1985).

487. Offences, penalties and exemptions. Any person who contravenes or fails to comply with any provision of the regulations relating to condensed milk and dried milk is guilty of an offence, for which penalties are prescribed[1]. Certain grounds of defence are made available to accused persons[2]. The regulations are enforceable by islands and district councils[3]. Certain provisions of the Food and Drugs (Scotland) Act 1956 are applied for the purposes of the regulations[4], some provisions of which do not apply to certain categories of condensed and dried milk[5].

1 Condensed Milk and Dried Milk (Scotland) Regulations 1977, SI 1977/1027, reg 10 (substituted by SI 1985/1068).
2 See ibid, reg 12.
3 Ibid, reg 11 (amended by SI 1983/270).
4 Condensed Milk and Dried Milk (Scotland) Regulations 1977, reg 13, applying the Food and Drugs (Scotland) Act 1956 (c 30), ss 41(2), (4), (5), 42(1)–(3), 44, 46(2) and 47, for which see paras 423–427 above.
5 Condensed Milk and Dried Milk (Scotland) Regulations 1977, reg 3.

(9) DAIRIES

488. Meaning of 'dairy'. The Milk and Dairies (Scotland) Act 1914 is principally concerned with the prevention of the transmission of bovine diseases to human beings, and with this objective in view it contains provisions about the inspection of dairies[1] and the making of dairy byelaws[2]. In that Act 'dairy' is defined as including any creamery, farm, farmhouse, cowshed, byre, milk store, milk shop or other premises from which milk[3] is sold or supplied for sale or in which it is kept for purposes of sale, or which are used for the making of butter, cheese or other milk products for human consumption for purposes of sale, but not as including premises from which a person sells milk only in small quantities and for their own consumption to persons in his employment or to neighbours[4]. This definition is, of course, musch wider than the dictionary definition of 'dairy'. A slightly less wide definition appears in the Food and Drugs (Scotland) Act 1956, in which 'dairy' includes any farm, byre, milk store, milk shop, creamery or other premises from which milk[5] is supplied on or for sale, or in which milk is kept or used for purposes of sale[6].

1 See paras 489 ff below.
2 See paras 492 ff below.
3 For the meaning of 'milk' in the Milk and Dairies (Scotland) Act 1914 (c 46), see para 443 above.

4 Ibid, s 2.
5 For the meaning of 'milk' in the Food and Drugs (Scotland) Act 1956 (c 30), see para 443 above.
6 Ibid, s 58(1).

489. Inspection of dairies. The proper officer of a local authority or any officer duly authorised in writing for the purpose must, from time to time and once at least in every year, inspect every dairy in the authority's district and report to the authority whether the dairy is in conformity with the Milk and Dairies (Scotland) Act 1914 and the dairy byelaws[1]. Where milk consigned from one local authority district to another is believed by the proper officer of the receiving district to be impure or likely to cause any infectious disease or other illness, he or a veterinary inspector may inspect the dairy from which the milk is consigned and the cattle there[2]. Where an official of a local authority proposes to inspect any dairy in the district of another local authority he must intimate his intention to the proper officer of that other authority so that, if circumstances permit, the officer or veterinary inspector of that other authority may be present[3].

1 Milk and Dairies (Scotland) Act 1914 (c 46), s 4(1) (amended by the National Health Service (Scotland) Act 1972 (c 58), s 64(2), Sch 7, Pt II, and the Local Government (Scotland) Act 1973 (c 65), s 214(1), Sch 27, Pt I, para 2(1)). For further powers of inspection, see para 444 above.
2 Milk and Dairies (Scotland) Act 1914, s 4(3) (amended by the National Health Service (Scotland) Act 1972, s 64(1), (2), Sch 6, para 61, Sch 7, Pt II, and the Local Government (Scotland) Act 1973, Sch 27, Pt I, para 2(1)).
3 Milk and Dairies (Scotland) Act 1914, s 6 (amended by the National Health Service (Scotland) Act 1972, Sch 6, para 62, Sch 7, Pt II, and the Local Government (Scotland) Act 1973, Sch 27, Pt I, para 2(1)).

490. Reports to the Secretary of State. Proper officers of local authorities, veterinary inspectors and other authorised officers are required to make such returns and special reports to the Secretary of State in such form and at such times as he may require[1].

1 Milk and Dairies (Scotland) Act 1974 (c 46), s 4(5) (amended by the National Health Service (Scotland) Act 1972 (c 58), s 64(2), Sch 7, Pt II, and the Local Government (Scotland) Act 1973 (c 65), s 214(1), Sch 27, Pt I, para 2(1)). As to the Secretary of State, see para 446, note 1, above.

491. Necessary alterations to leased dairy premises. The tenant of premises used by him, with the landlord's consent, as a dairy has power to make alterations or improvements, including the introduction of a sufficient water supply, such as are necessary to enable the premises to continue to be so used[1]. The cost of such alterations or improvements are contributed to by the landlord[1] provided the tenant has given notice in writing of his intention to carry them out, although the landlord may carry them out himself[2]. Questions whether the alterations or improvements are necessary, in what proportions the cost is to be met and any other matters in issue are, in default of agreement, to be settled by arbitration[3].

1 Milk and Dairies (Scotland) Act 1914 (c 46), s 29(1).
2 Ibid, s 29(1) proviso.
3 Ibid, s 29(2).

492. Dairy byelaws. It is the duty of every local authority[1] to make byelaws[2] for its district providing:
(1) for the inspection of cattle in dairies[3];
(2) for prescribing and regulating the structure, lighting, ventilation (including air and floor space), cleansing, drainage, washing and scalding facilities, and water supplies of dairies and their appurtenants[4];

(3) for the prevention of impurities in milk intended for human consumption and for securing the cleanliness of the persons and clothing of those engaged or assisting in the business, and of the milk, cows, dairies, sculleries, boiler houses and all utensils, vehicles and vessels used for the reception, conveyance, storage or sale of milk[5];

(4) for prescribing precautions to be taken by dairymen against infection or contamination[6].

Model dairy byelaws[7] were circulated to all local authorities by the Scottish Board of Health in 1926 and most authorities adopted them without alteration as byelaws for their areas. With the redrawing of local authority areas in 1973 and the transfer of functions relating to milk from burghs and districts of counties to islands and district councils, overlap of areas in which differing sets of byelaws may apply has emerged. No remedial measures have yet been taken to cure the difficulty, and dairies in some areas may thus have more than one set of byelaws to comply with — nominally at least. The byelaws made before local government reorganisation are still in operation. It is understood that most, if not all, local authorities made byelaws in terms the same or similar to the model byelaws, but to ascertain what byelaws are now in force in any authority's area it would be necessary to approach the particular authority direct or to seek information from the Secretary of State about the matter.

1 For the meaning of 'local authority', see para 444, note 3, above.
2 The provisions of the Local Government (Scotland) Act 1973 (c 65), s 202, as to byelaws (see LOCAL GOVERNMENT, vol 14, paras 279 ff) apply to dairy byelaws subject to the modification that the proper officer of the local authority must furnish on application a free copy of proposed byelaws to any dairyman within the district affected: Milk and Dairies (Scotland) Act 1914 (c 46), s 8(2) (amended by the Reorganisation of Offices (Scotland) Act 1939 (c 20), s 5, Schedule); Local Government (Scotland) Act 1973, ss 202(1)(c)(iii), 214(1), Sch 27, Pt I, para 2(1).
3 Milk and Dairies (Scotland) Act 1914, s 8(1)(a). For the meaning of 'dairy', see para 488 above.
4 Ibid, s 8(1)(b).
5 Ibid, s 8(1)(c). For the meaning of 'milk', see para 443 above.
6 Ibid, s 8(1)(d). For the meaning of 'dairyman', see para 444, note 8, above.
7 For an outline of the model byelaws, see para 493 below.

493. Outline of model byelaws. Under the model byelaws[1] the walls of every dairy are to be covered with specified materials in a manner laid down in the byelaws and to a stated height. The floors are to be paved with specified materials and are to be constructed so as to be impervious to liquids. At specified distances from feeding troughs the floor must have an adequate slope (fall) to the channels which are to be formed in a specified manner. There are provisions about lofts above dairies (none are to be permitted in dairies erected after a specified date), and about feeding troughs and stalls. Dairies must be properly lighted and ventilated and each must have specified air space and measurements of passages and channels and heights of walls. Floors and other areas must be cleaned at least every day and refuse removed, and the location and construction of dung steads and of deposits of dung are regulated.

Every dairy must have proper appliances for maintaining general cleanliness and adequate supplies of water and drainage facilities. The walls, ceilings, roofs, flooring and other parts of dairies must be kept clean. There are provisions about milk stores and about the keeping of materials such as bedding for cows, the grooming of cows, and the cleanliness of persons employed in dairies and of their clothing. The cleaning of utensils and equipment is dealt with, as are precautions to be taken against the infection or contamination of milk or milk products.

1 It is not thought profitable to specify any byelaw by the number it bears in the model. The byelaws in operation in any particular area should be consulted as a whole.

494. Registration of dairies and dairymen. Every local authority must keep a register of dairies and dairymen within its district to whom certificates of registration have been granted[1]. A person who carries on the trade of dairyman in any premises[2] without having obtained a certificate of registration in respect of the premises is guilty of an offence[3]. Application for a certificate must be in the form and be accompanied by the information prescribed by the authority[4], and must be lodged with the authority not less than one month before the premises begin to be occupied or used as a dairy[5]. In considering whether or not to grant a certificate the authority must first obtain a report from its proper officer or other officer authorised by it in writing[6], and must consider the report and any representations from interested persons, including any other local authority to whose district milk from the dairy is to be sent for sale[7]. The local authority must intimate its decision to the applicant within one month from the receipt of the application, and if it decides to refuse a certificate, must state its reasons[8]. A certificate may be granted provisionally on prescribed conditions which must be complied with before the certificate can take effect[9]. A certificate in respect of any person or premises may be refused or revoked if the dairyman is or becomes an unsuitable person to carry on the trade of a dairyman or if the premises are or become unsuitable to be used as a dairy[10].

Any person aggrieved by the grant, provisional grant, refusal or revocation of a certificate may appeal to the sheriff, whose decision is final[11]. If a dairyman is convicted of an offence against the Milk and Dairies (Scotland) Act 1914 or any order or byelaw made under it the sheriff, in addition to any penalty, may suspend or cancel his certificate, although the dairyman may appeal against the suspension or cancellation to the Court of Session[12].

1 Milk and Dairies (Scotland) Act 1914 (c 46), s 7(10). For the meaning of 'local authority', see para 444, note 3, above; for the meaning of 'dairy', see para 488 above; and for the meaning of 'dairyman', see para 444, note 8, above. The form of the register is prescribed by the Secretary of State (as to whom see para 446, note 1, above): s 7(10).
2 Where a person sells from a cart, van or other vehicle within a district milk supplied from without the district, the cart etc is deemed to be premises within the district: ibid, s 7(8).
3 Ibid, s 7(1), (9). As to the penalties, see para 447, note 1, above, and the text to note 12 below.
4 Ibid, s 7(2).
5 Ibid, s 7(3).
6 Ibid, s 7(3) (amended by the National Health Service (Scotland) Act 1972 (c 58), s 64(2), Sch 7, Pt II, and the Local Government (Scotland) Act 1973 (c 65), s 214(1), Sch 27, Pt I, para 2(1)).
7 Milk and Dairies (Scotland) Act 1914, s 7(5).
8 Ibid, s 7(3).
9 Ibid, s 7(4).
10 Ibid, s 7(6).
11 Ibid, s 7(7). However, a decision of the sheriff may be appealed to the sheriff principal: s 7(7).
12 Ibid, s 24(2) (amended by the Food and Drugs (Scotland) Act 1956 (c 30), s 60(1), Sch 2).

495. Registration of purveyors of milk. A requirement to keep a register of dairymen has effect as if it were a requirement to keep a register of retail purveyors of milk[1]. Every local authority by which a register of purveyors of milk is kept under or in pursuance of any enactment may, if satisfied that the public health is or is likely to be endangered by any act or default of any person registered or seeking to be registered as a retail purveyor of milk, give him seven days' notice with reasons stated to appear before it and show cause why he should not be refused a certificate or removed from the register, and if cause is not shown the authority may refuse to register him or remove him from the register[2]. An appeal to the sheriff is available within twenty-one days to any person aggrieved by the decision of the authority[3]. If a registered person is convicted of an offence against the Milk and Dairies (Amendment) Act 1922 or any other enactment relating to milk and dairies or any order or regulations made thereunder, the court may, on the application of the local authority, order the removal of his name from the register in addition to any other penalty[4].

Where the registration of a retailer is refused or a retailer is removed from a register, he is not liable to any action for breach of a contract for the purchase of further supplies of milk from a producer if he can prove that the refusal or removal was due to the quality of milk supplied by the producer[5].

1 Milk and Dairies (Amendment) Act 1922 (c 54), s 2(3). As to the registration of dairymen, see para 494 above.
2 Ibid, s 2(1). 'Local authority' means an islands or district council: s 2(4) (added by the Local Government (Scotland) Act 1973 (c 65), s 214(2), Sch 27, Pt II, para 61).
3 Milk and Dairies (Amendment) Act 1922, ss 2(1), 14(c). A decision to refuse registration or remove a person from the register does not have effect until the time for appealing has expired or, if an appeal is brought, until the appeal is determined: s 2(1).
4 Ibid, s 2(2).
5 Ibid, s 12.

3. SLAUGHTER OF ANIMALS

(1) INTRODUCTION

496. Meat produced from animals. The Slaughter of Animals (Scotland) Act 1980 consolidated certain enactments relating to slaughterhouses, knackers' yards and the slaughter of animals in Scotland[1]. The Act does not, of course, deal with anything more than the subjects covered by the Acts which it consolidates[2]. However, the long title of that Act and this part of the Encyclopaedia title are wide enough to include the killing (for whatever purpose) of every variety, species or breed of animal[3], domestic or wild.

The principal purpose of the provisions in the Act is to ensure, however, that the flesh of those animals (virtually all domestic animals) specified in it which is intended to be sold for human consumption is produced in conditions and by methods which will ensure that it will be fit and wholesome for that purpose. Other legislation having similar objects deals with the killing of animals not covered by the Act. The Slaughter of Poultry Act 1967, for example, is concerned with the killing ('humane slaughter') 'for the purposes of preparation for sale for human consumption' of turkeys, domestic fowls, ducks, geese and quails kept in captivity[4]. There are also statutory provisions about the sale of venison[5].

Of the animals of the many other kinds to which the 1980 Act is not specifically applied the best known perhaps are game, 'wild animals hunted by sportsmen'[6], though it may be doubted if the word 'slaughter' is apt to describe the killing of animals as a consequence of the success or gratification obtained in shooting. These are nonetheless usually, if not always, intended for human consumption. There is a large body of legislation relating to 'game' having different objects from those of the 1980 Act. Game has been the subject of legislation over the centuries. An early Act of the Scottish Parliament passed in 1427 established close seasons for the wildfowl to which it applied[7], but for the most part each Game Act applies to a different group of animals[8]. Briefly the Game Acts had two objects: first the protection of landowners' rights to kill animals on their land and secondly the maintenance of the value of the land for argicultural purposes.

Other animals to which the 1980 Act does not apply are seals not protected by the Conservation of Seals Act 1970 (c 30), stray dogs[9], dogs worrying livestock[10], troublesome animals[11], vermin[12] and cetaceous animals[13] and fish.

1 Slaughter of Animals (Scotland) Act 1980 (c 13), long title.
2 These include the Slaughter of Animals (Scotland) Act 1928 (c 29), the Slaughter of Animals (Pigs) Act 1953 (c 27), the Slaughterhouses Act 1954 (c 42), and the Slaughter of Animals (Amendment) Act 1954 (c 59): Slaughter of Animals (Scotland) Act 1980, s 24(2), Sch 3. See further para 303 above.
3 In the Slaughter of Animals Act 1980, 'animal' means every description of cattle, sheep, goat, swine or horse, and 'horse' includes ass and mule: s 22.
4 These are the birds to which the Slaughter of Poultry Act 1967 (c 24) applies: s 8(2) (added by the Animal Health and Welfare Act 1984 (c 40), s 16(1), Sch 1, para 1(6)).
5 As to the sale of venison, see para 433 above.
6 *Chambers 20th Century Dictionary.*
7 Wild Birds Act 1427 (1 March c 12).
8 The various Game Acts apply to various combinations of creatures: see GAME, para 802 below.
9 See the Dogs Act 1906 (c 32), s 3 (as amended), and ANIMALS, vol 2, para 105.
10 See the Dogs (Protection of Livestock) Act 1953 (c 28), and ANIMALS, vol 2, para 169.
11 Eg foxes, squirrels, moles, mink and coypu.
12 Eg rats and mice.
13 Eg whales.

497. Historical outline. At common law, in early times at least, the 'slaying and haughing of oxen, horses and other cattel' could be prosecuted as a crime punishable by death[1]. The severity of the penalty prompts the view that there was, in those days, more concern about the property involved (the animal) than with the cruelty to it. But from the middle of the nineteenth century onwards provisions for the prevention or avoidance of cruelty to animals appear in many statutes dealing with them. Provisions for ensuring that the flesh of animals killed in slaughterhouses (and in some circumstances, for example in emergencies, elsewhere) intended to be used for human consumption (formerly 'butcher's meat') was wholesome, hygienically produced and properly kept, gradually appeared either in statute or subordinate legislation[2]. Linked, these two subjects came to be regarded as part of the law of public health to be enforced by local authorities.

The Public Health (Scotland) Act 1867 was the first Act to consolidate (with amendments) the legislation which had been enacted under various titles before then and was scattered throughout the statute book. It, however, did little more than make it an offence to sell 'unwholesome meat'[3] and enact that the business of the slaughtering of cattle, horses or animals of any description was an 'offensive trade'[4]. That Act was replaced by the Public Health (Scotland) Act 1897 which included under a cross-heading 'Offensive Trades'[5] more detailed provisions about the control of slaughterhouses, knackers' yards and pigsties; and it also enacted a licensing system for slaughterhouses and knackers' yards (except those provided by the local authority)[6] and provided that local authorities might make byelaws regulating pigsties[7]. It applied in landward areas[8], since burghs had been catered for by the Burgh Police (Scotland) Act 1892[9]. Progressive authorities such as the councils of the cities of Edinburgh, Glasgow and Dundee had at earlier stages obtained powers in their own local legislation which enabled them to make provision for the use of hygienic practices in slaughterhouse premises, to provide slaughterhouses themselves (a facility followed for other authorities in the 1892 and 1897 Acts). This ensured so far as possible that their citizens were supplied with wholesome meat and that practices in knackers' yards were controlled so that, inter alia, the meat from them did not find its way on to the human food market.

The first Slaughter of Animals (Scotland) Act was passed in 1928 and was repealed, along with the Acts which had amended it, by the Slaughter of Animals (Scotland) Act 1980[10]. The first Slaughterhouses Act, passed in 1954, was also repealed by the 1980 Act, these two subjects being combined in that Act and, along with some provisions of the Food and Drugs (Scotland) Act 1956, the

1980 Act provides a statutory statement covering the whole field of the production for human consumption of wholesome meat derived from animals of the kinds to which it applies[11] and the prevention of cruelty to them.

1 Haughing is the severing of the tendons of the hind legs. This was made a statutory offence by the Killing and Maiming Cattle Act 1581 (c 14).
2 Cruelty to Animals (Scotland) Acts 1850 (c 92) and 1895 (c 13) (both repealed); Protection of Animals (Scotland) Act 1912 (c 14); Slaughter of Animals (Scotland) Act 1928 (c 29) (repealed); Slaughter of Animals (Amendment) Act 1954 (c 59) (repealed).
3 Public Helath (Scotland) Act 1867 (c 101), s 26 (repealed).
4 Ibid, s 30 (repealed).
5 Public Health (Scotland) Act 1897 (c 38), ss 32–37.
6 Ibid, ss 33, 34 (repealed).
7 Ibid, s 35 (still in force).
8 Landward areas were those areas of a county not within the boundaries of a city or burgh.
9 See the Burgh Police (Scotland) Act 1892 (c 55), ss 278–287 (repealed).
10 See para 496 above.
11 For these animals, see para 496, note 3, above.

498. Scope. This part of the title does not survey the common law, such as it is, relating to the slaughter of animals, and there is little case law. The part thus concerns itself principally with the provision of statutes and subordinate legislation, but not with those relating to cruelty to animals[1]. Of the statutory provisions those of the Slaughter of Animals (Scotland) Act 1980 (c 13) are the most important, but those of the Slaughter of Poultry Act 1967 (c 24) are also examined. The provisions of the relevant subordinate legislation are much more lengthy and wider in scope and include regulations the object of which is to harmonise Scots law with that of the European Community, particularly in its application to fresh meat exported from Scotland to any of the other member states and to the hygienic preparation of fresh meat and poultry meat. The regulations also cover the inspection of the animals or the birds from, and premises in, which fresh meat or poultry meat is produced[2].

The provisions of the statutes and the subordinate legislation are looked at below, though not in great detail, and both should be examined along with any related material in this title. Perhaps it should first be noted that the legislation which existed before the entry of the United Kingdom into the European Community remains in existence, while the harmonising regulations form a code which takes into account the earlier provisions but is more stringent in its requirements and is superimposed on the earlier[3]. It should also be noted that any animal[4] the meat to be derived from which is intended for sale for human consumption must be slaughtered in a slaughterhouse[5] and in no other place unless accident, illness or other emergency affecting the animal requires that it be slaughtered elsewhere[6]. Some modification of the requirements is permitted for slaughterhouse equipment and hygiene if the premises are situated in remote parts of certain local government areas[7]. In the case of poultry the occupier of premises used for the slaughter of the birds must hold a licence issued by the local authority[8]. The flesh of animals slaughtered in a knacker's yard may not be used as food for human consumption[9].

1 As to cruelty to animals, see ANIMALS, vol 2, paras 239 ff.
2 See the Poultry Meat (Hygiene) (Scotland) Regulations 1976, SI 1976/1221, and para 418 above; and the Fresh Meat Export (Hygiene and Inspection) (Scotland) Regulations 1987, SI 1987/800, and para 417 above.
3 See eg the partial savings of the Food (Meat Inspection) (Scotland) Regulations 1961, SI 1961/243, in the Fresh Meat Export (Hygiene and Inspection) (Scotland) Regulations 1987, reg 19, and the further savings of earlier regulations in regs 7(5), (6), 8(2) and 11. The 1961 regulations have been revoked and replaced by the Food (Meat Inspection) (Scotland) Regulations 1988, SI 1988/1484.

4 'Animal' is defined in similar terms to para 496, note 3, above: see para 404, note 1, above.
5 For the meaning of 'slaughterhouse', see para 404, note 2, above.
6 Food and Drugs (Scotland) Act 1956 (c 30), s 12(1), which is expressed to be subject to the other provisions of s 12 (see below) and to s 13 (see para 407 above).
7 Slaughterhouse Hygiene (Scotland) Regulations 1978, SI 1978/1273, reg 57, Sch 1.
8 Poultry Meat (Hygiene) (Scotland) Regulations 1976, reg 11: see para 418, note 3, above.
9 Food and Drugs (Scotland) Act 1956, s 12(2): see para 404 above.

(2) SLAUGHTERHOUSES AND KNACKERS' YARDS

499. Public slaughterhouses. A local authority[1] may provide and, if it thinks fit, operate a slaughterhouse. It may also, whether it operates the slaughterhouse or not, make charges in respect of its use by others and of services provided by it in connection with it[2]. A local authority which has provided or established a slaughterhouse may employ persons to slaughter or stun animals, and may make charges for the services of these persons[3]. Plant and apparatus for disposal of waste or for processing of by-products may also be provided by the authority[4], which may be authorised by the Secretary of State to acquire compulsorily land for slaughterhouse purposes[5]. A local authority may dispose of any slaughterhouse belonging to it[6].

1 Slaughter of Animals (Scotland) Act 1980 (c 13), s 1. 'Local authority' means an islands or district council, and 'slaughterhouse' means any building or place used for the killing of animals the flesh of which is intended for sale for human consumption: s 22. This definition of 'slaughterhouse' applies in the context of meat intended for sale for human consumption in the United Kingdom or in any country which is not a member state of the European Community; but in the context of provisions relating to the sale of fresh meat to member states 'slaughterhouse' means any premises used for slaughtering animals the flesh of which is intended for sale for human consumption, and includes any place used in connection therewith, but not a place used in connection with a slaughterhouse solely for the manufacture of bacon and ham, sausages, meat pies or other manufactured meat products or for the storage of meat used in such manufacture: Fresh Meat Export (Hygiene and Inspection) (Scotland) Regulations 1987, SI 1987/800, reg 2(1).
2 Slaughter of Animals (Scotland) Act 1980, s 3(1)(a).
3 Ibid, s 17.
4 Ibid, s 3(1)(b).
5 Ibid, s 2.
6 Ibid, s 1.

500. Private slaughterhouses. Premises may be used as a slaughterhouse by, and only by, a person who is registered in respect of the premises by the local authority[1]. An application for registration must be made to the authority by the person proposing to use the premises, and plans must be provided if the premises are yet to be erected or are to be reconstructed[2]. A certificate of registration must be issued to the user, specifying the kinds of animals that may be slaughtered in the premises[3]. However, the local authority must refuse to register premises or must cancel a registration if it appears to the authority that any enactment relating to slaughterhouses is not and is unlikely within a reasonable time to be complied with[4]. For the protection of the public health the authority may vary any registration[5]. Notice of any decision to refuse, cancel or vary a registration must be given to the applicant or person registered, and the notice must state the grounds of the decision and state that there is a right of appeal against it[6]. If no decision is given by the authority before the expiry of three months from the date of application, and in certain other circumstances, registration is deemed to have been refused[7]. Any appeal against a decision lies to the sheriff[8]. A separate registration is required for premises used for confinement of animals awaiting slaughter if the premises are outside the curtilage of the slaughterhouse[9]. A person who uses unregistered premises as a slaughter-house is guilty of an offence[10].

  1 Slaughter of Animals (Scotland) Act 1980 (c 13), s 4(1). 'Premises' means a building or any part
    thereof, and any forecourts, yards and places of storage used in connection therewith: s 22. For
    the meaning of 'slaughterhouse' and 'local authority', see para 499, note 1, above.
  2 Ibid, s 4(3).
  3 Ibid, s 4(4). For the meaning of 'animal', see para 496, note 3, above. If the premises are to be used
    for slaughtering horses the registration must expressly authorise such use: s 7(1)(b).
  4 Ibid, s 5(1).
  5 Ibid, s 5(2).
  6 Ibid, s 5(3).
  7 Ibid, s 5(4).
  8 Ibid, s 5(5). The appeal must be made within one month of the service of the notice: s 5(5).
  9 Ibid, s 7(2)(b).
 10 Ibid, s 4(2).

501. Knackers' yards. A person carrying on the business of slaughterman or knacker[1] may not use any premises[2] as a knackers' yard without a licence from the local authority, and if he does so he commits an offence[3]. Not less than twenty-one days before a new licence is granted the local authority must advertise notice of the intention to apply for it, and any person interested may show cause against the grant or renewal of the licence[4]. Seven days' notice of any objection to renewal must be served on the applicant[5]. Before granting a licence the authority must be satisfied as to compliance with any regulations as to the construction, layout and equipment of the premises[6]. Where renewal of a licence is refused, the person concerned may appeal to the Secretary of State, whose decision is final[7]. If premises are to be used for the slaughter of horses the licence must expressly authorise such use[8]. Where premises used for the con-finement of animals awaiting slaughter are situated outside the curtilage of the premises used for the slaughter, separate licences for each premises may be issued[9].

  1 'Slaughterman' means a person whose business it is to kill animals the flesh of which is intended
    for sale for human consumption, and 'knacker' means a person whose business it is to kill animals
    the flesh of which is not intended for such use: Slaughter of Animals (Scotland) Act 1980 (c 13),
    s 22.
  2 'Premises' has here the extremely wide meaning given by the Public Health (Scotland) Act 1897
    (c 38), s 3 (see PUBLIC HEALTH, vol 19, para 336, note 1), and 'knacker's yard' means any building
    or place used for the killing of animals the flesh of which is not intended for sale for human
    consumption: Slaughter of Animals (Scotland) Act 1980, s 22.
  3 Ibid, s 6(1). For the meaning of 'local authority', see para 499, note 1, above.
  4 Ibid, s 6(3). As to the duration of licences, and the fee, see s 6(2).
  5 Ibid, s 6(4).
  6 Ibid, s 7(3). For such regulations, see the Slaughter of Animals (Prevention of Cruelty) (Scot-
    land) Regulations 1955, SI 1955/1993, and the Slaughter of Animals (Stunning Pens) (Scotland)
    Regulations 1963, SI 1963/1888.
  7 Slaughter of Animals (Scotland) Act 1980, s 6(6).
  8 Ibid, s 7(1)(a).
  9 Ibid, s 7(2)(a).

502. Powers to make byelaws and regulations. A local authority may make byelaws to ensure the cleanliness and sanitary condition of slaughter-houses and their proper management[1]. Such byelaws must be confirmed by the Secretary of State[2]. However, regulations which are inconsistent with the byelaws will prevail[3].

The Secretary of State has power to make regulations for securing humane conditions and practices in connection with the slaughter of animals at slaugh-terhouses and knackers' yards and for securing their proper management[4].

Particular powers are available for these purposes, and there may be different provisions for different kinds of animals and in relation to premises used for different purposes in connection with slaughter[5]. The regulations may prescribe penalties for offences against them and may require occupiers of premises to ensure compliance with any provision made by them[6].

Power is also conferred on the Secretary of State to make regulations for securing the observance of sanitary and cleanly conditions and practices in connection with the sale of food for human consumption and for many other matters[7]. These powers have been exercised in relation to public and private slaughterhouses[8]. Export slaughterhouses are the subject of other regulations[9].

1 Slaughter of Animals (Scotland) Act 1980 (c 13), s 8(1) (amended by the Local Government (Miscellaneous Provisions) (Scotland) Act 1981 (c 23), ss 25, 41, Sch 2, para 37, Sch 4). For the meaning of 'local authority' and 'slaughterhouse', see para 499, note 1, above.
2 Slaughter of Animals (Scotland) Act 1980, s 8(2).
3 Ibid, s 8(3).
4 Ibid, s 9(1). For the meaning of 'knacker's yard', see para 500, note 2, above.
5 Ibid, s 9(1)(a), (b), (2). See the regulations cited in para 501, note 6, above.
6 Ibid, s 9(3).
7 See the Food and Drugs (Scotland) Act 1956 (c 30), s 13, and para 407 above.
8 Slaughterhouse Hygiene (Scotland) Regulations 1978, SI 1978/1273 (amended by SI 1984/842, SI 1985/1068, SI 1985/1856, SI 1986/1808 and SI 1987/1957).
9 Fresh Meat Export (Hygiene and Inspection) (Scotland) Regulations 1987, SI 1987/800: see para 417 above.

(3) METHODS OF SLAUGHTER; HYGIENE

503. Methods of slaughter. Animals slaughtered in a slaughterhouse or knackers' yard must be slaughtered instantaneously, by means of a mechanically operated instrument in proper repair unless (1) by stunning, effected by means of a mechanically operated instrument or an instrument for stunning by means of electricity, in proper repair, they are instantaneously rendered insensible to pain until death supervenes, or (2) by such other means as may be authorised by regulations, they are rendered insensible to pain until death supervenes and any conditions in the regulations are complied with[1]. The Secretary of State has power to make regulations after consultations with organisations concerned[2]. The regulations may be limited to a particular class of animal or a particular class of slaughterhouse or knacker's yard and may make incidental or consequential provisions[3]. In particular, these may include, in a case where a condition as respects the use of any means of rendering an animal insensible to pain consists in the giving of approval by a local authority, provision for securing a right of appeal to the sheriff against the withholding or withdrawal of approval[3]. These provisions do not apply to an animal slaughtered for the food of Jews or Muslims if the slaughter is carried out according to the Jewish or Muslim method of slaughter and no unnecessary suffering is inflicted[4].

No swine over twelve weeks old may be slaughtered in any place other than a slaughterhouse or knacker's yard otherwise than instantaneously by means of a mechanically operated instrument in proper repair unless by stunning, effected by means of a mechanically operated instrument or an instrument for stunning by means of electricity, it is instantaneously rendered insensible to pain until death supervenes[5]. This provision does not apply if the swine is slaughtered in a laboratory or research station for diagnosis of disease or for research[6].

Provisions for avoiding cruelty in connection with the confinement and treatment of animals awaiting slaughter are contained in regulations[7], which relate also to the construction and equipment of slaughterhouses and knackers' yards, including lairages[8], and the conditions to be observed in connection with the actual slaughter of the animals[9]. There are special provisions about knackers' yards[10] and the slaughter of horses[11]. Records of horses and carcases of horses received into a slaughterhouse and of all animals received into a knacker's yard must be kept, and notices of the number of horses slaughtered must be given to the local authority by the occupier of the slaughterhouse or yard where they were slaughtered[12].

1 Slaughter of Animals (Scotland) Act 1980 (c 13), s 10(1)(a), (b). For the meaning of 'animal', see para 496, note 3, above; for the meaning of 'slaughterhouse', see para 499, note 1, above, and for the meaning of 'knacker's yard', see para 501, note 2, above. No such regulations have been made.
2 Ibid, s 10(2).
3 Ibid, s 10(3). For the meaning of 'local authority', see para 499, note 1, above.
4 Ibid, s 11. However, the animal must be slaughtered by a person licensed under s 15 (for which see para 513 above): s 11.
5 Ibid, s 12.
6 Ibid, s 12 proviso.
7 See the Slaughter of Animals (Prevention of Cruelty) (Scotland) Regulations 1955, SI 1955/1993, Pt III (regs 4–9).
8 See ibid, Pt II (reg 3). See also the Slaughterhouse (Hygiene) (Scotland) Regulations 1978, SI 1978/1273, Pt II (regs 3–19).
9 See the Slaughter of Animals (Prevention of Cruelty) (Scotland) Regulations 1955, Pt IV (regs 10–14) (amended by SI 1963/1888).
10 See ibid, Pt VI (regs 16,17).
11 See ibid, Pt VII (regs 18–20).
12 See ibid, Pt VIII (regs 21, 22).

504. Hygiene regulations. The Slaughterhouse Hygiene (Scotland) Regulations 1978 are divided into four Parts, the first of which contains exhaustive interpretative provisions[1]. Part II deals with the construction and equipment of slaughterhouses[2] and Part III deals with hygienic practices in connection with premises and equipment, with slaughtering, with personal hygiene and the conduct of persons engaged in the handling of meat and with notification of certain diseases occurring amongst those persons[3]. Part IV contains miscellaneous provisions[4].

The regulations are to be enforced and executed in any area by the local authority[5]. In their application to slaughterhouses in specified remote areas the regulations have modified effect[6].

A person who fails to comply with the provisions of certain of the regulations[7] is guilty of an offence[8]. The owner or occupier of a slaughterhouse who fails to take all reasonable steps to secure that any person engaged in handling meat there complies with those provisions is also guilty of an offence[9], as is the owner of any slaughterhouse who fails to comply with requirements of the regulations of a structural character[10] or the occupier of a slaughterhouse who fails to take all reasonable steps to comply with or secure compliance with any other requirement[11] of the regulations[12]. Penalties are prescribed[13].

1 See the Slaughterhouse Hygiene (Scotland) Regulations 1978, SI 1978/1273, reg 2(1) (amended by SI 1987/1957).
2 Ibid, Pt II, comprises regs 3–19.
3 Ibid, Pt III, comprises regs 20–55.
4 Ibid, Pt IV, comprises regs 56–61.
5 Ibid, reg 56. 'Local authority' means the council of a district or islands area: reg 2(1).
6 See ibid, reg 57, Sch 1. 'Slaughterhouse' is defined in reg 2(1) in terms similar to those in the second definition of 'slaughterhouse' in para 499, note 1, above.
7 Ie ibid, regs 25, 42–54.
8 Ibid, reg 59(1).
9 Ibid, reg 59(2).

10 Ibid, reg 59(3).
11 Ie any requirement not mentioned in ibid, reg 59(2) or (3).
12 Ibid, reg 59(4).
13 See ibid, reg 60 (substituted by SI 1985/1068).

505. Construction and equipment of slaughterhouses. There are provisions about the dimensions, layout, lighting and flooring of lairages[1], and the
layout, design and arrangement of slaughterhouses, having regard particularly
to the location in which the several activities which take place in them are to be
carried out and the places within them where the parts of a carcase are, after
slaughter, to be kept[2]. The lighting, ventilation, construction of ceilings and
internal walls and the flooring of the slaughterhouse premises themselves are
also dealt with[3]. Prevention of infestation[4], cleaning of forecourts and yards[5]
and construction of dungsteads[6] are also mentioned.

Sufficient supplies of wholesome water must be piped to a slaughterhouse
under pressure[7]. There must also be adequate and wholesome supplies of piped
hot water[8], and water tanks must be covered[9]. Unwholesome water may be
used only for specified purposes[10]. The drainage system of a slaughterhouse
must comply with certain provisions[11]. Sanitary conveniences must have a
suitable water supply, must be adequately lighted and ventilated and have a
notice bearing specified wording prominently displayed[12]. Washbasins having a
supply of hot and cold water or warm water readily accessible to persons
working in a slaughterhouse must be provided[13]. Facilities for washing equipment and fittings (including receptacles, containers and scalding tanks) must
also be provided[14], and the equipment and fittings must be made of specified
materials[15].

1 Slaughterhouses Hygiene (Scotland) Regulations 1978, SI 1978/1273, regs 3, 9(1). 'Lairage'
   means any premises, yard or forecourt (but not field or pasture) used for confining animals
   awaiting slaughter: reg 2(1).
2 Ibid, regs 4, 5. As to the meaning of 'slaughterhouse', see para 504, note 6, above.
3 Ibid, regs 6–8, 9(2), (3).
4 Ibid, reg 10.
5 Ibid, reg 11.
6 Ibid, reg 12.
7 Ibid, reg 13(1).
8 Ibid, reg 13(2).
9 Ibid, reg 13(3).
10 Ibid, reg 14.
11 Ibid, reg 15.
12 Ibid, reg 16.
13 Ibid, reg 17.
14 Ibid, reg 18.
15 Ibid, reg 19.

506. Hygienic practice. The provisions of the Slaughterhouses (Scotland)
Regulations 1978 concerned with hygienic practices[1] (1) deal with the hygiene
of premises and equipment[2]; (2) deal with hygienic slaughtering practices[3];
(3) deal with personal hygiene and the conduct of persons engaged in the
handling of meat or who are liable to come into contact with meat[4]; and (4)
provide for the notification to the Chief Administrative Health Officer of the
Health Board of the area in which the slaughterhouse is situated that any person
engaged in the handling of meat there is suffering from or is a carrier of any of
the diseases listed in the regulations[5]. First aid materials must also be available[6].

1 Slaughterhouses Hygiene (Scotland) Regulations 1978, SI 1978/1273, Pt III (regs 20–55).
2 Ibid, regs 20–30.
3 Ibid, regs 31–41.

4 Ibid, regs 42–53.
5 Ibid, reg 54.
6 Ibid, reg 55.

507. Inspection of meat from animals slaughtered in slaughter-houses. The provisions for securing proper inspection in connection with the slaughter of animals are important and will be looked at in some detail.

An animal which is to be slaughtered in a slaughterhouse[1] must be subjected to an ante-mortem health inspection by an inspector[2]. Immediately after the animal has been slaughtered its body must be dressed[3] and the carcase must be subjected to a post-mortem inspection by an inspector[4], who, after the inspection, gives instructions as to the disposal of the offal and blood[5]. No part of the carcase or any offal may be removed from the slaughterhouse until it has been inspected for fitness for human consumption and duly marked[6]. A veterinary meat inspector directs into what portions he requires the carcase to be divided for inspection[7]. The inspector should, if practicable, make his inspection immediately after the offal has been removed[8]. Any offal or blood which shows evidence of disease or which for any other reason is suspected of being unfit for human consumption must be isolated, and a veterinary meat inspector must then examine them[9]. If he is satisfied that the carcase, offal or blood is unfit for human consumption or that the animal was suffering from any of certain specified diseases[10], the carcase or offal, or such part of it as is specified, or the blood, must not be disposed of for human consumption but is to be treated as unfit and disposed of accordingly[11]. If the owner of the meat is not satisfied that it is unfit, it is treated as suspected food[12].

More stringent provisions apply where the meat is sold or intended to be sold for export to a member state of the European Community[13].

1 'Slaughterhouse' means any premises used for slaughtering animals the flesh of which is intended for human consumption, and includes any place used in connection therewith: Food (Meat Inspection) (Scotland) Regulations 1988, SI 1988/1418, reg 2(1).
2 Ibid, reg 3(1), Sch 2. For an exception, see reg 3(2). 'Inspector' means a veterinary meat inspector or a meat inspector: reg 2(1). 'Veterinary meat inspector' means a veterinary surgeon who is appointed an inspector of meat for the purposes of the regulations or any person appointed under reg 13(2) to exercise the functions of a veterinary meat inspector; and 'meat inspector' means any person having any of the qualifications set out in Sch 6 and employed as a meat inspector by a local authority under reg 14(1): reg 2(1). See further para 512 below. 'Local authority' means an islands or district council: reg 2(1).
3 Ibid, reg 4(1).
4 Ibid, reg 5(1), Sch 3.
5 Ibid, reg 4(2).
6 Ibid, reg 5(2). As to health marking, see reg 6, Sch 4.
7 Ibid, reg 5(4).
8 Ibid, reg 5(3).
9 Ibid, Sch 3, Pt I, para 5 (1).
10 For these diseases, see ibid, Sch 3, Pt I, Annex.
11 Ibid, Sch 3, Pt I, para 5(2), (3).
12 Ibid, Sch 3, Pt I, para 5(4), applying the Food and Drugs (Scotland) Act 1955 (c 30), s 9, for which see paras 397, 398, above.
13 See para 510 below.

508. Inspection of meat from animals slaughtered elsewhere than in slaughterhouses. Where the animal to be slaughtered is a 'casualty animal' and is slaughtered elsewhere than in a slaughterhouse[1], similar, but not identical, provisions about hygiene apply. If the meat or blood is to be sold for human consumption, the carcase or, if the body has been dressed, the meat from the animal must be brought into a slaughterhouse for post-mortem inspection, but neither will be accepted there unless a statement signed by a veterinary surgeon containing specified information is provided[2]. There are restrictions on the moving of a carcase from one slaughterhouse to another[3].

1 Ie by reason of having been affected by an accident, illness or other emergency to which the Food and Drugs (Scotland) Act 1956 (c 30), s 12(1), applies: see para 404 above.
2 See the Food (Meat Inspection) (Scotland) Regulations 1988, SI 1988/1484, regs 7–9. The provisions of reg 5 as to post-mortem inspection (see para 507 above) are applied by reg 7(2).
3 See ibid, reg 10.

509. Functions of local authorities. The local authority has power to fix the days and hours during those days when slaughtering in a private slaughterhouse situated in its area may take place[1]. In certain emergency circumstances slaughtering at times other than those so fixed may be permitted[2].

Records of certain matters must be kept by the local authority[3]. The local authority may, after consultation, fix the charges to be made for the inspection of meat[4]. The persons obliged to pay these charges are specified[5].

The provisions as to the inspection of meat are to be executed and enforced in any area by the local authority for the area[6]. Contravention or failure to comply with those provisions is an offence for which penalties are laid down[7].

1 Food (Meat Inspection) (Scotland) Regulations 1988, SI 1988/1484, reg 11(1). For the meaning of 'local authority', see para 507, note 2, above.
2 Ibid, reg 11(2).
3 Ibid, reg 12, Sch 5.
4 Ibid, reg 15, Sch 7.
5 Ibid, reg 16.
6 Ibid, reg 18.
7 Ibid, reg 19.

510. Export slaughterhouses. An export slaughterhouse is premises approved by the Secretary of State as a slaughterhouse where animals, the fresh meat from which is intended for sale for export to a member state of the European Community for human consumption, are slaughtered[1]. An application for such approval must be made in writing by the occupier or intended occupier of the premises[2]. The application is notified to the local authority, and a veterinary officer of the Secretary of State inspects and reports on the premises[3]. The local authority may make written representations about the application, to which the applicant may respond[4].

Premises in respect of which such approval is sought must comply with specified requirements, and the method of operation in the premises must comply with other requirements[5]. If the Secretary of State is not satisfied about these matters he must refuse approval[6]. In considering the application he must have regard to the veterinary report and any local authority representations and any response thereto, and he must notify his decision to the applicant and the local authority, giving reasons if he refuses approval[7]. The Secretary of State must be consulted about proposed alterations to the premises or, as the case may be, the method of alteration[8]. When approval has been given the Secretary of State issues to the local authority the necessary equipment for applying a health mark[9], which may be applied only by an official veterinary surgeon and in the prescribed manner[10]. The mark may be used only in premises which have been approved[11].

Many of the conditions to be satisfied before the approval of premises as an export slaughterhouse can be given are difficult to achieve. This is principally due to the fact that the conditions which apply to public and private slaughterhouses are imported into those which apply to the export slaughterhouses[12].

Approval of any premises as an export slaughterhouse may be suspended or revoked in certain circumstances and after a specified procedure has been complied with, including notification to the local authority and the occupier of the premises[13]. Provision is made for termination of suspension[14]. The local authority is responsible for the performance of specified functions in relation to approved premises[15], and may make charges for the services so made available[16]. It must execute and enforce these provisions in its area[17], and provide such information to the Secretary of State as he requires[18].

There are also provisions about ante-mortem health inspection of animals to be slaughtered in an export slaughterhouse[19] and about the admission to the slaughterhouse of diseased or injured animals[20]. Powers of entry to export slaughterhouses are made available to the Secretary of State and the local authority[21]. There are also provisions about offences and penalties[22]. Local authority officers using their powers in good faith are protected against actions brought in respect of any use of the powers[23].

Provisions are also laid down about the approval of premises for use as export cutting premises[24], as export cold stores[25] and as transhipment centres[26]. Each of these types of premises is defined, along with related definitions[27]. Some of the provisions about those premises and their use are similar, if not the same, as those about export slaughterhouses.

1 See the Fresh Meat Export (Hygiene and Inspection) (Scotland) Regulations 1987, SI 1987/800, art 2(1). As to the Community provisions which these regulations implement, see para 417, note 1, above.
2 Ibid, reg 4(2).
3 Ibid, reg 4(3). 'Local authority' means an islands or district council: reg 2(1).
4 Ibid, reg 4(4), (5).
5 Ibid, reg 4(1)(a)(i), Sch 1, Sch 5, Pt I, Schs 6–8.
6 Ibid, reg 4(1)(b).
7 Ibid, reg 4(6), (7).
8 Ibid, reg 4(8).
9 Ibid, reg 4(9).
10 Ibid, reg 8(4), Sch 11. Under reg 8(6), if the meat is found to be fit for human consumption but not eligible for export to a member state, it is marked in accordance with what is now the Food (Meat Inspection) (Scotland) Regulations 1988, SI 1988/1484, reg 6, Sch 4.
11 Fresh Meat Export (Hygiene and Inspection) (Scotland) Regulations 1987, reg 8(10).
12 See eg ibid, Sch 1, para 1; Sch 2, Pt I, para 1; and Sch 2, Pt II.
13 Ibid, reg 6(1)–(4).
14 Ibid, reg 6(5).
15 Ibid, reg 12.
16 Ibid, reg 13.
17 Ibid, reg 17, which excepts regs 4 and 6 as being the responsibility of the Secretary of State.
18 Ibid, reg 16.
19 Ibid, reg 8(1), Sch 6.
20 Ibid, reg 11.
21 Ibid, reg 14.
22 Ibid, reg 18. The Food and Drugs (Scotland) Act 1956 (c 30), ss 45–47 (see paras 426–428 above), are applied by the Fresh Meat Export (Hygiene and Inspection) (Scotland) Regulations 1987, reg 20(1).
23 Ibid, reg 20(2), applying the Local Government (Scotland) Act 1973 (c 65), s 64(3).
24 Fresh Meat Export (Hygiene and Inspection) (Scotland) Regulations 1987, reg 4(1)(a)(ii), Sch 2, Pt I, Sch 5, Pt I, Sch 9.
25 Ibid, reg 4(1)(a)(iii), Sch 3, Sch 5, Pt III, Sch 13.
26 Ibid, reg 4(1)(a)(iv), Sch 4.
27 Ibid, reg 2(1).

511. Conclusion. It is perhaps desirable to end this section of the title with the following summary of the relationship of the two codes which have resulted from the harmonisation of Scots law with Community law. If the provisions of the Acts or regulations relating to the slaughter of animals, including provisions about the premises in which slaughter is carried out, whether they be a public, private or export slaughterhouse, or other place where emergency slaughter is permitted, with intent that the meat or blood derived from any animal so slaughtered is to be exported or sold for export to a member state of the European Community for sale for human consumption there, are complied with, then, if also all the provisions of regulations about cutting up, inspection, hygiene, sale, offer or exposure for sale and other relevant matters, specified in any Act, regulation, order or other subordinate legislation are complied with, such meat or blood may not only be so exported or sold for export but may also be sold, offered or exposed for sale within the United Kingdom. On the other hand, if the provisions of all such Acts and regulations, orders and other subordinate legislation as aforesaid, other than provisions which are enacted only by the Fresh Meat Export (Hygiene and Inspection) (Scotland) Regulations 1987, are complied with, the meat or blood may be sold, offered or exposed for sale in any part of the United Kingdom but must not be exported, or sold for export, to a member state.

(4) QUALIFICATIONS OF OFFICIALS, SLAUGHTERMEN AND KNACKERS

512. Veterinary meat inspectors and meat inspectors. A person appointed by a local authority as a veterinary meat inspector must be a veterinary surgeon[1] or, except for certain purposes, a registered medical practitioner appointed by the local authority if the Secretary of State gives his approval[2].

A person may not be employed by a local authority as a meat inspector unless he is a registered medical practitioner or a member of the Royal College of Veterinary Surgeons or holds a specified qualification[3].

1 Food (Meat Inspection) (Scotland) Regulations 1988, SI 1988/1484, reg 13(1). For the meaning of 'veterinary meat inspector' and 'local authority', see para 507, note 2, above.
2 Ibid, reg 13(2).
3 Ibid, reg 14(1), Sch 6. For the meaning of 'meat inspector', see para 507, note 1, above. In the Fresh Meat Export (Hygiene and Inspection) (Scotland) Regulations 1987, SI 1987/800, 'inspector' means a person so qualified and who is appointed by the local authority under reg 12(2): reg 2(1).

513. Slaughtermen and knackers. Every slaughterman or knacker must hold a licence granted by a local authority which enables him to slaughter or stun an animal in a slaughterhouse or knacker's yard, and no animal may be so slaughtered or stunned by any person except in accordance with such a licence[1], although this does not apply where the slaughter is carried out by an officer or employee of the Secretary of State under the Animal Health Act 1981[2]. An application for a licence must contain specified particulars[3]. A licence may be granted only to a male person of eighteen years or more who is, in the authority's opinion, a fit and proper person for the purpose[4]. A slaughterman must have passed ability tests and have had at least one year's experience[5]. If he has less experience, the licence may provide that he is not to slaughter an animal except under the supervision of a licensed person[5].

A licence granted by a local authority is valid only in the area of that authority and for a period not exceeding twelve months, although it may be renewed at the discretion of the authority, suspended for such period as the authority determines or revoked where the authority is satisfied that the holder of it is no longer a fit and proper person to hold it[6]. The authority may charge a fee for a licence and for a renewal of a licence[7], and there is a right of appeal to the sheriff against the refusal, suspension or revocation of a licence[8].

A licence specifies the kinds of animals which may be slaughtered or stunned by the holder and the types of instrument which may be used by him for the purpose[9]. Licences granted for the slaughter of animals by the Jewish or Muslim methods do not require to specify these matters[10]. But any licence may provide that a slaughterman who has not secured specified qualifications may slaughter an animal only under the supervision of a person holding a licence which is in force and not subject to a like condition[11]. Regulations may be made for the purpose[12]. A local authority may refuse to grant a licence, or may revoke or suspend it, if the applicant or holder has failed to comply with any licence conditions or has been convicted of any of certain offences relating to animals[13].

1   Slaughter of Animals (Scotland) Act 1980 (c 13), s 15(1). For the meaning of 'animal', see para 496, note 3, above; for the meaning of 'local authority' and 'slaughterhouse', see para 499, note 1, above, and for the meaning of 'slaughterman', 'knacker' and 'knacker's yard', see para 501, notes 1, 2, above.
2   Slaughter of Animals (Scotland) Act 1980, s 15(1) proviso (amended by the Animal Health Act 1981 (c 22), s 96(1), Sch 5, para 12).
3   Slaughter of Animals (Scotland) Act 1980, s 15(6).
4   Ibid, s 15(2).
5   Slaughter of Animals (Prevention of Cruelty) (Scotland) Regulations 1955, SI 1955/917, reg 15.
6   Slaughter of Animals (Scotland) Act 1980, s 15(3)(a)–(d).
7   Ibid, s 15(5).
8   Ibid, s 15(4). The appeal must be made within one month of intimation of the decision, and the sheriff's decision is final: s 15(4).
9   Ibid, s 16(1).
10   Ibid, s 16(2).
11   Ibid, s 16(1).
12   Ibid, s 16(3).
13   Ibid, s 16(4) (as amended: see note 2 above), which lists the offences. They include certain offences against the Protection of Animals Act 1911 (c 27), the Protection of Animals (Scotland) Act 1912 (c 14), the Slaughter of Animals Act 1958 (c 8), the Slaughterhouses Act 1974 (c 3), the Slaughter of Animals (Scotland) Act 1980 and regulations thereunder, and the Animal Health Act 1981.

(5) OFFENCES AND POWERS OF ENTRY

514. Offences. A person who slaughters or stuns or attempts to slaughter or stun an animal when unlicensed or other than in the authorised manner[1], or who knowingly makes a false statement for the purposes of obtaining a slaughterman's or knacker's licence, is guilty of an offence[2] unless he proves that by reason of accident or other emergency the contravention was necessary for preventing physical injury or suffering to any person or animal[3]. On conviction of certain offences licences or registrations may be cancelled in addition to any other penalty[4].

1   Ie in contravention of the Slaughter of Animals (Scotland) Act 1980 (c 13) s 10 or s 12 (see para 503 above) or s 15 (see para 513 above).
2   Ibid, s 18(1).
3   Ibid, s 18(2).
3   Ibid, s 18(3).

515. Powers of entry. Any officer of a local authority has the right, if he is authorised for that purpose by the authority, and on production of duly authenticated documents, if so requested, to enter any premises at all reasonable times so as to ascertain if there has been any contravention of the registration provisions[1] of the Slaughter of Animals (Scotland) Act 1980 or of byelaws, or generally for the purpose of the performance of the authority's functions thereunder[2]. If required to do so the officer must produce his authority to enter the premises[2]. The sheriff may grant a warrant to enter premises in certain circumstances³. An officer may take with him such persons as are necessary for the carrying out of the purpose for which he enters the premises and must leave the premises as effectively secured against unauthorised entry as he found them⁴.

Any constable, officer of the Secretary of State or person authorised in writing or appointed as a veterinary surgeon by the local authority⁵ has a right to enter any slaughterhouse or knacker's yard, at any time when business is or appears to be or is usually carried on there, for the purpose of ascertaining whether there is or has been any contravention of the provisions of that Act as to the method of slaughter or the licensing of slaughtermen and knackers⁶, or regulations under the Act⁷. Obstruction of such entry is an offence⁸.

The local authority also has a right to enter any knacker's yard, at any hour between 9 am and 6 pm or when business is usually carried on there, for the purpose of examining whether there is any contravention of the provisions of that Act as to the licensing of knackers' yards⁹ or of the Public Health (Scotland) Act 1897 (c 38) or byelaws thereunder¹⁰.

1 Ie the Slaughter of Animals (Scotland) Act 1980 (c 13), s 4: see para 500 above.
2 Ibid, s 13(1). For the meaning of 'local authority', see para 499, note 1, above, and for the meaning of 'premises', see para 500, note 1, above. Nothing in ss 13, 14, authorises any person, except with the permission of the local authority under the Animal Health Act 1981 (c 22), to enter any premises which are or are comprised in an infected place within the meaning of that Act (see s 17, and ANIMALS, vol 2, para 185): Slaughter of Animals (Scotland) Act 1980, s 13(4) (amended by the Animal Health Act 1981 (c 22), s 96(1), Sch 5, para 12).
3 Slaughter of Animals (Scotland) Act 1980, s 13(2).
4 Ibid, s 13(3).
5 Ibid, s 14(3).
6 Ie ibid, ss 10, 11 (see para 503 above), and s 15 (see para 513 above).
7 Ibid, s 14(1). See also note 2 above. For the meaning of 'slaughterhouse', see para 499, note 1, above, and for the meaning of 'knacker's yard', see para 501, note 2, above.
8 Ibid, s 14(2).
9 Ie ibid, s 6: see para 501 above.
10 Slaughter of Animals (Scotland) Act 1980, s 14(4).

(6) SLAUGHTER OF POULTRY

516. Introduction. The Slaughter of Poultry Act 1967 was not included in the measures consolidated in the Slaughter of Animals (Scotland) Act 1980 (c 13), and there thus exists a separate code dealing with the slaughter of birds to which the 1967 Act applies. These are turkeys kept in captivity, domestic fowls, guinea fowls, ducks, geese and quails so kept¹. After consultation with persons or bodies representative of the interests concerned the ministers² may by order extend the 1967 Act to the slaughter of birds of any kind kept in captivity³.

1 Slaughter of Poultry Act 1967 (c 24), s 8(2) (added by the Animal Health and Welfare Act 1984 (c 40), s 16(1), Sch 1, para 1(6)).
2 'The ministers' means the Minister of Agriculture, Fisheries and Food and the Secretaries of State for Wales and for Scotland acting jointly: Slaughter of Poultry Act 1967, s 8(1).
3 Ibid, s 7(1) (amended by the Animal Health and Welfare Act 1984, s 16(1), (2), Sch 1, para 1(5), Sch 2). Such an order, which may be varied or revoked by a subsequent order, must be made by statutory instrument a draft whereof has been approved by resolution of each House of Parliament: Slaughter of Poultry Act 1967, s 7(2), (3).

517. Method of slaughter. No bird to which the Slaughter of Poultry Act 1967 applies¹ may be slaughtered unless it is instantaneously slaughtered by decapitation or dislocation of the neck or some other approved method, or is by stunning, effected by means of an instrument of an approved kind in proper repair, instantaneously rendered insensible to pain until death supervenes². It is an offence for a person to employ any other method of slaughter of a bird unless he proves that by reason of accident or other emergency the use of another method was necessary to prevent physical injury or suffering to any person or animal[3].

The above provision as to the method of slaughter does not apply:

(1) to the slaughter, without the infliction of unnecessary suffering, of a bird by the Jewish method for the food of Jews, by a Jew licensed by the Chief Rabbi, or by the Muslim method for the food of Muslims, by a Muslim[4];

(2) to the slaughter of a bird in pursuance of powers conferred by or under the Animal Health Act 1981 (c 22)[5];

(3) to the slaughter of a bird in the course of a procedure duly authorised under the Animals (Scientific Procedures) Act 1986[6];

(4) to the slaughter of a bird, in the exercise of his profession, by a veterinary surgeon or a person registered in the supplementary veterinary register, or a person acting under his direction[7];

(5) to the slaughter of poultry chicks by a method approved by the ministers, without the infliction of unnecessary suffering[8].

Every local authority[9] must maintain a register of premises in its area, and if in premises in its area that are not registered a bird to which the 1967 Act applies is slaughtered by stunning, albeit by the approved method, the occupier of the premises is guilty of an offence[10] unless he proves that he took all reasonable steps and exercised all due diligence to avoid committing the offence[11].

The ministers may make regulations for the purpose of securing humane conditions and practices in connection with the slaughter of birds to which the 1967 Act applies[12], and, after consultation with persons or bodies representative of the interests concerned, may prepare, issue, print and distribute, and revise, codes of practice to provide practical guidance in respect of the Act and regulations under it[13]. Failure to follow such a code is not in itself an offence, but may be relied on in proceedings for a contravention of the Act or regulations as tending to establish guilt[14].

Regulations made under these powers contain provisions about the avoidance of unnecessary pain or unnecessary distress to a bird awaiting slaughter[15], about the lighting of premises[16], and about the actual slaughter[17]. Contravention or failure to comply with the regulations is an offence[18].

1 For the birds to which the Slaughter of Poultry Act 1967 (c 24) applies, see para 516 above.
2 Ibid, s 1(1) (amended by the Animal Health and Welfare Act 1984 (c 40), ss 5(1), 16(1), (2), Sch 1, para 1(2), Sch 2). Approval is by the ministers (as to whom see para 516, note 2, above): Slaughter of Poultry Act 1967, s 1(1).
3 Ibid, s 1(3).
4 Ibid, s 1(2), (4) (amended by the Slaughterhouses Act 1974 (c 3), s 46(1), Sch 3 para 4).
5 Slaughter of Poultry Act 1967, s 1(2A)(a) (added by the Animal Health and Welfare Act 1984, s 5(2)).
6 Slaughter of Poultry Act 1967, s 1(2A)(b) (as so added, and amended by the Animals (Scientific Procedures) Act 1986 (c 14), s 27(2), Sch 3, para 6).
7 Slaughter of Poultry Act 1967, s 1(2A)(c) (as so added).
8 Ibid, s 1(2B) (as so added). Such approval is by order made by statutory instrument subject to annulment in pursuance of a resolution of either House of Parliament: s 1(2B), (2C) (as so added).
9 'Local authority' means an islands or district council: ibid, s 8(1) (amended by the Local Government (Scotland) Act 1973 (c 65), s 214(2), Sch 27, Pt II, para 167).
10 Slaughter of Poultry Act 1967, s 2(1) (amended by the Animal Health and Welfare Act 1984, Sch 1, para 1(4), Sch 2).
11 Slaughter of Poultry Act 1967, s 2(2) (added by the Animal Health and Welfare Act 1984, Sch 1, para 1(4)).
12 Slaughter of Poultry Act 1967, s 3 (substituted by the Animal Health and Welfare Act 1984, s 6).
13 Slaughter of Poultry Act 1967, s 3A(1), (5) (added by the Animal Health and Welfare Act 1984, s 7). Such a code must be laid before Parliament and may not be issued if either House resolves that it be not issued: Slaughter of Poultry Act 1967, s 3A(2), (3) (as so added).

14 Ibid, s 3A(6), (7) (as so added).
15 Slaughter of Poultry (Humane Conditions) Regulations 1984, SI 1984/2056, regs 4, 5.
16 Ibid, reg 6.
17 Ibid, regs 7–11.
18 Ibid, reg 12.

518. Powers of entry. Where these powers of entry are exercisable in relation to any premises to which regulations for securing humane conditions of slaughter of poultry[1] apply, a person duly authorised by the Secretary of State or the local authority[2] may enter the premises to ascertain whether there is or has been there any contravention of the Slaughter of Poultry Act 1967 or any regulations or code of practice under it[3]. Where it appears to the person so authorised that the slaughter of birds to which the Act applies is in progress on the premises, the power of entry is exercisable at any time[4]. Where it appears to him that the slaughter of such birds has within forty-eight hours been in progress on the premises or that such birds are on the premises for the purpose of being slaughtered, the power may be exercised at all reasonable hours[5]. Obstruction of this power of entry is an offence[6].

1 Ie regulations under the Slaughter of Poultry Act 1967 (c 24), s 3: see para 517 above.
2 For the meaning of 'local authority', see para 517, note 9, above.
3 Slaughter of Poultry Act 1967, s 4(1) (substituted by the Animal Health and Welfare Act 1984 (c 40), s 8).
4 Slaughter of Poultry Act 1967, s 4(2) (as so substituted). For the birds to which the 1967 Act applies, see para 516 above.
5 Ibid, s 4(3) (as so substituted).
6 Ibid, s 4(4) (as so substituted).

519. Enforcement. Every local authority must execute and enforce in its area the provisions of the Slaughter of Poultry Act 1967 and regulations under it[1], and in particular, for the purpose of securing the execution of those provisions, must make arrangements for the supervision by suitably qualified persons of any premises in its area to which the regulations apply[2].

1 Slaughter of Poultry Act 1967 (c 24), s 6(1) (substituted by the Animal Health and Welfare Act 1984 (c 40), s 9). For the meaning of 'local authority', see para 517, note 9, above. The authority may not, of course, institute proceedings for any offence: Slaughter of Poultry Act 1967, s 6(4) (as so substituted).
2 Ibid, s 6(2) (as so substituted). Such arrangements must comply with directions given by the ministers (as to whom see para 516, note 1, above); s 6(3) (as so substituted).

520–600. Hygiene. Provisions designed to secure the hygiene of processes for the production, cutting up and storage of poultry meat intended for sale for human consumption have been discussed above[1].

1 See para 418 above.

FORESTRY

1. INTRODUCTION

601. Scope of the title. Forestry formerly in Scots Law meant the privileges of a royal forest. Forests were *inter regalia*; 'being places destinate for deer, for the King's use and pleasure in hunting'[1]. This title is concerned with the statute law of forestry in its more general sense of the science and art of forming and cultivating forests and the management of growing timber.

1 Stair *Institutions* II,3,67.

602. Legislation. Legislation arose from the need following the 1914–18 war for a national forest policy to ensure the maintenance of a strategic reserve of timber in the country, and by the Forestry Act 1919 there was established a Forestry Commission to promote afforestation and the production and supply of timber in the United Kingdom (subsequently restricted to Great Britain). By the 1919 Act and the Forestry (Transfer of Woods) Act 1923 there were transferred to the Forestry Commissioners many of the powers and duties of the Board of Agriculture and Fisheries, the Board of Agriculture for Scotland, the Department of Agriculture and Technical Instruction for Ireland and the Commissioners of Woods as regards the country's forest lands[1]. Both these Acts were subsequently amended, but the Forestry Acts 1919 to 1963 are now repealed[2] subject to limited exceptions and savings[3] and the law relating to forestry is now contained mainly in the Forestry Act 1967. There are also relevant provisions in the Countryside (Scotland) Act 1967[4] and the Plant Health Act 1967[5].

1 See the Forestry Act 1919 (c 58), s 3(2), and the Forestry (Transfer of Woods) Act 1923 (c 21), s 1 (both repealed).
2 Ie the Forestry Act 1919; the Forestry (Transfer of Woods) Act 1923; the Forestry Act 1927 (c 6); the Forestry Act 1945 (c 35); the Forestry Act 1947 (c 21); the Forestry Act 1951 (14 & 15 Geo 6, c 61); and the Forestry (Sale of Land) (Scotland) Act 1963 (c 23).
3 See the Forestry Act 1967 (c 10), s 50, Sch 6, Sch 7, Pt II.
4 See the Countryside (Scotland) Act 1967 (c 86), ss 58–60, 66, and paras 607, 609, 610, 617, 634–637, below.
5 See the Plant Health Act 1967 (c 8), ss 1–3, and para 608 below.

2. THE FORESTRY COMMISSION

(1) CONSTITUTION, POWERS AND DUTIES

603. Constitution. The Forestry Commissioners consist of a chairman and not more than ten other members appointed by Her Majesty, of whom three must be persons who have special knowledge and experience of forestry, at least one must be a person who has scientific attainments and a technical knowledge of forestry, and at least one must be a person who has special knowledge and experience of the timber trade[1].

The commissioners may act by three of their number and notwithstanding a vacancy in their number[2]. They also have the authority to regulate their own procedure[2]. There is an official seal which is officially and judicially noticed[3]; The seal must be authenticated by a Forestry Commissioner, or by the secretary to the commissioners, or by some person authorised by the commissioners to act on behalf of the secretary[4].

As a government department the Forestry Commission can sue and be sued in name of the Lord Advocate[5].

1 Forestry Act 1967 (c 10), s 2(1), (2) (amended by the Forestry Act 1981 (c 39), s 5).
2 Forestry Act 1967, s 2(4), Sch 1, para 3.
3 Ibid, Sch 1, para 4(1).
4 Ibid, Sch 1, para 4(2).
5 *Lord Advocate v Argyll County Council* 1950 SC 304, 1950 SLT 264, OH.

604. Documents. Every document purporting to be an order or other instrument issued by the Forestry Commissioners and to be sealed and authenticated[1], or to be signed by the secretary to the commissioners or anyone authorised by them to act for the secretary, must be received in evidence, and is deemed to be such order or instrument without further proof, unless the contrary is shown[2]. The mode of proving certain documents provided by the Documentary Evidence Act 1868[3] applies to documents issued by the commissioners[4].

1 As to authentication, see para 603 above.
2 Forestry Act 1967 (c 10), s 2(4), Sch 1, para 5(1).
3 Ie the Documentary Evidence Act 1868 (c 37), amended by the Documentary Evidence Act 1882 (c 9): see EVIDENCE.
4 Forestry Act 1967, Sch 1, para 5(2).

605. Staff. The Forestry Commissioners may appoint and employ such officers and servants as they think necessary and may remove any officer or servant so appointed or employed[1]. There must be paid to such officers and servants such salaries or remuneration as the ministers[2] may, with the approval of the Treasury, determine[3].

1 Forestry Act 1967 (c 10), s 2(4), Sch 1, para 6(1).
2 Ie the Minister of Agriculture, Fisheries and Food as respects England, and a Secretary of State as respects Wales and Scotland: ibid, s 49(1). The functions of the ministers under Sch 1, Pt I (paras 1–8), are exercised by them jointly, except in so far as they make arrangements that Sch 1, para 8, does not apply: Sch 1, para 8.
3 Ibid, Sch 1, para 6(2).

606. The general duty of the Forestry Commission. The Forestry Commissioners are charged with the general duty of promoting the interests of forestry, the development of afforestation and the production and supply of timber and other forest products in Great Britain[1]. This general duty includes that of promoting the establishment and maintenance of adequate reserves of growing trees[2]. In exercising their statutory functions, the commissioners must comply with such directions as are given to them by the ministers[3], and these directions must be given jointly except in so far as the ministers make arrangements otherwise[4].

In discharging their functions under the Forestry Acts 1967 and 1979[5] the commissioners must, so far as may be consistent with the proper discharge of those functions, endeavour to achieve a reasonable balance between (1) the development of afforestation, the management of forests and the production and supply of timber; and (2) the conservation and enhancement of natural beauty and the conservation of flora, fauna and geological or physiographical features of special interest[6].

1 Forestry Act 1967 (c 10), s 1(2).
2 Ibid, s 1(3).
3 Ibid, s 1(4). For the ministers, see para 605, note 2, above.
4 Ibid, s 1(5).
5 Ie the Forestry Act 1967 and the Forestry Act 1979 (c 21): s 3(1).
6 Forestry Act 1967, s 1(3A) (added by the Wildlife and Countryside (Amendment) Act 1985 (c 31), s 4). As to the national interest and conservation, see para 607 below.

607. The national interest and conservation. The ministers[1] are required in performing their functions under the Forestry Act 1967 to have regard to the national interest in maintaining and expanding the forestry resources of Great Britain[2], and, in exercising their functions relating to land, both ministers and commissioners must have regard to the desirability of conserving the natural beauty and amenity of the countryside[3].

1 For the ministers, see para 605, note 2, above.
2 Forestry Act 1967 (c 10), s 8A (added by the Forestry Act 1981 (c 39), s 4).
3 Countryside (Scotland) Act 1967 (c 86), s 66.

608. Management of forestry land. The Forestry Commissioners may manage, plant and otherwise use, for the purpose of the exercise of their statutory functions, any land placed at their disposal by the Secretary of State for Scotland, and these powers include the power to erect buildings or execute works on the land[1]. Any timber produced on land so placed at the commissioners[1] disposal belongs to the commissioners[2]. The commissioners may also (1) undertake the management or supervision or give assistance or advice in relation to the planting or management of woods and forests[3]; (2) purchase or otherwise acquire standing timber and sell or otherwise dispose of any timber belonging to them and generally promote the supply, sale, utilisation and conversion of timber[4]; (3) establish and carry on, or aid in the establishment and carrying on, of woodland industries[5]; (4) make an order requiring the owner and occupier of any land to afford facilities, subject to payment of reasonable rent and compensation for damage done, for the haulage of timber from any wood or forest to a road, railway or waterway[6]; (5) take steps to prevent damage to trees or tree plants by rabbits, hares and vermin and make orders for the control of timber pests and diseases[7]; (6) undertake the collection, preparation, publication of statistics relating to forestry and promote and develop instruction and training in forestry by establishing or aiding schools or other educational institutions or in such other manner as they think fit[8]; (7) make inquiries, experiments and research regarding forestry and its teaching, and publish the results[9]; and (8) with Treasury approval, make grants and loans out of the Forestry Fund to owners and lessees of land for and in connection with the use and management of the land for forestry purposes[10].

1 Forestry Act 1967 (c 10), s 3(1)(a).
2 Ibid, s 3(1)(b). For the purposes of s 3, 'timber' includes all forest products: s 3(4).
3 Ibid, s 3(2).
4 Ibid, s 3(3)(a).
5 Ibid, s 3(3)(b).
6 See ibid, s 6.
7 See ibid, s 7, and the Plant Health Act 1967 (c 8), ss 2, 3 (amended by the Criminal Justice Act 1967 (c 80), ss 92, 106(2), Sch 3, Pt II; the European Communities Act 1972 (c 68), s 4, Sch 4, para 8; the Customs and Excise Management Act 1979 (c 2), s 177(1), Sch 4, para 12, Table Pt I; and the Criminal Justice Act 1982 (c 48), s 42). For the purpose of the Plant Health Act 1967, the Forestry Commissioners are competent authorities as regards the protection of forest trees and timber, including all forest products, from attack by pests: see s 1(2)(a). As to the prevention of damage by rabbits, hares and vermin, see GAME, paras 866, 867, below.
8 Forestry Act 1967, s 8(a).
9 Ibid, s 8(b).
10 Forestry Act 1979 (c 21), s 1.

609. Byelaws and regulations. The Forestry Commissioners may, by statutory instrument, make byelaws with respect to any land which is under their management or control and to which the public has or may be permitted to have access[1].

The commissioners' authority is to make byelaws which appear to them to be necessary (1) for the preservation of any trees or timber on the commissioners' property; (2) for prohibiting or regulating any act or thing likely to injure or disfigure the land or its amenities; and (3) for regulating the reasonable use of the land by the public for the purposes of exercise and recreation[2]. In addition, subject to the commissioners' duty to consult with the Home Grown Timber Advisory Committee[3], they may, by statutory instrument, make regulations for prescribing anything which is authorised to be prescribed in regard to their powers to control felling[4].

1 See the Forestry Act 1967 (c 10), s 46 (amended by the Criminal Justice Act 1967 (c 80), ss 92, 106(2), Sch 3, Pt I; the Countryside (Scotland) Act 1967 (c 86), s 58(3); and the Criminal Procedure (Scotland) Act 1975 (c 21), s 289H, Sch 7D, para 25 (added by the Criminal Justice Act 1982 (c 48), s 54, Sch 6)).
2 Forestry Act 1967, s 46(2)(a)–(c). As to the provision of tourist, recreational or sporting facilities, see para 610 below.
3 As to the Home Grown Timber Advisory Committee, see para 612 below.
4 See the Forestry Act 1967, s 32. As to the control of felling, see paras 616 ff below.

610. Provision of tourist, recreational or sporting facilities. The Forestry Commissioners may on land placed at their disposal by the Secretary of State provide[1], or arrange for or assist in providing tourist, recreational or sporting facilities and any equipment, facilities or works ancillary thereto[2].

1 'Provide' includes manage, maintain and improve: Countryside (Scotland) Act 1967 (c 86), s 58(2).
2 See ibid, s 58(1)–(4).

(2) COMMITTEES

611. Appointment of committees. The Forestry Commissioners must by order appoint committees for England, Scotland and Wales respectively, consisting partly of commissioners or officers of the commissioners and other persons, not exceeding three in number, who are not commissioners or their officers[1]. The commissioners may delegate to these committees any of their functions, subject to such restrictions or conditions as they think fit[2]. Any such order creating a committee must make provision as to its constitution, quorum and procedure[3].

1 Forestry Act 1967 (c 10), s 2(3). Travelling and other allowances in respect of members who are not commissioners or officers of the commissioners are paid out of the Forestry Fund: see s 2(4), Sch 1, paras 7(2).
2 Ibid, s 2(3).
3 Ibid, Sch 1, para 7(1).

612. Central and regional advisory committees. For the purpose of advising them as to the performance of their functions in relation to the establishment and maintenance of adequate reserves of growing trees, the control of tree-felling and such other functions as they may determine, the Forestry Commissioners must maintain the central advisory committee for Great Britain known as the Home Grown Timber Advisory Committee and a regional advisory committee for each conservancy[1]. 'Conservancy' means any area in Great Britain which may for the time being be designated by the commissioners as a conservancy for the purposes of the performance of their functions[2].

In relation to the performance of their duty of promoting the establishment and maintenance of adequate reserves of growing trees, the commissioners must from time to time, and as a general rule not less than quarterly, consult with the Home Grown Timber Advisory Committee[3]. The commissioners also have the power to make regulations by statutory instrument authorised under the provisions of the Forestry Act 1967 for prescribing anything relating to the control and licensing of tree-felling[4]. This power may only be exercised after consultation with the Home Grown Timber Advisory Committee[5]. In considering whether to refuse a felling licence or grant it conditionally or unconditionally, and in considering whether to give felling directions, the commissioners must take into account any advice tendered by the appropriate regional advisory committee[6].

1 Forestry Act 1967 (c 10), s 37(1). As to the composition etc of advisory committees, see s 38. As to the control of tree-felling, see paras 616 ff below.
2 Ibid, s 35, applied by s 37(1)(b).
3 Ibid, s 37(2).

4 See ibid, s 32.
5 Ibid, s 37(2).
6 Ibid, s 37(3).

3. FORESTRY DEDICATION AGREEMENTS AND GRANT SCHEMES

613. Introduction. The dedication scheme was first introduced by the Forestry Act 1947 (c 21), now repealed. The scheme was devised to help rehabilitate the legacy of some 750,000 acres of devastated or felled woodlands following two world wars.

Private owners who dedicated their land to forestry were to receive financial assistance from the state to encourage systematic and efficient management of the dedicated land[1].

1 As to the taxation of forest, see paras 641 ff below.

614. Forestry dedication agreements. Since 1 July 1981 it has been the policy of the Forestry Commissioners not to enter into any new dedication agreements, but existing agreements will continue in effect for some years and are relevant for inclusion here. The commissioners' power to enter into dedication agreements continued under the Forestry Act 1967, allowing land to be devoted to forestry by means of agreements, entered into with the Commissioners[1]. These agreements have the effect that the land must not, except with the previous consent in writing of the commissioners or, in the case of dispute, under direction of the Secretary of State for Scotland, be used otherwise than for the growing of timber or other forestry products in accordance with the rules or practice of good forestry or for purposes connected therewith[1].

'Forestry dedication agreement' means an agreement to such effect entered into with the commissioners in respect of land in Scotland by a person who is the proprietor thereof for his own absolute use, or is the liferenter or the heir of entail in possession of the land, or a trustee[2]. A forestry dedication agreement recorded in the General Register of Sasines or the Land Register for Scotland may be enforced at the instance of the commissioners against any person having an interest in that land and against any person deriving title from him[3]. However, it is not enforceable against any third party who has in *bona fide* onerously acquired right (whether completed by infeftment or not) to his interest in the land prior to the agreement being recorded or against any party deriving title from such third party[4]. In practice, however, the form of agreement used contains more than the agreement as defined, and not only restricts the use of the lands described therein to forestry, echoing faithfully the wording of the Act, but also includes ancillary provision setting out terms and conditions for payment of grant. Such ancillary provisions cannot be so enforced. Release from dedication may be applied for at any time.

1 Forestry Act 1967 (c 10), s 5(1).
2 See ibid, s 5(1)(b), (4), Sch 2, para 4.
3 Ibid, s 5(3), and the Land Registration (Scotland) Act 1979 (c 33), s 29(2).
4 Forestry Act 1967, s 5(3) proviso.

615. The Forestry Grant Scheme. The Forestry Grant Scheme was introduced on 1 October 1981 in place of the dedication scheme, and was designed to retain the practical advantages of the earlier grant arrangements while reducing costs by simplifying the administrative and legal procedures[1]. There is no recordable agreement; the agreement comprises the application for entry to the scheme with the approval of the Forestry Commissioners indorsed thereon. As for dedication, applications are subject to approval by the commissioners after consultation as appropriate with relevant authorities on land use and environmental considerations[2].

From 15 July 1988 an applicant for grant aid for new forestry planting may be required to undertake a formal assessment of the effects that the proposed planting would be expected to have on the environment before the commissioners decide whether or not to make a grant[3].

1 The Forestry Grant Scheme was succeeded by the Woodland Grant Scheme in April 1988.
2 See generally paras 606 ff above.
3 See the Environmental Assessment (Afforestation) Regulations 1988, SI 1988/1207.

4. CONTROL OF THE FELLING OF TREES

(1) FELLING LICENCES

616. Application for a felling licence. Subject to certain exceptions which the Forestry Commissioners may by regulations modify, a felling licence granted by the commissioners is required for the felling of growing trees[1]. Application for a felling licence may be made to the commissioners in the prescribed manner by a person having such an estate or interest in the land on which the trees are growing as enables him, with or without the consent of any other person, to fell the trees[2]. On any such application the commissioners may grant the licence, or grant it subject to conditions, or refuse it, but they must grant it unconditionally except where it appears to them to be expedient to do otherwise (1) in the interests of good forestry or agriculture or of the amenities of the district; or (2) for the purpose of complying with their duty of promoting the establishment and maintenance in Great Britain of adequate reserves of growing trees[3]. In considering any such application, the commissioners must take into account any advice tendered by the appropriate regional advisory committee[4]. Any felling licence granted continues in force for such period of not less than one year from the date on which it is granted as may be specified in the licence[5].

If the commissioners do not within three months after receiving the application for a felling licence, or within such further time as may be agreed with the applicant, give notice to him of their decision on the application, it is to be treated as if it had been refused[6].

1 Forestry Act 1967 (c 10), s 9. For the exceptions, see para 617 below. As to the application of Pt II (ss 9–36) to Crown land, see s 33.
2 Ibid, s 10(1). For the prescribed form, see the Forestry (Felling of Trees) Regulations 1979, SI 1979/791, reg 4(a), Sch 2 (substituted by SI 1987/632). The application must be accompanied by an ordnance survey map: see reg 4(b) (as so substituted).
3 Forestry Act 1967, s 10(2).
4 Ibid, s 37(3). As to regional advisory committees, see para 612 above.
5 Ibid, s 10(3).
6 Ibid, s 13(1).

617. Exemption from requirement of a felling licence. A felling licence is not required for:
(1) the felling of trees with a diameter not exceeding 8 centimetres or, in the case of coppice or underwood, with a diameter not exceeding 15 centimetres[1]:

(2) the felling of fruit trees or trees standing or growing on land comprised in an orchard, garden, churchyard or public open space[2];

(3) the topping or lopping of trees or the trimming or laying of hedges[3];

(4) the felling by any person of trees on land in his occupation or occupied by a tenant of his (a) where the trees have a diameter not exceeding 10 centimetres and the felling is carried out in order to improve the growth of other trees; or (b) where the aggregate cubic content of the trees which are to be felled without a licence does not exceed 5 cubic metres in any quarter, and the aggregate cubic content of the trees so felled which are sold by that person whether before or after the felling does not exceed 2 cubic metres in any quarter, or such larger quantity as the Forestry Commissioners may in a particular case allow[4];

(5) the felling of any tree for the prevention of danger or the prevention or abatement of a nuisance[5];

(6) the felling of any tree in compliance with any obligation imposed by or under an Act of Parliament[6];

(7) the felling of any tree which is carried out by, or at the request of, an electricity board because the tree obstructs the construction by the board of a main transmission line or other electric line, or interferes or would interfere with the maintenance or working of such a line belonging to the board[7];

(8) the felling of any tree which is immediately required for the purpose of carrying out development authorised by planning permission granted or deemed to be granted under the town and country planning legislation[8].

The commissioners have the power to provide for additional exceptions by means of regulations and can also modify by regulation the relevant diameters of trees for exemption purposes or the relevant aggregate cubic contents[9].

1 Forestry Act 1967 (c 10), s 9(2)(a) (amended by the Forestry Act 1979 (c 21), s 2(1), Sch 1).
2 Forestry Act 1967, s 9(2)(b). 'Public open space' means land laid out as a public garden or used (otherwise than in pursuance of certain statutory provisions) for the purpose of public recreation, or land being a disused burial ground: s 9(6) (amended by the Countryside (Scotland) Act 1967 (c 86), s 58(5)).
3 Forestry Act 1967, s 9(2)(c).
4 Ibid, s 9(3) (amended by the Forestry Act 1979, Sch 1, and the Forestry (Modification of Felling Restrictions) Regulations 1985, SI 1985/1958). 'Quarter' means the period of three months beginning with the 1 January, 1 April, 1 July or 1 October in any year: Forestry Act 1967, s 9(6).
5 Ibid, s 9(4)(a).
6 Ibid, s 9(4)(b).
7 See ibid, s 9(4)(c), (6). See further ENERGY, vol 9, para 650.
8 Ibid, s 9(4)(d) (amended by the Town and Country Planning (Scotland) Act 1972 (c 52), s 276, Sch 21, Pt II).
9 See the Forestry Act 1967, s 9(5) (as amended: see note 1 above). References to the diameter of trees is to be construed as references to the diameter, measured over the bark, at a point 1.3 metres above the ground level: s 9(6) (as so amended). See also the Forestry (Exceptions from Restriction on Felling) Regulations 1979, SI 1979/792 (amended by SI 1981/1476; SI 1985/1572; SI 1986/1356; and SI 1988/970).

618. Compensation for refusal to grant a felling licence. The owner of trees, an application for the felling of which has been refused by the Forestry Commissioners, is entitled to compensation[1]. The compensation paid by the commissioners is for any depreciation in the value of the trees which is attributable to deterioration in the quality of the timber covered by the application in consequence of the refusal to grant a felling licence[2]. A claim for compensation must be made to the commissioners in the prescribed manner[3]. Claims may only be made for deterioration taking place after the refusal of a felling licence[4]. However, no claim may be made for deterioration which took place more than ten years before the date of the claim, and if the trees have been felled, no claim may be made after the expiration of one year from the date of the felling[5]. In calculating the compensation to be paid no account may be taken of deterioration in the quality of the timber which is attributable to neglect of the trees after refusal of a felling licence for them[6]. The value of the trees at any time is to be ascertained on the basis of prices current at the date of the claim[7]. Any question of disputed compensation will be determined by the Lands Tribunal for Scotland[8].

Compensation is not payable in a case where application is made for a licence for the felling of trees in accordance with a plan of operations or other working plan approved by the commissioners under a forestry dedication agreement or otherwise approved by them, and notice in the prescribed manner has been given by the applicant requiring them to buy the trees[9]. If the land on which the trees are growing is, or will be, in the opinion of the commissioners, managed in a manner approved by them, they may if they think fit and subject to Treasury approval, make advances by way of loan to persons interested in the land[10]. The loan will be upon such terms and subject to such conditions as the commissioners may determine[10]. Where a notice to buy trees has been given and the land on which the trees are growing is subject to a dedication agreement, no such loan may be made in respect of those trees, but the commissioners may nonetheless make advances in respect of any other trees on the land[11].

1 Forestry Act 1967 (c 10), s 10(4)(a). The commissioners must give notice in writing to the applicant of the grounds of the refusal: s 10(6). At any time after refusing a felling licence, the commissioners may give notice that they are prepared to grant a licence: see ss 10(5), 11(5). As to the application of Pt II (ss 9–36) to Crown land, see s 33.
2 Ibid, s 11(1). As to compensation where the interest of the owner of trees is for the time being subject to a heritable security, see s 29(2).
3 Ibid, s 11(2). For the form of application for claims for compensation, see the Forestry (Felling of Trees) Regulations 1979, SI 1979/791, reg 5, Sch 1, Form 2.
4 Forestry Act 1967, s 11(3).
5 Ibid, s 11(3)(a), (b).
6 Ibid, s 11(4)(a).
7 Ibid, s 11(4)(b).
8 See ibid, ss 11(6), 31.
9 See ibid, ss 10(4)(a), 14(1)–(4), 31. For the form of notice under s 14, see the Forestry (Felling of Trees) Regulations 1979, reg 6, Sch 1, Form 3. Where a felling licence is refused in respect of land subject to a forestry dedication agreement, no breach of the agreement is to be deemed to have occurred by reason of anything done or omitted in consequence of the refusal: Forestry Act 1967, s 10(7).
10 Ibid, s 10(4)(b).
11 See ibid, s 14(5).

619. Conditional felling licences. A felling licence may be granted subject to such conditions as the Forestry Commissioners, after consultation with the applicant, determine to be expedient for securing (1) the restocking or stocking with trees of the land on which the felling is to take place, or of such other land as may be agreed between the commissioners and the applicant; and (2) the maintenance of those trees in accordance with the rules and practice of good forestry for a period not exceeding ten years[1]. However, no conditions must be imposed on the grant of a felling licence where it is for trees on land subject to a forestry dedication agreement and the felling is in accordance with a plan of operations or other working plan approved by the commissioners and in force under the agreement[2]. If on granting a conditional licence it appears to the commissioners that the applicant is not entitled to an interest in land which would enable him to comply with those conditions, they may give notice in writing to that effect to the applicant and postpone consideration of the application until the person entitled to such an interest is joined as a party to the application[3].

1 Forestry Act 1967 (c 10), s 12(1). As to the application of Pt II (ss 9–36) to Crown land, see s 33.
2 Forestry Act 1967, s 12(2) (amended by the Trees Act 1970 (c 43), s 2).
3 Forestry Act 1967, s 13(2). Where the commissioners do not give notice of their decision within three months after the date on which such a person is joined as a party to the application, or within such further time as agreed with the applicant, the application is to be treated as refused: s 13(1), (2).

620. Trees subject to preservation orders. If an application is made to the Forestry Commissioners for a felling licence in respect of trees to which a tree preservation order[1] relates, and consent under the order is required for the felling of those trees, the commissioners, if they propose granting the licence, must give notice in writing to the authority by which the order was made and may in any case refer the application to that authority[2]. If within the prescribed period[3] after the receipt of the notice the authority objects to the commissioners' proposal, and that objection is not withdrawn, the commissioners may not deal with that proposal and, instead, must refer it to the Secretary of State so that it can be dealt with under the provisions of the Town and Country Planning (Scotland) Act 1972[4].

1 'Tree preservation order' means an order made or having effect as if made under the Town and Country Planning (Scotland) Act 1972 (c 52), s 58: Forestry Act 1967 (c 10), s 35 (amended by the Town and Country Planning (Scotland) Act 1972, s 276(1), Sch 21, Pt II).
2 See the Forestry Act 1967, s 15(1), (3), (5), (6).
3 Ie one month: see the Forestry (Felling of Trees) Regulations 1979, SI 1979/791, reg 7.
4 See the Forestry Act 1967, s 15(2), (4), (5)–(7), and Sch 3 (amended by the Town and Country Planning (Scotland) Act 1972, Sch 21, Pt II).

621. Review of refusal or conditions of a felling licence. Where the Forestry Commissioners refuse to grant a felling licence or grant it subject to conditions, a person aggrieved by that decision may by a notice request the Secretary of State to refer the matter to a committee appointed to review the commissioners' decision, and the Secretary of State must, unless he is of the opinion that the grounds for the request are frivolous, refer the matter accordingly[1]. No such request for review may be made in respect of the refusal to grant a felling licence unless a previous application for a licence in respect of the trees has been refused and the application to which the request relates is made after one of the following dates, that is (1) where a reference to a committee has been made in respect of a previous application, the third anniversary of the last such application in respect of which such a reference has been made, or (2) in any other case, the third anniversary of the first previous application[2]. The Secretary of State must, after considering the committee's report, confirm, reverse or modify the commissioners' decision on the application and direct the commissioners accordingly[3].

1 See the Forestry Act 1967 (c 10), s 16(1), (2)(a), and the Forestry (Felling of Trees) Regulations 1979, SI 1979/791, reg 8, Sch 1, Forms 4–6. As to the composition etc of committees of reference, see the Forestry Act 1967, s 27 (amended by the Forestry Act 1986 (c 30), s 1(b)).
2 Forestry Act 1967, s 16(4).
3 Ibid, s 16(2)(b), (3).

622. Unauthorised felling. Anyone who fells a tree without the authority of a felling licence, when such is required, is guilty of an offence and liable on summary conviction to a fine not exceeding level 4 on the standard scale or twice the sum which appears to the court to be the value of the tree, whichever is the higher[1].

Where a person convicted of an offence is a person having, as regards the land on which the felling which gave rise to the conviction took place, such an estate or interest in the land on which trees are growing as enables him, with or without the consent of any other person, to fell trees, the Forestry Commissioners may serve on him a restocking notice requiring him (1) to restock or stock with trees the land or such other land as may be agreed between the commissioners and him; and (2) to maintain those trees in accordance with the rules and practice of good forestry for a period, not exceeding ten years, specified in the notice[2]. A restocking notice must be served within three months after the date of the conviction or of the dismissal or withdrawal of any appeal against the conviction[3]. A person on whom a restocking notice has been served may request the Secretary of State to refer the matter to a committee for review[4].

1 See the Forestry Act 1967 (c 10), s 17(1), and the Criminal Procedure (Scotland) Act 1975 (c 21), ss 289F(8), 289G(2) (added by the Criminal Justice Act 1982 (c 48), s 54). At the date at which this volume states the law, level 4 is £1000: Increase of Criminal Penalties etc (Scotland) Order 1984, SI 1984/526, art 4. Proceedings may be instituted within six months from the first discovery of the offence by the person taking the proceedings, provided that no proceedings are instituted more than two years after the date of the offence: Forestry Act 1967, s 17(2).

2 Ibid, s 17A(1) (added by the Forestry Act 1986 (c 30), s 1(a)). This provision does not apply in relation to trees to which a tree preservation order relates or to trees the felling of which took place before the date the Forestry Act 1986 came into force (ie 8th September 1986): Forestry Act 1967, s 17A(4) (as so added). As to the matters to which the commissioners must have regard in considering whether to issue a restocking notice, see s 17A(3) (as so added). As to the enforcement of restocking notices, see s 17C (as so added).

3 Ibid, s 17A(2) (as so added).

4 See ibid, s 17B (as so added). As to the composition etc of committees of reference, see s 27 (amended by the Forestry Act 1986, s 1(b)). For the notice of objection, see the Forestry (Felling of Trees) Regulations 1979, SI 1979/791, reg 8A, Sch 1, Form 6A (added by SI 1987/632).

(2) FELLING DIRECTIONS

623. Power of Forestry Commissioners to direct felling. If it appears to the Forestry Commissioners that it is expedient in the interests of good forestry, or for purposes connected with their statutory duties, that any growing trees should be felled either (1) in order to prevent deterioration or futher deterioration in the quality of the timber, or (2) in order to improve the growth of other trees, they may give felling directions to the owner of the trees, requiring him to fell them within such period (being not less than two years after the directions have become operative) as may be specified in them[1]. Account must be taken by the commissioners of any advice tendered by the appropriate regional advisory committee[2], and, in considering whether to give felling directions, the commissioners must also have regard to the interests of agriculture and the amenity or convenience of any farm or dwellinghouse or park usually occupied with a dwellinghouse, or of any land held inalienably by the National Trust for Scotland[3]. Felling directions must contain a statement of the grounds upon which they are given[4]. In the case of trees to which a tree preservation order relates, directions given after the date on which the order comes into force is, notwithstanding anything in the order, sufficient authority for the felling[5].

1 Forestry Act 1967 (c 10), s 18(1). For the meaning of 'owner', see s 34. A person who is given felling directions may comply with them notwithstanding any lease, covenant or contract relating to the trees or land affected: s 18(4). As to the application of Pt II (ss 9–36) to Crown land, see s 33.

2 Ie under ibid, s 37(3): see para 612 above.

3 Ibid, s 18(2).

4 Ibid, s 18(3).

5 Ibid, s 18(5).

624. Restrictions on the Forestry Commissioners' power to give felling directions. Felling directions may not be given for the felling of (1) fruit trees or trees standing or growing on land comprised in an orchard, garden, churchyard or public open space[1]; or (2) trees on land which is subject to a forestry dedication agreement; or (3) trees which are being managed to the satisfaction of the Forestry Commissioners in accordance with a plan of operations or other working plan approved by them, but otherwise than under a forestry dedication agreement[2]. If the commissioners propose to give directions for the felling of trees to which a tree preservation order relates, they must give notice in writing of the proposal to the authority by which the order was made[3]. If, within the prescribed period after the receipt of the notice, the authority objects to the proposal and does not withdraw the objection, directions must not be given without the consent of the Secretary of State, who must consult with that authority before granting or refusing his consent[4].

1 For the meaning of 'public open space', see para 617, note 2, above.
2 Forestry Act 1967, s 19(1). As to the application of Pt II (ss 9–36) to Crown land, see s 33.
3 Ibid, s 19(3). If an application for a felling licence is made in respect of trees to which a tree preservation order relates and the commissioners refer the application under s 15 (see para 620 above) to the authority which made the order, then so long as the order remains in force no felling directions may be given in respect of the trees: s 19(2). As to felling licences, see para 616 ff above.
4 Ibid, s 19(3). The prescribed period is one month: Forestry (Felling of Trees) Regulations 1979, SI 1979/791, reg 9.

625. Review of felling directions. If a person to whom felling directions are given is aggrieved by them on the ground that the felling is not expedient in the interests of good forestry or for purposes connected with the Forestry Commissioners' duty of promoting the establishment and maintenance in Great Britain of adequate reserves of growing timber, he may, by a notice served within the prescribed time and in the prescribed manner, request the Secretary of State to refer the matter to a committee for report[1]. The committee's report is to be made to the person by whom the notice was served and to the commissioners, who must confirm, withdraw or modify the directions in accordance with that report[2].

1 Forestry Act 1967 (c 10), s 20(1). As to the composition etc of committees, see s 27 (amended by the Forestry Act 1986 (c 30), s 1(b)). The prescribed period is three months: Forestry (Felling of Trees) Regulations 1979, SI 1979/791, reg 10. For the form of notice, see Sch 1, Form 7. As to the application of the Forestry Act 1967, Pt II (ss 9–36) to Crown land, see s 33.
2 Ibid, s 20(2).

626. Persons adversely affected by felling directions. Where any person to whom felling directions are given claims that compliance with the directions would involve him in a net loss after taking into account any benefit arising therefrom in respect of other trees of which he is the owner, he may, by a notice given to the Secretary of State in the prescribed manner and within the prescribed period, (1) if he has the right to sell the trees for immediate felling, require the Forestry Commissioners to buy the trees to which the directions relate; or (2) in any case, require the Secretary of State to acquire his interest in the land affected by the directions[1]. Within the prescribed period after receipt of such notice, the Secretary of State may either accept the notice, refer it to a committee or revoke the directions to which it relates[2]. The committee to whom a matter is referred must make a report to the Secretary of State and to the person by whom the notice was given, stating whether in its opinion compliance with the felling directions would involve that person in such net loss, and, if so, what modifications (if any) of the directions would be sufficient to avoid that loss[3]. If the committee reports that compliance with the directions would not involve such net loss, the notice is of no effect, but in any other case the Secretary of State may, within the prescribed period after receiving the report, either accept the notice, or revoke the directions or modify the directions in accordance with the report[4].

Where a notice is accepted by the Secretary of State, the felling directions in respect of which the notice was given ceases to have effect[5]. If the notice requires the commissioners to buy the trees to which the directions relate, they are deemed to have contracted with that person to buy the trees on the date of acceptance of the notice at such price and on such terms (including terms as to the time within which they may fell and remove the trees) as may in default of agreement be determined by the Lands Tribunal for Scotland[6]. However, if the notice requires the Secretary of State to acquire that person's interest in the land affected by the directions, the Secretary of State is deemed to be authorised to acquire that interest compulsorily, and to have served a notice to treat in respect thereof on the date of the acceptance of that notice[7]. This notice to treat may not be withdrawn[8].

1   See the Forestry Act 1967 (c 10), ss 21(1), (2), 31. As to the application of Pt II (ss 9–36) to Crown land, see s 33. For the meaning of 'owner', see s 34. A notice under s 21 requiring the Secretary of State to acquire an interest in land is deemed to include an offer by the person entitled to that interest to convey such easement or servitude or other right for the benefit of the land over adjoining land in which that person has an interest: s 21(2). For the notices and prescribed periods under s 21, see the Forestry (Felling of Trees) Regulations 1979, SI 1979/791, reg 11, Sch 1, Form 8.

2   See the Forestry Act 1967, s 21(3), (6). As to the composition etc of committees, see s 27 (amended by the Forestry Act 1986 (c 30), s 1(b)).

3   Forestry Act 1967, s 21(4). In determining whether compliance with felling directions would involve a person in a net loss, regard must be had to any compensation received by that person under a tree preservation order in respect of a refusal of consent for the felling of the tree: s 21(7).

4   Ibid, s 21(5), (6).

5   Ibid, s 22(1), (2).

6   Ibid, s 22(3), 31(1)(b).

7   Ibid, s 22(4)(a). As to the power of the Secretary of State to acquire and dispose of land, see s 39, and paras 634, 635, below. The interest for this purpose includes such servitude or other right as the person is deemed to have offered in his notice to convey: s 22(4)(b).

8   Ibid, s 22(5).

627. Proceedings in respect of felling directions. A request for a review of felling directions[1] by a committee and a notice requiring the Forestry Commissioners to buy the trees or an interest in the land affected by the felling directions[2] may be made and given in respect of the same directions[3]. Regulations made by the commissioners may make provision for securing that in any such case proceedings respectively on the request and on the notice are taken concurrently and that the proceedings may be postponed until the expiration of the period within which such notice or request might be given or made in respect of those directions[4]. Felling directions are inoperative until the expiration of the period during which a request for a review or a notice requiring purchase may be made or given in respect of the directions and, where such request or notice is made or given, until the conclusion of any such proceedings arising therefrom[5].

1   Ie under the Forestry Act 1967 (c 10), s 20: see para 625 above.

2   Ie under ibid, s 21: see para 626 above.

3   Ibid, s 23(1). As to the application of Pt II (ss 9–36) to Crown land, see s 33.

4 Ibid, s 23(1)(a), (b). See also the Forestry (Felling of Trees) Regulations 1979, SI 1979/791, reg 12.
5 Forestry Act 1967, s 23(2).

(3) ENFORCEMENT

628. Compliance notice. If any works required to be carried out in accordance with conditions of a felling licence or a restocking notice are not so carried out or any felling directions given by the Forestry Commissioners are not complied with, notice may be given by the commissioners:

(1) in the case of works to be carried out in accordance with the conditions of a licence or notice to the owner of the land, or

(2) in the case of non-compliance with any felling directions to the owner of the trees,

requiring such steps as may be specified in the notice to be taken within the time (not being less than the prescribed period after the notice has become operative) as may be specified for remedying the default[1]. If, after the expiration of the time specified in the notice, any steps required thereby have not been taken, the commissioners may enter on the land and take those steps and may recover from the person to whom the notice was served any expenses reasonably incurred in connection with that power of entry[2]. Any person who without reasonable excuse fails to take any steps required by such notice is guilty of an offence and liable on summary conviction to a fine not exceeding level 5 on the standard scale[3].

1 Forestry Act 1967 (c 10), s 24(2), (2). As to the application of ss 24, 26(1), to restocking notices, see s 17C (added by the Forestry Act 1986 (c 30), s 1(a)). For the meaning of 'owner', see the Forestry Act 1967, s 34. A person who is required by notice to carry out works or take any steps may carry out those works or take the steps notwithstanding any lease, covenant or contract relating to the trees or land affected by the notice: s 24(5). As to the application of Pt II (ss 9–36) to Crown land, see s 33. The prescribed period is three months: Forestry (Felling of Trees) Regulations 1979, SI 1979/791, reg 13 (substituted by SI 1987/632).

2 Forestry Act 1967, ss 24(3), 26(1).

3 Ibid, s 24(4) (amended by the Criminal Procedure (Scotland) Act 1975 (c 21), s 289H, Sch 7D, para 24 (added by the Criminal Justice Act 1982 (c 48), s 54, Sch 6)). At the date at which this volume states the law, level 5 on the standard scale is £2000: Increase of Criminal Penalties etc (Scotland) Order 1984, SI 1984/526, art 4. Proceedings may be instituted within six months of the first discovery of the offence by the person taking the proceedings, provided that no proceedings must be instituted more than two years after the date of the offence: Forestry Act 1967, s 24(4).

629. Reference to committee of reference. If any person to whom notice has been given requiring compliance with the conditions of a felling licence, restocking notice or felling directions claims that the works in question have been carried out in accordance with the conditions of the felling licence or restocking notice or, in the case of felling directions, that they have been complied with, or that steps required by the notice are not required by the conditions, restocking notice or directions, he may by a notice served on the Secretary of State in the prescribed manner and within the prescribed period request him to refer the matter to a committee of reference for a report[1]. After consideration of the committee's report the Secretary of State must confirm or cancel the notice to which the reference relates[2].

The notice given by the Forestry Commissioners requiring compliance with conditions, directions or restocking notices is inoperative until the expiration of the period during which a request for reference to a committee may be made, and, where a request is made, until the conclusions of any proceedings following on from it[3].

1 Forestry Act 1967 (c 10), s 25(1), (3). As to the application of s 25 to restocking notices, see s 17C (added by the Forestry Act 1986 (c 30), s 1(a)). As to the application of the Forestry Act 1967, Pt II (ss 9–36) to Crown land, see s 33. The prescribed period is three months: Forestry (Felling of Trees) Regulations 1979, SI 1979/791, reg 14 (substituted by SI 1987/632). For the form of application, see Sch 1, Form 9 (as so substituted). As to the composition etc of committees, see the Forestry Act 1967, s 27 (amended by the Forestry Act 1986, s 1(b)).
2 Forestry Act 1967, s 25(4).
3 Ibid, s 25(2).

630. Expenses in connection with enforcement. The Forestry Commissioners may remove and either retain or dispose of trees felled by them in exercise of their powers to enter on land and take any steps required by a notice requiring compliance with licence conditions, restocking notices or felling directions[1]. If a claim in the prescribed manner is made by the owner of any trees so removed, they must pay to him a sum equal to the value of those trees, after deducting any expenses reasonably incurred by them in connection with the removal or disposal[2]. Unless there is an express agreement to the contrary, any expenses incurred by a person for the purpose of complying with a notice by the commissioners requiring compliance with licence conditions, felling directions or restocking notices, and any sums paid by a person in respect of the expenses of the commissioners in exercise of their powers to enter on land and take any steps required by such notice, are deemed to be incurred or paid by that person (1) where the notice relates to works required to be carried out in pursuance of conditions of a felling licence or restocking notice, for the use and at the request of the applicant for the licence or the person on whom the restocking notice was served; and (2) where the notice requires compliance with felling directions, for the use and at the request of the person to whom the directions were given[3]. Any sums recoverable by or from the commissioners in connection with enforcement may be recovered as a simple contract debt[4].

1 Forestry Act 1967 (c 10), s 26(1), (2). As to the application of Pt II (ss 9–36) to Crown land, see s 33.
2 Ibid, s 26(2). For the meaning of 'owner', see s 34. As to claims and payment of expenses under s 26 in respect of land subject to a heritable security, see s 29(2). For the prescribed form, see the Forestry (Felling of Trees) Regulations 1979, SI 1979/791, reg 15, Sch 1, Form 11.
3 Forestry Act 1967, s 26(3). As to the application of s 26(1), (3), (4), to restocking notices, see s 17C (added by the Forestry Act 1986 (c 30), s 1(a)).
4 Forestry Act 1967, s 26(4).

631. Identification of trees. Any person authorised by the Forestry Commissioners may take such steps, whether by marking or otherwise, as the commissioners consider necessary for identifying trees which are the subject of a felling licence or felling directions, or in respect of which a felling licence has been refused[1].

1 Forestry Act 1967 (c 10), s 28. As to the application of Pt II (ss 9–36) to Crown land, see s 33.

632. Service of documents. Any document required or authorised to be served relating to the power of the Forestry Commissioners to control the felling of trees may be served on a person either by delivering it to him, or by leaving it at his proper address, or by sending it through the post in a registered letter addressed to him at that address or in a letter sent by the recorded delivery service and so addressed[1]. Any such document required or authorised to be served upon an incorporated company or body is duly served if it is served upon the secretary or clerk of the company or body[2]. For this purpose, and the purpose of the Interpretation Act 1978[3], the proper address of any person upon whom such document is to be served is, in the case of the secretary or clerk of an incorporated company or body, that of the registered or principal office of the company or body, and in any other case the last known address of the person to be served[4]. However, where the person to be served has furnished an address for service, his proper address for service is the address furnished[5]. If it is not practicable to ascertain the name and address of an owner, lessee or occupier of land on whom any such document is to be served, the document may be served by addressing it to him by the description of 'owner', 'lessee' or 'occupier' of the land (describing it) to which it relates and by delivering it to some responsible person on the land[6]. If there is no such person on the land to whom it may be delivered, the document, or a copy of it, may be affixed to some conspicuous part of the land[7].

To enable them to serve or give any document or direction relating to their power to control felling of trees, the commissioners may require the occupier of any land and any person who, either directly or indirectly, receives rent in respect of any land, to state in writing the nature of his interest therein, and the name and address of any other person known to him as having an interest in it, whether as owner, or creditor in a heritable security, lessee or otherwise[8]. Anyone who, having been so required to give any information, fails to give it, or knowingly makes any misstatement in respect thereof, is liable on summary conviction to a fine not exceeding level 1 on the standard scale[9].

1 Forestry Act 1967 (c 10), s 30(1). Section 30 also applies to service of documents in respect of compulsory purchase: see s 40, Sch 5, para 2(2), 7(2), and para 634 below. As to the application of Pt II (ss 9–36) to Crown land, see s 33.
2 Ibid, s 30(2).
3 Ie the Interpretation Act 1978 (c 30), s 7: see s 22, Sch 2, para 3.
4 Forestry Act 1967, s 30(3).
5 Ibid, s 30(3) proviso.
6 Ibid, s 30(4). For the meaning of 'owner' in Pt II, see s 34.
7 Ibid, s 30(4).
8 Ibid, s 30(5).
9 See ibid, s 30(5), and the Criminal Procedure (Scotland) Act 1975 (c 21), ss 289F (8), 289G(2) (added by the Criminal Justice Act 1982 (c 48), s 54). At the date at which this volume states the law, level 1 on the standard scale is £50: Increase of Criminal Penalties etc (Scotland) Order 1984, SI 1984/526, art 4.

5. ACQUISITION AND DISPOSAL OF LAND

633. Introduction. Under the Forestry Act 1945 there was transferred to the Secretary of State the power of the Forestry Commissioners to acquire land in Scotland, and all land in Scotland vested in the commissioners at the date of the passing of that Act was thereby vested in the Secretary of State for Scotland, to be held by him subject to the same terms and conditions as it had been held by the commissioners[1]. But until he otherwise directed, the land was to be deemed to have been placed at the disposal of the commissioners[1]. The Secretary of State also replaced the Forestry Commissioners as the person to whom any estate, interest, rights, powers and liabilities of the Crown, Commissioners of Woods and any government department in woods and forests might be transferred by Order in Council[2]. In that context, 'woods and forests' included any land used or capable of being used for afforestation or for purposes in connection therewith[3].

1 See the Forestry Act 1945 (c 35), s 4 (repealed with savings: see the Forestry Act 1967 (c 10), s 50(2), (3), Sch 7, Pt II).
2 See the Forestry (Transfer of Woods) Act 1923 (c 21), s 1 (repealed), and the Forestry Act 1945, s 4(10)(a) (repealed).
3 Forestry (Transfer of Woods) Act 1923, s 7 (repealed).

634. Acquisition of land. The Secretary of State for Scotland may acquire by purchase, lease or exchange land which in his opinion is suitable for afforestation or for purposes connected with forestry, together with any other land which must necessarily be acquired therewith and may place it at the disposal of the Forestry Commissioners[1].

The power to acquire land by purchase includes a power of compulsory purchase[2] exercisable by means of a compulsory purchase order, and for that purpose certain provisions of the Lands Clauses Acts are incorporated into the Forestry Act 1967[3]. However, an order for compulsory purchase may not be made in respect of land:

(1) which is the site of an ancient monument or other object of archaeological interest[4];

(2) which forms part of a park, garden or pleasure ground, or which forms part of the home farm attached to, and usually occupied with, a mansion house, or is otherwise required for the amenity or convenience of a dwellinghouse[5];

(3) which is the property of a local authority[6];

(4) which has been acquired for the purpose of their undertaking by statutory undertakers[7];

(5) in respect of which a forestry dedication agreement is in force which is being used and managed in accordance with the provisions and conditions of a plan of operations approved by the Forestry Commissioners[8]; and

(6) which is held inalienably by the National Trust or by the National Trust for Scotland[9].

The power of acquisition of the Secretary of State includes the power to acquire land in proximity to land placed by him at the disposal of the commissioners where it appears to him that the land which it is proposed to acquire is reasonably required by them for the provision of tourist, recreational or sporting facilities which they are empowered to provide, arrange for, or assist in providing[10]. He may also acquire land which in his opinion ought to be used for planting trees in the interests of amenity, or partly for that purpose and partly for afforestation, together with any other land which must necessarily be acquired with it, and may place that land at the disposal of the commissioners[11].

---

1   Forestry Act 1967 (c 10), s 39(1). The Secretary of State may place any land acquired by him under s 39 at the disposal of the Forestry Commissioners: s 39(1). As to the procedure for the acquisition of land by agreement, see s 39(6), Sch 4, para 2.

2   Ibid, s 40(1).

3   As to the procedure for acquiring land by compulsory purchase, see ibid, s 40(5), Sch 5.

4   Ibid, s 40(2)(a).

5   Ibid, s 40(2)(b).

6   Ibid, s 40(2)(c)(ii) (amended by the Local Government (Scotland) Act 1973 (c 65), s 214(2), Sch 27, Pt II, para 166).

7   Forestry Act 1967, s 40(2)(d) (amended by the Gas Act 1986 (c 44), s 67(4), Sch 9, Pt I). 'Statutory undertakers' means persons authorised by an enactment, or by an order or scheme made under an enactment, to construct, work or carry on a railway, canal, inland navigation, dock, harbour, tramway, electricity, water or other public undertaking: Forestry Act 1967, s 40(2)(d) (as so amended).

8   See ibid, s 40(3). As to the compulsory purchase of land in respect of which an advance by way of grant has been made by the commissioners, see s 40(6).

9   Ibid, s 40(4) (substituted by the Forestry Act 1981 (c 39), s 2).

10   See the Countryside (Scotland) Act 1967 (c 86), s 59 (amended by the Forestry Act 1981, s 6(2), Schedule). As to the provision of these facilities, see the Countryside (Scotland) Act 1967, s 58, and para 610 above.

11   Countryside Act 1968 (c 41), s 24(2), applied to Scotland by s 50(5) (amended by the House of Commons Disqualification Act 1975 (c 24), s 10(2), Sch 3).

635. Disposal, management and use of land by the Secretary of State. The power of disposal in specific circumstances under the Forestry Act 1967[1] and the Countryside (Scotland) Act 1967[2] has been repealed. Instead, the Secretary of State may now dispose, for any purpose, of land acquired by him[3]. Any land required by him, and not for the time being placed at the disposal of the Forestry Commissioners for the exercise of their functions, may be managed and used by the Secretary of State for such purposes as he thinks fit[4]. He may let any such land or grant any interest or right in or over it[5].

Any instrument in connection with the management or disposal of land in Scotland acquired by the Secretary of State and for the time being placed at the disposal of the commissioners is, without prejudice to any other method of execution, deemed to be validly executed by him if it is executed on his behalf by an officer of the commissioners authorised by him for the purpose[6]. Any instrument so executed is for the purposes of the Reorganisation of Offices (Scotland) Act 1939[7] deemed to have been executed by an officer of the Secretary of State duly authorised by him[8].

1 Ie under the Forestry Act 1967 (c 10), s 39(2) (as originally enacted) (repealed).
2 Ie under the Countryside (Scotland) Act 1967, s 59 (repealed in part by the Forestry Act 1981 (c 39), s 6(2), Schedule).
3 Forestry Act 1967, s 39(2) (substituted by the Forestry Act 1981, s 1).
4 Forestry Act 1967, s 39(3)(a). This power includes the power of erecting buildings and other works on the land: s 39(3)(a).
5 Ibid, s 39(3)(b).
6 Ibid, s 39(5).
7 Ie the Reorganisation of Offices (Scotland) Act 1939 (c 20), s 1(8), (9).
8 Forestry Act 1967, s 39(5).

6. THE FORESTRY FUND

636. Payments into the Forestry Fund. The Forestry Fund established by the Forestry Act 1919[1] is continued by the Forestry Act 1967[2]. There is paid into it (1) out of money provided by Parliament, such annual amounts as Parliament may determine[3]; (2) all sums received by the Forestry Commissioners in respect of the sale of timber, or otherwise received by them in respect of transactions carried out by them in exercise of their statutory powers and duties[4]; (3) any sums received by the Secretary of State from the letting of or grant of any interest or right in or over land acquired and placed at the disposal of the commissioners[5]; and (4) any capital sums received by the Secretary of State from the sale, lease or exchange of land[6]. The commissioners may accept gifts[7].

1 Ie the Forestry Act 1919 (c 58), s 8 (repealed).
2 Forestry Act 1967 (c 10), s 41(1).
3 Ibid, s 41(2).
4 Ibid, s 41(4) (amended by the Countryside (Scotland) Act 1967 (c 86), s 58(6)(b)).
5 Forestry Act 1967, s 42(2)(b). As to the position in respect of land not placed at the disposal of the commissioners, see s 42(3).
6 Ibid, s 42(4).
7 Ibid, s 41(5).

637. Payments out of the Forestry Fund. There are paid out of the Forestry Fund (1) the salaries of the Forestry Commissioners and the salaries and remuneration of their officers and servants[1]; (2) the commissioners' expenses in carrying out their statutory functions, including the payment of allowances to members of committees[2]; (3) the administrative expenses of the Secretary of

State in respect of the commissioners' powers to control felling of trees[3]; and (4) the superannuation benefits payable to the commissioners and officers employed by them[4]. There must be paid out of the fund into the Consolidated Fund such sums as the ministers may from time to time with the approval of the Treasury direct[5]. Any capital payments made by the Secretary of State in acquiring land and his expenses in the acquisition, and rent and other outgoings payable in respect of such land for the time being placed at the disposal of the commissioners are defrayed out of the fund[6].

1 Forestry Act 1967 (c 10), s 41(3)(a).
2 Ibid, s 41(3)(b) (amended by the Countryside (Scotland) Act 1967 (c 86), s 58(6)(a)).
3 Forestry Act 1967, s 41(3)(c).
4 See ibid, s 2(4), Sch 1, Pt II (paras 9–13) (amended by the Superannuation Act 1972 (c 11), ss 28(1), 29(1), (4), Sch 6, paras 60–62, Sch 8; the Finance Act 1972 (c 41), s 134(7), Sch 28, Pt IV; and the Administration of Estates (Small Payments) (Increase of Limit) Order 1984, SI 1984/539, art 2(c)).
5 Forestry Act 1967, s 41(4A) (added by the Forestry Act 1981 (c 39), s 3). As to 'the ministers', see para 605, note 2, above.
6 Forestry Act 1967, s 42(1), (2)(a). As to the position where land has not been placed at the disposal of the commissioners, see s 42(3).

638. Regulation of the Forestry Fund. All payments into and out of the Forestry Fund, and all matters relating to the fund and money standing to the credit of the fund, must be made and regulated in such manner as the Treasury may, by minute laid before Parliament, direct[1].

1 Forestry Act 1967 (c 10), s 41(6).

639. Annual report and accounts. The Forestry Commissioners must, in respect of each financial year beginning with 1 April, prepare accounts showing sums paid into and the sums issued out of the Forestry Fund in that year[1]. The accounts must be in the form and manner which the ministers with the approval of the Treasury direct and must be sent to the ministers at such time as they, with Treasury approval, direct[2]. The ministers have the responsibility to transmit the accounts to the Comptroller and Auditor General, who, after examining and certifying them, must lay copies of them, together with his report, before both Houses of Parliament[3]. The commissioners must also make to the ministers an annual report which the ministers must lay before Parliament[4].

1 Forestry Act 1967 (c 10), s 44(1).
2 Ibid, s 44(2).
3 Ibid, s 44(3).
4 Ibid, s 45. As to 'the ministers', see para 605, note 2, above.

7. POWERS OF ENTRY AND ENFORCEMENT

640. Powers of entry and enforcement generally. An officer of the Forestry Commissioners or any other person authorised by them may enter on and survey land to ascertain its suitability for afforestation, or to inspect timber thereon, or for any purpose in connection with the exercise of the commissioners' statutory functions[1]. They may authorise their officers or servants to enforce their byelaws[2]. In particular, those officers and servants may be authorised to remove or exclude, after due warning, from any land covered by byelaws, a person who commits, or is reasonably suspected of committing, an offence under the Forestry Act 1967[3].

Anyone who obstructs such officers or servants in so enforcing, or otherwise in due exercise of any of, their powers or duties, is guilty of an offence and liable on summary conviction to a fine not exceeding level 3 on the standard scale[4].

1 Forestry Act 1967 (c 10), s 48(1). As to the commissioners' powers of enforcement in respect of felling licence conditions, felling directions and restocking notices, see paras 628 ff above.
2 See ibid, s 48(2). As to byelaws, see para 609 above.
3 Ibid, s 48(2).
4 Forestry Act 1967, s 48(3) (amended by the Criminal Procedure (Scotland) Act 1975 (c 21), s 289H, Sch 7D, para 26 (added by the Criminal Justice Act 1982 (c 48), s 54, Sch 6)). At the date at which this volume states the law, level 3 is £400: Increase of Criminal Penalties etc (Scotland) Order 1984, SI 1984/526, art 4.

8. TAXATION

(1) INTRODUCTION

641. The Forestry Commission. As a government department, the Forestry Commission is exempt from all taxation. The remainder of this discussion of the taxation aspects of forestry is therefore concerned with privately-owned woodlands.

(2) INCOME FROM FORESTRY

642. Former taxation under Schedule B. Before 15 March 1988, income tax was charged under Schedule B in respect of the occupation of woodlands in the United Kingdom managed on a commercial basis and with a view to the realisation of profits[1]. Schedule B differed from other income tax schedules in that the tax charge was not based on income or profits. Instead, tax was charged on an amount equal to one-third of the woodlands' annual value[2]. 'Annual value' meant the rent which the land might reasonably be expected to fetch if let in its unimproved state, instead of being woodlands, from year to year[3].

1 See the Income and Corporation Taxes Act 1988 (c 1), s 16 (repealed). Tax was charged on the 'occupier' of woodlands: see s 16(4)–(6) (repealed).
2 Ibid, s 16(3) (repealed).
3 See ibid, s 16(3) (repealed), and s 837.

643. Former election for taxation under Schedule D. The occupier of woodlands could elect to be assessed and charged to tax under Case I of Schedule D, instead of under Schedule B[1]. The combination of Schedule B and Schedule D election represented a very favourable tax regime. Where woodlands were immature and being run at a loss, an election for Schedule D could be made, creating losses offsettable against income from other sources. Once the woodlands became profitable, the basis of assessment under Schedule B, which was unrelated to income received, was generally favourable. The difficulty raised by the fact that a Schedule D election remained in force so long as the same person was in occupation[2] was in practice overcome by forming a partnership, or changing the composition of a partnership, when the woodlands came into profit[3].

1 Income and Corporation Taxes Act 1988 (c 1), s 54(1) (repealed). As to Schedule D, Case I, see, s 18.

2 See ibid, s 54(4) (repealed).
3 As to partnerships, see PARTNERSHIP, and REVENUE, vol 19, paras 1585 ff.

644. Post-1988 system. The Finance Act 1988 swept away the favourable treatment which arose by an election under Case I of Schedule D[1]. With effect from 15 March 1988, profits and losses arising from the occupation of commercial woodlands are not regarded as profits or losses chargeable under Schedule D[2], and Schedule B was abolished altogether[3]. The effect of this is that profits from the sale of timber are not taxable, and losses arising out of planting and growing trees are not allowable, although grants are available under various Forestry Commission schemes[4].

1 See para 643 above.
2 See the Finance Act 1988 (c 39), s 65, Sch 6, para 3(1), (2), (7).
3 See ibid, Sch 6, para 2, applying with effect from 6 April 1988.
4 Ie the Forestry Grant Scheme, the Broadleaved Woodland Grant Scheme (pure broadleaves only), and the Woodland Grant Scheme (pure and mixed woodland). Grants for broadleaved woodland are more generous.

645. Transitional provisions. There are transitional provisions applying to persons who were occupying commercial woodlands at 15 March 1988. For such persons, an election for Schedule D may be made for any profits or losses arising before 6 April 1993[1]. Elections must be made in writing within two years after the end of the chargeable period to which they relate and continue in force until revoked[2]. An election made prior to 15 March 1988 likewise continues in force unless revoked, subject again to the overriding limit of 6 April 1993[3].

1 See the Finance Act 1988 (c 39), s 65, Sch 6, paras 4(1), (2), 5.
2 Ibid, Sch 6, para 4(4)(a), (b). An election extends to all woodlands: Sch 6, para 4(4)(c).
3 Ibid, Sch 6, para 4(7), (9).

646. Capital allowances. Under the pre-1988 law, and under the transitional rules, capital allowances were and are available in respect of the construction of forestry buildings, fences or other works[1] and the purchase of machinery or plant[2]. This did not mean that occupation of woodlands was deemed to be a trade; rather, the profits were deemed to be the profits of a trade[3]. One consequence of this was that the timber was not trading stock; another was that the occupier was not liable to pay Classes 2 and 4 national insurance contributions[4].

1 See the Capital Allowances Act 1968 (c 3), s 68 (amended by the Finance Act 1978 (c 42), s 39(1)–(3), (5) (in respect of expenditure incurred after 11 April 1978); Finance Act 1985 (c 54), ss 62(1)–(3), 98(6), Sch 27, Pt VI. The Capital Allowances Act 1968, s 68, is repealed by the Finance Act 1986 (c 41), s 114(6), Sch 23, Pt VI, except with respect to expenditure incurred before 1 April 1986 and with respect to expenditure under existing contracts (defined in s 56(2)). For the provisions in respect of expenditure incurred after 31 March 1986, other than expenditure under existing contracts, see s 56(1), Sch 15.
2 See the Finance Act 1971 (c 68), s 41 (amended by the Finance Act 1985 (c 54), ss 55(1), (2)(a), Sch 27, Pt VI, with respect to capital expenditure incurred after, and to any chargeable period or its basis period ending after, 31 March 1985), and the Finance Act 1971, s 47(1) (amended by the Income and Corporation Taxes Act 1988 (c 1), s 844, Sch 29, para 32 Table).
3 *Coates v Holker Estates Co* [1961] TR 249, 40 TC 75.
4 See further SOCIAL SECURITY.

(3) PURCHASE AND SALE OF WOODLANDS

647. Introduction. The above discussion concerned the sale of standing or felled timber, with the occupier retaining land. By contrast, a sale of the woodlands in their entirety may give rise either to a charge to income tax[1] (if the seller carries on a trade of purchasing and selling woodlands) or to a charge to capital gains tax[2].

1　See para 648 below.
2　See para 649 below.

648. Charge to income tax. Where a charge to income tax arises, there must be disregarded so much of the cost of woodlands purchased as is attributable to trees or saleable underwood growing on the land[1]. Where the land is subsequently sold, so much of the price for the land as is equal to the amount so disregarded in respect of all or any of the trees or underwood still growing on the land is disregarded[2].

1　Income and Corporation Taxes Act 1988 (c 1), s 99(1)(a). This does not apply to a purchase made under a contract entered into before 1 May 1963: s 99(4).
2　Ibid, s 99(1)(b).

649. Charge to capital gains tax. Provided the person disposing of the woodlands was occupying them on a commercial basis and with a view to the realisation of profits, no charge to capital gains tax arises in respect of the consideration attributable to standing or felled trees[1]. This exemption extends to capital sums received under a policy of insurance against destruction of or damage to trees by fire or otherwise[2]. Accordingly, only the consideration attributable to the value of the land (as if unimproved) is chargeable, subject to the indexation allowance, to capital gains tax.

An anti-avoidance measure prevents allowable losses being created artificially. In computing the gain on disposal of woodlands, any expenditure attributable to trees growing on the land is disregarded[3]. It would otherwise be possible to purchase land with standing timber, sell the timber separately (exempt from tax) and then sell the land, minus trees, at a loss.

Relief for replacement of business assets ('roll-over relief') may be available in respect of the gain attributable to the land[4].

1　Capital Gains Tax Act 1979 (c 14), s 113(1)(a) (amended by the Finance Act 1988 (c 39), s 65, Sch 6, para 6(5), (9)). References in the Capital Gains Tax Act 1979, s 113, to trees include references to saleable underwood: s 113(5).
2　Ibid, s 113(1)(b) (as so amended). This provision has effect notwithstanding disposal arising on receipt of capital sum (as to which see s 20(1)): s 113(2).
3　Ibid, s 113(4).
4　See ibid, ss 115, 121(1)(b) (s 115 being amended by the Finance Act 1988, s 96, Sch 8, para 9, in relation to disposals after 5 April 1988).

(4) GRANT OF RIGHT TO FELL AND REMOVE TIMBER

650. Taxation of the grant of right to fell and remove timber. The grant of a right to fell and remove timber is a part disposal for capital gains tax purposes[1]. The chargeable gain is computed according to the formula in the Capital Gains Tax Act 1979, that is the fraction of expenditure deductible is

$$\frac{A}{A+B}$$

where A equals the consideration received for the felling rights, and B equals the market value of the land after the right is granted[2].

The grant is a standard-rated supply for the purposes of value added tax, if the seller is registered under the Value Added Tax Act 1983[3].

1 See generally the Capital Gains Tax Act 1979 (c 14), s 35 (amended by the Income and Corporation Taxes Act 1988 (c 1), s 844, Sch 29, para 15(b)).
2 Capital Gains Tax Act 1979, s 35(2).
3 See the Value Added Tax Act 1983 (c 55), ss 7, 17, Sch 6, Group 1, Item 1(e). As to value added tax generally, see CUSTOMS AND EXCISE.

(5) DEATH OF OWNER OF WOODLANDS

651. Introduction. The value of woodlands is prima facie included in the value of a person's estate immediately before death for inheritance tax purposes[1]. However, the person liable for the tax may elect to defer the charge, provided the deceased did not acquire the woodlands for value within five years before death[2]. An election must be made in writing within two years after the death, or later if the Commissioners of Inland Revenue allow[3]. The value of the trees and underwood is then left out of account in calculating the value transferred on death[4].

Where the recipient of woodlands upon which the tax has been deferred dies in turn without having disposed of the timber, no tax ever becomes payable in respect of the first death[5].

1 Inheritance tax was formerly known as capital transfer tax: see the Finance Act 1986 (c 41), s 100(1)(b), (2). As to inheritance tax generally, see WILLS AND SUCCESSION, vol 25, paras 999 ff.
2 See the Inheritance Tax Act 1984 (c 51), s 125(1).
3 Inheritance Tax Act 1984, s 125(3).
4 See ibid, s 125(2).
5 See ibid, s 126.

652. Inheritance tax deferred chargeable on subsequent disposal. Inheritance tax deferred becomes chargeable on a subsequent disposal by the person entitled (other than to his or her spouse), whether together with or apart from the land[1]. If the disposal is a sale for full consideration, tax is charged on the net proceeds of sale[2]. In the case of any other disposal, tax is charged on the net value of the timber at the time of the disposal[3]. Replanting expenses, including unrelieved expenses attributable to a previous disposal of timber, may be deducted if not allowable for income tax purposes[4]. The rate of tax is determined by assuming that the amount chargeable formed the highest part of the value of the estate of the person upon whose death tax was deferred, and tax is calculated at the rate current at the time of the disposal[5].

If the value of the timber would have attracted business property relief had tax not been deferred, the amount upon which tax is chargeable on the subsequent disposal is reduced by 50 per cent (regardless, seemingly, of whether business property relief would have been at the rate of 50 per cent or 30 per cent)[6]. If the chargeable disposal is a gift which itself gives rise to an inheritance tax charge, credit is given against the value thereby transferred for the amount of deferred tax which becomes payable[7].

1 See the Inheritance Tax Act 1984 (c 51), s 126.
2 Ibid, s 127(1)(a).
3 Ibid, s 127(1)(b).
4 See ibid, s 130.
5 See ibid, s 128. See also s 9, Sch 2, para 4 (amended by the Finance Act 1986 (c 41), ss 101, 114, Sch 19, para 37(6), Sch 23, Pt X). As to the rates of inheritance tax, see the Inheritance Tax Act 1984, s 7, Sch 1, and WILLS AND SUCCESSION, vol 25, para 1000.

6 See ibid, s 127(2). As to business property relief, see s 104, and WILLS AND SUCCESSION, vol 25, para 1012.
7 Ibid, s 129.

653. Advantages of deferring inheritance tax. It may or may not be advantageous to elect to defer tax on woodlands. Where woodlands have reached maturity and hence their highest value or, alternatively, where it is anticipated that they will not be disposed of during the lifetime of the person to whom they are bequeathed, an election is likely to be advantageous. On the other hand, where woodlands are immature and are expected to increase substantially in value prior to a disposal during the new owner's lifetime, it may be advisable to pay inheritance tax on their present low value, rather than risk a larger charge when the timber is later sold for a higher price.

654–700. Woodlands ancillary to agricultural land. The opportunity to defer inheritance tax does not apply to woodlands in the United Kingdom, the Channel Islands or the Isle of Man whose occupation is ancillary to that of agricultural land or pasture, such as shelter belts of trees[1]. Instead, agricultural property relief may be available on the agricultural value of such woodlands[2].

1 See the Inheritance Tax Act 1984 (c 51), s 125, and WILLS AND SUCCESSION, vol 25, para 1007.
2 See ibid, s 116, and WILLS AND SUCCESSION, vol 25, para 1013.

FRAUD

1. FRAUD IN RELATION TO JURISTIC ACTS

(1) GENERAL INTRODUCTION

701. Purpose of title. The purpose of this title is to examine the effect of fraud in relation to juristic acts. An attempt will be made to consider the consequences of fraudulent conduct in some major areas of Scottish private law. While the scope of the treatment is wide, it is not, of course, exhaustive. It is hoped to demonstrate not only the legal effects of fraudulent behaviour but also to illustrate how the conception of fraud varies according to the particular legal context in which it arises. The criminal law of fraud is dealt with elsewhere in this work[1].

1 See CRIMINAL LAW.

702. Meaning and effect of fraud. Erskine defined fraud as 'a machination or contrivance to deceive'[1]. Before the nineteenth century the scope of fraud was extensive, ranging from conduct deliberately intended to deceive to activities which were fraudulent only in the sense of being considered unfair. Whether behaviour was to be treated as fraudulent depended on the circumstances of the case. Conduct which was acceptable between businessmen contracting at arm's length could, for example, be regarded as fraudulent where the parties were law agent and client or parent and child. Given the wide meaning of 'fraud' at common law, it is not surprising that in time more specific rules evolved to deal with particular situations. Thus, for example, the doctrine of facility and circumvention was developed in relation to dealings with facile persons[2].

The matter has further been complicated by the emergence of doctrines which, while not developments from the common law concept of fraud are, in so far as they involve unfair practices, analogous to it. An example is the doctrine of 'fraud on a power'[3].

The two most important effects of fraud are, however, as a ground for the annulment of voluntary obligations and as a ground for delictual liability. The title therefore begins with a general treatment of those subjects. It continues with a survey of the effects of fraudulent — or quasi-fraudulent — conduct in specific areas of Scottish private law.

1 Erskine *Institute* III, 1, 16.
2 See paras 733 ff below.
3 '... the word "fraud" is used in a variety of senses. The extreme example perhaps is "fraud on a power" ': *Hartdegen v Fanner* 1980 SLT (Notes) 23 at 24, OH, per Lord Maxwell.

(2) VOLUNTARY OBLIGATIONS

(a) Introduction

703. Fraud and voluntary obligations. At the outset it is important to remember that voluntary obligations can be constituted both by the unilateral declaration of the will of the debtor and the consent of the parties to the obligation. However, as most of the case law is concerned with contracts, the treatment will proceed on the basis of the effect of fraudulent conduct on the consent of contracting parties. The categories of error and fraud overlap, and the wider the construction of error, the less need is there for a category of fraud as a factor vitiating consent[1].

While the nature of fraudulent conduct which will affect voluntary obligations is wider than that for which delictual liability will lie, it must nevertheless constitute some form of 'machination or contrivance to deceive'[2]. The major circumstances which will constitute such behaviour are discussed in detail below[3]. However, a false statement of fact or law made in good faith does not constitute fraud[4], unless 'it is destitute of all reasonable grounds, or which the least inquiry would immediately correct'[5].

1 See eg *Defective Consent and Consequential Matters* (Scot Law Com Consultative Memorandum no. 42 (1978)) vol 2, especially pp 92–102.
2 Erskine *Institute* III, 1, 16.
3 See paras 709–712 below.
4 *Brownlie v Miller* (1880) 7 R (HL) 66.
5 *Western Bank of Scotland v Addie* (1867) 5 M (HL) 80 at 87, per Lord Chelmsford LC. If so, the statement would not be made in good faith.

704. Averring fraud. Where fraud is alleged, specific averments of the conduct from which fraud can be inferred must be made[1]: 'general statements are not enough . . . We must know precisely what the things are, and what acts are alleged. What was it? Did he nod, or wink, or what was it that led them to believe?'[2]. Moreover, as fraud is always personal, in an action against a company 'the pursuers must therefore specify the individuals who are alleged to have committed the fraud for which the company is to be held responsible'[3]. Similarly, it is incompetent to sue a partnership for fraud without specifying the name of the partner or partners alleged to have committed the fraud[4].

1 *Sheddon v Patrick* (1852) 14 D 721 at 727, per Lord Fullerton; *Aitken & Co v Pyper* (1900) 8 SLT 258 at 259, per Lord McLaren.
2 *Drummond's Trustees v Melville* (1861) 23 D 450 at 463, per Lord President McNeil.
3 *Smith and Houston Ltd v Metal Industries (Salvage) Ltd* 1953 SLT (Notes) 73, OH, per Lord Birnam.
4 *Scott v Napier* (1827) 5 S 414 (NE 393); *Thomson & Co v Pattison, Elder & Co* (1895) 22 R 432 at 436, 437, 2 SLT 546, per Lord President Robertson.

(b) Fraud as a Factor preventing the Constitution of an Obligation

705. Fraud preventing *consensus*. Fraudulent conduct may operate to prevent the formation of a voluntary obligation. In the context of a contract, this will occur if the fraud has caused an error which prevents *consensus in idem* arising. Where there is an error in relation to the essentials of an ostensible agreement, which has been induced by fraud, the ordinary rules of offer and acceptance may not have been complied with and consequently no contract will have arisen. This situation has been conveniently described as one of *dissensus*[1].

The leading example of the operation of this principle in Scots law is *Morrisson v Robertson*[2]. The pursuer, Morrisson, negotiated with a rogue Telford, who fraudulently represented himself to be the agent (son) of a Mr Wilson of Bonnyrigg, a dairyman of good credit, with whom the pursuer had had previous dealings. Morrisson agreed to sell Wilson two cows and delivered them to Telford, who never paid the price and sold them to the defender, who took them in good faith. Telford was convicted of theft. The court held that there had never been a contract between Morrisson and Telford: Morrisson made his offer to Wilson of Bonnyrigg and this offer could only be accepted by him: this had not been done and therefore there had been no *consensus in idem* and no sale. Accordingly, Morrisson could recover the cows from Robertson because Telford had no title to them[3]:

> 'The owner, in this case the pursuer, does not contract with the fraudulent person who obtains the goods, because he never meant to contract with him. He thinks he is contracting with an agent for a different person altogether. He does not contract with the person with whom he in fact supposes he is making a contract, because that

person knows nothing about it and never intended to make an agreement; therefore there is no agreement at all'[4].

Where there is a case of *dissensus*, the purported contract is null. The general law of recompense will, however, operate to relieve the innocent party who has performed his obligations on the faith of the putative agreement[5].

1 For a full discussion, see eg T B Smith *A Short Commentary on the Law of Scotland* (1962) ch 37 at pp 818 ff, and *Constitution and Proof of Voluntary Obligations — Abortive Constitution* (Scot Law Com Consultative Memorandum no. 37 (1977)).
2 *Morrisson v Robertson* 1908 SC 332, 15 SLT 697.
3 As to the effects of fraud in relation to corporeal moveable property, see paras 761 ff below.
4 *Morrisson v Robertson* 1908 SC 332 at 339, 15 SLT 697 at 701, per Lord Kinnear.
5 *Wilson v Marquis of Breadalbane* (1859) 21 D 957: the defender's liability is *quantum lucratus*, not *quantum meruit*. The pursuer may also have recourse to an action in delict.

706. Test for *consensus*. However, cases where fraudulently induced error will prevent the formation of a contract are rare. This is because the test for *consensus in idem* is objective[1]. Accordingly, if an objective observer would conclude that, in spite of an error induced by the fraudulent conduct of one of the parties, there has, nevertheless, been a valid offer and acceptance, then a contract exists. While the contract may be capable of annulment, it will subsist unless and until it has been rescinded or reduced[2]. Where, for example, it is established that a seller was prepared to make an offer to — or accept an offer from — any person willing to purchase his goods, a fraudulent misrepresentation by a rogue as to his identity or creditworthiness will not usually prevent the formation of the contract, though it will afford a ground for its annulment[3]. The distinction was brought out by Lord McLaren in *Morrisson v Robertson*:

> 'If Telford, the man who committed the fraud, had by false representations as to his own character and credit obtained the cows from the pursuer on credit, then I think that would have been the case of a sale which, although liable to reduction, would stand good until reduced. But then that was not at all the nature of the case. The pursuer never sold his cows to Telford. He believed that he was selling the cows to a man Wilson of Bonnyrigg, whom he knew to be a person of reasonably good credit ... This belief that he was selling the cows to Wilson was induced by the fraudulent statement of Telford that he was Wilson's son. It is perfectly plain that in such circumstances there was no contract between Telford and the pursuer, because Telford did not propose to buy the cows for himself'[4].

Morrisson v Robertson was an exceptional case. As the Scottish Law Commission has observed:

> 'where the offeror and offeree are actually in each other's presence, the offeror's belief that the offeree was someone other than he in fact was would not normally prevent the conclusion of a contract: it would be only very rarely, it is thought, that a court would be able to hold that the offer was not in fact made to the person present before the offeror. The offeror's mistaken belief regarding the identity of the offeree would not, except in unusual circumstances, render nugatory the offer and acceptance ...'[5].

It should be emphasised that any misunderstanding or ambiguity arising from the fraudulent conduct of one of the parties could, in theory at least, prevent *consensus in idem*. The fraudulent behaviour would be an important factor which would be taken into account when determining, objectively, whether or not agreement had been reached. In determining this issue, the courts are not concerned with fraud *stricto sensu*: absence of good faith can suffice. Thus, an offeror will not be bound if the offeree knew that the 'offer' was made in terms which the offeror could not possibly have intended and had consequently 'accepted' the offer to take advantage of the offeror's error. In such circumstances an objective observer could conclude that there was never any *consensus in idem*[6]. This is a possible explanation of the early decision of *Sword v Sinclairs* [7]. There vendors were held justified in refusing to make delivery of tea which, through an error of their agent, was offered for sale at 2*s* 8*d* instead of 3*s* 8*d* per pound. In 1771 tea was a luxurious commodity, and a shilling was a considerable sum: 3*s* 8*d* was a realistic price, while 2*s* 8*d* was not. It could therefore be inferred that the offeree must have realised that the offeror could not have intended to offer the tea at 2*s* 8*d* per pound, and thus there was no *consensus in idem* when he purported to accept.

It must be stressed, however, that the test for *dissensus* is objective. It is not enough for the offeror merely to aver that he was under error as to the value or quality of the subject matter of a contract at the time when he made the offer. Only if it can be proved that the offeree was aware that the offer was made under such an error will the objective test for *dissensus* be satisfied[8]. And whatever the position in the eighteenth century when *Sword v Sinclairs* was decided, such knowledge will not be inferred merely because the offeror has made a bad bargain.

Thus while fraudulent conduct — including conduct *in mala fide* — may operate to prevent the formation of a contract, because the test for *consensus in idem* is objective, in practice proof of *dissensus* will be extremely difficult to establish.

1 *Muirhead and Turnbull v Dickson* (1905) 7 F 686, 13 SLT 151; *Mathieson Gee (Ayrshire) Ltd v Quigley* 1952 SC (HL) 38, 1952 SLT 239; *Steel's Trustee v Bradley Homes (Scotland) Ltd* 1972 SC 48, 1974 SLT 133.
2 See para 707 below.
3 See eg *MacLeod v Kerr* 1965 SC 253, 1965 SLT 358. In the view of the present writer, the fraudulent misrepresentation did not induce the contract of sale but rather the conveyance of the property. For a full discussion, see para 763 below.
4 *Morrisson v Robertson* 1908 SC 332 at 336, 15 SLT 697 at 700.
5 *Constitution and Proof of Voluntary Obligations — Abortive Constitution* (Scot Law Com Consultative Memorandum no. 37 (1977)) at pp 23, 24.
6 W M Gloag *The Law of Contract* (2nd edn, 1929) p 437; *Smith v Hughes* (1871) LR 6 QB 597; *Constitution and Proof of Voluntary Obligations — Abortive Constitution* (Scot Law Com Consultative Memorandum no. 37 (1977)) at pp 26 ff.
7 *Sword v Sinclairs* (1771) Mor 14241. See the approach of Lord Dunpark to this case in *Steel's Trustee v Bradley Homes (Scotland) Ltd* 1972 SC 48 at 55, 1974 SLT 133 at 135.
8 *Brooker-Simpson Ltd v Duncan Logan (Builders) Ltd* 1969 SLT 304, OH; *Steel's Trustee v Bradley Homes (Scotland) Ltd* 1972 SC 48, 1974 SLT 133.

(c) Fraud as a Factor vitiating Consent

707. Introduction. Where fraudulent conduct has not operated to prevent the formation of a contract, it may operate to allow the innocent party to annul the contract, that is to treat the contract as though it never has existed. The annulment of a contract in this situation is often described as 'rescission' or 'reduction'[1]. The important point to note is that, unless and until the contract is rescinded or reduced, the contract subsists between the parties[2].

Fraudulent conduct will amount to a ground of annulment if it has caused the innocent party to enter into the contract under error. The error may be *in substantialibus*, that is, an error which even in the absence of the fraud would have enabled the party under error to annul the contract. Error in substantials, according to Bell, includes error as to the subject matter of the contract, the person who undertakes the engagement, the price or consideration for the undertaking, the quality of the thing bargained for, if expressly or tacitly essential to the bargain, or the nature of the contract[3]. While the scope of error *in substantialibus*, in the context of uninduced error, is controversial[4], few of these uncertainties arise in the context of fraud.

Where an innocent party has been induced[5] as a result of fraudulent conduct to enter into a contract under error, then the error so induced is a ground for annulling the contract if it is material (essential). To constitute material error, the error need not be *in substantialibus*. It is sufficient if the error would have induced a reasonable man to enter into the contract[6]. An error *de minimis* will not suffice. In addition, it must be established that the material error did in fact induce the innocent party to enter into the obligation[7].

Fraud as a factor vitiating consent is, therefore, a particular aspect of error as a ground of annulment. Its effect is to extend the scope of operative error beyond the classic bounds of error *in substantialibus* to enable the innocent party to rescind or reduce a contract which he was induced to enter under a material error. This was recognised by Lord President Clyde when he held, in the *Westville Shipping* case, that:

> 'the quality of essential [material] error (for the purposes of a plea of essential error induced by innocent misrepresentation[8]) covers any error material to the entering into the contract, and the consequent acceptance of its rights and obligations. It involves no closer relation with the essentials of the contract itself (as defined, for instance, in Bell's Principles, section 11) *than is required in the case of fraudulent misrepresentation when pled as a ground for reducing a contract*'[9].

1 Actions of reduction fall within the exclusive jurisdiction of the Court of Session: see D M Walker *The Law of Civil Remedies in Scotland* (1974) p 141; *Young v Roberton* (1830) 9 S 59.
2 This can be important in relation to the rights of bona fide third parties.
3 Bell *Principles* s 11.
4 See eg T B Smith *A Short Commentary on the Law of Scotland* (1962) ch 37; D M Walker *The Law of Contracts and Related Obligations in Scotland* (2nd edn, 1985), ch 14; J M Thomson 'The Effect of Error in the Scots Law of Contract' 1978 Acta Juridica 135. See further OBLIGATIONS.
5 In spite of the views of Bell *Commentaries* I, 262, it is thought that Scots law has not adopted the distinction between fraud *quoad causam dedit contractui* and fraud *quod tantum in contractum incidit*.
6 *Hart v Fraser* 1907 SC 50, 14 SLT 381; *S Straker & Sons v Campbell* 1926 SN 31, 1926 SLT 262, OH; *Ritchie v Glass* 1936 SLT 591, OH; *McCulloch v McCulloch* 1950 SLT (Notes) 29, OH.
7 *M'Lellan v Gibson* (1843) 5 D 1032; *Burnett v Burnett* (1859) 21 D 813; *A W Gamage Ltd v Charlesworth's Trustee* 1910 SC 257, 1910 1 SLT 11.
8 See paras 715 ff below.
9 *Westville Shipping Co Ltd v Abram Steamship Co Ltd* 1922 SC 571 at 579, 1922 SLT 452 at 457, 458 (emphasis added). This approach was not disapproved of in the House of Lords (*Westville Shipping Co Ltd v Abram Steamship Co Ltd* 1923 SC (HL) 68, 1923 SLT 613).

708. The nature of relevant fraudulent conduct. There is a paucity of early cases on error induced by fraudulent conduct[1]. One reason for this is that until the mid-nineteenth century it was a principle of Scots law that parties when negotiating contractual obligations should act in good faith. Moreover, at common law, there was implied into the contract of sale warrandice as to the quality of the goods sold[2]. Liability for breach of warrandice was strict, and it was irrelevant that the seller did not know that the goods were not up to standard[3]. The seller's remedy was to rescind the contract and seek repetition of the price. Damages for breach of warrandice were prima facie not available[4].

Where, however, the seller knew of the defect, an action in damages was competent. While the matter is controversial, it is submitted that the action lay in delict[5]. Thus in *Stewart v Jamieson* Lord Justice-Clerk Inglis observed that if

> 'the seller knew there was a defect in the quality of the seed which he concealed from the purchaser, he is unquestionably answerable [in damages] for that is nothing short of fraud'[6].

But unless he sought damages as opposed to rescission or reduction, there was no need for the pursuer to aver that he had entered into the contract under an error induced by fraudulent conduct.

As a result of pressure from commercial interests, in the second half of the nineteenth century the Scots law of contract became influenced by the principle *caveat emptor*[7], and the significance of acting in good faith was increasingly eroded. Thus, as early as 1856, Lord Curriehill observed that

> '. . . it is not every kind and degree of fraud which is sufficient in law to annul a contract. In many of the bargains which are daily and hourly made in the business of life, there is practised a certain degree of cunning, craft, and even deceit, against which, although there be transgressions of the strict rules of morality, the law does not protect the contracting parties, but leaves them to protect themselves . . . mere disingenuousness, although it be at variance with strict moral principle, is not always and necessarily of such a kind, or to such an extent, as is sufficient in law to annul the transaction in which it may have been realised'[8].

The policy reasons for restricting the grounds on which contractual obligations could be annulled were expressly articulated by Lord McLaren in *Aitken & Co v Pyper*:

> 'No doubt there exists in our law a right of rescission of a contract on extrinsic grounds, such as error or fraud, but that right we know is strictly limited and defined, and any extension of these limits would tend to impair the validity and efficacy of contracts'[9].

There is therefore a tension in contemporary Scots law between the requirements of commerce, which demand certainty in relation to contractual obligations, and the interests of justice, which suggest that a party should be free to resile from contractual obligations in circumstances where it seems unfair to hold him to his bargain. To some extent these have been resolved by the incorporation into Scots law of the doctrine of innocent misrepresentation[10]. In general, however, the need for certainty has prevailed, and there are now specific rules on the circumstances in which a contract can be reduced or rescinded. These are narrower than would have been the case if the law had developed in accordance with the earlier principle of good faith. While it is probably too late to revert to the classical principles of Scots law, there is some evidence that an absence of bona fides may still amount to a ground of rescission and reduction[11]. But these cases do not lie easily with the general trend of developments during the last 150 years with their emphasis on freedom and sanctity of contract, and therefore must be treated with caution.

The circumstances which amount to fraudulent conduct for the purposes of rescission or reduction will now be considered. The treatment is not intended to be exhaustive, and for a full discussion the reader is referred to the title OBLIGATIONS[12].

1 See, however, *Defective Consent and Consequential Matters* (Scot Law Com Consultative Memorandum no 42 (1978)) vol 2, pp 92–102, which quotes extensively from the thesis of Dr W W McBride *Void, Voidable, Illegal and Unenforceable Contracts in Scots Law* (Glasgow, 1976).
2 See eg *Hill v Pringle* (1827) 6 S 229; *Begbie v Robertson* (1828) 6 S 1014; *Gilmer v Galloway* (1830) 8 S 420; *Deuchars v Shaw* (1833) 11 S 612; *M'Bey v Reid* (1842) 4 D 349; *Brown v Boreland* (1848) 10 D 1460; *Paterson v Dickson* (1850) 12 D 502; and *Jaffé Bros v Ritchie* (1860) 23 D 242.
3 See eg *Gilmer v Galloway* (1830) 8 S 420; *Brown v Boreland* (1848) 10 D 1460.
4 See *Gardiner v M'Leavy* (1880) 7 R 612. Classical Scots law did not accept the *actio quanti minoris*, but cf *Jaffé Bros v Ritchie* (1860) 23 D 242.
5 As to fraud as a delict, see paras 719 ff below.
6 *John Stewart & Sons v Jamieson* (1863) 1 M 525 at 529. Lord Neaves expressly stated at 532 that there was liability 'not upon warranty, but upon fraud'.

7 The process culminated in the Sale of Goods Act 1893 (c 71) (now replaced by the Sale of Goods Act 1979 (c 54)). See Lord Kilbrandon 'The Honest Merchant' (1967) 20 *Current Legal Problems* 1, and his *Scots Law Seen from England* (Child Lecture, 1980–81) 1, 5, 6.
8 *Gillespie v Russell* (1856) 18 D 677 at 686.
9 *Aitken & Co v Pyper* (1900) 8 SLT 258 at 259.
10 See paras 715 ff below.
11 See para 712 below.
12 See also *Defective Consent and Consequential Matters*, vol 2.

709. Fraudulent misrepresentations made by false statements. The paradigm of relevant fraudulent conduct is where a party has been induced to enter into a contract under a material error induced by the fraudulent misrepresentation of the other party to the contract or his agent[1].

The misrepresentation must be a false statement of fact. However, a false statement of the legal effect of a transaction has been held to be relevant[2], and a deed has been reduced when the granter had been induced to sign as a result of a solicitor's false representations of his rights and powers[3]. If the statement amounts to little more than an advertising puff it will generally be irrelevant[4]. As a general rule, a statement of opinion will not suffice[5]. If, however, the party expressing the opinion has much better knowledge of the facts on which it is based, he may be taken implicitly to have represented these facts[6]. Further, if the opinion was not honestly held, it will be treated as a fraudulent misrepresentation of fact, namely the representation that the person entertained an opinion which he did not in fact hold. Similarly, mere expressions of hope, expectation or intention are irrelevant[7], unless they were not honestly held at the time they were made[8].

To amount to a fraudulent misrepresentation, the representor must know that the statement is false or be in ignorance of whether it was true or false[9]. If it is made in good faith, prima facie it cannot amount to a fraudulent misrepresentation. However, if an untrue statement is made, founded upon a belief which is 'destitute of all reasonable grounds, or which the least inquiry would immediately correct, I do not see that it is not fairly and correctly characterised as misrepresentation and deceit'[10]. Thus a misrepresentation will be fraudulent not only when it is a deliberate lie, but also if there are no reasonable grounds at all on which it is based.

1 *Mair v Rio Grande Rubber Estates Ltd* 1913 SC (HL) 74, 1913 2 SLT 166. A principal is not liable for the misrepresentations of a third party unless he has adopted or ratified them: see *Thin and Sinclair v Archibald Arrol & Sons* (1896) 24 R 198, 4 SLT 222, and *Aitken & Co v Pyper* (1900) 8 SLT 258.
2 *Stewart v Kennedy* (1890) 17 R (HL) 25.
3 *Menzies v Menzies* (1893) 20 R (HL) 108. See also *Brownlie v Miller* (1880) 7 R (HL) 66.
4 However, there can be liability if a statement of verifiable fact has been included.
5 See eg *Flynn v Scott* 1949 SC 442, 1949 SLT 399, OH (van 'in good running order').
6 *Smith v Land and House Property Corpn* (1884) 28 Ch D 7; *Esso Petroleum Co Ltd v Mardon* [1976] QB 801, [1976] 2 All ER 5, CA.
7 See eg *Harvey v Seligmann* (1883) 10 R 680.
8 *Edgington v Fitzmaurice* (1885) 29 Ch D 459, CA.
9 *City of Edinburgh Brewery Co v Gibson's Trustee* (1869) 7 M 886 at 891, per Lord President Inglis.
10 *Western Bank of Scotland v Addie* (1867) 5 M (HL) 80 at 87, per Lord Chelmsford LC. Cf the approach of Lord President Inglis in *Lees v Tod* (1882) 9 R 807 at 853.

710. Fraudulent misrepresentations made by positive acts. A fraudulent misrepresentation can be made by positive acts of the misrepresentor. For example, in *Patterson v Landsberg*[1] the defenders had not expressly stated that their goods were antiques as opposed to modern copies. Lord Kyllachy held, however, that the appearance of the articles *per se* constituted misrepresentations, and since the defenders had not attempted to displace the inferences which to their knowledge the articles were bound to suggest to the buyer, their conduct amounted to fraud[2]. A representation made by conduct can also be made implicitly. For example, in the *Gamage* case, Lord Kinnear observed that:

'It has been repeatedly decided that to buy goods with the intention of not paying for them is a fraud going to the foundation of the contract, and, if that fraudulent intention were proved against the buyer, I apprehend it would not be necessary to go further and inquire into any particular statements and representations which may have been made by him to the vendor, because his conduct in buying is itself a representation that he intends to pay'[3].

However, it will be difficult to establish the requisite fraudulent intention on the part of the misrepresentor as the pursuer must show that at the time of the transaction the buyer had no intention of paying for the goods. Merely because the buyer was insolvent at the time does not constitute fraud if he honestly believed that he would be in a position to pay for the goods when called upon to do so[4]. Again, it must be established that the conduct was carried out with the requisite fraudulent intent[5].

1 *Patterson v H Landsberg & Son* (1905) 7 F 675, 13 SLT 62. An instance of fraud by conduct is apparent in the case of a 'whitebonnet' — a person who in collusion with the vendor takes part in an auction only to raise bids and with no intention to purchase: *Watson v Maule* (1743) Mor 4892; *Grey v Stewart* (1753) Mor 9560.
2 Lord Kyllachy took the view that the *res ipsa loquitur* principle applied, and the onus was on the defender to show that he had not acted fraudulently.
3 *A W Gamage Ltd v Charlesworth's Trustee* 1910 SC 257 at 264, 1910 1 SLT 11 at 14. See also *MacLeod v Kerr* 1965 SC 253, 1965 SLT 358.
4 *Ehrenbacher & Co v Kennedy* (1874) 1 R 1131: see para 777 below.
5 See eg *Panmuire Gordon v Watson and Montgomery* (1898) 6 SLT 274, OH, where a collie was bought on the strength of its dog show winnings. The seller had earlier fixed lozenges to its ears, but it was established that this was not done with the intention of deceiving the show judges; it was accepted practice for curing prick ears. Accordingly the dog had not been sold with a reputation obtained by fraud.

711. Fraudulent misrepresentations made by active concealment.
A fraudulent misrepresentation can be made by active concealment. For example, there will be a misrepresentation if a seller deliberately conceals defects in the articles sold[1]. Similarly, there will be a misrepresentation if a person obtains a discharge having concealed certain assets[2].

1 Cf *Gibson v National Cash Register Co Ltd* 1925 SC 500, 1925 SLT 377, where it was held that to sell reconditioned goods as new, without disclosure, could amount to concealment.
2 *Assets Co Ltd v Trustee* (1904) 6 F 676 at 692, 12 SLT 48. The decision was reversed on the basis that it was not established that full disclosure had not been made: *Bain's Trustees v Assets Co* (1905) 7 F (HL) 104, 13 SLT 147.

712. Fraudulent misrepresentations made by non-disclosure.
One of the most significant departures from the principle of good faith in contractual dealings is the acceptance by Scots law that, as a general rule, a contracting party is under no duty voluntarily to disclose any matter which could be material to the contemplated contract[1]. There are, however, exceptions to this rule.

First, where there is a fiduciary or quasi-fiduciary relationship between the parties, for example family arrangements[2], solicitor and client[3] or trustee and beneficiary[4], there is a duty of voluntary disclosure.

Secondly, where a person has made a representation which was believed to be true at the time it was made, but before the completion of the contract he discovers, either as a result of a change of circumstances or new information coming to his knowledge, that the statement is false, he has a duty of voluntary disclosure[5].

Thirdly, there is a duty of voluntary disclosure in relation to contracts *uberrimae fidei*. These include contracts of insurance[6] and contracts to enter into a partnership. The concept of *uberrimae fidei* contracts is of English origin, and the older Scottish authorities adhered to the term 'good faith'. It can be argued that the duty of voluntary disclosure which applies in relation to these contracts arises not because they are contracts *uberrimae fidei* but because, applying the concept of bona fides, an honest man would make full disclosure in these circumstances[7].

Fourthly, there remains a controversial residuary category of situations where a duty of voluntary disclosure may exist. If a person by his acts has knowingly misled another to believe that a certain state of facts exist, there is a duty to disclose the error[8]. Failure to do so will result in a fraudulent misrepresentation by conduct[9]. The controversial issue, however, is whether or not there is a duty to disclose where a person realises that another is acting under an error which has not been brought about by the former's actions. If the principle of good faith is applicable, it would appear that there would be a duty to do so. In *Steuart's Trustees v Hart*[10], the pursuer sold part of his land to the defender for £75, believing it to be burdened with the cumulo feu duty of £9 15s, so that when it was sold the pursuer would be relieved of paying feu duty in respect of the rest of the ground. The defender knew that the feu duty effeiring to the land in question was only 3s. In these circumstances the pursuer was held entitled to reduction and restitution.

The case can be taken as authority for the view that there is a duty of voluntary disclosure whenever one party knows that the other is acting under error[11]. However, this view of the case rests uneasily with the principle of *caveat emptor* which has permeated modern Scots law[12]. Indeed, the case has never been followed. It is submitted that the decision in *Steuart's Trustees v Hart* can be explained on other grounds. First, there was evidence that the defender had made representations to the pursuer's law agents to create a sense of false security so that they did not make full investigation of the titles. Secondly, it is the present writer's view that since the seller considered that the payment by the purchaser of the £9 15s feu duty was the more important part of the consideration, there was an error as to the price of the land, that is, an error *in substantialibus*, which even in the absence of fraudulent conduct on the buyer's part would have entitled the seller to have the contract reduced. The defender's conduct was simply evidence to establish that the vendor had indeed contracted under error *in substantialibus*. This view of the case proceeds, of course, on the assumption that unilateral error *in substantialibus* is a ground for rescission or reduction in Scots law[13].

Accordingly, it is submitted that where the error has not been perpetrated by his conduct, there is no duty of voluntary disclosure merely because a person knows that the other party is contracting under error: in the context of modern business ethics, this conduct does not amount to fraud. But if the error is *in substantialibus* and the formidable burden of proof can be discharged, the contract may be reduced or rescinded on the ground of unilateral error *in substantialibus*[14].

1 See eg *Gillespie v Russell* (1856) 18 D 677; *Wood v Edinburgh Magistrates* (1886) 13 R 1006; *Shankland & Co v John Robinson & Co* 1920 SC (HL) 103, 1920 2 SLT 96; *Park v Anderson Bros* 1924 SC 1017, 1924 SLT 689; *Walker v Greenock and District Combination Hospital Board* 1951 SC 464, 1951 SLT 329; and *Kelly v Kelly* 1986 SLT 101, OH.

2 *Woodward v Woodward* 1910 2 SLT 163, OH.

3 *M'Pherson's Trustees v Watt* (1877) 5 R (HL) 9.

4 *Dougan v Macpherson* (1902) 4 F (HL) 7, 9 SLT 439.

5 *Brownlie v Miller* (1880) 7 R (HL) 66 at 79, per Lord Blackburn; *Shankland & Co v John Robinson & Co* 1920 SC (HL) 103 at 108, 1920 2 SLT 96 at 99, per Viscount Finlay, and at 111 and at 101 per Lord Dunedin.

6 See eg *Standard Life Assurance Co v Weems* (1884) 11 R (HL) 48; *Equitable Life Assurance Society v General Accident Assurance Corpn* (1904) 12 SLT 348; and *The Spathari* 1925 SC (HL) 6, 1925 SLT 322.
7 *Defective Consent and Consequential Matters* (Scot Law Com Consultative Memorandum no. 42 (1978)) vol 2, para 3·68; M A Miller 'Fraudulent Disclosure' (1957) 74 SALJ 384.
8 *Patterson v H Landsberg & Son* (1905) 7 F 675, 13 SLT 62.
9 See para 710 above.
10 *Steuart's Trustees v Hart* (1875) 3 R 192.
11 See the approach of Lord Dunpark in *Steel's Trustee v Bradley Homes (Scotland) Ltd* 1972 SC 48, 1974 SLT 133.
12 See eg *Brooker-Simpson Ltd v Duncan Logan (Builders) Ltd* 1969 SLT 304, OH.
13 This issue is controversial: see *Stewart v Kennedy* (1890) 17 R (HL) 25 at 29, per Lord Watson; *Ellis v Lochgelly Iron and Steel Co Ltd* 1909 SC 1278 at 1282, 1909 2 SLT 224 at 226, per Lord President Dunedin; *Stein v Stein* 1914 SC 903 at 908, 1914 2 SLT 107 at 110, per Lord Skerrington. Cf *Steel's Trustee v Bradley Homes (Scotland) Ltd* 1972 SC 48 at 57, 1974 SLT 133 at 136, OH, per Lord Dunpark.
14 The error must go to the root of the contract; a small discrepancy in price, for example, will not suffice: *Seaton Brick and Tile Co Ltd v Mitchell* (1900) 2 F 550, 7 SLT 384. Cf *Hamilton v Western Bank of Scotland* (1861) 23 D 1033 with *Woods v Tulloch* (1893) 20 R 477. See generally J M Thomson 'The Effect of Error in the Scots Law of Contract' 1978 Acta Juridica 135.

713. Inducement of material error. Before a fraudulent misrepresentation is operative to allow the innocent party to rescind or reduce a voluntary obligation, it must have induced him to enter into the obligation under a material error.

The onus is on the innocent party to establish that he was in fact induced to enter the contract as a result of the fraudulent conduct[1]. If inducement cannot be proved, the action will fail[2]. However, the fraudulent misrepresentation need not be the sole inducing factor: it is sufficient if it was a reason which induced the innocent party to undertake the obligation[3].

The fraudulent conduct must have induced the innocent party to enter into the contract under error. The error need not be *in substantialibus* but it must be material (essential) in the sense that it would have induced a reasonable man to enter into the obligation[4]. The innocent party must also establish that he in fact entered into the obligation under such an error. Thus an action will fail if he, for example, relied on his own judgment[5] or realised that there was a misrepresentation[6].

1 See eg *National Exchange Co of Glasgow v Drew and Dick* (1860) 23 D 1 at 3, per Lord President McNeill; *Lees v Tod* (1882) 9 R 807 at 846, per Lord Shand; and *Spence v Crawford* 1939 SC (HL) 52, 1939 SLT 305.
2 See eg *Ehrenbacher & Co v Kennedy* (1874) 1 R 1131; and *A W Gamage Ltd v Charlesworth's Trustee* 1910 SC 257 at 268, 269, 1910 1 SLT 11 at 18, per Lord Johnston.
3 *Western Bank of Scotland v Addie* (1867) 5 M (HL) 80; *Lees v Tod* (1882) 9 R 807.
4 See para 707 above.
5 *Attwood v Small* (1838) 6 Cl & Fin 232, HL.
6 *Irvine v Kirkpatrick* (1850) 7 Bell App 186 at 237, HL, per Lord Brougham.

714. Remedies. Where a contract has been induced by an operative fraudulent misrepresentation, the innocent party may rescind or reduce the contract. The contract will be annulled and the innocent party may seek restitution in so far as the other party has been unjustifiably enriched; thus, in a contract of sale of goods, for example, he can rescind the contract and seek repetition of the price. When he rescinds, the innocent party must return any benefits he has received before the fraud was discovered[1]. But until it is rescinded or reduced, the contract subsists.

The right to rescind or reduce the contract will be precluded if *restitutio in integrum* is impossible[2]. In the case of fraudulent misrepresentation, however, the courts have not adopted a strict and literal application of the rule that annullment must be refused if specific restitution has become impossible. As Lord Wright observed in *Spence v Crawford*:

> 'The Court will be less ready to pull a transaction to pieces when the defendant is innocent, whereas in the case of fraud the Court will exercise its jurisdiction to the full in order, if possible, to prevent the defendant from enjoying the benefit of his fraud at the expense of the innocent plaintiff. But restoration is essential to the idea of restitution. To take the simplest case, if a plaintiff who has been defrauded seeks to have the contract annulled and his money or property restored to him, it would be inequitable if he did not also restore what he had got under the contract from the defendant. Though the defendant has been fraudulent, he must not be robbed nor must the plaintiff be unjustly enriched, as he would be if he both got back what he had parted with and kept what he had received in return. The purpose of the relief is not punishment, but compensation. The rule is stated as requiring the restoration of both parties to the *status quo ante*'[3].

Provided the substantial identity of the subject matter of the contract continues the courts will, in a case of fraudulent misrepresentation, go to considerable efforts to order restitution[4]. In particular, money may be awarded as a supplementary element in restitution to achieve equality between the parties[5].

There are, however, limits even in a case of fraudulent misrepresentation. Where the innocent party delayed seeking rescission or reduction for several years, rescission has been refused[6]. Similarly, *restitutio in integrum* was not possible where a shareholder had not rescinded before the company, in which he held shares, had been wound up[7]. In particular, where the rights of bona fide third parties have intervened, it is submitted that *restitutio in integrum* is no longer possible and the right to rescission or reduction will be barred[8]. The right to rescind or reduce a contract on the ground of fraudulent misrepresentation will not be precluded by the existence of an exemption clause, since a party cannot exempt himself from liability for fraudulent conduct[9].

1   See *Smyth v Muir* (1891) 19 R 81 at 89, per Lord Kinnear. The innocent party can elect to affirm the contract, but if he does so, he affirms all its terms.
2   *Graham v Western Bank of Scotland* (1862) 2 M 559; *Western Bank of Scotland v Addie* (1867) 5 M (HL) 80; *Robey & Co Ltd v John G Stein & Co* (1900) 3 F 278, 8 SLT 345; *Boyd and Forrest v Glasgow and South-Western Rly Co* 1915 SC (HL) 20, 1915 1 SLT 114.
3   *Spence v Crawford* 1939 SC (HL) 52 at 57, 1939 SLT 305 at 316.
4   See eg *M'Guiness v Anderson* 1953 SLT (Notes) 1. Rescission or reduction is still possible even if a contract for the sale of heritage has been executed: *S Straker & Sons v Campbell* 1926 SN 31, 1926 SLT 262, OH.
5   *Spence v Crawford* 1939 SC (HL) 52, 1939 SLT 305.
6   *Graham v Western Bank of Scotland* (1862) 2 M 559.
7   *Western Bank of Scotland v Addie* (1867) 5 M (HL) 80.
8   *MacLeod v Kerr* 1965 SC 253, 1965 SLT 358.
9   *Brownlie v Miller* (1880) 7 R (HL) 66; *Boyd and Forrest v Glasgow and South-Western Rly Co* 1911 SC 33, 1910 2 SLT 259 (revsd on a different point 1912 SC (HL) 93, 1912 1 SLT 476).

(d) Innocent Misrepresentation

715. Reduction or recission for innocent misrepresentation. The major difficulty facing a pursuer seeking to rescind or reduce a contract on the ground of fraudulent misrepresentation is to establish that the misrepresentation arose as a result of the defender's fraudulent conduct. But it is submitted that these difficulties have been alleviated as a result of the recent incorporation into Scots law of a doctrine of innocent misrepresentation[1]. The chief architect was Lord Watson, who held that a person would have a ground of rescission or reduction whenever he had been induced to enter into a contract under an error induced by the representations of the other contracting party[2]. In these circumstances it was irrelevant that the representation was not made fraudulently. The rationale for this development was expressly articulated by Lord Shaw of Dunfermline in *Mair v Rio Grande Rubber Estates Ltd*:

'Fraud is not far away from — nay, indeed, it must be that it accompanies — a case of any defendant holding a plaintiff to a bargain which has been induced by representations which were untrue; for it is contrary to good faith and it partakes of fraud to hold a person to a contract induced by an untruth for which you yourself stand responsible. It is elementary that a party cannot take advantage of a benefit derived from a contract sprung out of his own fraud, and I think it is equally sound that a party cannot take a benefit from a contract sprung out of a falsehood which he has placed before the party as an inducing cause'[3].

Thus, provided the representation was false, a party may rescind the contract even although the representor had no knowledge of the falsehood or, indeed, believed it to be true. In *Ferguson v Wilson* Lord Moncrieff held that:

'. . . if the pursuer has succeeded in proving that he was induced to agree to enter into partnership with the defender by misrepresentations made by the latter on matters material to the conduct and facts which were, or should have been, known to the defender, it is immaterial whether the misrepresentations were made innocently or not'[4].

1 For a full discussion, see P G Stein *Fault in the Formation of Contract in Roman and Scots Law* (1958) pp 140 ff.
2 *Stewart v Kennedy* (1890) 17 R (HL) 25 at 30; *Menzies v Menzies* (1893) 20 R (HL) 108 at 142.
3 *Mair v Rio Grande Rubber Estates Ltd* 1913 SC (HL) 74 at 82, 1913 2 SLT 166 at 170.
4 *Ferguson v Wilson* (1904) 6 F 779 at 784, 12 SLT 117 at 118. See also *Edgar v Hector* 1912 SC 348 at 352, 1912 1 SLT 93 at 94, per Lord Mackenzie.

716. Material error. At first the authorities were unclear whether the error induced by the misrepresentation had to be *in substantialibus*[1]. However, in the *Westville Shipping Co* case[2] it was accepted that the error so induced need involve 'no closer relation with the essentials of the contract itself . . . than is required in the case of fraudulent misrepresentation when pled as a ground for reducing a contract'[3]. Accordingly, it is sufficient if the error is material (essential), that is, would have induced a reasonable man to enter into the contract[4], and did in fact induce the misrepresentee to enter into the contract.

1 *Woods v Tulloch* (1893) 20 R 477 (however, it is submitted that there was no misrepresentation at all in this case as the discrepancy was only 7 acres in a contract of sale of '132 acres or thereby'); *Edgar v Hector* 1912 SC 348 at 353, 1912 1 SLT 93 at 95, per Lord President Dunedin.
2 *Westville Shipping Co Ltd v Abram Steamship Co Ltd* 1922 SC 571, 1922 SLT 452; affd 1923 SC (HL) 68, 1923 SLT 613.
3 1922 SC 571 at 579, 1922 SLT 452 at 457, 458, per Lord President Clyde.
4 *S Straker & Sons v Campbell* 1926 SN 31, 1926 SLT 262, OH; *Ritchie v Glass* 1936 SLT 591, OH; *McCulloch v McCulloch* 1950 SLT (Notes) 29, OH.

717. Statement must be of fact. To be operative, the misrepresentation must be a false statement of fact: mere opinion[1] or statements as to future intention[2] etc will not suffice. In general it must be express, but it may be implied; however, it will not be implied from silence unless there is a duty to disclose. Rescission and reduction will be precluded if *restitutio in integrum* is impossible. The requirement of *restitutio* will be more strictly applied than in the case of fraudulent misrepresentation, and liability for innocent misrepresentation can be excluded by a suitably drafted exemption clause.

1 *Brownlie v Miller* (1880) 7 R (HL) 66; *Woods v Tulloch* (1893) 20 R 477.
2 *Harvey v Seligmann* (1883) 10 R 680; *Ferguson v Wilson* (1904) 6 F 779, 12 SLT 117; *Bell Bros (HP) Ltd v Reynolds* 1945 SC 213, 1945 SLT 229.

718. Conclusion. It is therefore submitted that when a party seeks rescission or reduction of a voluntary obligation, as opposed to damages, it may be unnecessary to prove fraudulent misrepresentation, since a similar result may be obtained if material error induced by an innocent misrepresentation can be established.

2. FRAUD AS A DELICT

(1) INTRODUCTION

719. Development of the law. Fraud or *dolus* has long been recognised as a ground for delictual action in Scots law[1]. Erskine's definition of fraud as a 'machination or contrivance to deceive'[2] illustrates the potential width of the delict. But during the nineteenth century delictual liability for fraud came to be restricted to a narrow range of circumstances dependent on the *mens rea* of the defender, and there has been a tendency during the twentieth century to equate the Scottish delict of fraud with the English tort of deceit[3].

1 Stair *Institutions* I,9,9; IV,40,21.
2 Erskine *Institute* III,1,16.
3 The leading English case on the tort of deceit is *Derry v Peek* (1889) 14 App Cas 337, HL. It was held applicable to the Scots delict of fraud in eg *Boyd and Forrest v Glasgow and South-Western Rly Co* 1912 SC (HL) 93 at 99, 1912 1 SLT 476 at 479, per Lord Atkinson; *Romanes v Garman* 1912 2 SLT 104; and *Robinson v National Bank of Scotland* 1916 SC (HL) 154, 1916 1 SLT 336. However, this last case is of dubious authority: see *Hedley Byrne & Co Ltd v Heller & Partners Ltd* [1964] AC 465 at 489–491, [1963] 2 All ER 575 at 585, 586, HL, per Lord Reid.

720. Fraud and bad faith. At the outset, it should be appreciated that, while the concept of fraud as a factor vitiating consent in voluntary obligations is wide enough to include conduct which can be characterised as merely contrary to good faith[1], it does not follow that such conduct will be grounds for an action of reparation. Much confusion in the Scottish authorities has arisen from the failure to distinguish fraud for the purpose of rescission or reduction of a contract and fraud as a ground of liability in delict[2].

1 See para 712 above.
2 For a full discussion, see T B Smith *A Short Commentary on the Law of Scotland* (1962) pp 828 ff. See also *Defective Consent and Consequential Matters* (Scot Law Com Consultative Memorandum no. 42 (1978)) vol 2, p 93: 'In the context of delict it may be said that the categories of *dolus* as an aspect of *culpa* are never closed'.

721. Contractual and delictual remedies. The majority of reported decisions on fraud have been concerned with the situation where the pursuer has been induced to enter into a contract as a result of a fraudulent misrepresentation and has suffered loss thereby. In these circumstances it is important to distinguish the contractual and delictual remedies of the innocent party. In a contract for the sale of goods, for example, if the innocent party elected to affirm the contract, the common law of Scotland did not allow him to recover the difference in price between the goods contracted for and the goods delivered: this was because the *actio quanti minoris* was unknown to Scots law except in exceptional circumstances[1]. However, it has long been accepted that the innocent party could sue for such damages in delict[2]. An action for reparation is competent on the ground of fraudulent misrepresentation, even although the innocent party has not sought rescission or reduction of the contract[3] or if rescission or reduction is barred because *restitutio in integrum* is impossible[4]. Alternatively, the innocent party can rescind and sue in delict for any outstanding loss. The law was accurately summarised by Lord Anderson in *Bryson & Co v Bryson*:

> '. . . if there has been in the contract [for the sale of a business] some fraud on the part of the seller I think it is well settled that the buyer has a choice of two remedies: first, rescission of the contract involving the return of the subject-matter of the sale and a claim of damages; and second, a claim of damages without rescission or restitution'[5].

Where the fraudulent party sues for breach of contract, the defender's action in delict cannot proceed as a counterclaim[6].

1 *Gardiner v M'Leavy* (1880) 7 R 612; *Louttit's Trustees v Highland Rly Co* (1892) 19 R 791 at 800; *Bryson & Co v Bryson* 1916 1 SLT 361 at 363, OH, per Lord Anderson. See also R Brown *The Scale of Goods* (2nd edn, 1911) pp 62, 63.
2 *Hill v Pringle* (1827) 6 S 229; *Gilmer v Galloway* (1830) 8 S 420; *John Stewart & Sons v Jamieson* (1863) 1 M 525.
3 *Amaan v Handyside and Henderson* (1865) 3 M 526; *Brownlie v Miller* (1880) 7 R (HL) 66; *Manners v Whitehead* (1898) 1 F 171, 6 SLT 199; *Gibson v National Cash Register Co Ltd* 1925 SC 500, 1925 SLT 377; *Smart v Wilkinson* 1928 SC 383, 1928 SLT 243; *Smith v Sim* 1954 SC 357, OH.
4 *Robey & Co Ltd v John G Stein & Co* (1900) 3 F 278, 8 SLT 345; *Boyd and Forrest v Glasgow and South-Western Rly Co* 1911 SC 33, 1910 2 SLT 259 (revsd 1912 SC (HL) 93, 1912 1 SLT 476).
5 *Bryson & Co v Bryson* 1916 1 SLT 361 at 364, OH.
6 *Smart v Wilkinson* 1928 SC 383, 1928 SLT 243.

722. Procedural and evidential aspects. Fraud is always personal. Where an action is brought against a company or a partnership the pursuer must specify the individuals alleged to have committed the fraud for which the company[1] or partnership[2] is to be held responsible. The principle has been held to apply to an action brought against a government department[3]. The pursuer's allegations of fraudulent conduct must be specific. A general averment of fraud will not suffice[4]:

> 'A party alleging fraud must state specific acts, from which the fraud is to be inferred; he must explain in what the alleged fraud consists, and what are the particular acts of the persons whom he accuses, from which he seeks to draw the inference of fraud'[5].

A pursuer will not be allowed to prove averments of the defender's fraudulent conduct in respect of other persons, in order to establish that fraud was carried out on the pursuer[6].

1 *Smith and Houston Ltd v Metal Industries (Salvage) Ltd* 1953 SLT (Notes) 73, OH. Some decisions suggest that an action of damages for fraud should be brought against the directors personally: see *Western Bank of Scotland v Addie* (1867) 5 M (HL) 80, and paras 782, 783, below.
2 *Thomson & Co v Pattison, Elder & Co* (1895) 22 R 432, 2 SLT 546.
3 *H & J M Bennet (Potatoes) Ltd v Secretary of State for Scotland* 1986 SLT 665, OH (revsd 1988 SLT 390).
4 *Kyle v Allen* (1832) 11 S 87; *Gillespie v Russell* (1856) 18 D 677 at 682, per Lord President McNeill; *Drummond's Trustees v Melville* (1861) 23 D 450 at 462, per Lord President McNeill.
5 *Leslie v Lumsden* (1856) 18 D 1046 at 1070, per Lord Ardmillan.
6 *Inglis v National Bank of Scotland Ltd* 1909 SC 1038, 1909 1 SLT 518; *Hart v Royal London Mutual Insurance Co Ltd* 1956 SLT (Notes) 55, OH.

(2) THE NATURE OF RELEVANT FRAUDULENT CONDUCT

(a) Fraudulent Misrepresentation

723. What constitutes fraudulent misrepresentation. The paradigm of relevant fraudulent conduct is a fraudulent misrepresentation. It may be a false[1] statement of fact or law, but it can take the form of positive conduct, active concealment or failure to disclose where there is duty to disclose[2]. Where the defender's conduct gives rise to a prima facie inference of fraud, for example the supply of reconditioned as opposed to new cash registers, the principle *res ipsa loquitur* will apply and the onus will shift to the defender to show that the fact that the machines were reconditioned had been brought to the notice of the pursuer[3].

1 The statement must in fact be untrue: *MacDonald v Fyfe, Ireland and Dangerfield* (1895) 3 SLT 124, OH.
2 For a full discussion, see paras 709 ff above.
3 *Gibson v National Cash Register Co Ltd* 1925 SC 500, 1925 SLT 377.

724. Parties. Where a fraudulent misrepresentation is relied upon for the purposes of rescission or reduction, it has to have been made to the pursuer by a party to the contract or his agent[1]. However, where a person has been induced to enter into a contract as a result of a fraudulent misrepresentation made by a person who is not the other contracting party, while an action for rescission or reduction of the contract is not competent[2] the misrepresentor may be liable in delict for fraud[3]. Where the representation was not made directly to the pursuer, no action for damages will lie if the defender made his representation 'in confidence' to a third party without knowledge that it would be communicated to the pursuer[4].

1 See para 709 above.
2 *Aitken & Co v Pyper* (1900) 8 SLT 258.
3 *Thin and Sinclair v Archibald Arrol & Sons* (1896) 24 R 198, 4 SLT 222; *Gillies v Campbell, Shearer & Co* (1902) 10 SLT 289, OH; *Robinson v National Bank of Scotland* 1916 SC (HL) 154, 1916 1 SLT 336, where fraud was not established.
4 *J A Salton & Co v Clydesdale Bank Ltd* (1898) 1 F 110, 6 SLT 212.

(b) The *Mens Rea* of Fraud

725. Introduction. Where an action is brought for reparation on the grounds of fraud, the onus is on the pursuer to establish that the defender had the requisite mental element. This will always be difficult: 'In dealing . . . with the question of falsehood and fraud, you have to go into the minds of the parties making the statements'[1].

1 *Cullen's Trustee v Johnston* (1865) 3 M 935 at 937, per Lord President McNeill.

726. The requisite mental element. In a series of cases in the nineteenth century, the requisite mental element for fraud came to be crystallised[1]. The process culminated in the English decision of *Derry v Peek*[2], which was concerned with the tort of deceit, and which has influenced Scots law[3]. In that case Lord Herschell observed:

'First, in order to sustain an action of deceit [fraud], there must be proof of fraud, and nothing short of that will suffice. Secondly, fraud is proved when it is shewn that a false representation has been made (1) knowingly, or (2) without belief in its truth, or (3) recklessly, careless whether it be true or false. Although I have treated the second and third as distinct cases, I think the third is but an instance of the second, for one who makes a statement under such circumstances can have no real belief in the truth of what he states. To prevent a false statement being fraudulent, there must, I think, always be an honest belief in its truth . . . Thirdly, if fraud be proved, the motive of the person guilty of it is immaterial. It matters not that there was no intention to cheat or injure the person to whom the statement was made'[4].

1 See eg *Miller v Giels* (1848) 10 D 715; *Leslie v Lumsden* (1856) 18 D 1046; *Inglis v Douglas* (1861) 23 D 561; *Cullen's Trustee v Johnston* (1865) 3 M 935; *Lees v Tod* (1882) 9 R 807.
2 *Derry v Peek* (1889) 14 App Cas 337, HL.
3 See para 719 above.
4 *Derry v Peek* (1889) 14 App Cas 337 at 374, HL.

727. Statement made without belief in its truth. There is little difficulty where it can be shown that the defender knew that his statement was false: that is a deliberate lie and constitutes fraud[1]. However, fraud is also constituted where a statement is made without belief in its truth. To establish that the defender had no belief in the truth of his statement, evidence can be adduced to show that there was such an absence of reasonable grounds for the statement that it should be inferred that the defender — even in spite of his assertion to the contrary — could not have had a bona fide belief in the truth of his statement or was, at least, recklessly careless whether it was true or false[2]. As the Lord Chancellor, Lord Chelmsford, said in *Western Bank of Scotland v Addie*:

'. . . supposing a person makes an untrue statement, which he asserts to be the result of a *bona fide* belief of its truth, how can the *bona fides* be tested except for considering the grounds of such belief? And if an untrue statement is made, founded upon a belief *which is destitute of all reasonable grounds*, or which the least inquiry would immediately correct, I do not see that it is not fairly and correctly characterised as misrepresentation and deceit'[3].

In *Lees v Tod* Lord President Inglis took the view that there was no occasion to refer to the sufficiency or insufficiency of the grounds of the defender's belief 'unless they be so slender or flimsy as to destroy the idea of *bona fides*'[4].

The concept of a statement made without belief in its truth deserves fuller analysis. In *Lees v Tod* Lord President Inglis drew a distinction between (1) the situation where a person makes a statement which he believes to be untrue: this will amount to fraudulent conduct even if he does not positively know that the statement is false; and (2) the situation where a person merely makes a statement which he does not actually (that is, positively) believe to be true. Where the statement is on a matter of indifference to both the speaker and the listener, the latter situation will not amount to dishonesty. However,

'If the speaker, having no actual belief in the statement, though not believing it to be untrue, volunteers the statement, inconsistent with facts, to a person interested in the statement, and likely to act on it, he is dishonest and guilty of deceit, because he produces, and intends to produce, on the mind of the listener a belief which he does not himself entertain'[5].

In *H and J M Bennet (Potatoes) Ltd v Secretary of State for Scotland*, Lord Davidson relied on this passage to draw the conclusion that 'where both parties have an interest in what is said, the law regards it as dishonest for a person to make an assertion having no actual belief in its truth'[6]. The defender in that case had certified that seed potatoes were free from a particular pest, but Lord Davidson considered that the evidence established that because of the limitations of the tests carried out, he must have had serious doubts whether this was so[7]. While he did not positively know that the statement in the certificate was false, he did not have any actual belief that it was true. As Lord Davidson explained, 'in cases where fraud is in issue, the inquiry goes further than the knowledge of the person making the representation. In a case like the present an assertion is fraudulent if the person making it entertains no belief in its truth'[8].

1 *Brownlie v Miller* (1880) 7 R (HL) 66 at 79.
2 *Derry v Peek* (1889) 14 App Cas 337 at 369, HL, per Lord Herschell.
3 *Western Bank of Scotland v Addie* (1867) 5 M (HL) 80 at 87 (emphasis added).
4 *Lees v Tod* (1882) 9 R 807 at 854.
5 *Lees v Tod* (1882) 9 R 807 at 854, per Lord President Inglis.
6 *H & J M Bennet (Potatoes) Ltd v Secretary of State for Scotland* 1986 SLT 665 at 671, OH (revsd 1988 SLT 390).
7 The Lord Ordinary was overruled by the Inner House on this point: see *H & J M Bennet (Potatoes) Ltd v Secretary of State for Scotland* 1988 SLT 390 at 396, per Lord President Emslie, at 398 per Lord Brand and at 400 per Lord McDonald. However, Lord Davidson's analysis of the legal principles involved were not impugned.
8 *H & J M Bennet (Potatoes) Ltd v Secretary of State for Scotland* 1986 SLT 665, OH (revsd 1988 SLT 390).

728. Carelessness or unreasonableness. Not only must the evidence show that there was no reasonable grounds at all for the statement, but it must be emphasised that the evidence is being adduced to establish the state of the defender's mind, that is, that he could not have had a bona fide belief in the truth of his statement. If this inference cannot be drawn, fraud for the purpose of an action of reparation will not be established. Provided his statement was in fact made in good faith, a person is not guilty of fraud merely because he did not take reasonable care to ensure that his statement was consistent with the facts. As Lord Herschell observed in *Derry v Peek*:

'To make a statement careless whether it be true or false, and therefore without any real belief in its truth, appears to me to be an essentially different thing from making, through want of care, a false statement, which is nevertheless honestly believed to be true . . .'[1];

and in a later passage, he continued:

'A man who forms his belief carelessly, or is unreasonably credulous, may be blameworthy when he makes a representation on which another is to act, but he is not, in my opinion, fraudulent'[2].

This principle is consistent with the approach taken by the Court of Session in *Lees v Tod*, where Lord President Inglis maintained that if persons

'make statements in the *bona fide* belief that they are true, they are not guilty of fraudulent misrepresentation merely because in the judgment of the Court or of a jury they had not reasonable — which I understant to mean sufficient — grounds for believing the statements to be true; for this would be to make them answerable for the erroneous inference which they draw from the facts within their knowledge, which is only an error of judgment'[3].

1 *Derry v Peek* (1889) 14 App Cas 337 at 361, HL.
2 (1889) 14 App Cas 337 at 369, HL. See also *Romanes v Garman* 1912 2 SLT 104.
3 *Lees v Tod* (1882) 9 R 807 at 853, 854.

729. Conclusion. It is submitted that a fraudulent misrepresentation will be established if it can be proved that it was made by the misrepresentor:
(1) with the knowledge that the statement was false, or
(2) with the belief that the statement was false, or
(3) without actual belief that the statement was true where both parties have an interest in what was said.
The scope of category (3) is potentially very wide. Where, for example, a person has taken reasonable care to obtain grounds upon which to base a statement, he

could nevertheless be liable in fraud if he had doubts and did not actually believe the statement was true, albeit that he did not positively know that it was false. This result might well be thought to be far removed from the traditional concepts of *dolus* and *culpa* which are the foundations of the Scots law of delict.

(3) CAUSATION AND REMEDIES

730. Causation. The onus is on the pursuer to show that the fraudulent conduct caused him to sustain the loss for which he claims damages[1]. Where the pursuer seeks damages arising from a contract which he alleges he was induced to enter as a result of the defender's fraudulent misrepresentations, he must prove that the misrepresentation did induce him to make the contract[2].

1 See eg *Gillies v Campbell, Shearer & Co* (1902) 10 SLT 289, OH.
2 This will raise similar issues to those discussed in para 713 above in the context of fraudulent misrepresentation as a ground of rescission or reduction.

731. Remedies. Where a case of fraud has been established, the innocent party may obtain an award of damages. The pursuer is entitled to reparation for all losses which arose directly or naturally from the defender's fraudulent conduct[1]. It is submitted that in a case of fraud, the defender's liability is not restricted to those losses which were reasonably foreseeable by the defender at the time the fraudulent conduct took place: he is liable to compensate for all losses directly arising from the fraud, whether those losses were foreseeable or not.
   A person cannot exclude liability for fraud by use of an exemption clause[2].

1 *Thin and Sinclair v Archibald Arrol & Sons* (1896) 24 R 198, 4 SLT 222.
2 *Boyd and Forrest v Glasgow and South-Western Rly Co* 1911 SC 33, 1910 2 SLT 259 (revsd 1912 SC (HL) 93, 1912 1 SLT 476); *H and J M Bennet (Potatoes) Ltd v Secretary of State for Scotland* 1986 SLT 665, OH (revsd 1988 SLT 390).

(4) NEGLIGENT MISREPRESENTATION

732. Liability for negligent misrepresentation. It is accepted that in Scots law there is now general liability for *culpa* arising from a negligent misrepresentation[1]. Accordingly, while a person who has not taken reasonable care to ensure that his statement is consistent with the facts is not fraudulent if he believed in good faith that his statement was true[2], he may be liable for negligent misrepresentation[3].
   There was, however, no liability for *culpa* where the pursuer was induced by a negligent misrepresentation to enter into a contract with the person who made the representation[4]. The reason for this anomalous situation was the decision of the Inner House in *Manners v Whitehead*, where it was held that a person who has been induced to enter into a contract as a result of a misrepresentation made by the other party to the contract could seek rescission and restitution but could not obtain reparation unless fraud was proved[5]. The rule in *Manners v Whitehead* was abolished by the Law Reform (Miscellaneous Provisions) (Scotland) Act 1985, which provides:

'A party to a contract who has been induced to enter into it by negligent misrepresentation made by or on behalf of another party to the contract shall not be disentitled, by reason only that the misrepresentation is not fraudulent, from recovering damages from the other party in respect of any loss or damage he has suffered as a result of the misrepresentation; and any rule of law that such damages cannot be recovered unless fraud is proved shall cease to have effect'[6].

Consequently, there is no longer any need to establish fraud when an innocent party seeks reparation on the ground that he was induced to enter into a contract with the defender as a result of the defender's misrepresentation. The pursuer will, of course, have to prove inter alia that, in the circumstances, the defender owed him a duty of care[7] and that the misrepresentation was, in fact, made negligently.

In the light of these developments, often an action for negligent misrepresentation will now be competent where, previously, it was necessary to aver and prove fraud. Negligent misrepresentation will, of course, usually be less difficult to establish than fraud. However, unlike liability for fraud, liability for negligent misrepresentation can be excluded by an exemption clause or disclaimer[8].

1 *John Kenway Ltd v Orcantic Ltd* 1979 SC 422, 1980 SLT 46, OH, where the leading English decision in *Hedley Byrne & Co Ltd v Heller & Partners Ltd* [1964] AC 465, [1963] 2 All ER 575, HL, was followed. Cf *Robinson v National Bank of Scotland* 1916 SC (HL) 154, 1916 1 SLT 336, and comment thereon by Lord Reid in the *Hedley Byrne* case [1964] AC 465 at 489–491, [1963] 2 All ER 575 at 585, 586.

2 See paras 727, 728, above.

3 As to the general principles of liability for negligent misrepresentation, see OBLIGATIONS.

4 *Eastern Marine Services (and Supplies) Ltd v Dickson Motors Ltd* 1981 SC 355, OH; *Twomax Ltd v Dickson M'Farlane and Robinson* 1982 SC 113, 1983 SLT 98, OH.

5 *Manners v Whitehead* (1898) 1 F 171, 6 SLT 199. Although the *rationale* of this case would appear to be inconsistent with the general principles of liability for negligent misrepresentation laid down in the *Hedley Byrne* case, no attempt was made by the Scottish courts to apply the maxim *cessante ratione cessat ipsa lex* to free themselves from the case.

6 Law Reform (Miscellaneous Provisions) (Scotland) Act 1985 (c 73), s 10(1).

7 It is thought that where a professional person, at least, induces a person to enter into a contract with him, a duty of care will be assumed: see *Esso Petroleum Co Ltd v Mardon* [1976] QB 801, [1976] 2 All ER 5, CA.

8 *Hedley Byrne & Co Ltd v Heller & Partners Ltd* [1964] AC 465, [1963] 2 All ER 575, HL. Where the exemption clause is a contract term, then, in so far as it purports to exclude or restrict liability for breach of duty arising in the course of a business, it will be subject to the Unfair Contract Terms Act 1977 (c 50), s 16.

3. FACILITY AND CIRCUMVENTION

733. Introduction. Facility and circumvention as a ground of annulment of voluntary juristic acts developed from the common law concept of fraud. Because of the wide scope of that concept, it was not until the middle of the nineteenth century that facility and circumvention emerged as a separate plea. The exigencies of establishing fraud were, however, alleviated because, where facility and lesion were great, fraud would readily be inferred[1]. In the leading case of *Clunie v Stirling*[2] it was decided that separate issues should be granted as to facility and circumvention on one hand and fraud on the other. Nevertheless, the modern form of issue still refers to 'fraud and circumvention' or 'fraud or circumvention'. But in this context 'fraud' means, at most, taking unfair advantage of the facile person to his lesion[3]. As Lord Cockburn said in *Clunie v Stirling*, 'Circumvention sometimes amounts to fraud, and some cases of fraud are cases of simple circumvention; and the two pass into each other by such shadowy gradations, that they are often difficult to be distinguished'[4]. It is not necessary that anything amounting to moral fraud should be established. To make a relevant case it is necessary to make clear and specific averments of facility, lesion, and fraud or circumvention: it is also necessary to specify the person who took unfair advantage of the facile person.

1   See eg *Scott v Wilson* (1825) 3 Murr 518.
2   *Clunie v Stirling* (1854) 17 D 15.
3   Ie harm or loss to the facile person.
4   *Clunie v Stirling* (1854) 17 D 15 at 20.

734. Facility. The onus is on the pursuer[1] to establish that the person who entered into the obligation or granted the deed was in a weak or facile state of mind at the time he did so[2]. The state of facility is less than insanity, but does involve a state of mental weakness arising from, for example, old age[3], bodily infirmity[4], natural timidity or even distress as the result of bereavement[5]. As a result of the weakness, the person must be seriously liable to be influenced by advice, persuasion or intimidation so as to be unable to form an independent and balanced judgment.

It is competent to aver that the person was totally incapacitated mentally — when the juristic act would be null without proof of fraud and circumvention — and to aver facility and circumvention in the alternative[6].

1   Facility and circumvention can also be pleaded as a defence: see *Mackay v Campbell* 1967 SC (HL) 53, 1967 SLT 337, where the defender sought reduction *ope exceptionis*.
2   The pursuer may, of course, plead his own facility in respect of his own voluntary obligations or deeds.
3   *Munro v Strain* (1874) 1 R 522; *Horsburgh v Thomson's Trustees* 1912 SC 267, 1912 1 SLT 73.
4   This can include drunkenness: see *M'Callum v Graham* (1894) 21 R 824.
5   *MacGilvary v Gilmartin* 1986 SLT 89, OH.
6   See eg *Morrison v Maclean's Trustees* (1862) 24 D 625.

735. Lesion. Loss or harm suffered by the facile person as a result of the fraud or circumvention must be averred[1].

1   *Home v Hardy* (1842) 4 D 1184; *Clunie v Stirling* (1854) 17 D 15; *Mackay v Campbell* 1967 SC (HL) 53, 1967 SLT 337.

736. Fraud and circumvention. Proof of facility and lesion does not of itself establish a ground of annulment. In addition, fraud and circumvention or fraud or circumvention must be averred. While the institutional writers equated circumvention with deceit[1], it must be remembered that fraud was at that time considered to cover all conduct *in mala fide*. In *Clunie v Stirling*[2] it was emphasised that fraud in this context did not involve moral fraud.

Circumvention amounts to a course of conduct whereby a person is able to operate on the mind of a weak or facile person to bring that person entirely within his control. This can be done through persuasion or intimidation[3]. In determining whether the averments of fraud or circumvention are sufficient, the courts will consider them in the context of the averments of facility and lesion:

> 'the greater the weakness or facility the less fraud or circumvention is necessary, and the more pregnant the fraud or circumvention the slighter comparatively need be the weakness and facility . . .'[4].

Where facility or weakness of mind is satisfactorily averred and the juristic act is in favour of the alleged perpetrator, fraud or circumvention will often be assumed without proof of any specific act of coercion or dishonesty[5]. Where the facile person is dead, and the plea is raised in an action for reduction of a *mortis causa* deed, this principle will readily be applied since what actually passed between the perpetrator and the facile person will usually be unknown and properly a matter of inference from the circumstances of the case[6]. While it has been said that different considerations should not apply where the facile person is still alive[7], nevertheless such a distinction was drawn by Lord Guest in *Mackay v Campbell*[8]. There the defender had entered into missives for the sale of a farm when he was ill in hospital. On his recovery, he refused to implement the missives and sought reduction *ope exceptionis* on the ground that he had, while facile, entered into the missives as a result of the fraud or circumvention of the pursuer. In those — admittedly unusual — circumstances, Lord Guest held that because the allegedly injured person was alive and a party to the action, it was necessary to aver some facts of deceit or dishonesty from which circumvention could be inferred.

Accordingly, where the degree of facility and lesion is great and, in particular, if the facile person is dead, fraud or circumvention will be readily inferred: but if the facile person is alive and the parties have prima facie entered into a voluntary obligation at arm's length, proof that dishonest advantage had been taken of the obligor's condition will be necessary.

1 See eg Stair *Institutions* I,9,9.
2 *Clunie v Stirling* (1854) 17 D 15.
3 *Love v Marshall* (1870) 9 M 291 at 297, per Lord Kinloch.
4 *Munro v Strain* (1874) 1 R 1039 at 1047, per Lord Ormidale.
5 *Clunie v Stirling* (1854) 17 D 15; *Horsburgh v Thomson's Trustees* 1912 SC 267, 1912 1 SLT 73; *Mackay v Campbell* 1967 SC (HL) 53 at 61, 1967 SLT 337 at 338, per Lord Guest; *West's Trustee v West* 1980 SLT 6 at 7, OH, per Lord Stott; *MacGilvary v Gilmartin* 1986 SLT 89 at 90, OH, per Lord McDonald; *Wheelans v Wheelans* 1986 SLT 164n, OH.
6 *Mackay v Campbell* 1967 SC (HL) 53 at 61, 1967 SLT 337 at 338, per Lord Guest; *MacGilvary v Gilmartin* 1986 SLT 89 at 90, OH, per Lord McDonald.
7 *MacGilvary v Gilmartin* 1986 SLT 89 at 90, OH, per Lord McDonald.
8 *Mackay v Campbell* 1967 SC (HL) 53 at 61, 1967 SLT 337 at 338, per Lord Guest.

737. Remedies. Facility and circumvention operates as a factor vitiating the obligor's consent. It is therefore a ground for rescission of an *ex facie* valid obligation or reduction of an *ex facie* valid deed.

Where a person used fraud and circumvention to obtain a testamentary deed in favour of third parties, a decree of reduction was granted, although they were not implicated in any way in the alleged fraud[1]. Lord Justice-Clerk Inglis argued as follows:

'And the question is, is that a relevant ground of reduction against parties not implicated in [the perpetrator's] fraud? I think it is, and for this reason, that no party, however innocent, is entitled to take benefit by a fraud. I should be sorry if there was any doubt as to that. I do not say there is any clear authority on the point, but the rule is founded on so clear a principle of justice, that I should be sorry if it were not clearly understood to be the law'[2].

While this is acceptable in relation to *mortis causa* deeds, it is submitted that in relation to contractual obligations and the *inter vivos* transfer of property, different considerations apply. Unless the facility and circumvention has prevented the formation of the obligation[3] or has the effect that the transfer is null[4], it will operate only as a ground for rescission or reduction. These remedies will be barred if *restitutio in integrum* is impossible or, more importantly in this context, bona fide third parties have relied upon the *ex facie* valid contract or conveyance.

1 *Taylor v Tweedie* (1865) 3 M 928.
2 (1865) 3 M 928 at 930.

3 See paras 705, 706, above.
4 See para 763 below.

4. UNDUE INFLUENCE

738. Introduction. The common law concept of fraud was sufficiently wide
to include conduct which in the particular circumstances of the case amounted to
unfair actings. In particular, where a relationship of trust existed between the
parties, for example parent and child, conduct which abused that trust could be
regarded as fraudulent even if it would have been acceptable if the parties had
entered into the obligation at arm's length. In the nineteenth century, however,
there was a growing reluctance to stigmatise such conduct as fraud[1]. Instead,
adopting the concept from English law, the courts developed a plea distinct
from fraud, namely undue influence. The essence of the doctrine was explained
by Lord President Inglis in *Gray v Binney*:

> 'If. . . the relation of the parties is such as to beget mutual trust and confidence, each
> owes to the other a duty which has no place as between strangers. But if the trust and
> confidence, instead of being mutual, are all given on one side and not reciprocated,
> the party trusted and confided in is bound, by the most obvious principles of fair
> dealing and honesty, not to abuse the power thus put in his hands'[2].

Where a person has been induced to enter into a voluntary obligation or grant a
deed as a consequence of such an abuse of power, grounds exist for an action of
rescission or reduction. The onus rests on the pursuer to establish undue
influence: there is no presumption of undue influence arising from particular
relationships in Scots law. But where a relationship of trust is established, 'the
onus may be shifted with comparative ease'[3] and the defender will be called
upon to show there was no abuse of trust.

1 See *Gray v Binny* (1879) 7 R 332 at 347, per Lord Shand.
2 (1879) 7 R 332 at 342. Cf his approach in *Tennent v Tennent's Trustees* (1868) 6 M 840 at 876.
3 *Carmichael v Baird* (1899) 6 SLT 369, OH, per Lord Pearson.

739. The relationship between the parties. There must exist between the
parties a relationship which creates 'a dominant or ascendant influence' involving 'confidence and trust' between them[1]. Scots law has recognised parent and
child[2] and law agent and client[3] as such relationships, and there are *dicta* which
suggest that they could be extended to other relationships such as clergyman and
parishioner[4] or physician and patient[5]. However, the extent of the doctrine is
controversial, and in *Forbes v Forbes* Lord Guthrie suggested that it should be
kept within narrow bounds[6]. But in *Honeyman's Executors v Sharp*[7] Lord Maxwell held that where a person (here a fine art adviser) in pursuance of his
profession or calling undertook the giving of advice to another and where, as a
result, there developed a relationship between the adviser and the advised in
which as a matter of fact the advised placed trust and confidence in the adviser,
then the law recognised a moral duty on the adviser not to take advantage of the
advised, at least in relation to matters connected with the area to which the
advice related, and gave legal effect to that moral duty by applying the principle
of undue influence in appropriate cases.

1 *Gray v Binny* (1879) 7 R 332 at 347, per Lord Shand.
2 *Gray v Binny* (1879) 7 R 332; *Carmichael v Baird* (1899) 6 SLT 369, OH; *Allan v Allan* 1961 SC 200,
   OH; *MacGilvary v Gilmartin* 1986 SLT 89, OH.

3 *Logan's Trustees v Reid* (1885) 12 R 1094; *Forrests v Low's Trustees* 1909 SC (HL) 16, 1909 1 SLT 497; *Stewart v MacLaren* 1920 SC (HL) 148, 1920 2 SLT 134. The relationship of law agent and client involves a duty of voluntary disclosure in relation to contracts *inter se: M'Pherson's Trustees v Watt* (1877) 5 R (HL) 9. See para 712 above.
4 See eg *Munro v Strain* (1874) 1 R 1039.
5 See eg *Gray v Binny* (1879) 7 R 332 at 347, per Lord Shand.
6 *Forbes v Forbes's Trustees* 1957 SC 325, 1957 SLT 346, OH. See also *M'Kechnie v M'Kechnie's Trustees* 1908 SC 93, 15 SLT 419, where it was held that it did not apply to a man and his mistress.
7 *Honeyman's Executors v Sharp* 1978 SC 223, *sub nom Rodgers v Sharp* 1979 SLT 177, OH.

740. Material or gratuitous benefit. The pursuer must establish that a material or gratuitous benefit was received by the party who had the dominant or ascendant influence[1]. Where the obligation is gratuitous, undue influence will more readily be inferred[2], but it is sufficient if a benefit was obtained for a grossly inadequate consideration[3].

1 *Gray v Binny* (1879) 7 R 332 at 347, 348, per Lord Shand.
2 *Anstruther v Wilkie* (1856) 18 D 405 (gift to law agent); *MacGilvary v Gilmartin* 1986 SLT 89, OH.
3 *Gray v Binny* (1879) 7 R 332.

741. Absence of independent advice. The absence of independent advice is important. If independent advice was not made available, undue influence will be inferred unless the defender can show that the position of the obligor or granter was as good as if he had had independent advice[1]. An adviser who is common to both parties will not be considered independent for these purposes[2].

1 *Carmichael v Baird* (1899) 6 SLT 369, OH.
2 *Menzies v Menzies* (1893) 20 R (HL) 108. This was not, however, a case in which undue influence was pleaded.

742. Remedies. It is submitted that undue influence operates as a factor vitiating the obligor's consent. It is therefore a ground of rescission of an *ex facie* valid obligation or reduction of an *ex facie* valid deed[1]. In respect of the rights of third parties, it is submitted that a similar approach should be followed as in a case of facility and circumvention[2].

1 *Gray v Binny* (1879) 7 R 332; *MacGilvary v Gilmartin* 1986 SLT 89, OH.
2 As to remedies for facility and circumvention, see para 737 above.

5. SUCCESSION

743. Introduction. In this part of the title it is proposed to discuss the effects of fraudulent and quasi-fraudulent conduct in relation to the law of succession. At the outset it should be stressed that the treatment is not intended to be exhaustive, and for full discussion on particular points reference should be made to the title on WILLS AND SUCCESSION.

744. Wills. Although a will is normally embodied in a probative deed, an action of reduction lies if it can be established that the signature was a forgery[1] or that the testator was induced to sign it as a result of fraud[2]. The averments of fraud must be specific[3]. Where it can be shown that the testator was facile, the testamentary deed may be reduced on the ground of facility and circumvention[4]. Since the person upon whom the circumvention has been practised is dead it has been observed that 'In such a case if facility or weakness of mind is satisfactorily averred and the deed is impetrated in favour of the impetrator or his relatives, there is probably no need to aver or prove any specific act of circumvention . . . Circumvention would in such circumstances be assumed'[5]. It is irrelevant that the fraud or circumvention was practised from the best of motives[6].

A will can be reduced if it was made under undue influence[7]. While it is not the law of Scotland that a testamentary deed in favour of the law agent who drafted the will is null[8], the courts will exercise vigilance 'in seeing that the case, if he has to meet one, of undue influence is fully met or the knowledge of the testator is fully proved'[9]. In *Stewart v McLaren* Lord Dunedin took the view that the onus was on the law agent to 'clear himself from the idea that the gift in his favour was got by deception or undue influence, or that the testator did not know what he was about when making his will'[10].

It is not a bar to reduction of a testamentary deed on these grounds that the fraud was perpetrated by a person who was not a beneficiary under the will. Even although the beneficiaries were entirely innocent, they are not entitled 'to take benefit by a fraud'[11].

1 Where the will is holograph, the onus will be on the parties relying on the will to establish that the signature of the testator is genuine: a holograph document is not a probative deed *stricto sensu*.
2 *Hogg v Campbell* (1864) 2 M 848. Cf the views of Lord Deas, who dissented.
3 *Munro v Strain* (1874) 1 R 522.
4 As to facility and circumvention, see paras 733 ff above.
5 *Mackay v Campbell* 1967 SC (HL) 53 at 61, 62, 1967 SLT 337 at 339, per Lord Guest, approving *Clunie v Stirling* (1854) 17 D 15, and *Horsburgh v Thomson's Trustees* 1912 SC 267, 1912 1 SLT 73. See also *West's Trustee v West* 1980 SLT 6 at 7, OH, per Lord Stott.
6 *Munro v Strain* (1874) 1 R 1039.
7 As to undue influence, see paras 738 ff above.
8 *Grieve v Cunningham* (1869) 8 M 317.
9 *Forrests v Low's Trustees* 1909 SC (HL) 16 at 17, 1909 1 SLT 497 at 498, per Lord James of Hereford.
10 *Stewart v MacLaren* 1920 SC (HL) 148 at 153 (not reported on this point in 1920 2 SLT 134).
11 *Taylor v Tweedie* (1865) 3 M 928 at 930, per Lord Justice-Clerk Inglis, discussed in para 737 above.

745. Legal rights. Where a person attempts by a simulate *inter vivos* disposition to reduce his estate, his conduct will be regarded as *in fraudem* of those entitled to claim legal rights, and the transaction will be struck down by the courts[1]. However, the transaction must be nominal and fictitious, that is, the person must retain a beneficial interest in the property: a bona fide absolute transfer will not be struck down even if it was gratuitous[2].

1 *Buchanan v Buchanan* (1876) 3 R 556.
2 *Boustead v Gardner* (1879) 7 R 139.

746. Discharge. Where a person enters into a deed whereby he discharges his rights under a *mortis causa* settlement, there is a duty on the parties who benefit from the deed to ensure that the granter is aware of his rights under the settlement. This is particularly important where the deed is gratuitous. As Lord Justice-Clerk Moncrieff explained in *Dempsters v Raes*:

'Instead of there being no duty of disclosure, the most candid and full disclosure was incumbent on the defenders. The contract was not an ordinary one. It was a contract between parties who had an interest in a succession, and the proposal was that these interests, being entirely unequal, should *without consideration* be equalised. If the party who is to lose is in ignorance, and the party, who is to gain is well informed, and being aware of the ignorance of the other, takes advantage of that ignorance, it is a case of the grossest fraud'[1].

Nevertheless, in the absence of facility and circumvention or undue influence, the onus remains on the pursuer to establish the facts from which such an inference of fraud can be inferred[2].

1 *Dempsters v Raes* (1873) 11 M 843 at 846 (emphasis added).
2 *Ritchie v Ritchie's Trustees* (1866) 4 M 292; *Dempsters v Raes* (1873) 11 M 843.

747. Election. Although it has been said that 'in the absence of fraud or misrepresentation the Court is always slow to allow a grown man or woman to go back upon a formal agreement which he or she has signed with apparent deliberation'[1], nevertheless, a deed of election will be reduced if it is established that the granter did not have sufficient information upon which to make a choice between conventional provisions or legal rights. There is, in these circumstances, no need to aver fraud. As a general rule the granter should not be allowed by the trustees to make an election until he or she has received independent legal advice[2]; but where the election was not contrary to the pecuniary interests of the granter, reduction has been refused in spite of the absence of independent legal advice[3]. Because the courts are anxious that the granter, in particular a widow, should not be prejudiced as a result of a premature election, this is an area of the law where the parties are compelled to act honestly towards each other[4]. A delay of several years has been held not to bar reduction[5].

1 *Stewart v Bruce's Trustees* (1898) 25 R 965 at 984.
2 *Donaldson v Tainsh's Trustees* (1886) 13 R 967 at 971, 972, per Lord Justice-Clerk Moncreiff.
3 *Harvie's Executors v Harvie's Trustees* 1981 SLT (Notes) 126, OH.
4 *Inglis' Trustees v Inglis* (1887) 14 R 740 at 760, per Lord Shand.
5 *Donaldson v Tainsh's Trustees* (1886) 13 R 967.

748. Impersonation of heirs or legatees. Where a person fraudulently obtained service as heir, it was held that not only was the service reducible but, unless and until the prescriptive period had passed, all titles to property deriving therefrom were also subject to reduction[1]:

> 'a disposition granted by a person wrongly served as heir is of the nature of a conveyance *a non domino* and, therefore, will not support a right to property in the disponee unless fortified by prescription'[2].

While similar principles will apply today if a person obtains title to property directly, by impersonating the true heir or legatee, a measure of protection is afforded to those acquiring heritable property in good faith and for value from an executor. If the title was acquired directly or indirectly from the executor or a person deriving title directly from the executor, no challenge can be made to the acquirer's title on the ground that the executor's confirmation was reducible or has been reduced. Moreover, where title was acquired from a person who himself derived title directly from the executor, it is not competent to challenge the title, on the ground that the executor should not have transferred the title to the alleged heir or legatee[3].

1 See eg *Stobie v Smith* 1921 SC 894, 1921 2 SLT 189, discussed in para 759 below.
2 *Stobie v Smith* 1921 SC 894 at 904, 1921 2 SLT 189 at 192.
3 Succession (Scotland) Act 1964 (c 41), s 17: see WILLS AND SUCCESSION, vol 25, para 1110.

6. TRUSTS AND TRUSTEES

749. Introduction. There appear to be very few reported decisions on the effect of fraudulent conduct by trustees[1]. However, there are several issues which can conveniently be discussed in this part of the title.

1 See generally TRUSTS, TRUSTEES AND JUDICIAL FACTORS, vol 24.

750. Constitution of trusts. Where A has transferred property to B so that B holds the property on an *ex facie* valid irredeemable title, then if A, the alleged truster, seeks declarator that B is holding the property on trust for his (A's) benefit, proof of trust is restricted by the Blank Bonds and Trusts Act 1696 to B's (the alleged trustee's) writ or oath[1]. The 1696 Act will be excluded, however, if A was induced to consent to the title being taken in B's name as a result of B's fraudulent misrepresentation, that is, fraud in the inception of the transaction[2]. But, as Lord Justice-Clerk Inglis pointed out in *Marshall v Lyell,*

> 'while fraud in the constitution of the title will form a good ground, not for a declarator of trust, but for an action of reduction [of the title], and may be proved *prout de jure*, fraud, which consists merely in denying the existence of the trust alleged, will not prevent the operation of the statute; for every trustee who denies the existence of the trust is necessarily guilty of fraud'[3].

Where a third party alleges that the truster and trustee set up the trust for fraudulent purposes, proof of the fraud can be *prout de jure*, as the scope of the 1696 Act is restricted to issues between the alleged truster and alleged trustee[4]. It follows that where the truster alleges that the trustee had given an assurance that the trust property would be used for a particular purpose only, proof of such an arrangement will be restricted to the trustee's writ or oath, as any fraud on the trustee's part is not in relation to the constitution of the trustee's title to the property, and, as the issue is between the truster and the trustee, the 1696 Act should therefore apply[5].

Where the fraud of the alleged trustee consists in the destruction of a back bond or declaration of trust, it has been held that the 1696 Act does not apply and the alleged truster may prove the fraud *prout de jure*[6].

1 Blank Bonds and Trusts Act 1696 (c 25), The Act applies only as between truster and trustee. Third parties may prove *prout de jure*.
2 *Marshall v Lyell* (1859) 21 D 514; *Galloway v Galloway* 1929 SC 160, 1929 SLT 131.
3 *Marshall v Lyell* (1859) 21 D 514 at 521.
4 See eg *Lord Elibank v Hamilton* (1827) 6 S 69; *Wink v Speirs* (1867) 6 M 77.
5 *Tennent v Tennent's Trustees* (1868) 6 M 840 at 846, per Lord Barcaple, and at 859 per Lord Deas. Cf Lord President Inglis at 876 and Lord Ardmillan at 874. See generally W A Wilson and A G M Duncan *Trusts, Trustees and Executors* (1975) p 55.
6 *Marshall v Lyell* (1859) 21 D 514. See also *Pant Mawr Slate and Slab Quarry Co (Ltd) v Fleming* (1883) 10 R 457.

751. Trustee and trust estate. A trustee owes a very heavy fiduciary duty to the trust estate and the beneficiaries. Accordingly, the trustee must not act as *auctor in rem suam*. A contract between the trustee and trust estate is automatically voidable, even although it is a perfectly fair transaction. This principle has been applied, for example, in cases of sale by the trustee to the trust[1] or the purchase by the trustee of trust property[2].

1 *Aberdeen Rly Co v Blaikie Bros* (1854) 1 Macq 461, HL.
2 *Dunn v Chambers* (1897) 25 R 247, 5 SLT 345; *Davis v Davis* (1908) 16 SLT 380, OH.

752. Trustee and trust beneficiary. While a transaction between a trustee and a beneficiary under the trust is not automatically voidable, nevertheless since there is a fiduciary relationship between the parties, the onus rests on the trustee to establish that he made full and fair disclosure of all material facts and that the bargain was fair. If this cannot be established, the transaction can be reduced or rescinded[1].

1 See para 712 above.

753. Transactions in breach of trust. A transaction in breach of trust is voidable at the instance of the interested beneficiaries. If a beneficiary of full age consents to the transaction he cannot later challenge it, provided the consent is freely given in full knowledge of the facts and circumstances. However, a beneficiary will not be personally barred from challenging the transaction if the consent was obtained by abuse of the trustee's powers to influence him or given under error or fraud[1]. Where the trustee and beneficiary are parent and child, there will be a particularly heavy onus on the parent trustee to show that the consent of the child beneficiary was not obtained by undue influence, but, if the onus is discharged, the transaction will be upheld[2].

1 *Callander v Callander* 1975 SC 183 at 205, 1976 SLT 10 at 15, per Lord President Emslie.
2 1975 SC 183 at 211–213, 1976 SLT 10 at 18–20, per Lord Cameron.

754. Fraud on a power. Where a person (the donee) holds a power of appointment which has not been exercised, then if he buys the non-vested interest of the beneficiary who is the object of the power, he could exercise the power in his own favour. Moreover, since the power of appointment is unexhausted, the donee could put improper pressure on the beneficiary to consent to the transaction by indicating that if his consent is not forthcoming, the donee will not exercise the power in the beneficiary's favour. In these circumstances, the transaction can be cut down as a fraud on a power[1].

The donee is a trustee *quoad* the exercise of the power, and the purported transaction is prima facie in breach of the trust. In *Callander v Callander*[2] the Inner House held that while the transaction was in breach of trust it was voidable and not null. Consequently, the beneficiary could be personally barred if he consented to the transaction, provided consent was freely given and he had full knowledge of the facts and circumstances[3]. But, particularly where the parties are parent and child, the donee will have a formidable task to establish that consent was freely given: but it is important that such transactions are not regarded as null as this would inhibit changes in family arrangements which are necessary to alleviate the incidence of taxation[4].

1 *M'Donald v M'Grigor* (1874) 1 R 817.
2 *Callander v Callander* 1975 SC 183, 1976 SLT 10.
3 Cf *M'Donald v M'Grigor* (1874) 1 R 817, where the beneficiary did not know that the purchaser was the donee of the power.
4 *Callander v Callander* 1975 SC 183, 1976 SLT 10.

7. HERITABLE PROPERTY

755. Introduction. The purpose of this part of the title is to examine the effect of fraud on the transfer of the ownership of heritable property and the protection of the onerous bona fide acquirer of another's property.

756. Contract and conveyance: distinction between the principles of the law of obligations and property. Where, for example, parties enter into a contract for the sale of heritage, then provided the requisite formalities have been complied with, the buyer has a contractual right to have the seller implement the obligation. However, the ownership of the property (*dominium*) is not transferred to the buyer unless and until a disposition has been drawn up and the deed recorded in the General Register of Sasines or the interest in the property to which the deed relates is registered in the Land Register of Scotland[1]. Until recording or registration, the buyer has only a personal right *vis à vis* the seller for performance of his obligation: after recording or registration he has a real right in relation to the property. Fraud may affect both the antecedent obligation and the disposition, that is, the deed of conveyance.

1 Land Registration (Scotland) Act 1979 (c 33), s 3(1)(a).

757. Effect of fraud on antecedent obligation. Apart from the very rare cases where fraud will prevent the formation of the antecedent obligation[1], if the contract has been induced by a fraudulent misrepresentation, the innocent party will generally have the right to reduce the contract and claim restitution[2]. Similarly, reduction is possible if the innocent party was induced to enter into the obligation as a result of facility and circumvention[3]. Reduction is still possible even although the antecedent obligation has been executed[4].

1 See paras 705, 706, above.
2 In addition there may be a delictual remedy.
3 *Mackay v Campbell* 1967 SC (HL) 53, 1967 SLT 337.
4 *S Straker & Sons v Campbell* 1926 SN 31, 1926 SLT 262, OH; *McLeod v Cedar Holdings Ltd* 1989 SLT 620, where a husband forged his wife's signature in respect of a loan agreement, legal charge and standard security over his wife's *pro indiviso* share of the matrimonial home, and the court ordered partial reduction in so far as the wife's interests had been prejudiced.

758. Effect of fraud on the conveyance. Where a disposition has been granted in implement of an antecedent obligation which is vitiated by fraud, the disposition will itself be liable to reduction. Moreover, where a person is induced to grant a disposition as a result of fraud etc, then the disposition will also be liable to reduction. As Lord Murray observed in *Purdon v Rowat's Trustees*, 'There is nothing more important to the public, and to conveyancers themselves, than that the deeds of conveyances should be honestly and correctly prepared, and not fraudulently interpolated'[1].

An action of reduction of a disposition is not barred merely because the deed has been recorded in the General Register of Sasines or the interest to which it relates has been registered in the Land Register of Scotland[2]. However, unless and until the deed is reduced, it will have been effective to convey the ownership of the land to the disponee as soon as the conveyance was recorded or the interest was registered. Unless and until the deed is reduced, the disponee is the owner of the heritable property and is capable of transferring his interest in the land to a bona fide onerous acquirer, since such an acquirer is entitled to transact on the faith of the registers[3]. In these circumstances, reduction of the original deed is barred if the rights of bona fide onerous third parties would thereby be prejudiced[4]. Where, however, a deed is a forgery, the rights of bona fide onerous third parties will not bar reduction[5].

1 *Purdon v Rowat's Trustees* (1856) 19 D 206 at 222.
2 *Anderson v Lambie* 1954 SC (HL) 43, 1954 SLT 73.
3 *Williamson v Sharp* (1851) 14 D 127; *Nisbet v Cairns* (1864) 2 M 863.
4 *Anderson v Lambie* 1954 SC (HL) 43, 1954 SLT 73.
5 *Sereshky v Sereshky* 1988 SLT 426, OH *(obiter)*; *McLeod v Cedar Holdings Ltd* 1989 SLT 620.

759. Dispositions *a non domino*. Where a person fraudulently acquires heritable property by, for example, impersonating an heir or legatee, his title is subject to a radical defect, as the property was never intended to be conveyed to the disponee but to the person whom he was impersonating. Moreover, any conveyance by him to a bona fide onerous third party will be subject to reduction as a conveyance *a non domino*. As Lord Cullen observed in *Stobie v Smith*, there was, in these circumstances, 'no analogy between a disposition voluntarily granted by the true owner under the inducement of fraudulent misrepresentation and a service of the wrong person as heir. The service is fundamentally vitiated by falsity, and the analogy is rather that of a forged writ'[1]. Accordingly, the bona fide onerous acquirer is prima facie not protected because, as a result of the nature of the fraud, the deed forming the link in his title is *funditus null ab initio*, although, today he will often be protected by section 17 of the Succession (Scotland) Act 1964[2].

However, the title of a singular successor of the fraudulent party will become fortified by prescription[3]. If the interest of the singular successor was registered in the Land Register of Scotland, it is submitted that his title is unassailable without the need for prescription[4], and the 'true' owner is entitled to an indemnity from the Keeper[5].

1 *Stobie v Smith* 1921 SC 894 at 904, 905, 1921 2 SLT 189 at 192. See also *Sheddon v Patrick* (1852) 14 D 721; *Rocca v Catto's Trustees* (1876) 4 R 70; and *Mulhearn v Dunlop* 1929 SN 157, 1929 SLT 59, OH.
2 See the Succession (Scotland) Act 1964 (c 41), s 17, and WILLS AND SUCCESSION, vol 25, para 1110.
3 See the Prescription and Limitation (Scotland) Act 1973 (c 52), ss 1–5. Prescription does not operate if the deed is a forgery: s 1(1).
4 Prescription will be necessary, however, if the interest was registered with an exclusion of indemnity: ibid, s 1(1)(b) (amended by the Land Registration (Scotland) Act 1979 (c 33), s 10).
5 Ibid, s 12(1). But an indemnity will be excluded if the loss was the result of the claimant's 'fraudulent or careless act or omission': s 12(3)(n).

760. Dispositions by 'fraudulent' seller. A seller of land retains the owner-ship of the property until the purchaser records the disposition in the General Register of Sasines or registers his interest in the land to which the disposition relates in the Land Register of Scotland. Accordingly, if the seller grants a disposition to a third party who records the deed or registers his interest before the first purchaser has done so, the former acquires the *dominium* of the land and the first purchaser is left to his contractual remedies against the seller. As a matter of property law, it is not until the registration of the conveyance that the ownership of the property is transferred from the disponer to the disponee[1].

A disponee will, however, only be able to take advantage of this principle if he is acting in good faith when he records the deed or registers his interest[2]. As Lord Ormidale explained in *Stodart v Dalzell*:

> 'It would be unfortunate if the idea were to prevail that the public records, looked at by themselves, can in all circumstances be held as conclusive... It would be most inequitable if a man, in the full knowledge of a prior right, by merely having his title put first upon record could be in a position to ignore the prior right because it was not on record before his own. It would be allowing him to take advantage of his own fraud'[3].

To satisfy the criterion of good faith the disponee must not have been aware of the previous transaction: if he was, he is put on inquiry to determine whether any of the seller's obligations under the earlier transaction are still subsisting[4]. The law on this point was summarised by Lord Jamieson in *Rodger (Builders) Ltd v Fawdry*:

> 'In such circumstances the law is not in doubt. If an intending purchaser is aware of a prior contract for the sale of the subjects, he is bound to inquire into the nature and result of that prior contract, and his duty of inquiry is not satisfied by inquiry of the seller and an assurance by him that the contract is no longer in existence... fraud in the sense of moral delinquency does not enter into the matter. It is sufficient if the

intending purchaser fails to make the inquiry which he is bound to do. If he fails he is no longer *in bona fide* but *in mala fide*[5].

The principle only applies, however, where the seller's obligation constitutes an obligation relating to land which 'is capable of being made into a real right'[6] by the creditor in the prior transaction.

1 See K G C Reid 'Ownership on Registration' 1985 SLT (News) 280; and cf I Doran 'Ownership on Delivery' 1985 SLT (News) 165, which contains references to the considerable literature on the issue.
2 Land Registration (Scotland) Act 1979 (c 33), s 7(1), preserving the common law rules in respect of good faith.
3 *Stodart v Dalzell* (1876) 4 R 236 at 242.
4 *Petrie v Forsyth* (1874) 2 R 214 at 222, per Lord Ormidale; *Stodart v Dalzell* (1876) 4 R 236.
5 *Rodger (Builders) Ltd v Fawdry* 1950 SC 483 at 489, 1950 SLT 345 at 353.
6 *Wallace v Simmers* 1960 SC 255 at 259, 1961 SLT 34 at 37, per Lord President Clyde. See also *Morier v Brownlee and Watson* (1895) 23 R 67, 3 SLT 135.

8. CORPOREAL MOVEABLES

761. Introduction. The purpose of this part of the title is to examine the effect of fraud on the transfer of the ownership of corporeal moveables and the protection of the onerous bona fide acquirer of another's property.

762. Distinction between the principles of the law of obligations and of property. It is important at the outset to distinguish the respective spheres of the law of obligations and the law of property. Where, for example, a contract has been induced by a fraudulent misrepresentation, the innocent party will generally have the right to rescind the contract and claim restitution[1]. Rescission, however, is *res inter alios acta*. If the innocent party had intended to transfer the *dominium* of the property, a good title will have passed to the transferee provided the appropriate method for the transfer of rights in corporeal moveables has been followed. It is submitted that the rules of property law prevail over those applicable in the law of obligations. Accordingly the transfer of ownership will not be prevented by the invalidity of the antecedent contract, and until the conveyance is reduced, the *dominium* of the property remains with the transferee and is capable of transfer to bona fide subsequent acquirers for value[2].

1 In addition there may be a remedy in delict: see paras 719 ff below.
2 The conveyance can be reduced on any ground on which the antecedent obligation could have been reduced on *justa causa traditionis*: see T B Smith *A Short Commentary on the Law of Scotland* (1962) p 539 (where the SALJ reference should be 280), and T B Smith *Property Problems in Sale* (1978) p 87.

763. The effect of fraud on the transfer of *dominium*. Stair wrote:

'Yet in moveables, purchasers are not quarrellable upon the fraud of their authors, if they did purchase for an onerous equivalent cause. The reason is, because moveables must have a current course of traffic, and the buyer is not to consider how the seller purchased, unless it were by theft or violence which the law accounts as *labes reales*, following the subject to all successors, otherwise there would be the greatest encouragement to theft and robbery'[1].

It follows therefore that a *vitium reales* does not attach to corporeal moveables which have been obtained as a result of fraud. The fraudulent party will prima facie obtain the *dominium* of the property, which can then be transferred to a bona fide purchaser for value and the property cannot be vindicated by the original owner[2]. Instead, he will be left to his remedies in contract or delict against the fraudulent party.

Where, however, as a result of a fraudulent misrepresentation the antecedent contract is null, that is, a case of *dissensus, Morrisson v Robertson*[3] is authority that corporeal moveable property can be recovered from a bona fide purchaser for value. However, this decision is controversial[4], and can be explained on the basis that the pursuer never intended to transfer the property to the bogus agent, Telford, but to his named principal, Wilson of Bonnyrigg. Therefore Telford had no title to the cattle to pass to the defender[5].

Thus, as a general principle, where *dominium* has been transferred a good title will prima facie pass to the transferee, even though the antecedent contract and the transfer itself may be liable to rescission on the ground of the transferee's fraud. Until rescission the transferee has a good title which can be transferred to a bona fide purchaser for value. As Lord Kinnear has said, 'It is well settled law that a contract induced by fraud is not void, but voidable at the option of a party defrauded. In other words, it is valid until it is rescinded. It follows that when third parties have acquired rights in good faith and for value, these rights are indefeasible'[6]. In the leading case of *MacLeod v Kerr*[7] Kerr entered into a contract with a rogue, Galloway, for the sale of Kerr's motor car. Throughout the negotiations, Galloway had used a false name, L Craig. Kerr was induced to accept payment by cheque and parted with possession of the vehicle as a result of Galloway's fraudulent misrepresentation that the cheque would be honoured. Having determined that Kerr had intended to transfer the *dominium* to Galloway (the man who had answered the advertisement), the Inner House held that until the contract was rescinded Galloway had a good title to transfer to Gibson, a bona fide purchaser for value.

It is clear that if the innocent party rescinds or reduces the transfer or the antecedent obligation *before* title has been transferred to a bona fide purchaser for value, he should be able to recover his property. However, it would appear that such rescission would only be effective after judicial intervention[8]. Merely to inform the police of the fraud will not deprive a bona fide third party purchaser of protection[9]. Conversely, rescission is precluded if a bona fide purchaser for value has acquired the property before the action is brought[10].

1 Stair *Institutions* IV,40,21.
2 'Though the sale was tainted by fraud, the property had passed. The contract was not void [null], but only voidable. The remedy of rescission and recovery of the property is an equitable remedy, and, though as between seller and buyer a *brevi manu* operation may be effectual, it requires, when other interests are concerned, the interposition of the Court': *A W Gamage Ltd v Charlesworth's Trustee* 1910 SC 257 at 267, 1910 1 SLT 11 at 18, per Lord Johnston.
3 *Morrisson v Robertson* 1908 SC 332, 15 SLT 697, is discussed in paras 705, 706, above.
4 Cf W M Gloag *The Law of Contract* (2nd edn, 1929) pp 531 ff with J J Gow *The Mercantile and Industrial Law of Scotland* (1964) pp 52 ff; T B Smith *A Short Commentary on the Law of Scotland* (1962) pp 814 ff. See also para 706 above.
5 Alternatively the decision can be regarded as one of theft: cf, however, the views of Lord President Clyde in *MacLeod v Kerr* 1965 SC 253, 1965 SLT 358.
6 *Price and Pierce Ltd v Bank of Scotland* 1910 SC 1095 at 1106, 1107, *sub nom Laird v Bank of Scotland* 1910 2 SLT 126 at 128.
7 *MacLeod v Kerr* 1965 SC 253, 1965 SLT 358. This case is discussed by T B Smith (1967) 12 JLSS 206, by W A Wilson 1982 JR 268, 269, and by G H Gordon *The Criminal Law of Scotland* (2nd edn, 1978) p 492.
8 If a third party learned about the former owner's intention or attempt to rescind before acquiring the moveables, the acquisition would, it is submitted, be *in mala fide* and consequently the property could be recovered.
9 *MacLeod v Kerr* 1965 SC 253, 1965 SLT 358.

10 *Gloag* p 533; *A W Gamage Ltd v Charlesworth's Trustee* 1910 SC 257 at 267, 268, 1910 1 SLT 11 at 18; *MacLeod v Kerr* 1965 SC 253 at 257, 1965 SLT 358 at 363, per Lord President Clyde; D M Walker *The Law of Civil Remedies in Scotland* (1974) p 49. See also para 714 above.

764. The effect of fraud when less than *dominium* has been transferred. Hitherto it has been assumed that the original owner transferred full *dominium* to the fraudulent party. If, however, full *dominium* has not been transferred, a conflict arises between the principle *nemo dat quod non habet* and the policy of protecting the bona fide onerous purchaser of corporeal moveables. Since the middle of the nineteenth century, the Scottish courts have taken the view that where the fraudulent party has been given possession of moveables and has apparent authority to dispose of them, then the interests of the bona fide subsequent acquirer for value should prevail:

'if the true owner have knowingly conferred this ostensible title, although induced thereto by fraud, a *bona fide* purchaser cannot be required to restore what he has bought, on the ground of latent stipulations between the seller [the original owner] and his author . . . the loss . . . must fall on the party who put the wrongdoer in possession, and that conclusion must follow, although the possession was obtained by fraud, and although, in a question between [seller] and [buyer], the right of property had never been transferred'[1].

If the fraudulent party is acting as the agent of the original owner, *a fortiori* the loss will fall on the principal. The reason for this was expressly articulated by Lord Kinloch in the *Pochin* case:

'It is the broad ground of equity and common-sense, that where a man entrusts his agent either with the actual possession of his goods, or, which is the same thing, a document by which possession can be at any one moment obtained, and the agent, in abuse of his trust, raises money on his ostensible right from a *bona fide* lender, it is the employer of the agent who should suffer the loss, and not the innocent third party, with whom the agent was enabled to contract by the employer's own conduct'[2].

This protection only extends to onerous bona fide acquirers of the property.

'It is a recognised principle . . . that a gratuitous benefit conferred or obtained by one party and gained through the fraud of another cannot be retained by the person benefited, even though innocent of the fraud . . . But the principle is throughout the authorities limited to the case of benefits conferred or received gratuitously, and does not apply when a valuable consideration has been given . . . If the person resisting a claim of restitution is not only innocent of the fraud alleged, but has given some valuable consideration in the transaction, the person defrauded has no remedy against him'[3].

The legislature has, however, intervened to extend the protection to gratuitous as well as onerous bona fide acquirers of goods disponed to them by a person who had possession of the goods with the owner's consent[4]. In contrast, the buyer under a conditional sale agreement is deemed by statute not to be a person who has bought or agreed to buy goods[5], and consequently bona fide onerous acquirers of corporeal moveables from such buyers are not protected; but an exception is made for bona fide private purchasers of motor vehicles originally transferred under hire-purchase or conditional sale agreements[6].

The subsequent acquirer must act in good faith. This will depend on the circumstances of the particular case. Thus, for example, a proof before answer was allowed on the question whether a second hand car dealer was acting in good faith when he bought a car from a rogue who could not produce the car's registration book[7]. But it is not *in mala fide* to deal with a person who may be insolvent while the insolvency is still undeclared[8].

Where a fraudulent party has not been clothed by the true owner with apparent authority to dispose of moveable property, then the principle *nemo dat quod non habet* will apply. Thus the hirer of moveables cannot pledge or create a lien over the property in favour of a bona fide third party[9], unless the owner is personally barred from denying his authority to do so. As Lord President Clyde has said:

> '. . . in both pledge and lien the principle that the possessor of a moveable can give no better right therein or thereto to a third party than he has himself acquired from the owner applies, unless the owner has personally barred himself, by some actings of his own, from founding on the limited character of the title he actually gave to the possessor'[10].

The principle *nemo dat quod non habet* is enshrined in the Sale of Goods Act 1979[11], but is, of course, subject to the statutory exceptions already discussed.

1 *Brown v Marr* (1880) 7 R 427 at 435, 436, per Lord Justice-Clerk Moncreiff (pledge of jewellery obtained on sale or return basis; rights of bona fide pledgee prevailed), followed in *Bryce v Ehrmann* (1904) 7 F 5, 12 SLT 378.
2 *H D Pochin & Co v Robinows and Marjoribanks* (1869) 7 M 622 at 639. This approach was approved in *Vickers v Hertz* (1871) 9 M (HL) 65. Cf *M'Fadyean v Shearer Bros* 1952 SLT (Sh Ct) 12, where the sheriff equated the actions of a fraudulent agent to that of theft and allowed the principal to recover his property from a bona fide purchaser. It is submitted that this case was wrongly decided.
3 *Gibbs v British Linen Co* (1875) 4 R 630 at 634, OH, per Lord Shand. Cf the position of legatees under a testamentary deed vitiated by fraud or facility and lesion: see para 737 above.
4 Factors Act 1889 (c 45), ss 8, 9 (extended to Scotland by the Factors (Scotland) Act 1890 (c 40), s 1); Sale of Goods Act 1979 (c 54), ss 24, 25(1).
5 Ibid, s 25(2).
6 Hire Purchase Act 1964 (c 53), s 27 (substituted by the Consumer Credit Act 1974 (c 39), s 192(3), Sch 4, para 22, and amended by the Sale of Goods Act 1979, s 63(1), Sch 2, para 4).
7 *Wilkes v Livingstone* 1955 SLT (Notes) 20, OH.
8 *Price and Pierce Ltd v Bank of Scotland* 1910 SC 1095 at 1118, *sub nom Laird v Bank of Scotland* 1910 2 SLT 126 at 133, per Lord President Dunedin. Cf Lord Johnston (dissenting) at 1115 and at 131. See para 777 below.
9 *Mitchell v Heys & Sons* (1894) 21 R 600, 1 SLT 590; *Lamonby v Arthur G Foulds Ltd* 1928 SC 89, 1928 SLT 42.
10 *Lamonby v Arthur G Foulds Ltd* 1928 SC 89 at 95, 1928 SLT 42 at 46.
11 Sale of Goods Act 1979, s 21(1).

9. INCORPOREAL PROPERTY

765. Introduction. In this part of the title it is proposed to discuss the effect of fraud in relation to transactions concerned with the transfer of incorporeal property.

766. Assignation of voluntary obligations. Where the consent of a party to a voluntary obligation is vitiated on the ground of fraud, he remains entitled to annul the obligation even where the right of credit under it has been assigned for value to a bona fide third party. In the leading case of *Scottish Widows' Fund v Buist* Lord President Inglis said:

> 'It appears to me to be long ago settled in the law of Scotland – and I have never heard of any attempt to disturb the doctrine – that in a personal obligation, whether contained in a unilateral deed or in a mutual contract, if the creditor's right is sold to an assignee for value, and the assignee purchases in good faith, he is nevertheless

subject to all the exceptions and pleas pleadable against the original creditor. That is the doctrine laid down in all our institutional writers, and it has been affirmed in many cases . . . The doctrine does not apply to the transmission of heritable estate[1]; the doctrine does not apply in the sale of corporeal moveables[2]. But within the class of cases to which the doctrine is applicable – I mean the transmission to assignees of a creditor's right in a personal obligation – I know of no exception to the application of the doctrine'[3].

This doctrine can be summarised in the two Latin maxims, *resoluto jure dantis resolvitor jus accipientis* (where the cedent's right is annulled the transferee's right is also annulled) and *assignatus utitur jure auctoris* (the assignee can only assert as good a right as his cedent).

The Scottish Law Commission has taken the view that while there 'is a sound historical explanation of why onerous transferees of some classes of incorporeal property or obligations – by contrast with transferees of other property – should be liable to all exceptions and pleas competent against the cedent . . . it is possible to argue that apart from settled practice there are today no convincing reasons for making an exception to the general rule'[4]. Nevertheless, it is still the law of Scotland that, for example, where the debtor was induced to enter into a contract as a result of the fraudulent misrepresentation of the cedent, the debtor may seek rescission or reduction against an onerous bona fide assignee on the ground of the cedent's fraud. In the *Scottish Widows' Fund* case, where a life policy was reduced on the ground of the cedent's fraud, Lord Deas justified the decision on the ground that:

'. . . far greater inconvenience and far greater injustice would arise if it were to be held that as soon as a party, however fraudulently and however falsely, has obtained a policy upon his life, he may go into the market and sell it . . ., and then the insurance office must be liable for the whole sum insured'[5].

1 See paras 755 ff above.
2 See paras 761 ff above.
3 *Scottish Widows' Fund and Life Assurance Society v Buist* (1876) 3 R 1078 at 1082.
4 *Defective Consent and Consequential Matters* (Scot Law Com Consultative Memorandum no 42 (1978)) vol II, p 147.
5 *Scottish Widows' Fund and Life Assurance Society v Buist* (1876) 3 R 1078 at 1084.

767. General principles relating to negotiable instruments. In contrast to the rule in relation to the assignation of a debt, negotiable instruments, including bank notes[1], confer a good title on the recipient by mere delivery provided that he has taken in good faith, for value and without notice of any defect in the mode of acquisition from the true owner[2]. Thus, for example, if A was induced as a result of a fraudulent misrepresentation by B to sign a promissory note in B's favour, B's fraud cannot be pleaded against C, where C is a holder in due course, that is, has acquired the instrument in good faith and for value from B.

There is, however, an important limitation on the protection of the holder in due course of a negotiable instrument. There is no liability under a negotiable instrument if it is a forgery, unless the instrument is adopted by the debtor after the forgery has been discovered[3]. Inaction does not *per se* amount to adoption:

'It would be a most unreasonable thing to permit a man who knew the bank were relying upon his forged signature [as acceptor] to a bill to lie by and not to divulge the fact until he saw that the position of the bank was altered for the worse. But it appears to me that it would be equally contrary to justice to hold him responsible for the bill because he did not tell the bank of the forgery at once, if he did actually give the information, and if, when he did so, the bank was in no worse position than it was at the time when it was first within his power to give the information'[4].

1 A *vitium reale* does not apply to coins which are current legal tender: see MONEY, vol 14, paras
   1805 ff.
2 *Heritable Reversionary Co Ltd v Millar* (1892) 19 R (HL) 43. See generally COMMERCIAL PAPER.
3 See eg *Boyd v Robertson* (1854) 17 D 159.
4 *M'Kenzie v British Linen Co* (1881) 8 R (HL) 8 at 21, per Lord Watson. See also *British Linen Co v
   Cowan* (1906) 8 F 704, 13 SLT 941.

768. Cheques. If a cheque is forged, it does not operate as a valid assignment of
the drawer's funds[1]. A bank has therefore no authority to pay a forged cheque or
debit it to a customer's account and, if it does so, any loss falls on the bank, as the
bank should recognise when the purported signature of a customer is a forgery[2].
However, a customer owes his bank a duty (1) to refrain from drawing a cheque
in such a manner as may facilitate fraud or forgery[3], and (2) to inform the bank
of any forgery of a cheque purportedly drawn on account as soon as he, the
customer, becomes aware of it[4]. If the bank seeks greater protection it must do
so by express contractual terms brought to the notice of the customer. In the
absence of such terms, the bank will bear the loss if, for example, an employee
has defrauded his employer by forging the employer's signature on cheques
which were honoured by the bank before the forgeries were discovered by the
employer[5].

In the leading case of *Clydesdale Banking Co v Paul*[6], a clerk who had general
authority to represent his principal on the stock exchange entered into transactions for his own behalf in his principal's name, without the principal's
knowledge but for which the principal was bound. In order to meet a balance
due by the principal as a result of the clerk's speculations the clerk forged a
cheque which purported to be drawn by X in favour of the principal. The clerk
cashed the cheque at a bank and applied the proceeds to pay the balance. The
purported drawer of the forged cheque, X, was a customer of the Clydesdale
Bank. The bank was therefore liable to X for paying out on the forged cheque.
However, the Inner House held that the bank had recourse against the purported
payee, the principal, because the clerk had been acting as his representative on
the exchange and he had benefited from the fraud as he had not been declared a
defaulter on the exchange as the money which had been obtained by the fraud
had been used to pay the balance due. In the course of his judgment, Lord
President Inglis said:

> 'No doubt an agent will not be held to be authorised to commit a forgery or any
> other wrong; but if, in the course of doing his business of agent, he does commit a
> wrong or a crime, and if the principal is benefited, then he is liable to the extent to
> which he is benefited'[7].

However, a principal will not be liable if he did not benefit from his agent's fraud
and the agent was able to perpetrate the fraud as a result of the negligence of the
person defrauded. Thus, in *Robb v Gow Bros and Gemmell* a firm of stockbrokers
was not liable when its accredited clerk encashed cheques made payable to
bearer which the pursuer had sent as payment for shares. Lord McLaren
observed:

> 'The result is that it was through the pursuer's negligence that [the rogue] was
> enabled to perpetrate the fraud by paying these bearer cheques into his own bank
> account; and, as the loss is due to the pursuer's negligence, then in accordance with
> the rule, that it is the person whose negligence enables another to commit a fraud
> who should suffer, the pursuer ought to bear the consequences of that fraud'[8].

Similarly, if a person entrusts his agent with a cheque and the agent fraudulently
misapplies the money for the benefit of a third party, a claim for restitution will
fail if the third party was innocent of the fraud and gave valuable consideration
for the money. As Lord President Clyde has explained:

'In Scotland, in a case where as here an intermediary has been guilty of fraud in a question with two other innocent persons, it is well settled that a benefit obtained by one party through the fraud of another provided it is gratuitous cannot be retained by the party benefited even though innocent of the fraud. Considerations of equity demand that the latter should give up his gratuitous benefit. But, on the other hand, as Lord Shand put it in *Gibbs v British Linen Co*[9] "If the person resisting a claim for restitution is not only innocent of the fraud alleged, but has given some valuable consideration in the transaction, the person defrauded has no remedy against him"'[10].

1 *Dickson v Clydesdale Bank Ltd* 1937 SLT 585, OH.
2 *Tai Hing Cotton Mill Ltd v Liu Chong Hing Bank Ltd* [1986] AC 80 at 106, [1985] 2 All ER 947 at 956, PC.
3 *London Joint Stock Bank Ltd v MacMillan and Arthur* [1918] AC 777, HL. The liability is restricted to negligence in the manner in which the cheque is drawn.
4 *Greenwood v Martins Bank Ltd* [1933] AC 51, HL; *Tai Hing Cotton Mill Ltd v Liu Chong Hing Bank Ltd* [1986] AC 80 at 108, [1985] 2 All ER 947 at 958, PC.
5 *Tai Hing Cotton Mill Ltd v Liu Chong Hing Bank Ltd* [1986] AC 80, [1985] 2 All ER 947, PC. There is, eg, no obligation on the customer to check his bank statements.
6 *Clydesdale Banking Co v Paul* (1876) 4 R 626. For the earlier proceedings, see *Clydesdale Banking Co v Royal Bank of Scotland* (1875) 3 R 586.
7 *Clydesdale Banking Co v Paul* (1876) 4 R 616 at 628. Where an agent has very wide authority, the principal may be liable for his fraud on the basis that 'He who armed the deceiver with the power of deceiving ought to suffer rather then he who was deceived': *Union Bank of Scotland v Makin & Sons* (1873) 11 M 499 at 506, per Lord Ardmillan. In these circumstances the principal need not benefit from the fraud: see *Lloyd v Grace, Smith & Co* [1912] AC 716, HL, disapproving *Barwick v English Joint Stock Bank* (1867) LR 2 Exch 259. The extent of this principle in Scots law is controversial.
8 *Robb v Gow Bros and Gemmell* (1905) 8 F 90 at 107, 13 SLT 609 at 615. But cf *International Sponge Importers Ltd v Andrew Watt & Sons* 1911 SC (HL) 57, 1911 1 SLT 414, where the purchasers of goods had no reason to believe that a traveller was not entitled to receive payments in cash or uncrossed cheques: however, the principal had allowed him to do so for four years!
9 *Gibbs v British Linen Co* (1875) 4 R 630 at 634, OH.
10 *G M Scott (Willowbank Cooperage) Ltd v York Trailer Co Ltd* 1969 SLT 87 at 88, OH.

769. Documents of title. The general principles applicable to the transfer of corporeal moveable property apply in relation to the transfer of documents of title[1]. In particular, the law will operate to protect the interests of an onerous bona fide transferee of the documents from a fraudulent agent. Thus in the *Pochin* case Lord Kinloch referred to:

'... the long established principle of the law of Scotland ... that wherever a merchant entrusts his agent either with the actual possession of his goods, or with such documents as enables the agent at pleasure to obtain such possession, he thereby gives the agent power effectually to give over these goods to any one *bona fide* contracting with him, either for a purchase of the goods, or an advance on their security'[2].

This principle does not rest on any subtle distinctions between real and personal rights.

'It is the broad ground of equity and common-sense, that where a man entrusts his agent either with the actual possession of his goods, or, which is the same thing, a document by which possession can be at any one moment obtained, and the agent, in abuse of his trust, raises money on his ostensible right from a *bona fide* lender, it is the employer of the agent who should suffer the loss, and not the innocent third party, with whom the agent was enabled to contract by the employer's own conduct'[3].

1 See paras 761 ff above.
2 *H D Pochin & Co v Robinows and Marjoribanks* (1869) 7 M 622 at 638.
3 (1869) 7 M 622 at 639. See also eg *Vickers v Hertz* (1871) 9 M (HL) 65.

770. Heritable bonds. Where a person has obtained a benefit as the result of another's fraud, he cannot retain the benefit unless he gave consideration for it. Accordingly, when A granted a bond and disposition in B's favour as a result of a fraudulent misrepresentation by X that B had supplied the money for a loan to A, the bond was reduced when it was established that the money for the loan had been supplied by C and X had simply embezzled the money advanced by B[1]. Where the creditor's law agent embezzled a sum of money advanced by the debtor towards the repayment of the capital of the loan, it was held that while he was the creditor's agent for the receipt of interest, he had no authority to accept payments of capital: accordingly, in so far as the latter were concerned, he was acting as the agent of the debtor. In those circumstances, the loss fell on the debtor,

> 'for it was he who enabled the law agent to commit the fraud by placing the money in his hands, without ascertaining whether it ever reached his creditor'[2].

A forged discharge does not bind the creditor[3]; but a forged bond or discharge can be adopted by the debtor or creditor[4].

In relation to the effect of fraud when the subjects are realised, the law was stated by Lord Shand in *Gibbs v British Linen Co*:

> 'According to almost invariable practice, securities granted over heritable property contain a power of sale. If the debt be not paid the creditor after due intimation may sell the property, and if he be guilty of fraudulent misrepresentations in the sale he will be responsible for the consequences; or if he sell the property through an agent who is guilty of fraud he cannot retain the benefit of the contract. But if, in place of selling the property himself, he allows the debtor, the true proprietor, to effect the sale, the legal relations and consequences are entirely different. The contract of sale is then made between the purchaser and the proprietor; and the only agreement to which the creditor, as holder of the security, is a party, is a contract between him and his debtor to release the security for payment of his debt. It appears to me to make no difference in principle that the debt is so large as to absorb the whole price to be received for the subject of the security'[5].

1 *Traill v Smith's Trustees* (1876) 3 R 770, especially at 780 per Lord Justice-Clerk Moncreiff. See also *Richardson v MacGeoch's Trustees* (1898) 1 F 145, 6 SLT 226, where it was held that the discharge of a prior bond and disposition was ineffective if as a result of the agent's embezzlement the money advanced to pay the debt and discharge the bond never reached the creditor: see in particular per Lord Kinnear at 1 F 153.
2 *Peden v Graham* (1907) 15 SLT 143 at 144, OH, per Lord Salvesen.
3 *Bowie's Trustees v Watson* 1913 SC 326, 1912 2 SLT 458.
4 See eg *Muir's Executors v Craig's Trustees* 1913 SC 349, 1913 1 SLT 2, where it was held that constructive knowledge of the forgery was insufficient to result in adoption.
5 *Gibbs v British Linen Co* (1875) 4 R 630 at 633, OH.

771. Share certificates. Where share certificates have been fraudulently issued by an officer of a company, the company is barred from refusing to register the transfer of the certificates to a bona fide purchaser of the shares. A refusal to register the transferee as proprietor of the shares will render the company liable in damages[1]. In *Clavering, Son & Co v Goodwins, Jardine & Co*[2] the pursuer advanced money on the security of share certificates bearing that the debtor had a certain number of fully paid-up shares which had been fraudulently issued by the officers of the company. When the company refused to register the shares because they were not in fact fully paid up, the pursuer was held entitled to damages. In the course of his judgment Lord Young said:

> '[the company] cannot be permitted to allege that the 500 shares were not fully paid up, in the face of the certificate of their own directors and secretary that they were

fully paid up. I think they were estopped, or barred, or whatever term you choose to use, from pleading that they were not fully paid up. The pursuer proceeded, as he was entitled to do, in reliance upon a certificate under the hands of the proper officers of this mercantile company to the effect that they were fully paid up'[3].

1 See eg *Re Ottos Kopje Diamond Mines Ltd* [1893] 1 Ch 618, CA, and *Balkis Consolidated Co v Tompkinson* [1893] AC 396, HL. See further COMPANIES.
2 *Clavering, Son & Co v Goodwins, Jardine & Co* (1891) 18 R 652.
3 (1891) 18 R 652 at 662.

10. BANKERS' DOCUMENTARY CREDITS

772. The system of documentary credits. It has increasingly become common to finance international trading transactions through a system of documentary credits. A buyer of goods instructs his bank to issue credit for the price of the goods and either itself or more usually through a confirming bank to notify the credit to the seller and make payments to him or his order against presentation of stipulated documents, for example bills of lading or certificates of surveyors that the goods have been loaded. The confirming bank is under a contractual obligation to pay to the seller (the beneficiary) up to the amount of the credit on presentation of the stipulated documents, but will in turn be reimbursed by the issuing bank, on presentation of the documents. The seller and the confirming bank 'deal in documents and not in goods'[1]. Thus, as Lord Diplock has explained:

'If, on their face, the documents presented to the confirming bank by the seller conform with the requirements of the credit as notified to him by the confirming bank, that bank is under a contractual obligation to the seller to honour the credit . . . The whole commercial purpose for which the system of confirmed irrevocable documentary credits has been developed in international trade is to give to the seller an assured right to be paid before he parts with control of the goods that does not permit of any dispute with the buyer as to the performance of the contract of sale being used as a ground for non-payment or reduction or deferment of payment'[2].

Provided the seller presents the required documents, the confirming bank must honour the credit. The confirming bank will then be reimbursed against the documents by the issuing bank which, in turn, will be entitled to obtain payment against them from the buyer.

1 Uniform Customs and Practice for Documentary Credits (1974 revision) of the International Chamber of Commerce, art 8.
2 *United City Merchants (Investments) Ltd v Royal Bank of Canada* [1983] 1 AC 168 at 183, [1982] 2 All ER 720 at 725, HL.

773. Fraudulent documentary credits. Difficulties have arisen where the documents presented to the confirming bank are forgeries or include false statements which are intended to give them the appearance of regularity. It is the general rule that, provided on a reasonable examination of the documents they appear *on their face* to be in accordance with the terms and conditions of the letter of credit, the confirming bank is obliged and entitled to accept them. Accordingly, any loss arising from fraud will be borne by the buyer who may, of course, have recourse against the seller.

However, where the fraud or forgery is discovered before the realisation of the documentary credit, the confirming bank must not make the payment[1]. This principle operates within narrow confines. There must be evidence of blatant fraud; mere suspicion of fraud will not suffice. The bank is under no obligation to investigate an allegation of fraud[2]. Moreover, fraud can only effectively be raised against the party who has committed it. As Lord Diplock explained, 'The exception for fraud on the part of the beneficiary seeking to avail himself of the credit is a clear application of the maxim *ex turpi causa non oritur actio* or, if plain English is to be preferred, "fraud unravels all"'[3]. But it is not applicable if the seller is unaware of any forgery or fraudulent misstatement in the documents[4]. Provided the documents are *ex facie* in accordance with the terms and conditions of the credit, the bank cannot refuse payment to a bona fide seller even if it is aware that the documents contain a material misrepresentation which could entitle the buyer to reject the goods. To accept this as a ground for refusing to pay a bona fide seller would 'destroy the autonomy of the documentary credit which is its raison d'être'[5].

Concern has been expressed that, given the extent of fraud in recent times, for example the production of so-called bills of lading evidencing the shipment of non-existent cargo on a non-existent vessel, it is increasingly unsatisfactory that the loss should ultimately continue to fall on the buyer[6]. Indeed, the current prevalence of fraud in such transactions may well in the long run undermine the confidence of the business community in the very system itself.

1   The 'landmark' case is *Sztejn v J Henry Schroder Banking Corpn* 31 NYS 2d 631 (1941), approved in *Edward Owen Engineering Ltd v Barclays Bank International Ltd* [1978] QB 159, [1978] 1 All ER 976, CA, and in *United City Merchants (Investments) Ltd v Royal Bank of Canada* [1983] 1 AC 168, [1982] 2 All ER 720, HL.
2   See H C Gutteridge and M Megrah *The Law of Bankers' Commercial Credits* (6th edn, 1979) p 144, and cf R M Goode 'Reflections on Letters of Credit' 1980 JBL 291.
3   *United City Merchants (Investments) Ltd v Royal Bank of Canada* [1983] 1 AC 168 at 184, [1982] 2 All ER 720 at 725, HL.
4   *United City Merchants (Investments) Ltd v Royal Bank of Canada* [1983] 1 AC 168 at 184, [1982] 2 All ER 720 at 725, HL. Similarly, a holder in due course of a bill drawn under a documentary credit should not be enjoined from enforcing it by reason of the seller's fraud.
5   *United City Merchants (Investments) Ltd v Royal Bank of Canada* [1983] 1 AC 168 at 185, [1982] 2 All ER 720 at 726, 727, HL.
6   See eg E P Ellinger 'Fraud in Documentary Credit Transactions' 1980 JBL 258.

11. CAUTIONARY OBLIGATIONS

774. Cautionary obligation induced by fraud. A cautionary obligation is not a contact *uberrimae fidei*, demanding full disclosure between creditor and prospective cautioner. In *Young v Clydesdale Bank Ltd* Lord Adam said:

'... it is well settled that it is not the duty of a bank to give any information to a proposed cautioner as to the state of accounts with the principal... If the cautioner desires to know the state of accounts with the principal it is his duty to ask and inform himself, but no duty lies upon a party seeking security to give any information of that kind...'[1].

Lord Shand maintained:

'... nothing is better settled than this, that a bank-agent is entitled to assume that the cautioner has informed himself upon the various matters material to the obligation he is about to undertake. The agent is not bound to volunteer any information or statement as to the accounts, although if information be asked he is bound to give it, and to give it truthfully'[2].

A cautionary obligation must be in writing signed by the person undertaking it[3]. A fraudulent misrepresentation which induced the cautioner to enter into the cautionary obligation can be express[4] or by conduct[5]. While there is no duty of voluntary disclosure on the creditor[6], 'concealment may be undue, and void an obligation of cautionary, though it be not made with a fraudulent motive, if it be such as to cause the cautioner to view the case in a false light'[7].

1   *Young v Clydesdale Bank Ltd* (1889) 17 R 231 at 240.
2   (1889) 17 R 231 at 244. See also *Royal Bank of Scotland v Greenshields* 1914 SC 259, 1914 1 SLT 74.
3   Mercantile Law Amendment Act Scotland 1856 (c 60), s 6; *Clydesdale Bank Ltd v Paton* (1896) 23 R (HL) 22, 4 SLT 7; *Union Bank of Scotland Ltd v Taylor* 1925 SC 835, 1925 SLT 583.
4   See eg *Falconer v North of Scotland Banking Co* (1863) 1 M 704 at 716, per Lord Neaves.
5   *Broatch v Jenkins* (1866) 4 M 1030 at 1032, per Lord President McNeill.
6   See eg *Hamilton v Watson* (1845) 4 Bell App 67, HL, where it was held that a bank requiring security for a cash-credit is not bound to disclose voluntarily to the proposed cautioner the particular application to be made of the money to be advanced on credit.
7   *Royal Bank of Scotland v Ranken* (1844) 6 D 1418 at 1432, per Lord Mackenzie.

775. Duty of disclosure. Where caution is sought for the intromissions of an agent or employee, rather than as surety for a debt, there is an obligation to disclose to the proposed cautioner the reason why surety was demanded. In the words of Lord Eldon:

'if . . . a man or a body of men employing a number of agents find one whom they have reason to suppose not trustworthy, one who most likely owes them large sums of money, and call upon that man to give sureties, or cautioners as it is called in Scotland, both for his past and future dealings, thereby holding him out as a person trustworthy, when they know, or have strong grounds for suspecting, that he is not so, that would not bind the cautioners or sureties'[1].

This approach can be seen as an application of the need for bona fides between the parties where surety is sought for an employee or agent, but the application of this principle beyond this type of cautionary obligation is doubtful in the light of more recent cases[2].

1   *Smith v Bank of Scotland* (1813) 1 Dow 272, HL. These words do not appear in that report, but are quoted in *Smith v Bank of Scotland* (1829) 7 S 244 at 248, and again quoted in *Railton v Mathews* (1844) 6 D 536 at 553, per Lord Cockburn. This approach was approved by the House of Lords in *Railton v Matthews* (1844) 3 Bell App 56 at 65, 66, HL, per Lord Cottenham, and applied in *French v Cameron* (1893) 20 R 966 at 973, per Lord Trayner. See also *Wardlaw v Mackenzie* (1859) 21 D 940.
2   Cf eg *Royal Bank of Scotland v Ranken* (1844) 6 D 1418 with *Young v Clydesdale Bank Ltd* (1889) 17 R 231 and *Royal Bank of Scotland v Greenshields* 1914 SC 259, 1914 1 SLT 74.

12. INSOLVENCY AND BANKRUPTCY

776. Introduction. The purpose of this part of the title is to consider the circumstances in which the juristic acts of an insolvent person are reducible on the ground of fraud or unfairness to the general creditors of the insolvent person.

777. Voluntary obligations. Where it can be established that a person entered into a contractual obligation knowing that he would be unable to perform his obligation as a result of insolvency, the contract can be rescinded or reduced on the ground of fraud, as to enter into a contract in these circumstances is, *per se*, a fraudulent misrepresentation[1]. However, it is 'not fraud for persons in such a position [(insolvency)] to go on with their business and purchase goods with the purpose and intention of recovering their commercial position'[2]. Therefore proof of fraud in these circumstances will be difficult[3].

1 *A W Gamage Ltd v Charlesworth's Trustee* 1910 SC 257 at 264, 1910 1 SLT 11 at 14, per Lord Kinnear.
2 *Ehrenbacher & Co v Kennedy* (1874) 1 R 1131 at 1135, per Lord President Inglis.
3 *Muir v Rankin* (1905) 13 SLT 60, OH.

778. Corporeal moveable property. Although the antecedent voluntary obligation may be liable to annulment on the ground of fraud, where the innocent party has conveyed corporeal moveable property to the insolvent, prima facie the ownership of the property will have been transferred to him[1]. Until rescission or reduction, the insolvent will have title to the goods which can be transferred to a bona fide onerous third party. If this has been done, the rights of the bona fide onerous acquirer are indefeasible[2]. For these purposes it is not in mala fide to deal with a person suspected to be 'tottering', but not declared to be insolvent[3].

More problematic is the question whether the innocent party can obtain restitution of the property where title has remained with the insolvent but he has become sequestrated *before* rescission or reduction of the antecedent obligation or conveyance. In *Schuurmans v Goldie*[4], where the vendee deliberately concealed his imminent bankruptcy from the vendor to prevent him from exercising his right of stoppage *in transitu*, the Inner House refused to countenance such a fraud and held that the seller could recover the property in spite of the fact that the purchaser had become bankrupt. This decision was followed in *Watt v Findlay*[5], where a party who had purchased whisky to be paid on delivery induced the vendor to transfer ownership without full payment at a time when he was taking steps for his sequestration. But a change in approach is discernible in *Richmond v Railton*[6], where *Watt v Findlay* was explained as a special case where the specific conveyance of the property, as opposed to the antecedent obligation, had been induced by fraud. Where the vendor was seeking restitution on the ground that the antecedent obligation was tainted by fraud, the court took the view that he would be barred from obtaining restitution if the vendee had subsequently become sequestrated. Lord Justice-Clerk Hope explained:

'In a question as to restitution claimed by the sellers, arising under sequestration five or six months after the right of property had so passed by delivery voluntarily made on the part of the sellers, without any new fraud leading to and producing the actual delivery, and they taking a bill for the price, I should hold the point that the right of property had legally passed to the purchaser, to be conclusive, the delivery not being within the shadow and blight as it were of misrepresentation'[7].

An unpaid vendor can, of course, exercise his right of retention or stoppage *in transitu*[8], but, if this is not possible, it has been held that an insolvent buyer is entitled to reject the goods before the date of sequestration, and that this is not *in fraudem* of his general creditors[9]. Although there are *dicta* that an insolvent purchaser is under a legal as well as moral duty to reject the goods when he knows he is insolvent but not yet sequestrated[10], in *Ehrenbacher v Kennedy*[11] Lord President Inglis doubted whether this was so. It was subsequently held that it was not fraud for a purchaser to accept goods at a time when he knew that he was insolvent but hoped he could continue in business, and even though he could, in the circumstances, have lawfully rejected the goods[12].

While the authorities remain equivocal, it is nevertheless submitted that if an insolvent purchaser has not rejected the property before the date of the sequestration, then, as a general rule, restitution of the property will be barred by the subsequent sequestration of the insolvent party[13]. It is only where the insolvent's fraud specifically induced the transfer of the ownership of the property, which would not otherwise have passed, that the property will not fall to the trustee in bankruptcy[14]: otherwise, it would 'come very near to treating fraud in a contract as a *vitium reale*'[15].

 1 See paras 762, 763, above.
 2 *Price and Pierce Ltd v Bank of Scotland* 1910 SC 1095 at 1106, 1107, *sub nom Laird v Bank of Scotland* 1910 2 SLT 126 at 128, per Lord Kinnear.
 3 1910 SC 1095 at 1118, 1910 2 SLT 126 at 133, per Lord President Dunedin, approving the approach of Lord Mansfield in *Foxcroft* (1760) 2 Burr 931 at 942.
 4 *G Schuurmans & Sons v Goldie* (1828) 6 S 1110.
 5 *Watt v Findlay* (1846) 8 D 529.
 6 *James Richmond & Co v Railton* (1854) 16 D 403.
 7 (1854) 16 D 403 at 406.
 8 *Morton & Co v Alexander Abercromby & Co* (1858) 20 D 362, where, however, on the facts, the right had been lost; *Ehrenbacher & Co v Kennedy* (1874) 1 R 1131.
 9 *Inglis v Port Eglinton Spinning Co* (1842) 4 D 478; *Booker & Co v Milne* (1870) 9 M 314.
10 *Inglis v Port Eglinton Spinning Co* (1842) 4 D 478 at 480, 481, per Lord Justice-Clerk Hope; *Booker & Co v Milne* (1870) 9 M 314 at 321, per Lord Ardmillan, and at 323 per Lord Kinnear.
11 *Ehrenbacher & Co v Kennedy* (1874) 1 R 1131 at 1135.
12 *Clarke & Co v Miller & Son's Trustee* (1885) 12 R 1035.
13 *James Richmond & Co v Railton* (1854) 16 D 403; *A W Gamage Ltd v Charlesworth's Trustee* 1910 SC 257 at 267, 1910 1 SLT 11 at 18, per Lord Johnston.
14 *Watt v Findlay* (1846) 8 D 529.
15 *A W Gamage Ltd v Charlesworth's Trustee* 1910 SC 257 at 270, 1910 1 SLT 11 at 19, per Lord Johnston.

779. Transactions in fraud of creditors. At common law, an insolvent person is entitled to continue his trade until relieved of his estate. However, he has to regard himself as administering his estate for the benefit of his creditors to the extent that he cannot:

(1) voluntarily and gratuitously alienate his property or secretly set funds apart for his own use;

(2) voluntarily enter into schemes with a creditor, directly to confer a preference on the creditor, to the prejudice of other creditors[1].

While it is said that in these circumstances the insolvent is a trustee or *negotiorum gestor* for his creditors[2], it has been held that it is not a breach of trust for an insolvent to fulfil obligations which are due and prestable and, in particular, to pay in cash debts which are past due[3].

 1 *Nordic Travel Ltd v Scotprint Ltd* 1980 SC 1 at 10, 1980 SLT 189 at 193, per Lord President Emslie.
 2 Bell *Commentaries* II, 170.
 3 *Nordic Travel Ltd v Scotprint Ltd* 1980 SC 1 at 15, 1980 SLT 189 at 196, per Lord President Emslie.

780. Gratuitous alienations. A voluntary gratuitous alienation of property by an insolvent person is challengeable at common law as *in fraudem* of the insolvent's creditors. The onus rests on the challenger to prove that the debtor knew that he was insolvent at the date of the alienation[1] and that the disposal was not onerous. There is no need to prove that the debtor intended to defraud his creditors: it is his act which constitutes the fraud[2]. Even so the burden of proof on the challenger is formidable.

The Bankruptcy Act 1621 provided, however, that where an alienation was made to conjunct or confident persons, there was a rebuttable presumption (1) that the alienation was made without onerous consideration, and (2) that the debtor was insolvent at the time of the alienation[3]. The Act received a liberal construction because it was intended as a means of suppressing fraud[4]. Lord Allanbridge thought that 'the main consideration in interpreting the 1621 Act is to apply a liberal construction and one which accords with the principle which encouraged the passing of the Act by the Scottish Parliament'[5].

Nevertheless, doubts on the scope of the 1621 Act remained, and the opportunity was taken to reform the law in the Bankruptcy (Scotland) Act 1985, under which gratuitous alienations are challengeable if made (a) to an associate of the debtor within five years of the date of sequestration, and (b) to any other person within two years of the date of sequestration[6]. The onus is then on the person seeking to uphold the alienation to show (i) that the debtor was not insolvent at the date of the alienation or at any time thereafter or (ii) that the alienation was made for adequate consideration or (iii) that the alienation was a reasonable birthday, Christmas or other conventional gift or a reasonable gift for a charitable purpose[7]. 'Associate' includes the bankrupt's spouse, relatives, partners, employees or employer[8].

1 *M'Cowan v Wright* (1853) 15 D 494; *MacDougall's Trustee v Ironside* 1914 SC 186, 1913 2 SLT 431. It is, however, sufficient if the alienation under challenge made the debtor insolvent: *Abram Steamship Co Ltd v Abram* 1925 SN 19, 1925 SLT 243, OH.
2 Bell *Commentaries* II,184; *M'Cowan v Wright* (1853) 15 D 494.
3 Bankruptcy Act 1621 (c 18) (repealed): see BANKRUPTCY, vol 2, paras 1387 ff.
4 *Thomas v Thomson* (1865) 3 M 1160.
5 *Johnstone v Peter H Irvine Ltd* 1984 SLT 209 at 211, OH.
6 Bankruptcy (Scotland) Act 1985 (c 66), s 34(3).
7 Ibid, s 34(4).
8 See ibid, s 74(1), and BANKRUPTCY, vol 2, para 1390.

781. Fraudulent preferences. An anticipatory payment of a debt or an obligation is reducible at common law as an illegal or fraudulent preference if the challenger can prove (1) that it was the debtor's voluntary act, (2) that it was done when he was insolvent, and (3) that the debtor knew he was insolvent at the time[1]. There is no need to prove *animus fraudendi* on the debtor's part or collusion or concert on the part of the favoured creditor[2]. Payment of a debt or implement of an obligation which is due can be reduced on proof of collusion or concert between the debtor and the favoured creditor, establishing that they intended to defraud the other creditors, for example if the obligation was fictitious[3] or the price was inflated[4]. But while it is a fraudulent preference to give a creditor security for a debt while insolvent, it has been long accepted that, in the absence of collusion or concert, cash payments of debts or the implement of obligations[5] presently due in the ordinary course of trade are not reducible[5]. Moreover, it is irrelevant that the creditor knew that the debtor was irretrievably insolvent at the time of payment or implement of the obligation: in *Nordic Travel Ltd v Scotprint Ltd* Lord Cameron found that

> 'a long tract of binding authority leaves no room for doubt that where the only support for a claim to repetition of money paid in discharge of a lawful debt due and resting owing is to be found in the fact of "absolute" insolvency being known both to debtor and creditor at the time of payment, that is irrelevant and insufficient to support a subsequent claim for repetition at the instance of a trustee in bankruptcy or liquidation'[6].

By the Bankruptcy (Scotland) Act 1696, voluntary dispositions, assignations or other deeds made and granted by a person who was notour bankrupt at or after his becoming so or in the six months[7] before, in favour of any of his creditors for their satisfaction or further security in preference to other creditors were null and reducible at the instance of creditors or a trustee in sequestration or a liquidator[8]. Cash payments, so long as in bona fide and in the ordinary course of business[9], transactions in the ordinary course of trade and *nova debita* were, however, exempt from challenge under the 1696 Act. Similar provisions existed in relation to fraudulent preferences in the winding up of companies[10].

Nevertheless, doubts on the scope of the 1696 Act remained, and the opportunity was taken to reform the law in the Bankruptcy (Scotland) Act 1985, under which a transaction is challengeable as an unfair preference[11] when it has the effect of creating a preference in favour of a creditor to the prejudice of the general body of creditors, being a preference created not earlier than six months before:

(a) the date of sequestration of the debtor's estate (if, in the case of a natural person, a date within his lifetime); or

(b) the granting by him of a trust deed which has become a protected trust deed; or

(c) his death where, within twelve months after his death, his estate has been sequestrated, or a judicial factor has been appointed[12] to administer his estate and his estate was absolutely insolvent at the date of death[13].

However, the following transactions are excluded:

(i) a transaction in the ordinary course of trade or business;

(ii) a payment in cash for a debt which, when it was paid, had become payable, unless the transaction was collusive with the purpose of prejudicing the general body of creditors;

(iii) a transaction whereby the parties thereto undertake reciprocal obligations[14];

(iv) the granting of a mandate by a debtor authorising an arrestee to pay over the arrested funds or part thereof to the arrester where there has been a decree for payment or a warrant for summary diligence; and the decree or warrant has been preceded by an arrestment on the dependence of the action or followed by an arrestment in execution[15].

  1 *Whatmough's Trustee v British Linen Bank* 1934 SC (HL) 51 at 62, 1934 SLT 392 at 396, per Lord Thankerton.
  2 *Whatmough's Trustee v British Linen Bank* 1932 SC 525 at 543, 1932 SLT 386 at 399, per Lord President Clyde.
  3 *Coutts' Trustee and Doe v Webster* (1886) 13 R 1112.
  4 *Nordic Travel Ltd v Scotprint Ltd* 1980 SC 1 at 28, 1980 SLT 189 at 203, per Lord Cameron.
  5 *M'Cowan v Wright* (1853) 15 D 494; *Coutts' Trustee and Doe v Webster* (1886) 13 R 1112; *Whatmough's Trustee v British Linen Bank* 1932 SC 525, 1932 SLT 386; *Nordic Travel Ltd v Scotprint Ltd* 1980 SC 1, 1980 SLT 189.
  6 *Nordic Travel Ltd v Scotprint Ltd* 1980 SC 1 at 24, 1980 SLT 189 at 201.
  7 As originally enacted, the period was sixty days.
  8 Bankruptcy Act 1696 (c 5) (amended by the Companies Act 1947 (c 47), s 115(3)).
  9 See *Carter v Johnstone* (1886) 13 R 698; *Whatmough's Trustee v British Linen Bank* 1932 SC 525, 1932 SLT 386.
 10 Insolvency Act 1986 (c 45), s 243.
 11 In the Bankruptcy (Scotland) Act 1985 (c 66) the term 'unfair preference' replaces the older term 'fraudulent preference'.
 12 Ie under the Judicial Factors (Scotland) Act 1889 (c 39), s 11A (added by the Bankruptcy (Scotland) Act 1985, s 75(1), Sch 7, para 4): see BANKRUPTCY, vol 2, para 1451.
 13 Bankruptcy (Scotland) Act 1985, s 36(1)(a)–(c), (4).
 14 It is irrelevant whether the performance of the respective obligations occurs at the same time or different times: the transaction must not be collusive.
 15 Bankruptcy (Scotland) Act 1985, s 36(2)(a)–(d): see BANKRUPTCY, vol 2, para 1392.

13. COMPANIES

782. Introduction. The purpose of this part of the title is to discuss only one major aspect of fraud in the sphere of company law: liability in respect of prospectuses[1]. In particular, it is not intended to consider the law relating to fraudulent trading or the complex area of fraud on minority shareholders[2].

  1 See para 783 below.
  2 For full treatment of these and other related matters, see COMPANIES.

783. Liability in respect of prospectuses. Where a statement has been made fraudulently in a company prospectus and as a result a person subscribes for shares, the shareholder is entitled to bring an action against the company for reduction of the contract to take the shares[1]. However, reduction will be barred if *restitutio in integrum* is not possible, for example if the action is not brought until after the company has been wound up[2] or the shares are worthless at the time of the action[3].

In addition, an action in delict will lie against the person making the fraudulent misrepresentation[4]. More controversially, it is thought that an action in delict will lie against the company 'if any of its officers have knowledge that the statement is false'[5]. However, in *Houldsworth v City of Glasgow Bank*[6] the House of Lords held that an action in delict could not lie against a company in these circumstances, unless the allotment of shares is also rescinded. Thus no action in delict is possible against the company, as opposed to its directors, if *restitutio in integrum* is not possible and the allotment of shares cannot be reduced. If rescission is possible, the subscriber will be entitled to his money back with interest, and therefore little is to be gained by adding a claim for damages in delict.

The difficulty, of course, is to establish that the statement was made with the degree of fraudulent intent required by the House of Lords in *Derry v Peek*[7]. But specific statutory liability was introduced shortly after that decision by provisions in the Directors' Liability Act 1890 (c 64), later contained in the Companies Act 1985, under which compensation was payable to all those who subscribed for any shares or debentures on the faith of the prospectus for the loss or damage which they had sustained by reason of any untrue statement included in it[8]. While the company was not liable under this provision, liability extended to directors of the company at the time of the issue of the prospectus, those who authorised themselves to be named, and were named, as directors or had agreed to become directors, a promoter of the company and any person who had authorised the issue of the prospectus[9]. Thus once the pursuer had proved that he had sustained damage by reason of an untrue statement in the prospectus, his action would succeed unless the defender could disprove responsibility for the prospectus or show that he had reasonable grounds to believe, and did up to the time of allotment believe, that the statement in the prospectus was true[10].

The Financial Services Act 1986 has, however, introduced a new scheme of liability. Where listed securities are involved, 'listing particulars' (in effect a prospectus) must be published in accordance with Stock Exchange rules. The person or persons responsible for any listing particulars (or supplementary listing particulars) is liable to pay compensation to any person who has acquired any of the securities in question and suffered loss in respect of them as a result of any untrue or misleading statement in the particulars or the omission from them of any matter required to be included[11]. Thus, proof of reliance is not required, but the need to establish causation is retained. For the purposes of this liability, the persons responsible are (1) the issuer of the securities involved; (2) the directors of the issuer; (3) each person who has authorised himself to be named, and is named, in the particulars as a director or as having agreed to become a director; (4) each person who accepts, and is stated in the particulars as accepting, responsibility for all or any part of the particulars; and (5) any other person who has authorised all or part of the particulars[12]. Subject to certain conditions, it is a defence to establish that the defender reasonably believed, having made such inquiries (if any) as were reasonable, that the statement was true and not misleading or that the matter whose omission caused the loss was properly omitted[13]. A substantially identical set of provisions applies where unlisted securities are offered in a prospectus[14].

As an action in fraud is a personal action, 'the pursuers must therefore specify the individuals who are alleged to have committed the fraud for which the company is to be held responsible'[15].

1 *Mair v Rio Grande Rubber Estates Ltd* 1913 SC (HL) 74, 1913 2 SLT 166.
2 *Western Bank of Scotland v Addie* (1867) 5 M (HL) 80.
3 *Graham v Western Bank of Scotland* (1865) 3 M 617.
4 *Western Bank of Scotland v Addie* (1867) 5 M (HL) 80. An action is also competent against those, for example directors of the company, who were principals of those who issued it while acting within the scope of their authority: *Briess v Woolley* [1954] AC 333, [1954] 1 All ER 909, HL.
5 L C B Gower *Principles of Modern Company Law* (4th edn, 1979) p 372. Moreover, the directors, acting on behalf of the company, will normally have to accept responsibility for misstatements in the prospectus.
6 *Houldsworth v City of Glasgow Bank* (1880) 7 R (HL) 53.
7 *Derry v Peek* (1889) 14 App Cas 337, HL, discussed in paras 725 ff above. See also eg *Cullen's Trustee v Johnston* (1865) 3 M 935.
8 Companies Act 1985 (c 6), s 67(1) (repealed).
9 Ibid, s 67(2) (repealed).
10 See ibid, s 68 (repealed).
11 Financial Services Act 1986 (c 60), s 150(1).
12 Ibid, s 152(1)(a)–(e).
13 See ibid, s 151.
14 See ibid, ss 166–168.
15 *Smith and Houston Ltd v Metal Industries (Salvage) Ltd* 1953 SLT (Notes) 73, OH, per Lord Birnam.

14. THE LAW OF PERSONS

784. Introduction. Fraud does not feature prominently in the law of persons, but there are nevertheless some interesting — if disparate — situations where it has been important. These can conveniently be discussed in this part of the title.

785. Delictual liability. As a general principle, an action will lie in delict where the pursuer has suffered personal injury, for example nervous shock, as a result of the defender's fraudulent representations[1]. In this part of the title, however, it is intended to consider those aspects of delictual liability for fraud which are of particular relevance in the area of the law of persons.

1 See eg *Janvier v Sweeney* [1919] 2 KB 316, CA.

786. Seduction and fraud. Where the fraudulent representations have been made to induce a virgin to have sexual intercourse with the defender, he will be liable to be sued for seduction[1]. The essence of this delict is that the pursuer's consent to sexual intercourse has been obtained by deceit, and it is essential that she aver and establish that she was a virgin[2]. Where the deceit took the form of a promise to marry which the defender had no intention of implementing[3], the claim could formerly be combined with an action for breach of promise of marriage[4]. However, actions for breach of promise to marry are no longer competent[5]. Where the pursuer was not a virgin at the time the sexual intercourse took place, the ground of action is fraud not seduction.

1 See generally D M Walker *The Law of Delict in Scotland* (2nd edn, 1981) pp 698 ff.
2 Lord Fraser *Husband and Wife* (2nd edn, 1876) I, p 501.
3 See eg *M'Candy v Turpy* (1826) 4 S 520 (NE 527); *Walker v M'Isaac* (1857) 19 D 340; *Paton v Brodie* (1857) 20 D 258; *Forbes v Wilson* (1868) 6 M 770; *Cathcart v Brown* (1905) 7 F 951, 13 SLT 318.
4 *Forbes v Wilson* (1868) 6 M 770.
5 Law Reform (Husband and Wife) (Scotland) Act 1984 (c 15), s 1(1).

787. Entrapment: fraudulently inducing a void marriage. Where a person has been fraudulently induced to enter a void marriage, he or she may recover damages for the loss and injury suffered[1]. The most common example is where the pursuer is entrapped into a 'marriage' which is void because the defender is knowingly[2] a party to a prior subsisting marriage. Thus, for example, in *Burke v Burke*[3] the defender induced the pursuer to enter into a bigamous marriage. When the pursuer was pregnant, she discovered that the defender was a party to a prior subsisting marriage. She obtained a declarator of nullity of marriage and was awarded damages of £2,500 because she had been entrapped into marriage as a result of the defender's fraudulent representation that he had divorced his first wife. Moreover, Lord Allanbridge held that the defender could not seek to reduce the damages by suggesting that the pursuer should have been put on inquiry to find out if the defender was divorced[4].

It remains to be seen, however, whether recourse will still be made to this delict, now that it is competent for courts to make orders for financial provision on declarator of nullity of marriage[5].

1 *Clark v Fairweather* (1727) Hermand 95; *Morrison v Dunlop* (1756) Hermand 94; *Mackenzie v Macfarlane* (1891) 5 SLT 292, OH; *Polack v Shiels* 1912 2 SLT 329, OH; *Van Mehren v Van Mehren* 1948 SLT (Notes) 61, OH; *Burke v Burke* 1983 SLT 331, OH; E M Clive *The Law of Husband and Wife in Scotland* (2nd edn, 1982) p 116.
2 Another example is where the defender is recklessly indifferent to whether the earlier marriage subsists or not.
3 *Burke v Burke* 1983 SLT 331, OH.
4 *Burke v Burke* 1983 SLT 331 at 334, OH.
5 Family Law (Scotland) Act 1985 (c 37), s 17.

788. Marriage. While error as to the identity of the other contracting party[1] or as to the nature of the ceremony[2] renders a marriage null, any other type of error, for example error as to the qualities of the other contracting party, does not:

'Errors in qualities or circumstances vitiate not, as if one, supposing he had married a maid or a chaste woman, had married a whore'[3].

The reason is that spouses take each other 'for better or worse', and the courts will not imply resolutive conditions into the contract of marriage which would be inconsistent with this fundamental tenet of the institution[4]. Nor does it matter if the error as to quality was induced by the fraudulent representations or concealment of the defender.

In *Lang v Lang*[5], the Inner House held that neither a wife's fraudulent concealment that she was pregnant by another man, nor her fraudulent misrepresentation that the pursuer was the father of the child she was carrying, constituted grounds for declarator of nullity in Scots law. Accordingly, unless it has produced the appearance without the reality of consent, that is, has induced error as to the identity of the spouses or the nature of the ceremony, fraud has no effect on the validity of a marriage. The contract of marriage is thus an important exception to the general rule that when a party has been induced to enter into a contract as the result of a fraudulent misrepresentation, the contract can be rescinded or reduced if the fraudulent misrepresentation induced the innocent party to contract under material (essential) error[6].

Where a party has been induced to enter into a marriage as a result of a fraudulent misrepresentation as to the qualities of the other spouse, not only will this not constitute a ground of nullity, but it will not provide grounds of divorce under the provisions of the Divorce (Scotland) Act 1976 relating to behaviour[7]. This is because those provisions only apply to the defender's behaviour 'since the date of the marriage' and therefore fraudulent conduct before the marriage is irrelevant[8]. The innocent party may, therefore, have to wait for five years before he or she has grounds for divorce[9].

Given that society's perception of the institution has drastically altered since *Lang v Lang* was decided in 1921, it is difficult to see why marriage should continue to be an exception to the general rule that fraudulent misrepresentation operates as a factor vitiating consent. However, the simplest solution to the hardship inherent in the present law would be to amend the Divorce (Scotland) Act 1976 to include the defender's conduct before as well as after the marriage.

1 Stair *Institutions* I,9,9; *Lang v Lang* 1921 SC 44, 1920 2 SLT 353.
2 *Brebner v Bell* (1904) 12 SLT 2, OH; *S G v W G* 1933 SC 728, 1933 SLT 543. Cf *Ford v Stier* [1896] P 1.
3 *Stair* I,4,6. But such an error did entitle a person to resile from a contract of engagement: *Fletcher v Grant* (1878) 6 R 59 (concealment by a woman that she had had an illegitimate child eleven years previously).
4 *Lang v Lang* 1921 SC 44 at 58, 59, 1920 2 SLT 353 at 362, per Lord Dundas. There is, of course, one exception: the incurable impotency of either spouse, which is the only ground upon which a marriage is voidable in Scots law.
5 *Lang v Lang* 1921 SC 44, 1920 2 SLT 353, overruling *Stein v Stein* 1914 SC 903, 1914 2 SLT 107.
6 For a full discussion, see para 707 above.
7 See the Divorce (Scotland) Act 1976 (c 39), s 1(2)(b), under which a marriage is taken to have irretrievably broken down if since the date of the marriage the defender has at any time behaved in such a way that the pursuer cannot reasonably be expected to cohabit with the defender.
8 Contrast the position in English law where, eg, pregnancy *per alium* renders a marriage voidable under the Matrimonial Causes Act 1973 (c 18), s 12(f).
9 Ie under the Divorce (Scotland) Act 1976, s 1(2)(e) (no cohabitation for a continuous five-year period after the marriage and immediately preceding the bringing of the action).

789–800. Pupils and minors. As a general rule, transactions entered into on behalf of pupils and by minors are subject to challenge on the ground of minority and lesion. Reduction and restitution may be claimed until the expiry of the *quadriennium utile*[1]. However, a minor will be personally barred from seeking reduction on the ground of minority and lesion if he has induced the contract by fraudulently misrepresenting that he was of full age[2]. The fraud can be perpetrated not only by the minor positively representing himself as having reached majority[3], but also by his failure to disclose that he is not of full age, if his appearance suggests he is[4]. The other party must be able to demonstrate that he took reasonable steps to discover the minor's true status[5]. A minor may also be barred from reducing a contract if he fraudulently stated that his curator had consented[6].

1 Ie the four-year period after majority has been reached: Erskine *Institute* I,7.
2 *Wemyss v His Creditors* (1637) Mor 9025; *Kennedy v Weir* (1665) Mor 11658. If the recommendations of the Scottish Law Commission for a new statutory remedy to reduce the contracts of young persons are implemented, the bar of fraudulent misrepresentation is to remain: see *The Legal Capacity and Responsibility of Minors and Pupils* (Scot Law Com no 110; HC Paper (1987–88) no 151).
3 *Wemyss v His Creditors* (1637) Mor 9025.
4 *Wilkie v William Dunlop & Co* (1834) 12 S 506.
5 *Kennedy v Weir* (1665) Mor 11658.
6 *Harvie v M'Intyre* (1829) 7 S 561.

GAME

The General Editors and authors would like to thank Mr John A Wallace for permission to use his material on licensing.

1. INTRODUCTION

801. Historical background. The legislation protecting game in Scotland and regulating the periods within which they may be killed or taken dates back many centuries. Thus, the Scots Parliament in 1427 regulated the seasons during which wild fowl might legally be taken, including 'partricks, plovers, black-cocks, grey hennes, and muir cocks'[1]. An Act of 1457 which prohibited the killing of wild fowl and the destruction of their nests and eggs describes them generally as 'wild fowl and birds that gaines to eat for the sustenance of man, as partricks, plovers, wild ducks and such like foules'[2]. The Act of 1600 'against the slaughter of wild foules' prohibited, under a penalty of 100 pounds Scots, the shooting at and buying and selling of 'partridges, muir fowls, black cocks alth hennes, termigants, wild ducks, teilles and such kind of birds commonly used to be chased with halkes'[3]. These statutes have been repealed, but are of interest as indicating the species of birds regarded as game which it was thought necessary to protect by statute.

1 Wild Birds Act 1427 (c 12) (repealed).
2 Wild Birds Act 1457 (c 31) (repealed).
3 Game Act 1600 (c 34) (repealed).

802. Meaning of 'game'. 'Game', in the general sense, refers to all wild animals pursued and killed for sport and which are normally used as food for human consumption. There is no universal legal definition of 'game', and game are variously described in a number of statutes[1]. In order to ascertain whether a particular bird or animal is classed as game for the purpose of a statute it is necessary to examine the definition of 'game' in that statute: this has led to considerable confusion over the past two centuries, since some birds or animals may be game for the purpose of one statute but not for another[1]. Collectively, the birds and wild animals which are to be found under the definitions of 'game' in the various Acts are grouse, black game (including capercailzie), tarmigan, pheasant, partridge, woodcock, snipe, quail, landrail, wild duck, bustards, deer, hares and rabbits. The eggs of pheasant, partridge, grouse, black or moor game are protected by one statute only[2]. The definitions given by the various modern statutes will be considered later in this title.

1 See paras 805 ff below.
2 Poaching Prevention Act 1862 (c 114), s 1. It has been doubted whether lapwing or green plover were game: *Philip v Earl of Rosslyn* (1833) 5 SJ 433.

803. Common law game rights. All game, being wild animals, are *res nullius* in accordance with the principles of Roman law which were adopted by the Scots institutional writers; as *res nullius* they can be appropriated by any person who can capture them[1]. However, in modern times the principle has been largely eroded by the common law right of every proprietor to the exclusive use of his land and the consequent right to exclude members of the public and all others from his property. It is now well established at common law that, in the absence of statutory authority, no one has the right to enter upon the land of another in pursuit of game, without the permission of the owner, whether the land be enclosed or unenclosed[2]. The right of the landowner to take and kill the game on his land, and to exclude others from doing so, is now a valuable incident of landownership[3].

However, a landowner can only defend these rights by an action of interdict[4] and a claim for damage to trees, fences, structures, crop or stock, where this can be established. At common law, a landowner cannot defend his right of exclusion *brevi manu*, and a resort to force against a trespasser may result in criminal proceedings for assault and a claim for damages[5]. The lack of a simple and expeditious remedy for the landowner whose land is encroached upon by persons in pursuit of game has been filled as a result of a series of statutes collectively known as 'the game laws'[6].

1 Stair *Institutions* II,1,5. See also *Wilson v Dykes* (1872) 10 M 444.
2 *Livingstone v Earl of Breadalbane* (1791) 3 Pat 221, HL; *Welwood v Husband* (1874) 1 R 507.
3 *Birkbeck v Ross* (1865) 4 M 272. See generally PROPERTY.
4 An action of interdict is effective only against those specifically named: *Pattison v Fitzgerald* (1823) 2 S 536 (NE 468).
5 *HM Advocate v Kennedy* (1838) 2 Swin 213; *Bell v Shand* (1870) 7 SLR 267.
6 See paras 805 ff below.

804. Shooting of game on Sundays.   There would appear to be no legislation in force in Scotland prohibiting the shooting of game on Sundays, provided this is done outwith the close seasons. The Wildlife and Countryside Act 1981 prohibits the shooting of wild birds[1] on Sunday[2]. In England and Wales, the Game Act 1831 prohibits the taking of game on Sundays[3].

1 'Wild bird' means any bird of a kind which is normally resident in or is a visitor to Great Britain in a wild state, but does not include poultry or, except in the Wildlife and Countryside Act 1981 (c 69), ss 5, 16 (see ANIMALS, vol 2, paras 285, 292, 312), any game bird: s 27(1).
2 See ibid, s 2(1)–(3), and ANIMALS, vol 2, para 282. These provisions also prohibit shooting on Christmas Day.
3 Game Act 1831 (c 32), s 3.

2. THE GAME LAWS

(1) THE GAME (SCOTLAND) ACT 1772

805. Introduction.   The earliest statute which is not regarded as being in desuetude and remains unrepealed is the Game (Scotland) Act 1772[1].

1 Game (Scotland) Act 1772 (13 Geo 3 c 54).

806. Destruction etc of game.   Any person who wilfully destroys, carries, buys or has in his possession
(1) any muir fowl or tarmargan between 10 December and the following 12 August, or
(2) any heath fowl between 10 December and 20 August, or
(3) any partridge between 1 February and 1 September, or
(4) any pheasant between 1 February and 1 October,

is, on summary conviction, for every such bird, liable to a fine[1]. There are exemptions for birds[2] taken during the close seasons solely for breeding purposes[3].

 1 Game (Scotland) Act 1772 (13 Geo 3 c 54), s 1. At the date at which this volume states the law, the fine is one not exceeding level 1 on the standard scale, namely £50: see the Criminal Procedure (Scotland) Act 1975 (c 21), s 289C(4), (5) (added by the Criminal Law Act 1977 (c 45), s 63(1), Sch 11, para 5, and amended by the Criminal Justice Act 1982 (c 48), s 55(3)(a)), the Criminal Procedure (Scotland) Act 1975, s 289G (added by the Criminal Justice Act 1982, s 54), and the Increase of Criminal Penalties etc (Scotland) Order 1984, SI 1984/526, art 4.
 2 Ie pheasants or partridges: Game (Scotland) Act 1772, s 2.
 3 Ibid, s 2.

807. Custody of game. Any person not qualified[1] to kill game in Scotland, who has in his custody, or carries at any time of the year, any hares, partridges, pheasants, muir fowl, tarmargans, heath fowl or snipe, without the leave of the person qualified to kill the game, is liable to a fine[2]. This provision has only rarely been enforced in recent times[3].

 1 Formerly a 'qualified person' meant a person in right of a ploughgate of land (Hunting and Hawking Act 1621 (c 31) (repealed)), but now merely indicates the owner of the land at common law (see para 803 above). See also *Stevenson v Melville* (1863) 4 Irv 411.
 2 Game Act 1772 (13 Geo 3 c 54), s 3 (amended by the Statute Law Revision Act 1888 (c 3), and the Protection of Birds Act 1954 (c 30), s 15(2), Sch 6). At the date at which this volume states the law, the fine is one not exceeding level 1 on the standard scale, namely £50: see the Criminal Procedure (Scotland) Act 1975 (c 21), s 289C(4), (5) (added by the Criminal Law Act 1977 (c 45), s 63(1), Sch 11, para 5, and amended by the Criminal Justice Act 1982 (c 48), s 55(3)(a)), the Criminal Procedure (Scotland) Act 1975, ss 289E–289G (added by the Criminal Justice Act 1982, s 54), and the Increase of Criminal Penalties etc (Scotland) Order 1984, SI 1984/526, art 4. See also *Thomson v Romanes* (1865) 5 Irv 1.
 3 *Stevenson v Melville* (1863) 4 Irv 411; *Downes and Mercer v Stevenson* (1882) 4 Coup 567.

808. Powers of an agricultural executive committee. An agricultural executive committee has power to order the killing or destruction of game at any time within the close times[1].

 1 See the Agriculture (Scotland) Act 1948 (c 45), s 39, and paras 859 ff below. As to the close times under the Game (Scotland) Act 1772 (13 Geo 3 c 54), see s 1, and para 806 above.

809. Forfeiture. The Game (Scotland) Act 1772 contains no powers of forfeiture of game. An accused, having paid the penalty imposed, is entitled to delivery of the game[1].

 1 *Scott v Everitt* (1853) 15 D 288.

(2) THE NIGHT POACHING ACTS 1828 AND 1844

810. Taking or destroying game by night. If any person by night[1] unlawfully takes or destroys any game[2] or rabbits in any land[3], whether open or enclosed, or on any public road, highway or path, or at the sides thereof, or at the openings, outlets or gates of such land, public road, highway or path, or by night enters or is in any land, whether open or enclosed, with any gun[4], net or other instrument for the purpose of taking or destroying any game, he is guilty of an offence and liable to a fine[5]. To be in the company of a person who has a net for these purposes constitutes an offence[6].

The above provision contains two separate offences, namely that of taking any game or rabbits on any land, public road, pathway etc, and the offence of entering on any land (but not a public road, highway or path) with any gun, net etc for taking game[7].

1 For the meaning of 'night', see para 811 below.
2 'Game' is deemed to include hares, pheasants, partridges, grouse, heath or moor game, black game and bustards: Night Poaching Act 1828 (c 29), s 13.
3 A tenant farmer may be convicted of being unlawfully on his own land, by night, for the purpose of taking game: *Smith v Young* (1856) 2 Irv 402.
4 It is thought that 'gun' would include an airgun or similar weapon.
5 Night Poaching Act 1828, s 1 (extended by the Night Poaching Act 1844 (c 29), s 1, and amended by the Criminal Law Act 1977 (c 45), s 63(1), Sch 11, para 11). At the date at which this volume states the law, the fine is one not exceeding level 3 on the standard scale, namely £400: see the Criminal Procedure (Scotland) Act 1975 (c 21), s 289G(2) (added by the Criminal Justice Act 1982 (c 48), s 54, and amended by the Increase of Criminal Penalties etc (Scotland) Order 1984, SI 1984/526, art 4), and the Criminal Procedure (Scotland) Act 1975, Sch 7A (added by the Criminal Law Act 1977, Sch 11, para 11).
6 *HM Advocate v Granger* (1863) 4 Irv 432.
7 *Mains and Bannatyne v M'Lullich and Fraser* (1860) 3 Irv 533; *HM Advocate v Burns* (1863) 4 Irv 437; *HM Advocate v Duncan* (1864) 4 Irv 474. The second offence does not apply to rabbits.

811. Meaning of 'night'. An offence is committed by night if it occurs between the expiration of the first hour after sunset and the beginning of the last hour before sunrise, computed by reference to the time of sunset or sunrise at the place of the offence[1]. The actual hour of the offence must be libelled in the complaint[2].

1 Night Poaching Act 1828 (c 69), s 12.
2 *Drummond v Lathan* (1892) 3 White 166.

812. Powers of seizure and apprehension. A person found committing either of the above offences[1] on any land (but not a public road, highway or path) may be seized on such land and apprehended by the owner or occupier of the land, or his gamekeeper or servant, or, if he escapes, at any other place to which he may escape, and delivered to the custody of a constable[2]. If the intruder assaults or offers violence with any gun, crossbow, firearm, bludgeon, stick or any other offensive weapon[3] against any person authorised to apprehend him, he commits a further offence and is liable on summary conviction to a penalty of six months imprisonment or a fine or both[4]. These powers of seizure and apprehension are extended to the owner or occupier of land adjoining a public road, highway or path where the offender may be, and to the owner's or occupier's gamekeeper or servant and any person assisting them[5].

1 Ie the offences under the Night Poaching Act 1828 (c 69), s 1: see para 810 above.
2 Ibid, s 2 (amended by the Game Laws (Scotland) Amendment Act 1877 (c 28), s 10(2), and the Wild Creatures and Forest Laws Act 1971 (c 47), ss 1(4), 2(2), Schedule).
3 A stone and a fist have been held to be offensive weapons, as also a walking stick: *HM Advocate v M'Nab* (1845) 2 Broun 416; *HM Advocate v Mitchell* (1887) 1 White 321.
4 Night Poaching Act 1828, s 2 (amended by the Criminal Law Act 1977 (c 45), ss 15(4), 30(3), 65(4), Sch 12, para 1). At the date at which this volume states the law, the fine is one not exceeding level 4 on the standard scale, namely £1,000: see the Criminal Procedure (Scotland) Act 1975 (c 21), s 289G(2) (added by the Criminal Justice Act 1982 (c 48), s 54, and amended by the Increase of Criminal Penalties etc (Scotland) Order 1984, SI 1984/526, art 4).
5 Night Poaching Act 1844 (c 29), s 1.

813. Group offences. Where three or more persons together, by night, unlawfully enter or are on any land, whether open or enclosed, for the purpose of destroying game or rabbits, if any of such persons is armed with a gun, crossbow, firearm, bludgeon or any other offensive weapon, each and every such person is guilty of an offence and liable on summary conviction to imprisonment for a period not exceeding six months or to a fine not exceeding level 4 on the standard scale or to both[1]. It is sufficient for conviction if one of the group is armed[2].

1 Night Poaching Act 1828 (c 29), s 9 (amended by the Criminal Law Act 1977 (c 45), ss 15(4), 30(3), 65(4), Sch 12, para 2). As to level 4 on the standard scale, see para 812, note 4, above. It is thought that a 'gun' would include an airgun or similar weapon. For the meaning of 'game' and 'night', see para 810, note 2, and para 811 above.
2 *HM Advocate v Limerick* (1844) 2 Broun 1; *HM Advocate v Granger* (1863) 4 Irv 432.

814. Prosecutions. Prosecutions under the Night Poaching Acts 1828 and 1844[1] must be brought in the sheriff court at the instance of the procurator fiscal[2].

1 Ie the Night Poaching Act 1828 (c 69) and the Night Poaching Act 1844 (c 29).
2 See the Sheriff Courts and Legal Officers (Scotland) Act 1927 (c 35), s 12, and the Sheriff Courts (Prosecutions for Poaching) Order 1938, SR & O 1938/606.

(3) THE GAME (SCOTLAND) ACT 1832

815. Introduction. The Game (Scotland) Act 1832 (c 68) is commonly called the 'Day Trespass Act'. 'Game' is not defined in the Act but, in practice, the definition in the Night Poaching Act 1828 is accepted, that is hares, pheasant, partridge, grouse, heath or moor game, black game and bustards[1]. Capercailzie have also been found to be game for the purpose of the 1832 Act[2].

1 Night Poaching Act 1828 (c 69), s 13.
2 *Colquhoun's Trustees v Lee* 1957 SLT (Sh Ct) 50, 73 Sh Ct Rep 165.

816. Meaning of 'daytime'. For the purposes of the Game (Scotland) Act 1832, 'daytime' is deemed to commence at the beginning of the last hour before sunrise and to conclude at the expiration of the first hour after sunset[1].

1 Game (Scotland) Act 1832 (c 68), s 3. See also *Robertson v Adamson* (1860) 3 Irv 607.

817. Trespassing on land in search of game. Any person who in the daytime[1] trespasses by entering or being on any land, without leave of the proprietor, in search or pursuit of game, or of woodcock, snipe, wild ducks or conies, is guilty of an offence and may be summarily convicted before the sheriff upon the evidence of one or more credible witnesses, or on confession of the offence or other legal evidence, and will be liable to a fine and for the expenses of process[2].

If any person having his face blackened or coloured or otherwise disfigured for the purpose of disguise, or if five or more persons trespass in search of game or the above mentioned birds or conies, each person, on summary conviction by the evidence of one or more credible witnesses, or confession or other legal evidence, is liable to a fine and for the expenses of process[3].

Any person charged may prove by way of a defence any matter which would have been a defence to an action at law for such trespass[4].

1 For the meaning of 'daytime', see para 816 above.

2 Game (Scotland) Act 1832 (c 68), s 1 (amended by the Game Laws Amendment (Scotland) Act 1877 (c 28), s 10, Sch 1; Statute Law Revision (No 2) Act 1890 (c 51); Protection of Birds Act 1954 (c 30), s 15(2), Sch 6; Deer (Scotland) Act 1959 (c 40), s 36, Sch 3; and the Criminal Justice Act 1967 (c 80), ss 92, 106(2), Sch 3, Pt I). At the date at which this volume states the law the fine is one not exceeding level 1 on the standard scale, namely £50: see the Criminal Procedure (Scotland) Act 1975 (c 21), ss 289F, 289G (added by the Criminal Justice Act 1982 (c 48), s 54), and the Increase of Criminal Penalties etc (Scotland) Order 1984, SI 1984/526, art 4.
3 Game (Scotland) Act 1832, s 1 (as amended). At the date at which this volume states the law, the fine is one not exceeding level 3 on the standard scale, namely £400: see the Criminal Procedure (Scotland) Act 1975, ss 289F, 289G (added by the Criminal Justice Act 1982, s 54), and the Increase of Criminal Penalties etc (Scotland) Order 1984, art 4. See also *M'Adam v Laurie* (1876) 3 R (J) 20. Cf *Black v Bradshaw* (1875) 3 R (J) 18.
4 Game (Scotland) Act 1832, s 1 proviso.

818. Tenant farmers. A tenant farmer cannot be convicted under the Game (Scotland) Act 1832[1] for taking game on his own farm[2] but, as we have seen, where the game is taken by night he may be convicted under the Night Poaching Act 1828 (c 69)[3]. The protection afforded by the 1832 Act does not extend to the tenant farmer's family or servants, any of whom may be prosecuted[4].

However, as we shall see, a person who goes in search of rabbits or hares with written permission of the tenant under the Ground Game Act 1880 (c 47)[5], or who goes in search of rabbits with the permission of a tenant with a common law right to kill rabbits, is not guilty of an offence under the 1832 Act, unless the purported permission is invalid. Thus, a man who was hired by a tenant farmer was convicted for poaching rabbits when he had no written authority from the tenant and the rabbits were reserved to the landlord[6]. In the *Calder* case[7], where game was reserved to the landlord in the tenant farmer's lease and his farm servant shot rabbits on the tenant's instructions, the servant was acquitted, presumably on the ground of lack of *mens rea* as he was entitled to assume that his master had the common law right to kill rabbits and was under no duty to know the terms of his master's lease.

1 Ie under the Game (Scotland) Act 1832 (c 68), s 1: see para 817 above.
2 *Smellie v Lockhart* (1844) 2 Broun 194. However, see *Earl of Selkirk v Kennedy* (1850) Shaw Just 463; *Earl of Kinnoull v Tod* (1859) 3 Irv 501 (where a bench of seven judges reviewed the whole position); *Jack v Nairne* (1887) 1 White 350; *Morrison v Anderson* 1913 SC (J) 114, 1913 2 SLT 124 (game or rabbits); *Crawshay v Duncan* 1915 SC (J) 64, 1915 2 SLT 13 (rabbits).
3 See para 810, note 3, above.
4 *Black v Bradshaw* (1875) 3 R (J) 18; *James v Earl of Fife* (1879) 4 Coup 321; *Maxwell v Marsland* (1889) 2 White 176. However, see *Calder v Robertson* (1878) 4 Coup 131; *Earl of Selkirk v Kennedy* (1850) Shaw Just 463.
5 See paras 849 ff below.
6 *Richardson v Maitland* (1897) 24 R (J) 32.
7 *Calder v Robertson* (1878) 4 Coup 131. As to common law game rights, see para 803 above.

819. Meaning of 'trespass'. Trespass under the Game (Scotland) Act 1832[1] need not be actual and may be constructive. There is a contravention if a person remains on a road and sends his dog on to land to hunt game or rabbits[2], or if he prevents hares from escaping while others are hunting them with dogs[3]. However, where a gamekeeper sent his dog on to private land to retrieve a dead or moribund rabbit, he was acquitted[4]. It has been said *obiter* that a right of access on a private road or railway track does not entitle a person to pursue game thereon[5].

1 Ie under the Game (Scotland) Act 1832 (c 68), s 1: see para 817 above.
2 *Stoddart v Stevenson* (1880) 7 R (J) 11 (revsg *Colquhoun v Liddell* (1876) 4 R (J) 3).
3 *Wood v Collins* (1890) 17 R (J) 55.
4 *Macdonald v Maclean* (1879) 6 R 14; *Nicoll v Strachan* 1912 SC (J) 18, 1912 2 SLT 383.
5 *Colt v Webb* (1898) 1 F (J) 7, 6 SLT 183. As to killing hares on a public road, see *Mains and Bannatyne v M'Lullich and Fraser* (1860) 3 Irv 533.

820. Apprehension of trespassers. Where a person trespasses on any land in the daytime in search or pursuit of game or woodcock, snipe, wild ducks or conies, it is lawful for any person having the right of killing the game upon such land, or the occupier of the land or for any gamekeeper or servant of either of them, to require the trespasser to quit the land and to give his name and place of abode[1]. If he fails to provide this information, or continues to trespass, it is lawful for the party requiring it, or for any person acting under his authority or in his aid, to apprehend the offender[2]. Such offender, whether apprehended or not, on being summarily convicted at the instance of the owner or occupier or of the procurator fiscal, upon the evidence of one or more credible witnesses, or on confession or other legal evidence, is liable to a fine and for the expenses of process[3].

A person detained under these powers must not be detained for more than twelve hours before being brought before a sheriff, failing which he must be liberated for summons[4].

1 Game (Scotland) Act 1832 (c 68), s 2 (amended by the Protection of Birds Act 1954 (c 30), s 15(2), Sch 6). For the meaning of 'daytime', see para 816 above.
2 Game (Scotland) Act 1832, s 2.
3 Ibid, s 2 (amended by the Game Laws (Scotland) Amendment Act 1877 (c 28), s 10, Sch 1). The fine is one not exceeding level 1 on the standard scale: see para 806, note 1, above.
4 Game (Scotland) Act 1832, s 2 (as amended: see note 3 above).

821. Application to persons hunting. The provisions in respect of trespassers and their apprehension[1] do not extend to any person hunting or coursing upon any lands with hounds and being in pursuit of any hare or fox already started upon any other land on which such person was entitled to hunt or course[2].

1 Ie under the Game (Scotland) Act 1832 (c 68), ss 1, 2: see paras 817, 820, above.
2 Ibid, s 4 (amended by the Deer (Scotland) Act 1959 (c 40), s 36, Sch 3).

822. Forfeiture of game. Where any person is found trespassing upon any land in search or pursuit of game and has in his possession any game, it is lawful for any person having the right of killing the game on that land, or the occupier of that land or the gamekeeper or servant of either of them or any person acting by the order or in the aid of either of them, to demand possession of such game[1]. If the trespasser does not immediately give up the game, it may be seized and delivered to the person entitled to kill the game on such land[1].

1 Game (Scotland) Act 1832 (c 68), s 5.

823. Assault and obstruction. Any person in commission of a trespass who assaults or obstructs any person acting in execution of the Game (Scotland) Act 1832 may, on summary conviction by the evidence of one or more credible witnesses, or confession or other legal evidence, be liable to a fine[1].

1 Game (Scotland) Act 1832 (c 68), s 6. See also *Birrel v Jones* (1860) 3 Irv 546. The fine is one not exceeding level 1 on the standard scale: see para 806, note 1, above.

824. Prosecutions. Prosecutions must be commenced within three months of commission of the offence[1]. An information on oath must be submitted before a warrant to apprehend can legally be granted[2]. The prosecutor does not require to negative by evidence any authority or licence and the party founding thereon must prove it[3]. No latitude is allowed in libelling the *locus* of the offence[4]. The prosecutor's title (for example as a shooting tenant) may be proved by the evidence of one witness[5]. However, where no objection is taken to the prosecutor's title it has been held unnecessary to prove it[6]. Prosecutions may be undertaken at the instance of the owner or occupier or the procurator fiscal.

1 Game (Scotland) Act 1832 (c 68), s 11 (amended by the Statute Law Revision Act 1891 (c 67)). See also *Philip v Earl of Rosslyn* (1833) 5 SJ 433; *Blythe and Taylor v Robson* (1853) 1 Irv 235; *Murray v Allan* (1872) 11 M 147.
2 *Mackenzie v Maberly* (1859) 3 Irv 459; *Philip v Earl of Rosslyn* (1833) 5 SJ 433.
3 See the Game (Scotland) Act 1832, s 12.
4 *Cowie v Sandison* 1953 SLT (Notes) 54. See also *Mitchell v Campbell* (1863) 4 Irv 257.
5 *Lees v Macdonald* (1893) 20 R (J) 55.
6 *Saunders v Paterson* (1905) 7 F (J) 58, 13 SLT 251.

(4) THE HARES (SCOTLAND) ACT 1848 AND THE HARES PRESERVATION ACT 1892

825. Introduction. There is no close season for taking or killing hares[1]. The Hares (Scotland) Act 1848 (c 30), and the Hares Preservation Act 1892 (c 8) merely prohibit the selling of hares[2]. No special jurisdiction is conferred by the Acts, which will, therefore, lie only with the sheriff court.

1 See further para 826 below.
2 See para 827 below.

826. Killing hares. It is lawful for any person having the right to kill hares to do so by himself, or by a person authorised by him in writing, without obtaining an annual game certificate under the Game Licences Act 1860[1]. The hares must be found and killed upon his own land[2]. A person authorised as aforesaid has no power to authorise any other person to take or destroy a hare[3].

1 Hares (Scotland) Act 1848 (c 30), s 1 (amended by the Game Licences Act 1860 (c 90), s 6, and the Statute Law Revision Act 1891 (c 67)). As to prohibitions, see para 828 below. As to annual game certificates, see paras 829 ff below.
2 Hares (Scotland) Act 1848, s 1 first proviso.
3 Ibid, s 1 second proviso.

827. Selling and exposing hares for sale. It is unlawful at any time during the months of March, April, May, June and July to sell or expose for sale, in any part of Great Britain, any hare or leveret[1]. Any person contravening this provision is liable on summary conviction to a fine and for the costs of prosecution[2]. These provisions do not apply to foreign hares imported into Great Britain[3].

1 Hares Preservation Act 1892 (c 8), s 2.
2 Ibid, ss 2, 4. The fine is one not exceeding level 1 on the standard scale: see para 806, note 1, above.
3 Ibid, s 3. As to the restrictions on the importation of live hares into Great Britain, see ANIMALS, vol 2, para 214.

828. Prohibitions. It is unlawful for the purpose of injuring or destroying hares and game to put down any poison on any ground, whether open or enclosed, where game usually resort, or in any highway, or for any person to use any firearm or gun of any description, by night, for the purpose of killing any game or hares[1].

1 Hares (Scotland) Act 1848 (c 30), s 4 (amended by the Statute Law Revision Act 1891 (c 67)). 'Night' commences at the expiration of the first hour after sunset and concludes at the beginning of the last hour before sunrise: Hares (Scotland) Act 1848, s 5.

(5) THE GAME ACT 1831 AND THE GAME LICENCES ACT 1860

(a) Licences to Kill Game

829. Game licences generally. Every person before he takes, kills or pursues or aids or assists in any manner in so doing, or who uses any dog, net, gun or other engine for the purpose of taking, pursuing or killing any game, woodcock, snipe or coney or any deer must take out a licence to kill game[1]. A person contravening this provision is liable on summary conviction to a fine[2].

A licence to kill game taken out by a person in his own name, and not as a gamekeeper, is valid throughout the United Kingdom[3].

1 Game Licences Act 1860 (c 90), s 4 (amended by the Protection of Birds Act 1954 (c 30), s 15(2), Sch 6). 'Game' is not defined in the 1860 Act, but in practice the definition given in the Night Poaching Act 1828 (c 29) is adopted: see s 13, and para 810 above.
2 Game Licences Act 1860, s 4. At the date at which this volume states the law, the fine is one not exceeding level 2 on the standard scale, namely £100: see the Criminal Procedure (Scotland) Act 1975 (c 21), s 289C(4), (5) (added by the Criminal Law Act 1977 (c 45), s 63(1), Sch 11, para 5, and amended by the Criminal Justice Act 1982 (c 48), s 55(3)(a)), the Criminal Procedure (Scotland) Act 1975, s 289G (added by the Criminal Justice Act 1982, s 54), and the Increase of Criminal Penalties etc (Scotland) Order 1984, SI 1984/526, art 4.
3 Game Licences Act 1860, s 18.

830. Exceptions and exemptions. There is excepted from the requirement to hold a licence to kill game
(1) the taking of woodcock or snipe by nets or springs;
(2) the taking or destroying of conies by the landowner on enclosed land, or by the tenant thereof, either personally or by his direction or permission;
(3) the pursuing or killing of hares by hunting with hounds; and
(4) the taking or killing of deer on enclosed lands by the owner thereof or by the occupier, either personally or by his authority[1].

There are also certain exemptions from the licensing requirements, namely
(a) any member of the royal family;
(b) any gamekeeper appointed on behalf of the sovereign;
(c) any person assisting in killing or taking game, woodcock, snipe or conies or any deer in company with any person who holds in his own right a licence to kill game and does not act by virtue of any deputation or appointment; and
(d) any person authorised to kill hares[2] without a licence[3] to kill game[4].

1 Game Licences Act 1860 (c 90), s 5, exceptions 1–3, 5.
2 Ie under the Hares (Scotland) Act 1848 (c 30), s 1: see para 826 above.
3 Ie formerly known as an 'annual game certificate'.
4 Game Licences Act 1860, s 5, exemptions 1–4 (amended by the Statute Law Revision Act 1892 (c 19), and the Protection of Birds Act 1954 (c 30), s 15(2), Sch 6). For further exemptions, see the Ground Game Act 1880 (c 47), s 4 (see para 856 below), the Agriculture (Scotland) Act 1948 (c 45), s 53 (see para 865 below), and the Deer (Scotland) Act 1959 (c 40), s 14.

831. Production of licence. Where a person is discovered by an Inland Revenue officer[1], or by the gamekeeper of the land, or by any person who holds a licence to kill game, or the owner or occupier of the land, doing any act for which a licence to kill game is required, that officer, gamekeeper or person may demand production of a licence to kill game and may read and copy it[2]. If no such licence is produced the person challenged may be required to state his name and address[3]. Any failure to do so adequately and correctly constitutes an offence, for which a fine may be imposed[4].

1 By virtue of the Customs and Excise Management Act 1979 (c 2), s 177(1), Sch 4, para 1, 'Inland Revenue officer' is construed as a reference to an officer of Customs and Excise.
2 Game Licences Act 1860 (c 90), s 10.
3 Ibid, s 10. He may also be required to state the place at which he took out the licence: s 10.
4 Ibid, s 10. The fine is one not exceeding level 2 on the standard scale: see para 829, note 2, above.

832. Licence void on conviction of certain offences. If any person who has obtained a licence to kill game is subsequently convicted of an offence under the Game Act 1831[1] or the Game (Scotland) Act 1832 (c 68)[2], the licence to kill game is thereupon rendered null and void[3].

1 Ie under the Game Act 1831 (c 32), s 30. As to the application of the Act of Scotland, see para 833 below.
2 See paras 815 ff above.
3 Game Licences Act 1860 (c 90), s 11.

(b) Licences to Deal in Game

833. Introduction. Before any person may engage in trading in game[1] he must obtain first a gamedealer's licence from the islands or district council[2] and secondly a licence under the Game Licences Act 1860[3].

1 'Game' includes hares, pheasants, partridges, grouse, heath or moor game, black game: Game Act 1831 (c 32), s 2 (amended by the Protection of Birds Act 1954 (c 30), s 15(2), Sch 6). The provisions of the Game Act 1831 were extended to Scotland by the Game Licences Act 1860 (c 90), s 13.
2 See paras 834 ff below.
3 See para 842 below.

834. Grant of licence. Each islands or district council is authorised to grant a licence to deal in game to any person if it thinks fit, being a householder or keeper of a shop or stall within its area[1]. An innkeeper or person licensed to sell beer, or the driver, owner or guard of any mail coach, waggon or other public conveyance, or any courier or pedlar, or a person employed by any of the above mentioned may not be granted a licence[2]. The licence authorises the grantee to buy game at any place from any person who may lawfully sell game by virtue of the Game Act 1831, and also to sell game at any one house, shop or stall[2].

Every person so licensed to deal in game is required to affix to some part of the front of his house, shop or stall, and there keep, a board carrying in clear and legible characters his Christian name and surname, together with the words 'Licensed to deal in Game'[3]. Such licences continue in force for a year from the date of issue[4]. Two or more persons carrying on business in partnership from one house, shop or stall are not required to take out more than one licence in any one year[5].

1 Game Act 1831 (c 32), s 18 (amended by the Statute Law Revision (No 2) Act 1888 (c 57), and the District Courts (Scotland) Act 1975 (c 20), s 24(1), Sch 1, para 3). As to the form of the licence, see the Game Act 1831, Sch (A) (amended by the District Courts (Scotland) Act 1975, s 24, Sch 1, para 4, Sch 2). See also LOCAL GOVERNMENT, vol 14, para 525.

2 Game Act 1831, s 18.
3 Ibid, s 18 proviso.
4 Ibid, s 18.
5 Ibid, s 21.

835. Application to persons licensed to kill game. Every person licensed to kill game has power to sell game to any person licensed to deal in game[1]. However, a licence of less than £3 does not authorise a gamekeeper to sell game except on account of and with the written consent of his master[2].

1 Game Act 1831 (c 32), s 17. As to licences to kill game, see paras 829–832 above.
2 Ibid, s 17 proviso (amended by the Game Licences Act 1860 (c 90), s 6).

836. Innkeepers. An innkeeper may, without holding a licence to deal in game, sell game for consumption on his premises, provided he has obtained the game from a licensed dealer in game and not otherwise[1].

1 Game Act 1831 (c 32), s 26.

837. Offences. It is an offence for any person who has not obtained a licence to deal in game or a licence to kill game, to sell or offer for sale game to any person[1]. It is also an offence for any person authorised to sell game by virtue of holding a licence to kill game, to sell or offer to sell that game to any person who is not a licensed dealer in game[1].

If any person, not being licensed to deal in game, buys any game from any person, except one licensed to deal in game, or bona fide from a person who has displayed the statutory board purporting to convey that he is licensed to deal in game, that person is liable to a penalty and costs[2].

If any person licensed to deal in game buys or obtains from any person not authorised to sell game by virtue of a game dealer's licence or a licence to kill game, he is liable to a penalty and for expenses[3]. To sell or offer for sale at the licensed dealer's house, shop or stall, without exhibiting the statutory board at the time of selling, is an offence[3]. Further offences arise where the statutory board is affixed to more than one house, shop or stall, or where the game is sold from a place other than the house, shop or stall where the board has been exhibited; or where a person not licensed to deal in game pretends to be so by affixing the statutory board, or by offering any certificate or by any other device[3].

1 Game Act 1831 (c 32), s 25 (amended by the Game Laws (Scotland) Amendment Act 1877 (c 28), s 10, Sch 1). As to licences to kill game, see paras 829–832 above. The penalty is one not exceeding level 1 on the standard scale, namely £50: see the Criminal Procedure (Scotland) Act 1975 (c 21), s 289C(4), (5), (7A) (added by the Criminal Law Act 1977 (c 45), s 63(1), Sch 11, para 5, and amended by the Criminal Justice Act 1982 (c 48), s 55(3)(a)), the Criminal Procedure (Scotland) Act 1975, s 289G (added by the Criminal Justice Act 1982, s 54), and the Increase of Criminal Penalties etc (Scotland) Order 1984, SI 1984/526, art 4.
2 Game Act 1831, s 27 (as so amended). As to the statutory board, see para 834 above. The penalty is one not exceeding level 1 on the standard scale: see note 1 above.
3 Ibid, s 28 (as so amended). The penalty is one not exceeding level 1 on the standard scale: see note 1 above.

838. Buying and selling by employee of, or on behalf of, a licensed dealer. The buying or selling of game by any person employed by a licensed dealer in game, and acting in the usual course of his employment, and upon the premises where such dealing is carried on, is lawful in any case where the same would have been lawfully transacted by the licensed game dealer himself[1]. Any licensed dealer may sell any game which has been sent to him to be sold on account of any other licensed game dealer[1].

1 Game Act 1831 (c 32), s 29.

839. Prosecutions. Proceedings under the Game Act 1831 must be brought within three months of the commission of the offence[1]. The prosecutor does not require to negative by evidence any certificate, licence, consent or authority, and the party founding thereon is under burden of the proof thereof[2].

1 Game Act 1831 (c 32), s 41.
2 Ibid, s 42 (amended by the Statute Law Revision (No 2) Act 1888 (c 57)).

840. Prohibited periods for sale of game. If any person licensed to deal in game buys or sells any game bird (except live birds for exhibition or sale alive) after the expiration of ten days[1] from the respective dates in each year in which it becomes unlawful to kill or take such birds, or if any person not being licensed to deal in game buys or sells such game birds as aforesaid, he is liable to a penalty together with costs[2].

1 Ie one inclusive and the other exclusive: Game Act 1831 (c 32), s 4.
2 Ibid, s 4 (amended by the Game Laws Amendment (Scotland) Act 1877 (c 28), s 10, Sch 1, and the Game Act 1970 (c 13), s 1(1), (3)). The penalty is one not exceeding level 1 on the standard scale: see para 817, note 2, above.

841. Possession of game during the close season. Prior to the passing of the Game Act 1970[1], it was an offence to possess game during the close season. The introduction of sophisticated refrigeration processes made the enforcement of such provisions impracticable. It is now lawful for licensed dealers to freeze birds obtained outside the close season and to sell these during the following open season. It is important that records of the dates of acquisition and freezing be kept.

1 Ie the Game Act 1970 (c 13), s 1, which repealed the offence of possession of game during the close season.

842. Licence under the Game Licences (Scotland) Act 1860. Where a licence to deal in game has been granted by an islands or district council[1], it is necessary, before dealing in game, to take out a further licence which levies a duty under the Game Licences (Scotland) Act 1860[2]. Duty is levied by the islands or district council on the issue of the licence[2]. A person dealing in game without holding this further licence is guilty of an offence[3]. This licence cannot be granted except upon the production of a licence to deal in game[4].

1 Ie under the Game Act 1831 (c 32), s 18: see para 834 above.
2 Game Licences Act 1860 (c 90), s 14 (amended by the Local Government (Scotland) Act 1966 (c 51), s 44(1), and the Local Government (Scotland) Act 1973 (c 65), s 188(3)(j)). See further LOCAL GOVERNMENT, vol 14, para 525.
3 Game Licences Act 1860, s 14 (amended by the Statute Law Revision Act 1875 (c 66)). The penalty is one not exceeding level 2 on the standard scale: see para 829, note 2, above.
4 Game Licences Act 1860, s 15.

(6) THE POACHING PREVENTION ACT 1832

843. Meaning of 'game'. 'Game' is deemed to include any one or more hares, pheasants, partridges, eggs of pheasants and partridges, woodcock, snipe, rabbits, grouse, black or moor game, and eggs of grouse, black or moor game[1].

1 Poaching Prevention Act 1862 (c 114), s 1.

844. Powers of search, seizure and detention. It is lawful for any constable in any highway, street or public place to search a person whom he may have good cause to suspect of coming from any land where he has been unlawfully in search or pursuit of game, or any person aiding or abetting him, and having in his possession any game unlawfully obtained, or any gun, parts of a gun or any nets or engines used for killing game[1]. He may also stop and search any cart or other conveyance in or upon which the constable has good cause to suspect contains any such game or article[1]. The constable may seize and detain any such game or article so found[1]. If the person challenged has obtained the game by unlawfully going on any land in search or pursuit of game, or if he has used the article or thing for unlawfully killing game, or has been an accessory, he is on summary conviction liable to a fine and the game, article or thing may be forfeited[2].

The Poaching Prevention Act 1862 does not confer a power of arrest. It will be noted that the places where search may be made are limited. There is no power of search on private land. A search, provided it was within the limits allowed, may be lawful even though the suspicion later proves to be unfounded.

1 Poaching Prevention Act 1862 (c 114), s 2 (restricted by the Constables (Scotland) Act 1875 (c 47)). For the meaning of 'game', see para 843 above.
2 Poaching Prevention Act 1862, s 2 (amended by the Game Laws (Scotland) Amendment Act 1877 (c 28), s 10, Sch 1; Statute Law Revision Act 1893 (c 14); and the Criminal Justice Act 1967 (c 80), ss 92, 106(2), Sch 3, Pt I). The fine is one not exceeding level 3 on the standard scale, see para 817, note 3, above.

845. Oath of verity. The taking of an oath of verity by a constable is an essential preliminary to any proceedings under the Poaching Prevention Act 1862, and failure to do so is fatal to the proceedings[1].

1 See the Game (Scotland) Act 1832 (c 68), s 11 (preserved by the Statute Law Revision Act 1891 (c 67), s 1, as regards proceedings under the Poaching Prevention Act 1862 (c 114)); the Poaching Prevention Act 1862, s 3; and *M'Donald v Milne* (1897) 25 R (J) 41, 5 SLT 227.

846. Evidence. Where a person is found with poaching implements and game in his possession, this is sufficient to infer guilt under the Poaching Prevention Act 1862[1] even though he has not been actually seen on the land[2]. However, the mere possession of game, in the absence of other suspicious circumstances, will not suffice[2]. A ferret, a mesh needle and a quantity of twine were held not to be 'nets or engines'[4]. Where two men went on land for the purpose of shooting game with guns ready for firing, if opportunity offered, they were held to be 'using' the guns, although there was insufficient evidence to show whether the guns had actually been fired[5]. The evidence of one credible witness is sufficient to justify a conviction[6]. The complainer is a competent witness[7].

1 Ie under the Poaching Prevention Act 1862 (c 114), s 2: see para 844 above.
2 *M'Kenzie v Lockhart* (1890) 2 White 534. See also *Anderson and Holms v Cooper* (1868) 1 Coup 18; *Young v Jameson* (1891) 18 R (J) 20.
3 *Jameson v Barty* (1893) 1 Adam 91; *Scatterty v Barclay* (1898) 2 Adam 497.
4 *Gillan v Milroy* (1877) 3 Coup 551.
5 *Gray v Hawthorn* 1961 JC 13, 1961 SLT 11.
6 *Anderson v Macdonald* 1910 SC (J) 65, 1910 1 SLT 258.
7 *Scott v Anderson* (1868) 7 M 43.

847. Proceedings. Prosecution under the Poaching Prevention Act 1862 must be brought in the sheriff court at the instance of the procurator fiscal[1]. Penalties are to be recovered and enforced under the Game (Scotland) Act 1832[2]. This implies that proceedings under the 1862 Act must be commenced within three months of the commission of the offence[3].

1 See the Sheriff Courts and Legal Officers (Scotland) Act 1927 (c 35), s 12, and the Sheriff Courts (Prosecutions for Poaching) Order 1938, SR & O 1938/606.
2 See the Game (Scotland) Act 1832 (c 68), s 11 (preserved by the Statute Law Revision Act 1891 (c 67), s 1, as regards proceedings under the Poaching Prevention Act 1862 (c 114)), and the Poaching Prevention Act 1862, s 3.
3 See para 824 above.

(7) THE GAME LAWS (SCOTLAND) AMENDMENT ACT 1877

848. Prosecutions under the Game Acts. The Game Laws (Scotland) Amendment Act 1877 provides that all prosecutions under the Game Acts are to be brought in the sheriff court of the district in which the offence was committed[1]. Where any person has been or is prosecuted for any offence against any one or more of the Game Acts, he is not liable to be prosecuted again under another Game Act[2]. However, this does not apply to any prosecution under any enactment relating to the Inland Revenue[2].

1 Game Laws (Scotland) Amendment Act 1877 (c 28), s 10, Sch 1. As to the Game Acts, see paras 805 ff above.
2 Ibid, s 11.

(8) THE GROUND GAME ACT 1880

849. Introduction. The Ground Game Act 1880 deals only with ground game, which are defined as hares and rabbits[1].

1 Ground Game Act 1880 (c 47), s 8.

850. Right to take and kill ground game. Every occupier of land has, as incidental to and inseparable from his occupation of the land, the right to take and kill ground game on that land[1]. The occupier may only do so by himself or by persons authorised by him in writing[2]. Only the occupier and one other person authorised by him in writing may kill ground game by firearms[3]. The persons who may be authorised to take or kill ground game are limited to members of the occupier's household (including guests) resident on the land, persons in the occupier's service and any other one person bona fide employed by the occupier to take and kill ground game for reward[4]. A person so authorised will not commit an offence under the Game (Scotland) Act 1832, provided he does not pursue game other than hares or rabbits[5].

A person who has only a right in common to land or a right of pasturing of not more than nine months is not an occupier of the land for the purposes of the Ground Game Act 1880[6].

1 Ground Game Act 1880 (c 47), s 1. This is a concurrent right which may be exercised along with any common law right or right under contract. As to common law game rights, see para 803 above.
2 Ibid, s 1 proviso (1). As to the power of the agricultural executive committee to sanction written authorisations under s 1, see the Agriculture (Scotland) Act 1948 (c 45), s 48(2), and as to rabbit clearance areas, see the Pests Act 1954 (c 68), s 1(4), and para 851 below. See also *Richardson v Maitland* (1897) 24 R (J) 32.

3 Ground Game Act 1880, s 1 proviso (1)(a).
4 Ibid, s 1 proviso (1)(b). As to resident guests, see *Stuart v Murray* (1884) 12 R (J) 9, and as to bona fide, see *Bruce v Prosser* (1898) 2 Adam 487. See also *Niven v Renton* (1888) 1 White 578.
5 See para 818 above.
6 Ground Game Act 1880, s 1 proviso (2). As to common grazing, see para 858 below.

851. Powers of agricultural executive committees. An agricultural executive committee may sanction the authorisation of such persons additional to those authorised by an occupier[1], as the committee thinks reasonable[2]. In land forming part of a rabbit clearance area, the committee may also sanction the authorisation of additional persons to kill rabbits by firearms[3]. Persons so authorised are still subject to the requirement to produce their authority[4].

1 Ie under the Ground Game Act 1880 (c 47), s 1: see para 850 above.
2 See the Agriculture (Scotland) Act 1948 (c 45), s 48(2).
3 See the Pests Act 1954 (c 68), s 1(4). See also s 1(5). As to rabbit clearance orders, see paras 868 ff below.
4 See the Agriculture (Scotland) Act 1948, s 48(2), and the Pests Act 1954, s 1(4).

852. Concurrent right to take and kill ground game. Where there is a person having a concurrent right with the occupier to take and kill ground game on the same land (for example the owner or his sporting tenant) that person or anyone authorised by him may require any person purporting to be authorised by the occupier to produce his written authority[1]. If he fails to do so, he will be deemed not to be an authorised person[2].

1 Ground Game Act 1880 (c 47), s 1 proviso (1)(c). As to authorisation, see paras 850, 851, above.
2 Ibid, s 1 proviso (1)(c).

853. Moorland and unenclosed land. In the case of moorland and un-enclosed land (not being arable land) the occupier and the persons authorised by him may kill thereon hares and rabbits by any legal means, other than shooting, during the whole year, but by firearms only during the period 1 July to 31 March[1].

1 Ground Game Act 1880 (c 47), s 1 proviso (3) (amended by the Agriculture (Scotland) Act 1948 (c 45), s 48(1)). However, this provision does not apply to detached portions of moorland or unenclosed land adjoining arable land, where such detached portions are less than 25 acres in extent: s 48(1).

854. Common law right to kill ground game. Where an occupier has full power at common law to kill rabbits on the land and this power has not been competently restricted by contract with the owner or sporting tenant, then he may invite any number of persons to shoot the rabbits without the necessity of written permission[1]. However, if his only right to kill ground game is that conferred by the Ground Game Act 1880[2], the occupier may only authorise one person to shoot, and this permission must be in writing and the person author-ised must be one of those specified[3] in the Act[4].

1 *Stuart v Murray* (1884) 12 R (J) 9; *Inglis v Moir's Tutors and Gunnis* (1871) 10 M 204.
2 Ie under the Ground Game Act 1880 (c 47), s 1: see para 850 above.
3 Ie under ibid, s 1 proviso (1)(b): see para 850 above.
4 See ibid, s 2. See also *Stuart v Murray* (1884) 12 R (J) 9.

855. Agreements divesting or alienating occupier's right. Any agree-ment, condition or arrangement which purports to divest or alienate the right of an occupier of land[1], or gives him a consideration for refraining from exercising the right, is void[2].

1 Ie under the Ground Game Act 1880 (c 47), s 1: see para 850 above.
2 Ibid, s 3.

856. Exemption from game licences. The occupier and any person authorised[1] to kill ground game are exempt from the requirement to hold a licence to kill game, and they may sell the ground game killed[2].

1 Ie under the Ground Game Act 1880 (c 47), s 1: see para 850 above.
2 See ibid, s 4 (amended by the Local Government (Scotland) Act 1966 (c 51), s 48(2), Sch 6).

857. Instituting legal proceedings. Where a person who is not in occupation of the land (for example the owner or part owner of the land or a sporting tenant) has the sole right of killing game[1], he has the same authority to institute legal proceedings as if he were the exclusive owner[2].

1 However, this is subject to the exception of such right of killing and taking ground game as is by the Ground Game Act 1880 (c 47) conferred on the occupier as incident to and inseparable from his occupation: s 7.
2 Ibid, s 7.

858. Common grazing. It is lawful for landholders interested in a common grazing which has been apportioned[1] to appoint not more than two of their number and to authorise in writing one person bona fide employed by them for reward to kill and take ground game on the common grazing[2]. The two persons appointed are deemed to be the occupiers[3], but they have no right to authorise another person not bona fide employed to take or kill ground game[4]. The person authorised[5] is deemed to have been authorised by the occupier to kill the ground game by firearms or otherwise[6].

Similar provisions apply to the seven crofting counties of Scotland[7].

1 Ie apportioned under the Small Landholders (Scotland) Act 1911 (c 49), s 24(5): see AGRICULTURE, vol 1, para 853.
2 Small Landholders and Agricultural Holdings (Scotland) Act 1931 (c 44), s 23(1).
3 Ie for the purposes of the Ground Game Act 1880 (c 47): see paras 850 ff above.
4 Small Landholders and Agricultural Holdings (Scotland) Act 1931, s 23(2).
5 Ie authorised under ibid, s 23(1).
6 Ibid, s 23(2).
7 See the Crofters (Scotland) Act 1955 (c 21), s 27(5). As to apportionment, see AGRICULTURE, vol 1, paras 821, 822. As to the crofting counties, see AGRICULTURE, vol 1, para 797.

3. CONTROL OF RABBITS, HARES, BIRDS AND RODENTS

(1) PREVENTION OF DAMAGE BY INJURIOUS ANIMALS AND BIRDS

859. Requirement notice by the Secretary of State. The Secretary of State has certain enabling powers for the control of rabbits, hares, certain birds and rodents[1]. If it appears to the Secretary of State that it is expedient for the purpose of preventing damage to crops, pasture, animal or human foodstuff, livestock, trees, hedges, banks or any works on land, he may by notice in writing served on any person having the right to do so require that person to take such steps for the killing of such animals or birds, or the destruction of the eggs of such birds[2].

1 As to the animals and birds for which the Secretary of State may make a requirement notice, see para 860 below.
2 Agriculture (Scotland) Act 1948 (c45), s 39(1). A requirement notice may not be made if the killing would be prohibited by law: see para 860 below. The Secretary of State has delegated his functions under s 39 to agricultural executive committees: see the Agriculture (Scotland) (No 2) Regulations 1950, SI 1950/1552, and the Agriculture (Scotland) Regulations 1955, SI 1955/216. As to further powers of control by rabbit clearance orders, see paras 868 ff below.

860. Animals and birds for which a requirement notice may be made. The animals for which a requirement notice[1] may be made are rabbits, hares and other rodents, deer[2], foxes and moles[3]. The birds for which a notice may be made are, in relation to any area, wild birds other than those the killing or taking of which is for the time being prohibited[4] in that area[5]. 'Wild bird' means any bird of a kind which is ordinary resident in or is a visitor to Great Britain in a wild state[6]. It does not include poultry or, except for certain purposes[7], game birds[8].

1 Ie a notice under the Agriculture (Scotland) Act 1948 (c45), s 39(1): see para 859 above.
2 However, ibid, s 39, does not apply to red deer or sika deer or to any hybrid: see the Deer (Scotland) Act 1959 (c40), s 36, Sch 3, and the Deer (Amendment) (Scotland) Act 1982 (c19), s 15, Sch 3. As to the conservation and control of red and sika deer, see ANIMALS, vol 2, paras 296 ff.
3 Agriculture (Scotland) Act 1948, s 39(3).
4 Ie under the Wildlife and Countryside Act 1981 (c69), Sch 1, or any order made by the Secretary of State: Agriculture (Scotland) Act 1948, s 39(3) (amended by the Wildlife and Countryside Act 1981, s 72(4)). As to the conservation and protection of wild birds, see ANIMALS, vol 2, paras 282 ff.
5 Agriculture (Scotland) Act 1948, s 39(3) (as so amended).
6 Wildlife and Countryside Act 1981, s 27(1). See also ANIMALS, vol 2, para 282.
7 Ie for the purposes of ibid, ss 5, 16: see paras 880–883, 886, below.
8 Ibid, s 27(1).

861. Killing prohibited by law. A requirement notice[1] may not be made if the killing would be prohibited by law[2]. However, a notice may be made to kill game within the meaning of the Game (Scotland) Act 1772[3], at a time of year at which[4] the killing would be prohibited[5] by the 1772 Act[6]. The general effect of this, therefore, is that a notice cannot override the general law, except in regard to the killing of game in the close season under the 1772 Act.

1 Ie a notice under the Agriculture (Scotland) Act 1948 (c45), s 39(1): see para 859 above.
2 Ibid, s 39(2).
3 See para 806 above.
4 Ie apart from the Agriculture (Scotland) Act 1948, s 39(2) proviso.
5 Ie prohibited by the Game (Scotland) Act 1772 (13 Geo 3 c54), s 1: see para 806 above.
6 Agriculture (Scotland) Act 1948, s 39(2) proviso. For the purposes of s 39(1), a person is not to be deemed not to have the right to comply with a notice falling with s 39(2) proviso by reason only that apart from this proviso compliance with it would be prohibited: s 39(2) proviso.

862. Rabbits. A notice of requirement[1] may be given to any occupier of land in a rabbit clearance area, whether or not he has, apart from the notice, the right to take the required steps[2]. The requirement notice may deal specifically with rabbits and may specify the steps to be taken to destroy or reduce the breeding places and cover for rabbits, or to exclude rabbits from the land[2]. The notice is provisional and of no effect unless followed up by a second notice in writing[3].

1 Ie under the Agriculture (Scotland) Act 1948 (c 45), s 39(1): see para 860 above.
2 Pests Act 1954 (c 68), s 1(6), (14)(b).
3 Agriculture (Scotland) Act 1948, s 39(5) (added by the Pests Act 1954, s 2(1)). Where the occupier holds the land under a contract of tenancy, a copy of any notice must be served on any person to whom the occupier pays rent under the tenancy: Agriculture (Scotland) Act 1948, s 39(5) (as so added).

863. Failure to comply with a requirement notice. Failure to comply with a requirement notice is an offence involving a fine and a further fine of £5 for every day upon which the failure continues[1].

1 Agriculture (Scotland) Act 1948 (c 45), s 41(1). Section 41 does not apply to red deer or sika deer or to any hybrid: see para 860, note 2, above. At the date at which this volume states the law, the fine is one not exceeding level 2 on the standard scale namely £100: see the Criminal Procedure (Scotland) Act 1975 (c 21), s 289C(4), (5), (7) (added by the Criminal Law Act 1977 (c 45), s 63(1), Sch 11, para 5, and amended by the Criminal Justice Act 1982 (c 48), s 55(3)(a)), the Criminal Procedure (Scotland) Act 1975, s 289G (added by the Criminal Justice Act 1982, s 54), and the Increase of Criminal Penalties etc (Scotland) Order 1984, SI 1984/526, art 4.

864. Use of poisons. The use of poison gas or poisonous substances for the killing of animals[1] under the control provisions is permitted, provided it is placed in any hole, burrow or earth[2].

1 Ie the animals to which the Agriculture (Scotland) Act 1948 (c 45), s 39 applies: see para 860 above.
2 Ibid, s 49. The use of such gas or substance is generally prohibited by the Protection of Animals (Scotland) Act 1912 (c 14), s 7: see ANIMALS, vol 2, para 243.

865. Game licences. A person authorised or required to kill or take any bird or animal under the control provisions[1] does not require to obtain a licence to kill game and he may sell the birds or animals killed in pursuance of the requirement notice as though he in fact held a licence to kill game[2].

1 Ie under the Agriculture (Scotland) Act 1948 (c 45), s 39: see para 859 above.
2 Ibid, s 53 (amended by the Local Government (Scotland) Act 1966 (c 51), s 48(2), Sch 6).

(2) FORESTS

866. Prevention of damage by rabbits, hares and vermin. If they are satisfied that trees or tree plants are being or are likely to be damaged by rabbits, hares or vermin[1], owing to the failure of the occupier of the land[2] to destroy or control them, the Forestry Commissioners may exercise certain powers of entry to the land[3]. If so satisfied, the commissioners may authorise in writing any competent person to enter on the land and kill the rabbits, hares or vermin[4]. Before doing so, they must first give the occupier and owner of the land such opportunity as the commissioners think reasonable to kill or destroy the rabbits, hares or vermin, or to take steps to prevent damage[4].

1 'Vermin' includes squirrels: Forestry Act 1967 (c 10), s 7(5)(b).
2 The person entitled to kill rabbits, hares or vermin on any common land is deemed to be the occupier of the land: ibid, s 7(5)(a).
3 Ibid, s 7(1).
4 Ibid, s 7(2). The commissioners may recover from the occupier of the land the net cost incurred by them in connection with action taken by them: s 7(3).

867. Obstructing authorised persons. Any person who obstructs a person so authorised is liable, on summary conviction, to a fine[1]. The authorised person must, if required, produce his authority[2].

1 Forestry Act 1967 (c 10), s 7(4). At the date at which this volume states the law, the fine is one not
   exceeding level 2 on the standard scale, namely £100: see the Criminal Procedure (Scotland) Act
   1975 (c 21), ss 289F, 289G (added by the Criminal Justice Act 1982 (c 48), s 54), and the Increase of
   Criminal Penalties etc (Scotland) Order 1984, SI 1984/526, art 4.
2 Forestry Act 1967, s 7(4).

(3) RABBIT CLEARANCE ORDERS

868. Rabbit clearance areas. The Secretary of State has power to make rabbit
clearance orders designating specified areas as rabbit clearance areas to be freed,
so far as practicable, of wild rabbits[1].

1 Pests Act 1954 (c 68), s 1(1), (14)(a). Nothing in s 1(1) or in any such order confers on the occupier
   of land in a rabbit clearance area any additional right to authorise persons to kill rabbits on the
   land with firearms: s 1(3).

869. Occupiers' duties in rabbit clearance areas. The occupier[1] of any land
in a rabbit clearance area is required to take such steps as may from time to time
be necessary for the killing or taking of wild rabbits living on or resorting to the
land[2]. Where it is not reasonably practicable to destroy the wild rabbits, the
occupier is required to prevent damage by such rabbits[3]. He must comply with
such steps as may be specified in the rabbit clearance order or as to the time for
taking them[3].

1 'Occupier' in relation to unoccupied land means the person entitled to occupy the land: Pests Act
   1954 (c 68), s 1(13).
2 Ibid, s 1(2). Nothing in s 1(2) or in any order confers on the occupier of land in a rabbit clearance
   area any additional right to authorise persons to kill rabbits on the land with firearms: s 1(3).
3 Ibid, s 1(2).

870. Liability of authorised persons. A person authorised by the occupier to
kill wild rabbits for the purpose of complying with a rabbit clearance order, and
who acts in accordance with his authorisation, does not thereby commit any
offence under any enactment relating to the unlawful destruction or pursuit of
game[1].

1 Pests Act 1954 (c 68), s 1(7).

871. Failure to comply with a rabbit clearance order. The penalty for
failure to comply with a rabbit clearance order is, on summary conviction, a fine
and a further fine of £5 for every day upon which the failure continues[1].

1 Pests Act 1954 (c 68), s 1(9), applying the Agriculture (Scotland) Act 1948 (c 45), ss 39, 41, 53 (as
   to which see paras 859 ff above). The fine is one not exceeding level 2 on the standard scale, see
   para 863, note 1, above.

4. PROHIBITION OF SHOOTING AT
CERTAIN TIMES AND OF THE USE OF TRAPS,
SNARES, POISONS ETC

(1) PROHIBITIONS UNDER THE
AGRICULTURE (SCOTLAND) ACT 1948

872. Night shooting. A person is guilty of an offence if, between the expiration of the first hour after sunset and the first hour after sunrise, he uses a

firearm[1] for the purpose of killing rabbits and hares[2]. This prohibition does not apply to the owner of shooting rights on any land, or the occupier of any land[3]. However, unless he has exclusive right to the shootings, an occupier may not use a firearm unless he has first obtained the written permission of any other person entitled to kill game on the same land[4]. Such an occupier who is entitled to use a firearm may, subject to the provisions of the Ground Game Act 1880[5], authorise one other person to use a firearm on the said land and during the above period[6].

1 'Firearm' is not defined in the Agriculture (Scotland) Act 1948 (c 45). As to the further restrictions on the types of firearm which may be used for killing wild birds, including game birds, see the Wildlife and Countryside Act 1981 (c 69), s 5, and paras 880–882 below.
2 Agriculture (Scotland) Act 1948, s 50(1)(a) (substituted by the Pests Act 1954 (c 68), s 10). A person found guilty of an offence is liable to a fine: Agriculture (Scotland) Act 1948, s 50(2) (as so substituted and amended by the Criminal Law Act 1977 (c 45), s 63(1), Sch 11, para 13). At the date at which this volume states the law, the fine is one not exceeding level 3 on the standard scale, namely £400: see the Criminal Procedure (Scotland) Act 1975 (c 21), s 289G(2) (added by the Criminal Justice Act 1982 (c 48), s 54, and amended by the Increase of Criminal Penalties etc (Scotland) Order 1984, SI 1984/526, art 4), and the Criminal Procedure (Scotland) Act 1975, Sch 7C (added by the Criminal Law Act 1977, Sch 11, para 13).
3 Wildlife and Countryside Act 1981, s 12, Sch 7, para 2(1).
4 Ibid, Sch 7, para 2(2).
5 Ie the Ground Game Act 1880 (c 47), s 1: see para 850 above.
6 Wildlife and Countryside Act 1981, Sch 7, para 2(3).

873. Use, sale and possession of spring traps. Any person who, for the purpose of taking or killing animals, uses or knowingly permits the use of any spring trap, other than an approved trap, or uses or permits the use of an approved trap in circumstances for which it is not approved, is guilty of an offence[1]. The offering for sale of any spring trap, other than an approved trap, with a view to its being used in a manner which is unlawful, also constitutes an offence[2]. Any person who has in his possession a spring trap for a purpose which is unlawful under the above provisions is guilty of an offence[3]. A person found guilty of any of these offences is liable to a fine[4].

1 Agriculture (Scotland) Act 1948 (c 45), s 50(1)(b) (substituted by the Pest Act 1954 (c 68), s 10). This provision does not render unlawful the experimental use of a spring trap: see the Agriculture (Scotland) Act 1948, s 50(6) (as so substituted). Section 50(1) does not apply to spring traps specified by order of the Secretary of State as being adapted solely for the destruction of rats, mice or other small ground vermin: see s 50(7) (as so substituted). As to approved traps, see para 874 below.
2 Ibid, s 50(1)(c) (as so substituted).
3 Ibid, s 50(1)(d) (as so substituted).
4 Ibid, s 50(2) (as so substituted and amended by the Criminal Law Act 1977 (c 45), s 63(1), Sch 11, para 13). The fine is one not exceeding level 3 on the standard scale: see para 872, note 2 above.

874. Approved traps. An approved trap is one of a type and make specified in an order made by the Secretary of State as approved by him for the taking and killing of animals, and subject to conditions as to the animals which may be killed and the circumstances in which the trap may be used[1].

1 Agriculture (Scotland) Act 1948 (c 45), s 50(3) (substituted by the Pests Act 1954 (c 68), s 10). As to the traps approved and their specifications, see the Spring Traps Approval (Scotland) Order 1975, SI 1975/1722 (amended by SI 1982/91 and SI 1988/2213).

875. Inspection of traps. Any person who sets, or causes or procures to be set, any spring trap for the purpose of catching any rabbit or hare must inspect, or arrange for some competent person to inspect, the trap at least once every day[1].

1 Protection of Animals (Scotland) Act 1912 (c 14), s 9 (amended by the Wildlife and Countryside Act 1981 (c 69), s 73, Sch 17, Pt II).

876. Open trapping of hares and rabbits. A person who uses a spring trap for the taking of hares and rabbits elsewhere than in a rabbit hole is guilty of an offence and liable to a penalty[1]. This provision does not apply to spring traps used under licence by the Secretary of State[2]. Such a licence may be incorporated into a rabbit clearance order or into a notice of requirement[3].

These provisions are of universal application for the protection of the public. The proprietor or occupier of lands adjoining those lands where traps are set has no title to prosecute[4].

1 Agriculture (Scotland) Act 1948 (c 45), s 50A(1), (2) (substituted by the Pests Act 1954 (c 68), s 10, and amended by the Criminal Law Act 1977 (c 45), s 63(1), Sch 11, para 13). The penalty is one not exceeding level 3 on the standard scale: see para 872, note 2, above. See also *Duke of Bedford v Kerr* (1893) 20 R (J) 65, 1 SLT 32; *M'Douall v Cochrane* (1901) 3 F (J) 71, 9 SLT 58. As to what is a rabbit hole, see *Brown v Thomson* (1882) 9 R 1183; *Fraser v Lawson* (1882) 10 R 396.
2 Agriculture (Scotland) Act 1948, s 50A(3) (substituted by the Pests Act 1954, s 10).
3 Agriculture (Scotland) Act 1948, s 50A(4)(a) (as so substituted). Whether such licence is embodied or not, the licence may be revoked: s 50A(4)(b) (as so substituted). As to requirement notices, see paras 859 ff above, and as to rabbit clearance orders, see paras 868 ff above.
4 *Duke of Bedford v Kerr* (1893) 20 R (J) 65 at 67.

877. Myxomatosis. It is an offence for any person knowingly to use or permit the use of a rabbit infected by myxomatosis to spread the disease among unaffected rabbits[1]. However, this provision does not render unlawful any authorised procedure[2]. The penalty on summary conviction is a fine[3].

1 Pests Act 1954 (c 68), s 12.
2 Ibid, s 12 proviso (amended by the Animals (Scientific Procedures) Act 1986 (c 14), s 27(2), Sch 3, para 4), referring to a procedure authorised under the 1986 Act: see ANIMALS, vol 2, paras 251 ff.
3 Pests Act 1954, s 12 (amended by the Criminal Law Act 1977 (c 45), s 63(1), Sch 11, para 13). The fine is level 3 on the standard scale: see para 872, note 2, above.

(2) PROHIBITIONS UNDER THE WILDLIFE AND COUNTRYSIDE ACT 1981

(a) Introduction

878. Meaning of 'wild bird' and 'wild animal'. 'Wild bird' means any bird of a kind which is ordinarily resident in or is a visitor to Great Britain in a wild state, but does not include poultry or any game bird[1]. 'Wild animal' means any animal, other than a bird, which is or, before it was killed or taken, was living wild[2].

1 Wildlife and Countryside Act 1981 (c 69), s 27(1). However, for the purposes of ss 5, 16 (see paras 880–883, 886 below) 'wild bird' includes any game bird: s 27(1). 'Game bird' means any pheasant, partridge, grouse (or moor game), black (or heath) game or ptarmigan, and 'poultry' means domestic fowls, geese, ducks, guinea-fowls, pigeons and quails, and turkeys: s 27(1).
2 Ibid, s 27(1). Any reference to an animal of any kind includes, unless the context otherwise requires, a reference to an egg, larva, pupa, or other immature state of an animal of that kind: s 27(3).

879. Gin traps. The use of gin traps in Scotland was prohibited after 1 April 1973[1].

1 See the Agriculture (Spring Traps) (Scotland) Act 1969 (c 26) (repealed).

(b) Wild Birds

880. Prohibition of certain methods of killing or taking wild birds. Any person who:

(1) sets in position any of the following articles, being an article of such a nature and so placed as to be calculated to cause bodily injury to any wild bird coming in contact with it, namely any springe, trap, gin, snare, hook and line, or any electrical device for stunning or killing or frightening or any poisoned, poisonous or stultifying substance, or

(2) uses for the purpose of taking or killing any wild bird any such article, whether or not of such a nature or so placed as aforesaid, or any net, baited board, bird-lime or substance of a like nature to bird-lime, or

(3) uses for the purpose of taking or killing any wild bird:
    (a) any bow or crossbow,
    (b) any explosive other than ammunition for a firearm,
    (c) any automatic or semi-automatic weapon,
    (d) any shotgun of which the barrel has an internal diameter at the muzzle of more than $1\frac{3}{4}$ inches,
    (e) any device for illuminating a target or any sighting device for night shooting,
    (f) any form of artificial lighting or any mirror or dazzling device,
    (g) any smoke or gas not falling within heads (1) and (2), or
    (h) any chemical wetting agent, or

(4) uses as a decoy for the purpose of killing or taking any wild bird, any sound recording or any wild bird or animal whatever which is tethered, or which is secured by means of braces or other similar appliances, or which is blind, maimed or injured, or

(5) uses any mechanically propelled vehicle in immediate pursuit of a wild bird for the purpose of killing or taking it,

is guilty of an offence and liable to a special penalty[1].

1 Wildlife and Countryside Act 1981 (c 69), s 5(1)(a)–(e). For the meaning of 'wild bird', see para 878 above. A person guilty of an offence is liable on summary conviction to a special penalty not exceeding level 5 on the standard scale: s 21(1)(a). At the date at which this volume states the law, level 5 on the standard scale is £2,000: see the Criminal Procedure (Scotland) Act 1975 (c 21), s 289G(2) (added by the Criminal Justice Act 1982 (c 48), s 54), and the Increase of Criminal Penalties etc (Scotland) Order 1984, SI 1984/526, art 4. Where an offence was committed in respect of more than one bird, the maximum fine which may be imposed is to be determined as if the person convicted had been convicted of a separate offence in respect of each bird: Wildlife and Countryside Act 1981, s 21(5). As to forfeiture, see s 21(6).

881. Defences. It is a defence to any proceedings in respect of using certain prohibited methods to kill or take wild birds[1] to show that the article was set in position for the purpose of killing or taking, in the interest of public health, agriculture, forestry, fisheries or nature conservation, any wild animals which could lawfully be taken or killed by those means and that the accused took all reasonable precautions to prevent injury to wild birds[2].

1 Ie under the Wildlife and Countryside Act 1981 (c 69), s 5(1)(a): see head (1) in para 880 above. For the meaning of 'wild bird', see para 878 above.
2 Ibid, s 5(4).

882. Exemptions. Nothing in the provisions in respect of prohibited methods of killing or taking wild birds[1] is to make unlawful:

(1) to use any cage-trap or net by an authorised person for the purpose of taking certain birds[2];
(2) to use a net for taking wild duck in a duck decoy[3];
(3) the use of a cage-trap or net for the purpose of taking any game bird solely for breeding purposes[4].

However, the use of a net for taking wild birds in flight, or for taking birds on the ground, if projected or propelled otherwise than by hand, is forbidden[5].

1 Ie under the Wildlife and Countryside Act 1981 (c 69), s 5(1): see para 880 above. For the meaning of 'wild bird', see para 878 above.
2 Ie a bird included in ibid, Sch 2, Pt II: s 5(5)(a).
3 However, the duck decoy must be shown to have been in use immediately before the passing of the Protection of Birds Act 1954 (c 30) (repealed) (ie 1 December 1954): Wildlife and Countryside Act 1981, s 5(5)(b).
4 Ibid, s 5(5)(a)–(c).
5 Ibid, s 5(5).

883. Licences. The provisions prohibiting certain methods of killing or taking wild birds[1] do not apply to anything done:
(1) for scientific or educational purposes,
(2) for ringing or marking, or examining any ring or mark on, wild birds,
(3) for conserving birds,
(4) for protecting any collection of wild birds,
(5) for falconry or aviculture,
(6) for public exhibition or competition,
(7) for taxidermy,
(8) for photography,
(9) for preserving public health or public or air safety,
(10) for preventing the spread of disease, or
(11) for preventing serious damage to livestock, foodstuffs for livestock, crops, vegetables, fruit, growing timber or fisheries,
provided it is done under and in accordance with the terms of a licence granted by an appropriate authority[2].

The appropriate authority is (a) in respect of heads (1) to (3), either the Secretary of State or the Nature Conservancy Council; (b) in respect of heads (4) to (6), (8) to (10), the Secretary of State; and (c) in respect of head (7), the Nature Conservancy Council[3].

1 Ie under the Wildlife and Countryside Act 1981 (c 69), s 5: see paras 880–882 above. For the meaning of 'wild bird', see para 878 above.
2 Ibid, s 16(1)(a)–(k).
3 Ibid, ss 16(9)(a)–(d), 27(1).

(c) Wild Animals

884. Prohibition of certain methods of killing or taking wild animals. Any person who:
(1) sets in position any self-locking snare which is of such a nature and so placed as to cause bodily injury to wild animals[1] coming in contact with it,
(2) uses for the purpose of taking or killing any wild animal any self-locking snare, whether or not of such a nature or so placed, or any bow, crossbow or any explosive other than ammunition for a firearm, or
(3) uses as a decoy any live animal or bird,
is guilty of an offence[2].

Any person who:

(a) sets in position any trap or snare, any electrical device for killing or stunning or any poisonous, poisoned or stupefying substance, being an article which is of such a nature and so placed as to be calculated to cause bodily injury to any specified wild animal[3] which comes into contact with it,

(b) uses for the purpose of killing or taking any specified wild animal any such article mentioned in head (a), whether or not of such a nature and so placed, or any net,

(c) uses for the purpose of killing or taking any specified wild animal:
　　(i) any automatic or semi-automatic weapon;
　　(ii) any device for illuminating a target or sighting device for night shooting;
　　(iii) any form of artificial light or any mirror or other dazzling device; or
　　(iv) any gas or smoke not falling within heads (a) and (b);　·

(d) uses as a decoy, for the purpose of killing or taking any specified wild animal, any sound recording; or

(e) uses any mechanically propelled vehicle in immediate pursuit of any specified wild animal for the purpose of driving, killing or taking that animal,

is guilty of an offence[4].

Any person who sets in position any snare which is calculated to injure any wild animal, and fails without reasonable excuse, to inspect it at least once daily, is guilty of an offence[5].

1 For the meaning of 'wild animal', see para 878 above. For the purposes of the Wildlife and Countryside Act 1981 (c 69), s 11(1)(b), (c), (2)(b)–(e), an animal is presumed to have been a wild animal unless the contrary is shown: s 11(5).

2 Ibid, s 11(1)(a)–(c). For the purposes of an offence under s 11(1), (2), a person found guilty of an offence is liable on summary conviction to a fine: s 21(2). The fine is one not exceeding level 5 on the standard scale: see para 880, note 1, above. For the purposes of s 11, where an offence was committed in respect of more than one animal, the maximum fine which may be imposed is to be determined as if the person convicted had been convicted of a separate offence in respect of each animal: s 21(5). As to forfeiture, see s 21(6).

3 Ie specified in ibid, Sch 6: s 11(2)(a).

4 Ibid, s 11(2)(a)–(e). As to the penalty, see note 2 above.

5 Ibid, s 11(3). Any person guilty of an offence is liable on summary conviction to a fine: s 21(3). At the date at which this volume states the law, the fine is one not exceeding level 4 on the standard scale, namely £1,000: see the Criminal Procedure (Scotland) Act 1975 (c 21), s 289G(2) (added by the Criminal Justice Act 1982 (c 48), s 54), and the Increase of Criminal Penalties etc (Scotland) Order 1984, SI 1984/526, art 4.

885. Defences. As in the case of wild birds, it is a defence to a charge of using certain prohibited methods of killing or taking wild animals[1] to show that the article was set for the purpose of taking or killing, in the interests of public health, agriculture, forestry, fisheries or nature conservation, any wild animal which could lawfully be taken or killed by these means, and that the accused took all reasonable precautions to prevent injury to specified[2] wild animals[3].

1 Ie under the Wildlife and Countryside Act 1981 (c 69), s 11(2)(a): see para 884 above. For the meaning of 'wild animal', see para 878 above.

2 Ie specified in ibid, Sch 6.

3 Ibid, s 11(6).

886. Licences. The provisions in respect of the prohibition of certain methods of killing or taking wild animals[1] do not apply to anything done:

(1) for scientific or educational purposes,

(2) for ringing or marking, or examining any ring or mark on, wild animals,

(3) for conserving animals,

(4) for protecting any zoological collection,

(5) for photography,
(6) for preserving public health or public safety,
(7) for preventing the spread of disease, or
(8) for preventing serious damage to livestock, foodstuffs for livestock, crops, vegetables, fruit, growing timber or any other form of property or to fisheries,

provided it is done under and in accordance with the terms of a licence granted by an appropriate authority[2].

The appropriate authority is (a) in respect of heads (1) to (5), the Nature Conservancy Council; and (b) in respect of heads (6) to (8), the Secretary of State[3].

1 Ie under the Wildlife and Countryside Act 1981 (c 69), s 11(1), (2): see para 884 above. For the meaning of 'wild animal', see para 878 above.
2 Ibid, s 16(3).
3 Ibid, ss 16(9), 27(1).

5. RELATIONSHIP OF THE LANDLORD AND AGRICULTURAL TENANT

(1) COMMON LAW

887. Landlord's rights. The agricultural tenant may not inhibit or limit the right of the landlord, or someone deriving right from him, to pursue and kill game on the land occupied by the tenant[1]. The landlord may lease his game rights to a sporting tenant. Such rights of the landlord and his sporting tenant are a burden upon the agricultural tenant, except so far as modified by the agricultural lease. The agricultural tenant may not take the game, nor may he use any extraordinary methods to frighten it away[2].

1 As to common law game rights generally, see para 803 above.
2 *Wemyss v Gulland* (1847) 10 D 204. As to the tenant's rights at common law, see para 888 below.

888. Tenant's rights generally. The tenant's family and servants must not be endangered by the game operations of the landlord or his sporting tenant[1]. The tenant may kill rabbits to protect his crops, unless the right to kill them is reserved to the landlord[2]. If the right to kill rabbits is vested in the tenant under his lease, he may not recover from the landlord damages for injury to his crops by rabbits[2]. Where game are reserved to the landlord in the agricultural lease, this does not include rabbits[3], notwithstanding the Ground Game Act 1880[4]. The tenant may erect scarecrows but may not fire blank cartridges in order to protect his crop[5] and he may verbally authorise other persons to kill rabbits. If damage is unreasonably caused to the tenant's land or standing crops due to actions of the landlord or his sporting tenant, the agricultural tenant may recover damages[6].

1 *Wood v McRitchie* (1881) 2 Guthrie Select Cases 263, Sh Ct.
2 *Inglis v Moir's Tutors and Gunnis* (1871) 10 M 204 at 206; *Wood v Paton* (1874) 1 R 868; *Gowans v Spottiswoode* (1914) 31 Sh Ct Rep 30.
3 *Jack v Nairne* (1887) 1 White 350.
4 *Crawshay v Duncan* 1915 SC (J) 64, 1915 2 SLT 13. As to the Ground Game Act 1880 (c 47), see paras 849 ff above.
5 *Wemyss v Gulland* (1847) 10 D 204.
6 See the English case *Hilton v Green* (1862) 2 F & F 821.

889. Increase of game. Where the agricultural tenant can show that, during the lease, there has been a 'certain visible increase' over the game stock contemplated in the lease, or an 'extravagant increase in the numbers of game or rabbits', and this is attributable to the acts of the landlord, he may have a claim for any damage resulting to his crop[1]. The tenant must give timeous notice of any claim and a claim may be barred by payment of rent without deduction[2].

1 *Morton v Graham* (1867) 6 M 71; *Kidd v Byrne, Byrne v Johnson* (1875) 3 R 255; *Cadzow v Lockhart* (1876) 3 R 666.
2 *Eliott's Trustees v Eliott* (1894) 21 R 858, 2 SLT 66; *Emslie v Young's Trustees* (1894) 21 R 710, 1 SLT 615; *Ramsay v Howison* 1908 SC 697, 15 SLT 983.

(2) TENANT'S STATUTORY COMPENSATION FOR DAMAGE BY GAME

890. Compensation for damage by game. Where a tenant of an agricultural holding has sustained damage to his crops by game, the right to kill and take which is not vested in him, nor in any one under him, other than the landlord, and which the tenant has not permission to kill, he is entitled to compensation from his landlord for the damage, if it exceeds in amount the sum of 12 pence per hectare of the area over which it extends[1].

1 See the Agricultural Holdings (Scotland) Act 1949 (c 75), s 15(1) (amended by the Agriculture (Adaptation of Enactments) (Scotland) Regulations 1977, SI 1977/2007, reg 2, Sch 1). This provision applies to crofters: see the Crofters (Scotland) Act 1955 (c 21), s 3(3), Sch 2, para 10, and AGRICULTURE, vol 1, para 801.

891. Meaning of 'game'. For the purpose of obtaining compensation 'game' means deer, pheasants, partridges, grouse and black game[1]. Ground game is excluded because the tenant is entitled, under the Ground Game Act 1880, to protect himself against damage by ground game[2].

1 Agricultural Holdings (Scotland) Act 1949 (c 75), s 15(4). See also *Kidd v Byrne, Byrne v Johnson* (1875) 3 R 255.
2 As to the Ground Game Act 1880 (c 47), see paras 849 ff above.

892. Obtaining compensation. Compensation is not recoverable unless:
(1) notice in writing is given to the landlord as soon as may be after the damage is first observed, and opportunity for reasonable inspection is given (a) in the case of a growing crop, before it is reaped, raised or consumed; and (b) in the case of a crop already reaped or raised, before it is removed from the land; and
(2) notice in writing of the claim is given to the landlord within one month after the expiration of the calendar year[1] in respect of which the claim is made[2].
In default of agreement, the amount of the damage will be fixed by arbitration[3].

1 The notice may be given after such other period of twelve months as by agreement between the landlord and the tenant may be substituted: Agricultural Holdings (Scotland) Act 1949 (c 75), s 15(1) proviso (b).
2 Ibid, s 15(1) provisos (a), (b).
3 Ibid, s 15(2).

893. Indemnity against all claims for compensation. Where the right to kill the game is vested in some person other than the landlord, for example a sporting tenant, the landlord is entitled to be indemnified by that person against all claims by the agricultural tenant[1]. The agricultural tenant has no claim against the sporting tenant, since he has no contractual relationship with him[2].

1 Agricultural Holdings (Scotland) Act 1949 (c 75), s 15(3). See also *Kidd v Byrne, Byrne v Johnson* (1875) 3 R 255.
2 *Inglis v Moir's Tutors and Gunnis* (1871) 10 M 204; *Kidd v Byrne, Byrne v Johnson* (1875) 3 R 255.

894. Neighbouring land. Where the damage is caused by game from adjoining land, the landlord has no statutory right of relief from compensation against the neighbouring proprietor, but he may well have a claim at common law[1].

1 *Farrer v Nelson* (1885) 15 QBD 258.

6. RELATIONSHIP OF THE LANDLORD AND THE GAME TENANT

(1) THE NATURE OF THE SHOOTING LEASE

895. Introduction. The right to take game by shooting is normally, in modern practice, constituted by the grant of a lease of sporting rights, coupled with the right to enter upon the land for that purpose. It was at one time considered that a lease of shootings was a mere delegation of a right in the nature of a franchise. Thus, in the *Pollock* case it was held that a lease of shootings, including a shooting lodge, was not effectual against a singular successor of the landlord, even though he knew at the time of purchase of the existence of the lease[1].

1 *Pollock, Gilmour & Co v Harvey* (1828) 6 S 913.

896. The *Leith* case. The law in respect of shooting leases was intended to be settled by the Full Bench case of *Leith v Leith*[1]. This was a case involving the valuation of shootings for the purpose of an entail, but in the course of the judgment it was necessary to decide the true nature of a shooting lease. By a majority of six to five the court discarded the view expressed in the *Pollock* case[2] and held that shooting leases must be regarded as proper or real leases and therefore as valid against singular successors as agricultural leases. The decision in the *Leith* case was followed in the *Stewart* case[3]. Giving the leading judgment in that case, Lord President Inglis said:

> 'If, indeed, it were the law that a right of shootings was a mere personal franchise — as at one time the Court appeared inclined to hold — there would be a great deal to be said against the application of the words of the statute[4] to a lease of shootings; but I think it has now been laid down in a series of decisions that this is not the nature of a right of shootings, but that what the tenant receives under such a lease is a right of occupation of land'[5].

This statement of the law is particularly significant since Lord President Inglis was one of the five minority dissenting judges in the *Leith* case who favoured the older law as laid down in the *Pollock* case.

Although there have been a number of cases[6] (some dealing with pasturage and trout fishing) subsequent to the *Leith* case which appear to maintain the older law as laid down in the *Pollock* case, in none of these cases was the binding Full Bench decision in the *Leith* case referred to. Several text book writers also seem to accept the application of the law as decided in *Pollock* and to ignore

Leith[7]. One possible reason for this is that, despite its importance in the law of leases, the *Leith* case appears in the *Faculty Digest* under the heading of 'Expenses' and 'Entail' but not under 'Leases'.

While the matter may not be said to be beyond doubt and the weight and value of the narrow majority in the *Leith* case has not been further tested, it remains, in the author's opinion, the binding authority in favour of the modern view that a lease of shootings and of the right to enter upon land for that purpose, is a proper lease and valid against singular successors of the landlord. Support for this view is to be found in the case of *Palmer's Trustees*[8] which, although not referring to the *Leith* case, does found on the *Stewart* case which itself followed the *Leith* case.

1 *Leith v Leith* (1862) 24 D 1059.
2 *Pollock, Gilmour & Co v Harvey* (1828) 6 S 913: see para 895 above.
3 *Stewart v Bulloch* (1881) 8 R 381. See also *Farquharson v Farquharson* (1870) 9 M 66 at 75.
4 Ie the Diligence Act 1469 (c 12).
5 *Stewart v Bulloch* (1881) 8 R 381 at 383.
6 *Campbell v M'Lean* (1870) 8 M (HL) 40 (pasturage); *Earl of Galloway v Duke of Bedford* (1902) 4 F 851, 10 SLT 128 (trout fishing); *Beckett v Bisset* 1921 2 SLT 33 (right created by real burden).
7 See eg J Burns *Conveyancing Practice* (4th edn, 1957 ed F MacRitchie) p 180; G C H Paton and J G S Cameron *The Law of Landlord and Tenant in Scotland* (1967) p 80. The exception is J Rankine *The Law of Leases in Scotland* (3rd edn, 1916) pp 504, 505, who finally accepts the *Leith* case.
8 *Palmer v Brown* 1988 SCLR 499, 1989 SLT 128, OH.

897. Shooting rights. Shooting rights without land may not be conveyed as a separate heritable tenement either by way of disposition or under reservation as a real burden[1]. Again, such rights are not transmitted by an agricultural lease unless expressly stated or clearly implied in the lease[2]. The converse is the case in England.

1 *Beckett v Bisset* 1921 2 SLT 33.
2 *Copland v Maxwell* (1871) 9 M (HL) 1.

(2) GRANTERS OF SHOOTING LEASES

898. Who may grant shooting leases. Only the proprietor of the land or the party in right of the shootings under a proper lease may grant a lease of shootings[1]. In the case of joint proprietors of land all must concur in the grant of shootings[2]. Leases by liferenters and trustees holding for another are valid.

1 *Marquis of Huntly v Nicol* (1896) 23 R 610.
2 *Campbell and Stewart v Campbell* 24 Jan 1809 FC.

(3) NORMAL CLAUSES OF A SHOOTING LEASE

899. Introduction. In modern practice, particularly where it is desired to ensure that the tenant will be protected against singular successors under the Leases Act 1449 (c 6), the lease is drafted as a grant of the right to occupy the land, with the ancillary right of shooting over the same[1].

1 As to leases generally, see CONVEYANCING, INCLUDING REGISTRATION OF TITLE, vol 6, para 776.

900. Clauses in respect of control of, and right to kill, game. Clauses are usually incorporated requiring that a stock of game will be bred and that only a limited number of birds or animals will be shot in any one season. The right to kill game will frequently include hares and rabbits, but the right of any agricultural tenant of the land to kill rabbits and hares will be reserved. In any event the agricultural tenant has, under the Ground Game Act 1880 (c 47), a concurrent right to kill hares and rabbits along with the sporting tenant[1].

1 See paras 849 ff above.

901. Indemnifying the landlord against claims by the agricultural tenant. The lease will usually include a clause binding the shooting tenant to relieve the landlord of claims by the agricultural tenant for damage to crops by game or the operation of the lease[1]. However, the shooting tenant is not bound to indemnify the landlord for damage not claimed by the agricultural tenant[1]. The latter may not claim directly against the sporting tenant[2].

1 *Eliott's Trustees v Eliott* (1894) 21 R 858, 2 SLT 66.
2 *Inglis v Moir's Tutors and Gunnis* (1871) 10 M 204; *Kidd v Byrne, Byrne v Johnson* (1875) 3 R 255.

902. Assignation and subletting. The sporting tenant has no power to assign the lease or sublet the shootings unless expressly authorised by the lease or separate permission of the landlord[1].

1 *Earl of Fife v Wilson* (1864) 3 M 323 (approved in *Mackintosh v May* (1895) 22 R 345, 2 SLT 471).

903. Exclusive shooting rights. Where a lease provides for exclusive shooting rights, this excludes the right of the proprietor and of any other person to whom he may have given shooting rights. Breach of this provision or failure by the landlord to fulfil the terms of the lease may found a claim for damages[1].

1 *Critchley v Campbell* (1884) 11 R 475.

904. Fences. In the absence of express provision, the landlord is not bound to fence plantations or to maintain the fences in such a condition as to ensure that stock will be excluded[1].

1 *Patrick v Harris's Trustees* (1904) 6 F 985, 12 SLT 256.

7. VALUATION OF SHOOTING RIGHTS

(1) INTRODUCTION

905. Meaning of 'lands and heritages'. For the purposes of valuation, 'lands and heritages' originally extended to all lands, houses, shootings and deer forests which were actually let[1]. This definition was subsequently amended to delete the requirement that the shootings and deer forests should actually be let[2].

1 See the Lands Valuation (Scotland) Act 1854 (c 91), s 42 (as originally enacted). As to valuation for rating of shootings and deer forests generally, see VALUATION FOR RATING, vol 24, paras 736 ff.
2 See ibid, s 42 (amended by the Sporting Lands Rating (Scotland) Act 1886 (c 15), s 4). The 1886 Act also provided that 'lands and heritages' under the Poor Law (Scotland) Act 1845 (c 83), under which certain assessments were then made, should include shootings and deer forests: see s 1 (amended by the Sporting Lands Rating (Scotland) Act 1886, s 5) (repealed).

906. Entry of value of shootings and deer forests. In order to ascertain and assess the yearly value of shootings and deer forests in Scotland, it is the duty of the assessor to enter separately for each islands area or district, and in respect of each proprietor therein, the yearly value of the shootings over the lands and of the deer forests belonging to him in so far as situated within such islands area or district[1]. The effect of this provision is that sporting rights of shootings are liable to be rated at their annual value as fixed by the assessor, whether or not they are let.

  1   Sporting Lands Rating (Scotland) Act 1886 (c 15), s 6 (amended by the Local Government (Scotland) Act 1975 (c 30), s 38(1), Sch 6, Pt II, para 6). As to valuation of shootings and deer forests generally, see VALUATION FOR RATING, vol 24, para 740.

(2) BASIS OF VALUATION

907. Introduction. The net annual value of any lands and heritages is the rent at which the lands and heritages might reasonably be expected to let from year to year if no *grassum* or consideration other than the rent were payable in respect of the lease and if the tenant undertook to pay all the rates and to bear the cost of the repairs and insurance and other expenses, if any, necessary to maintain the lands and heritages in a state to command the rent[1].

If a sporting subject is let bona fide and the rent fixed represents the sum 'conditioned as the fair annual value thereof', the rent paid is conclusive of the value for rating purposes[2]. Where the lease is not bona fide, the assessor may ignore the rent and fix the annual value by some other method. The relationship of the parties may be relevant in determining bona fides but it is not conclusive[3]. If one of the parties has interest over or influence over the other, this may establish lack of bona fides and justify the assessor in ignoring the rent[4].

  1   See the Valuation and Rating (Scotland) Act 1956 (c 60), s 6(8), and VALUATION FOR RATING, vol 24, para 517.
  2   *Duke of Richmond* (1867) 11 M 978; *Lord Middleton v Ross-shire Assessor* (1882) 10 R 28, LVAC.
  3   *Bruce* (1868) 11 M 978; *Bowman v Inverbervie Assessor* (1900) 2 F 607, LVAC; *Marshall v Wigtownshire Assessor* 1929 SC 333, 1929 SLT 209, LVAC.
  4   *Higgins v Lanarkshire Assessor* 1911 SC 931, 1911 1 SLT 135, LVAC. See also *Bell v Edinburgh Assessor* (1904) 6 F 501, 12 SLT 18, LVAC: *Usher v Edinburgh Assessor* 1911 SC 912, 1911 1 SLT 200, LVAC.

908. Buildings. Where buildings are included in a lease of shootings, the buildings are a pertinent of the shootings and the entry in the valuation roll should be 'Shootings with buildings attached thereto'.

909. Assessing rateable value. The normal practice of assessing the rateable value of shootings is to take the rent for a particular season and to deduct such expenses (for example provision of gamekeepers, stalkers, beaters etc) as are properly chargeable against the rent[1]. There is no rule that, where rents have fluctuated over the years, the average of a number of years should be taken[2].

  1   *M'Kenzie v Aberdeenshire Assessor* 1924 SC 635, 1924 SLT 267, LVAC.
  2   *Macandrew v Sutherlandshire Assessor* 1925 SC 512, 1925 SLT 247, LVAC. However, as to where the court approved a valuation of an unlet deer forest based on the five years to 1939, less 33 per cent, see *Macdonald's Trustees v Inverness-shire Assessor* 1941 SC 268, 1941 SLT 264, LVAC.

910. Shootings used for other purposes. Shootings should be entered in the valuation roll separately 'along with pasture land' where de facto the same land is used for both purposes[1] However, where the land is used exclusively for one purpose or the other, only one entry should be made[2].

1 However, as to the problems which arise where land is used for other purposes, see VALUATION
FOR RATING, vol 24, para 738.

2 *Argyllshire Assessor v Stuart* (1888) 15 R 588 (unlet deer forest).

911. Reduction. Where a rent has been fixed and agreed for a number of
years, a general fall in the value of sporting rights, if proved by appropriate
evidence, may constitute grounds for reduction[1].

Where shootings in the Highlands could not be let in consequence of the
difficulty of finding tenants in wartime conditions, the previous annual value
was reduced by 50 per cent, on the basis that, although no rent was being
received, the shootings were still of substantial capital value to the proprietor[2].
The percentage of reduction to be allowed in cases of national difficulty in
letting will vary with the geographical situation of the subjects. Thus where
shootings were remote and situated far from rail and road communications
and no tenant could be obtained, the previous annual value was reduced by
66 per cent[3].

1 *Duke of Westminster v Sutherlandshire Assesor* 1924 SC 654 at 657, 1924 SC 287 at 289, LVAC, per
Lord Sands.

2 *Grant and Mackintosh v Inverness-shire Assessor* 1918 SC 620, 1918 1 SLT 146, LVAC. See also
Perrins v Ross-shire Assessor 1918 SC 602, LVAC.

3 *Mackenzie of Dundonell v Ross-shire Assessor* cited in *Grant and Mackintosh v Inverness-shire Assessor*
1918 SC 620 at 623n, 1918 1 SLT 146 at 149n, LVAC.

912. *Extra commercium* subjects. Where sporting rights and shooting lodges
have, by the legal actions of an appropriate authority been put *extra commercium*
and are therefore unlettable, they should be entered in the valuation roll at a nil
valuation or at least reduced[1]. The case of *Seafield's Trustees*, where a shooting
lodge was earmarked for billeting of evacuees during the war illustrates this
point[2].

1 As to *extra commercium* subjects generally, see VALUATION FOR RATING, vol 24, para 511.

2 *Seafield's Trustees v Inverness-shire Assessor* 1941 SC 271, 1941 SLT 270, LVAC.

913. Unlet sporting rights. Where subjects are legally capable of being let as
sporting rights (for example a deer forest) they will be valued as if they could be
so let. Thus in the *National Trust* case[1] the Trust purchased a deer forest for the
primary purpose of giving the public access to land, and let the grazing at £35 per
annum. The deer forest had previously been valued at £300. There was nothing
in the National Trust Order Confirmation Act 1935 (c ii), prohibiting the Trust
from letting the subjects as a deer forest. The court held that the subjects were, in
their actual state, a deer forest and could be let by the Trust as such since there
was nothing in the Act which indicated that the public should have unrestricted
right of access to land acquired by the Trust.

1 *National Trust for Scotland v Argyllshire Assessor* 1939 SC 291, 1939 SLT 177, LVAC.

914. Shooting rights attached to a house. Where a house goes with a right
to shootings, the presence of the shootings should attach an increased value to
the house[1]. The house should be assessed as a separate subject, leaving the
shootings to reflect their own proper annual value[2].

1 As to the rateable values of dwellinghouses and domestic subjects, see VALUATION FOR RATING,
vol 24, paras 607 ff.

2 *Scott v Kincardineshire Assessor* 1914 SC 655 at 660, 1914 1 SLT 8 at 9, 10, LVAC, per Lord
Johnston.

915. Carcases. While the normal method of valuing an unlet deer forest may be by reference to a fixed sum per stag killed, there is no general level at which that sum should be fixed. Thus, in the *Marquis of Breadalbane* case[1] the valuation committee fixed the sum of £20 per stag on the number killed in the season. The proprietor founded on previous decisions in Ross-shire and Inverness where a figure of £15 per stag had been fixed. The court sustained the committee's figure of £20 and held that there was no general principle applicable to the valuation for rating of deer forests in Scotland.

The case of *Broadlands Properties*[2] dealt with adjustment of the valuation of a let deer forest where the tenant was entitled under his lease to retain and dispose of the carcases. The assessor contended that the gross rental without deduction should be the basis of valuation. The proprietor argued that the gross rental should be regarded as including a payment made for the carcases. The valuation committee held that the assessor should have taken account of the value of the carcases retained by the tenant. On appeal, the court decided in favour of the assessor's view. The basis of the decision was that the deer, until killed, were *res nullius*, but became the property of the tenant on being shot. The provision in the lease did no more than confirm what was already the right of the tenant at common law[3]. Since he had the right to take the carcases without payment, no part of the rent could be attributed to the right conferred by the lease[4].

1 *Marquis of Breadalbane v Argyllshire Assessor* (1890) 17 R 837, LVAC.
2 *Argyll Assessor v Broadlands Properties Ltd* 1973 SC 152, 1974 SLT 265, LVAC.
3 As to common law game rights, see para 803 above.
4 As to a reservation of deer as a real burden in a feu contract, see *Hemming v Duke of Athole* (1883) 11 R 93.

8. MUIRBURNING

916. Introduction. The law[1] in regard to muirburning applies not merely to ground on which heath or heather grows but to all moors and uplands, whatever may grow there, though covered only with rank grass[2]. The one practical test furnished by the cases is that it must be a place to which moor game frequent for breeding[3].

1 The law which applies in Scotland is contained in the Hill Farming Act 1946 (c 73): see paras 917 ff below.
2 J Rankine *The Law of Land-ownership in Scotland* (4th edn, 1909) p 161. 'Muirburn' or 'moorburn' is the burning of heath or moorland, including the heather or grass on it. The exercise of the right is called 'making muirburn'.
3 *Rodgers v Gibson* (1842) 1 Broun 78.

917. Prohibition of muirburn at certain times. It is unlawful to make muirburn except before 16 April or after 30 September in any year[1]. However, there is an extension from 16 to 30 April for the proprietor of lands or for the tenant, provided he has the written authority of the proprietor or his factor[2]. For lands more than 450 metres above sea level, there is a further extension for the proprietor of land, or the tenant with authority as aforesaid, up to 15 May[3].

1 Hill Farming Act 1946 (c 73), s 23(1).
2 Ibid, s 23(1) proviso.
3 Ibid, s 23(2) (amended by the Agriculture (Adaptation of Enactments) (Scotland) Regulations 1977, SI 1977/2007, reg 2, Sch 2).

918. Powers of the Secretary of State. The Secretary of State may in any year, if it appears necessary or expedient, for the purpose of facilitating the making of muirburn, direct that the prohibition of making of muirburn at certain times[1] will not have effect as respects such lands as may be specified, as if for 16 April there were substituted such other date as he may deem proper, being a date not later than 1 May, or, in the case of lands more than 450 metres above sea level, 16 May[2]. Any such direction may be given as respects all land in Scotland, or as respects land in a county or any part of a county, or as respect any particular land or classes of land[3]. Notice of the direction (other than one for particular lands) must be published in one or more newspapers circulating in the locality[3].

1 Ie under the Hill Farming Act 1946 (c 73), s 23(1): see para 917 above.
2 Ibid, s 23(3) (amended by the Agriculture (Adaptation of Enactments) (Scotland) Regulations 1977, SI 1977/2007, reg 2, Sch 2).
3 Hill Farming Act 1946, s 23(3).

919. Offence of making prohibited muirburn. Any person who makes muirburn or causes or procures the making of muirburn prohibited under the Hill Farming Act 1946[1] is guilty of an offence[2].

1 Ie under the Hill Farming Act 1946 (c 73), s 23: see paras 917, 918, above.
2 Ibid, s 23(4). Any person found guilty of an offence is liable on summary conviction to a fine not exceeding level 3 on the standard scale: s 27 (amended by the Wildlife and Countryside Act 1981 (c 69), s 72(3)). At the date at which this volume states the law, level 3 on the standard scale is £400: see the Criminal Procedure (Scotland) Act 1975 (c 21), s 289G (added by the Criminal Justice Act 1982 (c 48), s 54), and the Increase of Criminal Penalties etc (Scotland) Order 1984, SI 1984/526, art 4.

920. Tenant's right to make muirburn. Where the tenant of any land is of the opinion that it is necessary or expedient for the purpose of conserving or improving that land to make muirburn thereon, it is, subject to the provisions of the Hill Farming (Scotland) Act 1946, lawful for him to make muirburn thereon notwithstanding any provision in the lease of such land prohibiting, whether absolutely or subject to conditions, or restricting in any way, the making of muirburn[1].

1 Hill Farming Act 1946 (c 73), s 24(1).

921. Notice of place and extent of muirburn. The tenant must give to the proprietor twenty-eight days' notice in writing of the place at which and the approximate extent to which he proposes to make muirburn[1]. If the proprietor is dissatisfied as to the places or extent to which the tenant proposes to make muirburn, he must, within seven days, give notice in writing to the tenant stating the grounds of his dissatisfaction, and must refer the matter to the Secretary of State for his decision; and, pending such decision, muirburning may not proceed[2].

1 Hill Farming Act 1946 (c 73), ss 24(2), 26(1).
2 Ibid, ss 24(2), 26(1). As to the decision of the Secretary of State, see para 922 below.

922. Decision of the Secretary of State. Upon any reference being made to him, the Secretary of State must make such inquiry as he sees fit, and after considering the representations of the parties, will give such directions as he deems proper for regulating the muirburning[1]. The decision of the Secretary of State is final[1].

1 Hill Farming Act 1946 (c 73), s 24(3).

923. Muirburning in accordance with an approved hill farming improvement scheme. It is lawful, subject to the provisions of the Hill Farming (Scotland) Act 1946, for the tenant of any land, notwithstanding any provision in his lease, to make muirburn if the work is done in accordance with an approved hill farming improvement scheme[1].

---

1 Hill Farming Act 1946 (c 73), s 24(4). The provisions of s 24(2), (3) (see paras 921, 922, above), do not apply to the making of such muirburn: s 24(4).

924. Regulation of muirburn. Any person who:
(1) commences to make muirburn between one hour after sunset and one hour before sunrise, or
(2) fails to provide at the place where he is about to make muirburn, or to maintain there while he is making muirburn, a sufficient staff and equipment to control and regulate the burning operations so as to prevent any damage to any woodlands on or adjoining the land where the operations are taking place, or to any adjoining land, march fences or other subjects, or
(3) makes muirburn on any land without having given the proprietor of the land, or of woodlands adjoining the land and, if he is the tenant, to the proprietor of the land, not less than twenty-four hours' notice in writing of his intention to make muirburning, and of the day on which and the approximate extent to which he intends to make muirburn, or
(4) makes muirburn on any land without due care so as to cause damage to any woodlands on or adjoining the land, or any adjoining land, woodlands, march fences or other subjects,
is guilty of an offence[1].
Any person found guilty of an offence is liable, on summary conviction, to a fine not exceeding level 3 on the standard scale[2].

---

1 Hill Farming Act 1946 (c 73), ss 25, 26(1).
2 Ibid, s 27 (amended by the Wildlife and Countryside Act 1981 (c 69), s 72(3)). As to level 3 on the standard scale, see para 919, note 2, above.

925. Negligence in the operations of muirburning. The operation of muirburning is one which, apart from statute, must be carried out with due care, and failure to do so may result in claims for damages either under the Hill Farming Act 1946 or at common law[1]. Where a party holding a servitude right of pasturage on another's muir burned the whole ground in one season, it was held that this could not be for the benefit of the pasture and he was found liable in damages to the proprietor whose sporting rights had been unduly interfered with[2]. The amount of care required will vary with the dryness of the season and the degree of incomplete extinction. Negligence or fault in the operation or control of muirburning must be proved[3].

---

1 *Mackintosh v Mackintosh* (1864) 2 M 1357. As to the Hill Farming Act 1946 (c 73), see paras 916 ff above.
2 *Robertson v Duke of Athole* (1814) 6 Pat 135. Cf *Grant v Gentle* (1857) 19 D 992.
3 *Robertson v Duke of Athole* (1814) 6 Pat 135. Cf *Grant v Gentle* (1857) 19 D 992. For an illustrative case where there was danger of muirburning spreading to the pursuer's adjoining plantation, see *Lord Advocate v Rodgers* 1978 SLT (Sh Ct) 31. This was an action in which the pursuer, as representing the Forestry Commission, sued for the cost of controlling and extinguishing muirburn which the defender had started on an adjoining estate. At no stage was damage actually done to the pursuer's property, though there was danger that the fire would spread to one of his

plantations. It was held by the sheriff principal on appeal that the pursuer had acted reasonably in an attempt to minimise his loss and in so doing any expense incurred by the pursuer stemmed directly from the actings of the defender.

9. DEER

(1) INTRODUCTION

926. Historical background. Unless they are farmed, deer are wild animals, *'ferae naturae'*, and therefore *'res nullius'* and capable of becoming the property of the first captor[1]. The only common law restriction upon the killing of deer arises from the landowner's right to the exclusive use of his own land. The red deer of Scotland are not, and have never been, 'royal' animals, *'regalia minora'*, although traditionally hunted by kings and considered to be 'game'.

  1 See generally ANIMALS, vol 2, paras 102, 103.

927. Meaning of 'game' with reference to deer. The popular meaning of 'game' is all wild land animals and birds killed for sport. There is no all embracing statutory definition of what constitutes 'game', and it is necessary to examine the particular statute to ascertain whether the particular animal or bird is included. The only early statute which originally referred to 'deer' was the Game (Scotland) Act 1832[1], although there is authority for concluding that the reference to 'hunting and halking' in the Act of 1621[2] includes deer of all sorts[3]. Otherwise the early Game Acts make no specific reference to 'deer'. The 1832 Act originally referred specifically to 'deer', in the context of trespassing on land, as well as to 'game', but the reference to deer was subsequently removed[4].

It has been conceded by the Crown that 'game' in the 1832 Act does not include deer, and the court has held that the inclusion of deer was not a tenable construction of 'game' when the history of the 1832 Act was examined[5].

  1 See the Game (Scotland) Act 1832 (c 68), s 1 (as originally enacted), with specific reference to 'trespass' on land.
  2 Ie the Hunting and Hawking Act 1621 (c 31) (repealed).
  3 J Rankine *The Law of Land-ownership in Scotland* (4th edn, 1909) p 148.
  4 See para 817, note 2, above.
  5 *Ferguson v MacPhail* 1987 SCCR 52.

928. Legislation. Legislation concerned with deer was passed in 1959[1] to provide for: (1) conservation and control[2], (2) close seasons[3], (3) poaching[4], (4) dealing in venison[5], and (5) enforcement[6].

  1 Ie the Deer (Scotland) Act 1959 (c 40).
  2 See paras 929, 931 ff below.
  3 See para 930 below.
  4 See paras 938 ff below.
  5 See paras 944 ff below.
  6 See paras 956 ff below.

(2) CONSERVATION AND CLOSE SEASONS

929. Conservation. The Deer (Scotland) Act 1959 (c 40) created the Red Deer Commission to conserve and control red and sika deer, their hybrids, and to a lesser extent roe and fallow deer[1]. The Commission advises the Secretary of State for Scotland on any deer related matter, has the power to advise land-owners regarding open hill management, stocking and culling levels and is able to support and carry out research[2]. It is regularly consulted by both public bodies and private individuals and issues authoritative guidelines and pamphlets.

1 See generally, ANIMALS, vol 2, paras 296 ff. As to control, see paras 931 ff below.
2 See ANIMALS, vol 2, para 296.

930. Close seasons. Deer are protected by close seasons during which period they may not be taken or wilfully killed[1]. Such close seasons do not apply to farmers who keep deer for the production of meat, skins or other by-products, or breeding stock[2]. Land used for this purpose must be enclosed by a deer-proof barrier[2] and the deer conspicuously marked[3].

1 For the close seasons, see ANIMALS, vol 2, para 300.
2 See the Deer (Scotland) Act 1959 (c 40), s 21(5A) (added by the Deer (Amendment) (Scotland) Act 1982 (c 19), s 7).
3 Deer (Scotland) Act 1959, s 21(5A) proviso (as so added).

(3) CONTROL

931. Introduction. The statutory provisions recognise that occupiers of land should be able legally to protect their livelihood from the ravages of wandering deer which, being wild and unenclosed, cannot otherwise be restricted or controlled.

932. Marauding deer. The Red Deer Commission has the power to authorise a competent person to follow and kill on any land specified in the authorisation red or sika deer which are causing serious damage to forestry or to agricultural production, including crops or foodstuffs[1].

1 See ANIMALS, vol 2, paras 297–299.

933. Control in the close seasons. To prevent serious damage at any time of the year, an occupier of agricultural land or enclosed woodlands is legally entitled in the close seasons to take or kill and to sell or dispose of the carcases of any species of deer found on any arable land, garden grounds, or land laid down in permanent grass (other than moor-land and unenclosed land) which forms part of his agricultural land or on enclosed woodland[1]. However, such action may only be taken by the occupier provided he has reasonable ground for believing that serious damage will be caused to his crops, pasture, trees or human or animal foodstuffs if the deer are not killed[2]. The occupier may also authorise in writing his own full-time employees or anyone normally resident on the land, or, if the occupier is a tenant, he may authorise the owner of the ground or the owner's full-time employees, to take the necessary action[3]. Any other person must receive authorisation from the Red Deer Commission[4]. Anyone authorised in writing by the Secretary of State for Scotland may take or kill deer during the close season for any scientific purpose[5].

The owner of land may at any time request the occupier to supply him with the numbers of red or sika deer shot by virtue of these provisions during the previous twelve months[6].

1 Deer (Scotland) Act 1959 (c 40), s 33(3) (substituted by the Deer (Amendment) (Scotland) Act 1982 (c 19), s 13(1)).
2 Deer (Scotland) Act 1959, s 33(3) proviso (as so substituted).
3 Ibid, s 33(3)(a)–(d) (as so substituted). As to the expiry of any authorisation under s 33(3), see s 33(3A) (as so substituted).
4 Ibid, s 33(3)(e) (as so substituted).
5 Ibid, s 33(3B) (as so substituted).
6 See ibid, s 33(4C) (as so substituted).

934. Prohibition of night shooting. The shooting of deer at night between the expiration of the first hour after sunset and the commencement of the last hour before sunrise is an offence except in certain circumstances[1]. It should be noted that the only lawful method of taking or wilfully killing or injuring deer in Scotland is by shooting[2], and shooting for this purpose means discharging a firearm as defined in the Firearms Act 1968[3].

1 Deer (Scotland) Act 1959 (c 40), s 23(1) (amended by the Deer (Amendment) (Scotland) Act 1982 (c 19), s 6(d)). Any person guilty of an offence is liable on summary conviction to a fine not exceeding level 4 on the standard scale per deer or to imprisonment not exceeding three months, or to both: Deer (Scotland) Act 1959, s 23(3) (amended by the Deer (Amendment) (Scotland) Act 1982, ss 8(2), 14(1), Sch 1). As to level 4 on the standard scale, see para 884, note 5, above. As to exceptions, see para 935 below.
2 Deer (Scotland) Act 1959, s 23(2) (amended by the Deer (Amendment) (Scotland) Act 1982, s 6(a)). As to the penalties, see note 1 above.
3 Deer (Scotland) Act 1959, s 23(2). For the meaning of 'firearm', see the Firearms Act 1968 (c 27), s 57(1): see FIREARMS AND EXPLOSIVES.

935. Permitted night shooting. The exceptions, when night shooting may be permitted, are:
(1) Red Deer Commission staff may shoot at night when dealing with marauding deer[1];
(2) any person may do any act to prevent suffering by an injured or diseased deer or by any deer calf, fawn or kid deprived of its mother[2]; and
(3) an occupier of agricultural land or of enclosed woodlands may, in person, carry out night shooting on his land of red or sika deer to prevent serious damage to his crops, trees etc on that land[3].
The occupier himself is empowered to carry out the shooting, and he cannot authorise others to do so[3].

The Commission may authorise in writing any competent person nominated by the occupier of agricultural land or enclosed woodlands to shoot any species of deer at night, provided the Commission is satisfied that such shooting is necessary to prevent serious damage to crops etc, and that there is no other adequate method of control available[4].

1 See the Deer (Scotland) Act 1959 (c 40), s 33(2) (substituted by the Deer (Amendment) (Scotland) Act 1967 (c 37), s 2(2)).
2 Deer (Scotland) Act 1959, s 33(1) (amended by the Deer (Amendment) (Scotland) Act 1967, s 2(1), and the Deer (Amendment) (Scotland) Act 1982 (c 19), s 12).
3 See the Deer (Scotland) Act 1959, s 33(4) (substituted by the Deer (Amendment) (Scotland) Act 1982, s 13(1). It should be noted that this provision does not apply to shooting other types of deer such as roe or fallow deer. The owner of the agricultural land or enclosed woodlands may request the occupier to inform him of the numbers of red or sika deer which have been shot within the period of twelve months: Deer (Scotland) Act 1959, s 33(4C) (as so substituted).
4 Ibid, s 33(4A) (as so substituted). Such authorisation is valid for such period as the Commission may specify: s 33(4B) (as so substituted). See also s 33(4C) (as substituted), and note 3 above.

936. Code of practice for night shooting. The Red Deer Commission is required to prepare and publish a code of practice for night shooting in respect of any authorisation[1] which it has given, and it is a condition of any authorisation that the authorised person complies with the relevant provisions of the code[2]. The latest version was issued in April 1986 and gives advice on general principles, methods of shooting and the equipment to be used and also specifies a number of obligatory conditions regarding safety precautions etc. The code of practice may be obtained from the Red Deer Commission in Inverness[3].

1 Ie any authorisation under the Deer (Scotland) Act 1959 (c 4), s 33(4A): see para 935 above.
2 Ibid, s 33(4D) (substituted by the Deer (Amendment) (Scotland) Act 1982 (c 19), s 13(1)).
3 Red Deer Commission, 'Knowsley', 82 Fairfield Road, Inverness IV3 5LK (Tel 0463 231751).

937. Permitted firearms and ammunition. The firearms permitted for killing deer in Scotland are prescribed, and include the specifications for rifles and ammunition and the use of shot guns in specified circumstances[1]. It is perhaps worth noting that a fundamental difference exists between the English and Scottish legislation, in that in England it is the calibre of the rifle itself that is the main criterion for lawful use, while in Scotland the criteria relate to the ammunition only, it being lawful to use any rifle which is capable of firing such ammunition. It is an offence to use any firearm or ammunition not so prescribed[2]. It is also an offence to use any firearm or ammunition for the purpose of wilfully injuring any deer[3].

Use of shotguns to shoot deer is permitted, but only in certain restricted circumstances where an occupier of agricultural land or enclosed woodlands believes serious damage will be caused to his crops if the deer are not killed[4]. In such cases only the occupier himself, his servants or other persons normally resident on the land (and authorised in writing by the occupier), or a person authorised by the Red Deer Commission, may use a shot gun with a gauge not less than 12 bore loaded with SSG ammunition (for any deer) or AAA or larger (for roe deer)[5].

1 See the Deer (Firearms etc) (Scotland) Order 1985, SI 1985/1168.
2 Deer (Scotland) Act 1959 (c 40), s 23A(3) (added by the Deer (Amendment) (Scotland) Act 1982 (c 19), s 10(1)). A person found guilty of an offence is liable on summary conviction to a fine not exceeding level 4 on the standard scale, in relation to each deer taken or killed, or to imprisonment for a term not exceeding three months, or to both: Deer (Scotland) Act 1959, s 23A(3) (as so added). As to level 4 on the standard scale, see para 884, note 5, above.
3 Ibid, s 23A(5) (as so added). A person found guilty of an offence is liable on summary conviction to a fine not exceeding level 4 on the standard scale for each deer in respect of which the offence was committed or to imprisonment for a term not exceeding three months, or to both: s 23A(5) (as so added). As to level 4 on the standard scale, see para 884, note 5, above.
4 See the Deer (Firearms etc) (Scotland) Order 1985, art 4.
5 Ibid, art 4. See also the Deer (Scotland) Act 1959, s 33(3)(c)–(e), and para 933 above.

(4) UNLAWFUL TAKING AND KILLING OF DEER

938. Poaching. It is an offence to take, wilfully to kill or to injure deer on any land without legal right or permission and to remove the carcase of any deer from any land without permission from someone having such legal right[1]. The latter part of this provision was necessitated by the decision in the *Miln* case[2] that the word 'take' here refers to the capture of a live deer and does not extend to the removal of a deer which has been killed. In that case the court quashed the conviction on the basis that the pannel could not be found guilty of the charge unless it was established that the deer, when alive, had been caught or wilfully killed. The Deer (Scotland) Act 1959 was as a result amended to include the removal of deer carcases from land as an offence[3].

A person will not commit the offence if the statutory exceptions apply[4]. If the deer is taken or killed on his neighbour's land a person will not be guilty of an offence provided he first shot and wounded the animal on his own land or over land on which he has permission to shoot.

1 Deer (Scotland) Act 1959 (c 40), s 22(1), (2) (amended by the Deer (Amendment) (Scotland) Act 1982 (c 19), s 6(c)(d)). Any person found guilty of an offence is liable on summary conviction to a fine not exceeding level 4 on the standard scale for each carcase or deer in respect of which the offence was committed or to imprisonment for a term not exceeding three months or to both and to the forfeiture of any carcase or deer: Deer (Scotland) Act 1959, s 22(1), (2) (amended by the Deer (Amendment) (Scotland) Act 1982, ss 6(c), 14(1), Sch 1). As to level 4 on the standard scale, see para 884, note 5, above. As to the aggravated offence of gang poaching, see para 939 below.
2 *Miln v Maher* 1979 JC 58, 1979 SLT (Notes) 10.
3 See note 1 above.
4 See the Deer (Scotland) Act 1959, s 33, and paras 933, 935, above.

939. Gang poaching. If two or more persons act together to commit an offence of poaching[1], unlawfully killing or injuring deer[2] or using prohibited ammunition[3] the offence becomes aggravated and the penalties are increased[4].

1 Ie under the Deer (Scotland) Act 1959 (c 40), s 22: see para 938 above.
2 Ie under ibid, s 23: see para 934 above, and para 940 below.
3 Ie under ibid, s 23A: see para 937 above, and para 940 below.
4 Ibid, s 24 (amended by the Deer (Amendment) (Scotland) Act 1982 (c 19), s 10(2)). Every person guilty of an offence is liable on summary conviction to a fine not exceeding in respect of each deer taken or killed the statutory maximum or to imprisonment for a term not exceeding six months or to both, and on conviction on indictment to a fine or to imprisonment not exceeding two years or to both: Deer (Scotland) Act 1959, s 24(a), (b) (amended by the Deer (Amendment) (Scotland) Act 1982, ss 14(1), 15, Schs 1, 3). On any conviction any deer illegally taken or killed by him or in his possession at the time of the offence is forfeited: Deer (Scotland) Act 1959, s 24 (amended by the Deer (Amendment) (Scotland) Act 1982, s 14(1), Sch 1). 'The statutory maximum' means the prescribed sum as defined in the Criminal Procedure (Scotland) Act 1975 (c 21), s 289B (added by the Criminal Law Act 1977 (c 45), s 63(1), Sch 11, para 5, substituted by the Criminal Justice Act 1982 (c 48), s 55(2), and amended by the Increase of Criminal Penalties etc (Scotland) Order 1984, SI 1984/526, art 3): Criminal Justice Act 1982, s 74(2). At the date at which this volume states the law, the prescribed sum is £2,000.

940. Unlawful methods. It is an offence to take or wilfully to kill or to injure deer:
(1) during the night[1];
(2) by any means other than shooting[2], for example traps, snares, crossbows, hunting with dogs etc.

1 See para 934 above. As to the exceptions, see para 935 above.
2 See para 934 above. Firearms and ammunition must comply with the statutory requirements: see para 937 above.

941. Aircraft and vehicles. It is an offence:
(1) to discharge a firearm or project a missile at any deer from an aircraft[1];
(2) to use an aircraft to transport live deer except in the interior of the aircraft or under veterinary[2] supervision[3];
(3) to use a vehicle to drive deer on unenclosed land with the intention of taking, killing or injuring the deer[4].

1 Deer (Scotland) Act 1959 (c 40), s 23(2A)(a) (inserted by the Deer (Amendment) (Scotland) Act 1982 (c 19), s 8(1)). For the penalties for offences under s 23(2A), see the Deer (Scotland) Act 1959, s 23(3), and para 934, note 1, above.
2 Ie a veterinary surgeon or practitioner: ibid, s 23(2B) (as so inserted). 'Veterinary practitioner' means a person who is for the time being registered in the supplementary register, and

'veterinary surgeon' means a person who is for the time being registered in the register of
veterinary surgeons: s 23(2C) (as so inserted).
3 Ibid, s 23(2A)(b) (as so inserted). This is intended to cover the situation where deer are lifted by
helicopter in a net, as is done in New Zealand.
4 Ibid, s 23(3A) (inserted by the Deer (Amendment) (Scotland) Act 1982, s 9). Any person guilty of
an offence is liable on summary conviction to a fine not exceeding level 4 on the standard scale or
to imprisonment for a term not exceeding three months or to both: Deer (Scotland) Act 1959,
s 23(3A) (as so inserted). As to level 4 on the standard scale, see para 884, note 5, above.

942. Exempted persons. The provisions in respect of unlawful taking, killing or injuring deer[1] do not prohibit persons having a legal right to take deer on
any land, or a person with permission in writing from any such person, from
taking a deer alive on that land in any manner which does not cause it unneces-
ary suffering[2]. Accordingly, deer farmers, estate managers etc can lawfully use a
vehicle to round up live deer.

1 Ie under the Deer (Scotland) Act 1959 (c 40), s 23: see paras 934, 941, above.
2 Ibid, s 23(5).

(5) UNLAWFUL POSSESSION OF DEER OR FIREARMS

943. Offences. If a person is found in possession of any deer or in circumstances affording reasonable grounds for suspecting that the possessor had
obtained possession of the deer as a result of his committing an offence during
the close seasons[1] or illegally taking, killing or injuring deer[2], that person may
be charged with unlawful possession of the deer[3]. Similarly, where it is suspected that a firearm or ammunition has been used to take, kill or injure deer
illegally[4], the possessor may be charged with unlawful possession of such
firearm or ammunition[5].
It is lawful to convict a person charged with possession of deer, firearms or
ammunition on the evidence of one witness[6].

1 Ie under the Deer (Scotland) Act 1959 (c 40), s 21: see para 930 above.
2 Ie under ibid, ss 22–24: see paras 934, 938, 939, 942, above.
3 Ibid, s 25(1). Where the court is satisfied that a person charged under s 25(1), (2), obtained
possession of deer as a result of his committing offences under ss 21–24, or, as the case may be,
that he has used any firearm or ammunition for the purpose of committing an offence under
ss 22–24, that person may be convicted of unlawful possession and dealt with in like manner as if
he had been convicted of the above offences: s 25(3).
4 Ie under ibid, ss 22–24: see note 2 above.
5 Ibid, s 25(2). See also s 25(3), and note 3 above.
6 Ibid, s 25(4).

(6) DEALING IN VENISON

(a) Licences to deal in Venison

944. Introduction. An islands or district council may grant to any person
whom it considers fit a licence to deal in venison[1]. 'Venison' means the carcase
or any edible part of the carcase of a deer, and 'deer' means deer of any species[2].

1 Deer (Scotland) Act 1959 (c 40), s 25A(1) (added by the Deer (Amendment) (Scotland) Act 1982
(c 19), s 11). The licence is known as a 'venison dealer's licence': Deer (Scotland) Act 1959,
s 25A(1) (as so added).
2 Ibid, s 25F (as so added).

945. Regulation of applications for venison dealers' licences. The Secretary of State has power by order to regulate applications for venison dealers' licences and the manner in which they are to be dealt with (including power to authorise islands and district councils to charge fees in respect of such applications)[1]. He may also regulate the procedure by which venison dealers' licences may be surrendered, and the procedure for the handing in of licences where a court has ordered their forfeiture or the holders have ceased to deal in venison[2].

  1 Deer (Scotland) Act 1959 (c 40), s 25A(2) (added by the Deer (Amendment) (Scotland) Act 1982 (c 19), s 11). As to the regulations made under this power, see the Licensing of Venison Dealers (Application Procedures etc) (Scotland) Order 1984, SI 1984/922.
  2 Deer (Scotland) Act 1959, s 25A(2) (as so added). For the purposes of s 25A(2), he may apply any provision of the Civic Government (Scotland) Act 1982 (c 45), Sch 1, as he thinks fit: Deer (Scotland) Act 1959, s 25A(2). See further LOCAL GOVERNMENT, vol 14, paras 529 ff.

946. Duration of venison dealers' licences. A venison dealer's licence is valid for three years, unless the dealer has been disqualified from holding a licence by reason of his conviction of an offence under the Deer (Scotland) Act 1959, and may be renewed provided that he is not at the time of application subject to such disqualification[1].

  1 Deer (Scotland) Act 1959 (c 40), s 25A(3) (added by the Deer (Amendment) (Scotland) Act 1982 (c 19), s 11).

947. Copies and returns to the Red Deer Commission. Every islands or district council which grants a venison dealer's licence must send a copy to the Red Deer Commission as soon as may be, and must also, as soon as may be after 1 January in each year, make a return to the Commission of the names and addresses of all the persons who on that day held venison dealers' licences issued by the council[1].

  1 Deer (Scotland) Act 1959 (c 40), s 25A(4), (5) (added by the Deer (Amendment) (Scotland) Act 1982 (c 19), s 11).

(b) Records

948. Records to be kept by licensed venison dealers. Every licensed venison dealer must keep a book recording in the prescribed form all purchases and receipts of venison by him and must enter in such book forthwith the prescribed particulars of such purchases and receipts[1].

  1 Deer (Scotland) Act 1959 (c 40), s 25B(1) (added by the Deer (Amendment) (Scotland) Act 1982 (c 19), s 11). 'Prescribed' means prescribed by order: Deer (Scotland) Act 1959 (c 40), s 25B(4). For the prescribed form, see the Licensing of Venison Dealers (Prescribed Forms etc) (Scotland) Order 1984, SI 1984/899. Notwithstanding the coming into force of the Deer (Amendment) (Scotland) Act 1982, s 11, the Deer (Scotland) Act 1959, ss 25B, 25C, 25D(1), (2), (5), (6), (8), do not apply to a registered venison dealer within the meaning of the Sale of Venison (Scotland) Act 1968 (c 38) until whichever is the earlier of (1) the date on which a venison dealer's licence is granted to that dealer, (2) the expiry of twelve months after the commencement of the Deer (Amendment) (Scotland) Act 1982, s 11; and the Sale of Venison (Scotland) Act 1968 is to continue to have effect in relation to such a registered venison dealer during the said period notwithstanding its repeal by the Deer (Amendment) (Scotland) Act 1982 (see ss 15, 16(4), Sch 3): Deer (Scotland) Act 1959, s 25E (as so added). The Deer (Amendment) (Scotland) Act 1982, s 11 and Sch 3 were brought into force on 1 January 1985, by a commencement order made 27 June 1984 (not a statutory instrument).

949. Inspection. Any person authorised in writing in that behalf by the Secretary of State or by the Red Deer Commission and showing his written authority when so requested, or any constable, may inspect any book required to be kept by a licensed venison dealer[1]. It is the duty of the dealer to produce for inspection by such authorised person or constable such book and also all venison in the dealer's possession or under his control, or on premises or in vehicles under his control, together with all invoices, consignment notes, receipts and other documents (including copies where the originals are not available) which may be required to verify any entry in such book, and to allow such authorised person or constable to take copies of such book or document or extracts therefrom[2].

1 Deer (Scotland) Act 1959 (c 40), s 25B(2) (added by the Deer (Amendment) (Scotland) Act 1982 (c 19), s 11). As to the transitional provisions which relate to the Deer (Scotland) Act 1959, s 25B, see para 948, note 1, above.
2 Ibid, s 25B(2) (as so added).

950. Retention of records and documents. Every book required to be kept by a licensed venison dealer[1] must be kept until the end of the period of three years beginning with the day on which the last entry was made in the book[2]. Any documents which may be required to verify any entry in such book[3] must be kept for a period of three years beginning with the date of the entry to which they refer[4].

1 Ie under the Deer (Scotland) Act 1959 (c 40), s 25B(1): see para 948 above.
2 Ibid, s 25B(3) added by the Deer (Amendment) (Scotland) Act 1982 (c 19), s 11). As to the transitional provisions which relate to the Deer (Scotland) Act 1959, s 25B, see para 948, note 1, above.
3 Ie any documents mentioned in ibid, s 25B(2): see para 949 above.
4 Ibid, s 25B(3) (as so added: see note 2 above).

951. Compliance. A licensed venison dealer who has purchased or received venison from another licensed venison dealer or from a 'licensed game dealer'[1] is to be deemed to have complied with the requirements as to keeping a record of purchases and receipts of venison[2] if he has recorded in his record book:
(1) that the venison was so purchased or received;
(2) the name and address of the other licensed venison dealer or of the licensed game dealer concerned;
(3) the date when the venison was so purchased or received;
(4) the number of carcases and sex of the venison; and
(5) the species of deer, provided that it is possible to identify it[3].

1 'Licensed game dealer' means a person licensed to deal in game under the Game Act 1831 (c 32) and the Game Licences Act 1860 (c 90), and includes a servant of such a person: Deer Act 1980 (c 49), s 2(4), applied by the Deer (Scotland) Act 1959 (c 40), s 25C (added by the Deer (Amendment) (Scotland) Act 1982 (c 19), s 11).
2 Ie under the Deer (Scotland) Act 1959, s 25B (as so added): see paras 948–950 above.
3 Ibid, s 25C(a)–(e) (as so added). As to the transitional provisions which relate to s 25C, see para 948, note 1, above.

(c) Offences

952. Selling, offering and exposing for sale venison not in accordance with licensing requirements. It is an offence for any person to sell, offer or expose for sale[1] or have in his possession, or transport or cause to be transported for the purpose of sale at any premises, any venison unless he is a licensed venison dealer[2], or he does so for the purpose of selling to a licensed venison dealer, or he has purchased the venison from a licensed venison dealer[3]. A person who is guilty of such an offence is liable on summary conviction to a fine not exceeding level 3 on the standard scale[4].

1 'Sale' includes barter, exchange, and any other transaction by which venison is disposed of for value: Deer (Scotland) Act 1959 (c 40), s 25F (added by the Deer (Amendment) (Scotland) Act 1982 (c 19), s 11).
2 'Licensed venison dealer' means the holder of a venison dealer's licence granted by the islands or district council within whose area the sale, offer or exposure for sale takes place, or where the premises concerned are situated: Deer (Scotland) Act 1959, s 25D(8) (as so added). As to the transitional provisions which relate to s 25D(1), (2), (8), see para 948, note 1, above.
3 Ibid, s 25D(1) (as so added).
4 Ibid, s 25D(2) (as so added). At the date at which this volume states the law, level 3 on the standard scale is £400: see the Criminal Procedure (Scotland) Act 1975 (c 21), s 289G(2) (added by the Criminal Justice Act 1982 (c 48), s 54), and the Increase of Criminal Penalties etc (Scotland) Order 1984, SI 1984/526, art 4.

953. Selling, offering and exposing for sale carcase of unlawfully killed deer. Any person who sells, offers or exposes for sale, or has in his possession for the purpose of sale, or purchases or offers to purchase or receives, the carcase or any part of the carcase of a deer which he knows or has reason to believe has been killed unlawfully, will be guilty of an offence[1], and liable on summary conviction to a fine not exceeding level 4 on the standard scale or to imprisonment for a term not exceeding three months or to both[2].

1 Deer (Scotland) Act 1959 (c 40), s 25D(3) (added by the Deer (Amendment) (Scotland) Act 1982 (c 19), s 11).
2 Deer (Scotland) Act 1959, s 25D(4) (as so added). As to level 4 on the standard scale, see para 884, note 5, above.

954. Failure to keep records and making false and misleading entries. Any licensed venison dealer who fails to comply with any of the provisions as regards the keeping of the prescribed records[1] or who knowingly or recklessly makes in any book or document, which he is required to keep[1], an entry which is false or misleading in any material particular, will be guilty of an offence and liable on summary conviction to a fine not exceeding level 2 on the standard scale[2].

1 Ie under the Deer (Scotland) Act 1959 (c 40), s 25B: see paras 948, 949, above.
2 Ibid, s 25D(5) (added by the Deer (Amendment) (Scotland) Act 1982 (c 19), s 11). At the date at which this volume states the law, level 2 on the standard scale is £100: see the Criminal Procedure (Scotland) Act 1975 (c 21), s 289G(2) (added by the Criminal Justice Act 1982 (c 48), s 54), and the Increase of Criminal Penalties etc (Scotland) Order 1984, SI 1984/526, art 4. As to the transitional provisions which relate to the Deer (Scotland) Act 1959, s 25D(5), see para 948, note 1, above.

955. Obstruction. Any person who obstructs a person entitled to inspect any book or document forming part of the prescribed records[1] or other thing in the making of such inspection will be guilty of an offence and liable on summary conviction to a fine not exceeding level 3 on the standard scale[2].

1 Ie under the Deer (Scotland) Act 1959 (c 40), s 25B(2): see para 949 below.

2 Ibid, s 25D(6) (added by the Deer (Amendment) (Scotland) Act 1982 (c 19), s 11). As to level 3 on the standard scale, see para 954, note 2, above. As to the transitional provisions which relate to the Deer (Scotland) Act 1959, s 25D(6), see para 948, note 1, above.

(7) ENFORCEMENT

956. Attempting or preparing to commit an offence. Any person who attempts to commit, or does any act preparatory to the commission of, an offence in respect of taking or wilfully killing deer during the close seasons[1] or the unlawful taking and killing of deer[2] is guilty of an offence and liable in the same manner as for the said offence, except that in the case of preparatory acts the penalty is a fine not exceeding level 4 on the standard scale or imprisonment for a term not exceeding three months or both[3].

1 Ie under the Deer (Scotland) Act 1959 (c 40), s 21: see para 930 above.
2 Ie under ibid Pt III (ss 22–25): see paras 934, 938–943, above.
3 Ibid, s 26 (amended by the Deer (Amendment) (Scotland) Act 1982 (c 19), s 14(1), Sch 1). This provision is expressed to be without prejudice to the operation of the Criminal Procedure (Scotland) Act 1975 (c 21), s 63, and the Summary Jurisdiction (Scotland) Act 1954 (c 48), s 2. As to level 4 on the standard scale, see para 884, note 5, above.

957. Search and seizure. The powers of search and seizure are as follows:
(1) a constable may seize any deer, firearm or ammunition, vehicle or boat liable to be forfeited on conviction of an offence under the Deer (Scotland) Act 1959[1];
(2) a sheriff or any justice of the peace may grant a search warrant to any constable, if satisfied there is reasonable suspicion that any of certain offences[2] have been committed and that evidence of the commission of the offence is to be found on any premises or in any vehicle or boat[3];
(3) a constable authorised by such a warrant, in addition to searching such premises, vehicle or boat, may also search every person found there or whom he reasonably suspects of having recently left or to be about to enter, and seize any article he has reasonable grounds to believe is evidence relating to the commission of the offence[4];
(4) in cases of urgency a constable, having reasonable grounds for suspicion that any of certain offences[5] have been committed, may stop and search any vehicle or boat[6] where he believes evidence may be found[7].

1 Deer (Scotland) Act 1959 (c 40), s 27(1) (amended by the Deer (Amendment) (Scotland) Act 1982 (c 19), s 15(1), Sch 2, para 2).
2 Ie under the Deer (Scotland) Act 1959, Pt III (ss 22–25) (see paras 934, 938–943, above), or s 25D(1) or s 25D(3) (see paras 952, 953, above): s 27(2) (amended by the Deer (Amendment) (Scotland) Act 1982, s 14(3)).
3 Deer (Scotland) Act 1959, s 27(2). The constable must search the premises within one week from the date of the warrant, and may enter, if necessary by force, the premises and every part of it or the vehicle or boat for the purpose of detecting the offence: s 27(2).
4 Ibid, s 27(3). Searches of females may only be conducted by other females: s 27(5).
5 See note 2 above.
6 This does not extend to a search of premises.
7 Deer (Scotland) Act 1959, s 27(4) (as amended: see note 2 above).

958. Powers of arrest. A constable may arrest any person found committing any offence under Parts III and IV[1] of the Deer (Scotland) Act 1959[2].

1 Ie under the Deer (Scotland) Act 1959 (c 40), Pt III (ss 22–25) (see paras 934, 938–943, above), and Pt IV (ss 26–31) (see paras 956, 957, above).
2 Ibid, s 28.

959. Cancellation of firearms certificates. In addition to its other powers, a court may cancel any firearm or shotgun certificate held by a person convicted of certain offences[1] under the Deer (Scotland) Act 1959[2].

    1   Ie under the Deer (Scotland) Act 1959 (c 40), Pt III (ss 22–25) (see paras 934, 938–943, above): s 28A(1) (added by the Deer (Amendment) (Scotland) Act 1982 (c 19), s 15(1), Sch 2, para 1).
    2   See the Deer (Scotland) Act 1959, s 28A (as so added). As to firearm and shotgun certificates, see FIREARMS AND EXPLOSIVES.

960. Disqualification from holding or obtaining a venison dealer's licence. The court by which any person is convicted of certain offences[1] may disqualify him from holding or obtaining a venison dealer's licence for such period as the court thinks fit[2].

    1   Ie under the Deer (Scotland) Act 1959 (c 40), Pt III (ss 22–25) (see paras 934, 938–943, above), and Pt IIIA (ss 25A–25F) (see paras 944 ff above): s 25D(7) (added by the Deer (Amendment) (Scotland) Act 1982 (c 19), s 11).
    2   Deer (Scotland) Act 1959, s 25D(7) (as so added).

961–1000. Disposal of deer. Where any deer seized is liable to forfeiture, the person by whom it is seized may sell it and the net proceeds of the sale are liable to forfeiture in the same manner as the deer sold[1].

    1   Deer (Scotland) Act 1959 (c 40), s 30. However, no person is subject to any liability on account of his neglect or failure to exercise the powers conferred on him: s 30 proviso.

GENERAL LEGAL CONCEPTS

1. INTRODUCTION

1001. Meaning of 'law'. 'Law' was defined by Lord Stair as the dictate of reason, but by Professors Erskine and Austin as the command of a sovereign[1]. Law, in its most general sense, was for Stair:

> 'the dictate of reason, determining every rational being to that which is congruous and convenient for the nature and condition thereof'[2].

So far as concerned the legal systems of human commonwealths, we may gather from Stair that these are founded on custom, which represents an experimental working out of the principles which determine rights and right conduct, and which determines the allocation of rule-making and adjudicative authority in the commonwealth. Although enacted rules of law do depend upon the will of a lawgiver and are frequently changeable, they can and should be understood as expressions of more fundamental principles grounded in human nature. And for that reason the study of law is capable of being a rational discipline, a science conducted according to rational principles[3].

1 Stair *Institutions* I,1,1; Erskine *Institute* I,1,2; J Austin *The Province of Jurisprudence Determined* (1954, ed H L A Hart) pp 1–5.
2 *Stair* I,1,1.
3 *Stair* I,1,17. Cf N MacCormick 'The Rational Discipline of Law' 1981 JR 146–160, but also N E Simmonds *The Decline of Juridical Reason* (1984).

1002. Rules of recognition. Stair's conception of law is preferable to those which stress the merely imperative and voluntaristic aspects of law. It is always the case that powers of commanding, rule-making and legislation presuppose (directly or indirectly) some customarily constituted and observed allocation of authority determining what are the criteria of validity for such acts. Following Professor H L A Hart, we may assign to this basis of authority the name of a 'rule of recognition' establishing criteria for validity of law and making it mandatory for those performing the role of judges to implement all such valid law in their judging[1]. Such custom involves the common (not necessarily universal) exercise of reason in respect of practical affairs, reason participating in the governance of human wills. It is proper to doubt whether this yields any so determinate a set of principles 'congruous and convenient for the nature and condition' of rational beings as Stair suggests. But it does not follow that within the indeterminacies of reason law can be supposed to be a simple manifestation of purely arbitrary will. Both at the level of law-making and at that of adjudication it is necessary at least to have some regard to the internal consistency and rational coherence of the rules which are made and thus of the principles which are elaborated in the process of rationally interpreting and applying the rules. Without this, the *systematic* quality of a legal system would be entirely absent, and law would descend into arbitrariness and chaos[2].

1 See H L A Hart *The Concept of Law* (1961) ch 6, pp 97–101, and cf N MacCormick *H L A Hart* (1981) pp 106–111.
2 On these conceptions of coherence and consistency, see N MacCormick *Legal Reasoning and Legal Theory* (1978) chs 7, 8. See also N MacCormick and O Weinberger *An Institutional Theory of Law* (1986) ch 9, and N MacCormick 'Coherence in Legal Justification' in W Krawietz et al (eds) *Theorie der Normen* (1984) pp 37–53.

1003. A legal system as a normative system. In this spirit, we may conclude that a legal system is a normative system, 'normative' in the sense that it contains 'dictates' determining right and wrong conduct, these 'dictates' addressing rational agents as guides to their conduct. This regulation of conduct is the primary element or most basic level of a legal system as a normative system, but does not exhaust all the ways in which law guides or regulates conduct. All sorts of exercises of legal authority, and the effecting of all manner of legal transactions, also require attention to the provisions of the law; but these are secondary elements of law and so consideration of them may for a time be deferred[1].

1 The distinctions here drawn parallel, without exactly reproducing, those drawn in H L A Hart *The Concept of Law* (1961) ch 5, between primary and secondary rules of law.

1004. General concepts of law. Both for the purposes of establishing and implementing a normative system and for those of describing it lucidly and economically, recourse may be had to a considerable range of general concepts whose meaning is primarily determined by their utility to these purposes. The more general of such concepts, for example principle and rule, wrongdoing and offence, duty and obligation, right and liberty, privilege and immunity, authority, capacity and power, liability and responsibility, along with many others, have uses throughout the whole range of practical human concerns, from moral and religious law to the laws of golf and of association football and the byelaws of public institutions. They are by no means peculiar to 'positive law', understood as law in that highly organised form of normative system with characteristically coercive modes of implementation and primarily territorial applicability which both belongs to and is constitutive of that special type of political association known as a 'state'[1]. It will be noted by inference from this that the legal system of Scotland for the moment exists as a system of positive law only by virtue of being a sub-system of that which constitutes the United Kingdom of Great Britain and Northern Ireland.

1 The concept of the state is here understood in terms similar to those proposed by H Kelsen *General Theory of Law and State* (trans A Wedberg 1945), but it is neither assumed nor implied that state law is the only kind of 'law' that there is. Cf R Cotterrell 'The Sociological Concept of Law' (1983) 10 Journal of Law and Society 241–255.

1005. Specialised concepts of law. These most general of normative concepts, albeit not exclusively applicable to the realm of positive law, have of course a particular and highly important application there; sometimes they acquire specialised senses for these legal purposes, but it is methodologically unsound to assume the existence of any specialised legal meanings of the terms in the absence of explicit and strong reasons for believing in them; such assumptions usually betoken unsound analyses by lawyers of common normative terms, the unsoundness of the analysis being such as would otherwise be obvious in virtue of its evident inapplicability to non-legal cases. There are, however, some cases in which a special legal analysis is needed. For, over and above these general normative concepts, there are many specialised legal concepts of general application in the context of positive law which lack application or are only loosely or metaphorically applicable in other contexts. Examples are provided by concepts such as contract, property, delict (tort), standard security (mortgage), corporation, testate and intestate succession and so forth. The task of this title in the Encyclopaedia is to provide an exhaustive explanation and analysis of the general normative concepts in their legal application, and to give such an account of the specialised legal concepts (most of them the subject of special discussion in other titles) as will facilitate locating them in the general conceptual framework of a legal system.

2. LAWFUL AND UNLAWFUL CONDUCT

1006. Law guides conduct. At the primary level of legal regulation, the most fundamental distinction is that between conduct which is 'unlawful' or 'legally wrongful' or 'wrong', and conduct which is not wrong by the standards of the law and thus at least minimally lawful. The fundamental idea that law *guides* conduct is here disclosed, for the most basic guidance is *to do no wrong*. Although a legal system which said no more than that would be, as Lord Cooper remarked in connection with the 'Dark Age of Scots Law', hopelessly lacking in any specificity of guidance[1], nothing would be a normative system at all which did not differentiate the wrongful or illicit from licit or permissible ways of acting, and which did not visit at least disapprobation and adverse judgment upon the former.

1 Lord Cooper *Selected Papers 1922–1954* (1957) p 219 at p 229 ('The Dark Age of Scottish Legal History').

1007. Approval and disapproval. How are we then to understand this most fundamental of distinctions? The answer must be in terms of human values — apprehensions, perhaps, of what is 'congruous and convenient' with human nature. Some states of being and states of affairs are approved and considered worthy of approval, the absence or negation of them being regarded with disapproval, this constituting the distinction between values and disvalues or goods and evils. Human dispositions which tend to realise or constitute such goods are in turn the objects of approval, while those which tend in the opposite direction are objects of disapproval. Here lies the distinction of virtue and vice, although as to vice a further distinction has to be drawn between vice in the sense of mere absence of disposition towards the good or indifference towards it and an active hostility to the good. In cases of such active hostility, mere vice shades over into viciousness, wickedness or depravity. Approval and disapproval have regard not only to dispositions; we also approve or disapprove of acts, types of act and modes of action or activity as respectively realising or tending towards good or evil.

1008. Plurality of values. Thus as to states of being and of affairs, as to human dispositions and as to human conduct we find a plurality of possible values or goods and of their opposites; and in those terms we can grade or evaluate on scales from the best or most admirable to the worst or most deplorable or reprehensible. To regard something as good is to regard it as worthy of pursuit and to suppose that pursuit of it is worthy of approval or even praise, while indifference to it is to be disapproved and activities hostile to it or in pursuit of its opposite are blameworthy and reprehensible to some high degree.

1009. Law as a body of rules. But where do we draw the line? And how do we draw a line? The 'how' question is easier to answer, for the answer is that we draw lines by having rules; and that the positive law at its primary level largely consists in a body of rules, whether established by custom or enshrined in authoritative precedents or (nowadays most commonly) explicitly enacted in legislation, which set the minimal requirements of lawful conduct[1]. Moreover, the specific feature of these rules is that breach of them is sanctioned by liability to punishments and penalties or (at the instance of an injured party) civil remedies, the sanctions themselves being coercively enforceable. There can also be direct enforcement of legal rules, as in the case of police action, for example to prevent pickets obstructing a highway, or by means of interdicts or injunctions. All this helps towards answering the 'where' question. For it can at least be said that the right and reasonable place to draw the legal line between what is merely unpraiseworthy or unadmirable and what is to be deemed actually *wrong* is the point at which such sanctioning or other coercive measures can be accepted as appropriate. It should be added that not all conduct which escapes legal sanctions or coercion of this sort is to be considered fully acceptable from a legal point of view. For example, wagering contracts or contracts for sexual gratification do not fall under the threat of civil or penal sanctions, but are unenforceable as contracts; there are not a few cases of such shadowy quasi-illegality, disapprobation through withholding of legal validity rather than by direct sanctions.

1 For further argument on this, see N MacCormick *HLA Hart* (1981) pp 40–44, 67–69. Cf J Raz *Practical Reason and Norms* (1975) pp 80–84, on the 'exclusionary' character of rules.

1010. Unlawful or legally wrongful conduct. One cannot, in any event, suppose that all the requirements of the law are in truth rightly and reasonably imposed. So in point of *legal analysis* one may properly say that whatever requirements of law have been established on the terms that their breach renders a person liable to anticipatory enforcement measures or to punishment or penalty or to the exaction of a civil remedy determine what is *unlawful* or *legally wrongful* conduct. The concept of the unlawful or legally wrongful in turn subdivides into criminal wrongs, comprising crimes and offences, and civil wrongs, which are infringements either of public or of private right. But, aside from formal legal analysis, it is important, both in theory and even more for practical purposes, to understand the conditions of intelligibility of the concept of the wrongful or unlawful. For the concept of the unlawful or legally wrongful is not exhausted by the enumeration of all the established rules determining relatively specific (and sometimes, in the rather special sense indicated below[1], somewhat arbitrary) requirements of conduct. To the extent that these rules, if rightly and reasonably established, determine a point on some scale of human value below which conduct is reasonably considered to be unacceptable and worthy of some potentially coercive counter-measure or sanction, they can be seen as embodying and giving detailed content to principles of conduct, by reference to which a legal judgment can be passed as to what is in principle wrongful, and what in principle tolerable or acceptable in the way of acts, actions, activities or (in general) conduct.

1 See paras 1119 ff below.

1011. Scots law founded on principles. Especially in relation to civil wrongs (not delicts only, but also breaches of contract and of trust, breaches of statutory duty and defects in the performance of public duties), the law of Scotland has always been represented, and correctly so, as founding more upon principles than upon precedents (or, one may suppose, rules of other sorts)[1]. Hence the Scots lawyer requires a clear conception of the nature of such principles. What is in fact needed is a conception of them as grounded in human values, drawing reasonable lines between the tolerable and the unacceptable in terms of these values, and providing a rationalisation of existing customary rules, case law rules (precedents) and statutory provisions[2]. Even in the criminal law, recent decisions indicate that the Lords Commissioners of Justiciary still conceive it appropriate to treat conduct which contravenes principles of criminal law to be legitimately punishable even if not previously subject to an express prohibition in some rule or ruling of law[3]. Even Lord Cockburn's famous, and eminently justified, protest against the excesses of the declaratory power enshrined in the majority opinion in the *Greenhuff* case[4] falls a fair way short of stipulating for express rules as necessary conditions of lawful penalties, and countenances the concept of a criminal law founded as much on principles as on rules determinative of misconduct.

1 See eg Lord Cooper 'The Common and the Civil Law — A Scot's View' (1950) 63 Harv LR 468 at 471; T B Smith 'Scottish Nationalism, Law and Self-Government' in N MacCormick (ed) *The Scottish Debate* (1970) p 34 at p 42; D M Walker *The Scottish Legal System* (5th edn, 1981) p 126.
2 N MacCormick *H L A Hart* (1981) pp 67–69.
3 *Khaliq v HM Advocate* 1984 JC 43, 1983 SCCR 483, 1984 SLT 137, where K and A were charged on indictment that they did 'culpably, wilfully and recklessly supply' to eighteen named children, aged variously from three to eighteen, glues and solvents together with various containers 'well knowing' that the children were buying them for purposes of inhalation and that this was or could be injurious to their health. On appeal against conviction, K and A argued that the indictment disclosed no crime known to the law; that statutes made it an offence to supply certain substances such as tobacco and alcohol to children, or dangerous drugs to anyone, but that in the absence of any statute law concerning solvent abuse or supply for glue sniffing, the

panel had committed no crime. For the Crown it was argued that what was libelled was not a new crime but merely a modern example of conduct which Scots law had always regarded as criminal. Lord Justice-General Emslie stated the legal foundation of the decision thus: 'The general principle... is that within the category of conduct identified as criminal are acts, whatever their nature may be, which cause real injury to the person' (1984 JC 23 at 32; 1983 SCCR 483 at 492; 1984 SLT 137 at 141). See also *R v HM Advocate* 1988 SCCR 254, 1988 SLT 623, where the court held that consensual sexual relations not involving sexual intercourse between a father and daughter amounted to the common law offence of shamefully indecent conduct. On the other hand, in *Grant v Allan* 1988 SLT 11 the court refused to recognise the existence of an offence of dishonest exploitation of confidential information.

4 *HM Advocate v Greenhuff* (1838) 2 Swin 236. For a discussion of the declaratory power of the High Court of Justiciary and the associated problems, cf G H Gordon *The Criminal Law of Scotland* (2nd edn, 1978) paras 1-15–1-43.

1012. Nulla poena sine crimine, nullum crimen sine lege. The commonly observed European principle of civil liberty that no person should be punished save for breach of an expressly pre-announced and prospective rule of the criminal law does not hold in Scots law. *Nulla poena sine crimine, nullum crimen sine lege* is with us faithfully observed only as to its first limb, that there be no punishment without prior charge and proof of the charge as libelled; as to the second, we do not require *lex* (*loi, Gesetz*, statute) but are satisfied with *jus* (principle of right conduct). It deserves to be more controversial than it is whether a principle of *nullum crimen sine jure* is a satisfactory foundation for civil liberty. That this is the principle of our law cannot be doubted, and the point is reinforced procedurally by the absence of any statutory requirements of recourse to *nomina juris* in the form of our indictments[1].

1 R W Renton and H H Brown *Criminal Procedure according to the Law of Scotland* (5th edn, 1983 by G H Gordon) para 6-82. Cf *Bewglass v Blair* (1888) 15 R (J) 45, 1 White 574, and the Criminal Procedure (Scotland) Act 1975 (c 21), s 44, re-enacting the Criminal Procedure (Scotland) Act 1887 (c 35), s 5 (repealed).

1013. Conclusion. This discussion has necessarily anticipated the elucidation of rules and principles which is continued extensively below[1]. For the moment, it suffices to conclude by repeating our analysis of 'wrong' and its cognates in law as the quality ascribed to conduct which infringes or fails to fulfil a requirement of the law which is either explicitly set by a rule for whose breach some punishment, penalty or civil remedy is provided, or justifiable by reference to a principle of criminal or civil law. Where some requirement is argued to be implicit in, rather than explicitly set by, a rule, the implication to be sound has to be justifiable by reference to relevant principle or principles. So even where principles alone are not sufficient to justify direct recourse to penalties or civil remedies, they may be necessary as adjuncts to unclear or ambiguous rules. Requirements of the sort whose breaches constitute wrongs are properly considered as 'categorical requirements'; this differentiates them from the hypothetical requirements we shall discuss in considering the concept of 'power'[2].

1 See paras 1119 ff below.
2 See paras 1059 ff below.

3. DUTIES AND BREACH OF DUTY

1014. Meaning of 'duty'. If the concept of that which is 'wrong' ('unlawful', 'legally wrongful' etc) is the simplest of legal concepts and practical concepts in general, the next simplest is that of 'duty', definable as that which one is categorically required to do or refrain from doing as occupant of some position or role. The most basic position or role known to ethics is that of the moral agent; and the most basic position or role known to law is that of the legal subject, namely that of a being whose conduct the law regulates. It is the duty of a legal subject to do no unlawful act, to commit no wrong; and this is trivially true. The triviality of this truth accounts for the fact that the concept of 'duty' plays only a small part in the criminal law. Persons are charged with, convicted of and punished for the wrongs (the crimes or offences) they commit, not for the breaches of the duty of a legal subject that they necessarily commit in doing wrong[1].

1 Cf A M Honoré 'Real Laws' in P M S Hacker and J Raz (eds) *Law, Morality and Society* (1979) p 99 at pp 117, 118; and N MacCormick *H L A Hart* (1981) p 60.

1015. Duty and criminal liability. There are, however, at least two respects in which the concept of duty and its breach plays a significant part in the criminal law. For there are some points of the criminal law where the commission of criminal wrongs presupposes acting in breach of a duty which itself exists apart from the criminal law. Thus, for example, one person's omission to take steps to save the obviously endangered life of another will constitute neither murder nor culpable homicide unless the former owed some duty to care for the latter, for example as a parent for a child, or had previously voluntarily undertaken such a duty[1]. And in the case of embezzlement or breach of trust, the *actus reus* necessarily involves an act in breach of the duty to use entrusted property only for another's benefit[2]. Conversely, acts which would otherwise involve the commission of a crime against person or property are lawful when justifiably done in pursuance of a duty of public or private law[3]. And even where such act exceeds the scope of the relevant duty, its having been done in pursuance of duty is a mitigating circumstance and may for example reduce what were otherwise murder to culpable homicide only[4].

1 G H Gordon *The Criminal Law of Scotland* (2nd edn, 1978), paras 3-33–3-37.
2 *Gordon* paras 17-01–17-04.
3 *Gordon* paras 13-11, 13-12.
4 *Gordon* para 25-06.

1016. Duty and civil liability. That the criminal law and statutes criminal or quasi-criminal[1] in character do in a trivial sense engage the duty to omit unlawful actions ceases to be trivial in connection with the civil law of reparation of injuries. For there is a common law right to the reparation of any injury caused by the act of another provided that such act involves breach of a duty owed by the actor to the injured party, and provided that the breach of duty was a sufficiently proximate cause of the injury inflicted[2]. For this purpose, the duty may be a duty created by statute or delegated legislation, even where the only sanction expressly established in the statute is one whereby failure to observe the statutory requirement is to constitute a crime or offence subject to prescribed punishments or penalties. In case of such 'breaches of statutory duty', a key question is whether the statute is purely penal or can properly be regarded as imposing a duty whose breach may also give rise to a civil remedy. The better view, it is submitted, treats it as decisive for answering this question that the intendment of the legislation should be not only to procure some common public benefit or good or to protect some common public interest or to avert some common public mischief, but also to procure for individuals affected by the legislation some benefit, or some protection of interest or protection from harm. Wherever such an element is within the intendment of the Act, civil remedies properly exist at common law for breach of the duties it imposes. More questionable, but happily here irrelevant, is whether or how far the conferment of statutory powers or discretions infers along with them a duty to exercise the power with reasonable care to avoid causing loss to private individuals[3].

1 As to the concept of 'quasi-criminal law', see Lord Devlin *The Enforcement of Morals* (1968) ch 2.
2 See eg *Bourhill v Young* 1942 SC (HL) 78, 1943 SLT 105, and D M Walker *The Law of Delict in Scotland* (2nd edn, 1981) pp 173–198.
3 See eg *Anns v Merton London Borough Council* [1978] AC 728, [1977] 2 All ER 492, HL, in contrast with earlier authorities such as *East Suffolk Rivers Catchment Board v Kent* [1941] AC 74, [1940] 4 All ER 527, HL. Since then there has, however, been a retrenchment from the *Anns* case: see eg *Yuen Kun Yeu v Attorney-General of Hong Kong* [1988] AC 175, [1987] 2 All ER 705, PC, and *Rowling v Takar Properties Ltd* [1988] AC 473, [1988] 1 All ER 163, PC.

1017. Duty of care in private law. These points may well serve to introduce that employment of the concept of duty which is perhaps most important and certainly most pervasive in the law, namely its employment in the context of the 'duty of care' of private law[1]. Here one considers *culpa*, in the sense of negligence as a ground of delictal (or, in an older incorrect usage, quasi-delictal) liability. As Lord Kinnear put it in the *Kemp* case:

'It is necessary for the pursuer in such an action to shew there was a duty owed to him by the defenders, because a man cannot be charged with negligence if he has no obligation to exercise diligence'[2].

In *Bourhill v Young* Lord Macmillan gave the following elucidation of the principle governing this duty:

'The duty to take care is the duty to avoid doing or omitting to do anything the doing or omitting to do which may have as its reasonable and probable consequence injury to others, and the duty is owed to those to whom injury may reasonably and probably be anticipated if the duty is not observed'[3].

1 See D M Walker *The Law of Delict in Scotland* (2nd edn, 1981) pp 173–198.
2 *Kemp and Dougall v Darngavil Coal Co Ltd* 1909 SC 1314 at 1319, 1909 2 SLT 181 at 183.
3 *Bourhill v Young* 1942 SC (HL) 78 at 88, 1943 SLT 105 at 108.

1018. Ascertainment of role of person owing duty of care. Actually to quantify that abstract duty of taking such care as is reasonable in principle requires first of all an ascertainment of the role or position being performed by the person in question (for example financial adviser, architect, driver, surgeon, or occupier of premises), and secondly a view of the particular circumstances of any given case of alleged negligence. The bearer of the duty has then to conduct himself or herself in accordance with the standard that a reasonable person or person of ordinary prudence bearing that role or position would observe, having regard to the various values and interests at stake in the given case. This necessitates the exercise of value judgment by the trier of fact in the case, but this judgment ought to be informed by reference to prevailing standards in the community, especially that of the members of any relevant calling; but such prevailing standards, though relevant, are not decisive and may, for example, be found to require less care than is properly to be deemed reasonable[1].

1 See D M Walker *The Law of Delict in Scotland* (2nd edn, 1981) pp 199–207, and cf N MacCormick 'On Reasonableness' in Ch Perelman and R Vander Elst (eds) *Les Notions à Contenu Variable en Droit* (1984) pp 131–156.

1019. *Culpa* as proximate cause of injury. However that may be, the duty itself is that which is constituted by the principle of law requiring all persons to use reasonable care to avoid causing injury, damage or loss to any persons or any members of any groups or classes of person of whom it is reasonably foreseeable that they are likely to suffer such injury, damage or loss in consequence of acts or omissions by the first party. Every breach of such a duty constitutes *culpa* or fault in the legal sense. Faulty or culpable acts are in a sense legally wrongful, but not in the sense that they are of themselves legally punishable (save by special statutory provision, as in the case of careless driving) or subject to civil remedies. For it is only in the case where a person's fault of action or omission is a sufficiently proximate cause of another person's legally reparable injury, damage or loss, that other being one among those towards whom the duty in question is owed, that the party in fault is liable to make reparation to the other[1]. And only in cases involving some serious apprehension of relevant injury, damage or loss would an interdict be appropriate to restrain some culpable course of acting or declarator to determine the rights of parties and (by implication) the required standard of care.

1 *Donoghue v Stevenson* 1932 SC (HL) 31 at 69–71, 1932 SLT 317 at 338, 339, HL, per Lord Macmillan. See D M Walker *The Law of Delict in Scotland* (2nd edn, 1981) pp 207–231, and cf H L A Hart and A H Honoré *Causation in the Law* (2nd edn, 1985).

1020. General duty of care to others. The point about the general duty of care for the safety of others is that a duty is incumbent on all persons in favour of any others within a relevant legally determined relationship (which will sometimes be, as in the case of of the care required in giving advice in business and financial matters, a special relationship[1]). It may become adjoined to a role or position or office in private or public law, thus requiring the office holder to exercise powers or fulfil official responsibilities with reasonable care for all parties affected[2]. But it is not in principle restricted in any way to the holders of such positions, some of whom may indeed enjoy special exemptions either from duty or from liability for certain breaches of duty. On the contrary, this duty is superimposed upon the ordinary intercourse and interchange of social existence and is equally as incumbent upon persons in unofficial as in official capacities.

1 See *Hedley Byrne & Co Ltd v Heller & Partners Ltd* [1964] AC 465, [1963] 2 All ER 575, HL. This is particularly pertinent where recovery is sought for 'pure' economic loss: see *Junior Books Ltd v Veitchi Co Ltd* 1982 SC (HL) 244, 1982 SLT 492. The decision in the *Junior Books* case has not, however, led to an extension of such liability: see eg *D and F Estates Ltd v Church Comrs for England* [1989] AC 177, [1988] 2 All ER 992, HL, and *Simaan General Contracting Co v Pilkington Glass Ltd (No 2)* [1988] QB 758, [1988] 1 All ER 791, CA.
2 *Anns v Merton London Borough Council* [1978] AC 728, [1977] 2 All ER 492, HL. See, however, the cases cited in para 1016, note 3, above.

1021. Special duties of care. In this respect the general duty of care contrasts with the numberless range of special duties constituted either by private or by public law such as the duties of contracting parties, the duties of executors, the duties of trustees, the duties of parents and of spouses, the duties of partners and of company officers and directors, the duties of councillors and of officials in regional, islands or district councils, the duties of reporters to the children's panels, the duties of health boards and of their members, the duties of sheriffs and of the members of all manners of public and quasi-public authorities, boards, commissions and committees.

1022. Circumstances giving rise to special duty of care. In all such cases one can understand the legal nature of the role (for example as spouse) or office (for example as company director) only by considering first by what process one acquires or is appointed to the position in question, what holding this position enables and permits one to do, and what is required of one as its holder. Those things which are required of one as its holder are the duties of the position (role or office). They are ordinarily specified by law in general terms, subject to further specification and, to some extent, variation in the exercise either of public authority or, as the case may be, of private right. In private law in particular private parties may be empowered quite largely to determine of their own free will the content and extent of the duties of position-holders such as, most noticeably, contracting parties and, to a somewhat less extent, trustees and executors. In such cases the specific duties of particular contractors, trustees or executors can be gathered only partly from the general provisions of the law and must be completed by reference to the particular terms of the contract or provisions of the deed or will (in the case of executors nominate).

In this light we may finally recur to the initial definition of duty stated above as 'that which one is categorically required to do or refrain from doing as occupant of some position or role'[1] — 'or office', one may now properly add. What has been noted already is that in the case of the general duty of care in private law, duties are enforceable primarily through action for their breach initiated by an injured party, it not being of the essence of breach of duty to be directly punishable or actionable. The same may be said *a fortiori* of the special duties of particular positions, roles or offices which we have most lately been considering.

1 See para 1014 above.

1023. Breach of duty gives rise to remedy. It is safe to affirm in the case of every breach of every duty of private law causing any injury, damage or loss to a party to whom the duty is owed that the law permits of some remedial action to be taken by the injured party, if only that of the administration of a warning by an employer to an employee in breach of a non-fundamental duty of his or her employment. And reparation is normally exigible for loss or damage arising in case of breaches of private duty. Where this has been deemed inadequate in either private or public interest or both (for there is commonly a public interest to prevent substantial, wilful and flagrant or dishonest invasions of private interests), the criminal law or the quasi-criminal law imposing penalties under conditions of strict liability has frequently been invoked. The case of embezzlement and breach of trust is merely one grand instance of this, already mentioned. Alternatively, or additionally, public bodies with 'watchdog' functions may be established and charged with the exercise of powers of conciliation and enforcement, as in the case of for example the Equal Opportunities Commission or the Office of Fair Trading.

1024. Enforcement of public duties. The enforcement of duties of a public nature may be yet more problematic. The breach of some such duties is, indeed, for constitutional reasons, exempt from all enforcement by ordinary legal process, as notably in the case of the duties of the members of the higher judiciary (Senators of the College of Justice, Lords Commissioners of Justiciary, the Lord President, the Lord Justice-Clerk and Lords of Appeal in Ordinary, so far as concerns Scotland), and in the case of ministers of the Crown, who are primarily subject to political rather than judicial discipline in respect of the discharge of their official duties; the scope of justiciability of breaches of statutory duty, or abuse of statutory discretion, by ministers of the Crown has, however, been substantially extended by judicial decision in the period since 1945. Such exemptions apart, it appears to be a general rule that any person who suffers at the hands of a public official or public body actual bodily injury or interference (including even medication with supposedly harmless substances) or deprivation of personal liberty or direct physical damage to or deprivation of property or some other invasion of some vested right, has a right to reparation therefor including any appropriate *solatium* if such injury arises from breach of a public duty, or, indeed, if it was inflicted otherwise than in performance of an express duty conferred in clear terms[1].

1   Cf *McColl v Strathclyde Regional Council* 1983 SLT 616, where it was held that a local authority empowered to provide a water supply had no implied right to add fluoride to the water supply albeit with a view to improving dental health, and that the ratepayer had a right not to be subjected to fluoride in her water supply. See further WATER SUPPLY, vol 25, para 509.

1025. Duty as the imposition of requirements. In the light of all this, it should be clear that what is constitutive of duty is the imposition of requirements upon persons as holders of roles, positions or offices, not the presence of any specific or direct sanctioning mechanism. In so far as legal duties are what categorical requirements of law require one to do, their breach or neglect is wrongful in law. Under various conditions such misconduct may be variously sanctioned or otherwise productive of adverse legal consequences. But what is essential is the notion of the requirement as partly definitive or constitutive of the position, role or office or annexed to the powers thereof; the sanctioning measures belong to the particular mode of wrongfulness of particular types of breach or neglect of duty; they are not constitutive of the concept of duty.

1026. Conclusion. Finally, it may be noted that although the treatment of duty here is somewhat narrower than that adopted by those jurisprudents who see fit to consider every legal requirement a duty and thus every legal wrong a breach of duty[1], it is exactly by that token the more faithful to the common usage of lawyers. It may further be noted that not every duty is imposed by a legal rule as such, and that a particularly important legal duty, namely the general duty of care, depends rather upon considerations of principle than upon any particular rule or rules, relevant though these may be to specifying its content in given instances. The present title is much indebted to Professor Hart as authority for representing duties as belonging at the primary level of law. But it rejects the supposition that the concept of legal duty could be fully elucidated in terms of a set of 'duty-imposing' 'primary rules' in Hart's sense; the title is accordingly opposed to the analysis of legal systems simply as systems of 'primary' and 'secondary' rules[2].

1   See eg J Austin *Lectures on Jurisprudence* (5th edn, 1885) chs 22–24; C K Allen *Legal Duties* (1931) pp 156–220; H L A Hart *The Concept of Law* (1961) pp 33–41, 54–58; A L Goodhart *English Law and the Moral Law* (1953) chs 1, 2; J W Salmond *Jurisprudence* (12th edn, 1966 ed P Fitzgerald) pp 100–104, 216, 217, 233, 234; G W Paton *A Textbook of Jurisprudence* (4th edn, 1972 ed D P Derham) pp 78–81, 297, 298; P M S Hacker 'Sanction Theories of Duty' in A W B Simpson (ed) *Oxford Essays in Jurisprudence, 2nd Series* (1973) ch 6. For a more refined view, see H L A Hart 'Legal and Moral Obligation' in A I Melden (ed) *Essays in Moral Philosophy* (1958) p 68, and J W Harris 'Trust, Power and Duty' (1971) 87 LQR 31. In *Institutions* I, 1, Stair does not offer analyses of the concepts of duty or obligation, but he clearly uses the terms in quite distinct ways.
2   As to this analysis, see H L A Hart *The Concept of Law* (1961) chs 5, 6.

4. OBLIGATIONS AND THE OBLIGATORY

1027. Meaning of 'obligatory'. The concept of that which is obligatory may be taken as identical in sense with that which has here been spoken of hitherto as 'categorically required'. If such and such a mode of action (for example wearing a seat belt while driving a car) is obligatory or categorically required by law, then failure so to act is wrong in law and *vice versa*; if refrainment from some other way of acting (for example driving one's car in excess of a certain speed) is obligatory, then so acting is wrong in law, and *vice versa*. These are tautologies. The concepts of the obligatory and of that which is wrong are fundamental to any normative order and are not susceptible of further analysis, though explicable by allusion and by exhibiting the point of the distinction drawn, as was attempted above[1].

1 See paras 1006 ff above.

1028. The concept of obligation. The primary level of law is that at which it is determined that certain lines of action or omission are wrong and unlawful or (to put it in simply converse terms) that certain lines of omission or action are obligatory. Not surprisingly, there therefore also exists a manner of speaking according to which whatever is obligatory is 'an obligation' and one is 'under an obligation' to do or refrain from all that the law categorically requires one to do or refrain from doing. This conception of obligation is perhaps especially common among moral philosophers, many of whom treat 'obligation' in ethics as signifying whatever it is morally obligatory for a person to do. Nor is so wide a usage unknown to jurisprudence, for Professor Hart takes the distinction between 'being obliged' (in the sense of coerced under danger or threat) and 'having an obligation' (where a rule requires some action of a person) to be fundamental to jurisprudence, and correspondingly refers to the rules which in his view constitute the primary level of law as 'primary rules of obligation'[1]. This broad use of the term 'obligation' commonly goes hand in hand with a broad use of the term 'duty', in which light 'duty' and 'obligation' become synonyms for each other, distinguishable only through established preferences for traditional phraseologies. This tendency to treat duty and obligation as equivalent can even be noted in the *dictum* of Lord Kinnear's in the *Kemp* case[2], where he argues that if there is a 'duty owed ... by the defenders' they must needs have an 'obligation to exercise diligence'.

1 H L A Hart *The Concept of Law* (1961) ch 5.2.
2 *Kemp and Dougall v Darngavil Coal Co Ltd* 1909 SC 1314 at 1319, 1909 2 SLT 181 at 183.

1029. Obligations as legal ties. There is also, however, a more specialised use of the term 'obligation', one which retains a certain vitality in Scottish legal usage, as signified by the time-hallowed phrase 'the law of obligations'. In this usage an obligation is, as Justinian first put it, a *vinculum juris*, 'a legal tie by which we may be necessitated or constrained to pay or perform something'[1] or (we may add) to refrain from some action or way of acting. What is more, as Gloag and Henderson have pointed out from their first edition onwards, 'Taking an obligation in the narrower sense of the word ... [it is] a legal tie by which one is bound to a specific creditor, or definite body of creditors'[2]. That is, an obligation is necessarily a link between persons (unlike duties, for there can be duties imposed in the general public interest, without any artificial personification of the public), and indeed between ascertained persons one of whom, the creditor (sometimes rather misleadingly styled 'the obligee'[3]), has in principle a discretion to call for or to waive or to let lapse the performance, payment or abstention required by law of the other party, the debtor or obligant (sometimes rather misleadingly styled 'the obligor'[3]).

1 Justinian *Institutes* III,13,pr. Cf Stair *Institutes* I,1,22: '... a legal tie, whereby the debtor may be compelled to pay or perform something, to which he is bound by obedience to God, or by his own consent and engagement'.

2 W M Gloag and R C Henderson *An Introduction to the Law of Scotland* (9th edn, 1987) para 3.3, following the 1st edn (1927) and subsequent editions.
3 Etymologically, 'obligee' suggests the idea of a person's being obliged, but in current usage this meaning is actually more commonly attached to the term 'obligor'; but where usage is neither logical nor securely established, one should avoid using potentially misleading expressions.

1030. The time span of an obligation.

Obligations in this sense as specific legal relations between ascertained parties ('legal ties' or *'vincula juris'*) have necessarily some degree of temporal endurance originating with some particular act or event — which we shall refer to as the 'institutive' act or event — and continuing until some 'terminative' act or event, such as performance, express waiver, novation, prescription by lapse of time, or (in certain cases) death of one or other party[1]. They are capable of being reified, that is, considered as a species of incorporeal thing; and as such may be subject to assignation on the creditor's part or transmissible on the death or bankruptcy of either party, save in the case of obligations involving purely personal services.

1 See N MacCormick 'Law as Institutional Fact' (1974) 90 LQR 102; and N MacCormick and O Weinberger *An Institutional Theory of Law* (1986) Introduction and chs 1, 2.

1031. Voluntary obligations.

It has been customary to classify obligations according to the nature of their institutive act or event. Voluntary obligations are those which are instituted by an act of the obligant with the actual or presumed intent to create a legal obligation and to determine wholly or in part the nature of the performance, payment or abstention which is its content. Conventional or consensual obligations may be considered a sub-class of voluntary obligations, concurrent wills of obligant and creditor being essential to their constitution and content. Contracts are, of course, the most important species of conventional obligation[1].

1 Cf Stair *Institutes* I,1,21, I,10, and D M Walker *The Law of Contracts and Related Obligations in Scotland* (2nd edn, 1985) chs 1–3.

1032. Non-voluntary obligations.

In contrast to such obligations arising by the will of man, Stair contradistinguished 'obediential obligations, flowing from the will of God'[1]. Theology apart, we may certainly identify as non-voluntary obligations all those instituted on the occurrence of an event, such as the birth of a child, engaging a parental obligation to aliment the child, or of an act of a sort neither actually nor presumptively intended to create an obligation, as where a payment of money under error gives rise to an obligation of restitution in the payee toward the original payer or where some conferment of benefit by one upon another gives rise to a non-contractual obligation in the beneficiary to recompense the benefactor to the extent of any gain received. Most important of the class of non-voluntary obligations are obligations of reparation. Here are involved both an act, namely some wilfully wrongful act or some breach of duty or of (for example contractual) obligation, and an event, namely the consequential occurrence of injury, damage or loss to a person other than the actor. The act in question may here be an intentional one, but it neither needs be, nor characteristically is, one intended to generate the consequential obligation. The occurrence of injury, damage or loss proximately caused by the wrongful act or breach of duty or obligation is of course essential to the existence of the obligation to make reparation for that injury, damage or loss, and it may occur some considerable time after the act in breach of duty etc. For example, a negligently manufactured article may lie in a store for some time before being incorporated in a machine which might in turn be put to use only after some space of time and only subsequently cause injury or damage[2]. The release into the market of supplies of a teratogenic drug must antedate by some time any doctor's decision to prescribe it to a pregnant patient, and some further space of time will elapse before actual harm is done to any developing foetus. In this case, moreover, no obligation of reparation arises until the live birth of the child[3].

1 Stair *Institutions* I, 10.
2 Cf *Watson v Fram Reinforced Concrete Co (Scotland) Ltd and Winget Ltd* 1960 SC (HL) 92, 1960 SLT 321. The question here was as to the Law Reform (Limitation of Actions &c) Act 1954 (c 36), s 6 (repealed), whereby an action for personal injuries had to be brought 'before the expiration of three years from the date of the act, neglect or default giving rise to the action'. The pursuer's injuries were due to a faultily manufactured part made by the defenders. Manufacture and sale by the defenders took place more than three years before the pursuer's action commenced. *Quid juris?* Lord Reid said: '. . . if the words which Parliament has used in section 6 are reasonably capable of meaning that the three-year period runs from the date when the right of action emerges, I would adopt that meaning' (1960 SC (HL) 92 at 107, 1960 SLT 321 at 326). And this was possible, because 'it appears to me that default in the sense of breach of duty must persist after the act or neglect until the damage is suffered' (at p 109 and at p 327). Accordingly, time only began to run against the pursuer when he was injured, that is when there arose a breach of duty which made its impact on him.
3 Cf *Liability for Antenatal Injury* (Scot Law Com no. 30; Cmnd 5371 (1973)).

1033. Prescription and limitation. Sometimes, by a fiction, it is said in these cases that the breach of duty itself occurs only upon the occurrence of the injury, damage or loss, or the birth of the child, or the time at which latent injury was first reasonably discoverable[1]. Resort to such a fiction may be necessary to overcome infelicities in legislation on prescription and limitation of actions or for other purposes. But it would be preferable for a clearer conceptual structure to be sustained in the law, for example by better draftsmanship of relevant legislation. What is properly subject to prescription or limitation is not the original breach of duty, but any obligation of reparation to which it gives rise[2].

Another way to put this point would be to say that the justice served by prescription and limitation of actions is that of not permitting persons to sleep upon rights of action, that is, remedial rights[3]. The right of an injured party to a remedy should be exercised or abandoned within a reasonable time, or be deemed to have lapsed; and the length of time should be the same for all persons who have a similar right grounded in a similar injury. But the space of time between breaches of duty as actually committed by wrongdoers and resultant occurrences of injury can be various. So if the statute happens to date prescription from the moment of a breach of duty, fiction has to be resorted to in order to secure the essential justice of the statutory scheme.

To have restated the matter in this alternative way is to have introduced the concept of 'right' to the present discourse. Plainly, the position of the creditor of an obligation is that of a right-holder. In voluntary obligations, the promisee has a right that the promiser perform (according to his obligation) the promised action or actions; in obligations of reparation, the injured party has a right to reparation of the injury suffered — a remedial right — and so on. It is at least characteristically, and perhaps even essentially, the case that such rights in respect of obligations imply a power of choice on the part of the creditor, namely choice as between demanding or insisting upon performance or explicitly or tacitly condoning non-performance, or even waiving the right to performance.

1 See *Watson v Fram Reinforced Concrete Co (Scotland) Ltd and Winget Ltd* 1960 SC (HL) 92, 1960 SLT 321, and para 1032, note 2, above, but see now also the Prescription and Limitation (Scotland)

Act 1973 (c 52), eg s 17. It is submitted that even the modern legislation on this topic is less clear than it might be as to the point taken in the text. This is a matter which the Scottish Law Commission considered in *Prescription and Limitation of Actions (Latent Damage and Other Related Issues)* (Scot Law Com no. 122) (Cm 790) (1989).

2 This obligation arises when harm occurs or becomes perceptible, not at the moment of the breach of duty.

3 'Right of action' is the phrase used in the Prescription and Limitation (Scotland) Act 1973. Cf Lord Reid's words cited in para 1032, note 2, above.

1034. Conclusion. This then implies that the particular legal relationship which we style 'obligation' in its special sense is that in which a particular party owes a particular duty to the other party, who has the power of demanding or waiving performance of the duty; that is, obligations are a particular species of duty — right relationship between ascertained parties. This is true in itself, and in it some have discovered the key to a complete analysis of the nature of rights[1]. But this is too bold a claim; a more exhaustive and wide-ranging analysis of rights is called for, and forms the subject matter of discussion below[2].

1 See eg H L A Hart 'Definition and Theory in Jurisprudence' (1954) 70 LQR 37; and H L A Hart *Essays in Jurisprudence and Philosophy* (1983) ch 1.

2 See paras 1073 ff below.

5. PERSONS AND PERSONALITY

1035. Active and passive aspects of personateness. Fundamental to the existence of a person are capability for rational and intentional action and capability to have interests and to suffer harm. The active aspect of personateness is manifest upon considering what has been called the primary level of law. In so far as law consists in categorical requirements which make acts and omissions obligatory and their converse wrong, it necessarily contemplates the existence of conscious rational beings who can make their intentional actions conform to these requirements by their own will and intention. Further, however, for law to consist in reasonable requirements of conduct, these requirements will inter alia have to have regard to protection of the interests of persons in their passive aspect. Laws are for the regulation of persons in their active aspect, with a view, at least in part, to protecting persons in their passive aspects, that is, to protecting them from harms (invasions of interests) and perhaps with a view also to advancing interests of theirs positively.

1036. Continuity of persons in time. Both active and passive aspects of the grounds of personateness imply the continuity of persons in time, and some degree of actual or imputed consciousness of this[1]. For intentionality in action entails an agent's anticipating in thought an action to be performed at some later moment by that same agent; and rational intentionality entails the capability to take decisions with a view to their coherence in an overall plan of life. And, on the other hand, the interests of rational beings are not confined to present and momentary states of gratification but include more significantly whatever is conducive to the overall well-being of the person through time. It follows that there has to be some criterion of personal identity through time, and some way of determining the temporal duration of any person's existence as such — all of which may be thought no more than an obscure way of saying that human beings are born, live and die, and in some sense remain the same person from birth to death.

1 J Locke *An Essay concerning Human Understanding* (1st edn, 1690 (many subsequent editions)) II,xxvii,9: 'To find out wherein personal identity consists, we must consider what *person* stands

for; which, I think, is a thinking intelligent being, that has reason and reflection, and can consider itself as itself, the same thinking thing, in different times and places...'. Concern with the problem of continuity has remained focal in subsequent philosophical discussion: see eg D Parfit *Reasons and Persons* (1984) ch 11, s 80, and the citations therein. Whether psychic continuity and self-consciousness can be considered essential to legal personality is plainly a doubtful point if the distinction between natural and artificial persons is taken in its common understanding; *sed quaere* if it should be so taken.

1037. Commencement of personate existence. Obscurity belongs more to these processes as affected by modern medical technology than to our way of speaking about them. Both for moral and for legal purposes, the question of the moment of commencement of the personate existence of a human being is a difficult and disputed one. In what circumstances, if at all, may the human foetus be aborted, or created and sustained *extra uterum* and there used for purposes other than implantation in the womb of an intending and otherwise infertile mother[1]? What, if any, duties of care are owed toward or in respect of the unborn or (in case of putative 'wrongful life' claims) unconceived foetus[2]? What, if any, rights can enure in favour of or vest in the child at birth in view of pre-natal events affecting it detrimentally or beneficially[3]? What, if any, rights may parents and others have in respect of injuries inflicted on a foetus *in utero* or of congenital defects against which genetic counselling or screening failed to produce due warning[4]? What, if any, rights accrue under 'surrogate parenthood' agreements[5]? These and other like questions all reflect a profound uncertainty as to how exactly, and with what consequences, the commencement of personality ought to be dated in the case of human beings as 'natural persons'[6]. The only ancient learning in such matters is that surrounding the brocard *nasciturus pro jam nato habetur quamdiu agitur de ejus commodo*. It is submitted that that maxim and its general applications justify the thesis that remedial rights or obligations of reparation can vest in or arise in favour of human beings at, and only at, birth, but may properly relate to harms and injuries previously inflicted. This implies that duties may be owed both to and towards the *nasciturus* and that breaches of such duty will be actionable on condition of live birth. This may be taken as implying that rights of a purely passive kind are vested in the foetus, and can be wrongfully invaded; hence some minimal form of personality exists from the moment of conception. What does not follow is that the same rights need hold in favour of the foetus against all parties to the same extent, in particular against the putative mother. Thus it is neither illogical nor conceptually absurd to insist on the rights of the foetus as against third parties while permitting (under certain conditions) the procurement of an abortion at the instance of the putative mother[7]. Whether this solution is morally right or morally wrong cannot properly be discussed here, and is a separate issue.

1 See M Warnock (ed) *A Question of Life* (1985) pp 29–35. This book is an expanded text of the *Report of the Committee of Inquiry into Human Fertilisation and Embryology* (the Warnock Report) (Cmnd 9314) (1984).
2 See *Liability for Antenatal Injury* (Scot Law Com no. 30; Cmnd 5371 (1973)); and cf the *Report of the Royal Commission on Civil Liability and Compensation for Personal Injury* (the Pearson Report) (Cmnd 7054–I) (1978) paras 1414–1453, 1478–1486. The Congenital Disabilities (Civil Liability) Act 1976 (c 28) does not extend to Scotland (s 6(2)), but, so far as concerns liability for fault causing damage to a foetus, the present principles of Scots law seem fully adequate to the case, as the Scottish Law Commission argues. As to 'wrongful life', see *McKay v Essex Area Health Authority* [1982] QB 1166, [1982] 2 All ER 771, CA, disallowing a claim for damages for 'wrongful life' as unsound in principle and contrary to public policy.
3 *Liability for Antenatal Injury*. See also T B Smith *A Short Commentary on the Law of Scotland* (1962) pp 245, 246; and *Elliot v Joicey* 1935 SC (HL) 57 at 70.
4 Cf *Soutar v Mulhern* 1907 SC 723, 14 SLT 862, and see D M Walker *The Law of Delict in Scotland* (2nd edn, 1981) pp 716, 717.

5 M Warnock (ed) *A Question of Life* (1985) pp 42–47. It would appear on principle to be contrary to public policy to enforce any of the provisions of a surrogacy agreement, although evidently unjust if a natural mother who had performed her part and acceded to adoption by surrogate parents were then unable to recover any payment agreed. Would it be in the interest of a child in such a case that it be at risk of being made a bargaining counter in the enforcement of a legally unenforceable agreement? On surrogacy generally, see *A v C* [1985] FLR 445, CA, and *Re C* [1985] FLR 846.

6 As to the computation of periods of age and the importance in that regard of the time of birth as entered in the register, see, however, Lord Fraser *Parent and Child* (3rd edn, 1906) p 200.

7 See *Paton v British Pregnancy Advisory Council Trustees* [1979] QB 276, [1978] 2 All ER 987, and *C v S* [1988] QB 135, [1987] 1 All ER 1230, CA. In England the courts have, however, refused to make a foetus a ward of court: *Re F (in utero)* [1988] P 122, [1988] 2 All ER 193, CA.

1038. Survival of human identity.

As to the continuing identity of persons through time, transplant surgery gives rise to conceptual problems whose solutions still lie at the level of science fiction and philosophical speculation[1]. But supposing a brain transplant were to occur in the case of wasting bodily disease of one party and some acute brain damage of another. Would the resulting being be Campbell, whose body survives with Cameron's brain in it, or Cameron, whose brain survives in Campbell's body? What if Cameron had been female and Campbell male? Can human identity survive change in sex? (And what about the continuing identity of trans-sexuals who undergo sex-change operations anyway? If such a person has been married, is the marriage nullified *ipso jure*, or must it be dissolved[2]? If there are children of the marriage, when do they acquire rights of succession to their 'father'?). If, as seems best, one treats psychic continuity as necessary (though perhaps of itself not sufficient) to the continuing identity of a person, this will solve or help in principle to solve some of the puzzles arising in such cases, But it will generate further puzzles. For if there can be 'split personality' cases such as those fictionally explored in James Hogg's *The Confessions of a Justified Sinner* (1824) or R L Stevenson's *The Strange Case of Dr Jekyll and Mr Hyde* (1886), it may appear to follow that one physical body can be the locus of, or 'belong to', two distinct persons. What is then the lawful, to say nothing of the just, result when one of the persons commits crimes which lead to lawful conviction and imprisonment whereupon the other petitions for liberation of 'his' or 'her' body from jail?

1 See D Parfit *Reasons and Persons* (1984) Pt III, especially chs 10, 11.
2 As to the nullity of a marriage between a man and a man who had undergone sex-change surgery and hormone treatment, cf *Corbett v Corbett* [1971] P 83. By parity of reasoning, a marriage would not be nullified *ipso jure* in the converse case. See also *X* 1957 SLT (Sh Ct) 61.

1039. Termination of personate existence.

The instance of organ transplantation has already implicitly introduced the topic of ascertaining the occurrence of death. It appears well established in principle, and now also by judicial precedent, that the correct method of ascertainment of death is through the concept of 'brain stem death'[1]. It follows that once a person has suffered brain stem death, no subsequent operation causing organic damage or such other event as the termination of heart beat or of lung-ventilation will constitute a legally relevant killing for any purpose. If this view is sound, it necessarily implies that, whatever else is true in our above hypothetical case of Campbell and Cameron[2], Campbell is in that case dead and cannot be deemed revived by the insertion of Cameron's brain; and, indeed, if the resultant person were not a continuing Cameron, there would seem to be no other solution than that Cameron has been killed, or even murdered. Yet if the argument is not sound, all those who engage in transplant surgery are guilty of, or accessories to, some form of unlawful homicide.

1 *Finlayson v H M Advocate* 1979 JC 33, 1978 SLT (Notes) 60.
2 See para 1038 above.

1040. Necessity for legal principles and rules. Albeit not pursued here to a final conclusion, such questions as these show that although it is a mere truism that all human beings are conceived, then born, then alive for some space of time at the end of which they die, it is not merely trivial truth that questions as to the commencement, endurance and termination of personality have to be answered by law according to some reasonable principles, and ideally reduced to rules for the avoidance of doubt and difficulty in areas such as those considered above. And in this respect there is a perfect analogy with other bearers of legal personality which are not individual human beings — bodies corporate, and whatever other objects or beings may be admitted to the class of 'juristic persons'. (Here, therefore, we follow Kelsen in declining to draw a distinction between 'natural' and 'juristic' persons; for the personality of human beings *in law* is no less, and no more, 'juristic' personality than that of any other entity[1].)

We may generalise and say of every type of legal person that legal rules and principles must exist to make some provision concerning the commencement of a person of any given type, concerning the duration and identity through time of any and every such person, and as to the final termination of the person, whether by natural or civil death, voluntary or involuntary liquidation, winding up or whatever. Moreover, of any legal person or class of legal person it must be possible to specify in general terms the passive and active capacities it enjoys or can exercise, and the types of limitation or qualification to which these are subject.

1 H Kelsen *The Pure Theory of Law* (trans M Knight, 1967) pp 168–192.

1041. The nature of personality; corporate actings. Introduction of the question of passive and active capacities of agents brings one back to the originally proposed criterion of, or rather ground for, personality, namely a 'capability for rational and intentional action and capability to have interests and to suffer harm'[1], and to a possible objection to this original proposal. The possible objection is that only individual humans satisfy the ground proposed since only they have a real capability either to act or to suffer. Hence every other 'person' would be one by mere fiction and by special creation or concession of law. Such an objection is false, for it turns upon a false view of acting and being acted upon. The key fact to note is that human beings are in their very nature collaborative and social beings and that there are some acts which can only be joint acts of collaborating individuals, like procreating a child or winning a game of football or playing Beethoven's Fifth Symphony. And likewise, there are some harms and misfortunes which are necessarily corporate, like the loss to a family through the death of one of its members, or being defeated in a game of football or a war, or being interrupted or shouted down while playing Beethoven's Fifth or performing *Hamlet*. The examples chosen are deliberately not, or not primarily, legal examples or ones necessarily involving any application of the law. Corporate actings are entirely natural to human beings, although indeed dependent on human convention, contrivance and organisation. For convention, contrivance and organisation are natural to human beings.

1 See para 1035 above.

1042. The attitude of the law to social collectivity. This is the kind of reality which has always been recognised in, for example, the Scots lawyers' acceptance of firms as having a reality over and above the partners of the moment, and hence of firms of partners as enjoying at least quasi-personality.

Only to be regretted in this instance is the rather absurd fact that in most of the points on which this sensible recognition of social reality might have been pushed home to real legal advantage, the law has held back from achieving this[1]. The fact of the matter surely is that the law's *non-personification* of certain types of social collectivity is far more a matter of fiction than its conferment of personality is in the case of others. The fiction is not that British Coal has corporate identity, but that the National Union of Mineworkers lacks it. Indeed, clubs, trade unions and other unincorporated associations often have (as Maitland noted[2]) much more reality than some such legally incorporated bodies as the one-man company in the celebrated case of *Salomon v Salomon and Co Ltd*[3]; and the various devices by way of manipulation of the law of trusts, of agency and of contract whereby the social realities are accommodated within the law make this sometimes very obvious[4]. This is not, however, to deny that resort to the fiction of non-incorporation may be grounded in consciously contemplated reasons of legislative policy, as in the case of trade unions; and that judicial circumvention of such policy[5], while understandable in terms of the social realities, may nevertheless sort ill with doctrines of legislative superiority, to say nothing of supremacy.

1 See P Hemphill 'The Personality of the Partnership in Scotland' 1984 JR 208. See generally PARTNERSHIP.
2 See F W Maitland 'Moral Personality and Legal Personality' in *Selected Essays* (1936, ed H D Hazeltine, G Lapsley and P H Winfield), ch 5, and Introduction to O Gierke *Political Theories of the Middle Ages* (trans F W Maitland, 1900) pp xviii–xliv. See also PUBLIC CORPORATIONS, vol 19, paras 213 ff.
3 *Salomon v Salomon & Co Ltd* [1897] AC 22, HL.
4 For an account of the way in which Scots law deals with unincorporated associations, see D M Walker *Principles of Scottish Private Law* (3rd edn, 1982) vol 1, ch 3.7. If one asks oneself why particular contractual rights and duties and trusts etc are implied in the case of a voluntary association, the answer is that the association exists, and those rights etc give effect to this fact rather than that the association exists in virtue of the rights etc.
5 This perhaps occurred in *Taff Vale Rly Co v Amalgamated Society of Railway Servants* [1901] AC 426, HL. However, at least since the enactment of the Trade Union and Labour Relations Act 1974 (c 52), s 2, this point has become merely historical.

1043. Imputing personality to corporate groups. To acknowledge that some human actions are corporate ones is not *eo ipso* to identify which ones are. And indeed in the realms of corporate personality it is a capital question to determine which human acts, decisions and intentions are imputable[1] to which corporate entities, and under what description and with what resultant variation in corporate rights and liabilities. Even apart from law, it is necessarily the case that the imputability of acts to groups and associations depends upon conventions and rules, for only organised groups can act or suffer as such, not merely as collectives of socially acting or suffering humans. And the organisation of groups and associations is organisation through and under conventions and rules which inter alia determine what interests are corporate interests and what acts of what people in what circumstances count as acts of the corporate group or association. What the law does is to establish a relatively clear framework of rules determining these matters in the case of those groups whose corporate identity is recognised as legal incorporation involving the conferment of juristic personality on the group in the same way that juristic personality is accorded to some human beings in all legal systems, and to all human beings in those systems which exclude chattel slavery and with it the reification (and, *pro tanto*, dehumanisation) of human beings.

1 For this concept of imputation, see H Kelsen *The Pure Theory of Law* (trans M Knight, 1967) pp 168–192 and cf (on 'attribution') J C Gray *The Nature and Sources of the Law* (2nd edn, 1921)

ch 2. See also H L A Hart 'Definition and Theory in Jurisprudence' in *Essays in Jurisprudence and Philosophy* (1983) ch 1 at pp 43–47, or (1954) 70 LQR 37 at 54–56.

1044. Legal corporate personality. In short, legal corporate personality is the device whereby in law certain acts or events constitute the coming into existence of a group enjoying personateness in law as distinct from any of the human beings who are in law its members, servants or agents, with the consequence that certain acts, decisions and intentions can be imputed to the group as its acts, decisions or intentions, that certain states of affairs can be deemed legally relevant interests of the corporation, and that human beings appropriately identified may act as agents or servants of the corporation; and whereby on the occurrence of certain acts or events the existence of the corporation as a person in law is brought to an end[1]. As with other persons, the law regulates in general and in particular the legal capacities to be enjoyed by corporate persons and classes and instances thereof.

1 Cf N MacCormick 'Law as an Institutional Fact' in N MacCormick and O Weinberger *An Institutional Theory of Law* (1986) ch 2, or (1974) 90 LQR 102.

6. THE CAPACITY OF PERSONS: PASSIVE AND ACTIVE CAPACITY

(1) PASSIVE CAPACITY

(a) Pure Passive Capacity

1045. The nature of passive capacity. Passive capacity is properly identified as the capability in law to be the beneficiary of some legal provision or provisions, in the sense that one's protection from harm or advancement in some interest or another is the presumed intendment of the law. This depends upon our conception of the justifying ground for some law or another; for example, if the law whereby assault is a punishable crime is justified as intending to protect human beings from the threat of or the actuality of physical violence to their bodies, then the presumed intendment is to protect humans, or some humans, from this harm. If the true justification were that these laws protect the public peace to the advantage of interests of state, then the presumed intendment is not the protection of humans, though the means to the true intendment of advancing the state's interest in peace is also advantageous to humans. On the other hand, the law prohibiting the demolition of historic buildings has as its presumed intendment advancing the cultural interests of humans, not the physical integrity of buildings (this latter being merely a means to the justifying end of the law). The case of laws against cruelty to animals is in this respect a disputable case, for on some views it is justified primarily as protecting the human interest in humane conduct, whereas on others it is justified primarily as protecting animals from suffering gratuitously inflicted.

1046. Identifying the beneficiary of the law. In these cases of purely passive protectedness, it is of course a matter of interpretation and of judgment to determine what is the beneficiary of the law and what the mere means to some ulterior presumed good. Furthermore, in cases in which the legal provisions in question are primarily criminal or quasi-criminal in character, so that the power and discretion over the law's enforcement processes vests (perhaps exclusively) in the Crown as represented by the Lord Advocate or other public agencies, it may appear to be a purely abstract and academic exercise to ascertain who has the capacity of being, and is, the beneficiary of some legal provision or provisions.

1047. Capacity to suffer legal wrong. Yet where the provisions in question are statutory in character, the question can arise, as was noted earlier, whether or not commission of the statutory offence can also constitute a 'breach of statutory duty' such that any injury, damage or loss sustained as a proximate consequence thereof gives rise to an obligation of reparation. For the purposes of resolving this question it is all-important to have a view whether or not committing the statutory offence does or can in principle involve wronging, inflicting a wrong upon, some other being. And that in turn requires that the being in question have the capacity for suffering legal wrongs and be, in the given case, a member of the class whose actual protection by the law is among the justifying ends of the law in question.

(b) Passive Transactional Capacity

1048. Beneficiaries in private law. Nor are these the only ways in which capacity to be the beneficiary of the law can be manifested. When it comes to private law, one may be able to be the beneficiary of a promise albeit incapable of making one or even of accepting the terms of a conditional offer. One may be capable of becoming an owner of property by gift, even if incapable of managing it. One may be capable of sustaining legally relevant injury by breach of some common law duty, and of acquiring thereupon some remedial right albeit incapable of exercising that right. One may be capable of being the beneficiary of the duties of a tutor or a trustee as such even while incapable of enforcing 'in one's own right' any breaches of duty.

1049. The capacity to be acted upon with legal effect. These illustrations draw attention to a second type of situation in which a person may, albeit wholly passively, take part in the drama of the law. For here we are considering various types of legal transactions. It is a feature of such transactions that not merely must the active part in them be taken by some person with appropriate capacity, but also the performance must be toward or for the behoof of some other, or effecting the imposition of some legal burden on another, that other being endowed with sufficient capacity for the transaction to take its intended effect. Capacity of this latter sort we shall call 'passive transactional capacity'. This is the capacity to be acted upon with legal effect through some form of legal transaction or act in the law, whether the effect be beneficial or detrimental. Those who doubt its significance may wish to reflect on the fact that a gift of property on trust for the benefit of a child is valid, whereas one for the benefit of a pet dog is not.

1050. Capacity to enforce legal rights etc. The moment one moves into the arena of civil wrongs (delicts) to persons with consequential obligations of reparation, or voluntary obligations to persons or the various sorts of legally protected rights to and in things, one necessarily further envisages a transition from passive over into active capacity. The legal ability to enforce, secure, uphold or vindicate — or waive or abandon — one's rights involves a capacity to perform 'juristic acts' or 'acts-in-the-law', that is to carry out what were above referred to as 'legal transactions'. If a person lacks such capacity, that person's purely passive rights outside the criminal law will surely tend to be neglected or even flouted for want of someone available and able to assert these rights with legal effect. It is exactly to this end that various devices of representation have been evolved or developed by law whereby to ensure that some person having active capacity in law is made responsible to act for the interest of the person endowed with purely passive capacity, albeit that in at least some such cases the will of the representative (tutor, guardian, trustee or agent or whatever) is attributed to or imputed to the party represented, the person under incapacity. We must therefore proceed to a consideration of active capacity; but before doing so we should note that passive capacity is fully conceivable as inhering in some being or entity wholly lacking in any active capacity; and that possession in some measure of some range of passive capacity is sufficient to existence as a legal person. Where some state of affairs is conceived of sufficient value to merit some legal protection for its own sake, it may even be the case that conferment of some minimal personate status even on inanimate objects can be considered a useful device. Thus it has even been suggested that environmental protection laws could be made much more effective if legal standing were to be conferred upon trees and the like[1]. No doubt this was a somewhat extravagant proposal, and half jocular in intent. But it is a useful reminder of the potential scope of legal personality; and of the fact that although legal capacities are ordinarily correlated with natural human or at least animal capabilities, this does not have to be so always.

1 See C Stone 'Should Trees have Standing? Towards Legal Rights for Natural Objects' (1972) S Cal Law Rev 450, and 'Should Trees have Standing? Revisited' (1985) 59 S Cal Law Rev 1.

1051. Personality involving both passive and active capacity. Finally, it should be noted that, probably *per incuriam*, some Scottish authorities, for example Erskine, as recently approved in the Inner House[1], deny that there is legal personality in the absence of any active capacity or of capacity to hold property, as in the case of the pupil child in Scots common law. Bell characterises pupillarity as 'in contemplation of law, a state of absolute incapacity'[2]. Such views of purely passive capacity as insufficient to constitute legal personality may seem to be fortified by discussion of the possibility that trees 'should . . . have standing', but it is submitted that the better view is that which acknowledges personality as extending over the capacity to suffer — to be legally wronged — as well as over the capacity to do; that is, over active capacity in its various forms. Moreover, as we shall see, active capacity presupposes, in some cases, a passive capacity in some persons (or all persons) to be affected by the exercise of powers, whether beneficially or onerously.

1 Erskine *Institute* I,7,14.
2 Bell *Principles* s 2067, approved and affirmed in *Finnie v Finnie* 1984 SLT 439, which concerned a rather intricate point of tax law dealing with the right to deduct tax before making certain sorts of alimentary payments. In this context the issue was whether a father's payment of money to his estranged wife as tutrix of the pupil children was a payment to or for the benefit of the children and thus subject to deduction of tax paid. Lord Cameron for the Division said (at 441): 'A pupil is incapable of acting on his own nor has he the capacity to consent. "[He] has no person in the legal sense of the word" (Erskine, *Institute*, I. vii. 14) . . . in our law a pupil is without personality: in effect this personality is subsumed in that of his tutor or tutrix'. That pupils lack transactional capacity, both active and passive, at common law is the point of the decision expressed in the terminology proposed in the present title; and doubtless a point which sufficiently disposes of the instant case. But it is submitted that when one considers pure passive capacity, and even a restricted sort of active capacity (capacity-responsibility), it is clearly too wide to say that pupils wholly lack capacity, far less that they lack personality altogether. That would be too paradoxical, not least because it would entail that pupillarity is not, after all, a legal status. That pupils are

not persons for the purposes of the law of property transactions, which is indeed the case, does not imply that they are not persons for any purposes of the law. But cf J M Halliday *Conveyancing Law and Practice in Scotland*, vol 1 (1985) para 2–03. The Scottish Law Commission clearly recognised the passive capacity of a pupil: *Legal Capacity and Responsibility of Minors and Pupils* (Scot Law Com Consultative Memorandum no. 65 (1985) para 1.3. See now *Legal Capacity and Responsibility for Minors and Pupils* (Scot Law Com no. 110 (HC Papers (1987–88) no. 151)), and the Age of Legal Capacity (Scotland) Bill (1989), cl 1(3)(e).

(2) ACTIVE CAPACITY

(a) Introduction

1052. Capacity-responsibility and transactional capacity. It is here envisaged that there are two forms or aspects of active legal capacity. The first, which will be called 'capacity-responsibility'[1], is the capacity to act in that sense of 'action' in which responsibility for results and consequences of acting is considered imputable to the being or entity whose bodily or mental activity is a proximate cause of the result or consequence under consideration. Such capacity for action normally entails also being able to incur liability for one's actions or their consequences, whether this be liability to punishment or penalty or liability to claims for civil reparation or other remedies. The second, which will be called 'transactional capacity', is the capacity to carry out legal transactions ('juristic acts', 'acts-in-the-law') with valid legal effect. Such capacity for transactions relates generally to transactions of a certain type, as in the case of contractual capacity, or capacity to vote in public elections, or to be a director of a company, or to grant a valid discharge for payments due, and so on.

  1 This follows H L A Hart *Punishment and Responsibility* (1968) ch 9, or (1967) 83 LQR 346.

1053. The nature of active capacity. In both forms of active capacity, what is involved is some standing feature or feature of persons in virtue of which they are treated in law as able to act (and also to be held liable for actions, as a matter of passive transactional capacity) or to transact and to have one's transactions of various sorts considered as valid. To put it another way round: the (active) legal capacities a person has are the conditions in law of his or her being able to act with full legal effect either in the way of committing some wrongful act or exercising some liberty of action, or in the way of effecting some legal transaction. These capacities are by law made dependent on enduring (though not necessarily permanent) features of a person which are either legally independent features of the person, such as age, sex or mental competence, or legally dependent features such as citizenship, legitimacy, matrimonial status or solvency, which are actually defined by law. Where capacity-determining features are legally independent, and in that sense 'natural', the ascription or non-ascription of capacities by the law is commonly justified as grounded in (and thus simply replicating) natural abilities and disabilities of persons of the given class. For example, the incapacities formerly affecting women and still affecting young children and those of unsound mind were represented as justified by the natural disabilities consequent on femininity, immaturity and insanity. The same kind of argument has been used in cases of racial qualifications and disqualifications. For present purposes it is assumed that such arguments are as well founded in the case of nonage and insanity as they are outrageous and ill-founded in the case of sex and race; but even this is disputed by some writers[1]. In the case of legally dependent incapacitating features such as bankruptcy and imprisonment, it is a part of the point of the institutions in question that they result in certain incapacities.

The concept of active capacity is at least implicitly present in any conception of law which envisages law as in any way guiding or regulating the conduct of conscious and rational agents by means of their awareness of the law's requirements. For this postulates an actual or at least possible awareness of the subjects of the law or of particular laws that their conduct is subject to this or that legal provision. Hence the law must contain, at least implicitly, some reference to the qualities of persons which bring them within the scope of given legal provisions. Some of these qualities will belong to the class of enduring features of the person, other to more transient roles, activities or circumstances (such as being an employer, driving a car, or labouring under error or the influence of drink or drugs or being a victim of fraud or duress). Qualities of the former sort are, as we have seen, those which are determinants of legal capacity and legal incapacity. In this light, it should be noted that what have here been identified as the two forms or aspects of active capacity match the two modes in which law is considered by leading jurists to regulate or guide conduct, namely the mode of imposing categorical requirements on conduct (making acts or omissions obligatory) or refraining from imposing requirements; and the mode of empowerment of persons to effect legal results by legal transactions subject to conformity with hypothetical requirements of law, or of restricting or withholding such empowerment. Some further remarks about capacity-responsibility and about transactional capacity are therefore called for.

1 See R Farson *Birthrights* (1978). However, for a cogent critique of this 'child libertarian' position, see R Adler *Taking Juvenile Justice Seriously* (1985) ch 3.

(b) Capacity-responsibility

1054. The nature of capacity-responsibility. It may appear that capacity-responsibility is in essence a more passive than active capacity, since it involves the question whether or not one can be subjected to criminal or civil liability to sanctions for one's acts. But, as we shall see below[1], capacity-responsibility also entails a capacity to have and to exercise active rights. And although capacity-for-liability is indeed a form of passive transactional capacity, what is important here is the distinction which exists between capacity to be held liable and capacity to do that to which liability attaches. In the case of children under the age of seven and in the case of insane persons[2], capacity for dole or *dolus* — the formation of criminal intent — is deemed absent in Scots law; hence it is impossible for persons of either class to be legally guilty of crimes, whether or not the public safety or the law justifies in that case other measures of constraint in cases of involvement in seriously harmful behaviour. It was also for some time a topic of discussion whether corporations were capable of forming a criminal intent and hence whether they were capable of committing any crime or offence involving dole (*mens rea*). The proper answer to this question is, of course, that the imputation of wrongous intent to bodies corporate may stand on somewhat different ground than in the case of natural persons, but is eminently as justifiable in this case, since intentions are definable as the results of decisions, and hence whoever takes the company's decisions *eo ipso* forms the company's intentions. So it is possible to regard a corporation as *capax doli*, that is, legally capable of criminal wrongdoing in its own person, as distinct from mere answerability vicariously for the wrongs of others. And so the law now holds, if less clearly in Scotland than in England[3].

1 See paras 1073 ff below.
2 On nonage, see Hume *Commentaries* I, 35, and on insanity, see G H Gordon *The Criminal Law of Scotland* (2nd edn, 1981) ch 10.

3 See *Gordon* paras 8-84 – 8-91. In England the position was settled in *Director of Public Prosecutions v Kent and Sussex Contractors Ltd* [1944] KB 146, [1944] 1 All ER 119, DC, and *R v ICR Haulage Ltd* [1944] KB 551, [1944] 1 All ER 691, CCA. If it is correct to say that intention results from decision, then necessarily corporate bodies as such can have intentions since they can make decisions. The only question is that of which decisions one should impute to corporations.

1055. Vicarious liability. As the case of vicarious liability in the civil law shows, it is possible to detach the obligation of reparation for harms wrongfully inflicted from the breach of duty or other wrongdoing upon which it is consequential. In those cases of employment, agency and the like in which vicarious liability is imposed on such grounds as that a delict was committed by an employee in the course of employment, one party's breach of duty or of obligation or other wrongful act causing harm legally results not merely in that party's incurring an obligation to make good the damage done but also in the employer's jointly and severally incurring an obligation of the same tenor to the same extent. And both employer and employee are liable to judicially imposed order for damages etc, and ultimately to coercive enforcement of these, if they each fail to satisfy the obligation of their own free will.

1056. Responsibility for harm occasioned by others. However, vicarious liability has to be distinguished from the case in which one person is at fault in his or her own person for failing to prevent harms occasioned by another. For example, young children may foreseeably make their way on to busy roads, and their presence there may cause vehicles to swerve and to cause or suffer damage, or both. In such a case, the adult in charge of the children may rightly be held to be in breach of the general duty of care by reason of the omission adequately to safeguard against the obvious risk in the case. But, depending on age and circumstances, the children in such a case may not have or not be in breach of any legal duty of their own, and certainly very young children wholly lack capacity-responsibility. The sole party at fault in that case is the adult in charge, who is the only relevant legal actor, having alone the capacity to be such[1]. The same goes for ineffectual confinement of animals: here there is no vicarious responsibility, but a breach of duty by the keeper, which the keeper must make good if the escaped animal does harm[2].

1 See *Carmarthenshire County Council v Lewis* [1955] AC 549, [1955] 1 All ER 565, HL, but note D M Walker *The Law of Delict in Scotland* (2nd edn, 1981) pp 87, 88: '. . . from about the age of five the capacity of the child with reference to the risk involved in his conduct and his ability to appreciate the danger caused has to be considered', citing *Crawford v Edinburgh Magistrates* (1906) 14 SLT 383, OH. See also *Harvey v Cairns* 1988 SCLR 254, 1989 SLT 107, OH, where a child of six was held to be two-thirds contributorily negligent. The position would not be affected by the Age of Majority (Scotland) Bill (1989), cl 1(3)(c). See further T B Smith 'The Age of Innocence' (1975) 49 Tulane Law Rev 311; and *Legal Capacity and Responsibility of Minors and Pupils* (Scot Law Com Consultative Memorandum no. 65 (1985)), especially Pt II, and *Legal Capacity and Responsibility of Minors and Pupils* (Scot Law Com no. 110 (HC Papers (1987–88) no. 151)).
2 *Henderson v John Stuart (Farms) Ltd* 1963 SC 245, 1963 SLT 22, OH.

1057. Capacity to act and capacity for legal liability distinguished. Hence in the case of potentially wrongful acts, both under criminal law and under civil law, it is clear that capacity to act — capacity-responsibility — is distinct from the passive capacity of being subject to legal proceedings, capacity for legal liability, which is a form of passive transactional capacity. Conversely, one may for some special reason have an incapacity to be held liable without its being supposed that one has no capacity to act. Diplomatic immunity is an example of this. Those who enjoy diplomatic immunity are not deemed incapable of action or of wrongful action, but merely incapable of being made subject to civil or criminal process[1]. The same point has been taken in some cases about legislation in respect of trade unions and trade disputes, which has been held not to affect the legal quality of certain acts, as in cases of picketing, but merely to confer on the actors an immunity from criminal or civil proceedings[2]. Whether this was a sound reading of the legislative principles is more than doubtful. Beyond doubt, however, is the logical soundness of the distinction drawn.

1 See the Diplomatic Privileges Act 1964 (c 81).
2 See *Broome v Director of Public Prosecutions* [1974] AC 587, [1974] 1 All ER 314, HL, and *Kavanagh v Hiscock* [1974] QB 600, [1974] 2 All ER 177, DC.

1058. Conclusion. The ability to act or abstain from acting in a legally relevant sense is fundamental to legal order as a rational ordering of rational beings. It is this ability which is essential to being judged a wrongdoer or one who does no wrong in respect of some given act or omission. It is this which differentiates acts and omissions from mere behaviour and from mere events. Hence capacity in the sense of 'capacity-responsibility' is fundamental in law and as an aspect of legal personality.

(c) Transactional Capacity

1059. The nature of transactional capacity. Transactional capacity is of equal significance in developed systems of law[1]. The concept here in view is that of ability to exercise legal power, that is, to perform some act which is deemed to bring about some valid legal effect. In what is analytically the simplest case, the effect in view will be either that of making wrongful what would otherwise be lawful, as where a person validly promises to do a certain act, whereupon performance of that act in favour of the promisee becomes obligatory (and non-performance wrongful); or *vice versa*, as where a person consents to what in the absence of consent would be an assault, as in a surgical operation, or where one grants a valid release from a promissory obligation. From these simplest cases of power, one can construct others more complex, for example when one person promises another to do a certain act if requested to do so in writing delivered not later than a certain date. In this case the promiser confers on the promisee a power the exercise of which results in the promiser either having an unconditional obligation to do the act in question or being free from any obligation in the matter. Thus there can be powers to confer powers as well as powers to incur or to impose obligations; there can also be powers to create, confer, transfer and terminate rights of all sorts, as will appear in due course.

1 The recognition of classes of transactions which persons are legally empowered to carry out can even be taken as an index of a development of law from its analytically simplest types, as in H L A Hart *The Concept of Law* (1961) ch 5.

1060. Valid legal effects of exercise of legal powers. What is in all cases crucial is the notion of 'valid legal effect' as attendant upon the due exercise of legal powers. The special significance of this lies in the judicial enforceability of sanctions for legal wrongs (this itself being dependent on the powers vested by law in judges as such), and in the judicial duty to give effect by enforcement to all validly established legal relations and institutions. This can even be viewed as a kind of reward: to those who have transactional capacity and who choose to exercise it in the forms and conditions prescribed by law, the reward is that the arrangements thus created are enforceable by due process of law[1].

1 See N MacCormick *H L A Hart* (1981) ch 6.

1061. Elements necessarily involved in the conferment of legal powers. Accordingly, legal provisions which confer powers are to be understood as prescribing that performance of a certain act is to engender a certain legal result, and this further requires that there be provision as to:

(1) the qualifications a person must have to be able to perform the act in a legally effectual way;

(2) any requirements as to the intention (for example intention to create legal relations) essential to effectual performance of the act;

(3) any special procedures which must be observed to secure validity of the act;

(4) any circumstances of action whose absence would deprive the act of validity and legal efficacity (for example 'jurisdictional facts' must exist in the case of an exercise of judicial or quasi-judicial power); and

(5) any vitiating circumstances whose presence will invalidate an otherwise valid and effectual act, or render it liable to subsequent nullification (for example cases of essential error and of consent fraudulently induced in the law of contract)[1].

These being the essential elements of power-conferring provisions in the law, we should observe that element (1) in effect picks out that which is essential to our concept of transactional capacity. In the case of powers exercisable by persons generally (for example contracts, transfers of property, declarations of trust and execution of wills), subject only to the possession of certain standing personal attributes (such as age, sex and soundness of mind), we properly ascribe 'capacity' — capacity for that act or transaction — to persons with the relevant attributes, that is, the legally required qualifications.

1 See N MacCormick and Z Bankowski 'Speech Acts, Legal Institutions and Real Laws' in N MacCormick and P B H Birks *The Legal Mind* (1986) ch 7.

1062. Special powers conferred on special persons. A different case is that in which special powers are conferred upon specially qualified persons, whether such special qualification be by succession (for example a monarch), by election (for example a president), or by appointment (for example ministers, judges, members of the Civil Service and of boards of nationalised industries and police officers). In such cases there may be conditions — in the way of 'passive transactional capacity' — as to who can be appointed or elected to given offices. But the fact of succession, election or appointment is what qualifies *this* person to exercise this range of powers. 'Competence', 'jurisdiction', even perhaps 'authority', are the terms we use to signify the investment of special power through such special qualifications. Although the illustrations so far chosen have been from the sphere of public law, and have concerned the competence or authority of office-holders in public law, it should be observed that there can also arise special powers by way of special appointments in private law, as when one person appoints another executor of his or her will, or trustee over certain property, or when a person is elected to be an official of a trade union or a director of a company or is appointed to a particular post within a business organisation, or is assumed into partnership in a firm. In all such cases, no doubt, a background circumstance is the appointee's passive transactional capacity to be appointed or elected to such a position or office, and no doubt only persons with appropriate active capacities would ever be appointed or elected. But what is conferred by election or appointment is not a general capacity but a special competence at law.

1063. Conclusion. To conclude these observations on capacity, then, we shall note again that possession of some at least minimal legal capacity or capacities is of the essence of personateness in law. To be a person is to be able to suffer and to act in law, to act and to be acted upon. Capacity is therefore differentiable into passive and active capacity. Pure passive capacity is the condition of being eligible to receive the protection of the law for one's own sake rather than as a means to some other end for its own sake. It is thus the minimum legal recognition that can be conferred on any being, and is that enjoyed by very young children and the incurably weak-minded. Other passive capacities, the transactional ones, concern rather the ability to be beneficially or onerously affected by legal acts; these are no less omnipresent a feature of law. Active capacity is either capacity-responsibility, conceptualised as the ability to act rightly or wrongly, or transactional capacity — the being qualified to exercise some legal power or powers. The fullest degrees of legal personality involve a full range of passive and active capacities. To be distinguished from capacities as such are special competences possessed by persons in virtue of succession, election or appointment to special positions.

(3) A NOTE ON THE CAPACITY OF CORPORATIONS

1064. Capacity of corporations generally. All that has been said about capacity is as much applicable to corporate persons as to other persons recognised by law. In so far as corporate status is explicitly conferred by law on particular appointed or elected bodies, and in so far as it results from incorporation by the statutory procedures (through exercises of power by persons with appropriate capacity) under the Companies Acts, the corporate persons which result therefrom have in principle the full range of capacity appropriate to their corporate character[1]. This implies some restriction as against human persons; for example, as to passive capacity, since corporations cannot in their nature be physically assaulted or killed, those branches of criminal and civil law which give protection against bodily harms do not apply — 'offences against the person' are not offences against *these* persons. But property crimes and defamation are of course possible here, and companies have capacity to be wronged in these ways — even without express statutory provision. So far as concerns capacity to be acted upon by way of exercise of power, there are some types of office to which in principle companies could not be appointed, such as that of judge (though some boards etc may exercise judicial or quasi-judicial powers), although such private law positions as that of trustee or executor can be assumed by corporations.

1 It is more common to speak of the 'powers' than of the 'capacities' of a body corporate, this being no doubt a reflection of the terms of the *ultra vires* rule; but here, as with 'natural' persons, it is surely better to distinguish the standing abilities a person has for various kinds of action or suffering from the perhaps momentary powers that person, being a person with those capacities, can exercise. The authority for the present conceptual analysis is D M Walker *The Law of Contracts and Related Obligations in Scotland* (2nd edn, 1985) ch 5, especially at 5.1, 5.2, 5.56–5.70.

1065. Active transactional capacity. In general, as to active capacity, so far as corporations can act, they can act wrongfully or within their rights, and the problems of imputing criminal intent and liability for *ultra vires* delicts or torts are at least theoretically resolved or resoluble. There is no reason either of conceptual logic or of legal principle why corporations cannot be considered as acting subjects, whether acting in the exercise of active rights or in the commission of legal wrongs[1]. As to transactional capacity, with such obvious exceptions as capacity to marry, to adopt children or to make a will, corporate persons have the full range of capacities proper to the nature of commercial, charitable or public corporations. But their special competence to act, and thus the competence of their officers to act, is in each case regulated by the incorporating statute or the incorporating instrument executed under statutory powers. How far acts beyond particular competence — *ultra vires* acts — are binding in the interest of third parties has been a much discussed and controversial question, concerning the fair balance of interest as between shareholders and 'outsiders' dealing in good faith with a corporation. But the current resolution of that matter in favour of outsiders acting in good faith does not destroy the distinction between the range of transactions over which in principle corporations have active capacity, and the specific competence of any particular corporation within that range[2].

1 As to delictal liability, see *Mersey Docks and Harbour Board Trustees v Gibbs* (1866) LR 1 HL 93, and *Houldsworth v City of Glasgow Bank* (1880) 7 R (HL) 53. For the position in criminal law, see G H Gordon *The Criminal Law of Scotland* (2nd edn, 1978) paras 8.84–8.91, and para 1054, text and note 3, above.
2 See the Companies Act 1985 (c 6), ss 35, 36(4), replacing the European Communities Act 1972 (c 68), s 9 (repealed).

1066. Conclusion. To have stressed the capacities — including passive capacities — of corporations is important. Especially as to the fundamental rights of persons, it should be noted that the most fundamental are *human* rights and hence primarily for the protection of each and every human person. No doubt the protection of humans sometimes requires the protection of corporations derivatively, and some human interests — for example in freedom of worship — are distinctively corporate rather than individualistic in kind. But in principle that passive protection which human rights constitute is protection for humans, and there should be no presumption of an extension of the protections thereof to corporate persons in their own right rather than as human instruments.

7. STATUS

1067. Differences in status. The legal concept of personal status is to be understood chiefly in light of the foregoing elucidation of capacity[1]. For differences of status are to be understood primarily as the grounds for differentiations of capacity; or perhaps it would be better in modern legal systems to say that status differentials are summations of sets of qualities which ground significant differentiations of passive or active capacity among different classes of person[2]. Standing features or qualities of persons which constitute the common grounds for numerous and interrelated capacities and/or incapacities, passive or active or both, are features or qualities also constitutive of some 'status' or another.

Thus a status is a summation of or ground for the legal grounds of various capacities or incapacities, for example in the case of age: in the period between conception and birth, only passive capacities exist, and all conditionally upon subsequent live birth, so far as concerns the capacity to have action taken on one's behalf by a representative in law; then the period of childhood is a period of restricted capacity in all legal systems — being in Scottish common law[3] divided into pupillarity (birth to age fourteen in males or twelve in females), in which only passive capacities exist, active capacity in civil law being wholly absent, and minority, a period of restricted active transactional capacity, but full active capacity at any rate so far as concerns matters criminal, albeit under the Social Work (Scotland) Act 1968 there is only restricted (and special) passive capacity in respect of the sanctions of lawbreaking; the age of capacity for dole being eight[4]; indeed, it must be acknowledged with regret that there is no overall systematic view of the status — or statuses — of childhood from the point of view of private law, criminal law and social welfare law taken all together.

Finally, there is the status of adulthood achieved at the age of eighteen, whereupon there vest in the individual the full range of passive and active capacities known to the law and ascribable to human persons. This full status is, however, enjoyed only by those of sound mind, and mental weakness as defined by statute or common law[5] may be deemed a status resulting in absence of or restriction in active capacities. Bankruptcy is another status which results in substantial diminution of the active capacities normally enjoyed by adults of sound mind.

1 See paras 1045 ff above.
2 For a firm identification of status as (conceptually) the ground of, or summation of, capacities, cf C K Allen *Legal Duties* (1931) ch 2, or G W Paton *A Textbook of Jurisprudence* (4th edn, 1972) ch 16, s 87. But cf T B Smith *A Short Commentary on the Law of Scotland* (1962) p 254. However, D M Walker *Principles of Scottish Private Law* (3rd edn, 1982) vol 1, ch 3.2, also follows Allen in linking status to capacity: 'Status is . . . belonging to a particular class of persons to all of whom the law assigns particular legal powers, capacities, liabilities or incapacities' (vol 1, p 198).
3 However, under the Age of Legal Capacity (Scotland) Bill (1989), in general the age at which transactional capacity is obtained would generally be sixteen (cl 1(1)). Persons below that age would be regarded as pupils for most purposes (cl 5(1)). The status of minority would be effectively abolished by cl 5(3).
4 See the Children and Young Persons (Scotland) Act 1937 (c 37), s 55, and the Criminal Procedure (Scotland) Act 1975 (c 21), ss 170, 369.
5 See MENTAL HEALTH, vol 14, paras 1401, 1402.

1068. Sex and family relationship. Differences of sex as between male and female are very commonly grounds of differential legal status. Happily, modern statute law has almost entirely elided this; and, with us, sexual difference no longer entails difference of legal status. As part of perhaps the same tendency in law, it has to be noted that familial relationships, both those between spouse and spouse and that between parent or parents and children, are nowadays barely recognisable as matters of status in the classical sense here identified. Nevertheless, since the active capacity of an adult to act on behalf of a child, and the passive capacity of a child to be acted for, is still largely regulated by family relationship, whether as legitimate child, illegitimate child, legitimated child or adopted child, these remain (albeit in attenuated form) matters of status; and likewise the capacity to take legal benefits under the law of succession, both testate and intestate. Further, since marriage bears upon parental relationships (and also upon the law of succession), it remains, even more attenuatedly, a status relation, not merely a specially regulated form of contract. And, of course, the doctrines of international private law which require personal status to be determined by domiciliary law classically have reference to such matters of familial status, and continue so to refer regardless of the noted attenuations[1].

1 See A E Anton *Private International Law* (1967) pp 267–276, 310, 342–353, and cf R H Graveson *Status in the Common Law* (1953). As to domicile, see PRIVATE INTERNATIONAL LAW, vol 17, paras 187 ff.

1069. Status in public law. The matters discussed so far have referred exclusively to status within private law — though this has sometimes had consequences in respect of public law also. But it should be noted that even apart from public law ramifications of status as determined by and in private law, there are some distinctions admissible as distinctions of status which belong purely or primarily to public law. Following Professor Walker's categorisations[1], we may here note citizenship or nationality as a status; nobility in its various grades, and the contrasting status of commoner; and the status of prisoner as against that of a person at liberty. All these statuses regulate capacities in public law, such as the capacity to cast a valid vote in elections to public office, or the capacity validly to be nominated as a candidate for election to public office or to be appointed to hold some appointive public office or position.

1 D M Walker *Principles of Scottish Private Law* (3rd edn, 1982) vol 1, ch 3.2.

1070. Decline in the importance of status as such. As is obvious, the differences of capacity and the different qualities of persons which ground differential capacities and incapacities have great importance. So also have the rights and duties directly determined by some or all of these qualities — consider here in particular those arising from family relationships. But the summation of these qualities as grounds of differential capacity into this or that named status: pupil, minor, adult; married or not; illegitimate, legitimate, legitimated or adopted; free or prisoner, and so on — these summations as such are of limited interest or importance as a topic in contemporary law. Status as such has declined in interest as a legal concept, notwithstanding the importance of the matters which we can sum up under 'status' as a rubric.

One may speculate why this is so. Sir Henry Maine argued that the movement of 'progressive societies' up to his time of writing had been 'from status to contract'[1]. This is perhaps best taken as implying that the whole of a person's legal position (rights etc) was in earlier periods determined largely via status as regulating above all the capacity to order people about — an active transactional capacity — or the (passive) capacity to be validly ordered about. One's rights and duties were settled by decision of familial or feudal superiors, not by one's own freely undertaken engagements. In turn, a move to contract implies an equalisation of status and with it of transactional capacities such that, in the end, one's rights and duties arise largely from the contracts one makes rather than from other legal grounds. The status of different persons becomes assimilated and the range of capacities — or of rights — determined by any particular status-defining quality is reduced. Hence status dwindles in interest and importance as a legal topic.

1 H S Maine *Ancient Law* (1931, ed F Pollock) ch 1.

1071. Protection of weaker parties. At the same time, however, differences both perceived and real in market strengths or social standing or ascribed gender roles may contrast with the equalised legal capacities whereby all persons are enabled to participate in the market. So a whole series of special and inexcludable terms comes to be implied into contracts in favour of the presumptively weaker party (in terms of economic strength), whether as passenger or consignor in relation to carrier of persons or goods, or as insured *vis à vis* insurer, consumer *vis à vis* retailer, employee *vis à vis* employer, shareholder *vis à vis* company or member *vis à vis* trade union[1]. Or women and members of ethnic minorities gain statutory protections against discrimination in favour of men or majorities. Whereas in earlier systems of common law (or of Pandect-based law) a small range of general and standing personal features qualified one in respect of a large range of capacities, nowadays a multiplicity of legally significant roles exists, each person playing several roles and enjoying rights or restrictions accordingly under some statutory scheme. Likewise in such fields as child law a series of statutory schemes directed at furthering each child's well-being creates a patchwork of different systems for the protection of those under incapacity, without any single age or other decisive qualification having general application. Childhood is a legal position overlaid by a multiplicity of statutory provisions with a variety of age qualifications and need-related criteria for intervention. Gone is the relative — and perhaps excessive — simplicity of the older all-purpose common law concepts of pupillarity and minority[2] — or infancy in English law.

Such developments have sometimes been said to amount to a new form of status, and thus to betoken a swing back from contract to status. But, as at least hinted above, statutory roles into and out of which one may step perhaps many times in a day or *a fortiori* in a lifetime are a far different thing from status. It would seem better to give Maine's apophthegm a further updating. Of societies which consider themselves progressive, the modern development has been from status to statute.

1 See D M Walker *The Law of Contracts and Related Obligations in Scotland* (2nd edn, 1985), chs 22, 23.
2 These statutory age provisions would continue under the Age of Legal Capacity (Scotland) Bill (1989): see cl 1(3)(d).

8. CORPORATE STATUS

1072. Significance of corporate status. The term 'status' has chiefly been applied to human persons, or so-called 'natural persons'. But all persons in law being juristic persons (some human, some corporate), there is no justification at all for such a restriction. Hence the phrase 'corporate status' is a fully appropriate usage, and in so far as it is of utility to envisage any person having a status, it is of use to acknowledge incorporatedness as a status distinguishing corporations of every sort from unincorporated associations and all the fictitious resort to agency, contract and trusts to which their legally unacknowledged existence gives rise. Furthermore, even among corporate persons, there can be differences of status such as, for example, those in current Scots law (and United Kingdom law generally) between companies incorporated by royal charter or letters patent, public corporations incorporated by Acts of Parliament, statutory companies, and the various types of company which may be incorporated under the Companies Acts, such as public limited companies, private limited companies and unlimited companies[1]; and Australian law even recognises that curious entity the 'no liability company'[2]. There are also so-called quasi-corporations enjoying, presumably, quasi-corporate status such as partnerships in Scots law and trades unions[3].

1 For a useful summary explicitly couched in terms of status, see D M Walker *The Law of Contracts and Related Obligations in Scotland* (2nd edn, 1985) ch 5.
2 This is a class drawn to the writer's attention by Mr Peter Hemphill as enshrined in the companies legislation of the State of Victoria, and there used in the highly speculative mining industry.
3 See T B Smith *A Short Commentary on the Law of Scotland* (1962) pp 273–277, and D M Walker *Principles of Scottish Private Law* (3rd edn, 1982) vol 1, chs 3.8, 3.9; but cf P Hemphill 'The Personality of the Partnership' 1984 JR 208.

9. RIGHTS

(1) RIGHTS IN GENERAL AND IN REGARD TO CONDUCT

1073. The nature of rights. Rights necessarily belong to or 'vest in' persons. They are here considered as positions of benefit or advantage secured to persons by law[1]. An alternative theory — that of Stair and of many subsequent thinkers — defines rights in terms of faculties or powers conferred on persons by law and exercisable in a person's discretion[2]. Such a 'faculty' theory (sometimes nowadays called a 'choice' or 'will' theory) appears to mistake the part for the whole. It is in this respect akin to those theories of personality which deny that personateness in law belongs to beings such as children who may wholly lack active legal capacities. Since this view of personality enjoys both institutional and recent high judicial support in Scotland[3], it may be of no little importance to exhibit the logical and practical absurdity of the view — it may for a time prevail *ratione imperii*, but *imperio rationis* it is entitled to no authority.

Consider the case of a serious and permanently disabling injury inflicted on a month-old child by some careless act of a medical practitioner. In such a case, the law would grant two distinct remedies against the doctor. On the one hand the parents, who would incur both extra costs in rearing and looking after the child and grief over their child's disability, would have a right to compensation and *solatium*. On the other hand, there would be payable in respect of the child compensation for damage done and *solatium* for pain and suffering and loss of the normal amenities of life. But these damages are not merely 'in respect of the child' — that phrase better characterises the rights of the parents to their reparation for their losses and suffering *in respect of* their child, as an object of their obligations and their affections. One could get similar damages in respect of one's domestic animals or even one's land or house. No. These damages and *solatium* are due *to* the child, or at least to be held on trust for him or her. They compensate the child's suffering for its sake, not as a ground for someone else's suffering. This is quite unintelligible save as a right *of the child's* to reparation for injury.

1 The argument for this general view of rights is stated in N MacCormick 'Rights in Legislation' in P M S Hacker and J Raz (eds) *Law, Morality and Society* (1979) ch 11, and N MacCormick 'Rights, Claims and Remedies' in M A Stewart (ed) *Law, Morality and Rights* (1983) pp 161–181. For the idea of rights as belonging to a class of legal 'advantages', cf A N Kocourek *Jural Relations* (2nd edn, 1928). On 'vesting' in the technical sense, see G Gretton 'What is Vesting?' (1986) 31 JLSS 148; G Maher 'The Rights and Wrongs of Vesting' (1986) 31 JLSS 396; and S C Styles 'Vesting and the Law of Property' (1989) 34 JLSS 338 (all three articles being further noted in para 1106, note 2, below). See also WILLS AND SUCCESSION, vol 25, paras 902 ff.

2 For this view of rights as essentially dependent on the 'choice' or 'will' of the right-holder, see Stair *Institutions* I,1,22: 'A right is a power, given by the law, of disposing of things, or exacting from persons that which they are due'. See also H L A Hart *Essays on Bentham* (1982) chs 7, 8, and N E Simmonds *Central Issues in Jurisprudence* (1986) ch 8. The dispute between this 'faculty', 'will' or 'choice' theory and the rival 'benefit' or 'interest' theory has ancient roots, first appearing in the mediaeval assimilation of *jus* and *dominium*: cf R Tuck *Natural Rights Theories* (1979).

3 Erskine *Institute* I,7,14, and Bell *Principles* s 2067. See also *Finnie v Finnie* 1984 SLT 439. See, however, the clear recognition of passive capacity of pupils in *Legal Capacity and Responsibility of Minors and Pupils* (Scot Law Com Consultative Memorandum no. 65 (1985)) 1.3, and, now, *Legal Capacity and Responsibility of Minors and Pupils* (Scot Law Com no. 110 (HC Papers (1987–88) no. 151)).

1074. Right depends on a relevant duty. Moreover, as was discussed earlier, no reparation at all is due save in case of injuries etc proximately caused by acts or omissions in breach of a relevant duty. But what makes a duty relevant? Only that it is *owed to* (not merely owed in respect of) the party whose injuries are supposed to be legally reparable. It is logically absurd to suppose that such a duty could be owed to X without its being the case that X has some right, namely the right to be treated with reasonable care. So, at least passively, X must here be deemed to have some right; and X as a legal right-holder is necessarily also a legal person.

1075. Capacity to have passive rights. To say this is to stress again the significance of the passive capacities of persons, which are indeed nothing other than capacities to have passive rights. And what makes such passive rights intelligible is this: that even beings incapable of performing legally relevant acts (though acts of others can be imputed to them) are capable of being recognised as having interests which it is wrong to invade and wrong not to protect. As sufferers, albeit not as doers, such beings can come within the protection of the law. Respect for persons in such cases is satisfied by acknowledging various goods as being the good of that person and securing that each such person's relevant good is protected. It is protected in the simplest way by counting as legally wrongful any act injurious of the relevant good of any relevant being. Such wrongs are wrongs to the person affected, and that is a significant part of their wrongfulness even if they are at the same time also counted as punishable public wrongs.

1076. Rights of *incapaces*. What sometimes makes this view seem unconvincing is that rights in the absence of any ability to take remedial action in cases of infringement seem to be but things writ upon water. To this, however, the simple reply is that legal systems do make provision whereby tutors and the like — persons of full (active) capacity — are enabled to take legal remedial action on behalf of the person under incapacity. Obligations of reparation owed to children and other *incapaces* are enforceable at the instance of whoever has the appropriate tutelary role; and damages paid have to be held in trust for the benefit of the *incapax*. What this shows, however, is not that the *incapax* lacks rights, but that special means have to be used to make his rights effectual. Since they are used, however, the idea that rights of such beings are rights writ on water is evidently false.

1077. Remedies and rights distinguished. Proponents of the faculty theory take this as support for their view. It shows, they say, that what is constitutive of a right as really existent is the existence of a power to enforce it at the discretion of a relevant enforcer[1]. The weakness of this view is, simply, that the powers in question are powers to enforce someone's rights, as distinct from, for example, powers to prosecute wrongs in their character as offences. They should not be considered as constitutive of that to which they are ancillary. That a motor car would be practically useless without tyres does not make tyres constitutive of cars; that rights would be practically useless without remedies does not make remedies constitutive of rights. Remediless rights might well, however, be deemed radically 'imperfect' rights, at any rate in the sense of legal rights. This is something of a point in favour of the choice or faculty theory. So in the end one must perhaps look to both theories for a full understanding, even if the benefit theory is the more fundamental.

1 See in particular H L A Hart 'Definition and Theory in Jurisprudence' in his *Essays in Jurisprudence and Philosophy* (1983) ch 1 at pp 33–35, and contrast N MacCormick *Legal Right and Social Democracy* (1982) ch 8.

1078. Recognition of active rights. However that may be, it is also true that in the case of any fully self-conscious rational agent, proper respect for that being includes recognition of the person as one capable of effectual action. A part of the insult historically offered to slaves and (only a little less grievously) to women was precisely a withholding of such recognition either entirely or in large measure. Among the most basic goods of personality is that of one's recognition as a responsibly acting subject. In this light, facultative provisions of law, whether simply acknowledging one's free and responsible agency or enabling one effectually to engage in and accomplish legal transactions, are properly considered also as right-conferring. In this sense, indeed, the facultative theory correctly identifies a feature central to the rights held by persons of full status. But still it mistakes the part for the whole in that it overlooks the purely passive aspect of the rights vested even in persons of full status and capacity. It would surely be Pickwickian to suppose that a sane adult's right to life is constituted by the power to demand (or waive) remedies in the event of wrongful actions causing death. Or is it thought that there was no right to life in the days when the maxim *actio personalis moritur cum persona* ruled and no remedy for wrongful death could transmit to successors[1]?

1 See *Smith v Duncan Stewart & Co Ltd* 1960 SC 329, 1961 SLT 2, and also now the Damages (Scotland) Act 1976 (c 13), s 2.

1079. Rights bearing on conduct. This discussion of passive and active aspects of rights indicates that rights can always be considered as bearing on conduct. They may bear on the conduct of persons other than the right-holder, and here rights are passive in form: rights to be treated in certain ways; rights not to be treated in other ways. Sometimes rights of this sort have been called 'rights *stricto sensu*', or 'claims' or 'claim-rights' or 'rights of recipience'[1]. Each such usage being subject to objections of real weight[2], it is here suggested that the term 'passive rights' be adopted to signify the particular types of right here in view. The point is that such a right is a right that some other person act or refrain from acting in a certain way towards the right-holder. Necessarily, the relevant act or abstention is obligatory for (or categorically required of) the other person. But it is not necessarily the case that a relevant other person is ascertainable whenever a right of this sort vests in a given person. For example, under the Succession (Scotland) Act 1964, the children of an intestate deceased have from the moment of his or her death a right to be given equal shares of the intestate estate[3]. This right has in due course to be honoured by an executor. But until one is confirmed, there is no individual upon whom it is yet obligatory to pay out the shares to the children.

1 See W N Hohfeld *Fundamental Legal Conceptions* (1923, ed W W Cook) chs 1, 2, where 'claim' is suggested as a possible alternative to 'right' in what Hohfeld considers its strictly correct sense, namely as correlative with 'duty'. 'Claim-right' is a term coined by some followers and critics of Hohfeld with the same sense. For a thorough survey of Hohfeld scholarship, see W J Kamba 'Legal Theory and Hohfeld's Analysis of a Legal Right' 1974 JR 249. A powerful restatement of the value of Hohfeldian analysis as a model both for legal and for ethical studies is C A Wellman *A Theory of Rights* (1985). Nevertheless, it is here submitted that objections to Hohfeld's typology such as those stated by Alan White as cited in note 2 below justify the present attempt to set out a new analytical approach. D D Raphael's terminology of 'rights of recipience' as contrasted with 'rights of action' (see 'Human Rights Old and New' in D D Raphael (ed) *Political Theory and the Rights of Man* (1967) pp 54–67) is also criticised there; and from a legal point of view 'right of action' is more suggestive of a remedial right than of what is here called an 'active right'. For the terminology and the idea, the present text owes much to M Dalgarno 'Reid's Natural Jurisprudence: the Language of Rights and Duties' in V Hope (ed) *Philosophers of the Scottish Enlightenment* (1984) pp 13–31.
2 For a thoroughgoing critique of these usages based on rigorous linguistic analysis, see A R White *Rights* (1984).
3 Succession (Scotland) Act 1964 (c 41), ss 2(1)(a), 6.

1080. Passive rights and correlative duties. It is sometimes said that passive rights always have 'correlative' duties[1]. But the example just given shows why any such thesis about correlativity has to be taken with some caution. For sometimes, when rights are conferred expressly by legislation on persons fulfilling certain qualifying conditions, we must envisage the exaction of duties from relevant others as consequential upon conferment of the right. In other cases, it is the general prohibiting of some kind of conduct — for example conduct wilfully, recklessly, or negligently endangering life — which entails the existence in persons generally of a right not to be killed by wilful, reckless or negligent actions of anyone else. And sometimes, where statutes impose statutory duties, it becomes a matter of anxious inquiry whether the intendment of the legislation properly understood was to confer rights as well as imposing duties.

What should be said is that essential to the existence of every passive right is either a prior or a resultant requirement on classes or individuals to act or abstain in favour of persons who qualify as holders of such a right. It is in this way that passive rights are properly seen as rights in regard to conduct; for that to which they have regard is the obligatoriness of acts or abstentions by others as necessary to securing some good for or interest of the right-holder.

1 See eg W N Hohfeld *Fundamental Legal Conceptions* (1923, ed W W Cook), for whom this is essential to them. The present criticisms of this view are counter-criticised in C A Wellman *A Theory of Rights* (1985) and N E Simmonds *Central Issues in Jurisprudence* (1986).

1081. Rights and personal conduct. The other sense in which rights may have regard to conduct is where that to which they have regard is the conduct of the right-holder himself or herself. Rights to do and rights not to do, and rights to do or not to do as one pleases, are obvious types of such active rights. The simpler form of active right is that sometimes called a 'liberty' or (misleadingly by W N Hohfeld) a 'privilege' or (misleadingly in legal terms by D D Raphael) a 'right of action'[1]. Here 'active right' is the preferred usage. Essential to the existence of such a right is the possession of capacity-responsibility together with absence of or exemption from any legal provision categorically requiring contrary conduct. Its not being obligatory for me to *v* is a condition of my having a right to refrain from *v*-ing; and its not being obligatory for me to refrain from *v*-ing is a condition of my having a right to *v*. In both cases, my possession of capacity-responsibility is a condition of my having any such a right; and for given instances of a right to *v*, further conditions and qualifications may have to be satisfied in order for it to be *my* right to *v*; for example *my* right to admit visitors to a particular building.

1 W N Hohfeld suggests 'privilege' (*Fundamental Legal Conceptions* (1923, ed W W Cook)), and D D Raphael suggests 'right of action' ('Human Rights Old and New' in D D Raphael (ed) *Political Theory and the Rights of Man* (1967)). For 'liberty', see G L Williams 'The Concept of Legal Liberty' in R S Summers (ed) *Essays in Legal Philosophy* (1968) p 121; cf J T Cameron 'Two Jurisprudential Case Notes' 1964 JR 155-158. For criticisms, see A R White *Rights* (1984).

1082. Rights and the absence of legal requirements. It is sometimes said that the law does not in any sense confer a right to *v* if all that is the case is some absence of law on the matter — that is, absence of a legal requirement in the opposite sense. Scots law containing no provisions whatever concerning entry upon the Moon, can it with any seriousness be said that Mr Neil Armstrong had under Scots law a right to land upon the Moon and walk about it as he chose? Further, it may be doubted whether in any sense, except, perhaps, some curious and Pickwickian sense, an absence of law amounts to a 'securing' of some 'good' to anybody.

Such objections, however, overlook certain points of some importance. First, they overlook the point that recognition of a person's active capacity is a precondition of anything's being deemed any sort of an act of a person; and such a recognition is undeniably a positive matter of positive law. Secondly, they overlook the point that whether or not foreigners count is of real significance in all systems of law, one by no means unimportant in view of any possible concern about human rights. Thirdly, and above all, they overlook the challengeability in principle of any act in any court. If we envisage some crank suing Mr Armstrong in a Scottish court for damage done by trespass upon the Moon, the absence of any prohibition in Scots law entails a (passive) right in Mr Armstrong that the action against him be summarily dismissed. But precisely this passive right is what 'secures' it to him that he may if he chooses — so far as Scots law goes — land on and walk about the Moon just as he likes. And so in all less fanciful or trivial cases. The liability of a person of full capacity to be judged as and sanctioned as a wrongdoer in case of any infringement of a legal requirement is quite properly balanced by a right to do whatever is not prohibited or to refrain from whatever is not required under legal rules and principles. And the protection which law does and should grant here is one's entitlement to judgment in one's favour whenever any actings are seriously but incorrectly challenged as wrongful. Further, the law does and must recognise one's active capacity (capacity-responsibility) precisely as being a capacity to have and to exercise active rights, and to have them declared as such when appropriate.

Whatever verb one substitutes for v, then, having a right to v or having a right not to v is conditional upon there being no contrary legal requirement. It does not follow, of course, that everything one does within one's (active) rights is a proper or admirable thing to do either morally or even legally. A part of the point of insisting upon the legal existence of active rights is that they create an area of personal discretion within which one cannot be called to account for doing the wrong thing[1]. All that is essential is that there be no contrary requirement. In a given case, this may be quite compatible with one's having a duty to do what one is not required not to do. It is a far from trivial truth that I can and should have a right to do whatever it is my duty to do; although one must here note that this holds good only provided that my duty in a given case is not overridden or cancelled by some higher order requirement. A soldier has no right to commit murder even if commanded to do so by his commanding officer; for in this case the normal duty to obey one's commander is overridden by the prior requirement of respect for human rights. Since the duties of an office are often accompanied by a sense of the honour of fulfilling that office, it is by no means surprising to find people so often speaking of what it is their 'right and duty' to do or — even more commonly, perhaps — to say.

---

1 For a discussion of the idea that, morally speaking, having a right to do something would be an empty idea if it did not make it possible for one to be able to act wrongly without being called to account for it, see J Waldron *Theories of Rights* (1984), Introduction.

1083. Rights and powers distinguished. Furthermore, where v is a verb signifying some legal transaction or act-in-the-law, one is properly said to have the right to v only if one is the person or a person authorised or empowered in law to v, and if one infringes no legal requirement in doing so. We must note that some exercises of power can be valid but wrongful, as where A having validly contracted to sell a piece of land to B proceeds to convey the same piece of land to C under a subsequent contract of sale, C acting in good faith and with no notice of B's prior right. Here A acts wrongfully towards B; but the conveyance, albeit not rightfully executed, is valid and effectual in C's favour. And there can be other cases in the sale of goods where a person has power to transfer property in goods without having the right to sell them — for example on account of having acquired them by fraud, and thus under a voidable title[1]. This sufficiently indicates that powers are not themselves rights, although one can only have a right to exercise a given power provided one has that power, and provided that the exercise in question is not on some ground a wrongful one[2].

1 On this point about unrightful exercises of power in general, see J Raz 'Voluntary Obligations and Normative Powers' (1972) 46 Aristotelian Society Supplementary Volume pp 79–102. As to the sale of goods, see the Sale of Goods Act 1979 (c 54), ss 21(2), 23, 25, and cf *MacLeod v Kerr* 1965 SC 253, 1965 SLT 358.
2 See J Raz *Practical Reason and Norms* (1975).

1084. Acting 'within one's rights'. The idea of being or of acting 'within one's rights' pertains to active rights. So long as one exercises any available legal powers in observation of all the conditions and hypothetical requirements governing the exercise of the power, and so long as one avoids committing any legal wrong, one is 'within one's rights' — as was, for example, said of Sir Stephen Gatty when he called up his bond on Maclaine of Lochbuie's estates in Mull, Lochbuie being then on active service in the trenches in Flanders. 'I confess I think the case a hard one,' said Lord Dunedin, 'but I think the pursuers are within their rights'[1]. In similar vein Lord Atkinson said: 'I do not think . . . that the conduct of Sir Stephen Gatty is very commendable, but at all events he cannot be deprived of his legal rights'[2]. These observations tie back in with the opening section of this title, in which the point was made that the law is primarily concerned to settle minimal requirements of conduct rather than the higher or even the most mediocre levels of what is 'commendable'. It is an important protection of a significant human good that one should be free from the law's coercion and entitled to exercise one's rights provided no wrong is done, and even if one fails to act commendably.

1 *Gatty v Maclaine* 1921 SC (HL) 1 at 10, 1921 1 SLT 51 at 56.
2 1921 SC (HL) 1 at 11, 1951 1 SLT 51 at 56.

1085. Rights contrasted with freedom, liberty and privilege. How is the concept of active right and of 'acting within one's rights' connected with the concepts of 'freedom', 'liberty' and 'privilege', with each of which it has occasionally been identified? There is certainly a normative use of the idea of 'being free to *v*' which is practically equivalent to that of 'having a right to *v*'. I am not free (in law, in morals, or by whatever normative standard one is judging) to do whatever I have no right to do; that is, whatever is obligatory on me or required of me not to do. Being free to *v*, accordingly, is governed entirely by the absence of contrary requirement, and no element of power enters into this concept. What I am free to do is not the same as what I am able to do, and *vice versa*. Sometimes 'being at liberty to *v*' is used as identical with being free to do it. But 'liberty' (*pace* Professor G Ll Williams[1]), even in law, normally implies an element of choice. To be at liberty in respect of *v*-ing requires being free either to *v* or not-*v* as one chooses. Furthermore, both freedom and liberty have vitally important non-normative senses. The constraints of legal requirement are one kind of constraint, but there are others, such as physical or psychological coercion or captivity. Being a free person, or being at liberty *sans phrase*, implies an absence of the actuality of coercion and captivity, and also an absence of threat of or liability to them. Hence to be (left at) liberty is the possible subject matter of a fundamentally important passive right. The use of 'liberty' in a plurality of senses, sometimes as the name for an active right and sometimes as the subject matter of a passive right, is inevitably misleading, and hence is not here recommended[2].

As for 'privilege', this would again be misleadingly used if used as denoting an active right *simpliciter*. Privileges, as Alan R White has shown[3], are positions of special advantage or favour, the content of special legal provisions for persons in special positions. Some privileges are indeed special exemptions from legal duties or requirements, as in the case of qualified or absolute privilege in defamation, or in the case of evidentiary privileges where one has a right to withhold items of evidence production of which is normally compellable. But other privileges, such as some of the privileges of Parliament and members of Parliament, are in the way of exceptional passive rights — and breach of parliamentary privilege normally involves infringement of such a right.

1 G Ll Williams 'The Concept of Legal Liberty' in R S Summers (ed) *Essays in Legal Philosophy* (1968) p 121.
2 For a fuller statement of this account of liberty, see N MacCormick *Legal Right and Social Democracy* (1982) ch 3.
3 See A R White *Rights* (1984) ch 11.

1086. Correlatives of active rights. Whether or not there are 'correlatives' of active rights is a discussable question. Hohfeld, who analysed the present topic in terms of person-to-person relations, supposed that wherever some individual A has a 'privilege' to *v* there must be another individual B who has no right that A refrain from *v*-ing[1]. This, surely, is correlativism carried to absurd extremes. Necessarily, if someone has a right that A refrain from *v*-ing, it is wrong for A to *v*; and if it is wrong for A to *v* then A cannot have a right (active right) to *v* — indeed, as it will be commonly said, 'A has no right to *v*'. So then conversely if A does have a right (active right) to *v*, then no one can have a (passive) right to his abstention from *v*-ing. But to say that no-one has such a right is surely different from ascribing to each of B, C, D . . . X, Y, Z etc a distinct 'no-right' that A should *v*. Legal usages which do violence to the common sense of ordinary speech should be adopted only where some striking gain in conceptual clarity is achieved. Here, nothing could be further from the case.

1 See W N Hohfeld *Fundamental Legal Conceptions* (1923, ed W W Cook) ch 1.

1087. Liability and power. The same goes for the supposition that 'liability' is a simple correlative of 'power'[1]. Especially in the case of official (public) powers, the idea that power is a one-to-one relation between some A and some B is evidently fatuous, and the idea that I have a liability to receive large money gifts from each of the millionaires in the world is nonsensical even though each of them is legally and economically able to make large gifts just as they please. Liability is a matter of the conditional divestability of rights, whether active or passive; and the conditional subjection of a person to duties at another's prescription. That failing to wear a seat belt while driving a car makes a person liable to a penalty means that whoever is proved to have done so can be validly deprived of the right not to pay money to the state; just as one who is liable to imprisonment can validly be deprived of the right to liberty, and so on. Whoever is in these positions is also exposed to the legal possibility of an imposed duty — the duty to pay the fine or to go to jail in obedience to some valid judicial order. In private law also, one's liabilities exist precisely in those cases where a duty to perform, pay or abstain is conditional upon somebody else's demand. In this sense, the law of obligations is also a law of liabilities.

1 See W N Hohfeld *Fundamental Legal Conceptions* (1923, ed W W Cook) ch 1.

1088. Passive rights conjoined with active rights of choice. Here again we are reminded that, in the case of persons of full (active) capacity, it is normally the case that passive rights are conjoined with active rights of choice — rights to demand or forgo observance of one's passive rights in one's own free discretion; and likewise in case of infringements of right, one has a right to demand or waive remedial action. Where such a demand is rejected, one's final sanctioning right is the right (and power) to sue for an appropriate remedy in an appropriate court. Here we return again to points taken by the facultative theory of rights — the passive right is only a right truly in so far as it is protected by such active rights. The error of this view has already been demonstrated; but the equipage of ancillary active rights and powers necessary to making effectual any passive right is a matter not to be overlooked; in the case of persons of restricted capacity, substitute enforcers have to be found, whose 'right and duty' it is to marshal remedial powers in support of the primary and remedial passive rights of the incapacitated. From a legal point of view, passive rights without effectual remedies would certainly be well described as 'imperfect' rights.

1089. Non-divestability of rights. A final and vitally important feature of the legal protection involved in having rights is that of their relative non-divestability[1]. This depends upon an absence of power on the part of others to divest the right-holder of either the primary right or its ancillary rights. In the case of constitutional entrenchments and international treaties guaranteeing human rights, such disempowerments are either absolute and universal, or at least cancellable only on stringent conditions. In other cases, all rights may be subjected to some liability to divestment, for example by legislation; but the range of persons enabled to divest is small and the conditions for allowing divestment fairly strict (even if only enshrined in constitutional conventions). This 'immunity against divesting' is a vital feature of that legal protection of individuals' goods or interests which is of the essence of rights. One can even conceive of a grading of the relative strength of rights according to the range, and to the liability to cancellation, of protective immunities against divesting by the unilateral acts of others.

   1 See A M Honoré 'Rights of Exclusion and Immunities against Divesting' (1959–60) 34 Tulane Law Review 453.

1090. Waiver, surrender and transfer of rights. Although it is commonly the case, as noted, that rights of persons of full status can be waived or even voluntarily surrendered or, in some cases, transferred to others by unilateral or bilateral act, there are some rights which not even such a person can either waive or abandon or alienate. Such are the right not to be enslaved and the statutory right to safe conditions of work in various forms of employment[1]. Here the disempowerment of the right-holder is in fact a further strengthening of the legal protection afforded to persons in respect of that right. That such disabling laws can strengthen rights must somewhat embarrass the 'faculty' theory of rights.

   1 Cf N MacCormick 'Rights in Legislation' in P M S Hacker and J Raz (eds) *Law, Morality and Society* (1979). As to safe conditions of work, see the Health and Safety at Work etc Act 1974 (c 37), Pt I (ss 1–54).

(2) RIGHTS IN REGARD TO STATES OF BEING AND STATES OF AFFAIRS

1091. Introduction. Hitherto we have considered rights as they have regard to the conduct of the right-holder (active rights) or of another person or persons (passive rights). All such rights can be stated in relatively specific terms; for once one has specified the person or class of persons in whom the right vests, and the act or type of act to which it is a right, and the person or persons or class against whom it avails, the right is as exactly specified as can be, subject always to the possible vagueness or open texture of language used in specifying acts and persons. All such rights are rights to *v* or be *v*-ed (or their negations), where *v* is a verb.

Now it is necessary to turn to rights of the form 'rights to *n*', where *n* stands for a noun or noun-phrase. Obvious cases are those of the 'right to life' or the 'right to a job' or the 'right to holidays with pay' or the right to 'freedom of conscience' or 'of association' or the 'right to privacy' or the 'right to fairness'. Such rights as these are all rights to, or in regard to, states of being — being alive, being in employment, being free to believe what seems true (or what one's fathers taught, or what one has always believed, or just anything) in matters of religion and morals, being free to associate with others who have the same freedom or being secluded from others; or they are rights in respect of states of affairs, such as statutory provisions under which employers make provision for annual paid vacations, or whatever amounts in given circumstances to fair treatment or 'fair play'.

1092. Difficulty of defining 'right to life'. Rights in regard to states of being and states of affairs are vague and unspecific for reasons quite other than the open-textured quality of language[1] (or, at least, additional to it). For the states of being or of affairs which we have mentioned are complex ones, especially in relation to the ways of acting which are required in order to secure respect for these rights. Even to take the ostensibly simplest of these: life — what is called for by way of respect for life? Does A H Clough's satirical couplet go to the heart of the matter:

> 'Thou shalt not kill but needst not strive
> Officiously to keep alive'?

Or is some degree of carefulness for the lives of others also required here? If there is a right to life, is there then even a duty to ensure medical aid and minimal income or food supplies for the destitute, sick and starving? And if so, what elaborate bureaucratic structures in the way of health services and social services must one create or support in order to avoid a culpable failure in respect for the right to life? It is obvious at a glance that such points are all disputable. The 'right to life' is one instance of what have been called 'essentially contested concepts', exactly because reasonable persons can reasonably support rival conceptions of what this concept really means or amounts to, subject to some restriction in the range of such conceptions, such as they must be related to the furtherance of 'life' in some sense of that also contested concept[2]. In this respect, the abortion controversy is obviously relevant.

1 On this phenomenon of 'open texture' in language, see H L A Hart *The Concept of Law* (1961) ch 7.
2 See W B Gallie 'Essentially Contested Concepts' (1955–56) 56 Procs Aristotelian Soc 169 — but probably not all of Gallie's criteria of essential contestedness apply here. For example, it is hardly a part of the point of appeals to the right to life that there should be dispute as to what this is. As for the contrast of 'concept' and 'conception', see J Rawls *A Theory of Justice* (1972) pp 4–6, and R M Dworkin *Taking Rights Seriously* (1978) ch 4. This distinction is not intended by those who draw it to express *essential* contestability.

1093. Difficulty of defining 'right to work'. The 'right to work' is at least as contested a concept. For a start, one can never be quite sure whether 'work' is here a verb or a noun, and even if it is a noun, should greater stress be given to maximising opportunities of job-seeking in market conditions which support only 'real jobs' or, rather, to using state or other collective agencies to the end of preserving or extending existing forms of employment under some protection from the perturbations of market forces. Proponents of each of these radically opposed views, focal as they are to the contemporary disputes of the political parties, may all be passionately sincere in their commitment to a 'right to jobs' or 'right to work'. But they do not share a common conception of what that right requires. Accordingly, they go on to disagree whether trade unions are on the whole beneficial towards or obstacles to securing all employable persons in enjoyment of this right. In turn, the question whether unions are really conspiracies in restraint of trade or are really bastions of the 'right to work' becomes entangled in the ambiguities of freedom of association.

1094. Difficulty of defining 'right to privacy'. As a final illustration of this point, it could be noted that some years ago the question of a 'right to privacy' was referred to the Younger Committee for consideration. The committee, having rightly noted that there are many rival versions of such a right, all vying for legislative or judicial adoption, concluded that the right was indefinable and thus not a fit topic for legislation in and of itself. This is a good case of deriving false conclusions from true premises. That there are disputes between rival conceptions of such a right is actually a reason for seeking to give it definite import by intelligent legislation based on some coherent conception of the right, not a reason for rejecting it as indefinable[1].

1 See N MacCormick 'A Note upon Privacy' (1973) 89 LQR 23, and 'Privacy: A Question of Definition?' (1974) 1 BJLS 74–78, both in criticism of the *Report of the Committee on Privacy* (the Younger Report) (Cmnd 5012) (1972).

1095. Necessity for specific quantification. What this tale in fact tells us is that rights to states of being or of affairs, while focussing on commonly admitted and perhaps in some cases undeniable human goods (namely good states of being or of affairs) do so in a necessarily inexact way. Thus in their implementation and concretisation through legislation or the judicial process, or both, they have to be specifically quantified in terms of more exact and specific provisions. A large part of this quantification and specification can and properly does take the form of rights in regard to conduct, both active and passive. Thus for example the (active) right to self-defence under attack is one concrete derivative of the abstract background right to life; and the fact that it is so justifies the way in which the right to defend oneself is restricted to taking only such steps as are reasonable in relation to the danger threatened. And the (active) right to procure an abortion can be both derived from and restricted by respect for right to life and to physical integrity, namely those of mother and of foetus (to the extent that we consider the foetus as having some passive capacity).

Similar competitions and specific resolutions of them arise in case of the right of free speech and of free association. So the derivative specific active and passive rights of individuals — to speak but not to be outraged or insulted or defamed or betrayed by others' speech; to associate, but not to be coerced by the associativeness of others — are rights which give concrete and always open-to-dispute resolutions of issues which have to be resolved if the right of free speech or of free association is to be given any more than merely rhetorical effect in the law.

1096. The place of abstract things in law. Perhaps the rights we have referred to never have more than rhetorical effect in law? Should we really reject these rights to states of being and of affairs from jurisprudence, assigning them purely to the realms of political and moral philosophy? No. For to do so would both be unfaithful to the tradition of fundamental human rights which, even in a United Kingdom which so far resists constitutional entrenchment of them, enjoy persuasive standing in the law at least since the accession of the United

Kingdom to the European Convention for the Protection of Human Rights and Fundamental Freedoms (1950). Although the provisions of the convention are, by the standard of domestic Bills of Rights and their like, remarkably precise and determinate, they are (it is submitted) best read as attempting to guarantee in fairly broad and general terms certain crucially important states of being and of affairs.

Further, and no less crucially from the standpoint of Scots law, it would be both to misunderstand and to underplay the important if indirect role which fundamental principles play in law, most particularly in our law. Of course a commitment in principle to such things as the protection of life, full employment and privacy, and to secure every individual so far as possible in enjoyment of these and like goods requires to be concretised or 'cashed out' in terms of more detailed provisions, including quite specific active and passive rights in regard to conduct. These are enshrined in the fine grain of a multitude of legal precedents, or in the even more bewildering multifariousness of statutes in such fields as employment or welfare law. But the principle as a guiding standard survives through changes at the level of detailed provisions and makes sense of them in their interplay. One is perhaps tempted to take the view that the 'right to life' or 'right to privacy' is no more than a name for a bundle of such provisions, and indeed 'bundle' theories of rights have never been in short supply. But this metaphor is unhelpful since it overlooks the quality of the abstract right as constituting the point or aim of the detailed provisions and thus expressing their organising principle, an organising principle or concept which survives shifts and changes at the level of detailed provisions for and conceptions of the right. So abstract rights to states of being or of affairs can play a part even in positive law, notably at the level of reasoning about basic principles of the law. A particularly clear illustration is that of the right to fairness and to a fair hearing, which has so often been found to be interstitially present even in the most arid stretches of detailed administrative provisions in public law[1].

They also provide a useful introduction to the idea of rights to things, as entirely distinct from rights to abstract states of being and of affairs, but as (crucially) sharing the feature of non-analysability in terms of simple 'bundles'.

---

1 On the right to a fair hearing, see eg *Malloch v Aberdeen Corpn* 1971 SC (HL) 85, 1971 SLT 245. The term 'abstract right' in this context is borrowed from R M Dworkin *Taking Rights Seriously* (1978) ch 4, but it is used in a somewhat different, and perhaps more exactly defined, sense.

1097. Rights to things. Hitherto, in considering 'rights to *n*', where '*n*' stands for a noun, we have considered only the possibility of quantifying the variable '*n*' in terms of abstract nouns signifying states of being and of affairs. But we can put other kinds of nouns and noun-phrases in place of *n* — for example 'right to Bucephalus (a horse)', 'right to 100 shares in the Carbolic Smoke-Ball Co Ltd', 'right to [the house at] 21 Encyclopaedia Circus', or whatever. In these cases, we are dealing with 'things' or *res* in the specific legal sense. Things are conceived as durable objects existing separately from and independently of persons, subject to being used, possessed and enjoyed by persons, and thus capable of being transferred from one person to another without loss of identity. 'Durability' requires temporal co-ordinates — there must be a space of time between some time $t1$ and some later time $t2$, or a space overlapping the $t1/t2$ interval, during which a given thing is conceived to exist. In the case of incorporeal things, only temporal duration is required for existence. In the case of corporeal things, each thing has spatial position as well, that is, at any given moment of its existence each thing has a particular spatial location; and in the case of immoveable corporeal things, this position is unchanging (that is, unchanging in its terrestrial geographical co-ordinates, subject to such specialities as *alluvio* and the like).

It is easy to suppose that corporeal things have existence naturally, while incorporeal ones exist only by legal fiction. 'Fiction' here, as so often, is a notion more misleading than helpful[1]. For while it is true that the existence, identity, and mutual separateness of incorporeal things such as copyrights, patents, company shares, servitude rights, contractual benefits and the like depend entirely on conventions of thought and speech constituted by legal rules, it cannot be supposed that the identity and separateness of corporeal things is something utterly independent of human conventions[2]. This is more spectacularly obvious in the case of immoveable (in Scotland often misleadingly referred to as 'heritable'[3]) property, each lot of which is identifiable only through elaborate conventions of land-measurement, boundary allocation, and co-ordinate-dependent naming. (Consider all the presuppositions involved in making use of '21 Encyclopaedia Circus' as an intelligible name for a fictitious subject of property rights, 'fiction' here being an appropriate concept: all these presuppositions are in real cases the real conventions for defining and identifying a specific immoveable corporeal *res* the subject of somebody's rights of, or rights akin to, property.)

And this individuation, naming or describing, and in some cases making, of moveable things is also conventionally constituted; *a fortiori* in the case of fungible corporeal moveables which are subject to being weighed and measured-out, the units and practices of weighing and measuring being conventional through and through. No doubt carboniferous strata are present in the earth's crust 'naturally', in the specific sense of 'independently of human action or convention'. 'A ton of Bilston Glen coal' does not, however, enjoy the same 'natural' existence. Of course, it is a natural object in the sense of being neither miraculous in its provenance nor unusual in its collocation. But the same is true of a block of shares in the Bank of Scotland. All the 'things' of law have their 'thinghood' or 'reality' defined by or under law, and, beyond law, by very basic cultural conventions. The modes of existence and identity of things are, by law, crucially different both as between moveables and immoveables and as between corporeals and incorporeals. The position in Scotland is further complicated by survival of an essentially feudal concept of 'heritability', which is not identical with 'immoveability'. It is certainly the case that corporeal things are conceived as part of the material world and as being some of its constituents, and so they have a radically different place among 'institutional facts'[4] from that of incorporeals. But that is a difference quite distinct from any wisely drawn differentiation of the real and the fictional or fictitious.

1 For a general discussion, see L L Fuller *Legal Fictions* (1967). J C Gray in *Nature and Sources of the Law* (2nd edn, 1921) distinguishes 'historical' from 'dogmatic' fictions. Like him, we may take the latter to be an essential part of legal thought; unlike him, we should reject the term 'fiction' as misleading. The error perhaps goes back to Bentham. For the view that when we use nouns otherwise than for referring to material objects we must be referring to fictitious ones, see C K Ogden *Bentham's Theory of Fictions* (2nd edn, 1951). This is an error both about nouns and about reference, as well as being rather arbitrary ontologically.

2 See paras 1113 ff below. See also N MacCormick 'Law as Institutional Fact' (1974) 90 LQR 102, and N MacCormick and O Weinberger *An Institutional Theory of Law* (1986) Introduction, ch 2.

3 *Corporeal Moveables — Some Problems of Classification* (Scot Law Com Consultative Memorandum no. 26 (1976)) at 21, 22, quotes relevant criticism and concludes that 'nothing would be lost, and much in the way of clarity would be gained, were "immoveable" to replace "heritable" in legal usage'. Except in relation to titles of honour, 'the category of "heritage" seems now obsolete or at least obsolescent in Scots law'.

4 See paras 1113 ff below.

1098. Things and abstract states of affairs distinguished. It is in their identity, mutual separateness, human possessability, and durability as between different possessors that the things of the law differ from abstract states of affairs. Hence rights to them, and even rights *in* them have a specificity and exactness quite absent in the case of the abstract rights. There is however this resemblance between rights *in* things and rights to states of being and of affairs, that both are complex and are the ground of more detailed provisions including active and passive rights in regard to conduct. Here, however, begins the task of differentiating rights *to* and rights *in* things in a technical sense. That distinction requires distinct treatment in the next part of the title[1].

1 See paras 1099 ff below.

(3) RIGHTS TO AND IN THINGS; PERSONAL AND REAL RIGHTS

1099. Rights to things; *jus ad rem.* A 'right *to* a thing', or '*jus ad rem*' in the traditional usage of the civilians[1], is an instance of what we have here been calling a 'right in regard to conduct', specifically a passive right to be given the thing or an active right to take it in default of voluntary giving by the obligant. In another well known usage, such a right is a personal right, good against some particular possessor of the thing in issue. Such rights commonly arise under some conventional or other voluntary obligation, such as contract or promise, where the creditor has a right that the obligant give or transfer some thing or some quantified lot of fungible things to him or her. Where there is a failure to fulfil this obligation, and if helping oneself to the thing is either unlawful or impossible, one is in such a case left to one's remedies for breach of obligation — including here the possibility of specific implement of, for example, a contract of sale.

1 Stair *Institutions* II,1,1 (speaking of God's gift to man of 'dominium or lordship over all . . . creatures'): 'This gift . . . was to mankind . . . and it did not import a present right of property, but only a right or power to appropriate by possession, or *jus ad rem*, not *jus in re*'. See also Erskine *Institute* III,1,2, and Bell *Principles* Introduction, para 3. For an incomparable modern restatement, see J M Halliday *Conveyancing Law and Practice in Scotland* vol 1 (1985) paras 1-09-1-13. Confusingly, common lawyers are apt to speak (with dubious latinity) of 'rights *in personam*' as contradistinguished from 'rights *in rem*'. This usage is now current in Scotland also.

1100. Event giving rise to right. The vesting of such rights to things always requires some particular title[1] over and above possession of the appropriate (at least passive) capacity. Some fact or event must obtain or occur whereby *this* person has a right to (receive, be given) *this* thing. The same fact or event sometimes serves to identify a particular other person or persons whose obligation it is to give or transfer the thing; this is so in the case of contracts, promises and the like. It is also the case in relation to beneficial rights under a trust, created under the same instrument as appoints trustees and defines their duties to and in respect of the beneficiaries. In other cases, for example rights of succession, most notably intestate succession, the event of death and the fact of relationship which vests in A a right to some share of D's estate does not itself identify any executor whose duty it is to satisfy those and other rights; even in testate succession, executors nominate require to be judicially confirmed, and are under no legal duty to accept the office of executor. Moreover, in so far as there are 'legal rights' of the spouse and family members to be satisfied even in a case of testate succession, that which vests those rights is not the same as that which appoints executors; for the will may even purport to override or simply ignore the legal rights. In any event, since things (as distinct from limbs and bodily organs, which become things in law only on being severed from a living body) do not have necessary links with particular persons, it follows that a person can have a legal right *to* this or that thing as against some other person only if he or she has some title which in law confers that right to that thing. And in any competition with any other, that title must be proved; and by that same title that same other must also be obligated to transfer the thing as sought; or some other title binding that person to that performance must be proved.

  1 See D M Walker *Principles of Scottish Private Law* (3rd edn, 1982) vol 1, ch 1.3, pp 38, 39.

1101. Rights in things; real rights. *A fortiori* in the case of rights *in* things, that is, real rights[1], such as ownership: these do not attach to persons naturally, nor do the things themselves. Even one's gloves, unlike one's hands, have to be put on, and can be quite as casually taken off. Only given some suitable title, therefore, does a real right in any particular thing vest in a particular person. By 'title' is meant some act, event or state of facts (or some combination of any two or all of these) implicating a particular person having particular capacity (at least passive, but normally also active and transactive) and having reference to a particular thing. Legal provisions of a sort which we may call 'investitive' or 'institutive' have the effect that for any person P having the capacity C, and for any thing T of type t, if the acts, events or facts A, E, F occur so as to implicate P and with reference to T, then the real right RR in T vests in P[2]. What constitutes title to a right of a particular type (ownership, tenancy, security rights, servitude rights etc) in a thing of a particular type (moveable or immoveable, corporeal or incorporeal, heritable or otherwise) is precisely the legally given set of acts, events and/or facts which suffice to vest that right in a particular person having given capacities[3].

  1 See D M Walker *Principles of Scottish Private Law* (3rd edn, 1982) vol 3, ch 5.1, p 4.
  2 See J Raz *The Concept of a Legal System* (2nd edn, 1980) pp 175–183.
  3 Cf N MacCormick 'Law as Institutional Fact' (1974) 90 LQR 102, and para 1114 below.

1102. Title to thing: *occupatio* etc. The simplest type of title conceptually is that of initial acquisition by taking of possession of a thing[1]. The act necessarily relates to the specific thing, that of which possession is taken, and to a particular person, the one who also takes possession. The act can be performed by anyone with capacity-responsibility, and provided capacity for ownership exists, the person becomes owner by the act of *occupatio*. The same goes, subject to somewhat more complexity, in the case of other original modes of acquisition (of which Scots law recognises accession, as where ownership of the newborn foal goes along with that of the mare; alluvion, where new soil is gradually washed on to land by a river or by the sea; specification, where a new article is made by irreversible alteration of raw materials, ownership going to the maker; and confusion or commixtion, inextricable mixing of liquids or solids, giving rise to joint ownership of the mixture)[2]. Even in the case of *occupatio*, however, the act has to be an act of taking possession, namely of taking physical control with intent to act as owner of the thing[3]. And the act must occur in certain circumstances, namely those of the thing being of a type admitting of possessory title and of its not being currently in another's ownership.

  1 As to *occupatio*, see Justinian *Institutes* II,1,12, and Stair *Institutions* II,1,29,33.
  2 See eg T B Smith *A Short Commentary on the Law of Scotland* (1962) pp 524, 536–538.
  3 *Smith* pp 461–464.

1103. Derivative modes of acquisition. In the case of derivative modes of acquisition, there is yet further complexity in that two parties are involved, so here two persons have to have appropriate capacity, the transferor has to have some legally sufficient title[1] to transfer the right in issue, and any legally stipulated procedures (for example writing and registration of deeds or of title) must be observed. Further, in order that acquisition should be perfect and irreducible there must be an absence of such vitiating circumstances as fraud, force and fear, or error, and all required circumstances must hold good. So establishing title may require establishment of complex acts and facts in such a case. In cases of acquisition by intestate succession, if ever that operates to transfer rights automatically, as formerly in the case of the heir at law, title is constituted by facts — of relationship to the deceased — and events, namely that person's death.

> 1 By 'some legally sufficient title' in this context it is intended to cover actual title as an owner or satisfaction of any legal provisions whereby acquisition *a non domino* by a purchaser in good faith is facilitated.

1104. Real rights as beneficial legal relations. Even if all this sufficiently accounts for the concept of titles to real rights, it hardly elucidates the real rights themselves. As to that, one may make first a general and then some special points. First, as Stair points out, real rights concern things directly, but persons indirectly, so far as they have meddled with things[1]. Although stated specifically as to dominion, or ownership, Stair's point holds quite generally. Real rights are beneficial legal relations as between particular persons and particular things; they are beneficial in that they imply enjoyment by the holder of the real right of certain active rights to the use and enjoyment of things, coupled with passive rights not to be impeded in or deprived of that use and enjoyment by anyone else, and (in some degree) immunity against unilateral divestment[2]. So much for the 'beneficial legal relations' between person and thing. But what of the relationship to persons 'indirectly . . . as they have meddled with . . . things'? This follows from the fact that any invasion of the passive right of the holder of the real right by any person, or any challenge to his or her active rights (as in the case of a prohibition to pass along a servitude right of way), or any purported overriding of immunities against divesting (for example by a purported act of 'compulsory purchase', or confiscation), must be an invasion, challenge or overriding by some distinct other person, or group of ascertainable persons. And against that person remedial rights to damages, interdict or declarator hold good. Consequential upon the holding of a real right are rights and powers to obtain legal remedies against any person who, as Stair puts it, 'meddles' in any way with the thing (or, indeed, with the right, as in purported overridings of immunities against divesting).

> 1 Stair *Institutions* I,1,22.
> 2 See A M Honoré 'Rights of Exclusion and Immunities against Divesting' (1959–60) 34 Tulane Law Review 453.

1105. Real rights involving consequential rights and powers. Secondly, as to the special points about real rights: it is of the nature of each real right, whether of ownership, tenancy (in systems where this is a real right), security or servitude that it entails as its consequences the holding of specific active and passive rights to the thing, and powers to regulate and license its use by others (exercise of which powers may involve investment in others of rights *to*, but not *in*, the thing in question). Each real right has its own special set of consequential active and passive rights and powers; and what makes it a 'real' right is that each of the consequential active and passive rights with ancillary remedial rights holds good against anyone simply upon proof of title to the real right, without proof of any special title obliging the given party to act in such or such a way towards the right-holder. Further, however, the consequences of holding a real right have not all themselves the character of rights or powers. Some of them are burdens, having the character of duties and liabilities, that is of restrictions upon active rights of use and abuse, as under planning or zoning laws, or under sumptuary laws prohibiting conspicuous consumption, further to which there may also be restrictions upon or exceptions in given cases to the powers consequential upon the holding of a real right in some type of thing. Examples here are provided by restrictions upon alienation, for example under certain forms of entail of landed property, or under the laws imposing strict conditions upon hire-purchase and credit sale agreements. Despite such burdens and restrictions, however, it remains the case that the holding of real rights is on the whole and on strongly predominant balance advantageous to the right-holder in all normal and ordinary circumstances and cases.

1106. Effect on real right of variation of consequential rights and powers. Nevertheless, for any given generic real right, the specific and detailed consequential provisions in the way of rights and powers (including remedial rights and powers), and in the way of duties, liabilities and disabilities, are variable; nor do variations change either the conceptual quality of the real right nor the vesting of it in particular persons over particular things. Owners of land in Scotland did not cease to own the very pieces of land they owned in the preceding moment when at a given moment in time the Town and Country Planning (Scotland) Act 1947 (c 51) came into force. Nor was landownership then abolished in Scots law. Existing rights of ownership remained undisturbed; but some of their consequences, or incidents, to use Honoré's valuable term[1], were altered. Specifically, active rights of use of land were restricted to existing modes of use of given pieces of land; but owners were empowered to seek of local authorities planning permission for changes of use, permission which the local authorities were then empowered to grant under statutory conditions.

It can reasonably be said that such legislation constitutes a shift in the legislature's conception of the proper rights and liabilities of landownership. It cannot reasonably be said that the concept of (private) ownership of land is thereby excised from Scots law. This exhibits why the theory of real rights as 'bundles' of other rights, or of personal rights, one each against every other citizen of the world[2], is a wholly inept notion. Real rights are grounds for a variable and shifting set of consequential rights, powers, duties, liabilities and disabilities, the rights being at least in reasonable measure protected with immunities against unilateral divesting without the free consent of the right-holder. The ground remains conceptually the same even as the consequences vary, either by legislation or by private act of the right-holder, exercising one of his powers to change (active) rights of use of a thing, as when a landowner licenses another to enter his property.

1 See A M Honoré 'Ownership' in A M Guest (ed) *Oxford Essays in Jurisprudence* (1961) ch 5.
2 This is, in effect, Hohfeld's theory of 'rights *in rem*' as sets of 'multital' rights — what is spoken of as one's right is in truth a set of rights having the same content in favour of one person against each other person: see W N Hohfeld *Fundamental Legal Conceptions* (1923, ed W W Cook) ch 2. G Maher in 'The Rights and Wrongs of Vesting' (1986) 31 JLSS 396 argues also for the Hohfeld theory of real rights as 'multital rights'; this by way of a critique of G Gretton 'What is Vesting?' (1986) 31 JLSS 148. The present argument shows reasons for preferring, with Gretton, continued use of the concept of 'real rights', being indebted both to Gretton and to S C Styles 'Vesting and the Law of Property' (1989) 34 JLSS 338.

1107. Divestment by transfer or termination. What can be invested in a person can be also divested from that person. Divestment takes two forms: transfer of the right from one to another, so that A's divestment is B's investment; and termination of the right, which may occur by abandonment or dereliction of the thing and of the right in it, or by death, destruction or other cessation of the thing, or by reason of the right having come to the end of a fixed term, whether or not termination of the right at its term calls for the exercise of some power or powers by one or more parties. It is in terms of modes of divestment or termination that one can best distinguish rights of property or ownership from other real rights; for it is of the nature of such rights that they are divested only either by voluntary abandonment or by transfer to another, whether by voluntary act as in gift or sale; or by involuntary act, as on death or expropriation, and terminable only upon destruction of the thing or abandonment of the right. Wherever real rights with consequential active rights of use and enjoyment and power to regulate use and enjoyment by others exist in a legal system and have the permanent duration which is signified by divestitive and terminative provisions such as those just noted, there we may say that rights of property are recognised; and these are rights of private property.

1108. Rights with fixed or limited terms. Rights of private property contrast with rights, such as tenancies, which, albeit conferring rights of use and enjoyment and at least some powers to regulate use by others, have fixed terms: that is, which terminate at a fixed date and then divest from the holder without transference to another, albeit that this effect may require also notice to quit given by the landlord of the property, in the absence of which a tacit relocation, that is, investment of the tenant with a new term of tenancy rights, may be provided for by law. They contrast also with usufructuary rights, such as liferents, which, although lacking a fixed term, necessarily both divest and terminate upon the death of the liferenter, leaving the owner in fee with full unencumbered enjoyment of previously overridden property rights. A further contrast is with rights of real security ('standard securities', 'mortgages', 'hypothecs', 'pledges' [of moveables] and the like). These rights presuppose some obligation owed by a debtor D to a creditor C, for security of which D grants C appropriate rights in security over some property owned by D. Whether or not such a security right is (or has to be by law) for a fixed term within which D must fulfil his obligation, it is always the case that upon some stated default of D's in respect of the obligation, C then has a right either to invest in himself D's full unencumbered rights of ownership or to exercise powers over the property such as will enable him to secure satisfaction of the full pecuniary value of the defaulted obligation. Such events necessarily terminate the security-right, divesting C of it; while at the same time D is divested of ownership of the property, whether or not that is then vested in C.

It is clear that all tenancies, liferents and real securities presuppose ownership in the sense both that they are all created by exercise of powers vested in owners as such, and, once created, constitute encumbrances upon property in that they restrict, qualify or cancel rights of use and disposal which the owner, if unencumbered, would otherwise have. On the other hand, in commercial societies, among the economic advantages ownership secures are the capabilities to let out property to tenants at favourable rents and to borrow money for investment upon the security of the property. That one who has reaped the advantage of property in these ways may have fewer advantages left to reap is scarcely a cause for grief or concern; or for amendment of our definitions.

1109. Servitudes. Finally, let it be noted that servitude rights of way, of light, of support and the like, ' praedial servitudes', are necessarily also real rights and do also presuppose ownership of landed property. For the duty to afford free passage to persons or to light or to sustain support becomes an incident of proprietorship of the servient tenement whoever be the owner of it, while the right to pass and re-pass freely upon a path or roadway, to receive light unimpeded, to have one's building supported, or whatever, is in each case a right conditional upon ownership of the dominant tenement, and not capable of being severed therefrom save at the cost of becoming a purely personal right in favour of its current holder as against its present granter. Further, it is a particular feature of servitude rights that they are automatically terminated as such if dominant and servient tenements both come to be owned by the same person.

1110. Different types of real right distinguished. In distinguishing various types of real right, one must look at each in a broad way, to see what sort of legally secured advantage is involved. Ownership, tenancy and liferent all have in common that they look to securing a person in enjoyment and use of some thing or asset — or 'property', as we commonly say and have said here. Ownership is differentiated from tenancy and liferent by an absence of specific term, as indicated in what was said above about provisions for divestment or termination. That distinction established, it is then demonstrable how tenancy and liferent are derivative rights, creatable only by exercise of proprietorial powers. Rights of real security in effect conditionally secure to the right-holder the economic value of the use and enjoyment of the subjects of the security; for to them the security-holder will have a prior right (deriving from the real right he has) in the event of default and (in particular) bankruptcy of the owner. Servitude rights enhance the beneficial incidents of ownership of one piece of land at the cost of an exactly equal increase in the burdensome incidents of ownership of adjoining land, the 'servient tenement' or *praedium serviens.*

The concepts of ownership, tenancy, liferent, real security and praedial servitude (as of other real rights, if any) are thus to be elucidated in terms of function as above, together with an explanation of the way in which each depends upon some *title* determined by institutive/investitive provisions of law, is accompanied by consequential incidents in the way of rights and powers over and duties, liabilities and disabilities in respect of, any thing owned, all of which have some relative immunity from unilateral involuntary divesting, and is governed also by divestitive/terminative provisions establishing the voluntary acts and involuntary events whereby persons may be divested of the given right, with or without its transfer to another, or whereby the right itself may be terminated. In all cases where rights are divested by being voluntarily or involuntarily transferred to another person, the same provisions are in one aspect divestitive (*quoad* the transferor), and in the other investitive (*quoad* the transferee).

Although structurally simple, the details of these aggregates of investitive/ terminative provisions are formidable, as all students of property law well know. Formidably detailed they have to be, for feudal societies and all post-feudal forms of government to date have been utterly dependent in their economic arrangements upon the property regimes that their lawyers and ruling authorities (including, latterly, democratic legislatures) have constructed. It is at this level of detail that different conceptions of property and of other rights become apparent, grounded in different political views of the proper moral and social — and economic — principles which ought to govern the interrelationships of civilised people.

1111. Real rights as titles of rights to things. As this suggests, just as there are acts, facts and events which, under law, constitute titles to rights of ownership of things, making particular persons owners of particular things (and likewise, *mutatis mutandis*, for other real rights), so too, in effect, ownership and other real rights constitute titles to particular rights *to* things, or are conditions of such titles. I have the right now to mark this paper with this pen, because each is mine. You can get a right to use my pen only by securing my agreement to lend or sell it, and only if I own it. The consequential provisions of real rights are far-reaching and ramified, and most particular rights to particular things are dependent on them.

1112. The alternative to private property. In principle, at least, one could abolish this by abolishing every form of private property, and prohibiting every use of every thing save such as licensed by public licensing authorities. Since that is in principle possible, it follows that a full socialisation of property is possible, and could still allow of the necessity that the actual use of particular things be by particular people. But whether it is at all desirable to wind up the devolution to particular discretions which private property secures is an entirely other question. Aside from complete socialisation, it can confidently be asserted that all legal systems allow of some forms of private property exercisable by some classes of persons (governed by status and capacity) over some types of things. And all forms of property and associated real rights can be understood in terms of the analysis here stated.

10. THINGS AND INSTITUTIONS

1113. Existence of entities through time. It is a characteristic of the law, hitherto noted on several occasions in this title, that under its provisions various types of entity may be said to exist through time, even if lacking in spatial position. In the case of persons, we noted that these must have commencement, duration and thus identity through time and finally cessation upon death or dissolution. The same, we saw, holds for things, most particularly for those 'incorporeal things' whose very existence seems so specially dependent on human convention. Finally, we have lately noted that real rights require investitive/institutive provisions, consequential provisions, and divestitive/terminative provisions if they are to be fully specified.

1114. Human arrangements and time. It is not surprising that this should be so. It is natural for human beings to make reasonably enduring arrangements with each other, of a sort which involves co-ordinating or otherwise regulating each others' activity (perhaps intermittently) over a period of time. Although in the nature of the case human beings are always located in space as well as time, the 'arrangements' they make have only temporal, not also spatial, co-ordinates. Making arrangements is one thing, and carrying them out is another. It is always some time after, and sometimes quite a long time after, the making of an arrangement that one carries it out. And at that stage of affairs, the fact that an arrangement was made a while ago comes to be itself a reason for what one is now doing; one which may even entirely survive the original reason for which the arrangement was made in the first place. The existence of an arrangement made some time ago becomes a reason for acting in certain ways now. But of course its 'existence' is not a matter of physical fact, for 'arrangements' are entirely abstract entities. A useful philosophical concept allows us to speak of their existence as a matter of 'institutional fact'[1].

1 See J R Searle *Speech Acts* (1969) pp 50–53; N MacCormick and O Weinberger *An Institutional Theory of Law* (1986) Introduction (especially pp 21–24) and chs 1, 2. See also N MacCormick 'Law as an Institutional Fact' (1974) 90 LQR 102.

1115. Legal arrangements and time. The law, of course, handles such matters somewhat more formally than most of us do in ordinary social intercourse. In the law, certainly, there are 'arrangements' like contracts, trusts, marriages and family settlements, as well as the incorporation of companies or the forming of partnerships, the acquisition and transfer of heritable property, the registration of a patent or issuance of a bonus issue of shares in a company, or indeed the issuance of a judicial order or the enactment of an Act of Parliament. And in the law all these and all such arrangements have the already noted feature of being durable in time and of providing people with reasons to do things. How they provide reasons for doing things in law is easy to say. There are rules and principles of law which set out requirements of conduct, requirements which are conditional upon the existence of a contract, a trust, a marriage, a partnership or whatever.

1116. Legal frameworks. On like conditions, there can be special exemptions from general requirements, so that one acquires special active rights (for example conjugal rights) through the existence of one of such 'institutions of law', to give special application to a vague usage of legal speech. So too there can be powers which are conditional upon the existence of some such institution, for example the powers of trustees to make advances of capital to beneficiaries. Rules of law which, within limits, require people to do all that is called for in order to implement or fulfil such of their arrangements as have been cast in the appropriate institutional form in effect create a framework within which persons can order their own and other duties and obligations, albeit within limits. The requirements and duties generally fixed by law are given detailed application and content in the terms of each set of private arrangements set up within the appropriate institutional framework. And these, or sets of, requirements or duties subsist during the whole existence of a particular set of institutional arrangements, a fact which in turn requires us to have some method for determining the point or points of time at which the arrangements terminate.

1117. Terminative rules. Since the special feature of legal requirements, duties and the like is that they can be coercively enforced (or at least, that remedies or penalties for their breach can be coercively enforced) by agencies of state at the instance of wronged parties, or even of prosecutors in some cases, it is plainly a matter of importance that there be clarity as to whether or not any instance of any such institution has been created or has come into existence. In any event, there develop clear provisions concerning the conditions required for the existence of any contract, trust, marriage, partnership, limited company, tenancy, mortgage (real security) or whatever. From the standpoint of those who wish to set up arrangements of a relevant sort with the sanction of the law, the conditions for setting them up are expressible as rules: rules indicating who is qualified (has 'capacity') to do so, by what act with what intentions and observing what (if any) formalities of procedure, subject to what circumstances and in the absence of what vitiating circumstances. Such rules, we have already noted, have the character of 'power-conferring' rules; they state hypothetical requirements, that is, requirements you must follow if you wish to bring into being a legally valid contract, trust, marriage, partnership, limited company, tenancy, mortgage or whatever. And since all human arrangements have a finite duration, some provisions must govern their termination, these being here envisaged as 'terminative rules' which either empower persons to bring particular arrangements to an end or which stipulate that certain events, independent of choice by persons, will end them. We must notice also that, in some cases, they can be brought into being by involuntary events or by acts not designed to create them, as in the case of intestate estates or obligations of reparation.

1118. Institutive and terminative rules. Thus it seems reasonable to conceive of the existence and duration in time of legal institutions, or instances of them, as depending upon institutive rules together with acts or events satisfying the conditions that these rules set; while their termination is regulated by terminative rules, and by acts and events as stipulated therein. Their existence as distinctively *legal* arrangements depends on the fact that sets of legal rules and principles regulate people's conduct whenever instances of such institutions are in being, imposing conditional duties, granting active and passive rights and powers, and so on. Here, however — and not for the first time — we are drawing a distinction between rules and principles. This calls for further explanation, which will be provided in the next part of the title.

11. RULES AND PRINCIPLES

1119. Necessity for rules. In considering the institutive conditions for legal institutions such as trusts, contracts, wills, marriages and the like, we can see reason why these should be laid down in rules. The reasons have to do with a certain arbitrariness involved in these conditions.[1] For what contracts will writing be required? What form of writing? Probative or not? How many witnesses? What form of attestation? The same, and other like questions, can be raised as to trusts, wills, forms of marriage and any other legal institution one cares to think of.

1 On the concept of the 'arbitrary' quality of rules, see N MacCormick *H L A Hart* (1981) pp 40–43.

1120. Desirability of and provision for certainty and clarity. Of course, it is not arbitrary to require some settlement of some such conditions. It is always desirable to have some reasonable certainty in human affairs. From the point of view of those seeking to arrange their affairs in a legally enforceable way, as well as from the point of view of those who have standing arrangements on foot, there needs to be clarity as to what has to be done, or clarity as to what the things already done amount to in law. To procure such clarity is desirable in principle. The only known way of procuring it is to have rules on the matter. One way to have rules is to have them made by express legislation (although it is to be noticed that this requires anterior clarity on how to legislate and on the — partly arbitrary — conditions of validity of legislation). Another way is to have courts or tribunals which can make rulings on disputed points — for example, it may be agreed that no trust exists until an effectual declaration of trust has been made, but this still leaves it open to dispute whether such a declaration has to be delivered to somebody other then the truster and, if so, to whom; and where two sides dispute the sufficiency of what was done in a given case, it is necessary to have some body authorised to make a ruling upon their dispute[1]. It is also reasonable, and almost inevitable, that such a ruling should be of at least persuasive authority for similar disputes on later occasions, and that a ruling which has been approved and often acted upon should be accepted by custom as a rule. Whether pure social customs, absent some such mode of achieving rulings on disputed points, could ever generate 'rules' in the specific sense is a matter of doubt. But it is beyond doubt that the strengthening of particular rulings into general rules requires the support of custom[2].

1 See eg *Allan's Trustees v Lord Advocate* 1971 SC (HL) 45, 1971 SLT 62.
2 This is because at least the 'ultimate rule of recognition' of a legal system must be grounded in custom: see H L A Hart *The Concept of Law* (1961) ch 6. In some ways the point at stake was already better taken in Stair *Institutions* I, 1, 16.

1121. Arbitrary nature of certain rules. However that may be, we have seen that there are some matters upon which it is desirable to have rules and at least two ways of having them, namely by legislation and by judicial rulings on disputed points. It is of the character of rules that they express legal require-ments in terms of clearly stated conditions and consequences; clarity of state-ment being at the price of a certain arbitrariness, in this sense: points which it is desirable to settle could quite reasonably be settled in more than one way, but one way must be chosen. The matter is then one of arbitrary choice between reasonable alternatives. This applies obviously in the case of hypothetical requirements such as the requirements of validity of a will or contract or declaration of trust or whatever. But it can also apply in the case of categorical requirements as the case of the 'rule of the road' indicates — it is vital that we make it obligatory for drivers on roads to keep to one or the other side, and highly reasonable to make some such rule; but arbitrary which we choose as between left and right.

Moreover, even in the case of the gravest crimes, where prohibitions (for example upon killing or assault or fraud and deceit) are grounded in the plainest considerations of principle and have as such no element of the arbitrary in them, it is by no means unreasonable to reduce matters to clarity by way of rules. For rules of criminal law, albeit primarily directives to citizens as to the things they must avoid doing, are secondarily to be viewed in a different light: the proven breach of the law by a citizen is a condition of his or her valid conviction and punishment at law. And the reduction of criminal law to rules, albeit this may draw somewhat arbitrary lines between acts in principle equally wrongful (for example, in English law, A wounds B who dies a year later — murder; while C wounds D who dies a year and two days later — not murder), nevertheless places stricter controls on the discretion of prosecutors, judges and juries than would be possible otherwise. An arbitrariness of rules guards against a risk of arbitrariness of decisions. The weakness of the *nulla poena sine lege* principle in Scots law reduces the former sort of arbitrariness in our criminal law, but at some risk of increasing the latter sort, or anyway opportunities for it.

1122. Danger of wholly arbitrary rules. The arbitrariness of rules which has here been noted does not necessarily imply unreasonableness. Indeed, as we have seen, there are many situations in which the only reasonable thing to do is to settle arbitrarily between reasonable alternatives. The trouble, however, is that the power to create rules which are in this sense arbitrary entails also the risk that rules will be made which are wholly arbitrary, lacking in sound reason or morality. Whether they remain then binding as laws is a disputed point[1]. Whatever be the sound view on that point, it is precisely an absence of supposed arbitrariness that gives principles their special nature and standing. Some things, we think, are not merely against the rules, but wrong in principle. To some things people have in principle a right, not merely by some technicality of law.

1 See H L A Hart *The Concept of Law* (1961) ch 8, and J M Finnis *Natural Law and Natural Rights*
   (1980) chs 10–12. Dworkin's suggestion is that such decisions at least lack 'gravitational force':
   R M Dworkin *Taking Rights Seriously* (1978) ch 4.

1123. Principles. Hence, to adhere to some norm or standard of conduct as a
principle is to conceive of it as in itself a ground of rightness or wrongness in
what one does. Since fine distinctions tend to be arbitrary (even if not always
unreasonably so), principles tend to be general. Since it is desirable that the right
prevail, it is trivially true that observance of principles of right conduct is
constitutive of a desirable or valuable state of affairs. Whether principles of
conduct determine rightness precisely because of the valued states of affairs their
observance engenders, or states of affairs are desirable only as being engendered
by right principles and their observance, is another disputed point whose
resolution is here inessential[1]. For on either view there is a necessary link
between principles and human values, such as respect for persons and their
bodily security, or fairness, or reasonableness, or good faith in interpersonal
dealings. In the next part of the title this will be illustrated with respect to good
faith.

1 See N MacCormick 'Coherence in Legal Justification' in W Krawietz et al (eds) *Theorie der
   Normen* (1984) pp 37–53. See also R M Dworkin *Taking Rights Seriously* (1978), especially
   chs 2–4, and J M Finnis *Natural Law and Natural Rights* (1980), chs 2, 3. See also R Dworkin *Law's
   Empire* (1986) *passim*.

1124. Interaction of rules and principles. Meantime, it is important to note
how principles and rules interact in the making and administration of law. At
the level of lawmaking, it is always at least a matter of aspiration that legislators
have some (however contested and contestable) view of the principles which
ought to guide and govern human interactions in all their manifold forms, and
which should govern the distribution of assets and goods among human beings.
To that extent at least, law as enshrined in legislative rules ought to be derived
from and to express some sort of a principled order of the right. And so too in
the judicial task of giving concrete rulings on the significance of the law, one
ought to aim at deriving this from some principled vision of the legal order. All
this *de lege ferenda*. Nevertheless, the law made is made largely in terms of rules
having at least that sort of reasonable arbitrariness we have noted. The whole
point of having such laws so made is that they engender clarity and reduce scope
for infinity of disputes. Therefore it is important that the rules be acknowledged
and implemented as binding in at any rate the great majority of cases, that is,
where not entirely unconscionable in content or effect.

In a considerable range of cases, therefore, the law which is most completely if
not always easily identifiable and important to know is the law as constituted of
rules made by legislation or evolved through case law. Yet what makes this vast
collocation or congeries of rules constitute a coherent and therefore reasonably
intelligible system is the fact that — or the extent to which — it is capable of
being considered as a concretisation of principles and values and of rights to
states of being and of affairs, as noted earlier. An understanding of the law, and
of each of its branches, requires not merely a knowledge of the rules, but also a
grasp of the principles that animate them[1].

1 See A W B Simpson 'The Common Law and Legal Theory' in A W B Simpson (ed) *Oxford Essays
   in Jurisprudence, 2nd Series* (1973) ch 4; N MacCormick *Legal Reasoning and Legal Theory* (1978)
   ch 7; R M Dworkin *Taking Rights Seriously* (1978) chs 2, 4.

12. GOOD FAITH

1125. 'Obedience, freedom and engagement'. Stair's three principles of equity — 'obedience, freedom, and engagement' — envisage, as to obedience, that some actions are wrong and must be eschewed; as to engagement, that we must 'stand to the faith of our pactions'; and as to freedom, that one has a rightful liberty of action provided one commits no wrong either in terms of the principle of obedience or in terms of breach of promise or of contract. Against this conception of rightful liberty he entertains, but rejects, the objection that, since all things must be done to the glory of God, there is no real freedom of choice; for every occasion of choice must be as between that which actually best serves God and that which is wrongful. As he says:

> '... it were a sad rack to the consciences of men, if their errors and mistakes in the matters of expediency were to lie as a guilt upon their consciences: but that *bona fides* or *conscientia illaesa*, so much spoken of in the law, is that which cleareth and acquitteth men in such mistakas'[1].

1 Stair *Institutions* I,1,20.

1126. Action justified by good faith. The principle then is, that one is not guilty of wrongdoing if one acts in pursuit of proper ends by the use of means which, given the facts as one honestly believes them to be, would be both legitimate means and reasonably effectual ones to the end in view. Even given that an act has a proper end and that one's choice of means is in both ways a proper one *on the facts as one believes them to be*, things may turn out badly. For the beliefs can be mistaken. Here, Stair's principle is that one who acts in good faith, or with unimpaired conscience, is not guilty of wrongdoing however untoward the outcome of the action. As a conception of conscientious action, this seems sound; though perhaps something needs to be added about the character of the beliefs upon which the action is grounded; at least in a certain sense of the 'reasonable', these ought to be reasonable beliefs, that is, beliefs formed with thoughtful regard to the evidence and with care of reflection proportional to the importance of the facts in respect of the action and its anticipated outcome. It would not show conscientiousness of action if, however honest one's beliefs, these beliefs were casually adopted without careful regard to evidence, in a case in which much must necessarily turn upon their truth or falsity, and where there is time enough for due deliberation. This is important, because the legitimacy of means is determined both by their own character and by their side effects. My belief that the means I use to a legitimate end will have side effects of an illegitimate kind makes my pursuit of that end by those means wrongful, and such that my pursuit of it by those means cannot be said to be in good faith. So too even when I did not believe that these side effects would occur or acted without adverting to their possibility — if such disbelief or non-adversion arises from inadequate thoughtfulness in all the circumstances of a case, then one remains guilty, and cannot set up one's good-faith beliefs as a defence.

1127. Qualification of the principle. These reflections require us to qualify the original statement of principle, which should now be stated in the terms: one is not guilty of wrongdoing if one acts in pursuit of proper ends by the use of means which, given the facts as one honestly and with adequate thoughtfulness believes them to be, would be both legitimate means and reasonably effectual ones to the end in view. Thus stated, no doubt, the principle is an equitable rather than a strictly legal one. As to law, while it doubtless states a sound principle of criminal law, that which takes dole or *mens rea* to be a precondition of criminal wrongdoing and liability to punishment, yet as to the civil law it does not constitute a sufficient ground of exemption from liability. One's actings can be in good faith and yet be in breach of a duty owed to some other person; so the obligation to make reparation will not be elided by the fact that one's injurious actions were performed in good faith.

1128. Good faith as a precondition. There are, however, other purposes of law for which good faith is an essential precondition of one's acquisition of rights, or retention of them against persons in particular or in general[1]. Thus there are various cases of potentially defective acquisitions of (rights in) things where the potential defect is cured by the good faith of the person acquiring; or perhaps a better way to state the point is that certain events are adequate to divest a prior right-holder of rights in things only upon condition that they are acquired in good faith by another person who has no knowledge of any defect in or burden upon his or her putatively acquired rights as owner. A case in point is where a purchaser P fraudulently induces a seller S to transfer certain property, for example by paying with a worthless cheque. Here, in case of moveables, P, notwithstanding the fraud, will generally acquire a voidable or reducible title to the goods. If a third party T then in good faith acquires the goods for value from P before S has taken any steps sufficient to reduce or avoid P's voidable title, T's right to the goods is then indefeasible. By contrast, in a case of theft, the original owner retains unimpaired rights in the thing and no ulterior transactions between the thief and an honest purchaser or any subsequent purchaser, however good their faith, suffices to divest the owner of his or her rights as such[2]; though their good faith will protect innocent intermediate handlers of the goods from actions of reparation or restitution, if not, in any case where a profit is made, of recompense, raised by the true owner[3].

Likewise, in the case of personal rights to particular things, as in the case of rights of beneficiaries under a trust, a person who acquires subjects in good faith and for onerous consideration from one who holds them as a trustee acquires them free of any rights of beneficiaries under the trust, the beneficiaries retaining remedial rights only against the trustee or trustees. But an acquirer who is not in good faith acquires the property subject to the trusts in question[4]. Similarly, one who possesses land in the honest and thoughtful belief that he possesses as of proprietary right is a good faith possessor of the land; and in this case fruits (for example harvests) which he gathers in or consumes become his own, whereas a possessor in bad faith has to account to the owner for ingatherings and fruits consumed; and the good faith possessor will be entitled to recompense for improvements to the subjects so far as these are actually profitable to the owner, but not so the bad faith possessor[5]. One may summarise all this as a general principle in the terms that one who acts in good faith with a view to acquiring things does so acquire except in a case where some other person has already indefeasible and unimpaired real rights in the thing or things in question.

 1 See T B Smith *A Short Commentary on the Law of Scotland* (1962) pp 296–299.
 2 See *Morrisson v Robertson* 1908 SC 332, 15 SLT 697, discussed in *Smith* pp 624–626; D M Walker 'Following Stolen Property' (1953) 69 SLR 1. See also FRAUD, paras 705, 706, above.
 3 See Stair *Institutions* I,7,11: '... he who *bona fide* did buy that which did belong to another, if while he hath it, it appeareth to be that other's, he must restore it without expectation of the price he gave for it, but as to that he must take himself to his warrandice, (express or implied) against the seller: but if *bona fide* he has sold it before he be questioned, he is free, and not obliged to restore it; though in so far as he is profited in receiving more for it than he gave, he be liable by the obligation of remuneration or recompense'. See also D M Walker *The Law of Delict in Scotland* (2nd edn, 1981) p 1006.
 4 See eg *Heritable Reversionary Co Ltd v Millar* (1892) R (HL) 43; and *Dunlop's Trustees v Clydesdale Bank Ltd* (1893) 20 R (HL) 59, 1 SLT 111.

5 *Stair* II,1,21; Erskine *Institute* II,1,25,26; *Marquis of Huntly's Trustees v Hallyburton's Trustees*
   (1880) 8 R 50; *Morrison v St Andrews School Board* 1918 SC 51.

1129. Conventional obligations and good faith. Conventional obligations
can themselves be considered as exigible simply on grounds of the requirements
of good faith. Each party to a contract necessarily engages the trust of the other,
hence no action by either which defeats the expectations in good faith formed by
the other is a fair or reasonable action. And indeed, when contractual liability
was in Roman law extended beyond various types of formally undertaken
obligation, it was to the four consensual contracts (of sale, hire, partnership and
mandate) which were deemed enforceable as a matter of good faith. What, if
any, extra or additional duties historically attached to the parties as special duties
of good faith in these cases is an obscure topic of no present concern[1]. The issue
in contemporary terms is how far, in principle, the concept of good faith which
lies at the foundation of the enforcement of all contracts ought to govern not
merely the fact but also the mode and extent of their enforcement.

  1 However, for scepticism about the classical concept and extent of the idea of 'good faith', see
     A F Rodger 'Concealing a Servitude' in P G Stein and A D E Lewis (eds) *Studies in Justinian's
     Institutes in Memory of J A C Thomas* (1983) p 134. See also 'L Fufius — Another Undeserving
     Winner' in N MacCormick and P B H Birks *The Legal Mind* (1986) p 185.

1130. The American Restatement. The furthest development of the view
that contracts remain founded in good faith is under the American Restatement[1]. Professor Summers has argued that under the Restatement there is a
general and residual duty of good faith contractual performance which may be
enforced in the absence of any more specifically exigible contractual provision
or statutory superimposition[2]. This view is not uncontested[3], even in the
United States, but is sustained both by relevant and persuasive authority and by
the reason and justice of the matter. From a Scots lawyer's point of view, the line
of development described by Summers may prompt historical regrets. For, as
Sir Thomas Smith has shown, the development of Scots law until the mid-
nineteenth century pointed in the direction of a generalisation from Roman and
native materials of general duties of good faith in conventional obligations[4].
What put a stop to this was the importation, largely at the instance of Scottish
mercantile interests, of English rules based on the *caveat emptor* principle. The
doctrine of freedom of contract became (almost) the doctrine that parties are free
to write their own contracts and that the law is not free to import any terms or
conditions other than those expressly agreed or necessarily implied by the
parties.

  1 *Second Restatement of Contracts* (1979) para 205.
  2 R S Summers 'The General Duty of Good Faith — its Recognition and Conceptualization' (1982)
     67 Corn L R 101.
  3 See S Burton 'Breach of Contract and the Common Law Duty to Perform in Good Faith' (1980)
     94 Harv L R 369; S Burton 'More on Good Faith Performance of a Contract: A Reply to
     Professor Summers' (1984) 69 Iowa L R 497. In his *Introduction to Law and Legal Reasoning* (1985)
     at p 90, Burton expresses doubt as to whether one can, by universalisation, extract any rule from
     the cases; discovering what good faith is requires a scrutiny of all the particulars of relevant cases.
  4 T B Smith *A Short Commentary on the Law of Scotland* (1962) pp 297, 298. See also Lord
     Kilbrandon 'The Honest Merchant' 1967 Current Legal Problems 1.

1131. Good faith and consumer contracts etc. Especially in consumer contracts, and especially in regard to exemption clauses and limitation of liability
clauses in favour of commercial parties operating through standard form contracts, these developments gave rise to approaches to the making and
implementing of contracts and to the rebutting of claims by injured parties

which can hardly be thought compatible with *conscientia illaesa*, unimpairment of conscience or any sort of good faith[1]. The idea that people were simply being held to the bargains they had freely made in full knowledge of material terms as agreed would have been laughable had it been advanced; of course, in cases where it is true that what is in issue is fidelity to a fair bargain freely made, as in the case of commercial parties dealing at arm's length, the requirement of good faith is precisely a requirement on parties to live with and honour their agreements made, however onerous they turn out to be.

Given the recent development of statutes rectifying in detailed terms some of the grosser abuses of market power, notably the Unfair Contract Terms Act 1977 (c 50), it would be fair to say, from the standpoint at least of Scots law, that a principle of good faith dealing has been at least partially restored in our law; and that, the principle being back in operation, it can legitimately be developed in the common law without need for further legislative intervention. Persuasive American authority is available to support such a development if undertaken. The argument in favour of the development is clear. It is that holding parties to obligations essentially grounded in good faith is the very nature of the business of enforcing contracts; and since good faith is of the essence of contract, no person should be able to assert contractual rights beyond the limits of good faith, and each party should have all these rights which the other ought in good faith to acknowledge and honour. The counter argument is that good faith is both an evaluative and a vague concept recourse to which unwisely enhances the scope for judicial discretions in contract litigation, thus both encouraging recourse to litigation and disastrously weakening certainty of law in a sphere in which for commercial societies it is more important that people clearly know their rights than that those rights conform to ideal justice. This second line of argument is one which supports the kind of detailed statutory intervention there has been, while also asserting that no further rights should be imputed to anyone beyond those which the statutes expressly envisage. Even if that view be accepted, the statutes all require interpretation, and that interpretation can either be or (unhappily) fail to be coherent and principled. The best way, it is submitted, for securing a coherent and principled approach to all the consumer protection and anti-exemption clause legislation would be the way of reading the specific provisions as but special instances of a general duty of good faith performance in contractual transactions.

1 See eg such cases as *M'Kay v Scottish Airways Ltd* 1948 SC 254, 1948 SLT 402, and *M'Cutcheon v David MacBrayne Ltd* 1964 SC (HL) 28, 1964 SLT 66. See in general T B Smith *A Short Commentary on the Law of Scotland* (1962) pp 755–757, and D M Walker *The Law of Contracts and Related Obligations in Scotland* (2nd edn, 1985) chs 20, 21.

1132. Principles requiring good faith. However that may be, we have seen that good faith as a concept figures in at least two and perhaps three sets of principles: as to the acquisition of rights in circumstances in which a putative acquirer lacks some of the normal requisites for good or unencumbered title, good faith is a normal condition (with or without others) for effectual acquisition. And, on the other hand, in contracts it may be in general and certainly is in particular instances true that contractors must perform up to the standard stipulated in terms of good faith. It is perhaps also found in substance in that maxim of criminal lawyers expressed by the English in the terms that *actus non facit reum nisi mens sit rea*.

1133. Good faith and personal bar. A fourth and further aspect of good faith is that evidenced by the doctrine of personal bar[1]. Here, what is envisaged is a purely personal disablement of one person from exercising an active right or advancing claims on the footing of a passive right, this disablement or barring being solely in regard to some other determinate person. The ground of the disablement is some prior communings between the parties in the light of which it would be inequitable and a breach of good faith for the party in whom reliance has been placed to disappoint the other's reliance. Sometimes the communings in question may primarily implicate the reliant party, as in *rei interventus*[2], where a party has incurred detriment in the faith of a formally imperfect contract — but here it is of the essence that the actings of the former party be in the full knowledge of the other and thus have had at least tacit approval. Sometimes, as in homologation[3], the primarily active party is the one in whom reliance is placed; and so too where personal bar arises out of some representation or assurance in some matter of fact or of particular right. Here again one cannot in good faith give the lie to one's own assurances, not, at least, in respect of the person to whom the assurance is made and who acts in reliance upon it. In all such cases, good faith sets a limiting condition upon the exercise of rights: one may not exercise one's rights, for example of ownership or of resiling from an imperfect contract, as against a party against whom one cannot so act without some breach of good faith and reasonable trust among persons.

1 See J Rankine *The Law of Personal Bar in Scotland* (1921). Lord Birkenhead LC gave a widely accepted general definition of personal bar in *Gatty v Maclaine* 1921 SC (HL) 1 at 7, 1921 1 SLT 51 at 54. Cf also T B Smith *A Short Commentary on the Law of Scotland* (1962) pp 292–296; D M Walker *Principles of Scottish Private Law* (3rd edn, 1982) vol 1, ch 1.2, pp 33–64; and PERSONAL BAR.

2 For a definition of *rei interventus*, see Bell *Principles* s 26, approved in *Mitchell v Stornoway Trustees* 1936 SC (HL) 56 at 63, 1936 SLT 509 at 512, per Lord Macmillan.

3 See Bell s 27, and *Gardner v Gardner* (1830) 9 S 138 at 140, per Lord Moncreiff.

1134. Good faith as an element of principles and rules. Taking account of all the ways in which good faith may enter into legal scrutiny, we can the better understand that there is no single principle of good faith. Rather, there are several principles of law — and many derived rules — in which good faith enters as an essential condition for some legal consequence or as an essential part of the definition of legal duties or disabilities. Thus it is like, for example, reasonableness[1], a value or virtue of signal importance in the operation of many legal provisions. What exactly are the particular requirements of good faith is a matter which must vary from general context to general context, and therein from particular case to particular case. But the general view is one under which good faith is an essential condition of certain otherwise irregular acquisitions of rights, in which it can be a condition upon the valid exercise of rights and upon the interpretation of duties undertaken by agreement, and in which the good faith in which actions are undertaken can be a ground of exemption from at least certain sorts of liability for untoward consequences of one's acts.

1 Cf N MacCormick 'On Reasonableness' in Ch Perelman and R Vander Elst (eds) *Les Notions à Contenu Variable en Droit* (1984) pp 131–156.

1135. The place of good faith in law. It would be an intolerable world in which all rights were conditional upon the virtue of their putative possessor; but only slightly more intolerable than one in which all acquisitions and exercises of right and every exaction of duty went forward wholly without regard to relevant virtue — in this case, good faith. A further difference between purely legal and more moralistic assessments of cases is that the law is not concerned with a person's generally virtuous or vicious character, but with the virtue — or, it might be better to say, the value — of particular actings. The law does not, probably cannot, and certainly should not seek to, make persons be or become persons of fidelity and good faith in the whole course of their lives. But it can require that they act in good faith in particular cases, or can reserve certain acquisitions of rights only for those who do so act. Thus do moral virtues transmute into legal values, and take their place in law as basic conditions in legal principles.

1136–1200. Conclusion. Here ends our exposition of the character of legal order and elucidation of its general concepts. A legal order systematically interweaves rules validated under reasonably precise criteria of validity, principles which express the underlying rationale of the rules, and values whose promotion is what makes the existence of legal order worthwhile. Only within this view of legal order can one render its general concepts intelligible. For the intellectual operations whereby rules, principles and values are put in operation, taken together with the actions they shape and attitudes they reinforce, are in truth constitutive of legal order. And the concepts we have investigated are the necessary working materials of those intellectual operations.

GUARDIANSHIP

1. INTRODUCTION

1201. Scope of the title. This title concerns itself with the law relating to the protection of those regarded as having no legal capacity of their own or having defective legal capacity, whether by reason of their age or mental condition. The mechanisms for the appointment of persons having duties and responsibilities for the administration of the affairs of the person who is under some incapacity, the nature of those duties and responsibilities and the means by which those persons may be called to account will be discussed. This title does not deal with the custody and care and control of children[1], except where statutory encroachment on the common law crosses the border with the notion of legal guardianship[2], nor with the subjects of adoption[3] or judicial factors[4].

1 See FAMILY LAW.
2 See paras 1229–1231 below.
3 See FAMILY LAW.
4 See TRUSTS, TRUSTEES AND JUDICIAL FACTORS, vol 24, paras 237 ff.

2. PROTECTION OF PERSONS UNDER LEGAL INCAPACITY

1202. Introduction. Legal incapacity, which the law seeks to protect, usually arises from one of two causes, that is to say either lack of age or mental disability. Absence abroad and physical illness, perhaps without mental disability, may also sometimes justify intervention on the part of a person by those concerned with the proper administration of his affairs.

In Scots law, the offices of those who have the charge of the interests of, or have responsibility for the obligations of such persons, are known as tutory and curatory. The resemblance to these offices in Roman Law is marked and significant[1].

Generally, the guardian of a pupil child is known as a tutor and the guardian of a minor child is known as a curator. According to the law of Scotland, pupillarity continues until the ages of fourteen and twelve in male and female children respectively, and minority from the end of pupillarity until the age of eighteen[2]. Statute has cut across this broadly simple classification, introducing specific age limits, for example, in respect of capacity to marry[3], questions of custody[4], local authority intervention in relation to the care of children[5] and in the area of criminal responsibility[6].

1 Stair *Institutions* I,6,1; Erskine *Institute* I,7,1; Bell *Principles* ss 2065–2068; Lord Fraser *Parent and Child* (3rd edn, 1906, ed J Clark) p 204.
2 See Erskine I,7,1; *Bell* s 2067; and the Age of Majority (Scotland) Act 1969 (c 39), s 1.
3 The age of capacity to marry is sixteen years of age: Marriage (Scotland) Act 1977 (c 15), s 1, and FAMILY LAW.
4 Ie under the Children Act 1975 (c 72), ss 47–55, the Law Reform (Parent and Child) (Scotland) Act 1986 (c 9), and the Family Law Act 1986 (c 55), Pt I, Ch I (s 1), Ch III (ss 8–18), Ch V (ss 25–32), and Ch VI (ss 33–43).
5 Ie under the Social Work (Scotland) Act 1968 (c 49): see paras 1229–1231 below.
6 The age of criminal responsibility is eight: see the Criminal Procedure (Scotland) Act 1975 (c 21), s 170 (solemn procedure), and s 369 (summary procedure).

1203. Status of pupillarity. The status of pupillarity denotes complete active incapacity: 'a pupil has no person in the legal sense of the word. He is incapable of acting, or even of consenting'[1]. His contracts are void, not merely voidable. Whether or not he has a tutor, he has no power to contract, and any agreement which he may make may neither be founded on nor enforced against him. However, the idea of complete incapacity in the legal sense is perhaps slightly misleading, for if necessaries have been sold and delivered to a pupil, he must pay a reasonable price for them[2].

1 Erskine *Institute* I,7,14; *Sinclair v Stark* (1828) 6 S 336; *Hill v City of Glasgow Bank* (1879) 7 R 68.
2 Sale of Goods Act 1979 (c 54), s 3(2).

1204. Status of minority. A minor has some active legal capacity. In particular, his contractual powers[1] depend on whether or not he acts along with a curator. If he has a curator, and contracts with his consent, then he is regarded as having full contractual capacity and powers, save that he may not grant a gratuitous disposition of heritable property[2]. On the other hand, contracts made by a minor without his curator's agreement are void, except for contracts of service[3] or contracts entered into in the course of a business carried on by the minor[4]. Contracts entered into by a minor who has a curator, but without the consent of the curator, are thus unenforceable against the minor. However, it is thought that such contracts are binding on other parties if to the advantage of the minor[5]. A minor can thus act legally to bind himself in relation to certain transactions, but often a curator must act with him.

1 For a full discussion of the contractual capacity of minors, see FAMILY LAW; OBLIGATIONS.
2 *Brown's Trustee v Brown* (1897) 24 R 962, 5 SLT 54.
3 *M'Feetridge v Stewarts and Lloyds Ltd* 1913 SC 773, 1913 1 SLT 325.
4 *O'Donnell v Brownieside Coal Co Ltd* 1934 SC 534, 1934 SLT 493.
5 T B Smith *A Short Commentary on the Law of Scotland* (1962) p 795.

1205. Reduction of minor's contracts. When a minor's contract is prima facie valid, it may, if subject to lesion or circumvention, be avoided or be open to subsequent repudiation after the minor attains the age of majority and within a period of four years of that date ('the *quadriennium utile*'). Such a contract may be reduced on proof of 'enorm lesion'.

Enorm lesion is presumed in gratuitous contracts. This means that if before reaching the age of twenty-two the person injuriously affected takes appropriate steps to have the contract set aside by an action of reduction he may do so and obtain restitution, upon proof that he has been materially disadvantaged by the provisions of the contract. Enorm lesion means some substantial injury to the estate of the minor, although a lesser injury may be treated as enorm when the minor has acted alone, without his curator[1]. There will be no defence to an action by a minor in such cases as gifts, the undertaking of obligations of guarantee or surety or the discharge of a debt for an inadequate sum[2].

Reduction is apparently competent in cases of loans to a minor and sales by him, if he has squandered the loan or price so that at majority his estate is diminished[3]. The Consumer Credit Act 1974 provides that it is an offence to send any document to a minor inviting him to borrow money[4]. A loan to a minor is not unlawful, but may be reduced on proof of lesion. Compromises of a minor's claims may be reducible if found not to be reasonably fair[5]. In the case of purchases by a minor, his contractual liability is recognised, it being held that lesion can only be shown if his purchase was extravagant considering the minor's position in life[6]. The Sale of Goods Act 1979 provides that where necessities are sold and delivered to a minor, he must pay a reasonable price for them[7]. Infants, who were included in the Sale of Goods Act 1893[8], are now excluded.

Reduction of contracts by a minor will be barred if there is proof of homologation after the age of majority, or if the minor contracts in the course of his trade or profession[9], or falsely holds himself out as being of full age[10].

1 *Cooper v Cooper's Trustees* (1885) 12 R 473.
2 Stair *Institutions* I,6,44.
3 *Harkness and Ranken v Graham* (1833) 11 S 760.
4 See the Consumer Credit Act 1974 (c 39), s 50, and CONSUMER CREDIT, vol 5, para 836.
5 *Robertson v S Henderson & Sons Ltd* (1905) 7 F 776, 12 SLT 113; *M'Feetridge v Stewarts and Lloyds Ltd* 1913 SC 773, 1913 1 SLT 325; *Faulds v British Steel Corpn* 1977 SLT (Notes) 18.
6 *Fontaine v Foster* (1808) Hume 409.
7 See the Sale of Goods Act 1979 (c 54), s 3.
8 See the Sale of Goods Act 1893 (c 71), s 2 (repealed).
9 *M'Feetridge v Stewarts and Lloyds Ltd* 1913 SC 773, 1913 1 SLT 325. In *O'Donnell v Brownieside Coal Co Ltd* 1934 SC 534, 1934 SLT 493, the court was not prepared to regard an industrial employee as a minor engaged in trade. 'Trade' does not include dealing on the Stock Exchange: *Dennistoun and Jardine v Mudie* (1850) 12 D 613. The case of *Hill v City of Glasgow Bank* (1879) 7 R 68 does not resolve the question of whether a minor who buys shares involving a later liability can reduce the contract for the purchase during the *quadriennium utile*.
10 *Wilkie v William Dunlop & Co* (1834) 12 S 506. Cf the position in England: *R Leslie Ltd v Sheill* [1914] 3 KB 607, CA.

1206. Welfare and benefit of the *incapax*. The concept of guardianship in modern Scots Law extends to the person of the *incapax* as well as to his estate. Accordingly, a factor *loco tutoris*, whose duties are administrative only, cannot act along with a tutor[1]. The emphasis of the law is on the protection of the *incapax*, and consequently the law looks to the guardian to exercise his powers for the benefit of the *incapax*, and not for the guardian's own interests. In any proceedings for the custody or upbringing of a pupil or the administration of any property belonging to him or held in trust for him, the court is to regard the welfare of the child as the first and paramount consideration[2].

1 *Speirs* 1946 SLT 203, OH. As to factors *loco tutoris* generally, see para 1216 below.
2 Law Reform (Parent and Child) (Scotland) Act 1986 (c 9), s 3(2).

1207. Functions of tutor and curator distinguished. The distinction between the functions of a tutor and those of a curator is expressed in the brocard *'tutor datur personae curator rei'*; the tutor acts *for* the pupil, while the curator acts *with* the minor, concurring with him in his acts and deeds. In bringing any action on behalf of the *incapax*, a tutor will sue as 'tutor and administrator-at-law' of the pupil child, while the minor brings or defends an action 'with the consent and concurrence' of the curator. The tutor may thus act without the consent and in spite of the opposition of his pupil, whilst the curator, if he cannot secure the co-operation of the minor, cannot continue in office and must obtain his discharge from the court. In such circumstances, it is thought that the court will then compel the minor to take another curator.

3. PARENTS AS GUARDIANS

1208. Introduction. The notion of guardianship of a pupil or minor child comprehends the proposition that the protection of the *incapax* is in the first place a family matter. Unless circumstances dictate otherwise, parents are left to bring up their children as they consider best. The parents' right to determine such matters as the religion, schooling, place of residence and medical treatment of their child are not generally the subject of legal regulation unless the child's welfare is seen as being at risk.

1209. Parental rights. As tutors and curators, parents derive their right to that office from the relationship of parent and child. So far as necessary, this wide spectrum of responsibility may be regulated by the court and may in extreme circumstances be taken away from the family altogether. At common law, a father was the natural guardian or administrator-at-law of his legitimate child so long as the child remained in minority. As such, he was *ex lege* the tutor to his legitimate pupil child and curator to his legitimate minor child. The Guardianship Act 1973 gave the mother of a legitimate child the same rights and authority of a guardian, equally with the father, and such rights were said to be exercisable by either parent without it being necessary to secure the consent and concurrence of the other[1]. The effect of this provision was to make the mother equally an administrator-at-law along with the father of a child in minority.

The position has been altered by the Law Reform (Parent and Child) (Scotland) Act 1986, which now provides that a child's mother is to have parental rights whether or not she is or has been married to the child's father, but that a child's father is to have parental rights *only* if he is married to the child's mother or was married to her at the time of the child's conception or subsequently[2]. Thus, both parents have parental rights if they are married at the date of the child's birth or were married at the date of the child's conception or marry subsequently. The term 'parental rights' has a wide scope. It means tutory, curatory, custody or access, as the case may require, and any right or authority relating to the welfare or upbringing of a child conferred on a parent by any rule of law[3]. Thus the whole spectrum of domestic situations where an adult may act or be required to act on behalf of, or along with, a child is covered in the modern legislation.

A father[4] who is not, and who does not become married to his child's mother may obtain a grant of parental rights by applying to the court[5]. However, in these proceedings the court is enjoined to regard the welfare of the child as the paramount consideration and may not make any order unless satisfied that it will be in the interests of the child to do so[6].

Where two persons have any parental rights, each of them may exercise that right without the consent of the other[7]. Any dispute will be settled by a court in accordance with the welfare principle[8].

1 See the Guardianship Act 1973 (c 29), s 10 (repealed).
2 Law Reform (Parent and Child) (Scotland) Act 1986 (c 9), s 2(1). 'Marriage' is deemed to include a union which is voidable or a union which is void, but believed in good faith by the father to have been valid at the time it was celebrated: s 2(2). In relation to a void marriage, it is irrelevant whether the father's belief was due to an error of fact or an error of law: s 2(2). Cf the common law putative marriage, where the error was restricted to one of fact: *Purves' Trustees v Purves* (1895) 22 R 513, 2 SLT 627.
3 Law Reform (Parent and Child) (Scotland) Act 1986, s 8.
4 Indeed, any person claiming interest: *M* 1988 GWD 38–1553, OH. Cf *AB* 1988 SLT 652, OH.
5 Law Reform (Parent and Child) (Scotland) Act 1986, s 3(1).
6 Ibid, s 3(2).
7 Ibid, s 2(4). However, this does not apply if any decree or deed conferring the right otherwise provides: s 2(4).
8 Ibid, s 3(1), (2).

1210. Divorce. A difficulty in respect of parental rights is immediately apparent in any dispute ending in divorce. Commonly in a divorce action one or other of the parents will obtain an order for custody of a child or children. Although forever the natural parent of that child, the non-custodial parent no longer enjoys the flexibility and freedom of a tutor; accordingly he no longer has discretion or power to regulate, or even contribute to, a decision concerning such matters as schooling, religion or medical treatment of the child. Professor J M Thomson suggests that as a practical matter these important regulatory rights are in fact enjoyed as an incident of the grant of custody to one parent; this cuts across the rights of one parent *qua* parent to act as tutor and curator, simply because of the blood relationship[1]. However, the exercise of parental rights is a different matter from the very existence of those rights themselves, although it is submitted that the learned author expresses a correct view when he says that pragmatically, the existence of the rights is of far less consequence without the power actually to exercise them.

This view of the practical status of parental rights does not sit happily with the failure of the Law Reform (Parent and Child) (Scotland) Act 1986 expressly to prescribe what is to happen to parental rights and the power to exercise them where an order of custody is made in favour of one or other parent. It is thought that, in practical terms, the rights of the custodial parent will prevail, so long as he or she exercises them properly[2], but the conundrum remains for closer examination.

1 J M Thomson *Family Law in Scotland* (1987) pp 159, 160.
2 Ie in accordance with the welfare of the child. As to court orders regarding custody in respect of consistorial causes, see para 1212 below.

1211. Tutor or curator on death of parent. Any person can be appointed to be a tutor or curator to a child following a parent's death provided the appointment is in writing and the grantor was the child's tutor or curator or would have been if he had survived until after the child's birth[1]. Such an appointment will remain in existence unless recalled (or its terms otherwise provide) until the attainment of majority, and includes the automatic assumption of the mantle of curatory when the child attains minority[2].

It is thought that such appointments are common enough among persons taking the trouble to regulate the succession to their means and estate, particularly where those persons are single parents, or are possessed of substantial means, or are partners in a married relationship the prospects for which appear to one partner to be poor. There will be an understandable, if not particularly laudable, desire to keep control of the child and his schooling away from the party perhaps responsible for the breakdown of the marriage. The writer perceives a difficulty in such circumstances if a dispute arose between an appointed, non-related tutor (perhaps a godparent) who came to office after a mother's death, on the one hand, and a divorced father living with his girlfriend or second wife on the other. The 'welfare principle' is all that the Law Reform (Parent and Child) (Scotland) Act 1986 gives to the court to assist its determination of such a dispute[3].

1 Law Reform (Parent and Child) (Scotland) Act 1986 (c 9), s 4(1).
2 Ibid, s 4(2).
3 See ibid, s 3(2), and para 1209 above.

1212. Court orders as to parental rights. Until the enactment of the Law Reform (Parent and Child) (Scotland) Act 1986, where parents and, *a fortiori*, an appointed guardian and a parent disagreed on any question affecting the welfare of a child, either of them could apply to the Court of Session, or to any sheriff court having jurisdiction, for directions[1]. Any order made subsequent to such an application could be varied or discharged by a subsequent order made on the application of either parent or guardian or any person disclosing a legitimate interest, or having the custody of the pupil or minor[2]. These provisions were not to be used to regulate custody of or access to the child[3].

However, proceedings must now be brought under the 1986 Act[4], which does not prevent the court regulating custody or access to the child. Where the custody of the child is in issue in such proceedings[5], the court may, if it appears that there are exceptional circumstances making it impracticable or undesirable for the child to be in the care of either of its parents or to any other individual, commit the care of the child to a specified local authority[6], so it should be noted that in respect of these proceedings it is irrelevant that the child was born within or outwith marriage.

There are provisions for the making of orders committing the care of a child to an individual or to a local authority where the court is deciding a consistorial cause, if that should be deemed necessary[7]. The court is enabled to require reports from advocates, solicitors or social workers as to the arrangements for the future care and upbringing of children[8], to require supervision of custody arrangements after any order is pronounced[9], and to obtain reports anent the operation of access if it seems to the court to be necessary and desirable for such reports to be obtained.

The widespread ordering of reports represents a considerable financial load upon the Legal Aid Fund, as it is almost invariably the party in receipt of legal aid who accepts responsibility for instructing and paying for such reports. However, the use of independent, speedily obtained reports remains a useful and much used weapon in the armoury of equipment available to the court. The opportunity for taking a person who has furnished a report to task concerning its contents is restricted by the limitations imposed in a Practice Note preventing the citing of such persons as witnesses without leave of the court[10]. However, this restriction does not apply to advocates or solicitors appointed to prepare such a report. It is thought that such instances are rare.

1 Guardianship Act 1973 (c 29), s 10(3) (repealed).

2 Ibid, s 10(5).
3 Ibid, s 10(4).
4 Ie under the Law Reform (Parent and Child) (Scotland) Act 1986 (c 9), s 3.
5 Ie proceedings other than an application to which the Matrimonial Proceedings (Children) Act
   1958 (c 40), Pt II (ss 7–15) applies: see the Guardianship Act 1973, s 11(1) (amended by the
   Children Act 1975 (c 72), s 48(3)).
6 Guardianship Act 1973, s 11(1)(a). It is arguable whether this provision could apply to a dispute
   concerning the exercise of parental rights if 'relating to custody'. It would not apply, for
   example, to an application to become the tutor or curator of the child.
7 Matrimonial Proceedings (Children) Act 1958 (c 40), s 10(1) (amended by the Law Reform
   (Parent and Child) (Scotland) Act 1986, s 10(2), Sch 2, and the Family Law Act 1986 (c 55),
   s 68(1), Sch 1, para 6).
8 See the Matrimonial Proceedings (Children) Act 1958, s 11 (amended by the Social Work
   (Scotland) Act 1968 (c 49), ss 95(1), (2), 97(1), Sch 8, para 43, Sch 9, Pt I; the Law Reform (Parent
   and Child) (Scotland) Act 1986, Sch 2; and the Family Law Act 1986, Sch 1, para 7).
9 See the Matrimonial Proceedings (Children) Act 1958, s 12 (amended by the Social Work
   (Scotland) Act 1968, s 95(2), Sch 9, Pt I, and the Local Government (Scotland) Act 1973 (c 65),
   s 214(2), Sch 27, Pt II, para 137).
10 *Practice Note* dated 6 June 1968.

1213. Duration of parental rights. Parental rights stemming from the
relationships of tutor and ward were thought to come to an end on the attainment of minority: *tutor datur personae rei*. Cases recognise the continued existence
of parental rights beyond pupillarity[1], and the encroachment of statutory provisions is further evidence of the continuation of parental rights to the age of
eighteen[2]. It is respectfully doubted how far the somewhat pontifical pronouncements in *Harvey v Harvey* are appropriate today[3], but the case remains a
leading authority.

On the thesis that parental rights are in reality an incident of the grant or
assumption of custody, they will survive until forisfamiliation or majority. The
right to counsel a child away from a prejudicial course of action is highlighted in
Harvey v Harvey, and is inseparable from the notion of the tutor's and curator's
position as being of a protective nature. Statute again impinges on the relationship in such areas as consent to sexual intercourse, employment, driving motor
vehicles, possessing firearms, betting, consenting to medical treatment and the
conduct of private homosexual acts between consenting males.

1 See eg *Harvey v Harvey* (1860) 22 D 1198. See also J M Thomson *Family Law in Scotland* (1987)
   pp 160 ff.
2 Law Reform (Parent and Child) (Scotland) Act 1986 (c 9), s 8. The Act does not specify in terms
   which rights may continue until the age of eighteen.
3 This is so particularly in the light of the decision in the English case of *Gillick v West Norfolk and
   Wisbech Area Health Authority and the Department of Health and Social Security* [1986] AC 112,
   [1985] 3 All ER 402, HL.

4. TUTORS

1214. Tutors testamentar or tutors nominate. The effect of the Guardianship Act 1973 was to make the mother of a child an administrator-at-law as well
as the father[1]. The effect of the Law Reform (Parent and Child) (Scotland) Act
1986 has been considered[2]. Both parents may now, therefore, nominate a
person to act after their death as tutor or curator to their child[3]. Such guardians
are known as tutors testamentar, or tutors nominate, and they enjoy preference
over other claimants to that office, but not, of course, over surviving parents.
They succeed, by their appointment, to the management and control of the
person and estate of the ward. A parent may make provision for such an
appointment in a will, which can be enforced by the court[4].

On the death of a parent, the surviving parent continues to be the guardian of the pupil child, and if the deceased has appointed a guardian in writing, the surviving parent acts along with him. If no appointment has been made, the court might appoint a guardian to act with the surviving parent, if circumstances so dictate. Where both parents nominate guardians, they act jointly. However, a surviving parent might refuse to act with the nominee of a predeceasing parent, and in that event the wishes of the surviving parent will prevail unless the nominee obtains an order from the court that he is to act jointly or as sole guardian. Where joint guardians cannot agree, they may apply for directions to the court, which will determine the issue according to the welfare principle[5].

The office of guardian is gratuitous, being presumed to be undertaken from natural affection or considerations of friendship or blood relationships. Such a person need not take the oath *de fideli administratione*, nor find caution unless the court so directs. His position is equiparated both with that of a tutor under the Judicial Factors Act 1849 (c 51), who is entitled to be reimbursed for all reasonable outlays made on behalf of the ward, and with the office of trustee within the meaning of the Trusts (Scotland) Acts 1921 and 1961[6].

As administrators-at-law the parents manage the estate of the pupil child and govern his person and are entitled to recover sums due to him and to grant discharges on his behalf. The discharge of a parent acting in this capacity is generally a sufficient protection to those who make payment of a sum due to the child, but there may be circumstances where, for example if such a person is aware that the parent is insolvent, it would be the duty of a person making such a payment to protect the child's interests by requiring the parent to find caution or refusing to make payment except under direction from the court. Where the child's interests dictate, the court may in such circumstances supersede a parent in the exercise of his guardianship and appoint a factor *loco tutoris*[7].

A stranger donating or bequeathing an estate to a pupil in a will may nominate someone other than a parent to manage the estate during pupillarity or minority. Although such a person is called a tutor, his powers extend only to the subject of the bequest and not to the person of the ward.

1 See the Guardianship Act 1973 (c 29), s 10 (repealed), and para 1209 above.
2 See para 1209 above.
3 See the Law Reform (Parent and Child) (Scotland) Act 1986 (c 9), s 4, and para 1211 above.
4 *Hogan* (1899) 7 SLT 22.
5 See the Law Reform (Parent and Child) (Scotland) Act 1986, s 3(1), (2), and para 1209 above.
6 See the Trusts (Scotland) 1921 (c 58), s 2 (amended by the Law Reform (Parent and Child) (Scotland) Act 1986, s 10(1), Sch 1, para 4 (re-enacting the Guardianship of Infants Act 1925 (c 45), s 10 (repealed)), and TRUSTS, TRUSTEES AND JUDICIAL FACTORS, vol 24, para 128. The law as set out in *Shearer's Tutor* 1924 SC 445 is altered. See also *Linton v Inland Revenue Comrs* 1928 SC 209 at 214, 1928 SLT 154 at 156, 157, per Lord President Clyde, and the *Cunningham's Tutrix* 1949 SC 275, 1949 SLT 357. The Trusts (Scotland) Acts 1921 and 1961 comprise the Trusts (Scotland) Act 1921 and the Trusts (Scotland) Act 1961 (c 57): s 7(1).
7 See further para 1216 below.

1215. Tutors at law or tutors legitim. In accordance with the principle of family solidarity, the nearest male agnate was by ancient statute, and as in Roman law, entitled to be appointed tutor in default of any appointed by the parents. Where a pupil has no tutor, which can since 1973 occur only where both parents are dead and there is no nominated tutor[1], or no nominated tutor prepared to act, the tutor at law may act as the guardian. He must be twenty-five years of age and fulfil the requirements of a brieve of tutory.

The ancient process of brieve of tutory is not now exercised[2], but when it was, the tutor at law obtained the office to which he was entitled by obtaining a brieve from Chancery on application to any judge with jurisdiction, and inquiry was carried out by a sworn inquest. The jury sitting had the task of finding that the applicant was the nearest male agnate of twenty-five years of age or more, and of carrying out any necessary inquiry. The nominee had to find caution which was lodged in the court granting the brieve and take the oath, and was subject to the court's supervision. In the same process the person being the mother or the nearest cognate who was to have custody of the pupil's person was ascertained. The tutor at law never obtained custody of the pupil *per se*, as he was by definition nearest to him in succession, but he was responsible for providing for the pupil's welfare. The tutor swore the oath *de fideli administratione* before a judge.

The ancient process of brieve of tutory was superseded by the method of applying for the appointment of a factor *loco tutoris*, an officer of the court[3]. A factor *loco tutoris* will not be appointed to act along with the mother[4]. Since the enactment of the Law Reform (Parent and Child) (Scotland) Act 1986, the appointment of a tutor can be made in an application for parental rights[5]. It will be recalled that the right to make such an application is not confined to blood relatives.

1 See para 1214 above.
2 However, the process is still competent: *Dick v Douglas* 1924 SC 787, 1924 SLT 578.
3 Ie under the Judicial Factors Act 1849 (c 51) (commonly referred to as 'the Pupils Protection Act'), and the Judicial Factors (Scotland) Act 1889 (c 39): see TRUSTS, TRUSTEES AND JUDICIAL FACTORS, vol 24, paras 237 ff.
4 *Speirs* 1946 SLT 203, OH.
5 See the Law Reform (Parent and Child) (Scotland) Act 1986 (c 9), s 3(1), and para 1209 above.

1216. Tutors dative and factors *loco tutoris*. In default of a tutor at law or tutor legitim, a tutor dative may be appointed by the court. Such a person formerly obtained office by presenting a signature to the Court of the Exchequer. The functions of that court have been transferred to the Court of Session, and the nomination, appointment and control of tutors dative are now within its jurisdiction and are exercised on application by petition to the Inner House.

The appointment of judicial factors on the estates of pupils not having a tutor for the purposes of regulating the administration of those estates is quite commonplace. No appointment as a tutor dative may be made until a year after a tutor at law might have served. As with a tutor at law, a tutor dative must take the oath and find caution, and is subject to the supervision of the Accountant of Court[1]. In modern practice a factor *loco tutoris* (who will not be appointed jointly with the mother) is almost invariably appointed, but the appointment of a tutor under the provisions of the old common law is still competent. A factor *loco tutoris* is appointed only to attend to the management of the pupil's affairs, and not to govern his person. He should be a disinterested person.

A tutor dative may be removed, on cause shown, and a factor *loco tutoris* may be appointed in his place. The impecuniosity of the factor is not of itself grounds for his removal, nor is the possibility of conflict between the interests of factor and child. A temporary appointment may be made if the court is dissatisfied with the performance of a tutor nominate.

A factor *loco tutoris* appointed to a pupil becomes his *curator bonis* when he attains minority, but that office terminates if the minor chooses curators. The action for the choosing of curators was abolished by the Administration of Justice (Scotland) Act 1933[2], and the usual procedure now is by petition to the Outer House[3]. A petition to the sheriff has been held competent[4].

1 See TRUSTS, TRUSTEES AND JUDICIAL FACTORS, vol 24, paras 237 ff.
2 See the Administration of Justice (Scotland) Act 1933 (c 41), s 12(1).

3 RC 189(a)(iii).
4 *Maclean* 1956 SLT (Sh Ct) 90.

1217. Pro tutors and pro curators. The descriptions 'pro tutor' and 'pro curator' apply to persons who assume to act as tutors or curators without legal title to the office. They do not enjoy the active powers or privileges of the office, such as to raise or defend actions or to grant discharges, but are liable to all the obligations of a duly appointed tutor or curator. Any sale of the property of the pupil or minor carried through by such persons is null and liable to reduction.

1218. Expiry of office of tutor. The office of tutor expires on the death of the pupil, or on his attainment of minority. If the tutor fails in his duty, or becomes incapable himself, or is somehow morally unsuitable or otherwise perceived to be unfit to hold his office, he may be removed by the Court of Session[1]. He may resign from office[2], although the common law did not permit him to do so after acceptance, without showing cause[3].

He is liable to account for intromissions with the estate of the pupil and for loss or damage sustained by the estate and resulting from his administration, where the pupil's position cannot be restored[4]. He is entitled to proper reimbursement of his outlays, and to exoneration and discharge which is now obtained by a petition to the court[5]. Claims against a factor *loco tutoris* no longer prescribe[6].

A person appointed tutor testamentar or tutor nominate automatically becomes curator of that child unless the appointment specifically provides otherwise[7]. A person appointed by a court to be a tutor to a child automatically becomes curator of that child unless the court orders otherwise[8]. A person appointed factor *loco tutoris* becomes ipso facto curator of the child unless the child chooses curators[9].

1 See the Judicial Factors Act 1849 (c 51), s 31, and the Law Reform (Parent and Child) (Scotland) Act 1986 (c 9), ss 3(1), 8 (as to which see para 1209 above). See also Erskine *Institute* I,7,29; Lord Fraser *Parent and Child* (3rd edn, 1906, ed J Clark) p 411.
2 See the Judicial Factors Act 1849, s 31, and the Trusts (Scotland) Act 1921 (c 58), s 3 (as to which see TRUSTS, TRUSTEES AND JUDICIAL FACTORS, vol 24, paras 164, 165).
3 *Lord Fraser* pp 408, 480.
4 Erskine *Institute* I,7,31,32.
5 See the Judicial Factors Act 1849, s 34, and RC 189. See also W W McBryde and N J Dowie *Petition Procedure in the Court of Session* (2nd edn, 1988), pp 1 ff.
6 See the Prescription and Limitation (Scotland) Act 1973 (c 52), ss 7, 16, Schs 3, 5.
7 Law Reform (Parent and Child) (Scotland) Act 1986, s 3(3).
8 Ibid, s 4(2).
9 See the Judicial Factors (Scotland) Act 1889 (c 39), s 11. See also *Ferguson v Blair* (1908) 16 SLT 284, OH. The action for the choosing of curators has been abolished: see para 1216 above.

5. CURATORS

1219. Introduction. A minor manages his own estate and property, and is legally able to transact himself, but only 'with the consent and concurrence' of his curator, *qua* adviser. A minor's powers of administration are unlimited, provided he acts with the concurrence of the curator: the curator cannot of course act himself in place of the minor. If the minor is resistant to the advice of the curator, the curator should properly apply to be relieved of his office.

1220. Appointment of curator. The right to appointment as a curator is very similar to the rights regarding the appointment of a tutor[1]. Both parents are curators of their minor child with the same rights and authority as each other[2]. Any nomination of a testamentary curator must be made by a deed executed *in liege poustie* (that is to say, not by a deed made on the parent's deathbed). A curator will only be imposed on a minor in the following instances:

(1) a curator may be appointed to manage a child's property. Where the parents are alive, they are of course *ipso jure* curators to the child. If a parent has given his consent, or if he has acted in violation of his duty or if there is a conflict of interest between him and the child, another curator may be appointed for the management of the child's property. It is thought this will be a very rare occurrence as the mother is now a curator as well as the father, but in the event of the failure of both parents, such an appointment is conceivable;

(2) under the Tutors and Curators Act 1696 (c 8), the father may by a deed executed *in liege poustie* nominate a curator.

The potential scope for the appointment of curators has been widened beyond those with an interest as a relative or a person concerned with the administration of the minor's estate by the Law Reform (Parent and Child) (Scotland) Act 1986, which permits a petition to be presented by any person claiming an interest for the appointment of a curator[3].

The court does not appoint curators to a minor *ex proprio motu*. It is sometimes arranged for particular sums of money obtained by a minor as a result of a court action, or following a bequest, to be held in trust for the minor until he attains majority. In those circumstances the court will appoint a *curator bonis*, but usually with the consent of the minor himself. A minor may present a petition to the court to have a curator appointed, if he so desires or requests[4]. These provisions overlap to some extent with the provisions of the Law Reform (Parent and Child) (Scotland) Act 1986, which may apparently be used by a minor for both the appointment and, it is thought, the removal of curators.

1 See paras 1214 ff above.
2 See the Law Reform (Parent and Child) (Scotland) Act 1986 (c 9), s 2, and para 1209 above.
3 Ibid, s 3(1).
4 See the Administration of Justice (Scotland) Act 1933 (c 41), s 12(1), and RC 189(a)(iii).

1221. Termination of office of curator. Curatory ends when the minor attains majority, or when he or the curator dies. The office may be brought to an end in the same circumstances as that of a tutor or factor *loco tutoris*[1]. The duty of a curator to account to the minor for his actings is similarly balanced by the entitlement of the guardian to recover outlays preferably expended for the minor in the course of the administration.

1 See paras 1216, 1218, above.

6. ADMINISTRATION BY TUTORS, FACTORS *LOCO TUTORIS* AND CURATORS

1222. Introduction. As already noticed, the function of the tutor is to administer and that of the curator to see to the administration of the ward's estate with a view to its preservation and sound management[1]. They are persons in a fiduciary position, and the general rule applies to them that they cannot be *auctores in rem suam*[2]. They must not use the office for the advancement of their private interests, and any benefit which accrues to them as a result of their office must be held by them as trustees and applied for the benefit of the estate. It must be accounted for as if it were the estate of the ward. They must not take personal profit from the estate, nor must they transact with it as individuals.

1 See para 1207 above.
2 See TRUSTS, TRUSTEES AND JUDICIAL FACTORS, vol 24, para 246.

1223. Administration by tutors and factors *loco tutoris*. In modern practice all tutors and factors *loco tutoris* must lodge with the Accountant of Court a rental of the lands and estate and a statement of the moveable property belonging to the pupil: in their administration of the estate, they are subject to the provisions of the Judicial Factors Acts and come under the supervision of the Accountant of Court[1]. Debts due to the estate must be recovered, and titles should be made up in the pupil's name.

As trustees within the meaning of the Trusts (Scotland) Acts[2], tutors are entitled to exercise the powers which are conferred by statute on trustees[3]. The Judicial Factors Acts prescribe the form of the rental and the inventory which tutors and factors must lodge after taking up office[4]; the next-of-kin must concur or be summoned and on their failure to appear the inventory is made up at the sight of the judge or of a delegate or commissioner appointed by him. Such a process is competent either in the Court of Session or the sheriff court.

It is the inventory with any necessary additions or eiks which forms the fund of which account has to be given. A guardian is liable for omissions in an action at the instance of the ward, who alone has the right to enforce the penalties against the guardian personally. Such penalties include liability for omissions from the inventory, the forfeiture of any exemptions from any joint liability and the refusal of any deduction for personal expenses or the expenses of litigation.

1 As to the Judicial Factors Act, see TRUSTS, TRUSTEES AND JUDICIAL FACTORS, vol 24, paras 237 ff, and as to supervision by the Accountant of Court, see vol 24, paras 242, 243, 255.
2 Ie the Trusts (Scotland) Act 1921 (c 58), and the Trusts (Scotland) Act 1961 (c 57): see TRUSTS, TRUSTEES AND JUDICIAL FACTORS, vol 24, para 128.
3 See TRUSTS, TRUSTEES AND JUDICIAL FACTORS, vol 24, paras 170 ff.
4 See the Judicial Factors Act 1849 (c 51), s 3 (amended by the AS (Appointment of Judicial Factors and Rules of Court Amendment No 2) 1967, SI 1967/487, art 2).

1224. Administration by curators. Administration by curators is somewhat different from that of tutors or factors *loco tutoris*.

> 'The law gives no right or title of management of a minor's estate to his curators, further than giving him their advice and concurrence to assist himself in managing'[1].

The curator is responsible to see that the minor applies similar standards to the performance of acts relative to his estate and to insist on like standards of administration. By definition curators do not have complete control, but

> 'Their duty is to see to the minor's affairs, that they get no detriment; and they must answer, not only for the deeds whereunto they consent, but for their omission, and for any detriment to the minor suffereth by their negligence'[2].

If the curator finds that the minor will not follow his advice or do what is necessary for the proper administration of the estate, he may apply to be relieved of his office.

The provisions of the Judicial Factors Acts[3] do not apply to a curator to a minor, but in the definition of 'trustee' in the Trusts (Scotland) Act 1921 factors and curators, and any person holding an appointment, be it judicial or otherwise, on another person's estate are embraced within the definition[4].

An important distinction is to be found between a curator to a minor and a *curator bonis*[5] appointed to a minor. A *curator bonis* is alone responsible to the

Accountant of Court and is bound to find caution for the exercise of his office[6]. His administrative duties generally are different[6].

> 'The distinction between a *curator bonis* and a curator to a minor is that the former acts in place of the minor in administering the estate, and the administration is subject to the control of the Accountant until the minor attains majority or has the curatory recalled and replaced, while the latter acts along with the minor'[7].

1 *Allan v Walker* (1812) Hume 586, per Lord Meadowbank.
2 Stair *Institutions* I,6,36,
3 As to the Judicial Factors Acts, see TRUSTS, TRUSTEES and JUDICIAL FACTORS, vol 24, paras 237 ff.
4 See the Trusts (Scotland) Act 1921 (c 58), s 2, and TRUSTS, TRUSTEES AND JUDICIAL FACTORS, vol 24, para 128.
5 Ie a curator appointed when a person through mental disability or otherwise is unable to administer his own estate: see paras 1232 ff below.
6 See further paras 1232 ff below.
7 *Maclean* 1956 SLT (Sh Ct) 90.

1225. Management. The standard of management adopted by the guardian, as in the case of all persons managing for others, must be 'good ordinary management' for the benefit of the *incapax* and his estate. He has power to apply to the court for authority, and would be wise to do so for any important or extraordinary step falling outside ordinary tutorial or curatorial administration. Such application, which had formerly to take the form of an action of declarator, soon came to take that of a petition to the *nobile officium*, and must now be presented to the Outer House[1]. Even acting with the authority of the court will not protect the tutor if there has been inaccurate representation of the facts in any petition.

Guardians are bound to recover all debts owing to the *incapax* if necessary by raising such actions as are necessary and doing diligence as soon as possible. Failure to follow up a hopeless debt is not a ground of fault. Funds in trade should be withdrawn in due course, as guardians are liable for loss sustained therefrom, but the retention of what appears to be a good heritable investment is not a ground of liability. A guardian must recover all writs and titles. Titles should be made up in the pupil's and not in the tutor's name. Money must be banked at once and invested within three months from the annual balance. In a position of trusteeship, the responsibility of the choice of investments rests with the guardian, but since the sufficiency of such investments may come for consideration by the Accountant of Court, guardians would neglect at their peril his rule of confining such investments to those prescribed by the Trusts Acts[2].

In the old law, the alienation of heritage was null as between tutor and pupil. Borrowing on heritable property was considered unwise. A tutor might carry on a lease, but should not enter into one as a new lease. It is thought preferable, where possible, to renounce existing leases. It would be necessary to apply for special powers to take an important step such as selling a house. Powers to trade will not be granted. A tutor has wider powers over moveable property much more akin to those of a proprietor.

The final sanction to the ward if a satisfactory accounting cannot be obtained is his power to reduce the actings of the guardian within the *quadriennium utile* on the ground of lesion[3].

It has been said that the liability of tutors and curators depends on their category — a father (or mother since 1973) would only be liable for gross negligence, while nominated tutors or curators must show the same diligence as in their own affairs, and curators chosen by a minor, tutors dative and tutors at law must show the 'exact' diligence of a provident man[4].

1 RC 189.
2 See TRUSTS, TRUSTEES AND JUDICIAL FACTORS, vol 24, para 207.
3 See para 1205 above.
4 Lord Fraser *Parent and Child* (3rd edn, 1906, ed J Clark) p 392; Stair *Institutions* I,6,21; Erskine *Institute* I,7,26.

7. CURATORS *AD LITEM*

1226. Appointment of curator *ad litem* generally. Where a pupil has no tutor or his tutor refuses to concur in his proposed course of action, he may institute proceedings and ask the court to appoint a curator *ad litem*[1] to protect his interests. If a pupil is sued, the court may appoint a curator *ad litem* even although no appearance has been entered[2]: the term 'tutor *ad litem*' is not appropriate. When a minor becomes involved in litigation, the court may also appoint a curator *ad litem* to guard his interests for the duration of the action.

A minor may, of course, commence proceedings without the consent of his curator, but in that event a defender may object to the proceedings continuing until the guardian joins in and signifies his assent, or until a curator *ad litem* is appointed by the court[3]. Such a curator will be routinely appointed where a defender, or prospective defender, is under a mental disability and is unable to conduct or respond to legal proceedings[4].

Although his designation is explicit, there is a common misconception that the rights of a curator *ad litem* extend beyond the subject matter of the action to the estate of the ward. They do not. His appointment is to safeguard the interests of the ward in the action, and the appointment terminates with the action.

The appointment of a factor to administer damages awarded to a pupil or minor is an appointment distinct from that of a curator *ad litem* and is regulated by Rules of Court[5].

1 *Ward v Walker* 1920 SC 80, 1920 1 SLT 2.
2 *Drummond's Trustees v Peel's Trustees* 1929 SC 484, 1929 SLT 450.
3 J A Maclaren *Court of Session Practice* (1916) p 172.
4 *Maclaren* p 185. See also the Divorce (Scotland) Act 1976 (c 39), s 11.
5 See RC 131–134. See also the Sheriff Courts (Scotland) Act 1907 (c 51), Sch 1, r 128 (substituted by AS (Ordinary Cause Rules, Sheriff Court) 1983, SI 1983/747).

1227. Appointment of curator *ad litem* in particular proceedings. In a special case presented to the Inner House[1] where the parties are agreed on the facts and are in dispute only on the law, a curator *ad litem* who is an advocate may be appointed if one of the parties is *incapax*, and he is charged by Rules of Court to consider the presentation of the case and to report[2].

In adoptions, the appointment and conduct of the curator *ad litem* is subject to detailed regulations. He is required to report in a specified way on a whole host of matters of importance before a court may consider an adoption petition[3]. It is understood that the preparation of such reports is carried out in a standard fashion, so far as possible, and subject to the supervision of one or a small number of sheriffs in each court, all in an effort to achieve and maintain uniform standards in this important area. It is also understood that sheriff clerks maintain lists of suitable solicitors who have indicated their willingness to act as curators and reporting officers in adoption cases.

The Ordinary Cause Rules provide for the special appointment of a curator *ad litem* in actions of divorce or separation only in such cases where it appears to the sheriff that a defender is suffering from mental disorder[4]. Presumably it would be competent to an opposing party to enrol a motion craving the appointment of a curator *ad litem* so that a sheriff could have a chance of making up his mind at an early stage in the action.

1 Ie presented under the Court of Session Act 1988 (c 36), s 27: see PROCEDURE, vol 17, paras 1428–1430.
2 See RC 266.
3 See RC 220–222, 224, 230. See generally P G B McNeill *Adoption of Children in Scotland* (2nd edn, 1986).
4 See the Sheriff Courts (Scotland) Act 1907 (c 51), Sch 1, r 133 (substituted by AS (Consistorial Causes) 1984, SI 1984/255, and the AS (Amendment of Ordinary Cause Rules) 1986, SI 1986/1230).

1228. Conduct of proceedings. A curator *ad litem* must exercise independent judgment[1]. He may conduct or compromise an action on behalf of a pupil without reference to the pupil, and is accordingly *dominus litis*[2]. By contrast, he may not conduct or settle an action raised by or defended by a minor without the minor's concurrence[3].

A curator *ad litem* is not personally responsible for expenses if he is unsuccessful in an action. It has been said that the normal rule applies, but it is clear from isolated cases that in relation to expenses a curator *ad litem* receives more favourable consideration[4], and where he is appointed to children in conflict with a parent, the parent is usually found liable for the costs of the curator *ad litem*, whether or not he is successful[5]. It is said that the court will always endeavour to secure his expenses out of whatever fund is available[6]. He is entitled to proper professional remuneration for perusal of papers, even if he decides not to enter an appearance[7]. A curator *ad litem* who lodges a minute[8] stating that he does not intend to lodge defences in a consistorial action is entitled to an order by the court providing that his fee and expenses are to be met by the pursuer[9].

1 *Dewar v Dewar's Trustees* (1906) 14 SLT 238, OH.
2 *M'Cuaig v M'Cuaig* 1909 SC 355 at 357, per Lord President Dunedin.
3 *Graham v Graham* (1843) 5 D 497.
4 See *Studd v Cook* (1883) 10 R (HL) 53, 8 App Cas 577; *Crum Ewing's Trustees v Bayly's Trustees* 1910 SC 994, 1910 2 SLT 174. See also RC 266(c).
5 *Smith v Smith's Trustee* (1900) 8 SLT 226, OH; *M'Neil's Judicial Factor v Brown* (1904) 11 SLT 522, OH.
6 *Rooney v Cormack* (1895) 23 R 11, 3 SLT 133; *Walker v Walker* (1903) 5 F 320, 10 SLT 551.
7 *Rennie* (1849) 11 D 1201; *Collie v Collie* (1851) 13 D 841.
8 Ie in terms of RC 167(1)(c).
9 *Practice Note* dated 10 February 1983.

8. LOCAL AUTHORITIES AS GUARDIANS

1229. Introduction. Necessarily, any review of the law of guardianship cannot avoid reference to the statutory encroachments made over the years to the common law, whereby the rights of parents as administrators-at-law of their children have been circumscribed to a greater or lesser extent. This finds its most important modern expression in the Social Work (Scotland) Act 1968[1], which provides that where a child under the age of seventeen has neither parent nor guardian, or is abandoned or lost, or where the parent or guardian is, for the time being or permanently, prevented by illness or mental disorder or other incapacity, or in any other circumstances, from providing for the child's proper accommodation, maintenance and upbringing, then the local authority has a duty to receive that child into its care, and to keep the child subject to the provisions of the Act until the child is eighteen and has therefore attained the age of majority[2]. This is a wide-ranging provision, giving local authorities jurisdiction to at least consider, and if thought advisable to implement, measures for taking children into care in a myriad of possible situations where they are threatened with, or have actually been inflicted with, some form of abuse, violence or distress, or even where the parents' suitability (because of some action or inaction by one or both of them) is called into question. In practice, the criteria employed in the use of such provisions may vary widely from locality to locality and depend, in some measure, upon the degree of enthusiasm and the extent of resources available to local authority social workers[3].

Throughout the legislation the 'welfare of the child' is deemed to be the determining criterion, although the Social Work (Scotland) Act 1968, its predecessors, and even more modern Acts[4] are silent as to any definition. Generally, in judicial proceedings, it is not a matter of great difficulty to determine where the welfare of a child lies, but without the judicial check it is at least legitimate to comment that standards may vary from place to place, depending on enthusiasm and resources, with a consequent effect on the numbers of children residing in local authority residential establishments.

1 See the Social Work (Scotland) Act 1968 (c 49), s 15 (amended by the Children Act 1975 (c 72), s 73, and the Health and Social Services and Social Security Adjudications Act 1983 (c 41), s 9, Sch 2, para 4).
2 Social Work (Scotland) Act 1968, s 15(1), (2). The local authority is the regional or islands council: s 1(2) (amended by the Local Government (Scotland) Act 1973 (c 65), s 214(2), Sch 27, Pt II, para 183).
3 See generally SOCIAL WORK, vol 22, paras 1 ff.
4 Eg the Law Reform (Parent and Child) (Scotland) Act 1986 (c 9).

1230. Vesting of relevant parental rights and powers. The Social Work (Scotland) Act 1968 provides that, subject to certain of its provisions[1], the local authority may resolve that there is to vest in it the relevant parental rights and powers in respect of a child who is in its care, or that such rights and powers may vest in certain prescribed voluntary organisations[2]. Such a resolution may be passed if it appears to the local authority either that the parents of the child are dead, and that he has no guardian, or that there exists in respect of a parent or guardian of the child certain circumstances[3] requiring the intervention of the local authority and its social workers[4]. 'Relevant parental rights and powers' are closely defined but do not include the power to consent to adoption[5].

Provision appears throughout for proper notice to be given to the natural parents or the guardian of the child in question where their whereabouts are known[6]. Such a person may take objection to the assumption of parental rights and, if the matter comes to dispute, provision is made for the resolution of that dispute before the sheriff[6]. Parental rights may also be assumed in respect of children in the care of voluntary organisations, and again, provision is made for the resolution of disputes by the sheriff[7].

The Act defines the effect of the assumption by a local authority of parental rights and permits fostering, the boarding of a child with a parent, guardian, relative or friend notwithstanding the assumption of parental rights, and adoption[8]. The assumption of parental rights by a local authority does not relieve a parent of his or her obligation to aliment the child[9].

A resolution to assume parental rights continues in force until the child attains the age of majority[10]. It may be rescinded during its currency if it appears to the local authority that that is in the child's interests[11]. A parent or guardian may apply for rescission of the resolution to the sheriff, who may determine the application or, instead, order that the child be placed in the care of the person making the application[12]. Children's interests in such proceedings may be safeguarded by the appointment of a person (usually a practising solicitor) known as a 'safeguarder', whose duty as *amicus curiae* is to represent the interests of the child independent of the interests of the local authority, the natural parents or any guardian[13]. The result of each case will nearly always turn upon its own circumstance, subject to the overriding injunction to regard the welfare of the child as the paramount consideration[14].

1 Ie the provisions of the Social Work (Scotland) Act 1968 (c 49), Pt II (ss 12–29).
2 See ibid, s 16(1)(a), (b) (substituted by the Children Act 1975 (c 72), s 74).
3 Ie the circumstances specified in the Social Work (Scotland) Act 1968, s 16(2) (as so substituted).
4 Ibid, s 16(1)(i), (ii) (as so substituted).
5 See ibid, s 16(3) (as so substituted).
6 See generally, s 16(5)–(13) (as so substituted, and amended by the Law Reform (Parent and Child) (Scotland) Act 1986 (c 9), s 10(1), Sch 1, para 9(1)).
7 See the Social Work (Scotland) Act 1968, s 16A (added by the Children Act 1975, s 75).
8 Social Work (Scotland) Act 1968, s 17(3) (amended by the Children Act 1975, s 108(1)(a), Sch 3, para 52).
9 Social Work (Scotland) Act 1968, s 17(6).
10 Ibid, s 18(1).
11 Ibid, s 18(2) (amended by the Children Act 1975, Sch 3, para 53).
12 See the Social Work (Scotland) Act 1968, s 18(3) (as so amended).
13 See ibid, s 18A (substituted by the Children Act 1975, s 78, and amended by the Health and Social Services and Social Security Adjudications Act 1983 (c 41), s 7(3)).
14 As to the welfare of the child, see para 1229 above.

1231. Care provisions. The scheme of the 1968 'care' provisions[1] is a very wide ranging one and, in conjunction with the duties of the reporter to local children's panels and the operation of the panels themselves, is thought to provide as comprehensive and detailed a framework as is necessary in current conditions, where the extent of urban deprivation and, unhappily, the increase in abuse and neglect of children in one form or another renders such watchdog and all encompassing provisions necessary. It is not thought that this title is the place to examine in detail the criteria applied by those responsible for the implementation of the measures[2], but some assistance can be obtained from a study of the few decided cases[3].

1 Ie under the Social Work (Scotland) Act 1968 (c 49), Pt II (ss 12–29), Pt III (ss 30–58).
2 See generally, LOCAL GOVERNMENT, vol 14, para 608, and SOCIAL WORK, vol 22, paras 17 ff. See further CHILDREN AND YOUNG PERSONS, and FAMILY LAW.
3 *Lothian Regional Council v S* 1986 SLT (Sh Ct) 37; *Central Regional Council v B* 1985 SLT 413; *Beagley v Beagley* 1984 SLT 202, HL; *Strathclyde Regional Council v T* 1984 SLT (Sh Ct) 18; *Lothian Regional Council v T* 1984 SLT 74; *Lothian Regional Council v B* 1984 SLT (Sh Ct) 83; *MacInnes v Highland Regional Council* 1982 SC 69, 1982 SLT 288, OH; *Lothian Regional Council v H* 1982 SLT (Sh Ct) 65; *Strathclyde Regional Council v M* 1982 SLT (Sh Ct) 106; *Strathclyde Regional Council v D* 1981 SLT (Sh Ct) 34; *Strathclyde Regional Council v McNair* 1980 SLT (Sh Ct) 16; *Central Regional Council v Mailley* 1977 SLT (Sh Ct) 36.

9. CURATORY OF THOSE UNDER MENTAL DISABILITY

1232. Introducton. Persons over the age of majority have, of course, a natural right to manage their own affairs and property. Before this right can be removed from them there must be a formal process of sufficient rigidity to ensure that the process is not abused, but of sufficient flexibility to ensure that it is capable of providing a relatively speedy, reliable and certain process whereby the means and estate of persons labouring under mental impairment may be properly, efficiently and safely administered if the person in right of the estate is not in a fit mental state.

In former times the method was known as cognition of the insane; a jury was convened, and if after inquiry a person was found to be jurious or furious or labouring under such unsoundness of mind as to render him incapable of managing his affairs, the nearest agnate was appointed curator in the absence of a living parent, who was preferred[1].

The procedure has fallen into disuse, but is still competent: without cognition the nearest male agnate may be appointed tutor dative[2] on a petition to the Outer House supported by two medical certificates[3]. This practice has itself been supplemented by the use of *curatores bonis*, whose appointment may be sought on petition to the Outer House[4].

1 Curators Act 1585 (c 18).
2 As to tutors dative, see para 1216 above.
3 As to medical certificates, see para 1233 below.
4 See further para 1233 below.

1233. Appointment of *curator bonis*. The appointment of a *curator bonis* may be sought on petition to the Outer House, supported by two medical certificates certifying the ward's inability to manage his own affairs or give instructions for their management[1]. The certificates must be dated within thirty days of the application, and detailed provision is made for safeguarding the interests of the *incapax*, for example by providing that service on the *incapax* may be dispensed with if it is certified that such a step would be injurious to health[2]. If special powers to sell heritable property belonging to the *incapax* are to be sought, the medical certificates must state that in the opinion of the examiner the *incapax* will never return to the house.

The medical certificates should be holograph of, or adopted as holograph by, the certifying doctor. They need not be on soul and conscience[3].

The petition may be at the instance of anyone disclosing an interest, for example a relative, the family solicitor, a neighbour, a local authority or the Mental Welfare Commission[4]. The criterion applied is that the person of unsound mind is incapable of managing his own affairs or of giving instructions for their management, not necessarily from the onset of insanity, but in the case of loss of vital faculties or the onset of *dementia*[5]. If a petition is opposed (perhaps by another relative, or the person who is the subject of the petition) the court will itself determine what inquiry or further certification should be made[6]. There is no right to insist on a cognition, and there is usually a remit to expert psychiatric examiners[7]. The petition should be served on all those interested or potentially interested in the estate of the *incapax*, and the *curator bonis* must not have an interest adverse to that of the *incapax*.

In a petition for the appointment of a *curator bonis*, the agent should always be clear, or as clear as possible, about the court's jurisdiction. It is thought that the court will always act to prevent abuse[8] or to protect the interests of, for example, a foreign *incapax* with property in Scotland, or a Scottish *incapax* with property abroad. The interlocutor of appointment has effect throughout the British Dominions[9]. The provisions relating to an application for an order respecting the tutory or curatory of a pupil or minor under the Family Law Act 1986[10] does not apply to petitions for the appointment of a *curator bonis* or to any application made by one (or by a facto *loco tutoris*).

Normally one person only is appointed, although appointments of more than one person are not unheard of, though rare[11]. Curators are normally professional people. If it is sought to appoint other than a professional person, the choice must be justified to the court, and the motion for the appointment will be starred. It is routine for a local authority finance officer to be appointed. A *curator bonis* must be a natural person; a limited company may not be a *curator bonis*[12]. An interim curator may be appointed if circumstances so dictate.

A *curator bonis* must find caution within one month of the interlocutor of appointment and before entering on the duties of his office[13]. The amount of any caution will depend in the first place on the inventory prepared by the petitioner.

1 RC 189.
2 RC 191(c). See also TRUSTS, TRUSTEES AND JUDICIAL FACTORS, vol 24, para 271.
3 *Practice Note* dated 6 June 1968.
4 As to the functions and duties of the Mental Welfare Commission, see the Mental Health (Scotland) Act 1984 (c 36), s 39, and MENTAL HEALTH, vol 14, para 1409.
5 *Kirkpatrick* (1853) 15 D 734; *Dowie v Hagart* (1894) 21 R 1052, 2 SLT 184; *Duncan* 1915 2 SLT 50. See also N M L Walker *Judicial Factors* (1974) ch IV, and TRUSTS, TRUSTEES AND JUDICIAL FACTORS, vol 24, para 271.
6 See TRUSTS, TRUSTEES AND JUDICIAL FACTORS, vol 24, para 271.
7 *CB v AB* (1891) 18 R (HL) 40; *Brown v Hackston* 1960 SC 27, OH; *Fraser v Paterson* 1987 SLT 562, OH (sequel 1987 SCLR 577, 1988 SLT 124, OH). See TRUSTS, TRUSTEES AND JUDICIAL FACTORS, vol 24, para 271.
8 *Fraser v Paterson* 1987 SLT 562, OH (sequel 1987 SCLR 577, 1988 SLT 124, OH).
9 See the Judicial Factors (Scotland) Act 1889 (c 39), s 13 (amended by AS (Appointment of Judicial Factors and Rules of Court Amendment No 2) 1967, SI 1967/487, art 3).
10 Ie the Family Law Act 1986 (c 55), s 16.
11 J C Irons *Judicial Factors* (1908) pp 32, 274.
12 *Brogan* 1986 SLT 420, OH.
13 See RC 200(c), and TRUSTS, TRUSTEES AND JUDICIAL FACTORS, vol 24, para 242. As to the duties of a *curator bonis*, see para 1234 below.

1234. Duties of *curator bonis*. The *curator bonis* must communicate with the Accountant of Court month by month[1]. Special powers may be sought in the petition, for example to sell heritage[2]. Once appointed, and having found caution, a curator must lodge an inventory with the Accountant of Court within six months[3]. His duty is to preserve the estate until the recovery or death of the *incapax*, not to alter his rights of succession or otherwise to dissipate the assets[4]. In *Macqueen v Tod* Lord President Robertson said:

> 'The most general of these principles [of the law of guardianship] is that the curator of an insane person is there to preserve the estate. He is to do so in the spirit of one whose ward may at any time come back to her full legal rights. He is therefore to keep things going, rather than to change; he is to do nothing that is irretrievable, unless in case of necessity; and he is to preserve, as far as possible, such options as are open in the management of the estate, reserving them for his ward if she convalesce, or, if not, then for her heirs'[5].

The primary concern of the court is the interest of the ward, and there are indications that the court favours a conservative policy, particularly in relation to persons of great age[6]. A curator may retain shares in a private company, notwithstanding that they are not authorised trustee investments[7].

A *curator bonis* may apply to the Accountant of Court for consent to take any of the steps desiderated in section 2 of the Trusts (Scotland) Act 1961[8]. If there are objections to the proposed course, the curator must lodge a note for special powers in terms of section 7 of the Judicial Factors Act 1849[9].

1 As to the role of the Accountant of Court, see TRUSTS, TRUSTEES AND JUDICIAL FACTORS, vol 24, para 265.
2 See TRUSTS, TRUSTEES AND JUDICIAL FACTORS, vol 24, paras 254 ff.
3 See TRUSTS, TRUSTEES AND JUDICIAL FACTORS, vol 24, para 245.
4 See generally TRUSTS, TRUSTEES AND JUDICIAL FACTORS, vol 24, paras 243 ff.
5 *Macqueen v Tod* (1899) 1 F 1069 at 1075.
6 See generally W W McBryde and N J Dowie *Petition Procedure in the Court of Session* (2nd edn, 1988), ch 9.
7 As to trustee investments generally, see TRUSTS, TRUSTEES AND JUDICIAL FACTORS, vol 24, para 207.
8 RC 200A. As to the Trusts (Scotland) Act 1961 (c 57), s 2(3), see TRUSTS, TRUSTEES AND JUDICIAL FACTORS, vol 24, paras 262, 263, 265.

9 See 'Notes for the Guidance of Judicial Factors issued by the Accountant of Court', *Parliament House Book*, pp M 301 ff. See also *Carmichael's Judicial Factor v Accountant of Court* 1971 SC 295, 1971 SLT 336 (powers sought too wide); *Bristow* 1965 SLT 225, OH (power to sell heritage found justified, but unnecessary). As to the Judicial Factors Act 1849 (c 51), s 7, see TRUSTS, TRUSTEES AND JUDICIAL FACTORS, vol 24, paras 254, 255, 261, 262, 265.

1235. Discharge of *curator bonis*. A judicial discharge of a *curator bonis* is not necessary. An informal system of writing off a curatory has been in operation for many years[1]. Expense is thus saved. However, a curator may apply by formal petition to the Outer House for exoneration and discharge[1]. Once final accounts of charge and discharge[2], and expenses, are prepared and taxed, the curatory funds are handed over to the executors of the ward. When the Accountant of Court has prepared and written his final report, it is placed before the court, which formally exonerates and discharges the curator[3].

Other processes may be envisaged. If a *curator bonis* dies, a new curator will be required[3]. A fresh petition is necessary, and it is the practice to seek exoneration and discharge of the *curator bonis* and his representatives[3]. If a ward recovers, he may present a petition for the exoneration and discharge of his curator supported by two medical certificates[4]. The thirty-day rule for the certificates does not apply[5]. An application may be presented by a *curator bonis* who no longer wishes to act, and in the same way he must be discharged and a substitute appointed[6]. If a process is transmitted from the sheriff court to the Court of Session it may be necessary to reappoint a *curator bonis* who, until the date of transmission, has been operating under an interlocutor pronounced in the lower court.

All these processes are governed by the supervision of the Accountant of Court, who may himself make a report to the court if he is dissatisfied with the management of a curatory[7].

1 See TRUSTS, TRUSTEES AND JUDICIAL FACTORS, vol 24, para 267.
2 As to accounts of charge and discharge generally, see TRUSTS, TRUSTEES AND JUDICIAL FACTORS, vol 24, para 246.
3 See TRUSTS, TRUSTEES AND JUDICIAL FACTORS, vol 24, para 267.
4 See TRUSTS, TRUSTEES AND JUDICIAL FACTORS, vol 24, para 271, text and note 29.
5 As to the thirty-day rule, see para 1233 above.
6 See TRUSTS, TRUSTEES AND JUDICIAL FACTORS, vol 24, para 267.
7 See TRUSTS, TRUSTEES AND JUDICIAL FACTORS, vol 24, para 250.

1236. Problems with the exercise of the office of *curator bonis*. The administration of curatories for persons labouring under a mental incapacity presents three difficulties, namely:
(1) the costs of setting up and administering curatories;
(2) the lack of power over the person of the *incapax*; and
(3) the lack of independent scrutiny of social security benefits and the management of patients' accounts by hospital authorities.

The cost of setting up and administering curatories is sufficiently great to make them inappropriate for sufferers whose day-to-day affairs require management but whose financial resources are limited or non-existent. It is understood that the Accountant of Court does not recommend a formal appointment of a *curator bonis* for estates valued at less than £15,000. This appears to be somewhat in conflict with the recommendations of the Mental Health Commission, which considers a curatory appropriate for estates over £10,000, and the general rule in hospitals, where formal appointments are usually sought for estates worth over £5,000[1]. It is generally agreed that the operation of a curatory may impose an unacceptable drain on a small estate. It is understood that some regional councils offer to undertake free curatory work on small estates with their finance officers acting as curator, and this is relatively common. When the cost of operation of an estate becomes an unacceptably large drain on its resources, that very fact conflicts with the principle of preservation of the estate[2]. There may, therefore, be an unacceptable restriction on a curator spending money in order to improve the care which a ward requires.

A *curator bonis* cannot take power over the person of his ward, and is, therefore, technically unable to make decisions about medical treatment, an appropriate place of residence or removal to institutional care.

A problem which commonly arises relates to the payment of social security benefits. It is common to find sufferers from mental disease in receipt of some form of state pension or allowance. If such a person cannot apply for or uplift the payments to which he or she is entitled, and no curator is appointed, anyone over eighteen can apply to the Department of Social Security to be appointed to act on his or her behalf, and the decision to appoint such a person is taken, not by a court, but by the local office of the department. The actions of such a person are not subject to any independent scrutiny. In the same way, hospital author-ities are entitled to receive and hold money and valuables on behalf of a patient who has no curator and who is unable to manage his or her own affairs. That money may be used by the hospital at its discretion for the benefit of the ward, although there appears to be no legal duty so to apply the funds. Again, there is no independent scrutiny here of the management of patients' accounts. Such an absence of supervision may lead to fraudulent misuse of funds going un-detected. It may also reduce the opportunity for identifying cases where hospital authorities fail to spend patients' money on their behalf, either through lack of time or interest or because patients are believed to be too disordered to obtain any benefit. There is in fact no legal requirement on a hospital authority to spend patients' money in any particular way, nor indeed any requirement to spend it at all. There is thus no incentive to do other than purchase small consumer items; and it is thought to be unlikely in the extreme that hospital officials, who are likely to be hard pressed and who are not subject to any form of external scrutiny, will be prepared to undertake major responsibility for dealing with insurance or arranging expenditure on a house. In the absence of a curator it may well be that patients are left inadequately protected, with no-one able or with legal authority to undertake such tasks on their behalf. It is submitted that this is a profoundly unsatisfactory state of affairs.

1 See MENTAL HEALTH, vol 14, para 1420.

1237. Proposals for reform. In relation to those suffering from mental illness it is submitted that any reform of the provisions relating to curatories should provide:

(1) that every person who is legally incompetent, or approaching incom-petence, should have a statutory legal right to comprehensive care and protection;

(2) that any compulsory intervention in the life of such a person should be the minimum necessary to provide sufficient care and protection; and

(3) that there should be a far more simple and cheap procedure geared to ensuring that expert and comprehensive consideration is given by persons possessed of the relevant experience to the needs of each person who requires care and protection.

The present curatory procedures adopt an approach which totally removes control from the ward without any consideration of whether he is still able to make or be informed about any of the vital decisions in respect of his life. At present, a court will not consider whether a person's personal care is being neglected; the court is required simply to have regard to whether or not the *incapax* is capable of managing his own affairs. There is no duty at present to investigate whether or not a person's affairs are being properly managed, until after the appointment of the curator, and the appearance of the first and subsequent reports to the Accountant of Court. Even then, scrutiny is restricted to study of and comment upon the curator's six-monthly report. There is no scrutiny at all of persons authorised to collect social security benefits, nor of hospital authorities who manage patients' finances[1].

It is conceived that it may be possible to create an essentially inquisitorial system, the duty of which is to establish the most appropriate form of care for a mentally disordered person. The full assessment of mentally disordered persons requires an expertise which judges do not possess. It has been suggested that the Scottish system of children's hearings[2] may provide a model for a new procedure, with the appointment of reporters charged with a function to receive and act on information about persons allegedly at risk by reason of their mental infirmity.

Whether or not an inquisitorial system is ever adopted, it is submitted that the existing procedure for the appointment of a *curator bonis* could be made quicker, cheaper and easier as regards estates under a specified financial limit. A do-it-yourself application form with a full explanatory leaflet might be made available to any person wishing to be appointed as a *curator bonis*. Stocks of the forms could be held by sheriff courts, citizens advice bureaux, solicitors, Department of Social Security offices, Social Work departments and Health Boards. An application on the form would be transmitted to the local sheriff court for consideration by a sheriff sitting in chambers. There would be a restricted cost for such an application. The form would contain information about the sufferer and be accompanied by medical certification of his condition. The form would also contain information about the applicant and a summary of the estate, accompanied by relevant documentation. Proper intimation to those with an interest or potential interest in the estate would be required, with any such person given a right to be heard as at present.

Provision ought to be made for the appointment of an *amicus curiae*[3]. The sheriff ought to be able to dictate the amount and extent of any further investigation which he considers necessary, and, if necessary, to summon parties or persons before him to testify as to matters such as mental capacity, the extent of an estate, and proposals for management.

The present emphasis is on the appointment of professional persons or local authority officials as curators. That emphasis, it is submitted, ought to be changed so that relatives or other persons caring for the ward could act as curators. Joint curatories — as for example a wife and son — might be encouraged. There would be no remuneration, but a curator would be entitled to reimbursement of necessary expenses. The court would retain a discretion to appoint a professional curator if, for example, the estate was unusually complex. A local authority might be obliged to make an appropriate application, and the Mental Welfare Commission might retain its existing discretion so to do. It would be for discussion whether an authority should be entitled to charge.

A problem which is of frequent occurrence is where a local authority finance officer who has been appointed curator moves to another appointment with the authority and no longer acts as guardian. Under the present procedure, with its emphasis on personal responsibility, it is necessary to petition the court for exoneration and discharge of the outgoing officer, and the appointment of his replacement. Such a procedure is time-consuming and, it is understood, can cost as much as £300. It is submitted that there can be no real objection to the appointment of a senior local authority official, such as the Chief Solicitor, as *curator bonis ex officio*. He or she would be less likely to move from post to post, but even if he did, his *ex officio* appointment would do away with the need for exoneration and reappointment. Similarly, where a person was detained in hospital, a Health Board could be required or given a discretion to apply for the appointment of one of its senior officials as a curator. Supervision of those suffering from a mental illness and living in private residential nursing homes might be assumed by a local authority.

The discretion vested in the Department of Social Security to permit the collection of benefits by a 'self appointed' person should be abolished, and the department obliged to inform local authorities when no independent curator came forward.

Curators would have a range of powers which would be specified and explained in the leaflet, with a discretion to the court to expand or restrict those powers as appropriate. A curator should have the power to apply in an informal way for an extension of the powers on demonstrating a material change of circumstances and after proper intimation. There is no reason why legal advice should not be available under the Legal Advice and Assistance Scheme to assist lay people in making such an application.

Overall financial supervision should be exercised by the Accountant of Court, who could require the curator to account at periodic intervals. The office of the Accountant of Court could be expanded to provide information and advice to curators. The Accountant would have the power of random inspection. Upon default of performance the Accountant would have the power to remit the matter to the sheriff for termination of the curatory, and, if so advised, for the initiation of criminal proceedings by passing the papers to the procurator fiscal. Provision should be made for the termination of curatories on cause shown both in respect of the failure to provide proper accounts and also failing to act in the best interests of the ward.

1 See para 1236 above.
2 See further CHILDREN AND YOUNG PERSONS.
3 Ie a friend of the court; one who argues at the request or with the leave of the court for an unrepresented party or in the public interest.

10. GUARDIANSHIP OF THE PERSON OF THE MENTALLY DISABLED

1238. Introduction. The general law governs the position of pupils who are suffering from mental disability[1]. The statutory law relating to the rights and duties of local authorities in respect of the care of children is also relevant[2]. Apart from this, there are two forms of 'guardianship' that are designed for persons (without any upper age limit) suffering from a mental disability: the appointment of a tutor dative[3] and the appointment of a guardian under the Mental Health (Scotland) Act 1984[4]. The two offices are quite distinct. The latter is *sui generis* and is a creation of statute[4].

In considering an application for appointment in either capacity a court should, however, consider whether an appointment has already been made in the other capacity in order to avoid a situation of overlap in respect of the specific powers given (by the court in the case of a tutor dative, and by statute in the case of a Mental Health Act guardian)[5].

1 See paras 1232 ff above.

4 See para 1240 below.

5 See the Mental Health (Scotland) Act 1984 (c 36), ss 36–57, and para 1240 below.

1239. Tutors dative. A tutor dative may be appointed following a petition to the Inner House. The appointment can be made even though there is a *curator bonis*[1]. There is no clear guidance in the case law as to the nature and degree of mental disability that must be shown before the court will make the appointment. Stair refers to tutors of 'idiots or furious persons'[2]. This classification related to an understanding of mental handicap and mental illness which does not exactly accord with the approach of medical science today[3]. As the tutor appointed has certain powers over the person of the *incapax*, the appropriate test would seem to be whether the patient has a level of understanding to take decisions about the aspects of his life to which these powers relate[4].

In modern practice a tutor-dative is given specific powers by the court on appointment and is not treated as being able simply by virtue of appointment *qua* tutor to exercise all the powers of a tutor. This seems to follow from the fact that the tutor dative is seen in such cases as under the control of the court[5]. It is also consistent with the situation that there can be a *curator bonis* different from the tutor-dative, and it is thought desirable, given the potentially contentious nature of decisions that might be taken, particularly those involving medical intervention. In the one modern reported application (which was undefended)[6] the appointment sought was for five years with a right to apply for variation on change of circumstances. The powers given were a general power to provide 'care, support and guidance' together, apparently, with specific powers inter alia to decide where the patient should live and the nature of any work, education or training he might undertake, and to consent to any health care that was in the best interests of the patient[7].

1 *Dick v Douglas* 1924 SC 787, 1924 SLT 578.

2 Stair *Institutions* I,6,6.

3 Erskine *Institute* I,7,48 (considering curatory).

4 Cf the condition required for appointment of a *curator bonis*: *Fraser v Paterson* 1987 SLT 562, OH.

5 *Dick v Douglas* 1924 SC 787 at 792, 1924 SLT 578 at 580, per Lord President Clyde.

6 A D Ward 'Revival of Tutors-Dative' (*Morris, Petitioner*) 1987 SLT (News) 69.

7 See *Ward* 1987 SLT (News) 69 at 71, 72.

1240. Guardianship under the Mental Health (Scotland) Act 1984. A guardian under the Mental Health (Scotland) Act 1984 is a person appointed by the sheriff court with certain powers and duties in respect of a mentally disordered person who is over sixteen[1] and has not been compulsorily detained in hospital on a long-term basis[2]. The institution is conceived as an aspect of community care. However, community care usually takes place without any such appointment[3]. Before 1983[4] these statutory guardians were effectively tutors[5]. Now the guardian merely has a number of limited powers and duties relating to the person of the *incapax*, and none relating to property[6]. The powers and duties are those set out in the relevant legislation[7] or necessarily implied in it. The guardian is not *in loco parentis*[8]. The procedure for appointment of a guardian under the Act (technically 'reception into guardianship'), its renewal and termination are dealt with elsewhere in this work[9].

The nature and degree of the mental disability that must be shown before a guardian can be appointed under the Act is laid down in the legislation. A necessary precondition is that the patient is suffering from 'mental disorder' as defined in the Act[10]. This may take the form of mental handicap or mental illness or both[11]. Most appointments that have been made have been in respect of mentally handicapped people. The sheriff must be satisfied by recommendations of two doctors[12] that the mental disorder is of a nature or degree which warrants the patient's reception into guardianship[13] and, in addition, must be satisfied in the light of evidence from a mental health officer[14] appointed by the relevant local authority for the area (in practice by its Social Work Department) that it is necessary in the interests of the welfare of the patient[15].

What these requirements amount to is a pragmatic consideration as to whether it is medically, and from a welfare point of view, appropriate that there should be a guardian. The court, it is submitted, should consider the matter in the light of the powers and duties given to Mental Health Act guardians by the legislation.

  1 See the Mental Health (Scotland) Act 1984 (c 36), s 37(1), and MENTAL HEALTH, vol 14, paras 1434, 1437.
  2 See ibid, s 50(7), and MENTAL HEALTH, vol 14, para 1448. This provision deals with people admitted to hospital on this basis who have been subject to guardianship. The Act does not specifically state that it is incompetent to appoint a guardian to a patient who is in hospital on this basis and has not had a guardian. However, in such a case it is likely that it would be impossible for the sheriff to be satisfied that the requirements for appointment are satisfied.
  3 Ibid, s 27 (as to which see MENTAL HEALTH, vol 14, para 1422), contains special provisions not involving guardianship relating to patients on leave of absence from hospital: *AB and CB v E* 1987 SCLR 419.
  4 Ie before the enactment of the Mental Health (Amendment) (Scoltand) Act 1983 (c 39).
  5 A D Ward 'Revival of Tutors-Dative' (*Morris, Petitioner*) 1987 SLT (News) 69.
  6 See the Mental Health (Scotland) Act 1984, s 41(3), and MENTAL HEALTH, vol 14, para 1439.
  7 See ibid, s 41, and the Mental Health (Specified Treatments, Guardianship Duties etc) (Scotland) Regulations 1984, SI 1984/1494, and MENTAL HEALTH, vol 14, paras 1409, 1425, 1441, 1442.
  8 It is a statutory offence for the guardian to administer corporal punishment: see the Mental Health (Scotland) Act 1984, s 41(4), and MENTAL HEALTH, vol 14, para 1439. This provision is for the avoidance of doubt and was included also in the earlier legislation, under which the guardian was effectively a tutor.
  9 See MENTAL HEALTH, vol 14, paras 1435–1438, 1440, 1446–1451.
 10 See the Mental Health (Scotland) Act 1984, s 1(2), and MENTAL HEALTH, vol 14, para 1402.
 11 See ibid, s 37(3)(a)(i), and MENTAL HEALTH, vol 14, para 1436.
 12 See ibid, s 37(3), and MENTAL HEALTH, vol 14, para 1436.
 13 See ibid, s 36(a), and MENTAL HEALTH, vol 14, para 1436.
 14 See ibid, s 37(3)(b), and MENTAL HEALTH, vol 14, para 1437. 'Mental health officer' means an officer of a local authority appointed to act as a mental health officer for the purposes of the Act: s 125(1).
 15 See ibid, s 36(b), and MENTAL HEALTH, vol 14, para 1437.

1241. Functions of Mental Health Act guardians and social work departments.

The position of the guardian is complicated in that the legislation imposes certain duties on the local authority, gives certain powers to the guardian, and imposes certain duties on the guardian towards the local authority. The details of these are covered elsewhere in this work[1].

The local authority has a duty of 'general supervision' in respect of the patient[2], and the guardian is required to advise the local authority of certain matters[3]. However, the guardian's powers are specific and given to him personally. He is not the agent of the local authority[4]. Accordingly the local authority does not have a power to direct the guardian with regard to these powers, that is to decide where the patient should live, to require the patient to attend for medical treatment (but there is no power to consent to that treatment), work, education or training of the *incapax*, and to require that people involved with the care of the patient have access to him. However, the local authority has certain duties which relate to these powers[5]. Where the local authority is itself the guardian these complications are avoided as the powers and duties are in the one body.

  1 See MENTAL HEALTH, vol 14, paras 1439, 1441, 1442.
  2 See the Mental Health (Specified Treatments, Guardianship Duties etc) (Scotland) Regulations 1984, SI 1984/1494, and MENTAL HEALTH, vol 14, para 1441.

3 See MENTAL HEALTH, vol 14, para 1442.
4 See the Mental Health (Scotland) Act 1984 (c 36), s 41, and MENTAL HEALTH, vol 14, para 1439.
5 See MENTAL HEALTH, vol 14, para 1441.

11. PROPOSALS FOR REFORM

1242. Introduction. In the Scottish Law Commission's *Report on the Legal Capacity and Responsibility of Minors and Pupils*[1], radical reform of the common law on guardianship and the legal capacity of children has been recommended[2]. The commission's major proposals will be discussed in this part of the title.

1 *Report on the Legal Capacity and Responsibility of Minors and Pupils* (Scot Law Com no 110 (1987)).
2 The Age of Legal Capacity (Scotland) Bill, which gave effect to the Scottish Law Commission's recommendations, was introduced in the 1988–89 parliamentary session but failed to obtain a second reading.

1243. Classification of pupils and minors and offices of tutor and curator to be abolished. The abolition of the existing classification of young people under the age of eighteen into the categories of pupils and minors is recommended. Instead there would be a new two-tier system whereby persons under the age of sixteen would have no legal capacity while those aged sixteen and seventeen would have full legal capacity. Similarly, the offices of tutor and curator would be abolished and replaced by a new office, the guardian of a person under the age of sixteen. The guardian of such a person would have, in relation to his person and his estate, the powers and duties which a tutor currently has in relation to a pupil. As at present, the guardian of a child under the age of sixteen would usually be his parents and the general principles in relation to parental rights laid down in section 2 of the Law Reform (Parent and Child) (Scotland) Act 1986 would be applicable[1]. The court would continue to have the power to appoint a curator *ad litem* to a person under the age of sixteen and a *curator bonis*, but the appointment of a factor *loco tutoris* would become incompetent. Applications for the appointment of a guardian to a person under the age of sixteen would have to be brought under section 3 of the 1986 Act[2]. Parents would, however, continue to have the right to appoint a testamentary guardian to a child under the age of sixteen under section 4 of that Act[3].

1 For the Law Reform (Parent and Child) (Scotland) Act 1986 (c 9), s 2, see para 1209 above.
2 For ibid, s 3, see para 1209 above.
3 For ibid, s 4, see para 1211 above.

1244. Legal capacity of children under sixteen. While as a general rule, a child under the age of sixteen would have no active legal capacity, he would have capacity to enter into transactions of a kind commonly entered into by persons of his age and circumstances provided these were not unreasonable. Moreover, persons over the age of twelve would have capacity to test or exercise powers of appointment. The consent of a person over the age of twelve would be required for the purpose of his or her adoption. If, in the opinion of a qualified medical practitioner, a child under the age of sixteen was capable of understanding the nature and possible consequences of any proposed surgical, medical or dental procedure or treatment, the child would have capacity to consent thereto. A girl under the age of sixteen would also have the legal capacity to exercise parental rights in relation to her own child.

1245. Legal capacity of children over sixteen. While a child over the age of sixteen would have full legal capacity to enter into legal transactions, the current statutory restriction on embarking on certain courses of conduct, for example, driving a motor car, would remain. The common law on reduction of minors' contracts on the grounds of minority and lesion would be abolished and replaced by a new statutory regime. It is proposed that when a person aged between sixteen and eighteen has entered into a prejudicial transaction, the transaction can be set aside by a court at any time until the young person reaches the age of twenty-one. A prejudicial transaction is one which:

(1) an adult, exercising reasonable prudence, would not have entered into in the circumstances of the young person at the time of the transaction; and
(2) has caused or is likely to cause substantial prejudice to the young person.

However, this remedy would not be available in respect of the exercise of testamentary capacity, a power of appointment, consent to an adoption order, the bringing or defending of civil proceedings, consent to surgical, medical or dental procedures or treatment, a transaction induced by the young person's fraudulent misrepresentation, a transaction ratified by the young person on reaching eighteen or by a court and any transaction in the course of the young person's trade, business or profession.

1246–1300. Conclusion. The major aim of the proposals of the Scottish Law Commission is simplification of the current law although — inevitably — there are numerous exceptions to the proposed general rule that a child would have no legal capacity under the age of sixteen but full legal capacity thereafter. The abolition of the distinction between pupils and minors and the offices of tutor and curator would, of course, remove one of the most distinctive features of the Scots law of parent and child: but, as the powers and duties of a guardian of a child under the age of sixteen are equated to those currently enjoyed by a tutor in relation to a pupil, the law of guardianship outlined in this title will not be rendered redundant if the proposals are enacted in their current form.

HARBOURS

1. INTRODUCTION

1301. Historical background. The development of the law relating to harbours has been much influenced by the economic history of Scotland. From the beginnings of maritime trade in the Middle Ages the rights of harbour were based on charters granted by the Crown, mostly but not exclusively to the royal burghs. It was the practice for these burghs to regulate the trading activities at their harbours, to receive the revenues and maintain such artificial works as there were. The Crown also gave grants to individuals of the right of harbour, often as a means of raising revenue. Although subsequent legislation has superseded many of these early grants, particularly at ports and harbours of economic significance, the existence of Crown charters and the law of free port which developed over the centuries are not to be overlooked. It is not unknown in relatively modern times for problems to arise which call for an examination of the terms of ancient grants and of the common law[1].

Substantial artificial harbour development[2] commenced at the mouth of the River Clyde in the second half of the eighteenth century as a response to the upsurge of trade with America and the West Indies. On the east coast, such development did not proceed until the early decades of the following century. The old system of ports maintained by royal burghs and individuals holding Crown grants was incapable of coping effectively with the increase in maritime trade. Revenues were insufficient to maintain, improve and extend harbour works in order to accommodate the ever increasing number of ships using them, and it was unlawful to augment dues in the absence of immemorial custom[3]. Conflict grew between the increasingly important manufacturing interests and the oligarchic burgh councils over the control of ports and harbours.

1 *Crown Estate Comrs v Fairlie Yacht Slip Ltd* 1979 SC 156. As to the common law, see paras 1304 ff below.
2 As to artificial harbours, see para 1305 below.
3 *Cowan v Edinburgh Magistrates* (1828) 6 S 586; *Christie v Landale* (1828) 6 S 813.

1302. The need for legislation. In the course of the eighteenth century it became the practice to obtain powers by Act of Parliament for the purpose of regulating the constitution of harbour authorities, for the construction of works, and for raising finance[1]. The first of a series of Clyde Navigation Acts was passed in 1759, and statutory harbour authorities at Port Glasgow and Greenock were established in 1772 and 1773 respectively. In 1815 a harbour authority was created for Dundee, followed in 1829 and 1838 by similar bodies for Aberdeen and Leith, and in due course a harbour authority was created for Glasgow. By the middle of the nineteenth century it was realised that, with the increasing number and size of ships and the advent of steam power, a comprehensive statutory framework was required for the establishment and running of harbours. It was in these circumstances that the Harbours, Docks and Piers Clauses Act 1847 (c 27) was passed, and this major piece of legislation remains in force in large measure to this day[2].

Some of the modern harbour authorities, like the Clyde Port Authority and the Forth Ports Authority, also possess important functions and exercise jurisdiction over large areas of the territorial sea. With the establishment of industry based on the discovery of oil reserves in the North Sea, it is interesting to see the resumption by local authorities of their earlier role as a harbour authority, notably in Orkney and Shetland, where sweeping powers have been granted for the control of shipping and the management of harbours[3]. In addition, important powers are vested in the Ministry of Defence in respect of dockyard ports which also cover extensive areas of the territorial sea[4].

In recent times, commercial exploitation of sheltered arms of the sea has taken place, notably on the west coast and in the islands. In response to demand, the Crown Estate Commissioners have pursued an active policy of leasing parts of the foreshore and seabed for the construction of slipways, jetties, piers, yacht marinas (a species of harbour), and of other structures such as fish farms, and for the laying of moorings, sometimes in groups of very large numbers[5]. This activity, unregulated by parliamentary powers or (at least so far as relating to the sea below low water mark) by planning powers[6], is a potential field of conflict with the common law rights of public navigation and of fishing, and possibly also with the law of nuisance[7].

1 *Milne Home v Allan* (1868) 6 M 189.
2 See paras 1308 ff below.
3 See the Orkney County Council Act 1974 (c xxx), and the Zetland County Council Act 1974 (c viii) (both amended).
4 See para 1319 below.
5 *Crown Estate Comrs v Fairlie Yacht Slip Ltd* 1979 SC 156.
6 *Argyll and Bute District Council v Secretary of State for Scotland* 1976 SC 248, 1977 SLT 33.
7 As to the common law rights of public navigation, see WATER AND WATER RIGHTS, vol 25, paras 306 ff; as to the common law rights of fishing, see FISHING AND FISHERIES, paras 1 ff above; and as to the law of nuisance generally, see NUISANCE, vol 14, paras 2001 ff.

1303. Expressions. In general terms the expressions 'port' and 'harbour' have the same meaning. They may be either natural, whereby ships can moor in safety against wind and weather on account of the configuration of the land; or artificial, whereby ships come to shelter within and lie alongside quays, piers or jetties[1]. The word 'harbour' is statutorily defined as meaning any harbour, whether natural or artificial, and any port, haven, estuary, tidal or other river or inland waterway navigated by seagoing ships, and includes a dock or a wharf[2]. 'Wharf' is defined by statute as meaning any wharf, quay, pier, jetty or other place at which seagoing ships can ship or unship or embark or disembark passengers[3].

A 'dock' may be said to be an artificial enclosure, generally but not always shut off by lock gates from the sea, a river or a harbour. It is defined by statute as a dock to be used by seagoing ships[4]. A 'wet dock' enables ships to lie alongside afloat. A 'dry dock' or 'graving dock' is a dock out of which water can be pumped so as to render possible the inspection and repair of vessels lying therein.

The construction of the word 'port' in essence is the same as for a harbour. However, its meaning may vary when considering the word in connection with shipping or commercial documents. It may be apt to consider whether it includes an open roadstead or whether it is merely confined to the limits of an artificial harbour[5]. For the purposes of determining the extent of admiralty jurisdiction, 'port' has been defined as meaning any port, harbour, river, estuary, haven, dock, canal or other place so long as a person or body of persons is empowered by or under an Act or charter to make charges in respect of ships entering it or using the facilities therein[6].

1 Bell *Principle.* s 654; *Burghead Harbour Co Ltd v George* 1906 8 F 982, 14 SLT 253.
2 See the Harbours Act 1964 (c 40), s 57(1) (amended by the Local Government (Scotland) Act 1973 (c 65), s 237(1), Sch 29), and the Merchant Shipping Act 1894 (c 60), s 742. See also *Macpherson v Mackenzie* (1881) 8 R 706 at 715, per Lord Justice-Clerk Moncreiff. For a further definition, see the Prevention of Pollution Act 1971 (c 60), ss 8(2), 29(1).
3 Harbours Act 1964, s 57(1). See also *Salt Union Ltd v Wood* [1893] 1 QB 370, DC.
4 Harbours Act 1964, s 57(1). See also the Merchant Shipping (Liability of Shipowners and Others) Act 1900 (c 32), s 2(4).
5 *Hunter v Northern Marine Insurance Co Ltd* 1888 15 R (HL) 72.
6 Administration of Justice Act 1956 (c 46), s 45(4). As to admiralty jurisdiction, see ADMIRALTY, vol 1, paras 401 ff.

2. THE COMMON LAW

1304. Natural harbours. Scotland is plentifully endowed with natural harbours, due to the nature of its coastline. These are places of shelter, whether bays, lochs, firths, river mouths or roadsteads, which have been used for the purpose of anchoring and of refuge and where it has been unnecessary to construct artificial works of protection. There is a public right of navigation to and from such places which at common law is subject to no restraint[1]. Incidental to that right is that of free anchorage[2]. The right to anchor as an incident of the public right of navigation is unburdened so long as anchoring is of a transient rather than of an extended or semi-permanent nature[3]. The public is not entitled as a matter of right to lay fixed moorings on the seabed for vessels. Such an act is not regarded as a proper or necessary incident of the right of navigation[3]. It is necessary to obtain a grant by the Crown acting through the Crown Estate Commissioners[4]. In addition to anchoring in natural harbours, there is a right to use the foreshore for the purpose of anchoring at appropriate states of the tide, for beaching a vessel, for the loading or unloading of goods, the taking on of ballast and like purposes[5]. The free use of natural harbours for these purposes in all circumstances cannot be assumed under modern conditions. The increase in economic activity and the considerable advance in boating and sailing for recreational purposes has led to a vigorous policy by the Crown Estate Commissioners of exploiting the commercial possibilities of natural harbours.

The rights of the Crown in the seabed within territorial waters are patrimonial, and accordingly the *solum* of the seabed is capable of alienation[6]. The practice of granting leases of the seabed for the purpose of laying fixed moorings, or structures connected with fish farms, or for pontoons for the purpose of marinas, may transform the appearance of natural harbours and restrict the public right of navigation[7]. It may also lead to a conflict between those patrimonial uses and the public's rights of navigation and of fishing which the Crown holds in trust. Such a conflict may be brought to a test by an action at the instance of the Lord Advocate as representing the public interest or by an *actio populares*[8].

In addition, the rights arising from the use of natural harbours may be subordinated to powers conferred by statute on the Ministry of Defence and on harbour undertakings[9].

1 Stair *Institutions* II, 1, 5.
2 *Stair* II, 1, 5; *Campbell's Trustees v Sweeney* 1911 SC 1319, 1911 2 SLT 194; *Denaby and Cadeby Main Collieries Ltd v Anson* [1911] 1 KB 171; *Leith-Buchanan v Hogg* 1931 SC 204, 1931 SLT 164; *Crown Estate Comrs v Fairlie Yacht Slip Ltd* 1979 SC 156.
3 *Crown Estate Comrs v Fairlie Yacht Slip Ltd* 1979 SC 156.
4 See the Crown Estate Act 1961 (c 55), s 1(4). See also *Crown Estate Comrs v Fairlie Yacht Slip Ltd* 1979 SC 156.
5 *Stair* II, 1, 5.
6 Craig *Jus Feudale* 1.15.13; Stair *Institutions* II, 1, 5; Erskine *Institute* II, 1, 6; Bell *Principles* s 639; *Lord Advocate v Trustees of the Clyde Navigation* (1891) 19 R 174.
7 *Walford v David* 1989 SLT 876, OH, where it was held that what amounted to a material inference in the public right of navigation due to the presence of a fish farm was a question of degree dependent on the circumstances of each case.
8 *Crown Estate Comrs v Fairlie Yacht Slip Ltd* 1979 SC 156 at 178, per Lord President Emslie. See also *Officers of State v Smith* (1846) 8 D 711.
9 See paras 1308 ff below.

1305. Artificial harbours. At common law a public harbour is held *inter regalia* in trust for the public[1]. From early times it was necessary for harbours artificially constructed to be subject to constitution and regulation. The Crown does not appear to have been involved directly in the creation of artificial harbours but in practice granted a right of harbour by charter. The grantees of the right were usually royal burghs or holders of seaboard baronies.

The charter of a royal burgh is a habile title to found a right of harbour by prescription[2]. A title was generally derived from a Crown charter, and any grant by a feudal superior proceeded upon the presumption that the superior had an original grant from the Crown. A grant of harbour which is obscure in its import and ambiguous in its terms can be explained by usage[3]. The geographical extent is not limited to the land and adjacent shore but may include deep water beyond the limits of artificial works. In so far as a charter does not define the boundaries of the harbour, its limits will be determined by prescriptive possession[4]. There is implied in a grant of harbour the right to construct walls or quays and adjacent roadways. A title to property comprised in such works cannot be inferred in the absence of an express grant except, possibly, by prescription[5].

1 Erskine *Institute* II, 1, 5; II, 6, 17.
2 *Macpherson v Mackenzie* (1881) 8 R 706.
3 *Wigton Magistrates and Town Council v M'Clymont and Glover* (1834) 12 S 289.
4 *Campbeltown Magistrates v Galbreath* (1844) 7 D 220.
5 *Ayr Harbour Trustees v Weir* (1876) 4 R 79.

1306. Free port. The grantee of an artificial harbour administers it for the public in right of the Crown and in that capacity is entitled to exact dues from vessels resorting there. The extent of the authority to do so may be ascertained by reference to the terms of the grant fortified by possession over the prescriptive period. When the charter is silent on the subject, dues may still be exacted on the basis of possession and by reference to custom and practice[1]. Failure to exact dues may result in the right to do so being lost by negative prescription[2].

The public has the right to use a free port on payment of the proper dues. Corresponding to the right by the grantee to levy dues is a duty to maintain the port in proper order for the reception of shipping[3]. A grant of port or harbour implies the duty to keep it in repair and properly furnished for the use of shipping resorting to it. It further implies that a grantee must apply any surplus revenue not only for repair and upkeep but for making such improvements as are found in ports of a like nature. If a grantee extends his harbour, these duties apply to that extension. However, a grantee is under no obligation to apply surplus revenue towards the building of an extension[4]. In so far as the revenue is insufficient to keep the harbour in a safe condition, a duty remains on the grantee to give warning to shipping of the existence of any danger[5]. It is not settled whether there is any obligation on the grantee to provide plant or machinery in connection with the accommodation of shipping. Furthermore it has still to be decided whether the duty of keeping a free port safe applies where no artificial works have been constructed[6].

Any person who constructs a pier within the curtilage of a free port is liable to pay dues to the Crown grantee for such use made of the pier. The independent loading or unloading of goods at such a place also renders those undertaking this task liable in dues to the grantee[7].

1 *Renfrew Magistrates v Hoby* (1854) 16 D 348; *Colquhoun v Paton* (1859) 21 D 996.
2 *Renfrew Magistrates v Hoby* (1845) 16 D 348 at 358; *Dundee Harbour Trustees v Dougall* (1848) 11 D 6.
3 Erskine *Institute* II,6,17; Bell *Principles* s 654.
4 *Officers of State and Lords of Admiralty v Christie* (1854) 16 D 454; *Home v Allan* (1868) 6 M 189.
5 *Firth Shipping Co Ltd v Earl of Morton's Trustees* 1938 SC 177, 1938 SLT 223.
6 *Firth Shipping Co Ltd v Earl of Morton's Trustees* 1938 SC 177 at 197, 1938 SLT 223 at 229, per Lord President Normand.
7 *Macfarlane v Edinburgh Magistrates* (1827) 5 S 665 (NE 620); *Edinburgh Magistrates and Council v Scot* (1836) 14 S 922; *Campbeltown Magistrates v Galbreath* (1844) 7 D 482.

1307. Private piers. The fact that a seaboard proprietor has created artificial works such as a pier or jetty as a part and pertinent of his property over part of the shore does not by itself confer on him a right of harbour and the right to exact dues. In principle the public rights take precedence over such private action[1]. Erections on the shore or seawards can be objected to by the Crown if they interfere with navigation or the enjoyment of the shore by the public[2]. Such works, whether on the foreshore or seawards, require the consent of the Crown[3] and, in practice, any grant by the Crown Estate Commissioners will be made under reservation of the public rights. A Crown grant will be necessary for any works below low water mark, but will not be required for works on the foreshore where the title is that of the seaboard proprietor.

Where boats have previously used the foreshore as part of the public right of navigation, a seaboard proprietor who has constructed a harbour or pier on that part of the foreshore may not exclude boatowners from the harbour or pier, nor may he exact harbour dues from them[4]. On the other hand, where there is no objection on the grounds of interference with public rights, the seaboard proprietor who has established a private pier is entitled to require payment from those whom he permits to land or disembark, as the public has no right to demand the use of the private pier[5].

1 Stair *Institutions* II,1,5; Erskine *Institute* II,6,17.
2 *Officers of State v Smith* (1846) 8 D 711.
3 As to the construction of harbours and piers and the constitution of harbour authorities, see paras 1309 ff below.
4 *Earl of Stair v Austin* (1880) 8 R 183.
5 *Colquhoun v Paton* (1859) 21 D 996.

3. STATUTE LAW

1308. Introduction. Most modern harbours are regulated by statute and commonly by private legislation. The Act of Parliament which authorises the construction or improvement of a harbour, dock or pier is called 'the special Act'[1], and in relation to any problem or occurrence which arises in relation to such harbours, it will be essential to consult the special Act to discover the extent of the powers conferred on 'the undertakers'[1], that is the harbour authority. In modern times these powers vary considerably from harbour to harbour. The provisions of the Harbours, Docks and Piers Clauses Act 1847 form a basic set of powers of harbour authorities. This Act extends only to such harbours, docks and piers as are authorised by any statute which declares that the Act is to be incorporated therewith[2]. All the clauses of the Act are to apply to the undertaking except in so far as they are expressly varied or excepted by the special Act[2]. Moreover, all the clauses of the Act (along with the clauses of every other Act incorporated therewith) are to form part of and are to be construed therewith as forming one Act[3].

Statutory provisions were enacted in the Harbours, Piers and Ferries (Scotland) Act 1937 which apply to many harbours and piers vested in local authorities or harbour authorities (but excluding the principal ports of the Clyde, the Forth, Aberdeen and Dundee)[4]. The main provisions relate to:

(1) the transfer of marine works[5] to local authorities;
(2) the compulsory acquisition of marine works by local authorities;
(3) statutory approval for the construction of minor works; and
(4) the responsibility of harbour authorities for the maintenance of marine works.

These provisions fall to be read, where applicable, along with those contained in the 1847 Act. In addition, the Harbours Act 1964[6] and the Docks and Harbours Act 1966[7] make important provision affecting a wide variety of aspects of harbour management. The interest of central government in the development and management of harbours in Scotland is reflected in the provisions of the Harbours Development (Scotland) Act 1972 (c 64). The aim of this Act is to enable the Secretary of State to develop, maintain and manage harbours in Scotland, or to authorise other persons to do so.

In approaching this subject, it is essential in every case where consulting the special Act to discover the extent to which the provisions of the 1847 Act are incorporated therein, and in addition to ascertain whether there are other special powers conferred on a particular harbour authority, whether by its own legislation or by any other statutory provisions incorporated expressly therein. It should also be borne in mind that a harbour authority may not act beyond the statutory powers expressly or impliedly conferred on it[8].

1 Harbours, Docks and Piers Clauses Act 1847 (c 27), s 2.
2 Ibid, s 1.
3 See ibid, ss 1, 5.
4 Harbours, Piers and Ferries (Scotland) Act 1937 (c 28), Sch 3 (substituted by the Local Government (Scotland) Act 1973 (c 65), s 154(1), Sch 19, para 13).
5 For the meaning of 'marine works', see para 1311 below.
6 Ie the Harbours Act 1964 (c 40), as amended in particular by the Transport Act 1981 (c 56): see paras 1312 ff below.
7 Ie the Docks and Harbours Act 1966 (c 28), Pt III (ss 36–50).
8 *D and J Nicol v Dundee Harbour Trustees* 1915 SC (HL) 7, 1914 2 SLT 418.

1309. Harbour authorities. Harbour authorities are bodies constituted by various statutes and are referred to as authorities, boards, commissioners or trustees, depending on the statute involved[1]. Membership of the governing body is generally drawn from representatives of local interests such as local authorities and from shipping, industrial, commercial and trade union interests. In addition, the Secretary of State for Scotland has powers to develop, maintain and manage harbours made or maintained by him by virtue of powers or duties vested in him by any Act or order, and compulsory purchase powers are conferred on him for the purposes of such development[2]. Any harbour or port thereof which is presently held and maintained by him may be transferred to a harbour trust together with all rights and liabilities pertaining thereto, and when that is done the harbour trust will become the harbour authority[3]. The Secretary of State has powers to make loans to a harbour authority with the consent of the Treasury where that authority is unable to meet a debt[4].

1 See the Merchant Shipping Act 1894 (c 60), s 742, and the Harbours Act 1964 (c 40), s 57(1).
2 See the Harbours Development (Scotland) Act 1972 (c 64), s 1.
3 See the Harbours (Scotland) Act 1982 (c 17), s 1.
4 See the Harbours (Loans) Act 1972 (c 16) (amended by the Transport Act 1981 (c 56), ss 15(2), 40(1), Sch 5, para 11, Sch 12, Pt II).

1310. Construction of harbours and piers. Private piers and jetties may be constructed without statutory powers in so far as not interfering with the public right of navigation and public rights on the foreshore. It will be necessary to obtain a grant or licence from the Crown Estate Commissioners, and also the consent of the Secretary of State for Trade and Industry for constructing, altering or improving any works on the seashore below low water mark[1]. If such works lie within the statutory limits of a harbour, it may be necessary to obtain a special licence from the harbour authority in accordance with the terms of that authority's special Act[2]. Planning permission will also be required so far as the development relates to land above low water mark[3].

1 See the Coast Protection Act 1949 (c 74), s 34 (amended by the Statute Law Revision Act 1953 (c 5), s 1, Sch 5, and the Merchant Shipping Act 1988 (c 12), s 36(1)–(4)). As to the licensing of tidal works by harbour authorities, see the Merchant Shipping Act 1988, s 37.
2 See eg the Forth Ports Authority Order Confirmation Act 1969 (c xxxiv).
3 *Argyll and Bute District Council v Secretary of State for Scotland* 1976 SC 248, 1977 SLT 33.

1311. Procedure for acquisition of powers. The procedure whereby powers in respect of proposed works are obtained may depend on whether or not the works in question are marine works. In Scotland, 'marine work' is defined as a harbour or boatslip which in the opinion of the Secretary of State for Scotland and the Secretary of State for the Environment is principally used or required for the fishing industry[1]. A work which is situated within defined areas in the Highlands and Islands, and which is principally used or required for the fishing or agricultural industries or for the maintenance of communications between any place in those areas of the Highlands and Islands and any other place in Scotland, is also a marine work[1]. However, exempted from this definition are works vested in the British Waterways Board, the British Railways Board, the Clyde Port Authority, the Forth Ports Authority and the harbour authorities of Aberdeen and Dundee[2].

If any proposed works are marine works, the procedure for obtaining the necessary powers is by application for authorisation by the Secretary of State for Scotland under the Harbours, Piers and Ferries (Scotland) Act 1937 or under the General Pier and Harbour Act 1861. Alternatively the procedure which can be followed, and which must be followed in relation to harbours or piers which are not marine works, is either under the Private Legislation Procedure (Scotland) Act 1936 (c 52) or by a harbour revision order or harbour empowerment order under the Harbours Act 1964. In practice the financial limits in relation to applications under the 1861 and 1937 Acts have the effect of confining them to relatively minor works. Where powers are sought in relation to major works or in relation to the establishment and management of harbour authorities, recourse will have to be made to the powers available under the 1936 or 1964 Acts.

When an application is made for authorisation under the Harbours, Piers and Ferries (Scotland) Act 1937, the Act gives details as to the procedure to be followed. If the Secretary of State for Scotland is satisfied that the cost of the necessary operations or marine works will not exceed £600,000 or such sum as may be subsequently substituted by statutory instrument[3], he may authorise the local or harbour authority to undertake the works in accordance with the prescribed procedure[4].

The General Pier and Harbour Act 1861 makes provision for any person, including companies and corporations, to apply to the Secretary of State for Scotland for a provisional order for the construction of any pier, harbour, quay, wharf, jetty or excavation, provided that the expenditure does not exceed £100,000[5]. No such application may be entertained if the Secretary of State is satisfied that the objects of the application could be achieved either by a harbour revision order or a harbour empowerment order[6]. In so far as a local authority may seek powers under the 1861 Act for the construction of a marine work, the application for a provisional order is to be made to the Secretary of State for Scotland[7]. Any application by either a local authority or a harbour authority for a provisional order authorising the construction of any new works or the improvement of any existing works is also to be made to the Secretary of State for Scotland[8].

1 Harbours Act 1964 (c 40), s 57(1) (amended by the Local Government (Scotland) Act 1973 (c 65), s 154, Sch 19, para 16).
2 See the Harbours Act 1964, s 57(1) (amended by the Transport Act 1968 (c 73), s 156(2), Sch 16, para 8(1); the Local Government (Scotland) Act 1973, Sch 19, para 16; the Transport Act 1980 (c 34), s 69, Sch 9, Pt III; and the Transport Act 1981 (c 56), ss 14(1), 40(1), Sch 4, Pt I, para 1(2), Sch 12, Pt I), and the Harbours, Piers and Ferries (Scotland) Act 1937 (c 28), s 31, Sch 3 (substituted by the Local Government (Scotland) Act 1973, Sch 19, para 13).
3 See the Harbours, Piers and Ferries (Scotland) Act 1937, s 7(3)–(5) (added by the Harbours, Piers and Ferries (Scotland) Act 1972 (c 29), s 1(2)), and the Harbours, Piers and Ferries (Scotland) Act (Variation of Financial Limit) Order 1980, SI 1980/2038.
4 Harbours, Piers and Ferries (Scotland) Act 1937, s 7(1), (2) (amended by the Local Government (Scotland) Act 1973, Sch 19, para 9). For the prescribed procedure, see the Harbours, Piers and Ferries (Scotland) Act 1937, s 7(1), Sch 2.
5 General Pier and Harbour Act 1861 (c 45), s 3. As to the transfer of powers to the Secretary of State for Transport, see the Secretary of State for the Environment Order 1970, SI 1970/1681, art 2(1), Sch 1, para (a), and the Secretary of State for Transport Order 1976, SI 1976/1775, art 2(1), Sch 1.
6 See the Harbours Act 1964, s 17(3). As to harbour revision and empowerment orders, see paras 1312, 1313, below.
7 See the Harbours, Piers and Ferries (Scotland) Act 1937, s 4(a), and s 5 (amended by the Statutory Orders (Special Procedure) (Substitution) Order 1949, SR & O 1949/2393, and the Local Government (Scotland) Act 1973, Sch 19, para 8).
8 See the Harbours Act 1964, s 4(b), and s 5 (as so amended: see note 7 above).

1312. Harbour revision orders. A harbour revision order may be made by the appropriate minister[1] in relation to a harbour which is being improved, maintained or managed by a harbour authority in the exercise and performance of statutory powers and duties[2]. Among the objects for which the order may be made are:

(1) reconstructing the harbour authority or altering its constitution, or establishing as the harbour authority, in lieu of the existing one, an existing body designated or a body constituted for that purpose;

(2) regulating the procedure and fixing the quorum of the authority or any of its committees;

(3) varying or abolishing certain duties or powers imposed by statutory provision of local application;

(4) imposing or conferring on the authority duties or powers, including the power to make byelaws;

(5) transferring to or from one authority the property vested in another authority;

(6) settling the limits of jurisdiction of a harbour authority;

(7) altering the financial structure of the authority, including the power to levy charges;

(8) powers of compulsory acquisition of land[3].

Before a harbour revision order is made, written application must be made to the appropriate minister by the harbour authority or by a person or a body representative of persons appearing to the minister to have a substantial interest[4]. The minister must be satisfied that the making of the order is desirable in the interests of securing the improvement, maintenance or management of the harbour in an efficient and economical manner or of facilitating the efficient and economic transport of goods or passengers by sea[5].

1 In the Harbours Act 1964 (c 40), s 14 and in Sch 2, 'the appropriate minister' in the case of an order to be made in relation to a harbour not being a fishery harbour or a marine work means the minister; in the case of an order to be made in relation to a fishery harbour means the Minister of Agriculture, Fisheries and Food; and in the case of an order to be made in relation to a marine work means the Secretary of State (s 14(7)); and 'the minister' means the Minister of Transport (s 57(1)).

2 Ibid, s 14(1).

3 See ibid, s 14(1), Sch 2.

4 Ibid, s 14(2)(a). Harbour revision orders are subject to special parliamentary procedure: see para 1314 below.

5 Ibid, s 14(2)(b).

1313. Harbour empowerment orders. Where a person is desirous of securing the achievement of certain objects but neither he nor any other person has powers, or sufficient powers, to secure these objects, or to secure them effectively, he may apply in writing to the Secretary of State for the making by him of an order conferring on the applicant, some other designated person or a body to be constituted for the purpose by the order, all such powers as are requisite for enabling that object to be achieved[1]. This is known as a 'harbour empowerment order'[2]. These powers include powers to levy charges other than ship, passenger and goods dues[3]. The objects in question are:

(1) the improvement, maintenance or management of a harbour (whether natural or artificial) navigated by seagoing ships (not being a fishing harbour or a marine work) or of a port, haven, estuary, tidal or other river or inland waterway so navigated (not being a fishery harbour or a marine work)[4];

(2) the construction of an artificial harbour navigable by seagoing ships or an inland waterway so navigable, other than a harbour or waterway which, in the opinion of the Secretary of State, will, on completion, be a marine work[5];

(3) the construction, improvement, maintenance or management of a dock elsewhere than at a fishery harbour or marine work or of a wharf elsewhere than at such a harbour or work[6].

Similar provisions by way of application to the minister or the Secretary of State are made in relation to fishery harbours and marine works[7].

The minister and/or the Secretary of State may not make a harbour empowerment order unless he is or they are satisfied that the making thereof is desirable in the interests of facilitating the efficient and economic transport of goods or passengers by sea[8].

1 Harbours Act 1964 (c 40), s 16(1).
2 Ibid, s 16(4).
3 Ibid, s 16(1).
4 Ibid, s 16(1)(a).
5 Ibid, s 16(1)(b) (amended by the Secretary of State for the Environment Order 1970, SI 1970/1681).
6 Harbours Act 1964, s 16(1)(c).
7 See ibid, s 16(2) and s 16(3) (as amended: see note 5 above).
8 Ibid, s 16(5). A harbour empowerment order is subject to special parliamentary procedure: see para 1314 below.

1314. Special parliamentary procedure. Both harbour revision orders and harbour empowerment orders are subject to special parliamentary procedure in the manner prescribed[1]. Applications for harbour revision orders and harbour empowerment orders may not be entertained by the Secretary of State unless he is satisfied that the objects to be achieved by the order could not be achieved by an application for a provisional order under the General Pier and Harbour Act 1861 (c 45) to which Part II of the Harbours, Piers and Ferries (Scotland) Act 1937 applies[2].

1 Harbours Act 1964 (c 40), s 17(1), Sch 3, para 4B (added by the Transport Act 1981 (c 56), s 18, Sch 6, para 4(2)). For the prescribed procedure, see the Harbours Act 1964, Sch 3 (amended by the Secretary of State for the Environment Order 1970, SI 1970/1681, art 5(1), Sch 3, para 11; the Transport Act 1981, Sch 5, para 14(1), (2), (4), Sch 6, paras 4, 12, Sch 12, Pt II; and the Gas Act 1986 (c 44), s 67(4), Sch 9, Pt I), and the Statutory Orders (Special Procedure) Act 1945 (9 & 10 Geo 6 c 18), as amended in particular by the Statutory Orders (Special Procedure) Act 1965 (c 43).
2 Harbours Act 1964, s 17(4). As to provisional orders, see para 1311 above. The Harbours, Piers and Ferries (Scotland) Act 1937 (c 28), Pt II, comprises ss 4–7.

1315. Harbour reorganisation schemes. A scheme known as a harbour reorganisation scheme may be submitted to the Secretary of State by all or any of the authorities comprised in a group of harbours with a view to securing the efficient and economical development of that group[1]. The object of this provision is to reduce or eliminate a multiplicity of harbour authorities within a given area.

1 See the Harbours Act 1964 (c 40), s 18 (amended by the Docks and Harbours Act 1966 (c 28), s 43(1), and the Transport Act 1981 (c 56), ss 18, 40, Sch 6, paras 3, 6(1)–(3), Sch 12, Pt II). As to the procedure for confirming and making harbour reorganisation schemes, see the Harbours Act 1964, Sch 4 (amended by the Transport Act 1981, ss 15–18, 40, Sch 5, para 14(1), (4), (5), Sch 6, para 6(6), (7), Sch 12, Pt II).

1316. Acquisition of land and development by harbour authorities. The Harbours, Docks and Piers Clauses Act 1847 confers on harbour authorities powers to acquire land compulsorily, and these powers are subject to the provisions of the Lands Clauses Consolidation (Scotland) Act 1845 (c 19)[1]. Works may not commence unless plans have been duly deposited with the proper officer of the regional or islands council in whose area the works are situated[2]. Any errors, misstatements or wrong descriptions in plans or reference books may be corrected by a certificate of the sheriff lodged with the sheriff clerk and the proper officer of the regional or islands council[3]. No construction of harbours, docks or piers or connected works may take place on the seashore or in tidal navigable rivers without the consent in writing of the Crown Estate Commissioners or the Secretary of State for Trade and Industry[4]. It is further provided that nothing in the 1847 Act or the special Act is to extend so as to defeat the rights of the Crown and the powers vested in the Secretary of State (as successor to the Admiralty), Customs and Excise, and the Crown Estate Commissioners, or the jurisdiction of the Commissioners of Northern Lights[5].

Regional and islands councils may acquire compulsorily:
(1) land for the purpose of constructing, reconstructing, extending or improving a marine work;
(2) any harbour whose acquisition is considered by the council to be desirable in the interests of its area and whose maintenance is to be discontinued by its owner, or which is considered by the council to be in a poor state of repair[6].

The consent of the Secretary of State for Trade and Industry is required for the carrying out of new coast protection works, the excavation of materials on or under any part of the seashore and the construction of works or deposit of materials below high water mark[7].

The powers of planning authorities in relation to construction and development of harbours is restricted to land above low water mark[8], and is further restricted by the wide range of permitted developments enjoyed by harbour undertakings in terms of the Town and Country Planning (General Development) (Scotland) Order 1981[9]. Their powers in relation to statutory undertakers generally are set out in the Town and Country Planning (Scotland) Act 1972[10].

1 See the Harbours, Docks and Piers Clauses Act 1847 (c 27), s 6.
2 See ibid, s 8 (amended by the Local Government (Scotland) Act 1973 (c 65), s 154(1), Sch 19, para 3).
3 See the Harbours, Docks and Piers Clauses Act 1847, s 7 (amended by the Local Government (Scotland) Act 1973, Sch 19, para 2).
4 See the Harbours, Docks and Piers Clauses Act 1847, s 12 (amended by the Harbours Transfer Act 1862 (c 69), s 5; the Transfer of Functions (Shipping and Construction of Ships) Order 1965, SI 1965/145, arts 2, 3, Sch 1; and the Secretary of State for Trade and Industry Order 1970, SI 1970/1537, art 2), and the Crown Estate Act 1961 (c 55), s 1. Moreover, a Crown grant will be needed for the construction of works both below water mark and, unless the undertaker has a title to the foreshore, above it.
5 Harbours, Docks and Piers Clauses Act 1847, ss 99, 102.
6 Local Government (Scotland) Act 1973, s 154(3). See further LOCAL GOVERNMENT, vol 14, paras 443–447.
7 See the Coast Protection Act 1949 (c 74), ss 16–18, and LOCAL GOVERNMENT, vol 14, para 474.
8 *Argyll and Bute District Council v Secretary of State for Scotland* 1976 SC 248, 1977 SLT 33.
9 Town and Country Planning (General Development) (Scotland) Order 1981, SI 1981/830, art 3, Sch 1, Pt I, Classes X, XV.B (amended by SI 1983/1620).
10 Ie the Town and Country Planning (Scotland) Act 1972 (c 52), Pt XI (ss 221–230): see TOWN AND COUNTRY PLANNING.

1317. Byelaws. Harbour authorities are provided with the necessary powers to make byelaws for all or any of certain specified purposes. These purposes include:
(1) the regulation of the use of the harbour, dock and pier;
(2) the powers vested in the harbour master;
(3) the movement and good order of shipping;
(4) the loading and unloading of vessels and the removal of goods;
(5) the hours when the harbour is to be open;
(6) the conduct of employees and others;
(7) the use of fires and lights within the harbour;
(8) the prevention of damage to vessels or goods; and
(9) the use of equipment[1].
The byelaws have to be confirmed by the sheriff after due publication before coming into operation[2].

As far as any legal problems arising in connection with harbours, docks and piers are concerned, it is necessary not only to consult the special Act for its terms but also to ascertain in each case whether byelaws exist and, if so, what are their terms. Byelaws which go beyond the powers conferred by the enabling Act are *ultra vires*. A byelaw purportedly made to apply beyond the defined harbour limits is beyond the power of a harbour authority, as are byelaws which discriminate in an arbitrary way against users[3].

1 See the Harbours, Docks and Piers Clauses Act 1847 (c 27), s 83. See also the Harbours, Piers and Ferries (Scotland) Act 1937 (c 28), s 10 (amended by the Reorganisation of Offices (Adaptation of Enactments) Order 1939, SR & O 1939/782, art 1, Schedule, and the Local Government (Scotland) Act 1973 (c 65), ss 209(1), 237(1), Sch 25, para 16, Sch 29), and the Harbours, Piers and Ferries (Scotland) Act 1937, s 11 (amended by the Criminal Justice Act 1967 (c 80), ss 92, 106(2), Sch 3, Pt II).

2 See the Harbours, Docks and Piers Clauses Act 1847, ss 85, 86.

3 *Galloway Steam Packet Co v Kirkcaldy Harbour Comrs* (1888) 25 SLR 732, OH; *Kerr v Auld* (1890) 18 R (J) 12, 2 White 561; *Somerville v Leith Docks Comrs* 1908 SC 797, 15 SLT 1004; *Western Isles Islands Council v Caledonian MacBrayne Ltd* 1989 GWD 28-1301.

1318. Harbour charges. Until 1964, it was not unusual to find limitations such as a maximum limit imposed by statute on the discretion of a harbour authority in relation to charges. By legislation enacted in that year, it was provided that the only limitation on the harbour authority's discretion was that the charges should be reasonable[1]. The only important exceptions from this provision relate to ship, passenger and goods dues[2]. These are charges made payable in respect of any ship entering or leaving the harbour, and include:

(1) charges made on the ship in respect of marking or lighting the harbour;
(2) charges for any passengers embarking or disembarking at the harbour (but not including charges in respect of any of the services rendered or facilities provided for them); and
(3) charges in respect of goods brought into, taken out of or carried through the harbour by ship (but not including charges in respect of work performed, services rendered or facilities provided in respect of goods so bought, taken or carried)[3].

As regards these charges it is provided that, subject to certain exceptions, a harbour authority has power to demand, take and recover such ship, passenger and goods dues at such a harbour as it thinks fit[4]. A harbour authority may combine ship, passenger and goods dues into a single charge[5].

Persons having a substantial interest to do so may object in writing to ship, passenger and goods dues on various grounds:

(a) that the charge ought not to be imposed at all;
(b) that the charge ought to be imposed at a rate lower than that at which it is imposed;
(c) that certain classes of ship, passenger and goods should be excluded from the scope of the charge or treated in a special way[6].

1 See the Harbours Act 1964 (c 40), s 27(1). 'Charges' includes fares, rates, tolls and dues of every description: s 57(1). The 'reasonableness' of a charge may be challenged in the courts: *Midland Rly Co v Myers, Rose & Co Ltd* [1909] AC 13, HL.

2 Harbours Act 1964, s 27(2)(a).

3 Ibid, s 57(1) (meaning of 'ship, passenger and goods dues').

4 Ibid, s 26(2).

5 Ibid, s 27A (added by the Transport Act 1981 (c 56), s 18, Sch 6, para 8(1)).

6 See the Harbours Act 1964, s 31 (amended by the Fisheries Act 1981 (c 29), s 13(2), Sch 3, para 8(1), (2), (4), and the Transport Act 1981, ss 15–18, 40, Sch 5, para 10(2), (3), Sch 6, paras 8(3), 13(2), (4), Sch 12, Pt II).

1319. Dockyard ports. 'Dockyard port' is defined by statute as meaning any port, harbour, haven, roadstead, sound, channel, creek, bay or navigable river of the United Kingdom in, on, or near to which Her Majesty has inter alia a dock, dockyard, steam factory yard, victualling yard, arsenal, wharf, or mooring[1]. In relation to these naval establishments, regulations may be made by Order in Council for inter alia the following purposes:

(1) to prohibit the mooring or anchoring of vessels so as to obstruct navigation into, in, or out of the port;

(2) to appropriate any space as exclusive mooring or anchoring places for Her Majesty's ships;

(3) to regulate the maximum permitted speed of any vessel under power within specified areas of the port; and

(4) for certain specified safety purposes[2].

Power is given to the harbour master of any dockyard port, known as the Queen's harbour master, to move ships which do not obey his directions, or which have no person on board to attend to such directions, to an appropriate place[3]. He also has powers to search vessels, to remove wrecks which cause obstructions and to remove unseaworthy vessels from any part of a dockyard port[4].

The dockyard ports in Scotland are Rosyth, Holy Loch, Gareloch and Loch Long, and Cromarty Firth. Their limits are defined by Order in Council. The dockyard ports in the lochs adjacent to the Firth of Clyde are extensive in area.

1 Dockyard Ports Regulation Act 1865 (c 125), s 2.
2 See ibid, s 5.
3 See ibid, s 11.
4 See ibid, ss 12–15 (s 12 being amended by the Defence (Transfer of Functions) Act 1964 (c 15), ss 1(1)(a), (2), 3(2), (6)).

4. DUTIES AND LIABILITIES OF HARBOUR AUTHORITIES

1320. The harbour master. In all but the most primitive harbours, a harbour master is appointed to act on behalf of a harbour authority. Where the regulation of the harbour is governed by the relevant provisions of the Harbours, Docks and Piers Clauses Act 1847, statutory powers are vested in the harbour master. These powers include the giving of directions for regulating the time at which and the manner in which any vessel is to enter into, go out of or lie in or at the harbour, dock or pier; and also its position, mooring or unmooring, placing and removing, whilst therein[1]. The harbour master can regulate the position in which any vessel may load or unload cargo, or embark or disembark passengers[1]. He may give directions for removing unserviceable vessels and other obstructions from the harbour, dock or pier, and for keeping the same clear[1]. Penalties are imposed on shipmasters for not complying with the directions of the harbour master[2]. The harbour master has power to remove any vessel which is unserviceable, at the expense of the owner[3]. He is empowered to lay the vessel on any part of the strand or seashore, but he is not entitled thereby deliberately to destroy her. In beaching a vessel, the harbour master must do so in a way which, so far as reasonably practicable, gives the owner the chance of refloating her. He may cause any vessel whose master does not obey his directions regarding mooring, unmooring, placing or removal, or which has no person on board to attend to such directions, to be moved, and he may do so at the expense of the master or owner[4].

1 See the Harbours, Docks and Piers Clauses Act 1847 (c 27), s 52. See also *Macdonald v Mackenzie* 1947 JC 122, 1948 SLT 14; *The Guelder Rose* [1927] P 1, 136 LT 226, CA; *Pearn v Sargent* [1973] 2 Lloyd's Rep 141.

2 See the Harbours, Docks and Piers Clauses Act 1847, s 53.
3 See ibid, s 57 (amended by the Debtors (Scotland) Act 1987 (c 18), s 108(1), Sch 6, para 4). See also *Peterhead Harbours Trustees v Chalmers* 1984 SLT 130, OH.
4 See the Harbours, Docks and Piers Clauses Act 1847, s 58. As to the powers of the harbour master to remove any vessel due to repairs to the harbour or dock, if the master neglects or refuses to do so, see s 65.

1321. Safety of berths. The general position with regard to safety of berths may be said to be established by the common law. To that extent the ensuing discussion will concentrate upon the important judicial decisions. However, the possibility of special provisions made under the governing statute of a particular authority should never be overlooked.

There is no duty on a harbour authority to provide, irrespective of cost, berths at which vessels can be absolutely safe from the elements[1]. While an authority is not obliged to guarantee safety, it is under a duty to take reasonable care to see that a berth, pier, lock or dock is in a fit condition to receive a ship[2]. It must, therefore, guard against vessels being damaged by obstructions, submerged objects, accumulation of material on the seabed, and the like[3]. A harbour authority is under a duty to take steps to inform itself of dangers affecting the safety of ships at a berth and, if unable to remove them or otherwise render them harmless, to give warning of their existence to shipping[4]. If it is established that a vessel has been damaged by such a danger, the onus will pass to the harbour authority of showing that it took all reasonable steps to acquaint itself with the dangers and to see that the berth was in a satisfactory condition[5]. The liability of a harbour authority extends vicariously to the fault of the harbour master, dock master or other employee[6].

1 *Niven v Ayr Harbour Trustees* (1898) 25 R (HL) 42, 6 SLT 8; *Mair v Aberdeen Harbour Comrs* 1909 SC 721, 1909 1 SLT 253.
2 *Thomson v Greenock Harbour Trustees* (1876) 3 R 1194; *The Bearn* [1906] P 48, CA; *Robertson v Portpatrick and Wigtownshire Joint Committee* 1919 SC 293, 1919 1 SLT 86; *Cormack v Dundee Harbour Trustees* 1930 SC 112, 1930 SLT 229.
3 *Mersey Docks and Harbour Board Trustees v Gibbs* (1866) LR 1 HL 93; *Mackenzie v Stornoway Pier and Harbour Commission* 1907 SC 435, 14 SLT 730; *Bede SS Co v River Wear Comrs* [1907] 1 KB 310, CA; *SS Fulwood Ltd v Dumfries Harbour Comrs* 1907 SC 456, 14 SLT 680; *Walker v Duke of Buccleuch and Queensberry* 1918 1 SLT 223, OH.
4 *R v Williams* (1884) 9 App Cas 418, JC; *The Moorcock* (1889) 14 PD 64; *Robertson v Portpatrick and Wigtownshire Joint Committee* 1919 SC 293, 1919 1 SLT 86; *Firth Shipping Co Ltd v Earl of Morton's Trustees* 1938 SC 177, 1938 SLT 223.
5 *Cormack v Dundee Harbour Trustees* 1930 SC 112, 1930 SLT 229.
6 *Renney v Kirkcudbright Magistrates* (1892) 19 R (HL) 11; *Parker v North British Rly Co* (1898) 21 R 1059, 6 SLT 79; *The Bearn* [1906] P 48, CA.

1322. Approaches to harbours. Where the relevant provisions of the Harbours, Docks and Piers Clauses Act 1847 are incorporated in the special Act, harbour authorities are required to lay down buoys for the guidance of vessels within their limits in such places and of such character as may be directed by the Commissioners of the Northern Lights[1]. They may not erect any lighthouse or beacon or exhibit any light, beacon or seamark without the sanction of the commissioners[2].

There is a duty at common law to keep the harbour reasonably safe for vessels invited to use it. When the seaward approach to a harbour is difficult but can be navigated safely by someone who knows the locality and exercises reasonable care, a harbour authority is not bound to take steps involving expense out of all proportion to its means in order to improve access such as by the removal of a rock or shoal[3]. There is a conflict of authority as to whether there is an obligation at common law to indicate the limits of the navigable channel by means of buoys[4]. However, if the harbour authority does take steps to buoy a channel, there is a duty to take reasonable care to see that the buoys do not get out of position so as to become misleading and a source of danger. In such circumstances a notice disclaiming responsibility may not be sufficient to avoid liability[5].

While there is no general duty to light the approaches to a harbour, unless by statute, there is a duty on a harbour authority to provide leading lights marking the harbour entrance itself, this being an aspect of the common law duty to maintain the harbour[6].

Where a harbour authority holds out that there is a certain depth of water at a part of the harbour over which ships may have to pass, it must use reasonable care to see that the approach is kept at such depth, or at least give adequate warning if the depth is at any time insufficient[7].

Should the approaches to a harbour become obstructed by a stranded vessel, it is the duty of the master of that vessel to take steps to light the vessel during the hours of darkness[8]. A harbour authority is empowered (1) to take possession of, and raise, remove, or destroy a sunken, stranded or abandoned vessel or part of a vessel; (2) to light or buoy any such vessel until its raising, removal or destruction; and (3) to sell the vessel so raised or removed along with any property recovered, and out of the proceeds reimburse itself for the expenses incurred in this process[9].

These powers are additional to and not in derogation of any powers conferred on a harbour authority by other legislation[10]. Under the 1847 Act a harbour master may remove any wreck or other obstruction to the harbour, dock or pier, or to the approaches thereof, and the expenses of doing so are to be paid by the owner of such wreck or other obstruction[11]. The right to recover expenses from the owner is qualified in so far as the harbour authority may be liable at common law to the owner for loss in relation to the wreck or obstruction caused by its fault[12].

1 Harbours, Docks and Piers Clauses Act 1847 (c 27), s 77.
2 See ibid, s 78.
3 *Parker v North British Rly Co* (1898) 21 R 1059, 6 SLT 79; *Aktieselskabet Dampskibet Forto v Orkney Harbour Comrs* 1915 SC 743 at 753, 1915 1 SLT 307 at 308, per Lord Salvesen.
4 *Aktieselskabet Dampskibet Forto v Orkney Harbour Comrs* 1915 SC 743, 1915 1 SLT 307; *Mersey Docks and Harbour Board Trustees v Gibbs* (1866) LR 1 HL 93. Cf *The Neptun* [1938] P 21.
5 *Buchanan v Clyde Lighthouses Trustees* (1884) 11 R 531; *Aktieselskabet Dampskibet Forto v Orkney Harbour Comrs* 1915 SC 743, 1915 1 SLT 307; *Anchor Line (Henderson Bros) Ltd v Dundee Harbour Trustees, Ellerman Lines Ltd v Dundee Harbour Trustees* 1922 SC (HL) 79, 1922 SLT 137. Cf *The Ballyalton* [1961] 1 All ER 459, [1961] 1 WLR 929.
6 *Bruce v Aiton* (1885) 13 R 358.
7 *Bede SS Co v River Wear Comrs* [1907] 1 KB 310, CA; *Workington Harbour and Dock Board v Towerfield (Owners)* [1951] AC 112, [1950] 2 All ER 414, HL.
8 *Kidston v M'Arthur and Clyde Navigation Trustees, M'Arthur v Kidston* 1878 5 R 936.
9 See the Merchant Shipping Act 1894 (c 60), s 530.
10 Ibid, s 534.
11 See the Harbours, Docks and Piers Clauses Act 1847, s 56. For cases, see M Thomas and D Steel *Merchant Shipping Acts* (7th edn, 1976) (British Shipping Laws, vol 11).
12 *Greenock Port and Harbours Trustees v British Oil and Cake Mills Ltd* 1944 SC 70, 1944 SLT 293.

1323. Movement of ships within harbour limits. While under way in a harbour, there is a duty on masters of ships to obey any direction of a harbour authority's employees acting within the scope of their duty, such as the harbour master. However, such orders may be disregarded if compliance would put the ship in danger. The harbour authority will be liable for the negligence of the harbour master in giving directions which result in damage[1].

The owner, master or salvor of a vessel may be directed by a harbour master not to enter a harbour, or to leave a harbour, if in his opinion the condition of that vessel or the nature or condition of anything it contains is such that its presence in the harbour might involve grave and imminent danger to the safety of any person or property, or grave and imminent risk that the vessel may be sinking or foundering in the harbour, or prevent or seriously prejudice the use of the harbour by other vessels[2]. Such directions are subject to additional directions by the Secretary of State altering the directions of the harbour master[3].

Where there are local rules made by or on behalf of an appropriate harbour authority, these will prevail over certain international regulations as far as the prevention of collisions at sea is governed[4]. Such local rules are usually to be found in byelaws made under a special Act. The byelaws do not have the force of statute but form a code of conduct, so that an infringement of them will be held to be in law a fault and, if it leads to loss or damage, will infer liability[5].

1 *The Apollo* [1891] AC 499, HL; *East London Harbour Board v Caledonia Landing, Shipping and Salvage Co Ltd, East London Harbour Board v Colonial Fisheries Co Ltd* [1908] AC 271, JC; *Renney v Kirkcudbright Magistrates* (1892) 19 R (HL) 11; *Robertson v Portpatrick and Wigtownshire Joint Committee* 1919 SC 293, 1919 1 SLT 86.
2 See the Dangerous Vessels Act 1985 (c 22), s 1.
3 See ibid, s 3.
4 International Regulations for Preventing Collisions at Sea 1972, reg 1(b), contained in the Collision Regulations and Distress Signals Order 1977, SI 1977/982, Schedule.
5 *The Carlotta* [1899] P 223; *Pacific Steam Navigation Co v Anglo-Newfoundland Development Co Ltd* 1924 SC (HL) 66 at 72, 1924 SLT 291 at 293, per Lord Dunedin.

1324. Limitation of liability. Until 1 December 1986 the owners of any dock or a harbour authority or a conservancy authority[1] could limit their liability where, without their actual fault or privity, any loss or damage is caused to any vessel or vessels, or to any goods, merchandise, or other things whatsoever on board any vessel or vessels within the authority's area[2]. The liability is limited by the aggregate amount equivalent to 1,000 gold francs[3] for each ton of the tonnage of the largest registered British ship which has been within the authority's area during the five years previous to the occurrence. The whole loss or damage must arise within the area of the authority[4]. Dock owners who are also ship repairers may obtain benefit under the provision[5]. As already mentioned these provisions apply to any liability arising out of an occurrence which took place prior to 1 December 1986[6].

Since 1 December 1986, the Convention on Limitation of Liability for Maritime Claims 1976 has the force of law[7]. In particular article 4 of the convention has the effect of substituting for the test of 'actual fault or privity' that of proving that the loss has resulted from a personal act or omission with the intent to cause such loss, or recklessly and with the knowledge that such loss would probably result[8]. The method of calculating the limits of liability are also changed. The calculation is made by relating the tonnage of the ship to Units of Account, the latter being special drawing rights as defined by the International Monetary Fund and converted as at the appropriate day into the sterling equivalents at the date of the limitation fund[9].

1 'Conservancy authority' includes all persons or bodies of persons, corporate or unincorporate, being proprietors of, or intrusted with the duty or invested with the power of constructing, improving, managing, regulating, maintaining or lighting a harbour: Merchant Shipping Act 1894 (c 60), s 742.
2 See the Merchant Shipping (Liability of Shipowners and Others) Act 1900 (c 32), s 2 (amended by the Merchant Shipping Act 1979 (c 39), ss 47(2), 50(4), Sch 7, Pt I).
3 Merchant Shipping (Liability of Shipowners and Others) Act 1900, s 2(1) (amended by the Merchant Shipping (Liability of Shipowners and Others) Act 1958 (c 62), s 1(1)). The sterling equivalent of the gold franc is determined from time to time by statutory instrument.
4 For a discussion of case law, see M Thomas and D Steel *Merchant Shipping Acts* (7th edn, 1976) (British Shipping Laws, vol 11).
5 *The City of Edinburgh* [1921] P 274; *Owners of SS Ruapehu v R and H Green and Silley Weir Ltd* [1927] AC 523, HL.

6 See the Merchant Shipping Act 1979, s 19(4), and the Merchant Shipping Act 1979 (Commencement No 10) Order 1986, SI 1986/1052.
7 See the Merchant Shipping (Liability of Shipowners and Others) Act 1900, s 2 (amended by the Merchant Shipping Act 1979, s 19(1), Sch 5); the Merchant Shipping Act 1979, s 17(1); and the Merchant Shipping Act 1979 (Commencement No 10) Order 1986.
8 See the Convention on Limitation of Liability for Maritime Claims 1976 (London, 1 November 1976; Misc 31 (1978); Cmnd 7035), Part I, art 4, set out in the Merchant Shipping Act 1979, Sch 4.
9 See Convention on Limitation of Liability for Maritime Claims 1976, arts 6(1)(b), 8.

1325. Liability to persons due to dangerous state of the harbour. The duty to show care to persons derives from the provisions of the Occupiers' Liability (Scotland) Act 1960. The provisions apply not only to a person occupying or having control of land or other premises but also to a person occupying or having control of a vessel[1]. The extent of the duty of a harbour authority to persons resorting there is that which an occupier owes to all such persons, namely, that of taking such care as in all the circumstances of the case is reasonable to see that that person will not suffer injury or damage by reason of any dangers which are due to the state of the premises or to any thing done or omitted to be done on them for which he is responsible[2].

1 See the Occupiers' Liability (Scotland) Act 1960 (c 30), s 1(1), (3).
2 See ibid, ss 2, 3.

1326. Other statutory duties. Upon payment of the appropriate rates, a harbour, dock and pier must be open to all persons for the shipping and unshipping of goods and the embarking and landing of passengers[1]. The undertakers may construct such warehouses and other buildings as they deem necessary for the accommodation of goods, and may erect or provide such cranes and other equipment as they think necessary in connection with loading and unloading[2]. They have power to lease or grant the use or occupation of warehouses, buildings, wharfs, yards, cranes, machines or other conveniences, but unless provided otherwise in a special Act no lease is to endure for more than three years[3]. The undertakers or their lessees are under a duty to provide proper servants and labourers for working cranes at all reasonable times for the use of the public[4].

Where the responsibility for stevedoring has been delegated to a third party, the question whether the third party is under a statutory duty to handle goods for the benefit of the public has not as yet been resolved by the Scottish courts[5]. Penalties are provided for in the event of anyone acting on behalf of the undertakers, or the lessees of the undertakers, giving any undue preference or showing any partiality in the handling of goods[6]. Goods may not lie on quays longer than is allowed by the local byelaws, and power is given to the harbour master to remove them and keep them elsewhere until claimed upon tendering the expense of the removal[7]. If goods are unclaimed or the expense of removal is unpaid, the harbour master may sell the goods[7].

The harbour authority is under an obligation to take reasonable care to see that quays and warehouses are reasonably fit for goods deposited there[8]. It is also under a duty to provide plant or equipment which is free from defects and is liable for injuries consequent upon such defects[9].

1 Harbours, Docks and Piers Clauses Act 1847 (c 27), s 33. As to payment of dues, see para 1318 above. See also *Somerville v Leith Docks Comrs* 1908 SC 797, 15 SLT 1004; *London and North Eastern Rly Co v British Trawlers Federation Ltd* [1934] AC 279, HL; *Caledonian MacBrayne Ltd v Western Isles Islands Council* 1989 GWD 31-1456, OH.
2 Harbours, Docks and Piers Clauses Act 1847, s 21.
3 Ibid, s 23. This section has to be construed widely and not *ejusdem generis*: *Glebe Sugar Refining Co Ltd v Greenock Harbour Trustees* 1921 SC (HL) 72, 1921 2 SLT 26.

4 Harbours, Docks and Piers Clauses Act 1847, s 22. The services provided by a harbour authority have been described as essentially negative in character: *Wilsons and Clyde Coal Co Ltd v North British Rly Co* 1923 SC 68 at 79, 1923 SLT 2 at 7, per Lord President Clyde.

5 *Coutts v J M Piggins Ltd* 1982 SLT 213, OH, per Lord Robertson; cf 1983 SLT 320, OH, per Lord Ordinary Stewart.

6 Harbours, Docks and Piers Clauses Act 1847, s 67. See also *Coutts v J M Piggins Ltd* 1982 SLT 213, OH; further proceedings 1983 SLT 320, OH.

7 Harbours, Docks and Piers Clauses Act 1847, s 68.

8 *Liebigs Extract of Meat Co Ltd v Mersey Docks and Harbour Board and Walter Nelson & Son Ltd* [1918] 2 KB 381, CA.

9 *Smith v London and St Katharine Docks Co* (1868) LR 3 CP 326.

5. LIABILITIES OF OWNERS AND MASTERS OF SHIPS

1327–1400. Liability of ships for damage to a harbour or its waters. Apart from liability at common law for damage caused to a harbour or its waters by negligence, the owner of a ship or float of timber which damages the harbour, dock, pier, quays or works is answerable under statute to the undertakers for the damage done by such ship or float of timber, or by any person employed about the same[1]. This liability is for damage and not damages, which is therefore confined to physical damage and does not cover economic loss. Liability is absolute, subject to the qualification that the damage must be caused by a human agency and not by an 'act of God'. Contributory negligence is not a relevant defence to a statutory claim for damage caused by the ship to the harbour[2], but the shipowner may limit his liability for such damage. Limitation of liability is governed by the provisions of the Merchant Shipping (Liability of Shipowners and Others) Act 1958 in respect of occurrences taking place prior to 1 December 1986[3]. Since that date, the right to limit liability is subject to the provisions of the Convention on Limitation of Liability for Maritime Claims 1976[4].

The owner or master of a vessel from which oil or oil mixture is discharged into the waters of a harbour has a duty to report the occurrence to the harbour master or harbour authority[5]. If he fails to do so he is guilty of an offence[5].

1 See the Harbours, Docks and Piers Clauses Act 1847 (c 27), s 74. However, this does not extend to impose any liability in respect of a vessel which is in the charge of a duly licensed pilot: s 74 proviso.

2 *River Wear Comrs v Adamson* (1877) 2 App Cas 743, HL; *The Mostyn* [1928] AC 57, HL; *Workington Harbour and Dock Board v Towerfield (Owners)* [1951] AC 112 at 147, [1950] 2 All ER 414 at 434, HL per Lord Normand, at 155 and at 439 per Lord Morton of Henryton, and at 158 and at 441 per Lord Radcliffe.

3 Merchant Shipping (Liability of Shipowners and Others) Act 1958 (c 62), s 2(2), (4) (repealed).

4 See the Convention on Limitation of Liability for Maritime Claims 1976 (London, 1 November 1976; Misc 31 (1978); Cmnd 7035), set out in the Merchant Shipping Act 1979 (c 30), Sch 4, and the Merchant Shipping Act 1979 (Commencement No 10) Order 1986, SI 1986/1052.

5 See the Prevention of Pollution Act 1971 (c 60), s 11(1), (3), and ENVIRONMENT, vol 9, paras 1208 ff.

HEALTH SERVICES

The General Editors acknowledge with appreciation assistance received from Mr John R Griffiths, who was at the time with the Scottish Health Service Central Legal Office.

1. NATIONALISATION

1401. Introduction. A national health service in Scotland, available to all, was introduced on 5 July 1948[1], based on recommendations in the Beveridge Report[2]. Before that date health insurance facilities were available to many persons with financial and treatment benefits which varied according to contributions and the rules of the association involved. Institutional treatment was provided in voluntary hospitals and in hospitals provided by local authorities.

The statute which introduced the national health service in Scotland was the National Health Service (Scotland) Act 1947. Other National Health Service (Scotland) Acts followed, the current principal statute being the National Health Service (Scotland) Act 1978 (c 29), which consolidated provisions in earlier enactments. It has since been heavily amended. The Health Services Act 1980 (c 53) contains additional provisions relating to health services and private patients, and major changes, especially relating to dental and ophthalmic services, were made by the Health and Medicines Act 1988 (c 49).

By April 1990 the National Health Service and Community Care Bill had completed all its legislative stages through the House of Commons. This Bill implements many of the proposals contained in the White Paper *Working for Patients*, published in 1989. In particular, Part II of the Bill authorises the Secretary of State by order to establish bodies to be called national health service trusts which will assume responsibility for the ownership and management of hospitals or other establishments or facilities which were previously managed or provided by health boards or the Common Services Agency or to provide and manage hospitals or other establishments or facilities. As well as the broad functions already mentioned, a national health service trust will have the following specific powers:

(1) it may enter into national health service contracts;
(2) it may undertake and commission research and make available staff and provide facilities for research by other persons;
(3) it may provide training for staff employed or likely to be employed by the trust and also make facilities and staff available in connection with training by a university or other body providing training in connection with the health service;
(4) it may make arrangements for the carrying out, on such terms as seem to it to be appropriate, of any of its functions jointly with the health board, the Common Services Agency, another national health service trust or any other body or individual;
(5) depending on its functions, it may make accommodation or services or both available to patients who undertake to pay for such services at a rate to be determined by the trust;
(6) so as to make additional income available in order better to perform its functions, it may exercise certain powers specified in the Health and Medicines Act 1988[3].

The Bill also makes provision for staff who were employed formerly either by a health board or the agency and who worked at a hospital, establishment or facility which has been transferred to a national health service trust to have their contracts of employment transferred automatically to the trust, and once this has happened that contract will be deemed to have been made originally between the employee and the trust. Further, the Bill also empowers the Secretary of State by order to provide for the transfer to a national health service trust of such of the property, liabilities and obligations of a health board, the agency or the Secretary of State as, in his opinion, need to be transferred to the trust for the purpose of enabling it to carry out its functions.

The Bill will also permit any one or more medical practitioners who are providing general medical services to apply to the relevant health board for recognition as a fund-holding practice. Such recognition will only be granted if each of the practitioners concerned can satisfy the board that he fulfils such conditions as may be prescribed. If such recognition is granted the board will become liable to pay to the members of the fund-holding practice an allotted sum which will be determined in accordance with such factors as the Secretary of State may direct. Any such allotted sum may only be applied for purposes which will be specified in regulations. These regulations will make provision generally with respect to the operation of recognised fund-holding practices. However, the regulations may, in particular:

(a) require the members of the practice to reimburse the health board out of allotted sums for expenditure in respect of pharmaceutical services supplied pursuant to orders given by or in behalf of members of the practice;
(b) provide that the goods and services, other than general medical services, which are purchased by or on behalf of members of the practice out of allotted sums for individuals on the practice's list of patients will be such as may be specified in a list approved by the regulations;

(c) impose a limit on the amount which may be spent out of an allotted sum on
     the provision of goods and services for any one individual, being a limit
     above which the cost of any goods and services for that individual in the
     financial year in question will fall to be met by the relevant health board.
Health boards are also given additional powers under the Bill to set indicative
budgets for doctors' practices. In future, for each financial year a health board
must, by notice in writing, specify, by way of a budget, an amount of money
(the indicative budget) representing the basic price of the pharmaceutical services which, in the board's opinion, it is reasonable to expect will be supplied in
that year pursuant to orders given by or on behalf of the practice. This provision
will apply not only to medical practitioners who practise in partnerships but also
to a single medical practitioner who practises alone.
    There are also a number of consequential changes which are introduced by the
Bill. These changes only became apparent at the proof stage of this title. Thus,
for example, the Secretary of State will acquire the power to specify by order the
maximum number of medical practitioners with whom, in any one year, a
health board can enter into arrangements for the provision of general medical
services. The Bill will also abolish the Scottish Health Service Planning Council
and the national consultative committees. In addition, the Bill will also alter the
membership composition of the management committee of the Common
Services Agency by ensuring that the committee will consist of a chairman
appointed by the Secretary of State and such other members as the Secretary of
State may, after consultation with the health boards, appoint. Finally, the Bill
also repeals the power which the Secretary of State presently has to make orders
for the formation and functions of joint liaison committees.
    The introduction of the national health service involved a transfer to and
vesting in the Secretary of State for Scotland of voluntary and local authority
hospitals and the rights and liabilities relating thereto[4]. As from 5 July 1948 it
had become the duty of the Secretary of State to provide throughout Scotland,
to such extent as he considered necessary to meet all reasonable requirements,
hospital accommodation and medical, nursing and specialist services[5].

1 5 July 1948 was the appointed day for the purposes of the National Health Service (Scotland) Act
   1947 (c 27): s 80(1) (repealed); National Health Service (Scotland) Act (Appointed Day) Order
   1948, SI 1948/344.
2 *Report on Social Insurance and Allied Services* (the Beveridge Report) (Cmd 6404) (1942).
3 Ie the Health and Medicines Act 1988 (c 49), s 7(2). These include powers to acquire, produce,
   manufacture and supply goods, have dealing with land, supply accommodation, supply services, provide instruction, do incidental things and make appropriate charges.
4 National Health Service (Scotland) Act 1947, s 6 (repealed).
5 Ibid, s 3 (repealed).

1402. Administrative authorities. Provision was made for the appointment
of administering authorities, namely (1) regional hospital boards for the purpose
of exercising functions with respect to the administration of hospital and
specialist services[1]; (2) boards of management for the purpose of exercising
functions with respect to the control and management of individual hospitals or
groups of hospitals[2]; and (3) executive councils for the purpose of exercising
functions with respect to the provision of services relating to general medical
and dental services, pharmaceutical services and supplementary ophthalmic
services[3].

1 National Health Service (Scotland) Act 1947 (c 27), s 11(1) (repealed).
2 Ibid, s 11(4) (repealed).
3 Ibid, s 32 (repealed).

1403. Local health authorities. Local health authorities were constituted[1] with duties of providing certain health services in private houses or of providing preventative or caring or after-care facilities[2].

1 National Health Service (Scotland) Act 1947 (c 27), s 20 (repealed).
2 See ibid, ss 21–28 (repealed). These services included the care of mothers and young children, health visiting, home nursing, vaccination and immunisation, midwifery and domestic help.

1404. The Hospital Endowments Commission. There was constituted for a limited period a Hospital Endowments Commission with the duty to frame and submit to the Secretary of State schemes for the management of endowments transferred to boards of management and regional hospital boards[1]. Over a period of years schemes were framed and statutory instruments containing the schemes were approved by the Secretary of State for such endowments.

1 National Health Service (Scotland) Act 1947 (c 27), s 8 (repealed).

1405. Transfer and vesting of property in general. On 5 July 1948 there were transferred to and vested in the Secretary of State for Scotland all interests in or attaching to premises forming part of a voluntary hospital or used for the purposes of a voluntary hospital, and in equipment, furniture or other moveable property, being interests held by the governing body or trustees solely for the purposes of that hospital and all rights and liabilities to which the governing body or trustees were entitled or subject, being rights or liabilities acquired or incurred solely for the purpose of managing such premises or property or carrying on the business of the hospital but excluding any endowment[1]. Also transferred were all hospitals vested in a local authority and all property and liabilities held by a local authority or to which it was subject, being property and liabilities held or incurred solely for the purposes of those hospitals[2].

All property so transferred was vested in the Secretary of State free of any trust existing immediately before 5 July 1948, and the Secretary of State was authorised to use any such property for the purpose of any of his functions under the National Health Service (Scotland) Act 1947, but he was required so far as practicable to secure that the objects for which any such property was used immediately before 5 July 1948 were not prejudiced by the exercise of that power[3]. In an action in 1958 relating to two hospitals which had been set up, one as a maternity hospital, the other for treatment of women and children, but both to be staffed entirely by women, the word 'practicable' was held to require the Secretary of State to secure that a male doctor was not appointed unless and until the post had first been advertised as being open only to women medical practitioners and no woman suitable for the appointment had applied[4].

1 National Health Service (Scotland) Act 1947 (c 27), s 6(1) (repealed). As to 5 July 1948, see para 1401, note 1, above.
2 Ibid, s 6(2) (repealed).
3 Ibid, s 6(4) (repealed).
4 *Adams v Secretary of State for Scotland and South-Eastern Regional Hospital Board* 1958 SC 279, 1958 SLT 258.

1406. Transfer and vesting of endowments. On 5 July 1948 there were transferred to and vested in boards of management, free of any trust, all endowments of a voluntary hospital given upon trusts between 5 November 1946 and 5 July 1948, whether to the governing body of the hospital or to trustees, to be held by the board on trust for such purposes relating to the hospital or specialist services or to the functions of the board with respect to research as the board might think fit[1]. The board was required to secure, so far as was reasonably practicable, that the objects of the endowment and the observance of any conditions attaching thereto, including in particular conditions intended to preserve the memory of any person or class of persons, were not prejudiced by the exercise of that power[2].

On the same date there were also transferred to and vested in boards of management all other endowments of a voluntary hospital which, pending the coming into operation of a scheme made by the Hospital Endowments Commission, were to be held by the board on trust for the like uses and purposes as they were held before 5 July 1948[3]. Detailed provision was made for the apportionment of any property held in trust partly for a voluntary hospital and partly for other purposes[4].

On 5 July 1948 there was also transferred to and vested in boards of management all property held solely or partly for the purposes of a hospital vested in a local authority, which, if the hospital had been a voluntary hospital, would have been an endowment[5].

1 National Health Service (Scotland) Act 1947 (c 27), s 7(1) (repealed). As to 5 July 1948, see para 1401, note 1, above.
2 Ibid, s 7(1) proviso (repealed).
3 Ibid, s 7(2), (3) (repealed).
4 Ibid, s 7(7) (repealed).
5 Ibid, s 7(11) (repealed).

2. NATIONAL HEALTH SERVICE REORGANISATION

1407. General duty of the Secretary of State for Scotland. The national health service in Scotland was reorganised with effect from 1 April 1974 by the National Health Service (Scotland) Act 1972, which imposed a general duty on the Secretary of State to provide or secure the effective provision of an integrated health service in Scotland[1]. That provision was repealed by the National Health Service (Scotland) Act 1978, which provided that it continues to be the duty of the Secretary of State to promote in Scotland a comprehensive and integrated health service designed to secure (1) improvement in the physical and mental health of the people of Scotland, and (2) the prevention, diagnosis and treatment of illness, and for that purpose to provide or secure the effective provision of services in accordance with the provisions of the 1978 Act[2]. These services are to be free of charge except in so far as the making and recovery of charges is expressly provided for by or under any enactment[3].

1 National Health Service (Scotland) Act 1972 (c 58), s 1(repealed); National Health Service (Scotland) Act 1972 (Commencement No 4) Order 1974, SI 1974/145. See the White Paper *The Reorganisation of the Scottish Health Services* (Cmnd 4734) (1971). For a summary of the changes, see J B Stewart 'The National Health Service Restructured' 1974 SLT (News) 145.
2 National Health Service (Scotland) Act 1978 (c 29), s 1(1).
3 Ibid, s 1(2).

1408. Specific duties of the Secretary of State. It is the duty of the Secretary of State for Scotland to secure the provision of general medical, general dental and general ophthalmic services, and of pharmaceutical services, in accordance with the provisions of Part II of the National Health Service (Scotland) Act

1978[1]. It is also his duty to provide throughout Scotland, to such extent as he considers necessary to meet all reasonable requirements, hospital and other accommodation and services[2]. Further specific duties are imposed on him in relation to other services and facilities[3].

1 National Health Service (Scotland) Act 1978 (c 29), s 18. Part II comprises ss 18–35.
2 Ibid, s 36. See further para 1476 below.
3 See the rest of ibid, Pt III (which comprises ss 36–48), and paras 1476 ff below.

1409. Inquiries and default and emergency powers of the Secretary of State. The Secretary of State may cause an inquiry to be held in any case where he deems it advisable to do so in connection with any matter arising under the National Health Service (Scotland) Act 1978[1].

Where the Secretary of State is of the opinion, on representations made to him or otherwise, that any health board, the Scottish Medical Practices Committee or the Scottish Dental Practice Board has failed to carry out its functions under the Act, or in carrying them out has failed to comply with any relevant regulations, schemes, proposals or directions, he may, after holding an inquiry, by order declare it to be in default[2], whereupon the members of the body must forthwith vacate their office, and the order must provide for their replacement and may contain interim provisions pending the new appointments[3].

If the Secretary of State is of the opinion that an emergency exists he may if necessary direct that any function conferred by or under the Act on any person or body is, during the period of the emergency, to be performed by some other specified body or person[4].

1 National Health Service (Scotland) Act 1978 (c 29), s 76(1). As to the person appointed to hold the inquiry and report back, and the procedure at the inquiry, see s 76(2), Sch 12.
2 Ibid, s 77(1).
3 Ibid, s 77(2). The order may also contain necessary or expedient supplementary and incidental provisions: s 77(3).
4 Ibid, s 78.

1410. Health boards. The National Health Service (Scotland) Act 1972 provided that health boards, to be constituted by order of the Secretary of State, would administer from 1 April 1974 the hospital and specialist services which had been administered by regional hospital boards and boards of management; the general medical and dental services and pharmaceutical and supplementary ophthalmic services which had been administered by executive councils; the school health service; and the health services which had been administered by local authorities which included health visiting, home nursing and midwifery, maternity and child care, preventative medicine, nursing care and after-care, and vaccination and immunisation[1].

Under the National Health Service (Scotland) Act 1978 the Secretary of State is required by order to constitute health boards for the purpose of exercising such of his functions under that Act as he may by order determine and for the purpose of making arrangements on his behalf for the provision of the services mentioned in Part II of the Act[2].

A health board is a body corporate with a common seal[3]. It consists of a chairman appointed by the Secretary of State and such number of other members so appointed as the Secretary of State thinks fit after consultation with each local authority within the area, any university having an interest in the provision of health services there, organisations representing the various medical professions and other organisations concerned[4].

Fifteen health boards have been constituted[5], and orders have been made defining their functions[6]. Health boards are empowered to hold property on trust⁷, to receive capital or income from certain trustees⁸ and to raise money by appeals or collections⁹.

The provision of the Public Health (Scotland) Act 1897 which relates to the protection of local authorities and their officers applies in relation to a health board in like manner as it applies in relation to a local authority¹⁰.

1 National Health Service (Scotland) Act 1972 (c 58), s 13(1) (repealed).
2 National Health Service (Scotland) Act 1978 (c 29), s 2(1) (amended by the Health and Social Services and Social Security Adjudications Act 1983 (c 41), s 14, Sch 7, para 1). The National Health Service (Scotland) Act 1978, Pt II, comprises ss 18–35.
3 Ibid, s 2(1), (10), Sch 1, para 1.
4 Ibid, Sch 1, paras 2, 3. As to appointment, remuneration and terms of service and procedure, see Sch 1, paras 4, 4A, 5, 5A, 6, 6A, 7, 7A, 8–10 (amended by the Health Services Act 1980 (c 53), s 25(3), (4), Sch 6, para 7(2), (3), Sch 7; Health and Social Services and Social Security Adjudications Act 1983, Sch 7, para 4(1), (2); Dentists Act 1984 (c 24), s 51(1), Sch 5, para 14); National Health Service (Health Boards: Membership, Procedure and Payment of Subscriptions) (Scotland) Regulations 1975, SI 1975/197 (amended by SI 1981/147).
5 National Health Service (Determination of Areas of Health Boards) (Scotland) Order 1974, SI 1974/266, revoking and replacing the National Health Service (Determination of Areas of Health Boards) (Scotland) Order 1973, SI 1973/691.
6 National Health Service (Functions of Health Boards) (Scotland) Order 1983, SI 1983/1027. This order replaced earlier orders.
7 See the National Health Service (Scotland) Act 1978, s 83.
8 See ibid, s 84.
9 See ibid, s 84A (added by the Health Services Act 1980, s 5(2)).
10 National Health Service (Scotland) Act 1978, s 101, referring to the Public Health (Scotland) Act 1897 (c 38), s 166.

1411. The Common Services Agency. There was constituted by the National Health Service (Scotland) Act 1972¹ and reconstituted by the National Health Service (Scotland) Act 1978 a body called the Common Services Agency for the Scottish Health Service, to which the Secretary of State may by order delegate such of his functions under the Act as he considers appropriate². He may also by order provide for the performance of such functions as he may determine to stand referred to the agency and be discharged by it on behalf of any or all of the health boards³. The Secretary of State may withdraw from the agency any function so delegated or referred to it⁴. The agency must provide such services and carry out such tasks for bodies associated with the health service as the Secretary of State and those bodies may agree⁵.

The agency is a body corporate with a common seal⁶. Its affairs are managed by a management committee consisting of a chairman appointed by the Secretary of State, five members appointed by the Secretary of State, six members appointed by him on the nomination of the health boards acting jointly and such other members as he may appoint after consulting the health boards acting jointly⁷.

The Secretary of State has by order imposed a duty on the agency to undertake functions to provide accommodation; to procure equipment and supplies and provide related scientific, engineering and technical services; to provide health education services; to provide an ambulance service; to provide a blood transfusion and blood fractionation service; to arrange for pharmaceutical prescription pricing; to service the Scottish Dental Practice Board; to co-ordinate personnel policies and to provide training; to service the Scottish Medical Practices Committee; to arrange the collection and dissemination of epidemiological data; and to provide legal services to health boards⁸.

The provision of the Public Health (Scotland) Act 1897 which relates to the protection of local authorities and their officers applies in relation to the agency in like manner as it applies in relation to a local authority⁹.

1 National Health Service (Scotland) Act 1972 (c 58), s 19(1) (repealed).
2 National Health Service (Scotland) Act 1978 (c 29), s 10(1), (3) (amended by the Health Services Act 1980 (c 53), s 25(3), Sch 6, para 2).
3 National Health Service (Scotland) Act 1978, s 10(4).
4 Ibid, s 10(5).
5 Ibid, s 10(6).
6 Ibid, s 10(2), Sch 5, para 1.
7 Ibid, Sch 5, paras 2, 3. As to remuneration, staff and terms of service and procedure, see Sch 5, paras 3A, 4–12 (amended by the Health Services Act 1980, s 25(3), (4), Sch 6, para 8(2)–(4), Sch 7); National Health Service (Common Services Agency: Membership and Procedure) (Scotland) Regulations 1975, SI 1975/196.
8 National Health Service (Functions of the Common Services Agency) (Scotland) Order 1974, SI 1974/467.
9 National Health Service (Scotland) Act 1978, s 101, referring to the Public Health (Scotland) Act 1897 (c 38), s 166.

1412. Co-operation; joint liaison committees. In exercising their respective functions, health boards, local authorities and education authorities must co-operate with one another in order to secure and advance the health of the people of Scotland[1]. In relation to disabled persons, persons aged sixty-five or over and such other categories of persons as the Secretary of State may by order specify, this duty includes joint planning of and development of services for those persons (being services of common concern to health boards and either or both local authorities and education authorities), appropriate consultation with voluntary organisations providing similar services and the publication of joint plans[2].

After consultation with such health boards, local authorities, education authorities, associations of such authorities and other organisations and persons as appear appropriate, the Secretary of State may by order provide for the formation and as to the functions of joint liaison committees to advise health boards and local and education authorities on the performance of such of their duties under the above provisions as consist of co-operation in the planning and operation of services of common concern to health boards and such authorities[3]. Such an order may provide for the role of voluntary organisations in such committees[4].

1 National Health Service (Scotland) Act 1978 (c 29), s 13.
2 Ibid, s 13A (added by the National Health Service (Amendment) Act 1986 (c 66), s 5(1)). For the meaning of 'voluntary organisation', see para 1488, note 1, below.
3 National Health Service (Scotland) Act 1978, s 13B(1) (as so added).
4 Ibid, s 13B(2) (as so added).

1413. Rights, liabilities and privilege of health boards and the Common Services Agency. A health board and the Common Services Agency, notwithstanding that these bodies are exercising functions on behalf of the Secretary of State, are entitled to enforce any rights acquired and are liable in respect of any liabilities in the exercise of those functions in all respects as if acting as a principal, and all proceedings are to be brought by or against such body in its own name[1]. Such a body is not entitled to claim in any proceedings any privilege of the Crown in respect of the recovery or production of documents, without prejudice to any right of the Crown so to do on the ground that disclosure would be contrary to the public interest[2].

1 National Health Service (Scotland) Act 1978 (c 29), ss 2(8), 10(8).
2 Ibid, ss 2(9), 10(9).

1414. Dissolution of former administrative authorities; transfers. On 1 April 1974 regional hospital boards, boards of management, medical education committees, executive councils, the Scottish Health Services Council and joint ophthalmic services committees were dissolved[1], and all rights and liabilities of regional hospital boards and boards of management were transferred to or made enforceable against the new health boards[2]. There were transferred to and vested in the Secretary of State for Scotland all property, rights and liabilities of executive councils and the Scottish Dental Estimates Board[3], and of local health authorities and education authorities wholly or mainly relating to the purposes of local health authority health functions or school health functions[4]. Endowments held by regional hospital boards and boards of management were generally transferred to the new health boards, although provision was made for some endowments to be transferred in stated proportions between health boards[5]. Provision was made by order for the rights and liabilities of executive councils and joint ophthalmic services committees to be enforceable by or against health boards and for those of the Drug Accounts Committee to be enforceable by or against the Common Services Agency[6]. Other orders determined the manner in which property formerly held on trust by local health authorities for the purposes of their health functions was to be divided between health boards in cases where the area of an authority was divided by reorganisation of the health service[7], and made provision for property held by a local health authority or education authority which had undergone a change of use before 1 April 1974 and authorised the Secretary of State to exempt certain property from transfer[8].

1 National Health Service (Scotland) Act 1972 (c 58), s 24(1) (repealed); National Health Service (Scotland) Act 1972 (Commencement No 4) Order 1974, SI 1974/145.
2 National Health Service (Transfer of Rights and Liabilities of Regional Hospital Boards and Boards of Management) (Scotland) Order 1974, SI 1974/509.
3 National Health Service (Scotland) Act 1972, s 26(1)–(3).
4 Ibid, s 27.
5 National Health Service (Transfer of Hospital Endowments) (Scotland) Order 1974, SI 1974/510.
6 National Health Service (Enforceability of Rights and Liabilities of Executive Councils and Joint Committees of Executive Councils) (Scotland) Order 1974, SI 1974/521.
7 National Health Service (Transfer of Local Health Authority Trust Property) (Scotland) Order 1975, SI 1975/457.
8 National Health Service (Transfer of Local Authority Property — Change of Use and Exemption) (Scotland) Order 1974, SI 1974/471.

1415. The Scottish Medical Practices Committee. The Secretary of State is required to constitute a Scottish Medical Practices Committee for the purpose of considering and determining applications made for inclusion in any list kept by a health board of medical practitioners undertaking to provide general medical services in the board's area[1]. The committee consists of a chairman, who must be a medical practitioner, and five other members of whom three must be medical practitioners actively engaged in medical practice[2].

1 National Health Service (Scotland) Act 1978 (c 29), s 3(1). The committee was originally constituted under the National Health Service (Scotland) Act 1947 (c 27), s 35 (repealed). As to the general medical services, see the National Health Service (Scotland) Act 1978, s 19, and para 1427 below.
2 Ibid, s 3(2), Sch 2, para 1. All are appointed by the Secretary of State after consultation with organisations representative of the medical profession: Sch 2, para 2. As to the appointment of members, tenure and vacation of office, the committee's procedure and the procedure on applications and appeals to the Secretary of State, see Sch 2, paras 3–5, and the National Health Service (General Medical and Pharmaceutical Services) (Scotland) Regulations 1974, SI 1974/506, Pt III (regs 11–14) (amended by SI 1981/965).

1416. The Scottish Dental Practice Board. For the purpose of carrying out prescribed duties with respect to dental treatment and appliances, authority is given for regulations to provide for the constitution of the Scottish Dental Practices Board[1], formerly constituted as the Scottish Dental Estimates Board[2]. The board consists of a chairman, who must be a dentist, and seven other members of whom five must be dentists, all appointed by the Secretary of State after consultation with organisations representing dentists, and detailed provision is made for the appointment, tenure of office, resignation and removal of members and for the procedure of the board[3].

1 National Health Service (Scotland) Act 1978 (c 29), s 4(1) (amended by the Health and Medicines Act 1988 (c 49), ss 12(1), 25(2), Sch 3). As to the functions which regulations may give to the board, see the National Health Service (Scotland) Act 1978, s 4(1A)–(1C) (added by the Health and Medicines Act 1988, s 12(3)). No regulations have yet been made under this power.
2 National Health Service (Scotland) Act 1947 (c 27), s 39 (repealed); National Health Service (Scotland) Act 1978, s 4(1) (as originally enacted).
3 Ibid, s 4(1), (2); National Health Service (General Dental Services) (Scotland) Regulations 1974, SI 1974/505, Pt III (regs 9–18) (amended by SI 1974/2048 and SI 1985/1552).

1417. National advisory bodies. On the reorganisation of the national health service in 1972 there were established or recognised certain national advisory bodies, namely the Scottish Health Service Planning Council[1] and various national consultative committees representative of the professions engaged in the provision of care or treatment under the health service[2].

1 See the National Health Service (Scotland) Act 1972 (c 58), s 17 (repealed). See now para 1418 below.
2 See ibid, s 18 (repealed). See now para 1419 below.

1418. The Scottish Health Service Planning Council. The Scottish Health Service Planning Council is constituted with the duty of advising the Secretary of State on the exercise of his functions under the National Health Service (Scotland) Act 1978[1]. For that purpose the council is required to keep under review the development of the health service in Scotland as a whole and in the various parts of Scotland[2]. The council consists of a chairman appointed by the Secretary of State, one member appointed by each health board, one member appointed by each university in Scotland which has a medical school, not more than six officers of the Secretary of State appointed by him and such other members, not being officers of the Secretary of State, as may be appointed by him[3]. The council advises the Secretary of State on the identification of health priorities in relation to resources available and the measures necessary to meet them; the implementation, review and evaluation of health planning in the national health service in Scotland; and the integration of health care with other kinds of care to ensure a co-ordinated policy for the treatment of people in need. The council is required to make an annual report which the Secretary of State must lay before Parliament with such comments as he thinks fit[4].

1 National Health Service (Scotland) Act 1978 (c 29), s 5(1). As to the proposed abolition of the council, see para 1401 above.
2 Ibid, s 5(3).
3 Ibid, s 5(2), Sch 3, para 1. Further as to the appointment, tenure and vacation of office of members, and as to committees, assessors and the council's powers, see Sch 3, paras 2–7. No regulations have been made under the power contained in Sch 3, para 3.
4 Ibid, s 5(4).

1419. National consultative committees. The Secretary of State must recognise as a national consultative committee any committee which he is satisfied has been formed and is representative of any, some or all of the professions engaged in the provision of care or treatment and when he is satisfied that it is in the interests of the health service for the committee to be so recognised[1]. Provision is made for professional teaching interests to be represented on such committees and for consultation and advice by regulations[2]. There have been recognised the national medical consultative committee, the national central consultative committee, the national nursing and midwifery consultative committee, the national paramedical (therapeutic) consultative committee, the national pharmaceutical consultative committee, the national optical consultative committee and the national consultative committee of scientists in professions allied to medicine.

Each committee has a duty to advise the Scottish Health Service Planning Council on the provision of health services with which the particular committee is concerned, but not with matters of remuneration or conditions of service[3]. That council may consult with committees and ask them to undertake investigations on its behalf[4].

1 National Health Service (Scotland) Act 1978 (c 29), s 6(1). As to the proposed abolition of the committees, see para 1401 above.
2 Ibid, s 6(2). No such regulations have yet been made.
3 Ibid, s 6(4).
4 Ibid, s 6(6).

1420. Local advisory bodies. There have been established, constituted or recognised the local advisory bodies referred to in the next three succeeding paragraphs, namely local health councils[1], university liaison committees[2] and local consultative committees[3].

1 See the National Health Service (Scotland) Act 1972 (c 58), s 14 (repealed). See now para 1421 below.
2 See ibid, s 15 (repealed). See now para 1422 below.
3 See ibid, s 16 (repealed). See now para 1423 below.

1421. Local health councils. Local health councils are established in accordance with schemes submitted by health boards and approved, with or without modifications, by the Secretary of State[1]. The general function of such a council is to represent the interests of the public in the health service in the area for which it has been established[2].

1 National Health Service (Scotland) Act 1978 (c 29), s 7(1), (3). As to such schemes, see s 7(2), (4). As to allowances to members, see s 7(6), (7) (amended by the Health Services Act 1980 (c 53), s 25(3), Sch 6, para 1).
2 National Health Service (Scotland) Act 1978, s 7(1). Further as to its functions, see s 7(8), (9) (as so amended), and the National Health Service (Local Health Councils) (Scotland) Regulations 1974, SI 1974/2177.

1422. University liaison committees. The Secretary of State is authorised to constitute by order for the area of a health board or for the combined areas of two or more health boards a university liaison committee, for the purpose of advising such board or boards on the administration of the health service so far as relating to the provision of facilities for undergraduate or post-graduate clinical teaching or for research and on any other matter of common interest to them[1]. Not less than one-third of the members are to be appointed by the appropriate university or universities, an equal number are to be appointed by the appropriate health board or boards and the remaining members are to be appointed as provided for in the order constituting the committee[2].

1 National Health Service (Scotland) Act 1978 (c 29), s 8(1).
2 Ibid, s 8(1), Sch 4.

1423. Local consultative committees. Where, after consultation with the health board concerned, the Secretary of State is satisfied that a committee formed for the area of the board is representative of the medical practitioners, or of the dental practitioners, or of the nurses and midwives, or of the pharmacists or of the ophthalmic opticians, all of that area, the Secretary of State is required to recognise that committee[1], which is to be called the area medical committee, the area dental committee, the area nursing and midwifery committee, the area pharmaceutical committee or the area optical committee as the case may be[2]. The general function of such a committee is to advise the health board on the provision of the services in which the committee is concerned, but excluding questions of remuneration and conditions of service of practitioners or other persons of whom it is representative[3].

1 National Health Service (Scotland) Act 1978 (c 29), s 9(1)(a)–(e) (amended by the Health and Social Security Act 1984 (c 48), s 24, Sch 8, Pt I).
2 National Health Service (Scotland) Act 1978, s 9(2)(a)–(e).
3 Ibid, s 9(5).

1424. Trusts. Two Scottish national trusts have been constituted in relation to certain endowment funds and funds for research.

The Scottish Hospital Trust was constituted with the duty to hold and administer certain hospital endowments which had been transferred to the trust[1].

The Scottish Hospital Endowments Research Trust was constituted with the duty to hold and administer funds on trust for the purpose of assisting the conduct of research into any matters relating to the causation, prevention, diagnosis or treatment of illness or to the development of medical or surgical appliances, including hearing aids[2].

1 National Health Service (Scotland) Act 1978 (c 29), s 11(1), (3). For the constitution, see s 11(2), Sch 6 (amended by the Law Reform (Miscellaneous Provisions) (Scotland) Act 1985 (73), s 54), and the Scottish Hospital Trust Regulations 1972, SI 1972/390 (amended by SI 1974/859). The trusts were transferred under the Hospital Endowments (Scotland) Act 1971 (c 8), s 2 (repealed).
2 National Health Service (Scotland) Act 1978, s 12(1), (3). For the constitution, see s 12(2), Sch 7 (as so amended), and the Scottish Hospital Endowments Research Trust Regulations 1953, SI 1953/1918.

1425. The Tribunal. At the inception of the national health service there was constituted a Tribunal for the purpose of inquiring into cases where representations are made by a health board or any other person that the continued inclusion in any list of any practitioner, optician or pharmacist would be prejudicial to the efficiency of the service[1]. The Tribunal comprises a chairman and two other members[2]. The chairman must be a practising advocate or solicitor of not less than ten years' standing appointed by the Lord President of the Court of Session[3]. One of the other members must be appointed by the Secretary of State after consultation with a body representative of health boards[4]. The remaining member must be appointed by the Secretary of State from a panel of practitioners, opticians or pharmacists, as he considers appropriate, having regard to the profession or calling of the person whose case is being investigated[5].

1 National Health Service (Scotland) Act 1978 (c 29), s 29(1) (amended by the Health and Social Security Act 1984 (c 48), s 24, Sch 8, Pt I): see para 1521 below.
2 National Health Service (Scotland) Act 1978, s 29(2), Sch 8, para 1. As to the appointment, term and vacation of office of Tribunal members and the Tribunal's procedure, see the National

Health Service (Service Committees and Tribunal) (Scotland) Regulations 1974, SI 1974/504, Pt IV (regs 36–54), made under the National Health Service (Scotland) Act 1978, Sch 8, para 7.
3 Ibid, Sch 8, para 2.
4 Ibid, Sch 8, para 3.
5 Ibid, Sch 8, paras 4, 5 (as amended: see note 1 above).

1426. The Health Service Commissioner for Scotland. A commissioner, known as the Health Service Commissioner for Scotland, is appointed by Her Majesty by letters patent, and holds office during good behaviour[1], subject to being relieved at his own request or being removed from office by Her Majesty in consequence of addresses from both Houses of Parliament, but must in any case vacate office on completing the year of service in which he attains the age of sixty-five[2]. His office may be declared vacant on the ground of medical incapacity[3]. An acting commissioner may be appointed during a vacancy in the office[4]. The commissioner's function is to investigate complaints in relation to a body subject to investigation[5], namely a health board, the Common Services Agency and the Scottish Dental Practice Board[6].

1 National Health Service (Scotland) Act 1978 (c 29), s 90(1), (2) (amended by the Parliamentary and Health Service Commissioners Act 1987 (c 39), s 2(1)). As to the commissioner's salary and pension, see the National Health Service (Scotland) Act 1978, s 91. As to his officers and expenses, see s 92.
2 Ibid, s 90(3).
3 Ibid, s 90(3A) (added by the Parliamentary and Health Service Commissioners Act 1987, s 2(1)).
4 National Health Service (Scotland) Act 1978, s 92A (added by the Parliamentary and Health Service Commissioners Act 1987, s 6(3)).
5 National Health Service (Scotland) Act 1978, s 90(1).
6 Ibid, s 93(1) (amended by the Health Service Act 1980 (c 53), ss 9(5), 25(4), Sch 2, para 11, Sch 7, and the Health and Medicines Act 1988 (c 49), s 12(5)). See further para 1522 below.

3. GENERAL MEDICAL SERVICES

1427. Arrangements for general medical services. It is the duty of every health board to make as respects its area arrangements with medical practitioners for the provision by them of personal medical services for all persons in the area who wish to take advantage of the arrangements[1]. The services thus provided are known as 'general medical services'[2]. These arrangements are to be made in accordance with regulations[3].

1 National Health Service (Scotland) Act 1978 (c 29), s 19(1). 'Registered medical practitioner' means a fully registered person within the meaning of the Medical Act 1983 (c 54) (see s 55): Interpretation Act 1978 (c 30), s 5, Sch 1 (amended by the Medical Act 1983, s 56(1), Sch 5, para 18), applied by the National Health Service (Scotland) Act 1978, s 108(1) (amended by the Medical Act 1983, Sch 5, para 17).
2 National Health Service (Scotland) Act 1978, s 19(1).
3 Ibid, ss 19(1), (2), (4), (6), 22, 24 (s 19(1) being amended and s 19(6) added by the Health and Social Services and Social Security Adjudications Act 1983 (c 41), s 14, Sch 7, para 2, and s 19(4) being added by the Health Services Act 1980 (c 53), s 7). The principal regulations are the National Health Service (General Medical and Pharmaceutical Services (Scotland) Regulations 1974, SI 1974/506 (amended by SI 1975/696, SI 1976/733, SI 1976/1574, SI 1978/1762, SI 1981/56, SI 1981/965, SI 1982/1279, SI 1985/296, SI 1985/534, SI 1985/804, SI 1985/1625, SI 1985/1713, SI 1986/303, SI 1986/925, SI 1986/1507, SI 1986/2310, SI 1987/385, SI 1987/386, SI 1987/1382, SI 1988/1073, SI 1988/1454, SI 1988/2259, SI 1989/1883 and SI 1989/1990).

1428. Terms of service for doctors. The arrangements made with doctors for the provision of personal medical services must incorporate the terms of service contained or referred to in regulations[1].

1 See the National Health Service (General Medical and Pharmaceutical Services) (Scotland) Regulations 1974, SI 1974, SI 1974/506, reg 3, Sch 1, Pt I (as amended), and paras 1444 ff below.

1429. Application to provide general medical services. An application by a doctor for inclusion in a medical list kept by a health board of the names of medical practitioners undertaking to provide general medical services in the board's area must be made by delivering or posting to the board an application in writing which must include the information and undertakings specified[1]. Where necessary the practitioner must satisfy the board that he has the necessary knowledge of English[2]. The application must be referred to the Scottish Medical Practices Committee with a report by the health board[3], and any medical practitioner whose application is granted by that committee is entitled to have his name included in the medical list[4]. However, that entitlement is subject to a requirement of suitable experience[5], to refusal on the ground that the number of medical practitioners already undertaking to provide general medical services in the area is regarded by the committee as already adequate[6], and to the provisions as to the disqualification of practitioners[7].

Where an application is refused or granted subject to conditions there is a right of appeal to the Secretary of State, who may direct the committee to grant the application either unconditionally or subject to such conditions as he may specify[8].

1 National Health Service (General Medical and Pharmaceutical Services) (Scotland) Regulations 1974, SI 1974/506, reg 6(1) (amended by SI 1989/1990) and, as to contraceptive services, reg 6(3) (added by SI 1975/696). For the forms, see Sch 1, Pts II, III (Pt II substituted by SI 1989/1990, and Pt III added by SI 1975/696 and amended by SI 1982/1279).
2 National Health Service (Scotland) Act 1978 (c 29), s 20(1A) (added by the European Communities (Medical, Dental and Nursing Professions) (Linguistic Knowledge) Order 1981, SI 1981/432).
3 National Health Service (General Medical and Pharmaceutical Services) (Scotland) Regulations 1974, reg 6(2) (amended by SI 1981/695).
4 National Health Service (Scotland) Act 1978, s 20(1) (amended by the Health Services Act 1980 (c 53), s 25(3), (4), Sch 6, para 3, Sch 7, and SI 1981/432).
5 National Health Service (General Medical and Pharmaceutical Services) (Scotland) Regulations 1974, reg 6(4) (added by SI 1981/56). Such experience is prescribed in the National Health Service (Vocational Training) (Scotland) Regulations 1980, SI 1980/30 (amended by SI 1981/55, SI 1982/770, SI 1983/948, SI 1984/1258 and SI 1986/1657), made under the National Health Service (Scotland) Act 1978, s 21.
6 Ibid, s 23(1). The committee may grant an application subject to a condition excluding the doctor from practising in a part of the board's area: s 23(4).
7 Ibid, s 20(1) (as amended: see note 4 above). As to disqualification, see s 29.
8 Ibid, s 23(5) (amended by SI 1981/432, and the Health and Medicines Act 1988 (c 49), s 25(1), Sch 2, para 10). As to the appeal, see the National Health Service (General Medical and Pharmaceutical Services) (Scotland) Regulations 1974, reg 13 (amended by SI 1981/965).

1430. The medical list. A health board must prepare a list, called 'the medical list', of the names of doctors who are entitled to be included in it[1], and of doctors temporarily appointed to act in the place of doctors who have died, have retired or otherwise cease to be entitled to be included in the list[2]. The list must distinguish those doctors who have indicated a willingness to provide maternity medical services or contraceptive services in addition to general medical services, and those doctors who are included for the purpose of providing maternity medical services only or maternity medical services and contraceptive services only[3]. The list must show which doctors have been relieved of the responsibility to provide services during periods of absence, and against those names must show the doctors with whom the board have made arrangements for provision of services during such periods[4]. The list must show, in addition to the name of the doctor, the addresses where he undertakes to attend to treat persons and telephone numbers for receiving messages; the times at which he undertakes to be in attendance, particulars of the days and hours during which he operates an appointment system; the name of each partner or his principal; whether he participates as a member of a group practice and (if so) the name of each doctor in the group practice; and any condition as to his practice attached to the grant of his application by the Scottish Medical Practices Committee or on appeal by the Secretary of State[5]. The list must also show the geographical boundary of the doctor's practice area shown on a map of appropriate scale and, provided the doctor consents to its inclusion, his date of birth or, if he does not so consent, the date of his first full registration as a medical practitioner[6].

The board must keep the medical list revised and up to date and make a copy available at its offices and other convenient places[7]. The board must send a copy of the list to the Secretary of State, the Medical Practices Committee and the area medical and pharmaceutical committees, and inform each of them, within fourteen days, of any change[8]. The board requires to send a copy to all chemists providing pharmaceutical services, notifying them of alterations at intervals of not more than three months[8].

1 National Health Service (General Medical and Pharmaceutical Services) (Scotland) Regulations 1974, SI 1974/506, reg 4(1)(a) (substituted by SI 1985/1625). As to entitlement to be included in the list, see regs 6 and 13, and para 1429 above.
2 Ibid, reg 4(1)(b) (as so substituted). As to such doctors, see reg 20 (as so substituted). The names of doctors so included must be marked in the list accordingly: reg 4(3)(d) (as so substituted).
3 See ibid, reg 4(2), (3)(a), (b) (as so substituted).
4 Ibid, reg 4(3)(c) (as so substituted).
5 Ibid, reg 4(4)(a)–(d), (dd), (e) (reg 4(4)(dd) being added by SI 1989/1990). The list may also, if the board thinks fit, show the part of the area in which each doctor will provide treatment: reg 4(4).
6 Ibid, reg 4(4)(f), (g) (amended by SI 1989/1990).
7 Ibid, reg 33(1), (2).
8 Ibid, reg 33(3).

1431. Adequacy of services. A health board must, once a year or more often as the Scottish Medical Practices Committee may require, provide information to enable the committee to judge the adequacy of the medical services in the board's area or part of it[1].

A decision of the committee to grant an application for inclusion in the medical list on the ground that the number of practitioners in the area is not already adequate must be given in such manner as the committee determines[2]. If the Secretary of State is satisfied, after such inquiry as he thinks fit, that the doctors on the medical list are not such as to secure the adequate provision of the general medical service or that for any other reason any considerable number of persons is not receiving satisfactory services, he may authorise the health board to make such other arrangements as he may approve or may himself make other arrangements[3].

1 National Health Service (General Medical and Pharmaceutical Services) (Scotland) Regulations 1974, SI 1974/506, reg 7(1).
2 Ibid, reg 12(1). Inclusion in the list may be refused if there are already enough doctors practising in the area: see para 1429 above.
3 National Health Service (Scotland) Act 1978 (c 29), s 33(a).

1432. Removal from the medical list. A doctor may give notice to the health board at any time that he wishes to withdraw his name from the medical list, and his name will then be removed at the expiration of three months from the date of the notice or of such shorter period as the board may agree[1]. The notice may be revoked only with the board's consent[2]. However, a doctor may not seek the withdrawal of his name if representations have been made to the

Tribunal about him until the termination of the proceedings on the representations[3].

Where a health board has determined that a doctor on the list has for the preceding six months not provided general medical services personally for persons in the area, the board, after giving him twenty-eight days' notice of its intention, may remove his name from the list unless the Secretary of State directs to the contrary[4], but the board must first afford the doctor the opportunity of making representations in writing to the board or, if he so desires, orally to a committee appointed by the board, of which committee at least one-third of the members are doctors; and the board must also consult the area medical committee[5]. Within twenty-one days of receiving notice of the board's intention the doctor may appeal to the Secretary of State, and, pending the decision on any such appeal, the health board must not remove the doctor's name from the list[6].

1 National Health Service (General Medical and Pharmaceutical Services) (Scotland) Regulations 1974, SI 1974/506, Sch 1, Pt I, para 21(1) (substituted by SI 1975/696).
2 Ibid, Sch 1, Pt I, para 21(2) (as so substituted).
3 Ibid, Sch 1, Pt I, para 21(3) (as so substituted). As to such representations, see para 1521 below.
4 Ibid, reg 5(1), (1A) (substituted and added by SI 1985/1625).
5 Ibid, reg 5(2) (amended by SI 1985/1625).
6 Ibid, reg 5(3) (as so amended).

1433. Succession to vacant medical practice. A health board may, after consultation with the area medical committee, and must, if directed by the Scottish Medical Practices Committee, invite by press advertisement applications from doctors desirous of providing general medical services[1]. When a health board receives notice of the death of a doctor or of the withdrawal or removal of a doctor's name from the medical list, the board must, within fourteen days, inform that committee and furnish it with a report as to the need for filling the vacancy[2]; and the board may, and if that committee so directs must, by press advertisement, invite applications from doctors desirous of succeeding to the practice in whole or in part[3]. After consultation with the area medical committee, the board may select a doctor or doctors to succeed to the practice in whole or in part[4]. The board must notify the medical practices committee and each doctor who applied of its decision, informing each unsuccessful applicant of his right of appeal to the medical practices committee[4]. Any doctor may, within seven days of receipt of notification, appeal to the Scottish Medical Practices Committee, which may direct that any appellant is to succeed to the practice instead of or in addition to any doctor selected by the board[5]. The board and, on appeal, the committee must have regard to any desire expressed by an applicant to practise with other doctors providing general medical services and to any desire by such other doctors to take any applicant into practice with them[6].

1 National Health Service (General Medical and Pharmaceutical Services) (Scotland) Regulations 1974, SI 1974/506, reg 10.
2 Ibid, reg 7(2) (amended by SI 1985/1625).
3 Ibid, reg 8(1). The provisions of reg 8 do not apply where a doctor gives notice of desire to exchange his practice under reg 9 (see para 1434 below) or in the case of a temporary appointment under reg 20 (see para 1441 below): reg 8(6) (substituted by SI 1985/1625).
4 Ibid, reg 8(2).
5 Ibid, reg 8(3). The committee determines the appeal procedure: reg 8(4).
6 Ibid, reg 8(5).

1434. Exchange of practices. A doctor whose name is on the medical list may notify the health board that he desires to exchange practices with another doctor providing general medical services, whether in the same area or not[1]. After inquiry and after consulting the area medical committee the board may approve the exchange; thereafter both doctors and the Scottish Medical Practices Committee must be notified, and the doctors will then agree and notify a date for the exchange, which must generally be not earlier than three months after the notification[2]. If the board does not approve the exchange, either doctor, with the consent of the other, may appeal to the Scottish Medical Practices Committee[3].

1 National Health Service (General Medical and Pharmaceutical Services) (Scotland) Regulations 1974, SI 1974/506, reg 9(1).
2 Ibid, reg 9(1), (2).
3 See ibid, reg 9(3)–(5).

1435. Prohibition of sale of practices. At the inception of the national health service every medical practitioner whose name was entered on a medical list was paid compensation for the loss suffered by reason that he would be unable to sell the goodwill of his practice, in whole or in part[1]. Where the name of any medical practitioner has been at any time after 5 July 1948 entered in a medical list it is unlawful subsequently to sell the goodwill of the medical practice of that practitioner[2]. In an action in the sheriff court his illegality was held to taint a contract and render it unenforceable[3]. Any person who sells or buys goodwill contrary to that provision is liable on conviction on indictment to a fine or to imprisonment for a term not exceeding three months or to both such fine and imprisonment[4]. There are detailed provisions as to transactions which are to be deemed to be a sale of goodwill[5], and a procedure whereby any medical practitioner may apply to the Scottish Medical Practices Committee for its opinion whether a proposed transaction or series of transactions involves the sale of goodwill[6]. Where a practitioner who has ceased to be entered in any list practises in another area where he has never been on the medical list, he will not be prohibited from selling the goodwill of the other practice[7]. There is no prohibition of a sale by a practitioner whose name has never been entered in a medical list notwithstanding that part of the goodwill to be sold is attributable to a practice previously carried on by a person whose name was entered in such a list[8].

1 National Health Service (Scotland) Act 1947 (c 27), s 37 (repealed).
2 National Health Service (Scotland) Act 1978 (c 29), s 35(1).
3 *Freedlander v Bateman* 1953 SLT (Sh Ct) 105.
4 National Health Service (Scotland) Act 1978, s 35(1), Sch 9, para 1(1) (amended by the Criminal Justice Act 1982 (c 48), ss 77, 78, Sch 15, para 20, Sch 16).
5 National Health Service (Scotland) Act 1978, Sch 9, para 2.
6 Ibid, Sch 9, para 1(2)–(4).
7 Ibid, s 35(2).
8 Ibid, s 35(3).

1436. Selection of doctor. Application by a person to a doctor for acceptance and inclusion in that doctor's list is to be made in writing on the person's medical card or on a form of application approved by the Secretary of State[1]. The right to choose a doctor is to be exercised on behalf of any child under the age of sixteen by the mother or, in her absence, the father, or in the absence of both parents the guardian or other person who has care of the child; on behalf of any other person who is incapable on account of sickness or other infirmity of choosing a doctor, by a relative or any person who has the care of that person; and on behalf of any person under the age of eighteen in the care of a local authority by a person duly authorised by that authority[2]. However, the right to choose may not be exercised by the doctor to whom the application is made[3]. There are special provisions in relation to any child under the age of five[4].

A woman who, after a doctor has diagnosed that she is pregnant, desires the provision of maternity medical services, may arrange for them to be provided either by any doctor on a medical list who has indicated his willingness to provide maternity medical services or by the doctor in whose list her name is included[5].

1 National Health Service (General Medical and Pharmaceutical Services) (Scotland) Regulations 1974, SI 1974/506, reg 15(1). Application for acceptance as a temporary resident is made on a form supplied by the health board: reg 15(2).
2 Ibid, reg 35(a)–(c), made under the National Health Service (Scotland) Act 1978 (c 29), s 34, and amended by SI 1989/1990.
3 National Health Service (General Medical and Pharmaceutical Services) (Scotland) Regulations 1974, reg 35 proviso.
4 See ibid, reg 15(3)–(6) (added by SI 1989/1990).
5 Ibid, reg 24.

1437. Assignment of persons to doctors. A health board must delegate the following matters to a committee, which must include general practitioner members appointed by the area medical committee but which must have a majority of members who are members of the board[1]:

(1) the assignment to such doctor as it thinks fit of a person who applies for assignment to a doctor (whether or not that person is then on the list of another doctor) or who is deemed to have applied for assignment[2], and the notification to that person and the doctor or doctors of the assignment[3];

(2) the exemption from liability to have persons assigned to him of any doctor who applies for that purpose[4]; and

(3) the granting to a doctor who is elderly or infirm of relief from liability for night-time and weekend emergency calls from persons who are not his patients[5].

1 National Health Service (General Medical and Pharmaceutical Services) (Scotland) Regulations 1974, SI 1974/506, reg 16(1).
2 Ie deemed in accordance with ibid, Sch 1, Pt I, para 4(2), under which where a doctor refuses to accept for inclusion in his list a person who lives in his practice area, and informs that person of the name and address of a neighbouring doctor and of that person's right to apply to the health board for assignment, and gives that person any treatment he requires immediately, the doctor must notify the board of his refusal and that person is deemed to have applied to the board for assignment.
3 Ibid, reg 16(3) (substituted by SI 1981/56). The committee may authorise its chairman or another member to make assignments where necessary before a committee meeting can be held: reg 16(2).
4 Ibid, reg 16(4).
5 Ibid, reg 16(5), Sch 1, Pt I, para 5.

1438. Doctors' lists. A health board must prepare and keep revised up to date, in respect of each doctor on its medical list, a list of the patients in its area for whom each doctor is for the time being responsible, advising the doctor from time to time of persons added to or deleted from the list[1]. The name of a person accepted by a doctor for inclusion is to be included from the date on which notification of acceptance is received by the board[2]. Where a person dies, or is absent from the United Kingdom for a period of three months, or leaves the United Kingdom with the intention of being away for a period in excess of three months, or enlists in Her Majesty's forces, or is serving a prison sentence of more than two years, his name is to be deleted from the doctor's list as from the date on which the health board first received notification of the death, absence, departure, enlistment or imprisonment[3]. Any deletion from a doctor's list by the transfer of a person to the list of another doctor takes effect from the date on which the health board receives notification of the acceptance by the doctor to whom the person is being transferred or, subject to the consent of the board, on such date not being earlier than the date of such consent as may be agreed between the doctors[4]. Any other deletion from a doctor's list takes effect from the date on which notice of deletion is sent by the health board to the doctor or from such other date not being earlier than that date as may be specified in the notice[5].

1 National Health Service (General Medical and Pharmaceutical Services) (Scotland) Regulations 1974, SI 1974/506, reg 23(1).
2 Ibid, reg 23(2). For an exception in the case of succession to a practice or exchange of practices, see reg 18(4).
3 Ibid, reg 23(3)(a)–(e).
4 Ibid, reg 23(4). This does not apply to a deletion in accordance with a notice of the death of a doctor, or the withdrawal or removal of a doctor's name from the medical list, under reg 18(3) (substituted by SI 1985/1625), or a notice of succession to a practice or exchange of practices under reg 18(4): reg 23(4).
5 Ibid, reg 23(5).

1439. Limitation of persons in doctors' lists. The maximum number of persons a doctor may have on his lists in all areas in which he provides general medical services (adjoining health boards being required to consult in relation to this[1]) is 3,500 for a doctor practising on his own and 4,500 for a doctor carrying on practice in partnership (subject to an average of 3,500 for each of the partners in the practice)[2]. Where a doctor (or doctors in partnership) employs permanently one or more assistants, an addition of not more than 2,000 persons to the list in respect of each assistant may be allowed with the consent of the health board or, on appeal, the Scottish Medical Practices Committee[3]. Where a health board finds the number of patients on a doctor's list to be in excess of the maximum number allowed, it must notify the doctor, who is required, within two months from the date of notification, to take steps to reduce his list by entering into partnership, or employing an assistant, or giving notice to the health board of the names of the necessary number of patients he wishes removed from his list[4]. If at the end of the period of two months the list is not reduced to the number allowed, the health board must remove from the doctor's list the necessary number of names[5]. In special circumstances a health board, subject to the consent of the Secretary of State and to any conditions he may impose, may permit a doctor or partnership to have a greater number than otherwise allowed[6].

1 National Health Service (General Medical and Pharmaceutical Services) (Scotland) Regulations 1974, SI 1974/506, reg 17(8).
2 Ibid, reg 17(1). This does not prevent a doctor accepting temporary residents; nor does it exempt him from liability in respect of his responsibility to patients under Sch 1, Pt I, para 4: reg 17(10).
3 Ibid, reg 17(2).
4 Ibid, reg 17(4). As to removal from lists, see Sch 1, Pt I, para 7.
5 Ibid, reg 17(5).
6 Ibid, reg 17(9).

1440. Change of doctor. A person may apply to any doctor (other than the doctor in whose list he is included) who provides general medical services for acceptance in that doctor's list of patients[1]. A person who has applied for a change of doctor and has been refused acceptance by any doctor may apply to the health board in whose area he is resident to be allocated to any doctor whose name is included in the board's medical list[2].

Where a doctor dies or his name is withdrawn or removed from the medical list, the health board must as soon as is practicable make known the fact by sending individual notices to persons on the doctor's list[3].

Where one or more doctors have been selected to succeed to a practice following a vacancy or exchange of practice, the health board must send to persons on the list of the doctor who last carried on that practice a statement of the name and address of the successor doctor or doctors in whose list it is considered that the person may wish to be included, together with an intimation that the successor is willing to accept them and that they will be deemed to be included in his list as from the date given in the notice, unless within one month of that date they have applied to and been accepted by other doctors or have given notice in writing to the board of their desire not to be included[4]. Where no successor is appointed, the health board must give to persons on the previous doctor's list notice of their right to apply to another doctor on the medical list for acceptance[5].

Where a doctor who has performed a period of relevant service[6] in an emergency has returned to his practice at the end of that service and has advised a health board in writing within one month of his return that he has resumed practice, the board must give notice within seven days to every person who was on the doctor's list at the beginning of that service and who, although residing at the same address as before, has transferred to another doctor[7]. The notice states that the person's name will be restored to the previous doctor's list unless within fourteen days that person gives written notice to the board that he wishes his name to remain on the list of his new doctor[7]. On the expiry of the fourteen days the board must notify the doctors concerned of those persons whose names are restored and those who have elected to remain[7].

A woman who has arranged for the provision of maternity medical services may terminate the arrangements by giving written notice to that effect to the health board; or to the original doctor, who must within seven days give written notice to the board; or by making a new arrangement with another doctor, who must within seven days give written notice to the board of the new arrangement[8]. Where a board has received such notification it must within seven days give written notice to the original doctor that the arrangement with him has been terminated[9].

1 National Health Service (General Medical and Pharmaceutical Services) (Scotland) Regulations 1974, SI 1974/506, reg 18(1), (2) (substituted by SI 1989/1990).
2 Ibid, reg 18(2) (as so substituted).
3 Ibid, reg 18(3) (substituted by SI 1985/1625), which does not apply to women accepted by him for the provision of contraceptive services only.
4 Ibid, reg 18(4). As to women who were also on the previous doctor's list for the provision of contraceptive services, see reg 18(4A) (added by SI 1981/56 and substituted by SI 1985/1625).
5 Ibid, reg 18(4B) (added by SI 1985/1625), which does not apply to women accepted by him for the provision of contraceptive services only.
6 'Relevant service' means whole-time service in the armed forces in a national emergency as a volunteer or otherwise, or compulsory whole-time service in the forces, and certain other service: see ibid, reg 2(1).
7 Ibid, reg 18(6).
8 Ibid, reg 25(1) (substituted by SI 1989/1990).
9 Ibid, reg 25(2) (as so substituted). As to such arrangements, see reg 24, and para 1436 above.

1441. Temporary arrangements. Where a doctor dies or otherwise ceases to be entitled to be included in the medical list, or where his registration is suspended[1], the health board may, in consultation with the area medical committee, make temporary arrangements for the provision of the general medical services for which the doctor was or might have become responsible, consisting of or including the appointment of another doctor to undertake the provision of those services[2]. Where the doctor has died, any person may apply to the board within seven days of the death, on behalf of the doctor's estate, and the board, instead of appointing a doctor of its own choice, may authorise a doctor named by the applicant to undertake those services[3]. An appointment by the board under either of these powers is to be for such period as the board thinks fit but not exceeding one year unless the board thinks fit to continue it; in no case may it subsist beyond the date on which the relevant practice vacancy is permanently filled or any suspension giving rise to the vacancy ceases to have effect[4].

After consulting the area medical committee a health board may require the medical examination of a doctor on the medical list who appears to be incapable of carrying out his obligations adequately because of his physical or mental condition[5], and where, on these grounds or because of the doctor's continued absence, the board is satisfied that his obligations are not being carried out adequately, the board may after such consultation and with the consent of the Secretary of State make temporary arrangements for the provision of treatment, consisting of or including the appointment of doctors to give such treatment[6].

1 Ie under the National Health Service (Scotland) Act 1978 (c 29), s 19(7) (added by the Health and Social Services and Social Security Adjudications Act 1983 (c 41), s 14, Sch 7, para 2, and amended by the Medical Act 1983 (c 54), s 56(1), Sch 5, para 17), by direction of the Health Committee of the General Medical Council under the Medical Act 1983, s 37(1), for unfitness to practise by reason of physical or mental condition; or by an order of that committee for immediate suspension under s 38(1); or by interim order of the Preliminary Proceedings Committee under s 42(3)(b).
2 National Health Service (General Medical and Pharmaceutical Services) (Scotland) Regulations 1974, SI 1974/506, reg 20(1), (2)(a) (substituted by SI 1985/1625).
3 Ibid, reg 20(2)(b) (as so substituted).
4 Ibid, reg 20(4) (as so substituted). The Secretary of State must be notified of arrangements which are to continue for over a year: see reg 20(5) (as so substituted).
5 Ibid, reg 20(6) (as so substituted). As to the examination, see reg 20(10) (as so substituted).
6 Ibid, reg 20(7) (as so substituted).

1442. Temporary residents. A person who is residing temporarily in a district and whose name is not on the list of a doctor providing general medical services in that district may, if he requires treatment, apply to any doctor to be accepted by him as a temporary resident and if he is so accepted his name is not to be removed from the list of any doctor in which it is already included[1]. A person is to be regarded as temporarily resident in a district if when he arrives he intends to stay there for more than twenty-four hours but not more than three months[2]. If the stay of a person accepted as a temporary resident exceeds three months, he ceases to be regarded as a temporary resident[3]. A woman who is residing temporarily in any district may arrange with a doctor for the provision by him of maternity services or contraceptive services during her period of temporary residence without prejudice to her right to obtain such services in any other area in which she may become resident[4].

1 National Health Service (General Medical and Pharmaceutical Services) (Scotland) Regulations 1974, SI 1974/506, reg 22(1).
2 Ibid, reg 22(2).
3 Ibid, reg 22(3).
4 Ibid, reg 26, and reg 26A (added by SI 1975/696).

1443. Removal from doctors' lists. A person whose name is included in a doctor's list and who no longer wishes to avail himself of general medical services may at any time give notice to the health board that he wishes his name to be removed, and at the expiration of fourteen days from the date of the receipt of the notice the board must remove the name and inform the person and the doctor[1].

Where a health board, after due inquiry, including consultation in writing with the doctor concerned, is satisfied either that a person no longer resides in that part of the area of the board where the doctor has undertaken to provide services, or that the whereabouts of the person are no longer known to the board, and that the doctor in whose list the name of that person is included is no longer responsible for providing that person with general medical services, the board must remove the name of that person from the doctor's list[2] and inform the doctor and that person at his last known address[3]. Without prejudice to the foregoing, where a board consults a doctor in writing about the possible removal of the name of a person from his list, the board must, unless the doctor satisfies it that he is still responsible for providing general medical services for that person, remove that name six months after the consultation[4] and inform the doctor and that person at his last known address[5].

On receiving from a doctor providing general medical services for pupils or staff at a school or for residents or staff at a residential institution particulars of persons who are pupils or staff or residents, a health board must remove forthwith the names of all persons appearing in his list as pupils or staff or residents of such school or institution not shown in those particulars[6]. Where a board has requested such particulars and has not received them within the one month required in the doctor's terms of service, the board may remove the names of persons at the school or institution appearing on the doctor's list[7].

1 National Health Service (General Medical and Pharmaceutical Services) (Scotland) Regulations 1974, SI 1974/506, reg 21(1).
2 Ibid, reg 21(2).
3 Ibid, reg 21(4).
4 Ibid, reg 21(3).
5 Ibid, reg 21(4).
6 Ibid, reg 21(5)(a). The doctor is required by Sch 1, Pt I, para 18, to give these particulars.
7 Ibid, reg 21(5)(b).

1444. Doctors' rights and obligations under terms of service generally. The terms of service of a doctor[1] are deemed to include any provisions affecting the rights and obligations of doctors of:

(1) the National Health Service (General Medical and Pharmaceutical Services) (Scotland) Regulations 1974;

(2) any statement made by the Secretary of State relating to payments to doctors[2]; and

(3) any of certain provisions of the National Health Service (Service Committees and Tribunal) Regulations 1974[3].

With the approval of the Secretary of State a health board may alter the terms of service as from such date as he may approve, and must generally give notice of the alteration to each doctor[4]. Except in the case of an alteration resulting from an Act of Parliament or regulation or which has been approved by the Secretary of State after consultation with an organisation representative of the general body of doctors, the Secretary of State must consult the area medical committee[5]. If after such consultation the Secretary of State so directs, notice given to that committee is deemed to have been given to each doctor[6].

The detailed rights and obligations of doctors are discussed in the paragraphs which follow[7].

1 The terms of service are contained in the National Health Service (General Medical and Pharmaceutical Services) (Scotland) Regulations 1974, SI 1974/506, Sch 1, Pt I: reg 3; see para 1428 above, and paras 1445 ff below.

2	Ie a statement made under ibid, reg 31 (amended by SI 1975/696, SI 1982/1279 and SI 1985/1625).
3	National Health Service (General Medical and Pharmaceutical Services) (Scotland) Regulations 1974, Sch 1, Pt I, para 2. The provisions referred to are those of the National Health Service (Service Committees and Tribunal) Regulations 1974, SI 1974/504, Pt II (regs 3–21) (investigations, disputes, appeals etc).
4	National Health Service (General Medical and Pharmaceutical Services) (Scotland) Regulations 1974, Sch 1, Pt I, para 3(1).
5	Ibid, Sch 1, Pt I, para 3(2).
6	Ibid, Sch 1, Pt I, para 3(3).
7	See paras 1445–1450 below.

1445. Doctors' patients. 'Patient' is defined as a person for whose treatment a doctor is responsible under the terms of service[1], namely (1) all persons whom the doctor has accepted or agreed to accept for inclusion in his list and who have not been notified to him by a health board as having ceased to be on his list; (2) all persons whom he has accepted or agreed to accept as temporary residents; (3) all persons who have been assigned to him and who have not been notified to him by the board as having ceased to be on his list; (4) all persons for whom he may be required[2] to provide treatment pending their acceptance by or assignment to another doctor; (5) all persons for whom he may be required[3] to provide treatment which is immediately required in case of accident or other emergency; (6) all persons to whom he is required to give necessary treatment[4], being persons who claim to be on his list and who apply for treatment but who fail to produce their medical cards; (7) all persons for whom he has undertaken to provide general medical services under an arrangement approved by the Secretary of State for the provision of such services to workmen residing in camps; (8) all persons in respect of whom he is acting as a deputy[5]; (9) persons whom he has been appointed to treat temporarily during the period of a temporary appointment[6] when a doctor has ceased to practise; (10) in respect of contraceptive services and maternity medical services, women for whom he has undertaken to provide such services; and (11) during the hours agreed with the health board, any person whose own doctor has been relieved of responsibility during those hours[7], for whom he has accepted responsibility[8].

If a doctor refuses to accept for inclusion in his list or as a temporary resident a person who lives in his practice area who is not in the list of or has not been accepted as a temporary resident by another doctor in that area, he may inform that person of the name and address of any neighbouring doctor, and must inform him of the name and address of the health board and of his right to apply to it for assignment, and he must give that person any treatment which he may require until that person has been accepted by or assigned to another doctor[9].

If a doctor is requested to provide treatment, and is available, he must provide treatment immediately required, by reason of accident or other emergency, by a person who is not on the list of and who has not been accepted as a temporary resident by or assigned to any doctor practising in the locality, or who is on the list of or has been accepted as a temporary resident by or assigned to such a doctor but neither the doctor nor any deputy is available to treat the person[10].

No doctor is to be responsible under the terms of service for the treatment in hospital of a person admitted thereto for treatment by the staff of that hospital[11].

1	National Health Service (General Medical and Pharmaceutical Services) (Scotland) Regulations 1974, SI 1974/506, reg 3, Sch 1, Pt I, para 1(a), referring to responsibility under Sch 1, Pt I, para 4, for which see below.
2	Ie in terms of ibid, Sch 1, Pt I, para 4(2): see below.
3	Ie in terms of ibid, Sch 1, Pt I, para 4(3): see below.
4	Ie in terms of ibid, Sch 1, Pt I, para 8.
5	Ie under ibid, Sch 1, Pt I, para 12(2A) (added by SI 1982/1279).
6	Ie under ibid, reg 20: see para 1441 above.
7	Ie the hours specified in ibid, Sch 1, Pt I, para 5: see para 1437 above.

8 Ibid, Sch 1, Pt I, para 4(1)(a)–(k) (amended by SI 1975/696 and SI 1985/1625).
9 Ibid, Sch 1, Pt I, para 4(2).
10 Ibid, Sch 1, Pt I, para 4(3).
11 Ibid, Sch 1, Pt I, para 4(4).

1446. Doctors' services to patients. A doctor is required to render to his patients all necessary and appropriate personal medical services of the type usually provided by general medical practitioners[1]. This treatment includes:
(1) the administration of anaesthetics or the rendering of any other assistance at an operation performed by and of the kind usually performed by a general medical practitioner;
(2) where appropriate giving advice personally to patients, either individually or in groups, relating to their general health, and in particular on the significance of diet, exercise, the use of tobacco, the consumption of alcohol and the misuse of drugs and solvents;
(3) offering to patients consultations and, where appropriate, physical examinations for the purpose of identifying, or reducing the risk of, disease or injury;
(4) offering to patients, where appropriate, vaccination or immunisation against Measles, Mumps, Rubella, Pertussis, Poliomyelitis, Diphtheria and Tetanus;
(5) arranging for the referral of patients, as appropriate, for the provision of any other services provided under the National Health Service (Scotland) Act 1978 (c 29);
(6) giving advice, as appropriate, to enable patients to avail themselves of social work services provided by a local authority[2].
However, doctors are not required to provide to any person:
(a) services which involve the application of such special skill or experience of a degree or kind which general medical practitioners as a class cannot reasonably be expected to possess;
(b) the administration of an anaesthetic at an operation performed by a doctor in the course of providing maternity medical services;
(c) contraceptive services, child health surveillance services, minor surgery services nor, except in an emergency, maternity medical services, unless he has previously undertaken to provide such services to that person; or
(d) where he is a restricted services principal, any category of general medical services which he has not undertaken to provide[3].
There are also restrictions on the supply of certain drugs and other substances[4].
In relation to maternity medical services, all proper and necessary treatment includes the provision of all necessary medical services (other than those involving special skill or experience of a degree which general practitioners as a class cannot reasonably be expected to possess) during and following pregnancy and labour in respect of all conditions arising therefrom[5]. Such treatment includes in particular:
(i) antenatal services, namely full antenatal care, supervision and examination, including full medical and obstetric examination of the patient as soon as possible after the doctor's engagement to provide maternity services, and such further examinations as the condition of the patient requires;
(ii) services during the confinement and lying-in period, namely (A) attendance at some stage of labour, either before or at delivery, or at such early time thereafter as is reasonably possible in the light of clinical circumstances, (B) attendance within twelve hours of completion of labour or as soon thereafter as is practicable and as often as the condition of the patient or her child requires throughout a lying-in period of fourteen days, and (C) attendance at any time when summoned by the midwife attending the case;

(iii) post-puerperal services, namely medical and pelvic examination of the
patient at or about six weeks after confinement[6];

and, where he is not the doctor on whose list the name of the person is included:

(iv) compliance with any request by the doctor on whose list the name of the
woman is included to examine or give other assistance to the woman and
her child; and

(v) the issue of any certificate required[7] in relation to pregnancy, expected
confinement and confinement[8].

A doctor is required to provide proper and sufficient consulting and waiting
room accommodation for his patients, which accommodation must not, except
with the consent of the health board or, on appeal, the Secretary of State, be in
premises occupied by a chemist[9].

A doctor must attend and treat any patient who attends for the purpose at the
places and during the hours for the time being approved by the board[10]. In
particular, a doctor is required to render his services at his practice premises; or,
if the condition of the patient so requires, at the patient's residence, or at such
other place as the doctor has informed the patient and the health board that he
has agreed to visit and treat the patient if the patient's condition so requires, or,
in any other case, at some other place in the doctor's practice area[11]. Moreover, a
doctor must make himself available for consultations at such places and at such
times as have been approved by the board[12]. However, the above obligations do
not apply in the case of a patient who attends when an appointment system is in
operation and who has not previously made, and is not given, an appointment[13]. In such a case the doctor may decline to attend the patient during that
surgery period, if the patient's health would not thereby be jeopardised and the
patient is offered an appointment to attend within a reasonable time having
regard to all circumstances[13].

A doctor must inform a patient requiring treatment which is not within the
scope of the doctor's obligation but which to his knowledge is available under
the national health service and give advice to enable the patient to take advantage
of such treatment[14]; if desired he must recommend for ophthalmic treatment a
patient who requires it[15]; and he must issue free of charge the prescribed
certificates[16].

Subject to prescribed restrictions relating to scheduled drugs[17], a doctor is
required, by the prescribed procedure, to order drugs and appliances required
for any treatment given to a patient[18]. A doctor is required to supply any drugs
(other than scheduled drugs) or appliances for the immediate treatment of a
patient if such treatment is necessary before a supply can be obtained otherwise
(and may supply any other non-scheduled drug which he administers in person,
or a diagnostic reagent listed in the drug tariff or a pessary which is an
appliance)[19]; and to supply all requisite drugs (other than scheduled drugs) and
appliances to any patient, being a patient to whom the health board has required
the doctor to supply drugs[20], under certain restrictions[21]. Any drug supplied by
a doctor, unless administered by him in person, must be supplied in a suitable
container[22].

A doctor is required to keep records of the illnesses of his patients and his
treatments of them in such form as the Secretary of State may from time to time
determine, and to send such records with reasonable promptness when called
for by the health board or, upon knowledge of the death of a patient, within
seven days[23].

1 National Health Service (General Medical and Pharmaceutical Services) (Scotland) Regulations
1974, SI 1974/506, reg 3, Sch 1, Pt I, para 9(1) (substituted by SI 1989/1990).
2 Ibid, Sch 1, Pt I, para 9(1A)(a)–(f) (added by SI 1989/1990).
3 Ibid, Sch 1, Pt I, para 9(1B)(a)–(d) (as so added).

4 See ibid, Sch 1, Pt I, para 16A (added by SI 1985/296).
5 Ibid, Sch 1, Pt I, para 9(2).
6 Ibid, Sch 1, Pt I, para 9(2)(a)–(c).
7 It in terms of ibid, Sch 1, Pt I, para 10(5), for which see below.
8 Ibid, Sch 1, Pt I, para 9(3)(a), (b).
9 Ibid, Sch 1, Pt I, para 13(1).
10 The approval is given under ibid, Sch 1, Pt I, para 13(3).
11 Ibid, Sch 1, Pt I, para 10(3)(a), (b)(i)–(iii) (substituted by SI 1989/1990).
12 Ibid, Sch 1, Pt I, para 10(4) (as so substituted).
13 Ibid, Sch 1, Pt I, para 10(7) (added by SI 1989/1990).
14 Ibid, Sch 1, Pt I, para 10(1).
15 Ibid, Sch 1, Pt I, para 10(2).
16 Ibid, Sch 1, Pt I, para 10(5) (substituted by SI 1976/1574, and amended by SI 1982/1279, SI 1986/303 and SI 1987/386). The prescribed medical certificates are listed in Sch 4 (amended by SI 1976/1574, SI 1982/1279, SI 1985/1625, SI 1987/386 and SI 1988/1454).
17 See ibid, Sch 1, Pt I, para 16A (added by SI 1985/296). For a list of drugs etc not to be supplied by general medical practitioners, see Sch 2A (added by SI 1985/296 and amended by SI 1985/534, SI 1985/804, SI 1985/1713, SI 1986/303, SI 1986/925, SI 1986/1507, SI 1986/2130, SI 1987/1382, SI 1988/1073, SI 1988/2259, SI 1989/1883 and SI 1990/883). For a list of drugs to be supplied by general medical practitioners only in certain circumstances, see Sch 2B (added by SI 1985/296, substituted by SI 1985/1713 and amended by SI 1987/1382).
18 Ibid, Sch 1, Pt I, para 15 (amended by SI 1985/1296). The drug tariff is a statement prepared by the Secretary of State after consulting an organisation representing chemists, and includes inter alia the prices on the basis of which the payment for drugs commonly prescribed, and for appliances, is calculated, the standards of quality for drugs, and the list of approved drugs and appliances: see reg 32 (amended by SI 1987/385 and SI 1989/1883).
19 Ie under ibid, reg 30 (amended by SI 1985/296), which relates to the supply by doctors of drugs and appliances where the health board is satisfied that a person cannot conveniently obtain them from a chemist.
20 Ibid, Sch 1, Pt I, para 15(2) (substituted by SI 1985/296 and amended by SI 1985/804).
21 Ibid, Sch 1, Pt I, para 15(4).
22 Ibid, Sch 1, Pt I, para 17.

1447. Doctor's absences, deputies, assistants and partners. A doctor is responsible for ensuring the provision of services[1] to each of his patients throughout each day during which his name is included in the medical list[2]. Any doctor who was relieved by the health board of this responsibility in the past will continue to enjoy this relief for so long as his name is included in the medical list[3].

A doctor is required to give treatment personally, unless reasonable steps are taken to ensure continuity of treatment by a partner or assistant; by a deputy; or by a member of the doctor's staff who is competent to carry out the treatment which it is reasonable in the circumstances to delegate[4]. A doctor is to make all necessary arrangements for the treatment of his patients[5]. He must inform the health board of any standing deputising arrangements, and, when he proposes to be absent from the practice for more than two weeks, of the arrangements he has made for the provision of general medical services to his patients during his absence[6].

A doctor must notify the health board as soon as possible of the name of any assistant he employs and of the termination of such employment[7]. A doctor is not, without the consent of the board, to employ any one or more assistants for a total period of more than three months in any period of twelve months, and such consent is subject to periodic review and may be withdrawn; although any refusal or withdrawal of consent may be appealed to the Scottish Medical Practices Committee[8]. A doctor acting as deputy may treat patients at places and at times other than those arranged by the doctor for whom he is acting, due regard being had to the convenience of patients[9]. When signing a certificate, prescription or other document, a deputy or assistant (other than a partner or assistant on the medical list) must add the name of the doctor for whom he is acting[10].

A doctor on the medical list, when acting as deputy to another doctor on that list, is responsible for his own acts and omissions in relation to the obligations under the terms of service of the doctor for whom he is acting, and those of any person employed by him or acting on his behalf[11]. A doctor is responsible for all acts or omissions of any doctor acting as his deputy, whether or not he is a partner or assistant, or of any deputising service, while acting on his behalf[12]. Without the consent of the Secretary of State, a doctor must not employ as a deputy or assistant any doctor who is disqualified for inclusion in the medical list following a direction of the Tribunal[13].

1 Ie the services referred to in the National Health Service (General Medical and Pharmaceutical Services) (Scotland) Regulations 1974, SI 1974/506, Sch 1, Pt I, para 9: see para 1446 above.
2 Ibid, reg 3, Sch 1, Pt I, para 11(1) (substituted by SI 1989/1990).
3 Ibid, Sch 1, Pt I, para 11(2) (as so substituted).
4 Ibid, Sch 1, Pt I, para 12(1) (amended by SI 1985/1625 and SI 1989/1990). 'Partner' includes any partner otherwise deemed to be an assistant, and 'assistant' does not include such a person: Sch 1, Pt I, para 12(8). 'Assistant' means a doctor (including a trainee general practitioner) acting as assistant to a doctor on the medical list, and 'trainee general practitioner' means a doctor who is being trained in general practice under an arrangement approved by the Secretary of State: reg 2(1).
5 Ibid, Sch 1, Pt I, para 12(3) (substituted by SI 1986/1625).
6 Ibid, Sch 1, Pt I, para 12(3) (as so substituted). If he is absent for more than three months, he must before the expiry of the three-month period obtain the board's consent to the continuance of the arrangements: Sch 1, Pt I, para 12(3) (as so substituted). Before entering into regular or standing deputising arrangements, a doctor must obtain the consent of the health board, which may be given subject to conditions, and in respect of which appeal lies to the Secretary of State: Sch 1, Pt I, para 12A (added by SI 1978/1762).
7 Ibid, Sch 1, Pt I, para 12(4)(b).
8 Ibid, Sch 1, Pt I, para 12(4)(a).
9 Ibid, Sch 1, Pt I, para 12(6).
10 Ibid, Sch 1, Pt I, para 12(7).
11 Ibid, Sch 1, Pt I, para 12(2A) (added by SI 1982/1279).
12 Ibid, Sch 1, Pt I, para 12(2) (substituted by SI 1982/1279).
13 Ibid, Sch 1, Pt I, para 12(5). As to such disqualification, see the National Health Service (Scotland) Act 1978 (c 29), s 43, and para 1521 below.

1448. Practice area. A doctor may at any time with the consent of the health board or, on appeal, the Secretary of State alter the extent of his practice area[1]. However, a doctor may not, contrary to any condition imposed by the Scottish Medical Practices Committee or, on appeal, the Secretary of State[2], extend his practice area or open practice premises in any area where at the time of the application that committee is of opinion that the number of doctors undertaking to provide general medical services is already adequate[3].

1 National Health Service (General Medical and Pharmaceutical Services) (Scotland) Regulations 1974, SI 1974/506, reg 3, Sch 1, Pt I, para 14(1).
2 Ie under the National Health Service (Scotland) Act 1978 (c 29), s 23(4), or s 23(5).
3 National Health Service (General Medical and Pharmaceutical Services) (Scotland) Regulations 1974, Sch 1, Pt I, para 14(2).

1449. Doctor's continued absence or disability. Where a health board, after consultation with the area medical committee, is satisfied that, owing to the continued absence or bodily or mental disability of a doctor, his obligations under the terms of service are not being adequately carried out, it may, with the consent of the Secretary of State, give notice to the persons on his list that the doctor is for the time being in its opinion not in a position to carry out his obligations; or may, after consultation with the area medical committee, make such arrangements as the Secretary of State may approve, including the appointment of a deputy for and on behalf of the doctor, and may deduct the cost of the arrangements in part or whole from the remuneration of the doctor[1]. If a deputy is appointed for a doctor who is performing relevant service in an emergency, the board must deduct the cost of the arrangements from the practitioner's remuneration[2].

1 National Health Service (General Medical and Pharmaceutical Services) (Scotland) Regulations 1974, SI 1974/506, reg 3, Sch 1, Pt I, para 22.
2 Ibid, Sch 1, Pt I, para 22 proviso. For the meaning of 'relevant service', see para 1440, note 6, above.

1450. Acceptance of fees. A doctor is inhibited from demanding or accepting any fee, remuneration or charge other than payments due to him under regulations[1] (detailed in the following paragraph) in respect of any treatment rendered or any drug or appliance supplied, whether under the terms of service or not, to a patient of his or of his partner or assistant, except:
  (1) when a patient fails to produce his medical card;
  (2) from any statutory body for services rendered for the purpose of that body's statutory functions;
  (3) from any school, employer or body for the medical examination of persons for whose welfare that school, employer or body is responsible, such examination being either a routine medical examination or for the purpose of advising the school, employer or body of any administrative action it might take;
  (4) subject to certain conditions, for treatment, not included within the range of services required to be given under the terms of service[2], given to private patients[3] or in a registered nursing home which is not providing services under the National Health Service (Scotland) Acts;
  (5) for emergency treatment of anyone injured in connection with a road accident[4];
  (6) from a dental practitioner in respect of the provision at his request of an anaesthetic for a person for whom the dental practitioner is providing general dental services;
  (7) from a partner or assistant in respect of the provision of an anaesthetic to a patient of the partner or assistant;
  (8) for attending and examining (but not otherwise treating) a patient at his request at a police station;
  (9) for certain treatments consisting of an immunisation in connection with travel abroad;
  (10) for circumcising a patient for whom such an operation is requested on religious grounds and is not needed on any medical ground;
  (11) for providing a prescription for medicine for a patient who intends to take it abroad in case the medicine is required for an ailment that might occur there; and
  (12) for a medical examination to enable a decision to be made whether or not it is inadvisable on medical grounds for a person to wear a seat belt[5].

1 Ie the National Health Service (General Medical and Pharmaceutical Services) (Scotland) Regulations 1974, SI 1974/506 (see para 1451 below), and the National Health Service (Charges for Drugs and Appliances) (Scotland) Regulations 1989, SI 1989/326.
2 See the National Health Service (General Medical and Pharmaceutical Services) (Scotland) Regulations 1974, Sch 1, Pt I, para 9, and para 1446 above.
3 As to private patients, see para 1496 below.

4 See the Road Traffic Act 1988 (c 52), s 158.
5 National Health Service (General Medical and Pharmaceutical Services) (Scotland) Regulations 1974, reg 3, Sch 1, Pt I, para 20(1)(a)–(g), (i)–(m) (amended by SI 1975/696, SI 1981/56 and SI 1982/1279).

1451. Payments to doctors. For each financial year ending on 31 March a health board must make payments to doctors with whom arrangements exist for the provision of general medical services in its area, in accordance with such rates and subject to such conditions as the Secretary of State, in a statement, may determine, after consultation with such organisations as he may recognise as representing doctors with whom such arrangements exist[1]. The statement must make provision for:

(1) basic and supplementary practice allowance, and additional allowances for designated areas, seniority, and employment of assistants;
(2) standard capitation fees, capitation fees for elderly patients, and fees for night visits;
(3) fees for items of service, for temporary residents and for workmen residing in certain camps;
(4) fees and allowances for the supply of drugs and appliances and for rural practice, fees for contraceptive services and fees for maternity medical services;
(5) allowances for training doctors and for initial practice or inducement to practice;
(6) allowances for practice expenses and for improvement of premises;
(7) payments in relation to the making of arrangements for, and payments for, the temporary provision of general medical services;
(8) capitation fees in respect of patients who participate in a consultation as newly-registered patients;
(9) capitation fees in respect of patients to whom child health surveillance services are provided;
(10) capitation fees in respect of patients who are resident in deprived areas;
(11) a fee for each minor surgery session undertaken;
(12) fees in respect of the provision of health promotion clinics approved by the health board;
(13) target payments in respect of immunisation provided;
(14) target payments in respect of cervical cytology;
(15) allowances for the employment of locums by doctors during confinement, sickness or study leave;
(16) allowances for undergoing approved postgraduate education;
(17) allowances for the employment of doctors by isolated single-handed doctors;
(18) allowances in respect of providing placements in practices for undergraduate medical students; and
(19) transitional payments in consequence of changes to the terms of service[2].

The statement may be amended from time to time by the Secretary of State after consultation with such organisations[3]. Where a doctor is on the medical list of more than one health board, any payment due to the doctor may, where the statement so provides, be made by one board on behalf of all boards concerned[4].

1 National Health Service (General Medical and Pharmaceutical Services) (Scotland) Regulations 1974, SI 1974/506, reg 31(1) (amended by SI 1985/1625).
2 Ibid, reg 31(1)(a)–(s) (amended by SI 1975/696, SI 1982/1279, SI 1985/1625 and SI 1989/1990).
3 Ibid, reg 31(1).
4 Ibid, reg 31(2).

4. GENERAL DENTAL SERVICES

1452. Arrangements for general dental services. It is the duty of every health board to make as respects its area arrangements with dental practitioners under which any person for whom a dental practitioner undertakes in accordance with the arrangements to provide dental treatment and appliances is to receive such treatment and appliances[1]. The services thus provided are called 'general dental services'[1]. These arrangements are to be made in accordance with regulations[2]. The principal regulations relating to the provision of general dental services are the National Health Service (General Dental Services) (Scotland) Regulations 1974[3].

1 National Health Service (Scotland) Act 1978 (c 29), s 25(1).
2 Ibid, s 25(2) (amended by the European Communities (Medical, Dental and Nursing Professions) (Linguistic Knowledge) Order 1981, SI 1981/432, and by the Health and Medicines Act 1988 (c 49), s 25(1), Sch 2, para 1).
3 National Health Service (General Dental Services) (Scotland) Regulations 1974, SI 1974/505 (amended by SI 1974/2048, SI 1979/705, SI 1980/1220, SI 1981/900, SI 1984/1491, SI 1985/1552, SI 1986/1571, SI 1987/1634 and SI 1989/602).

1453. Terms of service for dentists. The arrangements made with dentists for the provision of general dental services must incorporate the terms of service scheduled to the National Health Service (General Dental Services) (Scotland) Regulations 1974[1]. Different terms apply to dentists undertaking to provide general dental services otherwise than as salaried dentists[2], to dentists undertaking to provide those services as salaried dentists[3], and to dentists undertaking to provide those services under capitation agreements[4].

1 National Health Service (General Dental Services) (Scotland) Regulations 1974, SI 1974/505, reg 3, Sch 1 (as amended). See paras 1456 ff below.
2 Ibid, reg 3(1)(a)(i) (substituted by SI 1984/1491), applying Sch 1, Pt I (paras 1–16) and Pt II (paras 17–23).
3 Ibid, reg 3(1)(b) (amended by SI 1981/900), applying Sch 1, Pt I (paras 1–16) and Pt III (paras 24–30).
4 Ibid, reg 3(1)(a)(ii) (substituted by SI 1984/1491), applying Sch 1, Pt IV (paras 31–37) (added by SI 1984/1491).

1454. The dental list. A health board must prepare a list called the 'dental list' which is to contain the names of the dentists who have undertaken to provide general dental services in its area and who are not disentitled on grounds of want of knowledge of English[1]; the address of any surgery or health centre at which a dentist undertakes to provide these services; particulars of the days and hours at which he is or will be usually in attendance; and where two or more dentists practise in partnership, the names of the partners[2]. If the health board thinks fit, the list may be so arranged as to show the part of the area in which each dentist will provide treatment[3].

The health board must send a copy of the list to the Secretary of State, the Scottish Dental Practice Board and the area dental committee, and, within fourteen days of any alterations which may from time to time be made, must inform each of them accordingly[4]. A copy of the dental list must be available for inspection at the offices of the health board and is to be kept revised and up to date[5].

A dentist who wishes to be included in the dental list must apply to the health board in the appropriate prescribed form or in a form to the like effect[6]. A dentist in the list must notify the health board within fourteen days of any change or addition affecting the entries in relation to him[7].

A dentist is entitled at any time to give notice in writing to the health board that he wishes to withdraw his name from the dental list, and except where representations have been made to the Tribunal his name must be removed from it at the expiration of three months from the date of that notice or of such shorter period as the health board may agree[8]. A health board must remove a dentist's name from the dental list where it has determined that the dentist in question has died or has ceased to be a registered dental practitioner[9], or has not for the preceding six months while his name has been in the list provided general dental services[10]. Before making any such determination that a dentist has not provided such services the health board must give him twenty-eight days' notice of its intention; afford him an opportunity of making representations in writing, or, if he so desires, orally to a committee appointed for the purpose; and, except where he is a salaried dentist, consult the area dental committee[11]. No such determination is to be made, where a dentist is called into service in the armed forces of the Crown or equivalent service in an emergency, until six months after the completion of that service[12]. Nothing in the foregoing prejudices the right of a dentist to have his name included again in the dental list[13].

1 Ie not disentitled under the National Health Service (Scotland) Act 1978 (c 29), s 25(2A) (added by the European Communities (Medical, Dental and Nursing Professions) (Linguistic Knowledge) Order 1981, SI 1981/432).
2 National Health Service (General Dental Services) (Scotland) Regulations 1974, SI 1974/505, reg 4(1)(a)–(d) (amended by SI 1981/432).
3 Ibid, reg 4(1).
4 Ibid, reg 4(4)(a). If so requested, the health board must also send a copy of the list, with periodic updates, to the area medical and pharmaceutical committees, the Common Services Agency and local chemists: reg 4(4)(b).
5 Ibid, reg 30.
6 Ibid, reg 4(2). For the form, see Determination V of the Statement of Dental Remuneration, as to which see para 1462 below.
7 Ibid, reg 4(3).
8 Ibid, reg 7. As to representations to the Tribunal, see para 1521 below.
9 Ibid, reg 6(1).
10 Ibid, reg 6(2).
11 Ibid, reg 6(3).
12 Ibid, reg 6(5).
13 Ibid, reg 6(4).

1455. Obtaining general dental services. A person requiring general dental services may apply to any dentist whose name appears on any dental list[1]. The application is to be made on behalf of any person under the age of sixteen by the mother or, in her absence, the father, or, in the absence of both parents, the guardian or other person who has the care of the child; on behalf of any other person who is incapable of making such an application by a relative or any person who has the care of that person; and on behalf of any person under the age of eighteen in the care of a local authority by a person duly authorised by that authority[2]. However, the application may not be made by the dentist to whom the application is made[3]. It is a condition of obtaining general dental services that a person must, if required by the Scottish Dental Practice Board or a health board, submit himself for examination by a dental officer employed by the Secretary of State[4].

1 National Health Service (General Dental Services) (Scotland) Regulations 1974, SI 1974/505, reg 19.
2 Ibid, reg 20(a)–(c).
3 Ibid, reg 20 proviso.
4 Ibid, reg 21.

1456. Dentist's services to patients. The detailed rights and obligations referred to in this paragraph apply to all dentists who have undertaken to provide general dental services, whether or not they are salaried dentists, but only some of the provisions apply to dentists providing general dental services under capitation arrangements[1].

In providing general dental services a dentist must employ a proper degree of skill and attention[2]. Except where the special form is used[3], or where treatment is by agreement restricted to 'limited treatment' or 'preventive treatment', he must provide the treatment necessary to secure dental fitness which the patient is willing to undergo and satisfactorily complete that treatment[4]. Where the treatment provided is preventive treatment, the dentist must provide and complete satisfactorily that treatment to the extent that the patient is willing to undergo it[5]. Subject to certain exceptions he must give all the treatment personally[6]. He must comply with any requirements as to the materials to be used and any restrictions on the purpose for which they may be used as set out in Determination III of the Statement of Dental Remuneration[7].

The 'limited treatment' referred to above is certain emergency treatment, certain repairs to dentures, the arrest of abnormal haemorrhage and domiciliary visits connected with the arrest of abnormal haemorrhage or certain emergency treatment[8]; and 'preventive treatment' is the application of topical fluoride preparations to persons under the age of sixteen where necessary to maintain dental health[9].

Provision of the services of a doctor or another dentist in respect of the administration of a general anaesthetic is the responsibility of the dentist who provides the treatment[10]. A dentist must visit and treat a patient whose condition requires a visit at any place where the patient may be which is not more than 5 miles from the surgery or such other limit as the health board and the dentist may agree[11]. If the condition of a patient is such as to require treatment which the dentist is unable to carry out, but the treatment is available from another dentist under general dental services or otherwise under the national health service, the dentist must inform the patient of this and, if the patient so wishes, is to take all necessary steps to enable the patient to receive the treatment[12].

A dentist may supply to any patient such listed drugs as are required for immediate administration or application or for use before a supply can be obtained on prescription[13]. He may personally administer to a patient any drug required for his treatment[14], and may issue a prescription ordering listed drugs requisite for the patient's treatment[15].

A dentist may arrange for treatment to be given by a dental auxiliary, and must ensure that such treatment is properly completed[16]. In any event, a dentist is required to complete treatment with reasonable expedition and (excepting orthodontic treatment) generally within six months from the date on which he accepted the patient for treatment or from the date on which any necessary prior approval is received by him[17]. If owing to any cause beyond the dentist's control or because a patient has been referred for treatment by another dentist[18], the dentist is unable to complete any treatment which has been commenced, he must forthwith notify the health board in writing of the treatment completed and of the reasons for not completing the remainder[19].

1 See para 1453 above. As to the application of these provisions to dentists providing general dental services under capitation arrangements, see para 1461 below.
2 National Health Service (General Dental Services) (Scotland) Regulations 1974, SI 1974/505, Sch 1, para 2(1)(a).
3 'Special form' means the special estimate form set out in Determination V of the Statement of Dental Remuneration or a form to the like effect: reg 2(1).

4 Ibid, Sch 1, para 2(1)(b) (amended by SI 1974/2048 and SI 1986/1571).
5 Ibid, Sch 1, para 2(1)(bb) (added by SI 1986/1571).
6 Ibid, Sch 1, para 2(1)(c), which is expressed to be subject to Sch 1, paras 3, 5, 14, 22.
7 Ibid, Sch 1, para 2(1)(d): see para 1462 below.
8 Ibid, Sch 1, para 2(2)(a)–(d).
9 Ibid, reg 2(1) (amended by SI 1986/1571), and Sch 1, para 9A (added by SI 1986/1571).
10 Ibid, Sch 1, para 3 (substituted by SI 1984/1491).
11 Ibid, Sch 1, para 4 (amended by SI 1974/2048).
12 Ibid, Sch 1, para 5.
13 Ibid, Sch 1, para 11(1).
14 Ibid, Sch 1, para 11(2).
15 Ibid, Sch 1, para 12. The prescription must be signed in ink: Sch 1, paras 12, 13.
16 Ibid, Sch 1, para 14. As to dental auxiliaries (formerly known as 'ancillary dental workers'), see MEDICAL AND ALLIED PROFESSIONS, vol 14, paras 1143–1146.
17 Ibid, Sch 1, para 8(4). Thus the period is twelve months for extractions and consequent provision of dentures: Sch 1, para 8(4) proviso.
18 Ie under ibid, Sch 1, para 5.
19 Ibid, Sch 1, para 10(1).

1457. Dentist's premises and records. A dentist is required to provide proper and sufficient surgery and waiting room accommodation for his patients; suitable equipment in the surgery; and suitable instruments in the treatment of his patients[1]. The records to be kept by the dentist[2] are his property, and he must retain records of treatment which required the prior approval of the Scottish Dental Practice Board for a period of four years, and records of other treatment for two years, both periods being after the end of the financial year ending 31 March in which payment was made in respect of the treatment; and must send the record or a certified copy within fourteen days of a requirement to do so to the board, a health board or a dental officer appointed by the Secretary of State[3].

1 National Health Service (General Dental Services) (Scotland) Regulations 1974, SI 1974/505, Sch 1, para 17(1), (2). On reasonable notice he must admit a dental officer appointed by the Secretary of State to inspect his surgery and waiting room: Sch 1, para 17(3).
2 As to these records, see ibid, Sch 1, para 6.
3 Ibid, Sch 1, para 18.

1458. Dentist's absences, deputies, assistants and partners. Where a dentist is prevented from providing treatment by reason of temporary absence from his practice through illness or other reasonable cause, treatment may be given by a deputy[1]. Where two or more dentists practise in partnership or as principal and assistant[2], treatment may at any time be given by a partner or assistant of the dentist if reasonable steps are taken to ensure continuity of treatment[3]; however, a dentist may not employ more than two assistants at any one time without the consent of the appropriate health board, or on appeal the Secretary of State, and before giving any consent the health board must consult the area dental committee[4]. A dentist must not employ as an assistant any dentist who is included in the dental list of a health board as a dentist undertaking to provide general dental services at a surgery or suite of surgeries at which the first dentist undertakes to provide general dental services[5]; or, without the consent of the Secretary of State, employ as a deputy or assistant any dentist who is disqualified by the Tribunal for inclusion in the dental list of a health board[6]. Where a dentist knowingly employs an assistant who is subject to a requirement to submit estimates to the Scottish Dental Practice Board for prior approval, he must not allow that assistant to carry out such treatment unless the prior approval has been obtained[7]. A dentist who is included in the dental list, when acting as deputy to another dentist, is responsible for his own acts and omissions in relation to the terms of service of the dentist for whom he acts[8]. A deputy or assistant who signs a dental estimate form on behalf of the dentist for whom he acts must sign his own name, and except where he is a partner whose name is included in the dental list must also insert the name of the dentist for whom he acts[9]. A deputy or assistant is required to sign his own name on a prescription for listed drugs, but must insert on the prescription the name of the dentist for whom he is acting[10]. A dentist must notify a health board of the employment of an assistant or the cessation of such employment within seven days of the first day of employment or of the cessation[11]; and of his intention to absent himself from the practice for more than twenty-one consecutive days and of any deputy or assistant responsible for providing general dental services during his absence[12]. Where the dentist intends to be absent from the practice for more than two months the notification must be in writing, and the dentist must not employ an assistant for more than two months of such absence without the consent of the health board[13].

 1 National Health Service (General Dental Services) (Scotland) Regulations 1974, SI 1974/505, Sch 1, para 22(1). 'Deputy' means a dentist (other than a partner) acting on behalf of another dentist, otherwise than in the capacity of an assistant, for the purpose of providing general dental services: reg 2(1).
 2 'Assistant' means any dentist employed either whole-time or part-time under a contract of service by another dentist for the purpose of providing general dental services on behalf of that dentist: ibid, reg 2(1).
 3 Ibid, Sch 1, para 22(2).
 4 Ibid, Sch 1, para 22(3). Consent must be reviewed at least annually: Sch 1, para 21(3) proviso.
 5 Ibid, Sch 1, para 22(7).
 6 Ibid, Sch 1, para 22(9). As to such disqualification, see para 1521 below.
 7 Ibid, Sch 1, para 22(8).
 8 Ibid, Sch 1, para 22(10).
 9 Ibid, Sch 1, para 20.
 10 Ibid, Sch 1, para 21.
 11 Ibid, Sch 1, para 22(4).
 12 Ibid, Sch 1, para 22(5).
 13 Ibid, Sch 1, para 22(6).

1459. Fees and remuneration. A dentist is paid prescribed fees or other remuneration by a health board in respect of any treatment which he has provided under general dental services[1]. Except as otherwise provided, a dentist must not demand or accept payment of any fee or remuneration in respect of any treatment which he is required to give or has provided under the general dental services; which has not been provided or for which a claim has already been submitted to the Scottish Dental Practice Board; for which payment is excluded by the provisions of the scale of fees precluding payment for services provided within a specified period of time, or for services provided without approval of the board; or which has been provided otherwise than in accordance with the prescribed conditions with respect to materials[2]. Any fee which would otherwise have been payable is to be reduced by the amount of the appropriate charge approved by the Scottish Dental Practice Board on submission of a dental estimate form, being a charge which the dentist is entitled to make and recover from or on behalf of the patient under the appropriate statutory provisions[3]; or as determined by the board as recoverable from the patient when the treatment involved is of a more expensive type than that which is clinically necessary for dental fitness[4]; or as determined by the health board for the replacement of a dental appliance necessitated by an act or omission on the part of the patient[5].

 1 National Health Service (General Dental Services) (Scotland) Regulations 1974, SI 1974/505, Sch 1, para 19(1).

2 Ibid, Sch 1, para 19(2)(a)–(d). As to the scale of fees, see para 1462 below. The prescribed conditions as to materials are set out in Determination III of the Statement of Dental Remuneration (see para 1462 below). These provisions do not apply to a claim made by a dentist in respect of loss of remunerative time resulting from a patient's failure to keep an appointment: Sch 1, para 19(2) proviso.

3 Ibid, reg 22(2), (5) (amended by SI 1979/705). The statutory provisions referred to are the National Health Service (Scotland) Act 1978 (c 29), ss 70, 71, 71A (amended by the Health and Medicines Act 1988 (c 49), ss 11(4)–(6), 25(1), (2), Sch 2, para 12, Sch 3).

4 See the National Health Service (General Dental Services) (Scotland) Regulations 1974, reg 23 (amended by SI 1980/1220).

5 See ibid, reg 24.

1460. Salaried dentists. A salaried dentist[1] must attend at such premises on such days and at such hours as may be agreed between him and the health board[2]. Without the board's permission he is not entitled to provide at such premises any treatment which is not part of general dental services[3]. The services of a salaried dentist may be terminated by either a health board or the salaried dentist giving to the other party three months' notice in writing, except that if a salaried dentist fails to comply with any of the terms of service a health board may terminate on one month's notice in writing[4]. A salaried dentist is to account for and pay over to the health board any charges he is required to make and recover from or on behalf of a patient[5]. The records which he must keep[6] are the property of the health board[7].

1 'Salaried dentist' means a dentist employed by a health board to provide general dental services at a health centre, or to provide such services consisting of emergency treatment at a hospital or other health board premises at weekends or on bank, public or local holidays, and who is remunerated in accordance with Determination VI of the Statement of Dental Remuneration (as to which see para 1462 below): National Health Service (General Dental Services) (Scotland) Regulations 1974, SI 1974/505, reg 2(1) (amended by SI 1981/900), by reference to reg 29A (added by SI 1981/900). For other terms of service applying to salaried dentists, see Sch 1, paras 3–16, and para 1458 above.

2 Ibid, Sch 1, para 24(1) (substituted by SI 1981/900).

3 Ibid, Sch 1, para 24(2) (as so substituted).

4 Ibid, Sch 1, para 30.

5 Ibid, Sch 1, para 28.

6 Ie under ibid, reg 6.

7 Ibid, Sch 1, para 26.

1461. Dentists under capitation arrangements. In providing general dental services under capitation arrangements[1] to a patient, a dentist[2] must (1) employ a proper degree of skill and attention; (2) provide the care and treatment necessary to secure dental health which the patient is willing to undergo; (3) regularly provide the care and treatment necessary to maintain dental health which the patient is willing to undergo; (4) when the dentist provides treatment for which fees (other than capitation fees) or other remuneration is payable and which the patient is willing to undergo, satisfactorily complete the treatment; (5) save as otherwise provided[3] give all care and treatment personally; and (6) comply with any prescribed requirements[4] as to materials to be used and any restrictions on their use[5].

The dentist must retain all films taken or obtained by him as part of care and treatment, and all records of a patient's dental needs and treatment for twelve months from the end of the last month in respect of which a capitation fee is payable, and during that twelve-month period must on request submit the films and records to the Scottish Dental Practice Board or to a dental officer appointed by the Secretary of State[6].

In accepting a person for care and treatment under capitation arrangements and upon providing such care and treatment the dentist must at the appropriate times complete or secure the completion of the relevant parts, as appropriate, of the acceptance form, the initial or other capitation fee claim form, the dental estimate form and the certificate of dental fitness[7] and duly submit them to the board[8]. Provision is made for withdrawal from the capitation arrangements[9].

1 'Capitation arrangements' means arrangements whereby a dentist is remunerated in accordance with Section X of Determination I of the Statement of Dental Remuneration (as to which see para 1462 below): National Health Service (General Dental Services) (Scotland) Regulations 1974, SI 1974/505, reg 2(1) (amended by SI 1984/1491).
2 Dentists providing general dental services under capitation arrangements are also subject to the terms of service set out in ibid, Sch 1, paras 1, 4, 13, 15, 16, 20, 21 and 23; and also (with the substitution of 'care and treatment' for 'treatment') those set out in Sch 1, paras 3, 5, 6(1), 8(5), (6), 11, 12, 14, 17, 19 and 22; and also, in relation to the provision of treatment for which a fee (other than a capitation fee) is payable, those set out in Sch 1, paras 8(1), (2), (3)(a), (b), (4) and 10: Sch 1, para 32(1)–(3) (added by SI 1984/1491).
3 Ie in ibid, Sch 1, paras 3, 5, 14 and 22.
4 See Determination III of the Statement of Dental Remuneration.
5 National Health Service (General Dental Services) (Scotland) Regulations 1974, Sch 1, para 31(a)–(f) (added by SI 1984/1491).
6 Ibid, Sch 1, para 33 (as so added).
7 Ibid, Sch 1, para 34(1) (as so added).
8 Ibid, Sch 1, para 34(3) (as so added).
9 Ibid, Sch 1, para 35 (as so added).

1462. Statement of Dental Remuneration. The Secretary of State, after consultation with such organisations as he recognises as representing dentists, must make, and from time to time amend, and publish a Statement of Dental Remuneration making provision in 'determinations' as follows:

Determination I: A scale of fees which prescribes the fees to be paid for the provision of items of dental treatment and for the provision of other services, as therein specified, in order to undertake dental treatment;

Determination II: Those items of treatment specified in Determination I which may not be provided without the prior approval of the Scottish Dental Practice Board;

Determination III: Conditions with respect to materials, specifying standards, restrictions and conditions for their use;

Determination IV: Seniority payments;

Determination V: Forms for use in the provision of general dental services; and

Determination VI: Rates and conditions of payment of remuneration for salaried dentists[1].

1 National Health Service (General Dental Services) (Scotland) Regulations 1974, SI 1974/505, reg 26(1), (2) (amended by SI 1980/1220 and SI 1981/900).

5. GENERAL OPHTHALMIC SERVICES

1463. Arrangements for general ophthalmic services. It is the duty of every health board to make as respects its area arrangements with medical practitioners having the prescribed qualifications, and with ophthalmic opticians, for securing the testing by such practitioners and opticians of the sight (1) of a child[1]; (2) of a person whose resources fall to be treated under regulations as being less than or equal to his requirements[2]; and (3) of a person of such other description as may be prescribed[3]. Services which a contractor[4] must provide under his terms of service[5] are known as 'general ophthalmic services'[6].

The arrangements referred to are to be made in accordance with regulations[7]. The principal regulations relating to the provision of general ophthalmic services are the National Health Service (General Ophthalmic Services) Regulations 1986[8].

1 'Child' means a person under sixteen or a person under nineteen who is receiving qualifying full-time education: National Health Service (Scotland) Act 1978 (c 29), s 26(1A) (added by the Health and Medicines Act 1988 (c 49), s 13(4)).

2 For such persons, see the National Health Service (General Ophthalmic Services) (Scotland) Regulations 1986, SI 1986/965, reg 14(2) (substituted by SI 1989/387).

3 National Health Service (Scotland) Act 1978, s 26(1) (amended by the Health and Social Security Act 1984 (c 48), s 1(7), Sch 1, Pt II, para 1, and the Health and Medicines Act 1988, s 13(4)). Other prescribed persons are (1) a person who requires to wear a complex appliance (ie an optical appliance at least one lens of which has a power in any meridian of plus or minus 10 or more dioptres or is a lenticular lens); (2) a person who because of blindness cannot perform work for which eyesight is essential and is registered accordingly; (3) a person suffering from diabetes or glaucoma; (4) a person aged 40 or over who is the parent, sibling or child of a person suffering from glaucoma: National Health Service (General Ophthalmic Services) (Scotland) Regulations 1986, reg 14(1) (substituted by SI 1989/387).

4 'Contractor' means a person who has undertaken to provide general ophthalmic services and whose name is included in the ophthalmic list: ibid, reg 2(1).

5 Ie under ibid, Sch 1, para 10 (substituted by SI 1989/387): see para 1467 below.

6 Ibid, reg 2(1) (amended by SI 1989/387).

7 National Health Service (Scotland) Act 1978, s 26(2) (amended by the Health and Social Security Act 1984, ss 1(5), (7), 24, Sch 1, Pt II, paras 2–4, Sch 8, Pt I.

8 National Health Service (General Ophthalmic Services) (Scotland) Regulations 1986, SI 1986/965 (amended by SI 1988/543, SI 1989/387 and SI 1989/1177).

1464. Qualifications of ophthalmic medical practitioners. The prescribed qualifications, referred to in the preceding paragraph, for a medical practitioner who wishes to establish his status as an ophthalmic medical practitioner, are to have had, at the date of consideration by the Ophthalmic Qualifications Committee, recent experience and either:

(1) (a) to have held an appointment in the health service with the status of consultant ophthalmologist, or an appointment for a period of not less than two years of equivalent status as ophthalmic surgeon or assistant ophthalmic surgeon on the staff of an approved ophthalmic hospital, and (b) to have had adequate experience; or

(2) (a) to have held an ophthalmic appointment or appointment in an approved ophthalmic hospital for a period totalling not less then two years, including tenure for a period of not less than six months of a residential appointment or an appointment with duties comparable with those of a residential appointment (such tenure being unnecessary for a doctor registered for at least seven years and having appropriate experience); and (b) to have obtained the Diploma in Ophthalmology awarded conjointly by the Royal College of Physicians of London and the Royal College of Surgeons of England, or any approved higher degree or qualification; and (c) to have had adequate experience; or

(3) to have had before 1 November 1951 adequate experience and either (a) obtained a diploma or certificate in respect of an approved academic or postgraduate course in ophthalmology; or (b) held for a period of not less than two years an appointment as an ophthalmic surgeon or assistant ophthalmic surgeon on the staff of an approved ophthalmic hospital; or (c) held for a period of not less than two years an approved appointment affording special opportunities for acquiring the necessary skill and experience of the kind required for the provision of general ophthalmic services[1].

A doctor with the prescribed qualification must apply to the Ophthalmic Qualifications Committee for approval of his qualifications and experience[2]. The committee must consider his application and within one month inform the applicant of its decision[3]. If the committee approves the qualifications and experience of the applicant he will be an ophthalmic medical practitioner[4].

Any person aggrieved by a decision of the committee that he is not qualified to be an ophthalmic medical practitioner may within one month from the date on which he received notice of that decision, or such longer period as the Secretary of State may at any time allow, appeal against the decision by sending to the Secretary of State a notice of appeal stating the facts and contentions on which he relies[5]. The appeal will be determined by an appeal committee of five persons appointed by the Secretary of State, of whom at least three are to be appointed after consultation with such bodies or organisations representing doctors as appear to him to be concerned[6].

1 National Health Service (General Ophthalmic Services) (Scotland) Regulations 1986, SI 1986/965, reg 3(1)(a)–(c).
2 Ibid, reg 4(1).
3 Ibid, reg 4(2).
4 Ibid, reg 4(3).
5 Ibid, reg 5(1).
6 Ibid, reg 5(2). For the procedure on the appeal, see reg 5(3)–(9).

1465. The ophthalmic list. Each health board must keep a list, called 'the ophthalmic list', of persons who have undertaken to provide general ophthalmic services[1]. The list is divided into two parts, the first relating to ophthalmic medical practitioners and the other to opticians[2]. Each part contains (1) the names of persons entitled to be included therein; (2) the addresses in the board's area where they have undertaken to provide general ophthalmic services; (3) the days and hours when those services will be provided there; and (4) the name of each ophthalmic medical practitioner or optician who is regularly employed as a deputy, director or employee in the provision of those services there[3]. The board must send a copy of the list to the Secretary of State, the area medical committee and the area optical committee, as appropriate, and within fourteen days inform them of any changes[4].

An ophthalmic medical practitioner or optician who wishes to be included in the list must send to the health board an application to that effect, indicating whether he is an ophthalmic medical practitioner, a registered ophthalmic optician or a body corporate carrying on business as ophthalmic opticians, and including an undertaking to provide general ophthalmic services and to comply with the terms of service, and the information referred to in heads (1) to (4) above which is to be contained in the list[5], and within fourteen days must notify the board of any change or addition affecting his entry[6].

A contractor may give the board written notice that he desires to withdraw from the list, and, with the board's permission, his name will then be removed at the expiration of three months or such shorter period as the board agrees[7]. Before agreeing to the withdrawal the board must be satisfied that proper arrangements have been made for the completion of any services which the contractor has undertaken to provide, and if representations have been made to the Tribunal a contractor may not withdraw, except with the consent of the Secretary of State, until the proceedings on the representations have been determined[8].

A health board must remove from the list the name of a contractor who has died or has ceased to be an ophthalmic medical practitioner or optician[9]. It must also remove a name where it determines, having given the contractor twenty-eight days' notice and an opportunity of making oral or written representations, and having consulted the area medical committee or, as the case may be, the area optical committee, that a contractor has not during the preceding six months, whilst his name was on the list, provided general ophthalmic services for persons in the board's area[10]. Nothing in these provisions prejudices a person's right to have his name included again in the list[11].

1 National Health Service (General Ophthalmic Services) (Scotland) Regulations 1986, SI 1986/965, reg 6(1) (substituted by SI 1988/543).
2 Ibid, reg 6(2) (as so substituted).
3 Ibid, reg 6(3)(a)–(d) (as so substituted). 'Deputy' means an ophthalmic medical practitioner or optician (whether or not himself a contractor as defined in para 1463, note 4, above) who provides such services on behalf of a contractor otherwise than as a director or salaried employee of that contractor: reg 2(1).
4 Ibid, reg 6(4) (as so substituted).
5 Ibid, reg 7(1) (amended by SI 1988/543).
6 Ibid, reg 7(2) (as so amended).
7 Ibid, reg 8 (as so amended).
8 Ibid, reg 8 proviso (as so amended). As to Tribunal proceedings, see para 1521 below.
9 Ibid, reg 9(1) (as so amended).
10 Ibid, reg 9(2), (3) (as so amended). Such a determination may not be made in the case of a person called into whole-time service in the armed forces or equivalent service in an emergency, until six months after the completion of the service: reg 9(5).
11 Ibid, reg 9(4).

1466. Obtaining general ophthalmic services. An eligible person[1] who wishes to have his sight tested under general ophthalmic services may apply to any contractor[2] on a form provided to contractors by the health board, on which the applicant declares that he is an eligible person[3]. Before making a sight test the contractor must satisfy himself of the person's eligibility, ensure that the person's particulars and the approximate date of his last sight test, if any, are included in a sight test form, and satisfy himself that a sight test is necessary[4]. The application must be made and signed:

(1) on behalf of any person under sixteen by either parent or, in the absence of both parents, by the guardian or other adult who has the care of the child;

(2) on behalf of any other person who is incapable of applying and signing, by an adult relative or any other adult who has the care of that person or any other adult competent to apply or sign in accordance with any rule of law; and

(3) on behalf of any person under eighteen in the care of a local authority or voluntary organisation, by a person duly authorised by that authority or organisation[5].

However, the application must not be signed by the contractor to whom the application is made[6].

General optical services no longer cover the supply of optical appliances[7], but are limited to the testing of sight.

1 As to who is eligible, see para 1463 above.
2 National Health Service (General Ophthalmic Services) (Scotland) Regulations 1986, SI 1986/965, reg 14A(1) (added by SI 1989/387). For the meaning of 'contractor', see para 1463, note 4, above.
3 Ibid, reg 14A(2) (as so added). In certain circumstances evidence of eligibility is required: see reg 14A(3), (5) (as so added). If a sight test on a non-eligible person reveals that he is in fact eligible, he counts as an eligible person: see reg 14B (as so added).
4 Ibid, reg 14A(4) (as so added).
5 Ibid, reg 15(1) (amended by SI 1989/387).
6 Ibid, reg 15(2).
7 The National Health Service (Scotland) Act 1978 (c 29), s 26(1) (as originally enacted), provided that the supply of optical appliances should rank as general ophthalmic services, but the appropriate part of that provision was repealed by the Health and Social Security Act 1984 (c 48),

ss 1(5), 24, Sch 8, Pt I, and the whole provision was substituted by the Health and Medicines Act 1988 (c 49), s 13(4). As to charges for optical appliances, the eligibility of certain persons for payment of those charges and the issue of vouchers by health boards to meet the charges, see the National Health Service (Payments for Optical Appliances) (Scotland) Regulations 1986, SI 1986/966 (amended by SI 1986/1192, SI 1988/463, SI 1988/464, SI 1988/545, SI 1988/546 and SI 1988/1425).

1467. Ophthalmic services to patients. A contractor must make all necessary arrangements for the provision of general ophthalmic services to his patients[1]. Having accepted an application for the testing of sight, a contractor must test the patient's sight to determine whether the patient needs to wear or use an optical appliance, and on so doing must fulfil the following duty[2]. He must perform specified examinations for the purpose of detecting signs of injury, disease or abnormality in the eye or elsewhere, and must then give the patient a written statement that he has carried out the examinations and that he is, or, as the case may be, is not, referring the patient to a doctor[3]. He must also give the patient either a prescription for an optical appliance or a signed statement that he does not need to wear or use an optical appliance[4]. Where the contractor is of opinion that the patient shows on examination signs of injury, disease or abnormality in the eye or elsewhere which may require medical treatment, or that the patient is not likely to attain a satisfactory standard of vision notwithstanding the application of corrective lenses, the contractor must so inform that patient's doctor[5]. Where a contractor tests the sight of a patient diagnosed as suffering from diabetes or glaucoma he must inform the patient's doctor of the results of the test[6].

A contractor must provide proper and sufficient consulting and waiting room accommodation and suitable equipment, which are subject to inspection[7]. Notices must be displayed there indicating the services available and giving certain information as to payment for services[8].

An ophthalmic medical practitioner may arrange for sight to be tested on his behalf by another ophthalmic medical practitioner, and an optician may arrange for sight to be tested on his behalf by another optician[9]. Regular arrangements for deputies must be notified to the health board[10]. A contractor is responsible for all acts and omissions of his deputy and his deputy's employee, and a deputy who is himself a contractor is jointly responsible to the same extent as the contractor for whom he is deputising[11]. An ophthalmic medical practitioner who employs a person for sight testing must employ only another ophthalmic medical practitioner; and an optician who employs a person for the testing of sight must employ only another optician or a person under his continuous personal supervision who is duly authorised to test sight[12]. A contractor who regularly employs persons must notify the health board accordingly[13]. A contractor is responsible for all acts and omissions of any employee[14].

A contractor must keep and retain for three years proper records in respect of each patient[15].

1 National Health Service (General Ophthalmic Services) (Scotland) Regulations 1986, SI 1986/965, reg 11, Sch 1, para 3. For the meaning of 'contractor', see para 1463, note 4, above.
2 Ibid, Sch 1, para 10(1) (substituted by SI 1989/1177).
3 Opticians Act 1989 (c 44), s 26(1); Sight Testing (Examination and Prescription) (No 2) Regulations 1989, SI 1989/1230, reg 3(1). This does not apply where the testing of sight is carried out by a doctor in a hospital or clinic in the course of diagnosing or treating injury or disease of the eye: reg 3(2).
4 Opticians Act 1989, s 26(2).
5 National Health Service (General Ophthalmic Services) (Scotland) Regulations 1986, Sch 1, para 10(2) (substituted by SI 1989/1177).
6 Ibid, Sch 1, para 10(3) (as so substituted).
7 Ibid, Sch 1, para 4 (amended by SI 1988/543).
8 Ibid, Sch 1, para 5 (amended by SI 1988/543 and SI 1989/387).

9 Ibid, Sch 1, para 7(1).
10 Ibid, Sch 1, para 7(2) (amended by SI 1988/543).
11 Ibid, Sch 1, para 7(3) (amended by SI 1988/543).
12 Ibid, Sch 1, para 8(1), (2). As to such authorisation, see the Opticians Act 1989, s 24(3).
13 National Health Service (General Ophthalmic Services) (Scotland) Regulations 1986, Sch 1, para 8(4) (amended by SI 1988/543).
14 Ibid, Sch 1, para 8(5) (substituted by SI 1988/543). As to the joint responsibility of an employee who is himself a contractor, see Sch 1, para 8(5A) (added by SI 1988/543).
15 Ibid, Sch 1, para 6 (amended by SI 1988/543).

1468. Payments for ophthalmic services. Any claim by a contractor for fees in respect of the provision of general ophthalmic services is made by completing a sight test form and sending it to the health board in whose area the services were provided within six months after the completion of the provision of the services[1]. After consultation with organisations representing contractors the Secretary of State must make provision in a determination (known as 'the Statement') as to the fees to be paid by a health board for the testing of sight by ophthalmic medical practitioners and opticians[2]. Each health board must make payments to contractors in accordance with the Statement[3]. A contractor may charge a patient in respect of loss of remunerative time resulting from the patient's failure to keep an appointment, or for home visits[4], but, save as otherwise provided in the appropriate regulations or the Statement, a contractor may not demand or accept from a patient any fee or other remuneration in respect of the provision of general ophthalmic services[5]. Nor may a contractor demand or accept from the health board any fee or other remuneration in respect of any item of service which he has not provided under the general ophthalmic services or for which a claim has already been submitted to the board[6].

1 National Health Service (General Ophthalmic Services) (Scotland) Regulations 1986, SI 1986/965, reg 11, Sch 1, para 9(1). For the meaning of 'contractor', see para 1463, note 4, above. As to signing the form, see Sch 1, para 9(2), (3).
2 Ibid, reg 10.
3 Ibid, reg 13 (amended by SI 1989/387).
4 Ibid, Sch 1, para 9(5).
5 Ibid, Sch 1, para 9(4).
6 Ibid, Sch 1, para 9(6).

6. PHARMACEUTICAL SERVICES

1469. Arrangements for pharmaceutical services. It is the duty of every health board to make, in accordance with regulations, as respects its area, arrangements for the supply to persons who are in that area of:

(1) proper and sufficient drugs and medicines and listed appliances which are ordered for those persons by a medical practitioner in pursuance of his functions in the health service, the health service for England and Wales, the Northern Ireland health service or the armed forces of the Crown (excluding forces of a Commonwealth country and forces raised in a colony);

(2) proper and sufficient drugs and medicines which are ordered for those persons by a dental practitioner in pursuance of the provision by that board of dental services; and

(3) listed drugs and medicines which are ordered for those persons by a dental practitioner in pursuance of the provision by him of general dental services[1].

Services so provided are referred to as 'pharmaceutical services'[2]. The principal regulations relating to the provision of these services are the National Health

Service (General Medical and Pharmaceutical Services) (Scotland) Regulations 1974[3]. Except as provided by or under regulations, no arrangements may be made by a health board with a medical or dental practitioner under which he is required or agrees to provide pharmaceutical services to any person to whom he is rendering general medical services or general dental services; and except as so provided no arrangements for the dispensing of medicines may be made with persons other than registered pharmacists or persons lawfully conducting a retail pharmacy business and who undertake that all medicines supplied by them under the arrangements will be dispensed either by or under the direct supervision of a registered pharmacist[4].

1 National Health Service (Scotland) Act 1978 (c 29), s 27(1)(a)–(c) (amended by the Health Services Act 1980 (c 53), s 20(2)). 'Listed' means included in a list approved for this purpose by the Secretary of State: National Health Service (Scotland) Act 1978, s 27(1).
2 Ibid, s 27(1).
3 The National Health Service (General Medical and Pharmaceutical Services) (Scotland) Regulations 1974, SI 1974/506, have been extensively amended: see para 1427, note 3, above.
4 National Health Service (Scotland) Act 1978, s 28(1), (2) (amended by the National Health Service (Amendment) Act 1986 (c 66), s 3(4)).

1470. The pharmaceutical list. The health board must prepare a list, called 'the pharmaceutical list', of the names of persons (other than doctors and dentists) who undertake to provide pharmaceutical services and of the address and opening times of premises within the board's area where they undertake to provide such services, stating the nature of the services to be provided and showing chemists as a separate category in the list[1]. The health board must make the list available for inspection, revised and up to date, as its offices[2].

An applicant wishing to be included in a pharmaceutical list, or a person already on the list who wishes to change his premises or the services provided, must send to the health board an application in the appropriate form[3]. An application will normally be granted only if the board is satisfied that the provision of the services at the premises named is necessary or desirable in order to secure adequate provision of pharmaceutical services in the neighbourhood[4].

The board may also prepare a provisional pharmaceutical list in which there is to be included the name of any person (other than a doctor or dentist) who undertakes provisionally to provide pharmaceutical services[5]. This list must contain the same particulars as discussed above in relaton to any such person, and also the provisional date from which such person undertakes to provide pharmaceutical services at the premises specified in the application[5].

1 National Health Service (General Medical and Pharmaceutical Services) (Scotland) Regulations 1974, SI 1974/506, reg 28(1) (substituted by SI 1987/385).
2 Ibid, reg 33(1)(b).
3 Ibid, reg 28(2), Sch 3, Pt III, Form A, Pt IV, Form A (all substituted by SI 1987/385).
4 Ibid, reg 28(4) (as so substituted). As to removal from the list, see reg 28A (added by SI 1987/385). As to withdrawal from the list, see Sch 3, Pt I, para 9, Pt II, para 8.
5 Ibid, reg 28A(1) (added by SI 1989/1883).

1471. Terms of service for chemists. The arrangements for the provision of pharmaceutical services must include arrangements for the supply of contraceptive substances and appliances and the provision of supplemental services[1]. These arrangements must incorporate the appropriate terms of service[2], which vary depending on whether the chemist undertakes to provide pharmaceutical services other than as a chemist employed by a health board at a health centre[3], or the chemist is employed by a health board to provide those services at a health centre[4]. 'Supplemental services' means (1) where a chemist regularly supplies drugs and medicines to be taken by persons resident in a home[5], the giving of advice by him or, where he is not a pharmacist, by a pharmacist employed by him, following a visit to that home in connection with procedures there for the safe keeping and correct administration of those drugs and medicines; (2) the keeping of records of such visits; (3) the keeping of records in connection with drugs and medicines supplied to or to be taken by any person who claims exemption from charges for drugs or appliances, or who, in the opinion of the pharmacist dispensing the drug or medicine, is likely to have difficulty understanding the nature and dosage of the drug or medicine dispensed and the times at which it is to be taken, in circumstances where the nature of the drug or medicine is such that, in the opinion of the pharmacist who dispenses it, the same or a similar drug or medicine is likely to be prescribed for that person regularly on future occasions[6].

1 National Health Service (General Medical and Pharmaceutical Services) (Scotland) Regulations 1974, SI 1974/506, reg 27(1)(a), (b) (substituted by SI 1989/1883).
2 Ibid, s 27(2) (as so substituted).
3 In this case ibid, Sch 3, Pt I (amended by SI 1989/1883), applies.
4 In this case ibid, Sch 3, Pt II (as so amended), applies.
5 'Home' means any of the following: (1) a nursing home within the meaning of the Nursing Homes Registration (Scotland) Act 1938 (c 73) (see para 1525 below); (2) a residential or other establishment within the meaning of the Social Work (Scotland) Act 1968 (c 49), Pt IV (ss 59–68) (amended by the Registered Establishments (Scotland) Act 1987 (c 40)); (3) a private hospital within the meaning of the Mental Health (Scotland) Act 1984 (c 36), Pt IV (ss 12–16) (see para 1525, note 3, below): National Health Service (General Medical and Pharmaceutical Services) (Scotland) Regulations 1974, reg 27(4)(a) (substituted by SI 1989/1883).
6 Ibid, reg 27(3)(a)–(c) (as so substituted). For the meaning of 'pharmacist' and 'records', see reg 27(4)(b), (c) (as so substituted).

1472. Pharmaceutical services for patients. A chemist must supply, with reasonable promptness, to any person who presents on a prescription form:
(1) an order for drugs, not being Scheduled drugs[1], or for appliances, signed by a doctor,
(2) an order for one of certain specified drugs[2], signed by and indorsed on its face with the reference 'S.2B' by a doctor,
(3) an order for listed drugs[3], or for drugs, not being Scheduled drugs, signed by a dentist,
such drugs (in a suitable container) and appliances as may be so ordered[4]. All drugs supplied for which a standard or formula is specified in the British Pharmacopoeia, the British Pharmaceutical Codex or the Drug Tariff must conform to that standard or formula, and in any other case must be of a grade or quality not lower than that ordinarily used for medical purposes; and all appliances supplied must conform to the specifications included in the Drug Tariff[5]. Where a prescription for drugs or listed drugs does not prescribe the quantity, strength or dosage the chemist must supply such strength and dosage as in the exercise of his professional skill, knowledge and care he considers appropriate and in a quantity he considers appropriate for a course of treatment not exceeding five days[6]. The dispensing of medicines must be performed by or under the direct supervision of a registered pharmaceutical chemist who must not, unless the Secretary of State otherwise consents, be disqualified by the Tribunal for inclusion in the pharmaceutical list[7].

A health board, after consulting the area pharmaceutical committee, must prepare a scheme for testing the quality and checking the amounts of drugs and appliances supplied[8] and a scheme, to be approved by the Secretary of State, for securing that one or more places of business on the pharmaceutical list in the board's area is open at all reasonable times[9].

1 'Scheduled drug' means a drug or other substance specified in the National Health Service (General Medical and Pharmaceutical Services) (Scotland) Regulations 1974, SI 1974/506, Sch 2A

(as added and amended: see para 1446, note 17, above) or, where the conditions in Sch 1, Pt I, para 16A(2) (added by SI 1985/296), are satisfied, in Sch 2B (as added, substituted and amended: see para 1446, note 17, above): reg 2(1) (amended by SI 1985/296).

2 Ie a drug specified in ibid, Sch 2B.

3 'Listed drug' means a drug or medicine included in a list approved by the Secretary of State under the National Health Service (Scotland) Act 1978 (c 29), s 27(1) (see para 1469, note 1, above): National Health Service (General Medical and Pharmaceutical Services) (Scotland) Regulations 1974, reg 2(1).

4 Ibid, Sch 3, Pt I, para 2(1), Pt II, para 2(1) (both substituted by SI 1985/296).

5 Ibid, Sch 3, Pt I, para 2(2), Pt II, para 2(2). As to the Drug Tariff, see para 1475 below.

6 Ibid, Sch 3, Pt I, para 2(1A), Pt II, para 2(1A) (both added by SI 1976/733).

7 Ibid, Sch 3, Pt I, para 4, Pt II, para 4. As to the Tribunal, see para 1521 below).

8 Ibid, reg 29(1).

9 Ibid, reg 29(2), (3) (amended by SI 1987/385). If the board and committee cannot agree on the scheme, it must be referred to the Secretary of State: reg 29(4) (as so amended). As to the amendment of schemes, see reg 29(5) (substituted by SI 1987/385).

1473. Services by chemists not employed at health centres. The following provisions apply to chemists who are not employed at health centres, in addition to the requirements set out in the preceding paragraph. Pharmaceutical services are to be provided at the premises specified in the application for inclusion in the pharmaceutical list and during the hours specified in the scheme made by the health board[1]. At each premises the chemist must exhibit a prescribed notice giving his name and opening hours and, when the premises are not open, a notice indicating the facilities available for securing the dispensing of medicines urgently required[2].

A chemist must not give, promise or offer to any person any gift or reward (whether by way of share of or dividend on his profits or by way of discount or rebate or otherwise) as an inducement to or in consideration of his presenting a prescription for drugs or appliances[3].

If so required by the health board, a chemist must furnish to the board the names of registered pharmaceutical chemists employed by him in dispensing medicines[4].

1 National Health Service (General Medical and Pharmaceutical Services) (Scotland) Regulations 1974, SI 1974/506, Sch 3, Pt I, para 3(1) (amended by SI 1987/385).

2 Ibid, Sch 3, Pt I, para 3(2) (substituted by SI 1987/385).

3 Ibid, Sch 3, Pt I, para 4.

4 Ibid, Sch 3, Pt I, para 5.

1474. Payment of chemists not employed at health centres. On dates to be appointed by the Secretary of State after consultation with an organisation which in his opinion is representative of the general body of chemists, a chemist must furnish to the health board, or as it may direct, the forms upon which the orders for drugs and appliances supplied by him were given, together with a statement of accounts containing such particulars as the health board with the approval of the Secretary of State requires[1]. The health board, if any chemist so requires, must afford him reasonable facilities for examining all or any of the forms together with particulars of the amounts calculated to be payable in respect of such drugs and appliances, and if he takes objection the health board must take that into consideration[2]. Similar facilities must be given to and consideration must be taken of any objection from any organisation which, in the opinion of the Secretary of State, is representative of the general body of chemists[3]. Payment will be made for drugs and appliances in the Drug Tariff at the prices specified therein and for drugs or appliances not in the tariff in the manner set forth therein; and payment will be made for containers and in respect of dispensing fees in the manner set forth in the tariff under deduction of an amount equal to any charge made or recoverable under regulations[4].

1 National Health Service (General Medical and Pharmaceutical Services) (Scotland) Regulations 1974, SI 1974/506, Sch 3, Pt I, para 7(1).
2 Ibid, Sch 3, Pt I, para 7(2).
3 Ibid, Sch 3, Pt I, para 7(3).
4 Ibid, Sch 3, Pt I, para 7(4). As to the tariff, see para 1475 below.

1475. The Drug Tariff. After consultation with an organisation representative of the general body of chemists the Secretary of State must cause to be prepared a statement, called 'the Drug Tariff', which is to include:

(1) the prices on the basis of which the payment for specified drugs commonly prescribed and appliances is to be calculated;
(2) the method of calculating the payment for drugs not specified in the tariff;
(3) the method of calculating the payment for containers;
(4) dispensing fees;
(5) arrangements for claiming fees, allowances and remuneration in connection with the making and implementation of arrangements for the provision of pharmaceutical services;
(6) the standards of quality for drugs;
(7) the list of drugs approved by him[1];
(8) the list of appliances approved by him[1] and the specifications therefor;
(9) the list of chemical reagents approved by him and the specifications therefor; and
(10) the method by which a claim may be made for compensation for financial loss in respect of oxygen equipment[2].

A chemist on the pharmaceutical list must on request supply the Secretary of State with any information which he requires for the purpose of conducting any inquiry into prices, payments, fees, allowances and remuneration[3].

1 Ie approved under the National Health Service (Scotland) Act 1978 (c 29), s 27(1): see para 1469, note 1, above.
2 National Health Service (General Medical and Pharmaceutical Services) (Scotland) Regulations 1974, SI 1974/506, reg 32(a)–(d), (dd), (e)–(i) (amended by SI 1989/1883).
3 Ibid, reg 32(j) (added by SI 1987/385).

7. HEALTH SERVICE HOSPITALS AND OTHER SERVICES

1476. Hospital and other accommodation and services. It is the duty of the Secretary of State to provide throughout Scotland, to such extent as he considers necessary to meet all reasonable requirements:

(1) hospital accommodation, including accommodation at state hospitals[1] (which are provided for persons requiring treatment under conditions of special security on account of their dangerous, violent or criminal propensities);
(2) premises other than hospitals at which facilities are available for any of the services provided under the National Health Service (Scotland) Act 1978; and
(3) medical, nursing and other services, whether in such accommodation or premises, in the patient's home or elsewhere[2].

Where accommodation or premises so provided afford facilities for the provision of general medical, general dental, general ophthalmic or pharmaceutical services, they are to be made available for those services on such terms and conditions as the Secretary of State determines[3].

1 As to state hospitals, SEE MENTAL HEALTH, vol 14, para 1472.

2 National Health Service (Scotland) Act 1978 (c 29), s 36(1)(a)–(c).
3 Ibid, s 36(2).

1477. Prevention of illness, care and after-care. The Secretary of State must make arrangements, to such extent as he considers necessary to meet all reasonable requirements, for the purpose of the prevention of illness, the care of persons suffering from illness or the after-care of such persons[1].

1 National Health Service (Scotland) Act 1978 (c 29), s 37.

1478. Care of mothers and young children. It is the duty of the Secretary of State to make arrangements, to such extent as he considers necessary, for the care, including in particular medical and dental care, of expectant and nursing mothers and of young children[1].

1 National Health Service (Scotland) Act 1978 (c 29), s 38.

1479. Schools' medical and dental services. It is the duty of the Secretary of State to provide for the periodical medical inspection, and for the medical supervision and treatment, of pupils in attendance at any school under the management of an education authority, and of all young persons in attendance at any junior college or other educational establishment under such management[1]. It is also his duty to provide, to such extent as he considers necessary to meet all reasonable requirements, for the dental inspection of those pupils and young persons, for their dental treatment and for their education in dental health[2].

It is the duty of every education authority to make arrangements for encouraging and assisting pupils and young persons to take advantage of such medical and dental treatment unless in any case the parent gives notice to the authority that he objects[3]; and to afford sufficient and suitable facilities for such medical inspection, supervision and treatment and dental inspection, treatment and education[4].

1 National Health Service (Scotland) Act 1978 (c 29), s 39(1) (amended by the Health and Medicines Act 1988 (c 49), ss 10(2), 25(2), Sch 3).
2 National Health Service (Scotland) Act 1978, s 39(2) (substituted by the Health and Medicines Act 1988, s 10(2)).
3 National Health Service (Scotland) Act 1978, s 39(3) (amended by the Health and Medicines Act 1988, s 10(2)).
4 National Health Service (Scotland) Act 1978, s 39(4) (as amended: see note 1 above).

1480. Vaccination and immunisation. The Secretary of State may make arrangements with medical practitioners for the vaccination or immunisation of persons against any disease, either by medical practitioners or by others acting under their direction and control[1], and must give every medical practitioner providing general medical services an opportunity of participating in this arrangement[2]. The Secretary of State may supply free of charge to medical practitioners providing these services vaccines, sera or other preparations[3].

1 National Health Service (Scotland) Act 1978 (c 29), s 40(1). See further PUBLIC HEALTH, vol 19, paras 500 ff.
2 Ibid, s 40(2).
3 Ibid, s 40(3).

1481. Family planning. It is the duty of the Secretary of State to make arrangements, to such extent as he considers necessary, for the giving of advice on contraception, the medical examination and treatment of persons seeking such advice, and the supply of contraceptive substances or appliances[1].

1 National Health Service (Scotland) Act 1978 (c 29), s 41.

1482. Health education. The Secretary of State has power to disseminate information relating to the promotion and maintenance of health and the prevention of illness[1]. Health education is one of the functions of the Common Services Agency[2].

1 National Health Service (Scotland) Act 1978 (c 29), s 42.
2 See para 1411 above.

1483. Control of spread of infectious disease. The Secretary of State may provide a service, including the provision of laboratories, for the control of the spread of infectious diseases, and may allow persons to use the services of these laboratories on such terms and conditions as he determines[1].

1 National Health Service (Scotland) Act 1978 (c 29), s 43. See also PUBLIC HEALTH, vol 19, paras 444 ff.

1484. Supplies of blood etc. Where the Secretary of State has acquired supplies of human blood for blood transfusion purposes or supplies of any other substances not readily obtainable, or has acquired any part of a human body for the purpose of or in the course of providing any service under National Health Service (Scotland) Act 1978, he may arrange to make such supplies available to medical practitioners and other persons who require them or for supplying that part to any person on such terms and conditions as he may determine[1], but only if and to the extent that he is satisfied that what he proposes to do will not to any significant extent:
(1) interfere with his performance of any duty imposed on him by the Act to provide any accommodation or services, and
(2) operate to the disadvantage of persons seeking or afforded admission or access to accommodation or services at health service hospitals otherwise than as private patients[2].

1 National Health Service (Scotland) Act 1978 (c 29), s 44(1).
2 Ibid, ss 44(2), 54(a), (b).

1485. Ambulances. It is the duty of the Secretary of State to make such provision as he thinks necessary for securing that ambulances and other means of transport are available for the conveyance of persons suffering from illness or expectant or nursing mothers or of other persons reasonably requiring such transport in order to avail themselves of any service under the National Health Service (Scotland) Act 1978[1]. This is a function of the Common Services Agency[2].

1 National Health Service (Scotland) Act 1978 (c 29), s 45.
2 See para 1411 above.

1486. Invalid carriages etc. The Secretary of State may provide invalid carriages[1] for persons appearing to him to be suffering from severe physical defect or disability and, at the request of such a person, may provide for him a vehicle other than an invalid carriage[2]. On such terms and conditions as he may determine he may adapt any such carriage or vehicle to suit the circumstances of that person, may maintain and repair it, insure it and pay the vehicle excise duty on it, and provide a structure for keeping it in[3]. He may also make grants towards costs incurred by that person in doing any of those things, in paying excise duties on fuel and in taking driving instruction[4].

1 'Invalid carriage' means a mechanically propelled vehicle specially designed and constructed, and not merely adapted, for the use of a person suffering from some physical defect or disability, and used solely by such a person: National Health Service (Scotland) Act 1978 (c 29), s 46(5).
2 Ibid, s 46(1).
3 Ibid, s 46(2).
4 Ibid, s 46(3).

1487. Educational and research facilities. It is the duty of the Secretary of State to make available such facilities, in any premises provided by him under the National Health Service (Scotland) Act 1978, as appear to him to be reasonably required for undergraduate and postgraduate clinical training and research, and for the education and training of persons providing services under the Act[1]. Without prejudice to his general powers and duties under the Scottish Board of Health Act 1919[2], he may conduct, or assist by grants or otherwise any person to conduct, research into any matters relating to the causation, prevention, diagnosis or treatment of illness, or into such other matters relating to the health service as he thinks fit[3].

1 National Health Service (Scotland) Act 1978 (c 29), s 47(1).
2 See eg the Scottish Board of Health Act 1919 (c 20), s 2, which imposes duties relating to the co-ordination of measures conducive to health, including measures for preventing and curing disease, the initiation and direction of research, the treatment of physical and mental defects, the collection, preparation and publication of statistics and the training of persons for health services.
3 National Health Service (Scotland) Act 1978, s 47(2).

1488. Residential and practice accommodation. The Secretary of State may provide, on such terms and conditions as may be agreed, residential accommodation for officers employed for the purposes of his functions under the National Health Service (Scotland) Act 1978 or for officers employed by a voluntary organisation[1] for the purpose of any service provided under Part III of the Act[2]. In any case, in view of special circumstances, he may provide, on such terms and conditions as may be agreed, residential accommodation for medical and dental practitioners providing general medical or general dental services, and practice accommodation for such medical and dental practitioners and for such other persons providing services under the Act as he thinks fit[3].

1 'Voluntary organisation' means a body the activities of which are carried on otherwise than for profit, but does not include any public or local authority: National Health Service (Scotland) Act 1978 (c 29), s 108(1) (amended by the Health Services Act 1980 (c 53), s 25(3), Sch 6, para 6).
2 National Health Service (Scotland) Act 1978, s 48(1). Part III comprises ss 36–48.
3 Ibid, s 48(2). 'Practice accommodation', in relation to a person providing any services, means accommodation suitable for the provision of those services: s 48(3).

1489. Accommodation for persons displaced by development. Where the carrying out of a scheme for the provision by the Secretary of State under the National Health Service (Scotland) Act 1978 or the Mental Health (Scotland) Act 1984 of accommodation or other facilities will involve the displacement from any premises of persons residing there, the Secretary of State may arrange with a local authority for the purposes of the Housing (Scotland) Act 1987, Scottish Homes, a housing association or housing trust or a development corporation under the new towns legislation for securing, in so far as it appears to him that no other suitable residential accommodation is available for those persons on reasonable terms, the provision of residential accommodation in advance of the displacements from time to time necessary as the carrying out of the scheme proceeds[1]. Arrangements so made may provide for payments by the Secretary of State, with Treasury consent, to the body concerned[2].

1 National Health Service (Scotland) Act 1978 (c 29), s 100(1) (amended by the Mental Health (Scotland) Act 1984 (c 36), s 127(1), Sch 3, para 39; the Housing (Scotland) Act 1987 (c 26), s 339(2), Sch 23, para 24; and the Housing (Scotland) Act 1988 (c 43), s 3(3), Sch 2, para 1).
2 National Health Service (Scotland) Act 1978, s 100(2).

1490. Patients' expenses attending hospitals. The Secretary of State must pay the whole or part of the travelling expenses necessarily incurred or to be incurred by a person (and, unless the health board determines that the patient need not be accompanied, the travelling expenses of a companion) in attending a hospital for the purpose of availing himself of hospital services provided under the National Health Service (Scotland) Act 1978 if it is determined under arrangements made by the Secretary of State that in the circumstances the payment of those expenses by the patient would involve hardship[1].

1 National Health Service (Expenses in attending Hospitals) (Scotland) Regulations 1974, SI 1974/486, reg 3.

1491. Holidays for and transfer or return of patients. The functions of the Secretary of State may be performed outside Scotland so far as they relate to holidays for patients, to the transfer of patients to or from England, Wales, Northern Ireland, the Isle of Man or the Channel Islands, or to the return of patients who have received treatment in Scotland to countries or territories outside the British Islands[1].

1 National Health Service (Scotland) Act 1978 (c 29), s 99A (added by the Health and Social Security Act 1984 (c 48), s 9(2)).

1492. Use by contractors and local authorities of premises, goods and services. The Secretary of State, a health board or the Common Services Agency may, on such terms and conditions as may be agreed:

(1) supply to persons providing general medical, dental or ophthalmic services or pharmaceutical services such equipment, goods or materials as may be prescribed[1];
(2) supply to local authorities, education authorities, government departments and such public bodies or classes of public bodies as the Secretary of State may determine any equipment, goods or materials of a kind used in the health service[2];
(3) provide local authorities and education authorities with any administrative, professional or other services of persons employed by or having contracts with the Secretary of State, a health board or the agency;
(4) permit such authorities to use health service premises;
(5) permit education authorities to use any vehicle, plant or apparatus belonging to a health board or the agency;
(6) permit education authorities, for the purpose of providing special education, to use certain premises or facilities[3];
(7) carry out maintenance work in connection with land or buildings for the maintenance of which a local authority or education authority is responsible[4].

The Secretary of State may by order provide that in relation to any vehicle made available by him under these provisions the statutory provisions as to vehicle excise and third party liabilities are to have modified effect[5].

1 For the goods which may be supplied, see the National Health Service (Supply of Prescribed Goods) (Scotland) Regulations 1974, SI 1974/773. The power under heads (1) and (2) to supply equipment, goods and materials includes power to arrange with a third party for them to supply them: National Health Service (Scotland) Act 1978 (c 29), s 15(2).
2 See ibid, s 15(2), and note 1 above.
3 Ie premises or facilities provided under ibid, s 36, for which see para 1476 above.
4 Ibid, s 15(1)(a)–(g) (amended by the Education (Scotland) Act 1980 (c 44), s 136(2), Sch 4, para 16, and the Health Services Act 1980 (c 53), s 3(2)).
5 National Health Service (Scotland) Act 1978, s 15(3).

1493. Use by voluntary organisations of premises, goods and services. The Secretary of State may assist any voluntary organisation[1] whose activities include the provision of a service provided under the National Health Service (Scotland) Act 1978 by permitting it to use premises belonging to him on such terms as may be agreed, and by making available goods, materials, vehicles[2] or equipment, whether by way of gift, loan or otherwise, and the services of any staff who are employed in connection with the premises or other things which he permits the organisation to use[3].

1 For the meaning of 'voluntary organisation', see para 1488, note 1, above.
2 The Secretary of State may by order provide that in relation to any vehicle so made available by him the statutory provisions as to vehicle excise and third party liabilities are to have modified effect: National Health Service (Scotland) Act 1978 (c 29), s 16(2). The National Health Service (Vehicles) (Scotland) Order 1974, SI 1974/1491, makes provision for vehicles made available to voluntary organisations.
3 National Health Service (Scotland) Act 1978, s 16(1).

8. PRIVATE PATIENTS

1494. Accommodation and services for private patients. If the Secretary of State is satisfied, in the case of a health service hospital, that it is reasonable to do so, he may authorise accommodation and services there to be made available, to such extent as he may determine, for patients undertaking to pay such charges as the Secretary of State may determine, and may make and recover such charges therefor as he may determine and calculate them on an appropriate commercial basis; but may do so only if and to the extent that he is satisfied that to do so will not to a significant extent:
(1) interfere with the performance by him of any duty imposed on him by the National Health Service (Scotland) Act 1978 to provide accommodation or services of any kind; and
(2) operate to the disadvantage of persons seeking or afforded admission or access to accommodation or services at health service hospitals, whether as resident or non-resident patients, otherwise than under this provision[1].
The Secretary of State may allow accommodation and services to which an authorisation under the above provision relates to be made available in connection with treatment, in pursuance of arrangements made by a medical or dental practitioner serving on the staff of a health service hospital for the treatment of the practitioner's private patients[2].
The Secretary of State must revoke such an authorisation only if and to the extent that he is satisfied that sufficient accommodation and facilities for the private practice of medicine and dentistry are otherwise reasonably available, whether privately or at health service hospitals, to meet the reasonable demand for them in the area served by the hospital in question[3].

1 National Health Service (Scotland) Act 1978 (c 29), s 57(1) (substituted by the Health and Medicines Act 1988 (c 49), s 7(11)).

2 National Health Service (Scotland) Act 1978, s 57(2) (as so substituted).
3 Ibid, s 57(3) (as so substituted).

1495. Private resident patients. The Secretary of State may authorise certain accommodation to be made available, to such extent as he may determine, for patients who give or for whom is given an undertaking to pay such charges for part of the cost as the Secretary of State may determine, and he may recover those charges[1]. The accommodation referred to is (1) accommodation in single rooms or small wards which are not for the time being needed by any patient on medical grounds; (2) accommodation in any hospital[2].

The Secretary of State may require any person who is a resident patient for whom he provides services under the National Health Service (Scotland) Act 1978 and who is absent during the day for the purpose of engaging in remunerative employment from the hospital where he is a patient, to pay such part of the cost of his maintenance and any incidental costs as seems reasonable to the Secretary of State having regard to the amount of that person's remuneration, and may recover that payment[3].

1 National Health Service (Scotland) Act 1978 (c 29), s 55(1).
2 Ibid, s 55(1)(a), (b).
3 Ibid, s 56.

1496. Use of facilities for private practice. Provision is made for the use of health service facilities by medical and dental practitioners, registered pharmacists and ophthalmic opticians who (in each case) provide health services under Part II of the National Health Service (Scotland) Act 1978, by other persons who provide pharmaceutical or ophthalmic services under Part II, and by chiropodists who provide services under the Act at premises where health services are provided under Part II[1]. Any such person who wishes to use any relevant health service accommodation or facilities[2] for the purpose of providing medical, dental, pharmaceutical, ophthalmic or chiropody services to non-resident private patients may apply in writing to the Secretary of State for permission to do so[3], specifying which of the relevant health service accommodation or facilities the applicant wishes to use and which of those kinds of services he wishes the permission to cover[4].

On receiving the application the Secretary of State must consider whether anything for which permission is sought would interfere with the giving of full and proper attention to persons other than private patients, and must grant permission unless in his opinion anything for which it is sought would so interfere[5]. If granted, the permission must be on such terms (including terms as to the payment of charges) as the Secretary of State from time to time determines[6].

1 National Health Service (Scotland) Act 1978 (c 29), s 64(5) (amended by the Health and Social Security Act 1984 (c 48), s 24, Sch 8, Pt I).
2 'Relevant health service accommodation or facilities' in relation to an applicant means any accommodation or facilities available at premises provided by the Secretary of State by virtue of the National Health Service (Scotland) Act 1978, being accommodation or facilities which the applicant is for the time being authorised to use for the purposes of Part II (ss 18–35), or, in the case of a chiropodist applicant, accommodation or facilities which he is for the time being authorised to use for purposes of the Act at premises where services are provided under Part II: s 64(6).
3 Ibid, s 64(1).
4 Ibid, s 64(2).

5 Ibid, s 64(3).
6 Ibid, s 64(4).

9. HEALTH SERVICE STAFFING

1497. Employment of staff generally. A health board and the Common Services Agency may employ such officers and servants on such terms as to remuneration and conditions of service as the board or agency may determine in accordance with regulations and any directions given by the Secretary of State[1].

Regulations provide that, subject to the provisions of any Act or order, the remuneration of any officer who belongs to a class of officers whose remuneration has been the subject to negotiations by a negotiating body[2] and has been approved by the Secretary of State after considering the result of the negotiations is to be neither more nor less than the remuneration so approved, whether or not it is paid out of money provided by Parliament[3]. Where conditions of service (other than conditions as to remuneration) of any class of officers have been similarly approved after negotiations, the conditions of service of any officer of that class must include the conditions so approved[4]. However, the Secretary of State may if he thinks fit authorise a health board or the Common Services Agency to vary the remuneration or the conditions of service so approved in the case of an individual officer or officers of a particular description[5].

Provision is made for the payment of compensation to or in respect of a person prematurely retired in the interests of the health service or made redundant[6].

1 National Health Service (Scotland) Act 1978 (c 29), ss 2(10), 10(2), Sch 1, para 5, Sch 5, para 7 (amended by the Health Services Act 1980 (c 53), s 25(3), (4), Sch 6, paras 7(2), 8(3), Sch 7).
2 'Negotiating body' means a body accepted by the Secretary of State as a proper body for negotiating remuneration and conditions of service: National Health Service (Remuneration and Conditions of Service) (Scotland) Regulations 1974, SI 1974/276, reg 2(1).
3 Ibid, reg 3(1).
4 Ibid, reg 3(2). In *Palmer v Inverness Hospitals Board of Mangement* 1963 SC 311, 1963 SLT 124, conditions in a departmental circular relating to disciplinary procedures were held to be binding.
5 National Health Service (Remuneration and Conditions of Service) (Scotland) Regulations 1974, reg 3(3).
6 See the National Health Service (Compensation for Premature Retirement) (Scotland) Regulations 1981, SI 1981/1785 (amended by SI 1985/2036).

1498. Consultants and community medicine specialists. An advisory appointments committee must be constituted by a health board or the Common Services Agency (acting through the Management Committee) to advise the board or agency on the selection of candidates for the appointment[1] of any registered medical or dental practitioner to the post of consultant and of any registered medical practitioner to the post of community medicine specialist[2], not being one of certain exempted appointments[3]. The exempted appointments include certain university and research appointments, a person who receives no remuneration other than a distinction award for the appointment, locum appointments for two years or less and transferred, redundant and honorary consultants[4].

Vacancies must be advertised[5] and applications referred to the advisory appointments committee for consideration, possible interview and report to the health board or agency[6], which makes the appointment from among the candidates selected by the committee[7].

1 'Appointment' includes any appointment to a post, whether existing or new, and whether whole-time or part-time: National Health Service (Appointment of Consultants and Community Medicine Specialists) (Scotland) Regulations 1986, SI 1986/944, reg 3(2).
2 'Community medicine specialist' means a Chief Administrative Medical Officer or a Specialist in Community Medicine: ibid, reg 2(1).
3 Ibid, regs 3(1), 6, 7.
4 Ibid, reg 4.
5 Ibid, reg 5.
6 Ibid, reg 8.
7 Ibid, reg 9.

1499. Health visitors. No person may be employed as a health visitor[1] unless that person holds the health visitors certificate issued by the Council for the Education and Training of Health Visitors, or, under conditions approved by the Secretary of State, holds the health visitors certificate issued either by the Royal Sanitary Association of Scotland or by the Royal Society for the Promotion of Health, or (with certain restrictions) was a health visitor immediately before 1 September 1965 or holds an approved foreign qualification[2].

1 'Health visitor' means a person employed by a health board (or by a voluntary organisation under arrangements with a health board) to visit people in their homes or elsewhere to give advice as to the care of young children, persons suffering from illness and expectant or nursing mothers, and as to preventing the spread of infection: National Health Service (Qualifications of Health Visitors) (Scotland) Regulations 1974, SI 1974/485, reg 1(2).
2 Ibid, reg 2. For dispensations in the case of qualified midwives, see reg 3.

1500. Members of supplementary professions. No person may be employed as an officer of a health board in the capacity of chiropodist, dietitian, medical laboratory technician, occupational therapist, orthoptist, physiotherapist, radiographer or remedial gymnast unless either he is registered under the Professions Supplementary to Medicine Act 1960 in respect of the profession appropriate to the work for which he is employed, or he was appropriately employed in that capacity immediately before 1 April 1974[1].

1 National Health Service (Professions Supplementary to Medicine) (Scotland) Regulations 1974, SI 1974/549, reg 3. As to registration under the Professions Supplementary to Medicine Act 1960 (c 66), see MEDICAL AND ALLIED PROFESSIONS, vol 14, para 1174.

1501. Speech therapists. The conditions necessary for appointment as a speech therapist are prescribed[1]. Provision was made for the transfer of certain speech therapists employed by education authorities to health boards and for the protection of the terms and conditions of service of persons so transferred[2].

1 National Health Service (Speech Therapists) (Scotland) Regulations 1974, SI 1974/667 (amended by SI 1985/208).
2 National Health Service (Transfer of Speech Therapists) (Scotland) Regulations 1974, SI 1974/469.

1502. Designated medical officers. Each health board must designate a medical officer or officers of the board to exercise certain statutory functions on behalf of local authorities[1]. Any such officer is known as 'the designated medical officer'[2]. The officers required to be so designated are the chief administrative medical officer and any district medical officers[3]. Before designating any other person the board must satisfy itself as to his experience and qualifications and give local authorities concerned the opportunity to comment[4]. A designated medical officer may exercise any power conferred by any enactment on an authorised officer of a local authority if the authority authorises him in writing to do so[5].

1 National Health Service (Scotland) Act 1978 (c 29), s 14(1). As to deputes, see s 14(4).
2 Ibid, s 14(2).
3 National Health Service (Designated Medical Officers) (Scotland) Regulations 1974, SI 1974/470, reg 3.
4 Ibid, reg 5.
5 National Health Service (Scotland) Act 1978, s 14(3).

1503. Superannuation and injury benefits. The principal regulations governing superannuation arrangements for the health service[1] set out a contributory superannuation scheme participation in which is generally compulsory for officers of an employing authority who have attained the age of eighteen[2] and medical and dental practitioners on health board lists who have not attained the age of seventy[3]. In general an officer who:

(1) in the case of a mental health officer[4] or a female who is a nurse, physiotherapist, midwife or health visitor, has not attained the age of sixty-five, or
(2) has not completed forty-five years' contributory service or forty-five years' contributing and non-contributing service and has not attained (a) in the case of a mental health officer or a female who is a nurse, physiotherapist, midwife or health visitor, an age of not less than sixty, or (b) in any other case, an age of not less than sixty-five years,

must pay contributions of an amount equal to 5 per cent of his remuneration if his employment is by way of manual labour, and 6 per cent in any other case[5]. In general 'contributing service' means continuing employment with a health authority, certain other employment (by virtue of transfer schemes between health service and local government and other authorities) and certain war service[6].

On ceasing to be employed an officer is in general entitled to receive from the Secretary of State an annual pension and a lump sum allowance if he has completed five years' service and is permanently incapable of discharging efficiently the duties of his employment by reason of physical or mental infirmity or he has attained the age of sixty, or in other prescribed circumstances[7]. In appropriate circumstances a death gratuity[8], a widow's pension[9], a widower's pension[10] or a child's pension[11] may be payable. Generally the pension payable other than to a practitioner providing general medical or dental services is a sum equal to one-eightieth of the highest of his last three years' remuneration in respect of each year of his contributing service[12]. A different formula applies to practitioners[13]. The other allowances are also related to average remuneration. Generally a widow's pension is one-half of the pension which her husband was receiving or would have received if he had retired[14].

Provision is made for the payment by the Secretary of State of injury benefits to or in respect of any person engaged in the health service whose earnings ability is reduced or who dies as a result of an injury suffered or disease contracted in the course of his duties[15].

1 Ie the National Health Service (Superannuation) (Scotland) Regulations 1980, SI 1980/1177 (amended by SI 1981/1018, SI 1981/1680, and SI 1983/272), made under the Superannuation Act 1972 (c 11), ss 10, 12. See also the National Health Service (Superannuation—Special Provisions) (Scotland) Regulations 1984, SI 1984/1970 (amended by SI 1986/701).
2 See the National Health Service (Superannuation) (Scotland) Regulations 1980, Pt II (regs 4–65).
3 See ibid, Pt III (regs 66–79).
4 For the meaning of 'mental health officer', see ibid, reg 3.
5 Ibid, reg 9(1), (2).

6 See ibid, regs 3, 31–34 (amended by SI 1983/272).
7 See ibid, reg 10(1) (as so amended).
8 See ibid, reg 15 (as so amended).
9 See ibid, reg 16 (as so amended).
10 See ibid, reg 20.
11 See ibid, reg 17 (amended by SI 1983/272).
12 Ibid, reg 11(1).
13 See ibid, reg 70(2). As to the calculation of practitioners' remuneration, see reg 68.
14 Ibid, reg 16(3).
15 See the National Health Service (Scotland) (Injury Benefits) Regulations 1974, SI 1974/1838 (amended by SI 1986/587).

10. PROPERTY AND LAND

1504. Purchase of land and moveable property. The Secretary of State may purchase by agreement any moveable property, and may purchase by agreement or compulsorily any land which he considers is required for the purposes of any service under the National Health Service (Scotland) Act 1978, and may use for those purposes any heritable or moveable property acquired by him or on his behalf under the Act[1]. Where he so acquires premises, he may acquire compulsorily any equipment, furniture or other moveable property used in or in connection with the premises[2]. These functions of the Secretary of State are included in the functions to be exercised by health boards with effect from 15 August 1983[3]. Any health board or the Common Services Agency may acquire on behalf of the Secretary of State any moveable property which may be required for the above purposes[4].

1 National Health Service (Scotland) Act 1978 (c 29), s 79(1). As to the incorporation of the Lands Clauses Acts and parts of the Railways Clauses Consolidation (Scotland) Act 1845 (c 33), for the purpose of the purchase of land by agreement, see the National Health Service (Scotland) Act 1978, s 79(4).
2 Ibid, s 79(2). For the procedure for the acquisition of property other than land, see Sch 13.
3 See the National Health Service (Functions of Health Boards) (Scotland) Order 1983, SI 1983/1027.
4 National Health Service (Scotland) Act 1978, s 79(3).

1505. Disposal of land. Without prejudice to any other power of disposal the Secretary of State may dispose of any land which he considers is no longer required for the purposes of any service under the National Health Service (Scotland) Act 1978, and where he has delegated any of his functions as to the acquisition, management or disposal of land to a health board or the Common Services Agency any instrument in connection with the exercise of those functions may validly be executed by an officer of the board or agency authorised by him for the purpose[1].

1 National Health Service (Scotland) Act 1978 (c 29), s 79(1A) (added by the Health and Social Services and Social Security Adjudications Act 1983 (c 41), s 14, Sch 7, para 3).

11. FINANCE, REMUNERATION AND CHARGES

1506. Expenses and receipts of the Secretary of State. Any expenses incurred by the Secretary of State under the health service Acts are to be defrayed out of money provided by Parliament, and all sums received by him under these Acts are to be paid into the Consolidated Fund[1].

In respect of each financial year sums must be paid by the Secretary of State not exceeding the amount allotted by him for that year to the following bodies towards meeting their expenditure in that year: the Scottish Health Service Planning Council, every health board[2], the Common Services Agency, the Medical Practices Committee, the Dental Practices Board, the Tribunal and every local health council[3]. This does not apply in respect of the expenditure of a health board attributable to the performance of its functions relating to the provision of services[4], but in that respect the Secretary of State must pay in respect of each financial year:

(1) such amounts as he may allot for any kind of expenditure attributable to reimbursement of expenses of persons providing such services; and

(2) sums equal to any other expenditure attributable to remuneration of persons providing such services[5].

The Secretary of State may give directions to any body listed above with respect to the application of the sums so paid to it, and it is its duty to comply with the directions[6].

It is the duty of each such body so to perform its functions as to secure that the expenditure attributable to the performance of its functions in each year does not exceed the aggregate of the amounts so allotted to it, any other sums received by it under the National Health Service (Scotland) Act 1978 and any sums received by it otherwise than under the Act for the purpose of enabling it to defray such expenditure[7], and the Secretary of State may give a body directions designed to secure compliance with this duty[8].

1 Health Services Act 1976 (c 83), s 21; National Health Service (Scotland) Act 1978 (c 29), s 85(6).
2 The expenditure of a university liaison committee is deemed to be the expenditure of the health board for whose area it is constituted: see the National Health Service (Scotland) Act 1978, s 85(3).
3 Ibid, s 85(1) (substituted by the Health Services Act 1980 (c 53), s 6(3), and amended by the Health and Social Security Act 1984 (c 53), s 24, Sch 8, Pt I). The payments must be made at such times, in such manner and subject to such conditions as the Secretary of State may determine: National Health Service (Scotland) Act 1978, s 85(4). The date on which an allotment under s 85(1) or s 85(2)(a) takes effect is the date on which the Secretary of State notifies the body receiving the allotment of its amount: s 85(1A) (added by the Health and Social Security Act 1984, s 6(3), and amended by the Health and Medicines Act 1988 (c 49), s 25(1), Sch 2, para 14).
4 Ie its functions under the National Health Service (Scotland) Act 1978, Pt II (ss 18–35).
5 Ibid, s 85(2)(a), (b) (as substituted (see note 1 above) and amended by the Health and Medicines Act 1988, s 16(3)).
6 National Health Service (Scotland) Act 1978, s 85(2A) (added by the Health Services Act 1980, s 6(3)).
7 National Health Service (Scotland) Act 1978, s 85A(1) (added by the Health Services Act 1980, s 6(4), and amended by the Health and Medicines Act 1988 (c 49), s 16(4)).
8 See the National Health Service (Scotland) Act 1978, s 85A(3), (6) (as so added and amended).

1507. Contributions to community service expenditure. A health board may if it thinks fit make payments to a regional, islands or district council towards the council's expenditure in connection with certain of its social work, education, housing and other functions relating to community services[1], and to any registered housing association, any development corporation, the Housing Corporation and Scottish Homes towards their expenditure in connection with the provision of housing accommodation[2]. Payments may also be made to a voluntary organisation which provides services similar to the functions referred to above[3].

Any such payments, whether in respect of capital or revenue expenditure, must be made in accordance with conditions prescribed for payments of that description by the Secretary of State in directions[4].

The Secretary of State may give to a voluntary organisation which provides certain services[5] assistance by way of grant or loan or both[6].

1 See the National Health Service (Scotland) Act 1978 (c 29), s 16A(1) (added by the Health Services Act 1980 (c 53), s 4, and substituted by the Health and Social Services and Social Security Adjudications Act 1983 (c 41), s 2).
2 See the National Health Service (Scotland) Act 1978, s 16A(2) (as so added and substituted, and amended by the Housing (Consequential Provisions) Act 1985 (c 71), s 4, Sch 2, para 41, and the Housing (Scotland) Act 1988 (c 43), s 3(3), Sch 2, para 1).
3 See the National Health Service (Scotland) Act 1978, s 16A(3) (as so added and substituted). For the meaning of 'voluntary organisation', see para 1488, note 1, above.
4 Ibid, s 16A(4) (as so added and substituted).
5 Ie a voluntary organisation whose activities consist in or include the provision of a service similar to a relevant service, the promotion or publicising of a relevant service or the giving of advice as to how such a service or a similar one can best be provided: ibid, s 16B(2) (added by the Health and Social Services and Social Security Adjudications Act 1983, s 3). 'Relevant service' means service which must or may, by virtue of the National Health Service (Scotland) Act 1978, be provided or the provision of which must or may, by virtue of that Act, be secured by the Secretary of State, or a service for the provision of which a health board is, by virtue of that Act, under a duty to make arrangements: s 16B(3) (as so added).
6 Ibid, s 16B(1) (as so added), under which such grants or loans may be made on such terms and subject to such conditions as the Secretary of State may with Treasury approval determine.

1508. Accounts. Every health board and the Common Services Agency must keep, in a form directed by the Secretary of State with Treasury approval, accounts of all money it receives or pays out, the accounts being audited by auditors appointed by the Secretary of State[1], and must prepare and transmit to him in respect of each financial year accounts in such form as he may with Treasury approval direct[2]. In respect of each such year the Secretary of State must prepare, in a form directed by the Treasury, summarised accounts of the health boards and the agency, and transmit them by 30 November to the Comptroller and Auditor General, who must examine and certify them and lay them, with his report on them, before each House of Parliament[3].

1 National Health Service (Scotland) Act 1978 (c 29), s 86(1). As to the appointment of a treasurer by each board and the agency, standing financial instructions, the submission of estimates to the Secretary of State, accounts and audit, see the National Health Service (Financial Provisions) (Scotland) Regulations 1974, SI 1974/468, which have effect as if made under the National Health Service (Scotland) Act 1978, s 86(2).
2 Ibid, s 86(3).
3 Ibid, s 86(4).

1509. Control of prices for medical supplies. The Secretary of State may by order provide for controlling maximum prices to be charged for any medical supplies required for the purposes of the National Health Service (Scotland) Act 1978[1].

1 National Health Service (Scotland) Act 1978 (c 29), s 49(1). 'Medical supplies' includes surgical, dental and optical materials and equipment: s 49(3).

1510. Remuneration for services. Regulations must make provision as to the remuneration to be paid to persons providing general medical services, general dental services, general ophthalmic services or pharmaceutical services under the National Health Service (Scotland) Act 1978, and may include provision for their remuneration in respect of the instruction of any person in matters relating to those services[1]. In general[2] remuneration may consist of payments by way of salary, fees, allowances and full or partial reimbursement of expenses incurred in connection with the provision of the services or instruction[3].

1 National Health Service (Scotland) Act 1978 (c 29), s 28A(1) (added by the Health and Social Security Act 1984 (c 48), s 7(2), and amended by the Health and Medicines Act 1988 (c 49),

s 15(1)). As to the contents of the regulations, see the National Health Service (Scotland) Act 1978, s 28B (as so added, and amended by the National Health Service (Amendment) Act 1986 (c 66), s 4(6), (7)). The power to make regulations has not yet been exercised.

2 This is subject to the National Health Service (Scotland) Act 1978, s 19(3), under which the remuneration of a practitioner providing general medical services must not normally consist wholly or mainly of a fixed salary which has no reference to the number of his patients; and s 25(3) (amended by the Health Services Act 1980 (c 53), s 25(3), (4), Sch 6, para 4, Sch 7), under which the remuneration to be paid to a dental practitioner providing general dental services otherwise than at a health centre must not consist wholly or mainly of a fixed salary unless either it is paid under arrangements made under the National Health Service (Scotland) Act 1978, s 33 (special arrangements where the services in the area are inadequate), or the services are provided in prescribed circumstances and the practitioner consents.

3 Ibid, s 28A(2) (as added (see note 1 above) and amended by the Health and Medicines Act 1988, s 15(2)).

1511. Charges. It has already been noted that the services provided under the general duty of the Secretary of State under the National Health Service (Scotland) Act 1978 are free of charge, except in so far as the making and recovery of charges is expressly provided for by or under any enactment, whenever passed[1]. Reference is made in the paragraphs which follow to the enabling statutory powers and the principal regulations which have been made thereunder.

1 National Health Service (Scotland) Act 1978 (c 29), s 1(2): see para 1407 above.

1512. Charges for drugs, medicines or appliances and pharmaceutical services. Regulations may provide for the making and recovery in such manner as may be prescribed of such charges as may be prescribed in respect of (1) the supply under the National Health Service (Scotland) Act 1978 (otherwise than under Part II[1]) of drugs, medicines or appliances, including the replacement and repair of those appliances, and (2) such of the pharmaceutical services referred to in Part II as may be prescribed[2]. The regulations may provide for the grant, cn payment of prescribed sums, of exemption certificates from charges[3].

No charge may be made under these powers in relation to (a) the supply of drugs, medicines and appliances to a hospital patient, or (b) the supply of any drug or medicine for the treatment of venereal disease, or (c) the supply of any appliance for a person who is aged under sixteen or who is under nineteen and is receiving qualifying full-time education, or (d) the replacement or repair of any defective appliance[4].

1 The National Health Service (Scotland) Act 1978 (c 29), Part II (ss 18–35), relates to the provision of services.

2 Ibid, s 69(1). See the National Health Service (Charges for Drugs and Appliances) (Scotland) Regulations 1989, SI 1989/326.

3 National Health Service (Scotland) Act 1978, s 69(2).

4 Ibid, s 69(3), Sch 11, para 1(1) (amended by the Health Services Act 1980 (c 53), s 25(2), Sch 5, para 5).

1513. Charges for optical appliances. Regulations may provide for the making and recovery in such manner as may be prescribed of such charges as may be determined by or in accordance with directions given by the Secretary of State in respect of the supply under the National Health Service (Scotland) Act 1978 of glasses and contact lenses[1], although no such charge may be made for the supply of any appliance otherwise than under the general optical services to a patient resident in a hospital[2]. Regulations may provide for the remission or repayment of charges otherwise payable by persons of low income[3]. Regulations have been made under these powers[4].

1 National Health Service (Scotland) Act 1978 (c 29), s 70(1) (amended by the Health and Medicines Act 1988 (c 49), s 25(2), Sch 3), and the National Health Service (Scotland) Act 1978, Sch 11, para 2(1) (substituted by the Health and Medicines Act 1988, s 25(1), Sch 2, para 15).

2 National Health Service (Scotland) Act 1978, s 70(3), Sch 11, para 2(3).
3 Ibid, Sch 11, para 5.
4 National Health Service (Optical Charges and Payments) (Scotland) Regulations 1989, SI 1989/392.

1514. Charges for dental appliances and dental treatment. Regulations may provide for the making and recovery in such manner as may be prescribed of charges calculated in the specified manner[1] in respect of the supply under the National Health Service (Scotland) Act 1978 of dentures and other dental appliances of prescribed descriptions[2]. A charge calculated in the specified manner may be made and recovered, in such manner as may be prescribed, in respect of any services provided as part of the general dental services (other than the repair of appliances other than prescribed appliances or the arrest of bleeding)[3]. However, no charge may be made to persons aged under eighteen (or under nineteen and receiving qualifying full-time education), expectant mothers or any person who has borne a child within the previous twelve months[4]. Regulations may provide for the remission or repayment of charges for dental treatment otherwise payable by persons of low income[5]; may vary the amount or maximum amount of any such charge, or may direct that it is not payable[6]; and may provide that, in the case of such special dental treatment as may be prescribed, being treatment provided as part of general dental services, such charges as may be prescribed may be made and recovered by the person providing the service[7]. Regulations have been made under these powers[8].

1 See the National Health Service (Scotland) Act 1978 (c 29), s 71A (added by the Health and Medicines Act 1988 (c 49), s 11(6)).
2 National Health Service (Scotland) Act 1978, s 70(1A) (added by the Health and Medicines Act 1988, s 11(4)).
3 National Health Service (Scotland) Act 1978, s 71(1) (amended by the Health and Medicines Act 1988, ss 11(5), (7), 25(2), Sch 3).
4 National Health Service (Scotland) Act 1978, Sch 11, para 3(4) (amended by the Health Services Act 1980 (c 53), s 25(2), (4), Sch 5, para 7(2), Sch 7).
5 National Health Service (Scotland) Act 1978, ss 70(3), 71(1), Sch 11, para 5 (amended by the Health and Social Security Act 1984) (c 48), s 24, Sch 8, Pt I).
6 National Health Service (Scotland) Act 1978, s 71(1), Sch 11, para 3(2).
7 Ibid, s 71(2).
8 See the National Health Service (Dental Charges) (Scotland) Regulations 1989, SI 1989/363.

1515. Charges for goods supplied at clinics. Regulations may provide for the recovery of such charges as may be prescribed:

(1) in respect of prescribed services relating to the prevention of illness, care and after-care, not being services provided in a hospital[1];

(2) in respect of prescribed articles or services provided, other than in a hospital, for mothers and young children, not being a drug, medicine or appliance of a type normally supplied[2];

(3) from persons availing themselves of any service relating to family planning, except advice on contraception[3].

The regulations may provide for the remission of any such charge, in whole or in part, in prescribed circumstances[4]. Regulations have been made under these powers[5].

1 National Health Service (Scotland) Act 1978 (c 29), s 72(a), referring to services provided under s 37, for which see para 1477 above.
2 Ibid, s 72(b), referring to articles or services provided under s 38, for which see para 1478 above.
3 Ibid, s 72(c), referring to services under s 41, for which see para 1481 above.
4 Ibid, s 72.
5 See the National Health Service (Supply of Goods at Clinics etc) (Scotland) Regulations 1976, SI 1976/540.

1516. Charges for more expensive supplies and for certain repairs and replacements. Regulations may provide for the making and recovery of such charges as may be prescribed:

(1) by the Secretary of State in respect of the supply, replacement or repair of an appliance or vehicle of a more expensive type than the prescribed type[1]; or

(2) by persons providing general dental services in respect of the supply, replacement or repair, as part of those services, of dental appliances of a more expensive type than the prescribed type[2].

Regulations have been made under these powers[3].

Regulations may also provide for the making and recovery of such charges as may be prescribed:

(a) by the Secretary of State in respect of the replacement or repair of any appliance or vehicle supplied by him[4], or

(b) by persons providing general dental services in respect of the replacement or repair of any dental appliance provided as part of those services[5],

if it is determined in the prescribed manner that the repair or replacement is necessitated by the act or omission of the person supplied[6].

1 National Health Service (Scotland) Act 1978 (c 29), s 73(a).
2 Ibid, s 73(b) (amended by the Health and Social Security Act 1984 (c 48), s 24, Sch 8, Pt I).
5 See the National Health Service (Charges for Appliances) (Scotland) Regulations 1974, SI 1974/1910.
6 National Health Service (Scotland) Act 1978, s 74(a).
7 Ibid, s 74(b) (as amended: see note 2 above).

1517. Remission, repayment or reduction of charges and payment of travelling expenses. Regulations may provide for the remission or repayment of charges in certain circumstances[1]. They may also provide for the reduction of sums otherwise payable by a health board to persons by whom certain services are provided by the amount of the charges authorised by regulations in respect of those services[2].

Regulations may provide in relation to prescribed descriptions of persons[3]:

(1) for the remission or repayment of the whole or part of certain charges otherwise payable by them[4];

(2) for the payment by the Secretary of State in prescribed cases of travelling expenses and, if necessary, overnight accommodation expenses (including those of a companion) incurred for the purpose of availing themselves of any services provided under the National Health Service (Scotland) Act 1978[5].

Regulations have been made under these powers[6].

1 See eg the National Health Service (Scotland) Act 1978 (c 29), s 72, and para 1515 above, and Sch 11, para 5, and para 1513 above.
2 See ibid, s 75 (amended by the Health and Social Services Act 1984 (c 48), s 24, Sch 8, Pt I).
3 The description of persons may be prescribed inter alia on the criteria of age, the fact that a prescribed person or body accepts them as suffering from a prescribed medical condition or that such a condition arose in prescribed circumstances, their or some other person's receipt or entitlement to receive benefit, and the relationship between their resources and their requirements (calculated in a prescribed manner): National Health Service (Scotland) Act 1978, s 75A(2), (3) (added by the Social Security Act 1988 (c 7), s 14(2)).
4 National Health Service (Scotland) Act 1978, s 75A(1)(a) (as so added, and amended by the Health and Medicines Act 1988 (c 49), s 25(1), Sch 2, para 13), referring to charges otherwise payable under the National Health Service (Scotland) Act 1978, s 69(1), s 70(1) or (1A) or s 71 (for which see paras 1512–1514 above).
5 Ibid, s 75A(1)(b), (c) (as so added).
6 See the National Health Service (Travelling Expenses and Remission of Charges) (Scotland) Regulations 1988, SI 1988/546 (amended by SI 1989/393).

1518. Charges to overseas visitors. Regulations may provide for the making and recovery in such manner as the Secretary of State may determine[1] of prescribed charges in respect of the provision of prescribed services under the National Health Service (Scotland) Act 1978 for prescribed persons not ordinarily resident in Great Britain, and may provide that the charges are only to be made in such cases as may be determined under the regulations[2]. Regulations have been made under this power[3].

1 The Secretary of State may calculate charges under this provision on any basis that he considers to be the appropriate commercial basis: National Health Service (Scotland) Act 1978 (c 29), s 98 (amended by the Health and Medicines Act 1988 (c 49), s 7(13), (14)).
2 National Health Service (Scotland) Act 1978, s 98 (as so amended).
3 See the National Health Service (Charges to Overseas Visitors) (Scotland) Regulations 1982, SI 1982/898 (amended by SI 1982/1743, SI 1983/362, SI 1984/295, SI 1985/383, SI 1986/516, SI 1986/924, SI 1987/387, SI 1988/13 and SI 1988/462).

1519. Evasion of charges. If any person, for the purpose of evading the payment or reducing the amount of any charge under the National Health Service (Scotland) Act 1978 knowingly makes any false statement or false representation, or produces or furnishes or causes or knowingly allows to be produced or furnished any document or information which he knows to be false in a material particular, the charge may be recovered from him as a simple contract debt by the person by whom the cost of the service in question was defrayed[1].

1 National Health Service (Scotland) Act 1978 (c 29), s 99.

12. COMPLAINTS

1520. Complaints against practitioners providing general services. Every health board must establish a medical service committee, a pharmaceutical service committee, a dental service committee and a joint services committee[1], and every joint ophthalmic committee must establish an ophthalmic service committee[2]. Complaints made against a doctor, chemist, dentist, ophthalmic medical practitioner or optician in respect of an alleged failure to comply with his terms of service must be investigated by the appropriate service committee[3]. Generally a complaint must be made in the case of a dentist within six months after completion of the treatment or within six weeks after the matter which gave rise to the complaint came to the complainer's notice, whichever was the sooner, and in all other cases within six weeks after the matter which gave rise to the complaint came to the complainer's notice, in writing stating the substance of the matter he wishes investigated[4]. The service committees must also investigate matters properly referred by the health board[5]. A service committee or joint services committee must comply with detailed prescribed procedure[6], which requires a service committee, after a hearing if necessary, to draw up a report stating such relevant facts as appear to be established by evidence and the inferences which in its opinion may properly be drawn from the facts, together with a recommendation as to the action, if any, which should be taken[7]. The committee must present the report to the health board or the joint ophthalmic committee, and where the report infers a breach of the terms of service, the committee may draw attention to any previous reports based on a finding of a breach of the terms of service in connection with the practitioner, chemist or optician and to any action taken by the Secretary of State on such reports, and may recommend that account should be taken thereof by the board or the joint ophthalmic committee in reaching its decision[8].

A health board or the joint ophthalmic committee must consider the report of a service committee and accept as conclusive any finding of fact contained in it[9]. The decision of the board or joint ophthalmic committee may include:

(1) the imposition of a special limit on the number of persons for whom the doctor concerned may undertake to provide treatment;

(2) the recovery from a practitioner, chemist or optician, as the case may be, of any expenses reasonably and necessarily incurred by any person owing to the failure of the practitioner, chemist or optician to comply with the terms of service, and the payment of any sum so recovered to that person;

(3) representations to the Secretary of State that, owing to the failure of the practitioner, chemist or optician to comply with his terms of service, an amount be withheld from his remuneration;

(4) representations to the Tribunal that the continued inclusion of the doctor, chemist, dentist, ophthalmic medical practitioner or optician on the appropriate list would be prejudicial to the efficiency of the services in question; and

(5) a requirement that, owing to the failure of a dentist to comply with his terms of service, he should be required until further notice, in respect of any treatment other than an examination or emergency treatment, to submit for prior approval to the Scottish Dental Practice Board estimates in respect thereof[10].

Any party aggrieved by such decision is entitled to appeal to the Secretary of State against any decision that is adverse to him[11]. The decision of the Secretary of State is final and conclusive[12].

The Secretary of State may direct a health board to recover from a practitioner, chemist or optician, such amount as he thinks fit, where (a) he is satisfied after a report by a service committee that a practitioner, chemist or optician has failed or neglected to comply with the terms of service applicable to him; or (b) he is satisfied after a report by a medical officer that a doctor has failed to comply with the terms of service applicable to him in relation to reports to the medical officer; or (c) he is satisfied after a report by a dental officer that a dentist has failed to keep records as required by the terms of service applicable to him[13].

Where it appears to a health board after an investigation by the area medical committee of the drugs and appliances ordered or supplied by general medical practitioners for persons on its lists and where it appears that, by reason of the character or quantity of the drugs or appliances so ordered or supplied, the cost is in excess of what was reasonably necessary for the adequate treatment of those persons, the health board may decide to recover from the doctor, by deduction from his remuneration or otherwise, such sum as it thinks fit, from which decision there is an appeal to the Secretary of State[14]. On a report from the Scottish Dental Practice Board, the Secretary of State may refer similar questions to the area dental committee for consideration, and if it is decided that a dentist has regularly provided excessive dental treatment that dentist may be required to submit to the Scottish Dental Practice Board for prior approval estimates of all or specific treatments for a period of twelve months[15]. The joint ophthalmic committee is required to give similar consideration from time to time, and where it appears that owing to excessive prescribing by an ophthamlic medical practitioner or optician a health board has incurred costs materially in excess of what was reasonably necessary for adequate treatment, the committee may impose a requirement that a sum should be recovered from the practitioner or optician, from which decision he may appeal to the Secretary of State[16].

1 National Health Service (Service Committees and Tribunal) (Scotland) Regulations 1974, SI 1974/504, reg 3(1). For the constitution of the committees, see reg 3(2).
2 Ibid, reg 23(1). For the constitution of the committee, see reg 23(2).

3 Ibid, regs 4, 24.
4 Ibid, regs 5, 25. As to late complaints, see regs 6, 26.
5 Ibid, regs 6, 27.
6 For this procedure, see regs 8, 28, Sch 1 (amended by SI 1974/1031).
7 Ibid, Sch 1, paras 1, 2(1)–(9) (as so amended).
8 Ibid, Sch 1, para 2(9).
9 Ibid, regs 9(1), 29(1).
10 Ibid, regs 9(1)(a)–(e), 29(1)(a)–(c). As to the Tribunal, see para 1521 below.
11 Ibid, regs 10(1), 30(1). For the procedure on the appeal, see regs 10–12, 30–32.
12 Ibid, regs 11(6), 31(6).
13 Ibid, regs 13(1), 33.
14 Ibid, regs 14, 15.
15 Ibid, reg 20.
16 Ibid, reg 34.

1521. Disqualification of practitioners. The Tribunal constituted for the purpose of inquiring into representations, made in the prescribed form[1], that the continued inclusion in a list of persons providing general medical, general dental or general ophthalmic services or pharmaceutical services would be prejudicial to the efficiency of the services in question[2] must inquire into any representations received from a health board or joint ophthalmic committee, and may inquire into any other representations received; and if it is of opinion that the continued inclusion of that person in any list would be prejudicial to the efficiency of those services, must direct that his name be removed from that list and may also, if it thinks fit, direct that his name be removed from or not included in any corresponding list kept by any other health board[3].

Regulations confer the requisite powers on the Tribunal and set out procedures for holding inquiries[4], reporting[5], appealing[6] and publishing Tribunal decisions[7], and procedures whereby persons whose names have been removed from any list may apply for reinstatement[8]. At the conclusion of any inquiry the Tribunal must, as soon as may be, issue a statement under the chairman's hand containing its findings of fact, the conclusion which it has reached and such directions as to removal from lists as it may give, and any order it makes as to expenses[9]. Against any such direction there is an appeal to the Secretary of State[10].

Any person whose name is removed from a list is disqualified for inclusion in any list to which the direction relates until the Tribunal or the Secretary of State directs to the contrary[11]. For the purpose of deciding whether to issue such a direction the Tribunal or the Secretary of State may hold an inquiry[12].

1 See the National Health Service (Service Committees and Tribunal) (Scotland) Regulations 1974, SI 1974/504, reg 39, Sch 3, Form 1.
2 See para 1425 above.
3 National Health Service (Scotland) Act 1978 (c 29), s 29(3), (6); National Health Service (Joint Ophthalmic Committees) (Scotland) Regulations 1974, SI 1974/503, reg 10.
4 See the National Health Service (Service Committees and Tribunal) (Scotland) Regulations 1974, regs 41–51.
5 See ibid, reg 54.
6 See ibid, regs 55, 56.
7 See ibid, reg 57.
8 See ibid, reg 52.
9 Ibid, reg 54(1). Copies are sent to the Secretary of State and the parties, and the Secretary of State sends copies to such health boards and joint ophthalmic committees as appear to be concerned: reg 54(2).
10 National Health Service (Scotland) Act 1978, s 29(4).
11 Ibid, s 30(1).
12 Ibid, s 30(2).

1522. Jurisdiction of the Health Service Commissioner. The Health Service Commissioner for Scotland has been appointed[1] to investigate, in relation to a health board, the Common Services Agency or the Scottish Dental Practice Board[2]:

(1) an alleged failure in a service provided by a board or the agency, or
(2) an alleged failure by a board or the agency to provide a service which it was its function to provide, or
(3) any other action taken by or on behalf of a board or the agency,

in a case where a complaint is duly made by or on behalf of any person that he has sustained injustice or hardship in consequence of the failure or in consequence of maladministration connected with the other action[3]. The commissioner is not to investigate any action:

(a) in respect of which the person aggrieved has or had a right of appeal, reference or review to or before a tribunal constituted by or under any enactment or by virtue of Her Majesty's prerogative, or
(b) in respect of which the person aggrieved has or had a remedy by way of proceeding in any court of law;

but the commissioner may investigate notwithstanding such a right or remedy if he is satisfied that in the particular circumstances it is not reasonable to expect the person aggrieved to resort or to have resorted to it[4]. Nor may the commissioner investigate any action:

(i) taken in connection with any general medical, dental or ophthalmic service or pharmaceutical services by a person providing the service;
(ii) taken in connection with the diagnosis of illness or disease or the care or treatment of a patient, being action which, in the commissioner's opinion, was taken solely in the exercise of clinical judgment, whether formed by the person taking the action or any other person; or
(iii) taken by a health board or joint ophthalmic committee in the exercise of functions under disciplinary regulations[5];
(iv) taken in respect of appointments or removals, pay, discipline, superannuation or other personnel matters;
(v) taken in matters relating to contractual or other commercial transactions, other than in matters arising from arrangements between a board or the agency and another body outwith the health service for the provision of services to patients by that other body;
(vi) which has been or is the subject of an inquiry under the National Health Service (Scotland) Act 1978[6]; or
(vii) in relation to which the protective functions of the Mental Welfare Commission for Scotland have been or are being exercised under the Mental Health (Scotland) Act 1984[7].

Nothing in these provisions authorises or requires the commissioner to question the merits of a decision taken without maladministration by a board or the agency in the exercise of a discretion vested in that body[8].

1 See the National Health Service (Scotland) Act 1978 (c 29), s 90(1), and para 1426 above.
2 Ibid, s 93(1) (as amended): see para 1426 above.
3 Ibid, s 93(2)(a)–(c). 'Action' includes failure to act: s 97(1).
4 Ibid, s 93(a), (b). 'Person aggrieved' means a person who claims or is alleged to have sustained such injustice or hardship as is mentioned in s 93(2): s 97(1).
5 Ie under the National Health Service (Service Committees and Tribunal) (Scotland) Regulations 1974, SI 1974/504, any regulations amending or replacing them, or any regulations revoked by such regulations.
6 Ie under the National Health Service (Scotland) Act 1978, s 78: see para 1409 above.
7 National Health Service (Scotland) Act 1978, s 93(4), Sch 14, paras 1–7 (amended by Health Services Act 1980 (c 53), s 25(3), (4), Sch 6, paras 3, 9, Sch 7, and the Mental Health (Scotland) Act 1984 (c 36), s 127(1), Sch 3, para 42). As to the Mental Health Welfare Commission, see MENTAL HEALTH, vol 14, paras 1407–1409.
8 National Health Service (Scotland) Act 1978, s 97(2).

1523. Complaint to the Health Service Commissioner. A complaint to the Health Service Commissioner for Scotland may be made by any individual or by any body of persons, whether incorporated or not, except (1) a local authority or other authority or body constituted for purposes of the public service or of local government or for the purpose of carrying on under national ownership any industry or undertaking, or (2) any other authority or body whose members are appointed by Her Majesty or any minister of the Crown or government department or whose revenues consist wholly or partly of money provided by Parliament[1]. In certain circumstances the health board, the Common Services Agency or the Scottish Dental Practice Board, being the body subject to investigation, may itself refer a complaint to the commissioner[2].

Unless the commissioner otherwise allows, the complaint must be made in writing to him by or on behalf of the person aggrieved not later than twelve months from the day on which the matters alleged first came to his notice[3]. In appropriate circumstances a complaint may be made by a personal representative or a person on behalf of the person aggrieved[4].

1 National Health Service (Scotland) Act 1978 (c 29), s 94(1).
2 Ibid, s 94(5) (substituted by the Parliamentary and Health Service Commissioners Act 1987 (c 39), s 9).
3 National Health Service (Scotland) Act 1978, s 94(3). For the meaning of 'person aggrieved', see para 1522, note 4, above.
4 Ibid, s 94(2).

1524. Investigation of complaint by the Health Service Commissioner. Before investigating a complaint, the Health Service Commissioner for Scotland must normally satisfy himself that it has been brought, by or on behalf of the person aggrieved, to the notice of the body subject to investigation, and that that body has been afforded a reasonable opportunity to investigate and reply to it[1].

Certain provisions of the Parliamentary Commissioner Act 1967 apply with necessary modifications to the procedure to be followed before the commissioner[2].

If the commissioner decides not to conduct an investigation, he must send a statement of his reasons for doing so to (1) the complainant, (2) any member of the House of Commons who, to the commissioner's knowledge, assisted in the making of the complaint (or, if he is no longer a member, to such other member as the commissioner thinks appropriate), and (3) the body subject to investigation[3]. If he conducts an investigation, he must send a report of the result of the investigation to those persons and bodies and also to any person who is alleged in the complaint to have taken or authorised the action or failure to act complained of, and to the Secretary of State[4].

Where at any stage of his investigation the commissioner forms the opinion that the complaint relates partly to a matter which could be the subject of an investigation by the Parliamentary Commissioner for Investigation or the Health Service Commissioner for England and Wales he must, if he considers it necessary, inform the complainant of the steps necessary to initiate a complaint to that other commissioner and consult that other commissioner[5].

If after an investigation it appears to the commissioner that injustice or hardship has been caused to the person aggrieved in the alleged failure or action[6], and that the injustice or hardship has not been or will not be remedied, he may if he thinks fit make a special report to the Secretary of State, who must lay it before each House of Parliament[7]. The Commissioner must make an annual report, and may make such other reports as he thinks fit, to the Secretary of State, who must lay them before each House[8], and the commissioner may lay before each House such reports as he thinks fit[9].

Any report or statement made, sent or laid under these provisions is absolutely privileged for the purpose of the law of defamation[10].

1 National Health Service (Scotland) Act 1978 (c 29), s 94(4). However, this does not apply to a complaint made by an officer of the body subject to investigation on behalf of the person aggrieved (defined in para 1522, note 4, above) if the officer is authorised under s 94(2) (see para 1523 above) to make the complaint: s 94(4).
2 Ibid, s 95, applying with modifications the Parliamentary Commissioner Act 1967 (c 13), s 7 (procedure in respect of investigations), s 8 (evidence), s 9 (obstruction and contempt) and s 11 (except s 11(4)) (secrecy of information): see TRIBUNALS AND INQUIRIES.
3 National Health Service (Scotland) Act 1978, s 96(3) (amended by the Parliamentary and Health Service Commissioners Act 1987 (c 39), s 5(3)).
4 National Health Service (Scotland) Act 1978, s 96(1) (amended by the Health Services Act 1980 (c 53), ss 9(5), 25(4), Sch 2, para 11, Sch 7, and the Parliamentary and Health Service Commissioners Act 1987, s 5(1)).
5 National Health Service (Scotland) Act 1978, s 95A (added by the Parliamentary and Health Service Commissioners Act 1987, s 4(5)).
6 Ie in the circumstances described in the National Health Service (Scotland) Act 1978, s 93(2): see para 1522 above.
7 Ibid, s 96(4) (amended by the Health Services Act 1980, Sch 2, para 11, Sch 7).
8 National Health Service (Scotland) Act 1978, s 96(5) (as so amended).
9 Ibid, s 96(6) (as so amended).
10 Ibid, s 96(7).

13. NURSING HOMES AND PRIVATE HOSPITALS

(1) NURSING HOMES

1525. Meaning of 'nursing home'. In the Nursing Homes Registration (Scotland) Act 1938, 'nursing home' means:
(1) any premises used, or intended to be used, for the reception of, and the provision of nursing for, persons suffering from any sickness, injury or infirmity;
(2) any maternity home[1]; and
(3) any premises not falling within head (1) or head (2) which are used, or intended to be used, for the provision of any of the following services: the carrying out of surgical procedures under anaesthesia; the termination of pregnancies; endoscopy; haemodialysis or peritoneal dialysis[2].
Excluded from the definition are:
(a) any hospital or other premises maintained by a government department or local authority or any other authority or body established or incorporated by or under any local Act or by royal charter;
(b) any private hospital within the meaning of the Mental Health (Scotland) Act 1984[3];
(c) any sanatorium provided at a school or educational establishment and used or intended to be used solely by students, staff and their families;
(d) any first aid or treatment room at factory premises, at premises to which the Offices, Shops and Railway Premises Act 1963 (c 41) applies or at a sports ground, show ground or place of public entertainment;
(e) any premises used or intended to be used, wholly or mainly, by a medical practitioner for the purpose of consultations with his patients, by a dental practitioner or chiropodist for treating patients, or for the provision of occupational health facilities;
(f) any premises used, or intended to be used, wholly or mainly as a private dwelling; and
(g) any premises excepted by regulations made by the Secretary of State[4].

1 'Maternity home' means any premises used or intended to be used for the reception of pregnant women or of women immediately after childbirth: Nursing Homes Registration (Scotland) Act 1938 (c 73), s 10(1).
2 Ibid, s 10(2) (added by the Health Services Act 1980 (c 53), s 16, Sch 4, para 14).
3 In the Mental Health (Scotland) Act 1984 (c 36), 'private hospital' means any premises used or intended to be used for the reception of, and the provision of medical treatment for, patients subject to detention under that Act, not being a hospital vested in the Secretary of State, a State hospital, or any other premises managed by a government department or provided by a local authority: s 12(2).
4 Nursing Homes Registration (Scotland) Act 1938, s 10(3)(a)–(g) (as added: see note 2 above).

1526. Offences relating to the registration of nursing homes. If any person carries on a nursing home without being duly registered in respect of it he is guilty of an offence and liable on summary conviction to a fine not exceeding the prescribed sum or, on conviction on indictment, to a fine[1], and if any person carries on a nursing home in contravention of a condition of his registration in respect of that home he is guilty of an offence under the Nursing Homes Registration (Scotland) Act 1938[2].

Where a company is convicted of an offence against the Act, the chairman and every director and every officer concerned in its management is guilty of the like offence unless he proves that the offence took place without his knowledge and consent[3].

1 Nursing Homes Registration (Scotland) Act 1938 (c 73), s 1(1) (amended by the Health Services Act 1976 (c 83), s 19(4)). The penalty on summary conviction is amended by the Criminal Procedure (Scotland) Act 1975 (c 21), s 289B (added by the Criminal Law Act 1977 (c 45), s 63(1), Sch 11, para 5, and substituted by the Criminal Justice Act 1982 (c 48), s 55(2)). The prescribed sum is £2000: Criminal Procedure (Scotland) Act 1975, s 289B(6) (as so added and substituted, and amended by the Increase of Criminal Penalties etc (Scotland) Order 1984, SI 1984/526, art 3).
2 Nursing Homes Registration (Scotland) Act 1938, s 1(1A) (added by the Health Services Act 1980 (c 53), s 16, Sch 4, para 7). A person guilty of an offence under the Nursing Homes Registration (Scotland) Act 1938 for which no other penalty is specified is liable on summary conviction to a fine not exceeding level 4 on the standard scale (ie £1000), and, in the case of a continuing offence, to a further fine not exceeding £2 for each day on which the offence continues after conviction: s 8(1) (amended by the Criminal Procedure (Scotland) Act 1975, s 289C, Sch 7C (added by the Criminal Law Act 1977, Sch 11, paras 5, 13); Criminal Penalties etc (Scotland) Order 1984, art 4.
3 Nursing Homes Registration (Scotland) Act 1938, s 8(2).

1527. Registration of nursing home. Application for the registration of a nursing home is to be made in writing to the health board in whose area the home is situated in the prescribed form, accompanied by a fee of £100[1]. On receipt of the application the board must register the applicant in respect of the home and issue a certificate of registration[2], except that it may by order refuse to register the applicant if it is satisfied that:

(1) he or any person to be employed at the home is not a fit person, by reason of age, conduct or otherwise, to carry on or be employed at the home[3]; or

(2) the home or any premises to be used in connection with it are not fit, because of situation, construction, state of repair, accommodation, staffing or equipment, to be used for a nursing home of the description in the application, or that they are to be used for purposes which are improper or undesirable[4]; or

(3) the home or premises include works executed in contravention of the provisions of the Health Services Act 1976 which control certain constructions and extensions[5]; or

(4) the use of the home or premises is in contravention of any term in an authorisation under that Act of such constructions or extensions[6]; or

(5) in the case of a nursing home other than a maternity home[7], (a) the home will not be in the charge of a registered medical practitioner or a qualified

nurse[8], or (b) any condition imposed by the health board by notice requiring the presence on duty at specified times of a specified number of qualified nurses is not or will not be fulfilled[9]; or

(6) in the case of a maternity home, (a) the home will not be in the charge of a registered medical practitioner or a certified midwife and qualified nurse, or (b) any condition imposed by the health board by notice requiring the presence on duty at specified times of a specified number of certified midwives is not or will not be fulfilled[10].

It is a condition of registration that the number of persons kept at any time in the home (excluding the staff and their families) must not exceed the number specified in the certificate of registration[11]. The health board may also include in the certificate conditions regulating the age, sex or other category of persons who may be received into the home[12]. On written application by the person registered the board may vary any condition either for a definite or an indefinite period[13].

The certificate of registration must be displayed in a conspicuous place in the home, and if it is not the person carrying on the home is guilty of an offence against the Nursing Homes Registration (Scotland) Act 1938[14].

1 Nursing Homes Registration (Scotland) Act 1938 (c 73), s 1(2) (amended by the National Health Service (Scotland) Act 1972 (c 58), s 64(1), Sch 6, para 71). For the form and as to the fee, see the Nursing Home Registration Regulations (Scotland) 1938, SR & O 1938/1505, reg 3, Sch 1 (both substituted by SI 1981/977). For the meaning of 'nursing home', see para 1525 above.
2 Nursing Homes Registration (Scotland) Act 1938, s 1(3) (as so amended).
3 Ibid, s 1(3) proviso (a).
4 Ibid, s 1(3) proviso (b).
5 Ibid, s 1(3) proviso (bb) (added by the Health Services Act 1976 (c 83), s 19(1), (2)), referring to a contravention of s 12(1) of the 1976 Act, for which see para 1541 below.
6 Nursing Homes Registration (Scotland) Act 1938, s 1(3) proviso (bc) (added by the Health Services Act 1980 (c 53), s 16, Sch 4, para 7), referring to a contravention of an authorisation under the Health Services Act 1976, s 13, for which see para 1538 below.
7 For the meaning of 'maternity home', see para 1525, note 1, above.
8 'Qualified nurse' in this paragraph means a nurse possessing such qualifications as may be specified in a notice served by the health board on the person carrying on the home: Nursing Homes Registration (Scotland) Act 1938, s 1(3A) (as added: see note 6 above). In preparing any such notice the board must have regard to the class of patients for whom nursing care is or is to be provided: s 1(3C) (as so added).
9 Ibid, s 1(3) proviso (c) (substituted by the Health Services Act 1980, Sch 4, para 7), referring to the condition mentioned in s 1(3B) (as so added). In preparing any such notice the board must have regard to the class and number of patients for whom nursing care is or is to be provided: s 1(3C) (as so added).
10 Ibid, s 1(3) proviso (d) (as so substituted), referring to the condition mentioned in s 1(3B) (as so added). See also s 1(3C), and note 9 above.
11 Ibid, s 1(3D) (as so added).
12 Ibid, s 1(3E) (as so added).
13 Ibid, s 1(3F), (3G) (as so added).
14 Ibid, s 1(4). For the penalty, see para 1526, note 2, above.

1528. Cancellation of registration of nursing home. A health board may at any time cancel the registration of a person in respect of a nursing home:

(1) on any ground which would entitle it to refuse an application for registration[1], or
(2) on the ground that the person has been convicted of an offence under the Nursing Homes Registration (Scotland) Act 1938, or that another person has been convicted of such an offence in respect of that home, or
(3) on the ground that any of the conditions of the registration[2] has not been complied with[3].

On the registration of a person being cancelled, the holder of the certificate of registration must forthwith deliver it up to the health board[4].

1 For the grounds for refusing registration, see para 1527 above. However, (1) where a person's registration was in force immediately before 1 August 1981, a health board may not cancel the registration on any ground mentioned in heads (5) and (6) in para 1527 before the expiry of three months from the service of the relevant notice referred to in those heads; and (2) in the case of a person registered in respect of a maternity home under any enactment repealed by the Nursing Homes Registration (Scotland) Act 1938 (c 73), a health board may not cancel the registration for non-compliance with the requirements of head (6) in para 1527 before the expiry of three months after it has given written notice requiring compliance: s 2(1) proviso (a), (b) (amended by the National Health Service (Scotland) Act 1972 (c 58), s 64(1), Sch 6, para 72, and the Health Services Act 1980, s 16, Sch 4, para 8).

2 Ie any condition imposed under the Nursing Homes Registration (Scotland) Act 1938, s 1(3D)–(3G), for which see para 1527 above.

3 Ibid, s 2(1) (as amended: see note 1 above).

4 Ibid, s 2(2) (amended by the National Health Service (Scotland) Act 1972, Sch 6, para 72).

1529. Notice of and appeal against refusal or cancellation of registration. Before making an order refusing or cancelling the registration of a nursing home the health board must give to the applicant or the person registered not less than fourteen days' notice of its intention to make the order and giving him the opportunity of showing cause why the order should not be made[1]. On making such an order the board must send a copy to the applicant or person registered[2]. Any person aggrieved by the order may within fourteen days after the copy order was sent to him appeal to the sheriff, whose decision is final[3]. The order does not come into force until the expiration of fourteen days after it was made or until any appeal has been decided or withdrawn[4].

1 Nursing Homes Registration (Scotland) Act 1938 (c 73), s 3(1) (amended by the National Health Service (Scotland) Act 1972 (c 58), s 64(1), Sch 6, para 72).

2 Nursing Homes Registration (Scotland) Act 1938, s 3(2) (as so amended).

3 Ibid, s 3(3) (as so amended).

4 Ibid, s 3(4).

1530. Conduct and inspection of nursing homes. The Secretary of State is empowered to make regulations as to the records to be kept at nursing homes and the notices to be given to the health board of deaths there[1], and as to the conduct and inspection of nursing homes and the production and inspection of their records[2].

1 Nursing Homes Registration (Scotland) Act 1938 (c 73), s 4(1). See the Nursing Homes Registration Regulations (Scotland) 1938, SR & O 1938/1505, reg 4, and reg 5 (amended by SI 1974/1182).

2 Nursing Homes Registration (Scotland) Act 1938, s 3A (added by the Health Service Act 1980 (c 53), s 16, Sch 4, para 9). See the Nursing Homes Registration Regulations (Scotland) 1938, reg 6 (added by SI 1981/977).

1531. Exemption of nursing homes. A health board may grant, in respect of any hospital or similar institution not carried on for profit, but subject to conditions, exemption from the operation of the Nursing Homes Registration (Scotland) Act 1938[1]. The exemption may be withdrawn at any time, but will normally be effective for one year[2]. Any person aggrieved by the refusal or withdrawal of the exemption, or by the conditions attached to it, may appeal to the Secretary of State[3].

The Secretary of State, if satisfied that a nursing home will be carried on in accordance with the practice and principles of the Church of Christ Scientist, may grant exemption from the operation of the Act[4] on condition that the home adopt and use the name of Christian Science house[5].

1 Nursing Homes Registration (Scotland) Act 1938 (c 73), s 6(1) (amended by the National Health Service (Scotland) Act 1972 (c 58), s 64(1), Sch 6, para 75).

2 Nursing Homes Registration (Scotland) Act 1938, s 6(2) (as so amended).
3 Ibid, s 6(3) (as so amended).
4 Ibid, s 7(1) (amended by the Health Services Act 1980 (c 53), s 16, Sch 4, para 12).
5 Nursing Homes Registration (Scotland) Act 1938, s 7(2).

(2) PRIVATE MENTAL HOSPITALS

1532. Obligation to register private mental hospitals. Every private hospital within the meaning of the Mental Health (Scotland) Act 1984[1] must be registered[2]. A person who carries on a private hospital which is not registered is guilty of an offence and liable on summary conviction to a fine not exceeding the statutory maximum or on conviction on indictment to a fine[3].

1 For the meaning of 'private hospital' in that Act, see para 1525, note 3, above.
2 Mental Health (Scotland) Act 1984 (c 36), s 12(1).
3 Ibid, s 16(1). 'The statutory maximum' means the prescribed sum (for which see para 1526, note 1, above): Interpretation Act 1978 (c 30), s 5, Sch 1 (amended by the Criminal Justice Act 1988 (c 33), s 170(1), Sch 15, para 58(b)).

1533. Registration of private mental hospitals. Application for the registration of premises as a private hospital must be made in writing to the Secretary of State by or on behalf of the person proposing to carry on the hospital, with a fee of £1[1]. The Secretary of State may (but is not obliged to[2]) register the premises and issue a certificate of registration[3], which must specify the maximum number of persons who may at any one time receive care or treatment in the hospital and such conditions as the Secretary of State considers appropriate[4], and which will lapse after five years but which is renewable on a fresh application[4]. However, he may not issue a certificate unless he is satisfied that:

(1) the person proposing to carry on the hospital is a fit person for the purpose having regard to his age, conduct and other relevant considerations;
(2) the premises are fit to be used for a private hospital;
(3) neither the hospital nor any premises to be used in connection with it include works executed in contravention of the provisions of the Health Services Act 1976 controlling certain constructions and extensions[6];
(4) the arrangements proposed for patients are suitable and adequate; and
(5) the medical and nursing staff proposed is adequate and suitably trained and qualified[7].

The certificate of registration must be kept fixed conspicuously in the hospital, and if it is not the person carrying on the hospital is guilty of an offence[8].

1 Mental Health (Scotland) Act 1984 (c 36), s 12(3). For the meaning of 'private hospital', see para 1525, note 3, above.
2 Ibid, s 13(2).
3 Ibid, s 12(4).
4 Ibid, s 12(5).
5 Ibid, s 12(6).
6 Ie the Health Services Act 1976 (c 83), s 12(1): see para 1541 below.
7 Mental Health (Scotland) Act 1984, s 13(1)(a)–(e).
8 Ibid, s 12(7). He is liable on summary conviction to a fine not exceeding level 1 on the standard scale and in the case of a continuing offence to a further fine of £2 for each day on which the offence continues after conviction: s 16(2). Level 1 is £50: Increase of Criminal Penalties etc (Scotland) Order 1984, SI 1984/526, art 4.

1534. Cancellation of registration of private mental hospitals. The Secretary of State may at any time cancel the registration of a private mental hospital on any ground on which he might have refused to register it, or on the ground that the person carrying on the hospital has been convicted of an offence under the Mental Health (Scotland) Act 1984[1]. On such cancellation the person carrying on the hospital must deliver up the certificate of registration to the Secretary of State[2]. Where at the time of the cancellation a patient is liable to be detained on the premises concerned, the registration continues in force for a period of twenty-eight days or until every such patient has ceased to be so liable, whichever first occurs[3].

1 Mental Health (Scotland) Act 1984 (c 36), s 15(1).
2 Ibid, s 15(2).
3 Ibid, s 15(3).

1535. Control of private mental hospitals. Any person carrying on a private mental hospital must:
(1) keep it open to inspection at all reasonable times;
(2) keep such registers as may be prescribed, and keep them open to inspection;
(3) ensure that the conditions specified in the certificate of registration are complied with; and
(4) afford to the Mental Welfare Commission for Scotland all facilities (including inspection facilities) as are necessary for the commission to exercise its statutory functions[1].
Failure to comply with these requirements is an offence[2].

The Secretary of State must ensure by regular inspection that the private hospital is being properly carried on, and persons authorised by him have powers of entry and inspection[3] and may interview any patient in private[4].

1 Mental Health (Scotland) Act 1984 (c 36), s 14(1)(a)–(d). As to the commission, see MENTAL HEALTH, vol 14, paras 1407–1409.
2 Ibid, s 14(1). For the penalty, see para 1533, note 8, above.
3 Ibid, s 14(2).
4 Ibid, s 14(3).

(3) HOSPITAL BUILDING CONTROL

1536. Notification of hospital building work. Except in the case of works that are to be executed or a change that is to be made by or on behalf of the Crown or for the purposes of a visiting force[1], any person who proposes to make (1) an application for planning permission for any notifiable works[2], or (2) a notifiable change[3], must, before doing so, notify the Secretary of State of the proposal by giving notice in the prescribed form[4]. The notice must contain prescribed information about the notifiable works and the purposes for which the hospital premises are to be used, or about the notifiable change[5]. On receipt of the notice the Secretary of State must issue a written acknowledgment stating the date of receipt and acknowledging that it complies with the statutory requirements[6]. This acknowledgment is to be conclusive evidence in any proceedings for an offence[7] of failing to comply with these requirements[8].

1 Health Services Act 1976 (c 83), s 14(6) (substituted by the Health Services Act 1980 (c 53), s 14(3)). For the meaning of 'visiting force', see the Health Services Act 1976, s 20.
2 'Notifiable works' means (1) works for the construction of hospital premises or an extension of hospital premises, or (2) works for converting any premises into hospital premises, not being, in either case, works for which an authorisation is required: s 14(7).
   'Hospital premises' means premises at which there are or are to be facilities for the provision of hospital services, and 'hospital services' means all or any of the following services, namely the

carrying out of surgical procedures under general anaesthesia; obstetrics; radiotherapy; haemo-dialysis or peritoneal dialysis; pathology or diagnostic radiology: ss 12(2), 20 (amended by the Health Services Act 1980, ss 12(1), 15, Sch 3, para 5).

'Extension', in relation to hospital premises, means works designed to extend, adapt or be used in conjunction with the hospital premises, or to extend, adapt or be used in conjunction with them: Health Services Act 1976, s 14(7). 'Authorisation' means an authorisation required by s 12(1) (for which see para 1537 below): s 20.

3 'Notifiable change' means (1) any change in the nature or extent of the hospital services provided at controlled premises, or (2) any change in the facilities or the number of beds provided at any premises which results in their becoming controlled premises: ibid, ss 14(7), 20 (amended by the Health Services Act 1980, s 14(4), Sch 3, para 5). 'Controlled premises' means hospital premises which provide or will provide beds for the use of patients, being hospital premises (a) in the case of which the number of beds which are or will be so provided is 120 or more, or (b) which are or are to be situated in an area designated by the Secretary of State under the Health Services Act 1976, s 12(2A) (added by the Health Services Act 1980, s 12(2)): Health Services Act 1976, s 12(2) (amended by the Health Services Act 1980, s 12(1)).

4 Health Services Act 1976, s 14(1) (amended by the Health Services Act 1980, ss 9(5), 14(1), Sch 2, paras 1, 3). For the prescribed form, see the Health Services (Notification) Regulations 1980, SI 1980/1201, Schedule.

5 Health Services Act 1976, s 14(2) (amended by the Health Services Act 1980, s 14(2)).

6 Health Services Act 1976, s 14(3) (amended by the Health Services Act 1980, Sch 2, para 1).

7 Ie an offence under the Health Services Act 1976, s 18(2)(a), for which see para 1541 below.

8 Ibid, s 14(4).

1537. Necessity for authorisation for hospital building work.

Subject to the two exceptions detailed below, no person may execute any controlled works[1] unless:

(1) he is authorised in writing by the Secretary of State to do so and the works are in accordance with the authorisation; or

(2) the works are executed in accordance with planning permission granted otherwise than by a development order either before 22 November 1976 or in consequence of an application for such permission made before 12 April 1976[2].

This does not, however, apply:

(a) in the case of works that are to be executed or a change that is to be made by or on behalf of the Crown or for the purposes of a visiting force[3], or

(b) in the case of works for the construction of a controlled extension[4] of controlled premises[5] if (a) the premises are situated elsewhere than in an area designated by the Secretary of State[6] and (b) the premises were constructed as controlled premises, or were converted into controlled premises, and (c) where the works will enable additional beds to be provided, the aggregate number of additional beds which will then have been provided at the premises since the beginning of the current three-year period (or, if later, the time when the premises were constructed or converted) will not exceed the permitted number[7].

1 'Controlled works' means (1) works for the construction of controlled premises or of a controlled extension of controlled premises, or (2) works for converting any premises into controlled premises: Health Services Act 1976 (c 83), ss 12(2), 20. 'Controlled premises' is defined in para 1536, note 3, above. 'Controlled extension', in relation to controlled premises, means works designed (a) to extend, adapt or be used in conjunction with the controlled premises, or (b) to extend or adapt works used in conjunction with them: s 12(2).

2 Ibid, s 12(1)(a), (b) (amended by the Health Services Act 1980 (c 53), ss 9(5), 13(1), Sch 2, para 1).

3 Health Services Act 1976, s 12(3).

4 For the meaning of 'controlled extension', see note 1 above.

5 For the meaning of 'controlled premises', see para 1536, note 3, above.

6 Ie designated under the Health Services Act 1976, s 12(2A) (added by the Health Services Act 1980, s 12(2)): see para 1539 below.

7 Health Services Act 1976, s 12(4)(a), (b) (added by the Health Services Act 1980, s 13(2)). 'Three-year period' means the three-year period beginning with 8 August 1980 and each

successive three-year period; and 'permitted number', in relation to a three-year period, means one-fifth of the number of beds provided at the premises in question at the beginning of that period or, if later, the time when the premises were constructed or converted: Health Services Act 1976, s 12(5) (as so added).

1538. Authorisation for hospital building work. An application for planning permission for works that consist of or include controlled works is of no effect unless it is accompanied by a copy of an authorisation in force for all of those works in the district of the planning authority[1].

An application for an authorisation must be made to the Secretary of State[2] in the prescribed form with the prescribed fee of £250[3]. Regulations provide for the procedure in connection with the application, the procedure at hearings held by persons appointed by the Secretary of State, and the making of decisions by the Secretary of State[4].

On receipt of the application the Secretary of State must consider whether the execution of the works:

(1) would to a significant extent interfere with his performance of any duty imposed on him by the National Health Service (Scotland) Act 1978 (c 29) to provide accommodation or services of any kind, or

(2) would to a significant extent operate to the disadvantage of persons seeking or affording admission or access to any accommodation or services provided by him under that Act (whether as resident or non-resident patients) otherwise than as private patients[5].

In considering these matters the Secretary of State must have regard to:

(a) how much accommodation and what facilities are or will be provided at, and what are or will be the staffing requirements of, relevant hospital premises[6] in the area or areas served by the health service hospital or hospitals concerned;

(b) how much accommodation or additional accommodation the works would provide;

(c) what facilities or additional facilities the works would enable to be provided; and

(d) what staffing requirements or additional staffing requirements the works would give rise to[7].

Unless the Secretary of State is satisfied that the execution of the works would do either or both of the things mentioned in heads (1) and (2) he must grant the authorisation[8].

An applicant or any other person who appeared and was heard at a hearing may within three months appeal to the Court of Session on a point of law against the refusal by the Secretary of State of an application for an authorisation, and any person who appeared and was heard at a hearing (other than an applicant) may similarly appeal on a point of law against the grant of an application[9].

1 Health Services Act 1976 (c 83), s 15(1), (2), (5). For the meaning of 'controlled works', see para 1537, note 1, above.

2 Ibid, s 13(1) (amended by the Health Services Act 1980 (c 53), s 9(5), Sch 2, para 2). For the meaning of 'authorisation', see para 1536, note 2, above.

3 Health Services (Authorisation) Regulations 1980, SI 1980/1241, reg 3, Schedule.

4 See ibid, regs 4–7.

5 Health Services Act 1976, s 13(2)(a), (b) (amended by the Health Services Act 1980, ss 9(5), 15, Sch 2, para 1, Sch 3, para 2(1)).

6 'Relevant hospital premises' means hospital premises (defined in para 1536, note 2, above) occupied otherwise than by or on behalf of the Crown or a visiting force: Health Services Act 1976, ss 12(2), 20 (amended by the Health Services Act 1980, s 12(1), Sch 3, para 5).

7 Health Services Act 1976, s 13(3)(a)–(d) (substituted by the Health Services Act 1980, Sch 3, para 2(2)).

8 Health Services Act 1976, 13(2) (amended by the Health Services Act 1980, Sch 2, para 2).
9 Health Services Act 1976, s 17(1), (2)(b), (3) (amended by the Health Services Act 1980, Sch 2, para 5). From the Court of Session appeal lies to the House of Lords: Health Services Act 1976, s 17(8).

1539. Designation of area. If on an application by a health board the Secretary of State is satisfied that relevant hospital premises[1] in the whole or part of its area provide or will provide, if taken together, 120 or more beds for the use of patients[2], he may, after consulting such persons and representative bodies as appear to him to be concerned, by regulations designate the whole or, as the case may be, that part of the area as an area in which all hospital premises[3] which provide or will provide beds for the use of patients are to be controlled premises[4]. The regulations, which may contain transitional provisions, have effect for such period not exceeding five years as may be prescribed[5].

1 For the meaning of 'relevant hospital premises', see para 1538, note 6, above.
2 In determining how many beds relevant hospital premises will provide he must not take into account the proposed execution of any works unless an authorisation for them has been granted (see para 1538 above) or a contract for them has been entered into: Health Services Act 1976 (c 83), s 12(2B) (added by the Health Services Act 1980 (c 53), s 12(2)).
3 For the meaning of 'hospital premises', see para 1536, note 2, above.
4 Health Services Act 1976, s 12(2A) (as added: see note 2 above). For the meaning of 'controlled premises', see para 1536, note 3, above. He may not exercise this power unless, having regard to the matters mentioned in the Health Services Act 1976, s 13(3)(a) (see head (a) in para 1538 above), he considers that the execution of works which, if the power were exercised, would be controlled works (defined in para 1537, note 1, above) would be likely to interfere as mentioned in s 13(2)(a) or operate as mentioned in s 13(2)(b) (see heads (1) and (2) in para 1538 above): s 12(2C) (as so added).
5 Health Services Act 1976, s 12(2A)(a), (b) (as so added).

1540. Inspectors. The Secretary of State may appoint inspectors for the purposes of the provisions relating to the control of hospital building (except so far as they relate to notifiable works or the making of any notifiable change)[1]. Such an inspector has powers of entry and inspection in respect of controlled premises and power to enter on land and inspect controlled works, may require appropriate persons to grant him assistance and facilities for these powers and may call for relevant documents[2].

1 Health Services Act 1976 (c 83), s 16(4) (amended by the Health Services Act 1980 (c 53), ss 9(5), 15, Sch 2, para 4, Sch 3, para 3); Health Services (Inspectors) Regulations 1980, SI 1980/1202, reg 3. For the meaning of 'notifiable works' and 'notifiable change', see para 1536, notes 2, 3, above.
2 Ibid, regs 4, 5. For the meaning of 'controlled premises', see para 1536, note 3, above, and for the meaning of 'controlled works', see para 1537, note 1, above. For offences relating to inspectors, see para 1541 below.

1541–1600. Offences. Any person executing controlled works without an authorisation is guilty of an offence and liable on summary conviction to a fine not exceeding the prescribed sum or on conviction on indictment to a fine[2]. A person is also guilty of an offence, and is liable on summary conviction to a fine not exceeding level 5 on the standard scale[3], if he:

(1) without reasonable excuse fails to give due notification[4] in relation to an application for planning permission for any notifiable works or the making of a notifiable change[5]; or

(2) knowingly or recklessly furnishes a notice relating to such works or change which is false in a material particular[6]; or

(3) intentionally obstructs an inspector in the exercise of his powers of entry and inspection[7]; or

(4) without reasonable excuse fails to comply with any requirement imposed by an inspector[8].

1 Ie any person contravening the Health Services Act 1976 (c 83), s 12(1), for which see para 1537 above.
2 Ibid, s 18(1) (amended by the Criminal Procedure (Scotland) Act 1975 (c 21), s 289B(1)) (added by the Criminal Law Act 1977 (c 45), s 63(1), Sch 11, para 5, and substituted by the Criminal Justice Act 1982 (c 48), s 55(2)). For the prescribed sum, see para 1526, note 1, above.
3 Health Services Act 1976, s 18(2), (3) (amended by the Criminal Procedure (Scotland) Act 1975, ss 289F, 289G (added by the Criminal Justice Act 1982, s 54)). Level 5 is £2000: Increase of Criminal Penalties etc (Scotland) Order 1984, SI 1984/526, art 4.
4 Ie fails to comply with the requirements of the Health Services Act 1976, s 14(1) or (2), for which see para 1536 above.
5 Ibid, s 18(2)(a) (amended by the Health Services Act 1980 (c 53), s 15, Sch 3, para 4). For the meaning of 'notifiable works' and 'notifiable change', see para 1536, notes 2, 3, above.
6 Health Services Act 1976, s 18(2)(b).
7 Ibid, s 18(3)(a). As to inspectors, see para 1540 above.
8 Ibid, s 18(3)(b).

HERALDRY

The General Editors and author express warm appreciation of the advice given on this title by Lord Jauncey of Tullichettle as consultant.

1. INTRODUCTION

1601. General. 'Heraldry is that Science, which teacheth us to give, or know Arms, suitable to the Worth or Intention of the Bearer'[1].

Heraldry is the study of armorial bearings or, as they are sometimes called, coats of arms, ensigns armorial or arms. The coat of arms derived from the surcoat worn by knights over their armour, on which they displayed a symbolic pattern, which distinguished one knight from another in battle. These devices were repeated on the knight's shield and banner and were incorporated in his other flags. Later, the device was produced conventionally on a shield as a design used to mark a man's property.

As heraldry arose from the identification of the more important personages in battle, the feudal trains, it was the monarchy which began to assume control over the use of coats of arms, not only to ensure that there was no duplication of design, but to restrict the wearing of coat armour to those of sufficient feudal rank. From this arose the idea that to be armigerous was to be noble. Indeed, by Act of Parliament of 1429 all lairds were required to have a seal of arms and to send a copy thereof to the local sheriff court for recording[2].

1 Mackenzie *The Science of Heraldry* (1680); Mackenzie *Works* (1722) II, 575.
2 Service of Inquests and Retours Act 1429 (c 21) (APS i, 575).

1602. Armorial records. The armorial records of Scotland from which the early coats of arms of individual families can be ascertained are first the seals of arms which have been preserved either on charters or on other documents[1], and later the armorial manuscripts of the heralds. The earliest roll of arms in which Scottish arms appear is the *Armorial de Gelré* executed by Gelré Herault d'Armes between 1334 and 1369. The finest Scottish armorial is that by Sir David Lindsay of the Mount executed about 1542, which has been published in facsimile, as have extracts of other Scottish rolls of arms[2]. However, the foundation of the Scottish record of arms is the Public Register of All Arms and Bearings in Scotland which was established in 1672 pursuant to the Lyon King of Arms Act 1672 (c 47). This manuscript is preserved in the Lyon Court and is one of the finest heraldic armorials in the world.

1 J H Stevenson and M Wood *Scottish Seals of Arms* (1934).
2 Facsimile by W and D Laing (1822) of *Sir David Lindsay of the Mount's Armorial*; R R Stodart *Scottish Arms* (1881).

ESCROL

STANDARD

BORDURE
(for difference)

INESCUTCHEON
(with label)

SUPPORTER

COLLAR

DECORATION

CREST

BANNER

WREATH

MANTLING

HELMET

CORONET

SHIELD
(quartered)

SUPPORTER

COMPARTMENT

2. THE ACHIEVEMENT OF ARMS

1603. General. The achievement of arms includes all the heraldic devices to which the armiger may be entitled. The actual entitlement will depend on the social rank of the armiger concerned, because certain of the additaments are restricted to certain ranks or offices. The different components of the achievement are shown on the drawing opposite and are described in the paragraphs which follow.

1604. The shield. The basis of any achievement is the shield of arms. Without a shield, none of the other armorial additions can exist. On the shield are displayed devices such as geometric shapes, animals, birds or other objects, known as the 'charges'. The background of the shield is normally of one colour ('tincture') and the principal charge or charges of another colour. These two principal colours, usually a metal[1] and a colour[2] are called the 'livery colours'. The reason for combining a metal and a colour rather than two colours in the livery is the purely practical one of identification since it is far easier to see a red lion on a gold or silver background, than it is to see such a lion on a green or blue background. No doubt for this reason some survival rafts during the last war were painted with alternative red and yellow squares to provide a striking visual contrast. Prior to the Restoration of Charles II, a gentleman was entitled only to a shield of arms, while feudal barons and persons of higher rank were allowed shields, crests, mottoes and, where appropriate, supporters. Today a shield *simpliciter*, perhaps with a motto, is usually granted to a corporation, local authority or other corporate body. The shape of the shield is a matter for artistic licence and can vary through any of the conventional shield shapes, through ovals, roundels to square. The arms of ladies are depicted upon a diamond shaped shield, called a 'lozenge', or an oval shield.

1 The metals are 'or' (gold) and 'argent' (silver).
2 The colours most used are 'gules' (red), 'azure' (blue), 'vert' (green), 'purpure' (purple) and 'sable' (black). A number of furs are also used, principally 'ermine' (white with black tails), 'counter-ermine' (black with white tails) and 'vair' (blue and white). The inside of the mantling in the drawing in para 1603 above is of ermine.

1605. The helmet, mantling and wreath. Above the shield is placed a 'helmet befitting his degree' with a mantling. Heraldic rules determine the attitude and make up of the helmet for each rank. A salade helmet is usually granted to companies. The mantling is the cloth trim suspended from the top of the helmet and held in place by the wreath, which was designed to absorb the heat of the sun. As the mantling was liable to get cut in battle, it has allowed artists to use the mantling in most elaborate flowing designs around the arms. The colour rules for mantling are that the outside is of the principal colour from the shield and the lining, technically called 'doubling', is of the principal metal. Further, the Sovereign's mantling is gold doubled ermine, and peers and officers of state have crimson doubled ermine. The wreath is a skein of two colours of silk twisted together conventionally showing six alternative twists of the principal metal and colour of the shield, technically described as 'a wreath of the liveries'.

1606. The crest. To the shield may be added a crest upon a wreath of the liveries or, for those of chiefly or peerage rank, the crest may be shown as issuing from a crest coronet[1]. The crest originates from the stuffed animal or other device worn on top of the helmet by tournament knights. While there are many examples of crests which would be virtually impossible to wear on a helmet (such as the rising sun, or stars), it is normally a device which can be worn on a helmet. The attitude and direction in which the crest faces are laid down in the grant. Ladies and clergymen are not granted crests unless they are 'representatives' of their house, name or clan, when a crest is assigned to them for the heirs in their arms.

1   Sir Thomas Innes of Learney *Scots Heraldry* (2nd edn, 1956) p 32. The popular usage of the word 'crest' as meaning the full coat of arms is of course quite incorrect.

1607. The coronet or chapeau. If an armiger is entitled to a coronet, it is depicted above the shield and below the helmet. Peerage coronets follow the English form, although prior to the Union of 1603 there was a distinctive Scottish format[1]. The feudal baronage are entitled to chapeaux in lieu of coronets[2] with gules (red) doubled ermine for barons in possession of their barony, azure (blue) doubled ermine for barons no longer in possession, with the ermine altered to contre-ermine for Barons of Argyll and the Isles or of the Ancient Earldoms. Following the reorganisation of local government by the Local Government (Scotland) Act 1973 (c 65), the Lord Lyon assigned particular designs of coronet for each of the regional, islands, district and community authorities[3]. Mural, antique or celestial coronets are occasionally granted to distinguish soldiers, sailors or airmen. Particular ecclesiastical hats or mitres are assigned to the clergy, depending on their church and their rank within that church[4].

1   Sir Crispin Agnew of Lochnaw 'Scots Peerage Coronets' Coat of Arms (1980) vol 4, p 114.
2   Sir Thomas Innes of Learney 'Robes of the Feudal Baronage' lxxiv Proceedings of the Society of Antiquaries of Scotland 1946 p 149; Sir Thomas Innes of Learney *Scots Heraldry* (2nd edn, 1956) p 31.
3   R M Urquhart *Scottish Civil Heraldry* (1979).
4   Sir Thomas Innes of Learney *Scots Heraldry* (2nd edn, 1956) p 35.

1608. Supporters. Supporters are the human or animal figures depicted on either side of the shield, or occasionally singly behind it, which support the shield. They stand upon a mound known as the 'compartment'. In Scotland, a grant of supporters is confined to (1) peers and heirs of the (pre-1587) feudal baronage, (2) chiefs of substantial clans or families or established branch clans or families, (3) Knights of the Thistle or Grand Cross[1], and (4) certain high officials or persons upon whom the Lord Lyon in the exercise of his prerogative determines for good reason to grant supporters. Exterior additaments are inanimate objects granted to stand on either side of the shield and are assigned to chiefs of substantial clans or houses who do not quite qualify for supporters[2]. Such additaments are to be distinguished from the specific heraldic insignia borne by the holders of high office[3].

1   *Elliot of Brugh* 1957 SLT (Lyon Ct) 6.
2   *Leask of that Ilk* (1968) Lyon Register vol 52, p 16.
3   See para 1610 below.

1609. Banners, standards, guidons and pinsels. A shield of arms displayed on a square or rectangular flag may be used as a banner by all armigers. The correct size of banner for each feudal rank has been laid down by the Lord Lyon[1]. The standard is a long flag with the saltire or owner's arms in the hoist and the badges and motto in the fly. It is granted only to those of peerage, baronial or chiefly rank and the length (ranging from 8 yards for a king to 4 yards for a baron), reflects the rank of the bearer. Guidons, which are similar in design, but limited to 2 yards in length, are granted to chieftains and those of lairdly rank. The pinsel is a flag granted to clan chiefs only, and is for use by their appointed representative, when the chief is not present, as a symbol of the chief's authority.

1 Sir Thomas Innes of Learney *Scots Heraldry* (2nd edn, 1956) p 42.

1610. Badges and insignia of office. A badge is used to identify property and persons loyal to the armiger. The badges of the Kingdom of Scotland are the thistle and the St Andrew's Cross. An armiger's badge and particularly that of chiefs or heads of families is usually the crest within a belt and buckle emblazoned with the motto, although certain persons do have a separate and distinctive badge either for themselves or for their heritable offices. The badge of office of the Lord High Constable, an arm holding the sword of justice, is well known. Badges may be granted to companies or corporations which require to use them as, or in the nature of, a trade mark. Identificatory badges are granted to local authorities for use by their citizens[1].

Certain heraldic additaments or insignia of office may be granted or confirmed to the holders of appropriate dignities or offices. The badges of baronets or orders of chivalry are displayed below the shield, while insignia such as the swords of justice of the Lord Justice-General, the keys of keepers of castles or batons or wands of office are displayed in saltire behind the shield[2].

1 *Glenrothes New Town* (1984) Lyon Register vol 62, p 106.
2 *Earl of Lauderdale* (1952) 1985 SLT (Lyon Ct) 13. 'Displayed in saltire' means that the insignia stand crosswise.

1611. The motto. The motto, which may be in any language — English, Latin, Gaelic and Maori have been used — is normally depicted above the crest. The positioning is determined by the grant. Certain persons are entitled to two mottoes, and those of chiefly or lairdly rank are sometimes granted a 'Slughorn', or battle cry, which is depicted being shouted by their Slughorn Shouter.

3. THE LAW OF ARMS

1612. General. The law of arms may be divided into two branches. The first — better, perhaps, described as the rules of heraldry — is peculiar to the subject itself, and deals with the format and design of the coat of arms, the blazoning or describing of the arms and the rules which attribute particular additaments to particular ranks and offices. The second branch concerns the law of heraldry in the wider sense as one of the branches of the civil law of Scotland. Sir George MacKenzie of Rosehaugh recognised this division, writing in 1680 in the preface to his *Science of Herauldry, Treated as part of the Civil Law, and Law of Nations*, that

'for some had treated this Science as mere Law, without understanding the Practice of Blazoning, as Bartolus, Chaffaneus, etc, whilst others handled it as a Part of the Civil Law, as Guilim, Menestrier, Colombier, and others, without being bred to the Law which requires a whole Man, and his whole Age. To reconcile which two, I was induced to write some Observations . . .'[1].

The first aspect is best left to the heraldic writers, but those interested can pursue the subject in the standard text books[2]. This title will deal with the latter aspect, as it is of relevance to practising lawyers in Scotland.

1 Mackenzie *Works* (1722) II, 574.

2 Sir Thomas Innes of Learney *Scots Heraldry* (2nd edn, 1956); J H Stevenson *Heraldry in Scotland* (1914). For a lighter view, see Sir Iain Moncreiffe of that Ilk and Don Pottinger *Simple Heraldry Cheerfully Illustrated* (1953). Caution should be exercised in referring to English books because, while much is similar, there are important differences between the Scottish and the English heraldic rules. Examples of English books are C Boutell *Heraldry* (1983, ed J P Brooke-Little) and A C Fox-Davies *Complete Guide to Heraldry* (1985).

1613. The nature of arms. In Scotland a coat of arms is incorporeal heritable property, governed, subject to certain specialities, by the general law applicable to such property. Lord Robertson observed in *M'Donnell v M'Donald* that a right to arms:

> 'would involve a question of property, which a right to bear particular ensigns armorial undoubtedly is'[1].

In contrast, in England it has been observed:

> 'that the right to bear arms is not a matter cognizable by the common law, which seems to show that there is no property in arms in the legal sense, otherwise the courts of law would protect them'[2].

Thus the Scots armiger is afforded a protection by the law which appears to be available to his English cousin either not at all or only in exceptional cases in the High Court of Chivalry.

Further, a coat of arms is a fief annoblissant, similar to a territorial peerage or barony, the grant of which determines that the grantee

> 'and his successors in the same are, amongst all Nobles and in all Places of Honour to be taken, numbered, accounted and received as Nobles in the Noblesse of Scotland'[3].

This ennoblement confers a status and a precedence on the holder of the arms, whether a person or a corporate body[4].

Exactly what device amounts to a coat of arms has yet to be determined, but the modern view of the Lords Lyon and of the Procurator Fiscals of the Lyon Court appears to be that any device other than letters or numerals, displayed on a shield, lozenge, cartouche or rectangular banner or set upon a wreath, crest, coronet or chapeau amounts to an armorial bearing the display of which is subject to the provisions of the Lyon King of Arms Act 1672 (c 47).

1 *M'Donnell v M'Donald* (1826) 4 S 371 at 372 (NE 374 at 376).
2 *Manchester Corpn v Manchester Palace of Varieties Ltd* [1955] P 133 at 147, [1955] 1 All ER 387 at 392, Ct of Chivalry, per Lord Goddard, Surrogate.
3 Nobility clause in any grant of arms.
4 *Law Society of Scotland* 1955 SLT (Lyon Ct) 2.

1614. The right to bear or use arms. In terms of the Lyon King of Arms Act 1672 no person or corporate body in Scotland is entitled to bear or use a coat of arms unless those arms are recorded in their right in the Public Register of All Arms and Bearings in Scotland. The penalty for a breach of the statute is a fine of £100 Scots, with all the goods on which those arms are illegally displayed being escheat to the Crown or alternatively for the offending arms to be erased or defaced from any building or monument[1].

Arms come to be recorded in the Public Register of All Arms and Bearings in Scotland by reason of grant, confirmation or matriculation, all of which methods will be considered later[2].

The grantee and his successive heirs in the principal arms are entitled to use the arms on apparency for three generations, but thereafter require to rematriculate those arms to make up their title[3]. Cadets or collaterals of the grantee falling within the destination in the original grant may not use the arms until they have matriculated them in their own name with a suitable difference in terms of the Act of 1672.

The heir apparent or heir presumptive is entitled to bear the undifferenced arms charged with a three-point label[4] during his heir apparency or heir presumptiveship, and similarly the next heir bears the arms charged with a five-point label. Daughters are entitled to bear their father's arms on a lozenge during their lifetime, but unless they are heraldic heiresses they do not transmit any right in those arms.

It should be noted that in Scotland a person may be in right of two separate and distinct coats of arms either of which he may use at his pleasure to suit the occasion. The Earl of Erroll is in right of the plain undifferenced arms of Hay and a quartered coat of arms, and the Duke of Buccleuch is entitled to a separate coat of arms as proprietor of Granton Harbour[5].

The holder of a foreign coat of arms, including English arms, if he desires to use them in Scotland requires to matriculate those arms in his own name with, if necessary, an appropriate difference to distinguish them from any recorded Scottish coat of arms, before they may be used in Scotland. A temporary visitor to Scotland, if armigerous, is allowed as a matter of courtesy to use his arms in Scotland during a brief stay.

Members of an armigerous corporation may display the corporation's arms as a means of demonstrating their membership of that corporation on ties, blazer badges or official cars and the like, but if they wish to use the arms in a way which might imply that they are their personal arms, then 'Member of X' must be written below the arms. Thus any firm of solicitors as members of the Law Society of Scotland may use the Society's arms on its writing paper with 'Member of the Law Society of Scotland' written underneath the arms.

There is a misconception to the effect that corporations which have recorded armorial type trade marks under the Trade Marks Act 1938 (c 22) may use them in Scotland without recording them in the Public Register of All Arms and Bearings in Scotland. Such a corporation requires to record its trade mark by matriculation before it may lawfully be used in Scotland.

1 Lyon King of Arms Act 1672 (c 47); *Macrae's Trustees v Lord Lyon King-of-Arms* 1927 SLT 285, OH.
2 See paras 1615–1617 below.
3 Sir Thomas Innes of Learney *Scots Heraldry* (2nd edn, 1956) p 117.
4 A three-point label is shown in the inescutcheon in the drawing in para 1603 above.
5 *Earl of Erroll* (1980) Lyon Register vol 64, p 77; *Buccleuch* (1866) Lyon Register vol 7, folio 4.

1615. Grant of arms. The entire prerogative to grant arms has by sundry statutes been conferred on the Lord Lyon,

> 'and since at least 1542 the King of Scots has never himself granted a coat of arms or augmentation, the invariable practice being a Royal Warrant addressed to the Lord Lyon directing him to "give and grant" the specified arms or augmentation to the favoured subject'[1].

In terms of the Lyon King of Arms Act 1672 (c 47) the Lord Lyon 'may give Armes to vertuous and well-deserving Persones'. The Lord Lyon will consider petitions for grants of arms from natural and corporate persons who are domiciled in Scotland or who own heritage in Scotland, from citizens of any country in the Commonwealth (except Canada[2]) of Scots descent or from aliens (particularly those in the United States of America of Scots descent) who can show that they require to bear arms in Scotland[3]. The exercise of the royal prerogative in this respect by the Lord Lyon is discretionary and not subject to any appeal at the instance of a dissatisfied petitioner. It is not unknown for the Lord Lyon to refuse to grant arms.

This right to grant arms extends to the whole range of armorial additaments including crests, supporters, flags, badges and coronets. In this respect the powers of the Lord Lyon are considerably more extensive than those of the English Kings of Arms, who require the warrant of the Earl Marshal of England permitting a grant of arms or a warrant to grant supporters[4].

A coat of arms with any additaments is granted to the grantee and the heirs specified in the grant. In modern practice the destination is usually but not invariably to 'the petitioner and the other heirs of his grandfather'. If there is no reference to heirs in either the grant, or in the entry in the Public Register of All Arms and Bearings in Scotland, the presumption is that the grant is to the grantee and his heirs including collaterals bearing the name of the grantee[5]. The early entries in the register often do not include the destination, which then requires to be determined by reference to an extract which may include a specific destination, by reference to the subsequent descent of the arms from which a tailzied destination may be inferred or, in the last resort, from the presumption.

1 Sir Thomas Innes of Learney *Scots Heraldry* (2nd edn, 1956) p 10.
2 Canada now has its own heraldic authority established by letters patent from the Queen of Canada dated 4 June 1988.
3 As to the claims of the College of Arms in England to a Commonwealth jurisdiction, see CONSTITUTIONAL LAW, vol 5, para 719.
4 Commission of Colin Cole Esq as Garter Principal King of Arms in England, granting him 'authority, power and licence, with the consent of the Earl Marshal of England . . . of granting and appointing to eminent men Letters Patent of Arms and Crests'. The power to grant supporters still requires to be specifically conferred on the English Kings of Arms but not on the Lord Lyon: see *Elliot of Brugh* 1957 SLT (Lyon Ct) 6.
5 J H Stevenson *Heraldry in Scotland* (1914) p 335.

1616. Confirmation of arms. Where a petitioner is apparently in right to a coat of arms, but either the original grant is not in existence or there is some potential weakness in his title, then the Lord Lyon will 'Maintain Ratify and Confirm' the coat of arms to the petitioner and his heirs. A confirmation of arms by the Lord Lyon is the equivalent of a Crown charter of *novodamus* in respect of dignities or heritage, and secures the recipient against any defect in his title to the arms and acts as an original grant.

A confirmation of arms is used where there is no record of the original arms, although the petitioner by virtue of his position (for example as clan chief) is undoubtedly armigerous[1], for example where arms can be proved or presumed to have been in use by the petitioner's progenitors before the passing of the Lyon King of Arms Act 1672 (c 47). A confirmation may also be used where the chiefship is vacant and either the clan *derbfine* has selected a successor for presentation to the Lord Lyon for confirmation as chief[2] or the chiefly line is apparently extinct and the next cadet seeks confirmation as chief[3], or where the chiefly line has been forfeit but the family has later been restored to its former position without a formal restoration of the arms[4].

1 *MacNeil of Barra* (1806) Lyon Register vol 2, p 5, and (1915) Lyon Register vol 22, p 60; *Nicolson of Scorrybreac* (1934) Lyon Register vol 31, p 21.
2 *Morrison of Ruchdi* (1967) Lyon Register vol 51, p 19.
3 *Macnab of Macnab* 1957 SLT (Lyon Ct) 2.
4 *Lord Macdonald* 1950 SLT (Lyon Ct) 8; *Grahame of Duntrune and Claverhouse* 1960 SLT (Lyon Ct) 2.

1617. Matriculation. Successive heirs to the principal or undifferenced arms regularly rematriculate these arms every few generations to make up title to the armorial bearings or to alter the arms or the destination to take account either of succession to a new quartering or of a change in the family circumstances to resettle the arms on a new series of heirs. A rematriculation by progress is analogous to a general retour as regards representation and a special retour as regards title and pedigree, and is of great value in establishing the succession to headship of ancient families, clan chiefships, peerages and baronetcies[1].

Every person who can fall within the destination of arms is entitled to seek a matriculation of those arms in his own name with an appropriate difference, which is determined by the Lord Lyon. The petitioner requires to prove his relationship to the grantee of the arms. The differenced coat of arms assigned to the petitioner then descends to his heirs as nominated or implied in the extract of matriculation. Illegitimate children, provided they are acknowledged by their father, are entitled to matriculate their father's coat of arms with the difference appropriate to a natural child. Although adopted children formerly required to obtain a grant of arms in their own name, they are now allowed a matriculation of their adoptive father's arms with a special difference called a 'canton voided' to denote absence of blood-descent[2].

1 *Grant of Grant* 1950 SLT (Lyon Ct) 17; *Earl of Selkirk* (1945) 1985 SLT (Lyon Ct) 2.
2 Sir Thomas Innes of Learney *Scots Heraldry* (2nd edn, 1956) p 100; *Stewart* 1951 SLT (Lyon Ct) 3. A canton is a square, one-ninth of the area of the shield, in the upper left-hand corner.

1618. Cadency. Cadency is the system whereby a coat of arms may be differenced from the principal coat to demonstrate that the holder is a cadet of the family. The usual Scottish system of differencing is by the addition of a bordure round the shield wherein the colours or edging of the bordure conform to a system devised by Lyon Clerk Stoddart, which indicate the cadet's approximate position in the family[1]. Alternative systems such as quartering[2], changing a charge or tincture of the shield or adding an ordinary such as a chief or a new charge are also used[3]. The inclusion of a baronet's badge does not effect a differencing[4]. The crest, supporters and motto also require to be differenced. The motto of a cadet is usually differenced so that it answers the motto of the chief.

The heir apparent, whose armorial rights are no more than those of an heir presumptive[5], or heir presumptive may use a plain label of three points as a mark of difference and the next heir a label of five points, during the lifetime of the holder of the principal arms. A label of three points charged with particular devices is the difference assigned to those who should have been entitled to the principal arms, but for some reason have been by-passed, or to the heir male, when the succession has passed to the heir of line[6].

The bordure compony, the bend or baton sinister are the differences normally assigned to illegitimate children[7]. Adopted children are assigned a voided canton to indicate that there is no blood connection. It should be noted that the use of a coat of arms differenced for illegitimacy or adoption does not necessarily mean that that person is illegitimate or adopted because once the differenced arms are assigned, they may well have descended to the lawful heirs of the first illegitimate or adopted holder[8].

1 Sir Thomas Innes of Learney *Scots Heraldry* (2nd edn, 1956) plate XXI, p 79.
2 *Stewart Mackenzie v Fraser-Mackenzie* 1922 SC (HL) 39, 1922 SLT 18.
3 A charge is anything placed upon a shield. It may be an 'ordinary' (ie a shape, such as a chief, cross or chevron) or any other device. The charges shown in the four quarters of the shield in the drawing in para 1603 above are (1) three oak leaves, (2) a bordure, (3) a mullet, and (4) a bend. A tincture is a colour, metal or fur. A chief is a band occupying the top third of a shield.
4 *Cuninghame v Cunyngham* (1849) 11 D 1139.
5 *Dunbar of Kilconzie* 1986 SLT 463, HL.
6 J H Stevenson *Heraldry in Scotland* (1914) p 300; *Lord Gray* 1959 SLT (Lyon Ct) 2; *Dunbar of Kilconzie* (1980) Lyon Register vol 60, p 98. A three-point label is shown in the inescutcheon in the drawing in para 1603 above.

7 *Innes* p 109. A bordure compony is a bordure divided into sections. The bordure in the second quarter of the shield in the drawing in para 1603 above is 'counter-compony', ie a bordure compony further divided parallel with the sides of the quarter.

8 *Sholto Douglas* 1953 SLT (Lyon Ct) 11; *Douglas* 1953 SLT (Lyon Ct) 13. A canton is a square, one-ninth of the area of the shield, in the upper left-hand corner.

1619. Succession to arms: heir of line v heir male. Where no specific destination is incorporated in the grant or matriculation of arms and the last holder dies without heirs male of the body, the question arises as to who is entitled to the coat of arms and the family representation. The matter is by no means clear, although there is a general presumption in favour of the heir of line[1]. Each case will require to be determined on its own merits[2]. While there is a general presumption that heritage for which there is no specific destination descends to heirs, in armorial succession the so-called Jeffrey principle enunciated by Lord Jeffrey 'that the chief armorial dignities should follow the more substantial rights and dignities of the families' is usually applied[3] where there are landed estates or other dignities. In the absence of such estates or dignities the right of the heir of line usually prevails. Where the succession opens to heirs portioner, the arms being indivisible fall to the eldest alone[4]. Where the succession opens to the heir female, he or she is required to adopt or retain the name appropriate to the arms, and if he or she does not, the right may be superseded in favour of the next heir[5].

1 J H Stevenson *Heraldry in Scotland* (1914) p 355.

2 *Maclean of Ardgour v Maclean* 1941 SC 613, 1938 SLT 49, 1941 SLT 339, at 1941 SC 635 and 1938 SLT 57, and at 1941 SC 680, 681, and 1941 SLT 344, 345, per Lord Justice-Clerk Aitchison; and at 1941 SC 694 and 1941 SLT 353 per Lord Mackay.

3 *Cuninghame v Cunyngham* (1849) 11 D 1139 at 1152, per Lord Jeffrey.

4 *Mackintosh of Mackintosh* 1950 SLT (Lyon Ct) 2.

5 *Farquharson of Invercauld* 1950 SLT (Lyon CT) 13. An heir female can, of course, be a male, having derived his right through a female. Thus a grandson deriving right through his mother is the heir female of his maternal grandfather.

1620. Tailzied arms. Arms subject to a tailzie or entailed destination descend to the heir of provision in terms of the deed. Where there are prohibitions or conditions in the tailzie such as to require the heir to bear and use the name and arms alone or to bear and use the arms (which implicitly allows them to be used in conjunction with other names or arms), it is a question of interpretation of the deed as to whether the conditions have been complied with sufficiently to allow a matriculation in the name of the heir[1]. Where the heirs of provision under the deed are exhausted, the succession opens to the heir of line of the last heir infeft under the tailzie rather than to the heir of line of the entailer[2]. Where an entail of land provides that the heir succeeding under the tailzie is to bear a particular coat of arms, but those arms have not properly been constituted by the Lord Lyon, the heir is required to seek a grant or matriculation of appropriate arms from the Lord Lyon[3].

1 *Hunter v Weston* (1882) 9 R 492; *Munro of Foulis* 1953 SLT (Lyon Ct) 15 (matriculation allowed); *Smollet of Bonhill* 1959 SLT (Lyon Ct) 3 (matriculation allowed); *Munro-Lucas-Tooth of Teaninich* 1965 SLT (Lyon Ct) 2 (matriculation refused).

2 *Mackintosh of Mackintosh-Torcastle* 1950 SLT (Lyon Ct) 5.

3 *Moir v Graham* (1794) Mor 15537.

1621. Armorial additaments demonstrative of succession to higher dignities or heritable great offices. Certain armorial additaments are inextricably linked to particular dignities such as peerages or heritable great offices such as the Lord High Constable of Scotland. The armorial additaments descend to the same series of heirs as that dignity or heritable office. Accordingly, the establishment before the Lord Lyon of the right to succeed to those particular armorial additaments is demonstrative of a succession to that higher dignity or heritable office. Thus peers of Scotland seeking to establish their right to a Scottish peerage may petition the Lord Lyon for a rematriculation of arms 'with the insignia appropriate' to them as holders of the peerage[1]. Such matriculations are normally sufficient evidence of entitlement to a peerage to allow the matriculator to claim a writ of summons to the House of Lords[2]. Claims to baronetcies, and in particular to baronetcies of Nova Scotia, are proved by seeking a rematriculation of arms with a canton of arms of Nova Scotia or of the arms of Ulster (argent, a hand gules) as appropriate[3]. Claims to heritable offices are established by matriculating the additaments appropriate to the office claimed[4].

1 *Lady Ruthven of Freeland* 1977 SLT (Lyon Ct) 2.
2 254 HL Official Report (5th series) cols 380–389 (19 December 1963) and cols 939–943 (22 January 1964); Crispin Agnew of Lochnaw 'Peerage and Baronetcy Claims in the Lyon Court' (1981) 26 JLSS 311.
3 *Grant of Grant* 1950 SLT (Lyon Ct) 17.
4 *Livingstone of Bachuil* 1951 SLT (Lyon Ct) 5; *Earl of Lauderdale* (1952) 1985 SLT (Lyon Ct) 13.

1622. Transfer of arms. A coat of arms may be transferred *inter vivos* between living persons by a deed of resignation *in favorem* recorded in the Lyon Court Books followed by a rematriculation in the name of the tanist[1]. The arms may be transferred to a new heir, or the destination altered, by a deed of registration *in favorem* into the hands of the Lord Lyon for a regrant. This may be executed formally by deed of registration[2] or constructively by testament[3]. The chief of a clan or the holder of the principal arms may nominate his successor from within his own family for confirmation by the Lord Lyon on a matriculation[4], but if he wishes to settle the arms on a stranger in blood he can do this only with the prior approval of the Lord Lyon, which is likely to be forthcoming only in the most exceptional circumstances[5]. An armiger who is the sole proprietor of a company may execute a redeemable conveyance of a differenced version of his arms to the company so that the company can use them as a trade mark or symbol[6].

1 *Lamont v Lamont* (1953) Lyon Register vol 39, p 119; *Macdonnell of Scotus* (1983) Lyon Register vol 66, p 88.
2 *Macnab of Macnab* 1957 SLT (Lyon Ct) 2.
3 *Macpherson of Pitmain* 1977 SLT (Lyon Ct) 18.
4 *MacLeod of MacLeod* (1962) Lyon Register vol 46, p 91 (nomination by Dame Flora MacLeod of MacLeod of her nephew John, being the second son of her second daughter, as next chief of the MacLeods).
5 Sir Thomas Innes of Learney *Scots Heraldry* (2nd edn, 1956) p 126.
6 *James B Rintoul (Edinburgh) Ltd* 1950 SLT (Lyon Ct) 12.

1623. Proof of pedigree in armorial succession. The general rules of evidence apply to the proof of pedigree in the Lyon Court, subject to certain specialities. The normal rules for admissibility, and in particular the admissibility of documents, is applied, although older family histories and genealogical charts will be admitted in respect of those parts which could reasonably have been within the knowledge of the compiler[1]. The proof involved in proving the extinction of a senior *stirps*, except in peerage and baronetcy claims, is not the rigorous proof demanded by the Committee for Privileges[2], but follows the older practice in general and special retours, where after due advertisement of the claim *non apparentibus non existentibus presumuntur*[3]. This long established criterion is accepted because a wrongfully excluded senior *stirps* can sue a reduction of the matriculation within the prescriptive period. Evidence of physical resemblance is not admissible[4].

Pedigrees may be recorded in the Public Register of all Genealogies and Birth Brieves in Scotland conform to an interlocutor of the Lord Lyon. Such recorded pedigrees are accepted by the Committee for Privileges as sufficient evidence of heirship in Scots peerage claims[5].

1 W G Dickson *The Law of Evidence in Scotland* (3rd edn, 1887) paras 237, 1220–1222.
2 *Viscountcy of Dudhope and Earldom of Dundee* 1986 SLT (Lyon Ct) 2, Committee for Privileges.
3 Stair *Institutions* III, 5, 35; *Macnab of Macnab* 1957 SLT (Lyon Ct) 2 at 4.
4 *Grant v Countess of Seafield* 1926 SC 274, 1926 SLT 144.
5 *Viscountcy of Oxfuird* 1986 SLT (Lyon Ct) 8 at 13, Committee for Privileges, per Lord Fraser of Tullybelton; *Earldom of Annandale and Hartfell* 1986 SLT (Lyon Ct) 18 at 20, [1986] AC 319 at 329, Committee for Privileges, per Lord Keith of Kinkel.

1624. Prescription of Lyon Court decrees. The question of prescription of Lyon Court decrees has never been fully investigated. It has been held that negative prescription (now, by virtue of the Prescription and Limitation (Scotland) Act 1973, twenty years[1]) applies to Lyon Court decrees[2], but that Act preserves:

> 'any right to be served as heir to an ancestor or to take any steps necessary for making up or completing title to any interest in land'[3],

'land' being defined as including heritable property of any description[4]. In the *Dunbar* case[5] it was held that where arms descend under a tailzied destination a matriculation did not prescribe against the emergence of a nearer heir, because the question was one of succession. As a matriculation of arms is analogous to a retour or general or special service, the law of prescription as applied to retours with all its difficulties and contraditions probably applies to a Lyon Court decree.

From this it is possible to deduce that a confirmation of arms or a matriculation of arms descending under a destination to heirs probably will prescribe against any claimant after twenty years. In contrast, a matriculation of arms descending under a tailzied destination will prescribe after twenty years probably only in favour of the matriculator, but when the succession next opens, the rightful heir will again be allowed to take up the representation[6].

1 Prescription and Limitation (Scotland) Act 1973 (c 52), s 7(1).
2 *Stewart Mackenzie v Fraser-Mackenzie* 1922 SC (HL) 39 at 45, 1922 SLT 18 at 20, per Lord Dunedin; *Macnab of Macnab* 1957 SLT (Lyon Ct) 2 at 4.
3 Prescription and Limitation (Scotland) Act 1973, s 7(2), Sch 3, para (h).
4 Ibid, s 15(1).
5 *Dunbar of Kilconzie* 1985 SLT (Lyon Ct) 6.
6 *Fullarton v Hamilton* (1825) 1 W & S 410, HL. Cf *Neilson v Cochrane's Representatives* (1837) 15 S 365; and Bell *Principles* s 2024.

1625. Conflict of heraldic law. Within the United Kingdom there are two heraldic authorities, the Lord Lyon in Scotland and the English Kings of Arms operating from the College of Arms in London. The latter include Norroy and Ulster King of Arms, who claims to exercise the prerogative of the former Ulster King of Arms in Northern Ireland, although the constitutional authority by which an English King of Arms acting under the warrant of the Earl Marshal of England claims a jurisdiction in Northern Ireland is somewhat questionable. Many European states have heraldic authorities, as do some overseas states, including the authorities established in Canada by letters patent of the Queen of Canada dated 4 June 1988 and in Zimbabwe by the Armorial Bearing, Uniforms, Badges and Heraldic Representations Act 1976. As each authority has different criteria for either exercising a jurisdiction to grant arms or for recognising foreign grants of arms, and because the concept of what are arms is different, difficulties sometimes arise as to the recognition of each other's jurisdiction[1]. Within the Scottish conflict of law rules, specific rules have evolved for recognising foreign grants of arms. Once they have been recognised, if the person concerned wishes to, he may record those arms in the Public Register of All Arms and Bearings in Scotland. Honorary grants of arms in England are not recognised for recording in Scotland. Further, a person who is subject to the Lord Lyon's jurisdiction for a grant of arms, who also has a foreign grant of arms, will be required to obtain a grant of arms from the Lord Lyon rather than to matriculate his foreign coat for use in Scotland.

The general principle is that the Lord Lyon will recognise a grant of arms provided it is substantive and not an honorary grant of arms, made to a person bona fide within the jurisdiction of the granting authority. There is no difficulty about a person's holding more than one grant of arms from different jurisdictions, in the same way that one person may be granted and hold a number of peerages from different jurisdictions.

1 Sir Crispin Agnew of Lochnaw Bt 'The Conflict of Heraldic Law' 1988 JR 61.

1626. Marshalling of arms generally. Different coats of arms may be grouped or coordinated together to indicate alliances. The principal forms of marshalling include impalement, quartering and inescutcheon. These are considered in the paragraphs which follow.

1627. Impalement. Impalement is effected by dividing the shield vertically in half with a coat of arms depicted in each half. Where a husband and wife are both armigerous, their arms are impaled to illustrate the union of marriage. No matriculation is required, as such marshalling is an automatic right of marriage. Where a particular office has a coat of arms, these may be impaled with the personal arms of the office bearer, the official arms being on the dexter (right-hand) side (or left-hand side as observed from the front). Thus the Governors of Edinburgh Castle, the Lords Lyon, Lords Provost, and presidents of armigerous corporate bodies may impale the official arms with their personal arms.

1628. Quartering. Quartering is effected by dividing a shield into four quarters[1], each of which in turn may be further quartered, to represent a union of two or more coats of arms on a permanent basis. Where a person requires right to two or more coats of arms, a rematriculation is acquired to marshall officially the arms quarterly. Quartering represents (1) two or more family arms inherited by the same person, (2) inheritance hereditarily of arms of an earldom, lordship or fief or hereditary office[2]. A typical example of one person's inheriting two or more family arms occurs in the case of the eldest son of an armiger and of an heiress. A person with a *cumulo* coat is authorised to use the principal quarter alone on those occasions when it is impractical to use the full coat[3].

1 The shield in the drawing in para 1603 above is quartered.
2 *Earl of Caithness* (1969) Lyon Register vol 54, p 11; *Forbes of Waterton, Constable of Aberdeen* (*circa* 1672) Lyon Register vol 1, p 149.
3 Knights of the Thistle Stall Plates, Thistle Chapel, St Giles High Kirk; *Earl of Erroll* (1980) Lyon Register vol 64, p 77.

1629. Inescutcheon. In Scotland the 'inescutcheon *en surtout*' displays (1) arms of augmentation, (2) arms of earldoms, lordships or fiefs etc, or (3) the paternal arms. Chiefs entitled to a quarterly coat often use the paternal arms *en surtout* to indicate chiefship[1]. If arms of a fief are used *en surtout* this is often a mark of difference or cadetship, unless the shield is coroneted[2]. In England an inescutcheon may be adopted by a man married to a heraldic heiress where the shield is adopted 'in pretence' of his wife's heirship[3].

1 *Scott of Buccleuch, Duke of Buccleuch* (1975) Lyon Register vol 60, p 7.
2 Sir Thomas Innes of Learney *Scots Heraldry* (2nd edn, 1956) p 140.
3 A C Fox-Davies *Complete Guide to Heraldry* pp 539–541.

1630. Trade marks. Armorial bearings and trade marks are fundamentally separate systems of identification. However, where a manufacturer wishes to use in Scotland a trade mark which is armorial in design he will require to have those armorial bearings first granted by the Lord Lyon. The Trade Marks Act 1938 provides that 'It shall not be lawful to register as a trade mark or part of a trade mark any matter the use of which . . . would be contrary to law . . .'[1]. In Scotland, therefore, to register as a trade mark arms to which the applicant is not entitled in Scotland would be 'contrary to law'. Where it is apparent on the face of an application to register a trade mark under the 1938 Act, that it is armorial and to be used in Scotland, the Registrar will refer the application to the Lord Lyon for confirmation that the arms have been recorded in Scotland.

1 Trade Marks Act 1938 (c 22), s 11.

1631. Crest badges and identificatory badges. The clan crest badge of the chief's crest within a strap and buckle is well known in Scotland. It is the chief's badge for identifying his clansmen. It may by implied authority be worn (but not otherwise used) by any member of the clan (that is, bearer of the clan or a sept name), unless that person has been specifically disallowed by the chief. Persons who are not clan members but who have been accepted as members of the clan by the chief may wear his badge with the chief's specific authority. A clan chief may determine the membership of his clan[1]. The crest badge may not be used by clansmen by displaying it on such things as writing paper, china or signet rings unless the words 'An Ceann Cirean Cinnidh' or 'Member of Clan . . .' are printed below the crest badge. Manufacture of the crest badge without the chief's licence and authority is an actionable wrong, and the manufacturer may be prosecuted or interdicted in the Lyon Court. Licences to manufacture crest badges in exchange for a small royalty are issued on behalf of the chiefs by the Secretary of the Standing Council of Scottish Chiefs.

Chiefs or armigers in their own right wear their crest within a circlet without belt or buckle, ensigned if appropriate with a coronet or chapeau. Chiefs wear three eagle's feathers, chieftains two and armigers one eagle's feather, usually depicted symbolically as small silver eagle's feathers.

Certain local authorities and new towns have been granted identificatory badges for use by the inhabitants of the area 'to indicate their identity with or affection for the said . . .' Such badges can be used on vehicles, blazer badges, ties, football club strips and the like[2].

1 F Adams *Clan Septs and Regiments of the Scottish Highlands* (7th edn, 1965, by Sir Thomas Innes of Learney) ch VI.
2 *Ayrshire Vehicle Badge* (1969) Lyon Register vol 50, p 80; *Glenrothes New Town* (1984) Lyon Register vol 62, p 106.

1632. The royal arms. The royal arms are ensigns of public authority representing sovereignty over the dominions to which they relate. They pass with that sovereignty either by conquest, succession or election. Accordingly, to use the royal arms is to imply sovereignty over the kingdom, and the improper use of the royal arms is arguably treason because it asserts a claim to sovereignty, for 'he who usurps his Prince's Arms loses his head'[1]. The royal arms fall under the provisions of the Lyon King of Arms Act 1672 (c 47), and have been recorded in the Public Register of All Arms and Bearings in Scotland[2]. No portion of the royal arms — and this includes the 'double tressure' in the first and fourth quarters of the royal arms as used in Scotland — may be granted by the Lord Lyon without a royal warrant directed to him by the sovereign[3]. Lords Lieutenant and the Great Officers of State, such as the Lord High Commissioner, the Lord High Constable and others, have the power *virtute officii* to display the Royal Banner of Scotland. The Trade Marks Act 1938 provides certain restraints in the use of the royal arms in connection with trade[4], but these are more applicable to England than to Scotland, where the restraints already exist by law.

The Union with England Act 1707 (c 7), incorporating the Union Agreement, provides that 'The Ensigns Armorial of the said United Kingdom be such as Her Majesty shall appoint'[5]. The Act for the Union of Great Britain and Ireland 1800 provides that 'the Ensigns, Armorial Flags and Banners thereof shall be such as His Majesty, by his Royal Proclamation, under the Great Seal of the United Kingdom shall be pleased to appoint'[6]. The present form of the royal arms for the United Kingdom was established by royal proclamation on 26 July 1837 by Queen Victoria. The form of the royal arms of the United Kingdom as used in Scotland were recorded in the Public Register of All Arms and Bearings in Scotland. The royal arms in the Scottish form were authorised by royal proclamation of 24 April 1902 for use in the seals of the Secretary of State, the Signet and the justiciary seals. The form of the royal arms as used in Scotland since the Union has been the subject of much controversy[7].

1 Mackenzie *Works* (1722) II, 583.
2 *Matriculation of Blazon of Royal Arms of Scotland* (1960) Lyon Register vol 42, p 1.
3 *Royal Scottish Academy of Painting, Sculpture and Architecture* (1978) Lyon Register vol 59, p 107.
4 Trade Marks Act 1938 (c 22), s 61 (amended by the Patents, Designs and Trade Marks Act 1986 (c 39), s 2(2), Sch 2, para 6).
5 Treaty of Union between Scotland and England 1707, art I.
6 Union with Ireland Act 1800 (c 67), s 1, art I.
7 See 'Royal Styles, Titles and Armorial Bearings' in THE CROWN.

1633–1700. Protection of armorial rights.
Ensigns armorial, once granted, are the exclusive property of the grantee and his successors. His rights of property are capable of protection. It is a real injury to use another person's coat of arms. Mackenzie states that:

> 'by the civil law he who bears and uses another man's arms to his prejudice *vel in ejus scandalum et ignominium* is to be punished arbitrarily at the discretion of the Judges'[1],

and

> 'real injuries are committed by hindering a man to use what is his own ... by wearing in contempt what belongs to another man as his mark of honour'[2].

Persons — including corporations — who have a right to a coat of arms, which is wrongfully used, may present a petition and complaint against the offender in the Lyon Court or a petition for interdict against further wrongful use in either the Court of Session or the Lyon Court. Further, an armiger wronged by the wrongful assumption of his arms would have the right to raise an action for damages[3]. Actions in the public interests are raised by the Procurator Fiscal of the Lyon Court against the wrongful assumption either of another person's coat of arms or of a coat of arms not properly constituted by a grant under the Lyon King of Arms Act 1672[4].

No armiger, including a corporation, may without the warrant of the Lord Lyon authorise others to bear his or its arms, for this would infringe the statutory authority of the Lord Lyon and amount to an attempt to defraud the Treasury of the statutory dues on a grant or matriculation of arms.

Where a person is found to have displayed or used arms without authority, the Lord Lyon may impose a fine of £100 Scots and escheat to the Crown all the articles upon which the arms appear or may order the removal or erasure of the unwarrantable arms from the heritable property[5].

1 Mackenzie *The Science of Heraldry* (1680) p 12; Mackenzie *Works* (1722) II, 583.
2 Mackenzie *Laws and Customs of Scotland in Matters Criminal* (1678) I, 30, 3; Mackenzie *Works* II, 170.
3 Lord Dunedin *Encyclopaedia of Scottish Legal Styles* vol 5, pp 289 ff.
4 Complaint by *Procurator Fiscal of the Lyon Court v Porsche (UK) Ltd* (but resolved without litigation) (1980) The Scotsman, 25 March; Complaint by *Procurator Fiscal of the Lyon Court v Dryborough Ltd* (1984) (but resolved without litigation); *MacDonald of Keppoch* 1989 SLT (Lyon Ct) 2.
5 *Macrae's Trustees v Lord Lyon King-of-Arms* 1927 SLT 285, OH.

HOTELS AND TOURISM

The General Editors and author acknowledge with appreciation the assistance received from Mr Eric Jolly, formerly of the Scottish Hotel School, University of Strathclyde.

1. HOTELS

(1) INTRODUCTION

1701. Origin of Scots law of hotelkeepers. The laws of Scotland relating to hotelkeepers have their origin in a series of enactments of the Parliament of

Scotland in the fifteenth century[1]. The object of these statutes was the protection of the traveller from the exactions of 'bands of ridaris and gangaris throu the cuntre'[2]. The Acts provided for the establishment in towns and along high roads of 'hostilaris'[3]. An obligation was imposed upon the keeper, or 'hostilar'[4], to provide travellers with bread and ale and all other foods at a reasonable price, based upon the market price prevailing in the locality[5]. Travellers on horse or on foot were not permitted to lodge in any other place than these 'hostilaris'[6].

1 Ie the Innkeepers Act 1424 (c 25), and the Travellers Acts 1425 (c 11), 1427 (c 3) and 1535 (c 23) (all repealed).
2 Innkeepers Act 1424.
3 'Hostilaris', and later 'hostel' and 'hostler-house' are old Scots words and are probably equivalent to the English 'common inn'. 'Hostel' is defined in Chambers *Dictionary* as a house of public entertainment. This form died out in England after the sixteenth century, but was revived by Scott and hence restored to England in the nineteenth century. See also *Scottish National Dictionary*, vol V, p 196: *Smith v Scott* (1832) 9 Bing 14 at 17, per Tindal CJ.
4 'Hostilar', 'hosteler' and 'hostler' were used in Scotland to refer to the hotelkeeper. 'Hostler' was formerly used in England: *Lovett v Hobbs* (1680) 2 Show 127.
5 Innkeepers Act 1424.
6 Travellers Act 1425 (repealed). There were excepted those who travelled with a large retinue who were allowed to lodge with their friends if they sent their horses and followers to the hostilaris.

1702. Edictal liability. The edict *'nautae, caupones, stabularii'*[1] lies at the root of the Scots law of reparation and of the liability of the hotelkeeper for the property of the guest brought to the hotel[2]. The edict was transplanted into Scots law, with some variations, at an early date[3]. The strict liability which it imposed was thought necessary as the traveller was considered to be vulnerable to theft by the hostilar or to his collusion with thieves[4]. Speaking of its adoption into the law of Scotland, Viscount Stair stated 'The evident expediency thereof cannot but make it acceptable where the least respect is had to the civil law'[5]. Although the edict was never part of English law, the principles which it sets forth were recognised in English law at an early date[6] and are at the root of the English law of bailment[7].

1 *'Ait Praetor: nautae caupones stabularii, quod cujusque sulvum fore receperint nisi restituent in eos judicium dabo'*: 'The Praetor announces: I will grant an action against shipmasters, innkeepers and stablekeepers if they fail to restore to any person any property of which they have undertaken the safekeeping': Justinian *Digest* IV,9,1. See also Mackintosh 'The Edict Nautae, Caupones Stabularii' (1891) 3 JR 306.
2 See further paras 1741 ff below.
3 Stair *Institutions* I,9,5; Erskine *Institute* III,1,28; Bell *Principles* ss 235, 236.
4 *Gooden v Murray* (1700) Mor 9237.
5 *Stair* I,9,5.
6 *Calye's Case* (1584) 8 Co Rep 32a.
7 *Coggs v Bernard* (1703) 2 Ld Raym 909. However, cf *Mustard v Paterson* 1923 SC 142, 1923 SLT 21.

1703. Statutory modifications. Most of the fifteenth-century statutes relating to hotelkeepers have been repealed[1]. The rights and obligations of the hotelkeeper at common law in respect of property left with him by a guest[2], the nature and extent of his liability for the property of a guest[3] and the billeting of members of the armed forces[4] have been amended by statutory provisions. Legislation in the field of licensing[5], consumer protection[6] and employment[7] may also have particular application to the business of the hotelkeeper.

1 Ie the Travellers Acts 1425 (c 11), 1427 (c 3), and 1535 (c 23): Statute Law Revision (Scotland) Act 1906 (c 38).
2 See the Innkeepers Act 1878 (c 38), and paras 1741 ff below.
3 See the Hotel Proprietors Act 1956 (c 62), and paras 1748 ff below.

4 See the Army Act 1955 (c 18), s 155, the Air Force Act 1955 (c 19), s 155, the Armed Forces Act 1971 (c 33), s 67, and ARMED FORCES, vol 2, para 771.
5 See paras 1760 ff below.
6 See paras 1779 ff below.
7 See paras 1790–1792 below.

1704. Case law. There are few cases on the law of hotelkeepers in Scotland, whereas in England it has been the subject of many judicial decisions[1]. Indeed, most of the Scottish authorities on the rights and obligations of hotelkeepers are *obiter dicta*. For example, there was no judicial authority in Scotland on the scope of the hotelkeeper's lien until 1983[2].

1 *Rothfield v North British Rly Co* 1920 SC 805 at 825, 826, 1920 2 SLT 269 at 276, per Lord Scott Dickson.
2 *Bermans and Nathans Ltd v Weibye* 1983 SC 67, 1983 SLT 299.

1705. Scots and English law. The origins and development of the law of hotelkeepers have been different in Scotland and England. In England the law is based upon the 'custom of the realm', and the general obligation of the 'innkeeper' is founded upon the principle of 'public trust' or 'public duty'[1]. Nevertheless, despite the distinction in regard to sources, the Scots law of hotelkeepers is substantially the same as the English law of innkeepers[2].

1 *Lamond v Richard and Gordon Hotels Ltd* [1897] 1 QB 541 at 545, CA, per Lord Esher MR, and at 547 per Chitty LJ.
2 See *Ewing v Campbells* (1877) 5 R 230; *Strathearn Hydropathic Co Ltd v Inland Revenue* (1881) 8 R 798; *Rothfield v North British Rly Co* 1920 SC 805, 1920 2 SLT 269. However, cf *Mustard v Paterson* 1923 SC 142 at 148, 1923 SLT 21 at 23, 24, per Lord Alness.

(2) DEFINITIONS AND SCOPE OF APPLICATION

1706. Meaning of 'hotel'. 'Hotel' means an establishment held out by the proprietor as offering food, drink and, if so required, sleeping accommodation, without special contract, to any traveller presenting himself who appears able and willing to pay a reasonable sum for the services and facilities provided and who is in a fit state to be received[1]. A hotel is a place of business and is not a dwellinghouse, even if the proprietor lives there[2]. The main occupation of the premises is for the purpose of carrying on the trade of hotelkeeping[3]. In English law, the term 'hotel' was distinguished from the ancient 'hostel' which was no more than a 'common inn'[4].

1 Hotel Proprietors Act 1956 (c 62), s 1(3). A hotel is deemed to be an inn: s 1(1).
2 In *Ewing v Campbells* (1877) 5 R 230, there was a prohibition in a feu charter against the erection on the lands feud of buildings other than dwellinghouses and the vassal was prohibited from keeping a 'public house or tavern' on the feu: this was held to prevent the erection of an inn or hotel on the feu. See also *Macdonald v Douglas* 1963 SC 374, 1963 SLT 191.
3 *Ewing v Campbells* (1877) 5 R 230 at 233, per Lord President Inglis.
4 *Smith v Scott* (1832) 9 Bing 14.

1707. Meaning of 'inn'. An inn was defined as a house the owner of which held out that he would receive all travellers and sojourners who were willing to pay a price adequate to the sort of accommodation provided and who were in a fit state to be received[1]. Thus a house might be an inn for the accommodation of travellers[2]. English law distinguished between an 'inn' or 'hotel'[3] and a 'common inn'. The keeper of a common inn was bound to receive any traveller who could properly be accommodated[4]. The term 'common inn' was never accepted into the law of Scotland[5], but it appears to have been identical to the Scots term 'hotel'[6].

There was little, if any, difference as to the legal liability imposed on the person who carried on the business of a hotelkeeper in Scotland with that imposed on the keeper of a common inn in England[7]. However, the matter now appears to be settled; any establishment which does not come within the definition of 'hotel' provided by the Hotel Proprietors Act 1956 is not deemed to be an 'inn'[8].

1 *Thompson v Lacy* (1820) 3 B & Ald 283 at 286, per Bayley J, and at 287 per Best J.
2 *Pidgeon v Legg* (1857) 29 LTOS 166.
3 *Formby v Barker* [1903] 2 Ch 539 at 548, 549, 72 LJ Ch 716 at 719.
4 See *Lane v Cotton* (1702) 12 Mod Rep 472 at 483, per Holt CJ; *Browne v Brandt* [1902] 1 KB 696 at 698, per Alverston CJ.
5 *Rothfield v North British Rly Co* 1920 SC 805 at 826, 1920 2 SLT 269 at 276, per Lord Scott Dickson.
6 See *Ewing v Campbells* (1877) 5 R 230 at 233, where Lord President Inglis used the term 'hotel'.
7 *Rothfield v North British Rly Co* 1920 SC 805 at 826, 1920 2 SLT 269 at 276, per Lord Scott Dickson.
8 Hotel Proprietors Act 1956 (c 62), s 1(1). For the meaning of 'hotel', see para 1706 above.

1708. Hydropathic establishments and temperance hotels. The keeping of a hydropathic establishment is regarded as the keeping of a hotel to which all the public are invited[1]. A hotel does not cease to be a hotel merely because it is not licensed for the sale of alcoholic liquor[1]. Thus, a temperance hotel may be a hotel[2].

1 *Ewing v Campbells* (1877) 5 R 230; *Strathearn Hydropathic Co Ltd v Inland Revenue* (1881) 8 R 798.
2 *Cunningham v Philip* (1896) 12 TLR 352. As to the change of a temperance hotel to a licensed hotel, see *Manz v Butler's Trustees* 1973 SLT (Lands Tr) 2.

1709. Residential and private hotels. The statutory definition of 'hotel' maintains the distinction between a 'hotel' or 'inn' and a 'private' or 'residential' hotel[1]. The keeper of a private hotel or residential hotel is not subject to the strict liability imposed on the hotelkeeper[2], since he is not bound to receive and accommodate all travellers[3].

1 Hotel Proprietors Act 1956 (c 62), s 1(1), following the recommendation of *The Second Report of the Law Reform Committee on Innkeepers' Liability for Property of Travellers, Guests and Residents* (the Jenkins Report) (Cmd 9161) (1954).
2 As to the strict liability imposed on hotelkeepers, see paras 1738 ff below.
3 As to the duty to receive and entertain guests, see paras 1719 ff below.

1710. Lodging houses and boarding houses. The lodging house keeper does not hold himself out as receiving all travellers in the same way as a hotelkeeper[1]. He makes a special contract with each lodger who comes, and therefore a lodging house keeper is not a hotelkeeper[2]. Whereas a lodging house keeper merely provides accommodation for his lodgers, the keeper of a boarding house provides board and accommodation[3] and may, in addition, provide communal rooms and ancillary services in exchange for an agreed periodical payment. It has been held in England that in order to constitute 'board' there must be the provision of something substantial[4]. However, recent Scottish decisions have accepted that the provision of a 'continental breakfast' served in a dining room, the cost of which was reflected in the rent, amounted to 'board'[5]. The keeper of a boarding house does not hold himself as receiving all persons: thus, although he may be regarded as a hotelkeeper for some purposes, his liability in respect of luggage is not co-extensive with the liability of the hotelkeeper[6].

1 See 24 *Halsbury's Laws of England* (4th edn) para 1210.
2 As to hotelkeepers, see para 1715 below.
3 However, see *Taylor v Fordyce* 1918 SC 824 at 833, 834, 1918 2 SLT 186 at 189, per Lord Johnston.
4 For an interpretation of the word 'board' under the Increase of Rent and Mortgage Interest (Restriction) Act 1920 (c 17) (repealed), see *Wilkes v Goodwin* [1923] 2 KB 86, CA.
5 *Holiday Flat Co v Kuczera* 1978 SLT (Sh Ct) 47. See also *Berry v Smith* 1983 SCCR 327, 1984 SLT 79.
6 *Rothfield v North British Rly Co* 1920 SC 805 at 832, 833, 1920 2 SLT 269 at 280, 281, per Lord Salvesen; *Tinsley v Dudley* [1951] 2 KB 18, [1951] 1 All ER 252, CA. However, cf *May v Wingate* (1694) Mor 9236.

1711. Motels. The physical connection between a 'motel' and a 'hotel' are sufficiently proximate to entitle the premises to constitute a 'hotel' within the meaning of the Licensing (Scotland) Act 1976[1]. However, if no food is provided at the motel, the establishment cannot be a hotel[2].

1 *Northern Constabulary Chief Constable v Lochaber District Licensing Board* 1985 SLT 410. For the meaning of 'hotel' under the Licensing (Scotland) Act 1976 (c 66), see ALCOHOLIC LIQUOR, vol 2, para 11.
2 *King v Barclay and Barclay's Motel* (1960) 24 DLR (2d) 418 (Can).

1712. Public houses. The term 'public house' was originally used in Scotland to denote an 'inn, a tavern or a hotel'[1]. A house is 'public' in that members of the public are not only invited but have a right to resort to it[2]. However, it is the purpose for which people visit a public house which distinguishes it from a hotel. People go to a public house for the purchase of alcoholic liquor, and to a hotel for accommodation as travellers[3]. It does not matter that a proprietor describes his establishment as a public house; if he provides food and accommodation for anyone able and willing to pay for it, it is a hotel[4]. An establishment may be a hotel and a public house[5]. Where a public house is attached to a hotel, and the only entrance is through the hotel, the public house is part of the hotel[6]. However, although a public house may be under the same roof as a hotel, if it has a separate entrance it is not a hotel, and the duties of a hotelkeeper do not attach to it[7].

1 See Sir John Sinclair of Ulbster *Observation on the Scottish Dialect* (London, 1782), and Jamieson's *Dictionary of the Scottish Language*.
2 *Ewing v Campbells* (1877) 5 R 230 at 234, per Lord President Inglis. However, they do not have a right to be served.
3 *Ewing v Campbells* (1877) 5 R 230 at 239, per Lord Shand. See also *Taylor v Fordyce* 1918 SC 824 at 833, 834, 1918 2 SLT 186 at 189, per Lord Johnston.
4 *Thompson v Lacy* (1820) 3 B & Ald 283.
5 *Pidgeon v Legg* (1857) 29 LTOS 166.
6 *Ex parte Harley* (1862) 5 All 264 (Can).
7 *R v Rymer* (1877) 2 QBD 136, CCR. A function room used for dancing is only ancillary to hotel premises as a whole and not inherently bound up in those premises: *Skilbeck v Beveridge* 1959 SC 313, 1959 SLT 342.

1713. Restaurants and refreshment rooms. Restaurants and refreshment rooms do not offer accommodation to travellers and the proprietor has the right to refuse whom he wishes[1]. Thus, these establishments are not hotels[2]. However, a restaurant or refreshment room which is under the same roof as a hotel and which can only be entered through the hotel premises would constitute part of the hotel[3]. Nevertheless, where there is a separate entrance the liabilities of a hotelkeeper do not attach to those premises[4].

1 However, this is subject to the provisions of the Sex Discrimination Act 1975 (c 65), ss 2(1), 29(1), (2)(b), (e), and the Race Relations Act 1976 (c 74), s 20(1), (2)(b), (e).
2 For the meaning of 'hotel', see para 1706 above.
3 *Ex parte Harley* (1862) 5 All 264 (Can).
4 *R v Rymer* (1877) 2 QBD 136, CCR. See also *Ultzen v Nicols* [1894] 1 QB 92; *Orchard v Bush & Co* [1898] 2 QB 284.

1714. Eventide homes. An eventide home is not a hotel, and the liabilities of the hotelkeeper do not attach to this type of establishment[1].

1 *Macdonald v Douglas* 1963 SC 374, 1963 SLT 191.

1715. Meaning of 'hotelkeeper'. A hotelkeeper is one who holds out his establishment as offering food, drink and, if so required, sleeping accommodation, without special contract, to any traveller presenting himself who appears to be able and willing to pay a reasonable sum for the services and facilities provided and who is in a fit state to be received[1]. The keeping of a hotel therefore involves the provision of sleeping accommodation for the traveller and not merely the supply of alcoholic liquor and other refreshments[2]. In England the term 'innkeeper'[3] is more commonly used, but the Hotel Proprietors Act 1956 refers to the 'proprietor of a hotel', and 'hotelkeeper' is more in keeping with modern usage[4]. The definition of a hotelkeeper extends to the keeper of a hydropathic establishment[5] and a motel[6]. The liabilities of the hotelkeeper do not extend to any public house, refreshment bar, restaurant, dance hall or function room of which he is also proprietor, but for which there is a separate entrance from the hotel[7].

1 The Hotel Proprietors Act 1956 (c 62) does not define 'hotelkeeper' but refers to the proprietor of a hotel: see s 1.
2 *Taylor v Fordyce* 1918 SC 824 at 833, 834, 1918 2 SLT 186 at 189, per Lord Johnston. See also *R v Rymer* (1877) 2 QBD 136, CCR; *R v Armagh Justices* (1897) 2 IR 57; *Sealey v Tandy* [1902] 1 KB 296, DC.
3 *Jones v Osborn* (1785) 2 Chit 484, where it was held that a hotelkeeper was subject to the same liability as an innkeeper but that he must be declared against as an innkeeper.
4 See 'The Hotel Proprietors Act, 1956' (1956) 222 LT 168.
5 *Strathearn Hydropathic Co Ltd v Inland Revenue* (1881) 8 R 798. As to hydropathic establishments, see para 1708 above.
6 *Northern Constabulary Chief Constable v Lochaber District Licensing Board* 1985 SLT 410. As to motels, see para 1711 above.
7 As to public houses, refreshment bars, restaurants, dance halls and function rooms, see paras 1712, 1713, above.

1716. Meaning of 'traveller'. The common law duty[1] to receive and accommodate guests attaches only in respect of those guests who are travellers[2]. A traveller is a person, being neither an inhabitant of the hotel nor a private guest of the hotelkeeper, who has come to the hotel to obtain such services, facilities and accommodation as it affords and for which he is willing to pay[3]. It does not matter which mode of transport is used by the traveller, nor whether he used any transport at all[4]. He may be a traveller, and therefore a guest, even though he does not stay overnight at the hotel[5]. The distance travelled may be material but not conclusive[6]. Not every guest at a hotel is a traveller; only those *in itinere*[7]. Transient boarders are not travellers[8].

1 See also the Innkeepers Act 1424 (c 25).
2 *Lamond v Richard and Gordon Hotels Ltd* [1897] 1 QB 541, CA.
3 *Orchard v Bush & Co* [1898] 2 QB 284 at 289, per Kennedy J. However, criminal statutes may have a different definition of a 'traveller' from that of the civil law: see CRIMINAL LAW.
4 *Rothfield v North British Rly Co* 1920 SC 805, 1920 2 SLT 269.
5 *Williams v Linnitt* [1951] 1 KB 565, [1951] 1 All ER 278, CA, where a local resident was held to be a traveller. However, a person living in the same town, 1200 yards from a hotel, and walking

about the town for his own recreation and amusement was held not to be a traveller: *R v Rymer* (1877) 2 QBD 136, CCR.

6   *Williams v Linnitt* [1951] 1 KB 565 at 583, 584, [1951] 1 All ER 278 at 289, CA, per Denning LJ. See also *Bennett v Mellor* (1793) 5 Term Rep 273. However, *The Second Report of the Law Reform Committee on Innkeepers' Liability for Property of Travellers, Guests and Residents* (the Jenkins Report) (Cmd 9161) (1954) recommended that the term 'traveller' should be confined to a person seeking accommodation for the night and not merely refreshments. This recommendation was adopted in respect of a hotelkeeper's liability for a guest's property: see the Hotel Proprietors Act 1956 (c 62), s 2(1), and paras 1741 ff below.

7   *Lamond v Richard and Gordon Hotels Ltd* [1897] 1 QB 541, CA.

8   *Oliver v Loudon* (1896) 23 R (J) 34, 3 SLT 264; *Light v Abel* (1866) 6 All 400 (Can).

1717. Meaning of 'guest'. A person may be a guest at a hotel even though he is not a traveller *in itinere*[1]. He may be a local resident using the hotel, restaurant, bar or other facilities[2]. However, a person is not a guest for the purpose of acquiring the peculiar remedies which the law confers against hotelkeepers unless he is also a traveller[3]. The relationship of hotelkeeper and guest arises as soon as the traveller enters the hotel with the intention of using it as a hotel and is received on that basis by the hotelkeeper[4]. However, the mere signing of a registration card does not necessarily imply that a person is a guest[5]. A person who has made a previous contract for accommodation but not for food and drink is not a guest but a lodger[6]. A traveller may be a guest even where he is only provided with a room in which to change, the room having been engaged by another guest who is to occupy it later that day[7]. A traveller may be a guest notwithstanding the fact that another person is responsible for the bill[8]. A non-paying guest is still a guest[9]. A person who arrives at a hotel at the invitation of a hotel guest may himself be considered to be a guest[10]. However, a traveller who illicitly stays in the room of another guest is not a guest[11].

1   *Lamond v Richard and Gordon Hotels Ltd* [1897] 1 QB 541, CA.

2   *Pidgeon v Legg* (1857) 29 LTOS 166. However, the term 'customer' may be more correct.

3   *Williams v Linnitt* [1951] 1 KB 565 at 577, 578, [1951] 1 All ER 278 at 285, 286, CA, per Asquith LJ. See also the Hotel Proprietors Act 1956 (c 62), s 2(1), and paras 1741 ff below.

4   *Wright v Anderton* [1909] 1 KB 209. However, see the Hotel Proprietors Act 1956, s 2(1), and paras 1741 ff below. See also *Strauss v County Hotel and Wine Co Ltd* (1883) 12 QBD 27.

5   *Ford v Seligman* [1954] OR 957, [1955] 1 DLR 796, Ont CA.

6   *Parker v Flint* (1699) 12 Mod Rep 254.

7   *Medawar v Grand Hotel Co* [1891] 2 QB 11, CA.

8   *Wright v Anderton* [1909] 1 KB 209. See also *Daniel v Hotel Pacific Pty Ltd* [1953] VLR 447 (Aust).

9   Mackintosh 'The Edict Nautae, Caupones Stabularii' (1891) 3 JR 306 at 311.

10 *Cryan v Hotel Rembrandt Ltd* (1925) 133 LT 395.

11 See *Whyte's Case* (1558) 2 Dyer 158b.

1718. Persons no longer travellers or guests. A person who was received at a hotel as a traveller does not necessarily continue to reside there in that capacity[1]. Whether at any time a person is still in that capacity is a question of fact[1]. One of the factors determining this fact is the length of his stay at the hotel[1]. However, mere length of time is not conclusive evidence that a guest has ceased to be a traveller[2]. A person may stay for a longer period than anticipated due to illness. Nevertheless a person who engages accommodation at a hotel for a considerable time, and on special terms, is a lodger and not a guest[3]. The Hotel Proprietors Act 1956 did not solve the question as to when a person ceases to be a guest and becomes a lodger. It is still a question of fact. A person who leaves property at a hotel after 'checking out' is no longer a guest[4].

1   *Lamond v Richard and Gordon Hotels Ltd* [1897] 1 QB 541, CA.

2   [1897] 1 QB 541 at 546, per Esher MR.

3   *Ford v Seligman* [1954] OR 957, [1955] 1 DLR 796, Ont CA. See also *Pidgeon v Legg* (1857) 29 LTOS 166.

4 *Gelley v Clerk* (1607) Cro Jac 188. However, see the Hotel Proprietors Act 1956 (c 62), s 2(1), and paras 1741 ff below.

(3) HOTELKEEPER'S DUTY TO RECEIVE AND ENTERTAIN GUESTS

1719. Hotelkeeper's general duty. The hotelkeeper must receive without favour[1] all travellers who present themselves[2] and who are prepared to pay for the facilities and services provided by the hotel[3].

1 *Rothfield v North British Rly Co* 1920 SC 805, 1920 2 SLT 269. 'I am not inclined to believe that a Roman caupo or nauta had a right to say to one person, you shall come into my inn or ship, and to another, you shall not': Mackintosh 'The Edict Nautae, Caupones Stabularii' (1891) 3 JR 306 at 311.
2 See *Hawthorne v Hammond* (1844) 1 Car & Kir 404, where it was held to be a question of fact whether or not a hotelkeeper who heard someone knocking at the door of the hotel during the night ought to have concluded that that person wished to be admitted as a guest.
3 *Ewing v Campbells* (1877) 5 R 230 at 233, per Lord President Inglis; *Rothfield v North British Rly Co* 1920 SC 805, 1920 2 SLT 269. See also *Thompson v Lacy* (1820) 3 B & Ald 283; *R v Ivens* (1835) 7 C & P 213.

1720. Duty to provide refreshments. The hotelkeeper is bound to provide reasonable refreshment to any traveller who is prepared to pay for it[1]. What amounts to 'reasonable refreshment' will vary according to the time of day and the type of hotel which the traveller has chosen to visit[2]. A traveller calling at a hotel in the early hours of the morning could not reasonably expect to be provided with a three-course meal. A traveller is entitled to be given reasonable refreshment during his stay at a hotel or as an accompaniment with a meal[3].

The hotelkeeper is only bound to provide such food and drink as he in fact possesses[4]. He is not bound to send out for food and drink. He may refuse to supply a traveller with food and drink if he has a 'reasonable excuse'[5]. Thus, it may be reasonable for a hotelkeeper to reserve his limited supplies of food or drink for existing guests[5]. However, this would not excuse an incompetent hotelkeeper who had failed to maintain adequate stocks of food and drink.

1 Innkeepers Act 1424 (c 25). See also *Ewing v Campbells* (1877) 5 R 230 at 233, per Lord President Inglis; *Rothfield v North British Rly Co* 1920 SC 805, 1920 2 SLT 269; *Thompson v Lacy* (1820) 3 B & Ald 283; *R v Higgins* [1948] 1 KB 165, [1947] 2 All ER 619, CA.
2 *R v Higgins* [1948] 1 KB 165, [1947] 2 All ER 619, CCA.
3 *Oliver v Loudon* (1896) 23 R (J) 34, 3 SLT 264. See also *Manz v Butler's Trustees* 1973 SLT (Lands Tr) 2. As to the right to refuse accommodation and/or refreshments, see para 1723 below. A traveller who visits a temperance hotel would not be entitled to demand to be supplied with alcoholic liquor.
4 Innkeepers Act 1424 (c 25).
5 *R v Higgins* [1948] 1 KB 165, [1947] 2 All ER 619, CCA.

1721. Duty to accommodate travellers. The Acts of the Parliament of Scotland which provided for the establishment of 'hostilaris' did not expressly confer a right on the traveller to be accommodated by the 'hostilar', but such a right is necessarily implied[1]. The keeping of a hotel involves the provision of accommodation for travellers and not merely the supply of refreshments[2]. However, the hotelkeeper is only bound to supply such accommodation for the traveller as he in fact possesses[3]. He is not bound to take anyone if there is no room for him in the hotel[4], that is, where all the rooms commonly used as bedrooms for guests are occupied[5]. The traveller is not entitled to select a particular apartment or to insist upon a bedroom for purposes other than that of accommodation[6]. The hotelkeeper has fulfilled his duty if he provides a bedroom which is a proper room for that purpose[7]. However, the duty is not fulfilled where a hotelkeeper unreasonably refuses accommodation at one hotel but offers to provide it at another of which he is also proprietor[8].

1 See para 1701 above.
2 *Taylor v Fordyce* 1918 SC 824 at 833, 1918 2 SLT 186 at 189, per Lord Johnston; *Oliver v Loudon* (1896) 23 R (J) 34, 3 SLT 264.
3 *Winkworth v Raven* [1931] 1 KB 652.
4 *Medawar v Grand Hotel Co* [1891] 2 QB 11, CA.
5 *Browne v Brandt* [1902] 1 KB 696.
6 *Fell v Knight* (1891) 8 M & W 269. As to the extent of the traveller's right, see *Rothfield v North British Rly Co* 1920 SC 805 at 828, 1920 2 SLT 269 at 277, per Lord Scott Dickson.
7 *Fell v Knight* (1891) 8 M & W 269.
8 *Constantine v Imperial Hotels Ltd* [1944] KB 693, [1944] 2 All ER 171.

1722. Duty to receive travellers' luggage. The hotelkeeper is bound to take in not only the traveller but also his luggage[1]. 'Luggage' is not confined to personal luggage, but extends to whatever the traveller may bring with him[2]. The hotelkeeper has no right to demand whether the traveller owns the luggage or not[3]. It has been held that he is also bound to receive a guest's motor car[4]. Where the traveller brings with him luggage which is unusual and unreasonable[5], or dangerous, the hotelkeeper is not bound to accommodate him or his luggage[6].

1 *Robins & Co v Gray* [1895] 2 QB 501, CA.
2 *Robins & Co v Gray* [1895] 2 QB 501, CA. See also *Bermans and Nathans Ltd v Weibye* 1983 SC 67 at 69, 70, 1983 SLT 299 at 301, per Lord President Emslie.
3 *Bermans and Nathans Ltd v Weibye* 1983 SC 67 at 71, 1983 SLT 299 at 302, per Lord President Emslie.
4 *Gresham v Lyon* [1954] 2 All ER 786 at 788, [1954] 1 WLR 1100 at 1103, per McNair J.
5 *Broadwood v Granara* (1854) 10 Exch 417 (piano).
6 *Robins & Co v Gray* [1895] 2 QB 501, CA.

1723. Right to refuse accommodation or refreshments. The right of the traveller to be received and provided with refreshments or accommodation is not an absolute one[1]. The common law duty to receive and accommodate a guest attaches only in so far as the guest is a traveller[2]. The hotelkeeper may refuse to accommodate a traveller if there is no room available at the hotel[3]. He may also refuse to receive a person whose conduct on previous occasions had given rise to comment and complaint from other guests[4].

He may reject a traveller:

(1) who is not in a fit state to be received[5];
(2) whose presence would endanger other guests[6];
(3) who is accompanied by objectionable friends, unreasonable or dangerous luggage[7], or by a savage or unsuitable dog[8];
(4) who appears unable to pay a reasonable price for the accommodation or refreshments available[9] or who refuses or fails to provide security for his bill, if requested to do so[10].

The hotelkeeper is obliged to reject an alien who fails to provide a statement as to his name, date of arrival, passport number, address and nationality[11]. He may not reject a guest without sufficient reason. He may not refuse to accommodate a traveller on grounds of race[12] or sex[13]. The fact that the traveller could have obtained accommodation elsewhere is not sufficient grounds for refusal to receive him[14].

1   *Strathearn Hydropathic Co Ltd v Inland Revenue* (1881) 8 R 798 at 800, per Lord President Inglis; *Rothfield v North British Rly Co* 1920 SC 805 at 828, 1920 2 SLT 269 at 277, per Lord Scott Dickson.
2   *Lamond v Richard and Gordon Hotels Ltd* [1897] 1 QB 541, CA.
3   *Medawar v Grand Hotel Co* [1891] 2 QB 11, CA; *Browne v Brandt* [1902] 1 KB 696.
4   *Rothfield v North British Rly Co* 1920 SC 805, 1920 2 SLT 269.
5   Hotel Proprietors Act 1956 (c 62), s 1(3).
6   Thus, a traveller with a highly contagious disease might be rejected. As to the special provisions in respect of contagious diseases, see PUBLIC HEALTH, vol 19, paras 482 ff.
7   *Robins & Co v Gray* [1895] 2 QB 501, CA.
8   *R v Rymer* (1877) 2 QBD 136, CCR.
9   *Thompson v Lacy* (1820) 3 B & Ald 283 at 287, per Best J.
10 *Fell v Knight* (1891) 8 M & W 269.
11 Immigration (Hotel Records) Order 1972, SI 1972/1689, art 4.
12 Race Relations Act 1976 (c 74), s 20. See also *Mandla v Lee* [1983] 2 AC 548, [1983] 1 All ER 1062, HL.
13 Sex Discrimination Act 1975 (c 65), s 29. See also *Gill v El Vino Co Ltd* [1983] QB 425, [1983] 1 All ER 398, CA.
14 *Pidgeon v Legg* (1857) 29 LTOS 166; *Rothfield v North British Rly Co* 1920 SC 805, 1920 2 SLT 269.

(4) CREATION AND PERFORMANCE OF THE HOTELKEEPER'S CONTRACT

1724. Introduction. The general principles of the law of contract apply to contracts between hotelkeeper and guest and will not be discussed in detail in this title[1]. However, a few issues merit attention[2].

1   See generally OBLIGATIONS.
2   See paras 1725–1727 below.

1725. Bookings, offer and acceptance. The contract of booking was held to have taken place at the reception desk[1]. Accordingly, a notice in the guest's room limiting the hotelkeeper's liability, which was not seen by the guest until after the booking formalities had been completed, was not incorporated into the contract. However, if an exception clause is incorporated into the contract, its effectiveness will be subject to the Unfair Contract Terms Act 1977 (c 50)[2].

1   *Olley v Marlborough Court Ltd* [1949] 1 KB 532, [1949] 1 All ER 127, CA.
2   See OBLIGATIONS. See also CONSUMER PROTECTION, vol 6, paras 99–102.

1726. Voluntary code of booking practice. The Hotel Industry Voluntary Code of Booking Practice was drawn up between the Department of Trade and the British Hotels, Restaurant and Caterers Association with other interested organisations. The code is not confined to hotels but includes residential hotels, private hotels, guest houses and similar establishments with four or more letting bedrooms. The code requires the hotelkeeper etc, to provide the guest with written details of the prices of accommodation (including the total charge he will be obliged to pay) at the earliest opportunity. The code has detailed provisions in respect of prices of accommodation and the services included. It also requires the hotelkeeper to inform a guest who is to be accommodated in unconnected premises or in a separate establishment of the location of that accommodation and any difference in comfort or amenity compared with accommodation in the main establishment. Breach of the code does not give rise to a legal action in the courts, but commercial sanctions are provided[1].

> 1 See also the Tourism (Sleeping Accommodation Price Display) Order 1977, SI 1977/1877, and the Immigration (Hotel Records) Order 1972/1689 (amended by SI 1982/1025).

1727. Breach of contract. Where a hotelkeeper is in breach of contract, it is submitted that damages can be recovered by a guest for the loss of benefit sustained not only by himself but also members of his family who were with him at the time, even though they were not *stricto senso* parties to the contract[1]. An element in the damages may be awarded for loss of enjoyment[2].

> 1 This is by analogy with *Jackson v Horizon Holidays Ltd* [1975] 3 All ER 92, [1975] 1 WLR 1468, CA.
> 2 See *Jarvis v Swans Tours Ltd* [1973] QB 233, [1973] 1 All ER 71, CA.

(5) THE GUEST'S BEHAVIOUR

1728. Introduction. The definition of 'guest' and the scope of the relevant law relating to such persons has already been discussed[1]. Similarly we have considered when a person ceases to be a guest[2].

> 1 See para 1717 above.
> 2 See para 1718 above.

1729. Guest's behaviour. The hotelkeeper is under a duty to receive and accommodate all travellers who present themselves and who are prepared to pay for the facilities and services which he provides[1]. The guest is under a duty to conduct himself properly whilst on the hotelkeeper's premises[2]. The hotelkeeper is bound to attend to the decency and order of his establishment, which may require him to reject a guest whose manners and habits, or whose moral character, would be objectionable to other residents and prejudicial to the hotelkeeper's business[3]. He is bound to attend to the health and salubrity of his premises, and that might lead to the rejection of certain guests[4], including guests accompanied by savage or unsuitable animals[5]. Similarly, a guest who brings objectionable friends to the hotel may himself be justifiably excluded from the premises. Although the hotelkeeper appears to have a wide discretion in the matter[6], he cannot eject a guest unless there was misconduct or impropriety on the part of the guest, or on some other sufficient reason[7].

> 1 *Ewing v Campbells* (1877) 5 R 230 at 233, per Lord President Inglis; *Rothfield v North British Rly Co* 1920 SC 805, 1920 2 SLT 269.
> 2 *R v Ivens* (1835) 7 C & P 213.
> 3 *Strathearn Hydropathic Co Ltd v Inland Revenue* (1881) 8 R 798 at 800, 801, per Lord President Inglis; *Rothfield v North British Rly Co* 1920 SC 805, 1920 2 SLT 269. See also the Hotel Proprietors Act 1956 (c 62), s 1(3) ('. . . who is in a fit state to be received').
> 4 *Rothfield v North British Rly Co* 1920 SC 805, 1920 2 SLT 269.
> 5 *R v Rymer* (1877) 2 QBD 136, CCR. However, he is not under a duty to forbid guests or customers who bring in dogs, or insist that they be kept on a lead, unless the dog was making a nuisance of itself: *Carroll v Garford* (1968) 112 Sol Jo 948.

6 *Strathearn Hydropathic Co Ltd v Inland Revenue* (1881) 8 R 798 at 800, 801, per Lord President Inglis.
7 *Pidgeon v Legg* (1857) 29 LTOS 166; *Browne v Brandt* [1902] 1 KB 696 at 698, per Lord Alvestone. See also *Lamond v Richard and Gordon Hotels Ltd* [1897] 1 QB 541, CA.

(6) REGISTRATION

1730. Registration generally. There are statutory provisions[1] which lay down the information to be supplied by visitors on registration[2] and the records to be maintained by hotelkeepers. The provisions apply in the case of any hotel or other premises, whether furnished or unfurnished, where lodging or sleeping accommodation is provided for reward, which have been certified by the chief officer of police of the area in which they are situated, not to be occupied for the purposes of a school, hospital, club or other institution or association[3].

Every person of or over the age of sixteen who stays[4] at any premises to which the provisions apply, must, on arriving at the premises, inform the keeper[5] of the premises of his full name and nationality[6]. In addition, a person who is an alien[7] must inform the keeper of the premises of the number and place of issue of his passport, certificate of registration[8] or other document establishing his identity and nationality and, on or before his departure from the premises, inform the keeper of the premises of his next destination and, if it is known to him, his full address there[9].

The keeper of the premises is required to keep a written record of such information which must be open to inspection to the police or other person authorised by the Secretary of State for a period of up to twelve months[10].

1 See the Immigration (Hotel Records) Order 1972, SI 1972/1689, made under the Immigration Act 1971 (c 77), s 4(4). See also *Baljinder Singh v Hammond* [1987] 3 All ER 829, [1987] 1 WLR 283, DC. 'Nationality' includes the status of a stateless alien: Immigration (Hotel Records) Order 1972, art 2(1). A person is guilty of an offence if, without reasonable excuse, he fails to comply with any requirement of an order under the Immigration Act 1971, s 4(4), and is liable to a fine not exceeding level 4 on the standard scale or with imprisonment for not more than six months: s 26(1)(f). At the date at which this volume states the law level 4 is £1,000: see the Criminal Procedure (Scotland) Act 1975 (c 21), ss 289F(8), 289G(2) (added by the Criminal Justice Act 1982 (c 48), s 54), and the Increase of Criminal Penalties etc (Scotland) Order 1984, SI 1984/526, art 4.
2 See *Ford v Seligman* [1954] OR 957, [1955] 1 DLR 796, Ont CA. The mere signing of a registration card does not necessarily imply that a person is a guest.
3 Immigration (Hotel Records) Order 1972, art 3.
4 'Stay' means lodge or sleep, for one night or more, in accommodation provided for reward: ibid, art 2(1).
5 'Keeper', in relation to any premises, includes any person who for reward receives any other person to stay in the premises, whether on his own behalf or as manager or otherwise on behalf of any other person: ibid, art 2(1).
6 Ibid, art 4(1).
7 'Alien' has the same meaning as in the British Nationality Act 1981 (c 61) (see ss 50(1), 51(4), and NATIONALITY AND CITIZENSHIP, vol 14, para 1956): Immigration (Hotel Records) Order 1972, art 2(1) (amended by SI 1982/1025).
8 'Certificate of registration' means a certificate issued, or treated as issued in pursuance of regulations from time to time in force under the Immigration Act 1971, s 4(3) (see IMMIGRATION AND EXTRADITION): Immigration (Hotel Records) Order 1972, art 2(1).
9 Ibid, art 4(2).
10 Ibid, art 5.

(7) SAFETY

1731. Occupiers' liability generally. The general law on occupiers' liability is applicable in relation to hotels[1].

1 See the Occupiers' Liability (Scotland) Act 1960 (c 30) (see OBLIGATIONS), and *Murdoch v A and R Scott* 1956 SC 309, 1957 SLT 11. See also *Wheat v E Lacon & Co Ltd* [1966] AC 552, [1966] 1 All ER 582, HL (paying guests in 'private rooms' of manager's living accommodation): *Campbell v Shelbourne Hotel Ltd* [1939] 2 KB 534, [1939] 2 All ER 351 (failure to light a passage in a hotel during the night).

1732. Compulsory fire certificates generally. The Fire Precautions Act 1971 strengthened and rationalised the law relating to fire precautions in public buildings and in certain kinds of residential establishments. The Act set out the uses of premises for which a fire certificate is necessary[1]. The Secretary of State is empowered to designate by order particular uses of premises, but may not so designate any particular use unless it falls within at least one of the specified classes, including use as, or for any purpose involving the provision of, sleeping accommodation, or use for any purpose involving access to the premises by members of the public, whether on payment or otherwise[2]. The order may provide that a fire certificate is not to be required for premises of any description specified in the order, notwithstanding that they are, or form part of, premises which are put to a designated use[3]. An order may also, as respects any designated use, specify descriptions of premises which qualify for exemption by a fire authority from the requirement for a fire certificate in respect of premises which are put to that use[4].

1 See the Fire Precautions Act 1971 (c 40), s 1 (amended by the Health and Safety at Work etc Act 1974 (c 37), s 78(1), (2), and the Fire Safety and Safety of Places of Sport Act 1987 (c 27), s 1(1), (2)).
2 Fire Precautions Act 1971, s 1(2)(a), (e). As to 'designated use', see para 1733 below.
3 Ibid, s 1(3).
4 Ibid, s 1(3A) (added by the Fire Safety and Safety of Places of Sport Act 1987, s 1(1), (2)). For exemptions, see the Fire Precautions Act 1971, s 5A (added by the Fire Safety and Places of Sport Act 1987, s 1(4)).

1733. Designated uses. The Fire Precautions (Hotels and Boarding Houses) (Scotland) Order 1972 sets out the types of hotels, boarding houses and other premises which are thereby classified as a 'designated use' and thus require a fire certificate[1]. The order specifies those premises where, in the course of carrying on the business of a hotel or boarding house keeper, sleeping accommodation for staff or sleeping, dining room, drawing room, ballroom or other accommodation for guests is provided[1]. The provisions do not have effect in relation to any premises unless:
(1) sleeping accommodation is provided in those premises for more than six persons, being staff or guests[2]; or
(2) some sleeping accommodation is provided in those premises for staff or guests on any floor above the first floor of the building which constitutes or comprises the premises[3]; or
(3) some sleeping accommodation is provided in those premises for staff or guests below the ground floor of the building which constitutes or comprises the premises[4].

1 See the Fire Precautions (Hotels and Boarding Houses) (Scotland) Order 1972, SI 1972/382, art 3.
2 Ibid, art 3, proviso (a). An occupier of premises in which he provides sleeping accommodation for more than six persons whose rent includes payment for breakfast requires a fire certificate: *Berry v Smith* 1983 SCCR 327, 1984 SLT 79.
3 Fire Precautions (Hotels and Boarding Houses) (Scotland) Order 1972, art 3, proviso (b).
4 Ibid, art 3, proviso (c).

1734. Application for fire certificate. Application for a fire certificate[1] must be made to the fire authority in the prescribed form[2]. The fire authority may require the applicant to furnish it with plans of the premises[3]. It is the duty of the fire authority to inspect the premises[4]. If the fire authority is satisfied that the means of escape, the means for fighting fire and the means of giving warning in case of fire are such as may reasonably be required in the circumstances of the case in connection with that use of the premises, and that the means of escape can be safely and effectively used at all material times, it must issue a fire certificate[5]. If the fire authority is not satisfied, it must issue a notice to that effect specifying the steps necessary to be taken before a fire certificate can be issued and the specified time within which those steps must be completed[6]. If a certificate is not issued within the time specified it is deemed to have been refused[7].

1   For the contents of fire certificates, see the Fire Precautions Act 1971 (c 40), s 6 (amended by the Fire Safety and Safety of Places of Sport Act 1987 (c 27), ss 15, 49, Sch 4).
2   See the Fire Precautions Act 1971, s 5(1). For the prescribed form, see the Fire Precautions (Application for Certificate) Regulations 1976, SI 1976/2008, reg 3, Schedule. As to fire authorities, see LOCAL GOVERNMENT, vol 14, paras 497, 498.
3   See the Fire Precautions Act 1971, s 5(2) (amended by the Fire Safety and Safety of Places of Sport Act 1987, s 8(2)(a)). Where an application is made for a fire certificate in respect to any premises it is the duty of the occupier to secure that, when the application is made and pending its disposal, (1) the means of escape in case of fire with which the premises are provided can be safely and effectively used at all material times; (2) the means for fighting fire with which the premises are provided are maintained in efficient working order; and (3) any persons employed to work in the premises receive instruction or training in what to do in case of fire: Fire Precautions Act 1971, s 5(2A) (added by the Fire Safety and Safety of Places of Sport Act 1987, s 8(2)(b)).
4   Fire Precautions Act 1971, s 5(3) (amended by the Fire Safety and Safety of Places of Sport Act 1987, s 1(3), Sch 4).
5   Fire Precautions Act 1971, s 5(3) (as so amended). As to change of conditions affecting adequacy of matters specified in the fire certificate, see s 8.
6   Ibid, s 5(4).
7   Ibid, s 5(4). The applicant may be allowed further time by the authority or by any order made by a court, on or in proceedings arising out of, an appeal against the notice: s 5(4). As to appeals, see para 1735 below.

1735. Appeal against decisions in respect of fire certificates. Appeal against a decision made by the fire authority in relation to a fire certificate, or in respect of notices served on the applicant, may be made within twenty-one days of 'the relevant date', that is, within twenty-one days of the date on which the applicant was served with the notice of refusal, direction, cancellation, amendment or matter in question[1]. The fire authorities, following a 'deemed refusal', must give actual notice to the applicant[2]. Thus, it has been held that where an applicant had failed to meet a requirement specified by the fire authority and seven days later received a letter informing him that his application was thereby refused, he was entitled to appeal within twenty-one days of the receipt of that letter[2].

1   See the Fire Precautions Act 1971 (c 40), s 9.
2   *McGovern v Central Regional Council* 1982 SLT (Sh Ct) 110.

1736. Miscellaneous matters in respect of fire precautions. The fire authority may, if it is satisfied that the risk to persons in case of fire is so serious that the use of the premises ought to be prohibited or restricted, serve a prohibition notice on the occupier of the premises[1]. The Secretary of State is empowered to make regulations about fire precautions[2]. There is no statutory duty imposed on the fire authority to recommend interim measures or to give additional advice to applicants[3].

1   See the Fire Precautions Act 1971 (c 40), s 10 (substituted by the Fire Safety and Safety of Places of Sport Act 1987 (c 27), ss 9, 49, Sch 5, para 4).

2 See the Fire Precautions Act 1971, s 12 (amended by the Health and Safety at Work etc Act 1974 (c 37), s 78(1), (5); Cinemas Act 1985 (c 13), s 24, Sch 2, para 9, Sch 3; and the Fire Safety and Safety of Places of Sport Act 1987, ss 13(b), 49, Sch 4).
3 *Hallett v Nicholson* 1979 SC 1.

1737. Health and safety at work. The general law relating to health and safety at work[1] is applicable to the hotel trade.

1 See generally EMPLOYMENT, vol 9, paras 404 ff.

(8) HOTELKEEPER'S LIABILITY

(a) Death and Personal Injuries

1738. Duty of reasonable care. At common law and under statute a hotel-keeper must take reasonable care for his guests in respect of the safety of the hotel premises[1] and wholesomeness of food and drink[2] supplied. The hotel-keeper is not an insurer of the person of the guest; he is only liable for injury to the guest if negligence is proved[3]. He is not liable if a guest is attacked by another guest or third person[4], although it might be argued that he was negligent in failing to keep order in his establishment and in failing to eject a person who was proving to be a nuisance or danger to other guests[5]. It is his duty to ensure that his premises are as safe as reasonable care and skill can make them[6]. There is an implied warranty to that effect given in the contractual relationship between hotelkeeper and guest or customer[7].

Passages and stairways should be adequately lit[8] and adequate fire pre-cautions[9] should be taken[10]. The guest should also take reasonable care for his own safety[11].

1 Ie under the Occupiers' Liability (Scotland) Act 1960 (c 30) (see OBLIGATIONS), and the Health and Safety at Work etc Act 1974 (c 37) (see EMPLOYMENT, vol 9, paras 404 ff).
2 Ie under the Food and Drugs (Scotland) Act 1956 (c 30) (see para 1779 below); the Food Hygiene (Scotland) Regulations 1959, SI 1959/413 (see para 1780 below); and the Control of Food Premises (Scotland) Act 1977 (c 28) (see para 1781 below).
3 *Maclenan v Segar* [1917] 2 KB 325 at 328, per McCardie J.
4 *Calye's Case* (1584) 8 Co Rep 32a.
5 See *Strathearn Hydropathic Co Ltd v Inland Revenue* (1881) 8 R 798 at 800, 801, per Lord President Inglis.
6 See *Beaudry v Fort Cumberland Hotel Ltd* (1971) 24 DLR (3d) 80 (Can).
7 *Maclenan v Segar* [1917] 2 KB 325.
8 *Campbell v Shelbourne Hotel Ltd* [1939] 2 KB 534, [1939] 2 All ER 351.
9 *Hallett v Nicholson* 1979 SC 1. See also paras 1732 ff above.
10 *Beaudry v Fort Cumberland Hotel Ltd* (1971) 24 DLR (3d) 80 (Can).
11 *Andrews v Pattullo* [1956] JPL 364; *Carroll v Garford* (1968) 112 Sol Jo 948.

(b) Third Persons

1739. Liability for acts of a guest. The hotelkeeper is not liable for the acts or omissions of his guests[1] or of a dog which the hotelkeeper has permitted the guest to bring onto the hotel premises[2].

1 *Calye's Case* (1584) 8 Co Rep 32a. However, see the opinion of Lord President Inglis in *Strathearn Hydropathic Co Ltd v Inland Revenue* (1881) 8 R 798 at 800, 801.
2 *Carroll v Garford* (1968) 112 Sol Jo 948. He may be liable where he permits a savage and dangerous dog to be present on the premises. As to the liability for injury and damage caused by animals generally, see ANIMALS, vol 2, paras 160 ff.

1740. Liability for guest's debts. A hotelkeeper is not liable for the unpaid debts of the guest unless he had expressly guaranteed such debts[1]. Possession that creates a lien is not necessarily sufficient to permit arrestment; accordingly a guest's luggage cannot be arrested in the hands of an hotelkeeper[2].

1 *Callard v White* (1816) 1 Stark 171 (unpaid laundry bills). The legal position may be different if the hotelkeeper was in the habit of discharging bills left unpaid by guests.
2 *Hume v Baillie* (1852) 14 D 821; *Hutchison v Hutchison* 1912 1 SLT 219, OH.

(c) Property of the Guest

(A) LIABILITY GENERALLY

1741. Edictal liability. Edictal liability[1] lies at the root of the hotelkeeper's liability for the loss[2] of property brought to the hotel by a guest[3]. This liability is strict and is incurred even though the guest cannot prove negligence on the part of the hotelkeeper[4]. However, the hotelkeeper is not liable if the loss arises from the negligence of the owner, natural and inevitable accident, an act of God, or an act of the sovereign's enemies[5]. The liability does not depend upon contract or deposit, but merely by a traveller entering a hotel[6]. It arises without express intimation to, or acceptance by, the hotelkeeper or his agent[7]. The liability probably does arise in respect of damage to a guest's goods, as distinct from loss or theft, if it can be established that it was due to the negligence or wilful act of the hotelkeeper or his servants[8].

1 As to edictal liability generally, see para 1702 above.
2 As to the meaning of 'loss', see *Williams v Owen* [1956] 1 All ER 104 at 105, [1955] 1 WLR 1293 at 1295, per Finnemore J. See also *Collingwood v Home and Colonial Stores Ltd* [1936] 3 All ER 200 at 203, 204, CA, per Lord Wright MR.
3 Stair *Institutions* I,9,5; Erskine *Institute* III,1,28; Bell *Principles* ss 235–242A. As to the hotelkeeper's statutory liability, see para 1743 below.
4 *Burns v Royal Hotel (St Andrews) Ltd* 1958 SC 354 at 362, 1958 SLT 309 at 312, 313, per Lord President Clyde. This strict liability was considered just and necessary in order to protect the traveller from dishonest hotelkeepers: Bankton *Institute* I,16,1,2. The argument that this strict liability should be reduced in modern times was rejected in *The Second Report of the Law Reform Committee on Innkeepers' Liability for Property of Travellers, Guests and Residents* (the Jenkins Report) (Cmd 9161) (1954). It was felt that it caused little hardship because of the universal practice of insurance and more especially as the proportion of the premiums attributable to hotelkeepers' liability was small. See also *Gooden v Murray* (1700) Mor 9237.
5 See paras 1745–1747 below.
6 *Erskine* III,1,11 and 28.
7 See Justinian *Digest* IV,9,1, and Mackintosh (1891) 3 JR 306 at 310.
8 *Maclenan v Segar* [1917] 2 KB 325 at 328, per McCardie J; *Williams v Owen* [1956] 1 All ER 104, [1955] 1 WLR 1293. However, see *Mackintosh* at 318.

1742. Liability confined to hotelkeepers. The strict liability for the loss of property brought to a hotel by a guest applies only to hotelkeepers[1]. It does not apply to the keepers of boardinghouses[2], lodginghouses[3], staff hotels[4], restaurants[5], refreshment rooms[6], public houses or garages[7]. Strict liability is imposed upon the hotelkeeper only in his capacity as a hotelkeeper and not as a restaurateur[8], garage proprietor or public house keeper[9].

1 For the meaning of 'hotelkeepers', see para 1715 above. See also the Hotel Proprietors Act 1956 (c 62), s 1.
2 *Grimston v Innkeeper* (1627) Het 49; *Scarborough v Cosgrove* [1905] 2 KB 805 at 814, CA, per Romer LJ; *Tinsley v Dudley* [1951] 2 KB 18, [1951] 1 All ER 252, CA. However, see *May v Wingate* (1694) Mor 9236.

3 *Scott v Yates* (1800) Hume 207; *Watling v M'Dowall* (1825) 4 S 83 (NE 86). However, see *May v Wingate* (1694) Mor 9236.
4 *Edwards v West Herts Group Hospital Management Committee* [1957] 1 All ER 541, [1957] 1 WLR 415, CA.
5 *Ultzen v Nicols* [1894] 1 QB 92.
6 *Strauss v County Hotel and Wine Co Ltd* (1883) 12 QBD 27.
7 *Central Motors (Glasgow) Ltd v Cessnock Garage and Motor Co* 1925 SC 796, 1925 SLT 563; *Sinclair v Juner* 1952 SC 35, 1952 SLT 181.
8 However, see *Orchard v Bush & Co* [1898] 2 QB 284 (dining room of a hotel).
9 Hotel Proprietors Act 1956 (c 62), s 1(1).

1743. Liability for guest's property within hotel premises. The strict liability of the hotelkeeper applies in respect of property brought onto the hotel premises by the guest[1]. It does not matter that the hotelkeeper was not aware of the contents of the guest's luggage[2]. However, he may not be liable where the guest has retained control of the property in such a way as to relieve the hotelkeeper from his liability in respect of that property.

The liability applies only in respect of property brought within the hotel premises or *hospitium* of the hotel. The *hospitium* consists of the hotel buildings and those precincts so intimately related to them as to be treated for this purpose as forming part of the hotel[3]. An area may form part of the *hospitium* of the hotel for some purposes but not for others[4]. The liability of the hotelkeeper extends to property brought by the guest and placed in that part of the premises in which such goods are usually placed[5] that is within the hotel buildings in the case of luggage[6].

The hotelkeeper does not incur strict liability for property left at the hotel on the guest's departure[7].

1 See the Hotel Proprietors Act 1956 (c 62), s 2(1), (2), (3)(c), and para 1748 below.
2 *Williamson v White* 21 June 1810 FC; *Meikle v Skelly* 16 Feb 1813 FC.
3 *Williams v Linnitt* [1951] 1 KB 565 at 580, 581, [1951] 1 All ER 278 at 287, CA, per Asquith LJ.
4 *Gresham v Lyon* [1954] 2 All ER 786, [1954] 1 WLR 1100. However, as to vehicles and property left in them and horses and live animals, see the Hotel Proprietors Act 1956, s 2(2), and para 1748 below.
5 *Williams v Linnitt* [1951] 1 KB 565 at 577, [1951] 1 All ER 278 at 285, CA, per Lord Tucker.
6 *Watson v People's Refreshment House Association Ltd* [1952] 1 KB 318 at 324, 325, [1952] 1 All ER 289 at 292, per Devlin J.
7 *Gelley v Clerk* (1607) Cro Jac 188; *Lynar v Mossop* (1875) 36 UCR 230 (Can).

1744. Extent of the hotelkeeper's liability. The standard of care which the hotelkeeper is required to exercise in respect of the guest's luggage is greater than that of an ordinary careful man. It is not sufficient for him to prove that he used all reasonable care or that he had taken the usual precautions[1], for upon that basis the main protection afforded by the edict[2] would be destroyed[3]. His liability is not restricted to negligence. Such negligence would, in many cases, be difficult to prove and would impose an impossible burden on the owner of the goods who does not, and usually cannot, know what precautions are taken by the hotelkeeper to protect them[4]. This liability includes liability for the acts of employees[5]. Thus, where loss occurs due to the failure of an employee to perform his duties properly, or by the wilful act of an employee, the hotelkeeper is liable[6].

Similarly, the hotelkeeper is liable if the property was stolen by another guest[7]. A hotelkeeper who fails to take adequate steps to prevent theft or to apprehend thieves is negligent[8]. It does not matter that the hotelkeeper was not aware of the contents of the guest's luggage; it is enough that he knew, or ought to have known, that certain effects had been brought to the hotel[9].

1 *Mustard v Paterson* 1923 SC 142 at 148, 149, 1923 SLT 21 at 24, per Lord Justice-Clerk Alness.

2 Ie the edict *'nautae, caupones, stabularii'*: see paras 1741, 1702, above.

3 *Burns v Royal Hotel (St Andrews) Ltd* 1958 SC 354 at 362, 1958 SLT 309 at 313, per Lord President Clyde.

4 *Burns v Royal Hotel (St Andrews) Ltd* 1958 SC 354, 1958 SLT 309.

5 See *Central Motors (Glasgow) Ltd v Cessnock Garage and Motor Co* 1925 SC 796 at 804, 1925 SLT 563 at 567, 568, per Lord Sands.

6 *Central Motors (Glasgow) Ltd v Cessnock Garage and Motor Co* 1925 SC 796, 1925 SLT 563; *Kott and Kott v Gordon Hotels Ltd* [1968] 2 Lloyd's Rep 228.

7 *Gooden v Murray* (1700) Mor 9237.

8 *Kott and Kott v Gordon Hotels Ltd* [1968] 2 Lloyd's Rep 228.

9 *Chisholm v Fenton* (1714) Mor 9241.

(B) EXCEPTIONS

1745. Guest's negligence. The hotelkeeper will escape liability if he can show that the guest had himself been negligent. It is technically inaccurate to speak of the guest's contributory negligence, for it is the guest's failure to take reasonable care of his own property[1]. The burden of proof that the guest had been negligent lies with the hotelkeeper[2]. He must establish that the loss would not have happened if the guest had used the ordinary care that a prudent man may reasonably be expected to have taken in the circumstances[3]. It has been settled from an early date that the innkeeper is not exonerated from liability if the property of a guest was lost or stolen from a room for which the guest had a key[4]. It is not *per se* negligent for a guest to fail to lock his door, in the case of a small hotel, where everyone was under the observation of the staff[5]. It has been held that a guest who placed a diamond ring in a jewel case and then placed it in her suitcase in her room was not negligent despite a notice advising guests to deposit valuables at the hotel office[6].

1 *Shacklock v Ethorpe Ltd* [1939] 3 All ER 372 at 374, HL, per Lord Macmillan.

2 *Wilson v Orr* (1879) 7 R 266; *Medawar v Grand Hotel Co* [1891] 2 QB 11, CA.

3 *Cashill v Wright* (1856) 6 E & B 891, per Erle J; *Gee, Walker and Slater Ltd v Friary Hotel (Derby) Ltd* (1949) 66 (pt 1) TLR 59, CA.

4 *Gooden v Murray* (1700) Mor 9237.

5 *Oppenheim v White Lion Hotel Co* (1871) LR 6 CP 515 at 522; *Shacklock v Ethorpe Ltd* [1939] 3 All ER 372, HL; *Brewster v Drennan* [1945] 2 All ER 705, CA.

6 *Carpenter v Haymarket Hotel Ltd* [1931] 1 KB 364, DC.

1746. Act of God. The hotelkeeper is not liable for the loss of the guest's property if that loss occurred due to an act of God[1]. The exception 'act of God', as used in Scots law with regard to the edict[2], has a wider significance that that given to it in other branches of the law[3]. Accidental fire may be an act of God[4]. However, it is not to be taken that any fire, not wilfully ignited, is a *damnum fatale*[5]. Fire is not necessarily considered an unavoidable accident[6]. An accidental fire is one which was neither the result of a deliberate act of the hotelkeeper nor the result of culpable acts or omissions by him[7]. The hotelkeeper must have taken all reasonable precautions against the occurrence of a fire[8].

In order to escape liability the hotelkeeper must prove that the fire occurred in such a way as excluded the possibility of any cause implying negligence on his part or on the part of his employees[9].

1 *Burns v Royal Hotel (St Andrews) Ltd* 1958 SC 354 at 362, 1958 SLT 309 at 313, per Lord President Clyde.

2 Ie the edict *'nautae, caupones, stabularii'*: see paras 1702, 1741, above.

3 *Mustard v Paterson* 1923 SC 142 at 153, 1923 SLT 21 at 26, per Lord Hunter.

4 *Gooden v Murray* (1700) Mor 9237; *McDonell v Ettles* 15 Dec 1809 FC. As to fire precautions, see paras 1732 ff above.

5 *Sinclair v Juner* 1952 SC 35 at 43, 44, 1952 SLT 181 at 185, per Lord President Cooper; *Burns v Royal Hotel (St Andrews) Ltd* 1958 SC 354 at 362, 1958 SLT 309 at 313, per Lord President Clyde.
6 *Forward v Pittard* (1785) 1 Term Rep 27.
7 *Sinclair v Juner* 1952 SC 35 at 43, 44, 1952 SLT 181 at 185, per Lord President Cooper.
8 *Burns v Royal Hotel (St Andrews) Ltd* 1958 SC 354, 1958 SLT 309.
9 *Burns v Royal Hotel (St Andrews) Ltd* 1958 SC 354, 1958 SLT 309. See also *Sinclair v Juner* 1952 SC 35 at 48, 1952 SLT 181 at 187, per Lord Keith.

1747. Act of the sovereign's enemies. The hotelkeeper is not liable for loss of the guest's property if that loss was due to an act of the sovereign's enemies. However, he would not escape liability if he had been negligent in dealing with advanced warnings of bomb threats or other hostile acts. He may be under an obligation to exclude from the hotel persons who pose as a threat to the wellbeing and safety of guests and of their property[1].

1 *Rothfield v North British Rly Co* 1920 SC 805, 1920 2 SLT 269.

(C) LIMITATION OF LIABILITY

1748. Limitation of the extent of the hotelkeeper's liability. The hotelkeeper is not liable to make good to any traveller any loss or damage to property which the traveller brought with him to the hotel unless, at the time of the loss or damage, sleeping accommodation at the hotel had been engaged for the traveller[1]. That loss or damage must have occurred during the period commencing with the midnight immediately preceding, and ending with the midnight immediately following, a period for which the traveller was a guest at the hotel and entitled to use the accommodation so engaged[2]. The hotelkeeper is no longer liable for loss or damage to vehicles or property left in them, or to any horse or other live animal, its harness or other equipment[3].

1 Hotel Proprietors Act 1956 (c 62), s 2(1)(a). This provision overruled *Winkworth v Raven* [1931] 1 KB 652; *Williams v Owen* [1956] 1 All ER 104, [1955] 1 WLR 1293. Thus, *Williams v Linnitt* [1951] 1 KB 565, [1951] 1 All ER 278, CA, is no longer good law, except in regard to negligence of the hotelkeeper or his employees: see paras 1741 ff above.
2 Hotel Proprietors Act 1956, s 2(1)(b).
3 Ibid, s 2(2). Thus, the decision in *Gresham v Lyon* [1954] 2 All ER 786, [1954] 1 WLR 1100, that a garage may form part of the *hospitium* of an inn *quoad* a car but not *quoad* luggage left therein is overruled in respect of strict liability.

1749. Limitation of liability by statutory notice. Where a hotelkeeper[1] is liable to make good the loss or damage to property brought to the hotel, then, provided a statutory notice is properly exhibited, his liability to any one guest will not exceed £50 in respect of any one article, or £100 in the aggregate[2]. However, the hotelkeeper is not entitled to this protection unless, at the time when the property was brought to the hotel, a copy of the statutory notice[3] was conspicuously displayed in a place where it could conveniently be read by his guests at or near the reception office or desk or, where there is no reception office or desk, at or near the main entrance to the hotel[4].

1 For the meaning of 'hotelkeeper', see para 1715 above.
2 Hotel Proprietors Act 1956 (c 62), s 2(3). However, this is subject to a number of exceptions: see para 1750 below.
3 For the statutory notice, see ibid, s 2(3) proviso, Schedule.
4 Ibid, s 2(3) proviso. See also *Shacklock v Ethorpe Ltd* [1937] 4 All ER 672, CA, involving a similar provision under the Innkeepers' Liability Act 1863 (c 41), s 3 (repealed).

1750. Circumstances excluding limitation of liability. The limitation of liability by statutory notice[1] will not apply where:

(1) the property was stolen, lost or damaged through the default, neglect or wilful act of the proprietor or some servant of his[2]; or

(2) the property was deposited by or on behalf of the guest expressly for safe custody with the proprietor or some servant of his authorised, or appearing to be authorised, for the purpose, and, if so required by the proprietor or that servant, in a container fastened or sealed by the depositor[3]; or

(3) at any time after the guest had arrived at the hotel, either the property in question was offered for deposit as aforesaid and the proprietor or servant refused to receive it, or the guest or some other guest acting on his behalf wished so to offer the property in question but, through the default of the proprietor or of his servant, was unable to do so[4].

1 See para 1749 above.
2 Hotel Proprietors Act 1956 (c 62), s 2(3)(a). See also *Kott and Kott v Gordon Hotels Ltd* [1968] 2 Lloyd's Rep 228. The burden of proof lies with the guest: *Whitehouse v Pickett* 1908 SC (HL) 31, 16 SLT 254.
3 Hotel Proprietors Act 1956, s 2(3)(b). As to the deposit of goods for safe custody, see para 1751 below.
4 Ibid, s 2(3)(c).

1751. Deposit of goods for safe keeping. Goods are deposited expressly for safe custody if something is said or done by the guest that would convey to the hotelkeeper that the goods were being deposited with him for safekeeping[1]. Intention by the depositor is not enough[2]. Thus, a bag containing jewels (the contents of which were undisclosed[3]) was not deposited for safe custody where it was merely handed to a porter to be placed in the hotel office, notwithstanding that the guest had frequented the hotel before and the hotelkeeper was aware that he was in the habit of carrying valuable jewels with him[4]. The mere handing over of property to the hotelkeeper is not an express deposit for safe custody[5]. A deposit may be proved *prout de jure*[6]. Where a deposit is proved, the onus of proving restoration lies with the depositary.

1 *Whitehouse v Pickett* 1908 SC (HL) 31 at 33, 16 SLT 254 at 255, per Lord Ashbourne.
2 1908 SC (HL) 31 at 32, 16 SLT 254 at 254, per Loreburn LC.
3 See *Hay v Williamson* (1704) Mor 9238. See also *Theeman v Fort Properties Pty Ltd* [1973] 1 NSWLR 418, where disclosure of the value of the property was not considered a pre-requisite.
4 *Whitehouse v Pickett* 1908 SC (HL) 31, 16 SLT 254.
5 1908 SC (HL) 31 at 35, 16 SLT 254 at 256, per Lord James of Hereford.
6 *Taylor v Nisbet* (1901) 4 F 79.

(9) REMEDIES

(a) Guest's Remedies

1752. Action for declarator of rights of travellers. An action for declarator of his rights may be competently brought by a traveller against a hotelkeeper who refuses to recognise them, either when the traveller legitimately and properly asked that they should be recognised and accorded to him, or, in the appropriate circumstances, puts forward a claim to have these rights declared[1]. An action for declarator is competent only in so far as it is merely ancillary to a claim for damages; but it would fail if that claim failed[2]. Thus, a practical question or particular dispute must lie behind an action for declarator[3].

1 *Rothfield v North British Rly Co* 1920 SC 805 at 827, 1920 2 SLT 269 at 277, per Lord Justice-Clerk Scott Dickson.

2 1920 SC 805 at 830, 1920 2 SLT 269 at 278, per Lord Dundas.
3 *Callender's Cable and Construction Co Ltd v Glasgow Corpn* (1900) 2 F 397 at 401, 7 SLT 332 at 333, 334, per Lord Adam; *North British Rly Co v Birrell's Trustees* 1918 SC (HL) 33 at 47, 1917 2 SLT 271 at 274, per Lord Dunedin.

1753. Refusal to receive a traveller. If a hotelkeeper refuses to receive and accommodate a traveller without lawful excuse the traveller may raise an action for damages. The action is not an action for breach of contract[1], and is maintainable without proof of special damage[2]. It is doubtful that an action for declarator as to the rights of the traveller is an essential preliminary conclusion for damages in such an action[3].

1 The traveller may have contractual remedies where there was a previous contract of booking or where hotel accommodation formed part of a package of travel and accommodation, although in the latter case the remedies may be against the tour operator or the travel agent: John J Downes 'The Tour Operator and the Law' 1984 SLT 281. See also paras 1724–1727 above.
2 *Constantine v Imperial Hotels Ltd* [1944] KB 693, [1944] 2 All ER 171.
3 *Rothfield v North British Rly Co* 1920 SC 805 at 827, 1920 2 SLT 269 at 277, per Lord Justice-Clerk Scott, and at 838 and at 283, 284, per Lord Ormidale. However, 'such a declaratory conclusion would be competent in so far as it is merely ancillary, by way of preface or prelude, to the demand for damages; but would fail if the latter failed': at 830 and at 278, per Lord Dundas.

1754. Remedy for loss or damage to property. The guest may raise an action against the hotelkeeper[1] for loss of, or damage to, his property[2]. The guest must have been a person for whom sleeping accommodation had been engaged[3]. It is necessary to plead that the hotelkeeper is a proprietor of a hotel within the meaning of the Hotel Proprietors Act 1956[4].

1 For the meaning of 'hotelkeeper', see para 1715 above.
2 As to the liability for the property of the guest, see paras 1741 ff above.
3 Hotel Proprietors Act 1956 (c 62), s 2(1)(a).
4 See ibid, s 1(1), (2).

1755. Remedy for personal injury; contractual remedies. The remedy for personal injury has already been discussed[1]. A guest also has a remedy for breach of contract, and this has also already been discussed[2].

1 As to the liability of the hotelkeeper for death and personal injury, see para 1738 above.
2 As to the creation and performance of the hotelkeeper's contract, see paras 1724–1727 above.

(b) Hotelkeeper's Remedies

1756. Action against guests. The hotelkeeper may raise an action against a guest for payment of the price of the accommodation and the goods and services supplied to him. He may raise action against any other person who has undertaken to pay for the guest so far as that undertaking extends[1].

1 *Wright v Anderton* [1909] 1 KB 209. See also *Daniel v Hotel Pacific Pty Ltd* [1953] VLR 447 (Aust).

1757. Hotelkeeper's lien. A hotelkeeper[1], when acting in that capacity[2], has a lien over all goods brought by a traveller[3] to the hotel as his luggage and received as such by the hotelkeeper. The goods of a traveller become liable to the lien as soon as the traveller enters the hotel with the intention of using it as such and is received on that basis by the hotelkeeper. However, the lien does not attach to the goods until a debt has been incurred[4]. The fact that some person other than the traveller is to pay for the accommodation does not affect the hotelkeeper's liability for and lien upon the traveller's goods[5]. This right of lien is not confined to possessions[6] and baggage owned by the traveller himself but extends to possessions in the ownership of third persons which were brought to the hotel by him[6]. Thus, the hotelkeeper has a lien against the true owner of the goods and not merely against the guest only[7]. The hotelkeeper's lien is not confined to goods of a kind ordinarily brought by travellers for use on their journey[8]. However, there is no right of lien over vehicles or any property left in them, or any horse or other live animal or its harness or other equipment[9].

1 For the meaning of 'hotelkeeper', see para 1715 above. However, boardinghouse keepers are not entitled to a hotelkeeper's lien: *Light v Abel* (1866) 6 All 400 (Can); *Newcombe v Anderson* (1886) 11 OR 665 (Can).
2 *Matsuda v Waldorf Hotel Co Ltd* (1910) 27 TLR 153.
3 For the meaning of 'traveller', see para 1716 above.
4 *Wright v Anderton* [1909] 1 KB 209.
5 *Wright v Anderton* [1909] 1 KB 209. See also *Bermans and Nathans Ltd v Weibye* 1983 SC 67 at 69–71, 1983 SLT 299 at 301, per Lord President Emslie.
6 *Bermans and Nathans Ltd v Weibye* 1983 SC 67, 1983 SLT 299. In this case a film company booked hotel accommodation for a number of actors who left the hotel without paying their bills, and it was held that the hotelkeeper could not exercise a lien over costumes hired to the company, which were stored in a number of chalets in the hotel grounds, as the costumes were not within the possession of any of the individual guests concerned.
7 *Robins & Co v Gray* [1895] 2 QB 501, CA.
8 *Bermans and Nathans Ltd v Weibye* 1983 SC 67, 1983 SLT 299. See also Bankton *Institute* I, 17, 1, 2.
9 Hotel Proprietors Act 1956 (c 62), s 2(2).

1758. Power to sell goods left at hotel. In addition to the hotelkeeper's right of lien[1], the landlord, proprietor keeper or manager of a hotel has the right absolutely to sell and dispose by public auction any goods, carriages[2], horses, wares or merchandise which may have been deposited with him or left in the hotel, coach house, stable, stableyard or other premises attached to the hotel[3]. This right of sale exists where the person depositing or leaving such goods, carriages etc, is indebted or will become indebted to the hotelkeeper[4] either for any board and lodging or for the keep and expenses of any horse or other animals left with or standing at livery in the stables or fields occupied by the hotelkeeper[5]. The debt for payment of which the sale is made must not be any other, or greater, debt than the debt for which the goods or other articles could have been retained under the hotelkeeper's lien[6].

1 See para 1757 above.
2 Ie motor vehicles or trailers: see the Road Traffic Act 1988 (c 52), s 191.
3 Innkeepers Act 1878 (c 38), s 1. This right of sale is also given to the landlord, proprietor, keeper or manager of a licensed public house: see s 1.
4 For the meaning of 'hotelkeeper', see para 1715 above. This is not confined to the hotel proprietors defined in the Hotel Proprietors Act 1956 (c 62), s 1(1), (3): see further para 1715 above.
5 Innkeepers Act 1878, s 1.
6 Ibid, s 1, second proviso.

1759. Sale of goods left at hotel. The sale of goods left at the hotel may not be made until they have been in the hotelkeeper's charge or custody, or in or upon his premises, for six weeks without the debt due to him from the person leaving them having been paid or satisfied[1]. At least one month before the sale, the hotelkeeper[2] must insert an advertisement, containing notice of the intended sale, in one London newspaper and one country newspaper circulating in the district where the goods or articles were deposited or left[3]. The notice must give a short description of the goods and articles to be sold, together with the name, if known, of the owner or person who deposited or left them[3]. The hotelkeeper must pay to that person on demand any surplus of the proceeds of sale after he has deducted the amount of debt due to him, together with the costs and expenses of the sale[4].

1 Innkeepers Act 1878 (c 38), s 1, first proviso. See also *Chesham Automobile Supply Ltd v Beresford Hotel (Birchington) Ltd* (1913) 29 TLR 584.
2 Ie the landlord, proprietor, keeper or manager of the hotel.
3 Innkeepers Act 1878, s 1, third proviso.
4 Ibid, s 1, first proviso.

(10) LICENSING

(a) Introduction

1760. Scope of licensing provisions in respect of hotelkeepers. This part of the title sets out an outline of the main provisions in respect of the regulation of the sale of alcoholic liquor as they affect the hotelkeeper[1].

1 As to the regulation of the sale of alcoholic liquor in more detail, see ALCOHOLIC LIQUOR, vol 2, paras 1 ff.

(b) Licensing Authorities

1761. Introduction. The Licensing (Scotland) Act 1976[1] made radical changes in the constitution of licensing authorities. Licensing courts were replaced by licensing boards for district and islands areas[2]. A right of appeal to the sheriff against a decision of the licensing authorities was introduced, with a further right of appeal to the Court of Session on a point of law[3]. Two new types of licence were introduced[4]. The wide discretion to refuse an application which was formerly enjoyed by the licensing courts is now restricted in respect of the licensing boards to those grounds specified in the statute[5]. The period of the currency of a licence was extended to three years, but the licensing board may order the suspension of a licence or closure of premises in certain circumstances[6].

1 The Licensing (Scotland) Act 1976 (c 66) is based on the recommendations of the *Report of the Departmental Committee on Scottish Licensing Law* (the Clayson Report) (Cmnd 5354) (1973): see ALCOHOLIC LIQUOR, vol 2, para 2.
2 See para 1762 below, and ALCOHOLIC LIQUOR, vol 2, paras 3 ff.
3 See para 1769 below, and ALCOHOLIC LIQUOR, vol 2, paras 85 ff.
4 Ie a refreshment licence and entertainment licence: see ALCOHOLIC LIQUOR, vol 2, paras 14, 15.
5 See ALCOHOLIC LIQUOR, vol 2, paras 53 ff.
6 See para 1773 below, and ALCOHOLIC LIQUOR, vol 2, paras 58, 62, 63.

1762. Licensing authorities. There are separate licensing boards[1] for each district and islands area and each licensing division[2]. Every licensing board must hold a meeting for the purpose of discharging its statutory functions in January, March, June and October of each year beginning on a date in each month fixed by the licensing board at least eight weeks prior to the meeting[3]. The licensing board may delegate decisions, except those expressly reserved to it[4], to a committee of the board, one or more members[5], the clerk of the board or any other person appointed to assist the clerk[6].

1 See the Licensing (Scotland) Act 1976 (c 66), s 1(2), and ALCOHOLIC LIQUOR, vol 2, para 3.
2 See ibid, s 1(2), (3), and ALCOHOLIC LIQUOR, vol 2, para 3.
3 See ibid, s 4, and ALCOHOLIC LIQUOR, vol 2, para 5. The board may also hold such other meeting as appear to the board to be appropriate: s 4(1)(b).
4 As to the matters which may not be delegated, see ibid, s 5(2). See also *Main v City of Glasgow District Licensing Board* 1987 SLT 305, OH.
5 As to membership of a licensing board, see ALCOHOLIC LIQUOR, vol 2, paras 3, 69.
6 See the Licensing (Scotland) Act 1976, s 5(1).

(c) Types of Licences

1763. Hotel licences. A hotel licence is granted in respect of a hotel specified in it, and authorises the holder of the licence to sell by retail alcoholic liquor for consumption on or off the premises[1]. For this purpose 'hotel' means
(1) in towns and suburbs, a house containing at least four apartments set apart exclusively for the sleeping accommodation of travellers;
(2) in rural districts and populous places not exceeding 1,000 inhabitants according to the census for the time being last taken, a house containing at least two such apartments[2].

1 Licensing (Scotland) Act 1976 (c 66), s 9(3), Sch 1. See further ALCOHOLIC LIQUOR, vol 2, para 11.
2 Ibid, s 139(1).

1764. Restricted hotel licence. A restricted hotel licence is a licence granted in respect of a specified hotel which
(1) is structurally adapted and bona fide used, or intended to be used, for the purpose of habitually providing the customary main meal at midday or in the evening or both for the accommodation of persons frequenting the hotel;
(2) so far as it is used or intended to be used for the purpose of providing meals to persons who are not residing there, is principally used, or intended to be used, for providing the customary main meal at midday or in the evening or both; and
(3) does not contain a bar counter[1].
This licence authorises the holder to sell by retail or supply alcoholic liquor to residents and their private friends bona fide entertained by them, and to non-residents as an ancillary to table meals taken on the premises[1]. 'Table meal' means a meal eaten by a person sitting at a table, or at a counter or other structure which serves the purpose of a table and is not used for the service of refreshments for consumption by persons not seated at a table or structure serving the purpose of a table[2].

1 Licensing (Scotland) Act 1976 (c 66), s 9(3), Sch 1. See further ALCOHOLIC LIQUOR, vol 2, para 12.
2 Ibid, s 139(1).

(d) Obtaining a Licence

1765. Application for a licence. The applicant for a licence or his agent must complete and sign the appropriate application form and lodge it with the clerk to the licensing board not later than five weeks before the first day of the meeting of the board at which the application is to be considered[1]. In the case of an application for the grant of a new licence, the applicant must also lodge a plan of the premises[2]. He must also display at the premises a notice in the prescribed form specifying the type of licence applied for[3]. In the case of an application for a new licence, the applicant must give notice to every occupier of the premises situated in the same building as the premises to which the application relates[4]. An application made otherwise than by an individual natural person must name both the applicant and the employee responsible for the day-to-day running of the premises[5].

Not later than three weeks before the first day of the meeting, the clerk is required to publish a list of competent applications to be considered at that meeting[6].

1 See the Licensing (Scotland) Act 1976 (c 66), s 10(1), (6), and ALCOHOLIC LIQUOR, vol 2, para 37. See also *Tait v City of Glasgow District Licensing Board* 1987 SLT 340, OH.
2 See the Licensing (Scotland) Act 1976, s 10(2)(a), and ALCOHOLIC LIQUOR, vol 2, para 38.
3 See ibid, s 10(2)(b), and ALCOHOLIC LIQUOR, vol 2, para 40.
4 See ibid, s 10(5), and ALCOHOLIC LIQUOR, vol 2, para 40.
5 See ibid, s 11, and ALCOHOLIC LIQUOR, vol 2, para 41.
6 See ibid, s 12, and ALCOHOLIC LIQUOR, vol 2, para 42.

1766. The hearing of the application. The licensing board may not at any meeting hear the case of applicants for new licences until all other cases have been disposed of[1]. The board may decline to consider an application if the applicant or his representative does not attend the meeting[2]. In considering the application the board may take into account any competent objection[3]. An objection may only be considered if it is relevant to one or more of the grounds for refusal[4].

1 See the Licensing (Scotland) Act 1976 (c 66), s 13(1), and ALCOHOLIC LIQUOR, vol 2, para 57. See also *Tait v City of Glasgow District Licensing Board* 1987 SLT 340, OH.
2 See the Licensing (Scotland) Act 1976, s 15(1), and ALCOHOLIC LIQUOR, vol 2, para 56.
3 As to competent objections, see ALCOHOLIC LIQUOR, vol 2, paras 49–52.
4 As to the grounds for refusal, see para 1768 below.

1767. Grant of a licence. An application for a new licence may not be entertained by the licensing board unless the applicant produces certificates from the appropriate authority as to the suitability of the premises in relation to planning, building control and food hygiene[1]. Before granting a licence the licensing board must consult the fire authority for the area[2]. When granting any type of licence the board may specify the type of liquor which may be sold by retail[3].

A new licence comes into effect on being granted by a licensing board, except that where there were objections at the hearing the licence does not come into effect until the time within which an appeal may be made has elapsed, or where an appeal has been lodged, the appeal has been abandoned or determined in favour of the applicant for the licence[4]. The licence continues in effect until the quarterly meeting three years after the grant[5].

1 See the Licensing (Scotland) Act 1976 (c 66), s 23(1), and ALCOHOLIC LIQUOR, vol 2, para 43. As to planning permission, building control and food hygiene certificates, see ALCOHOLIC LIQUOR, vol 2, paras 44–46.
2 See ibid, s 23(5), and ALCOHOLIC LIQUOR, vol 2, para 48.
3 See ibid, s 29(1), and ALCOHOLIC LIQUOR, vol 2, para 70. A distinction is drawn between the type of alcoholic liquor which may be sold under a full licence from that which may be sold under a restricted licence: s 29(1) proviso.
4 See ibid, s 30(1), and ALCOHOLIC LIQUOR, vol 2, para 58.
5 See ibid, s 30(3), and ALCOHOLIC LIQUOR, vol 2, para 58.

1768. Refusal of an application. The board may decline to consider an application if the applicant or his representative does not attend the meeting[1]. Otherwise it can only refuse to grant a licence on the grounds:

(1) that the applicant or prospective manager is not suitable; or
(2) that the premises are not suitable or convenient; or
(3) that the use of the premises for the sale of alcoholic liquor is likely to cause undue public nuisance, or a threat to public order or safety; or
(4) that to grant the application would result in over-provision of facilities[2].

In considering whether or not the applicant or prospective manager is a fit and proper person to hold a licence, the board may have regard to any misconduct on the part of that person which in the opinion of the board has a bearing on his fitness to hold a licence[3].

1 See the Licensing (Scotland) Act 1976 (c 66), s 15(1), and ALCOHOLIC LIQUOR, vol 2, para 56.
2 See ibid, s 17(1), and ALCOHOLIC LIQUOR, vol 2, para 53.
3 See ibid, s 17(3), and ALCOHOLIC LIQUOR, vol 2, para 53.

1769. Appeal against a decision of the licensing board. Applicants and objectors are entitled to be furnished with a written statement of the reasons for the decision of the licensing board[1]. An applicant refused a licence may appeal to the sheriff a competent objector may similarly appeal against a grant, and either may appeal against any conditions which may have been attached[2]. The appeal must be lodged within fourteen days from the date of the decision appealed against or within fourteen days from the receipt of any statement of reasons[3]. Further appeal, on a point of law, lies to the Court of Session[4].

1 See the Licensing (Scotland) Act 1976 (c 66), s 18, and ALCOHOLIC LIQUOR, vol 2, para 59.
2 See ibid, s 39, and ALCOHOLIC LIQUOR, vol 2, para 85 ff.
3 See ibid, s 39(2), (3), and ALCOHOLIC LIQUOR, vol 2, para 92.
4 See ibid, s 39(8), and ALCOHOLIC LIQUOR, vol 2, para 93.

1770. Renewal of a licence. An application for the renewal of a licence must be completed and signed by the applicant or his agent, and lodged with the clerk to the licensing board at which the application is to be considered[1]. Before granting the renewal of a licence the board must consult the fire authority for the area[2]. The board may require a plan of the premises to which a licence renewal application relates to be produced to it and lodged with the clerk of the board[3].

1 See the Licensing (Scotland) Act 1976 (c 66), s 10(1), (6)(a), and ALCOHOLIC LIQUOR, vol 2, para 37. As to non-attendance by the applicant, objections and grounds of refusal, see ss 15–17, and ALCOHOLIC LIQUOR, vol 2, paras 50, 51, 53, 56. See also *Hart v City of Edinburgh District Licensing Board* 1987 SLT (Sh Ct) 54.
2 See the Licensing (Scotland) Act 1976, s 24(1), and ALCOHOLIC LIQUOR, vol 2, para 48.
3 See ibid, s 24(2), and ALCOHOLIC LIQUOR, vol 2, para 38.

1771. Permanent transfer of a licence. An application for the permanent transfer[1] of a licence must be made and completed and signed by the applicant or his agent, and lodged with the clerk to the licensing board not later than five weeks before the first day of the meeting at which the application is to be considered[2], provided that the applicant is a new tenant or occupant[3]. A transfer of a licence can only take effect during its currency[4]. Where an employee, in a jointly held licence, ceases to have day-to-day responsibility for the premises, the licence will cease to have effect unless the transfer to another employee is made within eight weeks[5].

1 See the Licensing (Scotland) Act 1976 (c 66), s 25(1), (6), and ALCOHOLIC LIQUOR, vol 2, para 35.
2 See ibid, s 10(1), (6)(c), and ALCOHOLIC LIQUOR, vol 2, para 37. The application must also comply with ss 11, 13, 15–21: see ALCOHOLIC LIQUOR, vol 2, paras 37, 41, 49–51, 53, 56–59, 69.
3 See ibid, s 25(1), and ALCOHOLIC LIQUOR, vol 2, para 35. See also *Tayside Chief Constable v Angus District Licensing Board* 1980 SLT (Sh Ct) 31.

4 As to the currency of a licence, see ALCOHOLIC LIQUOR, vol 2, para 58.
5 See the Licensing (Scotland) Act 1976, ss 11, 25(3), 26, and ALCOHOLIC LIQUOR, vol 2, paras 33,
    41.

1772. Temporary transfer of a licence. A licensing board may transfer a
licence temporarily to an applicant who is a representative of the licence holder
where the licence holder has died[1] or become bankrupt, insolvent or incapable[2],
and where the applicant is in possession of the premises[3]. A licence so transferred continues to be valid until the next meeting of the licensing board or until
the time within which an appeal may be made has elapsed or until the appeal has
been abandoned or determined[4].

  1 Ie the executor, representative or disponee.
  2 Ie the trustee, judicial factor or *curator bonis.*
  3 See the Licensing (Scotland) Act 1976 (c 66), s 25(2), and ALCOHOLIC LIQUOR, vol 2, para 35. A
     licensing board may delegate to a committee, member of the board or official: see s 5(1), (2).
  4 See ibid, s 25(4), and ALCOHOLIC LIQUOR, vol 2, paras 37, 58, 61.

1773. Suspension of a licence. A licensing board may suspend a licence[1] on a
complaint made by a competent person or body[2], if it is satisfied that it is in the
public interest to do so[3]. Such a suspension may be ordered on one or both of the
following grounds: (1) that the licence holder is no longer a fit and proper
person; or (2) that the use of the premises has caused undue public nuisance or a
threat to public order or safety[4]. On receipt of a complaint the board must
decide whether or not to hold a hearing on the issue and must inform the
complainer of the board's decision in the matter[5]. The period of suspension
must be a fixed period, and the effect of the suspension is that the licence ceases
to have effect during the period of the suspension[6].

  1 As to the power of the licensing board to make closure orders, see the Licensing (Scotland) Act
     1976 (c 66), s 32, and ALCOHOLIC LIQUOR, vol 2, para 63.
  2 As to competent persons and bodies, see ibid, s 16(1), and ALCOHOLIC LIQUOR, vol 2, para 49.
  3 See ibid, s 31(1), and ALCOHOLIC LIQUOR, vol 2, para 62.
  4 See ibid, s 31(2), and ALCOHOLIC LIQUOR, vol 2, para 62. As to the factors which the licensing
     boards may take into consideration, see s 31(3), and ALCOHOLIC LIQUOR, vol 2, para 62.
  5 See ibid, s 31(4), (5), and ALCOHOLIC LIQUOR, vol 2, para 62.
  6 See ibid, s 31(7), and ALCOHOLIC LIQUOR, vol 2, para 62. As to the time that the suspension takes
     effect, see s 31(6), and ALCOHOLIC LIQUOR, vol 2, para 62.

1774. Seasonal licences. The holder of a hotel licence or restricted hotel
licence may apply to the licensing board to be permitted to close the premises for
part or parts of the year, but such part or parts must not exceed 180 days[1]. The
board must be satisfied that the requirements of the area make a seasonal licence
desirable[2]. It is achieved by inserting a condition in the licence that for part or
parts of the year there are to be no permitted hours in the hotel premises[2]. The
board may, nevertheless, permit the licence holder to operate the permitted
hours in respect of a bar or restaurant which is open to the public[3].

  1 See the Licensing (Scotland) Act 1976 (c 66), s 62(1), (2).
  2 Ibid, s 62(1).
  3 Ibid, s 62(1)(b).

1775. Permitted hours. The permitted hours for premises in respect of which
a hotel licence or restricted hotel licence is in force are, on weekdays, the period
between 11 am and 2.30 pm, and the period between 5 pm and 11 pm, and on
Sundays, the period between 12.30 pm and 2.30 pm and the period between
6.30 pm and 11 pm[1]. It is not an offence to sell or supply alcohol outwith those

hours to a resident of the premises in which the sale or supply took place, or to any private friends of a resident bona fide entertained by him at his own expense[2]. If, in granting a restricted hotel licence, it appears to the board that only a midday or evening meal is being provided, it can restrict the permitted hours to the midday period in the former case or to the evening period in the latter case[3]. The sale or supply of alcoholic liquor for consumption off the premises is not permitted from premises for which a restricted hotel licence is held, except to residents for consumption as an ancillary to a meal supplied at, but to be consumed off, the premises[4].

1 See the Licensing (Scotland) Act 1976 (c 66), s 53(1), (3), and ALCOHOLIC LIQUOR, vol 2, para 18.
2 See ibid, s 54(3)(c), (e), and ALCOHOLIC LIQUOR, vol 2, para 19. See also *Oliver v Loudon* (1896) 23 R (J) 34, 3 SLT 264; *Macdonald v Skinner* 1979 JC 29, 1978 SLT (Notes) 52.
3 See the Licensing (Scotland) Act 1976, s 55, Sch 1.
4 See ibid, s 53(4), and ALCOHOLIC LIQUOR, vol 2, para 18.

1776. Extension of permitted hours. An extension of permitted hours may be granted in respect of premises which to the satisfaction of the licensing board are structurally adapted and bona fide used for the purpose of habitually providing the customary main midday meal for the accommodation of persons frequenting the hotel[1]. Alcoholic liquor may be supplied up to 4 pm to persons taking a table meal[2] in a part of those premises usually set apart for the service of such persons, and supplied for consumption by such a person in that part of the premises as an ancillary to his meal[3]. The holder of the licence must give written notice to the chief constable fourteen days prior to the date on which it is intended to apply for the extension of permitted hours[4].

Similar provision is made in respect of an extension of permitted hours by two hours in the evening[5]. In the case of such an extension the premises must have been adapted and used for providing substantial refreshment to which the sale and supply of liquor is ancillary[6]. An extension of permitted hours may also be granted to permit the sale and supply of liquor with a meal on approval between 5 pm and 6.30 pm on Sundays[7].

1 See the Licensing (Scotland) Act 1976 (c 66), s 57(1) proviso, and ALCOHOLIC LIQUOR, vol 2, para 20.
2 'Table meal' means a meal eaten by a person sitting at a table, or at a counter or other structure which serves the purpose of a table and is not used for the service of refreshments for consumption by persons not seated at a table or structure serving the purpose of a table: ibid, s 139(1).
3 See ibid, s 57(2), (3).
4 See ibid, s 57(6)(d), and ALCOHOLIC LIQUOR, vol 2, para 20.
5 See ibid, s 58(2).
6 See ibid, s 58(1), (3).
7 See ibid, s 60.

1777. Regular extensions of permitted hours. The holder of a hotel licence may apply for a regular extension of permitted hours[1]. At the same time as the application is made a copy must be sent to the chief constable[1]. Any person or body entitled to object to the grant, renewal or transfer of a licence[2] may object to the application[3]. The objection must be made in writing and lodged with the clerk of the licensing board and a copy sent to the applicant not less than seven days before the quarterly meeting at which the application is to be considered[3].

The licensing board may only grant a regular extension if it considers it desirable to do so[4]. The application must be refused if it is likely to cause undue public nuisance or be a threat to public order or safety[5]. In granting an application, the licensing board may specify the period for which the regular extension is granted and the hours during which alcoholic liquor may be sold or supplied[6].

1 See the Licensing (Scotland) Act 1976 (c 66), s 64(1), and ALCOHOLIC LIQUOR, vol 2, para 24.
2 See ibid, s 16(1), and ALCOHOLIC LIQUOR, vol 2, para 49.
3 See ibid, s 64(7), and ALCOHOLIC LIQUOR, vol 2, para 24.
4 See ibid, s 64(3), and ALCOHOLIC LIQUOR, vol 2, para 24. There is no provision for appeal against a decision of the licensing board in respect of an application under s 64: *Sloan v North East Fife District Council Licensing Board* 1978 SLT (Sh Ct) 62.
5 See the Licensing (Scotland) Act 1976, s 64(8), and ALCOHOLIC LIQUOR, vol 2, para 24.
6 See ibid, s 64(3), and ALCOHOLIC LIQUOR, vol 2, para 24. If the licence holder or his employee or agent contravenes the conditions imposed by the licensing board he is guilty of an offence: see s 64(6), and ALCOHOLIC LIQUOR, vol 2, para 84.

1778. Reconstruction and alterations to premises. The licence holder may not reconstruct or alter premises without the consent of the licensing board[1]. The board may order the licence holder to make alterations, and failure to comply with such an order is an offence[2].

1 See the Licensing (Scotland) Act 1976 (c 66), s 35, and ALCOHOLIC LIQUOR, vol 2, para 36.
2 See ibid, s 36, and ALCOHOLIC LIQUOR, vol 2, paras 64, 84.

(11) CONSUMER PROTECTION

(a) Food

1779. Introduction. The Food and Drugs (Scotland) Act 1956 provides that food should not be injurious to health and should also be of the nature and quality demanded by the purchaser[1]. The Act provides for the control of food composition, labelling and hygiene by the issuing of regulations[2]. The Act sets out a number of offences including:
(1) selling, to the prejudice of the purchaser, any food which is not of the nature, substance or quality demanded[3];
(2) selling, offering or exposing for sale, or having in possession for the purposes of sale, any food which is intended for human consumption but which is in fact not fit for that purpose[4].
Defences are provided in the Act[5].

1 See FOOD, DAIRIES AND SLAUGHTERHOUSES, paras 341 ff above.
2 See FOOD, DAIRIES AND SLAUGHTERHOUSES, paras 359 ff, 407 ff above.
3 See the Food and Drugs (Scotland) Act 1956 (c 30), s 2 (as amended), and FOOD, DAIRIES AND SLAUGHTERHOUSES, paras 343 ff above.
4 See ibid, s 8, and FOOD, DAIRIES AND SLAUGHTERHOUSES, para 399 above.
5 See ibid, ss 45, 46, and FOOD, DAIRIES AND SLAUGHTERHOUSES, vol 2, paras 426, 428 above.

1780. Hygiene. Regulations set out detailed provisions for the enforcement of hygiene standards in premises where food is either stored, prepared or served[1]. The regulations deal with such matters as the cleanliness of premises and equipment, personal cleanliness, smoking, washing facilities, first aid materials, overclothing, protection of food from contamination, lighting, temperature and ventilation, sanitary conveniences, refuse, and water supply.

1 See the Food Hygiene (Scotland) Regulations 1959, SI 1959/413 (as amended), and FOOD, DAIRIES AND SLAUGHTERHOUSES, paras 407 ff above.

1781. Premises. Where a person is convicted of an offence under the food hygiene regulations[1] involving the carrying on of a food business at any insanitary premises, or in premises which are so situated or designed or in such a condition that food is exposed to the risk of contamination, the court[2], upon application by a local authority[3], may order the premises to be closed[4]. The court must be satisfied that the continuation of activities at the premises would be injurious to health[4]. Once an order has been granted it is effective until the danger has been removed to the satisfaction of the local authority[4].

1 See para 1780 above.
2 Ie the sheriff court.
3 Trading standards officers are responsible for the enforcement of these provisions.
4 See the Control of Food Premises (Scotland) Act 1977 (c 28), s 1(1), and FOOD, DAIRIES AND SLAUGHTERHOUSES, para 422 above.

(b) Trade Descriptions

1782. Trade descriptions generally. It is an offence for any person in the course of any trade or business to make a statement which he knows to be false[1] or recklessly[2] to make a statement which is false regarding:
(1) the provision of services, accommodation or facilities;
(2) the nature of any services, accommodation or facilities provided;
(3) the time at which, manner in which or persons by whom any services, accommodation or facilities are so provided;
(4) the examination, approval or evaluation by any person of any services, accommodation or facilities so provided; and
(5) the location or amenities of any accommodation so provided[3].
Statutory defences are provided[4].

1 See *Wings Ltd v Ellis* [1985] AC 272, [1984] 3 All ER 577, HL, and CONSUMER PROTECTION, vol 6, paras 124, 127, 129.
2 See the Trade Descriptions Act 1968 (c 29), s 14(2)(b), and CONSUMER PROTECTION, vol 6, para 127.
3 See ibid, s 14(1), and CONSUMER PROTECTION, vol 6, paras 126–128.
4 See ibid, s 24, and CONSUMER PROTECTION, vol 6, paras 135–138. See also *Wings Ltd v Ellis* [1985] AC 272 at 300, [1984] 3 All ER 577 at 594, HL, per Lord Templeman.

1783. Brochures. A brochure may play an important role, particularly where the guest booked accommodation at a travel agency or was provided with accommodation at a hotel as part of a holiday package. The guest may have relied upon the information contained in the brochure in selecting accommodation or a particular package. The brochure may have been prepared a considerable time before the guest arrived at the hotel, and services, accommodation or facilities may have changed in the interim period[1]. The statutory offence[2] does not apply to a statement unrelated to existing facts but which amounts to a promise about the future[3]. Nevertheless an offence may be committed where a brochure advertises accommodation which at the time of publication did not exist[4].

1 *Sunair Holidays Ltd v Dodd* [1970] 2 All ER 410, [1970] 1 WLR 1037.
2 Ie under the Trade Descriptions Act 1968 (c 29), s 14(1): see para 1782 above.
3 *R v Sunair Holidays Ltd* [1973] 2 All ER 1233, [1973] 1 WLR 1105, CA. Cf *British Airways Board v Taylor* [1976] 1 All ER 65, [1976] 1 WLR 13, HL, and CONSUMER PROTECTION, vol 6, para 130.
4 *R v Clarksons Holidays Ltd* [1972] Crim LR 653, CA.

(c) Weights and Measures

1784. Weights and measures generally. Detailed provisions in respect of weights and measures are also relevant in the context of hotels. These provisions are discussed in detail elsewhere in this work[1].

1 See CONSUMER PROTECTION, vol 6, paras 173 ff.

(d) Prices

1785. Introduction. The Tourism (Sleeping Accommodation Price Display) Order 1977 requires the display of overnight accommodation prices in residential establishments in Great Britain at which sleeping accommodation is provided by way of trade or business and which, for the purposes of letting, has not fewer than four bedrooms or eight beds[1]. The order does not apply to bona fide members' clubs, youth hostels, rooms in the same occupation for at least twenty-one consecutive nights, or establishments which provide facilities other than those of a normal hotel as part of the price[2].

1 See the Tourism (Sleeping Accommodation Price Display) Order 1977, SI 1977/1877, art 2. The reference to beds includes beds situated in dormitories: art 2(a).
2 Ibid, art 2. As to members' clubs, see ASSOCIATIONS AND CLUBS, vol 2, paras 803 ff.

1786. Notice of prices of accommodation. The prices of accommodation must be clearly displayed by means of a notice at the reception or in the hotel entrance[1]. The information which must be provided in the notice is:
(1) the price of a bedroom for occupancy by one adult person;
(2) the price of a bedroom for occupancy by two adult persons;
(3) the price of a bed, other than in a single or double bedroom, for occupation by an adult person, stating whether the bed is situated in a dormitory or room to be shared with other guests[2].
The maximum and minimum prices must be given[3]. Value added tax may be shown separately, but the element of value added tax in the price must be shown in some form or other[4]. The notice must also make clear whether the room price is inclusive of meals[5]. Additional information may be contained in the notice provided that it does not detract from the prominence to be given to the above information[6].

1 Tourism (Sleeping Accommodation Price Display) Order 1977, SI 1977/1877, art 3(1). The notice must be displayed in a prominent position where it can easily be read by a person seeking to engage sleeping accommodation at the hotel: art 3(1).
2 Ibid, art 3(1)(a)–(c).
3 Ibid, art 3(4). If prices for each of the categories specified are not standard throughout the hotel, it is sufficient to state the lowest and highest current price of accommodation for each category: art 3(4).
4 See ibid, art 3(2).
5 Ibid, art 3(3). If the price is inclusive of meals, the meals must be suitably identified: art 3(3).
6 Ibid, art 3(5).

1787. Enforcement and penalties. A duly authorised officer of the local weights and measures authority may, at all reasonable hours and on production, if required, of his credentials, enter and inspect any establishment within the authority's area for the purpose of determining whether the statutory provisions are being complied with[1]. Any person who obstructs a duly authorised officer in the exercise of his right of entry and inspection is guilty of an offence and liable on summary conviction to a penalty not exceeding a fine of £100[2].

Any person failing to display the required notice[3] is liable on summary conviction to a penalty not exceeding a fine of £200 unless he proves that he had reasonable excuse for the failure[4].

1 Tourism (Sleeping Accommodation Price Display) Order 1977, SI 1977/1877, art 5(1). Where a local weights and measures authority has made arrangements for the discharge of any of its functions by another local authority, the powers conferred by art 5(1) may also be exercisable by a duly authorised officer of that other local authority: art 5(1).
2 Ibid, art 5(2).
3 Ie a notice which complies with ibid, art 3: see para 1786 above.
4 Ibid, art 4.

1788. Corporate bodies. Where an offence is committed by a body corporate with the consent of, or connivance of, or is attributable to any neglect on the part of, any director, manager, secretary or other similar officer of the body corporate[1], or any other person who was purporting to act in such capacity, he as well as the body corporate will be guilty of an offence[2].

1 Where the affairs of a body corporate are managed by its members this provision will also apply in relation to acts and defaults of a member in connection with its functions of management as if he were a director of the body corporate: Tourism (Sleeping Accommodation Price Display) Order 1977, SI 1977/1877, art 6(2).
2 Ibid, art 6(1).

1789. Powers of the Secretary of State. The Secretary of State for Scotland may make regulations[1] to exclude from the definition of 'hotel'[2] any class of establishment and to make consequential amendments to the statutory provisions[3].

1 Ie in respect of hotels in Scotland.
2 Ie under the Tourism (Sleeping Accommodation Price Display) Order 1977, SI 1977/1877, art 2: see para 1785 above.
3 Ibid, art 7.

(12) WAGES AND CONDITIONS OF EMPLOYMENT

1790. Introduction. Until the enactment of the Wages Act 1986[1], the Licensed Residential Establishment and Licensed Restaurant Wages Council[2] regulated the minimum terms and conditions to be observed where persons are employed in the service or preparation of food and drink, in the provision of living accommodation, in the retail sale of goods, office work or any other work reasonably connected with any other service or amenity on any premises which are licensed for the sale of liquor, and which are either residential or used as a restaurant.

1 As to the Wages Act 1986 (c 48), see para 1792 below.
2 Formerly the Licensed Residential Establishment and Licensed Restaurant Wages Board, established in 1945 under the Catering Wages Act 1943 (c 24) (repealed), the Licensed Residential Establishment and Licensed Restaurant Wages Council became a wages council under the Terms and Conditions of Employment Act 1959 (c 26) (repealed) and was continued under the Wages Councils Act 1959 (c 69) (repealed and re-enacted as the Wages Councils Act 1979 (c 12) (repealed)).

1791. Regulation of wages and conditions of employment. The Wages Board (Licensed Residential Establishment and Licensed Restaurant) Order

1945[1], dealt with such matters as inter alia minimum remuneration; definition of grades and descriptions of workers; board and lodging[2]; hours of work; additional payments for Sunday and night work[3]; uniforms and protective clothing; rest intervals; rest days; holidays and holiday remuneration.

1 See the Wages Board (Licensed Residential Establishment and Licensed Restaurant) Order 1945, SR & O 1945/226 (amended by SI 1982/739, which excluded from the field of operation of the Licensed Residential Establishment and Licensed Restaurant Wages Council workers who are employed (1) by local authorities; or (2) as aircraft stewards or stewardesses). The 1945 Order is spent: see the Wages Act 1986 (c 48), s 24.
2 *Leech Leisure v Hotel and Catering Industry Trading Board* (1984) 81 LS Gaz 1052.
3 *English v Gunter & Co Ltd* [1957] 2 All ER 838, [1957] 1 WLR 915, CA.

1792. The Wages Act 1986. Since the enactment of the Wages Act 1986, wages councils are only entitled to set one minimum hourly rate of pay and one minimum hourly overtime rate applicable to all workers covered by an order[1]. A wages council can no longer set other rates of pay or remuneration; nor can it make an order dealing with other terms and conditions of employment. The only other power which a wages council retains is the right to set a limit on the amount which an employer can recover from a worker in respect of living accommodation which he had provided[2]. Moreover, no order of a wages council can apply to a worker under the age of twenty-one[3].

1 See the Wages Act 1986 (c 48), s 14(1)(a), (b). As to the application of s 14(1), see s 14(2)–(9), and Sch 3. As to the Act generally, see EMPLOYMENT, vol 9, paras 62 ff.
2 See ibid, s 14(1)(c).
3 Ibid, s 12(3).

2. TOURISM

(1) POWERS AND DUTIES OF LOCAL AUTHORITIES

1793. Promotion of tourism. Under earlier legislation, regional, islands and district councils had responsibility for promoting tourism in their areas[1]. However, following the recommendations of the Stodart Report[2], which had the general aim of avoiding concurrency of powers, provision was made which removed responsibilities for tourism from regional councils[3].

An islands or district council may, either alone or jointly with any other person or body:
(1) encourage persons, by advertisement or otherwise (and whether inside or outside the United Kingdom) to visit its area for recreation, for health purposes or to hold conferences, trade fairs and exhibitions in its area; and
(2) provide, or encourage any other person or body to provide, facilities for recreation, conferences, trade fairs and exhibitions, or improve or encourage any other person or body to improve, any existing facilities for those purposes[4].

The islands or district council may not do anything outside the United Kingdom in exercise of this power, without the express or general consent of the Secretary of State for Scotland or with the express consent of such body as he may direct the islands or district council to consult[5].

1 See the Local Government (Scotland) Act 1973 (c 65), s 90(1) (as originally enacted).
2 *Committee of Inquiry into Local Government in Scotland* (the Stodart Report) (Cmnd 8115) (1981).
3 As to the powers of regional councils to make financial contributions, see para 1794 below.

4 See the Local Government (Scotland) Act 1973, s 90(1)(a), (b) (as amended), and LOCAL GOVERN-MENT, vol 14, para 662.

5 See ibid, s 90(1) proviso, (2) proviso (as amended), and LOCAL GOVERNMENT, vol 14, para 662.

1794. Financial assistance. An islands or district council may contribute towards expenses incurred by any person or body in the promotion of tourism[1].

Although regional councils may not engage in tourism promotion directly, they may contribute towards expenses incurred by any person or body in the promotion of tourism[2]. Such a contribution may be made if the council considers that the thing done is, or would be, of benefit to its area or any part of it[3].

1 See the Local Government (Scotland) Act 1973 (c 65), s 90(2) (as amended), and LOCAL GOVERN-MENT, vol 14, para 662. As to the promotion of tourism, see para 1793 above.

2 Ie anything mentioned in ibid, s 90(1)(a) or (b): see para 1793 above.

3 See ibid, s 90(3) (as amended), and LOCAL GOVERNMENT, vol 14, para 663.

1795. Collaboration. After consultation with the Scottish Tourist Board[1], islands and district councils may prepare, or arrange for the preparation of, schemes, in which they may participate, providing for:

(1) the forming of organisations of such persons as carry on, or have powers or duties as regards, or appear to the councils (or the person preparing the scheme) to have an interest in, activities which relate to tourism; and

(2) the composition and functions of such organisations[2].

1 As to the Scottish Tourist Board, see paras 1796 ff below.

2 See the Local Government (Scotland) Act 1973 (c 65), s 90A (as added), and LOCAL GOVERNMENT, vol 14, para 664. This provision was designed to encourage collaboration between the councils and voluntary organisations, eg the Highlands and Islands Development Board (as to which see TRADE REGULATION).

(2) THE BRITISH TOURIST AUTHORITY AND THE SCOTTISH TOURIST BOARD

(a) Promoting the Development of Tourism

1796. Introduction. The Development of Tourism Act 1969 provided for the establishment of the British Tourism Authority (BTA) and tourist boards for Scotland, England and Wales[1]. The BTA and the tourist boards are given responsibility for promoting the development of tourism to and within Great Britain[2]. The BTA and the boards are also authorised to provide financial assistance for tourist projects[3]. Provision may be made for the registration of hotels and similar establishments and for ensuring that notification of the prices of accommodation is given to those who wish to avail themselves of it[4].

The Act also empowers the BTA and the tourist boards to promote or undertake research[5]. The tourist boards may foster and co-operate with regional and area tourist organisations and provide them with financial or other assistance[6].

1 There are proposals for radical reforms and for the abolition of the BTA and the tourist boards and for their replacement by a British Tourism Commission with Scottish, English and Welsh departments. The commission would have more extensive power than those conferred on the BTA under the Development of Tourism Act 1969 (c 51).

2 See ibid, s 2(1).

3 See paras 1803, 1804, below.

4 See paras 1811, 1812, below.

5 Development of Tourism Act 1969, s 2(2)(c).
6 See ibid, s 2(5), and para 1801 below.

1797. Establishment and composition of the British Tourist Authority and the tourist boards. The Development of Tourism Act 1969 established four bodies known respectively as the British Tourist Authority (BTA), the English Tourist Board, the Scottish Tourist Board and the Wales Tourist Board[1].

The BTA consists of a chairman and not more than five other members appointed by the Secretary of State, and the chairmen of the English, Scottish and Wales tourist boards[2]. The Scottish Tourist Board[3] consists of a chairman and not more than six other members appointed by the Secretary of State for Scotland[4].

1 Development of Tourism Act 1969 (c 51), s 1(1).
2 Ibid, s 1(2)(a), (b). As to incorporation and status etc of the tourist boards, see s 1(5), Sch 1. 'Tourist board' includes the BTA: s 1(6). As to the transfer of functions to the Secretary of State, see the Secretary of State for Trade and Industry Order 1970, SI 1970/1537, and the Transfer of Functions (Tourism and Small Businesses) Order 1985, SI 1985/1778.
3 References throughout this part of the title are to the Scottish Tourist Board. The provisions apply equally to the BTA and the English Tourist Board and to the Wales Tourist Board unless otherwise indicated.
4 Development of Tourism Act 1969, s 1(3).

(b) Functions and Powers

1798. Promoting tourism. It is the function of the British Tourist Authority (BTA):
(1) to encourage people to visit Great Britain and people living in Great Britain to take their holidays there; and
(2) to encourage the provision and improvement of tourist amenities and facilities[1] in Great Britain[2].
The Scottish Tourist Board has the like functions in respect of Scotland[3].

1 'Tourist amenities and facilities' means, in relation to any country, amenities and facilities for visitors to that country and for other people travelling within it on business or pleasure: Development of Tourism Act 1969 (c 51), s 2(9).
2 Ibid, s 2(1)(a), (b).
3 Ibid, s 2(1).

1799. Particular powers of the Scottish Tourist Board. The Scottish Tourist Board has, for the purpose of the functions conferred on it[1] the power:
(1) to promote or undertake publicity in any form;
(2) to provide advisory and information services;
(3) to promote and undertake research;
(4) to establish committees to advise it in respect of its functions;
(5) to contribute to or reimburse expenditure incurred by any other person or organisation in carrying out any activity which the board has power to carry on[2].
The board may carry on any activities outside the United Kingdom for the purposes of encouraging people to visit Scotland[3]. However, the board may only exercise this power with the consent of the Secretary of State for Scotland who, before giving or withholding consent, must consult the British Tourist Authority (BTA)[4]. The Secretary of State may impose conditions on the consent given[4]. This provision does not affect the BTA's power to carry on any

activities outside the United Kingdom for the purpose of encouraging people to visit Scotland, nor does it prevent the board from acting on the BTA's behalf[5] in this regard[6].

The board is not empowered[7] to give financial assistance for the carrying out of, or itself to carry out, any project for providing or improving tourist amenities in Scotland[8].

1 Ie under the Development of Tourism Act 1969 (c 51), s 2.
2 See ibid, s 2(2)(a)–(e).
3 Tourism (Overseas Promotion) (Scotland) Act 1984 (c 4), s 1(1).
4 Ibid, s 1(2).
5 Ie under the Development of Tourism Act 1969, s 2(3).
6 Tourism (Overseas Promotion) (Scotland) Act 1984, s 1(3).
7 Ie except as provided by the Development of Tourism Act 1969, ss 3, 4: see paras 1803, 1804, below.
8 Ibid, s 2(4).

1800. Incidental powers of the Scottish Tourist Board. The Scottish Tourist Board has the power to do anything which is incidental or conducive to the discharge of the functions conferred upon it[1]. It may charge for its services and receive contributions towards its expenses in carrying out any of its functions[2]. It may not borrow money except with the consent of the Secretary of State for Scotland and the Treasury[3].

1 Development of Tourism Act 1969 (c 51), s 2(2). However, this is subject to the provisions of s 2(3), (4): see para 1799 above.
2 Ibid, s 2(7).
3 Ibid, ss 1(6), 2(8).

1801. Co-operation with other bodies. In discharging its functions, the Scottish Tourist Board must have regard to the desirability of fostering and, in appropriate cases, co-operating with organisations discharging functions corresponding to those of the board in relation to particular areas of Scotland[1]. The board has power to provide such organisations with financial or other assistance[1]. The board must also have regard to the desirability of undertaking appropriate consultation with the other tourist boards and with persons and organisations[2] who have knowledge of, or are interested in, any matters affecting the discharge of its functions[3].

1 Development of Tourism Act 1969 (c 51), s 2(5).
2 These include those mentioned in ibid, s 2(5).
3 Ibid, s 2(6).

1802. Miscellaneous duties and powers. The British Tourist Authority (BTA) has a duty to advise ministers or any public body[1] on such matters relating to tourism in Great Britain as a whole as the minister or body may refer to it or as the BTA thinks fit[2]. The Scottish Tourist Board has a like duty as respects matters relating to tourism in Scotland[2]. Provision is made for the keeping of accounts and the provision of information to the Secretary of State for Scotland and the Treasury[3]. The board must, as soon as possible after the end of the financial year[4], make a report to the Secretary of State detailing its activities during that year, and he must lay a copy of that report before each House of Parliament[5].

1 'Public body' includes any local authority or statutory undertaker, and any trustees, commissioners, board or other persons, who, as a public body and not for their own profit, act under any enactment for the improvement of any place or the production or supply of any commodity or service: Development of Tourism Act 1969 (c 51), s 5(2).

2 Ibid, s 5(1).
3 See ibid, ss 1(6), 6.
4 'Financial year' means the period beginning with the commencement of the Development of Tourism Act 1969 (ie 25 August 1969) and ending with 31 March 1970, and each subsequent period of twelve months ending with 31 March: s 6(7).
5 Ibid, s 6(6).

1803. General schemes of financial assistance for tourist projects. The British Tourist Authority (BTA) may, after consultation with the Scottish, English and Wales Tourist Boards, prepare schemes for the provision of financial assistance by the boards for the carrying out of projects of such classes as may be specified in the schemes[1]. Projects may be so classified if, in the opinion of the BTA, they will provide or improve tourist amenities and facilities in Great Britain[2]. Any such scheme must be submitted to the Secretary of State who may by order confirm it with or without modification[3]. Financial assistance may be given by grant or loan or a combination of those methods[4]. In making a grant or loan the tourist board may impose such terms and conditions as it thinks fit including conditions for repayment of a grant in specified circumstances[5].

1 Development of Tourism Act 1969 (c 51), s 3(1). At the date at which this volume states the law this power had not been exercised.
2 Ibid, s 3(1).
3 See ibid, s 3(2), (6). As to the transfer of functions to the Secretary of State, see para 1797, note 2, above.
4 Ibid, s 3(3).
5 See ibid, ss 3(4), 19, and Sch 2 (amended by the Criminal Law Act 1977 (c 45), s 65(5), Sch 13). The scheme may be varied or revoked by a subsequent scheme: see the Development of Tourism Act 1969, s 3(5).

1804. Execution of particular tourist projects. The Scottish Tourist Board has power[1] to give financial assistance for any project which in the opinion of the board will provide or improve tourist amenities and facilities in Scotland[2]. The board itself may carry out such a project with the approval of the Secretary of State and the Treasury[3]. The method of assistance may be by grant or loan[4], and the board may impose such terms and conditions as it thinks fit[5].

Where the project is being or is to be carried out by a company incorporated in Great Britain, financial assistance may be given by way of subscribing for or otherwise acquiring shares or stock in the company[6]. The board may not dispose of any shares or stock so acquired without consultation with the company in which the shares or stock is held, and the approval of the Secretary of State and the Treasury[7].

1 Ie in accordance with arrangements approved by the Secretary of State and the Treasury: Development of Tourism Act 1969 (c 51), ss 1(6), 4(1)(a).
2 Ibid, s 4(1)(a).
3 Ibid, s 4(1)(b).
4 Ibid, s 4(2). Financial assistance may be by a combination of grants and loans: s 4(2).
5 See ibid, s 4(3), and Sch 2 (amended by the Criminal Law Act 1977 (c 45), s 65(5), Sch 13).
6 Ibid, s 4(2). Financial assistance may be by a combination of grant, loan or subscription for shares or stock: s 4(2).
7 Ibid, ss 1(6), 4(4).

(c) Financial Assistance for Hotel Development

1805. Introduction. The Development of Tourism Act 1969[1] provided for financial assistance out of public funds for hotel[2] development. This was provided by the Hotel Development Incentives Scheme, which was administered by the Scottish, English and Wales Tourist Boards. Grants and loans were made for buildings and fixed equipment. The scheme operated from 1970 to 1973 and provided a massive increase in investment in the hotel industry. The main objective was rapidly to increase the capacity and quality of hotel stock at a time when demand for hotel accommodation was exceeding supply in a number of locations. The objective was achieved beyond expectation. Two criticisms levied at the scheme were that it involved larger sums of public expenditure than was originally envisaged for investment that would probably have occurred anyway, and that the scheme led to much indiscriminate expansion and no special stimulus was provided for particular types of development and particular locations[3].

The scheme has not operated since 1973, and the information set out below is only relevant to those grants and loans which are still in force[4].

1 Ie the Development of Tourism Act 1969 (c 51), Pt II (ss 7–16).
2 An establishment must not be treated as a hotel unless its services and facilities are offered to the public generally, that is to say, to any person who wishes to avail himself of, and appears able and willing to pay a reasonable sum for, those services and facilities and is in a fit state to be received: ibid, s 16(2).
3 OECD Tourism in Member Countries Report 1970 *Hotel Prospects to 1985*, prepared for the Economic and Development Committee for Hotels and Catering.
4 See paras 1806 ff below.

1806. New hotels. A person who has incurred eligible expenditure[1] in providing a new hotel[2] in Scotland was entitled[3] to receive from the Scottish Tourist Board, after completion of the hotel, a grant in respect of the eligible expenditure which he had so incurred[4]. The hotel must satisfy certain requirements:

(1) the hotel must have not less than ten letting bedrooms and the sleeping accommodation must consist wholly or mainly of letting bedrooms;
(2) breakfast and evening meals must be provided at reasonable times on the premises for persons staying at the hotel;
(3) there must be a lounge[5] available on the premises for the common use, at all reasonable times, of persons staying at the hotel;
(4) hotel services appropriate to the establishment[6] must be provided for persons staying at the hotel; and
(5) the accommodation must be in a building or buildings of a permanent nature[7].

A hotel will be treated as complying with these requirements if it complies[8] with them throughout the period in each year between 1 April and 31 October[9].

1 Ie approved capital expenditure on constructional work and on the purchase and installation of fixed equipment: Development of Tourism Act 1969 (c 51), s 7(4).
2 As to the meaning of 'hotel', see para 1805, note 2, above.
3 Ie subject to the provisions of the Development of Tourism Act 1969.
4 Ibid, s 7(1).
5 Ie whether a room or part of a room: ibid, s 7(2)(c).
6 This must include in every case the cleaning of rooms and making of beds: ibid, s 7(2)(d).
7 Ibid, s 7(2)(a)–(e).
8 Ie even though it does not comply with them at other times: ibid, s 7(3).
9 Ibid, s 7(3).

1807. Hotel extensions and alterations. A person who has incurred eligible expenditure[1] in extending or altering an existing hotel[2] in Scotland was entitled[3] to receive from the Scottish Tourist Board, after completion of the extension or alteration, a grant in respect of the eligible expenditure which he has incurred[4].

The extension or alteration must have consisted of, or include the provision of, not less than five additional letting bedrooms[4]. The hotel must have complied with certain specified requirements[5].

Where the extension or alteration includes, but is not confined to, the provision of letting bedrooms and those bedrooms are provided by altering existing accommodation in the hotel, no grant is payable[6] in respect of expenditure which is not attributable to the provision of the bedrooms and any bathroom or bathrooms provided in association with the bedrooms[7].

1 Ie approved capital expenditure on constructional work and on the purchase and installation of fixed equipment: Development of Tourism Act 1969 (c 51), s 8(4).
2 As to the meaning of 'hotel', see para 1805, note 2, above.
3 Ie subject to the provisions of the Development of Tourism Act 1969: s 8(1).
4 Ibid, s 8(1).
5 Ibid, s 8(2). For the specified requirements, see s 7(2), and para 1806 above.
6 Ie unless the Scottish Tourist Board in any case otherwise determines: ibid, s 8(3).
7 Ibid, s 8(3). It is for the board to determine whether or not a bathroom is provided in association with a bedroom.

1808. Fixed equipment. A person who has incurred approved capital expenditure in purchasing and installing in an existing hotel in Scotland fixed equipment of a specified description[1] was entitled to receive from the Scottish Tourist Board, after completion of the installation, a grant in respect of the approved capital expenditure incurred[2]. No grant was payable unless the board was satisfied that on completion of the installation the hotel complied, or as from its opening thereafter complied, with certain specified requirements[3]. No grant was payable unless the applicant had incurred expenditure of £1,000 or more (within a complete financial year[4]) in respect of the purchase and installation of that equipment[5].

1 As to fixed equipment eligible for a grant, see the Development of Tourism Act 1969 (c 51), s 9(1), Sch 3.
2 Ibid, s 9(1).
3 Ibid, s 9(2). For the specified requirements, see s 7(2), and para 1806 above.
4 'Financial year' means the period of twelve months ending with 31 March: ibid, s 9(4).
5 See ibid, s 9(3).

1809. Recipient, rates and conditions of grant. The recipient must have been an occupier[1] or a lessor[2] of the hotel[3] at the relevant time[4]. No grants were available to a local authority[5] or nationalised industry[6]. The Development of Tourism Act 1969 sets out the rates of grant which were available[7].

The Scottish Tourist Board was empowered to impose such conditions[8] as it thought fit[9]. Conditions could provide for repayment of the grant in specified circumstances, in particular where the number of letting bedrooms in the hotel was reduced or the hotel ceased to comply with the specified requirements as to facilities and services[10] before the expiration of such period as specified in the conditions[11]. Different periods were specified in different classes of case[11].

1 Ie the person in possession of the hotel: Development of Tourism Act 1969 (c 51), s 10(1)(a).
2 Ie, in a case where the occupier is in possession of the hotel by virtue of a lease, a person holding the interest of landlord under any lease under which the hotel is let: s 10(1)(b), (4).
3 As to the meaning of 'hotel', see para 1805, note 2, above.
4 See the Development of Tourism Act 1969, s 10(1), (4). 'Relevant time' means (1) in relation to a grant under s 7 (see para 1806 above), the time when the hotel in respect of which the grant is to be made is first opened after completion; (2) in relation to a grant under ss 8, 9 (see paras 1807, 1808, above), the time when the extension, alteration or installation of equipment, as the case may be, in respect of which the grant is to be made is completed or, if the hotel in question is then closed, when it is first opened thereafter: s 10(3)(a), (b). As to expenditure incurred by a predecessor in title or lessor, see s 10(2), Sch 4.

5 'Local authority' means any regional, islands or district council, and any statutory authority, commissioners or trustees who have power to levy a rate or to issue a requisition for payment of money to be raised out of such a rate and includes any joint board or joint committee of such authorities appointed under any enactment, order or scheme: ibid, s 14(2)(b) (amended by the Local Government (Scotland) Act 1973 (c 65), s 214(1), Sch 27, Pt II, para 194).

6 Development of Tourism Act 1969, s 14(1).

7 See ibid, s 11 (amended by the Local Employment Act 1972 (c 5), s 22(1), Sch 3; the Industry Act 1972 (c 63), s 19(3), Sch 4, Pt I; and the Industrial Development Act 1982 (c 52), s 19, Sch 2, Pt II, para 5).

8 Ie subject to the Development of Tourism Act 1969 (c 51), s 19: see para 1813 below.

9 Ibid, s 12(1). As to securing compliance with conditions, see s 12(3), Sch 2 (amended by the Criminal Law Act 1977 (c 45), s 65(5), Sch 13).

10 Ie under the Development of Tourism Act 1969, s 7(2): see para 1806 above.

11 Ibid, s 12(2).

1810. Loans. The Scottish Tourist Board has been empowered[1] to make a loan or loans to any person for assisting him to provide a new hotel in Scotland or to extend or alter, or to provide or install fixed equipment in, an existing hotel in Scotland[2]. The hotel in question must have complied with specified requirements[3] on completion of the project or on its opening thereafter[4]. The total amount of the loan was subject to a maximum percentage of the eligible expenditure or £500,000[5]. Loans were made subject to the terms and conditions determined by the board[6]. The maximum period for repayment of the loan in respect of new hotels is twenty years or fifteen years in the case of extensions, alterations or installation of new equipment[7].

No loans were available to a local authority or nationalised industry[8].

1 Ie under the provisions of the Development of Tourism Act 1969 (c 51), and of any directions under s 19 (as to which see para 1813 below): s 13(1).

2 See ibid, s 13(1)(a), (b). As to the total eligible expenditure, see s 13(1).

3 Ie under ibid, s 7(2): see para 1806 above.

4 Ibid, s 13(2).

5 See ibid, s 13(3), (4). 'Eligible expenditure' means approved capital expenditure on constructional work and on the purchase and installation of fixed equipment: s 13(6).

6 See ibid, s 13(5), and s 19 (as to which see para 1813 below).

7 Ibid, s 13(5).

8 See ibid, s 14(1), (2)(b) (as amended): see para 1809, notes 5, 6, above.

(d) Miscellaneous Provisions

1811. Registration of tourist accommodation. Her Majesty may, by Order in Council, make provision for registration by the tourist boards of, or of any class of, hotels and other establishments in Great Britain at which sleeping accommodation is provided by way of trade or business[1]. The order may make provision:

(1) as to the form and contents of the register;
(2) as to the information to be furnished;
(3) for charging registration fees;
(4) for the issue and display of certificates of registration and the display of signs indicating that an establishment is registered;
(5) for the inspection of hotels, with powers of entry;
(6) for exemptions; and
(7) for penalties for non-compliance[2].

The order may contain supplementary provisions and may authorise the Secretary of State to make regulations in respect of Scotland for the purposes of the order[3]. The order and regulations may make different provisions for different

cases and, in particular, provision may be made for the order to come into force
at different times in relation to, or to different parts of, England, Scotland and
Wales respectively[4].

1 Development of Tourism Act 1969 (c 51), s 17(1). At the date at which this volume states the law
   the power under s 17 had not been exercised.
2 Ibid, s 17(2)(a)–(g). A tourist board maintaining a register may publish or make available for
   publication any information furnished to it: see s 17(7). As to the classification and grading of
   hotels entered in a register, see para 1812 below.
3 See ibid, s 17(4).
4 Ibid, s 17(5). An order may be annulled by resolution of either House of Parliament, and may be
   revoked or varied by a subsequent order: s 17(6).

1812. Classification and grading of hotels. The order making provision for
the registration of hotels and other establishments[1] may provide for the classification or grading of hotels and other establishments entered in the register[2]. The
order must also make provision for requiring the criteria in accordance with
which the classification or grading is carried out[3] to be determined from time to
time by the British Tourist Authority (BTA) after consultation with the tourist
boards and such other organisations as appear to the BTA to be representative of
trade and consumer interests likely to be affected[4]. Provision is also made for the
publication of such criteria[5] and for the person carrying on an establishment
registered with the board to make representations before any classification or
grade is accorded to the establishment, or before its classification or grade is
altered or cancelled[6].

1 See para 1811 above.
2 Development of Tourism Act 1969 (c 51), s 17(3).
3 Ie as far as not prescribed by the order: ibid, s 17(3)(a).
4 Ibid, s 17(3)(a).
5 Ibid, s 17(3)(b).
6 Ibid, s 17(3)(c).

1813. Ministerial directions. The Secretary of State may, after consultation
with the Scottish Tourist Board, give it directions of a general character as to the
exercise of its functions[1]. The Secretary of State may give directions as to
matters with respect to which the board must be satisfied before making a loan
and the terms and conditions subject to which loans or grants are made[2]. The
board must give effect to any such directions given to it[3].

1 Development of Tourism Act 1969 (c 51), ss 1(6), 19(1).
2 See ibid, s 19(2), (3).
3 Ibid, s 19(4).

(3) FINANCIAL PROVISION BY CENTRAL GOVERNMENT

**1814–1900. Financial provision in respect of expenditure by the Scottish
Tourist Board.** The Secretary of State may pay to the Scottish Tourist Board
such sums in respect of its expenditure as he may, with the consent of the
Treasury, determine[1]. Such sums[2] are defrayed out of money provided by
Parliament[3]. The board must pay to the Secretary of State any sums received
(1) in repayment of, or as interest on, any loan made by it; (2) in repayment of
any grant made by it; (3) as dividend on, or otherwise in respect of, any shares or
stock acquired by it[4].

1 Development of Tourism Act 1969 (c 51), ss 1(6), 20(1).
2 Ie those required by the Secretary of State for making payments under ibid, s 20(1): s 20(2).
3 Ibid, s 20(2).
4 Ibid, s 20(3)(a)–(c). The Secretary of State must pay such sums received into the Consolidated Fund: s 20(4).

HOUSING

The author expresses appreciation of assistance received from Ms Joanna Cherry in the preparation of part of this title.

1. INTRODUCTION

1901. Scope of the title. Despite some statutory initiatives which have confused the boundaries of its subject matter, housing law may, for the purpose of this title, be usefully regarded as *public sector* housing law. It may also be usefully regarded as that body of law whose principal primary source is the Housing (Scotland) Acts. Thus, it is at present the law deriving from the consolidating Housing (Scotland) Act 1987 (c 26) as subsequently amended, principally by the Housing (Scotland) Act 1988 (c 43)[1]. There are, however, a number of qualifications to the general identification of housing law as first, public sector housing law and, secondly, the law of the Housing (Scotland) Acts. As to 'public sector', this term has to be broadly understood. Housing law is not only the law relating to housing accommodation owned and managed in the public sector but also embraces the law relating to the housing functions of public authorities which substantially affect privately owned accommodation. This, therefore, includes functions such as making grants for house improvement[2] and other forms of financial assistance for housing[3]. However, definition by reference to the public sector raises questions about what constitutes the public sector and for what purposes this distinction between public and private is relevant. The distinction is not pressed here, but some pragmatic recognition is given to it in the allocation of material to this title. Thus, this title is not the place to discover the detailed law on landlord and tenant, which is placed elsewhere[4] and carries with it the law on assured tenancies. Acknowledgment of the application of much of the general law of landlord and tenant in the public sector is, however, made in this title[5]. More systematically treated in the title is the law relating to housing associations[6] because, despite their transfer into the regime of assured tenancies, registered associations fall under the jurisdiction of Scottish Homes and many 'public sector' rules applicable to secure tenancies will continue to apply to associations and their tenants for some time. On the other hand, some material relevant to the structure and operation of housing associations is also to be found elsewhere[7], as also is the general law on local authorities, their structure, functions and operation[8].

There is a general recognition in this title of the systematic treatment elsewhere of the law of town and country planning[9], building controls[10], public health[11] and compulsory purchase and compensation[12], which explains their cursory treatment in the paragraphs which follow. Most statutory terms are defined as necessary as they arise in the title. One, however, is selected for preliminary definition: 'house' is defined to include any part of a building, being a part which is occupied or intended to be occupied as a separate dwelling, and, in particular, it includes a flat, and includes also any yard, garden, outhouses and pertinents belonging to the house or usually enjoyed therewith[13].

1 See also the Housing Act 1988 (c 50), and the Local Government and Housing Act 1989 (c 42). Housing association law was consolidated in the Housing Associations Act 1985 (c 69). That Act, too, has been extensively amended. As to housing associations, see paras 1924 ff below.
2 See paras 2019 ff below.
3 See paras 2010 ff below.
4 See LANDLORD AND TENANT.
5 See especially para 1934 below.

6 See paras 1924 ff below.
7 See generally ASSOCIATIONS AND CLUBS, vol 2, paras 801 ff, and INDUSTRIAL, FRIENDLY AND PROVIDENT SOCIETIES.
8 See LOCAL GOVERNMENT, vol 14, paras 1 ff.
9 See TOWN AND COUNTRY PLANNING.
10 See BUILDING CONTROLS.
11 See PUBLIC HEALTH, vol 19, paras 301 ff.
12 See COMPULSORY ACQUISITION AND COMPENSATION, vol 5, paras 1 ff.
13 Housing (Scotland) Act 1987 (c 26), s 338(1), although this definition is expressed not to apply to Pt XIV (ss 257–303) (assistance for owners of defective housing: see para 1969 below). Under the definition, 'house' also includes any structure made available under the Housing (Temporary Accommodation) Act 1944 (c 36), s 1. For the meaning of 'house' in the context of overcrowding, see para 2001, note 1, below.

2. THE GOVERNMENT AND ADMINISTRATION OF HOUSING IN SCOTLAND

(1) CENTRAL ADMINISTRATION

1902. The Secretary of State for Scotland. Central government does not have responsibility for the direct provision and maintenance of housing accommodation — with the limited exception of accommodation for some of its own employees[1]. That general responsibility lies instead with the local authorities and other agencies whose functions are described in the paragraphs which follow. It is nevertheless the case that central government, principally in the shape of the Secretary of State for Scotland, his junior ministers and the Scottish Development Department of the Scottish Office[2], determines the thrust of housing policy in Scotland.

This is achieved, first and principally, through the power of central government to decide the content of the primary legislation passed by Parliament in which is contained the main instruments of housing policy. In recent years, the Tenants' Rights Etc (Scotland) Act 1980 (c 52) (and succeeding Acts since consolidated in the Housing (Scotland) Act 1987) and the Housing (Scotland) Act 1988 (c 50) have radically altered the shape of Scottish housing policy and administration.

Secondly, the Secretary of State reserves to himself, in that primary legislation, abundant powers to control the way in which the main beneficiaries of direct housing powers (principally the local authorities) carry out their functions. These controls frequently take the form of the power to make delegated legislation. At other points, they are a power to grant or withhold consent to specific local authority actions[3]. Many examples of these powers appear in all areas of housing law. Financial controls may be the most significant but are certainly not the only area of central government influence. One which is always in the background is the power to take action when a local authority is held to have failed to discharge its responsibilities[4]. The Secretary of State is also generally empowered to prescribe the form of notices, advertisements, statements and other documents[5], to dispense with the publication of such notices and advertisements[6], and, for the purposes of the execution of his powers and duties, to cause local inquiries to be held[7]. The Secretary of State is the confirming authority for any byelaws made by local authorities under the Housing (Scotland) Act 1987[8]. With local authorities, the Secretary of State has powers to authorise entry into houses, premises and buildings[9].

Thirdly, the Secretary of State retains a very limited number of powers to intervene directly. His power to assist first-time buyers is one example[10]. He is also empowered, with the consent of the Treasury, to give to a voluntary organisation assistance by way of grant or loan to enable or assist it to provide training or advice, to undertake research, or for similar purposes[11].

1 The occupation of such accommodation is relevant at the point of the exercise by a secure tenant of his right to buy. See the Housing (Scotland) Act 1987 (c 26), s 61(11), and para 1955 below.
2 As to the Secretary of State for Scotland and the Scottish Office generally, see CONSTITUTIONAL LAW, vol 5, paras 516 ff.
3 For a fuller discussion of relationships between the Secretary of State and local authorities, see LOCAL GOVERNMENT, vol 14, paras 101 ff.
4 Housing (Scotland) Act 1987, s 329. See also the Local Government (Scotland) Act 1973 (c 65), s 211 (amended by the Local Government and Housing Act 1989 (c 42), s 159(2), (3)); and see LOCAL GOVERNMENT, vol 14, paras 106, 117, 127, 267.
5 Housing (Scotland) Act 1987, s 330(1)(b).
6 Ibid, s 332.
7 Ibid, s 333.
8 Ibid, s 316. Powers to make byelaws are conferred by s 18 (management and use of houses: see para 1934 below), s 313 (houses in multiple occupation: see paras 2004 ff below); s 314 (accommodation for agricultural workers), and s 315 (accommodation for seasonal workers).
9 Ibid, s 317. See also s 318 (related offences of obstruction).
10 Ibid, s 222.
11 Ibid, s 197.

(2) LOCAL AUTHORITY ADMINISTRATION

(a) Introduction

1903. General. Whatever may be the eventual effect of the government's plans heralded in *Housing: The Government's Proposals for Scotland*[1] and implemented, in part, in the Housing (Scotland) Act 1988 (c 43), there seems no reason to believe that the principal agencies for the administration of general housing policy at the local level will cease to be the local authorities. In the historical development both of public sector provision of housing and intervention into the private sector to improve housing conditions, heavy reliance has been placed upon local authorities and their predecessors. Indeed, local authorities, especially in the major cities, were, in a period when there was no national statutory framework and no lead from central government, in the vanguard of housing policy and administration[2]. Up to the reorganisation of local government in May 1975[3], housing legislation, first consolidated in 1925[4] and again in 1950 and 1966[5], imposed primary administrative responsibilities upon the four counties of cities, the large and small burghs and, in the landward areas, the county councils[6]. There were, therefore, 234 local housing authorities which, for the Wheatley Royal Commission on Local Government in Scotland, constituted one of the most significant reasons for reform[7]. Under the two-tier system of local government proposed in the Wheatley Report, the housing function would have been placed with the upper (regional) tier[8]. In the government's own proposals for reform[9] and subsequently in the Local Government (Scotland) Act 1973, however, housing was remitted to the district councils and, in the islands areas, the islands councils[10]. It was considered that the lower tier of local government needed one, at least, of the major local authority functions — a view subsequently upheld by the Stodart Committee of Inquiry into Local Government in Scotland[11]. Thus, there are today fifty-three district councils and three islands councils which discharge the primary housing functions at the local level[12]. Regional councils do not have general housing powers and are not 'housing authorities'. They do, however, have the limited power, with the consent of the Secretary of State, to promote the provision of housing accommodation by district councils[13], and by housing associations[14]; and they have responsibilities, as social work authorities, for homeless persons[15]. The tenants of regional councils are secure tenants, and may have the right to purchase their houses[16]. In this title, unless a contrary intention is stated, the term 'local authority' may be taken to be restricted to the authorities with primary housing responsibilites, that is district and islands councils[17].

Local authorities have a special statutory power to delegate to a 'housing co-operative' certain of their own powers. An authority may, with the approval of the Secretary of State, make an agreement with a society, company or body of trustees (and so approved as a 'housing co-operative' by the Secretary of State for the purpose)[18]. Under the agreement, the co-operative may be authorised to exercise any of the authority's powers relating to land (or any interest in land) and to perform any of the authority's duties relating to such land (or interest)[18]. By the end of April 1990 more than a dozen such agreements with housing co-operatives had been concluded[19], although no central register of agreements is maintained. It appears that local authorities operate on the understanding that they have a 'blanket approval' from the Secretary of State to conclude these agreements.

1 Cm 242 (1987).
2 See especially the Glasgow Improvements Acts 1866–1897.
3 Local Government (Scotland) Act 1973 (c 65), s 1.
4 Housing (Scotland) Act 1925 (c 15).
5 Housing (Scotland) Acts 1950 (c 34) and 1966 (c 49).
6 See also the Local Government (Scotland) Act 1929 (c 25) and 1947 (c 43).
7 *Report of the Royal Commission on Local Government in Scotland* (the Wheatley Report) (Cmnd 4150) (1969), ch 12.
8 Ibid, ch 12, 23.
9 *Reform of Local Government in Scotland* (Cmnd 4583) (1971).
10 Local Government (Scotland) Act 1973, s 130(1).
11 *Report of the Committee of Inquiry into Local Government in Scotland* (the Stodart Report) (Cmnd 8115) (1981).
12 Local Government (Scotland) Act 1973, ss 1, 2, Sch 1: see LOCAL GOVERNMENT, vol 14, para 78.
13 Ibid, s 131(1).
14 Housing Act 1985 (c 68), s 59.
15 Housing (Scotland) Act 1987 (c 26), s 38: see para 2037 below.
16 Ibid, ss 44(1), (2), 61(2)(a)(ii): see paras 1936, 1955 below.
17 Ibid, s 338(1), defines 'local authority' as an islands or district council.
18 Ibid, s 22. Houses on land included in an agreement continue also to be included in an authority's housing revenue account (as to which see para 1916 below): s 22(5).
19 As to housing co-operatives as landlords, see paras 1936, 1955, 1966, below.

(b) General Duties and Powers

1904. Housing conditions and needs. One of the historically most signifi-cant functions of local authorities has been the direct provision of housing accommodation within their areas. This function continues to have pride of place in Part I of the Housing (Scotland) Act 1987[1]. It imposes a number of general duties starting with the requirement that every local authority must consider the housing conditions in its area and the needs of the area for further housing accommodation[2]. In doing so, the authority must review any infor-mation brought to its notice, including information resulting from surveys or inspections carried out pursuant to its duties in relation to sub-standard houses[3]. The Secretary of State is empowered to give notice to an authority requiring it, within three months, to prepare and submit to him proposals for the provision of housing accommodation[4]. In performing these general functions in relation to housing provision, local authorities must have regard to the special needs of chronically sick or disabled persons[5].

1 The Housing (Scotland) Act 1987 (c 26), Pt I, comprises ss 1–23.
2 Ibid, s 1(1). For the meaning of 'local authority', see para 1903 above.
3 Ibid, s 1(2), referring to surveys or inspections under s 85(3).
4 Ibid, s 1(3).
5 Ibid, s 1(4).

1905. The provision of housing accommodation. Although there is now no obligation to acquire or hold any houses or land for housing purposes at all[1], a local authority is empowered to provide housing accommodation (1) by the erection of houses on land it has acquired or appropriated; (2) by the conversion of any buildings into houses; (3) by acquiring houses; and (4) by altering, enlarging, repairing or improving a house or other buildings acquired by the authority[2]. The provision of housing accommodation includes the provision of hostels[3]. Local authorities continue to have powers available to them to supply the housing needs of their own area by the provision of accommodation in the area of another authority[4]. This requires an agreement with the other authority as to the terms and conditions on which works are to be executed[5]. Differences between authorities may be referred by either authority to the Secretary of State, whose decision is final and binding[6]. In exercising its powers to provide houses (or, indeed, in taking any action under the Housing (Scotland) Act 1987), a local authority must have regard to artistic quality in the lay-out, planning and treatment of the houses to be provided, the beauty of the landscape or country-side and the other amenities of the locality, and the desirability of preserving existing works of architectural, historic or artistic interest[7]. An authority may appoint a local advisory committee including representatives of architectural and other interests[8].

1 Housing (Scotland) Act 1987 (c 26), s 2(6) (added by the Local Government and Housing Act 1989 (c 42), s 161(2), as a precautionary measure in case a local authority disposed of all its housing stock): see para 1908 below.
2 Housing (Scotland) Act 1987, s 2(1)(a)–(d).
3 Ibid, s 2(4)(b). 'Hostel' is defined in s 2(5), in relation to a building provided or converted on or after 3 July 1962, as a building providing, for persons generally or for any class or classes of persons, residential accommodation (other than in houses) and either board or common facilities for the preparation of food adequate to the needs of those persons, or both. The provision of housing accommodation also includes the provision of a cottage with a garden of not more than 1 acre: s 2(4)(a).
4 Ibid, s 2(2).
5 See ibid, s 7.
6 Ibid, s 8.
7 Ibid, s 6(1).
8 Ibid, s 6(2).

1906. Ancillary powers. In addition to any other infrastructural responsibilities vested in a local authority[1], certain powers incidental to the provision of accommodation are conferred by the Housing (Scotland) Act 1987 itself. Thus, in connection with the provision of housing accommodation, an authority may provide and maintain (1) a building adapted for use as a shop; (2) recreation grounds; and (3) other buildings or land which in the opinion of the Secretary of State will benefit the persons for whom the accommodation is provided[2]. Such provision (which may be undertaken jointly with another person) of buildings or land requires the consent of the Secretary of State[3]. In addition, authorities have the power to provide their houses with furniture, fittings and conveniences and to sell furniture to occupants of the houses[4]. They also have the power to provide facilities for obtaining meals and laundry facilities and services[5].

1 Eg under the town and country planning legislation.
2 Housing (Scotland) Act 1987 (c 26), s 3(1)(a)–(c), (2).

3 Ibid, s 3(3), (4).
4 Ibid, s 4(1)(a). This includes supplying furniture under a hire-purchase or conditional sale agreement: s 4(1)(b), (2).
5 See ibid, s 5.

(c) The Acquisition and Disposal of Land

1907. Land acquisition. All local authorities enjoy general powers to acquire land in relation to the discharge of their statutory functions[1]. Specific powers are also conferred upon local housing authorities. Thus an authority may acquire (1) land as a site for the erection of houses, and (2) land proposed to be used for the ancillary purposes mentioned above[2]. It may also acquire houses and other buildings (which may be made suitable as houses) together with land occupied with such houses or buildings or any right or interest in them[3]. Finally, the authority may acquire land for the purposes of selling or leasing it with a view to the erection on it of houses by persons other than the authority itself[4]. Related to this last power are powers enabling acquisition for the purpose of selling or leasing the land to enable its development as a building estate; and to enable works of improvement to be carried out on an adjoining house, whether by the authority or, after sale or lease, by someone else[5]. The acquisition of any land by the authority may be either by agreement[6] or, when authorised by the Secretary of State, compulsorily[7]. An authority may acquire land notwithstanding that it is not immediately required for the permitted purposes[8].

1 See the Local Government (Scotland) Act 1973 (c 65), Pt VI (ss 70–77), COMPULSORY ACQUISITION AND COMPENSATION, vol 5, paras 35, 45, and LOCAL GOVERNMENT, vol 14, paras 316 ff.
2 Housing (Scotland) Act 1987 (c 26), s 9(1)(a), (b), referring to the ancillary purposes authorised by s 3 or s 5: see para 1906 above.
3 Ibid, s 9(1)(c). There are restrictions upon the purchase of agricultural land: see s 9(2).
4 Ibid, s 9(1)(d)(i). This is subject to the restrictions imposed by the Land Tenure Reform (Scotland) Act 1974 (c 38). 'Sell' and 'sale' include feu: Housing (Scotland) Act 1987, s 338(1). The Land Tenure Reform (Scotland) Act 1974, s 8, imposes limitations on the residential use of property let under long leases on and after 1 September 1974. In general such property may not be used as, or as part of, a dwellinghouse. Exceptions are made where use as a private dwellinghouse is ancillary to the principal use.
5 Housing (Scotland) Act 1987, s 9(1)(d)(ii)–(iv).
6 Ibid, s 10(1), applying the Local Government (Scotland) Act 1973, s 70, for which see LOCAL GOVERNMENT, vol 14, para 316.
7 Housing (Scotland) Act 1987, s 10(2), (4), Sch 1. See also COMPULSORY ACQUISITION AND COMPENSATION, vol 5, para 35.
8 Ibid, s 10(3).

1908. Powers of dealing with land acquired or appropriated (including voluntary disposals). Once acquired, land is available for use for the purposes already mentioned. In addition, however, local authorities are given further specific powers in relation to such land. These include, in particular, the power to sell or lease the land or excamb it for land better adapted for the authorised purposes, either with or without paying or receiving any money for equality of exchange, subject, in certain cases, to the consent of the Secretary of State[1]. An authority may also sell or lease houses, but for this it normally needs the consent of the Secretary of State if it is a house to which the housing revenue account relates[2]. Exceptions are (1) where the house is being sold to a tenant (or to a member of his family who normally resides with him, or to a tenant and member of his family jointly) and (2) where the house is, in the opinion of the authority, either surplus to its requirements or difficult to let because it has been continuously vacant for a period of not less than three months immediately prior to the date of sale and during that period it has been on unrestricted offer to any applicant on the authority's housing list[3]. Sales to some sitting tenants referred to in head (1) are not merely permitted but required under Part III of the Housing (Scotland) Act 1987, in which case the discounts also required under that Part are available to purchasers[4] and another exception is where the disposal is made pursuant to the 'change of landlord' provisions[5].

In other cases the general rule for the disposal of land by local authorities applies. Except with the consent of the Secretary of State, an authority must not dispose of land for a consideration less than the least that can reasonably be obtained[6]. The power of the Secretary of State to consent to the disposal of houses (or other buildings or land) on an authority's housing revenue account is accompanied by the power, in giving consent, to impose such conditions as he thinks just[7]. His powers were expanded by the Housing Act 1988 as part of a policy designed to encourage the wholesale disposal by local authorities of housing schemes to a new landlord. Specifically, the Secretary of State is permitted to have regard to particular matters when determining whether to consent to a sale and, if so, on what conditions. These are (a) the extent (if any) to which the intending purchaser is (or is likely to be) dependent upon, controlled by or subject to influence from the selling local authority (or any of its members or officers); (b) the extent (if any) to which the proposed disposal would result in the intending purchaser's becoming the predominant or a substantial owner in any area of housing accommodation let on tenancies or subject to licences; (c) the terms of the proposed disposal; and, more widely, (d) any other matters whatsoever which the Secretary of State considers relevant[8]. In addition, the Secretary of State was given specific powers to give directions, where consent to a disposal is given, as to the purpose for which any capital money received may be applied[9]. At the same time, a number of other provisions, intended to protect the interests of tenants, were enacted.

First, there is a requirement of consultation. Whenever there is to be a disposal by a local authority of houses let on secure tenancies and the Secretary of State is to consider whether to consent, regard must be had to the views of tenants liable to cease to be secure tenants[10]. Procedurally, this means that, before the Secretary of State may entertain an application for consent, the local authority must certify that the consultation with all tenants (or all tenants except those likely to have vacated their houses before the disposal[11]) has been carried out[12]. The requirements of such consultation include the service of notice on each tenant informing him or her of details of the disposal (including the identity of the person to whom the disposal is to be made), its likely consequences and its effects on the right to buy, and informing the tenant of the opportunity to make representations to the authority within a reasonable period specified in the notice, being of not less than twenty-eight days[13]. The local authority must then consider any representations made and serve a further written notice informing the tenant of any significant changes in its proposal and that he or she may communicate any objections to the Secretary of State and of the consequences if a majority of tenants are opposed to the disposal[14]. The Secretary of State, after requiring a further process of consultation if he wishes[15], may not consent to the disposal if it appears to him that a majority of tenants do not wish the disposal to proceed, but this is declared not to affect his general discretion to refuse consent on grounds of tenant support or on any other ground[16]. In making his decision, he may have regard to any information available to him, and the local authority must give him such information as to representations made to it by tenants and others and other relevant matters as he may require[17]. Despite the enactment of these requirements to consult, it is also provided that his consent to a disposal is not invalidated by a failure on his part or of the local authority to comply with the requirements[18].

The second protection for a tenant is in the form of the statutory preservation of his or her right to buy where the tenant ceases to be a secure tenant because of a disposal to a private sector landlord[19]. This preservation of the right to buy, which does not apply in certain circumstances which are to be prescribed, is to be achieved in accordance with regulations[20]. It does not, however, extend to the situation after a second disposal of the house, although some protections for former tenants of local authorities are provided at that stage. Thus, thirdly, the person acquiring a house under the circumstances described may not dispose of it without the written consent of the Secretary of State, which consent may be given in respect of a particular disposal or of disposals of any class or description, and either conditionally or subject to conditions[21]. Before giving his consent, the Secretary of State must satisfy himself that the person seeking consent has taken appropriate steps to consult every tenant of any affected land or house and must have regard to the responses of tenants to that consultation[22].

1 Housing (Scotland) Act 1987 (c 26), s 12(1)(b), (c), (5), (7) (amended by the Housing Act 1988 (c 50), s 140(1), Sch 17, para 77). The consent of the Secretary of State is required for the disposal of land consisting of a common or open space or used for allotments (Housing (Scotland) Act 1987 (c 26), s 12(5)), or for the sale or lease of any land to which the housing revenue account applies: s 12(7) (as so amended) and s 14(2) (amended by the Housing (Scotland) Act 1988 (c 43), s 56(11)).
2 Housing (Scotland) Act 1987, ss 12(1)(d), (5), (7), 14(2) (as severally amended: see note 1 above).
3 Ibid, ss 12(7), (8), 14 (as severally amended: see note 1 above).
4 Ibid, s 14(2)(a) (amended by the Housing (Scotland) Act 1988, s 56(11)). As to the tenant's right to buy, see paras 1954 ff below. The Housing (Scotland) Act 1987, Pt III, comprises ss 44–84A.
5 See ibid, s 14(2)(a) (as so amended). For the change of landlord provisions, see the Housing (Scotland) Act 1988, Pt III (ss 56–64), and paras 1971 ff below.
6 Housing (Scotland) Act 1987, s 14(1), applying the Local Government (Scotland) Act 1973 (c 65), s 74(2). As to consents (to sell subject to discount) and guidance (including encouragement to sell, with discount, to sitting tenants), see SDD Circular 30/1980 and Appendix (amended by SDD Circular 23/1983).
7 Housing (Scotland) Act 1987, s 13(1) (renumbered by the Housing Act 1988, s 132(3)).
8 Housing (Scotland) Act 1987, s 13(2)(a)–(d) (added by the Housing Act 1988, s 132(3)).
9 Housing (Scotland) Act 1987, s 13(3) (as so added). As to the application of receipts from the disposal of land under s 208, see para 1919 below.
10 Ibid, s 81B (added by the Housing Act 1988, s 135(1)).
11 In this case the application may not be determined before the houses have been vacated: see the Housing (Scotland) Act 1987, s 81B (as so added), Sch 6A, para 2 (added by the Housing Act 1988, s 135(2), Sch 16).
12 Housing (Scotland) Act 1987, Sch 6A, paras 1, 2 (as so added).
13 Ibid, Sch 6A, para 3(1), (2) (as so added).
14 Ibid, Sch 6A, para 3(3) (as so added).
15 Ibid, Sch 6A, para 4 (as so added).
16 ibid, Sch 6A, para 5(1) (as so added).
17 Ibid, Sch 6A, para 5(2) (as so added).
18 Ibid, Sch 6A, para 6 (as so added).
19 Ibid, s 81A(1) (added by the Housing Act 1988, s 128).
20 Housing (Scotland) Act 1987, s 81A(2), (3) (as so added). As at 1 May 1990 no regulations had been made under this power.
21 Ibid, s 12A(1), (2) (added by the Housing Act 1988, s 134).
22 Housing (Scotland) Act 1987, s 12A(3) (as so added).

(d) Housing Finance

1909. General. A number of different forms of legal regulation apply to the financial arrangements to be made by local authorities in carrying out their housing functions. The most important of these govern:

(1) the housing support grant which the Secretary of State is empowered to make to authorities in support of their housing functions[1], and

(2) the housing accounts (especially the housing revenue account) which all authorities are obliged to maintain[2].

Other financial rules apply to housing functions as they do to other functions of local authorities. In particular, housing accounts are subject to the general arrangements for external audit by the Commission for Local Authority Accounts in Scotland[3]. The capital expenditure of housing authorities is subject to the standard form of control by the Secretary of State although, administratively, the controls he imposes are handled separately[4]. The local authority financial year for housing purposes is the same as that for other purposes, and thus runs from 1 April to 31 March[5].

1 See paras 1910 ff below.
2 See paras 1915 ff below.
3 See LOCAL GOVERNMENT, vol 14, paras 882 ff.
4 See LOCAL GOVERNMENT, vol 14, para 613.
5 Housing (Scotland) Act 1987 (c 126), s 338(1), applying the Local Government (Scotland) Act 1973 (c 65), s 96(5) (substituted by the Local Government (Scotland) Act 1975 (c 30), s 18).

1910. Housing support grants. The legal basis upon which the Secretary of State has subsidised the revenue expenditure of local authorities in relation to the provision and maintenance of housing has always been different from that which applies to other local services. From 1985 the distinction was maintained in the exclusion of housing subsidies from the expenditure which is 'relevant' for the purposes of the rate support grants introduced by the Local Government (Scotland) Act 1966[1]. The same dichotomy is continued in the arrangements for revenue support grants payable since 1 April 1989 under the Abolition of Domestic Rates Etc (Scotland) Act 1987[2]. Two substantial changes affecting central government housing subsidies to local authorities have, however, occurred. One is that amounts of central government subsidy have declined. Some local authorities receive no general contribution at all to revenue expenditure on housing[3]. The other change was the substantial simplification of subsidy arrangements when housing support grants were introduced and earlier subsidies were swept away by the Housing (Financial Provisions) (Scotland) Act 1978[4].

1 See the Local Government (Scotland) Act 1966 (c 51), s 2(8)(b) (set out in amended form in the Rating and Valuation (Amendment) (Scotland) Act 1984 (c 31), Sch 1) (repealed).
2 Abolition of Domestic Rates Etc (Scotland) Act 1987 (c 47), s 23, Sch 4 (amended by the Local Government and Housing Act 1989 (c 42), s 145, Sch 6, paras 28, 29).
3 See eg the Housing Support Grant (Scotland) Order 1987, SI 1987/332 (in respect of 1987–88); Housing Support Grant (Scotland) Order 1988, SI 1988/547 (in respect of 1988–89); Housing Support Grant (Scotland) Order 1989, SI 1989/181 (in respect of 1989–90); and the Housing Support Grant (Scotland) Order 1990, SI 1990/196 (in respect of 1990–91).
4 Housing (Financial Provisions) (Scotland) Act 1978 (c 14), s 7 (termination of certain exchequer payments to housing authorities) (repealed).

1911. The aggregate amount of grants. Now contained in Part IX of the Housing (Scotland) Act 1987[1], the housing support grant rules are closely analogous to those which govern revenue support grants[2]. Thus, the scheme imposes, first, a duty upon the Secretary of State to make housing support grants for the purpose of assisting local authorities to meet reasonable housing needs in their areas[3]. Grants are made for each financial year[4], and the initial step is for the Secretary of State to estimate in respect of all local authorities two amounts: one is the aggregate amount of 'eligible expenditure' which it is reasonable for local authorities to incur for the year in question[4]. 'Eligible expenditure' is defined as the expenditure which authorities are statutorily required to debit to their housing revenue accounts[5]. The other amount is the aggregate amount of 'relevant income' (other than housing support grants themselves) which could reasonably be expected to be credited to housing revenue accounts during the year[6]. 'Relevant income' is defined as the income, payments, contributions (including contributions from general funds) and receipts which authorities are required to credit to their housing revenue accounts[7]. It has been held that, in making his estimates of 'relevant income', the Secretary of State is not restricted to certain sources for his figures and, in particular, is not obliged to assume that the contribution from an authority's general fund would be at the maximum permitted level[8]. The deduction of 'relevant income' from 'eligible expenditure' produces (subject to one qualification mentioned below) the aggregate amount of the year's housing support grants[9]. Before estimating the two amounts of income and expenditure, the Secretary of State is required to consult with such associations of local authorities as appear to him to be concerned (in practice, the Convention of Scottish Local Authorities) and to take into consideration (1) the latest information available to him as to the level of eligible expenditure and relevant income; (2) the level of interest rates, remuneration, costs and prices which, in his opinion, would affect the amount of eligible expenditure for the year; and (3) the latest information available to him as to changes in the general level of earnings which would affect the amount of relevant income for the year[10]. The Secretary of State is further authorised, when making the required estimates, to leave out of account the expenditure and income of an authority if (either or both) (a) he estimates that its income will exceed its expenditure; (b) he determines that no proportion of the aggregate amount of grant is to be paid to the authority[11]. As indicated above, there is room for a further adjustment in the course of the calculation of the aggregate amount of grants by the Secretary of State. He may take into account the extent to which the actual amount of eligible expenditure for a *previous* year differs (or is likely to differ) from the amount estimated for grant purposes for that year[12].

1   The Housing (Scotland) Act 1987 (c 26), Pt IX, comprises ss 191–202. The relevant provisions are ss 191–193, 198–202.
2   As to revenue support grant, see LOCAL GOVERNMENT, vol 14, paras 832, 833, and para 875, note 3.
3   Housing (Scotland) Act 1987, s 191(1). For the meaning of 'local authority', see para 1903 above.
4   'Financial year' has the same meaning as in the Local Government (Scotland) Act 1973 (c 65), s 96(5) (substituted by the Local Government (Scotland) Act 1975 (c 30), s 18) (ie the twelve months ending 31 March): Housing (Scotland) Act 1987, s 338(1).
4   Ibid, s 191(2)(a).
5   Ibid, s 191(10).
6   Ibid, s 191(2)(b).
7   Ibid, s 191(10) (amended by the Housing (Scotland) Act 1988 (c 43), s 72(1), Sch 8, para 4).
8   *Sutherland District Council v Secretary of State for Scotland* 1988 GWD 4–167, OH. As to general fund contributions to the housing revenue account, see para 1917 below.
9   Housing (Scotland) Act 1987, s 191(2).
10   Ibid, s 191(3)(a)–(c).
11   Ibid, s 191(5)(a), (b).
12   Ibid, s 191(4).

1912. Housing support grant orders. Adhering once again to the revenue support grant model, the aggregate amount of housing support grants, fixed as described above[1], is required to be set out in an order made by the Secretary of State with the consent of the Treasury[2]. A housing support grant order may not be made until laid in draft before and approved by resolution of the House of Commons[3]. The draft must be accompanied by a report of the considerations leading to the provisions of the order[3]. A housing support grant order also contains details of the apportionment of the aggregate amount of grant between authorities[4]. In some circumstances the contents of an order may be varied. The Secretary of State may (after consultation with the Convention of Scottish Local Authorities) re-estimate the amount of eligible expenditure originally calculated[5]. If it appears to him that expenditure has been or is likely to be substantially increased or decreased because of changes since the original estimate (and inadequate account of these was taken at that time), he may make a re-estimate[6]. This is done by means of an order made in the same way as the first[7].

1 See the Housing (Scotland) Act 1987 (c 26), s 191(2), and para 1911 above.
2 Ibid, s 191(7). For examples of orders, see para 1910, note 3, above.
3 Ibid, s 191(9).
4 See ibid, s 192, and para 1913 below.
5 See ibid, s 193(1), (2).
6 Ibid, s 191(3).
7 Ibid s 193(4). For examples of variation orders, see the Housing Support Grant (Scotland) Variation Order 1987, SI 1987/331, the Housing Support Grant (Scotland) Variation Order 1988, SI 1988/548, and the Housing Support Grant (Scotland) Variation Order 1990, SI 1990/195.

1913. Apportionment of housing support grants. The housing support grant order is, in addition to fixing the aggregate amount of grants, the vehicle by which the Secretary of State prescribes, after consultation with the Convention of Scottish Local Authorities, the method according to which he determines the proportion, if any, of the aggregate amount each local authority will receive[1]. He must include within the report which accompanies the housing support grant a table showing, in respect of each authority, (1) the estimated amount of grant payable to the authority, or (2) if no grant is payable, that fact[2]. In prescribing the method of determining the proportions payable to an authority, the Secretary of State, on the one hand, *may* take into account a substantial difference, in a previous year, between estimated and actual eligible expenditure[3], and, on the other hand, *must* have regard to any special needs affecting an authority's eligible expenditure[4]. He may, in addition, seek to secure that no reduction in grant payable will, from one year to the next, produce an unreasonable increase in the amount to be met from an authority's general fund[5].

1 Housing (Scotland) Act 1987 (c 26), s 192(1), (7).
2 Ibid, s 192(3)(a), (b).
3 Ibid, s 192(4).
4 Ibid, s 192(5).
5 Ibid, s 192(6) (amended by the Housing (Scotland) Act 1988 (c 43), s 72(1), Sch 8, para 5).

1914. Payment of grants. Housing support grants are payable at such times and in such manner as the Secretary of State may determine, and subject to such conditions as he may impose[1]. The making of a payment is subject to the making of application for payment in such form, and containing such particulars, as the Secretary of State may from time to time determine[2].

1 Housing (Scotland) Act 1987 (c 26), s 198(1).
2 Ibid, s 198(2).

1915. Housing accounts of local authorities. Local authorities are required to keep certain accounts in relation to their housing functions. Specific provision is made in the Housing (Scotland) Act 1987 for the keeping of a rent rebate account, a rent allowance account and a slum clearance revenue account[1]. Above all, however, each authority must keep a housing revenue account[2].

1 See the Housing (Scotland) Act 1987 (c 26), ss 205–207. As to rent rebates and rent allowances, see SOCIAL SECURITY. As to the slum clearance revenue account, see para 1918 below.
2 See ibid, s 203, and para 1916 below.

1916. The housing revenue account. The central significance of the housing revenue account arises because the statutory rules which govern payments in and out of the account determine where the financial burden of local authority housing is to lie—whether simply upon tenants, upon those who pay community charges or non-domestic rates or upon the Secretary of State (and, thereby, the national taxpayers). Subject to the power of an authority to include or exclude (with the consent of the Secretary of State) certain houses or properties, and subject also to the power of the Secretary of State to direct that a category of houses be included in or excluded from the account, the housing revenue account must be maintained in respect of the houses, buildings and land specified in Part I of Schedule 15 to the Housing (Scotland) Act 1987[1]. The Schedule contains a detailed specification of properties by reference to the statutory powers authorising the provisions of local authority housing since 12 February 1919, that is, Part I of the 1987 Act and its predecessors[2]. Other categories of houses and buildings included are those acquired for improvement in housing action areas, lodging houses and hostels[3]. Excluded, however, is any land the authority has provided expressly for sale for development by another person[4]. Part II of Schedule 15 to the 1987 Act specifies what amounts are to be credited and debited to the housing revenue account[5]. The two principal amounts to be credited to the account[6] are the income receivable from standard rents[7] and any housing support grant payable to the authority[8]. The principal debits are loan charges in respect of money borrowed for the provision, repair and improvement of houses to which the account relates; expenditure in respect of the repair, maintenance, supervision and management of houses; and arrears of rent which have been written off[9]. The terms of the Schedule may be amended by order by the Secretary of State, after consultation with the Convention of Scottish Local Authorities[10].

1 Housing (Scotland) Act 1987 (c 26), s 203(1)–(3), Sch 15, Pt I (para 1).
2 Ibid, Sch 15, para 1(1)(a). Part I of the 1987 Act comprises ss 1–23.
3 Ibid, Sch 15, para 1(1)(d), (e).
4 Ibid, s 203(4).
5 Ibid, Sch 15, Pt II, comprises paras 2–10.
6 This is subject to para 1917 below.
7 Housing (Scotland) Act 1987, Sch 15, para 2(1)(a): see para 1934 below.
8 Ibid, Sch 15, para 2(1)(c). As to housing support grant, see para 1910 above.
9 See ibid, Sch 15, para 3, especially para 3(a)(i)–(iii), (c), (e).
10 Ibid, s 203(6). An order made under s 203(6) must be made by statutory instrument, subject to annulment in pursuance of a resolution of either House of Parliament: s 203(7). Items of income or expenditure are to be included or excluded from the account by direction of the Secretary of State: Sch 15, para 8.

1917. Contributions to the housing revenue account from the general fund. If the housing revenue account of an authority shows a credit balance, it may be made available for any purpose for which the general fund of the local authority may be applied[1]. If, on the other hand, a deficit is shown, the authority must carry to the credit of the housing revenue account a contribution of equal amount from the general fund[2]. On its face, this provision would enable an authority which wished to do so to budget for a deficit on its housing revenue account (perhaps by increasing expenditure on repairs whilst maintaining rents at existing levels) and thus ensure the need for a contribution from the general fund — in effect from ratepayers and payers of community charges. The scope for such a subsidy from the general fund was, however, narrowed by the Rating and Valuation (Amendment) (Scotland) Act 1984[3]. Following the failure to achieve the same result by other means[4], the Secretary of State was given the power to ensure that authorities would be obliged to raise rent levels rather than seek increased contributions from their general funds. The Secretary of State may impose, by order, a limit to the amount of contribution out of its general fund which an authority (or class of authorities) may estimate that it will carry to the credit of its housing revenue account for the year specified in the order[5]. The limit may be expressed in whatever way the Secretary of State thinks fit[6]. To enable the Secretary of State to monitor the position, every authority must submit to him an estimate of all income and expenditure in relation to the housing revenue account for the following year[7]. Once the order limiting the amount of the contribution has been made (by statutory instrument subject to annulment in pursuance of a resolution of either House of Parliament) a local authority affected by it is obliged to estimate for its account in a way which does not exceed the contribution specified in it[8]. In *City of Edinburgh District Council v Secretary of State for Scotland*[9] the council was unsuccessful in its attempt to challenge the validity of the first order[10]. A default order[11] was subsequently made against the council by the Secretary of State.

1 Housing (Scotland) Act 1987 (c 26), s 203(5), Sch 15, para 9(1). As to the general fund, see the Local Government (Scotland) Act 1973 (c 65), s 93, and LOCAL GOVERNMENT, vol 14, para 803.
2 Housing (Scotland) Act 1987, Sch 15, para 9(2) (amended by the Housing (Scotland) Act 1988 (c 43), s 72(1), Sch 8, para 10).
3 Housing (Financial Provisions) (Scotland) Act 1972 (c 46), s 23A (added by the Rating and Valuation (Amendment) (Scotland) Act 1984 (c 31), s 8) (repealed).
4 For a brief account, see C M G Himsworth *Public Sector Housing Law in Scotland* (3rd edn, 1989) pp 9, 10.
5 Housing (Scotland) Act 1987, s 204(1). See the Housing Revenue Account General Fund Contribution Limits (Scotland) Order 1989, SI 1989/2310.
6 Housing (Scotland) Act 1987, s 204(2).
7 Ibid, s 204(4).
8 Ibid, s 204(1), (3).
9 *City of Edinburgh District Council v Secretary of State for Scotland* 1985 SLT 551.
10 Housing Revenue Account Rate Fund Contribution Limits (Scotland) Order 1985, SI 1985/3. For a note on the case, see C M G Himsworth 'Defining the Boundaries of Judicial Review' 1985 SLT (News) 369.
11 Ie under the Local Government (Scotland) Act 1973, s 211.

1918. Slum clearance revenue account. Every local authority is obliged to maintain a slum clearance revenue account[1]. This account is to include the income and expenditure of an authority in respect of houses and other property acquired or appropriated for the purposes of Part IV (sub-standard houses), Part V (repair of houses) and Part VI (closing and demolition orders) of the Housing (Scotland) Act 1987[2]. Details of the amounts to be credited and debited to the account are set out in Schedule 16 to the Act. Until the financial year 1988–89, one item to be credited to the account was the amount of slum clearance subsidy payable to the authority[3]. With effect from 1989–90, however, that subsidy was abolished and replaced by support through revenue support grant[4].

1 Housing (Scotland) Act 1987 (c 26), s 207(1), (3), Sch 16 (amended by the Housing (Scotland) Act 1988 (c 43), ss 67(8), 72(3), Sch 10). For the meaning of 'local authority', see para 1903 above.
2 Housing (Scotland) Act 1987, s 207(2)(a). Houses acquired under Pt IV to bring them (or other houses) up to the tolerable standard are excluded. For details of the powers under Pt IV (ss 85–107), Pt V (ss 108–113) and Pt VI (ss 114–134), see paras 1978 ff, 1993 ff, 1982 ff below respectively.

3 Ibid, s 207(2)(b) (as originally enacted). It was subsequently substituted by the Housing (Scotland) Act 1988, s 72(2), Sch 9, para 17. Slum clearance subsidy was payable under the Housing (Scotland) Act 1987, s 200 (repealed).
4 Housing (Scotland) Act 1988, s 67. That section similarly ended direct central subsidies for improvement and repairs grants under the Housing (Scotland) Act 1987, s 254 (repealed), and amenity improvement under s 255 (repealed), and payments under s 296 (repealed) in respect of defective dwellings.

1919. Capital expenditure and receipts. The principal legal control over capital expenditure by housing authorities is that which applies to capital expenditure by local authorities in respect of their functions as a whole. The Local Government (Scotland) Act 1973 provides that any local authority liability to meet capital expenses requires the prior consent of the Secretary of State[1]. As applied to housing, this power of control is used by the Secretary of State to allocate to authorities, on an annual basis, 'blocks' of capital within which an authority has some freedom to decide on their disposal[2]. Each authority is allocated two such 'blocks'. The housing revenue account block relates to expenditure (such as on building and improvement) in relation to houses subject to the housing revenue account. The non-housing revenue account block relates to local authority expenditure on private sector housing — principally improvement and repairs grants, loans for house purchase and environmental improvement. Allocations to the housing revenue account block may take account of capital receipts which the Secretary of State estimates to be forthcoming from the sale of houses (especially purchased to the tenant's right to buy). There is a general provision that money received from the disposal of land held on the housing revenue account (or on the slum clearance account) is to be applied for a purpose for which the land was held[3]. This restriction does not apply if either the Secretary of State approves the use of the money for another purpose or he has already made directions in relation to the 'large scale' disposal of housing stock[4].

1 Local Government (Scotland) Act 1973 (c 65), s 94. For the operation of s 94 in general, see LOCAL GOVERNMENT, vol 14, paras 805 ff. For local authority borrowing powers, see vol 14, paras 813 ff.
2 For a summary of this system as it then operated, see *Housing Capital Allocations* (Report of the Select Committee on Scottish Affairs) (HC Papers (1980–81) no. 112).
3 Housing (Scotland) Act 1987 (c 26), s 208(1), (3). Section 208(3) refers to the 'slum clearance account' rather than the 'slum clearance revenue account'.
4 Ibid, s 208(2) (amended by the Housing Act 1988 (c 50), s 132(6)). See also para 1908, text to note 9, above.

(3) NEW TOWNS

1920. The development corporations. Some of the principal functions of the developement corporations of the five new towns designated in Scotland are the acquisition of land for the provision of housing and its subsequent management[1]. New towns receive an annual grant to supplement their rental income[2]. Tenants of new town corporations as secure tenants will benefit from the 'tenants' charter' and, where qualified, have the right to purchase their houses[3]. A recently added specific power of the corporations has been the power to make improvements to the amenities of predominantly residential areas[4]. It has, however, been the long-standing policy of central government to reduce, and ultimately conclude, the role of development corporations as providers of housing[5]. This intention has been reaffirmed in statute by conferring the power on all corporations to sell, with the consent of the Secretary of State, their whole interest in any land held for housing purposes[6].

1 See the New Towns (Scotland) Act 1968 (c 16), s 3. As to the establishment of new town development corporations, see s 2 (amended by the New Towns (Scotland) Act 1977 (c 16), s 1(1)). See generally TOWN AND COUNTRY PLANNING.
2 Housing (Scotland) Act 1987 (c 26), s 194(1), and s 338(1) ('development corporation').
3 As to the secure tenant's right to buy, see paras 1954 ff below.
4 Housing (Scotland) Act 1987, s 23 (substituted by the Housing (Scotland) Act 1988 (c 43), s 3(3), Sch 2, para 8). For the corresponding powers of local authorities, see para 2033 below.
5 See eg *Housing: The Government's Proposals for Scotland* (Cm 242) (1987) paras 6.11–6.13, and *The Scottish New Towns: The Way Ahead* (Cm 711) (1989) ch 5. See also the Enterprise and New Towns (Scotland) Bill, which was passing through Parliament during the Spring of 1990.
6 New Towns (Scotland) Act 1968, s 18AA (added by the Housing (Scotland) Act 1988, s 71).

(4) SCOTTISH HOMES

1921. Introduction. The principal institutional innovation in the law and administration of housing in Scotland has been the creation of Scottish Homes. With effect from 1 April 1989 the Scottish Special Housing Association, which had become a substantial provider of public sector housing, ceased to exist[1], and the operations (principally in relation to housing associations) of the Scottish sector of the Housing Corporation terminated[2]. Pursuant to proposals formulated first in *Scottish Homes: A New Agency for Housing in Scotland*[3], and then in *Housing: The Government's Proposals for Scotland*[4], Scottish Homes, which was established under the Housing (Scotland) Act 1988[5], assumed the functions of those two organisations but was also given a more widely cast remit[6].

1 Housing (Scotland) Act 1988 (c 43), s 3(1); Housing (Scotland) Act 1988 (Specified Date) Order 1988, SI 1988/2192. The Housing (Scotland) Act 1988, s 3(1), transferred all heritable or moveable property and rights, liabilities and obligations of the Scottish Special Housing Association to Scottish Homes. Subject to some specific amendments in Sch 2, for any reference in any enactment, or in any instrument made under any enactment, to the Scottish Special Housing Association there is so substituted a reference to Scottish Homes: s 3(3), Sch 2, para 1.
2 The Housing Corporation continued in existence, but with powers, especially in relation to housing associations, adjusted by ibid, s 4, and by amendments made to the Housing Associations Act 1985 (c 69): see para 1924 below. All heritable or moveable property of the Housing Corporation in Scotland and its rights, liabilities and obligations in connection with housing associations in Scotland and land in Scotland held by unregistered housing associations were transferred to Scottish Homes by the Housing (Scotland) Act 1988, s 4(5).
3 Scottish Development Department 1987.
4 Cm 242 (1987).
5 Housing (Scotland) Act 1988, s 1.
6 See ibid, Pt I (ss 1–11).

1922. Constitution and proceedings. Scottish Homes is established as a body corporate with a common seal but without Crown status, immunity, or privilege[1]. Membership is of not more than nine persons appointed by the Secretary of State and, *ex officio*, the chief executive[2]. The first chief executive was appointed by the Secretary of State, but subsequent appointments are to be by Scottish Homes itself, with the approval of the Secretary of State[3]. The Secretary of State appoints one member of Scottish Homes to be chairman and may appoint one or more others to be deputy chairman or chairmen[4]. Provision is made for the terms of office of chairmen and members, the payment of remuneration, allowances and pensions, and their resignation and removal[5]. Scottish Homes is empowered to appoint employees below the level of chief executive as it thinks fit[6]. There is little statutory regulation of the manner in which Scottish Homes conducts its business, save in relation to the disclosure by members of their interest in contracts or other matters falling to be considered by Scottish Homes[7]. Scottish Homes may establish committees (which may include members who are not members of Scottish Homes) in connection with the discharge of its functions[8]. In respect of its actions as a landlord, Scottish Homes is subject to investigation by the Commissioner for Local Administration in Scotland (the 'local authority ombudsman')[9], whilst its other actions are within the jurisdiction of the Parliamentary Commissioner for Administration[10].

 1 Housing (Scotland) Act 1988 (c 43), s 1(1), (2), Sch 1, paras 1, 3.
 2 Ibid, Sch 1, para 4(1). The Secretary of State must satisfy himself, both on their appointment and subsequently from time to time, that members will not be affected be any conflict of interest: Sch 1, para 4(2).
 3 Ibid, Sch 1, para 9.
 4 Ibid, Sch 1, para 6.
 5 Ibid, Sch 1, paras 6–8.
 6 Ibid, Sch 1, para 10. The terms and conditions of employment require the approval of the Secretary of State and Treasury consent: Sch 1, para 10.
 7 Ibid, Sch 1, paras 15, 16.
 8 Ibid, Sch 1, para 17.
 9 Local Government (Scotland) Act 1975 (c 30), s 23(1)(g) (substituted by the Housing (Scotland) Act 1988, s 3(2), Sch 2, para 4). See LOCAL GOVERNMENT, vol 14, paras 133 ff.
10 Parliamentary Commissioner Act 1967 (c 13), Sch 2 (amended by the Housing (Scotland) Act 1988, Sch 2, para 2. See CONSTITUTIONAL LAW, vol 5, paras 437, 484.

1923. Powers and functions. The statutory powers of Scottish Homes are conferred in two stages. There are first the general functions of:
(1) providing, and assisting in the provision of, finance to persons or bodies intending to provide, improve, repair, maintain or manage housing;
(2) providing, improving, repairing, maintaining and managing housing (whether solely or in conjunction with any other person or body);
(3) promoting owner-occupation (especially by those seeking to purchase for the first time), the wider ownership of housing by its occupants and a greater choice of tenancy arrangements;
(4) promoting the provision and improvement of housing and the improvement of management of housing (whether by its occupants or otherwise);
(5) promoting and assisting the development of housing associations, maintaining a register of housing associations and exercising supervision and control over registered housing associations;
(6) undertaking, and assisting the undertaking of, the development, redevelopment and improvement of the physical, social, economic and recreational environment related to housing;
(7) such other general functions as are conferred upon Scottish Homes by or under the Housing (Scotland) Act 1988 or any other enactment[1].
It is then provided that Scottish Homes may do anything, whether in Scotland or elsewhere, which is calculated to facilitate or is incidental or conducive to the discharge of these general functions[2]. Without prejudice to the generality of that qualification, however, it is further provided that Scottish Homes may:
(a) make grants[3];
(b) make loans;
(c) acquire, hold and dispose of securities;
(d) guarantee obligations (arising out of loans or otherwise) incurred by other persons, or grant indemnities;
(e) provide or assist in the provision of advisory or other services or facilities for any person;
(f) acquire land by agreement or gift;
(g) acquire land (including servitudes or other rights in or over land by the creation of new rights) compulsorily;

(h) hold and manage land and dispose of, or otherwise deal with, land held by it;

(j) acquire and dispose of plant, machinery, equipment and other property;

(k) develop land or carry out works on land, and maintain or assist in the maintenance of any such works;

(l) make land, plant, machinery, equipment and other property available for use by other persons;

(m) appoint other persons to act as its agents;

(n) act as agents for other persons;

(o) form companies within the meaning of the Companies Act 1985 (c 6);

(p) form partnerships with other persons;

(q) promote, provide or assist in the provision of, training in matters relating to housing;

(r) carry out, commission or assist in the provision of, research and development;

(s) promote, or assist in the promotion of, publicity relating to its general functions and powers and to matters relating to housing;

(t) make such charge as it thinks fit for any of its services;

(u) accept any gift or grant made to it for the purposes of any of its general functions and powers and, subject to the terms of the gift or grant and to the provisions of the Housing (Scotland) Act 1988, apply it for those purposes;

(v) turn its resources to account so far as they are not required for the exercise of any of its general functions and powers[4].

The powers in heads (a) to (d), (m) and (o) may be exercised only with the approval (or general authority) of the Secretary of State given with the consent of the Treasury[5].

The powers in heads (e) to (l) (with the exception of the power under head (h) to dispose of land) may be exercised only in accordance with arrangements made between Scottish Homes and the Secretary of State[6]. The power conferred by head (h) to dispose of land may be exercised only with the consent of the Secretary of State[7].

In addition to these controls, the Secretary of State has a general power to give Scottish Homes general or specific directions as to the exercise of its general functions and powers, and Scottish Homes must comply with these directions[8]. The Secretary of State has further powers of control over the financial arrangements of Scottish Homes. Acting with the approval of the Treasury, he may determine the financial duties of Scottish Homes and make grants in respect of its expenses incurred in the exercise of its general functions and powers[9]. Borrowing by Scottish Homes may be from the Secretary of State or, with his consent given with the approval of the Treasury, from other sources. Subject to adjustment (up to a maximum of £1500m) by the Secretary of State, the aggregate amount outstanding by way of borrowing by Scottish Homes or guaranteed to it by the Treasury is subject to a limit of £1000m[10]. There is provision for the accounts required to be kept by Scottish Homes and for an annual report to the Secretary of State which is to be laid before each House of Parliament[11].

1 Housing (Scotland) Act 1988 (c 43), s 1(3)(a)–(g).
2 Ibid, s 2(1).
3 As to grants, see also para 1932 below (housing associations) and para 2019 below (house improvement grants).
4 Housing (Scotland) Act 1988, s 2(2)(a)–(v). For additional (separately conferred) powers of Scottish Homes, see paras 1924 ff, 1971 ff, below.
5 Ibid, s 2(3)(a).
6 Ibid, s 2(3)(b) (amended by the Local Government and Housing Act 1989 (c 42), s 179(b)).

7 Housing (Scotland) Act 1988, s 2(3A) (added by the Local Government and Housing Act 1989, s 179(c)), under which consent may be given in relation to particular cases or classes of case and may be subject to conditions.

8 Housing (Scotland) Act 1988, s 2(10).

9 Ibid, ss 5, 6.

10 Ibid, ss 7–10.

11 Ibid, s 11.

(5) HOUSING ASSOCIATIONS

1924. Definition and introduction. 'Housing association' is defined as a society, body of trustees or company (1) which is established for the purpose of, or amongst whose objects or powers are included those of, providing, constructing, improving or managing, or facilitating or encouraging the construction or improvement of, housing accommodation, and (2) which does not trade for profit or whose constitution or rules prohibit the issue of capital with interest or dividend exceeding such rate as may be prescribed by the Treasury, whether with or without differentiation as between share and loan capital; but does not include Scottish Homes[1].

For some purposes, it is necessary to distinguish a 'fully mutual' housing association whose rules restrict membership to persons who are tenants or prospective tenants of the association and preclude the granting or assignment of tenancies to others, and a 'co-operative housing association' which is a fully mutual association registered under the Industrial and Provident Societies Act 1965 (c 12)[2]. There is also to be distinguished a 'self-build society', which is a housing association whose object it is to provide, for sale to or occupation by its members, dwellings built or improved principally with the use of its members' own labour[3].

In the period since 1974, housing associations have become substantial providers of housing. The Housing Act 1974 gave substantial new powers to the Housing Corporation (operating throughout Great Britain) and in particular as to the registration and subsequent supervision of housing associations. Registration with the Housing Corporation was a prerequisite for housing associations to receive grants (housing association grant) from central government[4]. It was access to this form of grant aid that led to the blossoming of housing provision by associations. Since the creation of Scottish Homes on 1 April 1989[5], it has taken over from the Housing Corporation the responsibilities of that body for virtually all housing associations operating in Scotland[6].

In Wales, an equivalent body, Housing for Wales, was established[7]. In some ways the powers of Scottish Homes have been modified and, in particular, entirely new grant-giving powers have been conferred[8]. With effect from 2 January 1989, other statutory changes were made which affect the operation of housing associations. Since that date, new tenancies created by housing associations have not been secure tenancies carrying with them the right to buy, but assured tenancies under the Housing (Scotland) Act 1988[9]. It should also be borne in mind that housing associations may become the principal actors under the 'change of landlord'[10] and 'voluntary disposal'[11] provisions introduced by that Act and the Housing Act 1988[12].

1 Housing Associations Act 1985 (c 69), s 1(1) (amended by the Housing (Scotland) Act 1988 (c 43), s 3(3), Sch 2, para 6).

2 Housing Associations Act 1985, s 1(2). 'Assignment' is the equivalent of 'assignation', which is the more usual term in Scots law.

3 Ibid, s 1(3).

4 Housing Act 1974 (c 44), Pt I (ss 1–12) (and Sch 2), Pt II (ss 13–28), and Pt III (ss 29–35).

5 See para 1921 above.
6 Housing (Scotland) Act 1988, s 4. The exceptions are associations which, although operating in Scotland, have their registered offices in England. For the detailed powers of Scottish Homes in relation to housing associations, see para 1923 above.
7 Housing Act 1988 (c 50), ss 46, 47, Sch 5.
8 See para 1932 below.
9 Housing (Scotland) Act 1988, Pt II (ss 12–55) (especially ss 12, 43); Housing (Scotland) Act 1988 Commencement Order 1988, SI 1988/2038. As to assured tenancies generally, see LANDLORD AND TENANT.
10 See the Housing (Scotland) Act 1988, Pt III (ss 56–64).
11 See the Housing (Scotland) Act 1987 (c 26), s 81B, Sch 6A (added by the Housing Act 1988, s 135(1), (2), Sch 16).
12 See paras 1971 ff below, and para 1908 above respectively.

1925. Registration of housing associations. Scottish Homes is required to maintain a register of housing associations[1], and it is its responsibility to admit associations to the register and, where required, to remove them from it[2]. To be eligible for registration by Scottish Homes a housing association must be a society registered under the Industrial and Provident Societies Act 1965 (c 12) with its registered office, for the purposes of that Act, in Scotland[3]. The association must further satisfy a number of statutory conditions. The conditions are that the association does not trade for profit and is established for the purpose of, or has among its objects or powers, the provision, construction, improvement, or management of (1) houses to be kept available for letting, or (2) houses for occupation by members of the association, where the rules of the association restrict membership to persons entitled or prospectively entitled (as tenants or otherwise) to occupy a house provided or managed by the association, or (3) hostels; and that any additional purposes or objects are contained within a statutorily prescribed list[4]. The list (which may be extended by the Secretary of State by order[5]) includes the provision of land, amenities or services for residents; the acquisition, construction, or conversion of houses for sale or lease; and encouraging and giving advice on the formation of other housing associations and the running of such associations and other voluntary organisations concerned with housing[6]. It is further provided that a housing association is not ineligible for registration by reason only that its powers include any on another statutory list[7]. That list includes the power to acquire (and repair and improve) commercial premises or businesses as an incidental part of another project and to repair or improve houses or buildings after the tenants have exercised or claimed to exercise their right to buy[7]. Provided that a housing association is eligible in accordance with these criteria, Scottish Homes may register the association. Scottish Homes is required, however, to establish further criteria (which may be different from their equivalents in England and Wales) which should be satisfied by a housing association seeking registration and, in deciding whether to register an association, Scottish Homes must have regard to whether it satisfies those criteria[8].

When a housing association is registered, Scottish Homes must notify the registrar under the Industrial and Provident Societies Act 1965[9]. Thereafter Scottish Homes has the power to remove an association from the register in certain circumstances. If it appears to Scottish Homes that the association is no longer eligible for registration or that the association has ceased to exist or does not operate, Scottish Homes must, after at least fourteen days' notice to the association, remove it from the register[10]. In addition, a registered association may itself request Scottish Homes to remove it from the register if it has never been in receipt of grant, and Scottish Homes may remove such an association if it thinks fit[11]. In either case, Scottish Homes must notify the registrar under the

1965 Act [12]. There is a right of appeal to the Court of Session against removal from the register[13].

1 Housing Association Act 1985 (c 69), ss 2A(1), 3(1) (respectively added by the Housing Act 1988 (c 50), s 59(2), (3), Sch 6, para 1, and amended by Sch 6, para 3).
2 See the Housing Associations Act 1985, ss 5–7 (amended by the Housing Act 1988, Sch 6, paras 4–6).
3 Housing Associations Act 1985, s 2A(1) (as added: see note 1 above).
4 Ibid, s 4(1), (2).
5 Housing Act 1988, s 48(2)–(4).
6 See the Housing Associations Act 1985, s 4(3) (substituted by the Housing Act 1988, s 48(1)).
7 Housing Associations Act 1985, s 4(4) (as so substituted).
8 Ibid, s 5(1), and s 5(2) (substituted by the Housing Act 1988, Sch 6, para 4).
9 Housing Associations Act 1985, s 5(4) (as so substituted).
10 Ibid, s 6(2).
11 Ibid, s 6(4) (amended by the Housing Act 1988, Sch 6, para 5).
12 Housing Associations Act 1985, s 6(5).
13 Ibid, s 7 (amended by the Housing Act 1988, Sch 6, para 6).

1926. Disposal of land. Subject to the right to buy provisions[1], every registered housing association is empowered to dispose of land as it thinks fit[2]. However, save where the disposal is a letting under a secure tenancy or an assured tenancy, it requires the consent of Scottish Homes[3]. That consent may be given generally or to a particular association or description of association (and in relation to particular land or a particular description of land), and may be given subject to conditions[4].

1 As to the right to buy provisions, see paras 1954 ff below.
2 Housing Associations Act 1985 (c 69), s 8(1).
3 Ibid, s 9(1) (substituted by the Housing Act 1988 (c 50), s 59(2), (3), Sch 6, para 7(1)) (read with the Housing Associations Act 1985, s 2A(1) (added by the Housing Act 1988, Sch 6, para 1)); Housing Associations Act 1985, s 10(2) (amended by the Housing (Scotland) Act 1987 (c 26), s 339(2), Sch 23, para 31(2), and the Housing Act 1988, Sch 6, para 8(2)).
4 Housing Associations Act 1985, s 9(2).

1927. Control of payments to members. Statutory restrictions are imposed on the payments which may be made by registered housing associations to their members and others. A registered association may not, with only limited exceptions (which include certain payments to former members of fully mutual associations[1]), make a gift (or pay a dividend or bonus) to a person who is or has been a member of the association[2]. This restriction extends to members of the family of such a person and also to companies and firms of which such a person is a director or, as the case may be, a member[3]. Certain fees and expenses may, however, be paid to members, committee members and to officers (who are not employees), but these must be within limits which may be specified by Scottish Homes from time to time[4]. Further more specific restrictions are then imposed upon payments (or other benefits) made by registered associations to any committee members, officers or employees (and their close relatives) or persons (and their close relatives) who have held any such positions in the preceding twelve months or a business trading for profit with which any such person is a principal proprietor or in which he is directly concerned in its management[5]. Payments to these categories are limited to those contained in a list which includes payments under contracts of employment, expenses to committee members and to officers who are not employees, grants or renewals of tenancies by co-operative housing associations, and payments approved (by class of case) by Scottish Homes[6]. Exceptional rules apply to 'community-based' associations designated as such by Scottish Homes[7]. Such a designation may be made only if Scottish Homes considers that the activities of a housing association relate wholly or mainly to the improvement of dwellings (or their management) within a particular community (whether or not identified by reference to a geographical area entirely within any one administrative area)[8]. In the case of community-based associations, additional payments are permitted to be made to committee members and voluntary officers of the association (or their close relatives)[9].

1 Housing Associations Act 1985 (c 69), s 13(2). For the meaning of 'fully-mutual', see para 1924 above.
2 Ibid, s 13(1)(a).
3 Ibid, s 13(1)(b)–(d). As to who is a member of the family, see s 105.
4 Ibid, s 14 (amended by the Housing Act 1988 (c 50), s 59(2), (3), Sch 6, para 2), read with the Housing Associations Act 1985, s 2A(1) (added by the Housing Act 1988, Sch 6, para 1).
5 Housing Associations Act 1985, s 15(1).
6 Ibid, s 15(2) (amended by the Housing Act 1988, Sch 6, para 9).
7 Housing Associations Act 1985, s 15A(3) (added by the Housing (Scotland) Act 1986 (c 65), s 14, and substituted by the Housing Act 1988, Sch 6, para 10).
8 Housing Associations Act 1985, s 15A(4) (as so added and substituted).
9 Ibid, s 15A(1), (2) (as so added and substituted).

1928. Committee members, rules and dissolution. Housing associations are in general responsible for the management of their own affairs in accordance with their own constitutions. In certain situations, however, Scottish Homes is empowered to intervene in the operation of registered associations. These include the situation where a committee member has become apparently insolvent, or incapable of acting by reason of mental disorder, or has not acted or cannot be found, in which case Scottish Homes may, on fourteen days' notice to the member, order his removal, subject to appeal to the Court of Session[1]. There is also a power to appoint new members[2]. In addition, Scottish Homes has certain powers of control over changes of rules, amalgamation or dissolution proposed by registered housing associations[3]. More positively, Scottish Homes has powers to petition for the winding up of a housing association[4]. On the dissolution of a registered housing association, its net assets fall to be transferred to Scottish Homes or to another association as directed by Scottish Homes[5].

1 Housing Associations Act 1985 (c 69), s 16 (amended by the Housing Act 1988 (c 50), s 59(2), (3), Sch 6, para 2), read with the Housing Associations Act 1985, s 2A(1) (added by the Housing Act 1988, Sch 6, para 1), and the Bankruptcy (Scotland) Act 1985 (c 66), ss 7, 73(1), (9).
2 Housing Associations Act 1985, s 17.
3 Ibid, s 19 (amended by the Housing Act 1988, Sch 6, para 14).
4 Housing Associations Act 1985, s 22 (amended by the Housing Act 1988, Sch 6, para 16).
5 Housing Associations Act 1985, s 23.

1929. Accounts and audit. The Secretary of State may by order lay down accounting (and auditing) requirements for registered housing associations with which they must comply[1]. Copies of audited accounts must be lodged with Scottish Homes within six months of the end of the period to which they relate[2]. Individuals who are directly responsible for the preparation and audit of accounts are responsible also for securing compliance with the statutory requirements, failing which they become liable to prosecution[3].

1 Housing Associations Act 1985 (c 69), s 24(1)–(3), (5) (amended by the Housing Act 1988 (c 50), s 59(2), (3), Sch 6, paras 2, 17), read with the Housing Associations Act 1985, s 2A(1) (added by the Housing Act 1988, Sch 6, para 1).
2 Housing Associations Act 1985, s 24(4).
3 Ibid, s 27 (amended by the Housing Act 1988, Sch 6, para 18).

1930. Guidance by Scottish Homes. Scottish Homes has the power to issue guidance with respect to the management of housing accommodation by registered housing associations, and it is further specifically provided that in considering whether action needs to be taken to secure the proper management of an association's affairs or whether there has been mismanagement[1], Scottish Homes may have regard (among other matters) to the extent to which any such guidance has been followed[2]. Guidance may relate to different cases and, in particular, to different areas, different descriptions of accommodation and different descriptions of associations[3]. It may relate, inter alia, to (1) the housing demands for which provision should be made and the means of meeting the demands; (2) the allocation of accommodation between individuals; (3) the terms of tenancies and principles for the determination of rent levels; (4) standards of maintenance and repair and the means of achieving them; and (5) consultation and communication with tenants[4]. The issue of guidance to housing associations by Scottish Homes is subject to prior consultation with bodies representative of associations and to the prior approval of a draft by the Secretary of State[5].

1 See para 1931 below.
2 Housing Associations Act 1985 (c 69), s 36A(1) (added by the Housing Act 1988 (c 50), s 49), read with the Housing Associations Act 1985, s 2A(1) (added by the Housing Act 1988, s 59(2), (3), Sch 6, para 1).
3 Housing Associations Act 1985, s 36A(2) (as so added).
4 Ibid, s 36A(3)(a)–(e) (as so added).
5 Ibid, s 36A(4)(a), (b), (5) (as so added). Guidance may subsequently be revised (subject to the same procedure) or withdrawn: s 36A(4) (as so added).

1931. Inquiries into the affairs of housing associations. One power available to Scottish Homes in its role of supervising the conduct of housing associations is the power to appoint a person to conduct an inquiry into the affairs of a registered association and to report to Scottish Homes on such matters and in such form as it specifies[1]. The person appointed may not be a present or past member of the staff of Scottish Homes (or of the Housing Corporation or Housing for Wales)[2]. Once appointed, he or she has extensive powers to gather information. He or she may, by notice in writing served on the association concerned or on a person who is or was an officer, agent[3] or member of the association, require the production of such books, accounts and other documents relating to the association and the supply of other information considered necessary for the purposes of the inquiry[4]. Failure to supply information is a summary offence[5]. The appointed person is further permitted to take copies of documents produced to him or her[6]; to make one or more interim reports if he or she thinks fit[7]; and, if he or she considers it necessary for the purposes of the inquiry, to extend the inquiry into the business of any other body which, at a material time, was a subsidiary[8] or associate[9] of the association concerned[10]. For this purpose the request for information may be made to an officer, agent or member of such a subsidiary or associate[11]. For the purposes of an inquiry into the affairs of a housing association, Scottish Homes may order an extraordinary audit of the association's accounts and balance sheet[12].

Where, as a result of either an inquiry or audit, Scottish Homes is satisfied that there has been misconduct or mismanagement in the affairs of an association, it may take a number of remedial measures: (1) it may by order remove (following fourteen days' notice and subject to appeal to the Court of Session) a member of the committee of the association or any officer, agent or employee of the association responsible for or privy to the misconduct or mismanagement or who has by his or her conduct contributed to or facilitated it; (2) it may suspend (subject again to appeal) such a person for up to six months, pending a decision on removal; (3) it may freeze assets by ordering a bank holding money or securities not to part with them without approval; (4) it may restrict the transactions to be entered into by the association without approval[13]. These powers (with the exception of the power to remove) may also be exercised on the issue of an interim report by the appointed person[14]. There is an additional power which may be exercised following an inquiry and where Scottish Homes is satisfied either that there has been administrative misconduct or mismanagement or that the management of land belonging to the association would be improved if the land were transferred to Scottish Homes or to another association[15]. In these circumstances it may direct such a transfer[15].

1   Housing Associations Act 1985 (c 69), s 28(1) (amended by the Housing Act 1988 (c 50), s 59(2), (3), Sch 6, paras 2, 19), read with the Housing Associations Act 1985, s 2A(1) (added by the Housing Act 1988, Sch 6, para 1).
2   Housing Associations Act 1985, s 28(1) (amended by the Housing Act 1988, Sch 6, para 19).
3   'Agent' includes banker, solicitor and auditor, but not in such a way as to require a solicitor to disclose any privileged communication or an association's banker to disclose information as to the affairs of any other customer: Housing Associations Act 1985, s 28(5)(a), (b).
4   Ibid, s 28(2) (as amended: see note 2 above).
5   Ibid, s 28(3). A person convicted is liable to a fine not exceeding level 5 on the standard scale: s 28(3). Level 5 is £2,000: Increase of Criminal Penalties etc (Scotland) Order 1984, SI 1984/526, art 4.
6   Ibid, s 28(3A) (added by the Housing Act 1988, Sch 6, para 19).
7   Housing Associations Act 1985, s 28(3B) (as so added).
8   'Subsidiary' means (1) a company of which the association is a member and the composition of whose board of directors is controlled by the association; or (2) a company more than half of whose equity share capital is held by the association; or (3) a company which is a subsidiary within the meaning of the Companies Act 1985 (c 6) (see s 736) or the Friendly and Industrial and Provident Societies Act 1968 (c 55) (see s 15) of another company which, by virtue of the foregoing, is itself a subsidiary of the housing association: see the Housing Associations Act 1985, s 28(6)(a)–(c), (7) (as added: see note 6 above).
9   'Associate' means a body of which the association is a subsidiary and any other subsidiary of such a body ('subsidiary' here having the same meaning as in the Companies Act 1985 or the Friendly and Industrial and Provident Societies Act 1968, or, in the case of a body which is itself a housing association, the meaning in note 8 above); Housing Associations Act 1985, s 28(8) (as so added).
10   Ibid, s 28(1) (as amended: see note 2 above).
11   Ibid, s 28(2)(c) (as added: see note 6 above).
12   Ibid, s 29 (amended by the Housing Act 1988, Sch 6, paras 2, 20), read with the Housing Associations Act 1985, s 2A(1) (added by the Housing Act 1988, Sch 6, para 1).
13   Housing Associations Act 1985, s 30(1)(a)–(d), (2)–(4) (amended by the Housing Act 1988, Sch 6, paras 2, 21), read with the Housing Associations Act 1985, s 2A(1) (as so added).
14   Ibid, s 30(1A) (added by the Housing Act 1988, Sch 6, para 21).
15   Housing Associations Act 1985, s 32 (amended by the Housing Act 1988, Sch 6, para 2), read with the Housing Associations Act 1985, s 2A(1) (added by the Housing Act 1988, Sch 6, para 1).

1932. Housing association finance. Although the transfer of responsibilities for housing associations in Scotland from the Housing Corporation to Scottish Homes did not in itself involve major change in the substantive law governing the associations themselves, the rules on finance, and in particular on grants, were altered over the same period. A 'new financial regime'[1] was introduced in 1989 which marked a reduction in the extent of public funding of housing associations, which are expected instead to become more self-sufficient and, in particular, to derive greater income from rents set by themselves under assured tenancies[2]. For the most part, the rules of the 'new financial regime' are administrative in character and will not be treated in detail here. The few relevant legal rules are contained in the Housing (Scotland) Act 1988 and the Housing Act 1988 and the primary powers of Scottish Homes already referred to[3] reveal the degree of discretion conferred on that body. Replacing much more detailed statutory rules, the function of Scottish Homes is inter alia to 'make grants'[4], and it is upon this power, exercised with the approval of the Secretary of State with the consent of the Treasury, that the system of grants to housing associations is built. Otherwise, specific statutory powers are conferred upon Scottish

Homes, in circumstances to be determined by it, to reduce, suspend or cancel grant or to require repayment of grant[5]; and upon the Secretary of State to make grants affording relief from tax chargeable on housing associations[6].

1 See *New Financial Regime for Housing Associations in Scotland* (Circular 3/89 of the Housing Corporation in Scotland).
2 See para 1936 below. See also LANDLORD AND TENANT.
3 See para 1923 above.
4 Housing (Scotland) Act 1988 (c 43), s 2(2)(a).
5 Housing Act 1988 (c 50), s 52(1), (2).
6 Ibid, s 54(1).

1933. Central association. The Secretary of State has the power, if he thinks fit, to give recognition to a central association or other body established for the purposes of promoting the formation and extension of housing associations in Great Britain or in any part of Great Britain, and of giving them advice and assistance[1].

The Secretary of State may assist such an association with a grant of such an amount as he may, with Treasury approval, determine[2].

1 Housing Associations Act 1985 (c 69), s 33(1) (amended by the Housing Act 1988 (c 50), s 59(2), (3), Sch 6, para 23).
2 Housing Associations Act 1985, s 33(2). The Scottish Federation of Housing Associations is so recognised and assisted.

3. PUBLIC SECTOR LANDLORDS AND THEIR TENANTS

1934. Introduction. The general law of landlord and tenant is treated in this encyclopaedia in a separate title of its own, together with statutory developments concerning tenancies of houses in the private sector[1]. These include the terms of the Rent (Scotland) Act 1984 (c 58), under which were created protected tenancies and, latterly, the terms of Part II of the Housing (Scotland) Act 1988[2]. That introduced the assured tenancy which is now the standard form for tenancies of private landlords (including, for this purpose, housing associations) created after 21 January 1989[3]. Public sector tenancies, on the other hand, are governed in part by the general law and in part by statutory modifications made to it. Thus, it is provided that, in relation to local authority housing, the general management, regulation and control of houses held for housing purposes are to be vested in and exercised by the local authority[4]. This extends to the power to make byelaws[5]. It is further, more specifically, provided that a house held for housing purposes is to be at all times open to inspection by the local authority or by a duly authorised local authority officer[6]. More significantly, the rents to be charged by local authorities in respect of their houses are not subject to any direct statutory regulation. A local authority may charge such reasonable rents as it may determine[7]. However, in the determination of standard rents (to which its housing revenue account relates) it must take no account of the personal circumstances of the tenants[8]. Other special provisions relate principally to the 'secure tenancy' which was a creation of the Tenants' Rights, Etc (Scotland) Act 1980[9]. This is used as the vehicle for conferring additional general rights and protections on tenants, for conferring the 'right to buy'[10], and, more recently, for the introduction of the 'change of landlord' provisions in Part III of the Housing (Scotland) Act 1988[11]. These are all discussed in later paragraphs. It is first necessary, however, to go back to the stage immediately prior to the creation of the landlord and tenant relationship, that at which landlords in the public sector select their tenants and allocate houses to them.

1 See LANDLORD AND TENANT.
2 The Housing (Scotland) Act 1988 (c 43), Pt II, comprises ss 12–55.
3 Ibid, s 12, Sch 4, para 1; Housing (Scotland) Act 1988 Commencement Order 1988, SI 1988/2038.
4 Housing (Scotland) Act 1987 (c 26), s 17(1). For the meaning of 'local authority', see para 1903 above.
5 Ibid, s 18.
6 Ibid, s 17(2).
7 Ibid, s 210(1). A local authority may also make service charges for garages and other services provided: see s 211.
8 Ibid, s 210(3). As to housing revenue accounts, see paras 1916, 1917, above.
9 See the Tenants' Rights Etc (Scotland) Act 1980 (c 52), Pt II (ss 10–25) (repealed). See now paras 1936 ff below.
10 See now paras 1954 ff below.
11 The Housing (Scotland) Act 1988, Pt III, comprises ss 56–64.

1935. Allocation of houses. Apart from the background constraint of the possibility of the judicial review of the tenant selection decisions of public authorities[1], the only legal regulation of the allocation of houses is contained in Part I of the Housing (Scotland) Act 1987[2]. This circumscribes the freedom of landlords in three different ways.

In the first place, rules, which apply only to district and islands councils, concern any local authority 'housing list' — a list of applicants for local authority housing, which is kept by a local authority in connection with the allocation of housing[3]. They are designed to prevent a local authority refusing to admit applicants for housing to a housing list on certain grounds. Thus, an authority must, in admitting to a list, take no account of (1) the age of the applicant provided that he or she has attained the age of sixteen; or of (2) the income of the applicant and his or her family[4]; or of (3) whether, or to what value, the applicant or any of his or her family owns or has owned heritable or moveable property; or of (4) any outstanding liability (for payment of rent or otherwise) attributable to the tenancy of any house of which the applicant neither is, nor was when the liability accrued, a tenant; or of (5) whether the applicant is living with, or in the same house as, his or her spouse (or other person as husband and wife)[5]. There are also certain restrictions upon the use of a test of residence in the area of the local authority. Residence may not be used as a test of admission to a housing list if the applicant satisfies one or more of five criteria based on (a) employment in the area of the authority; (b) an offer of employment in the area; (c) a wish to move into the area to seek employment; (d) having attained the age of sixty, the wish to move into the area to be with a younger relative; or (e) special social or medical reasons for requiring to be housed in the area[6]. Rules governing the priority of applicants on housing lists are required to treat people satisfying any of these criteria no less favourably than tenants of the authority, with similar housing needs, seeking transfer to another house[7].

With regard to the actual process of tenant selection, the Act requires, in the first place, that 'reasonable preference' be given to persons occupying houses below the tolerable standard[8] or overcrowded houses[9], persons having large families or persons living under unsatisfactory housing conditions[10]; and also to persons to whom the authority owes a duty under the homeless persons provisions[11]. The Act goes on to forbid the use by an authority of certain criteria for allocation purposes. Thus, an authority must take no account of the length of time for which an applicant has resided in the area nor of any of the considerations of age, income, ownership of property or outstanding liabilities referred to above[12]. Those categories are further extended by the prohibition of any prerequisite for eligibility for allocation of housing based on either an application's being in force for a minimum period, or a divorce or judicial separation's being obtained or the applicant's no longer living with or in the same house as some other person[13].

The third provision is concerned with the publication of rules, and extends more widely than local authorities alone and requires that district councils, islands councils, Scottish Homes, development corporations (including urban development corporations) and registered housing associations should publish any rules they have governing admission of applicants to a housing list, priority of allocation of houses, transfer of tenants from the housing body's own houses to those of other bodies, and exchanges of houses[14]. Alterations to rules must be published within six months[15].

In the case of registered housing associations, they must send copies of their rules (and alterations), within six months of their being made, to the registering body (Scottish Homes or the Housing Corporation) and to every district or islands council within whose area there is a house let or to be let by the association under a secure tenancy[16]. For all the listed landlords, the requirement to publish means that rules must be available for perusal; on sale at a reasonable price; and available in summary form on request to members of the public at all reasonable times[17]. An applicant for housing is entitled on request to inspect any record kept by the landlord furnished by the applicant in connection with his or her application[18].

Although housing mobility is not exclusively related to the process of allocation of houses by public authorities or housing associations, it should be added that the Secretary of State has the power, with Treasury consent, to make contributions towards the cost of housing mobility: he may make grants or loans towards the cost of arrangements for enabling or assisting people to move and become (i) in England and Wales, tenants or licensees of dwellings and (ii) in Scotland, tenants of houses[19]. The grants or loans may be made subject to conditions[20].

1   For a discussion of judicial review of administrative action, see ADMINISTRATIVE LAW, vol 1, paras 345 ff. Another possibility for challenge to allocation decisions is by way of complaint to the Commissioner for Local Administration in Scotland (the 'ombudsman'): see LOCAL GOVERNMENT, vol 14, paras 133 ff.

2   The Housing (Scotland) Act 1987 (c 26), Pt I, comprises ss 1–23. As to the allocation of houses, see ss 19–21.

3   Ibid, s 19(4).

4   'Family' is not specifically defined for this purpose. However, ibid, s 83(1), provides that for the purposes of the Act a person is a member of another's family if (1) he is the spouse of that person or he and that person live together as husband and wife, or (2) he is that person's parent, grandparent, child, grandchild, brother, sister, uncle, aunt, nephew or niece. For the purposes of head (2), a relationship by marriage is to be treated as a relationship by blood; a relationship of the half-blood is to be treated as a relationship of the whole blood; the stepchild of a person is to be treated as his child; and a child is to be treated as such whether or not his parents are married: ss 83(2)(a)–(d), 338(1).

5   Ibid, s 19(1)(a)–(e).

6   Ibid, s 19(2)(a)–(e).

7   Ibid, s 19(3).

8   As to the tolerable standard, see ibid, s 86, and para 1979 below.

9   As to overcrowding, see ibid, ss 135–137, and paras 2000 ff below.

10   Ibid, s 20(1)(a).

11   Ibid, s 20(1)(b). As to homelessness, see paras 2037 ff below.

12   Ibid, s 20(2)(a).

13   Ibid, s 20(2)(b).

14   Ibid, s 21(1), (2) (amended by the Housing (Scotland) Act 1988 (c 43), s 3(3), Sch 2, para 1).

15   Housing (Scotland) Act 1987, s 21(2).

16   Ibid, s 21(2), (3) (amended by the Housing (Scotland) Act 1988, Sch 2, para 7). As to the registration of housing associations, see para 1925 above.

17 Housing (Scotland) Act 1987, s 21(4), (5). In the case of a local authority or development corporation, access to the rules is to be provided at its principal offices and its housing department offices and in any other case (Scottish Homes and housing associations) access to the rules is to be provided at its principal and other offices: s 21(4).
18 Ibid, s 21(6). See also the Access to Personal Files Act 1987 (c 37).
19 Local Government and Housing Act 1989 (c 42), s 168(1).
20 Ibid, s 168(2).

1936. Secure tenancies. Because many of the statutory rights of public sector tenants flow from their enjoyment of a 'secure tenancy'[1], it is necessary to take account of the circumstances in which such a tenancy is created. For this one must turn first to the consolidation of the law in Part III of the Housing (Scotland) Act 1987[2]. A secure tenancy is a tenancy (whenever created) of a house if (1) the house is let as a separate dwelling[3]; (2) the tenant is an individual and the house is his only or principal home[4]; and (3) the landlord is one of the following[5]: a district, island or regional council (including a joint board or committee or trust under the control of a council); a development corporation (including an urban development corporation); Scottish Homes; the Housing Corporation; a registered housing association[6]; a housing co-operative[7]; a police authority or a fire authority[8].

The list of relevant landlords has, however, been modified by the Housing (Scotland) Act 1988. Subject to certain qualifications, a tenancy entered into on or after 2 January 1989 cannot be a secure tenancy unless the landlord is one of those on a shorter list which does not include the Housing Corporation, registered housing associations and housing co-operatives[9]. Of these, much the most significant is housing associations. The effect of the change is to take virtually all tenancies entered into with housing associations on or after 2 January 1989 into the 'private sector' as assured tenancies. The exceptions are (a) where a tenancy was entered into pursuant to a contract made before 2 January 1989; (b) where a tenancy is granted to a person who, immediately before it was entered into, was the secure tenant of the same landlord; or (c) where the tenancy is granted to a person as the 'suitable accommodation' following an order for possession of his or her house (itself subject to a secure tenancy) when the sheriff directs that it is to be a secure tenancy[10].

1 For the extension of some of the rights of secure tenants to other tenants, see note 6 below and paras 1951–1953 below.
2 The Housing (Scotland) Act 1987 (c 26), Pt III, comprises ss 44–84.
3 'Separate dwelling' is not a term defined in the 1987 Act, although it has been extensively considered in relation to its use in the Rent Acts: see LANDLORD AND TENANT.
4 'Only or principal home' is also a term shared with the Rent Acts. See also, in connection with a claimed right to buy, *Galloway v Kirkcaldy District Council* 25 June 1986, Lands Trib (unreported).
5 Housing (Scotland) Act 1987 (c 26), s 44(1), (2), referring to s 61(2)(a). In addition to the landlords listed, the landlord of a secure tenancy may be a housing trust which was in existence on 13 November 1953: s 44(2).
6 As to the registration of housing associations, see para 1925 above. Tenants of registered 'co-operative housing associations' are not secure tenants, but provisions concerning security of tenure itself *do* apply to tenancies of co-operative housing associations which are *not* registered: ibid, s 45.
7 Housing co-operatives are the local authority co-operatives created under ibid, s 22: see para 1903 above.
8 Ibid, s 61(2)(a) (amended by the Housing (Scotland) Act 1988 (c 43), s 3(2)).
9 Ibid, s 43(3)(a); Housing (Scotland) Act 1988 Commencement Order 1988, SI 1988/2038.
10 Housing (Scotland) Act 1988, s 43(3)(b)–(d). As to the possession proceedings and 'suitable accommodation' referred to, see para 1947 below.

1937. Exceptions. Even though it satisfies the requirements discussed in the proceding paragraph, a tenancy will not be a secure tenancy if it is excluded by

Schedule 2 to the Housing (Scotland) Act 1987[1], which lists eight types of tenancy, discussed in the paragraphs which follow: (1) premises occupied under a contract of employment; (2) house temporarily let to a person seeking accommodation; (3) house temporarily let pending development; (4) house temporarily occupied during works; (5) house temporarily let to homeless person; (6) agricultural and business premises; (7) premises let by police or fire authority; and (8) house part of, or within the curtilage of, certain other buildings[2].

1 Housing (Scotland) Act 1987 (c 26), s 44(4).
2 Ibid, Sch 2, paras 1–8: see paras 1938–1945 below.

1938. Premises occupied under a contract of employment.

A tenancy is not a secure tenancy if the tenant (or one of joint tenants) is an employee of the landlord or of any local authority or development corporation, and his contract of employment requires him to occupy the house for the better performance of his duties[1]. For these purposes 'contract of employment' means a contract of service or apprenticeship, whether express or implied, and (if it is express) whether it is oral or in writing[2].

Since the question of whether or not a tenancy is a secure tenancy is crucial to the question of a tenant's right to buy[3], the 'contract of employment' exception is one which has figured frequently in cases before the Lands Tribunal for Scotland. The Lands Tribunal for Scotland has emphasised the importance of looking to the contract of employment as opposed to the tenancy agreement as the determinant of the existence of security of tenure and the right to buy. Thus, the literal interpretation of this exception must prevail over any existing judicial dicta in cases concerning service occupancies and tied tenancies[4].

> 'For a contract of employment is strictly distinct from one of tenancy and the parliamentary draftsman has clearly looked to the former rather than the latter as the basis for security of tenure'[5].

Having established this basic point the Lands Tribunal has proceeded to elaborate upon the interpretation of the statutory provision.

Where there is a specific condition in the contract of employment which obliges the employee to occupy the house in question as a consequence of his employment, the tribunal has held that it is necessary to consider whether this condition is indeed imposed for the better performance of the employee's duties. If, as is often the case, this is not expressly stated, the tribunal must consider whether it is implied or whether there could be some other reason why the employee should be required to live in this particular dwellinghouse as a term of the contract of employment[6].

The fact that the term itself may be implied in the contract of employment is not in dispute in view of the clear wording of the definition of 'contract of employment'[7]. However, the Lands Tribunal has stipulated that the onus of proving the existence of such an implied term is on the landlord, who must establish that the provision excluding security of tenure applies. The correct test is what a reasonable landlord and a reasonable tenant should be taken to have contemplated[8].

The Lands Tribunal has also offered interpretations of the word 'requires' and the phrase 'to occupy the house for the better performance of his duties'. Accordingly it seems that the imposition of such a requirement may be inferred either from a request of a formal nature, that is one expressed authoritatively or imperatively in writing, but this is not absolutely necessary, and such a requirement may also be inferred in less formal circumstances, for example when it has been expressed orally[9].

That such a requirement must be 'to occupy the house for the better performance of his duties' has been interpreted to mean that the Lands Tribunal must be satisfied that the employee's duties could not be so well performed if he lived elsewhere. It does not mean that the tribunal must be satisfied of the necessity of living in the particular house if the job is to be performed at all[10]. The practical circumstances which will be taken to imply a requirement to occupy for the better performance of duties *qua* employee are indicated in the case law of the Lands Tribunal in this area to date.

Although the existence of a service occupancy or a tied tenancy is not of itself conclusive, it does link the occupancy of the house with the employment[11]. The pre-existing case law on service occupancies and tied tenancies may be utilised as an indication of the facts and circumstances which point in the direction of an implied term to occupy for the better performance of duties *qua* employee[12]. However, as emphasised above, the wording of the statute must prevail over any conflicting judicial dicta[13].

The fact that the dwellinghouse in question has been purpose-built to house the occupant of a particular post has been held to be a significant point in favour of the application of this exemption from security of tenure, and hence the right to buy[14]. In another case the fact that the tenant was given freedom from rent and rates in connection with the performance of certain weekend duties was also held to be significant[15]. Indeed, the imposition of additional duties as a consequence of the tenant's occupation of the dwellinghouse in question is by far the most common factor leading to the application of this exemption in the case law to date.

In one important case[16] it was held that while the existence of a service tenancy might, depending on the circumstances, provide evidence of a link between the job and the house, what was also needed was a direct link between the occupation of the house during the continuation of the lease in connection with the tenant's local duties *qua* employee[17]. In contrast, the fact that a house is allocated to an employee by the employer is not enough to imply a term in the contract of employment to occupy for the better performance of his or her duties in a situation where the house 'goes with the job' merely as a matter of convenience or as an inducement to take the job[18]. Similarly, where an employee is allocated by chance, rather than design, a house which happens to be situated in close proximity to the place of work, this is not enough to imply a condition to occupy for the better performance of the duties in his contract of employment[19].

It should also be noted that where there is an express term in an earlier contract of employment to occupy for the better performance of duties but later contracts of employment entered into as a result of promotion do not include such a term and the nature of the duties performed under the contract of employment has changed, then such a term cannot be implied[20]. Nor will the Lands Tribunal imply such a term where it has been expressly deleted[21].

Finally, the Lands Tribunal has held that the refusal or reluctance of tenants to accept conditions of let which imposed duties additional to those in their contract of employment even in the face of a discounted rent meant that terms to occupy their houses for the better performance of their duties *qua* employees could not be implied. The onus was upon the council to insist upon the new conditions or to adjust the rent accordingly[22].

1 Housing (Scotland) Act 1987 (c 26), s 44(4), Sch 2, para 1(1). Where a tenancy is excluded from being a secure tenancy by reason only of the operation of Sch 2, para 1, the provisions of ss 53–60 (leases; subletting; repairs and improvements) nevertheless apply to the tenancy as if it were a secure tenancy: s 44(5).
2 Ibid, Sch 2, para 1(2).
3 As to the right to buy, see paras 1954 ff below.
4 *Douglas v Falkirk District Council* 1983 SLT (Lands Trib) 21 at 24, 25.
5 *Docherty v City of Edinburgh District Council* 1985 SLT (Lands Trib) 61 at 63.
6 *Neillie v Renfrew District Council* 7 January 1985, Lands Trib (unreported).

7 *Douglas v Falkirk District Council* 1983 SLT (Lands Trib) 21 at 22, referring to the Tenants' Rights Etc (Scotland) Act 1980 (c 52), Sch 1, para 2(2) (repealed), which corresponds to the Housing (Scotland) Act 1987, Sch 2, para 1(2).

8 *Douglas v Falkirk District Council* 1983 SLT (Lands Trib) 21 at 22, 23.

9 *Docherty v City of Edinburgh District Council* 1985 SLT (Lands Trib) 61.

10 *Douglas v Falkirk District Council* 1983 SLT (Lands Trib) 21.

11 *Douglas v Falkirk District Council* 1983 SLT (Lands Trib) 21; *Docherty v City of Edinburgh District Council* 1985 SLT (Lands Trib) 61; *Neillie v Renfrew District Council* 7 January 1985, Lands Trib (unreported).

12 *Douglas v Falkirk District Council* 1983 (Lands Trib) 21; *Milne v City of Dundee District Council* 28 October 1985, Lands Trib (unreported).

13 *Douglas v Falkirk District Council* 1983 SLT (Lands Trib) 21.

14 *Douglas v Falkirk District Council* 1983 SLT (Lands Trib) 21; *Campbell v Western Isles Islands Council* 1988 SLT (Lands Trib) 4.

15 *Kinghorn v City of Glasgow District Council* 1984 SLT (Lands Trib) 9.

16 *Docherty v City of Edinburgh District Council* 1985 SLT (Lands Trib) 61.

17 *Naylor v City of Glasgow District Council* 12 January 1983, Lands Trib; *Neillie v Renfrew District Council* 7 January 1985, Lands Trib; *Milne v City of Dundee District Council* 28 October 1985, Lands Trib; *Sturrock v City of Dundee District Council* 28 October 1985, Lands Trib; *Anderson v City of Dundee District Council* 28 October 1985, Lands Trib; *Paterson v City of Dundee District Council* 28 October 1985, Lands Trib; *Logan v East Lothian District Council* 10 April 1986, Lands Trib; *Bruce v Borders Regional Council* 25 May 1988, Lands Trib (all unreported).

19 *MacDonald v Strathclyde Regional Council* 1990 SLT (Lands Trib) 10.

20 *Little v Borders Regional Council* 2 March 1989, Lands Trib (unreported).

21 *Fisher v Fife Regional Council* 1989 SLT (Lands Trib) 26 at 27.

22 *Gilmour v City of Glasgow District Council* 1989 SLT (Lands Trib) 74.

1939. Temporary letting to person seeking accommodation. A tenancy is not a secure tenancy if the house was let by the landlord expressly on a temporary basis to a person moving into an area in order to take up employment there, and for the purpose of enabling him to seek accommodation in the area[1].

Some guidance as to the construction to be put upon this exception was given by the Lands Tribunal for Scotland in *Campbell v Western Isles Islands Council*[2]. Mr and Mrs Campbell were granted the tenancy of a schoolhouse on Harris following Mrs Campbell's appointment to a peripatetic teaching post on the island. They signed a missive of let which stipulated that the tenancy was to be for just under two years. Together with the offer to let, the council had sent a covering letter which said that the offer was made in terms of provisions of the Tenants' Rights Etc (Scotland) Act 1980[3] which were the forerunner of this exception. The sole issue in dispute between the parties was whether or not this covering letter had the effect of bringing the tenancy within the terms of this exception. The Lands Tribunal based its decision on the law of contract and a narrow interpretation of the exception. It found that the terms of let were to be found within the four corners of the missive of let. Material in the covering letter was extraneous to the missive of let and therefore could not qualify or amend the terms therein[4]. Furthermore, although it was obvious that the council's intention was to exclude the tenancy from being a secure tenancy by bringing it within the terms of the exception, the Lands Tribunal held that the legislature's use of the words 'let ... *expressly* on a temporary basis' required that such intention be explicitly stated in the lease in order for it to be effective. The dictionary meaning of 'expressly' was 'not merely implied but distinctly stated in plain language'. Therefore, in the absence of an express clause in the lease bringing the tenancy within the terms of the exception, the council had failed to make its intentions legally effective.

1 Housing (Scotland) Act 1987 (c 26), s 44(4), Sch 2, para 2.

2 *Campbell v Western Isles Islands Council* 1988 SLT (Lands Trib) 4.

3 Ie the Tenants' Rights Etc (Scotland) Act 1980 (c 61), Sch 1, para 3 (repealed).

4 See *Inglis v John Buttery & Co* (1878) 5 R (HL) 87; *Norval v Abbey* 1939 SC 724, 1939 SLT 549.

1940. Temporary letting pending development. A tenancy is not a secure tenancy if the house was let by the landlord to the tenant expressly on a temporary basis, pending development affecting the house[1]. An approach similar to that taken in relation to the exception in the preceding paragraph was taken in the interpretation of this exception in *Shipman v Lothian Regional Council*[2], where a council opposed the application to buy the former governor's house within the grounds of a former old people's home. The applicant was the former principal of the house and the council opposed his application on the basis that the house had latterly been let to him on a temporary basis pending development.

Although the Lands Tribunal for Scotland accepted that such was clearly the council's intention and that indeed the applicant had been aware of this, it stated that nonetheless the use of the words 'let . . . *expressly* on a temporary basis' must be held to require explicit reference in the lease to the terms of the exception. In the absence of such an express reference in the lease the applicant was free to buy despite the fact that it was obvious from the evidence that he had deliberately engineered the situation in the knowledge of the council's intentions otherwise.

  1 Housing (Scotland) Act 1987 (c 26), s 44(4), Sch 2, para 3, in terms of which 'development' has the meaning assigned to it by the Town and Country Planning (Scotland) Act 1972 (c 52), s 19.
  2 *Shipman v Lothian Regional Council* 1989 SLT (Lands Trib) 82 at 87.

1941. Temporary accommodation during works. A tenancy is not a secure tenancy if the house is occupied by the tenant while works are being carried out on the house which he normally occupies as his home, and if he is entitled to return there after the works are completed either by agreement or by virtue of an order of the sheriff[1] in possession proceedings[2].

  1 Ie an order under the Housing (Scotland) Act 1987 (c 26), s 48(5), for which see para 1947 below.
  2 Ibid, s 44(4), Sch 2, para 4.

1942. Accommodation for homeless persons. A tenancy is not a secure tenancy if the house is being let to the tenant expressly on a temporary basis, in the fulfilment of a duty imposed on a local authority by the provisions[1] relating to homelessness[2].

  1 Ie the Housing (Scotland) Act 1987 (c 26), Pt II (ss 24–43): see paras 2037 ff below.
  2 Ibid, s 44(4), Sch 2, para 5.

1943. Agricultural and business premises. A tenancy is not a secure tenancy if the house (1) is let together with agricultural land[1] exceeding 2 acres in extent; (2) consists of or includes premises which are used as a shop or office for business, trade or professional purposes; (3) consists of or includes premises licensed for the sale of exciseable liquor; or (4) is let in conjunction with any purpose mentioned in head (2) or head (3)[2].

  1 'Agricultural land' is not defined, but for the meaning of 'agriculture', see the Housing (Scotland) Act 1987 (c 26), s 338(1).
  2 Ibid, s 44(4), Sch 2, para 6(a)–(d).

1944. Police and fire authorities. A tenancy is not a secure tenancy if the landlord is either:
(1) a police authority[1] and the tenant (a) is a constable of a police force[2] who, in pursuance of regulations[3], occupies the house without obligation to pay rent

or rates, or (b) (where head (a) does not apply) is let the house expressly on a temporary basis pending its being required for the purposes of a police force[4]; or

(2) a fire authority[5] and the tenant (a) is a member of a fire brigade[6] who occupies the house in consequence of a condition in his contract of employment that he live in close proximity to a particular fire station, or (b) (where head (a) does not apply) is let the house expressly on a temporary basis pending its being required for the purposes of a fire brigade[7].

1 Housing (Scotland) Act 1987 (c 26), s 61(2)(a)(viii).
2 Ie within the meaning of the Police (Scotland) Act 1967 (c 77): see s 50(c).
3 Ie under ibid, s 26.
4 Housing (Scotland) Act 1987, s 44(4), Sch 2, para 7(a)(i), (ii); Abolition of Domestic Rates Etc (Scotland) Act 1987 (c 47), s 26(2). These exceptions were added to the original list in the Tenants' Rights Etc (Scotland) Act 1980 (c 52), Sch 1, by the Housing (Scotland) Act 1986 (c 65), s 12, Sch 1, para 18 (repealed).
5 Housing (Scotland) Act 1987, s 61(2)(a)(ix).
6 Ie a fire brigade maintained in pursuance of the Fire Services Act 1947 (c 41).
7 Housing (Scotland) Act 1987, Sch 2, para 7(b)(i), (ii). See also note 4 above.

1945. Houses part of, or within the curtilage of, certain other buildings. A tenancy is not a secure tenancy if the house forms part of, or is within the curtilage of, a building which mainly (1) is held by the landlord for purposes other than the provision of housing accommodation, and (2) consists of accommodation other than housing accommodation[1]. This exception was added to the original list in the Tenants' Rights Etc (Scotland) Act 1980 by the Housing (Scotland) Act 1986[2] to curtail the right to buy in some circumstances not covered by the contract of employment exception[3]. The concept of 'curtilage' has not, however, been without difficulty.

It should first be noted that the test for exclusion under this exception is a two-stage test[4], although not both stages of the test need be used in every case. The questions to be asked are whether the dwellinghouse in question (a) forms part of a building, or (b) is within the curtilage of a building which (i) is held by the landlord mainly for non-housing purposes or (ii) consists of accommodation other than housing accommodation.

The majority of cases heard to date have concerned purely the curtilage question. However, the Lands Tribunal for Scotland has heard four cases[5] in which the dwellinghouse concerned has actually been a part of the same structure as the building which the landlord claims is covered by head (1) or head (2) of the exception. In these cases the Lands Tribunal has stated that the mere fact that a dwellinghouse is semi-detached[6] or part of a terrace[7] is not enough to bring it within the meaning of the phrase 'forms part of'. The test is rather whether such a dwellinghouse is nonetheless capable of forming a separate independent unit[7]. If it is, it does not 'form part of' the adjoining building within the terms of the exception. Nor in such a case is the structurally supportive function of the dwellinghouse enough to bring it within the curtilage of the adjacent building[8]. In practice the two questions concerning whether a dwellinghouse forms part of a building or is within such a building's curtilage are integrally linked and usually treated together[9].

There is no definition of the word 'curtilage' in the Housing (Scotland) Act 1987, and the Lands Tribunal has turned to dicta of Lord Mackintosh in an old Court of Session case, *Sinclair-Lockhart's Trustees v Central Land Board*[10], in order to inform its approach. The effect of Lord Mackintosh's dicta is that the curtilage of a building is ground which is used for the comfortable enjoyment of that building so as to form an integral part of it[11].

The fact that the dwellinghouse has its own enclosure which separates it off from the other building which belongs to the landlord may be an indication that it is not within the curtilage of that other building. However, it is not conclusive[12]. The key consideration is whether or not the dwellinghouse serves any useful purpose in relation to the other building.

There may be cases where the enclosure of both the dwellinghouse and the building are such that there could be said to be two separate curtilages, but the connection in usage between the two is such as to create a single all-embracing curtilage. However, once such a connection is severed, in that the dwellinghouse no longer serves the other building any useful purpose, there remain only the two separate curtilages[13]. An example of such a situation, typical of the majority of cases heard up to the end of 1989 by the Lands Tribunal which have concerned former schoolhouses, would be where a schoolhouse is situated adjacent to a school building, although separated by boundary walls. As long as the schoolhouse continues to serve a useful purpose in connection with the school as a home for the school teacher, it is held to be within the curtilage of the school building or to 'form part of' the school building if it is indeed part of the same structure. However, if the school shuts down or the schoolhouse is let to a tenant unconnected with the school, the connection in use is severed and the two are held to have separate curtilages or to be separate independent units[14].

A different sort of situation is where the dwellinghouse in question is claimed by a landlord to be within the curtilage of a group of buildings forming an institution, as opposed to a single building. In the only such case before the Lands Tribunal[15], an approach based on a literal interpretation of the exception was adopted. The case concerned a dwellinghouse in the grounds of a former old people's home. The tribunal stated that in the exception the words 'building' and 'curtilage' were used in the singular and therefore indicated a small area of ground attached to a building or perhaps a composite building but not a group of buildings; 'the word "curtilage" has not escaped from its diminutive suffix'[16]. The tribunal's approach in that case was supported by an English case[17], in which the Court of Appeal took a similarly restrictive view of the use of the word 'curtilage' in the singular. It held that a lecturer's house standing within the 160-acre grounds of an agricultural college was not within the curtilage of any one building. The Lands Tribunal has also held that a curtilage cannot exist fragmented on either side of a public road[18].

It may be concluded that the Lands Tribunal's overall approach to the interpretation and application of this exclusion has been characterised by its observation in an early case[19] that the underlying intention of the exclusion and the exclusions to secure tenancies in general is to exclude only the minimum number of houses consistent with the particular landlord's functions. The tribunal has also refused to be swayed by considerations of problems that may be faced in the future by local authorities and other public sector landlords as a result of particular decisions of the tribunal[20].

1 Housing (Scotland) Act 1987 (c 26), s 44(4), Sch 2, para 8(a), (b). Where a tenancy is excluded from being a secure tenancy by reason only of the operation of Sch 2, para 8, the provisions of ss 53–60 (leases; subletting; repairs and improvements) nevertheless apply to the tenancy as if it were a secure tenancy: s 44(5). For a valuable and wide-ranging discussion of 'curtilage', see P Q Watchman and E Young 'The Meaning of "Curtilage"' 190 SLT (News) 77.

2 Tenants's Rights Etc (Scotland) Act 1980 (c 52), Sch 1, para 9 (added by the Housing (Scotland) Act 1986 (c 65), s 12, Sch 1, para 18).

3 Ie the Housing (Scotland) Act 1987, Sch 2, para 1: see para 1938 above.

4 *Allison v Tayside Regional Council* 1989 SLT (Lands Trib) 65.

5 See *Pratt v Strathclyde Regional Council* 22 November 1988, Lands Trib (unreported); *Allison v Tayside Regional Council* 1989 SLT (Lands Trib) 65; *MacDonald v Strathclyde Regional Council* 1990 SLT (Lands Trib) 10.

6 *Allison v Tayside Regional Council* 1989 SLT (Lands Trib) 65.

7 *Pratt v Strathclyde Regional Council* 22 November 1988, Lands Trib (unreported).
8 *Allison v Tayside Regional Council* 1989 SLT (Lands Trib) 65.
9 This is obvious from the tribunal's approach in *Pratt v Strathclyde Regional Council* 22 November 1988, Lands Trib (unreported), and *Allison v Tayside Regional Council* 1989 SLT (Lands Trib) 65.
10 *Sinclair-Lockhart's Trustees v Central Land Board* 1951 SC 258 at 264, 1951 SLT 121 at 123.
11 See *Barron v Borders Regional Council* 1987 SLT (Lands Trib) 36.
12 *Richardson v Central Regional Council* 19 February 1988, Lands Trib (unreported).
13 *Burns v Central Regional Council* 1988 SLT (Lands Trib) 46.
14 See *Barron v Borders Regional Council* 1987 SLT (Lands Trib) 36; *Richardson v Central Regional Council* 19 February 1988, Lands Trib (unreported); *Burns v Central Regional Council* 1988 SLT (Lands Trib) 46.
15 *Shipman v Lothian Regional Council* 1989 SLT (Lands Trib) 82. For a more detailed discussion of this case, see para 1940 above.
16 *Shipman v Lothian Regional Council* 1989 SLT (Lands Trib) 82 at 89.
17 *Dyer v Dorset County Council* [1989] QB 346, CA.
18 *Fisher v Fife Regional Council* 1989 SLT (Lands Trib) 26 at 29.
19 See *Barron v Borders Regional Council* 1987 SLT (Lands Trib) 36; and *Pratt v Strathclyde Regional Council* 22 November 1988, Lands Trib (unreported).
20 *Allison v Tayside Regional Council* 1989 SLT (Lands Trib) 65.

1946. Security of tenure. The principal characteristic of a secure tenancy is the actual security of tenure conferred on the tenant. In the period prior to the introduction of secure tenancies in the Tenants' Rights Etc (Scotland) Act 1980 (c 52), it was uncertain to what extent a decision by a public authority to evict a tenant was subject to enforceable restrictions[1]. Such protection apart, however, public sector tenants, in contrast with their counterparts in the private sector, by virtue of the Rent Acts[2], were, in law, vulnerable to a notice to quit from their landlords on any grounds. By virtue of restrictions imposed originally by that Act, a secure tenancy may be brought to an end only in certain defined circumstances. These are (1) by the death of the tenant (or, where there is more than one, of any of them) where there is no 'qualified person'[3]; (2) by the operation of the succession rules regarding 'qualified persons'[4]; (3) by written agreement between the landlord and the tenant; (4) by the abandonment of the tenancy[5]; (5) by order of the sheriff for recovery of possession[6]; or (6) by four weeks' notice given by the tenant to the landlord[7].

1 See eg *City of Edinburgh District Council v Parnell* 1980 SLT (Sh Ct) 11, and *City of Aberdeen District Council v Christie* 1983 SLT (Sh Ct) 57.
2 As to the Rent Acts, see generally LANDLORD AND TENANT.
3 Ie a qualified person within the meaning of the Housing (Scotland) Act 1987 (c 26), s 52, for which see para 1949 below.
4 Ie by the operation of ibid, s 52(4) or (5), for which see para 1949 below.
5 Ie by the operation of ibid, s 50(2), for which see para 1948 below.
6 Ie by order under ibid, s 48(2), for which see para 1947 below.
7 Ibid, s 46(1)(a)–(f).

1947. Proceedings for possession. As already indicated[1], the most significant guarantee of security of tenure for a secure tenant (as with a protected or assured tenant in the private sector) is that the landlord is entitled to recover possession only on specified grounds and in accordance with a specified procedure[2]. The relevant rules are contained in the Housing (Scotland) Act 1987[3]. Thus the landlord may not raise proceedings for possession (by summary cause in the sheriff court of the district in which the house is situated[4]) unless (1) he has first served a notice of proceedings in the prescribed form[5] (setting out the ground for recovery and a date not earlier than four weeks from service of the notice on which proceedings may be raised[6]); (2) the proceedings are raised on or after the date specified in the notice; and (3) the notice is still in force when they are raised[7]. The powers of the court and the nature of the proceedings then depend on the ground which is the basis of the landlord's action. The sixteen grounds themselves are set out in Part I of Schedule 3 to the Act and may usefully be divided into three groups: grounds 1 to 7 (sometimes called 'conduct grounds'), grounds 8 to 15 ('management grounds'), and ground 16[8]. In summary form the grounds are:

(1) rent lawfully due has not been paid or another obligation of the tenancy has been broken;

(2) the tenant (or a joint tenant or other person residing or lodging with him or her or a sub-tenant) has been convicted of using the house (or allowing it to be used) for immoral or illegal purposes;

(3) the condition of the house (or any common parts) has deteriorated owing to acts of waste by, or the neglect or default of, the tenant (or, in some circumstances, of a lodger or sub-tenant if reasonable steps have not been taken by the tenant to remove them);

(4) the condition of any furniture provided has similarly deteriorated;

(5) the tenant and his or her spouse have been absent from the house without reasonable cause for a continuous period exceeding six months or have ceased to occupy the house as their principal home;

(6) the tenant is the person to whom the tenancy was granted and the landlord was induced to grant it by a false statement made knowingly or recklessly by the tenant;

(7) the tenant (or a joint tenant, or other person residing or lodging with him or her or a sub-tenant) has been found guilty of conduct in or in the vicinity of the house which is a nuisance or annoyance and it is not reasonable in all the circumstances that the landlord should be required to make other accommodation available to him[9];

(8) as in (7) but where, in the opinion of the landlord, it is appropriate in the circumstances to require the tenant to move to other accommodation;

(9) the house is overcrowded[10] in such circumstances as to render the occupier guilty of an offence;

(10) it is intended within a reasonable period of time to demolish[11], or carry out substantial work on, the building or a part of the building which comprises or includes the house, and such demolition or work cannot reasonably take place without the landlord's obtaining possession of the house;

(11) the house has been designed or adapted for occupation by a person whose special needs require accommodation of the kind provided, and (a) there is no longer a person with such special needs occupying the house; and (b) the landlord requires it for occupation (whether alone or with other members of his family[12]) by a person who has such special needs;

(12) the house forms part of a group of houses (sheltered housing) designed, or provided with facilities, for persons in need of special social support and the house is required as in head (11);

(13) the landlord is a housing association which has as its object the housing of persons in a special category by reason of age, infirmity, disability or social circumstances and the tenant has ceased to be in the special category or the house is no longer suitable and the accommodation is required for someone who is in a special category;

(14) the landlord's interest is as a lessee and either the lease has terminated or will terminate within six months;

(15) the landlord is an islands council[13] and the house is both held for education authority purposes and required for the accommodation of a person who is or will be employed for those purposes and the council cannot reasonably provide a suitable alternative house for the person and the tenant (or predecessor) is or was employed by the council for education authority purposes and such employment has terminated;

(16) the landlord wishes to transfer the secure tenancy of the house to (a) the tenant's spouse (or former spouse); or (b) a person with whom the tenant has been living as husband and wife who has applied to the landlord for such a transfer; and either the tenant or the other person no longer wishes to live together with the other in the house[14].

Where proceedings have been commenced[15] under any of heads (1) to (7) or (16), the court may, as it thinks fit, adjourn them for a period of periods with or without imposing conditions as to payment of outstanding rent or other conditions[16]. Subject to that possibility of adjournment[17], the court must make an order for recovery of possession if it appears that the landlord has a ground for recovery based on any of heads (1) to (7) and that it is reasonable[18] to make the order[19]. Alternatively, recovery of possession must be ordered if one of the grounds in heads (8) to (15) is established and other suitable accommodation will be available for the tenant when the order takes effect[20]. For these purposes, the suitability of alternative accommodation is to be determined in accordance with rules in Part II of Schedule 3 of the 1987 Act[21]. Accommodation is there stated to be suitable if it consists of premises which are to be let as a separate dwelling[22] under a secure, protected or assured tenancy, and it is reasonably suitable to the needs of the tenant and his family[23]. In determining whether accommodation is reasonably suitable, regard is to be had to (a) its proximity to the place of work (including attendance at an educational institution) of the tenant and of other members of his family, compared with his existing house; (b) the extent of the accommodation required by the tenant and his family; (c) the character of the accommodation offered compared to his existing house; (d) the terms on which the accommodation is offered to the tenant compared with the terms of his existing tenancy; (e) if any furniture was provided by the landlord for use under the existing tenancy, whether furniture is to be provided for use under the new tenancy which is of a comparable nature in relation to the needs of the tenant and his family; and (f) any special needs of the tenant or his family[24]. It is further provided that if the landlord has made an offer in writing to the tenant of new accommodation which complies with the requirement that it be premises let as a separate dwelling under a secure, protected or assured tenancy and which appears to be suitable, specifying the date when the accommodation will be available and the date (not being less than fourteen days from the date of the offer) by which the offer must be accepted, the accommodation is deemed to be suitable if either the landlord shows that the tenant accepted the offer within the time limit; or alternatively the landlord shows that the tenant did not accept the offer, and the tenant does not satisfy the court that he acted reasonably in failing to accept the offer[25].

Finally, recovery of possession must be ordered if it appears to the court that the ground in head (16) is established and both that it is reasonable to make the order and that other suitable accommodation will be available[26]. If the possession proceedings are based on the ground in head (10) (the need for demolition or substantial work) and it appears to the court that it is the landlord's intention (i) that substantial work is to be carried out on the building which comprises or includes the house, and (ii) that the tenant should return to the house after the work is completed, the court must make an order entitling him to return to the house after the work is completed[27]. Any order for recovery of possession must appoint a date for recovery and has the effect of terminating the tenancy[28], and giving the landlord the right to recover possession of the house, at that date[29].

---

1 See para 1946 above.
2 An attempt to rely on other grounds or another procedure will be unsuccessful: see *Monklands District Council v Johnstone* 1987 SCLR 480, Sh Ct.

3 See the Housing (Scotland) Act 1987 (c 26), ss 47, 48, Sch 3.

4 Ibid, s 47(1).

5 For the prescribed form, see the Secure Tenancies (Proceedings for Possession) (Scotland) Order 1980, SI 1980/1389.

6 Housing (Scotland) Act 1987, s 47(3).

7 Ibid, s 47(2). A notice ceases to be in force if withdrawn or on the expiry of six months from the date specified in it: s 47(4).

8 Ibid, s 48(1), (2).

9 See *Scottish Special Housing Association v Lumsden* 1984 SLT (Sh Ct) 71 at 74, where it was held that a tenant could be held responsible for the nuisance caused by his wife, even though he himself was in prison. See also *City of Glasgow District Council v Brown* 1988 SCLR 433, Sh Ct, and *City of Glasgow District Council v Brown (No 2)* 1988 SCLR 679, Sh Ct. See also note 18 below.

10 Ie within the meaning of the Housing (Scotland) Act 1987, s 135, for which see para 2001 below.

11 Reconstruction may count as demolition: see ibid, s 338(3).

12 As to references to members of the family, see para 1935, note 4, above.

13 See also para 1963 below.

14 Housing (Scotland) Act 1987, Sch 3, Pt I, paras 1–16. For fuller discussion of the circumstances addressed under head (16) and its relationship to the rules contained in the Matrimonial Homes (Family Protection) (Scotland) Act 1981 (c 59), see 'Husband and Wife' in FAMILY LAW.

15 See *City of Edinburgh District Council v Davis* 1987 SLT (Sh Ct) 33.

16 Housing (Scotland) Act 1987, s 48(1).

17 On the earlier use of the power to adjourn, see M Adler, CMG Himsworth and S Kerr *Public Housing, Rent Arrears and the Sheriff Court* (Scottish Office CRU, 1985), and M Adler and CMG Himsworth 'Tenants in arrears: a new role for the Sheriff Court' in *Scottish Government Yearbook 1985* (ed D McCrone).

18 Thus 'the court is empowered to apply as an ultimate test, the test of reasonableness': *City of Glasgow District Council v Brown (No 2)* 1988 SCLR 679 at 681, Sh Ct. See also *Nairn v City of Edinburgh District Council* 1983 SCOLAG 44.

19 Housing (Scotland) Act 1987, s 48(2)(a).

20 Ibid, s 48(2)(b).

21 Ibid, s 48(3).

22 In *Charing Cross and Kelvingrove Housing Association v Kraska* 1986 SLT (Sh Ct) 42 at 46 it was held that the accommodation must be actually *intended to be* let as a separate dwelling under a secure (or protected etc) tenancy, and not merely likely to become so by operation of law.

23 Housing (Scotland) Act 1987, Sch 3, Pt II, para 1(a), (b).

24 Ibid, Sch 3, Pt II, para 2(a)–(f).

25 Ibid, Sch 3, Pt II, para 3(a), (b). For a discussion of this procedure, its permissive character and its effect of shifting to the tenant the burden of proving lack of suitability, see *Charing Cross and Kelvingrove Housing Association v Kraska* 1986 SLT (Sh Ct) 42 at 44.

26 Housing (Scotland) Act 1987, s 48(2)(c).

27 Ibid, s 48(5)(a), (b). The temporary occupation of the other house may not be brought to an end before the house originally occupied is again available, unless the secure tenancy has been brought to an end: see s 46(2). For a discussion of the 'demolition situation' and the 'decanting situation', see *Charing Cross and Kelvingrove Housing Association v Kraska* 1986 SLT (Sh Ct) 42 at 45.

28 This does not apply in the case of an order on the ground in head (10) (substantial work): Housing (Scotland) Act 1987, s 48(5).

29 Ibid, s 48(4)(a), (b).

1948. Abandonment of a secure tenancy. As mentioned above[1], another way in which a secure tenancy may be terminated is following its abandonment[2]. The circumstances in which, and the procedure according to which, this may occur are set out in the Housing (Scotland) Act 1987[3]. The landlord must have reasonable grounds for believing both that the house is unoccupied and that the tenant does not intend to occupy it as his or her home[4]. The landlord must then serve a notice on the tenant stating these facts, requiring the tenant to inform him in writing within four weeks if he or she intends to occupy the house as his or her home, and informing the tenant that, if it appears to the landlord at the end of the four weeks that the tenant does not intend to occupy the house, the tenancy will be terminated forthwith[5]. Provision is then made for the conditions under which the termination of the tenancy may take place, for the tenant's right to appeal to the sheriff within six months of the termination of the tenancy, and for the safe custody but eventual disposal of the tenant's property[6].

1 See para 1946 above.
2 Housing (Scotland) Act 1987 (c 26), s 46(1)(b).
3 See ibid, ss 49–51.
4 Ibid, s 49(1). The landlord is entitled to enter the house, by force if necessary, to secure the house and any fittings, fixtures or furniture against vandalism: s 49(2), (3).
5 Ibid, s 50(1)(a)–(c).
6 Ibid, ss 50(2)–(4), 51. For the procedure governing the disposal of a tenant's property, see the Secure Tenancies (Abandoned Property) (Scotland) Order 1982, SI 1982/981.

1949. Succession to a secure tenancy. An important characteristic of a secure tenancy is that it may pass by operation of law, on the death of the tenant, to a 'qualified person'[1]. The 'qualified person', in the first place, is the tenant's spouse (or other person living with the tenant as husband and wife) provided that his or her only or principal home at the time of the tenant's death was the house under the tenancy[2]. In the case of a joint tenancy, a 'qualified person' is a surviving tenant, provided again that the house was his or her only or principal home[3]. Failing a qualified person in either of these categories, a member of the tenant's family[4] who has attained the age of sixteen may be a qualified person where the house was his or her only or principal home throughout the period of twelve months immediately preceding the tenant's death[5].

These rules may produce the situation in which there is more than one qualified person. In that case, the tenancy passes to the qualified person (or two or more jointly) as may be decided by agreement between all or, failing agreement within four weeks of the tenant's death, as decided by the landlord[6]. If there is no qualified person, the tenancy is terminated[7]. If there is a qualified person entitled to the benefit of succession to the tenancy, he or she may decline the tenancy by giving written notice to the landlord within four weeks of the tenant's death[8]. In that case, the tenancy is terminated and the qualified person must vacate the house within three months, paying rent for the period of occupation[9]. Succession to a secure tenancy may occur only once. A tenancy which has passed once will be terminated on the death of the succeeding tenant, save that the secure tenancy of a joint tenant is not ended where he or she continues to use the house as his or her only or principal home[10]. When a secure tenancy is terminated in this way but there is a qualified person, he or she is entitled to continue as tenant (but not under a secure tenancy) for a period not exceeding six months[11].

1 Housing (Scotland) Act 1987 (c 26), s 52(1). As to succession to a tenancy in relation to the right to buy, see para 1955, text to note 22, below.
2 Ibid, s 52(2)(a).
3 Ibid, s 52(2)(b).
4 Family membership is defined in ibid, s 83: see para 1935, note 4, above.
5 Ibid, s 52(2)(c).
6 Ibid, s 52(3).
7 Ibid, s 52(1).
8 Ibid, s 52(4).
9 Ibid, s 52(1), (4).
10 Ibid, s 52(5).
11 Ibid, s 52(6).

1950. Written lease and variation of terms. Every secure tenancy must be constituted in writing (either probative or holograph of the parties[1]), and it is the landlord's duty to draw up the required documents, to ensure that they are duly executed before the commencement of the tenancy and to supply a copy of them to the tenant[2]. The tenant must not be required to pay any fees in respect of these duties[3]. Once constituted, the terms of a tenancy may be varied only in statutorily prescribed ways, notwithstanding anything contained in the agreement itself[4]. One such way is by agreement between the landlord and tenant[5]. Another relates only to the rent or other charge payable, which may be increased[6] with effect from the beginning of any rental period by written notice given by the landlord not less than four weeks before the beginning of the rental period[7]. A third case involves recourse to the sheriff and arises where the landlord wishes to vary the terms or conditions of a secure tenancy and the tenant refuses or fails to agree, or alternatively where the tenant wishes to vary a term but the landlord refuses or fails to agree. In respect of a tenant his or her wish must be to vary a term of the tenancy which restricts his or her use or enjoyment of the house on the ground that (1) by reason of changes in the character of the house or of the neighbourhood or other circumstances (which the sheriff may deem material) the term is or has become unreasonable or inappropriate; or (2) the term is unduly burdensome compared with any benefit which would result from its performance; or (3) the existence of the term impedes some reasonable use of the house[8]. It is for the landlord or, as the case may be, the tenant, to make summary application in the sheriff court[8]. In such proceedings the sheriff may make such order varying a term of the tenancy (other than in relation to the rent or a charge payable) as he thinks reasonable in the circumstances, having particular regard to the safety of any person and to any likelihood of damage to the house or other premises[9]. The sheriff may include an order that the tenant pays compensation to the landlord for patrimonial loss occasioned by the variation[9]. Before making any order for the benefit of a tenant, the sheriff may order the tenant to serve a copy of his or her application on any person who, as owner or tenant of any land, may be affected, whether beneficially or adversely, by the change[10].

1 Housing (Scotland) Act 1987 (c 26), s 53(1). Sections 53 and 54 also apply to tenancies excluded from being secure by reason only of Sch 2, para 1 or para 8 (see paras 1938, 1945, above): s 44(5).
2 Ibid, s 53(2).
3 Ibid, s 53(3).
4 Ibid, s 54(1).
5 Ibid, s 54(1)(a). An agreement must satisfy the same requirements (of writing etc) as the tenancy agreement itself: s 54(6).
6 This is subject to the Rent (Scotland) Act 1984 (c 58), s 58 (phasing of progression to registered rent).
7 Housing (Scotland) Act 1987, s 54(2).
8 Ibid, s 54(3).
9 Ibid, s 54(4).
10 Ibid, s 54(5).

1951. Subletting and assignation. It is a required term of every secure tenancy that the tenant must not assign, sublet or otherwise give up to another person possession of the house or any part of it, or take in a lodger, except with the consent in writing of the landlord, which must not be unreasonably withheld[1]. The landlord may refuse his consent if a payment (other than reasonable rent or a deposit) has been or is to be received by the tenant in consideration of the assignation, subletting or other transaction[2]. The procedure according to which a tenant gives notice to the landlord of his or her wish to assign or sublet, the landlord responds, and, in the event of his refusal, the dispute is referred to the sheriff court, is statutorily prescribed[3]. An assignation, subletting or other transaction is neither a protected nor a statutory tenancy under the Rent (Scotland) Act 1984, nor, under that Act, a Part VII (furnished house) contract, nor an assured tenancy under the Housing (Scotland) Act 1988[4]. Once the landlord's consent to an assignation or subletting has been given, the tenant may not thereafter increase the sub-tenant's rent if the landlord objects[5]. Related to the right to assign a tenancy has been the introduction of administrative schemes designed to assist house exchanges and tenant mobility generally[6].

1 Housing (Scotland) Act 1987 (c 26), s 55(1). Sections 55 and 56 also apply to tenancies excluded from being secure by reason only of Sch 2, para 1 or para 8 (see paras 1938, 1945, above): s 44(5).
2 Ibid, s 55(2).
3 See ibid, s 55(6), Sch 4.
4 Ibid, s 55(4) (amended by the Housing (Scotland) Act 1988 (c 43), s 72(2), Sch 9, para 10). The Rent (Scotland) Act 1984 (c 59), Pt VII, comprises ss 62–81.
5 Housing (Scotland) Act 1987, s 56.
6 See the Tenants' Exchange Scheme and National Mobility Scheme. See also para 1935, text to notes 19, 20, above.

1952. Repairs and improvements. The general repairing obligations falling upon landlords and tenants, whether in the public or private sector, are considered elsewhere[1]. What follows in this paragraph and the next are specific statutory rules applicable to secure tenancies.

It is a required term of every secure tenancy that the tenant must not carry out work, other than interior decoration, in relation to the house without the written consent of the landlord which must not, in turn, be unreasonably withheld[2]. 'Work', for these purposes, means the alteration, improvement or enlargement of the house or its fittings or fixtures; the addition of new fittings or fixtures; or the erection of a garage, shed or other structure, but does not include repairs or maintenance of any of these[3]. Provision is made for the reference of disputes to the sheriff court[4] and also to empower the landlord, on the termination of a secure tenancy, to reimburse the cost of work undertaken by the tenant and which has materially added to the value of the house[5]. Such an increase in value must not be taken into account when calculating the price of the house if the tenant exercises his or her right to buy[6], nor in the assessment of rent payable during the tenancy[7].

1 See LANDLORD AND TENANT.
2 Housing (Scotland) Act 1987 (c 26), s 57(1). Sections 57–59 also apply to tenancies excluded from being secure by reason only of Sch 2, para 1 or para 8 (see paras 1938, 1945, above): s 44(5).
3 Ibid, s 57(2).
4 Ibid, s 57(3), Sch 5, paras 5–7.
5 Ibid, s 58(1). Any payment is restricted to the cost of work done after deduction of any improvement grant paid or payable: s 58(2). See paras 2019 ff below. If termination is due to the tenant's death, the payment may be made to his personal representative: s 58(3).
6 Ibid, s 62(2).
7 Ibid, s 59.

1953. Right to repair. Statutory power has been given for the creation of a secure tenant's 'right to repair'. To bring this into effect it falls to the Secretary of State to make a scheme by regulations[1], something which, by 1 May 1990, he had not done. If made, such a scheme would entitle a tenant to carry out repairs to the house which the landlord is himself under an obligation to carry out, and then to recover a prescribed amount of the cost from the landlord[2].

1 Housing (Scotland) Act 1987 (c 26), s 60(1)–(4). Section 60 also applies to tenancies excluded from being secure by reason only of Sch 2, para 1 or para 8 (see paras 1938, 1945, above): s 44(5).
2 Ibid, s 60(1)(a), (b).

4. THE SECURE TENANT'S RIGHT TO BUY

1954. Introduction. When the concept of the secure tenancy was introduced to the law of Scotland by the Tenants' Rights Etc (Scotland) Act 1980[1], security of tenure for tenants was only a subsidiary purpose of the government. The main objective was the use of the secure tenancy as a springboard from which a tenant might end the landlord and tenant relationship by the purchase of his or her own house. The rules introduced in 1980 now appear as amended and consolidated in sections 61 to 84A (the latter sections of Part III) and Part XIV (assistance for owners of defective housing) of the Housing (Scotland) Act 1987[2].

1 See the Tenant's Rights Etc (Scotland) Act 1980 (c 52), Pt I (ss 1–9) (repealed).
2 The Housing (Scotland) Act 1987 (c 26), Pts III, XIV, comprise ss 44–84 and ss 257–303. They have been amended by the Housing (Scotland) Act 1988 (c 43), the Housing Act 1988 (c 50) and the Local Government and Housing Act 1989 (c 42).

1955. The right to buy. Subject to certain statutory qualifications but notwithstanding anything contained in any agreement, the tenant of a house to which these provisions of the Housing (Scotland) Act 1987[1] apply has the right to purchase the house[2]. The house must be let under a secure tenancy[3], which means that the statutory conditions must be satisfied and that a tenancy falling within one of the exceptions set out in Schedule 2 to the Act is not secure and the right to buy is precluded[4]. As already indicated, the most significant disputes over these exceptions have arisen at the point at which a tenant seeks to exercise his or her right to buy. It should also be borne in mind that the Housing (Scotland) Act 1988 restricted the list of qualifying landlords for secure tenancies. Most importantly, a housing association tenancy entered into after 2 January 1989 will not normally be a secure tenancy[5]. Only tenants under tenancies created at an earlier date are secure and, prima facie, have the right to buy.

There are, however, other restrictions affecting the tenants of registered housing associations. Thus, the tenant of an association which has never received grants from public funds does not have the right to buy[6]; nor the tenant of an association with charitable status[7]; nor the tenant of a housing association where, within a neighbourhood, the house concerned is one of a number (not exceeding fourteen) let by the association where it is the practice of the landlord to let at least a half of the houses for occupation by any or all of (1) persons suffering (or who have suffered) from mental disorder, physical handicap or addiction to alcohol or other drugs; (2) persons who have been released from prison or other institutions; or (3) young persons who have left the care of a local authority, and, in any case, a social service is, or special facilities are, provided for the purpose of assisting these persons[8]. A separate but related exception is that of a house (not necessarily belonging to a housing association) which is one of a group provided with facilities (including a call system and the services of a warden) specially designed or adapted for the needs of persons of pensionable age or disabled persons[9]. Another limb in the test of entitlement to purchase is that the landlord be the heritable proprietor of the house or that, in the case of a landlord who is a housing co-operative, the local authority must be the heritable proprietor[10]. In the early days of the operation of the right to buy procedures, certain difficulties were encountered in situations where the landlord (notably the Scottish Special Housing Association) was not in a position to sell houses under the right to buy because the heritable proprietor was a district council. The Secretary of State subsequently took powers to vest, by order, the whole of the interest of the heritable proprietor in such a case in the landlord[11].

The final characteristic empowering a tenant to purchase is that, immediately prior to the date of service of the application to purchase[12], the tenant must have been for not less than two years in occupation of a house[13] (which will include his or her present house) or of a succession of houses provided by any of the following persons or bodies[14]:

(a) a regional, islands or district council in Scotland; any local authority in England and Wales or in Northern Ireland; and the statutory predecessors of any such council or authority, or the common good of any such council, or any trust under the control of any such council;

(b) the Commission for the New Towns;

(c) a development corporation, an urban development corporation; and any development corporation established under corresponding legislation in England and Wales or in Northern Ireland; and the statutory predecessors of any such authority;

(d) Scottish Homes and the Scottish Special Housing Association;

(e) a registered housing association;

(f) the Housing Corporation;

(g) a housing co-operative[15];

(h) the Development Board for Rural Wales;

(i) the Northern Ireland Housing Executive or any statutory predecessor;

(j) a police authority[16] or the statutory predecessors of any such authority;

(k) a fire authority[17] or the statutory predecessors of any such authority;

(l) a water authority in Scotland; any water authority constituted under corresponding legislation in England and Wales or in Northern Ireland; and the statutory predecessors of any such authority;

(m) the Secretary of State, where the house was at the material time used for the purposes of the Scottish Prison Service or of a prison service for which the Home Office or the Northern Ireland Office has responsibility;

(n) the Crown, in relation to accommodation provided in connection with service whether by the tenant or his spouse as a member of the regular armed forces of the Crown;

(o) the Secretary of State, where the house was at the material time used for the purposes of a health board[18] or for the purposes of a corresponding board in England and Wales, or for the purposes of the statutory predecessors of any such board; or the Department of Health and Social Services for Northern Ireland, where the house was at the material time used for the purposes of a Health and Personal Services Board in Northern Ireland, or for such purposes of the statutory predecessors of any such board;

(p) the Secretary of State, or the Minister of Agriculture, Fisheries and Food, where the house was at the material time used for the purposes of the Forestry Commission;

(q) the Secretary of State, where the house was at the material time used for the purpose of a State Hospital provided by him[19] or for the purposes of any hospital provided under corresponding legislation in England and Wales;

(r) the Commissioners of Northern Lighthouses;

(s) the Trinity House;

(t) the Secretary of State, where the house was at the material time used for the purposes of Her Majesty's Coastguard;

(u) the United Kingdom Atomic Energy Authority;

(v) the Secretary of State, where the house was at the material time used for the purposes of any function transferred to him under the Defence (Transfer of Functions) Act 1964[20] or any function relating to defence conferred on him by or under any subsequent enactment;

(w) such other person as the Secretary of State may by order made by statutory instrument subject to annulment in pursuance of a resolution of either House of Parliament prescribe[21].

The forms which 'occupation' may take for the purposes of the Housing (Scotland) Act 1987 are further specified. Thus, occupation includes occupation (i) in the case of joint tenants, by any one of them; (ii) by a person occupying the house rent-free; (iii) as the spouse of the tenant or joint tenant; (iv) as the child (or spouse of a child) of a tenant who has succeeded²² directly or indirectly to the rights of that person in a qualifying house, but only in relation to any period when the child (or spouse of a child) is at least sixteen years of age; or (v) as a member of the family of a tenant who has succeeded as in head (iv), but again only for the time over the age of sixteen²³. It is also provided that (A) any interruption in occupation of twelve months or less does not affect its continuity; that (B) an interruption of between twelve and twenty-four months may, at the discretion of the landlord, be regarded as not affecting its continuity; and that (C) there is to be added to the period of occupation of a house by a joint tenant any earlier period during which he or she was at least sixteen years of age and occupied the house as a member of the family of the tenant or of one or more of the joint tenants of the house²⁴.

1   Ie the Housing (Scotland) Act 1987 (c 26), s 61.
2   Ibid, s 61(1).
3   Ibid, s 61(2).
4   For ibid, Sch 2, and the rules relating to secure tenancies, see paras 1936 ff above.
5   See para 1936 above.
6   Housing (Scotland) Act 1987, s 61(4)(b) (amended by the Housing (Scotland) Act 1988 (c 50), s 140(1), Sch 17, para 79). The types of grant are listed in the subsection and include, most significantly, the various forms of grant formerly available under the Housing Associations Act 1985 (c 69), the Housing Act 1974 (c 44), which it replaced, and earlier legislation.
7   Housing (Scotland) Act 1987, s 61(4)(d), (e), (8), (9) (amended by the Housing (Scotland) Act 1988 (c 43), s 3(3), Sch 2, para 9(a)–(c)).
8   Housing (Scotland) Act 1987, s 61(4)(f) (amended by the Housing (Scotland) Act 1988, s 72(1), Sch 7, para 2). These descriptions of persons may be amended or added to by the Secretary of State by order: Housing (Scotland) Act 1987, s 61(7).
9   Ibid, s 61(4)(a). See also the possibility of a right of pre-emption in the case of 'amenity' housing, and para 1958 below. For authority that the statutory references to a call system and a warden are definitive of 'sheltered housing', see *Crilly v Motherwell District Council* 1988 SLT (Lands Trib) 7; *Heenan v Motherwell District Council* 6 August 1987 (Lands Trib) (unreported); and *Martin v Motherwell District Council* 9 October 1989 (Lands Trib) (unreported).
10 Ibid, s 61(2)(b). 'Housing co-operative' here means one created under s 22, for which see para 1903 above. 'Heritable proprietor' in relation to a house includes any landlord entitled under the Conveyancing (Scotland) Act 1924 (c 27), s 3 (disposition of the dwellinghouse etc by persons uninfeft) to grant a disposition of the house: Housing (Scotland) Act 1987, s 82. For the extension of the right to buy to the tenant of a landlord who is a lessee, see para 1968 below.
11 Ibid, s 77. The original provision was contained in the Tenants' Rights Etc (Scotland) Act 1980 (c 52), s 1A (added by the Local Government (Miscellaneous Provisions) (Scotland) Act 1981 (c 23), s 35) (repealed). For an example of its use, see the Scottish Special Housing Association (Vesting of City of Glasgow District Council Land) (Scotland) Order 1981, SI 1981/1860.
12 See para 1957 below.
13 This includes accommodation referred to in head (n) below.
14 Housing (Scotland) Act 1987, s 61(2)(c). The requirement of occupation of a house for two years does not apply where the tenant occupies the house under the 'defective dwelling' provisions (for which see s 282(2), (3), and para 1969 below): s 61(3)(a) (amended by the Local Government and Housing Act 1989 (c 42), s 194(1), Sch 11, para 93). As to deemed qualifying occupation of the house of a registered housing association prior to its registration, see the Housing (Scotland) Act 1987, s 61(2A) (added by the Housing (Scotland) Act 1988, s 72(1), Sch 8, para 1).
15 Ie within the meaning of the Housing (Scotland) Act 1987, s 22, or the equivalent in England and Wales (the Housing Act 1985 (c 68), s 27B (added by the Housing and Planning Act 1986 (c 63), s 10)).
16 Ie a police authority or joint police committee under the Police (Scotland) Act 1967 (c 77) (see ss 2(1), 19(2)(b), (9)(b)), or police authorities under corresponding legislation in England and Wales or Northern Ireland: Housing (Scotland) Act 1987, s 82.
17 Ie a fire authority or joint committee under the Fire Services Acts 1947 (c 41), 1951 (c 27) and 1959 (c 44): Housing (Scotland) Act 1987, s 82.
18 Ie constituted under the National Health Service (Scotland) Act 1978 (c 29), s 2: see HEALTH SERVICES, para 1410 above.
19 Ie under the Mental Health (Scotland) Act 1984 (c 36), s 90: see MENTAL HEALTH, vol 14, para 1472.

20 Ie under the Defence (Transfer of Functions) Act 1964 (c 15), s 1(2) (former functions of the Minister of Defence, the Secretary of State for War, the Secretary of State for Air or, with certain exceptions, the Admiralty).

21 Housing (Scotland) Act 1987, s 61(11)(a)–(w) (s 61(11)(d) being substituted by the Housing (Scotland) Act 1988, Sch 2, para 9(d)).

22 As to succession to secure tenancies, see para 1949 above. Succession may be only on the death of the tenant: *Robb v Kyle and Carrick District Council* 1989 SLT (Lands Trib) 78.

23 Housing (Scotland) Act 1987, s 61(10)(a)(i)–(v) (amended by the Local Government and Housing Act 1989, ss 176(1)(a), 194(4), Sch 12, Pt II).

24 Housing (Scotland) Act 1987, s 61(10)(b) (amended by the Local Government and Housing Act 1989, s 176(1)(b)).

1956. The price and discount. A vital part of the right to buy is the price, which is calculated, as at the date of service of the application to purchase[1], according to a statutory formula. The price to be paid is the market value of the house less a discount[2]. The market value itself is to be determined as if the house were available for sale on the open market with vacant possession at the date of service of the application to purchase, and the valuation is made by either a qualified valuer nominated by the landlord and accepted by the tenant or the district valuer, as the landlord thinks fit[3].

No account may be taken of any element in the market value of the house reflecting an increase in value as a result of improvements whose cost would qualify for reimbursement by the landlord[4].

The basic discount to be deducted from the market value is 32 per cent except where the house is a flat, in which case it is 44 per cent[5]. To that basic discount is added a further 1 per cent, or for a flat, 2 per cent, for every year beyond the minimum qualifying period of two years of continuous occupation by the 'appropriate person' of a house or succession of houses provided by any specified person or bodies[6]. The maximum discount is 60 per cent of the market value, or 70 per cent for a flat, which is reached after thirty-six years of continuous qualifying occupation, or fifteen years for a flat[7]. The same rules relating to continuity of occupation for the purposes of discount apply as they apply for the calculation of the minimum qualifying period[8]. The 'appropriate person' referred to is the purchasing tenant him or herself but, if it would produce a higher discount, it may instead be the tenant's spouse (provided that they are cohabiting at the date of service of the application to purchase)[9]. In the case of joint purchase by joint tenants, the 'appropriate person' is whichever tenant (or spouse) has the longest occupation[9]. The Secretary of State has powers (as yet unexercised) to adjust by order (with Treasury consent) the statutory entitlements to discount[10].

One general adjustment to the calculation of discount is made in respect of houses provided (or other costs incurred) within the five years prior to application to purchase: the allowable discount must not reduce the price below that calculated in accordance with rules contained in a determination promulgated by the Secretary of State[11] (the 'cost floor').

1 Housing (Scotland) Act 1987 (c 26), s 62(2). As to the application to purchase, see para 1957 below.

2 Ibid, s 62(1) (amended by the Housing (Scotland) Act 1988 (c 43), s 65(1), and the Local Government and Housing Act 1989 (c 42), s 194(1), Sch 11, para 94).

3 Housing (Scotland) Act 1987, s 62(2) (amended by the Housing (Scotland) Act 1988, s 72(1), Sch 8, para 2).

4 Housing (Scotland) Act 1987, s 62(2). Reimbursement is under s 58. For the right of a secure tenant to undertake repairs and improvements under ss 57, 58, see para 1952 above.

5 Ibid, s 62(3)(a). 'Flat' means a separate and self-contained set of premises, whether or not on the same floor and forming part of a building from some other part of which it is divided horizontally: s 338(1). In the case of the purchase of a house or flat following 'defective housing' proceedings (see s 282(2), (3), and para 1969 below), the minimum discounts are 30 or 40 per cent

(s 62(3)(a)), ie taking account of the absence of the requirement of a minimum qualifying period of two years' occupation (see para 1955 above).

6 Ibid, s 62(3)(b). The specified persons and bodies are those listed in s 61(11), for which see para 1955 above.

7 Ibid, s 62(3).

8 Ibid, s 61(10): see para 1955 above.

9 Ibid, s 62(4) (as amended: see note 3 above).

10 See ibid, s 62(5), (6).

11 Ibid, s 62(6A), (6B) (substituted by the Housing (Scotland) Act 1988, s 65(2)). For the determination in force on 1 January 1990, see Scottish Development Department Circular 32/1988. The expression 'cost floor' is not statutory, but is used in the side note to the Housing (Scotland) Act 1988, s 65.

1957. The application to purchase. In order to exercise his or her right to purchase, the tenant must adhere to the statutory procedure, the first step of which is service upon the landlord of a formal application to purchase[1]. This must be in the prescribed form which contains (1) notice that the tenant seeks to exercise the right to purchase; (2) a statement of the periods of occupancy of houses relied upon to establish entitlement to purchase and to discount; (3) the name of any proposed joint purchaser[2]. The landlord is then required to respond either by making an offer to sell or, in defined circumstances, by refusing to sell[3]. An offer must be served within two months of the application to purchase and must contain (a) the market value of the house (determined under the statutory rules[4]); (b) the discount; (c) the price; (d) any conditions the landlord intends to impose[5]; and (e) the actual offer to sell to the tenant (and joint purchaser where relevant)[6].

1 Housing (Scotland) Act 1987 (c 26), s 63(1).

2 Ibid, s 63(1)(a)–(c). For the prescribed form, see the Right to Purchase (Application Form) (Scotland) Order 1986, SI 1986/2138.

3 Housing (Scotland) Act 1987, s 63(2). As to refusal to sell, see para 1963 below.

4 See ibid, s 62(2), and para 1956 above.

5 See ibid, s 64, and para 1958 below.

6 Ibid, s 63(2)(a)–(e).

1958. Conditions of sale. The landlord's power to insert conditions into an offer to sell is not unlimited. Conditions must be 'reasonable', and must further comply with certain more specific statutory requirements[1]. Thus conditions must have the effect of ensuring that the tenant has as full enjoyment and use of the house as owner as he or she had as tenant[2]. They must secure to the tenant such additional rights as are necessary for the reasonable enjoyment and use of the house as owner (including common rights in any part of the building of which the house forms part), and must impose on the tenant any necessary duties relative to such rights[3]. Conditions must also include such terms as are necessary to entitle the tenant to receive a good and marketable title to the house[4]. A condition which imposes a new charge or increase of an existing charge for the provision of a service must provide for the charge to be in reasonable proportion to the cost to the landlord of providing the service[5]. Certain types of conditions must not be imposed. One is a condition which has the effect of requiring the tenant to pay any expenses of the landlord[6]. Another is a condition which requires the tenant (or a successor in title) to offer to the landlord or to another person an option to purchase the house in advance of resale to a third party[7]. There are, however, limited exceptions to this prohibition upon the reservation of rights of pre-emption. One applies in the case of a house (sometimes known as 'amenity housing') which has facilities substantially different from an ordinary house and which has been designed or adapted for occupation by a person of pensionable age or a disabled person whose special needs require accommodation of the kind provided by the house[7]. When an option to purchase in the case of such a house comes to be exercised, the price is to be determined by the district valuer, who must have regard to the market value of the house at the time of the purchase and also to any discount due to be repaid to the landlord[8]. The other exception may arise in relation to certain houses in rural areas. An islands or district council may designate a 'rural area' (a term not further defined) where, on the council's application, the Secretary of State makes an order to that effect[9]. Such an order may be made where (1) within the area more than one-third of all relevant houses (that is, those owned either by the council on 3 October 1980 or by a registered housing association on 7 January 1987[10]) have been sold either under the right to buy or otherwise[11], and (2) the Secretary of State is satisfied that an unreasonable proportion of the houses sold consists of houses which have then been resold and are not (a) being used as the only or principal homes of the owners or (b) subject either to regulated or assured tenancies[12]. Any conditions securing a right of pre-emption in such a designated rural area may not have effect for more than ten years from the date of conveyance[13]. The price payable is calculated in the same way as for amenity housing as stated above[13].

1 Housing (Scotland) Act 1987 (c 26), s 64(1). For Lands Tribunal decisions on the reasonableness of the conditions, see para 1959 below.
2 Ibid, s 64(1)(a).
3 Ibid, s 64(1)(b).
4 Ibid, s 64(1)(c).
5 Ibid, s 64(2).
6 Ibid, s 64(3).
7 Ibid, s 64(4).
8 Ibid, s 64(5). As to repayment of discount, see s 72, and para 1965 below.
9 Ibid, s 64(6). As to the parallel designation of rural areas for the purposes of the change of landlord provisions, see para 1972 below.
10 Ibid, s 64(8).
11 Ibid, s 64(7)(a) (amended by the Housing (Scotland) Act 1988 (c 43), s 72(2), Sch 9, para 11(a)).
12 Housing (Scotland) Act 1987, s 64(7)(b) (substituted by the Housing (Scotland) Act 1988, Sch 9, para 11(b)).
13 Housing (Scotland) Act 1987, s 64(9).

1959. Variation of conditions. When the tenant receives an offer to sell, he or she may wish to proceed with the purchase but subject to conditions different from those stipulated by the landlord. The tenant may consider a proposed condition to be unreasonable or may wish another new condition to be included[1]. If this is the case, the tenant may, by serving on the landlord, within one month after service of the offer to sell, a notice requesting the landlord to strike out or vary a condition or insert a new one, and if the landlord agrees, it must serve an amended offer to sell within a further month[2]. If the landlord refuses and the tenant is aggrieved by the refusal (or by a failure to serve an amended offer within a month) he or she may (again within one month or, with the landlord's written consent given within the month, two months) refer the matter to the Lands Tribunal for Scotland[3]. The same procedure for requesting from the landlord an amended offer to sell (and reference thereafter to the Lands Tribunal) applies where the tenant wishes either to add a joint purchaser or to delete a joint purchaser originally proposed[4].

When a question relating to a condition is thus referred to the Lands Tribunal, the tribunal may, as it thinks fit, uphold a condition or strike it out or vary it or, where appropriate, insert a new condition[5]. Where a variation in the terms of the offer to sell results from the tribunal's determination, it must order the landlord to serve an amended offer within two months[5]. The tribunal's powers in relation to conditions attached to sales have been exercised in a number of cases.

Many of these have focussed upon the statutory requirement that conditions be reasonable, which, in this context, has been held to require that the interests of both the purchasing tenant and of the landlord are to be taken into account[7]. There is no clear onus of proof on either party[8]. One type of condition held to be unreasonable is a condition which derogates from the express statutory requirements. Thus conditions must not be imposed which tend to relieve the landlord from the duty to secure the tenant a marketable title or requiring the tenant to accept the title as it stands[9].

Similarly, a condition forbidding the future occupation of a house 'by separate families' could not stand, as that would leave the purchaser less free to sublet than he was as tenant — another form of derogation from the statutory conditions[10]. However, conditions may certainly range more widely than those statutorily identified although, on the other hand, they must not be too vague or ambiguous[11] and must 'fairly and reasonably relate to the sale'. They must not be designed to achieve a purpose unrelated to the sale of the house. Thus a condition could not be used to restrict the future resale of the house to a person resident in the area or 'who, by nature of their employment or other interest in the economic well-being of the area, requires to reside therein'[11]. It has also been held that conditions should not be used by the landlord merely to duplicate or strengthen protections provided for it elsewhere in the right to buy legislation[12].

One general interest of landlords which may be safeguarded by conditions, however, is that of protecting the amenity of a housing scheme as a whole. Thus conditions requiring future maintenance of the house may be imposed, but not, as in one case, a condition requiring compliance with the landlord's chosen colour scheme[13]. Particular problems arose when a landlord authority sought to protect remaining participants in a district heating scheme[14]. One inappropriate use of conditions was identified when the Lands Tribunal held that a tenant could not, as a condition of sale, require the landlord to carry out repairs prior to the sale which the tenant claimed to be an obligation under the lease[15].

On the other hand, the tribunal also struck down an attempt by a landlord to impose a condition requiring repayment of a central heating grant previously paid to the tenant[16]. Another restriction on the use of conditions is that they may not be used in such a way as to affect the extent of the actual land or other property to be sold[17]. Perhaps the most difficult problems have arisen where the rights of neighbours have had to be considered at the time of a sale. As far as the land to be purchased by the tenant is concerned, it has been held that this should be sold free from any condition purporting to give effect to an informal agreement between the purchaser and a neighbour under which the neighbour enjoyed a right of access[18]. The same has been held to apply even where the right of access has been formally conferred upon the neighbour under an earlier disposition pursuant to the right to buy[19]. This may leave the landlord in the difficulty of having conferred upon one neighbour rights whose corresponding burdens cannot be imposed on another. It is not, however, a problem capable of resolution (by the landlord or the Lands Tribunal in right to buy proceedings) at the time of the second sale[20]. More broadly, however, the Lands Tribunal will uphold conditions designed to protect the interests of neighbours in relation to shared facilities such as common drying greens by ensuring that exclusive access to previously shared areas is not given to the purchasing tenant[21]. On the other hand, land, even if subject during a tenancy to some shared use or to management by the landlord, should not be excluded from the sale if included in the lease. A condition enabling the landlord to undertake continued maintenance could, where appropriate, be imposed[22].

---

1 Housing (Scotland) Act 1987 (c 26), s 65(1)(a), (b). For the separate power of the Secretary of State to give directions to modify conditions of sale, see para 1967 below.

2 Ibid, s 65(1).
3 Ibid, s 65(2).
4 Ibid, s 65(1)(c), (d), (2).
5 Ibid, s 65(3).
6 See ibid, s 64(1), and para 1958 above.
7 *Clark v Shetland Islands Council* 14 June 1982, Lands Trib (unreported).
8 See eg *Pollock v Dumbarton District Council* 1983 SLT (Lands Trib) 17 at 18.
9 *Keay v Renfrew District Council* 1982 SLT (Lands Trib) 33.
10 *Mackenzie v City of Aberdeen District Council* 10 March 1982, Lands Trib (unreported).
11 *Pollock v Dumbarton District Council* 1983 SLT (Lands Trib) 17 at 20.
12 An example is *Lewis v Renfrew District Council* 7 May 1982, Lands Trib (unreported).
13 *Keay v Renfrew District Council* 1982 SLT (Lands Trib) 33 at 37.
14 *Irvine v Midlothian District Council* 12 May 1982, Lands Trib (unreported).
15 *Miller v Livingstone Development Corpn* 24 March 1986, Lands Trib (unreported).
16 *Brookbanks v Motherwell District Council* 1988 SLT (Lands Trib) 72.
17 *Fullerton v Monklands District Council* 1983 SLT (Lands Trib) 15. See also *Hannan v Falkirk District Council* 1987 SLT (Lands Trib) 18. However, as to consideration by the Lands Tribunal of the extent of subjects to be sold, see para 1964 below.
18 *Arnott v Midlothian District Council* 21 June 1983, Lands Trib (unreported).
19 *Popescu v Banff and Buchan District Council* 1987 SLT (Lands Trib) 20 at 22.
20 For discussion of the similar problem which may arise if subjects of the wrong extent have already been sold to a purchasing tenant next door, see para 1964 below.
21 *Porter v City of Aberdeen District Council* 10 March 1982, Lands Trib (unreported).
22 *Neave v City of Dundee District Council* 1986 SLT (Lands Trib) 18 at 21.

1960. Notice of acceptance. The procedural step which follows the landlord's offer to sell is the service of a notice of acceptance by the tenant. This is required whenever the tenant wishes to exercise his or her right to purchase and either does not dispute timeously the terms of the offer to sell by serving a notice requesting a variation of conditions[1] or by referring the matter to the Lands Tribunal[2], or any dispute arising has been resolved[3]. The tenant has two months within which to serve the notice of acceptance[3]. Normally the period of two months runs from service of the offer to sell or amended offer to sell but, otherwise, from a relevant finding or determination of the Lands Tribunal or decision in relation to a loan[4]. Once the notice of acceptance has been duly served on the landlord, a contract of sale of the house is constituted between the landlord and tenant on the terms contained in the offer (or amended offer) to sell[5].

1 Ie under the Housing (Scotland) Act 1987 (c 26), s 65(1): see para 1959 above.
2 Ie under ibid, s 71(1)(d): see para 1964 below.
3 Ibid, s 66(1)(a), (b).
4 See ibid, s 66(1)(i)–(vii). For decisions by the landlord or the court on loan applications, see para 2014 below.
5 Ibid, s 66(2). For the enforcement of a contract constituted under this provision by the executors of a deceased tenant, see *Cooper's Executors v City of Edinburgh District Council* 1989 GWD 31–1435, OH, upheld 1990 GWD 6-327. Appeal to the House of Lords is pending.

1961. House loans to tenants. Accompanying the statutory right to a discount in the calculation of the purchase price[1] there is a scheme of mandatory loans to tenants to assist financially with the purchase. Details of the scheme, including the application and appeal procedures, are discussed below[2].

1 See para 1956 above.
2 See para 2014 below.

1962. Fixed price option. Where an offer or amended offer to sell has been served on a tenant but the tenant is unable to obtain a house loan of the amount applied for by reason of the application of the appropriate regulations[1], he or she may, within two months of the offer of a loan (or of the date of declarator by the sheriff if later), serve on the landlord a notice requesting a fixed price option[2]. The notice must be accompanied by a payment of £100[2]. The effect of such a request is that the tenant is entitled to delay further progress with the purchase[2]. A notice of acceptance may be served at any time within two years[3] of the original service of application to purchase[4], although the existence of the option to purchase does not preclude the landlord from recovering possession of the house during the option period, in which event the option is terminated and the £100 is recoverable by the tenant[5]. It is also to be repaid to the tenant on purchase of the house or at the expiry of the two-year period, or to the tenant's personal representatives if the tenant dies without purchasing the house[6].

1 Ie regulations under the Housing (Scotland) Act 1987 (c 26), s 216(3): see para 2014 below.
2 Ibid, s 67(1).
3 The period is extendable, if a loan application is made, until two months after a decision: ibid, s 67(1) proviso.
4 Ibid, s 67(1).
5 Ibid, s 67(3).
6 Ibid, s 67(2).

1963. Refusal of applications. Essential to the tenant's right to purchase is the absence of any general right of the landlord to refuse to sell. There are, however, some circumstances (two general and two more specific) in which the landlord is entitled to refuse to proceed. The first general case is where the landlord disputes the tenant's right to purchase at all, perhaps on the ground that the tenant is not a secure tenant. In such a case the landlord must, within one month of the tenant's application to purchase, serve a notice of refusal[1]. The application may be refused *simpliciter* or the landlord may offer instead a voluntary sale[2]. Such a sale carries no statutory entitlement to a discount or loan for the tenant. The other general circumstance in which a landlord may refuse to sell is where after reasonable inquiry (including reasonable opportunity for the tenant to amend the application) the landlord is of the opinion that information contained in the application is incorrect in a material respect[3]. In this case the landlord must issue a notice of refusal within two months of the application[3]. A notice of refusal issued in either of these two circumstances must specify the grounds on which the landlord disputes the tenant's right to purchase or, as the case may be, the accuracy of the information[4]. The tenant may within one month of service of the notice of refusal apply to the Lands Tribunal for Scotland for a finding that he has a right to purchase, on such terms as the tribunal determines[5]. It is in the exercise of this power that the tribunal has made many of its decisions on the right to purchase[6].

The first of the two specific circumstances in which a landlord may refuse to sell arises where the application to purchase relates to a house (first let on a secure tenancy before 1 January 1990[7]) which has facilities substantially different from those of an ordinary house and which has been designed or adapted for occupation by a person of pensionable age whose special needs require accommodation of the kind provided by the house[8]. The landlord may, within one month of service of the application to purchase, make an application to the Secretary of State specifying the facilities and features of design or adaptation which, in the landlord's view, cause the house to be one to which the special rules apply[9]. If the house then appears to the Secretary of State to be such a house, he must authorise the landlord to serve on the tenant a notice of refusal as soon as is practicable, and in any event within one month[10]. Such a notice of refusal must specify the relevant special facilities and features and state that the authority of the Secretary of State has been obtained[11]. Where the Secretary of State refuses the landlord's application, the landlord must serve on the tenant an offer to sell[12].

The other special circumstance where a refusal to sell is permitted is restricted to situations where an islands council is the landlord[13].

Where (1) a house which is the subject of an application to purchase is held by an islands council for the purposes of its functions as education authority and is required for the accommodation of a person who is or will be employed by the council for those purposes, and (2) the council is not likely to be able reasonably to provide other suitable accommodation for such a person, and (3) the tenant would otherwise have the right to purchase the house, the council may, nevertheless, within a month of service of the application, serve a notice of refusal on the tenant[14]. Such a notice must contain sufficient information to demonstrate that the conditions mentioned in heads (1) and (2) are fulfilled in relation to the house[15].

1 Housing (Scotland) Act 1987 (c 26), s 68(1).
2 Ibid, s 68(1)(a), (b). For the general power of local authorities to sell houses, see s 14, and para 1908 above.
3 Ibid, s 68(2).
4 Ibid, s 68(3).
5 Ibid, s 68(4). The time at which a tenant 'applies for a finding' is when he or she first intimates to the Lands Tribunal a wish to apply, rather than the date when a completed form of application for a finding is submitted: see *Robb v Kyle and Carrick District Council* 1989 SLT (Lands Trib) 78.
6 See para 1959 above.
7 Housing (Scotland) Act 1987, s 69(1A) (added by the Local Government and Housing Act 1989 (c 42), s 177).
8 Housing (Scotland) Act 1987, s 69(1).
9 Ibid, s 69(2), (3).
10 Ibid, s 69(4).
11 Ibid, s 69(5).
12 Ibid, s 69(6).
13 Ibid, s 70(1). An attempt to argue that Strathclyde Regional Council was, in its islands areas, an 'islands council' was made in *MacDonald v Strathclyde Regional Council* 1990 SLT (Lands Trib) 10.
14 Housing (Scotland) Act 1987, s 70(1)(a)–(c).
15 Ibid, s 70(2). There does not appear to be a right of appeal to the Lands Tribunal against this form of refusal to sell.

1964. The Lands Tribunal for Scotland. The functions of the Lands Tribunal for Scotland in relation both to questions concerning conditions and to notices of refusal have already been discussed[1]. The tribunal is, however, also given powers in situations where a tenant complains that, in one way or another, the landlord is failing to comply with the statutory procedures[2]. Thus, where (1) a landlord fails to respond timeously[3] to an application to purchase by issuing either an offer to sell (even if it is 'defective' in the sense discussed below) or a notice of refusal[4], or (2) a landlord fails to issue an amended offer after an earlier determination of the Lands Tribunal varying the terms of the offer[5], or (3) a landlord fails to respond in time to a finding of the tribunal following a notice of refusal (or an order following a 'defective' offer)[6], the tenant (together with any joint purchaser) may refer the matter to the Lands Tribunal by serving on the clerk to the tribunal copies of relevant documents and a statement of his or her grievance[7]. The Lands Tribunal must consider whether, in its opinion, one of the forms of failure or delay has indeed occurred[8]. If it so finds, the tribunal may give any consent, exercise any discretion or do anything available to the landlord under the right to buy provisions[9], and issue such notices and undertake such other steps as may be required to complete the procedure leading to an offer to sell, to vary conditions, to complete the contract of sale or to make a fixed price option[10]. Any such action taken is to have effect as if taken by the landlord[10].

In other circumstances, the tenant's complaint may arise not from a complete failure to act or a delay on the part of the landlord but from an offer to sell which is, in some respect, defective. If a landlord has served an offer whose contents do not conform with the statutory requirements relating to (a) the determination of the market value of the house, (b) the calculation of the discount, (c) the fixing of the price, (d) the conditions intended to be imposed, or (e) the offer (to tenant and any joint purchaser) itself, the tenant may refer the matter to the Lands Tribunal[11]. The reference may also be based upon a complaint that the contents of the offer were not obtained in accordance with the statutory provisions[12]. Where a reference on any of these grounds is upheld, the Lands Tribunal may order the landlord to serve on the tenant an offer to sell, in proper form, within such time, not exceeding two months, as it may specify[13]. Using its powers to examine offers claimed to be defective in the ways described, the Lands Tribunal has decided cases relating to the calculation of discount and price[14] and also to the extent of the subject to be sold[15]. Particularly difficult problems have arisen where a purchasing tenant claims that he or she is entitled to purchase land already contained in a disposition to a neighbouring former tenant. The landlord may be ordered to offer to sell to one tenant land already sold to another[16].

An appeal lies from the Lands Tribunal to the Inner House of the Court of Session[17]. Despite the importance of these enforcement provisions under which the Lands Tribunal is given powers to compel landlords to comply with the right to buy provisions, it is specifically provided that they are not to affect the operation of the provisions of any other enactment relating to the enforcement of a statutory duty[18]. The principal such provision having general application to local authorities is in the Local Government (Scotland) Act 1973. This enables the Secretary of State to declare, following inquiry, an authority to be in default and to order it to rectify the position[19]. Another means available for the enforcement of a statutory duty is by obtaining a decree of specific performance from the Court of Session[20].

1 See paras 1959, 1963, above.
2 The individual obligations imposed on landlords are accompanied by a general obligation to make provision for the progression of applications: see the Housing (Scotland) Act 1987 (c 26), s 74, and para 1966 below.
3 The Lands Tribunal has taken a strict view of the timetable. An offer, even if only a few days late, is not timeous and is, therefore, subject to its jurisdiction: see eg *Fullerton v Monklands District Council* 1983 SLT (Lands Trib) 15 at 16.
4 Housing (Scotland) Act 1987, s 71(1)(a).
5 Ibid, s 71(1)(b).
6 Ibid, s 71(1)(c).
7 Ibid, s 71(1).
8 Ibid, s 71(2)(a).
9 Ie ibid, ss 61–84.
10 Ibid, s 71(2)(a).
11 Ibid, s 71(1)(d), by reference to s 63(2)(a)–(e), for which see para 1957 above.
12 Ibid, s 71(1)(d).
13 Ibid, s 71(2)(b).
14 See *Motherwell District Council v Gliori* 1986 SLT 444 (on appeal from the Lands Tribunal to the Inner House); *McEwan v Annandale and Eskdale District Council* 1989 SLT (Lands Trib) 95.
15 See eg *Neave v City of Dundee District Council* 1986 SLT (Lands Trib) 18; *Allison v Tayside Regional Council* 1989 SLT (Lands Trib) 65 (a case primarily concerned with whether the tenancy was secure on 'curtilage' grounds); *Quinn v Monklands District Council* 7 February 1989, Lands Trib (unreported).
16 *Morrison v Stirling District Council* 1987 SLT (Lands Trib) 22 at 24.
17 Tribunals and Inquiries Act 1971 (c 62), s 13(1), Sch 1, para 39. Such appeals are governed by RC 290, 292, and an appeal by stated case is inappropriate: see *Motherwell District Council v Gliori* 1986 SLT 444, and *Campbell v Western Isles Islands Council* 1989 SLT 602 at 605.

18 Housing (Scotland) Act 1987, s 71(3).
19 Local Government (Scotland) Act 1973 (c 65), s 211 (amended by the Local Government and Housing Act 1989 (c 42), s 159): see LOCAL GOVERNMENT, vol 14, para 117. Default orders arising out of failures to implement the right to buy provisions have included orders against the City of Dundee District Council and Stirling District Council in 1981 and against East Lothian District Council in 1982. An order against the City of Glasgow District Council in 1989 required it to reverse the effects of a practice adopted by the council requiring tenants to sign undertakings not to buy their houses as a precondition of works of improvement or modernisation being carried out: see *Lord Advocate v City of Glasgow District Council* 1989 GWD 35–1626.
20 Court of Session Act 1988 (c 36), s 45, replacing the Court of Session Act 1868 (c 100), s 91, for which see ADMINISTRATIVE LAW, vol 1, paras 305, 335, 346, and LOCAL GOVERNMENT, vol 14, paras 118, 123, 124.

1965. Recoverability of discount. Although there are no general restrictions upon the freedom of a purchasing tenant subsequently to dispose of the house which he or she has bought, a purchaser may be penalised by the obligation to repay a proportion of the discount originally deducted from the purchase price. With only limited exceptions, a purchaser (or successor in title) who sells or otherwise disposes of the house before the expiry of three years from the date of service of notice of acceptance is liable to repay to the landlord a proportion of the difference between the original market value and the price of the house[1] (that is, a proportion of the discount). The proportion of that difference repayable is 100 per cent where the disposal occurs within the first year; 66 per cent where it occurs in the second year; and 33 per cent where it occurs in the third year[2]. This obligation to repay applies even though the disposal is of a part of the house only (thus, in an extreme case, the duty to repay could not be avoided if only a small part of the garden were retained by the vendor), *except* where the disposal is by one of the parties to the original sale to one of the other parties, or the remainder of the house continues to be the only or principal home of the person disposing of the part[3]. On the other hand, where there is more than one disposal of the house (or of part) within the three-year period, the obligation attaches only to the first such disposal[4]. Provision is made for the protection of a landlord's securing of the liability to repay discount and for the order of its priority in relation to other forms of security[5]. The liability to make a repayment cannot be imposed as a real burden in a disposition of any interest in the house[6]. The specific exceptions to the general obligation to repay discount are three: (1) a disposal by the executor of a deceased owner acting in that capacity; (2) a disposal as a result of a compulsory purchase order; and (3) a disposal which is to a member of the owner's family[7] who has lived with the owner for a period of twelve months before the disposal and is for no consideration[8]. This last exception is accompanied by the proviso that if the disponee further disposes of the house before the expiry of the original three-year period, the obligations apply to him or her as if this were the original disposal and as if he or she were the original purchaser[9].

1 Housing (Scotland) Act 1987 (c 26), s 72(1). As to the discount, see para 1956 above.
2 Ibid, s 72(3)(a)–(c).
3 Ibid, s 72(2)(a), (b).
4 Ibid, s 72(4).
5 See ibid, s 72(5), (6).
6 Ibid, s 72(7).
7 As to references to members of a family, see ibid, s 83, and para 1935, note 4, above.
8 Ibid, s 73(1)(a)–(c), (2).
9 Ibid, s 73(2) proviso.

1966. Duties of landlords. In the light of what has already been said, it will be clear that the right to buy provisions impose a substantial number of duties upon landlords which must be discharged if the rights of tenants are to be brought fully to fruition. For the avoidance of doubt, it is further expressly enacted that it is the duty of landlords to make provision for the progression of applications to purchase in such manner as may be necessary to enable tenants who wish to exercise their rights to do so, and to comply with regulations made by the Secretary of State[1]. For the more specific protection of tenants, it is provided that no person exercising or seeking to exercise a right to purchase may be obliged, notwithstanding any agreement to the contrary, to make any payment or lodge any deposit with the landlord which would not otherwise have been required[2]. Likewise, landlords are required neither to enter into, nor to induce (or seek to induce) any person to enter into, any such agreement or into one which purports to restrict the person's rights under the right to buy provisions[3]. A specific duty of a different kind requires landlords to alert intending secure tenants to circumstances which may affect their right to buy. Thus, where a new secure tenancy is to be created but the landlord is not the heritable proprietor of the house[4], or the house is one statutorily excluded from the right to buy provisions, or the 'cost-floor' provisions[5] may affect the purchase price, the landlord must inform the prospective tenant by written notice[6]. A similar obligation applies where the landlord ceases, during a secure tenancy, to be the heritable proprietor[7] or the house becomes one excluded from the right to purchase[8]. In addition, a landlord is obliged to give immediate written notice to a purchasing tenant[9] of the passing or making of an enactment which will subsequently come into force with the result of changing the law relating to the calculation of the price of the house[10]. The notice must state the nature of the change of the law and how it will affect the price and suggest that the tenant should seek appropriate advice[10].

1 Housing (Scotland) Act 1987 (c 26), s 74.
2 Ibid, s 75(1)(a). This prohibition does not apply to expenses in any court proceedings: s 75(2).
3 Ibid, s 75(1)(d).
4 Nor, since the insertion of ibid, s 84A, by the Local Government and Housing Act 1989 (c 42), s 178)(2) (see para 1968 below), the holder of the interest of the landlord under a registered lease. These requirements do not, in any case, apply to a landlord which is a housing co-operative (see the Housing (Scotland) Act 1987, s 22, and para 1903 above), where the heritable proprietor (defined in para 1955, note 10, above) (or landlord under a registered lease) is a local authority: s 76(3) (amended by the Local Government and Housing Act 1989, s 178(1)).
5 See the Housing (Scotland) Act 1987, s 62(7), (8), and para 1956 above.
6 Ibid, s 76(1)(a)–(c) (amended by the Local Government and Housing Act 1989, s 178(1)).
7 Or the landlord under a registered lease: see note 4 above.
8 Housing (Scotland) Act 1987, s 76(2) (as amended: see note 6 above).
9 Ie where an application to purchase has been served (and has neither been withdrawn nor refused) and no contract of sale has been constituted.
10 Housing (Scotland) Act 1987, s 76(4), (5) (added by the Local Government and Housing Act 1989, s 181).

1967. Powers of the Secretary of State. At many points during the procedures described above, the extensive influence of the Secretary of State has been evident. He has the power inter alia to prescribe relevant forms[1]; to add to the list of public sector landlords qualifying for discount purposes[2]; to vary rates of discount[3]; to regulate by determination the effect of the cost-floor provisions[4]; and to approve or not the designation of rural areas[5]. In addition to these, the Secretary of State is given further powers. They may be listed as follows:

(1) He may, where necessary, order that, where a landlord is not the heritable proprietor of land on which there are houses otherwise subject to the right to buy, the whole of the heritable proprietor's interest in the land is to vest in the landlord[6]. This power was enacted (and subsequently used) to remove

technical barriers from the exercise of the right to buy of certain secure tenants[7].

(2) The Secretary of State has the power to give directions to landlords (in general or in particular) requiring them not to include in offers to sell conditions which he considers to be unreasonable[8]. This power supplements the powers of intervention in specific cases available to the Lands Tribunal for Scotland[9].

(3) The Secretary of State is empowered to give financial or other assistance to tenants and purchasers in relation to proceedings under the right to buy provisions where either the case would raise a question of principle and the public interest requires that the assistance be given or some other special consideration applies[10].

(4) The Secretary of State is given wide powers to require landlords (or their designated officers) to supply to him documents and information relevant to the exercise by him of powers under the right to buy provisions[11].

1 See the Housing (Scotland) Act 1987 (c 26), s 63(1), and para 1957 above.
2 See ibid, s 61(11)(w), and para 1955 above.
3 See ibid, s 62(5), and para 1956 above.
4 See ibid, s 62(7), (8), and para 1956 above.
5 See ibid, s 64(6), and para 1958 above.
6 Ibid, s 77. For the meaning of 'heritable proprietor', see para 1955, note 10, above.
7 See para 1955, note 11, above.
8 See the Housing (Scotland) Act 1987, s 78.
9 See para 1964 above.
10 See the Housing (Scotland) Act 1987, s 79.
11 See ibid, s 81.

1968. Right to buy where landlord is lessee. It has already been explained that one prerequisite of the exercise of the right to buy is that the landlord be heritable proprietor of the house[1]. It has, however, been recently provided that the right to buy provisions[2] apply, with modifications, to enable the acquisition by a secure tenant of the landlord's interest in a house as lessee under a registered lease[3] of the house (or of land which includes it) or as assignee of that interest[4]. The equivalent right to obtain a loan is also provided[5]. References in the right to buy provisions to the purchase of sale of a house are to be construed as references to the acquisition or disposal of the landlord's interest by way of a registered assignation[6]. Appropriate modifications are made to the right to buy provisions defining the landlord's interest, the market value and price of the house, and the conditions (including rights of pre-emption) which may be attached[7].

1 See para 1955 above. See also para 1967, above (vesting in landlord of interest of heritable proprietor).
2 Ie the Housing (Scotland) Act 1987 (c 26), ss 61–84, but not s 76 (landlord's duty to provide information to secure tenants: see para 1966 above), nor s 77 (vesting in landlord of heritable proprietor's interest: see paras 1955, 1967, above); and s 216 (loans).
3 'Registered lease' means a lease (1) which is recorded in the General Register of Sasines, or (2) in respect of which the lessee's interest is registered in the Land Register of Scotland under the Registration of Leases (Scotland) Act 1857 (c 26): Housing (Scotland) Act 1987, s 84A(7) (added by the Local Government and Housing Act 1989 (c 42), s 178(2)).
4 Housing (Scotland) Act 1987, s 84A(1)(a) (as so added).
5 Ibid, s 84A(1)(b) (as so added).
6 Ibid, s 84A(2). 'Registered assignation' means an assignation of a registered lease which is registered or recorded as mentioned in note 3 above: s 84A(7) (as so added).
7 See ibid, s 84A(3)–(6) (as so added).

1969. Defective housing. Part XIV of the Housing (Scotland) Act 1987[1] reproduces the text of the Housing Defects Act 1984 which, although it set up an elaborate statutory code, was intended to respond to a specific problem which arose in the early years of the operation of the right to buy. It is a response which is also time-limited in its effect. General defects in the construction and condition of houses sold under the right to buy are expected to be handled in the normal way at the time of purchase by survey and determination of the price[2]. However, because some forms of structural infirmity may not be discoverable at the time of sale on account of latent defects in construction (especially in the case of certain types of prefabricated concrete buildings) the government was persuaded that a major hardship might be caused to tenants purchasing in ignorance of the defect. The 1984 Act went some way to providing a remedy. Although the provisions now contained in Part XIV of the 1987 Act could be extended to any class of buildings (consisting of a dwelling or dwellings which are defective by reason of their design or construction and, by virtue of those circumstances having become generally known, the value of some or all of the dwellings concerned has been substantially reduced[3]), only a limited number of types of building have been designated by the Secretary of State. They are certain types of prefabricated reinforced concrete buildings designed (but not necessarily built) before 1960[4].

The provisions of Part XIV of the 1987 Act are activated by a written application made to the local authority by a person eligible for assistance[5]. To be eligible a person must be the owner of the dwelling and must be either (1) an individual who is not a trustee, or (2) a trustee if all the beneficiaries are individuals, or (3) a personal representative[6].

One of two sets of conditions have then to be fulfilled. The first is that (a) there was a disposal by a public sector authority[7] of the owner's interest before a cut-off date set at 26 April 1984[8], and (b) there has been no disposal for value by any person on or after that date[9]. The second, alternative, set of conditions is that (i) the applicant acquired the owner's interest in the dwelling for value within twelve months of the cut-off date, and (ii) he or she was unaware on that date of the defect, and (iii) the price did not take any or any adequate account of the defect, and, finally, (iv) if the cut-off date had fallen immediately after the disposal, the *first set* of conditions would have been satisfied[10]. A person is not eligible to apply if remedial works have been carried out[11], and an application for assistance may not be entertained if an application has also been made for an improvement grant to cover relevant works of reinstatement[12].

The application is made to the appropriate district or islands council, and if it decides (as soon as reasonably practicable) that the applicant is eligible, assistance is to be either by way of reinstatement grant paid by the authority or by repurchase[13]. Assistance is required to be (on the determination of the authority, again as soon as reasonably practicable) by way of repurchase if either it would be unreasonable to expect the applicant to secure or await the carrying out of reinstatement works[14] or if the dwelling is a flat[15]. Otherwise the applicant is entitled to assistance by repurchase only if certain conditions (which lead to assistance by reinstatement grant) are not satisfied. Those conditions relate primarily to the value for money obtainable on reinstatement[16]. If the house is repurchased, the price is fixed at 95 per cent of the value at the time of the repurchasing authority's offer[17]. There is provision for the owner of the house to be given a tenancy — normally a secure tenancy of the house which was the subject of the repurchase[18]. If, on the other hand, a reinstatement grant becomes payable, this is to be paid in respect of 'qualifying work' (which may subsequently be varied) as required to ensure that the dwelling becomes likely to provide satisfactory housing accommodation for at least thirty years, and of any 'associated arrangement' entered into in connection with the work which is likely to contribute towards the dwelling being acceptable security on a loan[19].

The rate of grant is 90 per cent (or 100 per cent in cases of financial hardship) of the amount originally determined by the authority, or of that amount as varied by it or, if less, of the actual expenditure incurred or, again if less, a prescribed maximum amount[20].

In addition to the main obligations of authorities to repurchase or to pay grant, they have a number of other duties and powers. These include the obligation to provide information about rights to assistance[21] and also warnings to those purchasing defective dwellings of their lack of entitlement to assistance[22]. There is also provision for the reference of disputed questions to the sheriff court[23], and for the designation of defective dwellings under local schemes[24].

1 The Housing (Scotland) Act 1987 (c 26), Pt XIV, comprises ss 257–303.
2 See para 1956 above.
3 Housing (Scotland) Act 1987, s 257(1). The anomalous use of the term 'dwelling' derives from its original appearance in the Housing Defects Act 1984 (c 50) (repealed). It is now defined as any house, flat or other unit designed or adapted for living in: Housing (Scotland) Act 1987, s 302(1). The definition goes on to distinguish, contrary to standard Scottish practice, the horizontal division of buildings into 'flats' but the vertical division into 'houses': see s 302(2).
4 Ibid, s 257(1), (3)–(5); Housing Defects (Prefabricated Reinforced Concrete Dwellings) (Scotland) Designation 1984 (annexed to Scottish Development Department Circular 31/1984).
5 Housing (Scotland) Act 1987, s 262.
6 Ibid, ss 259(1), (2).
7 'Public sector authority' means a regional, islands or district council or its predecessor (or a joint board or joint committee), a water authority, the Housing Corporation, Scottish Homes, a registered housing association (other than a co-operative housing association), a development corporation, the British Coal Corporation, the United Kingdom Atomic Energy Authority, or a body corporate or housing association specified by the Secretary of State: ibid, s 300(1); Coal Industry Act 1987 (c 3), s 1(3); Housing (Scotland) Act 1988 (c 43), s 3(3), Sch 2, para 1.
8 See the designation cited in note 4 above.
9 Housing (Scotland) Act 1987, s 259(3)(a), (b).
10 Ibid, s 259(4)(a)–(d).
11 Ibid, s 260.
12 Ibid, s 263. As to improvement grants, see paras 2019 ff below.
13 Ibid, ss 264, 265.
14 Ibid, s 265 (amended by the Local Government and Housing Act 1989 (c 42), s 166(2)).
15 Housing (Scotland) Act 1987, s 266(1)(a). See also note 3 above. The applicant for assistance must be the owner of the house. Conclusion of missives is not sufficient: see *McSweeney v Dumbarton District Council* 1987 SLT (Sh Ct) 129.
16 See the Housing (Scotland) Act 1987, s 266(1)(b)–(d).
17 See ibid, s 275, and Sch 20 (amended by the Housing (Scotland) Act 1988, s 72(1), Sch 7, para 29). There is also provision for repurchase by an authority other than the local authority: see the Housing (Scotland) Act 1987, s 276 (amended by the Housing (Scotland) Act 1988, Sch 7, para 20).
18 See the Housing (Scotland) Act 1987, s 282 (amended by the Housing (Scotland) Act 1988, Sch 7, para 22). A house let under a secure tenancy under this provision becomes subject to the right to buy provisions but without the requirement of the minimum period of two years' occupation by the tenant: see the Housing (Scotland) Act 1987, s 61(3) (amended by the Local Government and Housing Act 1989, s 194(1), Sch 11, para 93), and para 1955 above.
19 See the Housing (Scotland) Act 1987, ss 266–269 (s 267 being amended by the Local Government and Housing Act 1989, s 166(3)).
20 Housing (Scotland) Act 1987, s 271(1), (2).
21 Ibid, s 290.
22 Ibid, s 291.
23 Ibid, s 299 (amended by the Housing (Scotland) Act 1988, Sch 7, para 26).
24 Housing (Scotland) Act 1987, ss 287–289 (s 289 being amended by the Local Government and Housing Act 1989, s 166(4), (5)).

1970. Voluntary disposals and the right to buy provisions. The right to purchase is a statutory right assured to secure tenants in accordance with the rules discussed in the preceding paragraphs. Further specific provisions apart, therefore, it is not a right which survives the disposal of the landlord's interest in a house to another landlord. If a tenant thereby ceases to be a secure tenant, the statutory right to buy is also lost. Two different situations are usefully distinguished. If the landlord's interest is transferred to another landlord under the 'change of landlord' provisions, there is no general survival of a right to buy unless the disposal is to Scottish Homes itself[1]. The right to buy is lost unless preserved in contractual form under the tenant's new lease. Since, however, the change of landlord provisions cannot be implemented without the tenant's consent, this operates to protect the tenant's interests. Where, on the other hand, the disposal is 'voluntary', the tenant's consent is not a prerequisite, although certain rights to be consulted are preserved[2]. For such a tenant's further protection, the right to buy provisions do continue to apply in relation to the private sector landlord in terms of a scheme to be prescribed by the Secretary of State[3]. There is no statutory preservation of the right to buy if a second disposal to a further private landlord takes place.

1 As to change of landlord, see paras 1971 ff below.
2 For discussion of such voluntary disposals and the consultation required, see para 1908 above.
3 Housing (Scotland) Act 1987 (c 26), s 81A (added by the Housing Act 1988 (c 50), s 128).

5. CHANGE OF LANDLORD: SECURE TENANTS

1971. Introduction. The previous part of this title[1] was concerned with the exercise by secure tenants of their right to buy, a right originally enacted by the Tenants' Rights Etc (Scotland) Act 1980 (c 52)[2]. More recently, the Housing (Scotland) Act 1988 introduced what has been popularly described as the tenant's 'right to choose' a new landlord. Although, under the provisions contained in Part III of the Act[3], 'Change of Landlord: Secure Tenants', the safeguard permitted to tenants may be construed as an indirect right to choose a new landlord, the more evident purpose of the provisions is to confer on certain bodies and under certain conditions the right to acquire houses from landlords in the public sector. It will be seen that the procedures laid down are closely modelled upon those applicable to the right to buy. It should also be borne in mind that they were introduced in parallel with other changes made by the Housing (Scotland) Act 1988 and the Housing Act 1988 (c 50) concerning the 'voluntary' disposal of houses by public sector landlords[4].

1 See paras 1954 ff above.
2 See para 1954 above.
3 The Housing (Scotland) Act 1988 (c 43), Pt III, comprises ss 56–64.
4 For 'voluntary disposals', see paras 1908, 1970 above. The other main change was the introduction by ibid, Pt II (ss 12–55), of assured tenancies in the private sector (including housing associations) with 'open market' rents: see LANDLORD AND TENANT.

1972. The right to acquire. There is conferred on certain persons the right to acquire from a 'public sector landlord' a house which on 'the relevant date' is occupied by a 'qualifying tenant' and of which, on the same date, the landlord is heritable proprietor[1]. The terms used in the definition of this right to acquire need further elaboration. As to the persons with the right to acquire, these are Scottish Homes or a person approved by Scottish Homes, which cannot be a public sector landlord or a regional council[2]. A public sector landlord, from whom houses are acquired, is an islands or district council[3], a development corporation[4], the Housing Corporation and Scottish Homes[5]. The relevant date is the date on which an application is made seeking to exercise the right to acquire[6]. A qualifying tenant is any secure tenant except one obliged to give up possession of the house pursuant to a court order[7]. Finally, 'heritable proprietor' is defined to include any person entitled under the Conveyancing (Scotland) Act 1924[8] to grant a disposition[9]. It should further be noted that the right to acquire extends not only to a house alone. For these purposes the term 'house' extends also to other heritable property of which the landlord is heritable proprietor and which will reasonably serve a beneficial purpose in connection with the occupation of any house[10]. There are, however, excluded from houses subject to the right to acquire, sheltered housing, amenity housing, certain houses held by islands councils for educational purposes and housing in designated rural areas[11].

1 Housing (Scotland) Act 1988 (c 43), s 56(1).
2 Ibid, s 57(1). The exclusion of regional councils is specifically required because they are not, for this purpose, defined as public sector landlords (see below). The exclusion extends also to joint boards or joint committees of two or more regional councils or a trust under the control of a regional council: s 57(1). Approvals by Scottish Homes may be given to particular persons or to persons of a particular description; may be given generally or in relation to particular acquisitions; may specify a maximum number of acquisitions; and may be given subject to conditions: s 57(2)(a)–(d). An approval may be revoked by Scottish Homes, but without prejudice to any transaction previously completed: s 57(3).
3 This includes a joint board or joint committee of an islands or district council, or the common good of or any trust under the control of such a council: ibid, s 56(3)(a).
4 Ie a development corporation within the meaning of the New Towns (Scotland) Act 1968 (c 16) (see s 2), including an urban development corporation within the meaning of the Local Government, Planning and Land Act 1980 (c 65), Pt XVI (ss 134–172) (see s 135): Housing (Scotland) Act 1988, s 56(3)(b).
5 Ibid, s 56(3)(a), (b), (d), (e).
6 Ibid, s 56(10). As to applications, see para 1973 below.
7 Ibid, s 56(4).
8 Ie under the Conveyancing (Scotland) Act 1924 (c 27), s 3.
9 Housing (Scotland) Act 1988, s 56(2).
10 Ibid, s 56(1).
11 See ibid, s 56(5)–(9). The rules relating to these exclusions closely parallel those applicable to the right to buy: see para 1958 above.

1973. Application to acquire. In order to exercise the right to acquire, the applicant (whether Scottish Homes or an 'approved person'[1]) must serve on the landlord an application in the prescribed form containing a statement that the applicant is seeking to exercise the right to acquire, accompanied by the consent in writing of the qualifying tenant to an approach being made to the existing landlord[2]. For this purpose the reference to the qualifying tenant includes his or her spouse (including a person living with the tenant as husband or wife) occupying the house as the spouse's only or principal home[3]. It is the requirement to obtain the consent of the tenant which represents this first formal, though indirect, 'right' of the tenant to choose the new landlord. The tenant is entitled to receive a copy of the application (as is Scottish Homes, where Scottish Homes is not the applicant)[4], and an application ceases to have effect if, at any time, the qualifying tenant withdraws his or her consent by notice served on the landlord[5]. The application also lapses if the applicant withdraws it[6].

Otherwise, unless the landlord serves a notice of refusal[7], it must, within two months of service of the application, serve on the applicant an offer to sell notice[8]. A copy must also be served on the qualifying tenant[9]. The notice itself must state (1) the market value of the house on the date of service of the application, and (2) any conditions the landlord intends to impose, and must then contain an offer to sell the house to the applicant at a price equal to the market value and under those conditions[10].

The market value is to be determined by either a qualified valuer nominated by the landlord and accepted by the applicant or by the district valuer, as the landlord thinks fit[11]. Statutory assumptions are laid down about the determination of the market value. It is to be the price of the house if sold on the open market by a willing seller assuming (a) that it was subject to the tenancy of the qualifying tenant but otherwise with vacant possession; (b) that it was to be conveyed with the same rights and subject to the same burdens; (c) that the only prospective purchasers were Scottish Homes or persons approved by it; and (d) that the applicant would, within a reasonable period, carry out repairs necessary to comply with the landlord's repairing obligations[12]. These assumptions have evinced statutory recognition of the possibility that the appropriate market value and price may be nil or even a negative amount and that, in some transactions, it may be necessary for the landlord rather than the applicant to make the payment[13].

Conditions attached to the offer to sell may be such conditions as are reasonable provided that (i) they do not reduce the tenant's enjoyment and use of the house as tenant of the applicant from that of tenant of the landlord, and (ii) they include such terms as are necessary to entitle the applicant to receive a good and marketable title to the house[14]. More specifically, a condition imposing a new or increased charge for the provision of a service must provide for the change to be in reasonable proportion to the cost to the landlord of providing the service[15]. No condition may have the effect of requiring either the applicant or the tenant to pay any expenses of the landlord[16].

1 Ie a person approved under the Housing (Scotland) Act 1988 (c 43), s 57: see para 1972, text and note 2 above.
2 Ibid, s 58(1)(a), (b). For the prescribed form, see the Right to Purchase From A Public Sector Landlord (Application Form) (Scotland) Regulations 1989, SI 1989/423.
3 Housing (Scotland) Act 1988, s 58(2).
4 Ibid, s 58(3).
5 Ibid, s 58(4)(b).
6 Ibid, s 58(4)(a).
7 See para 1976 below.
8 Housing (Scotland) Act 1988, s 58(5).
9 Ibid, s 58(9).
10 Ibid, s 58(5).
11 Ibid, s 58(6).
12 Ibid, s 58(7)(a)–(d).
13 Ibid, s 58(8).
14 Ibid, s 58(1)(a), (b).
15 Ibid, s 58(11).
16 Ibid, s 58(12).

1974. Variation of conditions. If, having received an offer to sell, an applicant considers a condition to be unreasonable or wishes to have a new condition included, the applicant may make a request to the landlord and, if necessary, refer the matter to the Lands Tribunal for Scotland in the same manner as is available to an acquiring tenant under the right to buy provisions[1].

1 See the Housing (Scotland) Act 1988 (c 43), s 59. For discussion of the equivalent right to buy provisions, see para 1959 above.

1975. Notice of acceptance. There is similarly parallel provision for the service by the applicant of a notice of acceptance on the landlord, at which point a contract of sale of the house concerned is constituted[1]. The one significant addition is that a notice of acceptance is of no effect unless the qualifying tenant and the applicant have concluded a lease of the house for a period immediately subsequent to its sale, conditional upon the sale proceeding[2]. This is the final point, prior to the sale itself, at which the tenant's compliance with its terms and with the basis of his or her future legal relationship with the purchasing landlord is required[3].

1 See the Housing (Scotland) Act 1988 (c 43), s 60(1). For the equivalent provision in relation to the right to buy, see para 1960 above.
2 Ibid, s 60(2).
3 It is the point at which, for instance, a contractual right to buy might be preserved. As to the loss of the statutory right to buy, see para 1977 below. See also para 1970 above.

1976. Refusal of applications and references to the Lands Tribunal. To complete the procedural scheme for the exercise of the right to acquire, there is provision for the service of notices of refusal by landlords and for their reference in contested cases to the Lands Tribunal for Scotland in the same way as in the case of the right to buy provisions[1]. Similarly there is provision for the reference to the Lands Tribunal of complaints that the landlord has failed to comply with the statutory timetable or has issued an offer to sell which does not comply with statutory requirements[2].

1 Housing (Scotland) Act 1988 (c 43), s 61. For the equivalent right to buy provision, see para 1963 above.
2 Ibid, s 62. See, again, para 1964 above.

1977. Subsequent disposals. It will be appreciated that, although a similar right might be contractually guaranteed, a tenant whose landlord changes under the foregoing provisions will normally lose the statutory right to buy his or her house. The tenant will, except in the case of an acquisition by Scottish Homes itself, cease to be a secure tenant[1]. Hence the concern, notwithstanding the loss of the right to buy, to ensure that the consent of an affected tenant is obtained both to the initiation of the procedure and to the terms of the tenancy which will follow the sale. Tenants do, however, remain vulnerable to possible further change in the future and, in particular, if the acquiring landlord subsequently disposes of his interest. There is no assurance that the disposal will be to an 'approved' landlord, nor is the tenant, at this later stage, given any power of veto. There is, however, some protection in the form of a statutory requirements that Scottish Homes must consent to a subsequent disposal[2]. Such consent may be in relation to a particular disposal or to a class or description of disposals, and may be unconditional or subject to conditions[3]. Before giving its consent for this purpose, Scottish Homes must satisfy itself that the person seeking the consent has taken appropriate steps to consult the tenant or tenants of the house or houses concerned and must have regard to the response of such tenant or tenants to that consultation[4].

1 See para 1936 above.
2 Housing (Scotland) Act 1988 (c 43), s 63(1). 'Disposing of property' for these purposes includes (1) granting or disposing of any interest in property; (2) entering into a contract to dispose of such property or such an interest; and (3) granting an option to acquire property or any such interest: s 63(4)(a)–(c).
3 Ibid, s 63(2).
4 Ibid, s 63(2A) (added by the Housing Act 1988 (c 50), s 140(1), Sch 17, para 89).

6. SUB-STANDARD HOUSES

(1) GENERAL

1978. Introduction. Complementing the provision of new housing accommodation are the powers and duties of local authorities to improve the general quality of the housing stock in their areas. Not all of these powers are conferred by legislation contained within 'housing' law, and are better viewed as aspects of planning law, public health law, or building control[1]. Several substantial parts of the Housing (Scotland) Act 1987 are, however, devoted to local authority powers in relation to sub-standard housing. They fall into various categories and are discussed in the paragraphs which follow. Although these start with aspects of Part IV of the Act[2] (which is itself headed 'Sub-Standard Houses'), the order of treatment of material does not follow absolutely that adopted in the Act. Thus, after the introduction of the 'tolerable standard'[3], subsequent paragraphs deal with closing and demolition orders (Part VI of the Act)[4], improvement orders (from Part IV)[5] and repair notices (Part V)[6] before moving on to housing action areas (from Part IV)[7].

1 See BUILDING CONTROLS; PUBLIC HEALTH, vol 19 (especially paras 346 ff and paras 467 ff); and TOWN AND COUNTRY PLANNING.
2 The Housing (Scotland) Act 1987 (c 26), Pt IV, comprises ss 85–107.
3 See ibid, s 86, and para 1979 below.
4 Ibid, Pt VI, comprises ss 114–134. See paras 1982 ff below.
5 See ibid, s 88, and paras 1990 ff below.
6 Ibid, Pt V comprises ss 108–113. See paras 1993 ff below.
7 See ibid, ss 89–93, and paras 1996 ff below.

1979. The tolerable standard. Essential to the statutory scheme under which local authorities are empowered to take action against sub-standard housing is a statement of the standard according to which the condition of a house is to be judged. Since the Housing (Scotland) Act 1969, when the unspecific standard of 'unfitness for human habitation' was finally discarded[1], the concept of the 'tolerable standard' has taken its place[2]. The Housing (Scotland) Act 1987 now provides that a house meets the tolerable standard for the purposes of the Act if it:
(1) is structurally stable;
(2) is substantially free from rising or penetrating damp;
(3) has satisfactory provision for natural and artificial lighting, for ventilation and for heating;
(4) has an adequate piped supply of wholesome water available within the house;
(5) has a sink provided with a satisfactory supply of both hot and cold water within the house;
(6) has a water closet available for the exclusive use of the occupants of the house and suitably located within the house;
(7) has an effective system for the drainage and disposal of foul and surface water;
(8) has satisfactory facilities for the cooking of food within the house;
(9) has satisfactory access to all external doors and outbuildings[3].
Any reference to a house not meeting the tolerable standard or being brought up to the tolerable standard is to be construed accordingly[4]. The Secretary of State is empowered to vary, extend or amplify by order the defining criteria of the tolerable standard[5]. He may do this either generally or, after consultation with a particular local authority, in relation to its district or any part of its district[5].

1 See the Housing (Scotland) Act 1969 (c 34), s 69, Sch 7, repealing the Housing (Scotland) Act 1966 (c 49), s 5.
2 See the Housing (Scotland) Act 1969, ss 1, 2, and thereafter the Housing (Scotland) Act 1974 (c 45), ss 13, 14 (repealed).
3 Housing (Scotland) Act 1987 (c 26), s 86(1)(a)–(i). Section 86 is without prejudice to s 114, which enables certain underground rooms to be treated as houses not meeting the tolerable standard (see s 114(4), and para 1982 below): s 86(3).

4 Ibid, s 86(1).
5 Ibid, s 86(2).

1980. General duty of local authorities. The concept of the tolerable standard is incorporated into a widely-drawn general duty of all authorities in relation to sub-standard houses. It is the duty of every local authority to secure that all houses in its district which do not meet the tolerable standard are closed, demolished or brought up to the tolerable standard within such period as is reasonable in all the circumstances[1]. In determining what period is reasonable, regard is to be had to alternative housing accommodation likely to be available for persons displaced from houses as a result of action proposed by the authority in carrying out its general duty[2]. Authorities are required from time to time to cause to be made such survey or inspection of their districts as may be necessary for the purposes of performing these duties[3]. A further provision (surely of only slight contemporary significance?) enables the proper officer of an authority to make an official representation in writing to the authority whenever he is of the opinion that a house in the district does not meet the tolerable standard[4]. The authority must 'as soon as may be' take into consideration any such official representation[5].

  1 Housing (Scotland) Act 1987 (c 26), s 85(1). For the meaning of 'local authority', see para 1903 above.
  2 Ibid, s 85(2).
  3 Ibid, s 85(3).
  4 Ibid, s 87(1), (3). 'Proper officer' in relation to any purpose of a local authority means an officer appointed for that purpose by the local authority: s 338(1). Prior to local government reorganisation in 1975, the reference to the 'proper officer' was a reference to the medical officer of health: see the Housing (Scotland) Act 1966 (c 49), s 180 (repealed).
  5 Housing (Scotland) Act 1987, s 87(2).

1981. Specific functions of local authorities. In addition to its relevance to the general duty described above[1], the tolerable standard figures in the more specific functions of housing authorities. Thus, in relation housing action areas, the tolerable standard is important both for the purpose of defining the circumstances in which an action area may be declared and also the standard to which houses subject to improvement must be raised[2]. The tolerable standard also defines the susceptibility of a house to the making of a closing order (with special adaptation of the standard for underground rooms)[3], a demolition order[4], or improvement order (where the standard is also adjusted to incorporate the need for a fixed bath or shower)[5]. The tolerable standard is further incorporated into the criteria for the making of a (mandatory) improvement grant for the provision of standard amenities[6], and for the making of a house loan[7].

  1 See para 1980 above.
  2 See para 1996 below.
  3 See para 1982 below.
  4 See para 1983 below.
  5 See para 1990 below.
  6 See para 2023 below.
  7 See para 2011 below.

(2) CLOSING AND DEMOLITION ORDERS

1982. Closing orders. Historically, the most significant of the orders a local authority may direct towards individual sub-standard houses are the closing order and the demolition order. Dating from the nineteenth century[1], they are now the subject matter of Part VI of the Housing (Scotland) Act 1987[2]. In that Part, they are joined by the procedure to require by resolution the demolition of an obstructive building[3]. The necessary prerequisite of the making of either a closing order or a demolition order is an official representation or report of the proper officer of the authority or other information in the authority's possession[4]. If, on consideration of that representation, report or information, the authority is satisfied that a house[5] does not meet the tolerable standard[5] and that it ought to be demolished, and the house forms only part of a building and that building does not comprise only houses below the tolerable standard, the authority may make a closing order[7]. Such an order prohibits the use of the house for human habitation[7]. It comes into effect on the date specified in it, being not less than twenty-eight days from the date it comes into operation[8].

1 An early power to order premises 'to be shut up or to be demolished' is contained in the Artizans and Labourers Dwellings Act 1868 (c 130), s 18 (repealed).
2 The Housing (Scotland) Act 1987 (c 26), Pt VI, comprises ss 114–134.
3 See para 1989 below.
4 Housing (Scotland) Act 1987, ss 114(1), 115. For the meaning of 'proper officer', see para 1980, note 4, above. Prior to local government reorganisation in 1975, the reference to the 'proper officer' was a reference to the sanitary inspector: see the Housing (Scotland) Act 1966 (c 49), s 15(1) (repealed).
5 In the Housing (Scotland) Act 1987, s 114, 'house' includes any room habitually used as a sleeping place, the surface of the floor of which is more than 3 feet below the surface of the street adjoining or nearest to the room ('an underground room'): s 114(3). An underground room does not meet the tolerable standard if (1) it is not an average of 7 feet high, or (2) it does not comply with such regulations as the local authority may make to secure proper ventilation and lighting and protection against dampness, effluvia or exhalation; s 114(4)(a), (b). The Secretary of State may require an authority to make such regulations, and if it does not do so, he may himself make them: s 114(5) (amended by the Housing (Scotland) Act 1988 (c 43), s 72(1), Sch 7, para 3). In the Housing (Scotland) Act 1987, Pt VI (except ss 125, 126, 132), any reference to a 'house' or 'building' includes a reference to premises occupied by agricultural workers although such premises are used for sleeping purposes only: s 133(1).
6 As to the tolerable standard, see para 1979 above.
7 Housing (Scotland) Act 1987, s 114(1). For the form of the order, see the Housing (Forms) (Scotland) Regulations 1974, SI 1974/1982, Schedule, Form 2.
8 Housing (Scotland) Act 1987, s 114(2).

1983. Demolition orders. If, on consideration of the representation, report or information referred to in the preceding paragraph, the local authority is satisfied that a building[1] comprises only a house which does not meet, or houses which do not meet, the tolerable standard[2], and that the house or houses ought to be demolished, it may make a demolition order requiring (1) that the building be vacated within a specified period of not less than twenty-eight days from the date on which the order comes into operation, and (2) that it be demolished within six weeks after the expiration of that period or, if later, within six weeks after it is vacated[3].

This power is subject to the further provision that where (apart from this further provision) an authority would be empowered to make a demolition order[4] with respect to a building in relation to which a building preservation order[5] is in force or which is a listed building[6], the authority must not make a demolition order but may instead make a closing order or orders[7]. If a demolition order has already been made in respect of such a building it must be revoked, and the authority may then make a closing order or orders[8].

1 As to references to buildings, see para 1982, note 5, above.
2 As to the tolerable standard, see para 1979 above.

3 Housing (Scotland) Act 1987 (c 26), s 115(a), (b). For the form of the order, see the Housing (Forms) (Scotland) Regulations 1972, SI 1972/1982, Schedule, Form 1. As to the date of operation of the order, see para 1985 below.

4 Ie under the Housing (Scotland) Act 1987, Pt VI (ss 114–134).

5 Ie under the Town and Country Planning (Scotland) Act 1972 (c 52), s 56.

6 Ie within the meaning of ibid, s 52(7).

7 Housing (Scotland) Act 1987, s 119(1).

8 See ibid, s 119(2). As to revocation, see para 1984 below.

1984. Revocation and suspension of closing and demolition orders. If, following the making of a closing or demolition order, the local authority is satisfied, on an application made by the owner or a person appearing to have reasonable cause for making the application, that the house or houses concerned have been brought up to the tolerable standard, it must make an order revoking the closing or demolition order[1]. It is also open, in some circumstances, to the authority to suspend (rather than revoke) a closing or demolition order. This arises when the owner (or person holding a heritable security over the property) gives a written undertaking (normally within twenty-one days of the service of the initial order) that he will carry out such works as will, in the opinion of the authority, bring the house or houses up to the tolerable standard or, in the case of a building subject to a demolition order, that no house in it will be used for human habitation[2]. If such an undertaking is given, the authority must, as soon as may be, either accept the undertaking and make an order suspending the earlier order or reject it and serve notice accordingly[3]. Such a suspension order ceases to have effect after one year unless renewed at the discretion of the authority, and further such renewals may be made[4]. If, at any time, the local authority has reasonable cause to believe that there has been a breach of the undertaking given, it may revoke the suspension order[5].

1 Housing (Scotland) Act 1987 (c 26), s 116. As to the tolerable standard, see para 1979 above.

2 Ibid, s 117(1).

3 Ibid, s 117(2). As to the effect on the date of operation of the order, see s 117(5).

4 Ibid, s 117(3).

5 Ibid, s 117(4).

1985. Service of orders and notices. Any order made or notice issued under the above provisions relating to closing and demolition orders[1] must be served upon (1) the person having control[2] of the house; (2) the owner of the house; (3) any person holding a heritable security over it; and (4) in the case of a revocation order, any person who applied for the order to be made[3].

1 Ie any order or notice under the Housing (Scotland) Act 1987 (c 26), ss 114–117: see paras 1982 ff above.

2 As to the person having control, see ibid, s 338(2).

3 Ibid, s 118(1)(a)–(d). References to an owner of, and to any person holding a heritable security over, a building are to be construed as including references to an owner of, and a person holding a heritable security over, any part of the building: s 118(2). As to the owner of a croft or landholding, see s 133(2). For consideration of the somewhat similar English provision, see *Pollway Nominees Ltd v Croydon London Borough Council* [1987] AC 79, [1986] 2 All ER 849, HL.

1986. Appeals. Any person aggrieved by (1) a closing order, or (2) a refusal to determine such an order, or (3) a demolition order, or (4) a refusal to determine such an order, may appeal to the sheriff by giving notice of appeal within twenty-one days after the date of service or of refusal[1]. A local authority may take no enforcement proceedings while such an appeal is pending[2]. In cases where an undertaking has been given, the sheriff may consider the undertaking and, if he thinks it proper to do so, may direct the authority to make a suspension order[3]. In the absence of an appeal, an order becomes operative on the expiration of twenty-one days after the date of service, and is final and conclusive as to any matters which could have been raised on appeal[4]. If, on the other hand, an appeal is made, an order (to the extent that the sheriff confirms it) becomes operative from the date of determination of the appeal[5].

1 Housing (Scotland) Act 1987 (c 26), s 129(1)(a), (b) (amended by the Housing (Scotland) Act 1988 (c 43), s 72(1), Sch 7, para 4), which is expressed to be subject to the general provisions of the Housing (Scotland) Act 1987, s 324(3)–(7), in relation to appeals to the sheriff. The phrase 'refusal to determine' is anomalous. There was a failure to convert it to 'refusal to revoke' when the latter term was adopted in ss 116 and 119 at the time of consolidation. It is not absolutely clear, therefore, that an effective appeal now lies against a refusal to revoke.
2 See ibid, s 129(2), which forbids an appeal by a person who occupies the premises under a lease or agreement which has less than six months unexpired. It is possible, however, that such a person might seek judicial review of the decision in the Court of Session. In relation to the equivalent position in England and Wales, see *R v Maldon District Council, ex parte Fisher* (1986) 18 HLR 197.
3 Housing (Scotland) Act 1987, s 129(3).
4 Ibid, s 130(1).
5 Ibid, s 130(2).

1987. Powers of acquisition. Where a building consists wholly of houses subject to closing orders which are all operative (and none of which is revoked or suspended) the local authority may revoke the closing orders and substitute for them a demolition order[1]. Alternatively, the authority may purchase the land by agreement, or, with the consent of the Secretary of State, compulsorily[2]. Where either a closing or demolition order has been made and it appears to the local authority, having regard to the existing condition of the house or building and to the needs of the area for the provision of further housing accommodation, the authority may purchase it[3]. Notice of such a determination to purchase a house or building must be served on all the persons on whom a closing or demolition order must be served[4]. There is the same right of appeal to the sheriff[5]. Purchase may be by agreement or, with the authority of the Secretary of State, compulsory[6]. Once a house or building is purchased, the authority must carry out such works as are, in its opinion, required for rendering or keeping it capable of being continued in use as housing accommodation[7]. The authority has the same powers and duties in respect of any house it has purchased under these provisions as it has in respect of its other housing stock[8].

1 Housing (Scotland) Act 1987 (c 26), s 120(1)(a).
2 Ibid, s 120(1)(b). The Acquisition of Land (Authorisation Procedure) (Scotland) Act 1947 (c 42) applies to any such compulsory purchase under the Housing (Scotland) Act 1987, s 120 or s 121 (see below), the compensation being assessed by the Lands Tribunal for Scotland under the Land Compensation (Scotland) Act 1963 (c 51), but subject to the Housing (Scotland) Act 1987, s 120(4), (5), or s 121(6), (7): ss 120(2), (3), 121(4), (5). See COMPULSORY ACQUISITION AND COMPENSATION, vol 5, paras 36 ff.
3 Ibid, s 121(1), (2).
4 Ibid, s 121(3), by reference to s 118(1), for which see para 1985 above.
5 Ibid, s 129(1)(c): cf para 1986 above.
6 Ibid, s 121(3). See further note 2 above.
7 Ibid, s 121(8).
8 Ibid, s 121(9). See paras 1904–1908 above.

1988. Other consequences of a closing or demolition order. Any person who, knowing that a closing order has become operative, uses or permits the use of the premises for human habitation without the consent of the local authority is guilty of an offence[1]. The same is true of someone who knows that an undertaking not to use premises for human habitation has been accepted by the local authority[2]. A person found guilty of an offence is liable on summary conviction to a fine not exceeding level 5 on the standard scale or to imprisonment for up to 3 months or both[3]. A continuing offence attracts a further fine of £5 for every day (or part day) on which the premises are used[4].

When a demolition order has become operative, the owner of the building must demolish it within the time required by the order[5]. If the building is not demolished in that time, the local authority may enter and demolish the building and sell the material[5]. The authority may recover the expenses of demolition from the owner, but must correspondingly pay to him any surplus following the sale of materials[6]. Special provision is made for the position where a building is jointly owned[7]. If, following its demolition of a building, a local authority is unable to recover its expenses because the owner cannot be found, it may be authorised by the Secretary of State to acquire the site compulsorily[8]. In circumstances where either a closing or a demolition order has become operative, the local authority must serve on the occupier of any building or house (or part of building or house) a notice, which must (1) state the effect of the order, (2) specify the date by which vacation of the building or house is required, and (3) require the occupier to remove before that date or, if later, before the expiration of twenty-eight days from the service of the notice[9]. If, at any time after that date, any person is in occupation of the building or house, the local authority or any owner of the building or house may make summary application to the sheriff for removal and ejection[10]. Warrant for ejection may be granted to give vacant possession within a period (between two and four weeks) to be determined by the sheriff[11]. Expenses incurred by an authority in obtaining possession are normally recoverable from the owner[12]. By virtue of a provision almost directly complementing that which applies following a closing order, any person who, with knowledge that a demolition order has become operative, enters (or permits another to enter) into occupation of the affected building after the date on which its vacation is required commits an offence[13]. Penalties are the same as stated above[13].

1 Housing (Scotland) Act 1987 (c 26), s 122(1)(a). For discussion of the knowledge required to constitute an offence under the corresponding English enactment, see *Barber v Shah* (1985) 17 HLR 584, DC.
2 Housing (Scotland) Act 1987, s 122(1)(b).
3 Ibid, s 122(2)(a). As to level 5, see para 1931, note 5, above.
4 Ibid, s 122(2)(b).
5 Ibid, s 123(1).
6 Ibid, s 123(2). Powers are available under s 131, Sch 9, to make a charging order in favour of the authority.
7 See ibid, s 123(3).
8 See ibid, s 124, which applies the Acquisition of Land (Authorisation Procedure) (Scotland) Act 1947 (c 42). See also COMPULSORY ACQUISITION AND COMPENSATION, vol 5, paras 36, 37, 56 ff.
9 Housing (Scotland) Act 1987, s 127(1)(a)–(c).
10 Ibid, s 127(2). Nothing in the Rent (Scotland) Act 1984 (c 58) or in the Housing (Scotland) Act 1988 (c 43), Pt II (ss 12–55) (assured tenancies), is deemed to affect these proceedings for possession: see the Housing (Scotland) Act 1987, s 128 (amended by the Housing (Scotland) Act 1988, s 72(2), Sch 9, para 13). For the impact on relations between landlords and tenants, see the Housing (Scotland) Act 1987, s 132(2), and cf *Beaney v Branchett* (1987) 19 HLR 471, [1987] 2 EGLR 115, CA.
11 Housing (Scotland) Act 1987, s 127(3).
12 See ibid, s 127(4), (5).
13 See ibid, s 127(6).

1989. Demolition of obstructive buildings. An obstructive building is one which, by reason only of its contact with, or proximity to, other buildings is injurious or dangerous to health[1]. The local authority may serve notice upon the owner of a building which appears to be an obstructive building, requiring inter alia a statement of the name and address of the superior and of any person holding a heritable security[2]. The owner and any such person are entitled to be heard when the authority considers the question of demolishing the building[3]. If the authority is satisfied that the building is indeed obstructive and that it ought to be demolished, it may pass a resolution accordingly[4]. Thereafter the same provisions relating to obtaining possession, imposing penalties for unlawful occupation and permitting appeals apply to such resolutions as they apply to demolition orders[5]. There is, however, an additional requirement imposed upon the authority that it be bound to purchase the building (and thereafter demolish it) if the owner offers to sell it[6]. This applies only if the offer is made before the expiry of the period within which vacation is required and the acquisition of the owner's interest would enable the authority, without a resolution, to demolish the building[7]. If no offer to sell is made within the prescribed period, the local authority must, as soon as may be, demolish the building[8]. It has the right to sell the materials[8].

1 Housing (Scotland) Act 1987 (c 26), s 125(6). This does not include a building which is the property of public undertakers unless used for the purposes of a dwelling, showroom or offices, or which is the property of a local authority: s 125(7). 'Public undertakers' means any corporation, company, body or person carrying on a railway, canal, inland navigation, dock, harbour, tramway, gas, electricity, water or other public undertaking: s 338(1).
2 Ibid, s 125(1), (2). Failure to provide information is an offence: see s 125(5).
3 Ibid, s 125(3).
4 Ibid, s 125(4).
5 Ibid, ss 127(1), 129(1)(b), 130(1): see paras 1986, 1988, above.
6 See ibid, s 126(1), (2). The offer to sell is to be at a price assessed by the Lands Tribunal for Scotland in accordance with the Land Compensation (Scotland) Act 1963 (c 51) (as modified by the Housing (Scotland) Act 1987, Sch 1) as if it were compensation for compulsory purchase: s 126(4). See COMPULSORY ACQUISITION AND COMPENSATION, vol 5, paras 105 ff.
7 Ibid, s 126(3).
8 Ibid, s 126(5).

(3) IMPROVEMENT ORDERS

1990. General. The power to make an improvement order was first introduced by the Housing (Financial Provisions) (Scotland) Act 1978[1] and is now contained in the Housing (Scotland) Act 1987. The power is exercisable where a local authority is satisfied that a house (outwith a housing action area[2]) does not meet the tolerable standard[3]. For these purposes, this includes a house which does not have a fixed bath or a shower[4]. If an authority is so satisfied, it may make an order requiring the owner of the house to improve the house by executing works (1) to bring it up to the tolerable standard, and (2) to put it into a good state of repair[5]. Where the authority is also satisfied that the house has a future life of not less than ten years, it may in addition require the execution of further works to ensure that the house will be provided with all the standard amenities[6]. The order must stipulate that the required works be completed within a period of 180 days[7] but, if they have not been completed within that period, and, if the authority either (a) considers that satisfactory progress has been made, or (b) has been given a written undertaking that the works will be completed by a date it considers satisfactory, it may amend the order to require completion of the works within a further period which it may determine[8].

1 Housing (Scotland) Act 1974 (c 45), s 14A (added by the Housing (Financial Provisions) (Scotland) Act 1978 (c 14), s 10, and amended by the Tenants' Rights Etc (Scotland) Act 1980 (c 52), ss 71, 72) (repealed).
2 As to housing action areas, see paras 1966 ff below.

3 Housing (Scotland) Act 1987 (c 26), s 88(1). As to the tolerable standard, see para 1979 above.
4 Ibid, s 88(2).
5 Ibid, s 88(1)(a), (b). As to the exclusion of houses controlled by the Crown, except with the consent of the appropriate authorities (usually the Crown Estate Commissioners or a government department), see s 105.
6 Ibid, s 88(1). For the standard amenities, see para 2023 below.
7 Ibid, s 88(1).
8 Ibid, s 88(3).

1991. Notices and appeals. Notice of the making of an improvement order must be served on (1) the person having control[1] of the house, (2) any other person who is an owner of the house, and (3) any person holding a heritable security over the house[2]. The same provision is made for improvement orders as it is for closing and demolition orders to enable a person aggrieved by an order to appeal to the sheriff[3].

1 As to the person having control, see the Housing (Scotland) Act 1987 (c 26), s 338(2).
2 Ibid, s 88(5), applying s 118(1)(a)–(c), for which see para 1985 above.
3 Ibid, s 88(6), applying s 129, for which see para 1986 above.

1992. Other provisions. To assist the owner of a house to comply with an improvement order, the local authority is obliged to make an improvement grant towards meeting the cost of the required works[1]. The owner may also apply to the authority for a loan. The rules governing the making of such a loan are the same as those which apply to loans on houses to be improved in housing action areas[2]. The authority also has the same general power to execute works of improvement by agreement with the owner and at his expense[3]. If, however, the works have not been completed by the owner within the prescribed period of 180 days (or such further period determined as above), the local authority may, to enable it to carry out the works itself, acquire the house by agreement or, by authority of the Secretary of State, compulsorily[4].

1 Housing (Scotland) Act 1987 (c 26), s 88(7). See also s 214(1)(d). As to improvement grants, see paras 2019 ff below.
2 Ibid, s 88(8), applying s 217(2)–(9), for which see para 2015 below.
3 Ibid, s 106.
4 Ibid, s 88(4), which also applies the Acquisition of Land (Authorisation Procedure) (Scotland) Act 1947 (c 42) in relation to any such compulsory purchase. See generally COMPULSORY ACQUISITION AND COMPENSATION, vol 5.

(4) REPAIR NOTICES

1993. General. Powers to enable local authorities to deal with individual houses in need of repair were conferred by the Housing (Scotland) Act 1969[1]. Now the power to serve a repair notice is contained in the Housing (Scotland) Act 1987. This power may be exercised where a local authority is satisfied that a house in its district is in a state of serious disrepair[2]. For these purposes 'house' includes a building which comprises not only a house or houses but also other premises[3]. If a local authority is of the opinion that a house, although not in a state of serious disrepair, is nevertheless in need of repair and likely to deteriorate rapidly or to cause material damage to another house if nothing is done to repair it, the authority may treat it as being in a state of serious disrepair[4]. A repair notice is to be served upon the person having control of the house[5], and must require that person to execute works necessary to rectify such defects as are specified within such period, being not less than twenty-one days, as is specified[6]. The notice must state that, in the authority's opinion, the rectification of the specified defects will bring the house up to such a standard of repair as is reasonable having regard to the age, character and location, but disregarding the internal decorative repair, of the house[7]. The power to serve a repair notice is stated to be without prejudice to any other powers of the authority or any legal remedy available to the tenant of a house against his landlord[8].

1 Housing (Scotland) Act 1969 (c 34), s 24 (repealed).
2 Housing (Scotland) Act 1987 (c 26), s 108(1). See also the related powers in the Building (Scotland) Act 1959 (c 24), s 13 (amended by the Local Government (Scotland) Act 1973 (c 65), s 134(2), Sch 15, para 10) (see BUILDING CONTROLS), and in the Civic Government (Scotland) Act 1982 (c 45), s 87 (amended by the Housing (Scotland) Act 1987, s 339(2), Sch 23, para 28) (see PUBLIC HEALTH, vol 19, para 351). As to the recovery of expenses, see the Civic Government (Scotland) Act 1982, s 108 (as so amended).
3 Housing (Scotland) Act 1987, s 108(8).
4 Ibid, s 108(7).
5 Ibid, s 108(1). As to the person having control, see s 338(2).
6 Ibid, s 108(2)(a).
7 Ibid, s 108(2)(b).
8 Ibid, s 108(6).

1994. Appeals. Any person aggrieved by a repair notice may appeal to the sheriff by giving notice of appeal within twenty-one days after the date of service of the notice, and no proceedings may be taken by the local authority to enforce the notice while an appeal is pending[1]. If no appeal is brought against a notice, it becomes operative on the expiration of twenty-one days after service, and is final and conclusive as to matters which might have been raised on appeal[2]. If there is an appeal, the notice, if and so far as it is confirmed by the sheriff, becomes operative from the date of the determination of the appeal[3].

1 Housing (Scotland) Act 1987 (c 26), s 111(1)(a). The grounds to be considered in an appeal under the corresponding English legislation were discussed in *Kenny v Kingston-upon-Thames Royal London Borough Council* (1985) 17 HLR 344, 274 EG 395, CA.
2 Housing (Scotland) Act 1987, s 112(a).
3 Ibid, s 112(b).

1995. Other provisions. A person served with a repair notice may apply to the local authority for a repairs grant and, if the application is duly made, the authority must approve the application so far as it relates to the execution of works required by the notice[1]. Additionally, where the person having control of the house is willing to carry out the works necessary to rectify the defects specified in the notice, he may, not later than twenty-one days after the date of service of the notice (or determination of an appeal) apply to the authority for a loan[2]. If an application is made, the same rules apply as they do to an application for a loan to meet the expenses of improvement in a housing action area (or pursuant to an improvement order)[3].

The authority may, by agreement with the owner of a house and at his expense, execute or arrange the execution of works of repair which the authority and owner agree are necessary or desirable[4]. Additionally, once the time specified in the notice (or a period of twenty-one days after the determination of an appeal, or longer period ordered by the sheriff) has expired, if the notice has not been complied with, the authority may itself execute the works required[5]. It may also execute further works found to be necessary for the purpose of bringing the house up to the required standard of repair but which could not reasonably have been ascertained to be required prior to the service of the notice[6]. Any question as to whether further works are necessary (or could not have been reasonably ascertained) is to be determined by the sheriff, whose decision is final[7]. Expenses incurred by the authority in executing works (together with interest) may be recovered from (1) the person having control of the house, or (2) if he receives the rent (for example in his capacity as trustee or agent) from some other person, from that other person, or (3) in part from one and in part from the other[8]. Provision is made for payment by instalments[9]. The local authority may make a charging order in respect of expenses incurred[10]. A person aggrieved may appeal to the sheriff against a demand for expenses, an order requiring payment by instalments, or a charging order[11]. In any such appeal, however, no question may be raised which might have been raised on an appeal against the original repair notice[12]. There is provision for the determination (with recourse to the sheriff if necessary) of the liability of a landlord whose tenant has borne the expense of compliance with a repair notice[13].

1 Housing (Scotland) Act 1987 (c 26), s 248(1): see para 2025 below.
2 Ibid, s 218(1). As to the person having control, see s 338(2).
3 Ibid, s 218(2), applying s 217(2)–(8), for which see para 2015 below.
4 Ibid, s 106.
5 Ibid, s 108(3)(a), (5).
6 Ibid, s 108(3)(b), (5).
7 Ibid, s 108(4). As to appeals where the sheriff's decision is final, see PROCEDURE, vol 17, para 1278.
8 Ibid, s 109(1)(a)–(c). As to the person having control, see s 338(2). As to apportionment of the expenses, see s 109(2). For problems in recovery from the 'owner' under the Civic Government (Scotland) Act 1982 (c 45), s 99, see *Purves v City of Edinburgh District Council* 1987 SLT 366.
9 See the Housing (Scotland) Act 1987, s 109(3).
10 See ibid, s 109(5), Sch 9.
11 Ibid, s 111(1)(b)–(d).
12 Ibid, s 111(2). In relation to a similar provision in the Edinburgh Corporation Order Confirmation Act 1967 (c v), see *City of Edinburgh District Council v Round and Robertson* 1987 SLT (Sh Ct) 117.
13 See the Housing (Scotland) Act 1987, s 110. See also ss 318, 319, which make obstruction of the officers of a local authority or of the Secretary of State or of the owner or his representatives or employees a criminal offence.

(5) HOUSING ACTION AREAS

1996. General. The powers and procedures relating to the treatment of sub-standard housing on an area basis are to be found in Part IV of the Housing (Scotland) Act 1987[1]. Local authorities may declare areas to be housing action areas — successors to the slum clearance areas and housing treatment areas of earlier legislation[2]. Resolutions declaring such areas are subject to procedural requirements both for the notification of those affected and for publication generally[3]. They are also subject to modification or veto by the Secretary of State. Once action areas are declared, housing authorities acquire new responsibilities within them — including powers to purchase and duties to give financial assistance for housing improvement.

There are three types of action areas. The first is the action area for demolition where the authority is satisfied that the houses (or the greater part of the houses) in the area do not meet the tolerable standard and that the most effective way of dealing with the area is by securing the demolition of all the building within it[4]. An action area for demolition cannot include the site of a building unless at least a part of the building consists of a house below the tolerable standard[5]. On the other hand, there may be excluded any part of a building in the area which is used for commercial (rather than residential) purposes[6]. In relation to a housing action area of any of the three types, a house which is subject to a closing order is deemed to be a house which does not meet the tolerable standard[7].

The second type of action area is the housing action area for improvement. Here the authority must be satisfied that the houses (or the greater part of the houses) in the area either lack one or more of the standard amenities or do not meet the tolerable standard and that the most effective way of dealing with the area is by ensuring their improvement[8]. An action area for improvement cannot include the site of building unless at least a part of the building consists of a house which is sub-standard in the sense that it either lacks one or more standard amenities or does not meet the tolerable standard or is not in a good state of repair (disregarding internal decorative repair) having regard to the age, character and locality of the house[9]. The authority has to specify a standard to be reached by houses in an action area for improvement[10]. This must require all houses both to meet the tolerable standard and to be in a good state of repair (as above) and, where the authority is satisfied that the houses in the area have a future life of not less than ten years, it may also specify that all houses are to be provided with all the standard amenities[11].

The third type of action area combines features of the first two and is the housing action area for demolition and improvement. This may be declared in the same conditions as for an area for improvement but where the authority is satisfied that the most effective way of dealing with it is by securing the demolition of some buildings but the improvement of others[12]. The same restrictions upon buildings which may be included (and the circumstances in which they may be demolished) and the same provisions as to the fixing of a standard of improvement apply as they do in the other types of area[13].

1 The Housing (Scotland) Act 1987 (c 26), Pt IV, comprises ss 85–107. See especially ss 89–93. Housing action areas, in their present form, were introduced by the Housing (Scotland) Act 1974 (c 45), Pt II (ss 13–36) (repealed).
2 See the Housing (Scotland) Act 1966 (c 49), Pt III (ss 34–57), and the Housing (Scotland) Act 1969 (c 34), ss 4–16 (all repealed).
3 See para 1997 below.
4 Housing (Scotland) Act 1987, s 89(1).
5 Ibid, s 89(2)(a). As to the tolerable standard, see para 1979 above.
6 Ibid, s 89(2)(b).
7 Ibid, s 89(3). As to closing orders, see para 1982 above.
8 Ibid, s 90(1). For the standard amenities, see para 2023 below.
9 Ibid, s 90(4).
10 Ibid, s 90(2).
11 Ibid, s 90(3).
12 Ibid, s 91(1).
13 See ibid, s 91(2)–(5).

1997. Procedure. The declaration of an action area of any type follows the same procedural pattern. The Housing (Scotland) Act 1987 requires, first, that a local authority, when considering whether to declare an action area, must have regard to any directions (general or particular) given by the Secretary of State with regard to the identification of suitable action areas[1]. Another way in which the Secretary of State may be involved at this stage is that he may, on the application of an authority and when satisfied that in all the circumstances it is reasonable to do so, direct that in relation to an action area for improvement, or for demolition and improvement, the requirement that the greater part of the houses be sub-standard may be waived[2].

The formal means by which an action area is initially declared is by draft resolution in such form as may be prescribed by the Secretary of State[3]. The draft resolution must specify, where appropriate, the standard of improvement to be attained in an area and must identify buildings which are to be demolished, houses which are to be improved to the specified standard, and houses forming part of a building which are below that standard and which require to be integrated with other parts of the building[4]. In each case the action area is also defined on a map[5]. There are special provisions which apply to listed buildings in housing action areas and also to the making of rehabilitation orders in relation to houses affected by clearance areas and housing treatment areas under earlier legislation[6].

As soon as may be after the passing of a draft resolution, it is to be submitted along with the map to the Secretary of State, who must acknowledge receipt of them in writing[7]. He is not obliged to take any further action but, if it appears to him appropriate to do so, he may, within twenty-eight days of his acknowledgment of receipt, either direct the authority to rescind the draft resolution, or notify the authority that he does not propose to direct rescission, or notify the authority that he requires a further period for consideration[8]. In that event he must direct the authority as soon as practicable thereafter to rescind the draft resolution or notify it of his intention not to require rescission[9]. If the authority is directed to rescind the draft resolution, it must do so as soon as may be after the Secretary of State's notification[10]. If, however, the authority is told that the Secretary of State is not proposing to direct rescission or if the period of twenty-eight days expires without notification from him, then the authority must publish in two or more newspapers circulating in the locality (including, if practicable, a local newspaper) a notice of the making of the draft resolution[11]. The notice must also name a place or places and times at which a copy of the resolution and the map may be inspected[11].

The authority must also serve on every owner, lessee and occupier of premises to which the draft resolution relates a notice stating the effect of the resolution[12]. The Secretary of State may prescribe the form, contents and manner of serving of such a notice[13]. The notice must, in any event, state that its recipient may, within two months of service, make respresentations to the authority concerning the draft resolution or its contents[14]. The authority must have regard to any such representations and must, within a further period of two months from the expiry of the first, either pass a final resolution confirming the draft with or without modifications (which may not extend the area defined in the resolution) or rescind the draft[15]. A final resolution must contain the same information as is required for a draft resolution, and the same requirements apply both as to general publicity and as to service of notice upon relevant owners, lessees and occupiers[16]. A copy of the resolution (with map) must be sent to the Secretary of State[17].

1 Housing (Scotland) Act 1987 (c 26), s 92(1).
2 Ibid, s 92(2).
3 Ibid, s 92(3); Housing (Forms) (Scotland) Regulations 1974, SI 1974/1982, Schedule, Forms 37, 47.
4 Housing (Scotland) Act 1987, s 92(4).
5 Ibid, ss 89(1), 90(1), 91(1).
6 See ibid, s 93, Sch 7 (amended by the Housing (Scotland) Act 1988 (c 43), s 72(1), Sch 7, para 28).
7 Housing (Scotland) Act 1987, s 94(1), (2).
8 Ibid, s 94(3)(a)–(c).
9 Ibid, s 94(3)(c).
10 Ibid, s 94(4).
11 Ibid, s 94(5)(a).
12 Ibid, s 94(5)(b). If appropriate names cannot, after reasonable inquiry, be ascertained, service may be upon the 'owner' etc or by affixing a notice or copy to a conspicuous part of the house: see s 95(1), Sch 8, para 2.
13 Ibid, s 94(6). See the Housing (Forms) (Scotland) Regulations 1974, Schedule, Forms 39, 49.
14 Housing (Scotland) Act 1987, s 94(7).
15 Ibid, Sch 8, paras 1, 2(1)–(3). For forms of final resolution, see the Housing (Forms) (Scotland) Regulations 1974, Schedule, Forms 40, 50.

16 Housing (Scotland) Act 1987, Sch 8, para 2(4), applying s 92. However, no notice of a final resolution may be served in respect of Crown property save with the consent of the Crown Estate Commissioners or the government department concerned: see s 105.

17 Ibid, Sch 8, para 2(3).

1998. Acquisition of land. One of the aims of the treatment of sub-standard housing by the declaration of a housing action area is to provide the local authority with enlarged powers of land acquisition. These begin at the point when the statutory notice of the making of the draft resolution has been published and served. The authority has the power thereafter to purchase land by agreement in the area to which the resolution relates in order to undertake or otherwise secure the demolition or improvement of the affected houses or buildings[1]. This power to purchase extends to another part of a building if it is identified as necessary for the integration of parts of a building mentioned above[2]. It also extends to any land surrounded by or adjoining the action area if the acquisition is reasonably necessary for the purpose of securing an area of convenient shape and dimensions or is reasonably necessary for the satisfactory development or use of the action area[3]. The power to acquire land in an action area for demolition, or for improvement and demolition, is not restricted by the fact that buildings within the area have been demolished since the declaration of the housing action area[4]. Acquisition by agreement for the purposes of housing action areas takes place under the general powers local authorities have to acquire land by agreement[5].

The authority may also be authorised by the Secretary of State to purchase land compulsorily for the same purposes as purchase by agreement[6]. Where notice of a final resolution declaring an action area has been published and served, a compulsory purchase order must be submitted to the Secretary of State for his consideration within six months in the case of an action area for demolition and within nine months (and not less than three months) in the case of an area for improvement or demolition and improvement[7]. The Secretary of State may allow periods longer than the six and nine months as he thinks appropriate[8]. Otherwise the compulsory acquisition of land within an action area follows the standard rules of the Acquisition of Land (Authorisation Procedure) (Scotland) Act 1947 with necessary modifications[9]. The principal adjustments to that standard procedure are that different forms for that order and associated notices are to be prescribed; the order must identify houses in the action area which do not meet the tolerable standard (or which do not meet the standard specified) and the land proposed to be purchased outside the area; the order may not, if confirmed by the Secretary of State, with modifications, authorise purchase on less favourable terms than if no modification had been made; and the Secretary of State may modify the order to exclude any land if of the opinion that it ought not to have been included in the action area[10]. Separate provision is made for the extinction of rights of way and also in relation to the apparatus of public undertakers[11].

An authority which has purchased land in connection with a housing action area may thereafter dispose of it. If the land was purchased for the purpose of bringing houses up to a specified standard of improvement, any such house may be sold or leased subject to the condition that the house be brought up to that standard and any other restriction or condition the authority thinks fit[12]. Other land may be sold or leased (again subject to such restrictions or conditions as the authority thinks fit), or it may be appropriated by the authority for any purpose for which it is authorised to acquire land[13].

1 Housing (Scotland) Act 1987 (c 26), s 95(2), Sch 8, para 3(1).

2 Ibid, Sch 8, para 3(2).

3 Ibid, Sch 8, para 4.

4 Ibid, Sch 8, para 5(1).
5 Ibid, Sch 8, para 5(2), applying the Local Government (Scotland) Act 1973 (c 65), s 70, for which see LOCAL GOVERNMENT, vol 14, para 316.
6 Housing (Scotland) Act 1987, Sch 8, para 5(3).
7 Ibid, Sch 8, para 5(4)(a), (b).
8 Ibid, Sch 8, para 5(4).
9 Housing (Scotland) Act 1987, Sch 8, para 5(3): see COMPULSORY ACQUISITION AND COMPENSATION, vol 5. For the right to rehousing, see s 98.
10 See ibid, Sch 8, para 5(3)(a)–(h).
11 See ibid, Sch 8, paras 9, 10.
12 Ibid, Sch 8, para 8(a).
13 Ibid, Sch 8, para 8(b), by reference to the Local Government (Scotland) Act 1973, s 73, for which see LOCAL GOVERNMENT, vol 14, para 319.

1999. Other action area provisions. Where a local authority owns land (whether by purchase or otherwise belonging to it) in a housing action area on which there are buildings which, under the resolution, are required to be demolished, the authority may postpone demolition if the building is, or contains, a house which in the authority's opinion must be continued in use as housing accommodation for the time being[1]. The authority must carry out such works on such a building as are in its opinion from time to time required for rendering or keeping the house capable of being continued in use as housing accommodation pending its demolition[2].

Otherwise, however, it is important that the authority has powers to control the occupation of certain houses within a housing action area. Once it has received notification from the Secretary of State that he is not to require rescission, or the statutory twenty-eight-day period has elapsed, the authority may make an order prohibiting the occupation of houses identified for demolition or integration except with its consent[3]. Such an order must be followed within twenty-eight days by the service of notice in the prescribed form (in relation to each relevant house) upon the person having control of the house and any other person who is an owner or occupier of the house[4]. The notice must state that the order has been made and indicate its effect[4]. The prohibition on occupation does not apply to a person occupying the house on the date of the service of the notice[5], but any other person who occupies or permits to be occupied a house included in the order is guilty of an offence and liable, on summary conviction, to a fine not exceeding level 5 on the standard scale or to imprisonment for up to three months or both[6]. In the case of a continuing offence, a further fine may be imposed of £5 per day (or part day) of occupation of the house[6].

Where an owner or person having control of a house considers that it is unreasonable in all the circumstances that the order should continue to apply to the house he may apply to the authority to revoke the order in respect of that house, failing which he may appeal to the sheriff within twenty-one days of the authority's refusal[7]. A control order ceases to have effect if revoked; if the draft resolution is rescinded or if the final resolution changes the house into a house of improvement rather than demolition; or if the Secretary of State refuses to confirm or modifies a compulsory purchase order in relation to the house[8].

More positively, in the case of houses designated for improvement in an action area, improvement and repairs grants are available at enhanced levels[9]. In addition the authority may be obliged to offer loans to meet the expenses of improvement. An owner or lessee willing to carry out improvement works required to bring a house up to the specified standard may apply to the authority for a loan within nine months of the final resolution[10]. If the authority is satisfied that the applicant can reasonably be expected to meet the obligations of a loan, the authority must offer a loan of the amount applied for (or a smaller amount) up to the estimated value of the house as improved[11]. The loan is to be secured by a standard security[11] and must be made subject to the condition that the amount lent be reduced in the light of the making of an improvement or repairs grant[12]. On the other hand, an authority must not offer a loan at all unless satisfied (1) that the applicant's estate or interest in the house amounts to ownership or a lease extending beyond the date for final repayment, and (2) that the principal of the loan does not exceed the improved value of the subjects secured[13]. The rate of interest on any loan is the variable rate applicable to other forms of local authority home loan[14]. Subject to the provisions above, a loan is to be subject to such reasonable terms as the authority may offer[15]. These may include those relating to repayment (by instalments and otherwise) specified for home loans in general[16].

An authority may by agreement with the owner of a house and at his expense execute required works of improvement or repair[17].

In some cases, notice of an action area resolution given to a landlord will affect his tenants. If an owner of a house is willing to comply with a notice requiring demolition, works of integration or improvement but his tenant is unwilling to give up possession or, as the case may be, to consent to works or to a temporary evacuation of the premises, the landlord may apply to the sheriff for an appropriate order, which may be made subject to such conditions as the sheriff thinks just and reasonable[18]. Nothing in the Rent (Scotland) Act 1984 (c 58) or in the assured tenancies provisions of the Housing (Scotland) Act 1988[19] is to restrict an order for possession which may be made by the sheriff[20]. If the sheriff refuses to make any order applied for, this does not affect the validity of the housing authority's resolution[21].

1 Housing (Scotland) Act 1987 (c 26), s 96(1).
2 Ibid, s 96(2). Otherwise the authority has the same powers and duties as are conferred by Pt I (ss 1–23) (provision of housing: see paras 1905 ff above): s 96(3).
3 Ibid, s 97(1). As to the notification and the twenty-eight-day period, see s 94(3) and para 1997 above.
4 Ibid, s 97(2). For the form of notice, see the Housing (Forms) (Scotland) Regulations 1974, SI 1974/1982, Schedule, Form 76.
5 Housing (Scotland) Act 1987, s 97(3).
6 Ibid, s 97(4). As to level 5, see para 1931, note 5, above.
7 Ibid, s 97(5), (6).
8 Ibid, s 97(7).
9 See paras 2031, 2032, below.
10 Housing (Scotland) Act 1987, s 217(1).
11 Ibid, s 217(2), (3).
12 Ibid, s 217(4).
13 Ibid, s 217(5)(a), (b).
14 Ibid, s 217(6): see s 219, and para 2013 below.
15 Ibid, s 217(7).
16 See ibid, s 217(8), Sch 17, paras 4–7.
17 Ibid, s 106.
18 See ibid, ss 99–102.
19 See the Housing (Scotland) Act 1988 (c 43), Pt II (ss 12–55).
20 Housing (Scotland) Act 1987, s 103 (amended by the Housing (Scotland) Act 1988, s 72(2), Sch 9, para 12).
21 Housing (Scotland) Act 1987, s 104.

7. OVERCROWDING

2000. Introduction. Since they were first imposed in the nineteenth century[1], statutory restrictions upon overcrowding have been used in efforts to improve housing conditions. Now contained in Part VII of the Housing (Scotland) Act

1987[2], they should be seen as accompanying other parts of the housing code and, in particular, Part VIII of the Act relating to multiple occupation[3]. The principal purpose of Part VII is to define 'overcrowding' and then to create criminal offences which are committed by certain occupiers of houses who cause or permit overcrowding. Subsidiary offences may be committed by landlords. Some responsibilities for monitoring and enforcement are given to local authorities[4].

1 See eg the inclusion within the definition of 'nuisance' in the Public Health (Scotland) Act 1867 (c 101), s 16(f) (repealed), of 'Any house or part of a house so overcrowded as to be dangerous or injurious to the health of the inmates'. This was repeated in the Public Health (Scotland) Act 1897 (c 38), s 16(7): see PUBLIC HEALTH, vol 19, para 336.

2 The Housing (Scotland) Act 1987 (c 26), Pt VII, comprises ss 135–151.

3 Ibid, Pt VIII, comprises ss 152–190: see paras 2004 ff below. As there noted, the legislation relating to multiple occupation and, therefore, more broadly, to overcrowding, was at the end of 1989 under review by the Scottish Development Department.

4 The relevance of overcrowding to the determination of homelessness (see para 2049 below) and to the general process of house allocation by local authorities (see para 1935 above) should also be borne in mind.

2001. Meaning of 'overcrowding'. For the purposes of the Housing (Scotland) Act 1987, 'overcrowding' is defined by reference to the number of persons sleeping in a house[1]. For overcrowding to occur, that number of persons must contravene either 'the room standard' or 'the space standard'[2]. The room standard is straightforward and is contravened when the number of persons sleeping in a house and the number of rooms available as sleeping accommodation is such that two persons of opposite sexes (other than children under the age of ten)[3] who are not living together as husband and wife must sleep in the same room[4]. The space standard (which also combines within it a 'room standard') is contravened when the number of persons sleeping in a house is in excess of the permitted number, having regard to the number and floor area of the rooms of the house available as sleeping accommodation[5]. The permitted number of persons (for which purpose children under the age of one do not count and those aged one or over but under ten are reckoned as one-half[6]) is whichever is the less of (1) a specified number[7] in relation to the number of rooms available as sleeping accommodation, and (2) the aggregate for all such rooms of specified numbers in relation to each room of a specified floor area[8]. The Secretary of State may prescribe inter alia the means of calculating floor areas[9], and may increase by order the permitted number of persons temporarily[10].

1 The definition of 'house' for these purposes has recently been changed. 'House' is defined in the Housing (Scotland) Act 1987 (c 26), s 151(1), as meaning 'any premises used or intended to be used as a separate dwelling, *not being premises which are entered in the valuation roll last authenticated at a rateable value exceeding £45*'. The italicised words, criticised in particular for their retention of the reliance on the much outdated rateable value and their possible incorporation into the definition now contained in s 24(3)(d) and in ss 31, 32, concerned homelessness (see paras 2068–2070 below), were repealed by the Housing (Scotland) Act 1988 (c 43), s 72(1), (3), Sch 8, para 3, Sch 10.

2 Housing (Scotland) Act 1987, s 135.

3 Ibid, s 136(2)(a).

4 Ibid, s 136(1). A room is defined as available as sleeping accommodation if it is of a type normally used in the locality either as a bedroom or as a living room: s 136(2)(b).

5 Ibid, s 137(1). A room is defined as available as sleeping accommodation if it is of a type normally used in the locality either as a living room or as a bedroom: s 137(2)(b).

6 Ibid, s 137(2)(a).

7 Ie, for one room, two persons; for two rooms, three persons; for three rooms, five persons; for four rooms, seven and one-half persons; and for five or more rooms, two persons for each room: ibid, s 137(3), Table I. A room with a floor area of less than 50 sq ft does not count as a room: s 137(3).

8 Ibid, s 137(3)(a), (b). The specified room floor areas and number of persons are, for 110 sq ft or more, two persons; for 90 sq ft or more but less than 110 sq ft, one and one-half persons; for 70 sq ft or more but less than 70 sq ft, one person; and for 50 sq ft or more but less than 70 sq ft, one-half person: s 137(3), Table II. A room with a floor area of less than 50 sq ft does not count as a room: s 137(3).

9 Ibid, s 137(4), (5): see the Housing (Computation of Floor Area) (Scotland) Regulations 1935, SR & O 1935/912.

10 See the Housing (Scotland) Act 1987, s 138.

2002. Offences. The occupier of a house who causes or permits it to be overcrowded after an appointed day is guilty of an offence[1]. To this general rule are exceptions which apply (1) in certain circumstances where the overcrowding occurs simply by reason of a child attaining the age of one or ten; (2) in relation to temporary visitors; (3) where a licence to exceed the normal limit has been granted in exceptional circumstances by the local authority; or (4) where the local authority has by resolution authorised higher levels of occupation to provide a seasonal increase of holiday visitors in the area[2]. The landlord of a house is guilty of an offence if after an appointed day he lets or agrees to let it to any person without giving the person a written statement in a prescribed form of the permitted number of persons in relation to the house[3]. On the other hand, if the occupier is guilty of an offence because of overcrowding, nothing in the Rent (Scotland) Act 1984 (c 58) or in the assured tenancies provisions of the Housing (Scotland) Act 1988[4] prevents the landlord from obtaining possession[5]. Furthermore, the local authority may, in the same circumstances, take the same steps, following notice to the landlord, to terminate the tenancy as the landlord is entitled to take[6].

1 Housing (Scotland) Act 1987 (c 26), s 139(1). An offender is liable on summary conviction to a fine not exceeding level 1 on the standard scale: s 139(3). Level 1 is £50: Increase of Criminal Penalties etc (Scotland) Order 1984, SI 1984/526, art 4. This offence takes place and can be committed only after a day appointed in a statutory instrument for the locality by the Secretary of State under the Housing (Scotland) Act 1966 (c 49), s 99, or earlier legislation: Housing (Scotland) Act 1987, s 151(2) (amended by the Housing (Scotland) Act 1988 (c 43), s 72(1), Sch 7, para 6), the terms of which preclude the appointment of new days after the repeal of the 1966 Act by the Housing (Scotland) Act 1987, s 339(3), Sch 24. There is some uncertainty about the extent (if any) to which days were appointed under the 1966 Act and preceding legislation, and, with the reorganisation of local government under the Local Government (Scotland) Act 1973 (c 65), as to their territorial effect.

2 Housing (Scotland) Act 1987, s 139(2) (amended by the Housing (Scotland) Act 1988, Sch 7, para 5), by reference to the Housing (Scotland) Act 1987, ss 140–143.

3 Ibid, s 144(1), and s 151(2) (as amended: see note 1 above). As to the appointed day, see note 1 above. For the form of statement, see the Housing (Forms) (Scotland) Regulations 1974, SI 1974/1982, Schedule, Form 22. An offender is liable on summary conviction to a fine not exceeding level 1 on the standard scale: Housing (Scotland) Act 1987, s 144(2).

4 Ie the Housing (Scotland) Act 1988, Pt II (ss 12–55).

5 Housing (Scotland) Act 1987, s 145(a) (amended by the Housing (Scotland) Act 1988, s 72(2), Sch 9, para 14).

6 Housing (Scotland) Act 1987, s 145(b).

2003. Powers and duties of local authorities. In addition to the responsibilities for the avoidance of overcrowding which are imposed directly upon occupiers and landlords, certain related powers and duties (though little invoked in practice) are given to local authorities. These include duties of inspection of their districts to identify overcrowded houses[1]; the power to require, on pain of prosecution, information from occupiers of houses as to the number, ages and sexes of the persons sleeping there[2]; the duty to inform landlords and occupiers of the permitted number of persons[3] and to publish information generally for the assistance of landlords and occupiers as to their rights and duties relating to overcrowding[4]; and the duty to enforce the overcrowding provisions[5].

1 Housing (Scotland) Act 1987 (c 26), s 146(1). The inspection must be made at such time as the local authority considers necessary or as the Secretary of State directs (s 146(2), (6)), and must be followed by a report to the Secretary of State (s 146(3)–(5)).

2 Ibid, s 147(1). An occupier who defaults in complying, or who gives false information, is liable on summary conviction to a fine not exceeding level 1 on the standard scale (for which see para 2002, note 1, above): s 147(2).

3 Ibid, s 148.

4 Ibid, s 149.

5 Ibid, s 150.

8. HOUSES IN MULTIPLE OCCUPATION

2004. General. Complementing in some respects the provisions of Part VII (overcrowding)[1], Part VIII of the Housing (Scotland) Act 1987[2] is concerned with what the title of the Part calls 'Houses in Multiple Occupation'. This is not, however, a term used in the text of the Act itself[3]. Although Part VIII appears to be quite substantial, its provisions are not widely used in practice and they will, therefore, be reviewed very selectively[4]. This contrasts with the position in England and Wales where the equivalent provisions in Part XI of the Housing Act 1985 are more frequently involved[5].

1 The Housing (Scotland) Act 1987 (c 26), Pt VII, comprises ss 135–151: see paras 2000 ff above.

2 Ibid, Pt VIII, comprises ss 152–190.

3 See eg ibid, s 152(1), and para 2005 below. See also the related but not identical definition used in s 171(1) and referred to in para 2006, note 1, below. For convenience, the term 'house in multiple occupation' is used in the paragraphs which follow.

4 As with overcrowding, not all legislation which relates to houses in multiple occupation is contained within housing law as such. For instance, potentially significant powers are conferred on local authorities by the Public Health (Scotland) Act 1897 (c 38), ss 72, 92, to make byelaws relating to houses in multiple occupation and common lodging houses: see PUBLIC HEALTH, vol 19, paras 467, 472. The power to make byelaws under s 72 is extended by the Housing (Scotland) Act 1987, s 313. A recent review of both law and policy in this area is contained in a Scottish Development Department consultation paper of 25 July 1988, *Houses in Multiple Occupation*.

5 The Housing Act 1985 (c 68), Pt XI, comprises ss 345–400. Some, at least, of the difficulties (see eg para 2006, note 1, below) to be encountered in the application of Part VIII of the Housing (Scotland) Act 1987 may be ascribed to its most inelegant adoption into the law of Scotland. Its provisions originally applied only to England and Wales and were contained in the Housing Act 1961 (c 65), ss 12–23 (repealed). It was only by virtue of the Housing Act 1964 (c 56), s 71 (repealed), that they were, with modifications, applied to Scotland.

2005. Registration schemes. The first group of provisions enable a local authority to make and submit to the Secretary of State for confirmation a registration scheme authorising the authority to compile and maintain a register for its district[1]. Such a register is to be of (1) houses which, or a part of which, are let in lodgings, or which are occupied by members of more than one family[2]; and (2) buildings which comprise separate dwellings, two or more of which lack either or both of (a) a sanitary convenience accessible only to those living in the dwelling, and (b) personal washing facilities so accessible[3]. The Secretary of State may, if he thinks fit, confirm the scheme, with or without modification[4]. Public notice must be given both of an authority's intention to submit a registration scheme and, if the scheme is confirmed, of that confirmation[5]. Once a scheme is in operation the authority acquires powers to require the provision of information relevant to the registration process[6].

1 See the Housing (Scotland) Act 1987 (c 26), ss 152–155. For the meaning of 'local authority', see para 1903 above.

2 Ibid, s 152(1)(a). As to members of a family, see para 1935, note 4, above.
3 Ibid, s 152(1)(b). It appears that 'personal washing facilities' may include a hot water supply: see *McPhail v Islington London Borough Council* [1970] 2 QB 197, [1970] 1 All ER 1004, CA.
4 Housing (Scotland) Act 1987, s 152(1). For subsidiary provisions, see s 152(2)–(5). As to proof of the scheme, see s 154.
5 Ibid, s 153.
6 Ibid, s 155.

2006. Management code. If it appears to a local authority that a house in multiple occupation is in an unsatisfactory state in consequence of failure to maintain proper standards of management, the authority may invoke the terms of regulations known as the 'management code' and apply them to the house[1]. The regulations themselves are made by the Secretary of State and may make provision for the purpose of ensuring that the person managing a house[2] to which they are applied observes proper standards, including standards of repair, maintenance, cleansing and good order of water supply and drainage, roof and windows, common staircases, yards and gardens[3]. The regulations may, inter alia, make different provision for different types of house, impose duties on owners, occupiers and others and authorise the local authority to obtain information as to numbers of people accommodated in a house[4]. To apply the code to a particular house, the authority makes an order to that effect, after not less than twenty-one days' notice of its intention to do so[5]. Once made, the order takes immediate effect[6], and a copy must be served on the owner and any known lessee[7]. Any such person may appeal to the sheriff on the ground that the order was unnecessary[8]. A person who knowingly contravenes or without reasonable excuse fails to comply with the code is guilty of an offence punishable with a fine not exceeding level 3 on the standard scale[9].

1 Housing (Scotland) Act 1987 (c 26), s 157(1). A house in multiple occupation is defined for these purposes in language almost identical to that used in s 152(1) (see para 2005 above), save that it is extended to include also a building which is not a house but comprises separate dwellings, two or more of which are wholly or partly let in lodgings or occupied by members of more than one family: s 171(1). The definitions in ss 152(1), 171(1) (and also in s 172) raise potentially acute problems (largely avoided by the lack of use in practice made of these sections) of the interpretation of 'house', 'building', 'dwelling', 'tenement' and 'flat'.
2 This is normally the owner or lessee who receives rent from tenants or lodgers: see s 156(5). See also ss 176, 177.
3 Ibid, s 156(1), (2)(a)–(f). See the Housing (Management of Houses and Buildings in Multiple Occupation) (Scotland) Regulations 1964, SI 1964/1371.
4 See the Housing (Scotland) Act 1987, s 156(3).
5 Ibid, s 157(2).
6 Ibid, s 157(3). An order applying the management code, and a notice revoking the order, must each be recorded in the General Register of Sasines or registered in the Land Register of Scotland: s 159.
7 Ibid, s 157(4).
8 Ibid, s 158(1). An appeal also lies against a refusal to revoke an order (a power available to an authority under s 157(5)): s 158(4).
9 Ibid, s 156(4). Level 3 is £400: Increase of Criminal Penalties etc (Scotland) Order 1984, SI 1984/526, art 4. It has been explained in *City of Westminster v Mavroghenis* (1983) 11 HLR 56, DC, that (in the equivalent (English) Housing Act 1985 (c 68), s 369(5)) two separate criminal offences are created. There is no requirement to establish knowledge of the regulation in order to secure a conviction under the second head. See also *Wandsworth London Borough v Sparling* (1987) 20 HLR 169, DC, where it was held that the owner of a house in multiple occupation was not the manager, since the rents were being received directly by the local authority.

2007. Powers to require works. Another consequence of the application of the management code to a particular house is that if, in the opinion of the local authority, the condition of the house is defective in consequence of neglect to comply with the code[1], the authority may serve on the person managing the house[2] a notice specifying works required to make good the neglect within a specified period of not less than twenty-one days[3]. Two further related powers to require works may be invoked even though the management code has not been applied to the house concerned. The first is a general power to require a house in multiple occupation to comply with standards corresponding to those which may be applied by the management code where the house is considered so defective (in respect of any such standard, having regard to the number of individuals or households accommodated) as not to be reasonably suitable for occupation[4]. The other, more specific, power is that of serving a notice specifying works required to provide a means of escape from fire where it appears to the authority that such a means of escape is necessary[5]. This power should be considered alongside the important right to improvement grants for the provision of fire escapes[6]. An appeal lies to the sheriff, on specified grounds, against the service of any of these three types of notice[7]. Failing compliance with a notice requiring works, the local authority is empowered to carry out the works itself, with an accompanying power to recover expenses[8]. The final means of enforcement is by prosecution. Wilful failure to comply with a notice is punishable by a fine not exceeding level 3 on the standard scale, or level 4 for fire escape notices[9].

1 Housing (Scotland) Act 1987 (c 26), s 160(1)(a). This includes neglect to comply with corresponding standards during a period prior to the application of the code to the house: s 160(1)(b).
2 As to the person managing the house, see para 2006, note 2, above.
3 Housing (Scotland) Act 1987, s 160(1), (3). As to service of the notice where the identity of the person managing the house cannot be established, see s 160(2).
4 See ibid, s 161. Provisions similar to those in s 160 govern matters of service etc.
5 See ibid, s 162.
6 See ibid, s 249, and para 2028 below.
7 See ibid, s 163. For discussion of the equivalent provision of the Housing Act 1985 (c 68), s 367, see *Berg v Trafford Borough Council* (1988) 20 HLR 47, CA.
8 See the Housing (Scotland) Act 1987, s 164.
9 See ibid, s 165. Levels 3 and 4 are £400 and £1000: Increase of Criminal Penalties etc (Scotland) Order 1984, SI 1984/526, art 4.

2008. Overcrowding and general. In addition to the powers so far described (and apart from the power to make control orders[1]), the Housing (Scotland) Act 1987 contains a number of further provisions concerning houses in multiple occupation. The most important group of provisions enable a local authority (subject to appeal to the sheriff[2]) to give directions to prevent or reduce overcrowding[3]. The authority may fix a limit to the number of individuals who may live in a house[4], with breach of the limit punishable by fine[5]. In addition, authorities are given powers to obtain warrants for entry into premises to carry out their powers in relation to houses in multiple occupation[6].

1 See para 2009 below.
2 See the Housing (Scotland) Act 1987 (c 26), s 170.
3 See ibid, ss 166, 167. As to the power to require information, see s 168, and as to the revocation and variation of directions, see s 169. These powers may be invoked even though the occupation of the premises by the people living there is only temporary: *Thrasyvoulou v Hackney London Borough* (1986) 18 HLR 370, CA (interpreting the similar but not identical provisions of the (English) Housing Act 1985 (c 68), Pt XI (ss 345–400)).
4 Housing (Scotland) Act 1987, s 166(1).
5 Ibid, s 166(5).
6 Ibid, s 173 (amended by the Housing (Scotland) Act 1988 (c 43), s 72(1), Sch 7, para 7). Obstruction is a criminal offence: see the Housing (Scotland) Act 1987, ss 318, 319.

2009. Control orders. The most stringent of the measures available to local authorities is the control order. Such an order may be made in relation to a house in respect of which either (1) a notice has been served requiring the execution of works[1] (other than for a fire escape), or (2) a direction limiting the number of occupants[2] has been given, or (3) an order[3] applying the management code is in force, or (4) it appears that the state or condition of the house is such as to call for the taking of any such form of action, and, in all cases, it appears that living conditions in the house are such that it is necessary to make the control order in order to protect the safety, welfare or health of persons living in the house[4]. Provision is made for the service of copies of the order and an accompanying notice on, inter alia, a person managing or having control of the house and the owner[5]. There is a right of appeal, on specified grounds, to the sheriff[6], but otherwise an order comes into force when made and the authority is required to take steps pursuant to the order as soon as is practicable thereafter[7]. It must similarly cause the control order to be recorded in the General Register of Sasines or registered in the Land Register of Scotland[8]. The general effect of a control order, once it is in force (until revoked on appeal or on the initiative of the authority or on the expiry of five years[9]) is to give the authority the right to possession of the premises and then the right to do and to authorise others to do anything which a person having an estate or interest in the premises would be entitled to do[10]. Further provision is made to govern the detailed consequences of this comprehensive form of local authority intervention. In outline, the rights and liabilities of occupants of the house continue unaffected but with the local authority substituted for the lessor[11]; the authority is obliged to maintain proper standards of management and to take action needed to remedy defects (against which it would, the control order apart, have taken other forms of enforcement action)[12]; a management scheme must be prepared[13]; and compensation becomes payable to dispossessed proprietors[14].

1 Ie the Housing (Scotland) Act 1987 (c 26), s 160 or s 161: see para 2007 above.
2 Ie under ibid, s 166: see para 2008 above.
3 Ie under ibid, s 157: see para 2006 above.
4 Ibid, s 178(1)(a)–(d). For a discussion of these grounds and their relationship to a subsequent compulsory purchase order, see *R v Secretary of State for the Environment, ex parte Royal Borough of Kensington and Chelsea* (1987) 19 HLR 161.
5 Housing (Scotland) Act 1987, s 178(4), (5).
6 See ibid, s 186. As an important example of an attempt (albeit unsuccessful) to use judicial review proceedings to challenge a control order in the English courts, see *R v Southwark London Borough, ex parte Lewis Levy Ltd* (1983) 8 HLR 1, [1984] JPL 105.
7 Housing (Scotland) Act 1987, s 178(3).
8 Ibid, s 178(6).
9 See ibid, ss 187, 188.
10 See ibid, s 179 (amended by the Housing (Scotland) Act 1988 (c 43), s 72(1), Sch 7, para 8).
11 See the Housing (Scotland) Act 1987, s 180 (amended by the Housing (Scotland) Act 1988, s 72(2), Sch 9, para 16).
12 See the Housing (Scotland) Act 1987, s 182.
13 See ibid, s 184, Sch 11.
14 See ibid, s 183.

9. HOUSE LOANS AND OTHER FINANCIAL ASSISTANCE

2010. Introduction. Part XII of the Housing (Scotland) Act 1987[1] has brought together a number of different powers (and in some cases duties) enabling local authorities (and other bodies) to assist in the financing of private sector housing. Some involve the making of loans; some concern other forms of financial assistance. Some powers are cast in quite general terms. Others are related to specific action taken by an authority as a part of its statutory housing functions.

1 The Housing (Scotland) Act 1987 (c 26), Pt XII, comprises ss 214–235.

2011. General. A local authority has a general power to advance money to any person for the purpose of (1) acquiring a house; (2) constructing a house; (3) converting another building into a house or acquiring a building for conversion; (4) altering, enlarging, repairing or improving a house; or (5) facilitating the repayment of the amount outstanding on a previous loan made for the above purposes[1]. In this last case, the authority must be satisfied that the primary effect of an advance would be to meet the housing needs of the applicant by enabling him either to retain an interest in the house or to carry out works eligible for an advance under head (3) or head (4)[2]. In all cases the power to make advances applies to houses or buildings whether or not they are in the area of the authority[3]. An authority must have regard to advice given from time to time by the Secretary of State[4]. Before advancing money for the purpose of acquiring a house, the local authority must, in any event, be satisfied that the house will meet the tolerable standard[5].

1 Housing (Scotland) Act 1987 (c 26), s 214(1)(a)–(e). References in s 214 to a house (defined in para 1901 above) include references to any part share of it: s 214(7). For the meaning of 'local authority', see para 1903 above.
2 Ibid, s 214(4).
3 Ibid, s 214(2).
4 Ibid, s 214(3). General advice was given in Scottish Development Department Circular 29/1980.
5 Housing (Scotland) Act 1987, s 215(1). The same applies in relation to houses to be constructed, altered, improved etc: s 215(2). As to the tolerable standard, see para 1979 above.

2012. Conditions relating to house loans. A number of general conditions apply to loans made under the powers discussed in the previous paragraph[1]. These include the requirements that an advance is to be preceded by a valuation on behalf of the local authority[2]; that the advance with interest thereon is to be secured by a heritable security[3]; and that the amount of the principal is not to exceed the value of the subjects (after improvement, where applicable)[4]. Repayment may be by instalment or by lump sum[5].

Attempts have been made by some borrowers who have encountered difficulties following purchase of their houses to ascribe liability to the lending local authority. In *Hadden v City of Glasgow District Council*[6], however, the purchasers were unsuccessful in their claim that the council owed them a duty of care and were liable for the defects and extensive building repairs which were subsequently required. Similarly, in *Vaughan v City of Edinburgh District Council*[7], the purchaser was unsuccessful in proceedings based on delict and misrepresentation when the house which was the subject of the loan was shortly included within the scope of a housing action area for demolition declared by the lending authority itself. There was no duty on the council to volunteer information in relation to planning proposals which might affect the house.

1 See the Housing (Scotland) Act 1987 (c 26), s 214(8), Sch 17.
2 Ibid, Sch 17, para 9.
3 Ibid, Sch 17, para 2.
4 Ibid, Sch 17, para 3.
5 Ibid, Sch 17, para 4.
6 *Hadden v City of Glasgow District Council* 1986 SLT 557, OH.
7 *Vaughan v City of Edinburgh District Council* 1988 SLT 191, OH.

2013. Rates of interest. Since new arrangements were introduced by the Tenants' Rights Etc (Scotland) Act 1980[1], all advances under the powers discussed above[2] are variable interest home loans[3]. In respect of such loans, a local authority must normally[4] charge a rate of interest equal to the higher of (1) the standard rate for the time being declared by the Secretary of State (who, when he declares the rate, must take into account rates charged by building societies in the United Kingdom and any movement in these rates[5]) and (2) the locally determined rate[6]. That rate is determined by the local authority for six-month periods and is the rate necessary to service loan charges on money to be applied to home loans during each six-month period plus one-quarter per cent to cover administration costs[7]. Provision is made for the service by the authority of notice to the borrower of any change in interest rates to be charged[8].

1 See the Tenants' Rights Etc (Scotland) Act 1980 (c 52), s 30 (repealed).
2 See para 2011 above.
3 Housing (Scotland) Act 1987 (c 26), s 219(1)(a). The same applies (1) to other powers to make loans for like purposes; (2) to sums secured, on the sale of a house by a local authority (see para 2014 below), by a standard security; and (3) to sums secured under any security taken over under s 229 from a building society (see para 2017 below): s 219(1)(a)–(c). The rules do not affect the power to make the interest-free loans described in para 2016 below.
4 This is subject to an overriding power of the Secretary of State to direct that a different rate be paid, if he considers that an authority is charging the wrong rate: see ibid, s 221.
5 Ibid, s 219(5).
6 Ibid, s 219(4)(a), (b).
7 Ibid, s 219(6), (7).
8 See ibid, s 220.

2014. Loans to tenants exercising their right to buy. An essential component of a tenant's right to purchase his house from a public sector landlord[1] is his entitlement to a loan to assist the purchase. Whenever a tenant (with, where appropriate, a joint purchaser) has received an offer to sell, he may apply to the selling authority[2] for a loan of an amount not exceeding the price fixed for the house[3]. The application (which must be in a form prescribed by the Secretary of State[4] and include details of the amount of loan sought, the applicant's income and liabilities, and a statement that he has applied for but been unable to obtain a sufficient building society loan[5]) must be served on the authority (or other body), with supporting evidence, within one month after service of the offer to sell[6] (or within one year and ten months after the application to purchase if the tenant has a fixed price option[7]). The authority, provided that it is satisfied on reasonable inquiry (including opportunity for the applicant to amend his application) that the information supplied is correct, must, within two months, serve an offer of a loan specifying a maximum amount calculated in accordance with regulations made by the Secretary of State[8]. Alternatively, the authority may, within the period, refuse the application on the ground that information contained in it is incorrect in a material respect[9]. If an offer is made, the applicant, if he wishes to accept it, must do so along with his acceptance of the landlord's offer to sell[10]. An agreement is thereby constituted under which the lending body must lend either the statutory maximum or the amount sought, whichever is the lesser, on the execution by the applicant of a standard security[11]. If, on the other hand, the applicant is aggrieved either by the refusal of a loan, failure to comply with the procedure or by the calculation of the maximum amount of the loan, he may, within two months, raise proceedings for a declarator by summary application in the sheriff court[12]. If the sheriff grants declarator that the applicant is entitled to a loan, it has effect as if it were an offer of a loan as above[13].

1 As to the right to buy, see paras 1954 ff above.
2 Where the selling landlord is a development corporation, application is made to the corporation; where the landlord is Scottish Homes or a housing association registered with it, it is made to Scottish Homes; where the landlord is the Housing Corporation or a housing association registered with it, it is made to the Housing Corporation; and in any other case it is made to the local authority: Housing (Scotland) Act 1987 (c 26), s 216(1)(a), (b), (bi), (c) (amended by the Housing (Scotland) Act 1988 (c 43), s 3(3), Sch 2, para 13).
3 Housing (Scotland) Act 1987, s 216(1). The price is fixed under s 62: see para 1956 above.
4 See the Right to Purchase (Loan Application) (Scotland) Order 1980, SI 1980/1492, Schedule.
5 Housing (Scotland) Act 1987, s 216(2)(b).
6 Ibid, s 216(2)(a)(i), (c).
7 Ibid, s 216(2)(a)(ii). See s 67, and para 1962 above.
8 Ibid, s 216(3), (4)(a); Right to Purchase (Loans) (Scotland) Regulations 1980, SI 1980/1430. The regulations define the maximum amount of loan as the amount of the applicant's 'available annual income' multiplied by the 'appropriate factor' (reg 2), both of which terms are defined (regs 3, 12).
9 Housing (Scotland) Act 1987, s 216(4)(b).
10 Ibid, s 216(5). For acceptances of offers to sell, see ss 66, 67, and paras 1960, 1962, above.
11 Ibid, s 216(6).
12 Ibid, s 216(7).
13 Ibid, s 216(8).

2015. Loans in respect of houses in housing action areas or subject to an improvement order or a repair notice. The other circumstances in which a positive duty to offer a loan arises are where a house is required to be improved or repaired in terms of a housing action area resolution, an improvement order or a repair notice[1]. Where the owner or lessee of a house in an action area is willing to carry out required improvement works he may, within nine months of the date of publication and service of notice of the final resolution, apply to the local authority for a loan[2]. The owner of a house subject to an improvement order may similarly apply[3] and the same option is open to a person having control of a house subject to a repair notice, who must apply not later than twenty-one days after service of the notice[4].

Subject in all cases to certain qualifications, the authority must, if satisfied that the applicant can reasonably be expected to meet the obligations of the loan, offer a loan of the amount of expenditure to which the application relates[5]. The loan must be secured by a standard security[6], and the rate of interest is the normal variable rate[7]. The loan may be made subject to such reasonable terms as the authority may specify[8]. One standard condition which is required in all offers is that, if an improvement or repairs grant becomes payable in respect of the relevant works, the amount of the loan will not exceed the amount of expenditure remaining after deduction of the grant[9]. Further pre-conditions of a loan are that the applicant's estate or interest in the house will not expire before final repayment and that, according to a valuation made on behalf of the authority, the amount of the principal of the loan does not exceed the estimated value of the house after improvement or repair[10].

1 The principal rules are contained in the Housing (Scotland) Act 1987 (c 26), s 217. These relate to housing action areas. Section 217(2)–(9) are applied to improvement orders by s 88(8), and s 217(2)–(8) are applied to repair notices (with a modification in s 217(5)) by s 218(2). For discussion of housing action areas, see paras 1996 ff above, and for discussion of improvement orders and repair notices, see paras 1990 ff, 1993 ff above.
2 Ibid, s 217(1).
3 Ibid, s 88(8).
4 Ibid, s 218(1).
5 Ibid, s 217(2). If the authority is not so satisfied, it may offer a smaller loan: s 217(3).
6 Ibid, s 217(2).

7 Ibid, s 217(6). See para 2013 above.
8 Ibid, s 217(7). The offer may include any of the conditions in Sch 17, paras 4–7, as to repayment of principal and interest: s 217(8).
9 Ibid, s 217(4). Account is to be taken of grant payments by instalments: s 217(9).
10 Ibid, s 217(5).

2016. Assistance for first-time buyers. The Home Purchase Assistance and Housing Corporation Guarantee Act 1978 (c 27) introduced a new scheme for the assistance of first-time purchasers of house property in Great Britain. It was a scheme which largely lost its practical significance because it was overtaken by other developments in the financing of house purchase and because the financial limits incorporated into the scheme were not adequately updated. The scheme nevertheless remains on the statute book in the Housing (Scotland) Act 1987[1], although provision has now been made for the winding-up of the scheme and repeal of the legislation by order of the Secretary of State[2]. As presently enacted, however, the essential elements of the scheme are that the Secretary of State may make advances to recognised lending institutions to enable them to provide assistance to first-time purchasers of house property[3]. The recognised lending institutions are building societies, local authorities, new town development corporations, Scottish Homes, banks, insurance companies, friendly societies and other bodies which the Secretary of State may add, by order, to the list[4]. These lending institutions may assist a first-time purchaser where (1) he intends to make his home in the property, (2) finance for the purchase (and improvements, if any) is obtained by secured loan from the institution, and (3) the purchase price is within prescribed limits[5].

The assistance takes three forms: (a) the secured loan, to the extent of £600, may be financed by the Secretary of State; (b) £600 of the total loan may be made free of interest and of any obligation to repay principal for up to five years; (c) the institution may provide the purchaser with a tax-exempt bonus on his savings up to a maximum of £110 towards the purchase or expenses arising in connection with it[6]. Preconditions are that, in relation to heads (a) and (b), the purchaser has been saving with a recognised savings institution for the two preceding years; has had at least £300 in savings throughout the preceding twelve months; and has, at the time of application for assistance, accumulated at least £600[7]. In relation to head (c), the first two of the conditions apply[8]. A further general restriction is that no assistance may be given unless the amount of the secured loan is at least £1,600 and amounts to not less than 25 per cent of the purchase price of the property[9].

1 See the Housing (Scotland) Act 1987 (c 26), ss 222–227.
2 See the Local Government and Housing Act 1989 (c 42), s 171, and the Home Purchase Assistance (Winding Up of Scheme) Order 1990, SI 1990/374.
3 Housing (Scotland) Act 1987, s 222(1).
4 Ibid, s 224 (amended by the Housing (Scotland) Act 1988 (c 43), s 3(3), Sch 2, para 1). National Westminster Home Loans Ltd was added by the Home Purchase Assistance (Recognised Lending Institutions) Order 1982, SI 1982/976.
5 Housing (Scotland) Act 1987, s 222(1)(a)–(c). Prescribed price limits are fixed by order made by statutory instrument, which may prescribe different limits for different areas: s 222(2), (3). The orders are made periodically. See eg the Home Purchase Assistance (Price-limits) Order 1989, SI 1989/137, setting a limit, for Scotland, of £34,900.
6 Housing (Scotland) Act 1987, s 223(1)(a)–(c).
7 Ibid, s 223(2)(a)–(c).
8 Ibid, s 223(2). The recognised savings institutions are building societies, local authorities, banks, friendly societies, the Director of Savings, the Post Office, recognised savings institutions for the purposes of the corresponding provisions of the (English) Housing Act 1985 (c 68), ss 445–449,

and of the Housing (Northern Ireland) Order 1981, SI 1981/156, Pt IX, and institutions added to the list by order of the Secretary of State: Housing (Scotland) Act 1987, s 225.

9 Ibid, s 223(4).

2017. Other assistance. Three other forms of financial assistance towards house purchase may be mentioned. Under the first, a local authority may, with the approval of the Secretary of State, enter into an agreement with a building society or other recognised body[1] under which the authority binds itself to indemnify the society or body in respect of (1) the whole or any part of any outstanding indebtedness of a borrower, and (2) loss or expense to the society or body resulting from the failure of the borrower to perform any obligation imposed by a heritable security[2].

The second form of assistance relates to what is known as a 'homesteading scheme'. Pursuant to such a scheme approved by the Secretary of State, a local authority may assist a person acquiring a house in need of repair or improvement by making provision for waiving or reducing, for a period of up to five years, interest due on sums advanced under certain forms of home loan[3]. Thus, together with loans to first-time purchasers[4], arrangements under such a scheme form partial exceptions to the rules governing variable interest home loans[5].

The third form of assistance has recently been enacted in Part III of the Local Government Act 1988[6]. Under that Act, a local authority has the power to provide a person with financial assistance for the purposes of, or in connection with, the acquisition, construction, conversion, rehabilitation, improvement, maintenance or management of any property which is, or is intended to be, privately let as housing accommodation[7]. The financial assistance may take the form of a grant, loan, guarantee, indemnity or acquisition of share or loan capital[8]. To qualify as 'privately let', the property concerned must be occupied as housing accommodation in pursuance of a lease or licence of any description or under a statutory tenancy and the immediate landlord of the occupier must be a person other than a public-sector landlord[9]. Financial assistance may be given only in accordance with a consent given by the Secretary of State[10].

1 Any such recognised body must be designated by the Secretary of State by order: Housing (Scotland) Act 1987 (c 26), s 229(6). See the Local Authorities (Recognised Bodies for Heritable Securities Indemnities) (Scotland) Order 1987, SI 1987/1388, which designates the Bank of England and the Post Office, insurance companies to which the Insurance Companies Act 1982 (c 50), Pt II (ss 15–71) applies, authorised institutions under the Banking Act 1987 (c 22), and friendly societies and branches thereof which are registered within the meaning of the Friendly Societies Act 1974 (c 46).

2 Housing (Scotland) Act 1987, s 229(1), replacing the Tenants' Rights Etc (Scotland) Act 1980 (c 52), s 31 (repealed), which itself replaced with modifications the unused Housing (Financial Provisions) (Scotland) Act 1968 (c 31), s 50 (repealed).

3 Housing (Scotland) Act 1987, s 230(1), referring to home loans under s 219, for which see para 2013 above.

4 See para 2016 above.

5 See para 2013 above.

6 The Local Government Act 1988 (c 9), Pt III, comprises ss 24–26.

7 Ibid, s 24(1).

8 Ibid, s 24(2). In the case of a loan, the Housing (Scotland) Act 1987, s 219 (home-loan interest rates), does not apply: Local Government Act 1988, s 24(4).

9 Ibid, s 24(3). 'Statutory tenancy' has the same meaning as in the Rent (Scotland) Act 1984 (c 58) (see ss 3, 115(1)); and 'public-sector landlord' means a regional, islands or district council, joint board or joint committee or any trust under the control of any such body, a development corporation or Scottish Homes: Local Government Act 1988, s 24(6) (amended by the Housing (Scotland) Act 1988 (c 43), s 3(3), Sch 2, para 1).

10 See the Local Government Act 1988, ss 25, 26 (s 25 being amended by the Local Government and Housing Act 1989 (c 42), s 194(1), (4), Sch 11, para 96, Sch 12, Pt II). Guidance on the use of the powers has been given in Scottish Development Department Circular 22/1988.

10. GRANTS FOR IMPROVEMENT, REPAIR AND CONVERSION

(1) INTRODUCTION

2018. General. Part XIII of the Housing (Scotland) Act 1987[1] brings together a number of powers under which local authorities may give financial assistance to owners and occupiers of houses to enable them to be improved, repaired or converted. The various forms of grant assistance are discussed in the paragraphs which follow, for the most part in the order adopted in Part XIII. Whilst an accurate statement of the existing law is aimed at, it should be noted that the government has made radical proposals for change[2]. One significant amendment to the law has already been made by the Housing (Scotland) Act 1988, under which the local authority powers described below are to be extended to Scottish Homes[3]. The Act also contains provisions designed to prevent duplication of grant, under which the Secretary of State may give directions (with which the recipients must comply) to a local authority, to local authorities generally and to Scottish Homes as to the circumstances in which they, or any of them, may or may not exercise their grant-making powers, or are or are not to perform their duties in respect of those powers[4].

An extension of the powers of assistance available to the public was made by the Local Government and Housing Act 1989, under which a relevant authority (defined as a regional, islands or district council[5]) has the power to provide professional, technical and administrative services for owners or occupiers of houses in connection with their arranging or carrying out relevant works[6]. Alternatively, a relevant authority may provide those services to encourage or facilitate the carrying out of such works, whether or not on payment of charges determined by the authority[7]. Further related powers are given (1) to relevant authorities to give financial assistance to housing associations, charities and other approved bodies[8], and (2) to the Secretary of State to give financial assistance in connection with the provision of services[9].

1 The Housing (Scotland) Act 1987 (c 26), Pt XIII, comprises ss 236–256.
2 See *Housing: The Government's Proposals for Scotland* (Cm 242) (1987), and the Scottish Development Department consultation paper *Private Housing Renewal: The Government's Proposals for Scotland* (1988).
3 Housing (Scotland) Act 1988 (c 43), s 2. The Housing (Scotland) Act 1987, Pt XIII (except ss 253–255), applies to Scottish Homes as it applies to a local authority: s 256A (added by the Housing (Scotland) Act 1988, s 2(9)).
4 Housing (Scotland) Act 1987, s 239A (added by the Housing (Scotland) Act 1988, s 2(8), and amended by the Local Government and Housing Act 1989 (c 42), s 194(1), Sch 11, para 95).
5 Local Government and Housing Act 1989 (c 42), s 170(9).
6 Ibid, s 170(1). 'Relevant works' are such works as are specified in regulations made by the Secretary of State: s 170(2).
7 Ibid, s 170(1), (3).
8 See ibid, s 170(4), (5), (9).
9 See ibid, s 170(6)–(8).

(2) IMPROVEMENT GRANTS

2019. General. Subject to other provisions in Part XIII of the Housing (Scotland) Act 1987[1], a local authority may give assistance by making an improvement grant in respect of (1) works required for the provision of houses by the conversion of houses or other buildings, and (2) works required for the improvement of houses[2]. 'Improvement' is defined to include, in relation to any house, alteration and enlargement and, in relation to a house for a disabled occupant, the doing of works required for making it suitable for his accommodation, welfare or employment[3]. A house for a disabled occupant is a house which is the only or main residence when application for a grant is made, or is likely to become, after a reasonable period from the completion of the works, the only or main residence, of a person who is substantially handicapped by illness, injury or congenital deformity and for whose benefit the improvement is proposed to be made[4]. 'Works required for the provision or improvement of a house' include works of repair or replacement needed in the opinion of the local authority for the purpose of enabling the house to attain a good state of repair[5].

1   The Housing (Scotland) Act 1987 (c 26), Pt XIII, comprises ss 236–256.
2   Ibid, s 236(1). For the meaning of 'local authority', see para 1903 above, and for the meaning of 'house', see para 1901 above. As to improvement grants in housing action areas, see para 2031 below.
3   Ibid, s 236(2)(a).
4   Ibid, s 236(3).
5   Ibid, s 236(2)(b). However, such works do not include works specified by or ancillary to a fire escape notice under s 162 (see para 2007 above and para 2028 below): s 236(4). As to repair grants, see paras 2025 ff below.

2020. Applications and approvals. An application for an improvement grant must be in the prescribed form and contain full particulars of (1) the works to be carried out, together with plans and specifications, (2) the land, and (3) the expenses (including professional fees, and apportioned between houses where appropriate) estimated to be incurred[1]. It is then open to the local authority to approve the application (in which case it must make a grant) or refuse to approve it[2]. In making its decision, a local authority must comply with any directions given to that authority or to authorities generally by the Secretary of State[3]. He may require that a particular application or class of applications should not be approved except with his consent and subject to any conditions he may impose[3]. A local authority must not approve an application for grant unless satisfied that the owner of any land[4] on which the works are to be carried out has consented in writing to the application and to being bound by any conditions imposed[5]. An application must also be refused if the specified works have been begun, unless the authority is satisfied that there were good reasons for beginning the works before the application was approved[6].

There are other restrictions. First, there must be no approval of an application (other than one for the provision of standard amenities[7]) unless the authority is satisfied that the house or houses to which the application relates will provide satisfactory housing accommodation for such period and conform with such requirements as to construction, physical condition and the provision of services and amenities as may be specified by the Secretary of State[8]. With the approval of the Secretary of State, however, an authority may disregard any such requirement where, in the authority's opinion, conformity would not be practicable at a reasonable expense[9]. The authority must be further satisfied that, in a case where the house or houses concerned is or are comprised in a building containing more than one house, the works to be carried out will not prevent the improvement of any other house in the building[10].

Secondly, an authority must not approve an application in respect of a house provided after 15 June 1964 subject to waiver, in a particular case or in general, by the Secretary of State[11].

Thirdly, in many cases there is a rateable value restriction. The general rule is that if an application for grant is made by the owner of the house (or by a member of his family[12]) and the house or any part of it is to be occupied by the owner (or member of his family) after completion of the works, the application must be refused if the rateable value of the occupied premises exceeds the prescribed amount or if, in the case of a conversion of two or more houses, the aggregate of the rateable values exceeds the prescribed limit[13]. The rule does not apply where the application relates to a part of a house which, after completion of the works, will be self-contained and will not be occupied by the owner or a member of his family[14]. Prescribed limits of rateable value are determined by the Secretary of State with consent of the Treasury by statutory instrument subject to annulment by either House of Parliament, and different limits may be prescribed for different cases and classes of case[15]. The Secretary of State also has power to vary by order (again by statutory instrument subject to annulment) the rules on rateable value restrictions as a whole[16]. The rules must now be read subject to the provision of the Abolition of Domestic Rates Etc (Scotland) Act 1987 which specifies how rateable values will be calculated on domestic subjects removed from rating[17]. The rateable value restrictions do not, in any event, apply to certain types of application. These are (1) where the house is in a housing action area[18] and listed for improvement or integration, or (2) where the house is subject to an improvement order[19], or (3) where the application is for the conversion of a building which does not, at the date of the application, consist of or include a house, or (4) where the house is to be occupied by a disabled person and the application is in respect of works which his disability renders necessary[20].

Where a local authority approves an application, it must notify the applicant (and, where appropriate, the owner) of the amount of the estimated expense approved as attributable to each house (the 'approved expense') and the amount of grant payable expressed as a percentage of the approved expense and as a cash amount[21]. In approving an application, the authority may require, as a condition of payment of grant, that the works be carried out within a specified period (of not less than twelve months) or within such further period as the authority may allow[22]. Where a local authority either refuses an application or approves an application but fixes the amount of grant below the maximum awardable, it must notify the applicant in writing of the grounds of its decision[23]. There is no provision for appeal against the refusal of an application for an improvement grant, but aggrieved applicants have made frequent use of the procedure for complaint to the Commissioner for Local Administration in Scotland[24]. In England (but not, so far, it seems in Scotland) there has been some recourse to judicial review as a means of challenge[25].

1 Housing (Scotland) Act 1987 (c 26), s 237(a)–(c). For the prescribed form, see the Housing (Forms) (Scotland) Regulations 1980, SI 1980/1647, Schedule, Form 2.
2 Housing (Scotland) Act 1987, s 238. For the difficulties caused by a purported 'approval in principle' and the court's refusal to treat it as a fully operative approval, see _Margrie Holdings Ltd v City of Edinburgh District Council_ 5 February 1987, OH (unreported).
3 Housing (Scotland) Act 1987, s 239.
4 This does not apply to land proposed to be sold or leased under ibid, s 12(4): s 240(1)(a) (amended by the Housing (Scotland) Act 1988 (c 43), s 72(1), Sch 7, para 10).
5 Housing (Scotland) Act 1987, s 240(1)(a). For conditions, see para 2024 below.
6 Ibid, s 240(1)(b).
7 As to the standard amenities, see para 2023 below.
8 Housing (Scotland) Act 1987, s 240(2)(a)(i).
9 Ibid, s 240(6).
10 Ibid, s 240(2)(a)(ii).
11 Ibid, s 240(2)(b).
12 As to members of the family, see para 1935, note 4, above.
13 Housing (Scotland) Act 1987, s 240(2)(c).
14 Ibid, s 240(2) provisio.
15 Ibid, s 240(4). See the Housing (Limits of Rateable Value for Improvement Grants and Repairs Grants) (Scotland) Order 1985, SI 1985/297.

16 Housing (Scotland) Act 1987, s 240(5).
17 See the Abolition of Domestic Rates Etc (Scotland) Act 1987 (c 47), s 5 (amended by the Local Government Finance Act 1988 (c 41), s 137, Sch 12, para 12).
18 As to housing action areas, see paras 1996 ff above.
19 As to improvement orders, see paras 1990 ff above.
20 Housing (Scotland) Act 1987, s 240(3)(a)–(d).
21 Ibid, s 241(1); see para 2021 below.
22 Ibid, s 241(2). For other conditions, see para 2024 below.
23 Ibid, s 241(3).
24 As to the commissioner, see LOCAL GOVERNMENT, vol 14, paras 133 ff.
25 Recent examples include *R v Camden London Borough, ex parte Christey* (1987) 19 HLR 420; *R v Oldham Metropolitan Borough Council, ex parte Garrity* (1987) 20 HLR 229, CA; and *R v Hackney London Borough, ex parte Gransils Investments Ltd* (1988) 20 HLR 313.

2021. Amount of grant. Subject to special rules relating to grants for the provision of standard amenities[1], the amount of an improvement grant must be determined by reference to prescribed maximum levels: the grant to be paid must not exceed 50 per cent[2] of the approved expense, but that approved expense is subject to a maximum value per house (fixed at present at £12,600) prescribed by the Secretary of State[3].

There are a number of qualifications to this general rule. First, the authority may, after approval of an application and if satisfied that, owing to circumstances beyond the control of the applicant, the expense of the works will exceed the estimate, substitute a higher amount of approved expenses — but not so as to exceed the maximum amount of (at present) £12,600[4]. If, on the other hand, the authority is satisfied that, in a particular case, there are good reasons for fixing an amount higher than the prescribed maximum, it may be exceeded by such amount as may be approved by the Secretary of State[5]. Such approval may be given either with respect to a particular case or a particular class of case[5]. Similar provision is made to permit larger payments where the expense of executing works is materially enhanced by measures taken to preserve the architectural or historic interest of the house or building[6].

Secondly, the authority may pay additional amounts of grant to allow for works of repair and replacement needed, in its opinion, to enable the house to attain a good state of repair[7]. There are two different situations. One is where an application relates wholly or partly to the provision of any or all of the standard amenities[8] and either (1) on completion of the works the house is likely to be available for use as a house for at least ten years, in which case a further maximum approved expense of (at present) £3,450 or 50 per cent of the approved expense for the improvement works, whichever is greater, is allowable, or (2) the house is likely to be available for less than ten years, in which case a maximum approved expense of (at present) £345 for each standard amenity is allowable, subject to a prescribed maximum of (at present) £1,380[9]. The second situation is where the application does not relate to the provision of standard amenities, in which case an additional maximum approved expense not exceeding 50 per cent of the approved expense of executing the improvement works is allowable[10].

The third general qualification affecting the total grant payable applies in situations when an earlier grant has been paid in respect of the same house. If an improvement grant or repairs grant has already been made[11], or assistance given under the Hill Farming Act 1946[12] or the Crofters (Scotland) Act 1955[13] and within ten years of the date of payment (or, where appropriate, the date of the last instalment[14]) an improvement grant [15] is made, the amount payable must, when added to any unrepaid amount of the previous grant, not exceed the total permitted percentage of the maximum approved expense[16].

There is also provision for ensuring that conditions attached to a new grant include afresh those attached to an earlier one[17].

1 See para 2023 below.
2 This percentage is subject to adjustment by the Secretary of State by order: Housing (Scotland) Act 1987 (c 26), s 242(1), (7), (10).
3 Ibid, s 242(1), (9), (10); Housing (Improvement and Repairs Grants) (Approved Expenses Maxima) (Scotland) Order 1987, SI 1987/2269. In the case of the rehabilitation of a pre-1914 tenement in a housing action area, the order fixes a maximum (instead of £12,600) of £17,100 or, if the rehabilitation is carried out by a housing association, £19,700.
4 Housing (Scotland) Act 1987, s 242(2).
5 Ibid, s 242(4)(a).
6 Ibid, s 242(4)(b).
7 Ibid, s 242(3).
8 As to the standard amenities, see para 2023 below.
9 Housing (Scotland) Act 1987, s 242(3)(a)(i), (ii); Housing (Improvement and Repairs Grants) (Approved Expenses Maxima) (Scotland) Order 1987.
10 Housing (Scotland) Act 1987, s 242(3)(b). This percentage is subject to adjustment by the Secretary of State by order: s 242(1), (7), (10).
11 Ie whether, in either case, under the Housing (Scotland) Act 1974 (c 45) (repealed) or the Housing (Scotland) Act 1987.
12 Ie under the Hill Farming Act 1946 (c 73), s 1.
13 Ie under the Crofters (Scotland) Act 1955 (c 21), s 22(2): see AGRICULTURE, vol 1, para 819.
14 As to instalment payments, see para 2022 below.
15 Ie other than one in respect of standard amenities or for the benefit of a disabled occupant.
16 Housing (Scotland) Act 1987, s 242(5).
17 See ibid, s 242(6) (amended by the Housing (Scotland) Act 1988 (c 43), s 72(1), Sch 7, para 11).

2022. Payment of grant. An improvement grant must be paid within one month of the date on which, in the opinion of the local authority, the house first becomes fit for occupation after the completion of the works[1]. Alternatively it may be partly paid in instalments from time to time as the works progress and with final settlement within one month of their completion, but the aggregate of instalments paid must not, at any time before completion of the works, exceed 50 per cent[2] of the aggregate approved expense of the works executed up to that time[3]. All payments, whether by instalments or otherwise, are conditional upon the works being executed to the satisfaction of the local authority[4]. If an instalment of grant is paid before completion and the works are not then completed within twelve months of the date of the instalment, then that instalment, together with any further instalment paid, becomes repayable, with interest, on being demanded by the authority[5].

1 Housing (Scotland) Act 1987 (c 26), s 243(1)(a).
2 Another percentage may be prescribed by the Secretary of State by order: see ibid, ss 242(1), 243(1)(b).
3 Ibid, s 243(1)(b) (amended by the Housing (Scotland) Act 1988 (c 43), s 72(1), Sch 7, para 12).
4 Housing (Scotland) Act 1987, s 243(2). In *Curran v Northern Ireland Co-ownership Housing Association Ltd* [1987] AC 718, [1987] 2 All ER 13, HL, the House held that the obligation under equivalent Northern Ireland legislation to execute works to the satisfaction of the authority (the Northern Ireland Housing Executive) did not create a duty of care to the grant recipients to ensure the proper execution of the works.
5 Housing (Scotland) Act 1987, s 243(3).

2023. Grants for standard amenities. Special rules apply when an application for an improvement grant relates to the execution of works required to provide a house with standard amenities[1]. These amenities are statutorily defined as follows, together with the 'maximum eligible amount' for each:

Fixed bath or shower	£450
Hot and cold water supply at a fixed bath or shower.............	£570
Wash-hand basin	£170
Hot and cold water supply at a wash hand basin	£305
Sink...	£450
Hot and cold water supply at a sink	£385
Water closet	£680[2]

If an application is made in relation to the provision of one or more standard amenities which a house presently lacks, a local authority must, subject to other provisions to be mentioned, make the grant if in the opinion of the authority the house will, on completion of the works, (1) be provided with all the standard amenities for the exclusive use of its occupants, and (2) meet the tolerable standard[3]. As with other grants, the authority must not make a grant in respect of one house in a building unless satisfied that the works will not prevent the improvement of any other house in the building[4]. If a standard amenity is, in the authority's opinion, essential to the needs of a disabled occupant, this may be provided even if the house already has such a standard amenity[5]. The prerequisite that the house should, on completion of the works, be provided with all standard amenities for the exclusive use of its occupants does not apply in the case of a grant in respect of a house which is not likely to be available for use as a house for a period of at least ten years[6] (thus single amenities can be approved). The amount of improvement grant payable is 50 per cent of the approved expense[7]. The total approved expense, in relation to any application, is the sum of the maximum eligible amounts (set out above) for each amenity to be provided[8]. These amounts may, however, be exceeded if the authority is satisfied that an increased estimate for the works is justifiable[9].

1 Housing (Scotland) Act 1987 (c 26), s 244, Sch 18.
2 Ibid, s 244(6), (11), Sch 18, Pt I (amended by the Housing (Improvement and Repairs Grants) (Approved Expenses Maxima) (Scotland) Order 1987, SI 1987/2269).
3 Housing (Scotland) Act 1987, s 244(1)(a), (b), the requirements of which may be varied by order made by the Secretary of State: s 244(1)(a), (13). As to the tolerable standard, see s 244(9), applying s 86, for which see para 1979 above.
4 Ibid, s 244(2).
5 Ibid, s 244(3).
6 Ibid, s 244(4).
7 Ibid, s 244(7). The amount is subject to amendment by order made by the Secretary of State: s 244(12), (14).
8 Ibid, Sch 18, Pt II, paras 1, 2. The percentage may be varied by order made by the Secretary of State: s 244(10)(b), (12) (amended by the Housing (Scotland) Act 1988 (c 43), s 72(1), Sch 7, para 13).
9 Housing (Scotland) Act 1987, Sch 18, Pt II, para 3.

2024. Conditions. When an application for an improvement grant has been approved, certain conditions will normally apply for a period of five years with effect from the date when, in the opinion of the local authority, the house first becomes fit for occupation after the completion of the works[1]. Such conditions are deemed to be part of the terms of any lease or tenancy and may be enforced accordingly[1]. The conditions are (1) that the house will not be used for purposes other than as a private dwelling house[2], (2) that the house will not be occupied by the owner or a member of his family[3] except as his only or main residence[4], and (3) that all such steps as are practicable will be taken to secure the maintenance of the house in a good state of repair[5]. On being required to do so by the local authority, the owner of the house must certify that these conditions are being observed and, for this purpose, he may require any tenant to furnish him with information[6]. A local authority must not, as a prerequisite of approving a grant, require the observance of any conditions or obligations other than those specified in the Housing (Scotland) Act 1987 or other statutory obligations[7]. The primary method of enforcement of grant conditions is a requirement to repay grant in the event of breach[8]. Detailed rules are contained in Schedule 19 to the 1987 Act which includes, on the one hand, provisions permitting relaxation of the requirement to repay[9] but, on the other, the enforcement of conditions by interdict in the sheriff court[10] and by the making of a charging order in favour of the local authority[11]. A local authority is also required[12] to cause to be recorded in the General Register of Sasines or registered in the Land Register of Scotland a notice specifying the conditions to be observed, the period for which they are to be observed, and the provisions of Schedule 19 under which grant may be repayable by the owner[13]. Expenses incurred in recording or registering the notice are repayable to the authority by the applicant for grant[14]. The owner of a house (or holder of a heritable security over it) may at any time repay to the authority the amount which would become so repayable under Schedule 19 in the event of breach in which case, in the terms of that Schedule, observance of the conditions ceases to be required[15].

1 Housing (Scotland) Act 1987 (c 26), s 246(1). For consideration of the problems of determining the date of completion of improvement works under the equivalent (rather differently worded) English legislation, see *R v Westminster City Council, ex parte Hazan* (1987) 20 HLR 205, [1988] 1 EGLR 29, CA.

2 However, it may be, in part, used as a shop or office or for business, trade or professional purposes: Housing (Scotland) Act 1987, s 246(2)(a).

3 As to members of the family, see para 1935, note 4, above.

4 Ie within the meaning of the Capital Gains Tax Act 1979 (c 14), Pt V (ss 101–114) (see especially s 101(5), (6)).

5 Housing (Scotland) Act 1987, s 246(2)(a)–(c).

6 Ibid, s 246(3).

7 Ibid, s 246(4).

8 Ibid, s 246(5), Sch 19, para 1.

9 Ibid, Sch 19, paras 2, 3.

10 Ibid, Sch 19, para 5.

11 Ibid, Sch 19, para 7.

12 This does not apply where the applicant was and remains a tenant at will, in which case the authority must simply keep a written record: ibid, s 246(8).

13 Ibid, s 246(7), (9)(a)–(c). For the form of notice, see the Housing (Forms) (Scotland) Regulations 1980, SI 1980/1647, Schedule, Form 5.

14 Housing (Scotland) Act 1987, s 246(10).

15 See ibid, s 247.

(3) REPAIRS GRANTS

2025. General. It has been seen that an improvement grant may itself include an amount in respect of works of repair. Since the Housing (Financial Provisions) (Scotland) Act 1978[1], however, local authorities have been able to make grants solely in respect of such repair works. That provision is now made in the Housing (Scotland) Act 1987[2], which creates, in effect, two parallel grant schemes. They relate, on the one hand, to applications for grant in cases where no repair notice[3] has been served and, on the other hand, to applications relating to words required by a repair notice.

In the case of an application which is not related to a repair notice, the authority is empowered, on receipt of an application duly made to it, to approve the application in such circumstances as it thinks fit[4]. It must not, however, approve an application unless satisfied that the house will provide satisfactory housing accommodation for such period as it considers reasonable[5]. In considering whether to approve an application, an authority must normally also have regard to the question whether, in its opinion, the owner would, without undue hardship, be able to finance the works without grant assistance[6].

In the case of an application pursuant to a repair notice, it must be approved in so far as it relates to the works required by the notice[7].

A grant may relate to premises other than a house specified in a repair notice, but the authority must be satisfied that such premises form part of a building which contains a house or houses which will provide satisfactory accommodation for a reasonable period[8].

1   Housing (Scotland) Act 1974 (c 45), s 10A (added by the Housing (Financial Provisions) (Scotland) Act 1978 (c 14), s 8) (repealed).
2   Housing (Scotland) Act 1987 (c 26), s 248. As to repairs grants in housing action areas, see para 2032 below.
3   As to repair notices, see paras 1993 ff above.
4   Housing (Scotland) Act 1987, s 248(1)(b).
5   Ibid, s 248(2).
6   Ibid, s 248(3). However, this does not apply in such cases as may be prescribed: s 248(3) proviso.
7   Ibid, s 248(1)(a).
8   Ibid, s 248(6)(a).

2026. Amount of grant. A repairs grant must not exceed 50 per cent[1] of the approved expense of the works up to a maximum (at present) of £5,500 for each house (or premises)[2].

1   Some other percentage may be prescribed by the Secretary of State by order: Housing (Scotland) Act 1987 (c 26), s 248(4), (8), (9).
2   Ibid, s 248(4), (10); Housing (Improvement and Repairs Grants) (Approved Expenses Maxima) (Scotland) Order 1987, SI 1987/2269.

2027. Procedural and other provisions. The procedures for the making of improvement grants are made broadly applicable to the making of repairs grants[1]. They include provision for application forms, the pre-conditions of approval, and the general requirements for payment and the imposition of conditions on payment. Whilst the principal rules on amounts of grant are different[2], the provisions authorising authorities to permit the expense of works (and grant) to exceed estimates and to make increased grants (with the approval of the Secretary of State or in respect of buildings of architectural or historic interest) apply also to repairs grants.

1   See the Housing (Scotland) Act 1987 (c 26), s 248(5) (amended by the Housing (Scotland) Act 1988 (c 43), s 72(1), Sch 7, para 14, Sch 8, para 6), applying the Housing (Scotland) Act 1987, ss 242(1), (3), (5), (7)–(10), 244, for which see paras 2021, 2023, above.
2   Cf paras 2021, 2026, above.

(4) GRANTS FOR FIRE ESCAPES

2028. General. Introduced for the first time by the Local Government and Planning (Scotland) Act 1982[1] was the duty to make grants for the provision of fire escapes. Where an application is made for a grant for a fire escape in a house in multiple occupation, a local authority must approve the application in so far as it relates to the execution of works specified in a notice served under the Housing (Scotland) Act 1987[2]. The authority may also approve an application in respect of works which, whilst not specified in such a notice, are required in connection with works so specified[3]. The local authority must not approve any

Para 2028   *Vol 11. Housing*   696

application unless satisfied that, on completion of the works, the house will be in reasonable repair (disregarding internal decoration) having regard to its age, character and location[4].

1 Housing (Scotland) Act 1974 (c 45), s 10B (added by the Local Government and Planning (Scotland) Act 1982 (c 43), s 52) (repealed).
2 Housing (Scotland) Act 1987 (c 26), s 249(1)(a). This obligation does not arise if the notice is served on a regional, islands or district council or other prescribed public body: s 249(1)(a), (7). The notice is served under s 162, for which see para 2007 above.
3 Ibid, s 249(1)(b).
4 Ibid, s 249(2).

2029. Amount of grant. When an application for a grant for a fire escape is approved, the local authority determines the maximum amount of expenses it thinks proper to be incurred for the relevant works subject to a maximum amount (at present) of £9,315 for the specified works and £3,340 for ancillary works[1]. The normal amount of grant payable is then 75 per cent[2] of these maximum amounts of proper expenses[3]. If, however, it appears to the authority that the applicant would not without undue hardship be able to finance the cost of the non-grant-aided works, it may increase the percentage normally payable up to a maximum of 90 per cent of the maximum amounts[4].

1 Housing (Scotland) Act 1987 (c 26), s 249(3), (8); Housing (Improvement and Repairs Grants) (Approved Expenses Maxima) (Scotland) Order 1987, SI 1987/2269.
2 Another percentage may be prescribed by the Secretary of State by order: Housing (Scotland) Act 1987, s 249(4), (9), (10).
3 Ibid, s 249(4).
4 Ibid, s 249(5).

2030. Procedural and other provisions. As with repairs grants, most of the provisions generally applicable to improvement grants are extended to fire escape grants[1]. Principal exceptions (other than the rules on amounts of grant) are the preconditions of approval[2].

1 Housing (Scotland) Act 1987 (c 26), s 249(6) (amended by the Housing (Scotland) Act 1988 (c 43), s 72(1), Sch 7, para 15, Sch 8, para 7), applying the Housing (Scotland) Act 1987, ss 242(1), (3), (5)–(10), 244, for which see paras 2021, 2023, above.
2 Ie those contained in ibid, s 240, for which see para 2020 above.

(5) GRANTS FOR HOUSES IN HOUSING ACTION AREAS

2031. Improvement grants. By a process of modification of the general provisions which apply outwith housing action areas[1], rules contained in the Housing (Scotland) Act 1987 permit and require a more generous system of grants to be made available for the improvement of houses specified by resolution of the local authority within such areas. Thus, the general level of grant is raised from 50 per cent of maximum approved expense[2] to 75 per cent[3], and this may be further raised to a maximum level of 90 per cent if it appears to the authority approving the application that the applicant (who must, for this purpose, be the owner of the land) will not without undue hardship be able to finance the cost of the non-grant-aided works[4]. There is no general power to refuse an application for grant in respect of houses subject to a housing action area resolution, and grants in respect of standard amenities are not, as such, available. An authority must, however, make a grant to the owner of a house in a housing action area in respect of the improvement works required to bring the house up to the standard specified in the resolution[5], but not if the works on one house in a building would prevent another house in the same building from being brought up to the specified standard[6].

1 As to housing action areas, see paras 1996 ff above.
2 See the Housing (Scotland) Act 1987 (c 26), ss 242(1), 243(1), and paras 2021, 2022, above.
3 Ibid, s 250(1)–(3).
4 Ibid, s 250(5).
5 Ibid, s 250(6).
6 Ibid, s 250(6) proviso.

2032. Repairs grants. The general provisions regarding repairs grants[1] are similarly modified in the case of houses in housing action areas[2], in particular so as to raise the standard level of grant from 50 per cent to 75 per cent of the approved expense of works[3].

1 As to repairs grants, see paras 2025 ff above.
2 See the Housing (Scotland) Act 1987 (c 26), s 250(7).
3 See ibid, s 248(4), modified by s 250(7)(b) (amended by the Housing (Scotland) Act 1988 (c 43), s 72(1), Sch 7, para 16).

(6) IMPROVEMENT OF AMENITY GRANTS

2033. Improvement of amenity. For the purpose of securing the improvement of the amenities of a predominantly residential area in its district, a local authority may (1) carry out works on land it owns and assist (by grants, loans or otherwise) in carrying out works on land it does not own; (2) with the owner's agreement carry out or arrange the carrying out of works on his land (whether at the expense of the authority or of the owner or at shared expense); and (3) acquire land by agreement, or, with the authority of the Secretary of State, compulsorily[1].

1 Housing (Scotland) Act 1987 (c 26), s 251(1)(a)–(c). By virtue of s 251(2), the Acquisition of Land (Authorisation Procedure) (Scotland) Act 1947 (c 42) applies to any such compulsory purchase of land: see COMPULSORY ACQUISITION AND COMPENSATION, vol 5, paras 56–80.

(7) CONTRIBUTIONS FROM CENTRAL GOVERNMENT

2034. Central government financial contributions towards improvement, repairs and improvement of amenity grants. Although grants are paid, in the first instance, by the local authorities concerned, the authorities receive financial support from central government. Until 1 April 1989, this was in the form of specific exchequer contributions payable under the Housing (Scotland) Act 1987[1]. Since that date a substituted form of contribution is provided through the revenue support grant[2]. These arrangements do not extend to grants payable to an authority's own tenants which are financed from its housing revenue account[3].

1 See the Housing (Scotland) Act 1987 (c 26), s 254 (improvement, repairs and fire escape grants), and s 255 (with the Housing (Improvement of Amenities of Residential Areas) (Scotland) Order 1988, SI 1988/10) (improvement of amenity grants). See also the Housing (Scotland) Act 1987, s 240 (slum clearance subsidy), and s 296 (contributions in respect of defective dwellings). Sections 254, 255 and 296 were repealed by the Housing (Scotland) Act 1988 (c 43), s 72(3), Sch 10, and by virtue of s 67(1) no subsidy or contribution could be made under the Housing (Scotland) Act 1987, ss 240, 254, 255 or 296, in respect of any expense or expenditure incurred on

or after 1 April 1989. Transitional arrangements were made by the Housing (Scotland) Act 1988, ss 67(2)–(7), 72(1), Sch 7, paras 10, 17, 18, 25, Sch 8, para 8.

2 As to revenue support grant, see the Abolition of Domestic Rates Etc (Scotland) Act 1987 (c 47), s 23(2), (3), Sch 4 (amended by the Local Government Finance Act 1988 (c 41), s 137, Sch 12, para 41, and the Local Government and Housing Act 1989 (c 42), s 145, Sch 6, para 29): see LOCAL GOVERNMENT, vol 14, para 875.

3 As to the housing revenue account, see para 1916 above.

(8) GRANTS FOR THERMAL INSULATION

2035. General. The Homes Insulation Act 1978 (c 48) introduced a new sys-tem for the offering of financial inducements to encourage the improvement of thermal insulation of dwellings. Using powers now contained in the Housing (Scotland) Act 1987, the Secretary of State prepares and publishes a homes insulation scheme under which local authorities must make grants towards the cost of insulation works[1]. Schemes must be laid before Parliament and must specify (1) the descriptions of dwellings and insulation works qualifying for grants, and (2) the persons from whom applications may be entertained[2]. A scheme may also provide for grants to be made only to persons applying on grounds of special need (by reference to matters such as age, disability, bad health and inability without undue hardship to finance the cost of the works) or to be made in those cases on a higher scale[3]. Amounts of grant (as a percentage of the cost of works or as a money sum, whichever is the less) are prescribed by the Secretary of State[4]. Finance for the making of grants by local authorities is provided by the Secretary of State[5], and an authority has no power to make grants in any year beyond the level of finance committed to that authority in that year[6]. The Secretary of State must also contribute towards the administrative expenses of the authorities[7]. Finally, the Secretary of State may, after consul-tation with their representative organisations, give to authorities directions[8], including directions as to (a) the way in which applications for grants are to be dealt with and priorities to be observed, and (b) the means of authenticating applications[9].

1 Housing (Scotland) Act 1987 (c 26), s 252(1).
2 Ibid, s 252(2)(a), (b). See the Homes Insulation Scheme 1987 (Scottish Development Department Circular 25/1987 (amended by Circular 15/1988)).
3 Housing (Scotland) Act 1987, s 252(4).
4 Ibid, s 252(3), (5), (6). The present maximum grant payable is £144: see para 2036 below.
5 Ibid, s 253(1).
6 Ibid, s 253(2).
7 Ibid, s 253(5).
8 Ibid, s 253(3).
9 Ibid, s 253(4)(a), (b).

2036. The current order, scheme and directions. Under the framework described above[1], the current Homes Insulation Grants Order restricts payment of grants to persons in receipt of housing benefit, income support or family credit and specifies the amount of grant as 90 per cent of the cost of qualifying works or £144, whichever is less[2]. The current Homes Insulation Scheme[3] inter alia restricts qualifying dwellings to those provided before 1 January 1976 and defines the qualifying works. The current Homes Insulation Directions[4] pro-vide for the system of application, waiting lists, priorities, approval of appli-cations, payment of grant and subsequent inspection of works.

1 See para 2035 above.
2 Homes Insulation Grants Order 1987, SI 1987/2185 (amended by the Homes Insulation Grants Order 1988, SI 1988/1239).

3 Homes Insulation Scheme 1987 (Scottish Development Department Circular 25/1987 (amended by Circular 15/1988)). The scheme was effective from 1 February 1988, and the amendment was effective from 15 August 1988.
4 The directions accompany the scheme: see note 3 above.

11. HOMELESSNESS

(1) GENERAL

2037. Relationship between homeless persons' provisions and housing law. The obligations imposed in respect of homeless persons are found in the Housing (Scotland) Act 1987[1]. The legislation is identical to that found in the Housing Act 1985 (c 68) (as amended) for England and Wales, except for one difference in the definition of homelessness[2]. Specific obligations are imposed on local authorities[3] to certain homeless people applying to them for accommodation. These involve securing that accommodation be made available to those homeless applicants who satisfy the local authority that they meet the tests imposed under the legislation[4].

The legislation is unequivocal as to the existence of housing duties towards qualifying homeless applicants[5]. However, some authorities initially were confused as to the relationship between the specific obligations towards homeless people and the restrictions placed on local authorities in selecting tenants[6]. The law requires local authorities to secure that a reasonable preference is given to persons occupying houses which do not meet the tolerable standard, who are occupying overcrowded houses, who have large families or who are living under unsatisfactory housing conditions, and to homeless persons[7]. This does not have the effect of downgrading the statutory obligation on local authorities to homeless applicants, but simply adds to the groups of persons to be considered for allocation of housing from the general housing stock. This is in addition to their duties to ensure that homeless applicants are dealt with as a priority.

In order to clarify how an authority should carry out its obligations, the legislation provides that the Secretary of State may give guidance either generally or to a specified description of authorities[8]. This has taken the form of a Code of Guidance issued in September 1980 which, at the end of 1989, was in course of being updated. The local authority must have regard to its content when implementing the legislation[9]. This has been accepted by the courts as meaning that the authority must consider the guidance in the Code, but they may choose not to follow it[10]. This has been the approach taken in Scotland, England and Wales[11]. However, there is Scottish authority for the view that failure to have regard to the guidance in the Code amounts to inadequate inquiries and flaws a decision[12].

Where a local authority requests another local authority in Great Britain, a development corporation, a registered housing association, Scottish Homes, a social work authority or a social services authority to assist it in the exercise of its functions relating to homeless persons, or to exercise certain functions, that other authority is under an obligation to render such assistance as is reasonable[13].

1 Housing (Scotland) Act 1987, Pt II (ss 24–43). These provisions were derived from the Housing (Homeless Persons) Act 1977 (c 48) (repealed). For further details, see P Watchman and P Robson *Homelessness and the Law* (1983), and P Watchman and P Robson *Homelessness and the Law in Britain* (1989).

2 See the Housing (Scotland) Act 1987, s 24(3)(d), and para 2049 below. See also para 2038 below.
3 For the meaning of 'local authority', see para 1903 above.
4 See the Housing (Scotland) Act 1987, ss 28, 31, 32.
5 See ibid, s 31(2).
6 Commissioner for Local Administration in Scotland *Report of a Complaint against Bearsden and Milngavie District Council* dated 21 March 1980, quoted in Watchman and Robson *Homelessness and the Law* p 134.
7 Housing (Scotland) Act 1987, s 20(1)(a)(i)–(iv), (b). As to the tolerable standard, see para 1979 above.
8 Ibid, s 37(1), (2).
9 Ibid, s 37(1).
10 *Mazzaccherini v Argyll and Bute District Council* 1987 SCLR 475 at 478, OH.
11 *De Falco v Crawley Borough Council* [1980] QB 460 at 478, [1980] 1 All ER 913 at 921, CA.
12 *Kelly v Monklands District Council* 1986 SLT 169 at 172, OH.
13 See the Housing (Scotland) Act 1987, s 38.

2038. Background to the current legislation. The treatment of homeless people in the past has ranged from criminalisation and incarceration to treating them as a problem for social services departments[1]. Until 1948 the Poor Law made bleak institutional provision for those without housing. After the 1939–45 War, Part III of the National Assistance Act 1948[2] provided temporary accommodation for 'persons who are in urgent need thereof'[3]. This was provided by the social services or social work departments rather than as a function of the housing department. This situation was far from satisfactory. The modern legislation providing rights for homeless people was introduced in 1977 by the Housing (Homeless Persons) Act 1977, which came into force in Scotland on 1 April 1978, five months after it commenced in England and Wales[4]. This Act has now been incorporated into the consolidation of Scottish housing legislation in the Housing (Scotland) Act 1987. The only changes between the 1977 legislation and that currently in force is the change to the definition of 'homelessness'. This was amended following pressure from SHELTER (Scotland) to overcome a decision in the House of Lords[5]. In this case the House of Lords took the view that a person was not homeless if he had any accommodation, however poor its condition[6]. The amendment secured by the Housing (Scotland) Act 1986 differs substantially from that which was passed for England and Wales at the same time in the Housing and Planning Act 1986[7]. The implications of this difference apparently were not appreciated at the time by those legislators supporting the amendments[8].

1 P Watchman and P Robson *Homelessness and the Law in Britain* (1989) pp 26 ff.
2 The National Assistance Act 1948 (c 29), Pt III, comprises ss 21–36.
3 Ibid, s 21(1)(b) (repealed).
4 Housing (Homeless Persons) Act 1977 (c 48), s 21(3) (repealed).
5 *R v Hillingdon London Borough Council, ex parte Puhlhofer* [1986] AC 484, *sub nom Puhlhofer v Hillingdon London Borough Council* [1986] 1 All ER 467, HL.
6 [1986] AC 484 at 517, [1986] 1 All ER 467 at 474, HL, per Lord Brightman.
7 Housing (Homeless Persons) Act 1977, ss 1(2)(d), 4(7) (added by the Housing (Scotland) Act 1986 (c 65), s 21(2), (3), respectively). Cf the Housing Act 1985 (c 68), s 58(2A), (2B) (added by the Housing and Planning Act 1986 (c 63), s 14(2)).
8 Interview with Lord Pitt, Chairman of SHELTER, November 1986.

2039. Applications. A duty arises under the homelessness provisions of the Housing (Scotland) Act 1987 only when an application is made, as opposed to inquiries being made about the likely attitude of the local authority if the applicant should become homeless[1]. Local authorities must provide a proper service to enable applications to be made at all reasonable times, which in heavily populated areas means a twenty-four-hour service[2]. Applications may be made individually, and this is likely to occur where the applicant is seeking to establish non-acquiescence in actions or omissions amounting to intentional homelessness[3]. An applicant may make multiple applications to different authorities, and the nature of the decision-making process may result in different assessments. Coupled with the concept of local connection this means that authority A may determine an applicant intentionally homeless and yet have to house that person because authority B comes to a different decision. Whether authorities at the receiving end of a local connection referral must accept this position[4] depends on the quality of the original decision and whether there has been additional investigation[5]. In addition, there may be repeat applications to a single authority where there has been any change in circumstances[6].

1 *R v Hillingdon London Borough, ex parte Tinn* (1988) 20 HLR 305.
2 *R v Camden London Borough, ex parte Gillan* (1988) 21 HLR 114, DC.
3 *R v Penwith District Council, ex parte Trevena* (1984) 17 HLR 526.
4 *R v Slough Borough Council, ex parte Ealing London Borough Council* [1981] QB 801, [1981] 1 All ER 601, CA.
5 *R v Tower Hamlets London Borough, ex parte Camden London Borough* (1988) 21 HLR 197, 87 LGR 321.
6 Contrast *Delahaye v Oswestry Borough Council* (1980) Times, 29 July, with *R v Ealing London Borough Council, ex parte McBain* [1986] 1 All ER 13, [1985] 1 WLR 1351, CA.

2040. Inquiries. If a person applies to a local authority for accommodation or for assistance in obtaining accommodation and the authority has reason to believe that the applicant may be homeless or threatened with homelessness, then the authority must make inquiries[1]. Initially it must make such inquiries as are necessary to satisfy itself as to whether the applicant is homeless or threatened with homelessness[1]. If it is satisfied as to homelessness or the threat of homelessness it must then make further inquiries to satisfy itself (1) whether the applicant is in priority need[2], and (2) whether he became homeless or threatened with homelessness intentionally[3]. The authority may, if it thinks fit, also make inquiries as to whether he has a local connection with another local authority in Great Britain[4]. The onus is on authorities to make the proper inquiries rather than on the applicant to prove his case for assistance[5]. The Code of Guidance suggests a variety of issues which local authorities should cover in the inquiry process, such as the size and structure of the household, the nature and location of the accommodation last occupied, the reasons for leaving it and the prospects of return, the question of availability of accommodation elsewhere, any particular problems such as illness or handicap, the need for accommodation located some distance from a violent partner, and the length of time the applicant intends to stay in the area[6]. Other relevant information might include the place and type of employment, family connections or attendance at hospitals and schools[7]. The Secretary of State advises that inquiries should be carried out quickly and sympathetically, and in many cases it should be possible for all the issues to be dealt with in a single interview[8]. In the event of inquiries taking further time, not only should applicants be kept fully informed of what is happening[8], but if the authority has reason to believe that an applicant may be homeless and in priority need it must ensure that temporary accommodation is provided[9].

After an initial reticence about the extent and nature of inquiries that are required[10], the courts have made it clear that the authority must obtain such information as will enable it to make a proper decision[11], even if such inquiries are complex[12]. If the authority has failed to make inquiries as to whether accommodation in fact is available to an applicant, any finding of intentional homelessness or that the applicant is not homeless would be unlawful and subject to judicial review[13]. Similarly, where an applicant has lost accommodation because of mortgage arrears it is incumbent on the authority to investigate whether the non-payment was deliberate[14]. Issues which are crucial to the tests of homelessness, priority need and intentional homelessness must be investigated or there must be material on which the authority can base its decision[15].

The inquiries must be carried out fairly and the applicant given the right to a fair hearing[16], although this does not require the applicant to be heard personally[17]. It is not necessary for an applicant to raise matters with an authority where it is evident from the applicant's conduct that further inquiries are required[18]. Similarly, where there is evidence put forward which suggests on the face of it that the applicant is entitled to accommodation under the homelessness provisions of the Housing (Scotland) Act 1987, then the authority, if it has doubts about the evidence, may not reject it without further inquiry[19] unless it is highly implausible[20].

1 Housing (Scotland) Act 1987 (c 26), s 28(1).
2 Ibid, s 28(2)(a). As to priority need, see paras 2051 ff below.
3 Ibid, s 28(2)(b). As to intentional homelessness, see paras 2057 ff below.
4 Ibid, s 28(2). As to local connections, see para 2066 below.
5 *R v Woodspring District Council, ex parte Walters* (1984) 16 HLR 73.
6 Code of Guidance, para 2.2. As to the Code, see para 2037 above.
7 Ibid, para 2.3.
8 Ibid, para 2.4.
9 Housing (Scotland) Act 1987, s 29(1). This duty arises irrespective of any local connection which an applicant may have with another local authority: s 29(2).
10 *Miller v Wandsworth London Borough Council* (1980) Times, 19 March; *Lally v Kensington and Chelsea Royal Borough* (1980) Times, 27 March.
11 *R v Reigate and Banstead Borough Council, ex parte Paris* (1984) 17 HLR 103; *R v Dacorum Borough Council, ex parte Brown* (1989) 21 HLR 405.
12 *R v Tower Hamlets London Borough Council, ex parte Rouf* (1989) 21 HLR 294.
13 *R v Westminster City Council, ex parte Ali* (1983) 11 HLR 83.
14 *R v Wyre Borough Council, ex parte Joyce* (1983) 11 HLR 73.
15 *Krishnan v Hillingdon London Borough Council* 1981 LAG Bulletin 137.
16 *Afan Borough Council v Marchant* 1980 LAG Bulletin 16.
17 *R v West Somerset District Council, ex parte Blake* 10 July 1986, QBD (unreported).
18 *R v West Dorset District Council, ex parte Phillips* (1984) 17 HLR 336.
19 *R v Bath City Council, ex parte Sangermano* (1984) 17 HLR 94.
20 *R v Gillingham Borough Council, ex parte Loch* 17 Sept 1984, QBD (unreported).

(2) MEANING OF 'HOMELESS'

2041. Introduction. Part II of the Housing (Scotland) Act 1987[1] defines the situations in which a person is homeless[2]. There are four situations where a person is homeless according to the Act: rooflessness; no right to accommodation; accommodation inadequate for the family unit; and accommodation the occupation of which is unacceptable for a variety of reasons[3].

1 The Housing (Scotland) Act 1987 (c 26), Pt II, comprises ss 24–43.
2 Ibid, s 24.
3 See paras 2042 ff below.

2042. Rooflessness. A person is homeless if he has no accommodation in Scotland, or England or Wales[1]. This would apply to someone who was living rough. It also includes someone living in temporary refuge accommodation such as night shelters[2] and women's refuges[3]. It would also include someone who had accommodation outside Great Britain. However, as we shall see, where applicants have accommodation elsewhere they may be regarded as having become homeless intentionally and so qualify only for temporary assistance[4].

1 Housing (Scotland) Act 1987 (c 26), s 24(1).
2 *R v Waveney District Council, ex parte Bowers* (1982) Times, 25 May (revsd [1983] QB 238, [1982] 3 All ER 727, CA, on the issue of vulnerability under the Housing (Scotland) Act 1987, s 25(1)(c), for which see para 2054 below).
3 *R v Ealing London Borough Council, ex parte Sidhu* (1982) 80 LGR 534, 2 HLR 45; *R v Broxbourne Borough Council, ex parte Willmoth* (1989) 21 HLR 415.
4 As to intentional homelessness, see paras 2057 ff below.

2043. No right to accommodation. There are also situations where a person ostensibly has somewhere to stay but has no right of occupation. A person does not have a right to accommodation if that person had a right in the past which has been lost[1], nor if the occupancy is dependent upon an employment relationship[2].

1 *R v Woodspring District Council, ex parte Walters* (1984) 16 HLR 73.
2 *R v Kensington and Chelsea Royal Borough, ex parte Minton* (1988) 20 HLR 648.

2044. Accommodation inadequate for the family unit. A person is treated as having no accommodation if there is no accommodation which he has the right or permission to occupy along with any other person who normally resides with him as a member of his family[1]. The right or permission can be express or implied, and it may stem from a rule of law or enactment[1], such as the rights of occupancy of a non-entitled spouse or cohabitee under the Matrimonial Homes (Family Protection) (Scotland) Act 1981[2]. The courts have accepted that the right of a cohabitee to apply for a declaration of occupancy rights has the status of a right to remain in occupation[3], despite the fact that his right is inchoate in that it depends on satisfying the sheriff that the couple are living together as man and wife[4]. The Housing (Scotland) Act 1987 indicates that an applicant needs to be able reasonably to reside with any person who normally resides with him as a member of his family[5]. This is a factual question and goes wider than simply close blood relatives. The Code of Guidance suggests that the phrase should be taken to include people living together as if they were members of a family, such as cohabiting couples and adults with foster children[6]. The wording of the Act is wide enough to cover a companion or housekeeper for an elderly or disabled person. The extent of the family can be determined depending on past living arrangements. However, there is case law to suggest that an authority would not be bound to house the family in a single unit if this were impracticable[7]. In addition, the wording includes those who would normally live with the applicant, so that this covers situations where the parties have not been living together because of lack of accommodation. In a controversial House of Lords case it was indicated by Lord Brightman that any accommodation would suffice provided it could physically accommodate the family[8]. As long as an applicant had accommodation it did not need to be 'reasonable', 'adequate' nor 'suitable' as earlier case law had suggested[9]. Lord Brightman summed up the matter thus: 'There are no rules'[10]. This interpretation would not have allowed successful challenges by applicants in the situation which one family had found themselves in an earlier case — a family of seven in a room 12 feet by 10 feet[11]. This limited approach has now been expressly augmented by a change to the definition of 'homelessness' to cover overcrowded accommodation which is a threat to the health of the occupants[12].

1 Housing (Scotland) Act 1987 (c 26), s 24(2).
2 See the Matrimonial Homes (Family Protection) (Scotland) Act 1981 (c 59), s 1 (spouses) and s 18 (cohabitees) (amended by the Law Reform (Miscellaneous Provisions) (Scotland) Act 1985 (c 73), s 13).
3 *McAlinden v Bearsden and Milngavie District Council* 1986 SLT 191, OH.
4 Matrimonial Homes (Family Protection) (Scotland) Act 1981, s 18(2).
5 Housing (Scotland) Act 1987, s 24(2).

6 Code of Guidance, para 2.13a. As to the Code, see para 2037 above.
7 *R v Lambeth London Borough, ex parte Ly* (1986) 19 HLR 51.
8 *R v Hillingdon London Borough Council, ex parte Puhlhofer* [1986] AC 484 at 517, *sub nom Puhlhofer v Hillingdon London Borough Council* [1986] 1 All ER 467 at 474, HL.
9 See para 2049 below.
10 *R v Hillingdon London Borough Council, ex parte Puhlhofer* [1986] AC 484 at 517, *sub nom Puhlhofer v Hillingdon London Borough Council* [1986] 1 All ER 467 at 474, HL.
11 *R v Westminster City Council, ex parte Ali* (1983) 11 HLR 83.
12 See para 2049 below.

2045. Unacceptable accommodation. There are four ways under the legislation in which a person who actually has accommodation can still be regarded as homeless: (1) if he cannot secure entry to it; (2) if occupation of it will probably lead to violence or threats of violence from another resident; (3) if it is a moveable structure and there is no place where he can keep it and reside in it; and (4) if it is overcrowded and may endanger the occupants' health[1].

1 See the Housing (Scotland) Act 1987 (c 26), s 24(3)(a)–(d), and paras 2046–2049 below.

2046. Unable to secure access. A person is homeless if he has accommodation but he cannot secure entry to it[1]. This would cover situations where the landlord had forcibly evicted the tenant and there was no immediate prospect of re-entry. The fact that one has a housing right which may not be put into effect is recognised in the homelessness provisions of the Housing (Scotland) Act 1987 as amounting to homelessness. It would also cover housing which had been made the subject of a closing order[2], thus rendering the right of ownership or tenancy inoperable. The courts have, however, taken a lax view of the problems faced by partners following a marital breakdown. In the *Cadney* case[3] the court was not prepared to hold that no reasonable council could reach the decision that a women was not homeless where she left the marital home to live with another man. Several months later the new relationship broke up and the wife approached the local authority for assistance under the homeless persons legislation. It declined to offer her accommodation on the basis that she had accommodation — the former matrimonial home of which she was joint tenant.

1 Housing (Scotland) Act 1987 (c 26), s 24(3)(a).
2 As to closing orders, see para 1982 above.
3 *R v Purbeck District Council, ex parte Cadney* (1985) 17 HLR 534.

2047. Probability of violence from another resident. A person who has accommodation is also homeless if it is probable that occupation of it will lead to violence from some other person residing in it[1], or to threats of violence from another resident and that person is likely to carry out the threats[2]. This provision is limited to threats from another resident in the property. It does not deal with two common problems: violence or threats from neighbours[3]; and violence from members of the household who have moved out of the property or never lived in it[4]. However, these two limitations in the legislation can be dealt with by the change made to the English legislation in 1986[5], which provides that a person is not to be treated as having accommodation unless it is such as would be reasonable for him to continue to occupy[6].

1 Housing (Scotland) Act 1987 (c 26), s 24(3)(b). See *R v Broxbourne Borough Council, ex parte Willmoth* (1989) 21 HLR 415.
2 Housing (Scotland) Act 1987, s 24(3)(b).
3 *R v Vale of White Horse District Council, ex parte Preen* 18 April 1983, QBD (unreported) (Glasgow); *R v Warwick District Council, ex parte Wood* 15 August 1983, QBD (unreported)

(Glasgow). For details, see P Watchman and P Robson *Homelessness and the Law in Britain* (1989) p 117. These cases were dealt with as questions of intentional homelessness, but illustrate the existence of the phenomenon of violent threats of neighbours.

4 This problem was pointed out by Scottish Women's Aid, and there are draft proposals at the time of writing to alter the legislation to take account of this unfortunate omission.

5 *R v Kensington and Chelsea Royal London Borough Council, ex parte Hammell* [1989] QB 518 at 535, [1989] 1 All ER 1202 at 1212, CA.

6 See the Housing Act 1985 (c 68), s 58(2A) (added by the Housing and Planning Act 1986 (c 63), s 14(2)).

2048. No place to park a moveable structure or moor a boat. Where a person lives in either a mobile home or a boat there are circumstances where they may be treated as homeless if there is no place where the mobile home or boat can lawfully be placed and lived in[1]. This covers moveable structures, vehicles or vessels which are either designed or adapted for human habitation[1]. No case law yet exists on the interpretation of this provision, although there have been cases where homeless applicants have occupied cars[2], caravans[3] and boats[4] prior to applying to a local authority as homeless.

1 Housing (Scotland) Act 1987 (c 26), s 24(3)(c).
2 *Hynds v Midlothian District Council* 1986 SLT 54, OH.
3 *Smith v Wokingham District Council* 1980 LAG Bulletin 92.
4 *R v Preseli District Council, ex parte Fisher* (1984) 17 HLR 147.

2049. Bad housing conditions. Between 1977 and 1986 various standards were operated by the courts to indicate that applicants who occupied housing in bad condition were also to be regarded as homeless[1]. The standards applied included 'reasonable in all the circumstances'[2], 'unsuitable for human habitation'[3] and 'inappropriate accommodation'[4]. These interpretations, including as they did a House of Lords decision, were rejected by the House of Lords in 1986[5]. This was a doubtful authority in Scotland since there was already authority from a House of Lords appeal in a Scottish case on the need for accommodation to be 'reasonable'[6]. However, rather than rely on this technical argument[7] a campaign was initiated to restore what had been the status quo by inserting a clear test in the legislation.

The campaign led by SHELTER (Scotland) resulted in a specific test that a person is homeless if he has accommodation but it is statutorily overcrowded[8] and may endanger the health of the occupants[9]. There are two requirements in the test. The provisions for statutory overcrowding are found in Part VII of the Housing (Scotland) Act 1987[10]. At the time of the change to the law it was pointed out that the statutory overcrowding provisions were limited in their application to housing below a certain rateable value[11]. This restriction was removed in the Housing (Scotland) Act 1988[12]. In addition, the local authority must be satisfied that the overcrowded accommodation may endanger the health of the occupants. This is a narrower test than that introduced in England and Wales. The difference can produce greater variations in decision-making in England. One early case in England saw an authority reject an application by an occupant of an overcrowded property which was a fire risk. The Divisional Court was not prepared to overturn this decision[13]. In another case in England the authority's decision on homelessness was successfully challenged. The authority had taken the view that since the accommodation was not overcrowded it could not be unreasonable[14]. The local authority had applied the overcrowding test mechanically, rather than looking to the wider English question of 'reasonable . . . to continue to occupy'[15].

1 See P Watchman and P Robson *Developments in Homelessness and the Law 1983–85* (1986) pp 28–31.
2 *Brown v Hamilton District Council* 1983 SC (HL) 1 at 17, 1983 SLT 397 at 403, per Lord Wheatley.

3 *R v South Hereford District Council, ex parte Miles* (1983) 17 HLR 82.
4 *R v Preseli District Council, ex parte Fisher* (1984) 17 HLR 147.
5 *R v Hillingdon London Borough Council, ex parte Puhlhofer* [1986] AC 484, *sub nom Puhlhofer v Hillingdon London Borough Council* [1986] 1 All ER 467, HL.
6 *Brown v Hamilton District Council* 1983 SC (HL) 1, 1983 SLT 397.
7 P Robson *Life after Puhlhofer* Scottish Housing Law News (1986) Issue 1, p 1.
8 Ie within the meaning of the Housing (Scotland) Act 1987 (c 26), s 135, for which see para 2001 above.
9 Ibid, s 24(3)(d).
10 Ibid, Pt VII, comprises ss 135–151.
11 T Mullen 'The New Law on Homelessness' 1987 SCOLAG 7.
12 Housing (Scotland) Act 1987, s 151(1) (definition of 'house') (amended by the Housing (Scotland) Act 1988 (c 43), s 72(1), Sch 8, para 3, so as to delete the reference to rateable value): see para 2001, note 1, above.
13 *R v Blackpool Borough Council, ex parte Smith* 29 July 1987, QBD (unreported).
14 *R v Westminster City Council, ex parte Alouat* (1989) 21 HLR 477.
15 Housing Act 1985 (c 68), s 58(2A) (added by the Housing and Planning Act 1986 (c 63), s 14(2)).

2050. Threatened with homelessness. A person is threatened with homelessness if it is likely that he will become homeless within twenty-eight days[1]. This covers those who have tenancy rights but which are likely to be lost through a successful possession action in the courts. It also covers situations where permission to stay is withdrawn, as by a parent from a child. It formerly covered the situation of spouses who were either asked or forced to leave by their partners. Those who are neither tenants nor owners, 'non-entitled spouses', now may rely on the occupancy rights provided for under the Matrimonial Homes (Family Protection) (Scotland) Act 1981[2]. This category also includes, according to an Outer House decision[3], partners living together as man and wife where the non-entitled spouse has the right to seek a declaration of occupancy rights[4].

1 Housing (Scotland) Act 1987 (c 26), s 24(4).
2 Matrimonial Homes (Family Protection) (Scotland) Act 1981 (c 59), s 1(1) (amended by the Law Reform (Miscellaneous Provisions) (Scotland) Act 1985 (c 73), s 13).
3 *McAlinden v Bearsden and Milngavie District Council* 1986 SLT 191, OH.
4 Matrimonial Homes (Family Protection) (Scotland) Act 1981, s 18(1) (as amended: see note 2 above).

(3) PRIORITY NEED

2051. Introduction. The major limitation on whether a homeless person can expect assistance under the Housing (Scotland) Act 1987 is priority need. This is defined in the Act under four distinct headings: pregnancy; dependent children; vulnerability; and emergency[1], although the Secretary of State has power to vary these categories and add new ones[2].

1 See the Housing (Scotland) Act 1987 (c 26), s 25(1)(a)–(d), and paras 2052–2055 below.
2 See ibid, s 25(2)–(4), and para 2056 below.

2052. Pregnancy. Priority is given to pregnant women[1]. The Housing (Scotland) Act 1987 does not state any minimum duration of pregnancy. Alternatively a person with whom the pregnant woman resides qualifies as being in priority need[1]. This allows a partner to make an application. This might occur where the partner is in waged work and the local authority wishes to offer a tenancy to the working partner. Also included are those who might reasonably be expected to reside with the pregnant woman[1].

1 Housing (Scotland) Act 1987 (c 26), s 25(1)(a).

2053. Dependent children. A person with whom dependent children reside has a priority need[1]. Where the children are not living with the applicant they nonetheless have a priority need if they might be expected to reside with them[1]. The Code of Guidance suggests that a distinction should be made between situations where the children are not living with the applicant because of lack of accommodation and where there is some other reason, such as when they are in care because of risk of violence. In the latter case where it is unreasonable for the children to live with the applicant the Code of Guidance indicates that they should be excluded from the priority category[2]. The term 'dependent children' is not defined in the legislation. The Code of Guidance states that no custody order is necessary[2], and this approach has been adopted in the courts[3]. The term 'dependents' is to be construed widely, according to the Code of Guidance, to include grandchildren, adopted or foster children[4]. Dependency is to be assumed where the children are either under sixteen or in full-time education or training or otherwise unable to maintain themselves up to the age of nineteen[4]. The changes introduced by the Social Security Act 1988 mean that many sixteen- and seventeen-year-olds will not be entitled to income support in their own right for a period after leaving school[5]. They are assumed to be living with their parents. Certain individuals come within a limited range of exceptions. These include lone parents and registered blind[6].

1 Housing (Scotland) Act 1987 (c 26), s 25(1)(b).
2 Code of Guidance, para 2.13a. As to the Code, see para 2037 above.
3 *R v Ealing London Borough Council, ex parte Sidhu* (1982) 80 LGR 543, 2 HLR 45.
4 Code of Guidance, para 2.13a.
5 Social Security Act 1986 (c 50), s 20(3) (amended by the Social Security Act 1988 (c 7), s 4(1)).
6 See the Income Support (General) Regulations 1987, SI 1987/1967, reg 8, Sch 1, paras 1, 8; D Killeen *Estranged* (1988).

2054. Vulnerability. Persons who are vulnerable have a priority need for accommodation[1]. Within the category of vulnerability the legislation mentions four specific conditions: old age, mental illness, mental handicap and physical disability[1]. In addition, a person may be vulnerable as a result of any other special reason[1]. There has been extensive litigation on the vulnerability aspect of the priority need test. The general test of vulnerability according to the Court of Appeal depends on whether a person is 'less able to fend [for himself] so that injury or detriment will result when a less vulnerable man will be able to cope without harmful effects'[2]. It has been suggested that vulnerability should be concerned with housing, although this view seems unduly restrictive[3]. The principal practical question at issue has been the mechanism whereby local authorities assess those who may be vulnerable. Where confronted by someone who is on the face of things vulnerable an authority may not reject the application without seeking proper advice[4]. Local authorities must not simply rubber stamp the views of other authorities on vulnerability[5], nor those of professional advisers[6]. They should seek relevant advice. This may include consulting with social work departments[7] and taking medical opinion[8] and that of housing specialists where appropriate[9]. Where professional advice conflicts, the authority may choose which advice it will follow[10]. Vulnerability as a result of old age should be looked at broadly and should include not only those of retirement age but those approaching those ages[11]. Not all mental illness will result in an applicant being assessed as vulnerable[12]. The authority, properly advising themselves, must decide. The same considerations apply in relation to mental handicap and physical disability. It should be noted that the suggestion in the Code of Guidance that a person in the mental or physically disabled category must be substantially disabled[13] is contrary to the wording of the legislation. It has been expressly disapproved by the courts[14].

As far as other special reason is concerned, the Code of Guidance suggests that two categories of applicants should be considered vulnerable on this ground by local authorities: battered women without children who are at risk, and young people at risk of financial, sexual or other exploitation[15]. Vulnerability does not arise from age alone[16]. However, according to Lord Ross in a case involving a sixteen-year-old girl, not every sixteen-year-old is vulnerable, but when you find a girl of that age 'who has no assets, no income and nowhere to go and who has apparently left home because of violence, I am of opinion that no reasonable authority could fail to conclude that she was vulnerable'[17].

 1 Housing (Scotland) Act 1987 (c 26), s 25(1)(c).
 2 *R v Waveney District Council, ex parte Bowers* [1983] QB 238 at 244, 245, [1982] 3 All ER 727 at 730, CA, per Waller LJ.
 3 *R v Reigate and Banstead Borough Council, ex parte Di Dominico* (1987) 20 HLR 153.
 4 *R v Bath City Council, ex parte Sangermano* (1984) 17 HLR 94.
 5 *R v Wandsworth Borough Council, ex parte Banbury* (1986) 19 HLR 76.
 6 *R v Lambeth London Borough, ex parte Carroll* (1987) 20 HLR 142.
 7 *Kelly v Monklands District Council* 1986 SLT 169 at 172, OH, per Lord Ross.
 8 *R v Bath City Council, ex parte Sangermano* (1984) 17 HLR 94.
 9 *R v Lambeth London Borough, ex parte Carroll* (1987) 20 HLR 142.
10 *R v Tandridge District Council, ex parte Hayman* 29 September 1983, QBD (unreported).
11 Code of Guidance, para 2.13c. As to the Code, see para 2037 above.
12 *R v Bath City Council, ex parte Sangermano* (1984) 17 HLR 94.
13 Code of Guidance, para 2.13c.
14 *R v Waveney District Council, ex parte Bowers* [1983] QB 238 at 245, [1982] 3 All ER 727 at 730, CA, per Waller LJ; *R v Lambeth London Borough, ex parte Carroll* (1987) 20 HLR 142.
15 Code of Guidance, para 2.12c.
16 *Kelly v Monklands District Council* 1986 SLT 169 at 171, OH, per Lord Ross.
17 1986 SLT 169 at 171, OH, and cf 172.

2055. Emergency. An applicant is in priority need if he is homeless or threatened with homelessness as a result of an emergency such as flood, fire or any other disaster[1]. Apart from the disasters specifically mentioned it has been decided in the Court of Appeal that the service of a demolition order is not covered by this provision[2].

 1 Housing (Scotland) Act 1987 (c 26), s 25(1)(d).
 2 *Noble v South Hereford District Council* (1983) 17 HLR 80, CA.

2056. Power of the Secretary of State to specify further categories of priority need. The Secretary of State has the power to specify further descriptions as having a priority need as well as to amend or repeal the existing categories[1]. Appropriate prior consultation is required[2]. No such alteration has yet been made and none is envisaged by the Scottish Office[3].

 1 Housing (Scotland) Act 1987 (c 26), s 25(2). The power is exercised by order made by statutory instrument (s 25(2)), a draft of which must be approved by each House of Parliament (s 25(4)).
 2 Ibid, s 25(3).
 3 Scottish Office letter to COSLA reported in *Inside Housing* 13 October 1989.

(4) INTENTIONAL HOMELESSNESS

2057. The background. A person becomes homeless intentionally if he deliberately does or fails to do anything in consequence of which he ceases to occupy accommodation which is available for his occupation and which it would have been reasonable for him to continue to occupy[1]. The Private Member's Bill introduced by Stephen Ross MP made no mention of this limitation on the rights of homeless applicants to accommodation. Parallel with this restriction is one on those who are threatened with homelessness intentionally[2]. This occurs where an applicant deliberately does or fails to do anything the likely result of which is that he will be forced to leave accommodation which is available for his occupation and which it would have been reasonable for him to continue to occupy[2]. As a result of the late stage at which homeless people generally present themselves to authorities this latter test has not been the subject of extensive litigation[3].

The introduction of the intentionality concept allows local authorities to limit their obligations to homeless persons in priority need[4] to provide accommodation for such a period as they consider will give him a reasonable opportunity of himself securing that accommodation becomes available for his occupation[5]. Authorities find about 10 per cent of priority homeless applicants to be intentionally homeless[6]. Actions which have resulted in the loss of accommodation and a finding of intentionality include wilful non-payment of rent[7]; voluntarily terminating a tenancy[8]; giving up a job with 'tied accommodation'[9]; failing to maintain a satisfactory tenancy[10]; moving from abroad without ensuring that there is accommodation available in Great Britain[11]; and moving from another part of the United Kingdom without ensuring that permanent accommodation is available[12].

1 Housing (Scotland) Act 1987 (c 26), s 26(1).
2 Ibid, s 26(2).
3 See *Zold v Bristol City Council* (1981) LAG 287, and *Jones v Bristol City Council* (1981) LAG 163, discussed in P Watchman and P Robson *Homelessness and the Law* (1983) p 76.
4 As to priority need, see paras 2051 ff above.
5 Housing (Scotland) Act 1987, s 31(3)(a): see para 2068 below.
6 Scottish Development Department Statistical Bulletin, June 1987.
7 *Robinson v Torbay Borough Council* [1982] 1 All ER 726; *Hynds v Midlothian District Council* 1986 SLT 54, OH.
8 *Dyson v Kerrier District Council* [1980] 3 All ER 313, [1980] 1 WLR 1205, CA; *Mazzaccherini v Argyll and Bute District Council* 1987 SCLR 475, OH.
9 *Lewis v North Devon District Council* [1981] 1 All ER 27, *sub nom R v North Devon District Council, ex parte Lewis* [1981] 1 WLR 328; but cf *R v Kensington and Chelsea Royal Borough, ex parte Minton* (1988) 20 HLR 648.
10 *Mackenzie v West Lothian District Council* 1979 SC 433; *R v Salford City Council, ex parte Devenport* (1983) 82 LGR 89, 8 HLR 54, CA.
11 *R v Tower Hamlets London Borough, ex parte Monaf* (1988) 20 HLR 529, 86 LGR 709, CA.
12 *R v Peterborough District Council, ex parte McKernan* 17 July 1987, QBD (unreported); *R v Vale of White Horse District Council, ex parte Preen* 18 April 1983, QBD (unreported).

2058. Accommodation must exist and have been available for occupation. As far as intentional homelessness is concerned, accommodation is to be regarded as available for the applicant's occupation only if it is available for occupation both by him and by any other person who might reasonably be expected to reside with him[1]. There is no minimum standard as to what amounts to accommodation in Scotland, although the question of reasonableness to continue to occupy imports a relative standard[2]. The local authority must consider the question of whether or not there is available accommodation and not start off with the assumption that the applicant must have done deliberate acts which result in the current state of homelessness[3]. The fact that accommodation was previously available cannot displace the requirement to make inquiries at the time of application[4]. Accommodation offered but never accepted by the applicant is not available for occupation[5].

1 Housing (Scotland) Act 1987 (c 26), s 41.
2 See ibid, s 26(4).
3 *R v Reigate and Banstead Borough Council, ex parte Paris* (1984) 17 HLR 103.
4 *R v Westminster City Council, ex parte Ali* (1983) 11 HLR 83.
5 *R v Westminster City Council, ex parte Chambers* (1982) 6 HLR 24, 81 LGR 401; *R v Ealing London Borough Council, ex parte McBain* [1986] 1 All ER 13, [1985] 1 WLR 1351, CA.

2059. Accommodation must have been reasonable to continue to occupy.

The local authority must have regard to the housing conditions which led the applicant to give up the accommodation[1]. Overcrowded conditions and damp unhealthy conditions may lead to a finding that it would not have been reasonable for him to continue to live in that accommodation[2]. In deciding whether or not it would have been reasonable to continue to occupy the available accommodation the authority may look at the general circumstances prevailing in relation to housing in the district of the local authority[3]. In addition to looking at the housing suitability, factors personal to the circumstances of the applicant are relevant[4]. These have been held to include lack of employment prospects[5], marital breakdown[6], threats of violence from outwith the household[7], medical problems of the applicant[8], and the unavailability of welfare benefits[9]. Local authorities often take the view that it is up to the applicant to put up with inconvenience, particularly where the applicant has prior knowledge[10].

1 *R v Eastleigh Borough Council, ex parte Beattie* (1983) 10 HLR 134.
2 Cf *R v Westminster City Council, ex parte Ali* (1983) 11 HLR 83 (overcrowding), with *R v Westminster City Council, ex parte Lester* 22 February 1984, QBD (unreported) (dampness).
3 Housing (Scotland) Act 1987 (c 26), s 26(4); *Formosa v Manchester City Council* (1980) Roof 27. 'Roof' is a magazine published by SHELTER.
4 *R v Hammersmith and Fulham London Borough Council, ex parte Duro-Rama* (1983) 81 LGR 702.
5 *R v Kensington and Chelsea Royal Borough, ex parte Cunha* (1988) 21 HLR 16.
6 *R v Basingstoke and Deane Borough Council, ex parte Bassett* (1983) 10 HLR 125.
7 *R v Vale of White Horse District Council, ex parte Preen* 19 April 1983, QBD (unreported).
8 *R v Wycombe District Council, ex parte Homes* 1 December 1988, QBD (unreported).
9 *R v Hammersmith and Fulham Borough Council, ex parte Duro-Rama* (1983) 81 LGR 702.
10 *Fezoui v Torbay Borough Council* 27 July 1983, CA (unreported).

2060. Applicant must have ceased to occupy accommodation as a result of his or her own acts or omissions.

There must be a direct link between the actions of the applicant and the loss of accommodation, and the homelessness must by a consequence of these actions[1]. Local authorities are entitled to look back to events in the past which triggered off the current state of homelessness[2]. The authority must look at the question of causation at the date the applicant became homeless rather than at the date of the application[3]. The disadvantages of intentional homelessness will not be avoided by an applicant's giving up accommodation and obtaining other temporary accommodation[4]. Accommodation which has failed to break the chain of causation includes off-season holiday lets[4], holiday lets[5], staying with friends or relatives[6], lodgings without security of tenure[7] and bed and breakfast accommodation[8]. The effect of obtaining one of the newer post-1980 tenancies without security of tenure[9] is not fully settled[10]. If, however, another cause intervenes to result in the loss of accommodation where, but for this occurrence, the applicant would have been intentionally homeless, the same principle applies. The applicant cannot be then deemed intentionally homeless[11].

1 See the Housing (Scotland) Act 1987 (c 26), s 26(1), and para 2057 above.
2 *Hynds v Midlothian District Council* 1986 SLT 54, OH; *Mazzaccherini v Argyll and Bute District Council* 1987 SCLR 475, OH. These cases apply the English authorities originating with *De Falco v Crawley Borough Council* [1980] QB 460, [1980] 1 All ER 913, CA.
3 *Din v Wandsworth London Borough Council* [1983] 1 AC 657, [1981] 3 All ER 881, HL.
4 *Dyson v Kerrier District Council* [1980] 3 All ER 313, [1980] 1 WLR 1205, CA.

5 *Lambert v Ealing London Borough Council* [1982] 2 All ER 394, [1982] 1 WLR 550, CA.
6 *De Falco v Crawley Borough Council* [1980] QB 460, [1980] 1 All ER 913, CA.
7 *Mazzaccherini v Argyll and Bute District Council* 1987 SCLR 475, OH; *R v Merton London Borough, ex parte Ruffle* (1988) 21 HLR 361.
8 *R v Harrow London Borough, ex parte Holland* (1982) 4 HLR 108, CA.
9 As to these tenancies, see the Rent (Scotland) Act 1984 (c 58), s 9 (short tenancies, introduced with effect from 1 December 1980 by the Tenants' Rights Etc (Scotland) Act 1980 (c 43), s 34 (repealed)), and the Housing (Scotland) Act 1988 (c 43), s 32 (short assured tenancies, with effect from 2 January 1989).
10 *R v Christchurch Borough Council, ex parte Conway* (1987) 19 HLR 238.
11 *R v Gloucester City Council, ex parte Miles* (1985) 83 LGR 607, 17 HLR 292, CA.

2061. Acts or omissions must have been deliberate. A distinction must be drawn between those actions and omissions which are covered by intentionality which are deliberate and those which are non-deliberate. The Code of Guidance indicates that where an act or omission is involuntary or largely attributable to external factors this should not be regarded as being deliberate. The Secretary of State specifically mentions failure to keep up mortgage or rent payments because of real personal or financial difficulties, arrears of a partner, victims fleeing domestic violence, pregnant women deemed intentionally homeless on account of their pregnancy, people no longer able to afford rent or mortgage payments and living conditions which have degenerated to a point where they cannot reasonably be expected to be lived in[1]. Non-deliberate actions and omissions accepted by the courts have included failing to pay rent or mortgage payments through financial hardship[2], leaving accommodation early where there is no effective defence to a possession action[3], and fleeing violence and threats of violence from political opponents[4]. However, included within deliberate actions and omission have been moving but failing to make arrangements before leaving settled accommodation[5], as well as coming to Britain from abroad without making appropriate arrangements for permanent accommodation[6].

1 Code of Guidance, paras 2.16, 2.17. As to the Code, see para 2037 above.
2 *R v Wyre Borough Council, ex parte Joyce* (1983) 11 HLR 72.
3 *R v Portsmouth City Council, ex parte Knight* (1984) 82 LGR 184 (tied accommodation and dismissal); *R v Surrey Heath Borough Council, ex parte Li* (1984) 16 HLR 79 (licensees).
4 *R v Westminster City Council, ex parte Iqbal* 21 October 1988, QBD (unreported). See also the treatment of household 3 in *R v Hammersmith and Fulham London Borough, ex parte P* (1989) 22 HLR 21.
5 *Dyson v Kerrier District Council* [1980] 3 All ER 313, [1980] 1 WLR 1205, CA; *R v Vale of White Horse District Council, ex parte Preen* 18 April 1983, QBD (unreported).
6 *R v Westminster City Council, ex parte Rahman* 9 June 1983, QBD (unreported); *R v Peterborough District Council, ex parte McKernan* 17 July 1987, QBD (unreported). See, however, *R v Wandsworth London Borough Council, ex parte Rose* (1983) 11 HLR 105; *R v Hammersmith and Fulham London Borough, ex parte P* (1989) 22 HLR 21.

2062. Acts or omissions in good faith and in ignorance of a relevant fact are not deliberate. The Housing (Scotland) Act 1987 specifically states that certain acts or omissions are not to be treated as deliberate. This occurs where the acts or omissions are in good faith made by a person who was unaware of any relevant fact[1]. The Secretary of State has indicated that examples of persons who might be regarded as unaware of a relevant fact are those who get into rent arrears unaware of their entitlement to welfare benefits and those who leave rented accommodation on receipt of a notice to quit unaware of their rights of security of tenure[2]. There is, however, an obiter view from the House of Lords to the effect that there is a difference between what the statute recognises, namely ignorance of a fact, and ignorance of rights, which is a matter of law[3]. In practice the courts do not seem to have operated this distinction. They have accepted in this category a woman who assumed that the earlier availability of accommodation for her brothers meant that she would be treated the same by her father on her entry into Britain[4]; a tenant who failed to appreciate the need as indicated in correspondence to respond promptly in order to secure a tenancy renewal[5]; and a young woman who did not believe her father's threats to refuse her re-entry to the family home if she stayed with her mother while pursuing a higher education course away from home[6]. The acceptance of a mistaken belief is subject to the proviso that the belief must be intrinsically reasonable[6]. This seems to be related to the nature of the relationship between the parties[7].

1 Housing (Scotland) Act 1987 (c 26), s 26(3).
2 Code of Guidance, para 2.18. As to the Code, see para 2037 above.
3 *Brown v Hamilton District Council* 1983 SC (HL) 1, 1983 SLT 397.
4 *R v Wandsworth London Borough, ex parte Rose* (1983) 11 HLR 105.
5 *R v Christchurch Borough Council, ex parte Conway* (1987) 19 HLR 238.
6 *Wincentzen v Monklands District Council* 1987 SCLR 712, 1988 SLT 259, OH; 1989 SCLR 190, 1988 SLT 847, IH.
7 Contrast *R v Wandsworth London Borough, ex parte Rose* (1983) 11 HLR 105, and *Wincentzen v Monklands District Council* 1987 SCLR 712, 1988 SLT 259, OH; 1989 SCLR 190, 1988 SLT 847, IH, with *R v Wandsworth London Borough Council v Wells* 23 November 1983, QBD (unreported).

2063. Acts or omissions may be by either the applicant or a member of the family unit. Although it has been pointed out that the legislation refers to an applicant[1], it has been suggested in the courts that the legislation, in practice, deals with the family unit[2]. This means that all members of the family unit are assumed to be party to the acts of one member. Accordingly, if these acts lead to a finding of intentionality then this covers all the members of the family unit[3]. There are, however, situations where the actions or omissions are not to be treated as being the responsibility of the family unit[4].

1 *Hynds v Midlothian District Council* 1986 SLT 54 at 56, OH, per Lord Ross.
2 *Lewis v North Devon District Council* [1981] 1 All ER 27, *sub nom R v North Devon District Council, ex parte Lewis* [1981] 1 WLR 328.
3 *R v Swansea City Council, ex parte John* (1982) 9 HLR 56.
4 See para 2064 below.

2064. Acts or omissions are not the responsibility of the applicant where there is non-acquiescence. In outlining the notion of family unit responsibility it was noted that there were some situations where it would be unreasonable to assume that, for example, one partner acquiesced in the actions or omissions amounting to intentionality[1]. The courts have recognised non-acquiescence in such situations as when the husband failed to heed the wife's urgings to pay the rent[2] or mortgage[3], and the surrender of the tenancy by the wife when leaving her husband where there was a later reconciliation[4]. It is not enough simply to assert non-acquiescence[5]. However, this will be much easier to establish where there is some tangible evidence of non-acquiescence, such as making payments towards paying off rent arrears[6].

1 *Lewis v North Devon District Council* [1981] 1 All ER 27 at 31, *sub nom R v North Devon District Council, ex parte Lewis* [1981] 1 WLR 328 at 333.
2 *R v West Dorset District Council, ex parte Phillips* (1984) 17 HLR 336; *R v East Northamptonshire District Council, ex parte Spruce* (1988) 20 HLR 508.
3 *R v Eastleigh Borough Council, ex parte Beattie* (1983) 10 HLR 134.
4 *R v Penwith District Council, ex parte Trevena* (1984) 17 HLR 526.

5 *R v East Hertfordshire District Council, ex parte Bannon* (1986) 18 HLR 515; *Stewart v Monklands District Council* 1987 SCLR 45, 1987 SLT 630, OH.
6 *R v Thanet District Council, ex parte Groves* 19 December 1988, QBD (unreported).

2065. Reviewing intentional homelessness. Where a local authority lawfully determines that an applicant is homeless intentionally, its decision may be altered either by the authority itself or by the decision of another authority. Authorities are urged to review cases from time to time[1]. According to the Secretary of State, they should do this where there is evidence of changed behaviour, such as reducing rent arrears[1]. In addition, the proposition has been accepted that local authorities must accept a different assessment by another authority on intentionality[2] where the applicant is referred back under the local connection provisions[3] unless there is no sound basis for the rejection of the original decision[4]. Where one authority makes a negative decision on intentionality and the unsuccessful homeless person applies elsewhere, the second authority normally must make its own investigations into the question of intentionality. It cannot simply assume the first authority's decision is correct without having grounds for such a belief[5].

1 Code of Guidance, para 2.21. As to the Code, see para 2037 above.
2 *R v Slough Borough Council, ex parte Ealing London Borough Council* [1981] QB 801, [1981] 1 All ER 601, CA.
3 See the Housing (Scotland) Act 1987 (c 26), s 33(2), and para 2066 below.
4 *R v Tower Hamlets London Borough, ex parte Camden London Borough* (1988) 21 HLR 197, 87 LGR 321.
5 *R v South Hereford District Council, ex parte Miles* (1983) 17 HLR 82.

2066. Local connection. Local authorities have a power to investigate whether an applicant has a local connection with the district of another local authority in Scotland, England or Wales[1]. In determining what having a local connection with a district means there are four issues to be considered: (1) past normal voluntary residence there; (2) employment there; (3) family associations there; and (4) any special circumstances[2]. Residence is not deemed to be of a person's choice where that person or any person who might reasonably be expected to reside with him was serving in the regular armed forces of the Crown or was in prison or was detained under the mental health legislation[3]. The Secretary of State adds nothing by way of guidance as to the interpretation of these four issues[4]. Some assistance can be obtained from the approach taken by the courts to the Agreement on Procedures for Referrals of the Homeless[5]. The courts, including the House of Lords, have accepted that decisions taken in strict conformity with the guidelines laid down in this document are lawful[6]. In addition the House of Lords has suggested that, whilst a local connection not founded upon one of the four grounds is irrelevant, an applicant does not have a local connection simply through satisfying one or more of the grounds: local connection is not established simply through either one or more of these factors being present. It is these which spell out a local connection in real terms[7]. It must be built up and established, and this is done through either residence, employment, family associations or other special circumstances[8].

Normal residence has been interpreted following strictly the guidelines in the Agreement[9], which equates this phrase with six months' residence during the past twelve months or three years' residence during the previous five years. Longer periods of residence have not been recognised where the character of the residence did not denote permanence[10]. It is possible for an applicant's circumstances to alter and so provide the basis for a local connection. This occurred in an early case where an applicant obtained work in an area after being rejected for lack of local connection[11]. Other than this, problems regarding the interpretation of 'employment' and 'family associations' have not reached the courts, although the Agreement has been utilised[12] under the system set up under the administrative arrangements under the legislation[13]. The general category of special circumstances has not been accepted as covering the tenant's desire to stay in a particular area[14], nor membership of local institutions or organisations[15].

If the authority establishes in its inquiries in respect of a homeless applicant with a priority need, where it is not satisfied that the applicant became homeless intentionally, that there is local connection elsewhere, the question of referral arises[16]. Pending agreement or referral elsewhere, the responsibility for housing the applicant remains with the original authority[17]. The conditions of referral affect both the applicant and any person who might reasonably be expected to reside with him[18]. The referral can operate in respect of another local authority where the original authority is satisfied that there is no local connection with its district and there is one with the district of the other authority[19]. This is subject to the overall test that neither the applicant nor that person will run the risk of domestic violence in the district of the other authority[20]. A person runs the risk of domestic violence if he (or more usually she) runs the risk of violence from a person with whom, but for the risk of violence, he or she might reasonably be expected to reside or from a person with whom he or she formerly resided[21]. Alternatively a person runs the risk of violence if he or she runs the risk of violence from a partner or ex-partner and these threats are likely to be carried out[22]. The legislation does not at present cover threats from partners with whom the person has never resided. However, the government has responded positively to the call from Scottish Women's Aid to remedy this situation[23]. Only domestic violence is covered, and not threats of violence from others such as neighbours[24].

The decision as to whether the conditions for referral are satisfied is to be dealt with either by mutual agreement between local authorities or, in default of agreement, in accordance with arrangements made by the Secretary of State by order made by statutory instrument[25]. It is lawful for an authority to refer an applicant to an authority with whom the applicant has no local connection provided all parties find such an arrangement to be acceptable[26]. Where applicants are entering Britain from abroad they are to be treated as having a local connection with the authority to which they apply[27]. If there is a local connection outwith Great Britain the local authority may refer the applicant back, exercising its power[28] of securing accommodation from some other person. The local authority must be satisfied that such a reference would not cause the applicant to run the risk of domestic violence[29].

1 Housing (Scotland) Act 1987 (c 26), s 28(2).

2 Ibid, s 27(1)(a)–(d).

3 Ibid, s 27(2)(a). The Secretary of State may by order specify other circumstances: s 27(2)(b).

4 Code of Guidance, para 2.23. As to the Code, see para 2037 above.

5 Agreement on Procedures for Referrals of the Homeless (Association of District Councils; Association of Metropolitan Authorities; London Boroughs Association) 6 June 1979, reproduced in A Arden *Homeless Persons; The Housing Act 1985, Part III* (LAG, 1988).

6 *R v Eastleigh Borough Council, ex parte Betts* [1983] 2 AC 613, *sub nom Eastleigh Borough Council v Betts* [1983] 2 All ER 1111, HL; *R v Waltham Forest Borough Council, ex parte Koutsoudis* 1 September 1986, QBD (unreported).

7 *R v Eastleigh Borough Council, ex parte Betts* [1983] 2 AC 613, *sub nom Eastleigh Borough Council v Betts* [1983] 2 All ER 1111, HL.

8 [1983] 2 AC 613 at 627, [1983] 2 All ER 1111 at 1119, HL.

9 *R v Eastleigh Borough Council, ex parte Betts* [1983] 2 AC 613, *sub nom Eastleigh Borough Council v Betts* [1983] 2 All ER 1111, HL.

10 *Brooks v Midlothian District Council* 12 December 1985, OH (unreported).

11 *Wyness v Poole Borough Council* [1978] Journal of Social Welfare Law 368.
12 Digest of Referees' Decisions (Department of the Environment).
13 Housing (Homeless Persons) (Appropriate Arrangements) Order 1978, SI 1978/69; Housing (Homeless Persons) (Appropriate Arrangements) (No 2) Order 1978, SI 1978/661.
14 *R v Islington London Borough Council, ex parte Adigun* 20 February 1986, QBD (unreported).
15 *R v Vale of White Horse District Council, ex parte Smith and Hay* (1984) 17 HLR 160, 83 LGR 437, DC.
16 See the Housing (Scotland) Act 1987, s 33(1).
17 *R v Beverley Borough Council, ex parte McPhee* Times, 27 October 1978, DC.
18 Housing (Scotland) Act 1987, s 33(2).
19 Ibid, s 33(2)(a), (b).
20 Ibid, s 33(2)(c).
21 Ibid, s 33(3)(a).
22 Ibid, s 33(3)(b); *R v Islington London Borough Council, ex parte Adigun* 20 February 1986, QBD (unreported).
23 Inside Housing 15 October 1989.
24 *R v Hillingdon London Borough Council, ex parte H* (1988) 20 HLR 554.
25 Housing (Scotland) Act 1987, s 33(4). See note 13 above.
26 *Parr v Wyre Borough Council* (1982) 2 HLR 71, CA.
27 *R v Hillingdon London Borough Council, ex parte Streeting* [1980] 3 All ER 413, [1980] 1 WLR 1425, CA.
28 See the Housing (Scotland) Act 1987, s 35(1)(b).
29 *R v Bristol City Council, ex parte Browne* [1979] 3 All ER 344, [1979] 1 WLR 1437, DC.

2067. Notification of decision and reasons. On completing its inquiries the local authority must notify the applicant of the decision as to whether he is homeless or threatened with homelessness[1]. If he is considered homeless or threatened with homelessness then he must be notified of its decision as to whether he has priority need[2]. If in turn he is deemed to be in priority need he must be notified of the decision as to whether he became homeless or threatened with homelessness intentionally[3]. In addition, any homeless applicant in priority need must be informed if the authority has referred or intends to refer his application to another local authority on the grounds of local connection[4].

In certain circumstances where the decision denies the applicant accommodation in that area reasons must be given. Thus, if the authority notifies the applicant that either (1) it is not satisfied that he is homeless or threatened with homelessness or has a priority need, or (2) it is satisfied that he became homeless or threatened with homelessness intentionally, or (3) it has already or intends to refer him to another authority on the ground of local connection, then it must at the same time notify him of its reasons[5].

The notice given to the applicant must be in writing[6]. However, the notice does not need to be given to the applicant personally where it is made available at the authority's office for a reasonable period for collection by him or on his behalf[6]. As far as the adequacy of reasons is concerned, the extensive case law from other areas suggests that reasons must be intelligible and deal with substantive points[7]. This does not always seem to have been considered of great importance for homelessness decisions[8]. The giving of an inadequate notice involves the authority's requiring to reformulate its defective decision in proper form[9], and, despite misleading newspaper law report headlines[10], the substantive decision remains intact.

1 Housing (Scotland) Act 1987 (c 26), s 30(1).
2 Ibid, s 30(2). As to priority need, see paras 2051 ff above.
3 Ibid, s 30(3)(a).
4 Ibid, s 30(3)(b).
5 Ibid, s 30(4)(a)–(c).
6 Ibid, s 30(5).

7 *Westminster City Council v Great Portland Estates plc* [1985] AC 661 at 673, *sub nom Great Portland Estates plc v Westminster City Council* [1984] 3 All ER 744 at 752, HL, per Lord Scarman (a town planning decision).

8 *R v Swansea City Council, ex parte John* (1982) 9 HLR 56.

9 *R v Tower Hamlets London Borough, ex parte Monaf* (1988) 20 HLR 529, 86 LGR 709, CA.

10 See the headings for the *Monaf* case in The Times, The Independent and The Guardian on 28 April 1988, and compare them with the action of the council as reported in The Daily Telegraph on the same day.

(5) PROVISIONS OF ACCOMMODATION ETC

2068. Interim accommodation. Whilst inquiries are being carried out[1], the local authority to whom the applicant applies, if it has reason to believe that an applicant may be homeless and have a priority need[2], must secure that accommodation is made available for his occupation until a decision is finally made[3]. This duty arises irrespective of any local connection with the district of another authority[4]. The standard of this interim accommodation need not be as high as that required of permanent accommodation[5].

Homeless applicants who are in priority need but who are deemed to have become homeless or threatened with homelessness intentionally must be provided with accommodation for such period as the authority considers will give them a reasonable opportunity to secure accommodation for their occupation[6]. The amount of time for which accommodation must be provided in these circumstances varies with the availability of alternative housing[7].

Accommodation let expressly on a temporary basis in fulfilment of an authority's obligation to secure that accommodation becomes available to homeless persons cannot be either a secure tenancy[8] or an assured tenancy[9].

1 As to inquiries, see para 2040 above.

2 As to priority need, see paras 2051 ff above.

3 Housing (Scotland) Act 1987 (c 26), s 29(1).

4 Ibid, s 29(2). As to local connections, see para 2066 above.

5 *Brown v Hamilton District Council* 1983 SC (HL) 1 at 47, 1983 SLT 397 at 417, per Lord Fraser of Tullybelton.

6 Housing (Scotland) Act 1987, s 31(3)(a). The authority must also give him advice and appropriate assistance: see s 31(3)(b), and para 2070 below.

7 *Lally v Kensington and Chelsea Royal Borough* (1980) Times, 27 March.

8 Housing (Scotland) Act 1987, s 44(4), Sch 2, para 5: see para 1942 above.

9 Housing (Scotland) Act 1988 (c 43), s 12(2), Sch 4, para 11A (added by the Housing Act 1988 (c 50), s 140(1), Sch 17, para 90).

2069. Permanent accommodation. Subject to the local connection referral procedures[1], where a local authority is satisfied that an applicant is homeless and in priority need and not intentionally homeless it must secure that accommodation becomes available for his occupation[2]. It may do this (1) by making accommodation available from its own housing stock, or (2) by securing that he obtains accommodation from some other person, or (3) by giving such advice and assistance as will secure that he obtains accommodation from some other person[3]. The accommodation provided must not be statutorily overcrowded[4]; nor may it endanger the health of the occupants[5]. This is a different standard from that adopted under the equivalent English legislation, which requires the accommodation to be provided to be 'suitable accommodation'[6].

1 See the Housing (Scotland) Act 1987 (c 26), s 33, and para 2066 above.

2 Ibid, s 31(2).

3 Ibid, s 35(1)(a)–(c).

4 Ie within the meaning of ibid, s 135, for which see para 2001 above.

5 Ibid, s 32(5).

6 See the Housing Act 1985 (c 68), s 69(1) (substituted by the Housing and Planning Act 1986 (c 63), s 14(3)).

2070. Advice and assistance. Those who are intentionally homeless, in addition to being provided with temporary accommodation[1], must be provided with advice and such assistance as the local authority considers appropriate in all the circumstances in any attempts the applicant may make to secure that accommodation becomes available for his occupation[2]. The same level of advice and assistance must be given to those homeless applicants who are not in priority need[3].

1 See para 2068 above.
2 Housing (Scotland) Act 1987 (c 26), s 31(3)(b).
3 Ibid, s 31(4).

2071. Charging for accommodation. A local authority may require a person to whom it provides either interim or permanent accommodation to pay such reasonable charges as it may determine for that accommodation[1]. There is also equivalent provision for the payment of charges in respect of sums paid by the authority for accommodation which the authority secures from another person for the applicant[2].

1 Housing (Scotland) Act 1987 (c 26), s 35(2)(a).
2 Ibid, s 35(2)(b).

2072. Protection of property. Where a local authority has reason to believe that an applicant is homeless or threatened with homelessness and that there is a danger of loss or damage to his moveable property because of his inability to protect it or deal with it and that no other suitable arrangements have been made, it must take certain action[1]. It must take reasonable steps to prevent the loss of moveable property or prevent or mitigate damage to it, and if it has not become subject to such a duty it may take any steps it considers reasonable for the purpose of protecting the applicant's property[2]. The authority has power to enter at all reasonable times any premises which are or were the usual residence of the applicant and deal with moveable property in any way that is reasonably necessary[3]. This would normally involve providing or arranging for storage. The authority can impose certain conditions, such as the making and recovery of reasonable charges for the actions taken, or the disposal of items[4]. The authority ceases to have any obligation when in its opinion there is no longer any reason to believe that there is a danger of loss or damage to the applicant's moveable property, although this does not affect the duty to property already in store[5]. Where the authority ceases to be under an obligation it must notify the applicant[6] either by delivering a notification to him or leaving it or sending it to him at his last known address[7].

1 Housing (Scotland) Act 1987 (c 26), s 36(1). References to the applicant's moveable property include references to the moveable property of any person who might reasonably be expected to reside with him: s 36(8).
2 Ibid, s 36(2).
3 Ibid, s 36(3).
4 Ibid, s 36(4).
5 Ibid, s 36(5).
6 Ibid, s 36(6).
7 Ibid, s 36(7).

(6) OFFENCES AND REMEDIES

2073. Offences. In connection with a homelessness application, where a person knowingly or recklessly makes a statement which is false in a material particular or knowingly withholds information, then the legislation makes this an offence in certain circumstances[1]. The information must have been reasonably required by the authority[1]. There must be an intent by the applicant to induce the local authority to believe that he is homeless or threatened with homelessness, or has a priority need, or did not become homeless or threatened with homelessness intentionally[2]. Where there is a change of material facts after application but prior to notification of the authority's decision, this must be notified to the authority as soon as possible[3]. Failure to notify material changes is an offence unless the applicant can establish that the local authority failed in its duty[3] to explain to every applicant, in ordinary language, this obligation or that he had some other reasonable excuse for failing to comply[4]. A person found guilty of this offence is liable on summary conviction to a fine not exceeding level 5 on the standard scale[5].

1 Housing (Scotland) Act 1987 (c 26), s 40(1).
2 Ibid, s 40(1)(a)–(c).
3 Ibid, s 40(2).
4 Ibid, s 40(3).
5 Ibid, s 40(4). As to level 5, see para 1931, note 5, above.

2074. Remedies. There is no direct right of appeal against a decision of a local authority relating to homelessness; nor is there provision for a ministerial default power as found in the legislation covering homelessness prior to the introduction of the Housing (Homeless Persons) Act 1977[1]. The applicant can, however, seek judicial review of the authority's action in the Court of Session[2]. The standard rules for judicial review[3] apply, and a significant number of the petitions for judicial review relate to homelessness[4]. Damages may also be sought as part of the review process[5]. Provided an authority accepts that it is under a duty it is also possible to seek damages in the sheriff court[6]. Interdict proceedings are also competent where relevant. As the obligations towards homeless people fall on local authorities, it follows that assistance may be sought from the Commissioner for Local Administration in Scotland[7].

1 See the National Assistance Act 1948 (c 29), s 36(1) (repealed).
2 *Brown v Hamilton District Council* 1983 SC (HL) 1, 1983 SLT 397.
3 See RC 260B, ADMINISTRATIVE LAW, vol 1, paras 345–348, and PROCEDURE, vol 17, para 1419.
4 J Burns 'Application for Judicial Review: Some Preliminary Findings' (1986) 31 JLSS 361.
5 *Mallon v Monklands District Council* 1986 SLT 347, OH.
6 *Purves v Midlothian District Council* 1986 SCOLAG 144.
7 As to the commissioner, see the Local Government (Scotland) Act 1975 (c 30), Pt II (ss 21–32), and LOCAL GOVERNMENT, vol 14, paras 133 ff. See especially s 23(1)(a).

INDEX

FISHERIES

Abstraction of water
salmon fishings, 6
Access
fisheries, to—
  British fisheries, 131, 132
  powers of entry, 25
  United Nations Convention on the Law of the Sea, 109
salmon fishing rights, 8
Alcoholic liquor
supply within North Sea limits, 129
Alveus
river, of, interference with, 6
Anglers
representation on district salmon fisheries boards, 35, 37
Angling right
not accessory to agricultural tenancy, 49
Annual close time
See CLOSE TIME
Arrest, powers of
salmon fishing offences, 28

Bag net
salmon fishing by, 11
Baits
illegal, 12
Baselines
See TERRITORIAL SEA
Bays
territorial waters, baseline system, 78
Behring Sea Award Act (1894), 217
Black fish
meaning, 2*n*
Body corporate
inshore fishing, offences in relation to, 143
sea fishing, offences in relation to, 153
Brown trout
brown trout fishing rights, 5, 48
  salmon fishing rights include, 5
fish farms, 58
See also TROUT
Bull trout
River Tweed, 40
Byelaws
district salmon fisheries boards, enforcement by, 38
England and Wales, inshore fisheries, 133
Fishery Acts implemented by, 117

Cameron Report, 112
Channel Islands
territorial sea, 76
Clams
early legislation, 118
Close season
North-East Atlantic Fisheries Commission powers, 95
Close time
annual, 14, 15, 32
  annual close time order, 15
  buying salmon, 16
  cruives and other equipment, 16
  obstruction of fish, 19
  offences relating to, 16
  River Esk, 46
  River Tweed, 42, 43
  Secretary of State's powers, 23
  selling salmon or exposing for sale, 16
  shipping or exporting salmon, 16
  trout, 53
seal fishing, 216, 217
weekly, 14, 17, 32
  introduction of principle, 2
  River Esk, 46
  River Tweed, 42, 43
  Secretary of State's powers, 23
Coast guards
British sea-fisheries officers, as, 126*n*
Coble
meaning, 3*n*
net and coble, *see* NET AND COBLE
Compensation
damage relating to fisheries, for, 176
Conservation
Conservation of Seals Act (1970), 220
definition, 90
European Community, 67
exclusive economic zone, 107
exploration and exploitation of natural resources interfering with, 85
high seas, fish stocks in, 89, 90
international fishery commissions, 67
landing of foreign-caught fish, 144, 150
making and maintaining shellfish beds, 157
nets and gear, regulations and conventions, 89, 146
salmon—
  act or omission relating to salmon, salmon roe or salmon eggs, 13, 43

References are to paragraphs

Conservation—*contd*
salmon—*contd*
 Convention for the Conservation of
  Salmon in the North Atlantic
  Ocean, 103
 North Atlantic, 67, 101–105
 North Atlantic Salmon Conservation
  Organisation, 67, 104, 105
 stocks of, 89, 90
 scientific research, 68
 sea fish, of, 144–154
  bodies corporate, offences by, 153
  enforcement, 154
  foreign-caught sea fish, regulation of
   landing, 144, 150
  high seas, stocks in, 89, 90
  increase or improvement of marine
   resources, measures for, 151
  restrictions on fishing for sea fish, 148
  size limits for fish, 144, 145
  trans-shipment of fish, prohibition on,
   44, 147, 149
 Sea Fish (Conservation) Act (1967), 144
 seals, 220
 shellfish fisheries, 161, 162
 trans-shipment of fish, 144, 147, 149
 United Nations Convention on the Law
  of the Sea, 82, 84, 106–109
Continental Shelf
Convention on the Continental Shelf—
 conflicts with other uses of the sea, 85
 generally, 82
 natural resources, rights to, 83, 84
installations constructed on, 85
outer limit, 82
**Convention on Conduct of Fishing
 Operations in the North Atlantic
 (1967),** 173
**Convention for Regulating the Pol-
 ice of the North Sea Fisheries,** 124
British sea-fisheries officers' powers, 126
**Convention respecting the Liquor
 Traffic in the North Sea,** 129
Crabs
prohibition on taking and sale of certain,
 168
size limits, 145*n*
Crown
proprietary right to sea bed vested in, 61
right of catching salmon vested in, 3, 3*n*
salmon fishing—
 provision binding on, 39
 rights, grant of, 4
Cruives
annual close time, 16

Cruives—*contd*
byelaws relating to, failure to comply
 with, 19
charter rights, 11
meaning, 2*n*
prohibition in tidal waters, 2
regulations as to, 32
Secretary of State's powers, 23
when permitted, 11
Customs officers
British sea-fisheries officers, as, 126*n*

Dam
examination of, 25
meaning, 25*n*
obstruction of passage of salmon, 19
Secretary of State's powers, 23
Damage
relating to fisheries, compensation for,
 176
Disease
control in fish farms—
 inland farms, 60
 marine farms, 61
District boards, 32
District salmon fishery boards, 35
application for changes in legislation, 38
byelaws, enforcement of, 38
clerk, appointment of, 38
defect in appointment or qualification of
 member, 39
duties, 38
election procedure, 35
financial powers and duties, 38
fishery assessments, 38
heritable property, purchase of, 38
mandatories, 37
maximum number of members, 35
may sue and be sued, 38
powers, 38
proprietors, 35
report, 38
salmon anglers, 35
statement of accounts, 38
tenant netsmen, 35
vacancies, 35, 39
water bailiffs, appointment of, 38
where no salmon in district, 39
Dragging
salmon fishing by, 11*n*

Eels
freshwater fish, as, 5*n*
fry, 5*n*
Electrical device
fishing with prohibited, 12
illegal use in trout fishing, 54

References are to paragraphs

References are to paragraphs

Fisheries—*contd*
inshore—*contd*
  prohibition of sea fishing in specified
    areas, 136
  salmon nets, prohibition of fishing
    near, 139
  sea-fishery officers, powers of, 141
  Secretary of State's powers, 135
international legal framework—
  Common Fisheries Policy, 70
  conservation, 67, 68
  development of, 70
  jurisdictional zones, 66
  need for, 65
  resolution of conflicts, 69
  scientific research, 68
  territorial limits, *see* TERRITORIAL SEA
  United Nations Conferences on the
    Law of the Sea, 65, 70, 73, 76, 80
  United Nations Convention on the
    Law of the Sea, 82, 84, 106–109
landing of foreign-caught fish, 144, 150
licensing—
  after 1983 ... 115
  before 1983 ... 114
  pressure stocks, 115
limits, 130–132
net mesh size, 95, 144
North-East Atlantic Fisheries Commission, 92–96
Northwest Atlantic Fisheries Commission, 92, 97–100
open access to high seas fisheries, problems of, 89
over exploitation, 65
pressure stocks, 115
quotas, European Community, 181
regulation of conduct of operations—
  compensation for damage, 176
  fine in relation to, 174
restrictions, 144
sea, *see* SEA FISHERIES
sea-fishery officers, *see* SEA FISHERIES
shellfish, *see* SHELLFISH
size limits for fish, 144, 145
statutory instruments, fisheries Acts
  implemented by, 117
territorial sea, *see* TERRITORIAL SEA
trans-shipment of fish, 144, 147, 149
unqualified fishing boats, 183
United Kingdom laws—
  access to British fisheries, 131, 132
  bodies corporate, offences by, 143, 153
  Cameron Report, 112
  conservation of sea fish, 144–154
  consolidating legislation, need for, 116

Fisheries—*contd*
United Kingdom laws—*contd*
  Convention for Regulating the Police
    of the North Sea Fisheries, 124
  early legislation, 118–29
  European Community measures, con-
    flict with, 113
  fisheries Acts, implementation of, 117
  fishery limits, 130–32
  foreign-caught sea fish, regulations on
    landing, 150
  general purposes and objectives, 110
  inshore fisheries—
    bodies corporate, offences by, 143
    discarding of illegally caught fish,
      137
    England and Wales, 133, 134
    police powers, 142
    prohibitions, 136, 138, 139
    Scotland, 135–143
    sea-fishery officer's powers, 141
    water bailiff's powers, 142
  licensing—
    after 1983 ... 115
    before 1983 ... 114
  marine resources, increase or
    improvement of, 151
  purposes and objectives, 110
  regulatory techniques, 111
  sea fisheries, 169–182
  shellfish, 155–168
  size limits for fish, 145
  trans-shipment of fish, prohibition on,
    147, 149
Fisheries Act (1705), 119
Fisheries Committee
functions of, 39
Fishery assessments
district salmon fisheries boards' powers,
  38
Fishery Board for Scotland, 32
Fishing boats
abandoned at sea, 198
accidents, reporting, 207
certificates, 201
construction rules, 202
equipment requirements, 203
fines, 187
fishing vessel, meaning, 188*n*
foreign, meaning, 196*n*
gear lost or abandoned at sea, 198
injury to boat or gear, inquiry into, 199
joint ownership, 128
jurisdiction of flag state over, 88
letters and numbers on, 197
licensing, 195

References are to paragraphs

References are to paragraphs

Navigation
exclusive economic zone, 107
high seas, rights on, 87
interference with rights, 7
    exploration and exploitation of natural
        resources, caused by, 85
trout fishing, and, 50
Net and coble
annual close time, 15
bag net, 11
coble, meaning, 3*n*
definition, 11
fly net, 11
lease of fishings, 9
River Tweed, 43
salmon fishing, 3, 5, 11, 188
stake net, 11
Nets
bag, 17*n*
    River Tweed, 43
Behring Sea Award Act (1894), 217
drift, 12, 12*n*
fly, River Tweed, 43
freshwater fishing by, 11
gill, 12, 12*n*
inshore fishing, 138
mesh size, 12, 12*n*, 23, 32
    high seas, 89
    North-East Atlantic Fisheries Com-
        mission powers, 95
    sea fishing, 144, 146
paidle—
    meaning, 45
    Solway Firth, 45
prohibited use, 12, 42
prohibition of fishing near, 139
proposed review of salmon net fishing,
    39
River Tweed, 42, 43
seine, 12
stake, River Tweed, 43
trawl, 12
**North Atlantic Salmon Conser-
    vation Organisation (NASCO),**
    67, 104, 105
North Atlantic salmon convention,
    103
North Sea Fisheries Act (1893), 129
**North-East Atlantic Fisheries Com-
    mission (NEAFC),** 67, 89, 92
after 1981 ... 94
before 1982 ... 93
enforcement, 96
powers, 95
**North-East Atlantic Fisheries Con-
    vention,** 89

**Northwest Atlantic Fisheries Com-
    mission (NAFC),** 67, 89, 92, 97–
    100
**Northwest Atlantic Fisheries Organ-
    isation,** 99
Noxious substance
fishing with, 12, 21

Obstruction
enforcing officer, of, 29
Obstructions
examination of, 25
regulations as to, 32
salmon, obstructing passage of, 14, 19,
    23
Otterboards
illegal use in trout fishing, 54
Overflight
exclusive economic zone, 107
Oysters
Oyster Fisheries (Scotland) Act (1840),
    121
prohibition on sale of, 167
Sea Fisheries Act (1883), 125

Pentland Firth
territorial sea, 76
Poaching
brown trout, 51
forfeiture of fish or other articles, 11, 27
freshwater fish, 10
salmon, 10, 11
Poinding and sale
boat, gear or catch, of, 174
Poison
fish farms, controlling pollution from,
    62
fishing with prohibited, 12, 21
illegal use in trout fishing, 54
Police
authority to enforce legislation, 24
inshore fishing, powers as to, 142
obstruction of, 29
powers of entry, 25
powers of search, 26
Pollution
discharge of pollutants into river, 6
fish farms, 62
Prescriptive possession
salmon fishing rights, 4
Proprietor
definition, 34
different proprietor on each river bank—
    salmon fishing, 5
    trout fishing, 48

References are to paragraphs

References are to paragraphs

References are to paragraphs

References are to paragraphs

References are to paragraphs

References are to paragraphs

FOOD, DAIRIES AND SLAUGHTERHOUSES

References are to paragraphs

References are to paragraphs

References are to paragraphs

References are to paragraphs

Food—*contd*
labelling—*contd*
  early legislation, 304
  EEC Council Regulations, 383
  false, 350
  fancy confectionery, 383
  Her Majesty's forces or visiting forces,
    food for consumption of, 383
  immediate consumption, food for,
    383, 388
  ingredients, list of, 383, 385
    low content of particular ingredient,
      383
  instructions for use, 383, 386
  manner of, 392
  meat, 432
  milk, *see* MILK
  mineral water, 383
  misleading, 383, 394
  name and address of manufacturer,
    packer or seller, 383
  names required by law, 384
  offences, 396
  place of origin, 383
  prepacked in special materials, 383
  prepared meals, 388
  preservatives, food containing, 377
  prohibited and restricted claims, 393
  regulation of, 383
    power to make regulations, 306
  small packages, 383, 389
  specific foods, of, 359–370
  storage instructions, 383
  unprepacked food, 383, 387
  vending machine, food sold from,
    383, 388, 390, 396
  wine, word used in composite name,
    393, 395
lead, restriction on use of, 382
legislation—
  byelaws, 322
  cognate law, 325, 326
  Crown, application to, 307
  early, 301–303
  emergency powers, 320
  European Communities Act (1972),
    305
  local, alteration of, 308–310
  milk, 302
  principal regulations, 306
  saving for pre-1956 subordinate legis-
    lation, 323
  Scottish, 304–307
  Secretary of State's powers, 321
  slaughterhouses, 303

Food—*contd*
legislation—*contd*
  subordinate, 321–334
    regulations and orders, procedure
      for making, 324
manufacture—
  drainage and sanitation, 408
  equipment and utensils, 408, 409
  infested food, 317
  refuse, disposal of, 408
manufacturer or packer, notification of
  sampling, 338
meaning, 311
  excluded items, 311
milk, *see* MILK
mineral hydrocarbons, 375
names required by law, 384
not of kind demanded, sale of, 343–349
  extraneous matter, 343
  false representation, 346
  nature, substance or quality of food,
    343
  notice to purchaser, 345
  question of fact, 347
  sale to prejudice of purchaser, 344
  standard of quality, 348
  statutory defences, 349
noxious ingredients, 325
packaging, 407. *See also* labelling, above
pesticides, powers as to import, sale and
  use of, 319
premises—
  alteration, apportionment of expenses
    of, 435
  closing order, 422
  drainage, 419
  first aid equipment, 419
  forecourts and yards, 419
  hygiene regulations, 407, 408, 419–22
  infestations, 419
  lighting, 419
  registration, 420, 421
  sanitary provisions, 419
  sinks or other washing facilities, 419
  sleeping places or bedrooms, 419
  storage, 419
  ventilation, 419
  water supply, 419
  where prepared, 407, 420, 421
  where sold or offered, 407, 420, 421
preparations, 407
  apparatus, 407
  early legislation, 304
  premises, regulation of, 407
preservatives, 377
  early legislation, 301

References are to paragraphs

Food—*contd*
price—
 marking of, 314
 subsidies to reduce, limit or prevent
  increase of, 314
prize or reward, offered as, 400
prosecutions and penalties, 423–430
 act or default of other person, contravention due to, 428
 certificates of analysis, evidence of,
  424
 Government Chemist, analysis by,
  425
 nature of, 423
 offences in relation to, 427
 place of, 423
 presumptions, 429
 warranty—
  as defence, 426
  offences in relation to, 427
public analyst, *see* PUBLIC ANALYST
purchaser—
 false representation to, 346
 notice to, 345
 sale to prejudice of, 344
regulations—
 appeal against, 434
 composition or treatment of food, as
  to, 352, 354–358
 food standards, 353
 power to make, 306
reheating, 408, 410
safety, early legislation, 304
sale of—
 advertisement, *see* ADVERTISEMENT
 clothing of persons selling, 407
 cognate law, 326
 early legislation, 304
 emergency powers, 320
 excisable liquor, 315
 exposure for, 407
 false representation, 346
 fish, close seasons, 312
 food not of proper nature, substance or
  quality, 343
 food supplied not of kind demanded,
  343–349
 game, 312
 hares, 312
 implied conditions of, 326
 infested food, 317
 injurious food, 341
 labelling, *see* labelling, above
 measures, by, 313
 notice to purchaser, 345
 number, by, 313

Food—*contd*
sale of—*contd*
 pesticides, 319
 prejudice of purchaser, to, 344
 premises where sold or offered, 407
 price control, 314
 prosecutions and penalties, 423–430
 salmon, 312
 sea trout, 312
 Secretary of State's powers to obtain
  particulars of, 351
 shellfish, 312, 403, 407
 trade descriptions, 316
 trout, 312
 unfit for human consumption, 397–
  402
 unsound food, 399
 value added tax, 314
 venison, 312
 weight, measure or number, by, 313
 wild birds, 312
samples, analysis of, *see* analysis of **sam**-
 ples, above
sampling officer—
 authorisation of, 334
 authority of, 337
 direction to take samples, 335
 division and disposal of samples, 338
 duty, 333, 334
 milk, sampling of, 336
Secretary of State's powers, 321, 351, 407
shellfish, 407
 cleansing of, 312, 403
solvents, containing, 378
stabilisers, 373
statutory sources, 301–303
 Scottish legislation, 304–307
statutory standard of quality, 348, 353,
 359–370
storage, 407, 408
 infested food, 317
supplied otherwise than by sale, 342,
 342*n*
sweeteners, 379
trade descriptions, 316
trade marks, 384
transit, in, examination of, 401
transport of, 407
 infested food, 317
treatment of, regulations as to, 352, 354–
 358
unfit for human consumption, 397–402
 condemnation, 398
 examination of, 397
  food in transit, 401

References are to paragraphs

References are to paragraphs

References are to paragraphs

Reward
food offered as, 400

Salad cream
advertisement, 367
composition, 367
labelling, 367
Sale
food, of, *see* FOOD
Salmon
close season, buying, selling or exposing
    for sale during, 312
Salt
raw and unprocessed meat, added to,
    374n
Sampling officer
See FOOD
Sandwiches
labelling, 388
Sanitary inspector
food unfit for human consumption, 402
Sausages
skin, 358
School
food supplied by, 342n
Scottish Food Hygiene Council
abolition, 328
Sea trout
close season, buying, selling or exposing
    for sale during, 312
Seals
Slaughter of Animals (Scotland) Act
    (1980) not applicable to, 496
Secretary of State
food, powers in relation to, 321, 351
    food hygiene, 407
milk—
    dairies, inspection of, 490
    licences, 458, 461–436
    price control, 467
    provision of facilities for treatment of,
        456
    special designations, 452, 453
slaughterhouses, regulations as to, 502
Sheep
milk, 438
Shellfish
cleansing of, 403
food, preparation and sale as, 312
regulations as to, 407
Ship
entry, powers of, in relation to Food and
    Drugs (Scotland) Act (1956), 340
Slaughterhouses
byelaws and regulations, 502
ceilings, 505

Slaughterhouses—*contd*
cleansing, 505
confinement and treatment before
    slaughter, 503
construction, 505
diseases, persons handling meat, of, 506
drainage, 505
early legislation, 303, 304
entry, powers of, 515
equipment, 505
export, animals slaughtered for, 510, 511
first aid materials, 506
floors, 505
hygiene, 504, 506
infestation, prevention of, 505
inspection of meat, 507
Jewish slaughter, 503, 513
knacker's yard, *see* KNACKER'S YARDS
lighting, 505
local authorities, functions of, 509
local authority provision, 499, 499n
meaning, 404n, 499n
meat inspector, 507, 507n
methods of slaughter, 503
Muslim slaughter, 503, 513
offences, 514
private, 500
    certificate of registration, 500
    confinement of animals, separate
        premises used for, 500
    registered person, 500
public, 499
    disposal of, 499
    employees, 499
    plant and apparatus, 499
Secretary of State's powers in relation to,
    321
unregistered premises used as, 500
ventilation, 505
veterinary meat inspector, 507, 507n
walls, 505
water supply, 505
See also ANIMALS
Slaughtermen
qualification and licensing, 513
Smoking
meat and food handlers, hygiene regu-
    lations, 415
Snipe
Game Acts, 496n
Snuff
meat and food handlers, hygiene regu-
    lations, 415
Solvents
food containing, 378
meaning, 378n

References are to paragraphs

South Devon cattle
regulations as to, 466
Spitting
meat and food handlers, 415
prohibited in premises where food sold,
    407
Stabilisers
food, in, 373
Stall
food sold from—
    hygiene regulations, 408, 409, 411
Sterilisation
cream, 355, 479
ice cream, 354
milk, 459
Suet
food standard, 353
Sugar products
dextrose, 369
labelling, 369
white, use of word, 369
Swan
Game Acts, 496n
Sweeteners
food containing, 379

Tea
colouring matter not permitted, 372
Tenant
leased dairy, alterations to, 491
Tetrachloroethylene
content in olive oil, 370, 370n
Tobacco
meat and food handlers, hygiene regu-
    lations, 415
Tomato ketchup
food standard, 353
Trade descriptions
food, in relation to, 316
Trade marks
may not be substituted for real name of
    food, 384
Transport
food in transit, examination of, 401
meat, of, hygiene regulations, 416, 417
Trout
close season, buying, selling or exposing
    for sale during, 312
Tuberculosis
cow suffering from, notification of, 447
Turkeys
slaughter of, 516

Ultra heat-treatment
cream, 479
milk, 459

Value added tax
food—
    catering, supplied for, 314
    price control, 314
    zero-rated, 314
Vehicle
food sold from—
    entry, powers of, 340
    hygiene regulations, 408, 409, 411
Vending machine
food sold from, 396
    labelling, 338n, 383, 388, 390, 396
    soft drinks, 368
Venison
regulations as to preparation and sale,
    312, 433
slaughter of, 496
Veterinary inspector
inspection of cattle, 444, 444n
Veterinary meat inspector
generally, 507, 507n
qualification, 512

Warranty
sale of food, in relation to, 426, 427
Water
food premises, supply to, 419
ingredient, where, 385
is not food, 311
mineral, labelling, 383
Weights and measures
bread, 359
food, sale by weight, measure or num-
    ber, 313
Welfare food and milk
applications to obtain, 432
meaning, 432n
Wild animals
meat from, 496
Wine
preservatives, 377
use of word in composite names, 383,
    393, 395
Wrapper
food, 350

References are to paragraphs

FORESTRY

Agricultural land
capital gains tax deferral on woodlands, 654
Ancient monument
compulsory purchase order exemption, 634
Archaeological interest
site of, compulsory purchase order exemption, 634

Byelaws
Forestry Commission—
enforcement, 640
power to make, 609

Capital gains tax
grant of right to fell and remove timber, 650
woodlands, 649
Churchyard
felling trees in, 617
Compensation
felling licence, for refusal to grant, 618
Conservancy
Home Grown Timber Advisory Committee, 612
meaning, 612
Conservation
Forestry Commission, duty of, 606, 607

Danger
trees felled to prevent, 617
Dedication agreements
ancillary provisions, 614
effect of, 613, 614
existing agreements, continuation of, 614
form, 614
generally, 613, 614
grant schemes replacing, 615
meaning, 614
recording of, 614
release from, 614

Evidence
Forestry Commission documents, 604

Felling of trees
danger, to prevent, 617
enforcement of provisions as to—
committee of reference, 629
compliance notice, 628
expenses of, 630
identification of trees, 631
service of documents, 632

Felling of trees—*contd*
felling directions—
agricultural interests to be considered, 623
committee of reference, 629
farm or dwellinghouse, interests to be considered, 623
Forestry Commission's power to direct, 623
restrictions of, 624
identification of trees, 631
interests to be considered, 623
persons adversely affected by, 626
proceedings in respect of, 627
review of, 625
Secretary of State's powers, 624–626
statement of grounds to be given, 623
felling licence—
application for, 616
committee of reference, 629
conditional, 619
review of conditions, 619
enforcement, 628–632
exemption from requirement, 617
felling without authority of, 622
generally, 612, 616
identification of trees, 631
preservation orders, trees subject to, 621
public open space, trees growing on, 617
refusal to grant—
compensation for, 618
deterioration of timber after, 618
review of, 621
nuisance, to abate, 617
obstruction, to remove, 617
restocking notice, *see* RESTOCKING NOTICE
unauthorised, 622
Forestry Commission
byelaws—
enforcement, 640
power to make, 609
committees—
advisory, 611
appointment of, 611
central, 611
regional, 611
conservation, 606
national interest and, 607
constitution, 603
documents, 604
proof of, 604
receipt in evidence, 604

References are to paragraphs

Forestry Commission—*contd*
entry and enforcement, powers of, 640
establishment, 602
general duty, 606
government department, as, 603
grant schemes, approval of, 615
grants and loans, *see* FORESTRY FUND
Home Grown Timber Advisory Committee, 609, 612
management of forestry land, 608
membership, 603
obstruction of officers or servants of, 640
official seal, 603
proceedings, 603
quorum, 603
regulations, powers to make, 609, 612, 616, 617
sporting or recreational facilities, provision of, 610
staff, 605
statute law, generally, 601, 602
statutory functions, exercise and discharge of, 606
taxation, exemption from, 641
tourist facilities, provision of, 610
Forestry dedication agreement
compulsory purchase exemption, 634
Forestry Fund
generally, 608
gifts to, 636
payments into, 636
payments out of, 637
regulation, 638
report and accounts, 639
Forestry grant scheme
dedication scheme replaced by, 615
procedure, 615
Fruit trees
felling of, 617

Garden
felling trees in, 617
Gift
Forestry Fund, to, 636

Hedges
laying of, licence not required, 617
Home Grown Timber Advisory Committee
consultation with, 609, 612
maintenance by Forestry Commissioners, 612
regional advisory committees, 612

Income tax
woodlands, 642–648

Income tax—*contd*
woodlands—*contd*
abolition of previous system, 644
capital allowances, 646
election to be charged under Schedule D, 643
former taxation under Schedule B, 642
transitional provisions, 645
Inheritance tax
woodlands, 651–654
deferral of tax, 651
advantages of, 653
agricultural land, 654
subsequent disposal, 652

Land
acquisition of—
compulsory purchase, 634
exceptions, 634
proximity, land in, 634
generally, 633
Secretary of State's powers, 633–635
disposal of, 635
management of, 635
use of, 635
Lands Tribunal for Scotland
disputed compensation claims, 618
Licence
tree-felling, *see* FELLING OF TREES
Lopping
licence not required, 617

National Trust for Scotland
land held inalienably by—
compulsory purchase order exemption, 634
felling directions and, 623
Nuisance
trees felled to abate, 617

Obstruction
trees felled to remove, 617
Orchard
felling trees in, 617

Pests
protection of trees and forest products from, 608, 608n
Preservation order
meaning, 620n
trees subject to, felling, 620
Proof
Forestry Commission documents, 604
Public open space
meaning, 617n
trees growing on, felling licence not required, 617

References are to paragraphs

Regulations
Forestry Commission power to make, 609, 612, 616, 617
Restocking notice
committee of reference, 629
compliance with, 628
contents, 622
expenses in connection with, 630
review, reference for, 622
service, 622

Secretary of State
acquisition of land, powers as to, 633–635
felling directions, powers as to, 624–626
Sport and recreation
Forestry Commission, provision of facilities by, 610
Standing timber
purchase of, 608

Taxation
forestry, income from—
    abolition of previous system, 644
    capital allowances, 646
    election to be charged under Schedule D, 643
    former taxation under Schedule B, 642
    transitional provisions, 645
Forestry Commission exempt from, 641
grant of right to fell and removed timber, 650
woodlands—
    death of owner, 651

Taxation—*contd*
woodlands—*contd*
    inheritance tax deferment, 652–654
    purchase and sale of, 647
        capital gains tax, 649
        income tax, 648
Timber
deterioration after refusal of felling licence, 618
meaning, 608*n*
ownership of, 608
right to fell and remove, grant of, 650
sale, 608
standing, purchase of, 608
utilisation, 608
Topping trees
licence not required, 617
Tourism
Forestry Commission, provision of facilities by, 610
Trees
felling of, *see* FELLING OF TREES
restocking notice, *see* RESTOCKING NOTICE

Woodlands
broadleaved, grants for, 644*n*
capital allowances, 646
commercial, profits and losses arising from, 644, 645
death of owner, 651
    deferral of inheritance tax, 651–654
Forestry Commission schemes, 644
purchase and sale, taxation on, 647
    capital gains tax, 649
    income tax, 648

FRAUD

Alienation
gratuitous, 780

Bad faith
conduct contrary to good faith, 720
fraud and, 720
Bankers' documentary credits
fraudulent, 773
system of, generally, 772
Bankruptcy
See INSOLVENCY
Bond
heritable, fraud, obtained by, 770

Carelessness
fraud, whether constituting, 728
Causation
proof of inducement, 730
Cautionary obligation
See OBLIGATION
Cheques
forged, 768
Circumvention
See FACILITY AND CIRCUMVENTION
Company
prospectus, fraudulent misrepresentation in, 782, 783
    directors, liability of, 783

Company—*contd*
prospectus, fraudulent misrepresentation in—*contd*
  listed securities, 783
  unlisted securities, 783
Concealment
active, fraudulent misrepresentation by, 711
Conduct
carelessness, 728
fraudulent, nature of, 708, 723–729
  fraudulent misrepresentation, 723, 724
  mens rea of fraud, 725–729
unreasonableness, 728
Consensus in idem
dissensus, 705
fraud preventing, 705
test for, 706
Consent
fraud as factor vitiating, 707–714
  active concealment, 711
  conduct, nature of, 708
  false statements, 709
  material error, inducement of, 713
  non-disclosure, 712
  positive acts, 710
  remedies, 714
Contract
contractual remedies for fraud, 721
fraudulent misrepresentation, induced by, 707–714
law of obligations and law of property, distiction between principles of, 756
marriage, *see* MARRIAGE
minor, reduced by, 789
Conveyance
fraud on the, effect of, 758
law of obligations and law of property, distinction between principles of, 756
Credit
documentary, *see* BANKERS' DOCUMENTARY CREDITS
Creditors
transactions in fraud of, 779

Debt
fraudulent preference, payment by, 781
gratuitous alienation, 780
insolvency and bankruptcy, 776–781
transactions in fraud of creditors, 779
Deed
mortis causa, action for reduction of, 736
Delict
fraud as—
  bad faith, fraud and, 720

Delict—*contd*
fraud as—*contd*
  contractual and delictual remedies, 721
  delictual liability, 785
  development of law, 719
  procedural and evidential aspects, 722
Director
company, fraudulent misrepresentation in prospectus, liability as to, 783
Disclosure
duty of—
  cautionary obligations, 775
  in *uberrimae fidei* contracts, 712
voluntary, 712
  cautionary obligations, 774
Documentary credits
fraudulent, 773
system of, generally, 772

Error
contract entered under, 712, 713
in substantialibus, 712, 713, 716
inducement of material, 713
material, 716

Facility and circumvention
circumvention—
  fraud and, generally, 736
  meaning, 736
dishonest advantage, proof of, 736
facility, meaning, 734
lesion, 735
mortis causa deed, plea raised in action for, 736
plea of, generally, 733
remedies—
  reduction, 737
  rescission, 737
  restitutio in integrum impossible, where, 737
False statement
fraudulent misrepresentation by, 709, 717
Forgery
cheques, 768
negotiable instruments, 767
Fraud
antecedent obligations, effect on, 757
averring fraud, 704
bad faith, and, 720
bankers' documentary credits, 772, 773
bankrputcy, *see* INSOLVENCY
causation, 730
cautionary obligations induced by, 774
duty of disclosure, 775

References are to paragraphs

Promissory note
inducement to sign by fraudulent mis-
    representation, 767
Property
corporeal moveables, *see* MOVEABLES
dominium, *see* MOVEABLES
gratuitous alienation, 780
heritable, *see* HERITABLE PROPERTY
incorporeal, *see* INCORPOREAL
Prospectus
company, fraudulent misrepresentation
    in, 782, 783
Pupil
transactions on behalf of, 789

Seduction
action for, 786
Share certificate
fraud, obtained by, 771
Statement of fact
false, fraudulent misrepresentation by,
    709, 717
Succession
discharge of rights, 746
election, reduction of deed of, 747
fraud in relation to, generally, 743
heirs, impersonation of, 748, 759
legal rights, 745
legatees, impersonation of, 748, 759
simulate *inter vivos* disposition, 745
wills, 744
    fraudulent inducement to sign, 744
    innocent beneficiary, position of, 744
    undue influence, made under, 744
See also HERITABLE PROPERTY

Title
documents, of, fraud in relation to, 769
Trusts
constitution of, 750

Trusts—*contd*
fraud, proof of, 750
generally, 749
power, fraud on a, 702, 754
transactions in breach of, 753
trustee—
    fiduciary duty of, 751
    must not act as *auctor in rem suam*, 751
    trust beneficiary and, transaction
        between, 752
    trust estate, and, 751

Uberrimae fidei
contracts—
    fraudulent misrepresentation by non-
        disclosure, 712
Undue influence
essence of doctrine, 738
generally, 738
independent advice, absence of, 741
material or gratuitous benefit to domi-
    nant party, 740
parties, relationship between, 739
remedies, 742
trust, relationship of, 738
will made under, 744
Unfair preference
fraudulent preference replaced by, 781*n*
Unlisted security
fraudulent misrepresentation in prospec-
    tus, 783
Unreasonableness
fraud, whether constituting, 728

Voluntary obligations
insolvency, 777

Wills
See SUCCESSION

GAME

Agricultural executive committee
close times, powers as to, 808
ground game, powers as to, 851
Agriculture
agricultural tenant, *see* TENANT
hill farming improvement scheme, 923
muirburning, 923
wild birds or animals killed or taken in
    interests of, 881, 883, 885, 886

Air safety
taking or killing wild birds in interests of,
    883
Aircraft
hunting deer from, 941
transporting live deer in, 941
Animals
game, *see* GAME
injurious, control of, 859–865

References are to paragraphs

References are to paragraphs

Deer—*contd*
unlawful possession, 943
unlawful taking and killing, 938–942
　arrest, powers of, 958
　attempting or preparing to commit offence, 956
　cancellation of firearms certificate, 959
　exempted persons, 942
　search and seizure, powers of, 957
vehicles, driving deer with, 941, 942
venison, *see* VENISON

Detention
Poaching Prevention Act (1832), 844

Disease
taking or killing wild birds or animals in interests of, 883, 886

Dogs
hunt deer with, 940

Duck
wild—
　duck decoys, 882
　game, as, 802
　trespass in search of, 817

Educational purposes
taking or killing wild birds or animals in interests of, 883, 886

Electrical device
wild birds or animals taken or killed with, 880, 884

Evidence
Poaching Prevention Act (1832), 846

Explosives
wild birds or animals taken or killed with, 880, 884

Falconry
taking or killing wild birds, 883

Fences
maintenance of, 904

Firearms
certificate, cancellation of—
　offences under Deer (Scotland) Act (1959), 959
Night Poaching Acts, 810, 813
night shooting of ground game, 872
unlawfully used to kill or injure deer, 943
wild birds or animals taken or killed with, 880, 884

Fisheries
wild birds or animals killed or taken in interests of, 881, 883, 885, 886

Foodstuffs
prevention of damage by injurious animals or birds, 859

Footpath
public, Night Poaching Acts, 810

Forestry
prevention of damage by rabbits, hares and vermin, 866, 867
valuation, entry of, 906
wild birds or animals killed or taken in interests of, 881, 883, 885, 886

Forestry Commission
prevention of damage by rabbits, hares and vermin, 866, 867

Forfeiture
deer, of, 961
game, of, 809, 822

Foxes
hunting, application of Day Trespass Act, 821
requirement notice to control, 860–863

Game
agricultural executive committee powers, 808
breeding purposes, catching for, 882
Christmas Day, shooting on, 804*n*
close seasons, wilful destruction during, 806
common law game rights, 803
custody of, by unqualified person, 807
damage by—
　compensation for, 889–894
　game from neighbouring land, 894
　increase of game, 889
Day Trespass Act, 815–824
　apprehension of trespassers, 820
　assault, 823
　daytime, meaning, 816
　disguise or blackened face, 817
　forfeiture of game, 822
　hunting, application to, 821
　obstruction, 823
　prosecutions, 824
　tenant farmers, position of, 818
　trespass—
　　meaning, 819
　　in search of game, 817
forfeiture—
　Game (Scotland) Act (1772), 809
　Game (Scotland) Act (1832), 822
　Night Poaching Acts, 809
game laws, 803, 805–858
　Game Act (1831), 829–842
　Game Laws (Scotland) Amendment Act (1877), 848
　Game Licences Act (1860), 829–842
　Game (Scotland) Act (1772), 805–809
　Game (Scotland) Act (1832), 815–824

References are to paragraphs

References are to paragraphs

Hares—*contd*
spring traps—
  approved, 874
  inspection of, 875
  open trapping, 876
  use, sale and possession of, 873
trespass in search of, 817
unenclosed land, 853
Heath fowl
close season, 806
custody of, by unqualified person, 807
Heath game
Game (Scotland) Act (1832), 815
trespass in search of, 817
Hedges
prevention of damage by injurious animals or birds, 859
Heritages
See LANDS AND HERITAGES
Highway
public, Night Poaching Acts, 810
Hunting
Day Trespass Act, application to, 821

Innkeeper
game, sale of, 836

Land
entry of, in pursuit of game, 803, 817
landowner, *see* LANDOWNER
neighbouring, damage caused by game
  from, 894
occupier, *see* OCCUPIER
trespass, generally, *see* TRESPASS
trespass in pursuit of game, 803
  damage caused by, 803
  landowners' remedies, 803
Land works
prevention of damage by injurious animals or birds, 859
Landlord
agricultural tenant, relationship with—
  common law, 887–889
  compensation, tenant's right to, 889,
    890, 892–894
  increase of game, 889
  landlord's rights, 887
  tenant's rights, 888
fences, maintenance of, 904
game tenant, relationship with—
  normal clauses of, 899–904
  shooting lease—
    granters of, 898
    nature of, 895–897
neighbouring land, damage caused by
  game from, 894

Landowner
deer, 926
ground game, 854
  concurrent right to take and kill, 852
seizure, powers of, 812
Landrail
game, as, 802
Lands and heritages
meaning, 905
valuation—
  assessing rateable value, 909
  buildings, 908
  entry of, 906
  net annual value, 907
  shooting rights, 907–915
Licence
game, licence to deal in, 833–842
  application to person licensed to kill
    game, 835
  buying and selling on behalf of
    licensed dealer, 838
  close times, 840, 841
  employee of licensed dealer, 838
  frozen game, 841
  grant of, 834
  innkeepers, 836
  offences, 837
  prosecutions, 839
  two or more persons in partnership,
    834
game, licence to kill, 829–832
  exceptions and exemptions, 830
  ground game, 856
  person authorised under control pro-
    visions, 865
  production of, 831
  valid throughout United Kingdom,
    829
  void on conviction, 832
sale of—
  close times, 840, 841
  frozen game, 841
  licence to deal in game, 833–842
venison, to deal in, 944–947
  applications, 945
  copies and returns, 947
  disqualification from holding, 960
  duration, 946
  grant of, 944
wild birds, killing or taking, 883
Liferenter
shooting lease by, 898
Lighting, artificial
wild birds or animals taken or killed
  with, 880, 884
Livestock
prevention of damage to, 859, 883, 886

References are to paragraphs

References are to paragraphs

References are to paragraphs

Venison
dealing in—
　dealers' records, 948–951, 954, 955
　inspection of, 948, 955
　licences, 944–947
　　disqualification from holding, 960
　offences, 952–954
　Red Deer Commission, copies and
　　returns to, 947
meaning, 944
selling, offering and exposing for sale,
　offences as to, 952–955
unlawfully killed deer, selling, offering
　or exposing for sale, 953
Verity
oath of, 845
Vermin
forests, prevention of damage to, 866,
　867

Wild animals
meaning, 878
mechanically propelled vehicles used in
　pursuit of, 884
prohibited methods of taking or killing,
　884
　defences, 885
　licences, 886
res nullius, 803

Wild birds
conservation, 883
game birds, 878, 878n
injurious, control of, 859–865
meaning, 804n, 860, 878
mechanically propelled used in pursuit
　of, 880
prohibited methods of killing or taking,
　880
　defences, 881
　exemptions, 882
　licences, 883
requirement notice to control, 860–863
ringing or marking, 883
shooting on Sunday or Christmas Day,
　804, 804n
Wildlife and Countryside Act (1981)
gin traps, prohibition of use, 879
wild animal, meaning, 878
wild bird, meaning, 878
Woodcock
game, as, 802
nets or springs, taken by, 830
Poaching Prevention Act (1832), 843
trespass in search of, 817

Zoological collection
taking or killing wild animals, 886

GENERAL LEGAL CONCEPTS

Abortion
right to procure, 1095
Acquisition
derivative modes of, 1103
Animals
laws against cruelty to, 1045

Bankruptcy
obligation, transmission on, 1030
status diminished by, 1067
Beneficiary
passive capacity, 1048

Capacity
corporations, of, *see* CORPORATION
incapax, rights of, 1075
passive rights, to have, 1075
persons, of, *see* PERSONS AND PERSONALITY
status, 1067

Care
duty of, *see* DUTY
Case law
Scots law founded on principles, 1011
Children
capacity, 1067
family relationships, 1063, 1068
incapacity of, 1053, 1054
parent's duty of care, 1015
rights of, 1075
status, concept of, 1068, 1071
vicarious liability for actions of, 1056
Citizenship
status of, 1069
Civil liberty
principle of, 1012
Civil service
special legal powers, 1062
Conduct
approval and disapproval of, 1007

References are to paragraphs

Conduct—*contd*
law as guide, 1006
lawful and unlawful, 1006–1013
legally wrongful, 1010
rights in regard to, 1073–1090
   personal conduct, 1081
values, plurality of, 1008
virtue and vice distinguished, 1007
Contract
good faith, and, 1129, 1132
   American Restatement, 1130
   consumer contracts, 1131
obligation, as, 1031
sexual gratification, for, 1009
specialised concept of law, as, 1005
unenforceable, 1009
wagering, 1009
Corporate actings
firms, 1042
personality, and, 1041–1043
Corporate personality
corporate actings, 1041–1043
imputing to corporate groups, 1043
legal, 1044
Corporation
capacity of, 1064–1066
   active, 1065
   passive, 1065
capax doli, 1054
corporate status, 1072
powers of, 1064*n*
specialised concept of law, as, 1005
Creditor
obligee, as, 1029
Criminal law
Scots law founded on principles, 1011
Criminal liability
duty, and, 1015
Culpa
proximate cause of injury, as, 1019

Damage
obligation of reparation, 1032
Damages
injury, for, 1073
Death
ascertainment of, 1039
obligation, transmission on, 1030
Debtor
obligor, as, 1029
Delict
specialised concept of law, as, 10095
Dolus
capacity for, 1054

Duty
breach of—
   constitutional reasons, for, 1024
   embezzlement, 1015
   gives rise to remedy, 1023
   obligations of reparation, 1032–1034
care, of, 1015
   ascertainment of role of person owing,
     1018
   general, 1020
   private law, in, 1017
   special, 1021, 1022
   unborn or unconceived foetus, 1032,
     1037
   vicarous liability, 1056
civil liability, and, 1016
criminal liability, and, 1015
culpa as proximate cause of injury, 1019
enforcement of duties, 1022
imposition of requirements, as, 1025
injured party, remedial action by, 1023
judiciary, 1024
legal subject, 1014
meaning, 1014
Ministers of the Crown, 1024
moral agent, 1014
obligation, and, 1028, 1034
public duties, enforcement of, 1024
public interest, imposed in, 1029
rights depend on relevant, 1074

Election
capacity to stand for public office, 1069
capacity to vote at, 1069
Embezzlement
breach of duty, 1015
Engagement
principle of equity, as, 1125
Error
whether restitution obligatory, 1032

Family relationships
capacity, and, 1068
status, and, 1068
Firm
reality over and above partners, 1042
Foetus
unborn or unconceived, 1032, 1037
Freedom
principle of equity, as, 1125
rights contrasted, 1085

General legal concepts
act or abstain from acting, capacity to,
   1058
animals, laws against cruelty to, 1045

References are to paragraphs

References are to paragraphs

Rights—*contd*
title, 1101
transfer, 1090, 1107
waiver, 1090
work, right to, 1091, 1093

Seat belts
obligation to wear, 1027
Self-defence
right to, 1095
Servitudes
praedial, 1109, 1110
real rights, as, 1101, 1109, 1110
Sex discrimination
incapacity as argument for, 1053
status, concept of, 1068, 1071
Speed restrictions
obligation to observe, 1027
Standard security
rights of, 1108
specialised concept of law, as, 1005
Status, concept of
adulthood, 1067
bankruptcy, 1067
capacity, 1067
childhood, 1067
citizenship, 1069
commoner, 1069
corporate, 1072
decline in importance of, 1070
differences in status, 1067
elections—
     candidature for election, 1069
     capacity to vote at, 1069
family relationships, 1068
nationality, 1069
nobility, 1069
prisoners, 1069
public law, 1069
sex, differences of, 1068

Status, concept of—*contd*
unsound mind, persons of, 1067
weaker parties, protection of, 1071
Support
right of, 1109

Tenancy
tenancy rights, 1101, 1108, 1110
Testate succession
specialised concept of law, as, 1005
Things
existence of entities through time, 1113
incorporeal, 1113
rights in and to, *see* RIGHTS
Time
continuity of persons in, 1036
existence of entities through, 1113
human arrangements and, 1114
human identity, survival of, 1038
institutive rules, 1118
legal arrangements and, 1115
obligation, time span of, 1030
overall well-being of person through,
     1036
terminative rules, 1117, 1118
Title
rights, 1102
Trans-sexual
children of, 1038
marriage, 1038
persons and personality, 1038
Trust
breach of, 1015

Women
former incapacities affecting, 1053
Work
right to, 1091, 1093

GUARDIANSHIP

Accountant of Court
curator bonis, communication with, 1234

Child
over sixteen, legal capacity, 1245
under sixteen, legal capacity, 1244
Contract
'enorm lesion', 1205
minor acting with curator, 1204

Contract—*contd*
pupil incapable of entering into, 1203
quadriennium utile, 1205
reduction of minor's, 1205
Criminal responsibility
age of, 1202*n*
Curator
ad litem—
     adoption proceedings, 1227

References are to paragraphs

References are to paragraphs

References are to paragraphs

HARBOURS

References are to paragraphs

References are to paragraphs

HEALTH SERVICES

References are to paragraphs

References are to paragraphs

Diabetes
diagnosis of, 1467
person suffering from, ophthalmic services, 1463*n*

Diet
advice as to, 1446

Dietitian
employment of, 1500

Diphtheria
vaccination against, 1446

Disability
physical, provision of invalid carriages, 1486

Doctor
absence of, 1447, 1449
accident, provision of immediate treatment for, 1445
advice as to general health given by, 1446
anaesthetics, administration of, 1446
assignment of persons to, 1437
assistants, 1447, 1447*n*
budgets, health boards, set by, 1401
change of, 1440
    application for, 1440
    death of doctor, 1440, 1441
    temporary arrangements, 1441
    withdrawal or removal from medical list, 1440, 1441
complaints against, 1520
consultants, 1498
consultations, 1446
consulting room accommodation, regulations as to, 1446
deputies, 1447, 1449
disability, 1449
disqualification of, 1521
doctors' lists—
    applications for acceptance on, 1436
    limitation of persons in, 1439
    removal from, 1438, 1443
    revision, 1438
    schools and residential institutions, 1443
    temporary residents, 1442, 1445
    transfers, 1438
drugs and other substances, *see* DRUGS
duties and obligations, 1447
elderly or infirm, relief from certain duties, 1437
emergency treatment, 1445
    fees for, 1450
exchange of practices, 1434
fees, when acceptable, 1450
fund-holding practice, application for recognition as, 1401

Doctor—*contd*
general practitioners' drugs budgets, 1401
hospital care, purchase of, 1401
maternity medical services, 1446
medical list—
    application for inclusion, 1429, 1431
        appeal against decision, 1429
        consideration of, 1415
        refusal of, 1429
    contraceptive services, willingness to provide, 1430
    copies, availability of, 1430
    English, necessary knowledge of, 1429
    maternity medical services, willingness to provide, 1430
    reinstatement, application for, 1521
    removal from, 1432, 1521
        appeals, 1432
    revision, 1430
    Tribunal, inquiry by, 1425
    withdrawal from, 1432
medical service committee, 1520
ophthalmic treatment, 1464
    ophthalmic list, 1465
    recommendation of patient for, 1446
partners, 1447, 1447*n*
patients—
    obligations with regard to, 1445, 1446
    See also PATIENT
payments to, 1451
physical examination by, 1446
practice area, 1448
practice funds, 1401
records, requirement to keep, 1446
referral to other services, 1446
sale of practices prohibited, 1435
selection of, by patients, 1436
social work services, advice as to, 1446
temporary residents, 1442, 1445
terms of service, 1428
    alteration of, 1444
    rights and obligations under, 144
trainee medical practitioner, 1447*n*
treatment, requirement to given personally, 1447
treatment not within scope of doctor's obligations, 1446
vacant medical practice, succession to, 1433
vaccination and immunisation by, 1446
waiting room accommodation, regulations as to, 1446
Working for Patients White Paper, 1401

Drugs
medical—
    charges for, 1512

References are to paragraphs

Drugs—*contd*
medical—*contd*
checking amount supplied, 1472
Drug Tariff, 1446n, 1472, 1474, 1475
general practitioners' drugs budgets, 1401
listed, 1472, 1472n
restrictions on supply, 1446, 1446n, 1472
scheduled, 1446, 1472, 1472n
standards or formulas, 1472
supply to patients, 1472
testing quality, 1472
See also PHARMACEUTICAL SERVICES

Education
clinical training and research, 1487
health, provisions as to, 1482
Education authority
health service joint liaison committees, 1412
medical and dental services, duty in connection with, 1479
school health service, 1410, 1450, 1479
Employer
medical services supplied to, fees for, 1450
Employment
National Health Service staffing, *see* NATIONAL HEALTH SERVICE
Endowments
nationalisation, arrangements made during, 1404
Scottish Hospital Endowments Research Trust, 1424
Expectant and nursing mothers
care of, 1478

Family planning
contraceptive substances and appliances, supply of, 1471, 1481
provisions as to, 1481

General dental services
accommodation, health service provision, 1476
administrative authorities, 1402
anaesthetics, provision of—
dental practitioner, for, 1450, 1456
fees for, 1450
application for, 1455
area dental committee, 1423
arrangements for, 1452
charges for dental appliances and treatment, 1514, 1516
complaints, 1520

General dental services—*contd*
dental auxiliary, treatment by, 1456
dental list, *see* DENTIST
dental service committee, 1520
dentist, *see* DENTIST
executive councils, 1402
fees, 1459
health boards, administration by, 1410
obtaining general dental services, 1455
private practice, health service facilities used for, 1496
records, 1457
schools, provision in, 1479
Scottish Dental Practice Board, *see* SCOTTISH DENTAL PRACTICE BOARD
Statement of Dental Remuneration, 1462
surgeries, 1457
treatment must be completed with reasonable expedition, 1456
waiting rooms, 1457
General medical services
accommodation for provision of, 1476
adequacy of services, 1431
administrative authorities, 1402
ambulances, provision of, 1485
application to provide, 1429
blood supplies, 1485
complaints against practitioners—
appeals, 1520
disqualification of practitioners, 1521
generally, 1520
developments, persons displaced by, 1489
doctor, *see* DOCTOR
educational and research facilities, 1487
executive councils, 1402
family planning, *see* FAMILY PLANNING
health boards—
duty to provide general medical services, 1427
administration by, 1410
health education, 1482
infectious disease, control of spread, 1483
invalid carriages, provision of, 1486
meaning, 1427
medical list, *see* DOCTOR
practice—
exchange of, 1434
sale of prohibited, 1435
vacant, succession to, 1433
remuneration for, 1510
residential and practice accommodation, 1488
schools health service, 1410, 1450, 1479

General ophthalmic services

accommodation, provision for, 1476
administrative authorities, 1402
area optical committee, 1423
arrangements for, 1463
charges for optical appliances, 1513
complaints, 1520
contractor—
 deputies, 1465, 1465n, 1467
 duties, 1467
 records of, 1467
disqualification of practitioner, 1521
doctor, referral to, 1467
executive councils, 1402
health boards, administration by, 1410
national optical consultative committee, 1419
obtaining, 1466
ophthalmic list, 1465
 application for inclusion, 1465
 copies of, 1465
 medical practitioners, 1465
 opticians, 1465
 reinstatement, application for, 1521
 removal from, 1465, 1521
 Tribunal, inquiry by, 1425
 withdrawal from, 1465
ophthalmic medical practitioners, qualifications of, 1464
Ophthalmic Qualifications Committee, 1464
opthalmic service committee, 1520
patients, services to, 1467
payments for, 1468
prescriptions, 1467
private practice, health service facilities used for, 1496
remuneration for, 1510
specified examinations, 1467
 written statements as to, 1467
testing of sight, 1466
use of health service premises, goods or services, 1492

General practitioner

See DOCTOR

Glaucoma

diagnosis of, 1467
ophthalmic services for sufferers, 1463n

Health boards

accounts, 1508
adequacy of medical services, report on, 1431
budgets for doctors' practices set by, 1401
community service expenditure, contributions to, 1507

Health boards—*contd*

complaints as to, investigation of, 1426, 1522–1524
constitution, 1410
dental list, preparation of, 1454
dental services committee, 1520
doctors, payments to, 1451
doctors' lists, duties in relation to, 1438, 1439, 1443
expenses, 1506
functions, 1410
fund-holding practice, applications for recognition as, 1401
general dental services, duties as to, 1452
general medical services, provision of, 1427
general ophthalmic services, arrangements as to, 1463
joint liaison committees, 1412
joint services committee, 1520
liabilities, 1413
medical list, preparation of, 1430
medical service committee, 1520
membership, 1410
nursing homes, registration of, 1527, 1528
ophthalmic list, preparation of, 1465
ophthalmic services, payments for, 1468
pharmaceutical service committee, 1520
pharmaceutical services, duties as to, 1469
privilege of, 1413
rights, 1413
vacant medical practice, powers as to succession, 1433

Health education

provisions as to, 1482

Health Service Commissioner for Scotland

acting, 1426
appointment, 1426
complaint to, 1523, 1524
function, 1426
jurisdiction, 1522

Health visitor

employment of, 1499
health visiting, administration by health boards, 1410
meaning, 1499n
qualification, 1499

Home nursing

health boards, administration by, 1410

Hospital Endowments Commission

nationalisation, duties with regard to, 1404, 1406

References are to paragraphs

Hospitals
administrative authorities, 1402
boards of management, 1402
building, accommodation of persons displaced by development of, 1489
building control—
    authorisation of works, 1537, 1538
        application for, 1538
    designation of area, 1539
    inspectors, appointment of, 1540
    notification of building work, 1536
    offences in relation to, 1541
    planning permission, 1536
controlled premises, 1536n, 1539, 1540
controlled works, 1537, 1537n, 1540
default, in, 1409
expenses for attending, 1490, 1517
    companion's expenses, 1490, 1517
functions, failure to carry out, 1409
hospital care, purchase by general practitioners, 1401
mental, private, see PRIVATE HOSPITAL
national health service trust, ownership and management by, 1401
opting out of health authority control, 1401
patients—
    returning from outside British Isles, 1491
    transfer within British Isles, 1491
premises, goods and services used by contractor or local authority, 1492
premises, meaning, 1536n
private patients—
    accommodation and services for, 1494
    facilities used for, 1496
    resident patients, 1495
private, see PRIVATE HOSPITAL
regional hospital boards, 1402
residential and practice accommodation, 1488
Scottish Hospital Trust, 1424
Secretary of State's duty to provide, 1476
self-governing, 1401
state, provision of accommodation at, 1476

Immunisation
See VACCINATION AND IMMUNISATION
Infectious disease
control of spread, 1483
Invalid carriages
provision of, 1486

Laboratory technician
medical, employment of, 1500

Local authority
health service joint liaison committees, 1412
use of health service premises, goods or services, 1492
Local consultative committees
function, 1420, 1423
Local health authorities
duties, 1403
Local health council
function, 1420, 1421

Maternity care
See MIDWIFERY, MATERNITY AND CHILD CARE
Maternity home
meaning, 1525n
nursing home, as, 1525
Measles
vaccination against, 1446
Medical list
See DOCTOR
Medical practitioner
disqualification of, 1521
fund-holding practice, application for recognition as, 1401
health boards, powers of, 1401
health service facilities—
    contractors, use by, 1492
    private practice, used for, 1496
health service staffing, 1497, 1498
ophthalmic, 1464
    complaints against, 1520
    ophthalmic list, see GENERAL OPHTHALMIC SERVICES
Scottish Medical Practices Committee, see SCOTTISH MEDICAL PRACTICES COMMITTEE
trainee, 1447n
See also DOCTOR
Medical services
See GENERAL MEDICAL SERVICES
Medical supplies
control of prices for, 1509
Mental hospital
private, see PRIVATE HOSPITAL
Mental Welfare Commission for Scotland
inspection of private mental hospitals, 1535
Midwifery, maternity and child care
area nursing and midwifery committee, 1423
health boards, administration by, 1410
maternity medical services—
    doctors' obligations as to, 1446
    termination of, 1440

References are to paragraphs

References are to paragraphs

References are to paragraphs

Patient—*contd*
hospital—
    return from outside British Isles, 1491
    transfer within British Isles, 1491
hospital attendance, expenses incurred,
    1490
medical card, failure to produce, 1450
ophthalmic services, 1467
pharmaceutical services for, 1472
police station, doctor attending and
    examining at, 1450
private—
    fees for treating, 1450
    health service facilities used for, 1496
    national health service accommo-
        dation and services used for, 1494,
        1495
records on, 1446
return from outside British Isles, 1491
temporary residents, 1442, 1445
transfer within British Isles, 1491
Pertussis
vaccination against, 1446
Pharmaceutical services
accommodation, provision for, 1476
administrative authorities, 1402
area pharmaceutical committee, 1423,
    1472
arrangements for, 1469
charges for, 1512
chemist, *see* CHEMIST
complaints, 1520
drugs and medicines—
    proper and sufficient supply of, 1469
    See also DRUGS
executive councils, 1402
health boards—
    administration by, 1410
    duties as to, 1469
meaning, 1469
national pharmaceutical consultative
    committee, 1419
patients, for, 1472
pharmaceutical list—
    reinstatement, application for, 1521
    removal from, 1521
pharmaceutical service committee, 1520
private practice, health service facilities
    used for, 1496
remuneration for, 1510
Tribunal, inquiry by, 1425
use of health service premises, goods or
    services, 1492
See also DRUGS
Physiotherapist
employment of, 1500

Planning permission
hospital building control, 1536
Police station
doctor attending and examining patient
    at, 1450
Poliomyelitis
vaccination against, 1446
Preventative medicine
arrangements for, 1477
health boards, administration by, 1410
research into, 1487
Private hospital
meaning, 1525*n*
mental hospitals—
    control of, 1535
    inspection, 1535
    registration, 1532, 1533
        application for, 1533
        cancellation, 1534
        certificate of registration, display of,
            1533

Radiographer
employmnent of, 1500
Remedial gymnast
employment of, 1500
Road accident
emergency treatment given at, 1450
Rubella
vaccination against, 1446

School
medical services supplied to, fees for,
    1450
Schools medical and dental services
health boards, administration by, 1410
provision of, 1479
Scottish Dental Practice Board
alleged failure by, investigation into,
    1522–1524
chairman, 1416
Common Services Agency, service by,
    1411
default, in, 1409
expenses, 1506
functions, 1416
    failure to carry out, 1409
investigation of complaints as to, 1426
members, 1416
**Scottish Health Service Planning
    Council**
annual report, 1418
chairman, 1418
constitution, 1418
expenses, 1506
members, 1418

References are to paragraphs

Scottish Health Service Planning Council—*contd*
national consultative committees, role of, 1419
National Health Service reorganisation, 1417
prospective abolition, 1401
Secretary of State, duty to advise, 1418
Scottish Hospital Endowments Research Trust
duty, 1424
Scottish Hospital Trust
duty, 1424
Scottish Medical Practices Committee
chairman, 1415
Common Services Agency, service by, 1411
default, in, 1409
expenses, 1506
functions, 1409
medical list, consideration of applications for membership, 1415
members, 1415
Seat belt
medical examination in connection with, 1450
Secretary of State
Common Services Agency, delegation of functions to, 1411
complaints against practitioners, appeals, 1520
doctors' remuneration, conditions as to, 1451
Drug Tariff, 1475
expenses and receipts in relation to health service, 1506
hospital building control, appointment of inspectors, 1540
hospitals and other services, duties in connection with, 1476–1493
medical supplies, control of prices for, 1509

Secretary of State—*contd*
nursing homes, regulations as to, 1530
ophthalmic services, determination of fees for, 1468
property and land, purchase and disposal for National Health Service, 1504, 1505
Scottish Health Service Planning Council advice, 1418
Statement of Dental Remuneration, 1462
Sight
testing, *see* OPHTHALMIC SERVICES
Social work services
doctors' obligation to advise on, 1446
Speech therapist
employment of, 1501
State hospital
provision of accommodation at, 1476
Statutory body
medical services supplied to, fees for, 1450

Tetanus
vaccination against, 1446
Tobacco products
medical advice as to use, 1446

University liaison committee
function, 1420, 1422
members, 1422
Tribunal, 1506*n*

Vaccination and immunisation
doctors' obligations as to, 1446
health boards, administration by, 1410
provisions as to, 1480
travel abroad, in connection with, 1450
Voluntary organisation
use of health service premises, goods or services, 1493

***Working for Patients* White Paper**
National Health Service nationalisation, 1401

HERALDRY

Achievement of arms
badges and insignia of office, 1610
banners and flags, 1609
chapeau, 1607
components of, generally, 1603
coronet, 1607
crest, 1606

Achievement of arms—*contd*
helmet, 1605
mantling, 1605
motto, 1611
shield, 1604
supporters, 1608
wreath, 1605

References are to paragraphs

References are to paragraphs

References are to paragraphs

References are to paragraphs

Shield—*contd*
crest, addition of, 1606
generally, 1604
gentleman's entitlement, 1604
helmet above, rules as to, 1605
ladies, arms of, 1604, 1606
livery colours and metals, 1604*n*
lozenge, 1604
mantling, 1605
oval, 1604
roundel, 1604
shape, variation of, 1604
square, 1604
supporters, 1608
tincture, 1604
wreath, 1605
Slughorn
grant of, 1611
shouter, 1611
Standard
display in, 1610*n*
grant of, 1609
Standing Council of Scottish Chiefs
.licences to manufacture badges, 1631
Stranger
transfer of arms to, 1622
Succession to arms
heir of line and male heir, 1619
Jeffrey principle, 1619

Supporters
compartment, 1608
exterior additaments, 1608
grant of, generally, 1608
shield, of, 1608

Tailzie
arms subject to, generally, 1620
matriculation of appropriate arms, 1620
name and arms conditions, 1620
prescription of tailzied arms, 1624
Tincture
shield background, 1604
Trade marks
armorial in character, 1630
recording, 1614
restraint of use of royal arms, 1632
use in Scotland, 1614
Transfer of arms
inter vivos, 1622
stranger, to, 1622

Ulster
baronetcies of, 1621
questionable jurisdiction of English King
    of Arms, 1625

Wreath
liveries, of, 1605, 1606

HOTELS AND TOURISM

Accommodation
generally, 1721
prices, display of, 1786
provision of, 1721, 1723
right to refuse, 1723
tourist, registration of, 1811
Act of God
hotelkeeper not liable for, 1746
Alcoholic liquor
hotels, sale in, *see* LICENSING
Alien
accommodation of, 1723, 1730*n*
Animals
dogs, *see* DOGS
limitation of hotelkeeper's liability, 1748
no right of lien over, 1757

Board
meaning, 1710
Boarding house
hotel distinguished, 1710

Boarding house—*contd*
liability, 1742
    luggage, for, 1710
lodging house distinguished, 1710
meaning, 1710
Bookings
breach of contract for, 1727
hotel, 1723–1727
offer and acceptance, 1725
voluntary code of practice, 1726
British Tourist Authority (BTA)
See TOURISM
Brochures
accuracy of contents, 1783

Car
See MOTOR VEHICLE
Consumer protection
generally, 1779–1789
See also FOOD; PRICES

References are to paragraphs

References are to paragraphs

References are to paragraphs

Permitted hours
sale of alcohol, for, 1775
  extension of, 1776
  regular extensions, 1777
Personal injury
hotelkeeper's liability, 1738
Prices
corporate bodies, offences by, 1788
display of, 1786
enforcement and penalties, 1787
generally, 1785
maximum and minimum, 1786
Secretary of State's powers, 1789
value added tax, 1786
Private hotel
keeper not subject to strict liability, 1709
Public house
hotel distinguished, 1712
liability, 1742
meaning, 1712
part of hotel, as, 1712

Refreshment room
hotel distinguished, 1713
liability, 1742
part of hotel, as, 1713
Refreshments
hotelkeeper's duty to provide, 1720
provision of, 1720
  refusal to provide, 1723
refreshment licence, 1761n
refreshment room, see REFRESHMENT
  ROOM
right to refuse, 1723
See also FOOD
Residential hotel
keeper not subject to strict liability, 1709
Restaurant
hotel distinguished, 1713
liability, 1742
part of hotel, as, 1713

Safe custody
deposit of goods for, 1751
proof of deposit and restoration, 1751
Safety
fire precautions, see FIRE
health and safety at work, 1737
occupiers' liability, generally, 1731
Sale of goods
goods left at hotel, 1758, 1759
Scottish Tourist Board
See TOURISM
Secretary of State
hotels, exclusion of establishments, 1789

Table meal
meaning, 1764
Temperance hotel
generally, 1708
Theft
guest's property, of, liability for, 1744,
  1745
Tourism
British Tourist Authority—
  duty of, 1802
  establishment, 1797
  financial assistance for tourist projects,
    1803
  functions and powers, 1798
  membership, 1797
  promotion of tourism, 1796, 1798
collaboration between districts, 1795
financial assistance to aid, 1794, 1805–
  1810
local authorities' powers and duties,
  1793–1795
promotion of, 1793, 1796, 1797
registration of tourist accommodation,
  1811
Scottish Tourist Board—
  co-operation with other bodies, 1801
  duties, 1802
  establishment, 1797
  expenditure by, financial provision in
    respect of, 1814
  functions, 1798
  powers, 1799–1804
  promotion of tourism by, 1796, 1798
  tourist projects, execution of, 1804
tourist boards, generally, 1796, 1797
Tourist accommodation
registration of, 1811
Trade descriptions
brochures, 1783
generally, 1782
offences, 1782
Traveller
declarator of rights of travellers, action
  for, 1752
discontinuance of status as, 1718
early statutes, 1701
generally, see GUEST
hotelkeeper's duty towards, 1719–1723.
  See also HOTELKEEPER
luggage, see LUGGAGE
meaning, 1716, 1716n
refusal to receive, 1723, 1753

Value added tax
notice of prices of accommodation, 1786

References are to paragraphs

Wages
generally, 1790
regulation of, 1791
Wages Act (1986), 1792

Wages—*contd*
wages councils, powers of, 1792
Weights and measures
hotels, in relation to, 1784

HOUSING

Access
inability to secure, amounting to homelessness, 2045, 2048
tolerable standard, 1979
Acquisition of land
local authority, by, 1907, 1908
Agriculture
agricultural premises, tenancy not
secure, 1937, 1943
Alcoholic liquor
premises licensed for sale of, tenancy not
secure, 1937, 1943
Amenities
central government contributions, 2034
improvement of, grants for, 2033, 2034
local authority provision, 1906
standard, definition, 2023
Amenity housing
secure tenant's right to acquire, exclusion
from, 1972
Assignation
secure tenancies, 1951
Assured tenancy
conversion of secure tenancy into, 1936

Boat
no place to park amounting to homelessness, 2045, 2048
Building preservation order
demolition orders, 1983
Business premises
tenancy not secure, 1937, 1943
Byelaws
local authority power to make, 1902

Central government
contributions—
improvement of amenity grants, 2034
improvement grants, 2034
repairs grants, 2034
Children
priority housing needs, 2051, 2053
Closing order
acquisition, local authority powers of,
1987
appeal against, 1986

Closing order—*contd*
consequences of generally, 1988
demolition order—
replaced by, 1983
substitution of, 1987
effect of, 1982
generally, 1982, 1983
renewal, 1984
revocation, 1984
service, 1985
suspension, 1984
using or permitting use of building for
human habitation, 1988
vacation, notice requiring, 1988
Co-operative housing associations,
1924
Contract of employment
occupancy dependent upon, 2043, 2057
premises occupied under, tenancy not
secure, 1937, 1938, 1947
Cooking facilities
tolerable standard, 1979
Curtilage
house within curtilage of certain other
buildings, 1937, 1945

Damp
tolerable standard, 1979
Demolition
housing action areas, 1996, 1998
Demolition order
appeal against, 1986
building preservation order, 1983
closing order in place of, 1983
compulsory acquisition of site, 1988
consequences of, 1988
demolition by local authority, 1988
expenses, recovery of, 1988
generally, 1983
listed buildings, 1983
local authority powers, 1983, 1987
obstructive buildings, 1989
offences with regard to, 1988
requirements, 1983
revocation, 1984
service, 1985

References are to paragraphs

Demolition order—*contd*
substitution for closing order, 1987
suspension, 1984
time for demolition, 1988
vacation, notice requiring, 1988
Development corporations
allocation of houses, 1935
reduction of powers, 1920
Disaster
homelessness as result of, 2055
Disposal of land
housing association, by, 1926
local authority, by, 1908
District council
See LOCAL AUTHORITY
Drainage
tolerable standard, 1979

Emergency
homelessness as result of, 2055
Employment
contract of, premises occupied under,
    2043, 2057
  tenancy not secure, 1937, 1938, 1947
Excisable liquor
premises licensed for sale of, tenancy not
    secure, 1937, 1943

Fire
homelessness as result of, 2055
Fire authority
landlord, as, 1937, 1944
Fire escapes
grants for—
  amount, 2029
  generally, 2028
  procedural and other provisions, 2030
Flood
homelessness as result of, 2055
Furniture, fittings and conveniences
local authority housing, provision in,
    1906

General Register of Sasines
multiple occupation control orders,
    recording in, 2009
Grants
amenities, to improve, 2033
central government, 2034
fire escapes, to install, 2028–2030
housing support grants, 1910–1914
improvement, *see* IMPROVEMENT GRANT
repair, *see* REPAIR GRANT
Scottish Homes, power to make, 1923
thermal insulation, for, 2035, 2036

Health
accommodation which may endanger,
    2045, 2049
Heating
tolerable standard, 1979
Homelessness
access to accommodation, inability to
    secure, 2046
accommodation, provision of—
  advice and assistance as to, 2070
  charges, 2071
  interim, 2068
  permanent, 2069
  protection of property, 2072
  tenancy not secure, 1937, 1942
applications for housing, 2039
bad housing conditions, 2045, 2049
boat, no place to moor, 2048
Code of Guidance, 2037, 2040, 2044,
    2053, 2054
disaster, as result of, 2055
fire, as result of, 2055
flood, as result of, 2055
generally, 2037–2040
homeless, meaning—
  generally, 2041
  inadequate accommodation for family
    unit, 2044
  no right to accommodation, 2043
  rooflessness, 2042
  unacceptable accommodation, 2045–
    2049
illness or handicap, 2040
inquiries by local authority, 2040
intentional, 2040
  acts or omissions of applicant, 2060–
    2064
  availability of accommodation, 2058,
    2059
  decisions as to, 2071
  examples, 2057
  generally, 2057
  limitation of local authorities' obli-
    gations, 2057
  local considerations, issues to be con-
    sidered, 2066
  review of, 2066
judicial review of decisions as to, 2074
legislation, development of, 2038
local authorities, duties of, 2037
local connections, issues to be con-
    sidered, 2040, 2066
mobile home, no place to park, 2048
mortgage arrears, due to, 2040
obligations in respect of, 2037
offences with regard to, 2073

References are to paragraphs

References are to paragraphs

Housing—*contd*
public sector tenancies, *see* PUBLIC
  SECTOR TENANCIES
repair notices—
  appeals, 1994
  generally, 1993, 1995
repairs grant, *see* REPAIRS GRANT
scope of title, 1901
Scottish Homes, *see* SCOTTISH HOMES
secure tenants, *see* SECURE TENANT
sub-standard, *see* SUB-STANDARD HOUSES
thermal insulation, grants for, *see* THER-
  MAL INSULATION
underground rooms, 1981, 1982*n*
Housing action area
declaration of, 1996, 1997
demolition, area for, 1996, 1998
demolition and improvement, area for,
  1996
generally, 1996
house loans, 2015
improvement, area for, 1996
improvement grants, 2031
improvement orders, 1992
land, acquisition of, 1998
local authority—
  loans, 1992
  powers, 1999
notice, service of, 1997
repairs grants, 2032
revocation of order, application for, 1999
sub-standard housing, 1978
types of, 1996
Housing association
accounts and audit, 1929
allocation of houses, 1935
assets, freezing of, 1931
central association, 1933
change of landlord, 1924
co-operative, 1924, 1927
committee members, 1928
community-based, designation of, 1927
definition, 1924
disposal of land, 1926
dissolution, 1928
expenses, 1927
extraordinary audit ordered, 1931
fees, 1927
finance, 1932
fully mutual, 1924
generally, 1924
housing lists, 1935
inquiries into affairs of, 1931
members—
  appointment, 1928
  becoming insolvent, 1928

Housing association—*contd*
members—*contd*
  control of payments to, 1927
  incapacity due to mental disorder,
    1928
  removal or suspension, 1931
misconduct or mismanagement of
  affairs, 1931
objects of, 1925
payments to members, control of, 1927
registration, 1925
  admission to, 1925
  eligibility for, 1925
  removal from register, 1925
    appeals against, 1925
restriction on transactions, 1931
right to buy, restrictions on, 1955
rules, 1928
Scottish Homes, guidance by, 1930
security of tenure, 1955
self-build society, 1924
sheltered housing, 1955
special categories of tenant, 1947, 1955
tenancies after 1988 ... 1936, 1955
trading for profit prohibited, 1925
transfer of land to Scottish Homes or
  other association, 1931
voluntary disposal, 1924
Housing Corporation
functions of Scottish sector assumed by
  Scottish Homes, 1921
Housing list
generally, 1935
  rules for admitting applicants to, 1935
housing associations, 1935
priority of applicants, 1935
publication of rules governing admission
  to, 1935
reasonable preference to be given to certain categories, 1935
tenant selection, 1935
Housing support grants
aggregate amounts, 1911, 1912
apportionment, 1913
generally, 1910
housing support grant order, 1912
payment of, 1914
Housing treatment areas
housing action areas replacing, 1996

Improvement
housing action areas, 1996
meaning, 2019
Improvement grant
amount of, 2021
  additional amounts, 2021

Local authority—*contd*
housing action areas—*contd*
  revocation of order, application for,
    1999
  types of, 1996
improvement of amenity grants, 2033
improvement grants, *see* IMPROVEMENT
  GRANT
improvement orders—
  appeals, 1991
  generally, 1990, 1992
  mandatory improvement grants, 1992
  notices, 1991
intentional homelessness, local author-
    ities' obligations, 2057, 2057–2067
laundry service, facilities for, 1906
loans, *see* house loans, above
meals, facilities for obtaining, 1906
multiple occupation, housing in—
  control orders, 2009
  directions to prevent or reduce over-
    crowding, 2008
  limits fixed by local authority, 2008
  management code, 2006, 2007
  powers to require works, 2007
  registration schemes, 2005
overcrowding—
  licence to exceed limit, 2002
  powers and duties as to, 2003
  seasonal increases allowed, 2002
repair notice, *see* REPAIR NOTICE
repairs grant, *see* REPAIRS GRANT
sub-standard housing, powers as to,
    1978–1981
  general duty, 1980
  specific functions, 1981
  See also SUB-STANDARD HOUSING
thermal insulation, grants for, 2036
Lodgers
multiple   occupation   registration
  schemes, 2005
public sector housing, 1951

Meals
facilities for obtaining, local authority
  provision, 1906
Mobile home
no place to park amounting to homelessness, 2045, 2048
Mobility
housing, 1935
Multiple occupation
housing in—
  control orders, 2009
  generally, 2004, 2008
  management code, 2006

Multiple occupation—*contd*
housing in—*contd*
  overcrowding, *see* OVERCROWDING
  registration schemes, 2005
  works, power to require, 2007
    appeals, 2007
    enforcement, 2007
    wilful failure to comply, 2007

New towns
annual grant, 1920
development corporations, 1920
rental income, 1920

Obstructive building
demolition of, 1989
meaning, 1989
Occupation
multiple, *see* MULTIPLE OCCUPATION
Office
tenancy not secure, 1937, 1943
Overcrowding
amounting to homelessness, 2045, 2049
calculation of areas, 2001
endangering health of occupants, 2049
generally, 2000, 2008
homelessness, and, 2049
house, meaning, 1901n
local authority licence to exceed limit,
  2002
meaning, 2001
multiple occupation, *see* MULTIPLE OCCU-
  PATION
offences, 2002
  exceptions to rule, 2002
powers and duties of local authorities,
  2003
public sector housing list, affecting, 1935
room standard, 2001
seasonal increases allowed, 2002
secure tenancies, 1947
space standard, 2001
See also MULTIPLE OCCUPATION

Police authority
landlord, as, 1937, 1944
Pregnancy
priority housing needs, 2051, 2052
Public sector tenancies
agricultural premises, 1937, 1943
allocation of houses, 1935
business premises, 1937, 1943
change of landlord provisions, 1934
contract of employment, premises occupied under, 1937, 1938
fire authority as landlord, 1937, 1944

Public sector tenancies—*contd*
generally, 1934
homeless persons, accommodation for, 1937, 1942. *See also* HOMELESSNESS
houses part of, or within curtilage of, certain other buildings, 1937, 1945
housing lists, 1935
  priority of applicants, 1935
  publication of rules governing admission to, 1935
  rules for admission to, 1935
  tenant selection, 1935
inspection of house, 1934
local authority powers, 1934
police authority as landlord, 1937, 1944
private sector landlord, disposal to, 1908
right to buy, *see* SECURE TENANT
secure tenancy, 1903, 1934, 1936
  abandonment of tenancy, 1948
  after 1988, 1936
  assignation, 1951
  assured tenancy, conversion into, 1936
  change of landlord, 1971–1977
  creation of, 1936
  disposal by local authority of houses let on, 1908
  exceptions, 1937–1945
  improvements, 1952
  landlords of, 1936
  lease must be in writing, 1950
  lodgers, 1951
  meaning, 1936
  possession, proceedings for, 1947
  repairs, 1952, 1953
  right to buy, *see* SECURE TENANT
  security of tenure, 1946
  subletting, 1951
  succession to, 1949
  variation of terms, 1950
  See also SECURE TENANT
temporary letting—
  during works, 1937, 1941
  pending development, 1937, 1940
  person seeking accommodation, to, 1937, 1939

Recreation ground
local authority provision of, 1906
Rent
wilful non-payment, 2057
Repair notice
appeals–1, 1994
arrangement and execution of works by local authority, 1995
generally, 1993, 1995
local authority loan, 1995, 2015

Repair notice—*contd*
power to serve, 1993
repair grant, *see* REPAIR GRANT
serious disrepair, house in, 1993
tenant bearing expense, 1995
time for execution of works, 1993
Repairs
secure tenancy, 1952, 1953
Repairs grant
additional to improvement grant, 2021, 2025
amount, 2026
application for, 1995, 2025
approval, 2025
central government contributions, 2034
gererally, 2025
housing action areas, 2032
local authority house loans, and, 2015
procedural and other provisions, 2027
Right to buy
See SECURE TENNANT
Rooflessness, 2042
Room standard
overcrowding, calculation of, 2001
Rural area
designated, 1972

Sanitary conveniences
improvement grants, 2023
multiple occupation, housing in, 2005
tolerable standard, 1979
Scottish Homes
accounts, 1923
acquisition on change of landlord, 1972–1977
allocation of housing, 1935
annual report, 1923
chairman, appointment of, 1922
community-based associations, designation of, 1927
constitution, 1922
creation of, 1921
establishment, 1921
functions, 1923
housing associations, 1924
  admission and removal of associations from register, 1925
  control of payments by, 1927
  extraordinary audit, order of, 1931
  finance, powers as to, 1932
  guidance of, 1930
  inquiries into affairs of, 1931
  management guidelines, 1930
  operation of, 1928
  registration of, 1925
  remedial measures, powers as to, 1931

References are to paragraphs

Secure tenant—*contd*
right to buy—*contd*
  prescribed form, 1957
  price, calculation of, 1956
    fixed price option, 1962
  prior occupation by tenant, 1955
  prohibitions, 1958
  reasonable, must be, 1958
  recoverability of, 1965
  refusal of, 1963
  regional council as landlord, 1903
  restrictions, 1955
  Secretary of State, powers of, 1967
  statutory conditions, to be satisfied, 1955
  statutory requirements, compliance with, 1958
  variation, 1959
  voluntary disputes, 1970
security of tenure, generally, 1946
sheltered housing, 1947
special needs, house adapted for, 1947
subletting, 1951
succession to, 1949
temporary letting—
  during works, 1937, 1941
  pending development, 1937, 1940
  person seeking accommodation, to, 1937, 1939
variation—
  of conditions, 1959
  of terms, 1950
waste, neglect or default by tenant, 1947
Security of tenure
landlord's interest as lessee, 1947
Self-build society
housing associations, 1924
Service occupancy
tenant, 1948
Sheltered housing
restriction on right to buy, 1955
secure tenant's right to acquire, exclusion from, 1972
security of tenure, 1947
Shop
local authority provision, 1906
tenancy not secure, 1937, 1943
Slum clearance
revenue account, 1918
slum clearance areas replaced by housing action areas, 1996
Space standard
overcrowding, calculation of, 2001
Special needs
housing adapted for, 1947

Spouse
public sector secure tenancy transferred to, 1947
Standard amenities
meaning, 2023
Stodart Committee of Inquiry
housing, recommendations as to, 1903
Structural stability
tolerable standard, 1979
Sub-standard housing
closing order, *see* CLOSING ORDER
demolition order, *see* DEMOLITION ORDER
generally, 1978
improvement grants, 1981
improvement orders, 1981
local authorities—
  general duties, 1980
  powers as to, 1978–1981
  specific function, 1981
tolerable standard, 1978, 1979
underground rooms, 1981
Subletting
secure tenancies, 1951
Succession
secure tenancy, to, 1949

Temporary letting
pending development, 1937, 1940
persons seeking accommodation, to, 1937, 1939
works, during, 1937, 1941
Tenant
assured, 1936
contract of employment, premises occupied under, 1937, 1948
public sector tenancies, *see* PUBLIC SECTOR TENANCIES
repair notice, bearing expense of, 1995
right to buy, *see* SECURE TENANT
secure, *see* SECURE TENANT
service occupancy, 1948
temporary lettings—
  pending development, 1937, 1940
  person seeking accommodation, to, 1937, 1939
  works, during, 1937, 1941
tied, 1948
Thermal insulation
current order, scheme and directions, 2036
finance, 2036
grants for, 2035, 2036
homes insulation scheme, 2035
Tied tenancy
premises occupied under, 1948, 2057
Tolerable standard
homelessness, and, 2037

References are to paragraphs

Tolerable standard—*contd*
housing, of, 1978, 1979
improvement orders, 1990
underground rooms, 1981, 1982*n*

Underground rooms
closing orders, 1981, 1982*n*
Unfit for human habitation
concept of tolerable standard, replaced
    by, 1979

Ventilation
tolerable standard, 1979
Violence
probability of, amounting to homeless-
    ness, 2045, 2047

Violence—*contd*
violent partner, 2040
Vulnerable persons
priority housing needs, 2051, 2054

Washing facilities
improvement grants, 2023
improvement orders, 1990
multiple occupation, housing in, 2005
tolerable standard, 1979
Water closet
See SANITARY CONVENIENCES
Water supply
tolerable standard, 1979
Wheatley Royal Commission
housing, recommendations as to, 1903